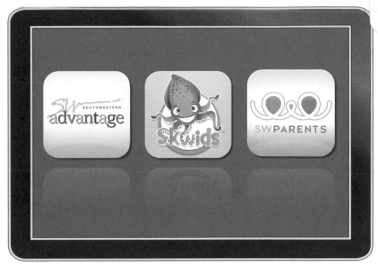

Web Sites

- How-to videos help students understand and solve homework problems
- Hundreds of character-building and parenting articles and videos
- Sites for everyone from preschool through parenthood

SOUTHWESTERN
advantage
Learning System

Software

- Younger education packages introduce children to computers and give them games to encourage learning
- Older students can use the software to edit and research reports, practice revision techniques, and write practice papers
- The College Prep Pack is specially designed to help college-bound students

Books

- Essential tools to help students excel in school as well as prepare for life
- Easily accessible, yet authoritative for the most important academic subjects
- Designed to teach children through exciting activity-based learning

www.SWadvantage.com

Sharing the Advantage

Southwestern Advantage is an effective learning system and an important key to a better education and achieving success in life. Our mission is to share education and learning skills with every child and every family, regardless of their circumstances, through qualified nonprofit partnerships and local community involvement with organizations focused on helping young people. Southwestern Advantage will also donate one SWadvantage.com membership for each one purchased.

Thank you for helping us Share the Advantage!

SOCIAL STUDIES & LANGUAGE

SOUTHWESTERN

www.SWadvantage.com

SOCIAL STUDIES
& LANGUAGE

www.SWadvantage.com

SOUTHWESTERN
advantage

Southwestern Advantage

Henry Bedford
Chief Executive Officer, Southwestern/Great American, Inc.

Dan Moore
President, Southwestern

Dave Kempf
President, Southwestern Publishing Group, Inc.

Sales Directors

Chris Adams	Robin Mukherjee
Dave Causer	Mark Rau
Lester Crafton	Tim Ritzer
Grant Greder	Chris Samuels
Kevin Johnson	Nate Vogel

Editorial

Executive Editor and President
Dan Moore

Editorial Director
Mary Cummings

Managing Editor
Judy Jackson

Senior Editor
Barbara J. Reed

Editor
Alison Nash

Section Editors
Julee Hicks
Cathy Ropp
Tanis Westbrook

Design

Senior Art Directors
Steve Newman
Starletta Polster

Senior Designer
Travis Rader

Composition and Production Design
Jessie Anglin
Sara Anglin

Production

Production Manager
Powell Ropp

Production Coordinator
Wanda Sawyer

Preface

Welcome to *Southwestern Advantage Social Studies & Language*. We are pleased to bring you this unique, user-friendly reference book. It has been designed in such a way that students can spend "more time learning, less time looking." The pages are open and inviting and organized into information boxes, bulleted lists, and other easily usable and understandable pieces.

Now You Know boxes are used frequently to briefly summarize the information on the preceding few spreads. **The Basics** boxes outline information essential to the topic at hand. **Watch Out** boxes alert students to things that might be easily confused or that might give students difficulty. **FYI** boxes give additional small nuggets or bits of information.

Time lines are used widely to encapsulate visually events that were occurring at the same time in various parts of the world. They can help students correlate what they may be studying in several different areas of their schoolwork.

Students (or their parents) can also go to **SWadvantage.com**, where they will find additional, more in-depth information on a wide range of subject matter.

We hope you will find this book both useful and enjoyable. Every effort has been made to ensure that the information in this book is as accurate as possible. If errors should be found, however, we would appreciate hearing from you. Please send your comments or suggestions to editor@southwestern.com or to Editor, The Southwestern Company, P.O. Box 305142, Nashville, TN 37230.

How to Use Southwestern Advantage

How to Use This Book

These books have been designed so that information can be accessed easily. Social Studies has been divided into six "strands": United States History; Canadian History; Government; Economics; World History; and Geography. Language has likewise been divided into six strands: Grammar; Writing and Research; Vocabulary; Reading; Speaking; and Literature. Each strand is then divided into smaller units.

The first navigational tool is the detailed, color-coded Table of Contents. The contents pages also indicate separately where the special features of the book can be found, such as the Table of Shakespeare's Plays and the history time lines.

UNITED STATES HISTORY

CANADIAN HISTORY

GOVERNMENT

ECONOMICS

WORLD HISTORY

GEOGRAPHY

Next, above the heading on the right-hand text pages, you will see color bars that tell you exactly where you are in the book. The bar that extends all the way to the edge of the page is the color of the unit you are in; the other bar denotes the strand you are in. The strand color is repeated in a tab at the bottom of the page. When the book is closed, you can tell at a glance where each strand and unit begins and ends.

When the book is open, headings on the pages also help to tell you exactly where you are in the book, for example, the Nile Valley section of World History.

↑
Strand color bar

fyi!

Though the Stone Age in the Near East ended in about 3000 BC, not all societies left it behind at once.

How to Use Southwestern Advantage Online (www.SWadvantage.com)

An integral part of Southwestern Advantage is the accompanying Web site. Organized by subject areas, it is a comprehensive suite of online study helps, additional in-depth subject matter, tips for parents, and coaching for students on how to get better at life.

GRAMMAR

WRITING AND RESEARCH

VOCABULARY

READING

SPEAKING

LITERATURE

SPECIAL ADVANTAGES

THE ROSETTA STONE

For over 1,000 years, scholars tried but failed to decipher the writing system of ancient Egypt. Then, in 1799, a rock slab with ancient Greek and Egyptian writing was found outside Rosetta, a city near Alexandria.

↑ **Features**

THE NILE VALLEY   WORLD HISTORY

↑ **Unit within World History**

↑ **Name of strand World History strand**

↑ **Unit color bar**

ALEXANDER THE GREAT

356–323 BC

As one of the greatest generals in history, Alexander the Great was responsible for the spread of Greek culture throughout western Asia and Egypt.

- He was educated by the famous Greek philosopher Aristotle.

THE **basics**

WORLD WAR II: CAUSES AND BEGINNINGS

✔ Worldwide economic depression during the 1930s helped create military dictatorships in Europe and Asia.

WATCH OUT!

Set a goal for each writing session. Whether it's one paragraph or one page, having a goal will help you focus on that particular section.

!

✔ The end of the Ice Age, about 11,500 years ago, marked the beginning of the Neolithic era.

→ **Strand color tab**

We gratefully acknowledge the invaluable contributions of these educators and writers to the development and production of this book. Their academic awards are testament to their breadth of knowledge and excellence in the classroom, and the accomplishments listed here are merely highlights from their careers.

Joan Brummond

M.A., Lesley College
B.A., University of Wyoming
26 years as a classroom teacher, K–Grade 3; Wyoming Teacher of the Year; developed new programs in guided reading; coached and consulted for a migrant workers education program; developed a before-school early-bird library program; tutors middle school students; coaches early literacy teachers

Kent Crippen

Ph.D., M.Ed., and B.S., University of Nebraska
Associate professor, Curriculum and Instruction, UNLV; coauthor of "Computer Uses in Chemical Education" in *The New ChemSource*; associate editor of the *Journal of Science Education and Technology*; associate director, Center for Mathematics and Science Education, University of Nevada, Las Vegas; his research involves the design and implementation of Web-based learning systems to support self-regulated learning

Denise Croker

M.Ed., Peabody College of Vanderbilt University
B.A., University of Kansas
more than 20 years as a classroom teacher, in English and Journalism; advisor to award-winning student newspaper and news site; frequent contributor to such scholarly publications as the *English Journal*, which gave her their Paul and Kate Farmer writing award; State Media Adviser of the Year; named a Dow Jones Newspaper Fund Special Recognition Adviser; frequent speaker at regional and national conferences

Arthur R. Echerd, Jr.

Ph.D., M.A., and B.A., University of North Carolina
25 years as a classroom teacher, in European History, AP Comparative Government, AP U.S. Government, World Religions; Tennessee Humanities Council Outstanding Teacher Award; Presidential Scholar's Inspirational Teacher Award; past holder of the Ellen Bowers Hofstead Chair in the Humanities

Jesus Garcia

Ed.D. and M.A., University of California, Berkeley
B.A., San Francisco State University
Professor, Curriculum and Instruction, UNLV; coauthor of *Field Experience: Strategies for Exploring Diversity in School, Social Studies for Children: A Guide to Basic Instruction*, and *Contexts of Teaching: Methods for Middle and High School Instruction*; past president, National Council for the Social Studies

Sherri Gould

M.Ed. and B.S., University of Maine
28 years as a classroom teacher, in English and Literacy; department chair; Maine Teacher of the Year; UMPI Alumni Educator of the Year; frequent speaker at conferences and workshops; former secretary and former vice president of National State Teachers of the Year Association; supervisor and trainer of preservice teachers

Pat Graff

B.S., Oklahoma State University
29 years as a classroom teacher, in Journalism, Humanities, and Social Studies; New Mexico Teacher of the Year; Governor's Award for Outstanding New Mexico Woman; Distinguished Service Award, National Council of Teachers of English; Medal of Merit, Journalism Education Association

Dale A. Grote

Ph.D., University of Wisconsin
M.A., University of Iowa
B.S., Cornell University
Associate professor, Classics, University of North Carolina; author of *A Comprehensive Guide to Wheelock's Latin*; president of the North Carolina Classical

Association; frequent speaker at education conferences; conducts study tours to Greece and Rome

Barry Hertz
M. Ed, University of Alberta
M.S. and B.S., South Dakota State University
21 years as a classroom teacher, in Biology, Chemistry, Physics, and IB (International Baccalaureate) Biology; Prime Minister's Award for Teaching Excellence

Keil Hileman
M.S. and B.S., University of Kansas
more than 20 years as a classroom teacher, Social Studies/Museum Studies; Kansas Teacher of the Year; 2004 National Teacher of the Year finalist; creator of the Museum Connections class, which has amassed more than 20,000 teaching artifacts; teaches museum courses for other social studies teachers

Rollie J. Myers
Ph.D., University of California
M.S. and B.S., California Institute of Technology
Emeritus professor, Chemistry, University of California, Berkeley; Guggenheim Fellow; ACS International Award Fellow; former visiting professor, Harvard University; former faculty senior scientist, Lawrence Berkeley National Laboratory; author of, among other books, *University Chemistry* and *Molecular Magnetism and Magnetic Resonance Spectroscopy*

James A. Roe
Ph.D., University of California, Berkeley
B.S., Williams College
Associate professor, Chemistry and Biochemistry, Loyola Marymount University; contributor to such scholarly publications as *Journal of Biological Chemistry* and *Free Radical Biology and Medicine*

Edna Rogers
M.S. and B.S., University of Tennessee
33 years as a classroom teacher, in Pre-K, Grade 2, and Grade 5; Tennessee Teacher of the Year; National Teachers Hall of Fame; Tennessee Educators Association Friend of Education Award; Presidential

Award for Excellence in Science and Mathematics; Governor's Outstanding Tennessean Award; on the boards of, among others, the Dollywood Foundation and Berkshire Education Scholarship Foundation; director of Dolly Parton's Chasing Rainbows Award

Ernest Schiller
Ph.D. and M.S., University of Iowa
B.S., Iowa State University
33 years as a classroom teacher, in Biology and Advanced Biology; Iowa Teacher of the Year; Outstanding Young Iowan Educator Award; Excellence in Teaching Science Award; Presidential Award in Secondary Science; Christa McAuliffe Award

Michael Seidel
Ph.D., M.A., and B.A., University of California, Los Angeles
Emeritus Jesse and George Siegel Professor in the Humanities, Columbia University; Department Chair; associate editor of *Columbia History of British Fiction*, *Columbia World of Quotations*, and *The Works of Daniel Defoe*; author of, among other books, *Epic Geography: James Joyce's Ulysses* and *Streak: Joe DiMaggio and the Summer of '41*; frequent contributor to such scholarly publications as *Eighteenth-Century Fiction* and *James Joyce Quarterly*

Mary Elizabeth Spalding
Ph.D., Indiana University
M.A. and B.A., West Virginia University
Editor, *Journal of Teacher Education*; frequent contributor to such scholarly publications as *Educational Forum, English Education, English Journal,* and *Teaching and Teacher Education;* member, executive committee, Conference on English Education of the National Council of Teachers of English; her research interests include performance and portfolio assessment, learning communities in teacher education, and secondary English teaching and teachers

Contents

UNITED STATES HISTORY

CANADIAN HISTORY

www.SWadvantage.com

Contents

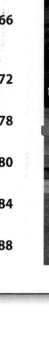

SPECIAL ADVANTAGES

Contents

WORLD HISTORY

GEOGRAPHY

Contents

VOCABULARY

READING

SPEAKING

LITERATURE

Social Studies
Advantage

United States History
Canadian History
Government
Economics
World History
Geography

FIRST AMERICANS

The First Native Americans arrived in North America some 10,000 to 20,000 years ago. These first Americans were probably big game hunters and fishermen who migrated from Siberia to Alaska by way of a land bridge that disappeared about 8000 BC. From Alaska, they moved southward over much of the continental United States, as well as into Central and South America, and gradually established many different types of societies.

Native American Groups

Modern research suggests that 2,000 different tribes, or groups, of Native Americans once lived in North America. Geography was the main factor in determining the way of life of these tribes.

Indian Land Regions

In the area that would become the contiguous United States, there were five land regions that were home to five major cultural groups of Indians. Different tribes developed different cultures, largely influenced by the characteristics of the land regions in which they made their homes. ▶

Native American Groups. Almost every Indian group had its own name. For example, the Delaware Indians of eastern North America called themselves Lenape, which means "genuine people." Today, many Indians refer to themselves as Native Americans.

The Pacific Northwest area ran along the Pacific coast, from southern Alaska through present-day Oregon and Washington. In the mild, wet climate, wild berries and other foods grew easily and plentifully. Pacific Northwest tribes were well provided with food and the materials needed for shelter.

The California-Intermontaine region included what are now California and the Great Basin. The mild climate of California made it suitable for farming and for gathering foods that grew wild, such as berries, acorns, and roots. In the Intermontaine area, however, the climate was dry and not good for farming. Winters in the mountains were harsh, and finding food was nearly impossible.

The Southwest region was marked by steep-walled canyons, few rivers, and stretches of flat desert land, yet the Indians who settled here, including the Hopi, Zuni, Navajo, and Apache, were able not only to survive, but also to develop highly organized and comfortable societies.

The Plains were flatlands covered by tough grass. The Plains Indians lived mostly in villages along streams and rivers. During the harsh winters, they stayed in villages. In summer, they lived as nomads on long buffalo hunts.

The Eastern Woodland area was the largest land region, characterized by inland waterways and coastal waters, forests filled with game, and good soil. In this environment, the tribes of the area became hunters and farmers.

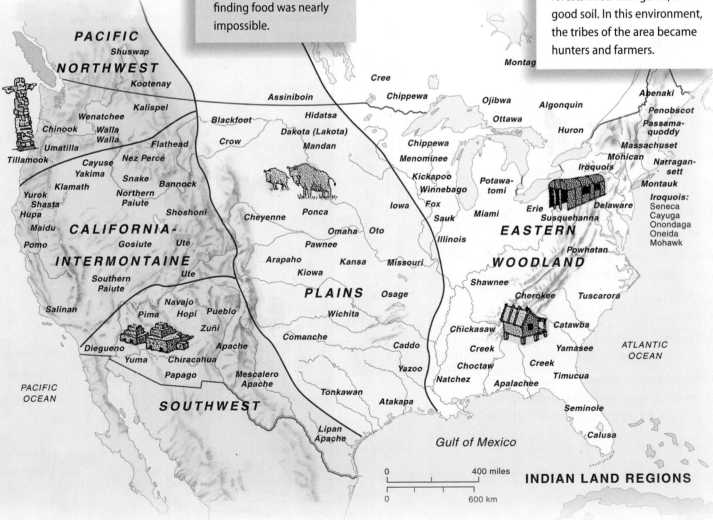

INDIAN LAND REGIONS

About a million Native Americans lived in the area that has since become the United States and Canada. (See also pages 240–243.) European settlers arrived in the late 1500s and early 1600s. The rise of farming had encouraged a more stable way of life, promoted greater social organization, and fostered development of crafts and art forms among Native Americans.

Government

For the most part, the Indians of the Americas lived in small groups and shared in making important decisions. Some Indians, including the Aztec in Mexico and the Inca in Peru, developed complicated systems of government. But most tribes had no need for such systems.

FORMS OF NATIVE AMERICAN GOVERNMENT

Bands
- Ranged in size from about 20 people to as many as 500.
- The size resulted mainly from the number of people that the nearby area could support.

Tribes
- Larger than bands.
- All members lived in the same general area.
- Forms of leadership varied; tribes might have one or more chiefs, or leaders.

Confederacies
- Made up of several tribes joined together.
- The Five Civilized Tribes (Southwest) built towns with up to 2,000 residents.
- The Iroquois Confederacy (Great Lakes region) promoted peace between member tribes and provided for common defense from enemies.

The Pueblo Indians of the Southwest developed a thriving village culture. They constructed large multistory housing complexes of sun-dried bricks (adobe).

WRITING SYSTEMS

It is estimated that at the time of their highest population, Native Americans in North America spoke at least 200 different languages. Many of these languages have been lost, but we know the following:

- Some tribes used pictures or wampum (a type of bead) to keep records.

- Pictures drawn on animal skins or bark showed events in a person's life or a tribe's history.

- The Indian tribes of the Plains spoke many languages and needed some means of communicating with one another. From this need came a series of commonly understood gestures called sign language.

Symbols painted on animal skins recorded the passage of time for tribes in parts of North America. ▶

Ways of Life

Native American tribes adapted their lifestyles to the regions and climates in which they lived. For example, the forests of the Pacific Northwest provided plenty of lumber for log buildings. On the treeless plains, Indians built portable tipis covered in animal skins.

NATIVE AMERICAN RELIGION

Indians had no one religion, but certain religious beliefs were widespread. Most important was the belief in a mysterious force in nature. The Indians depended upon this unseen spirit power for success in the search for food and in healing the sick, as well as for victory in war.

	Pacific Northwest	California-Intermontaine	Southwest	Plains	Eastern Woodland
Clothing	 Tlingit	 Hupa	 Hopi	 Sioux	 Iroquois
Buildings and shelters	 Haida plank house; Kwakiutl plank house	 Tipai summer shelter; Monache bark house; Hupa plank house	 Pueblo adobe village; Navajo hogan; Apache brush lodge	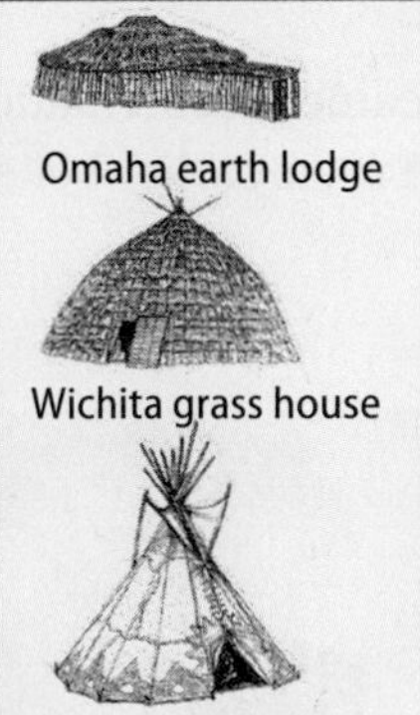 Omaha earth lodge; Wichita grass house; Sioux buffalo-hide tipi	 Kickapoo wigwam; Iroquois longhouse
Crafts and weapons	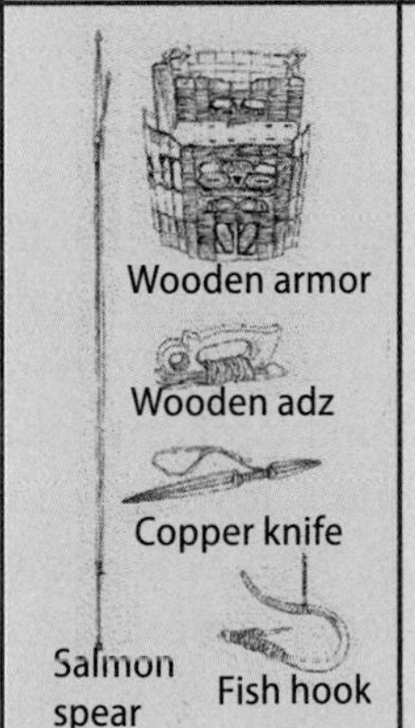 Wooden armor; Wooden adz; Copper knife; Salmon spear; Fish hook	 Wicker seed beater; Yew bow; Rod armor; Woven basket	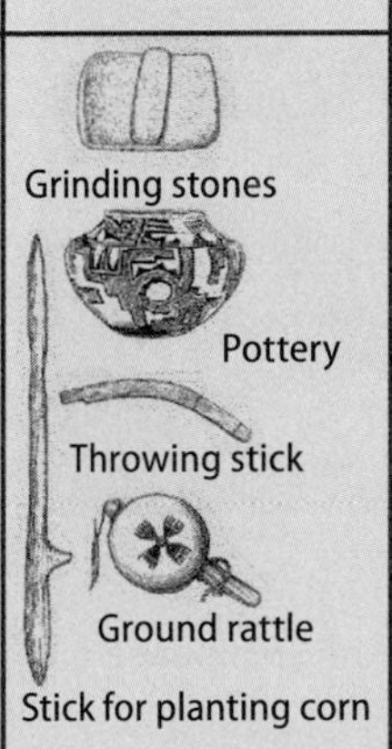 Grinding stones; Pottery; Throwing stick; Ground rattle; Stick for planting corn	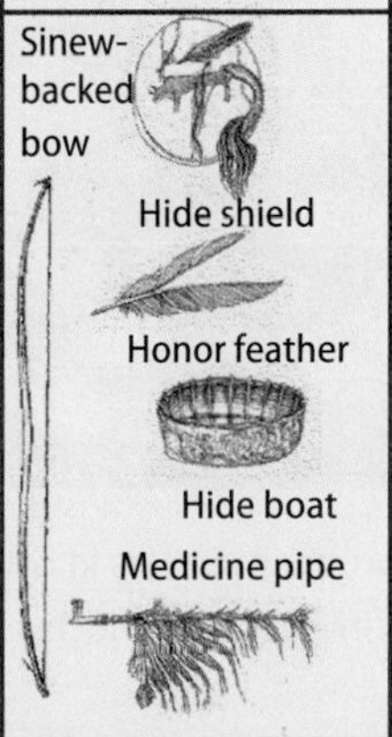 Sinew-backed bow; Hide shield; Honor feather; Hide boat; Medicine pipe	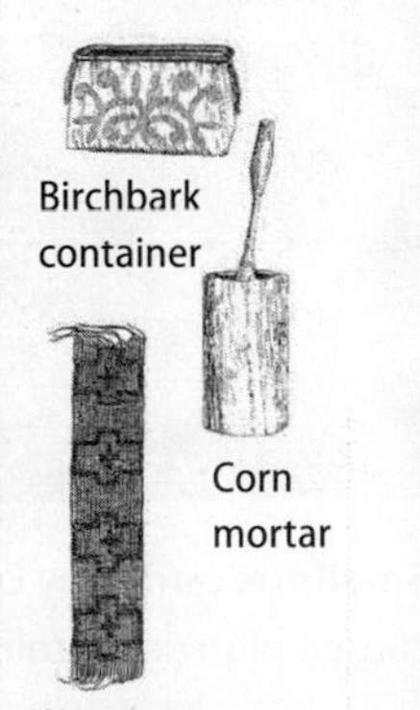 Birchbark container; Corn mortar; Wampum

When European colonists began arriving in the late 1500s and early 1600s, most of the million or so Native Americans in the United States lived east of the Mississippi River. Though some tribes were more warlike than others, Indians generally coexisted peacefully.

First Contact

The Caribbean people were the first Indians to come into permanent contact with Europeans, when Christopher Columbus explored the region on his four voyages. Spanish explorers followed him. Many Caribbean Indians died of diseases or as slaves. Whole tribes were wiped out, and others fled to remote areas to escape the white people. Soon, only a few Indian groups remained. But even these no longer lived as they had before the Europeans arrived.

- Food was not so plentiful as it once had been, because the Europeans had driven the Indians onto poor land.

- The Indians no longer made pottery or wove cloth. They used whatever European manufactured goods they could afford.

- Their religion became a combination of the Roman Catholic faith and their earlier beliefs.

▲ **William Penn,** founder of Pennsylvania, agreed to pay the Indians for most of the land he claimed in the territory.

Early Interactions

Native Americans initially had fairly peaceful relations with colonist groups, especially in the Northeast. At the Jamestown Colony in Virginia and the Plymouth Colony in Massachusetts, Native Americans provided colonists with food when the colonists' supplies ran short. They even taught the colonists how to plant corn and other New World crops. Spanish colonists taught the Plains tribes how to ride horses; soon, horse-mounted Plains warriors became fierce fighters.

Disease and Decline. European explorers and colonists brought over diseases that the native peoples had never been exposed to. As a result, contagious diseases like smallpox devastated whole tribes. Disease and poor nutrition—and later, the Indian Wars—caused a decline in the total Native American population which lasted until about 1900, at which point there were only about 250,000 Native Americans.

Smallpox carried by European settlers in colonial Massachusetts caused high death tolls in local tribes such as the Wampanoag.

Land Conflicts

At first, the colonists respected the Native Americans' sovereignty over their tribal land, but conflict became inevitable as the colonies grew and

▲ **Powhatan,** a powerful chief in what is now Virginia, at first called the colonists his allies.

the number of colonists increased. The first wars between Native Americans and colonists started in the 1600s. In Jamestown, the **Powhatan War** (1622–1644) killed most of the Native Americans in the area, and the settlers took over nearly all their land. In Connecticut, the **Pequot War** (1637) ended with the slaughter of nearly all Pequot Indians. (See also page 43.)

K **now you Know!**

✔ The earliest Native Americans in North America came from Siberia and arrived on the continent 10,000–20,000 years ago, traveling across a now-vanished land bridge.

✔ Geography was the main factor in determining the way of life of Native American groups as they spread across the continent.

✔ Five land regions of what are now Canada and the United States gave rise to five cultural groups of Native Americans: Pacific Northwest, California-Intermontaine, Southwest, Plains, and Eastern Woodland.

✔ The development of agriculture resulted in a stable way of life and promoted social and cultural advances among Native Americans.

✔ European colonization drastically affected the Native American way of life through introduction of diseases against which Native Americans had no natural immunity and through their takeover of Native American lands.

BUFFALO ON THE PLAINS

When European settlers encountered the Plains Indians, they brought two things with them: horses and guns. These greatly changed life on the Plains.

- With the horse, Indians could leave their villages and follow the buffalo herds—which they could not do on foot.

- Buffalo meat became their main food. The meat could be roasted over a fire, dried in the sun to make jerky, or pounded, together with berries and suet, to make pemmican.

- The Indians used buffalo skins to make clothing, bedding, and tipis. They made the bones and horns into tools and utensils and used dry buffalo manure for fuel.

The widespread killing of buffalo, particularly by white hunters, threatened to wipe out the great beasts. By 1890, the buffalo herds had almost disappeared—and with them, the Plains way of life.

Plains Indians tribes held many ceremonies aimed at assuring a large enough supply of buffalo.

EXPLORERS AND COLONISTS

In the late 1400s, the kingdoms of Europe were seeking to expand. They explored both land and sea in search of treasure, trade, and new territories. In seeking a better route to Asia, they discovered the Americas. (See also pages 502–505.)

European Explorers

Motives for Exploration

Political. Following the Middle Ages, nations like England, France, Spain, Portugal, and the Netherlands had been organized and strengthened by strong monarchs. In Spain, for example, the marriage in 1469 of King Ferdinand of Aragon (1452–1516) and Queen Isabella of Castile (1451–1504) began the unification of the Spanish state. The Spanish monarchs sponsored the expeditions of Christopher Columbus, an Italian. His discoveries gave Spain an advantage in gaining an overseas empire.

ATTEMPTED ROUTES TO THE EAST INDIES

- South along the western coast of Africa, around the Cape of Good Hope
- Northwest across the Atlantic
- Southwest across the Atlantic
- South across the Atlantic and along the eastern coast of South America, around Cape Horn

The Age of Discovery. Improvements in navigation, increased knowledge about the world beyond Europe (gained during the late Middle Ages), and successful voyages along the African coast all helped set the stage for a rapid succession of voyages of discovery. ▼

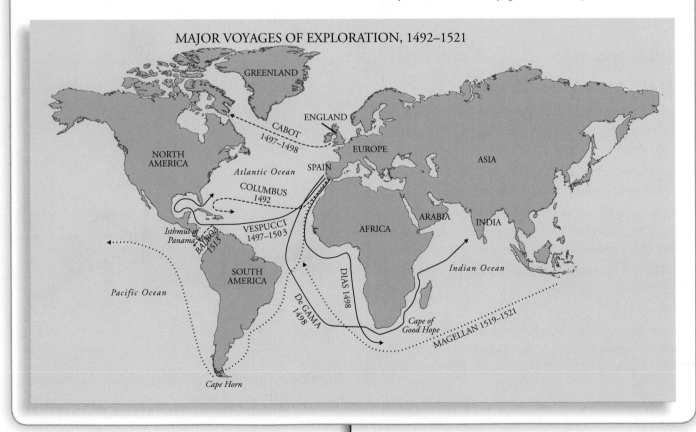

MAJOR VOYAGES OF EXPLORATION, 1492–1521

Economic. The Crusades of the 1100s and 1200s had acquainted Europeans with the useful and beautiful goods of the Middle East and Asia—spices, silks, polished steel, perfumes, and fine pottery. The overland routes to these regions were slow, expensive, and often dangerous. Merchants and sailors were looking for faster and more economical sea routes. By the late 1400s, a new merchant class had become increasingly important, and it was eager to extend its buying and selling powers to new markets and products.

Religious. In addition to seeking better trading options and valuable goods, Europeans also hoped to make converts to Christianity. In Europe, religious upheaval would later send some groups across the ocean in order to escape persecution.

 *One of the most famous explorers from the Age of Exploration is the Portuguese prince,* Henry the Navigator (1394–1460).

- *He wanted to increase Portuguese trading options and sponsored many expeditions to the African coast.*

- *Despite his nickname, he never went on a single sea expedition.*

THE TECHNOLOGY OF EXPLORATION

Three inventions helped to make the explorations of the 1400s and 1500s possible.

The astrolabe (*right*) consisted of a metal disk mounted on a circular frame. A navigator could rotate the disk to line up with a star, then read the star's elevation using marks on the frame. This enabled sailors to determine latitude more accurately.

The quadrant is an instrument used to measure angles up to 90 degrees. It is one-quarter (or quadrant) of a circle, with a plumb level (weighted cord) that determines direction. Combined with the astrolabe, it helped to measure latitude.

By 1500, ship designers in these countries had made long voyages possible by designing a new kind of ship, known as the caravel. **The caravel** (*right*) combined square sails with the triangular lateen sails used by Arabs. ▶

New technology such as the astrolabe (*left*) and the caravel ship (*below*) made it possible for explorers in the 1400s and 1500s to travel farther than ever before.

European Explorers

Where They Came From

Norway, Sweden, Denmark. The Vikings sailed westward into the Atlantic Ocean from the 800s on. After settling Iceland and Greenland, their travels took them to present-day Newfoundland and Labrador. Repeated attacks by the native populations prevented them from establishing settlements there.

Portugal. During the early 1400s, Portuguese explorers concentrated their attention on the west coast of Africa. Their expeditions south along the coast of Africa resulted in the discovery of a sea route to India, which other nations soon followed.

Spain. Christopher Columbus believed he could find a sea route to the East by sailing west. When his voyages took him to several islands in the Caribbean Sea, he was convinced he'd reached Asia. Later Spanish expeditions led by explorers such as Hernando de Soto and Francisco Coronado also went west, landing in Mexico, Central America, South America, and North America.

France. In 1524, the king of France sent Giovanni da Verrazano to explore the North American coast and find a "Northwest Passage" through North America to Asia. Verrazano did not find this passage, but on the basis of his explorations, France laid claim to North America. Later French expeditions traveled deeper into North America.

England. England had begun sending its explorers to North America as early as 1497. Many were traveling in search of a Northwest Passage. They were unsuccessful, but explorers such as John Cabot claimed the "new-found-land" for England.

▲ **Christopher Columbus** arrived at the island now called Hispaniola, in the Caribbean.

IMPACTS

The age of exploration brought great wealth to Europe and catastrophe to the native tribes living in the New World. Explorers and colonists brought foreign diseases that devastated whole Indian tribes. Friendly relations gave way to violent conflicts over land. In South America, conquered tribes were enslaved and stripped of their wealth.

Francisco Pizarro of Spain conquered the Incas of Peru. In this image, the Inca ruler Atahualpa pleads for mercy; Pizarro later had Atahualpa killed anyway. ▶

Key Explorers and Expeditions

Name	Sailed For	Dates	Expedition
Bartholomeu Dias	Portugal	1487–1488	• Sailed down the western coast of Africa, near the southern tip of the continent
Vasco da Gama	Portugal	1497–1498	• Followed Dias's route • Continued through the Indian Ocean, and on to India
Christopher Columbus	Spain	1492–1504	• Sought a westward path to Asia • Traveled with three ships—the *Niña*, the *Pinta*, and the *Santa Maria* • Landed on the islands of San Salvador, Hispaniola, and Cuba, believing they were part of Asia
Juan Ponce de León	Spain	1513	• Found gold in Puerto Rico • Explored the coasts of Florida seeking a legendary "Fountain of Youth"
Ferdinand Magellan	Spain	1519–1522	• Searched for a westward route to the Spice Islands • Killed in 1521 in the Philippines • His expedition circumnavigated, or traveled completely around, the globe in 1522
Hernando de Soto	Spain	1539	• Sought gold • Expeditions began in Florida, went through the Carolinas • Traveled as far west as present-day Oklahoma
Francisco Coronado	Spain	1539–1542	• Inspired by tales of wealth from explorer Alvar Nuñez Cabeza de Vaca • Explored the U.S. Southwest, including the Grand Canyon
Jacques Cartier	France	1535–1536	• Failed to find a Northwest Passage • First European to see the St. Lawrence River
René-Robert Cavelier, Sieur de la Salle	France	1643–1687	• Traveled down the Mississippi River to its mouth at the Gulf of Mexico • Claimed the entire region drained by the Mississippi for France and named it Louisiana in honor of King Louis XIV
John Cabot	England	1497–1498	• Explored the coast of North America in search of a water route across North America to Asia • Claimed the land for England
Henry Hudson	Netherlands	1607–1611	• Traveled deep into Canada searching for a Northwest Passage • Claimed the region along the Hudson River (into present-day New York) for the Dutch

European Settlement

In the 1400s and 1500s, Western European nations sent expeditions across the seas seeking treasure, land, and trade. After their explorers arrived in the "New World" of North, South, and Central America, these nations began to found permanent settlements in the lands they had claimed.

Why Colonize?

The Europeans had many economic reasons for colonizing the lands they had discovered. A colony could supply raw materials to a mother country and provide markets for goods that the mother country produced. In that way the mother country could become self-sufficient and eliminate the need to buy from other nations.

EUROPEAN SETTLEMENTS in North America

Eventually, the English established settlements along the continent's east coast, while the French claimed land in the interior and around the Great Lakes. Spanish settlements arose in the south, in present-day Florida, Texas, and Mexico.

1565: St. Augustine

- In 1565, the Spanish founded the first permanent European settlement in the present-day United States: the fort and village of St. Augustine, along the Atlantic coast of Florida. Future settlements would be along the Pacific coast of present-day California.

1604: New France

- Jacques Cartier and the French explorers who followed him found vast riches in fish and fur in the territory along the northern coast of North America. The territory, which they called New France, included the St. Lawrence River valley, the Great Lakes, and the Mississippi River valley. In 1604, Pierre du Gua (or du Guast), Sieur de Monts, and Samuel de Champlain established Acadia along the Atlantic coast. Champlain founded the settlement of Quebec along the St. Lawrence River in 1608.

RELIGIOUS CONFLICT IN EUROPE

Many groups that came to the American colonies were fleeing some form of religious persecution. The persecution came from a series of European religious upheavals.

The Reformation. In 1517, a theologian named Martin Luther begins to develop Protestantism, a form of Christianity, in response to abuses by the Catholic Church. Catholic princes throughout Europe attempt to crush the Protestant movement. (See page 500.)

Church of England. In 1534, King Henry VIII is excommunicated from the Roman Catholic Church for divorcing his first wife. In response, he creates his own church, the Church of England. He then persecutes all who oppose the new church.

Anglicanism. After a brief Catholic revival in England, Queen Elizabeth I (reign: 1558–1603) establishes a moderate form of Protestantism that becomes known as Anglicanism. The Puritans oppose it, demanding additional reforms to the church. Catholicism is officially banned in England.

1607: Jamestown

- A group of about 120 settlers founds a community called Jamestown, in present-day Virginia. The first winter, two-thirds of the settlers die.

- In 1608, Captain John Smith takes charge of the colony. Smith leads the settlers through starvation, disease, and conflicts with the Powhatan Indians.

- Jamestown becomes England's first permanent settlement in the New World.

1620: Plymouth

- A group of 102 Pilgrims, fleeing religious persecution in England, heads for Virginia.

- Their ship, the *Mayflower,* is blown off-course and lands on the coast of Massachusetts. Before landing, the Pilgrims draw up a plan of government called the Mayflower Compact. Under the leadership of William Bradford, they found the Plymouth settlement.

- Like the settlers at Jamestown, the Pilgrims face great hardships in that first winter. Half of them die; the rest survive with the help of friendly Indians.

1628: Massachusetts Bay Colony

- Eight years after the Pilgrims, a group called the Puritans comes to Massachusetts in search of religious freedom.

- They establish their first community at Salem in September of 1628 and soon found other settlements in Massachusetts, including Boston. The colony thrives.

- In 1632 Boston becomes the colony's capital, and Plymouth joins the colony in 1691.

Martin Luther, a German theologian, helped develop the Protestant religion. Clashes between Protestant and Catholic powers would lead many to flee for the New World.

now you **Know!**

✔ In the 1400s and 1500s, European nations increasingly looked beyond their continent to advance their individual interests. The nations launched numerous sea expeditions to gain power and prestige.

✔ European nations had political, economic, and religious motives for exploration. Such nations as Spain were newly unified and could apply resources to expansion. A growing merchant class sought both new markets for its goods and new sources of raw materials. Some nations desired to introduce Christianity where it was not known.

✔ Such technological developments as the astrolabe and quadrant (navigational devices) and the caravel (a type of ship) encouraged sea expeditions.

✔ The major colonizers of the Americas were the English, French, and Spanish. Between the late 1500s and early 1600s, each of these nations had established American settlements and claimed vast stretches of American territory.

THE THIRTEEN COLONIES

The Spanish and French explorers who came to North America in the 1400s and 1500s were interested in sending furs, gold, and other riches back to Europe. Many English settlers, however, wanted to set up permanent homes. Struggles in England over religious beliefs resulted first in a group known as the Puritans. Out of the Puritans arose a group called the Pilgrims. Members of these groups founded and joined American colonies and strongly influenced colonial culture.

Pilgrims and Puritans

COLONIAL FOUNDERS AND KEY FIGURES

Who They Were	Where They Lived
John Smith	Jamestown
William Bradford	Plymouth
John Winthrop	Massachusetts Bay
George Calvert, Lord Baltimore	Maryland
Roger Williams	Rhode Island
Anne Hutchinson	Rhode Island

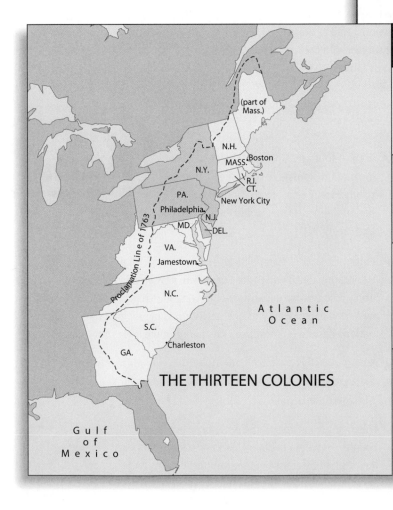

THE THIRTEEN COLONIES

Region	Colony	First Permanent Settlement
New England	Massachusetts	1620
	New Hampshire	1623
	Connecticut	1633
	Rhode Island	1636
Middle Colonies	New York	1624
	Delaware	1638
	Pennsylvania	1643
	New Jersey	1660
Southern Colonies	Virginia	1607
	Maryland	1634
	North Carolina	1650
	South Carolina	1670
	Georgia	1733

◀ **From Maine to Georgia.** By the 1750s, the population of the 13 colonies stood at about a million and a half people.

John Smith
(c. 1580–1631)

Arrived in Jamestown in 1607, and led the colony beginning in 1608. According to his own story, Smith was taken prisoner by the Indian chief Powhatan; his life was saved by Powhatan's daughter, Pocahontas.

George Calvert,
Lord Baltimore
(c. 1580–1632)

Former English statesman and founder of Maryland. After converting to Catholicism, he hoped to establish a Catholic-friendly colony. Unfortunately, the charter for Maryland was only issued after his death.

William Bradford
(1590–1657)

Governor of Plymouth colony from 1622 to1656. Bradford arrived with other Pilgrims on the *Mayflower* in 1620. He was part of the group that established the Mayflower Compact, organizing Plymouth's government.

Roger Williams
(c. 1603–1683)

Puritan minister who supported religious and political freedom. Disagreements with the Massachusetts Bay Colony leadership led to his banishment from the colony in 1636. He fled into the wilderness, later founding the settlement of Providence. From 1654 to 1657, Williams was president of the Rhode Island colony.

John Winthrop
(1588–1649)

First governor of the Massachusetts Bay Colony. A Puritan, he established a government-by-clergy. From 1630 to 1649, he was elected governor 12 times. As governor, he supported the banishments of Roger Williams and Anne Hutchinson.

Anne Hutchinson
(1591–1643)

Religious leader in Boston who supported religious liberty. Her doctrine conflicted with the doctrines of Governor John Winthrop and other powerful church leaders. Banished from Massachusetts, she formed a settlement in the new Rhode Island colony founded by Roger Williams.

The English government colonized the New World by giving out charters, or grants of land, to parts of the territory England had claimed. The corporations and individuals who received these grants then recruited settlers, established the colonies, and hoped the colonies would become profitable. Between 1607 and 1730, thirteen English colonies were established along the Atlantic coast, stretching from Maine (then a part of Massachusetts) in the north to Georgia in the south.

New England

The founding of much of New England came, in part, from trouble in Massachusetts. The Puritan leaders there demanded that people living in Massachusetts follow Puritan beliefs and practices. As a result, some groups left Massachusetts Colony in search of greater religious or political freedom and began their own colonies. The New England area was characterized by rocky soil, plentiful fishing, and woodlands.

Colony	Early Events
Massachusetts	Begins with settlements founded by the Pilgrims (1620) and Puritans (1628). Strict Puritan laws and codes.
New Hampshire	Charter granted to John Mason and Sir Ferdinando Gorges in 1622. Originally consisted of New Hampshire and Maine, but the land is divided in 1629. Made part of Massachusetts in 1641. But in 1680, King Charles II of England made New Hampshire a separate province.
Connecticut	Dissenters from Massachusetts, led by Thomas Hooker, establish a town called Hartford. Hartford joins with Windsor and Wethersfield in 1636 to form Connecticut Colony.
Rhode Island	Begins with settlement in Providence, founded after Roger Williams is banished from Massachusetts.

Baptism of Virginia Dare.

THE LOST COLONY

One of the earliest English settlement attempts ended with a mystery that is still unsolved. In 1585 and 1587, English adventurer Sir Walter Raleigh sent expeditions to Virginia. The settlers landed on Roanoke Island, off the coast of present-day North Carolina. Their ship sailed back to England for supplies, but was delayed there. When the ship returned in 1591, nothing remained of the colony except the word Croatoan—the name of a local friendly Indian tribe—carved into a tree. All of the colonists had disappeared.

Virginia Dare. This image shows the baptism of Virginia Dare, the first English child born in North America. Dare disappeared along with the rest of Roanoke Colony.

The Middle Colonies

The first settlers in this area had been Dutch, and much of the region was claimed by the Netherlands. The English seized control of New Netherland in 1664. This area had richer soil than the New England region and therefore was home to more farming.

Colony	Early Events
New York	Initially the Dutch settlement of New Amsterdam.
	Dutch settlers did not resist the English takeover in the late 1600s, due to their dislike of the current Dutch governor, Peter Stuyvesant.
	Renamed New York, after the English king appointed the Duke of York as its proprietor.
Delaware	Originally settled by the New Sweden Company in 1638.
	Taken over by the Dutch in 1655.
	The English take control of the area in 1664.
Pennsylvania	Created by William Penn, a Quaker, in response to religious persecution.
	Charter granted in 1681; government established the following year.
	Advertised by pamphlets throughout the countries of Western Europe.
	The colony granted religious freedom to Quakers, Protestants, Catholics, and Jews.
New Jersey	Given by the Duke of York to two of his friends, Lord John Berkeley and Sir George Carteret.
	Initially divided into East Jersey and West Jersey, but eventually combined into a single colony.

The Southern Colonies

In this region, rich soil, flat land, and a warm climate combined to promote large-scale agriculture.

Colony	Early Events
Virginia	The first permanent English settlement, dating back to Jamestown in 1607.
Maryland	Founded to offer religious freedom to Roman Catholics, who were persecuted in England.
	In 1649, the Maryland Toleration Act granted religious freedom to all Christians who settled there.
North and South Carolina	Began as a single large colony called Carolina, under the control of eight proprietors.
	Conflicts with the Spanish and the Indians, and within the colony itself, led to it being controlled by the English Crown.
Georgia	Last of the 13 colonies to be established.
	Founded as a place where people in debt could start over, instead of going to debtors' prison in England.

By the 1750s, about a million and a half people were living in colonies on the Atlantic coast. Cities like Philadelphia, Boston, New York, and Charleston had begun to grow (but even the largest of them, Philadelphia, still had fewer than 20,000 people). The colonists were overwhelmingly from the British Isles.

The Search for Freedom

Life in the American colonies was full of risk and hardship. In the earliest settlements, huge numbers of colonists died of starvation or diseases. Communities were often at risk of attacks from the native Indian populations in their areas.

Religious and Political Freedom. Some of the colonists, beginning with the Pilgrims in 1620, came to the New World to create communities where they could worship in their own way. Throughout the colonial period, many groups, including the ones below, headed for the colonies to escape persecution for their religious beliefs.

- Quakers and Roman Catholics from England

- Huguenots (a Protestant group) from France (See page 501.)

- Moravians from Germany

- Jews from throughout Europe

Economic Freedom. People looked to the New World as a place where they could buy land or find employment and eventually better themselves. Land ownership made people independent and promised a better standard of living for them and their children. Some people also came to the colonies to escape their debts—the colony of Georgia was founded specifically as a land where debtors could make a fresh start.

RELIGION IN THE COLONIES

Many colonists came to America seeking religious freedom. As a result, religion was a major force in colonial life.

Jonathan Edwards

- In the 1730s, a new crop of Protestant preachers began a series of religious revivals throughout the colonies. Preachers such as Jonathan Edwards and George Whitefield gave stirring, emotional sermons, filled with vivid images of heaven and hell. These revivals came to be called the First Great Awakening.

- While Protestants dominated New England and the Middle colonies, French and Spanish settlers had established strong Catholic communities in the south. Spanish missionaries would eventually establish missions throughout the south and southwestern territories—all the way to California.

Colonial Missions. Spanish Catholics set up missions, like the one shown here, throughout their territory. The missions often housed and fed Indians who agreed to convert to Catholicism. ▶

The Colonial Economy

The economy created by the colonists was based largely on agriculture. The type of farming and other economic pursuits differed from section to section.

New England	
Land and climate	● Frequently rocky soil, plenty of forests
Industries	● Small-scale farming (generally not more than about 10 acres per farm) ● Shipbuilding (using wood from the forests) ● Fishing (cod, haddock)
Trade	● Merchants traded with Europe, Africa, and China, as well as with other colonies

Middle Colonies	
Land and climate	● Richer soil than New England; mild climate in colonies such as Virginia and Maryland
Industries	● Large-scale farming (especially wheat) ● Manufactured fine goods (hats, furniture, wigs, carriages, etc.)
Trade	● Centered in port cities such as New York and Philadelphia

Southern Colonies	
Land and climate	● Rich soil, flat land, warm climate
Industries	● Large-scale plantation farming (tobacco, rice, cotton, and indigo)
Trade	● Traded agricultural products for manufactured goods from England and other colonies

SERVITUDE AND SLAVERY

The large Southern plantations needed an inexpensive source of labor in order to be profitable. In the earliest days of colonization, this labor was often provided by *indentured servants*. These were people who agreed to work as servants for a period of time, in return for their passage to America and for some land and tools. Once they had finished this period, the servants were free.

In 1619, Africans were brought to Jamestown in Virginia as indentured servants, but by the late 1600s Africans were being brought to American shores as slaves, to work for masters for their entire lives. All of the colonies were involved in this: most African slaves went to the Southern colonies, but New England slave traders brought them to America.

Most slave ship voyages across the Atlantic took several months. The slaves were chained below deck all day and all night except for brief periods of exercise. Their crowded conditions led to the chief horrors of the Middle Passage—filth, stench, disease, and death.

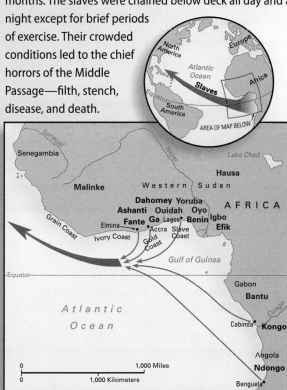

Slave Trade Routes. This map shows the areas along the west coast of Africa, near the Gulf of Guinea, where most of the African slave trade occurred. The globe shows the path across the Atlantic Ocean. The red type indicates the groups from which most slaves were taken. The groups that captured the most Africans for European and American slave traders are shown in bold black type.

The desire for representative government ran strong in the colonies, but all of the colonial governments were subject to some control by the English Crown. The British Parliament passed some laws for the colonies, especially ones regulating trade. British officials reviewed—and could reject—all laws passed by colonial legislatures. This system helped create resentment between the colonies and Britain.

In the Spanish and French territories, governments followed systems closer to feudalism, with landholders having direct authority over their tenants.

Systems of Government

Systems of government varied throughout the colonies. The government of each colony was partly determined by the kind of colony it was.

Royal Colonies
• New Hampshire, Massachusetts, New York, New Jersey, Virginia, North Carolina, South Carolina, and Georgia
• under the direct authority of the king
Proprietary Colonies
• Maryland, Delaware, and Pennsylvania
• under the authority of one or more proprietors
Self-governing Colonies
• Rhode Island and Connecticut
• had no direct supervision

All of the colonies had a governor, a council to advise the governor, and a legislature or assembly.

Voting. Not all adult colonists were permitted to vote—generally, only property owners were qualified. Slaves could not vote in any colony. Laws and custom usually kept women from voting as well. Some requirements restricted voting to members of certain religious faiths.

- Membership in the Puritan church was a requirement for voting in Massachusetts.

- The governor of Connecticut had to be "always a member of some approved congregation."

- Voters in Connecticut were required to take an "oath of fidelity" before being allowed to vote.

The governments established in the British colonies would later serve as models for the government of the new United States.

- *The Jamestown general assembly served as a template for the U.S. Congress.*

- *The U.S. Constitution would take some of its language from colonial constitutions.*

The English Pilgrims arrived at a place they called Plymouth in 1620. Their plan of government, called the Mayflower Compact, established majority rule in the new settlement.

Colonial Governments

The governments of the different colonies reflected the different needs and beliefs of their residents. However, many of their elements—such as freedom of religion and representative government—would eventually become important parts of the government of the United States.

House of Burgesses

- Formed in Virginia in 1619. The burgesses were the elected representatives of the Virginia colonists.
- Determined laws and taxation for the colony.

Mayflower Compact

- Plan of government drafted by the Pilgrims arriving in Massachusetts in 1620.
- Promised to make "just and equal laws . . . for the general good" and abide by the will of the majority.
- The compact established a pattern of "government by law and not by men."

The Fundamental Orders

- Drawn up in Connecticut in 1639, based on an earlier Massachusetts plan.
- Provided for the election of a governor and representatives.

Unlike the Massachusetts plan, the Connecticut plan did not make membership in the Puritan church a requirement for voting. It did restrict the governorship to members "of some approved congregation."

King George II of England, who ruled from 1727 to 1760, granted many of the charters for the 13 colonies. Though each colony had its own government, all were still under the king's authority.

COLONIAL CRIME AND PUNISHMENT

Laws in many colonies were strict, and punishment was direct and swift.

- Men and women convicted of adultery, gossip, slander, petty theft, drunkenness, or disturbing the peace faced fines, whipping, or shaming.
- Common forms of shaming included the pillory and the stocks (*left*).
- More severe crimes, such as murder, rape, or burglary, carried a death sentence.

In the stocks, the holes held the victim's legs, and sometimes also the arms. Prisoners were locked into the holes for a certain time. A pillory held the prisoner's arms and head. These devices were often used in a public area for all to see.

When settlers began to arrive in the American colonies, they encountered the Native Americans whose tribes already occupied the land. Native Americans and colonists had fairly good relations at first. As the 13 colonies expanded and became more populated, however, the relationship between the colonists and the Native Americans grew more strained. Eventually, the conflicts led to a series of bloody wars. (See also pages 26–27.)

Early Cooperation

Agriculture. At the Jamestown Colony in Virginia and the Plymouth Colony in Massachusetts, Native Americans provided colonists with food when supplies ran short. They even taught the colonists how to plant corn and other New World crops.

Trade and Cultural Exchange. The settlers introduced the Indians to metal pots and tools, textiles, and other goods. The colonists traded these products with the Indians in return for hides and furs, chiefly deer skins and beaver pelts. Many European fur traders lived in Indian villages and married Indian women. Some Indians living near or among colonists worked as laborers for the Europeans or sold them baskets and other crafts.

Land and Treaties. At first, the colonists respected the Native Americans' sovereignty over their tribal land. For example, William Penn, the founder of Pennsylvania Colony, paid for the land he claimed. He also established a treaty of friendship with the local tribes. In Plymouth, a 1621 peace treaty lasted for over 50 years.

Felt hats were enormously popular during the 1500s. The booming fur trade in North America helped to supply Europe with pelts for this kind of fashionable clothing.

THE FUR TRADE

The fur trade was one of the earliest and most important industries in North America. It began in the 1500s, when French explorers offered to trade with the Indians they met in the North American interior. By the end of the century, the fur trade had grown rapidly.

The then-current style in Europe was for men to wear hats made of felted fur. Beaver skins, plentiful in Canada, provided the best fur. Fox, marten, mink, and otter also were traded.

IMPORTANT DATES in relations between colonists and Native Americans

1616	A smallpox epidemic nearly wiped out Indians along the New England coast.
1621	Squanto, a Patuxet Indian, showed the Plymouth colonists how to plant corn.
1626	Peter Minuit, a Dutch colonial governor, purchased the island of Manhattan from the Indians.
1675–76	The Wampanoag Indians and several other tribes led by King Philip (Indian name Metacom) fought King Philip's War to resist colonial expansion in New England. The Indians were eventually defeated.
1763	The British issued the Proclamation of 1763, which outlawed colonial settlement west of the Appalachian Mountains. That region was to be reserved for the Indians.
1768	Northern Indian commissioner Sir William Johnson signed the Treaty of Fort Stanwix with the Iroquois, acquiring much of the land between the Tennessee and Ohio rivers for colonial settlement.

Conflicts

The rapid expansion of the English colonies in the 1600s led to conflict with the American Indian tribes whose lands were being absorbed by English settlements. The battles that followed came to be known as the Indian Wars.

Powhatan War. The settlements of Virginia and Maryland had maintained friendly relations with the tribes of the Powhatan Confederacy, until the death of Powhatan in 1618. In 1622, however, the settlements were attacked by Powhatan's successor. The attack killed more than 300 colonists. The colonists fought back, but in 1644, the confederacy launched another, more devastating attack. This time the colonial response was overwhelming. It led to the destruction of the confederacy and the seizure of much of the Powhatans' remaining lands.

Pequot War. In New England, growing friction between the Indians and settlers led to a year of conflict known as the Pequot War. The war led to the near destruction of the Pequot Indians of eastern Connecticut and brought an end to over 50 years of peace.

King Philip's War. In 1675, Plymouth authorities executed three Wampanoag men for the murder of a Christian Indian. Within a few days, fighting flared up; soon it engulfed New England. The Indian side was led by King Philip, or Metacom, leader of the Wampanoags and head of a confederacy of Indian tribes stretching from Maine to Connecticut. The war led to the destruction of Indian power in New England and opened the way for rapid colonial settlement in the region.

Pontiac, an Ottawa chief, was forced to sign a treaty of peace with the British in 1766 after his attempted rebellion failed. ▶

SOUTHERN CONFLICTS

American Indians also faced dislocation in the Southern colonies.

The Tuscarora War (1711) in Carolina led to the defeat of the Tuscaroras. The survivors migrated to New York and became the sixth tribe of the Iroquois Confederacy.

The Yamassee War (1715) of lower Carolina was an initially successful war against English settlers, but the Yamassee Indians eventually were defeated and driven into Florida.

PONTIAC'S REBELLION

One of the last conflicts during this period was known as Pontiac's Rebellion.

Indian tribes living in the upper Ohio Valley opposed British expansion. In 1763, the Ottawa chief Pontiac launched an uprising against English outposts in the region.

They captured eight British military posts, but in the end were unable to counter British force. To avoid costly future wars, the British government issued a proclamation in October of 1763, prohibiting colonial expansion to the west of the Appalachian Mountains.

England vs. France

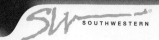

As the American colonies expanded into the West, their claims began to conflict with the lands claimed by the French. This rivalry led to a series of wars, fought from 1689 to 1763, which came to be called the French and Indian Wars. (See also pages 252–257.)

The French and Indian Wars, 1689–1763

War	Causes and Events	Results
King William's War (1689–1697)	• Named after King William III of England. • In New York, Indian allies of the English challenged French control of the fur trade. • In New England, Indian allies of the French resisted English expansion. • War broke out between England and France.	• Fighting in North America was inconclusive. • Treaty of Ryswick (1697) restored all conquered lands to their original owners. • France stepped up settlement in the Ohio and Mississippi river valleys.
Queen Anne's War (1702–1713)	• Named after Queen Anne of England. • Britain went to war against France to prevent France from gaining control of the Spanish throne. • English colonists attacked and burned Spanish-held St. Augustine (1702), captured all but one of the 14 missions in northwestern Florida (1704), and captured Port Royal, Nova Scotia (1710). • The colonists failed to take Quebec (1711).	• The American phase of the war went in favor of the English colonists. • Treaty of Utrecht (1713) gave Britain Hudson Bay, Newfoundland, and Nova Scotia. • France became determined to develop its western holdings.
King George's War (1744–1748)	• Named for King George II of Britain. • Fighting in North America began when the French tried to regain Nova Scotia. • The greatest battle of the war occurred in 1745, when New England colonial troops captured the French fortress of Louisbourg on Cape Breton Island.	• The Treaty of Aix-la-Chapelle, which ended the war, gave back to Britain and France the territory each side had lost in the war.
The French and Indian War (1754–1763)	• The final conflict between England and France in North America. • The French moved to gain control of the Ohio Valley. • In 1754, a Virginia force was sent to order French withdrawal and establish a fort at the site of present-day Pittsburgh, but the French had already established Fort Duquesne. • Virginia forces established Fort Necessity nearby at Great Meadows but were forced to withdraw.	• After initial French successes, the tide of war turned against them. • The British took forts Duquesne (1758) and Ticonderoga (1759) and captured Quebec (1759) and Montreal (1760). • The Treaty of Paris (1763) ended the war. France surrendered all its territories east of the Mississippi River, except for New Orleans.

The French and Indian Wars eventually led to the end of France's colonial power in North America. This map shows the location of several key battles.

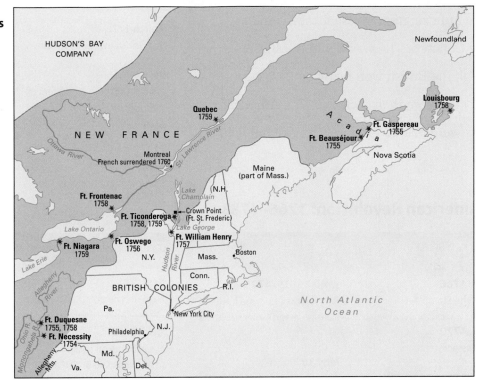

British possession

French possession

—— Colonial boundary

✳ Major battle

▪ Fort

• City

0   200 Miles
0   200 Kilometers

✔ Some colonizers of North America were interested mostly in the opportunities the colonies offered to build wealth. Other colonizers, such as the English Puritans and Pilgrims, were primarily interested in the opportunities the colonies offered to create societies based on their religious beliefs.

✔ The colonies of the Atlantic coast fell into groups according to geography: New England, in the north, Middle colonies, and Southern colonies. From 1607 to 1730, 13 colonies became established in the region.

✔ The colonial economy was largely agricultural. Small farms were characteristic of New England, whereas conditions in the Middle and Southern colonies supported large-scale farming of such crops as cotton, tobacco, and wheat.

✔ Government of the colonies varied with their types. The monarch ruled royal colonies; one or more proprietors (owners) governed proprietary colonies; and some colonies were self-governing.

✔ Such parts of colonial government as the House of Burgesses, a form of legislature, in Virginia, and the Fundamental Orders of Connecticut, a type of constitution, would serve as models for similar parts of the government of the United States.

✔ Native Americans and colonists largely coexisted at first. However, as the colonies began to prosper and take over more and more Native American land, the coexistence turned into conflict. Wars between colonists and Native Americans took place from the early 1600s through the early 1700s.

✔ The English and French fought for control of territory in what are now Canada and the United States in the French and Indian Wars. The wars erupted periodically from the late 1600s through the mid-1700s. At the end of the wars, the English controlled much more territory than the French.

INDEPENDENCE

The Revolutionary War began on April 19, 1775, when British soldiers and American patriots clashed at Lexington, Massachusetts, and at nearby Concord. The war would last 8 years. Although the British won many battles, they gained little from their victories. The American patriots were able to form new forces and fight on.

The Revolutionary War

March 1776
The British evacuate Boston

July 4
Declaration of Independence adopted by Continental Congress in Philadelphia

Sept. 15
Occupation of New York City by the British

Jan. 3, 1777
Washington gains a victory at the Battle of Princeton, NJ

April 25–26
British raid and burn Danbury, CT

Sept. 11
British victory at the Battle of Brandywine, PA

The American Revolution: 1766–1783

1766–1774

March 8, 1766
Repeal of the Stamp Act

March 5, 1770
Boston Massacre

June 9, 1772
Burning of the customs schooner *Gaspé*

Dec. 16, 1773
Boston Tea Party

Sept. 5, 1774
First Continental Congress (to Oct. 6, 1774)

1775

April 18–19, 1775
Paul Revere's ride and battle of Lexington and Concord

May 10
American forces under Ethan Allen and Benedict Arnold capture Ticonderoga

June 17
Battle of Bunker Hill: The British, under Gov. Thomas Gage, drive the Americans back

July 3
Washington assumes command of the Continental Army at Boston

July
Siege of Boston (to Mar. 1776)

Sept. to Dec.
American invasion of Canada

Nov. 12
American forces capture Montreal

1776

Sept. 22
Nathan Hale executed as a spy

Oct. 11–13
Naval battle on Lake Champlain: The British defeat American forces led by Benedict Arnold

Nov. to Dec.
Washington's forces retreat through New Jersey

Dec. 25
Washington's forces cross the Delaware River

Dec. 26
Battle of Trenton, NJ: Washington's troop defeats Hessian (German) mercenaries in a surprise attack

1777

Sept. 19
Continental Congress flees from Philadelphia to York, PA

Sept. 26
British occupy Philadelphia

Oct. 4
Washington's forces defeated at Battle of Germantown, PA

Oct. 17
Surrender of the British Army at Saratoga, NY, by Sir John Burgoyne. The victory, a turning point in the war, inspires the French to commit their support to the Americans.

Nov. 15
Articles of Confederation submitted to the states for ratification

Dec. 19
Washington's army encamps at Valley Forge, PA (to June 17, 1778)

Feb. 6, 1778
Franco-American treaty of alliance signed in Paris

June 18
British evacuate Philadelphia

July 4
British forces defeat American troops in what comes to be called the Wyoming Massacre (in PA)

Jan. 29 , 1779
British conquest of Georgia succeeds

Feb. 25
Capture of Vincennes, IN, by American forces

June 21
Spain declares war on Great Britain

May 12, 1780
British siege of Charleston, SC, ends in American surrender

July 10
Arrival of French troops under Rochambeau at Newport, RI

July 25
Gen. Horatio Gates assumes command of American army in the South

March 1, 1781
Articles of Confederation become effective

Sept. 28 to Oct. 19, 1781
Siege of Yorktown, VA

Oct. 19, 1781
The British surrender at Yorktown, VA, to forces led by George Washington, ending the war

1778	1779	1780	1781–1783

July 11
Arrival of French fleet under Comte d'Estaing off Sandy Hook, NY

Nov. 11
Cherry Valley Massacre (in PA) by Indians led by Chief Joseph Brant, allied with the British

Dec. 29
Capture of Savannah, GA, by British general Robert Howe

July 5
Plundering and burning of New Haven, CT, by British forces

Sept. 23
The *Bonhomme Richard*, an American ship, captures the British *Serapis* in a naval battle

Oct. 9
American forces launch an assault on Savannah. Washington's aide-de-camp, Casimir Pulaski, is killed.

Aug. 16
Battle of Camden, SC, ends in a British victory under Lord Cornwallis

Sept. 21
Benedict Arnold's treason uncovered

Dec. 4
Gen. Nathanael Greene assumes command of the American army in the South

July 11, 1782
British evacuate Savannah, GA

Nov. 30, 1782
Preliminary Treaty of Peace between the United States and Great Britain signed in Paris

Dec. 14, 1782
British evacuate Charleston, SC

Sept. 3, 1783
The United States and Great Britain sign the definitive Treaty of Paris

Nov. 25, 1783
British evacuate New York City

Dec. 4, 1783
Washington delivers his Farewell Address to his officers in Fraunces Tavern, New York City

Dec. 23, 1783
Washington resigns as commander in chief of the American army

A Famous Crossing. The image below is a depiction of Washington and his troops crossing the Delaware River on December 25, 1776.

First Struggles

For 150 years, the people of the American colonies had lived in relative freedom. British rule over them had been lax, and representative government had thrived. Following the French and Indian War, however, Britain began to tighten its hold on the colonies and to raise taxes to help pay off the war debts. Colonial resentment soon came to a boil. The colonists pushed back harder with each new set of British restrictions. Eventually, an organized resistance formed.

The Stamp Act. Engraved stamps, such as the ones shown here, were used on various documents or publications in the colonies.

The Grenville Acts (1764–1765)

Action

Passed by Lord George Grenville, Britain's prime minister and Chancellor of the Exchequer.

- **The Sugar Act (1764)** imposed new duties on many goods shipped to the colonists from Britain.
- **The Quartering Act (1765)** required colonial governments to provide housing and supplies for British troops stationed in the colonies.
- **The Stamp Act (1765)** required the purchase of a tax stamp for every legal document, newspaper, pamphlet, or broadside issued in the colonies. Even playing cards and dice required a tax stamp.

Colonial Response

American protest against the Grenville Acts was immediate and loud.

- Colonial merchants complained that the Sugar Act duties were more than they could afford. Colonial governments refused to obey the Quartering Act.
- The Stamp Act caused the most anger. In Virginia's House of Burgesses, Patrick Henry condemned the Act and the English king, saying of his defiance, "If this be treason, make the most of it!"
- Groups of angry colonists organized the Sons of Liberty, who openly defied the act by attacking stamp tax collectors.
- In October of 1765, representatives from nine colonies formed a Stamp Act Congress, which sent a formal protest to King George III. "Taxation without representation is tyranny," they cried.

Results

- The hated Stamp Act was repealed in 1766, following protests and the colonists' widespread refusal to buy or use the stamps.
- Parliament passed a law declaring the colonies to be subordinate to the British government, which had "full power and authority" to make laws concerning them.

The Townshend Acts

Action

Passed by Charles Townshend, Grenville's successor. In 1767, Townshend persuaded the British Parliament to place a new set of revenue-producing duties on glass, lead, paper, paints, and tea brought into the colonies.

Colonial Response

The colonists saw these duties as thinly disguised taxes.

- Boycotts and smuggling increased.
- The Virginia House of Burgesses passed the Virginia Resolves, stating that only the colonial government had the authority to tax its citizens.
- Boston became a hotbed of resistance.

Results

- Imports of the listed goods went down by 50 percent.
- Britain stationed troops in Boston to keep the peace and enforce the duties.

The Intolerable Acts

Action

Early in 1774, in response to the Boston Tea Party (see page 51), Parliament began passing a series of Coercive Acts, called "Intolerable Acts" in America.

- The Boston Port Bill closed Boston Harbor to all shipping. This threatened the people of Boston with shortages of food and with business failures.
- Another act placed the Massachusetts government under British rule.
- The Acts forced colonists to get written permission from the governor to hold any town meeting other than the annual meeting held to elect selectmen or other local officials.

Results

- The British government intended for these acts to punish and isolate Massachusetts, but the other colonies rallied to its defense.

THE ZENGER CASE

Colonial resistance was fueled in part by the press, which published works critical of British actions. They could do so, without punishment, because of John Peter Zenger. In 1735, Zenger, a newspaper publisher, was placed on trial for printing articles criticizing the British governor of New York. He was acquitted and the principle of freedom of the press was established in the colonies.

The Zenger case was a key milestone for the free press. In this image, British troops and government officials are shown burning newspapers printed by Zenger.

Growing Resistance

The Boston Massacre had both immediate and long-term effects. It resulted in the repeal of several unpopular laws. Additionally, two of the British soldiers involved in the incident were convicted of manslaughter. In the long term, it was also one step closer to full revolution.

The Boston Massacre

The Boston Massacre was the first conflict between Britain and the colonies to become violent. Still, it was not truly a massacre; the term was used to create anti-British sentiment in the colonies.

Action

- British troops were stationed in Boston after protests against the Townshend Acts (see preceding page).
- Under the Quartering Act, the citizens of Boston were forced to provide housing for the troops.

Colonial Response

- On March 5, 1770, the Bostonians' anger exploded into violence. As a crowd of Bostonians taunted red-coated soldiers standing guard near the Customs House, a shot rang out, and the soldiers opened fire on the crowd. When the smoke cleared, five of the colonists lay dead or dying in the snow.

Results

- Word of this "Boston Massacre" spread quickly through the colonies. In the next month, the British government repealed all the Townshend duties except the one on tea. It left that as an indication of its right to tax the colonists.

Organized Resistance

Organized resistance took a few different forms, with the colonies gradually forming a large united front against British actions.

Movement	Characteristics	Actions
Committees of Correspondence	Started by Samuel Adams after the Boston Massacre. Soon there were Committees in nearly every colony. Members included John Hancock and James Otis of Massachusetts, and Patrick Henry and Thomas Jefferson of Virginia.	• Kept tabs on British actions in the colonies • Passed information along to other colonists • Encouraged opposition to British actions
First Continental Congress (1774)	Included representatives of all the colonies (except Georgia). The Congress met to draw up a united protest against British acts.	• Declared the Coercive Acts null and void • Pledged that their colonies would not buy goods from Britain • Urged the colonists of Massachusetts not to pay any taxes to their military government • Encouraged Massachusetts to organize a militia • Sent a formal protest to King George III • Planned to meet again the following May
Second Continental Congress (1775)	Met after military clashes at Lexington and Concord. Included colonists from every colony. Among the representatives: George Washington, John Adams, Benjamin Franklin, Thomas Jefferson, and John Hancock.	• Petitioned the king to repeal the Intolerable Acts • Authorized the creation of the Continental Army • Named George Washington commander of the Continental Army's forces

THE BOSTON TEA PARTY

In 1773, the British passed the Tea Act, which favored the East India Company, a British tea-selling company, and threatened to put colonial tea merchants out of business. In the dark of night on December 16, 1773, some 50 Sons of Liberty disguised as Indians stole aboard three ships anchored in Boston Harbor that were loaded with tea from the hated British tea company. They threw all of the tea overboard. This "Boston Tea Party" enraged the British government.

The Boston Tea Party brought immediate backlash from Britain: the Intolerable Acts. (See page 49.)

Revolutionary Ideas

The Enlightenment

Sometimes called the Age of Reason, the Enlightenment was an intellectual movement in Europe and America that championed rationalism, natural laws, and science. Enlightenment thinkers challenged conventional social, religious, and political doctrines. The ideas and spirit of this age gave impetus to both the American and French revolutions.

American colonists who resisted British control were reacting to political and economic restrictions, but they were also acting on new ideals about individual liberty, human dignity, and government. These ideals fueled the American Revolution and helped to form the new nation. (See also pages 512–514.)

ENLIGHTENMENT PHILOSOPHERS and the American Revolution	
Name	**Contributions to the Revolution**
John Locke (1632–1704) **English philosopher**	• Disagreed with the divine right of kings to rule. • Believed that government gains its legitimacy from the consent of the governed. • Urged toleration of differing religious and political views.
Charles-Louis Montesquieu (1699–1755) **French historian and philosopher**	• Wrote *De l'Espirit des Lois* (The Spirit of Laws) in 1748. • Preferred the independent freedom enjoyed by the legislative, executive, and judicial powers in England during his time. • Ideas on law greatly influenced the framers of the U.S. Constitution.
William Blackstone (1723–1780) **British jurist**	• Published *Commentaries on the Laws of England* (4 volumes, 1765–1769). • The colonists used it as their chief source of information about English law.
Jean-Jacques Rousseau (1712–1778) **Swiss-born French philosopher**	• Outlined institutions he believed were necessary to establish a democracy in which all citizens would participate. • Believed that laws should express the general will of the people.

✔ In debt because of the French and Indian Wars, the British government increased taxes and placed new taxes on the colonies. After years of relative freedom in doing business, the colonists strongly resisted the new British laws.

✔ Two events hastened the American Revolution. In 1770, British soldiers fired on people in Boston protesting British taxes; five colonists died in the event labeled the Boston Massacre. In 1773, reacting to a British threat against local tea merchants, men boarded ships in Boston Harbor and threw their load of tea overboard in an action known as the Boston Tea Party.

✔ The American Revolutionary War extended from 1775, with the battles at Lexington and Concord in Massachusetts, to its official conclusion with the signing of the Treaty of Paris in 1783.

✔ Ideas about individual liberty and proper government arising from the Age of Reason, or the Enlightenment, of the 1600s and 1700s contributed to the colonists' drive toward independence. These ideas influenced the thinking of such founding fathers as Thomas Jefferson and John Adams.

now you Know!

Philosophies of the Founders

The leaders of the revolutionary movement in the colonies drew on Enlightenment ideas about government and freedom—though they did not always agree on how a free government should look.

Thomas Paine. Paine's strong belief in reason and his opposition to monarchy put him at the front of the revolutionary movement. His first popular pamphlet, *Common Sense* (1776), demanded an immediate declaration of independence. He enlisted in the colonial army that year and also began a pamphlet series, *The Crisis*. He would later use these ideals to argue in favor of the French Revolution (1789–1799), as well.

Thomas Jefferson. Jefferson's ideal was rule by the people with minimal government interference. Fearing the possible tyranny of a strong federal government, he was in constant conflict with Alexander Hamilton. He argued for freedom of speech, of the press, and of religion, and pressed for the addition of a bill of rights to the Constitution of the United States.

James Madison. In many ways, Madison was Jefferson's close political partner. He felt strongly that tyranny must be resisted. In an essay for *The Federalist*, he wrote that tyranny existed whenever all power was concentrated "in the same hands, whether of one, a few, or many, and whether hereditary, self-appointed, or elective."

Alexander Hamilton. The opposite of Jefferson in many ways, he supported the establishment of a strong federal government and believed that the U.S. Constitution should be interpreted loosely to give the government greater powers.

John Adams. Adams got his political start by helping to lead the protests against the British. When asked to write the Massachusetts Constitution of 1780, he echoed the ideas of the Mayflower Compact, stating that it would be a "government of laws, and not of men." The United States Constitution would later reflect many of Adams's beliefs.

Spotlight on... PATRICK HENRY

1736–1799

- American Revolutionary leader and speaker, famous for his anti-aristocratic views.

- In 1765, he was elected to the Virginia House of Burgesses, where he spoke against the Stamp Act and supported the colonies' right to self-government: "If this be treason, make the most of it."

- In 1775, his fiery speech—including the famous line, "Give me liberty or give me death"—led to the creation of the Virginia militia.

- Leader in the move to adopt a bill of rights.

THE DECLARATION OF INDEPENDENCE

By 1775, major military conflicts had already broken out between colonists and the British—at Lexington and Concord in April, and at Bunker Hill in July. Still, the Continental Congress did not call for total revolution against Britain. Many Americans were still loyal to the British Crown. They simply wanted to end what they saw as Britain's unfair and wrongful actions toward them.

Toward Revolution

After years of conflict, a series of events finally brings, the colonies to the point of revolution.

- **July 1775.** Congress sends a conciliatory petition, known as the Olive Branch Petition, to the king in hopes of restoring peace.
- **September 1775.** The colonists learn that the king has refused the petition. He declares the colonies to be in revolt, and that Britain will take military action against them.
- **May 1776.** The Second Continental Congress meets once more and declares, "It appears absolutely irreconcilable to reason and good conscience for the people . . . to support any government under the Crown of Great Britain."
- **June 1776.** Richard Henry Lee of Virginia brings a motion before the Continental Congress: "Resolved, that these United Colonies are, and of right ought to be, free and independent States." A committee of delegates begins to prepare a declaration of this motion.
- **July 4, 1776.** The Congress adopts the Declaration of Independence.

Declaration of Independence

The Continental Congress began meeting in 1774. The Congress would approve the Declaration of Independence, lead the nation through the Revolutionary War, and establish the Articles of Confederation—the nation's original plan of government.

The Declaration

Structure. This historic document was composed of two parts: a preamble that justified the colonists' rights as God-given, and a list of grievances against the tyrannical King George III.

Philosophy. The Declaration laid out the beliefs and ideals of the new country and its founders:

- All men are equal.
- Governments rule only by the consent of the governed.
- People have the right to change or overthrow unjust governments.

The Committee	
Thomas Jefferson	Delegate from Virginia; does most of the actual writing.
Benjamin Franklin	Delegate from Philadelphia. Warned that the signers must work to remain united, he replies, "Yes, we must indeed all hang together, or assuredly we shall all hang separately."
John Adams	Delegate from Massachusetts. He also works with the Congress to coordinate the Continental Army and pushes for George Washington to be its leader.
Robert R. Livingston	Delegate from New York.
Roger Sherman	Delegate from Connecticut. The only person who signed all four of these great documents: ● Articles of Association (1774) ● Declaration of Independence (1776) ● Articles of Confederation (1777) ● Constitution of the United States (1787)

THE DECLARATION OF INDEPENDENCE [excerpts]

Adopted by the Continental Congress, July 4, 1776

When in the Course of Human Events, it becomes necessary for one People to dissolve the Political Bands which have connected them with another, and to assume among the Powers of the Earth, the separate and equal Station to which the Laws of Nature and of Nature's God entitle them, a decent Respect to the Opinions of Mankind requires that they should declare the causes which impel them to the Separation.

We hold these Truths to be self-evident, that all Men are created equal, that they are endowed by their Creator with certain unalienable Rights, that among these are Life, Liberty, and the Pursuit of Happiness—That to secure these Rights, Governments are instituted among Men, deriving their just Powers from the Consent of the Governed, that whenever any Form of Government becomes destructive of these Ends, it is the Right of the People to alter or to abolish it, and to institute new Government, laying its Foundation on such Principles, and organizing its Powers in such Form, as to them shall seem most likely to effect their Safety and Happiness. Prudence, indeed, will dictate that Governments long established should not be changed for light and transient Causes; and accordingly all Experience hath shewn, that Mankind are more disposed to suffer, while Evils are sufferable, than to right themselves by abolishing the Forms to which they are accustomed. But when a long Train of Abuses and Usurpations, pursuing invariably the same Object, evinces a Design to reduce them under absolute Despotism, it is their Right, it is their Duty, to throw off such Government, and to provide new Guards for their future Security. Such has been the patient Sufferance of these Colonies; and such is now the Necessity which constrains them to alter their former Systems of Government.

[A list of grievances against the King and the British government appeared next, omitted here.]

We, therefore, the Representatives of the UNITED STATES OF AMERICA, in GENERAL CONGRESS, Assembled, appealing to the Supreme Judge of the World for the Rectitude of our Intentions, do, in the Name, and by Authority of the good People of these Colonies, solemnly Publish and Declare, That these United Colonies are, and of Right ought to be, FREE AND INDEPENDENT STATES; that they are absolved from all Allegiance to the British Crown, and that all political Connection between them and the State of Great-Britain, is and ought to be totally dissolved; and that as FREE AND INDEPENDENT STATES, they have full Power to levy War, conclude Peace, contract Alliances, establish Commerce, and to do all other Acts and Things which INDEPENDENT STATES may of right do. And for the support of this Declaration, with a firm Reliance on the Protection of divine Providence, we mutally pledge to each other our Lives, our Fortunes, and our sacred Honor.

THE REVOLUTIONARY WAR

THE REVOLUTIONARY WAR began with violent clashes between the Americans and the British in 1775. After the Americans declared their independence, they had to win it by force. Some Americans, called Loyalists, remained true to Britain, but a growing number of Americans supported the fight for independence. The war would go on for 8 years before the British were defeated and recognized the United States as an independent nation.

(See also page 514.)

From Rebellion to War

When the Declaration of Independence was signed on July 4, 1776, the Revolution was more than a year old. King George had declared the colonies in official rebellion in 1775. Fighting had already begun in Massachusetts, Canada, and the Chesapeake colonies.

Early battles were concentrated in the New England and Middle colonies. Later, the fighting would shift to the south.

Valley Forge. The bitter winter of 1777–78, shared by George Washington and his troops at Valley Forge, Pennsylvania, was a time of starvation and disease. Yet they endured. Thanks to military drill and training, they emerged a stronger army than before.

War in the Northern Colonies		
Early Battles	**Location**	**Events and Results**
Lexington and Concord (April 1775)	Massachusetts	• British soldiers attempted to capture a storehouse of American weapons at Concord. • Eight militia fighters, or "Minutemen," were killed at Lexington. • At Concord, the British troops confronted 400 Minutemen and destroyed the militia's supplies. • A total of 3,700 Minutemen sniped at the retreating British troops. British casualties were almost 300 dead, wounded, or missing.
Bunker Hill (June 1775)	Massachusetts	• General Gage sent 2,400 troops to drive the Americans out of Breed's Hill and Bunker Hill, north of Boston. • After three charges, the British troops drove the Americans out. • This victory in the Battle of Bunker Hill cost the British about 1,000 casualties.
Trenton and Princeton (1776)	New Jersey	• On Christmas night, Washington and 6,000 troops crossed the Delaware River for a surprise attack on the British garrison at Trenton, New Jersey. • The British forces quickly surrendered. • At Princeton, Washington's men captured two British regiments with their guns and supplies. • The American army retook much of New Jersey.

Patriots and Loyalists

Even as the war began, as many as a third of the people sympathized with Britain. They called themselves Loyalists. The revolutionaries, or Patriots, made up less than a third of the population.

Turning Points

Britain nearly conquered the Patriots several times during the fighting in the North, which lasted from 1775 to 1778. But British generals failed to carry out their strategy effectively, and in 1778, the war began changing course.

The Battle of Saratoga proved to be the turning point of the American Revolution in two ways:

- It weakened the British and strengthened American morale.

- It hclpcd to convince France that the Americans could win the war. The French decided to support the Americans with troops and supplies.

War in the Middle Colonies		
Battles	**Location**	**Events and Results**
Brandywine and Germantown	Pennsylvania	• British general Howe moved his troops toward Pennsylvania. • Howe's troops defeated Washington's at Brandywine. • Two weeks later, the British captured Philadelphia. • Howe's troops win again at Germantown, Pennsylvania.
Saratoga	New York	• Forces led by British general John Burgoyne moved south from Canada and into New York. • Burgoyne's troops were outnumbered in the first and second Battles of Freeman's Farm. • The Continental Army surrounded them and forced their surrender at Saratoga on October 17, 1777.

CANADA
ME. (Mass.)
(VT.)
N.Y.
N.H.
Lexington-Concord April, 1775
Saratoga Oct., 1777
MASS.
CONN.
R.I.
PA.
N.J.
Valley Forge Winter, 1777-78
New York surrenders to the British Sept., 1776
Trenton Dec., 1776
MD.
DEL.
British evacuate Philadelphia June, 1778
1775-1778
1778-1781
British surrender at Yorktown October, 1781
VA.
THE AMERICAN REVOLUTION
British invade Virginia May, 1781
N.C.
Kings Mtn. Oct., 1780
S.C.
ATLANTIC OCEAN
British capture Charleston May, 1780
GA.
British capture Savannah Dec., 1778

0   200 miles
0   300 km

MAJOR BATTLES OF THE REVOLUTION

This map shows the shift in fighting from the Northern colonies (1775–1778) to the Southern colonies (1778–1781).

The American Revolutionary War fell roughly into two periods: One from 1775 to 1778, which was marked by British victories, and the second from 1778 to 1781, which saw the war turn in the Americans' favor.

Fight for Liberty

War in the Southern Colonies

In 1778, the British developed a new military plan: attack the Southern colonies and then march northward.

War in the Southern Colonies	
Battle	**Events and Results**
Savannah, Georgia	• In December of 1778, British forces attacked Savannah, the major port of Georgia. • The attack succeeded, and the British soon took control of most of the colony.
Charleston, South Carolina	• In 1780, British forces under the command of General Charles Cornwallis sailed into the South Carolina port of Charleston and captured it. • British troops soon began the march north to capture the Carolinas. However, groups of Patriots began to attack their supply lines, as well as the Loyalists that Britain expected to control the region.
Kings Mountain, North Carolina	• Cornwallis's men reached Kings Mountain in North Carolina on October 7, 1780. • There, a few hundred Kentucky and Tennessee riflemen wiped out half of Cornwallis's army.

In the months following Kings Mountain, the British lost additional battles in the Carolinas to Americans under the command of generals Nathanael Greene and Daniel Morgan. In the end, the British were able to hold onto Savannah and Charleston but nothing else.

General Charles Cornwallis surrendered to the Americans at Yorktown. This British defeat signaled the birth of a new nation. ▶

The End of the War

By 1781, the fighting was concentrated in Virginia. The British believed that their Southern strategy was failing—Cornwallis's troops hadn't been able to control the Carolinas—and they planned to move troops back to the North.

Yorktown. After a stalemate between Cornwallis and the American force under the command of the Marquis de Lafayette, Cornwallis made camp at Yorktown, Virginia, on the Chesapeake Bay. He waited there for a British fleet to resupply him with fresh troops, ammunition, and provisions. At this point,

• Washington and his army, along with French troops commanded by Marshal Rochambeau, moved south to Virginia to attack by land.

• the French fleet arrived to blockade Chesapeake Bay, cutting off any possibility of resupply or escape by sea for the British.

Surrounded and cut off, Cornwallis and his force of over 7,000 men surrendered on October 19, 1781. Sporadic fighting continued in the colonies for the next year, but essentially the American Revolution was over.

Establishing a New Nation

The Treaty of Paris was drawn up by British representatives and the Americans Benjamin Franklin, John Adams, and John Jay. The treaty was signed on September 3, 1783. Through it, the British recognized American independence. The Americans also persuaded the British to cede their rights to the rich Ohio Valley.

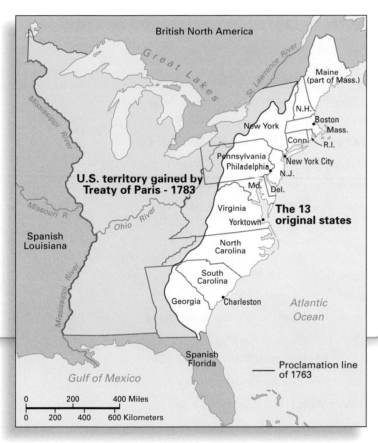

The New United States. Under the terms of the Treaty of Paris, the United States stretched from Canada to Spanish Florida and from the Atlantic coast to the Mississippi River.

AID FROM ABROAD

The Continental Congress. Vital support for the American cause came from France, Spain, and the Netherlands.

1776 to 1778: France gave the American government loans, gifts of money, and weapons.

1778: France and America signed a treaty of alliance. Thereafter, France also provided the patriots with troops and warships.

Revolutionary War Soldiers

The American Colonies entered the Revolutionary War without an army or a navy—only militia units in the various colonies. Soldiers often went without pay, food, and proper clothing because the Continental Congress was so poor.

Equipment. The flintlock musket was the chief firearm of the Revolutionary War. This diagram shows a Continental Army soldier loading a musket.

1 Release gunpowder from cartridge.

2 Pour powder into firing pan.

3, 4 Gunpowder and lead ball pushed into barrel.

5 Flintlock is cocked.

6 Ready to fire.

1779: Spain entered the war as an ally of France.

1780: The Netherlands joined the war.

The British army hired professional German soldiers, called Hessians, to aid their army.

Freedom Fighters

The events of the American Revolution created military heroes and political leaders. Some would go on to play key roles in the new nation's government and society; others would continue the fight for liberty elsewhere. Many came from the Patriots' overseas allies to aid the struggling Continental Army.

Native Americans and the Revolution

During the American Revolution, Native American tribes fought on both sides.

American: Stockbridge and Mashpee Indians (Massachusetts); Catawba Indians (South Carolina)

British: Mohawks, Senecas, Cayugas, and Onondagas (all of the Iroquois League)

Military and Political Leaders

GEORGE WASHINGTON

- Military career began in the French and Indian War (1754–1763)
- Member of the Virginia House of Burgesses (1759–1774) and the first and second Continental Congresses (1774, 1775)
- Appointed commander in chief of the American forces after the outbreak of the Revolution (1775)
- Guided the American troops until the British surrender at Yorktown (1781)
- Elected first president of the United States (1789) (See also page 88.)

JOHN ADAMS

- Public career began with protesting British colonial policies
- Served in the Continental Congresses (1774, 1775); signed the Declaration of Independence
- During the war, served as chairman of the Continental Board of War and Ordnance
- Went to France in 1778; secretly negotiated the peace treaty with Britain
- Elected second president of the United States (1797) (See also page 89.)

MARQUIS DE LAFAYETTE

- French nobleman; defied royal objections to fight with the colonists
- Barely 20 years old, he was virtually adopted by George Washington, whom he idolized
- Led the army that defeated Cornwallis at Yorktown in 1781
- During the French Revolution, became the most powerful man in France, as popular leader of the moderates and commander of the national guard (1789–1791)

THADDEUS KOSCIUSZKO

- Polish general and patriot
- Fought as a volunteer with the American colonists
- Rewarded with citizenship and the rank of brigadier general
- Returned to Poland (1784) and joined the army to fight for Polish independence from Russia

CASIMIR PULASKI

- Polish nobleman; forced into exile in 1772 for conspiring to capture the king of Poland
- Met Benjamin Franklin in France and offered to serve in the American army
- Made a brigadier general of cavalry for distinguished service at the Battle of Brandywine
- Organized an independent cavalry unit, the Pulaski Legion
- Mortally wounded at Savannah in 1779

African Americans and the Revolution

Some African Americans, hoping liberty for the country would bring liberty to them as well, supported the resistance and the Revolution.

Phillis Wheatley was the first important African-American poet. In her poetry, she praised General Washington and contrasted her status as a slave with the Colonies' call for independence.

Crispus Attucks was an African-American patriot killed in the Boston Massacre. He is thought to have been a runaway slave.

In all, about 5,000 African Americans fought on the Patriot side in the war. Many were slaves who had been promised freedom in exchange for military service.

Women and the American Revolution

Colonial women contributed to the Revolutionary War effort in many different ways.

- **New roles at home** while husbands, fathers, and brothers were away at war
- **Raised funds** for the military
- **Fought** in the army and militias—disguised as men

Martha Washington

Martha Washington, wife of George Washington, stayed with her husband and his troops during the long, harsh winter at Valley Forge.

Mercy Otis Warren wrote satirical plays about the British government to stir up support for the revolution. After the war, she wrote the three-volume *History of the Rise, Progress, and Termination of the American Revolution* (1805).

✔ The British surrender after the battle at Yorktown in Virginia in 1781 effectively ended the American Revolutionary War. The Treaty of Paris, by which the British recognized American independence, was not signed until 1783.

✔ The involvement in the Revolutionary War on the side of the Americans of such figures as the Marquis de Lafayette, from France, and Thaddeus Kosciuszko and Casimir Pulaski, from Poland, was critical to the American victory.

✔ Such heroes of the American Revolution as George Washington and John Adams later took key roles in the government of the new nation—in Washington and Adams's cases as first and second presidents, respectively.

BUILDING A NEW NATION

After the signing of the Treaty of Paris in 1783, the newly independent United States—which had been at war for 8 years—needed a way to govern itself in peacetime.

The Articles of Confederation

Shortly after adopting the Declaration of Independence in 1776, the Second Continental Congress drew up a plan of government. The Articles of Confederation were adopted by Congress on November 15, 1777, and ratified on March 1, 1781.

The Articles

- provided for the continuation of Congress, with state delegates appointed and paid by each state
- gave Congress the right to declare and carry on war and build a navy
- gave Congress the right to manage all foreign and Indian affairs
- gave Congress the right to settle interstate disputes, coin money, and create post offices

Weaknesses. The Articles attempted to balance an effective national government with the traditional independence of each state. They placed limits on the powers of Congress.

- Congress could not levy or collect taxes; it could only ask states for funds.
- Any change required a unanimous vote from all 13 states.
- This meant any one state could block a measure, even if it were supported by the other 12.

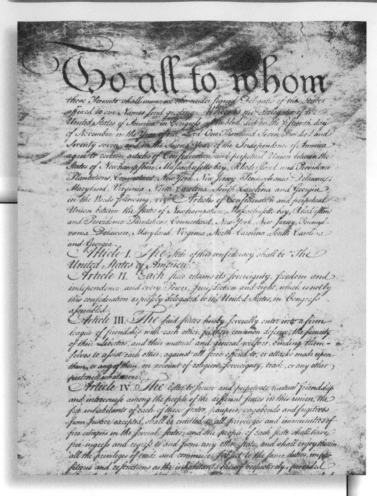

The Articles of Confederation, the first page of which is shown here, served as the plan of government both during and immediately after the Revolutionary War. They could not, however, solve many of the problems faced by the new nation.

Many national leaders, such as James Madison and Alexander Hamilton, thought that the agreement did not give Congress enough power to operate effectively.

The requirement for a unanimous vote on any amendment made the document very difficult to change for the better. Before long, Madison and Hamilton began working to establish a new plan for the nation's government.

NORTHWEST ORDINANCE

Congress did complete one major task under the Articles: managing the Northwest Territory, the land gained under the Treaty of Paris. The Northwest Ordinance of 1787 created a method for adding states to the Union.

Northwest Ordinance (1787)	
Provisions	• Allowed states into the Union when their populations reached 60,000 • Prohibited slavery in the new states (did not apply to fugitive slaves from other states, or existing slaves in the territory)
States added	Ohio (1803), Indiana (1816), Illinois (1818), Michigan (1837), and Wisconsin (1848)

THE WANDERING NATIONAL CAPITAL

Several different cities served as the nation's capital during the early years of American independence.

New York City was the temporary capital when George Washington was elected president in 1789.

Philadelphia became the capital in 1790.

Washington, D.C., the current capital, was chosen by George Washington in 1800. It was a compromise between the interests of the Northern and Southern states.

The Capitol Building, on Capitol Hill in Washington, D.C., is the building where the United States Congress meets. Congress first met there in 1800. ▼

Congress, under the Articles of Confederation, did not have enough power to settle disputes among the states or to deal with foreign affairs. In 1787, Congress called a convention to correct the weaknesses of the Articles. The outcome was the U.S. Constitution, a document that governs the country to this day.

The Constitutional Convention

In May 1787, fifty-five delegates from 11 states met in Philadelphia (Rhode Island was absent, and New Hampshire's delegates arrived later). Among them were some of the nation's most prominent leaders: George Washington (chosen to be president of the convention), James Madison, Alexander Hamilton, Benjamin Franklin, and Gouverneur Morris.

As delegates to the Constitutional Convention (1787) worked to design a new system of government, delegate James Madison declared, "In framing a system which we wish to last for ages, we should not lose sight of the changes which ages will produce." The genius of the federal government is that it has been so adaptable to changing circumstances.

The Constitution of the United States was officially adopted in Philadelphia on September 17, 1787. This image depicts many of the members of the Constitutional Convention.

Issues	Solutions
Balance of power between central and local governments	● a *Federal System*, in which the national government would share power with the state governments
Balance of power between states with large and small populations	The Connecticut Compromise (Roger Sherman): ● The House of Representatives: representation on the basis of population (large states would have more representatives than small states) ● The Senate: equal representation from each state, large or small
Slavery questions: ● Whether or not slaves would be counted in the population ● Whether Congress would have the power to outlaw the slave trade	● Only 3/5 of a state's slaves would be counted ● Congress would not be allowed to regulate the slave trade until 1808

Spotlight on... **BENJAMIN FRANKLIN**

1706–1790

A writer, scientist, and statesman, Franklin would almost certainly be on any list of the half-dozen greatest Americans.

Writer, Printer, Publisher. Franklin opened a printer's shop in Philadelphia in 1730. There, he published the *Pennsylvania Gazette*, a newspaper, and the popular *Poor Richard's Almanack*. He also authored his (unfinished) *Autobiography*.

Scientist. Franklin's inventions included the Franklin stove, bifocal eyeglasses, and a type of clock. In 1752, his famous kite experiments with electricity brought him international recognition.

Statesman. Active in colonial politics, Franklin was sent twice to represent the colonies in England (1757 and 1762). In 1775, he returned to America and helped draft the Declaration of Independence. In 1776, Franklin went to France, where his charm and wit made him immensely popular—and helped him secure France's military assistance in the Revolutionary War. Returning home, nearly 80 years old, he helped draft the U.S. Constitution.

INFLUENCES

The delegates to the Constitutional Convention relied greatly on past experience and examples.

Magna Carta (1215): an English constitutional document that limited royal power—even the king had to obey the law. (See page 462.)

Jamestown (1619): the settlement set up the first elected assembly in the New World.

State Constitutions: All American states established constitutional governments after they declared their independence from the United Kingdom in 1776.

Especially influential documents were:

- **New York Constitution,** written in 1777 by John Jay
- **Massachusetts Constitution,** written by John Adams in 1780

The Albany Plan of Union: a plan, proposed by Benjamin Franklin in 1754, to unite the 13 colonies under a central government.

fyi!

- *The youngest person to sign the Constitution was Jonathon Dayton, age 26.*
- *The oldest person to sign was Benjamin Franklin, age 81.*
- *Gouverneur Morris, a diplomat and statesman from New York, was responsible for much of the actual writing.*

Ratifying the Constitution

On September 17, 1787, the delegates adopted the Constitution. Now they had to go back to their states to convince the state governments to ratify it (vote for its adoption). Two-thirds of the states would need to ratify the Constitution before it became law.

Supporters. Support for the Constitution came from a group called the Federalists—supporters of strong central government, among other things. Alexander Hamilton, James Madison, and John Jay defended the Constitution in a series of letters called *The Federalist Papers.*

Opposition. The Constitution met with opposition in the various states, even from some prominent patriots. Many feared that a strong central government would lead to tyranny. This group eventually became known as the Anti-Federalists.

Ratification. Gradually, the states began ratifying the Constitution. Massachusetts would only ratify it after assuring that a bill of amendments would be added. (These were incorporated into the first 10 amendments, or Bill of Rights.) On June 21, 1788, the ninth state (New Hampshire) voted and made the Constitution "the supreme law of the land."

Major Opponents	Objections
Patrick Henry, Samuel Adams, Elbridge Gerry	Created too strong a central government
Thomas Jefferson	Lacked a "bill of rights" to protect citizens' personal liberties (for example, freedom of speech, press, and religion)
George Mason	Senate was potentially too aristocratic; also, lacked a bill of rights

Samuel Adams, one of the Sons of Liberty, opposed the new Constitution and joined the Anti-Federalists.

RATIFYING THE CONSTITUTION

Over 2$\frac{1}{2}$ years, all 13 states eventually approved the Constitution.

Delaware	December 7, 1787
Pennsylvania	December 12, 1787
New Jersey	December 18, 1787
Georgia	January 2, 1788
Connecticut	January 9, 1788
Massachusetts	February 6, 1788
Maryland	April 28, 1788
South Carolina	May 23, 1788
New Hampshire	June 21, 1788
Virginia	June 25, 1788
New York	July 26, 1788
North Carolina	November 21, 1789
Rhode Island	May 29, 1790

Federalism

The Constitution divided power between the central and state governments through federalism. In a federalist system, the central government and state governments share powers.

Federalists and Anti-Federalists

In 1789, a political division appeared between those who favored a strong federal government and those who opposed it. These groups came to be known as the Federalists and the Anti-Federalists—America's first political parties.

Alexander Hamilton

Thomas Jefferson

The Federalists

During the ratification of the Constitution in 1787 and 1788, a group of statesmen—Alexander Hamilton, James Madison, and John Jay—wrote a series of 85 letters to various newspapers, arguing for ratification. These letters were later collected into a book called *The Federalist*.

The Federalist Party. After the Constitution took effect, Hamilton and the other Federalists formed an official group, The Federalist Party, which

- favored a strong and active federal government.
- opposed limiting government powers strictly to those granted in the Constitution.
- supported the idea of a national bank.

The Anti-Federalists

This group included Patrick Henry, Thomas Jefferson, and George Mason. It formed first in opposition to the Constitution, and then in opposition to the policies pushed by Hamilton. The Anti-Federalist group

- wanted to limit federal power.
- supported strong state powers.
- defended the interests of farmers over the interests of commerce.

The Democratic-Republican Party. The Democratic-Republican party, headed by Thomas Jefferson (himself an Anti-Federalist), pushed many of the policies supported by Anti-Federalists.

FEDERALISM IN ACTION

Under a federalist system, federal, state, and local governments both divide up and share power and responsibility. In the United States Constitution, federal laws take precedence over state laws.

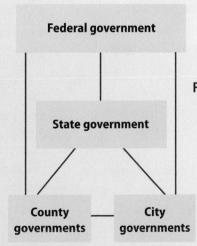

Federal government

State government

County governments — **City governments**

Functions of federal government
(broad national issues)
Regulating interstate trade
Defense

Functions of state, county, and city governments
(local matters)
Education
Safety
Welfare

Shared functions
(overlapping)
Education
Health
Raising revenues (taxes)
Welfare

The writers of the Constitution had thrown off a government they found oppressive. They were very concerned about the same oppression developing in the new nation. At the same time, they needed a government with enough power to address the needs of a large—and still growing—nation.

Principles

The Constitution aims to spell out both the responsibilities of the United States government and the structure of that government.

The purposes of the government are laid out in the Constitution's first section, or Preamble:

- "establish justice"—mediate between citizens
- "ensure domestic tranquility"—protect citizens
- "provide for the common defense"—conduct foreign affairs
- "promote the general welfare"—provide services for citizens
- "secure the blessings of liberty"—promote prosperity.

Structure

The Preamble is followed by seven sections, called Articles:

- Article I – The Legislative Branch
- Article II – The Executive Branch
- Article III – The Judicial Branch
- Article IV – Relation of the states to each other, Federal-state relations
- Article V – Amending the Constitution
- Article VI – National Debts
- Article VII – Ratifying the Constitution

Following the Articles is a section of Amendments—additions or changes to the Constitution—made since 1787.

The Constitution Since 1787

The Constitution remains effective to this day because it can be amended, or changed, to meet the nation's changing needs.

Amendments. Amendments address issues missing from the original—for example, how to fill a vacant vice president's seat (25th amendment)—or extend rights to formerly excluded groups. Among other things, constitutional amendments have:

- Granted citizenship to former slaves
- Granted the right to vote to women
- Lowered the voting age for all citizens

The Bill of Rights. The first 10 amendments to the Constitution are called the Bill of Rights. These amendments, added in 1791, protect individual liberties such as freedom of speech, religion, and the press.

ESSENTIALS OF THE CONSTITUTION

Separation of Powers. The responsibilities of the government are carefully divided among the three branches: the legislative, the executive, and the judicial.

Checks and Balances. The Constitution provides for checks and balances that offer each branch protection against the others.

- The president (executive branch) has the power of veto over acts of Congress; he or she may simply refuse to sign into law a bill Congress has passed.
- The Congress (legislative branch) may override a presidential veto, if both the House and the Senate vote to override by a two-thirds majority.
- The judiciary (judicial branch) determines the constitutionality of laws passed by Congress and signed by the president.

The ultimate check in this system is that the president, the vice president, and federal judges are subject to impeachment and removal for violation of their oaths of office. (See also page 340.)

Constitution of the United States

Preamble

We the people of the United States, in order to form a more perfect union, establish justice, insure domestic tranquility, provide for the common defense, promote the general welfare, and secure the blessings of liberty to ourselves and our posterity, do ordain and establish this Constitution for the United States of America.

Note: The titles and annotations in this column are aids to understanding. They are not part of the Constitution itself.

Article I

Section 1. All legislative powers herein granted shall be vested in a Congress of the United States, which shall consist of a Senate and House of Representatives.

The Legislative Branch

Section 2. The House of Representatives shall be composed of members chosen every second year by the people of the several States, and the electors in each State shall have the qualifications requisite for electors of the most numerous branch of the State legislature.

House of Representatives

No person shall be a Representative who shall not have attained to the age of twenty-five years, and been seven years a citizen of the United States, and who shall not, when elected, be an inhabitant of that State in which he shall be chosen.

Representatives and direct taxes shall be apportioned among the several States which may be included within this Union, according to their respective numbers, which shall be determined by adding to the whole number of free persons, including those bound to service for a term of years, and excluding Indians not taxed, three-fifths of all other persons. The actual enumeration shall be made within three years after the first meeting of the Congress of the United States, and within every subsequent term of ten years, in such manner as they shall by law direct. The number of Representatives shall not exceed one for every thirty thousand, but each State shall have at least one Representative; and until such enumeration shall be made, the State of New Hampshire shall be entitled to choose three; Massachusetts, eight; Rhode Island and Providence Plantations, one; Connecticut, five; New York, six; New Jersey, four; Pennsylvania, eight; Delaware, one; Maryland, six; Virginia, ten; North Carolina, five; South Carolina, five; and Georgia, three.

This section set up the national census to determine how many representatives in Congress each state would have. Originally, slaves and Indians were not counted "whole persons" in the census, but the 14th Amendment gave former slaves the full rights of citizenship. The number of congressmen from each state is still determined by the number of people in the state, but the total membership of the House is limited to 435.

When vacancies happen in the representation from any State, the executive authority thereof shall issue writs of election to fill such vacancies.

The House of Representatives shall choose their Speaker and other officers, and shall have the sole power of impeachment.

"Impeachment" means accusing an official of wrong conduct in office. The House of Representatives makes these charges, and the Senate acts as the court where they are tried (see Section 3).

The Constitution

Senate

Since the 17th Amendment was passed in 1913, senators have been chosen by direct popular vote, not by the legislatures.

This clause set up a system of staggered elections to the Senate. All senators now have 6-year terms, but the terms expire at different times.In one election year, only one-third of the senators are up for election; the others still have 2 or 4 more years to serve. This gives the Senate more continuity than the House, where all members are up for election every 2 years.

Since there is always an even number of senators, tie votes are possible, and so the vice president was given the power to break ties.

Congressional Elections

The 20th Amendment changed this meeting time to noon, January 3.

Procedures

Section 3. The Senate of the United States shall be composed of two Senators from each State, chosen by the legislature thereof for six years; and each Senator shall have one vote.

Immediately after they shall be assembled in consequence of the first election, they shall be divided as equally as may be into three classes. The seats of the Senators of the first class shall be vacated at the expiration of the second year, of the second class at the expiration of the fourth year, and of the third class at the expiration of the sixth year, so that one-third may be chosen every second year; and if vacancies happen by resignation, or otherwise, during the recess of the legislature of any State, the executive thereof may make temporary appointments until the next meeting of the legislature, which shall then fill such vacancies.

No person shall be a Senator who shall not have attained the age of thirty years, and been nine years a citizen of the United States, and who shall not, when elected, be an inhabitant of that State for which he shall be chosen.

The Vice President of the United States shall be President of the Senate, but shall have no vote, unless they be equally divided.

The Senate shall choose their other officers and also a President pro tempore, in the absence of the Vice President, or when he shall exercise the office of President of the United States.

The Senate shall have the sole power to try all impeachments. When sitting for that purpose, they shall be on oath or affirmation. When the President of the United States is tried, the Chief Justice shall preside; and no person shall be convicted without the concurrence of two-thirds of the members present.

Judgment in cases of impeachment shall not extend further than to removal from office, and disqualification to hold and enjoy any office of honor, trust, or profit under the United States; but the party convicted shall nevertheless be liable and subject to indictment, trial, judgment and punishment, according to law.

Section 4. The times, places, and manner of holding elections for Senators and Representatives shall be prescribed in each State by the legislature thereof; but the Congress may at any time by law make or alter such regulations, except as to the places of choosing Senators.

The Congress shall assemble at least once in every year, and such meeting shall be on the first Monday in December, unless they shall by law appoint a different day.

Section 5. Each House shall be the judge of the elections, returns, and qualifications of its own members, and a majority of each shall constitute a quorum to do business; but a smaller number may adjourn from day to day, and may be authorized to compel the attendance of absent members, in such manner, and under such penalties, as each House may provide. Each House may determine the rules of its proceedings, punish its members for disorderly behavior, and with the concurrence of two-thirds, expel a member.

Each House shall keep a journal of its proceedings, and from time to time publish the same, excepting such parts as may in their judgment require secrecy, and the yeas and nays of the members of either House on any question shall, at the desire of one-fifth of those present, be entered on the journal.

Neither House, during the session of Congress, shall, without the consent of the other adjourn for more than three days, nor to any other place than that in which the two Houses shall be sitting.

Section 6. The Senators and Representatives shall receive a compensation for their services, to be ascertained by law and paid out of the Treasury of the United States. They shall, in all cases except treason, felony, and breach of the peace, be privileged from arrest during their attendance at the session of their respective Houses, and in going to and returning from the same; and for any speech or debate in either House they shall not be questioned in any other place.

No Senator or Representative shall, during the time for which he was elected, be appointed to any civil office under the authority of the United States, which shall have been created, or the emoluments whereof shall have been increased during such time; and no person holding any office under the United States shall be a member of either House during his continuance in office.

Section 7. All bills for raising revenue shall originate in the House of Representatives; but the Senate may propose or concur with amendments as on other bills.

Every bill which shall have passed the House of Representatives and the Senate shall, before it become a law, be presented to the President of the United States; if he approve he shall sign it, but if not he shall return it, with his objections, to that House in which it shall have originated, who shall enter the objections at large on their journal and proceed to reconsider it. If after such reconsideration two-thirds of that House shall agree to pass the bill, it shall be sent, together with the objections, to the other House, by which it shall likewise be reconsidered, and if approved by two-thirds of that House, it shall become a law. But in all such cases the votes of both Houses shall be determined by yeas and nays, and the names of the persons voting for and against the bill shall be entered on the journal of each House respectively. If any bill shall not be returned by the President within ten days (Sundays excepted) after it shall have been presented to him, the same shall be a law, in like manner as if he had signed it, unless the Congress by their adjournment prevent its return, in which case it shall not be a law.

Every order, resolution or vote to which the concurrence of the Senate and House of Representatives may be necessary (except on a question of

In addition to the *Congressional Record*, which is published every day, both houses of Congress keep a record of their proceedings.

Payment and Privileges
These privileges are called "congressional immunity."

"Emoluments" are salaries. This section prevents federal officials from being members of Congress at the same time.

Relation to Executive

This section describes the president's veto power. Even if a bill has been passed by both the Senate and the House, the president can veto it, or turn it down, instead of signing it and making it a law. However, a two-thirds vote by both houses can pass the bill over his veto. Simply holding the bill when Congress is about to adjourn is a "pocket veto."

adjournment) shall be presented to the President of the United States; and before the same shall take effect shall be approved by him, or being disapproved by him, shall be repassed by two-thirds of the Senate and House of Representatives, according to the rules and limitations prescribed in the case of a bill.

Specific Powers

Section 8. The Congress shall have power to lay and collect taxes, duties, imposts and excises, to pay the debts and provide for the common defense and general welfare of the United States; but all duties, imposts and excises shall be uniform throughout the United States;

To borrow money on the credit of the United States;

To regulate commerce with foreign nations, and among the several States, and with the Indian tribes;

To establish an uniform rule of naturalization, and uniform laws on the subject of bankruptcies throughout the United States;

To coin money, regulate the value thereof, and of foreign coin, and fix the standard of weights and measures;

To provide for the punishment of counterfeiting the securities and current coin of the United States;

To establish post offices and post roads;

This section allows Congress to pass laws about patents and copyrights.

To promote the progress of science and useful arts by securing for limited times to authors and inventors the exclusive right to their respective writings and discoveries;

To constitute tribunals inferior to the Supreme Court;

To define and punish piracies and felonies committed on the high seas, and offenses against the law of nations;

Only Congress can declare war, but the president, as commander in chief, can order the armed forces to act.

To declare war, grant letters of marque and reprisal, and make rules concerning captures on land and water;

To raise and support armies, but no appropriation of money to that use shall be for a longer term than two years;

To provide and maintain a navy;

To make rules for the government and regulation of the land and naval forces;

To provide for calling forth the militia to execute the laws of the Union, suppress insurrections, and repel invasions;

To provide for organizing, arming and disciplining the militia, and for governing such part of them as may be employed in the service of the United States, reserving to the States respectively the appointment of the officers, and the authority of training the militia according to the discipline prescribed by Congress;

This gave Congress the authority to establish and govern the District of Columbia.

To exercise exclusive legislation in all cases whatsoever over such district (not exceeding ten miles square) as may, by cession of particular States and the acceptance of Congress, become the seat of the government of the United States, and to exercise like authority over all places purchased by the consent of the legislature of the State in which the same shall be, for the erection of forts, magazines, arsenals, dockyards, and other needful buildings;—And

To make all laws which shall be necessary and proper for carrying into execution the foregoing powers, and all other powers vested by this Constitution in the Government of the United States, or in any department or officer thereof.

Section 9. The migration or importation of such persons as any of the States now existing shall think proper to admit shall not be prohibited by the Congress prior to the year one thousand eight hundred and eight, but a tax or duty may be imposed on such importation, not exceeding ten dollars for each person.

The privilege of the writ of habeas corpus shall not be suspended, unless when in cases of rebellion or invasion the public safety may require it.

No bill of attainder or ex post facto law shall be passed.

No capitation or other direct tax shall be laid, unless in proportion to the census or enumeration herein before directed to be taken.

No tax or duty shall be laid on articles exported from any State.

No preference shall be given by any regulation of commerce or revenue to the ports of one State over those of another; nor shall vessels bound to or from one State be obliged to enter, clear or pay duties in another.

No money shall be drawn from the Treasury but in consequence of appropriations made by law; and a regular statement and account of the receipts and expenditures of all public money shall be published from time to time.

No title of nobility shall be granted by the United States; and no person holding any office of profit or trust under them shall, without the consent of the Congress, accept of any present, emolument, office, or title of any kind whatever from any king, prince, or foreign state.

Section 10. No State shall enter into any treaty, alliance, or confederation; grant letters of marque and reprisal; coin money; emit bills of credit; make anything but gold and silver coin a tender in payment of debts; pass any bill of attainder, ex post facto law or law impairing the obligation of contracts, or grant any title of nobility.

No State shall, without the consent of the Congress, lay any imposts or duties on imports or exports, except what may be absolutely necessary for executing its inspection laws; and the net produce of all duties and imposts, laid by any State on imports or exports, shall be for the use of the Treasury of the United States; and all such laws shall be subject to the revision and control of the Congress.

No State shall, without the consent of Congress, lay any duty of tonnage, keep troops or ships of war in time of peace, enter into any agreement or compact with another State or with a foreign power, or engage in war, unless actually invaded or in such imminent danger as will not admit of delay.

This is sometimes called the "elastic clause," as it can be interpreted to give many powers not actually mentioned in the Constitution.

Limitations on Congress
This paragraph set up a waiting period for action on the slave trade; Congress did abolish it in 1808.

Habeas corpus guards against unjust imprisonment by requiring a judge or court to decide if a person may be held.

An *ex post facto* law applies to acts committed before the law was passed. The 16th Amendment allowed the income tax, which is not related to the census.

In fact, presidents often exchange gifts with important foreign visitors, but the gifts are considered as gifts to the country.

Limitations on States

The Constitution

The Executive Branch
The President

The system for electing the president has been changed a great deal since the Constitution was written, primarily because of the rise of political parties. The so-called "electoral college" still meets, though under the 12th Amendment electors vote separately for the president and vice president. Originally, the candidate who came in second in the presidential race became vice president. Since electors now are pledged to support a party's candidates, election results are actually known before the electors meet.

The 25th Amendment (1967) makes further provisions for succession to the presidency and for cases when the president is ill.

Article II

Section 1. The executive power shall be vested in a President of the United States of America. He shall hold his office during the term of four years, and together with the Vice President, chosen for the same term, be elected as follows:

Each State shall appoint, in such manner as the legislature thereof may direct, a number of Electors, equal to the whole number of Senators and Representatives to which the State may be entitled in the Congress; but no Senator or Representative, or person holding an office of trust or profit under the United States, shall be appointed an Elector.

The Electors shall meet in their respective States and vote by ballot for two persons, of whom one at least shall not be an inhabitant of the same State with themselves. And they shall make a list of all the persons voted for, and of the number of votes for each; which list they shall sign and certify, and transmit sealed to the seat of the government of the United States, directed to the President of the Senate. The President of the Senate shall, in the presence of the Senate and House of Representatives, open all the certificates, and the votes shall then be counted. The person having the greatest number of votes shall be the President, if such number be a majority of the whole number of Electors appointed; and if there be more than one who have such majority, and have an equal number of votes, then the House of Representatives shall immediately choose by ballot one of them for President; and if no person have a majority, then from the five highest on the list the said House shall in like manner choose the President. But in choosing the President the votes shall be taken by States, the representation from each State having one vote; a quorum for this purpose shall consist of a member or members from two-thirds of the States, and a majority of all the States shall be necessary to a choice. In every case, after the choice of the President, the person having the greatest number of votes of the Electors shall be the Vice President. But if there should remain two or more who have equal votes, the Senate shall choose from them by ballot the Vice President.

The Congress may determine the time of choosing the Electors and the day on which they shall give their votes, which day shall be the same throughout the United States.

No person except a natural-born citizen, or a citizen of the United States at the time of the adoption of this Constitution, shall be eligible to the office of President; neither shall any person be eligible to that office who shall not have attained to the age of thirty-five years, and been fourteen years a resident within the United States.

In case of the removal of the President from office, or of his death, resignation, or inability to discharge the powers and duties of the said office, the same shall devolve on the Vice President, and the Congress may by law provide for the case of removal, death, resignation, or inability, both of the President and Vice President, declaring what officer shall then act as President, and such officer shall act accordingly until the disability be removed or a President shall be elected.

The President shall, at stated times, receive for his services a compensation, which shall neither be increased nor diminished during the period for which he shall have been elected, and he shall not receive within that period any other emolument from the United States or any of them.

Before he enter on the execution of his office he shall take the following oath or affirmation:

"I do solemnly swear (or affirm) that I will faithfully execute the office of President of the United States, and will to the best of my ability preserve, protect, and defend the Constitution of the United States"

Section 2. The President shall be Commander-in-Chief of the Army and Navy of the United States, and of the militia of the several States when called into the actual service of the United States; he may require the opinion, in writing, of the principal officer in each of the executive departments, upon any subject relating to the duties of their respective offices, and he shall have power to grant reprieves and pardons for offenses against the United States, except in cases of impeachment.

He shall have power, by and with the advice and consent of the Senate, to make treaties, provided two-thirds of the Senators present concur; and he shall nominate, and, by and with the advice and consent of the Senate, shall appoint ambassadors, other public ministers and consuls, judges of the Supreme Court, and all other officers of the United States whose appointments are not herein otherwise provided for, and which shall be established by law; but the Congress may by law vest the appointment of such inferior officers, as they think proper, in the President alone, in the courts of law, or in the heads of departments.

The President shall have power to fill up all vacancies that may happen during the recess of the Senate, by granting commissions which shall expire at the end of their next session.

Section 3. He shall from time to time give to the Congress information of the state of the Union, and recommend to their consideration such measures as he shall judge necessary and expedient; he may, on extraordinary occasions, convene both Houses, or either of them, and in case of disagreement between them with respect to the time of adjournment, he may adjourn them to such time as he shall think proper; he shall receive ambassadors and other public ministers; he shall take care that the laws be faithfully executed, and shall commission all the officers of the United States.

Section 4. The President, Vice President and all civil officers of the United States shall be removed from office on impeachment for and conviction of treason, bribery, or other high crimes and misdemeanors.

Presidential Powers

This is the only mention of the cabinet made in the Constitution; the first three cabinet secretaries—state, treasury, and war—were named in 1789.

The Senate must approve presidential appointments to important posts, such as cabinet members, ambassadors, and Supreme Court justices.

Relation to Congress

The president traditionally delivers the "State of the Union" message at the start of each session of Congress. He can suggest legislation at any time.

Impeachment

All federal judges are appointed for life and can be removed only by impeachment and conviction or by resigning.

The Judicial Branch
Courts

Jurisdiction

Certain kinds of cases are taken directly to the Supreme Court. The Court can also review cases that have been tried in other federal or state courts.

Treason

Relations Between the States
Full Faith and Credit

Contracts and other legal documents written in one state are valid in all other states.

Other Obligations

Extradition is the process by which a fugitive from justice in one state is handed over to the state in which the crime was committed.

Article III

Section 1. The judicial power of the United States shall be vested in one Supreme Court, and in such inferior courts as the Congress may from time to time ordain and establish. The judges, both of the Supreme and inferior courts, shall hold their offices during good behavior, and shall, at stated times, receive for their services a compensation, which shall not be diminished during their continuance in office.

Section 2. The judicial power shall extend to all cases, in law and equity, arising under this Constitution, the laws of the United States, and treaties made, or which shall be made, under their authority; to all cases affecting ambassadors, other public ministers, and consuls; to all cases of admiralty and maritime jurisdiction; to controversies to which the United States shall be a party; to controversies between two or more States; between a State and citizens of another State; between citizens of different States; between citizens of the same State claiming lands under grants of different States, and between a State, or the citizens thereof, and foreign states, citizens, or subjects.

In all cases affecting ambassadors, other public ministers and consuls, and those in which a State shall be party, the Supreme Court shall have original jurisdiction. In all the other cases before mentioned the Supreme Court shall have appellate jurisdiction, both as to law and fact, with such exceptions and under such regulations as the Congress shall make.

The trial of all crimes, except in cases of impeachment, shall be by jury; and such trial shall be held in the State where the said crimes shall have been committed; but when not committed within any State, the trial shall be at such place or places as the Congress may by law have directed.

Section 3. Treason against the United States shall consist only in levying war against them, or in adhering to their enemies, giving them aid and comfort. No person shall be convicted of treason unless on the testimony of two witnesses to the same overt act, or on confession in open court.

The Congress shall have power to declare the punishment of treason, but no attainder of treason shall work corruption of blood or forfeiture except during the life of the person attainted.

Article IV

Section 1. Full faith and credit shall be given in each State to the public acts, records, and judicial proceedings of every other State. And the Congress may by general laws prescribe the manner in which such acts, records, and proceedings shall be proved, and the effect thereof.

Section 2. The citizens of each State shall be entitled to all privileges and immunities of citizens in the several States.

A person charged in any State with treason, felony, or other crime, who shall flee from justice, and be found in another State, shall, on demand of the executive authority of the State from which he fled, be delivered up, to be removed to the State having jurisdiction of the crime.

No person held to service or labor in one State, under the laws thereof, escaping into another, shall, in consequence of any law or regulation therein, be discharged from such service or labor, but shall be delivered up on claim of the party to whom such service or labor may be due.

Section 3. New States may be admitted by the Congress into this Union; but no new State shall be formed or erected within the jurisdiction of any other State; nor any State be formed by the junction of two or more States or parts of States, without the consent of the legislatures of the States concerned as well as of the Congress.

The Congress shall have power to dispose of and make all needful rules and regulations respecting the territory or other property belonging to the United States; and nothing in this Constitution shall be so construed as to prejudice any claims of the United States or of any particular State.

Section 4. The United States shall guarantee to every State in this Union a republican form of government, and shall protect each of them against invasion, and on application of the legislature, or of the executive (when the legislature cannot be convened) against domestic violence.

Article V
The Congress, whenever two-thirds of both Houses shall deem it necessary, shall propose amendments to this Constitution, or, on the application of the legislatures of two-thirds of the several States, shall call a convention for proposing amendments, which, in either case shall be valid to all intents and purposes as part of this Constitution, when ratified by the legislatures of three-fourths of the several States, or by conventions in three-fourths thereof, as the one or the other mode of ratification may be proposed by the Congress; provided that no amendment which may be made prior to the year one thousand eight hundred and eight shall in any manner affect the first and fourth clauses in the Ninth Section of the First Article; and that no State, without its consent shall be deprived of its equal suffrage in the Senate.

Article VI
All debts contracted and engagements entered into, before the adoption of this Constitution, shall be as valid against the United States under this Constitution as under the Confederation.

This Constitution, and the laws of the United States which shall be made in pursuance thereof, and all treaties made, or which shall be made, under the authority of the United States, shall be the supreme law of the land; and the judges in every State shall be bound thereby, anything in the constitution or laws of any State to the contrary notwithstanding.

The Senators and Representatives before mentioned and the members

This paragraph provided that runaway slaves should be returned; the 13th Amendment abolished slavery.

New States

Federal Guarantees

Constitutional Amendments

Federal Supremacy
John Marshall, first chief justice, gave broad interpretations to many sections of the Constitution during his tenure from 1801 to 1835. He interpreted this clause to mean that the Supreme Court had the power to review the constitutionality of acts of Congress, since, as stated here, the Constitution is the "supreme law of the land."

The Constitution

of the several State legislatures, and all executive and judicial officers both of the United States and of the several States, shall be bound by oath or affirmation to support this Constitution; but no religious test shall ever be required as a qualification to any office or public trust under the United States.

Ratification

The Constitution was signed by 39 delegates to the Constitutional Convention, representing 12 of the 13 colonies—all except Rhode Island.

Article VII

The ratification of the conventions of nine States shall be sufficient for the establishment of this Constitution between the States so ratifying the same.

Done in convention by the unanimous consent of the States present, the seventeenth day of September in the year of our Lord one thousand seven hundred and eighty-seven, and of the independence of the United States of America the twelfth. In witness whereof we have hereunto subscribed our names.

The Bill of Rights (1791)

The first 10 amendments to the Constitution were proposed—and adopted—together at the request of the states. This Bill of Rights has become an integral part of the Constitution, and its guarantees to individuals are still significant today.

Amendments to the Constitution

The conventions of a number of the States having, at the time of their adopting the Constitution, expressed a desire, in order to prevent misconstruction or abuse of its powers, that further declaratory and restrictive clauses should be added, and as extending the ground of public confidence in the Government will best insure the beneficent ends of its institution;

Resolved, by the Senate and House of Representatives of the United States of America, in Congress assembled, two-thirds of both Houses concurring, that the following articles be proposed to the Legislatures of the several States, as amendments to the Constitution of the United States; all or any of which articles, when ratified by three-fourths of the said Legislatures, to be valid to all intents and purposes as part of the said Constitution, namely:

Freedom of Religion, Speech, Press, Assembly, and Petition

Amendment 1. Congress shall make no law respecting an establishment of religion, or prohibiting the free exercise thereof; or abridging the freedom of speech or of the press; or the right of the people peaceably to assemble, and to petition the government for a redress of grievances.

Right to Bear Arms

This amendment is often cited by those opposed to gun-control laws.

Amendment 2. A well-regulated militia, being necessary to the security of a free State, the right of the people to keep and bear arms shall not be infringed.

Quartering Soldiers

Amendment 3. No soldier shall, in time of peace, be quartered in any house without the consent of the owner, nor in time of war, but in a manner to be prescribed by law.

Searches and Seizures

Police and other officials must have ▶

Amendment 4. The right of the people to be secure in their persons, houses, papers, and effects, against unreasonable searches and seizures, shall not be violated, and no warrants shall issue but upon probable cause, supported by oath or affirmation, and particularly describing the place to be searched, and the persons or things to be seized.

Amendment 5. No person shall be held to answer for a capital, or otherwise infamous crime, unless on a presentment or indictment of a grand jury, except in cases arising in the land or naval forces, or in the militia, when in actual service in time of war or public danger; nor shall any person be subject for the same offense to be twice put in jeopardy of life or limb; nor shall be compelled in any criminal case to be a witness against himself, nor be deprived of life, liberty, or property, without due process of law; nor shall private property be taken for public use without just compensation.

Amendment 6. In all criminal prosecutions, the accused shall enjoy the right to a speedy and public trial, by an impartial jury of the State and district wherein the crime shall have been committed, which district shall have been previously ascertained by law, and to be informed of the nature and cause of the accusation; to be confronted with the witnesses against him; to have compulsory process for obtaining witnesses in his favor, and to have the assistance of counsel for his defense.

Amendment 7. In suits at common law, where the value in controversy shall exceed twenty dollars, the right of trial by jury shall be preserved, and no fact tried by a jury shall be otherwise re-examined in any court of the United States, than according to the rules of the common law.

Amendment 8. Excessive bail shall not be required, nor excessive fines imposed, nor cruel and unusual punishments inflicted.

Amendment 9. The enumeration in the Constitution of certain rights shall not be construed to deny or disparage others retained by the people.

Amendment 10. The powers not delegated to the United States by the Constitution, nor prohibited by it to the States, are reserved to the States respectively, or to the people.

Amendment 11. The judicial power of the United States shall not be construed to extend to any suit in law or equity, commenced or prosecuted against one of the United States by citizens of another State, or by citizens or subjects of any foreign state.

Amendment 12. The Electors shall meet in their respective States and vote by ballot for President and Vice President, one of whom, at least, shall not be an inhabitant of the same state with themselves; they shall name in their ballots the person voted for as President, and in distinct bal-

Rights of Defendants
Several legal protections are included here—the need for a grand jury hearing; protection against "double jeopardy"; and the right not to testify against oneself in a trial or hearing. The right of the government to take private property for public use is called the "right of eminent domain."

Jury in Criminal Cases
A 1963 Supreme Court decision ruled that the basic constitutional right to legal counsel in felony cases applies whether or not the accused person can afford a lawyer. If the accused cannot, the court must appoint a lawyer.

Jury in Civil Cases

Excessive Penalties

Other Rights
Amendments 9 and 10 protect against a too-powerful federal government.

Suits Against States (1795)

Presidential Elections (1804)
This amendment changed the election process so that electors voted separately for president and vice president.

specific search warrants when they make investigations of people, homes, or private property.

lots the person voted for as Vice President, and they shall make distinct lists of all persons voted for as President and of all persons voted for as Vice President, and of the number of votes for each; which lists they shall sign and certify, and transmit sealed to the seat of the government of the United States, directed to the President of the Senate. The President of the Senate shall, in the presence of the Senate and House of Representatives, open all the certificates and the votes shall then be counted. The person having the greatest number of votes for President shall be the President, if such number be a majority of the whole number of Electors appointed; and if no person have such majority, then from the persons having the highest numbers not exceeding three on the list of those voted for as President, the House of Representatives shall choose immediately, by ballot, the President. But in choosing the President the votes shall be taken by States, the representation from each State having one vote; a quorum for this purpose shall consist of a member or members from two-thirds of the States, and a majority of all the States shall be necessary to a choice. And if the House of Representatives shall not choose a President whenever the right of choice shall devolve upon them, before the fourth day of March next following, then the Vice President shall act as President, as in case of the death or other constitutional disability of the President.

The person having the greatest number of votes as Vice President shall be the Vice President, if such number be a majority of the whole number of Electors appointed; and if no person have a majority, then from the two highest numbers on the list the Senate shall choose the Vice President; a quorum for the purpose shall consist of two-thirds of the whole number of Senators, and a majority of the whole number shall be necessary to a choice. But no person constitutionally ineligible to the office of President shall be eligible to that of Vice President of the United States.

Abolition of Slavery (1865)

The 13th and 14th Amendments were added after the Civil War. The 13th abolished slavery in the United States. The 14th gave the rights of citizenship to former slaves.

Amendment 13

Section 1. Neither slavery nor involuntary servitude, except as a punishment for crime whereof the party shall have been duly convicted, shall exist within the United States, or any place subject to their jurisdiction.

Section 2. Congress shall have power to enforce this article by appropriate legislation.

Rights of Citizens (1868)

This section extends Bill of Rights protection to matters under state jurisdiction. It is the basis for important court decisions and legislation protecting civil rights of minorities.

Amendment 14

Section 1. All persons born or naturalized in the United States, and subject to the jurisdiction thereof, are citizens of the United States and of the State wherein they reside. No State shall make or enforce any law which shall abridge the privileges or immunities of citizens of the United States; nor shall any State deprive any person of life, liberty, or property, without due process of law; nor deny to any person within its jurisdiction the equal protection of the laws.

Section 2. Representatives shall be apportioned among the several States according to their respective numbers, counting the whole number of persons in each State, excluding Indians not taxed. But when the right to vote at any election for the choice of Electors for President and Vice President of the United States, Representatives in Congress, the executive and judicial officers of a State, or the members of the legislature thereof, is denied to any of the male inhabitants of such State, being twenty-one years of age, and citizens of the United States, or in any way abridged except for participation in rebellion or other crime, the basis of representation therein shall be reduced in the proportion which the number of such male citizens shall bear to the whole number of male citizens twenty-one years of age in such State.

This section gave the right to vote to black men; the 19th Amendment allowed women to vote; the 26th lowered the voting age to 18.

Section 3. No person shall be a Senator or Representative in Congress, or elector of President and Vice President, or hold any office, civil or military, under the United States or under any State, who, having previously taken an oath as a member of Congress, or as an officer of the United States, or as a member of any State legislature, or as an executive or judicial officer of any State, to support the Constitution of the United States, shall have engaged in insurrection or rebellion against the same, or given aid or comfort to the enemies thereof. But Congress may, by a vote of two-thirds of each House, remove such disability.

The idea of this clause was to keep former Confederate officials out of the federal government. Special acts of Congress later allowed some to serve.

Section 4. The validity of the public debt of the United States, authorized by law, including debts incurred for payment of pensions and bounties for services in suppressing insurrection or rebellion, shall not be questioned. But neither the United States nor any State shall assume or pay any debt or obligation incurred in aid of insurrection or rebellion against the United States, or any claim for the loss or emancipation of any slave; but all such debts, obligations, and claims shall be held illegal and void.

This clause forbade both the federal government and the states to pay any debt the Confederacy owed.

Section 5. The Congress shall have the power to enforce, by appropriate legislation, the provisions of this article.

Amendment 15
Section 1. The right of citizens of the United States to vote shall not be denied or abridged by the United States or by any State on account of race, color, or previous condition of servitude.

Black Voting Rights (1870)
This amendment was added to strengthen the 14th Amendment.

Section 2. The Congress shall have power to enforce this article by appropriate legislation.

Amendment 16
The Congress shall have power to lay and collect taxes on incomes, from whatever source derived, without apportionment among the several States, and without regard to any census or enumeration.

Income Taxes (1913)
An amendment to allow an income tax was needed because the Constitution did not allow any direct tax.

The Constitution

Senatorial Elections (1913)

Prohibition (1919)
The Prohibition amendment was ineffective and so was repealed in 1933 by the 21st Amendment.

Women's Suffrage (1920)

Terms of Office (1933)
This is known as the "lame duck" amendment because it shortened the time between congressmen's elections and the date that they took office. "Lame ducks" were defeated members who, under the old system, remained in Congress long after being defeated in an election.

Amendment 17
Section 1. The Senate of the United States shall be composed of two Senators from each State, elected by the people thereof, for six years; and each Senator shall have one vote. The electors in each State shall have the qualifications requisite for electors of the most numerous branch of the State legislatures.

Section 2. When vacancies happen in the representation of any State in the Senate, the executive authority of such State shall issue writs of election to fill such vacancies: Provided, that the legislature of any State may empower the executive thereof to make temporary appointments until the people fill the vacancies by election as the legislature may direct.

Section 3. This amendment shall not be so construed as to affect the election or term of any Senator chosen before it becomes valid as part of the Constitution.

Amendment 18
Section 1. After one year from the ratification of this article the manufacture, sale or transportation of intoxicating liquors within, the importation thereof into, or the exportation thereof from the United States and all territory subject to the jurisdiction thereof, for beverage purposes, is hereby prohibited.

Section 2. The Congress and the several States shall have concurrent power to enforce this article by appropriate legislation.

Section 3. This article shall be inoperative unless it shall have been ratified as an amendment to the Constitution by the legislatures of the several States, as provided in the Constitution, within seven years from the date of the submission hereof to the States by the Congress.

Amendment 19
Section 1. The right of citizens of the United States to vote shall not be denied or abridged by the United States or by any State on account of sex.

Section 2. Congress shall have power to enforce this article by appropriate legislation.

Amendment 20
Section 1. The terms of the President and Vice President shall end at noon on the 20th day of January, and the terms of Senators and Representatives at noon on the 3d day of January, of the years in which such terms would have ended if this article had not been ratified; and the terms of their successors shall then begin.

Section 2. The Congress shall assemble at least once in every year, and such meeting shall begin at noon on the 3d day of January, unless they shall by law appoint a different day.

Section 3. If, at the time fixed for the beginning of the term of the President, the President-elect shall have died, the Vice President-elect shall become President. If a President shall not have been chosen before the time fixed for the beginning of his term or if the President-elect shall have failed to qualify, then the Vice President-elect shall act as President until a President shall have qualified; and the Congress may by law provide for the case wherein neither a President-elect nor a Vice President shall have qualified, declaring who shall then act as President, or the manner in which one who is to act shall be selected, and such person shall act accordingly until a President or Vice President shall have qualified.

Section 4. The Congress may by law provide for the case of the death of any of the persons from whom the House of Representatives may choose a President whenever the right of choice shall have devolved upon them, and for the case of the death of any of the persons from whom the Senate may choose a Vice President whenever the right of choice shall have devolved upon them.

Section 5. Sections 1 and 2 shall take effect on the 15th day of October following the ratification of this article.

Section 6. This article shall be inoperative unless it shall have been ratified as an amendment to the Constitution by the legislatures of three-fourths of the several States within seven years from the date of its submission.

Amendment 21
Section 1. The eighteenth article of amendment to the Constitution of the United States is hereby repealed.

Repeal of Prohibition (1933)

Section 2. The transportation or importation into any State, territory, or possession of the United States for delivery or use therein of intoxicating liquors, in violation of the laws thereof, is hereby prohibited.

Section 3. This article shall be inoperative unless it shall have been ratified as an amendment to the Constitution by conventions in the several States, as provided in the Constitution, within seven years from the date of the submission hereof to the States by the Congress.

Amendment 22
Section 1. No person shall be elected to the office of President more than twice, and no person who has held the office of President, or acted as

Presidential Terms (1951)
This amendment was passed after the death of Franklin D. Roosevelt, ▶

who had been elected four times. Its purpose was to prevent subsequent presidents from serving more than two terms.

President, for more than two years of a term to which some other person was elected President shall be elected to the office of President more than once. But this Article shall not apply to any person holding the office of President when this Article was proposed by Congress, and shall not prevent any person who may be holding the office of President, or acting as President, during the term within which this Article becomes operative from holding the office of President or acting as President during the remainder of such term.

Section 2. This article shall be inoperative unless it shall have been ratified as an amendment to the Constitution by the legislatures of three-fourths of the several States within seven years from the date of its submission to the States by the Congress.

District of Columbia Voting Rights (1961)

Before this amendment, residents of the District of Columbia could not vote.

Amendment 23

Section 1. The District constituting the seat of Government of the United States shall appoint in such manner as Congress may direct:

A number of electors of President and Vice President equal to the whole number of Senators and Representatives in Congress to which the District would be entitled if it were a State, but in no event more than the least populous State; they shall be in addition to those appointed by the States, but they shall be considered, for the purposes of the election of President and Vice-President, to be electors appointed by a State; and they shall meet in the District and perform such duties as provided by the twelfth article of amendment.

Section 2. The Congress shall have power to enforce this article by appropriate legislation.

Poll Tax Prohibited (1964)

Poll taxes had been used to prevent or discourage black voters from registering or voting.

Amendment 24

Section 1. The right of citizens of the United States to vote in any primary or other election for President or Vice President, for electors for President or Vice President, or for Senator or Representative in Congress, shall not be denied or abridged by the United States or any State by reason of failure to pay poll tax or other tax.

Section 2. The Congress shall have power to enforce this article by appropriate legislation.

Presidential Succession (1967)

Amendment 25

Section 1. In case of the removal of the President from office or of his death or resignation, the Vice President shall become President.

Section 2. Whenever there is a vacancy in the office of the Vice President, the President shall nominate a Vice President who shall take office upon confirmation by a majority vote of both Houses of Congress.

Section 3. Whenever the President transmits to the President pro tempore of the Senate and the Speaker of the House of Representatives his written declaration that he is unable to discharge the powers and duties of his office, and until he transmits to them a written declaration to the contrary, such powers and duties shall be discharged by the Vice President as Acting President.

Section 4. Whenever the Vice President and a majority of either the principal officers of the executive departments or of such other body as Congress may by law provide, transmit to the President pro tempore of the Senate and the Speaker of the House of Representatives their written declaration that the President is unable to discharge the powers and duties of his office, the Vice President shall immediately assume the powers and duties of the office as Acting President.

Thereafter, when the President transmits to the President pro tempore of the Senate and the Speaker of the House of Representatives his written declaration that no inability exists, he shall resume the powers and duties of his office unless the Vice President and a majority of either the principal officers of the executive department or of such other body as Congress may by law provide, transmit within four days to the President pro tempore of the Senate and the Speaker of the House of Representatives their written declaration that the President is unable to discharge the powers and duties of his office. Thereupon Congress shall decide the issue, assembling within forty-eight hours for that purpose if not in session. If the Congress, within twenty-one days after receipt of the latter written declaration, or, if Congress is not in session, within twenty-one days after Congress is required to assemble, determines by two-thirds vote of both Houses that the President is unable to discharge the powers and duties of his office, the Vice President shall continue to discharge the same as Acting President; otherwise, the President shall resume the powers and duties of his office.

Amendment 26

Voting Age (1971)

Section 1. The right of citizens of the United States, who are eighteen years of age or older, to vote shall not be denied or abridged by the United States or by any State on account of age.

Section 2. The Congress shall have power to enforce this article by appropriate legislation.

Amendment 27

Congressional Salaries (1992)

No law varying the compensation for the services of the Senators and Representatives shall take effect, until an election of representatives shall have intervened.

The New Economy

The Revolutionary War had left the United States government deeply in debt, both to American citizens and to foreign governments. The nation also needed many costly internal improvements—roads, for example. Different leaders disagreed on how to solve these problems.

Economics in the Constitution

The Constitution provided some guidance for managing the nation's economy. For example, it called for the government to coin (or print) a national currency and collect taxes.

In the first years of the new government, however, Alexander Hamilton (then Secretary of the Treasury) and Thomas Jefferson (then Secretary of State) were split on how the government could influence economics and banking.

Hamilton: The ability to levy new taxes and establish a national bank fell under the Constitution's "implied powers."

Jefferson: Since the Constitution did not mention a national bank, the federal government could not create one.

Another Rebellion. This 19th-century illustration depicts whiskey-tax protestors parading a tarred and feathered tax collector before the mob. ▼

The U.S. Economy

- The United States economy developed as a mixed, but basically free-market, economy. (See page 361.)

- Decisions relating to production and pricing are left to the private sector—businesses and individuals.

- However, the government will intervene when the system does not act in the best interests of society as a whole.

- Many people disagree on the amount of influence the government should have on the U.S. economy.

WHISKEY REBELLION

Political leaders such as Jefferson, Adams, and Hamilton weren't the only people to disagree over the government's role in the economy—the public also resisted some of the changes.

In 1791, a new law was passed, allowing the government to tax whiskey makers. Frontier farmers in Pennsylvania and elsewhere assembled quickly to protest the law and threatened tax inspectors.

- In the summer of 1794, the federal government ordered the arrest of the Pennsylvania ringleaders.

- Rebel farmers in western Pennsylvania prevented the arrests.

- The rebels exchanged gunfire with government representatives, burned property of tax inspectors, and marched on Pittsburgh.

- Several people were killed and wounded before President George Washington raised an army of nearly 13,000 soldiers who put down the rebellion. Two rebels were convicted of treason, but they were later pardoned.

Spotlight on... **ALEXANDER HAMILTON**

1755–1804

Born in the West Indies, he was sent by his family to study in New York. Hamilton played many different roles in the early years of the United States and was known for his intelligence. He died tragically in a duel with Aaron Burr (see below).

Founding Father

- George Washington's aide, 1777–1781
- Delegate to the Constitutional Convention
- One of the authors of *The Federalist Papers*, an essay series defending the Constitution

Secretary of the Treasury

- First to hold the position
- Established the First Bank of the United States

The First Bank of the United States, proposed by Alexander Hamilton, was founded in 1791, despite Jefferson's objections.

THE HAMILTON-BURR DUEL

In 1795, Alexander Hamilton resigned from his position as Secretary of the Treasury, but he did not abandon politics entirely. In the end, a political disagreement would lead to his death.

Hamilton's policies often clashed with those of Thomas Jefferson. For a time, the two men struggled bitterly to drive each other from the cabinet. In the 1800 election, Burr and Jefferson tied for the presidency, and the U.S. House of Representatives had to break the tie. Ironically, because he hated Aaron Burr more, Hamilton was forced to support Jefferson for president in 1800.

Burr and Hamilton clashed again when Burr ran for governor of New York in 1804. Hamilton opposed him, criticizing his character. Charging slander, Burr challenged Hamilton to a duel. Hamilton accepted, was mortally wounded with one shot, and died the following day.

▲ **Duel to the Death.** On July 11, 1804, Aaron Burr and Alexander Hamilton faced each other with pistols in Weehawken, New Jersey. Hamilton was killed; Burr's reputation never fully recovered.

A New Jersey grand jury indicted Burr for murder, but he was never arrested. He presided over the Senate as vice president until his term ended. Later, he recruited a group of men to detach part of the country's southwestern frontier or to invade Mexico. He was tried for treason but acquitted.

EARLY PRESIDENTS

The presidents of the United States are the only officials who are elected by all the people of the country. From the beginning, presidents have had considerable prestige and power, especially in times of national crisis. Four early presidents—George Washington, John Adams, Thomas Jefferson, and James Monroe—set precedents for decision-making and use of executive power that are heeded even today.

Spotlight on... GEORGE WASHINGTON

1732–1799

- Born in Westmoreland County, Virginia, the son of a planter
- Educated at home; worked briefly as a surveyor and a militia officer
- Served in the French and Indian War
- His family estate, Mount Vernon, was his proudest possession
- Married Martha Custis in 1759

Washington and Adams

George Washington

In three important ways, George Washington helped shape the United States. First, he commanded the Continental Army that won American independence from Britain in the Revolutionary War. Second, he served as president of the convention that wrote the United States Constitution. Third, he was elected the first president of the United States.

Presidency (1789–1797). On February 4 (the first Wednesday in February), 1789, the Electoral College chose Washington as president of the United States and John Adams as vice president. They took office on April 30.

Influence. Washington's administration set several important precedents.

- Stepping down after two terms (tradition broken only by Franklin D. Roosevelt in 1940)
- Appointing a cabinet
- Giving an inaugural address

In his Farewell Address (1796), Washington also urged the country to avoid political parties; however, this advice would not be followed.

Challenges. Washington's two administrations faced both domestic and foreign challenges.

Domestic	Foreign
• Heavy debts from the costs of the Revolutionary War. • Whiskey Rebellion (1794): Farmers and distillers revolt against Hamilton's new tax on liquor manufacturers. Washington sends troops, ending the rebellion and reinforcing federal authority.	• Conflict between France and Britain; U.S. attempted to stay neutral. • Harassment of U.S. shipping by the French and British. • Impressment of U.S. sailors by the British. • French minister to the U.S., Edmond Genêt, undermines U.S. neutrality by organizing expeditions against British territories.

John Adams

John Adams guided the young United States through some of its most serious troubles. He served under George Washington as the first vice president and followed him as the second president.

Presidency (1797–1801). In 1797, John Adams, a Federalist, became president. He continued Washington's negotiations with foreign governments—especially France, which had broken off diplomatic relations with the U.S. after the Jay Treaty (1794). By this time, the U.S. had two political parties: the Federalists and the Democratic-Republicans.

Major Events	Causes and Details	Effects
XYZ Affair	• Adams sent diplomats to France. Talleyrand, the French minister of foreign affairs, refused to see them. • Talleyrand sent three French agents (referred to only as X, Y, and Z) to bribe the U.S. into a peaceful settlement.	• The Federalists demanded that the U.S. declare war on France. • Navy Department established in 1798. • 1778 alliance with France repealed. • Undeclared naval war began.
Alien and Sedition Acts	• **Alien Act:** Deportation for any potentially threatening foreigner. • **Sedition Act:** Fines and imprisonment for anyone opposing government measures. • **Naturalization Act:** 14 years of residency for citizenship. • **Alien Enemies Act:** Prison or deportation for alien subjects of an enemy nation in time of war.	• The Democratic-Republicans accused the Federalists of a "reign of terror." • Kentucky and Virginia passed resolutions in 1798 denying the federal government any powers not explicitly given by the Constitution.

Spotlight on...

JOHN ADAMS

1735–1826

- Born in Braintree (now Quincy), Massachusetts
- Began his public career working for American independence
- Initially Thomas Jefferson's political enemy; later, the two would become friendly
- Married to Abigail Smith
- Died on July 4, 1826—the same day as Thomas Jefferson

THE WORLD OF ADAMS

During John Adams's presidency...

1799
- The first organized strike—by Philadelphia shoemakers—in the United States took place.
- Napoleon began to rule France as a dictator.

1800
- The Library of Congress was established.
- The federal government moved to Washington, D.C., from Philadelphia.

Jefferson and Monroe

Thomas Jefferson

In the presidential election of 1800, Federalist John Adams was defeated by Thomas Jefferson, and the Democratic-Republicans took over. Jefferson was a firm believer in limited government and was in constant conflict with Federalist leader Alexander Hamilton over the government's power. (See page 67.)

Presidency (1801–1809). Jefferson's first term was a time of growth and prosperity. The United States increased greatly in size, and its economy expanded. Before his second term was over, however, conflict overseas nearly pushed the nation into war.

THE WORLD OF JEFFERSON

1803
- Dalton's Theory of the Atom, one of the foundations of chemistry, was developed.

1804
- Napoleon crowned himself emperor of France.
- Richard Trevithick, an English engineer, invented the steam-powered locomotive.

1807
- American inventor Robert Fulton began the first successful steamboat service.

Spotlight on... THOMAS JEFFERSON

1743–1826
- Designed the Virginia Capitol, the University of Virginia, and his home at Monticello
- His library was the basis of the Library of Congress
- Wrote the first draft of the Declaration of Independence
- Served as vice president under John Adams

Major Events	Causes and Details	Effects
Tripolitan War (1801–1805)	• Tripoli (a Barbary State on the coast of north Africa) demanded increased tributes to protect American ships in the Mediterranean. • Jefferson refused to pay and blockaded the Tripoli port; war followed.	• A peace settlement ended the tributes to Tripoli. • The U.S. paid tribute to other Barbary States until 1815.
The Louisiana Purchase (1803)	• Napoleon offered to sell the vast area between the Mississippi River and the Rocky Mountains for only $15 million. • In 1810, West Florida was also annexed.	• The U.S. doubled in size. • Congress extended the Mississippi Territory and created the Michigan and Illinois territories.
Embargo Act (1807)	• Britain and France had interfered with American ships for years. • The Embargo Act forbade American ships to call on foreign ports.	• The Act hurt American traders and did not stop British and French interference. • Trade resumed with all nations except Britain and France in 1809.

Major Events	Causes and Details	Effects
"The American System"	• In 1817, Congress passed a bill to help finance the construction of "a perfect system of roads and canals." • The Erie Canal was approved by the New York legislature, but not by Congress.	• Completed in 1825, the Canal ran from Albany to Buffalo on Lake Erie. • Opened a shipping passage from the Atlantic Ocean to the Great Lakes. • Aided the growth of industry and the westward movement of settlers.
Seminole War	• In 1817, fighting broke out between Georgia settlers and Seminole Indians in Spanish Florida, partly because the Americans were not honoring treaties. • Monroe ordered Major General Andrew Jackson to attack the Indians.	• Jackson captured Pensacola, Spanish Florida's capital. • In 1819, the Adams-Onis Treaty gave Florida to the United States in return for the cancellation of $5 million in Spanish debt to the U.S.

James Monroe

In 1816, the Democratic-Republican candidate, James Monroe of Virginia, won the presidency. Monroe became president after more than 40 years of public service.

Presidency (1817–1825). Following the War of 1812, America took its place as a full-fledged nation in the world. At home, there was a growing sense of unity and nationalism. As a result of this, the two terms of Monroe's presidency are often referred to as "the Era of Good Feelings."

THE MONROE DOCTRINE

This foreign policy declaration became firmly established as part of the nation's political practice.

• In the early 1800s, Spanish colonies in Latin America began declaring their independence.

• Monroe and (Secretary of State) John Quincy Adams worried that Spain and its European allies might attempt to reclaim the colonies.

• In 1823, Monroe recognized the colonies' independence and warned Europe against any attempt at conquest or colonization in the Western Hemisphere.

Spotlight on... JAMES MONROE

1758–1831

• Studied law under Thomas Jefferson

• With James Madison and Thomas Jefferson, helped form the Democratic-Republican party

• As U.S. minister to France, helped arrange the Louisiana Purchase

THE WAR OF 1812

Less than 30 years after the American Revolution, tensions between Britain, France, and the United States caused the U.S. to declare war on Britain again. Fighting continued from 1812 until January of 1815. In December of 1814, the Treaty of Ghent ended the war, but did not solve any of the conflicts that caused it—those conflicts simply faded away on their own. The end of the war marked a new era of peace between the U.S. and Britain, both of whom claimed to have won the war.

Back to War

The Battle of New Orleans was a victory for the Americans, but neither side knew that peace had already been declared.

MAJOR EVENTS—WAR OF 1812

1812	1813	1814	1815
June 18 President James Madison and Congress declare war. Britain, involved in war with France, can spare few troops to fight the war.	**April 27** The Americans capture York (now Toronto), the capital of Upper Canada. They burn some public buildings.	**Aug. 24** The British attack Washington, D.C., and burn the White House.	**Jan. 8** General Andrew Jackson defeats a British attack on New Orleans. The British suffered some 2,000 casualties, but American losses were only 8 dead and 13 wounded. Neither side knows that the war has already ended.
Aug. 19 The USS *Constitution* ("Old Ironsides") defeats the British *Guerriere* in sea battle.	**Sept. 10** Captain Oliver Hazard Perry scores a naval victory on Lake Erie and forces the British to leave Detroit.	**Sept. 13** The British bombard Fort McHenry near Baltimore.	
Oct. 13 British forces win the Battle of Queenston Heights in Canada. A three-pronged American attack on British-held Canada fails.	**Oct. 5** General William Henry Harrison attacks British troops retreating from Detroit and their Indian allies. The Indian leader Tecumseh is killed, and the Indians desert the British cause.	**Dec. 24** The Treaty of Ghent is signed in Belgium, ending the War of 1812.	

Causes

In 1793, the French government went to war with Britain and Spain. France expected American support, but President Washington proclaimed that the nation would remain strictly neutral. This proved difficult.

- Both French and British ships harassed American shipping.
- The British began taking American sailors off their ships and impressing (or forcing) them into the British navy.

Actions

- **Jay Treaty.** John Jay negotiated this treaty in 1794. It did not end British impressment, but it did promise that British troops would be removed from the Northwest Territory. This reduced the threat of war in North America.
- **Embargo Act.** In 1807, President Jefferson persuaded Congress to pass a law forbidding American ships to call on foreign ports. He hoped this loss of American goods would make Britain and France stop their interference, but it only hurt American traders. In 1809, trade was resumed with all nations but Britain and France.

Results

In 1809, James Madison succeeded Jefferson as president. By then, in addition to harassing American ships, the British were also encouraging Indians along the western frontier to attack American settlers. Some members of Congress, called "war hawks," demanded a declaration of war on Britain. Congress declared war on June 18, 1812.

Consequences

The 1814 peace treaty, the Treaty of Ghent, marked the beginning of better relations between the United States and Britain. The European wars had finally ended, so interference with American shipping ended too. This new peace allowed the United States to enter a long period of uninterrupted westward expansion and development.

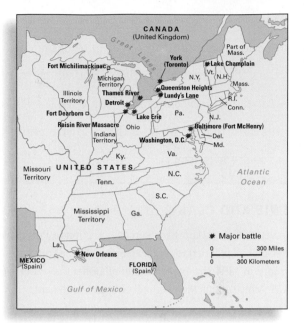

War of 1812. This map shows where the major land and sea battles of the war took place.

"THE STAR-SPANGLED BANNER"

- Written by Francis Scott Key while he watched the bombardment of Fort McHenry
- Became the national anthem in 1931
- Original flag from Fort McHenry displayed at the Smithsonian Institution in Washington, D.C.

Star-Spangled Banner. The American flag flown at the Battle of Fort McHenry, shown here, has been preserved and restored.

FROM SEA TO SHINING SEA

No sooner was the United States an independent nation than it began to expand its borders. The Treaty of Paris (1783), which ended the American Revolutionary War, gave the United States control over most of the land stretching west to the Mississippi.

New Lands

Shifting Borders

A series of treaties and purchases, both large and small, more than doubled the size of the United States by 1820. By the 1850s, the national borders would stretch to the Pacific Ocean. The growth would bring new wealth, but it would also create political conflict—especially over the issue of slavery in the new lands. (See also page 112.)

LEWIS AND CLARK

Even before the Louisiana Purchase was made, President Jefferson had planned to send explorers into the Louisiana Territory. In 1804, the expedition set off under the leadership of U.S. Army captain Meriwether Lewis and lieutenant William Clark.

- The expedition traveled a total of about 8,000 miles (12,800 kilometers).
- The group returned in 1806.
- The expedition's journals describe about 180 plants and 125 animals that had not yet been reported to scientists.

Equipment

The group set off in a large flat-bottomed boat called a *keelboat*. The keelboat carried

- supplies, including food, medicine, scientific instruments, and weapons.
- presents for the Indians they expected to meet, including brass kettles, colored beads, knives, pipes, pocket mirrors, scissors, sewing needles and thread, and tobacco.

The Lewis and Clark expedition left a camp near St. Louis in 1804, journeyed up the Missouri River, and crossed the Rocky Mountains. The explorers reached the Pacific coast in 1805. ▼

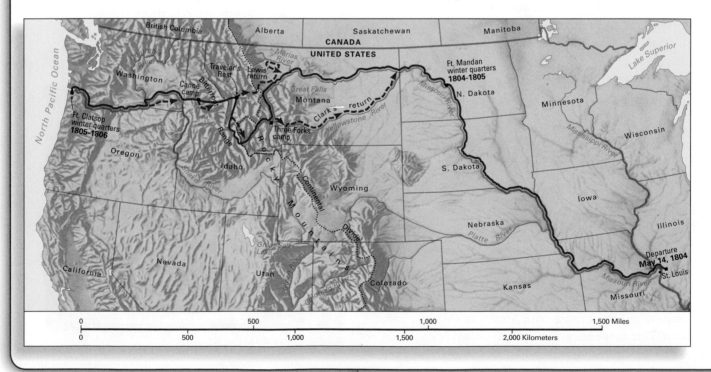

Sacagawea, depicted above with Meriwether Lewis and William Clark, was a Shoshone Indian woman who accompanied the Lewis and Clark expedition in 1805 and 1806. She joined the expedition in what is now North Dakota, after her husband was hired as an interpreter.

Approval and Funding

The Lewis and Clark expedition was partly initiated by a secret message to the United States Congress from President Jefferson in 1803, asking Congress to authorize a grant for an expedition to the Pacific Ocean.

- Meriwether Lewis and William Clark each received 1,600 acres of land as rewards.
- The rest of the men got double pay and 320 acres.
- The trip's interpreter, Toussaint Charbonneau, received an additional $533.33 for his services. His wife Sacagawea got nothing.

Northwest Ordinance. The Ordinance of 1787, also called the Northwest Ordinance, determined the future of the area west of the colonies and north of the Ohio River.

- It provided for the formation of no less than three or more than five states in the territory.
- Each new state could be admitted into the Union when its population reached 60,000.
- Slavery was forbidden in the area, but this provision did not affect fugitive slaves from other states, or slaves already in the territory.
- Five states were formed from this territory—Ohio (1803), Indiana (1816), Illinois (1818), Michigan (1837), and Wisconsin (1848).

Louisiana Purchase. In 1803, President Jefferson was offered an opportunity to double the size of the United States.

- France (under Napoleon's rule) was in need of money after years of warfare in Europe.
- Jefferson was concerned that French control in Louisiana and Florida would hurt American shipping and trade, so he sent diplomats to negotiate the purchase of New Orleans and West Florida.
- Napoleon instead offered to sell the Louisiana Territory, a vast area between the Mississippi River and the Rocky Mountains, for only $15 million (a few cents an acre). The diplomats, Robert R. Livingston and James Monroe, snapped up the offer.
- Eventually all or parts of 15 states were formed out of this region.

The Adams-Onis Treaty. The area that is now the state of Florida joined the Union in two parts.

- In 1810, West Florida, which Jefferson viewed as part of Louisiana but which was considered by Spain to be part of Spanish Florida, was also annexed.
- In 1819, the Adams-Onis Treaty gave America control of Spanish Florida.

Economics of Expansion

Development of Regional Economies

By the end of President James Monroe's second term in 1825, the nation was developing three distinct economic sections—the North, the South, and the West. The different priorities and demands of these regions created heated political divisions.

Political Effects. By the election of 1824, the "Era of Good Feeling"—marked by national unity and optimism—enjoyed under Monroe was drawing to a close. That year, four candidates—John Quincy Adams of Massachusetts, William Crawford of Georgia, Henry Clay of Kentucky, and Andrew Jackson of Tennessee—vied for the presidency. Each region favored a different candidate for different reasons.

- The industrial North wanted high tariffs on manufactured goods entering the United States to reduce competition from imported goods.

- The agricultural South, which had to buy (rather than make) most of its manufactured goods, favored low tariffs.

- The West, the newest and least developed section, favored federal spending on roads and other improvements; the other sections resisted the higher taxes this would require.

- The South believed its economy was thoroughly dependent on slavery and therefore defended it strongly. Elements in the North, however, objected to slavery just as strongly.

The Industrial North

Region: The New England and Mid-Atlantic states

The many waterways in the North supplied a ready source of available energy to power factory machines. In 1790, Samuel Slater built a cotton-thread spinning mill in Pawtucket, Rhode Island. Within the next 25 years, textile mills sprang up all over New England, and the American factory system was born.

The labor to run the North's growing industries brought on rapid population growth. Immigrant workers came by the thousands. Between the 1820s and the 1850s

- the population of the North more than doubled.

- Philadelphia's population tripled.

- New York City's and Boston's populations quadrupled.

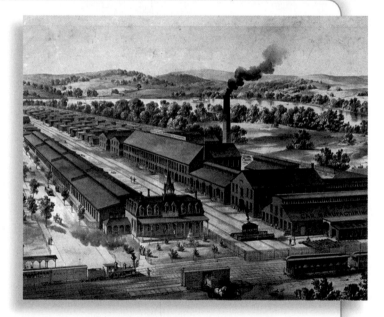

The factory production system gave rise to other industries. Iron and steel were needed for factory and farm machines. Coal mining provided fuel for factory machines and iron/steel production.

THE COTTON GIN

Prior to 1793, cotton had been a very expensive crop to produce: because it was hand-cleaned, one worker produced only 1 pound of cotton per day. The cotton gin (short for engine), invented by Massachusetts-born Eli Whitney in 1793, made it possible for one worker to clean 50 pounds of cotton a day. Cotton gins, manufactured in Connecticut, suddenly made cotton a profitable crop and the cornerstone of the Southern economy.

The Agricultural South

Region: The Southern states, especially the new states of Louisiana, Alabama, and Mississippi

The economic system of the South was largely agricultural, thanks to fertile soil and a warm climate. The chief crop was cotton.

- Planters in search of cheap land established large plantations in western Georgia, Alabama, and Mississippi, and even farther west.
- Gradually, the South became the producer of two-thirds of the world's supply of cotton.

Southern farms sold their cotton to Northern shippers, who sent it to Northern mills. Northern manufacturers then sold finished goods to the South, which lacked manufacturing of its own. The cotton gin, for example, was produced in the North.

Plantation Labor. Planters relied largely on slaves for their labor force. In 1790, the number of slaves in the United States was almost 700,000. By 1820, the number was more than 1.5 million, and by 1860, more than 3.9 million.

The Frontier West

Region: West of the Appalachian Mountains; Kentucky, Tennessee, Iowa, Missouri, and beyond

As droves of settlers crossed the Appalachian Mountains following the War of 1812, the fertile prairie soil of the West became the new breadbasket.

- Western farm products included corn, wheat, beef, pork, and poultry.
- Settlement was encouraged by federal government policies and increased transportation (canals, railroads).
- The development of the agricultural West made greater industrialization of the nation possible.
- The West provided the food the North needed to feed its ever-growing numbers of industrial workers.

Frontier Farming. The Land Acts of 1796, 1800, and 1820 made it easier for farmers—especially immigrant farmers from Ireland, Germany, and Scandinavia—to buy parcels of land cheaply.

Politics of Expansion

Andrew Jackson's election ushered in a period that came to be known as the "Era of the Common Man." During this time, Jackson extended suffrage (voting rights) and attacked government policies that he thought protected privileged groups.

Politics

The Party System

After the election of 1824, the Republican Party split along ideological lines.

National Republicans: John Quincy Adams and his supporters named their party to reflect a belief in strong national government.

Democrats: Jackson and his supporters named their party to stress their concern for the common man. They painted the National Republicans as the "aristocratic" party of the wealthy.

Spotlight on... ANDREW JACKSON

1767–1845

- First president born in a log cabin
- At age 13, was a prisoner of war in the American Revolution
- Military hero in the War of 1812 and the Seminole War
- Nicknamed "Old Hickory" for his toughness and rough frontier manners

THE ELECTION OF 1824

In the election of 1824, four candidates—John Quincy Adams, William Crawford, Henry Clay, and Andrew Jackson—ran for the presidency.

- Jackson won the popular vote, but not the electoral college vote.
- The election was thrown into the House of Representatives, where Henry Clay gave his support to Adams, who was then chosen president.
- Adams subsequently made Clay his secretary of state.
- Jackson became Clay's enemy, and many in the West felt betrayed.

THE ELECTION OF 1828

Several factors favored Jackson's election over Adams in 1828.

- Extension of the right to vote to more of "the common men" to whom Jackson appealed.
- Jacksonians in Congress passed the Tariff of 1828, called the "Tariff of Abominations." Enraged, Southern voters turned on Adams and supported Jackson.
- Jackson won by a landslide in the electoral college, tallying up 178 votes to 83 for Adams.

National Parties. By the 1832 election, the National Republicans and the Democrats had become national parties. They were joined by the Anti-Masonic Party, which sprang from investigations of corruption in the Freemasons. The Anti-Masons introduced the first national convention and the first party platform.

Election of 1832		
Party	**Candidate**	**Votes**
National Republicans	Henry Clay	Electoral: 49 Popular: 530,189
Democrats	Andrew Jackson [Winner]	Electoral: 219 Popular: 687,502
Anti-Masonic Party	William Wirt	Electoral: 7

Spoils System. Jackson believed that people shouldn't serve too long in public office. He also began replacing people who opposed him with supporters. This "spoils system" had long been a part of state politics, and other presidents had also rewarded friends and supporters with positions. Later presidents would extend the system, causing a massive turnover of officeholders with each new administration.

William Henry Harrison, who had defeated several Indian tribes in the Battle of Tippecanoe, was portrayed as an Indian-fighting hero of the people. His campaign slogan was "Tippecanoe and Tyler, Too."

POLITICS OF THE EXPANSION ERA

Economic woes and political divisions that arose during Andrew Jackson's presidency continued to shake the nation for many years.

Panic and Depression: In an attempt to control rampant inflation and borrowing, President Jackson had returned the nation to the use of gold or silver instead of paper money. This dealt a severe blow to the economy. As President Martin Van Buren took over, mortgages were going unpaid, banks were failing, and factories were closing. This Panic of 1837 led to the worst depression in the nation's history to date.

Elections: The financial gloom helped to defeat Van Buren's bid for reelection in 1840.

- Henry Clay and the National Republicans joined together with many of Jackson's enemies, including John C. Calhoun, to form the Whig Party.
- The Whig candidate in 1840 was William Henry Harrison. Harrison won the election in a landslide, but died of pneumonia just 1 month after taking office.
- His vice president, John Tyler, succeeded him.

Economics

Two major economic issues—nullification and the national bank—characterized Jackson's presidency. Both would have far-reaching effects on the nation.

Issue	Causes and Events	Effects
Nullification	• The South viewed the "Tariff of Abominations" as a violation of states' rights. • In Congress, Daniel Webster (Massachusetts) and John C. Calhoun (South Carolina) debated federal vs. state authority. Webster supported federal authority; Calhoun supported the states. • A new tariff in 1832 caused South Carolina to draft an Ordinance of Nullification. • The Ordinance declared that the tariff was null in South Carolina, and that the state would secede if forced to honor it.	• President Jackson opposed the tariff, but still issued a warning to South Carolina. • Congress passed the Force Bill, giving the president authority to enforce the tariff. • Henry Clay, "the Great Compromiser," passed a 10-year decrease in tariffs. • The issues of state and federal authority—and divisions between North and South—remained unresolved.
The bank fight	• Jackson felt the Second Bank of the United States favored rich stockholders at the expense of the poor and small businesses. • He gradually crippled the Bank by withdrawing funds and refusing to make deposits. • He instead deposited funds into Democrat-owned state banks, which came to be called "pet banks."	• The Second Bank could no longer restrain the printing of currency. • A boom of rampant speculation and inflation followed. • The boom ended with the Panic of 1837. • After 1837, the Second Bank failed.

Manifest Destiny

As Americans filled up the Ohio and Mississippi valleys, the nation looked west. Said writer John Louis Sullivan in 1845, "Our manifest destiny is to overspread the continent allotted by Providence . . ." But the land was not simply the Americans' for the taking. Not only were there hundreds of thousands of American Indians there—many of them driven westward by earlier American settlement—but other nations were also laying claim to the West.

Travelers on the Oregon Trail typically used covered wagons made from farm wagons. The wagons were fitted with four to six wooden bows that arched from side to side over the wagon bed. Then, canvas or some other sturdy material was stretched over the bows.

The wagons were packed with household essentials, such as cookware and clothing. Settlers also had to bring with them enough flour, cornmeal, bacon, salt, and other staples to last for at least 6 months.

Manifest Destiny. By the middle of the 19th century, the U.S. would extend its borders to the Pacific Ocean. ▼

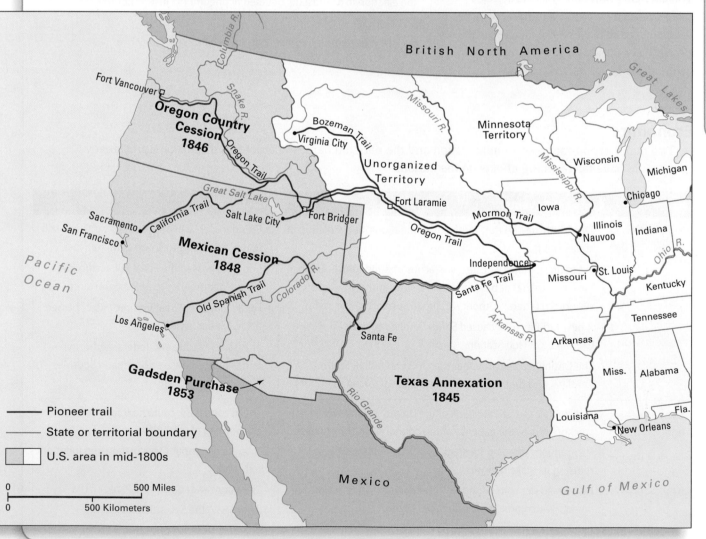

Mountain Men and the Oregon Trail

The first non-Indians to come to the Oregon Territory were the so-called "mountain men"—hunters and trappers after animal furs, especially beaver.

By the 1830s, the mountain men had eliminated most of the beavers. They instead began leading wagon trains of American settlers to the fertile land west of the Rockies. The route they followed was the Oregon Trail.

- The trail began in Independence, Missouri, and stretched as far as Portland, Oregon.

- More than 50,000 people used it between 1841 and 1860.

- Even today, travelers can see the deeply rutted road cut by wagon wheels along sections of the trail.

Covered wagons took many settlers to the West on the Oregon Trail. The journey took 6 months and was extremely dangerous. ▶

The western lands sought by the United States during the mid-1800s were owned by Britain and Mexico.

"Fifty-four Forty or Fight!" In 1818, the United States and Britain had agreed to share the rights to the Oregon Territory, which included what are now Oregon, Washington, Idaho, and part of Canada.

- Before long, though, American settlers in the Oregon Territory vastly outnumbered the British.

- Expansionist-minded Americans wanted the United States to take over the entire Pacific Northwest, up to the parallel 54°40'. "Fifty-four forty or fight" became their rallying cry.

- For a time, war threatened, but neither nation wanted war.

- The Oregon Treaty of 1846 divided the Oregon Territory at the 49th parallel, a continuation of the boundary between Canada and the United States. (See also page 270.)

California. California, which had been part of New Spain, became Mexican in 1821. The Spanish had sparsely settled the area, mainly with a chain of missions founded by Franciscan friars along the California coast.

Presidents Jackson and Tyler had both tried unsuccessfully to buy California from Mexico, but in 1845, President James K. Polk tried a different tactic.

- He encouraged Americans in California to rebel against the Mexican government. (By 1845, there were about 700 Americans living in California.)

- On June 14, 1846, American rebels proclaimed the California Republic and raised their flag which depicted a grizzly bear and a lone star.

- On July 7, U.S. naval forces landed at Monterey and declared California a part of the United States.

U.S. Army captain John C. Frémont took command of the Californian forces and drove all Mexican troops out of California.

War with Mexico

Texas

In 1821, Mexico gained its independence from Spain and wanted to make Texas—formerly Spanish-claimed—its northern province. The Mexican government granted permission to Moses Austin and 300 other American settlers to start a colony in Texas. By the end of the 1820s, there were about 20,000 Americans living there, versus 4,000 Mexicans.

Texan Independence. It was not long before there was severe friction between the Texans and the Mexican government.

Causes

- **Religion:** The Mexicans were Roman Catholics, and the Americans predominantly Protestants.

- **Language:** The Spanish-English language barrier caused misunderstandings.

- **Slavery:** The Americans were mainly Southerners who had brought slaves with them; the central government later outlawed slavery.

Mexico tried to maintain its weakening control over the region, but most of its attempts only made the problem worse. In 1833, Antonio López de Santa Anna established himself as dictator of Mexico and sent troops to restore control in Texas. Armed clashes followed in 1835.

Spotlight on... ANTONIO LÓPEZ DE SANTA ANNA

1795–1876

- Mexican soldier and politician
- Served as president of Mexico 11 times
- Often declared himself a dictator, but always overthrown

Annexation

In 1837, Sam Houston applied for permission for Texas to enter the United States. President Jackson saw two problems: probable war with Mexico and the admission of a slave state that would tip the delicate balance between North and South. Jackson refused to support annexation.

Statehood. In 1843, Houston again approached the United States government. President John Tyler, eager for American expansion, was able to put a joint resolution through Congress authorizing annexation. On December 29, 1845, Texas became the Union's 28th state. Mexico broke off diplomatic relations with the United States.

REMEMBER THE ALAMO!

In February of 1836, Santa Anna and an army of about 6,000 advanced into Texas. On February 23, he began a siege of the Alamo, at San Antonio, garrisoned by some 189 Texan volunteers.

- On March 6, the Alamo fell and Santa Anna had all of its defenders killed.

- The defense of the Alamo gave General Sam Houston time to gather more forces for the independence movement. "Remember the Alamo!" became their battle cry.

- On April 21, Santa Anna was defeated, captured by Houston's forces, and forced to agree to Texan independence.

- In October, Sam Houston became president of independent Texas.

Battle of the Alamo. Among the Texans defending the Alamo were famous frontiersmen James Bowie and Davy Crockett.

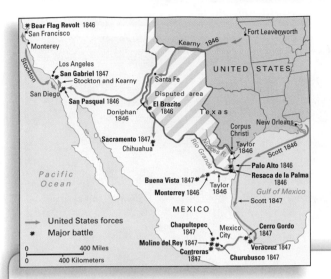

The American military strategy called for four moves. General Taylor was to hold the Rio Grande; General Winfield Scott was to land at the Mexican port of Veracruz and advance on Mexico City, the capital; Colonel Stephen Kearny was to take and hold New Mexico, then push on to California to join the forces there under Captain Frémont; and Commodore Robert F. Stockton was to position a fleet in the Pacific off the California shore. All four campaigns were successful.

Mexican War (1846–1848)

Eager to see the nation stretch across the continent, several American presidents had offered to buy the Mexican lands of the West and Southwest, but Mexico refused to sell. To many, war seemed to be the only way to get the lands once and for all.

Zachary Taylor. On February 22, 1847, a force of about 5,000 Americans led by Zachary Taylor defeated a Mexican army of about 20,000. The Battle of Buena Vista raged for 2 days.

Causes		Results	
Call for expansion	The American government wanted the Mexican territory between the current United States and the Pacific. Western and Southern states responded enthusiastically. Many in the Northern states, however, were critical of the government's actions, fearing the extension of slavery into new territory.	**Treaty of Guadalupe Hidalgo**	• Ended the war. • Settled the border question: The Rio Grande would be Texas's southwestern boundary. • Ceded to the United States, for $15 million, the territories now known as California, Utah, Arizona, and New Mexico. • The United States now stretched "from sea to shining sea."
Texan border	The immediate cause of the war was the issue of Texas's boundary. Texas claimed that the Rio Grande was its southwestern boundary. Mexico claimed the region as far north and east as the Nueces River. In May 1845, President Polk sent General Zachary Taylor and his troops to the disputed border, and in July the American forces advanced to the Rio Grande. On April 25, 1846, Mexican forces crossed the Rio Grande and attacked the American troops, killing 16. On May 13, 1846, Congress declared war on Mexico, and Mexico's formal declaration followed.	**Political and economic effects**	• General Zachary Taylor's victory over Mexican General Santa Anna at the Battle of Buena Vista made Taylor the hero of the war—and put him in the White House in 1849. • Gold was soon discovered in the Sacramento Valley. In the gold rush that followed, some 80,000 prospectors, called "Forty-Niners," arrived in California in 1 year. • The new territory revived debates over slavery; these debates would become an underlying cause of the American Civil War.

As westward expansion by white settlers became more intense, the U.S. government at first tried buying Native American land and setting aside enclaves for the original Americans. Eventually, though, fighting between whites and Native Americans became frequent. (See also pages 138–139.)

Removal, Resettlement, and Resistance

Under the U.S. Constitution, treaties with Native American tribes were as legally binding as agreements with other nations. But many of the treaties were broken as increasing numbers of settlers entered lands reserved for the Indians.

Indian Removal Act (1830). Under this act, the U.S. military forced about 100,000 Native Americans from east of the Mississippi into Indian Territory. This territory, from the Missouri River to the Oregon Territory, was to belong to the Native Americans "as long as the rivers shall run." The "Five Civilized Tribes" of the Southeast resisted, to no avail.

Reservation Policy (1851). Under this policy, the American government restricted the Indians to designated areas (often the poorest ones, which the settlers did not want), allowing settlers to take over the rest. However, if a reservation area became attractive, the Indians were driven off again.

Black Hawk and Son. The Black Hawk War failed to return Indian lands to their original inhabitants.

Resistance. Several tribes fought the continued demands from land-hungry settlers.

- In 1832, Sauk chief Black Hawk attempted to reclaim land in Illinois, but was defeated.
- The Sioux Wars began in Wyoming in 1854.
- By the 1860s, Cheyenne, Apache, and other tribes also resisted attempts to take their land or force them onto reservations.

The Indian Territory was land set aside by the U.S. government for Indians from about 1825 to 1906. It covered most of present-day Oklahoma. Among the tribes forced to live on the land were the Cherokee, Chickasaw, Choctaw, Creek, and Seminole.

After the Black Hawk War, Black Hawk told his story to a French-American interpreter. The account was published as Life of Ma-ka-tai-me-she-kia-kiak, or Black Hawk (1833).

A 50-foot (15-meter) statue of Black Hawk by American sculptor Lorado Taft stands beside the Rock River near Oregon, Illinois.

The Trail of Tears

In 1828, the state of Georgia attempted to take over the land of the Cherokee Indians and relocate them west of the Mississippi River.

- The Cherokees challenged Georgia's authority over their lands in the Supreme Court (*Worcester v. Georgia*) in 1832.

- The court declared that "the Cherokee Nation . . . is a distinct community, occupying its own territory, with boundaries accurately described, in which the laws of Georgia can have no force."

- President Andrew Jackson agreed with Georgia. "[Chief Justice] John Marshall has made his decision," Jackson remarked. "Now let him enforce it."

As a result, the entire Cherokee nation was marched westward, under U.S. Army guard.

Trail of Tears. The 15,000 Cherokees called their march westward the Trail of Tears. About 4,000 Cherokees died from sickness and exhaustion. About one-quarter of the Native Americans from all tribes sent to the Indian Territory during the 1830s died en route.

NATIVE AMERICAN ACTIVISM

The violent resistance of Indian tribes in the late 19th century led to many deaths on both sides, but little gain for the tribes. In the 20th century, many Native Americans resorted to legal and political action instead of violence to resist white domination.

The movement began making some important strides in the early 1900s, and progress continued throughout the century.

- In 1911, the Society of American Indians was organized to promote collective action by the tribes.

- In 1944, The National Congress of American Indians was founded to promote Native American rights through legislative action.

In 1973, AIM activists occupied the Wounded Knee massacre site in protest. The protest led to a standoff with government officials that lasted 71 days and claimed three lives.

- In 1946, the Indian Claims Commission began reviewing land transactions in which tribes claimed they had been cheated. By the time the commission finished in the 1970s, it had awarded about $800 million in compensation to Native Americans for stolen lands and broken treaties.

The civil rights and counterculture movements of the 1960s brought about a new, more militant phase in Indian activism. The American Indian Movement (AIM) of 1968, led by Dennis Banks, was among the militant groups that promoted civil disobedience. The group staged several protests to draw attention to the problems faced by Indians.

Gold Rush

The Gold Rushes

A "gold rush" is a rapid movement of people to a site where gold has been discovered. The discovery of gold fields has long attracted large numbers of prospectors and other people because of the traditionally high value of gold. Gold rushes played an important role in the development of the American West.

Gold in California. On January 24, 1848, gold was discovered on the property of John Augustus Sutter in the Sacramento Valley. The news spread through the U.S. just as the Treaty of Guadalupe Hidalgo, which ended the Mexican War (see page 103), made California an American territory. The Sutter's Mill discovery set off a gold rush to California.

The "Forty-Niners." By 1849, some 80,000 "Forty-Niners" had arrived in California. Towns developed overnight, transportation networks were hacked out of the wilderness, and new territories were born within months. San Francisco, the nearest port, grew from a small town to a city of about 25,000 in a year's time as people arrived from all over the world. By 1850, California had enough people to be admitted to the Union as a state.

Mining Camps and Settlements. California set the pattern for other gold rushes throughout the West.

- The Pikes Peak gold rush in 1859 opened Colorado, launched the city of Denver, and started a great mining industry.

- Gold rushes also brought people to Alaska, Arizona, Idaho, Montana, Nevada, New Mexico, South Dakota, Utah, and Wyoming.

Some mining districts and camps died within a year, but others lasted more than a hundred years. These districts include several mining areas in Colorado and the Homestake mine near Lead, South Dakota. Gold rushes led to clashes between white settlers and Indians, and to permanent cities, states, transportation systems, and varied economies.

The California gold rush brought tens of thousands of people to the region. Here, miners are shown washing for gold in the Sierra foothills. ▼

THE YUKON GOLD RUSH

Gold rushes were not confined to the American West. A large gold rush in 1897–1898 led to the development of Canada's Yukon territory. The rush began in the Klondike area.

- On August 17, 1896, near the settlement of Dawson, George W. Carmack, his Indian wife Kate, and her relatives found a large quantity of gold in the gravel of a creek he named the Bonanza.

- When news of the rich strike reached the outside world in July 1897, it brought a stampede of prospectors to the Klondike in the fall of 1897, and an even greater one in 1898.

- Few of the men made fortunes. The good claims were staked before most prospectors arrived.

Residents of the town of Dawson now celebrate August 17 as "Discovery Day," and it is a territorial holiday.

Searching for Gold. One common gold-mining tool was a *sluice*, or a series of long, water-filled wooden boxes, that separated gold from gravel. ▼

Jack London, an American author, prospected for gold during the Yukon gold rush. Many of his works, such as *Call of the Wild* and *Son of the Wolf*, vividly recount the harsh conditions faced by those seeking their fortune in the Klondike. ▼

Industrialization

As early as the late 1700s, the Industrial Revolution, which was already well established in Britain, was coming to life in the United States. The 1800s brought significant new technologies to manufacturing, transportation, communication, and agriculture.

Manufacturing

The manufacturing base of the United States was largely concentrated in the northern states. There, the developing factory system led to the growth of cities such as Boston, Philadelphia, and New York City.

Mass Production. In 1798, Eli Whitney developed a new method of manufacture when producing muskets: machines that produced uniform, interchangeable parts. Now, relatively unskilled workers could produce an enormous number of muskets. Soon other products were being made using these mass-production principles.

New and Growing Industries. The emerging factory production system gave impetus to many other industries. Iron and steel were needed for factory and farm machines. In the 1850s, a British engineer named Sir Henry Bessemer invented an inexpensive way of making steel. Shortly afterward, an American named William Kelly invented a similar process. Production and use of steel spread rapidly.

The need for steel, iron, and coal followed the rise of factories. This blast furnace was associated with the steel industry.

Age of the Steamboat. Steamboats made it easier and less expensive to transport people and goods throughout the country. By the 1820s, steam navigation was common on the rivers and lakes of the North.

Transportation and Communication

New, growing industries demanded improved transportation. During the period from the 1820s to the 1850s, new canals and roads were being built, and new forms of transportation were appearing. Better transportation helped fuel the growth of the West and of cities such as St. Louis, Cincinnati, and Chicago.

On the Water. The development of the steam engine helped American industry take advantage of the nation's many lakes and rivers. In 1802, John Stevens demonstrated a propeller-driven steam ferry on the Hudson River, and in 1807, Robert Fulton developed a practical steamboat.

Over the Land. While steamboats populated American waterways, the railroad was spreading across dry land. In 1826, John Stevens installed a steam locomotive on a circular track at his New Jersey home. In 1830, there were about 28 miles (45 kilometers) of railroad track in the United States. By 1840, the mileage increased to 2,800 (4,500 kilometers), and by 1860, to more than 30,000 (48,270 kilometers). Two-thirds of the mileage was in the North, and Chicago was the rail center of the nation.

THE TELEGRAPH SYSTEM

While steamboats and railroads helped move people and goods, new communication technology helped move information. In 1837, Samuel Morse developed the first practical telegraph machine.

- The machine sent electric signals over a wire in the form of a dot or a dash.
- A code of dots and dashes—Morse code—was used to spell out words.
- The first telegraph line ran from Washington to Baltimore and cost $30,000.
- By the late 1800s, organizations such as Western Union, the Associated Press, and Reuters were sending news and financial information all over the world.

McCormick's reaper increased American wheat production. Other farm machines, including seeders, cultivators, and threshers, continued to revolutionize American agriculture.

Agriculture

As Americans moved westward into new territories during the 1800s, cheap land rates and new agricultural technologies led to the rise of farming in the prairies of the Midwest.

Plowing and Reaping. The prairie land was fertile, but thick grasses and sticky sod made traditional plowing difficult. This problem was solved by the steel plow, developed by John Deere in 1837. Another boost to American agriculture came in 1831 when Cyrus Hall McCormick developed the first successful reaper. McCormick patented his reaper in 1834 and began large-scale production in 1847. Soon the Midwest was producing enough grain for export.

now you **Know!**

- ✔ In the years after the American Revolutionary War, the nation began expanding its boundaries.
- ✔ Three regional economies soon developed: the industrial North, the agricultural South, and the frontier West.
- ✔ Manifest Destiny inspired Americans to claim new territories in the West.
- ✔ A war with Mexico in 1846 gave the United States control over Texas, California, Utah, Arizona, and New Mexico.
- ✔ The invention of railroads, steamboats, and new farming equipment made expansion possible.

A DIVIDED NATION

Sectional differences between North and South dated from colonial times. Gradually, the political and cultural attitudes created by the South's plantation culture and the North's industrialized economy contributed to a deep rift between North and South.

Diverging Economies

As the United States grew and developed, the North became more industrialized and urbanized. The South maintained a very different character, remaining agricultural and rural. It also developed an economic system and a social structure that differed from that of the North. (See also pages 96–97.)

Cultural Composition of the United States, 1860		
Element	**North**	**South**
Labor force in agriculture	40% (down 30% from 1800)	80% (constant)
Concentration in urban areas	25%	10%
School attendance	Twice the Southern rate	Half the Northern rate
Illiteracy	6%	50% (incl. slaves)

Plantation Culture. The South's agricultural economy developed, in part, due to its warm climate and fertile soil. Planters in search of cheap land gradually left the seaboard states and established large plantations in western Georgia, Alabama, Mississippi, and even farther west.

Cotton. The economic system of the South was dominated by the production of cotton. Prior to 1793, cotton had been a very expensive crop to produce. In 1793, Eli Whitney's invention of a "cotton gin" (short for cotton engine) made it possible for one worker to clean 50 pounds of cotton a day. Cotton was suddenly profitable. The South became the producer of two-thirds of the world's supply of cotton.

Slavery. Labor was needed to work the plantations, and the planters relied on slaves. Slavery, an institution that had been diminishing somewhat in the South, experienced a burst of growth. In 1790, the number of slaves in the United States was almost 700,000. By 1820, the number was more than 1.5 million, and by 1860, more than 3.9 million.

Issue	North	South
Economic and political interests	• Manufacturing (textiles, finished goods); small farms • Protectionist tariffs (taxes on imported goods)	• Plantation farming (cotton and tobacco) • Opposition to tariffs • Strong support of states' rights
Labor force	• Slavery diminished by the 1800s • Free workers hired themselves out for wages • Large immigrant population increased the workforce	• Based heavily on enslaved workers • Generally accepted that plantations could not be profitable without slaves
Attitudes toward slavery	• Many came to view slavery as wrong	• Some considered slavery a necessary evil • Many considered it a positive good

Slavery in the United States

The first Africans to settle in North America were indentured servants, not slaves. After working for a few years, they were freed. By the late 1600s, however, American colonies began to pass laws establishing automatic, lifelong slavery exclusively for these people. (See also page 39.)

Life Under Slavery. African slaves were subject to appalling conditions as soon as they were put on ships to America. Slave traders crowded hundreds of people below decks, fed them poorly, and left them in stifling and unsanitary conditions. Many slaves did not survive the trip, known as the Middle Passage. Once they arrived, they faced new hardships.

Working Conditions

- Worked from sunrise to sunset
- Cleared land, tended fields, harvested crops
- Toiled as household servants
- Could be beaten for resisting

Living Conditions

- Basic food rations of salt pork and corn (sometimes planters might provide other foods)
- Clothing often coarse and poorly made
- Slaves or their family members could be sold to other owners at any time

While many of the working and living conditions of northern laborers, both industrial and agricultural, resembled those of slaves, the critical difference was freedom. Northern laborers toiled with the knowledge that they owned themselves. Through education and hard work, they could hope to rise into the middle class, or higher. Slaves knew no such hope.

Resistance. Slaves protested against their condition by destroying property, running away, pretending illness, and disobeying orders. Major slave protests included armed revolts and mutinies. The religion of the slaves, combining African and Christian beliefs, also helped them survive the brutality. Slaves sometimes fled west or north, or joined Native American tribes.

Free Blacks. Besides former slaves freed by law, free blacks included those who had been freed by their masters, who had bought their freedom, or who had been born of free parents. By 1860, the nation had about 490,000 free blacks. Most faced severe discrimination, and were little better off than the slaves.

CULTURE UNDER SLAVERY

The oppressive conditions of slavery and racism limited, but did not eliminate, African Americans' culture. Dancing and music became especially important common cultural links between black slaves of various African tribes.

Slave musicians played traditional African instruments like drums, banjos, and xylophones (bafalos), which they made themselves. A number of free blacks won widespread recognition, despite discrimination, including

- Jupiter Hammon and Phillis Wheatley, poets.
- Benjamin Banneker, mathematician.
- Samuel Cornish and John Russwurm, editors.

Lawmakers Decide

As the South became increasingly dependent on slave labor, Northern attitudes toward slavery were shifting in the opposite direction. Northern states had both political and moral reasons to oppose slavery.

Slavery and the Territories

New lands gained in the West during the 1840s and 1850s worsened the tensions between North and South. The South wanted to extend slavery into the new areas; the North objected.

Whether new states would be admitted to the Union as slave or free states was a frequent point of contention in the Senate. Neither North nor South wanted the other side to have more states—and therefore more senators to promote one region's interests over the other's.

Legislative Actions

From the 1820s to the 1860s, Congress passed a number of laws and compromises in an attempt to solve the issue of slavery in the territories.

THE SLAVERY QUESTION— OUTSIDE THE U.S.

By the time the slavery issue began to dominate U.S. politics, several other nations had taken steps to end the practice.

United Kingdom: Activists such as William Wilberforce, Granville Sharp, and former slave Olaudah Equiano worked to ban slavery. In 1833, slavery was banned throughout the British Empire.

Latin America: During the early 1800s, most of Spain's Latin American colonies won wars of independence. These newly independent countries immediately abolished slavery or adopted laws for gradual emancipation of slaves.

Legislation	Details	Effects
Missouri Compromise (1820)	• Proposed in Congress by Henry Clay of Kentucky • Admitted Maine as a free state and Missouri as a slave state • Forbade slavery in any other territory of the Louisiana Purchase	• Maintained the balance between Northern and Southern states in Congress
Wilmot Proviso (1846)	• President Polk hoped to pass a bill compensating Mexico for lands annexed by the U.S. • Congressman David Wilmot of Pennsylvania introduced an amendment stating, "neither slavery nor involuntary servitude shall ever exist" in lands acquired from Mexico.	• Failed in Congress • Became the key issue for the Free-Soil and Republican parties
Compromise of 1850	• Also proposed by Henry Clay • Admitted California as a free state, but allowed New Mexico and Utah to choose their own free state or slave state status • Included a Fugitive Slave Act to help slave owners recapture slaves who escaped to the North	• Briefly ended the debate in Congress • Opposition to the Fugitive Slave Act increased Northern antislavery feelings
Kansas-Nebraska Act (1854)	• Proposed by Senator Stephen A. Douglas • Created two new territories—Kansas and Nebraska—and allowed them to decide for themselves whether to have slavery	• Repealed the Missouri Compromise • Pro- and antislavery forces sent armed settlers to the territories, especially Kansas • Resulted in violent clashes (see following page)

Sectionalism and Politics

The growing conflict between slave and free states affected not only Congress, but also the presidential elections of the time. Parties split, new parties formed, and sectional divisions became even deeper.

Election of 1848. Slavery in the territories became the key issue in the national election of 1848. At the time, the main parties were the Democratic Party and the Whig Party.

- The Democrats nominated Lewis Cass, who supported popular sovereignty—letting territories determine their own free or slave status.

- The Whig Party nominated General Zachary Taylor, the hero of the Mexican War and a slaveholder.

- Antislavery factions called the Barnburners and the Free-Soil Party nominated Martin Van Buren.

- Taylor won the election with 163 electoral votes to 127 for Cass. Van Buren won no electoral votes, but his candidacy cost Cass the election.

Election of 1856. Divisions within the Whig Party had grown as sectional strains had worsened, and the Kansas-Nebraska Act tore the party apart.

- In July 1854, antislavery forces from both the Whig and the Democratic parties formed the Republican Party.

- In 1856, they ran John C. Frémont for president.

- His Democratic opponent, James Buchanan, won by 174 electoral votes to 114.

- Millard Fillmore, nominated by the virtually dead Whig Party and the American, or "Know-Nothing," Party, won eight electoral votes.

- The "Know-Nothing" Party, based in various secret societies, was antiforeigner, anti-Catholic, and short-lived.

BLEEDING KANSAS

The Kansas-Nebraska Act left the decision of whether or not to permit slavery up to the territories. When it came time to vote for representatives to the Kansas legislature,

- proslavery Missourians crossed the border, voted illegally, and gave the proslavery party an overwhelming victory.

- antislavery settlers, calling it a stolen election, set up their own legislature.

- violence broke out, especially along the Missouri border.

- for the next 4 years, a state of civil war existed in "Bleeding Kansas."

DRED SCOTT V. SANDFORD

On March 6, 1857, the Supreme Court handed down a momentous decision in the ongoing slavery debate. A black man named Dred Scott had filed a lawsuit insisting that because he had lived in a free state (Illinois), he was a free man rather than a slave.

The Supreme Court declared

- slaves or those of slave ancestry could not be citizens of the United States.

- slaves were "property" to be transported from state to state.

- Congress could not prohibit slavery in the territories and was bound by the Constitution to protect it.

The Dred Scott decision delighted the South. Northerners were outraged, and the Republican Party called for congressional legislation against the slavery in the territories. ▶

During the 1700s, noted philosophers and religious leaders in Europe and North America began to condemn slavery. They declared that slavery violated human rights and God-given law. From this sentiment grew a movement to abolish, or ban, slavery.

The Abolitionist Movement

There had always been some moral qualms about slavery in the nation. In 1696, Quakers in Pennsylvania took the first action against slavery by banning the importation of slaves into the colony. But opposition to slavery did not attract real support until the American Revolution brought questions about liberty and justice squarely before the colonists.

Effects of the Revolution. Some 5,000 African Americans had fought with the colonists against the British during the Revolutionary War. Prominent leaders of the American revolutionary movement, including Thomas Jefferson (himself a Southern slaveholder), Patrick Henry, and Thomas Paine, spoke out against slavery. The drafting of the Constitution again raised the issue of abolishing slavery. However, Southern states, whose economy depended on slavery, refused to abolish it.

Organizations and Leaders. In 1833, William Lloyd Garrison helped organize the American Anti-Slavery Society. He served as its president for two decades. One of the most effective speakers of the 1,000-chapter Anti-Slavery Society was Frederick Douglass. Douglass and Sojourner Truth, another freed slave, sought to influence public opinion by telling the stories of their own lives.

Voice of Liberation. *The Liberator* was perhaps the best known of the abolitionist newspapers.

ABOLITIONISTS IN PRINT

Throughout the early 1800s, abolitionist books and newspapers helped to stir antislavery feelings throughout the country.

1827 John Russworm, a former slave, founds *Freedom's Journal*, the first African-American newspaper.

1829 David Walker, a free black, publishes *The Appeal*, urging black Americans to strike for their freedom.

1831 William Lloyd Garrison begins publishing a newspaper called *The Liberator*, in which he demands freedom for slaves, claiming that the Declaration of Independence forbids slavery.

1847 Former slave and famous antislavery orator Frederick Douglass founds the newspaper *North Star*.

▲ **William Lloyd Garrison's** printed attacks on slave dealers caused him to be jailed for 7 months.

Sojourner Truth (born Isabella Baumfree) was the first black female orator to speak out against slavery. Born a slave, she became free when New York State outlawed slavery in 1828.

UNCLE TOM'S CABIN

In 1852, author Harriet Beecher Stowe published *Uncle Tom's Cabin*, a novel. The work described the cruelties of slave life and the desperation of the slaves who fled from it. It quickly became a best-seller in the United States and Great Britain. In the North, it stirred antislavery feelings to a fever pitch; in the South, Stowe became a hated figure.

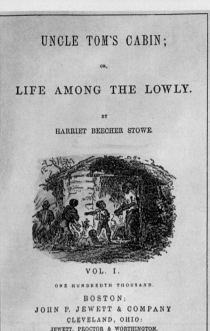

UNCLE TOM'S CABIN;

OR,

LIFE AMONG THE LOWLY.

BY

HARRIET BEECHER STOWE.

VOL. I.

ONE HUNDREDTH THOUSAND.

BOSTON:
JOHN P. JEWETT & COMPANY
CLEVELAND, OHIO:
JEWETT, PROCTOR & WORTHINGTON.
1852.

MORE FAMOUS ABOLITIONISTS

- Poets John Greenleaf Whittier and James Russell Lowell
- Reformers Wendell Phillips and Theodore Weld
- Women's rights activist Lucretia Mott
- Angelina and Sarah Grimke, wealthy sisters from the South who had left South Carolina in protest against slavery

In 1840, abolitionists formed the Liberty Party and ran a presidential candidate. In 1854, the antislavery factions within the nation's major political parties—the Whigs and the Democrats—split from their parties and formed the Republican Party.

Spotlight on... **FREDERICK DOUGLASS**

1818?–1895

- U.S. writer and speaker, a leading voice of the abolitionist movement.

- Born a slave, Douglass learned to read and write from his owner's wife. His eloquent *Narrative of the Life of Frederick Douglass, an American Slave* (1845), is a classic.

- In 1838, he escaped to New York and became a speaker for the Massachusetts Anti-Slavery Society. To avoid reenslavement, he went to England to lecture on slavery and women's rights.

- On his return, he founded the antislavery weekly *North Star*, published until 1860.

- After the Civil War, Douglass involved himself in the issues of Reconstruction and held federal office.

Seeking Freedom

The Underground Railroad

While advocating for the end of slavery, many abolitionists also acted to free slaves by helping them escape. Slaves seeking freedom would travel by night, following the North Star to make their way up to Northern states or to Canada, which prohibited slavery. Abolitionists along the way hid the fleeing slaves in their homes and farms by day. This informal system was called the Underground Railroad, because of the swift, secret way in which the slaves escaped. (See also page 273.)

A Dangerous Escape. The Underground Railroad had no formal organization. Some whites and free blacks provided runaways with food, clothing, directions, and places to hide. Some enslaved people in the South also helped fugitives escape. Thanks to the Fugitive Slave Law, passed in 1850, those who helped slaves escape or hid them from authorities faced harsh punishment. Escaped slaves in the North could be captured and returned to slavery. Several thousand people who walked, ran, swam, and sailed to freedom successfully reached their destinations. Many others did not.

Effects. The Underground Railroad showed the determination of a small group of Americans to end slavery. Its success angered many and contributed significantly to the hostility between North and South that led to the American Civil War (1861–1865).

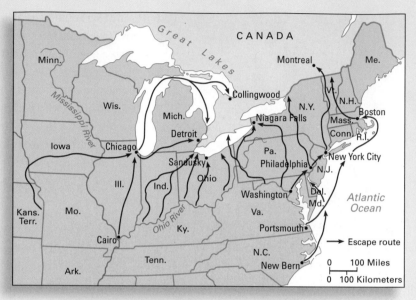

The Road to Freedom. This map shows the network of routes that made up the Underground Railroad. These routes led from slave states to free states and to Canada.

HARRIET TUBMAN

1820?–1913

- Called the "Moses of her people," Tubman risked her life leading groups of escaped slaves to the North along the Underground Railroad.

- Born into slavery, she escaped in 1849 and fled to Philadelphia.

- She made 19 trips to and from the South via the Underground Railroad.

- Despite large rewards offered for her capture, Tubman succeeded in bringing out more than 300 fugitive slaves.

- After the Civil War began, she worked as a nurse, a scout for Union soldiers, and a spy.

HARPER'S FERRY UPRISING

In 1855, antislavery activist John Brown moved to Kansas, where clashes with proslavery forces from Missouri had turned violent.

- After a bloody attack at Lawrence, Kansas, on May 21 by proslavery men, Brown and six others attacked a proslavery encampment on the Pottawatomie Creek and killed five people.

- In August, he and a small band of antislavery fighters battled against a much larger force of proslavery men, gaining Brown even more notoriety.

- Finally, on the night of October 15, 1859, Brown and a small band of followers attacked and took the federal armory at Harper's Ferry, Virginia. They hoped to steal weapons for a slave revolt.

President Buchanan ordered U.S. Marines to retake the armory and capture Brown. After a 2-day siege, the Marines succeeded. Brown was tried for treason and hanged on December 2, 1859. He became a martyr to the abolitionist movement, memorialized in the Civil War song "John Brown's Body."

HARPER'S FERRY.

Harper's Ferry. After John Brown's attack, many in the South felt that their survival as slaveholding states might require separation from the Union.

Finishing the Revolution Against Tyranny

As the 1850s drew to a close, many Southerners began to regard their struggles against the North as an extension of the American Revolution. Even as abolitionists and slaves sought freedom for African Americans, Southerners sought freedom from what they perceived as the tyranny of a central government infringing upon their rights as sovereign states.

One of the central tensions surrounding the creation of the United States was the power assigned to the federal government. The first attempt to resolve this tension, the Articles of Confederation (1781), failed because the bonds of union weren't strong enough. States were largely free to enact their own policies. When the Constitutional Convention met, much debate was held on how to strengthen the central government without reimposing a tyranny similar to a monarch's. (See also pages 64–65.)

The compromises between federal and state authority struck in the Constitution did not entirely satisfy the Southern states. That dissatisfaction simmered during the first half of the 19th century. Its primary manifestation became the issue of extending the institution of slavery into territories and states admitted into the Union. Are states free to choose slavery or does the federal government have the authority to limit slavery?

As the political turmoil increased—as grand bargains such as the Missouri Compromise were negotiated, political parties foundered or established themselves, and rhetoric became heated on both sides—that question was recast as a choice.

- Will the country choose to be a nation, a larger entity that does not allow a minority to rend it asunder whenever it chooses?

- Or does the country choose to curtail the power of the central government and restore freedom to the states because the states have rights and powers that the federal government cannot legally deny?

The latter, sometimes known as state sovereignty or states' rights, became a rallying cry of Southerners who firmly and passionately believed they were finally completing the Revolution.

THE CIVIL WAR

Between December of 1860 and February of 1861, six states seceded (withdrew) from the United States. They banded together to form the Confederate States of America. (Five more would leave the Union and join the Confederacy in March and April 1861.) In April 1861, Confederate forces bombarded Fort Sumter. After decades of conflict, war had finally broken out between the North and the South. At the beginning of the war, the North and South each hoped to gain victory in a short war—90 days perhaps. But the war would last 4 years.

Union artillery fires upon advancing Confederate troops during the Battle of Gettysburg (July 1–3, 1863). This Pennsylvania battle is considered a turning point in the war. ▼

The Civil War: Time Line

Nov. 6
Abraham Lincoln, running as the candidate of the Republican Party, is elected president. ▼

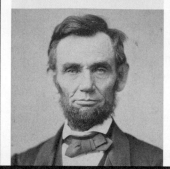

1860

Dec. 20
South Carolina secedes from the Union. Five other states of the lower South—Mississippi, Florida, Alabama, Georgia, and Louisiana—follow suit.

Feb. 9
Representatives of the six states that seceded meet in Montgomery, AL, to form a new nation: the Confederate States of America. They elect as president Jefferson Davis of Mississippi.

1861

Feb. 22
Davis inaugurated at Montgomery, AL.

March 2
Texas joins the Confederacy.

Legend

 Union victory

 Confederate victory

 Draw

(U) Union general
(C) Confederate general
(k) killed
ital victorious general

◄ July 21

The first battle of Bull Run (First Manassas): Union forces marching from Washington, D.C., clash with Confederate troops at Manassas Junction in Virginia. The Union army is forced to retreat. Irvin McDowell (U); *J. E. Johnston* and *P. G. T. Beauregard (C).*

Jan. 19

Battle of Mill Springs (or Logan's Cross Roads), KY: *G. H. Thomas (U)*; G. B. Crittenden (C).

Feb. 6

Fall of Fort Henry, TN: *Ulysses S. Grant (U)*; L. Tilghman (C).

April 6–7

At Shiloh, TN, a Confederate attack on General Grant's Union army fails. The Confederate troops withdraw after 2 days of bloody fighting. *Ulysses S. Grant (U)*; A. S. Johnston (k) and P. G. T. Beauregard (C).

April 16

First Confederate Conscription Act.

1862

March 4

Abraham Lincoln is inaugurated.

April 12–13

The Confederates attack federally held Fort Sumter in the harbor of Charleston, SC, triggering the Civil War.

April 19

Blockade of Southern ports declared by President Lincoln.

May

Virginia, Tennessee, Arkansas, and North Carolina join the Confederacy. The Confederate capital moves from Montgomery, AL, to Richmond, VA, on May 21.

Aug. 10

Battle of Wilson's Creek, MO: Nathaniel Lyon (U)(k); *Ben McCulloch (C).*

Oct. 21

Battle of Ball's Bluff, VA: C. P. Stone (U); *N. G. Evans (C).*

Nov. 7

Battle of Belmont, MO: Ulysses S. Grant (U): *L. Polk (C).*

Nov. 8

Union seizure of Confederate commissioners James Mason and John Slidell from the British steamer *Trent.*

Dec. 9

Creation of Committee on the Conduct of the War by Union Congress.

Feb. 14–16

Siege and surrender of Fort Donelson, TN: *Ulysses S. Grant (U)*; S. B. Buckner (C).

March–June 9

Jackson's Valley campaign (VA): N. P. Banks (U); *T. J. Jackson (C).*

March 9

The Union warship *Monitor* forces the Confederate ship *Merrimack* to a draw. The *Merrimack* retires. This is the first battle in history between ironclad warships.

April 5–May 4

Siege of Yorktown, VA: *G. B. McClellan (U)*; J. B. Magruder and J. E. Johnston (C).

May 1

Surrender of New Orleans, LA: *B. F. Butler (U)*; Mansfield Lovell (C).

May 31–June 1

Battle of Seven Pines (or Fair Oaks), VA: *G. B. McClellan (U)*; J. E. Johnston and G. W. Smith (C).

June 1

Robert E. Lee appointed to command the Confederate Army of Northern Virginia.

June 25–July 1

Seven Days battles, VA: G. B. McClellan (U); *Robert E. Lee (C).*

July 17
Second Union Confiscation Act passed.

Aug. 29–30
The Second Battle of Bull Run (Second Manassas) takes place as Union troops, trying to capture the Confederate capital at Richmond, VA, are defeated by Confederate troops. John Pope (U); *Robert E. Lee (C).*

Oct. 3–4
Battle of Corinth, MS: *W. S. Rosecrans (U)*; E. Van Dorn (C).

Oct. 8
Battle of Perryville, KY: D. C. Buell (U); Braxton Bragg (C). Draw.

Jan. 1
Lincoln signs the Emancipation Proclamation, declaring all slaves in Confederate states free.

Jan. 1
Galveston, TX, recaptured: I. S. Burrell (U); *J. B. Magruder (C).*

April 11–May 4
Siege of Suffolk, VA: *John J. Peck (U)*; James Longstreet (C).

May 1–May 4
At the Battle of Chancellorsville, in Virginia, Lee's troops defeat another Union attempt on Richmond. "Stonewall" Jackson is wounded and dies on May 10. Joseph Hooker (U); *Robert E. Lee (C).*

1863

Sept. 17
At Antietam Creek in Maryland, Confederate troops marching to attack Pennsylvania are stopped by Union troops at the Battle of Antietam (Sharpsburg). They retreat to Virginia. *G. B. McClellan (U)*; Robert E. Lee (C).

Sept. 19
Battle of Iuka, MS: *W. S. Rosecrans (U)*; Sterling Price (C).

Sept. 24
President Lincoln suspends the writ of *habeas corpus* rights in the Union.

Dec. 13
At Fredericksburg, VA, Union forces are defeated again as they try for Richmond. A. E. Burnside (U); *Robert E. Lee (C).*

Dec. 20
Holly Springs, MS, depot captured and burned; R. C. Murphy (U); *E. Van Dorn (C).*

Dec. 31– Jan. 2, 1863
Battle of Stones River (or Murfreesboro), TN: W. S. Rosecrans (U); Braxton Bragg (C). Draw. ▶

Feb. 25
Union National Bank Act effective.

March 3
Union Federal Draft Act.

June 9
Cavalry battle of Brandy Station, VA: Alfred Pleasanton (U); *Jeb Stuart (C).*

A greater proportion of men were killed, wounded, or captured during the Battle of Stones River than in any other Civil War battle.

June 20
West Virginia admitted to Union.

June 23–30
Tullahoma, TN, campaign:
W. S. Rosecrans (U);
Braxton Bragg (C).

July 13–16
In March, Congress had instituted the first national military draft. Because only the wealthy could escape conscription by paying $300 or hiring a substitute, the act became known as the poor man's draft. It triggers 4 days of bloody July riots in New York City.

Feb. 3–March 5
Meridian, MS, campaign:
W. T. Sherman (U); L. Polk (C).
No decision.

Feb. 20
Battle of Olustee (or Ocean Pond), FL: Truman Seymour (U);
Jos. Finegan (C).

May 4
The campaign to take Atlanta begins in Chattanooga. In a series of chesslike maneuvers, W. T. Sherman (U) pushes J. E. Johnston and J. B. Hood (C) southeast toward Atlanta.

1864

July 1–3
At Gettysburg, Lee's march into Pennsylvania is repulsed, and he retreats to Virginia. This loss marks the beginning of the end for the South.
George G. Meade (U);
Robert E. Lee (C).

May 19–July 4
Siege and surrender of Vicksburg, MS. The campaign started in November 1862.
Ulysses S. Grant (U);
John C. Pemberton (C).

May 27–July 9
Siege and surrender of Port Hudson, LA. Together with the fall of Vicksburg, this victory placed the Mississippi River under Union control.
N. P. Banks (U);
Franklin Gardner (C).

Sept. 19–20
In the Battle of Chickamauga, Confederate forces overwhelm the Union forces.
W. S. Rosecrans (U);
Braxton Bragg (C).

Sept. 21–Nov. 25
Siege of Chattanooga, TN, begins on Sept. 21. The Battle of Chattanooga takes place from Nov. 23 to Nov. 25: *Ulysses S. Grant (U)*; Braxton Bragg (C).

Nov. 17–Dec. 4
Siege of Knoxville, TN: *A. E. Burnside (U)*; J. Longstreet (C).

Nov. 19
Lincoln delivers the Gettysburg Address at the battlefield in Gettysburg, PA.

March 9
Ulysses S. Grant is appointed lieutenant general of Union armies.

March 10–May 22
Red River, LA, campaign:
N. P. Banks (U);
Richard Taylor (C).

April 12
Capture of Fort Pillow, TN:
L. F. Booth (U)(k); *N. B. Forrest (C)*.

May 5–6
Battle of the Wilderness, VA:
Ulysses S. Grant (U);
Robert E. Lee (C).

May 8–19
Operations about Spotsylvania Court House, VA:
Ulysses S. Grant (U);
Robert E. Lee (C).
No decision.

May 11
Cavalry battle at Yellow Tavern, VA: *P. H. Sheridan (U)*;
Jeb Stuart (C)(k).

May 15
Battle of New Market, VA:
Franz Sigel (U);
J. C. Breckinridge (C).

May 25–26
Battle of New Hope Church, GA:
J. Hooker (U); *J. E. Johnston (C)*.

Aug. 5
Naval battle in Mobile Bay, AL: *D. G. Farragut (U)*; Percival Drayton (C).

June 1–3
Battle of Cold Harbor, VA: Ulysses S. Grant (U); *Robert E. Lee (C)*.

Aug. 7–Oct. 25
Union forces under Philip H. Sheridan invade the Shenandoah Valley. Grant charges Sheridan with flushing Jubal Early out of the valley and removing the threat to Washington, D.C.

Oct. 23
Battle of Westport, MO: *S. R. Curtis (U)*; Sterling Price (C).

June 10
Battle of Brice's Cross Roads, MS: S. D. Sturgis (U); *N. B. Forrest (C)*.

Nov. 8
Lincoln reelected president.

Jan. 13–15
Battle of Fort Fisher, NC: *A. H. Terry (U)*; W. H. Whiting (C)(k).

Feb. 3
Hampton Roads, VA, peace conference.

1865

June 20
Siege of Petersburg, VA, begins as part of the Union effort to cut off Richmond's supply lines. Trench warfare, a precursor to WWI tactics, lasts until April 1865.

Sept. 1
Atlanta falls to Union forces and the city is evacuated. *W. T. Sherman (U)*; J. B. Hood (C).

Nov. 15–Dec. 21
"Sherman's March to the Sea" begins as Union troops under the command of General Sherman cut a path of destruction from Atlanta to Savannah, GA. Savannah falls on December 21.

Feb. 6
Robert E. Lee is appointed general in chief of all Confederate forces.

Feb. 17
Columbia, SC, captured and destroyed by fire: *W. T. Sherman (U)*.

June 19
Naval battle between the *Alabama* and *Kearsarge,* off the French coast; *John A. Winslow (U)*; Raphael Semmes (C). ▶

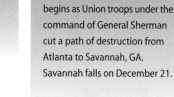

Feb. 18
Charleston, SC, evacuated by Confederate troops.

March 4
Abraham Lincoln inaugurated for second term.

July 5–12
Early's raid on Washington, D.C.: *Ulysses S. Grant (U)*; J. E. Early (C).

July 9
Battle of Monocacy, MD: Lew Wallace (U); *J. E. Early (C)*.

Oct. 19
Toward the end of the Shendandoah Valley campaign, Sheridan inflicts a crushing defeat upon Early at the Battle of Cedar Creek, VA. *P. H. Sheridan (U)*; J. E. Early (C).

Nov. 30
Battle of Franklin, TN: *J. Scofield (U)*; J. B. Hood (C).

Dec. 15–16
Battle of Nashville, TN: *G. H. Thomas (U)*; J. B. Hood (C).

April 1

Battle of Five Forks, VA: *P. H. Sheridan (U)*; G. E. Pickett (C).

April 2

Capture of Selma, AL: *J. H. Wilson (U)*; N. B. Forrest (C).

April 12

Capture of Mobile, AL: *E. R. S. Canby (U)*; D. H. Maury (C).

April 15

Death of President Lincoln. Andrew Johnson inaugurated as president. ▶

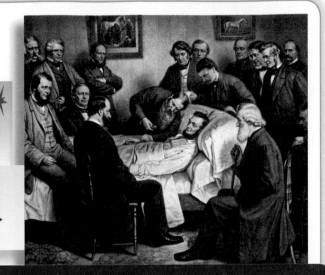

April 2

The Siege of Petersburg ends as Union forces pierce the city's defenses and Confederate forces evacuate after nightfall. The Confederate government evacuates Richmond, the capital, the same day.

April 3

Union forces occupy Richmond.

April 9

Lee surrenders to Grant in the house of Wilmer McClean, in Appomattox Court House, VA. ▶

April 26

Confederate surrender at Durham, NC: *W. T. Sherman (U)*; J. E. Johnston (C).

May 4

Surrender of Confederate forces in Louisiana: *E. R. S. Canby (U)*; R. Taylor (C).

May 10

Jefferson Davis captured at Irwinsville, GA.

May 26

Surrender of Trans-Mississippi Dept.: *E. R. S. Canby (U)*; Kirby Smith (C).

June 2

Surrender of Galveston, TX: H. K. *Thatcher (U)*; Kirby Smith (C).

Nov. 6

Final Confederate surrender— *Shenandoah,* Capt. James Waddell, to British authorities at Liverpool, England.

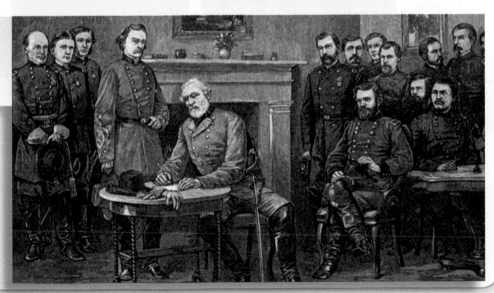

Appomattox Court House.

Lee, always considerate of his men, knew only senseless slaughter awaited them after Grant pursued him deep into Virginia. In this depiction, the two great generals sign the surrender terms in the McLean home.

Davis, Lincoln, and War

THE LINCOLN-DOUGLAS DEBATES

In 1858, Abraham Lincoln ran against Stephen A. Douglas for the Senate. He challenged Douglas to a series of debates on the question of slavery.

- Douglas defended "popular sovereignty"—the right of each state's voters to decide the slavery issue for themselves.

- Lincoln argued that slavery was a moral wrong, and that popular sovereignty would make it permanent.

- Lincoln lost the election, but the Lincoln-Douglas debates brought him national prominence.

The Election of 1860

By the end of the 1850s, compromises between the sides were fraying. Many in the South felt their only option lay in separation from the Union. With Southern states considering secession and violent confrontations in "Bleeding Kansas," the entire nation anxiously awaited the 1860 presidential election.

Nominations. The Democratic Party had split into Northern and Southern factions. The Southern Democrats nominated John C. Breckinridge of Kentucky. The Northern Democrats nominated Senator Stephen A. Douglas of Illinois. The Republicans nominated Abraham Lincoln, also from Illinois.

Election of 1860	Electoral Votes	Popular Votes
Abraham Lincoln (Republican)	180	1,865,908
Stephen A. Douglas (Northern Democrat)	12	1,380,202
John C. Breckinridge (Southern Democrat)	72	848,019
John Bell (Constitutional Union)	39	590,901

Lincoln's Victory. Thanks to the split in the Democratic Party, Lincoln won the election easily. However, he won only 40 percent of the popular vote. All of his electoral votes—and most of his popular votes—came from the North.

Lincoln's platform did not push abolition of slavery but did restrict its extension into territories. The platform also favored a tariff and a homestead act for Western lands, strengthening its appeal to the North and the West. In his inaugural address, Lincoln denied that he had any intention of interfering with slavery in states where the Constitution protected it. He urged the preservation of the Union.

Division and War

Before the 1860 presidential election, some Southern leaders had urged that the South secede from the Union if Lincoln should win. The Republican Party had been founded by abolitionists from the Whig and Democratic parties. Despite Lincoln's stated intentions, Southerners closely associated the Republicans with abolition.

Secession. The secession of Southern states began before Lincoln officially took office. South Carolina led the movement, declaring itself a free and independent state on December 20, 1860. By February 1861, five other states—Mississippi, Florida, Alabama, Georgia, and Louisiana—had taken similar action.

Confederacy. On February 4, delegates from these six states met in Montgomery, Alabama, to form the Confederate States of America. Five days later they elected Jefferson Davis of Mississippi as president and Alexander H. Stephens of Georgia as vice president. The Confederate constitution stressed state sovereignty, prohibited high protective tariffs (import taxes), and recognized "the institution of Negro slavery as it now exists in the Confederate States."

Fort Sumter and War. The young Confederacy took over many federal forts and arsenals in the South. Lincoln, hoping to avoid war and keep the states of the upper South—Virginia, Arkansas, Tennessee, and North Carolina—from seceding, had not acted to oppose the takeovers until the siege of Fort Sumter in April 1861.

- On April 11, the Confederates ordered the commander of the garrison, Major Robert Anderson, to surrender the fort.
- Anderson refused to comply; he let it be known that in a few days the lack of supplies would force him to evacuate anyway.
- On April 12, Confederates began bombarding the fort. After 33 hours of bombardment, Anderson surrendered. The first shots of the Civil War had been fired.
- On April 15, Lincoln called for Union troops to regain the fort.

Lincoln's inauguration took place on March 4, 1861—2 days after Texas left the Union. Lincoln had left politics after one term in Congress. Opposition to the Kansas-Nebraska Act (1854) brought him back.

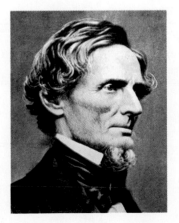

◀ **Jefferson Davis** (*left*) and Alexander H. Stephens had actually opposed secession, but defended slavery and southern states' rights. (See page 117.)

Preparations

Mobilization

The day after the surrender of Fort Sumter, both sides began preparations for full-scale war.

- President Lincoln issued a proclamation calling for 75,000 troops.

- Within a month, four more states had gone over to the Confederacy. Virginia seceded, but its western section remained loyal to the Union and was admitted to the Union as the state of West Virginia. Arkansas, Tennessee, and North Carolina followed.

- President Davis licensed Southern privateers to seize U.S. vessels.

- Lincoln proclaimed a blockade of Southern ports.

States Secede from the Union	
State	**Month/Year**
South Carolina	December 1860
Alabama	January 1861
Florida	January 1861
Georgia	January 1861
Louisiana	January 1861
Mississippi	January 1861
Texas	March 1861
Arkansas	April 1861
North Carolina	April 1861
Tennessee	April 1861
Virginia	April 1861

In Kentucky and Missouri—states that were members of the Union—secessionist groups set up separate state governments and sent representatives to the Confederate Congress.

Membership in the Confederacy and the Union					
Confederate States of America (11 states)		**Union (23 states plus 7 territories)**			
Alabama	Tennessee	California	Maine	New York	**Territories**
Arkansas	Texas	Connecticut	Maryland	Ohio	Colorado
Florida	Virginia	Delaware	Massachusetts	Oregon	Dakota
Georgia		Illinois	Michigan	Pennsylvania	Nebraska
Louisiana		Indiana	Minnesota	Rhode Island	Nevada
Mississippi		Iowa	Missouri	Vermont	New Mexico
North Carolina		Kansas	New Hampshire	Wisconsin	Utah
South Carolina		Kentucky	New Jersey		Washington

Unequal Sides

By December 1861, 600,000 men were in the Union army. In the South, the call for volunteers met with equal success. However, the Confederate army would reach peak strength in 1863, and then decline, while the Union army kept growing. All in all, the sides were unevenly matched.

Civil War Commanders

The South had many brilliant commanders, some of whom—like Robert E. Lee—had originally been part of the U.S. Army. Lincoln had a harder time recruiting commanders who met his expectations.

Many of the officers had trained together at West Point and served together in the Mexican War but now found themselves on opposite sides of the conflict.

Comparing North and South in 1861			
Resource	**North**	**South**	**Advantage**
Military talent	Struggled to find strong commanders at first	Many talented U.S. Army officers resigned to serve in the Confederacy	South
Population (general)	23 million	9 million (including 4 million slaves)	North
Population (military age)	4 million	1 million	North
Factories	110,000	18,000	North
Railroads	27,000 miles (43,000 km) of track	8,400 miles (13,500 km) of track	North

Ulysses S. Grant

Thomas J. "Stonewall" Jackson

William T. Sherman

James Longstreet

Generals Declare Loyalties	
North	**South**
Ambrose E. Burnside	Pierre G. T. Beauregard
Ulysses S. Grant	Braxton Bragg
Henry W. Halleck	Jubal E. Early
Joseph Hooker	Nathan Bedford Forrest
George B. McClellan	Ambrose Powell (A. P.) Hill
Irvin McDowell	Daniel Harvey (D. H.) Hill
George G. Meade	Thomas J. "Stonewall" Jackson
John Pope	Albert Sidney Johnston
William S. Rosecrans	Joseph E. Johnston
Philip H. Sheridan	Robert E. Lee
William T. Sherman	James Longstreet
George H. Thomas	J. E .B. Stuart

The Anaconda Plan

The South planned to wear the North down with a defensive war. The North, on the other hand, planned to invade and isolate the South with General Winfield Scott's Anaconda Plan (named after the python that crushes its victims). The plan would split the South into three parts.

1. Capture the Mississippi River valley and isolate states west of it.

2. Split the Confederacy east and west of the Appalachians.

3. Strangle the South with a naval blockade extending from Virginia to Texas.

BATTLE OF THE IRONCLADS

In 1861, the Confederates had raised a sunken federal ship, the *Merrimack*, off Norfolk, Virginia, covered the wooden vessel with iron plates, and renamed it the *Virginia*. On March 8, 1862, the *Virginia* attacked the Northern ships at Hampton Roads, a channel in Virginia. It destroyed two Northern vessels and grounded three others. When the ship returned the next day to finish the job, it faced the *Monitor*, an ironclad ship designed especially for the Northern Navy. History's first battle between ironclad warships followed. Although neither ship won, the *Monitor* proved to be the superior vessel. Later, the U.S. Navy built a large ironclad fleet modeled after it.

Early Battles

Several early battles were fought in an attempt by the North to capture the Confederate capital, Richmond. Union forces hoped the capture would demoralize the South.

First Bull Run. In July 1861, the Union advance was stopped by General Thomas Jonathan Jackson, who earned his nickname "Stonewall" in this battle by standing (it was later claimed) calmly in the midst of the fighting, like a stone wall.

Second Bull Run. Union forces under General John Pope joined with General George B. McClellan's forces and marched on Richmond in the summer of 1862. But like the Union army of 1861, they too were stopped at Bull Run in a battle on August 29 and 30.

General Robert E. Lee hoped to invade Maryland and wreak havoc—cut off roads and rail lines, take prisoners, capture supplies, and demoralize the North. ▶

Antietam. While the Union tried to capture Richmond, Lee set out to invade the border state of Maryland. On September 17, 1862, Union and Confederate forces met in the bloodiest single-day battle of the war, at Antietam Creek in Maryland. Almost 5,000 died and more than 18,000 were wounded. McClellan fought the Confederate army to a draw, but allowed Lee's army to retreat.

Fredericksburg and Chancellorsville. Union troops under General Ambrose E. Burnside made another attempt on Richmond in mid-December 1862. Lee's smaller army stopped the Union Army at Fredericksburg. General Joseph "Fighting Joe" Hooker marched on Richmond in late April 1863, but only got as far as Chancellorsville. The Union defeat came with 17,000 dead, wounded, or missing.

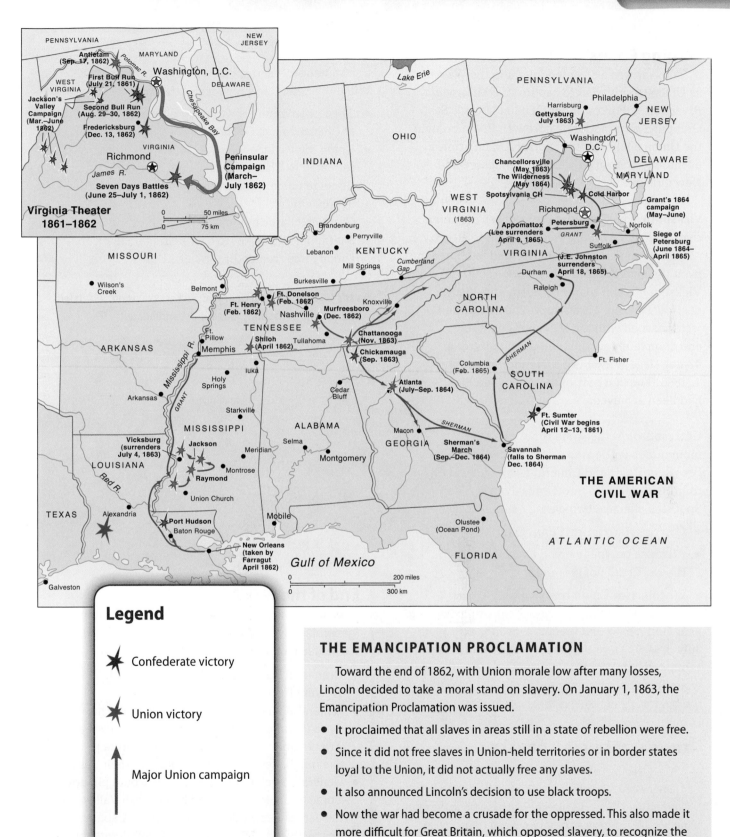

Virginia Theater 1861–1862

Antietam (Sep. 17, 1862)
First Bull Run (July 21, 1861)
Jackson's Valley Campaign (Mar.–June 1862)
Second Bull Run (Aug. 29–30, 1862)
Fredericksburg (Dec. 13, 1862)
Washington, D.C.
Richmond
James R.
Seven Days Battles (June 25–July 1, 1862)
Peninsular Campaign (March– July 1862)
PENNSYLVANIA
MARYLAND
NEW JERSEY
WEST VIRGINIA
DELAWARE
VIRGINIA
Potomac R.
Chesapeake Bay

0   50 miles
0   75 km

THE AMERICAN CIVIL WAR

Lake Erie
PENNSYLVANIA
Harrisburg
Philadelphia
Gettysburg July 1863
NEW JERSEY
Washington, D.C.
DELAWARE
MARYLAND
Chancellorsville (May 1863)
The Wilderness (May 1864)
Spotsylvania CH
Cold Harbor
Grant's 1864 campaign (May–June)
Richmond
Appomattox (Lee surrenders April 9, 1865)
Petersburg
Norfolk
Suffolk
Siege of Petersburg (June 1864– April 1865)
GRANT
OHIO
INDIANA
WEST VIRGINIA (1863)
VIRGINIA
(J.E. Johnston surrenders April 18, 1865)
Durham
Raleigh
Brandenburg
Perryville
Lebanon
KENTUCKY
Mill Springs
Cumberland Gap
Burkesville
MISSOURI
Wilson's Creek
Belmont
Ft. Donelson (Feb. 1862)
Ft. Henry (Feb. 1862)
Nashville
Murfreesboro (Dec. 1862)
Knoxville
NORTH CAROLINA
Ft. Pillow
Memphis
TENNESSEE
Shiloh (April 1862)
Tullahoma
Chattanooga (Nov. 1863)
Chickamauga (Sep. 1863)
Columbia (Feb. 1865)
Ft. Fisher
ARKANSAS
Mississippi R.
GRANT
Iuka
Holy Springs
Arkansas
Starkville
MISSISSIPPI
Jackson
Meridian
Selma
ALABAMA
Cedar Bluff
Atlanta (July–Sep. 1864)
SOUTH CAROLINA
SHERMAN
Ft. Sumter (Civil War begins April 12–13, 1861)
Vicksburg (surrenders July 4, 1863)
Raymond
Montrose
Union Church
LOUISIANA
Red R.
Montgomery
GEORGIA
Macon
Sherman's March (Sep.–Dec. 1864)
SHERMAN
Savannah (falls to Sherman Dec. 1864)
TEXAS
Alexandria
Port Hudson
Baton Rouge
Mobile
Olustee (Ocean Pond)
FLORIDA
ATLANTIC OCEAN
New Orleans (taken by Farragut April 1862)
Gulf of Mexico
Galveston

0   200 miles
0   300 km

Legend

✶ Confederate victory

✴ Union victory

↑ Major Union campaign

THE EMANCIPATION PROCLAMATION

Toward the end of 1862, with Union morale low after many losses, Lincoln decided to take a moral stand on slavery. On January 1, 1863, the Emancipation Proclamation was issued.

- It proclaimed that all slaves in areas still in a state of rebellion were free.
- Since it did not free slaves in Union-held territories or in border states loyal to the Union, it did not actually free any slaves.
- It also announced Lincoln's decision to use black troops.
- Now the war had become a crusade for the oppressed. This also made it more difficult for Great Britain, which opposed slavery, to recognize the Confederacy.

Battles and Campaigns

Turning Points

The war was also being fought in the West, as Union troops tried to capture the Mississippi River valley. Forces under General Ulysses S. Grant and Commodore Andrew H. Foote brought the Union a number of victories. Union armies eventually controlled western Tennessee and New Orleans.

Vicksburg. The Confederate defenses high on a river bluff at Vicksburg were difficult to attack. After several failures, Grant decided to approach from the east. After landing troops south of Vicksburg, Grant marched north and east to destroy Jackson, Mississippi. Then he turned west, clashed with the Vicksburg garrison, and completely surrounded the city. After a 47-day siege, Vicksburg surrendered on July 4, 1863. The first part of the Anaconda Plan had been achieved.

Gettysburg. At the same time, another momentous battle was raging in the East. President Davis and General Lee had decided to bring the war up into Pennsylvania. The Southern plan had two parts.

- Capture Harrisburg, Pennsylvania
- Advance on Philadelphia and New York if the North did not surrender

Lincoln sent Union troops under General George C. Meade to stop Lee. The two forces met near Gettysburg and fought from July 1 through July 3, 1863. Here the South met defeat. The estimated number of Union and Confederate dead, wounded, and missing was 51,000. This marked the beginning of the end for the South.

THE GETTYSBURG ADDRESS

On November 19, 1863, President Lincoln spoke at a ceremony dedicating the Gettysburg battlefield to those who had died there. His speech, which is among the most memorable in American history, defined the nation as dedicated to equality.

Chickamauga. A series of battles set the stage for General William T. Sherman's march to Atlanta and the sea.

- The Confederate army overwhelmed the Union forces at Chickamauga, Georgia.
- Union forces under General William S. Rosecrans retreated to Chattanooga. General Braxton Bragg's Confederate forces occupied high ground surrounding the city.
- Grant, in charge of the western armies, rushed with Sherman and Hooker to Chattanooga; the combined Union forces routed Bragg's army.

Pickett's Charge. General George C. Pickett's division, which led a final charge at Gettysburg, was almost annihilated. ▼

End of the War

General Grant was appointed lieutenant general (general in chief) of all Union armies in March 1864. He devised a three-point plan to end the war.

- Grant and his troops were to march from Washington and capture Richmond.
- General William Tecumseh Sherman and his forces were to march from Chattanooga, Tennessee, to Atlanta and then sweep through Georgia to Savannah, destroying everything in their path.
- Generals Sigel, Butler, and Banks would pin down Confederate forces in the Shenandoah Valley, on the James Peninsula, and at Mobile, Alabama (respectively), thus preventing Confederate forces from consolidating against Grant and Sherman.

CIVIL WAR SOLDIERS

The Civil War was fought primarily by foot soldiers, most of them untrained. Compared with today's standards, they had a hard life. Both sides paid their soldiers poorly. Blue-clad Union soldiers were called "bluecoats," while the homespun-clad Confederate soldiers were known as "butternuts."

Uniforms and Weapons. Most Civil War soldiers carried muzzle-loading rifles. These were more accurate than previous types of rifles.

Union Victory. The Shenandoah campaign was successful after General Sheridan replaced Sigel, but Butler and Banks both failed utterly. Grant and Sherman prevailed nonetheless. On April 9, 1865, after General Lee's Army of Northern Virginia was worn down and finally trapped by Grant's forces, Lee surrendered to General Grant at Appomattox Court House in southwestern Virginia.

Death of Lincoln. On the night of April 14, five days after Lee's surrender, President Lincoln attended a performance of a play entitled *Our American Cousin* at Ford's Theater in Washington, D.C. At about 10 o'clock, a shot rang out. John Wilkes Booth, a popular actor and Confederate sympathizer, had shot Lincoln in the head. As he leaped down to the stage, Booth shouted, "Sic semper tyrannis!" ("Thus ever to tyrants"—the Virginia state motto). The president died of his wound the next morning.

Vice President Andrew Johnson of Tennessee, a southern Democrat who had remained loyal to the Union, became the 17th president of the United States.

now you Know!

- ✔ By 1860, the nation was deeply divided on the question of slavery. Violence had even broken out between proslavery and antislavery forces.

- ✔ In 1860, Abraham Lincoln became president of the United States, and Southern states began to secede from, or leave, the Union.

- ✔ Eleven states seceded and formed the Confederate States of America in 1861.

- ✔ The Civil War between the Union and the Confederacy began on April 15, 1861, at Fort Sumter in South Carolina.

- ✔ The war lasted from 1861 to 1865 and ended with a Union victory.

- ✔ In 1865, five days after Lee's surrender, Abraham Lincoln was assassinated. Andrew Johnson became president.

CIVIL WAR AFTERMATH

Once the Civil War had finally ended, the nation faced many difficult problems. Much of the American South lay in ruins. Political leaders on both sides were unsure of how the Confederate states would reenter the Union. The period following the war, in which the nation worked to solve these and other problems, is known as Reconstruction.

Reconstruction

"All Men Are Created Equal"

The Emancipation Proclamation (1863) sharpened the focus of the American Civil War into a fight to abolish slavery. When the war ended, three amendments to the Constitution became the foundation for African-American freedom and civil rights. (For the full text of these amendments, see pages 80–81.)

The 13th Amendment

The 13th Amendment legally abolished slavery— "involuntary servitude"—in the United States. Slaves had been freed after the Union's victory in the Civil War, but this confirmed the change and gave Congress the power to enforce it.

Ratification. President Andrew Johnson demanded that former Confederate states ratify, or approve, the amendment. By December 6, 1865, 27 states had ratified it, making it law.

Reconstructing the Nation. This photograph captures a scene of destruction typical throughout the South. Here, the Northeastern Railroad Depot in Charleston, South Carolina, has been destroyed by the Union forces of General Sherman. Rebuilding transportation, reforging political bonds, and reviving citizenship were the main tasks of Reconstruction.

The 14th Amendment

After the war, a number of the reorganized state governments drew up laws called Black Codes, which denied blacks many rights of citizenship. Partly in response to this, Congress proposed the 14th Amendment in 1866. The amendment

- granted citizenship rights to blacks (as well as to anyone born in the United States). This overturned the Supreme Court decision *Dred Scott v. Sandford* (1857), which had declared that black slaves were not citizens.

- declared that no state could deny a citizen any rights without due process, or proper legal procedures.

- granted equal protection under the law to all citizens.

- granted the right to vote to any male citizen over 21 years old.

- forbade Confederate officers from serving in the federal government. It also forbade the federal and state governments from paying Confederate debts.

Ratification. President Johnson opposed the 14th Amendment as a violation of states' rights. He encouraged states not to ratify it. This backfired, however, and Congress eventually made approval of the 14th Amendment a requirement for readmitting a state to the Union.

The 15th Amendment

The 14th Amendment had given blacks the right to vote when it extended voting rights to all men over age 21. The 15th Amendment, proposed in 1869 and ratified in 1870, forbade states from denying voting rights based on race. It was meant to strengthen and emphasize black voting rights.

Ratification. Amendment 15 was ratified on February 3, 1870. Seven Southern states tried to bypass it by adding grandfather clauses to their constitutions. One such clause gave the right to vote to people who could vote on January 1, 1867, and to their family descendants. In 1915 and 1939, the Supreme Court of the United States declared "grandfather clauses" unconstitutional.

LIFE AFTER SLAVERY

The Union victory in the Civil War ended the practice of slavery in the United States. Constitutional amendments protected African Americans' citizenship and voting rights. Still, life remained desperate for many newly free slaves, or freedmen.

The Black Codes were laws passed by some states that denied the freedmen many rights of citizenship. They forbade blacks from carrying arms, required that they serve an apprenticeship while under age, governed their employment, and instituted curfews.

Sharecropping became the only option for some former slaves. Often they worked a plot of their former masters' lands and lived no better than they had before.

The Freedmen's Bureau, established by Congress in March 1865, offered funds for food, education, and legal protection.

◀ **African-American students and teachers** gather outside a Freedmen's Bureau school in Beaufort, South Carolina.

Reconstruction

Conflicting Plans

The debate over Reconstruction had begun as early as 1861. In the end, several different plans emerged.

Lincoln's Plan. Lincoln had wanted to restore civil government to the South as quickly as possible. Under his plan, each formerly rebellious state had to meet two conditions.

- First, 10 percent of its citizens who had voted in 1860 had to swear an oath of allegiance to the United States. (High-ranking Confederate leaders, former U.S. congressmen and judges who supported the rebellion, and military officers would not be pardoned.)

- Second, the state had to abolish slavery.

Radical Reconstruction. In Congress, a group of so-called "Radical Republicans" believed that Lincoln's plan was far too lenient. In 1864, they pushed through the Wade-Davis Bill, a harsher plan.

- First, more than 50 percent of white males had to swear allegiance.

- Second, anyone who wanted to vote or take part in government had to swear never to have supported the Confederacy.

- Third, the state government not only had to abolish slavery, but to repudiate Confederate debts and its act of secession.

Johnson's Plan. President Andrew Johnson had been a bitter opponent of secession, but he did not share the Radical Republicans' views. Johnson's plan demanded that reorganized states

- repudiate Confederate debts and acts of secession.

- legally end slavery by ratifying the 13th Amendment.

Johnson's plan offered a full pardon to anyone who would swear allegiance to the Constitution, including many former Confederate officials.

Legislative Sparring

Johnson and Congress fought over legislation as well as Confederate pardons. Johnson vetoed several bills.

- A bill to renew the Freedmen's Bureau and extend its powers to protect blacks (1866)

- The Civil Rights Act, which declared that freedmen were U.S. citizens entitled "to full and equal benefit of the laws" (1866)

- The Reconstruction Act of 1867, which divided the South into five military districts, each under the control of a military commander

In each case, Congress passed new bills or overrode Johnson's vetoes.

Carpetbaggers. Northerners who had moved to the South following the war were often derided as "carpetbaggers," especially after they began to exert some power in Southern state governments.

Impeachment

Due to these conflicts, Congress worked to limit Johnson's role in Reconstruction.

- The Tenure of Office Act denied the president the right to dismiss civilian government officials without Senate approval.

- In 1867, Johnson came into conflict with Secretary of War Edwin M. Stanton; on February 21, 1868, Johnson removed Stanton from office.

- Radical Republicans saw this as an opportunity to get rid of Johnson, so the House voted to bring articles of impeachment against him on February 24, 1868.

From March 30 to May 26, Johnson stood trial. In two votes, 35 senators voted Johnson guilty— one vote short of the necessary two-thirds majority.

HOW A PRESIDENT IS IMPEACHED

In the impeachment process, the House draws up charges against a federal official. If the House votes to impeach, the official is tried in the Senate with the chief justice of the Supreme Court presiding as judge. A two-thirds majority vote is required to remove the official from office.

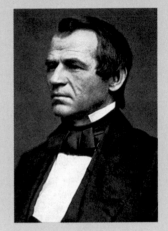

After impeachment, President Johnson could remain in office, but his power was greatly diminished.

Reconstruction Ends

As time wore on, Reconstruction came to an end. By 1871, all the former Confederate states had reorganized their governments, under generally Republican domination, and had been readmitted to the Union. Gradually, however, Southern governments moved out of Republican hands and into Democratic ones. Unfortunately, racial tensions survived Reconstruction and would continue to plague the country.

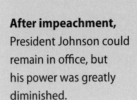

✔ During the era of Reconstruction, leaders debated over the best ways of bringing the Confederate states back into the Union.

✔ Radical Republicans in Congress wanted harsh requirements for Confederate states; Andrew Johnson fought them by vetoing many of their laws.

✔ The 13th, 14th, and 15th Amendments abolished slavery, granted civil rights to African-American citizens, and gave voting rights to African-American males over 21 years old.

Former Confederate States Readmitted to the Union			
State	**Year**	**State**	**Year**
Tennessee	1866	South Carolina	1868
Alabama	1868	Georgia	1870
Arkansas	1868	Mississippi	1870
Florida	1868	Texas	1870
Louisiana	1868	Virginia	1870
North Carolina	1868		

CLOSING THE FRONTIER

In the early 19th century, settlers moving west to the Pacific Ocean mostly ignored the "Last West," the area made up of the Great Plains and the basins, plateaus, and mountains of the Rocky Mountain region. Early explorers called the dry, treeless plains the Great American Desert. Settlers moved through it as quickly as they could and on to California and the Pacific Northwest. During the 1850s, though, settlers began coming to the Last West in large numbers.

Settling the West

Farming the Frontier

Initially, the Great American Desert seemed like a bad place for agriculture. It lacked rainfall, and the tough prairie grasses made plowing difficult. All of this began to change in the mid-1800s.

- Improvements in farm machinery made the Great Plains much easier to farm.
- The Homestead Act made land available at very little or no cost.

As a result, by the 1880s, Kansas and Nebraska were covered with wheat fields. Farm production from the newly settled area soared.

The Homestead Act. In 1862, Abraham Lincoln signed the Homestead Act into law. Under the act

- the government offered settlers 160-acre (65-hectare) plots of land at no cost, if they lived on the land and developed it for 5 years.
- farmers could also buy plots for $1.25 an acre after living on them for only 6 months.

Pioneer Living. Families started life on the frontier with simple housing and a few pieces of (usually handmade) furniture.

PIONEER LIFE

Once their long, difficult journey west was finished, pioneers were faced with the job of building homes and settlements.

Temporary shelters often consisted of a framework of poles covered in mud and branches. They typically had only three walls.

Log cabins were the typical pioneer homes in Kentucky, Tennessee, and many other wooded regions. The pioneers cut trees into logs and then chopped notches close to the ends. The notches held the logs to each other when they were fitted together to form the sides of the cabin.

Pioneer women were typically responsible for making the family's clothing, helping with farming tasks, preparing food for the family (and sometimes the community), and raising children.

New Industries

While some settlers came to the West in search of cheap or free land, others were drawn by the rise of two industries: mining and cattle.

Mining. Prospectors in the Rocky Mountains quickly discovered that the region was rich in precious ores.

- In 1859, a gold strike near Denver, Colorado, caused the Pikes Peak gold rush. Fifty thousand prospectors arrived in just a few months.

- Also in 1859, the greatest deposits of gold and silver ever found were discovered in the Comstock Lode, near Virginia City, Nevada, drawing 20,000 prospectors.

- In 1861, a gold strike at Last Chance Gulch in Montana brought thousands of settlers.

- In 1875, gold was discovered in the Black Hills of the Dakotas, creating the Homestake Mine near Deadwood. (See also page 106.)

Cattle. A growing cattle industry was also bringing in settlers. Millions of longhorns, descendants of cattle brought by the Spanish settlers, roamed lower Texas. Cowboys rounded up the cattle and moved them northward on "the long drive" to such railroad towns as Abilene and Dodge City in Kansas. From these towns, the cattle could be shipped to meatpacking houses in Chicago.

Buffalo soldiers won 13 Medals of Honor between about 1870 and the mid-1890s.

BUFFALO SOLDIERS

After the Civil War and the end of slavery, African Americans played a larger part in the settlement of the American West.

- Formed in 1866, the African-American 9th and 10th cavalries were sent to the West in 1867 to fight Indians.

- The Indians gave the troops the name Buffalo Soldiers, probably because they thought their short, dark, curly hair resembled the mane of the buffalo.

- The soldiers were also assigned to protect settlers and capture outlaws.

Cows and Cowboys. The growing population in the East led to a growing demand for meat and other food. The western range helped meet the demand.

To many Native American tribes, the Last West was their last home. Some Plains Indian tribes had lived there for centuries or longer, but many were driven there by white settlement and the Indian Removal Act of 1830. (See page 104.)

Shrinking Territory

By the 1850s, the resettled Native Americans again faced pressure from land-hungry settlers moving westward. In the 1850s alone, the U.S. government negotiated treaties, many times by unfair means, for 174 million acres of Indian land.

Reservations. In 1851, the American government launched a reservation policy. Under this policy

- Indians were restricted to designated areas.
- settlers were allowed to take over the rest of the land.

Fighting Back. For the next 25 years, clashes erupted between protesting Indians and the U.S. Army. There were bloody massacres by both sides. For example, at Sand Creek, Colorado, American troops attacked a peaceful Indian camp; the Sioux, Cheyenne, and Arapaho Indians retaliated and killed many Americans.

THE BATTLE OF LITTLE BIGHORN

The Battle of Little Bighorn was one of the worst defeats the United States Army ever suffered against American Indian warriors.

- In late 1875, the U.S. government decided to ignore an 1868 treaty with the Sioux and take control of the Black Hills region, where gold had been found.
- The U.S. Army sent three columns to force the Sioux onto reservations.
- On the morning of June 25, Lieutenant Colonel George A. Custer's scouts found an Indian village in the valley along the Little Bighorn River in Montana.
- As Custer headed north, the Sioux and Cheyenne warriors overwhelmed his cavalry unit and killed all 264 men, Custer included.

 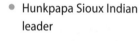

SITTING BULL

1834?–1890

- Hunkpapa Sioux Indian leader
- His forces defeated Custer at Little Bighorn.
- After Little Bighorn, he was driven into Canada, but returned to the United States in 1881.
- In 1890, he encouraged the Ghost Dance spiritual movement.
- Thinking the Ghost Dance posed a threat, the government tried to arrest Sitting Bull. He and his son were killed in the process.

The Battlefield at Little Bighorn. The group of Sioux and Cheyenne warriors at Little Bighorn was one of the largest Indian fighting forces in history. Its leaders included Crazy Horse, Gall, and Sitting Bull.

New Indian Policies

In 1871, Congress concluded that the tribes were no longer separate, independent governments. This action freed the United States from the need to make treaties with the Indians. From then on, government policies would change the way Native Americans lived.

The Dawes Act. The most significant policy was the Dawes Severalty Act of 1887. This act dissolved Indian tribes by law and divided the reservation land among individual Indians. The government wanted to weaken the tribes' collective power and prevent resistance.

A New Way of Life. From the late 1800s, the federal government actively tried to suppress the Native Americans' tribal culture. The government wanted to make Native Americans self-sufficient, educate them, and bring them into non-Indian society.

- The Dawes Act tried to make Native Americans farmers. Each family received 160 acres of reservation land.

- Many Indian children were sent to boarding schools away from their homes. They were not allowed to practice Indian customs or speak Indian languages.

- The Bureau of Indian Affairs (BIA) banned certain religious ceremonies.

As it worked out, many Native Americans had little interest in joining non-Indian society. The Native American landowners first rented, then sold, their land to whites. By 1934, when the system was abolished, tribal holdings had been reduced by nearly two-thirds.

WOUNDED KNEE

The Wounded Knee massacre of 1890 was the final tragedy of the conflicts between Native Americans and the U.S. Army. Soldiers massacred over 200 Sioux who were camped at Wounded Knee Creek, on the way to the Pine Ridge Reservation.

▲ **Geronimo.** In 1886, the capture and imprisonment of the Apache chief Geronimo (shown here with his family) all but ended military resistance by the Indians.

Indian reservations were often located in the poorest areas, which the white settlers did not want. If a designated area became attractive, however, the Indians were driven off.

INDUSTRIAL MIGHT

After the Civil War, U.S. industry changed dramatically. A new nationwide network of railroads distributed goods far and wide. Inventors developed new products the public wanted, and businesses made them in large quantities. Investors and bankers supplied the huge sums of money that industrial leaders needed to expand their operations. Many big businesses grew up. They included coal mining, petroleum, railroad, and manufacturing companies. The industrial growth had major effects on American life.

Rise of Railroads

Beginning in about 1830, the first steam locomotives began serving passengers in the United States. By 1850, rail lines served every U.S. state east of the Mississippi River. In 1857, the Baltimore and Ohio Railroad reached from Baltimore, on the east coast, to St. Louis, just west of the Mississippi.

The Rail Acts

By the 1850s, the American government was eager to link the nation with a transcontinental railroad. Unfortunately, with the nation torn over slavery and the threat of war, the project stalled. Then, in 1861, the Civil War began. Suddenly the Union needed a way to carry people and supplies between the North and the West.

On July 1, 1862, President Abraham Lincoln signed the Pacific Railroad Act. The act

- provided low-cost loans to private railroad companies.
- granted the companies huge tracts of government-owned land.
- required them to use the money made by selling the land to build new railroads.

In 1864, another act was passed, doubling the land grants to the railroads.

THE PONY EXPRESS

Before railroads and telegraphs crisscrossed the nation, there was the Pony Express. This mail delivery service operated between St. Joseph, Missouri, and Sacramento, California, in 1860 and 1861. It consisted of relays of men riding fast ponies or horses across a 1,966-mile (3,164-kilometer) trail. These riders could deliver mail to California in 10 days or less, faster than any other mail service of that time.

◀ **Pony Express** riders braved many dangers as they rode through lonely territory, carrying valuable mail.

The Transcontinental Railroad

With money and land available, the race was on! Two companies were given responsibility for finishing the rail line.

- Central Pacific would begin construction in Sacramento, California, and go east.
- Union Pacific would begin in Omaha, Nebraska, and go west.

Central Pacific began their work in 1863; the Union Pacific crews started in 1865. On May 10, 1869, the two sets of tracks met at Promontory, Utah. It was now possible to cross the nation in only a matter of days. By 1890, the entire Last West could be crossed by such railroads as the Great Northern, the Northern Pacific, and the Southern Pacific.

Effects

Transportation was transformed with the massive expansion of the railroads. Trains now moved people and cargo quickly across tremendous distances and spurred economic growth. Rail company owners such as Cornelius Vanderbilt and Jay Gould made tremendous fortunes.

Industry	• Mining companies used railroads to ship raw materials to factories. • Manufacturers distributed finished products by rail throughout the country.
Agriculture	• Railroad companies sold off land and advertised the sales across the East and Europe to attract new farmers. • Wheat, corn, beef, and poultry could be shipped from the Great Plains to the East.
Cities	• Railroad extension aided the growth of cities such as St. Louis, Cincinnati, and Chicago. • Electric trolley cars, elevated trains, and subways enabled cities to expand beyond all previous dreams.

CHINESE-AMERICANS AND THE RAILROADS

Chinese immigrants began flocking to California during the gold rushes of the mid-1800s.

- They found plenty of work, especially once railroad construction took off.
- The gold rush had created a serious labor shortage because many able-bodied people were busy prospecting for gold.
- The Chinese immigrants worked long hours for low pay as miners, cooks, laundry workers, shopkeepers, and laborers in factories and mills.
- By 1860, the United States had a Chinese population of about 35,000, most of whom lived in California.

Later, Chinese people came in large numbers to work on railroad construction gangs. The Central Pacific part of the transcontinental railroad became the first big railroad construction project to use Chinese labor, employing perhaps 14,000 between 1858 and 1869.

Chinese rail workers were essential to the building of rail lines across the American West.

Rise of Big Business

Between 1890 and 1920, the United States changed from a pioneer nation to a world power. New business activity drew record numbers of people to urban areas. Some Americans amassed huge fortunes from the business boom, but others lived in poverty. The sharp contrast between rich and poor stirred widespread discontent and led to, among other things, measures to control the size and power of big business.

Growth of Industry

Four circumstances led to the nation's phenomenal industrial growth.

Natural Resources. The U.S. had vast reserves of coal, iron ore, oil, copper, zinc, gold, and silver, as well as supplies of lumber and excellent conditions for agriculture.

Growing Markets and Workforces. From 1870 to 1920, immigration and rising birth rates increased the population from 38 million to 106 million. This provided a vast industrial and agricultural workforce and an enormous number of customers for American goods.

Pro-Industry Government. Business enjoyed the benefits of high tariffs (taxes on imports) and government reluctance to curb the excesses of industry.

Innovative Industrial Leaders. Talented inventors, resourceful business organizers, and ingenious investment bankers emerged to create, lead, and finance new industry.

All of these forces combined to cause American industrial production to grow fivefold by 1900.

Spotlight on... ANDREW CARNEGIE

1835–1919

- Scottish-born U.S. industrial magnate Andrew Carnegie was known for his phenomenal accumulation of wealth in the iron and steel business and for his philanthropy.
- Introduced the sleeping car to American railways
- Began the use of iron in bridge building
- Founded the Carnegie Steel Company (which became, in 1901, part of U.S. Steel)
- From the 1880s on, he endowed hundreds of Carnegie libraries and established foundations for education and peace.
- After retiring in 1901, he spent about $300 million on philanthropy.

Corporations. Before 1865, most businesses had been owned by a single proprietor or by a few partners. As businesses grew, though, it became apparent that many small, competing businesses were not necessarily the most efficient way to turn a profit. Instead, financiers formed large corporations by buying and merging small firms.

- Andrew Carnegie assembled all of the elements of steel production—coal and ore mining, shipping to steel plants, steelmaking, shipping to customers— into one vast enterprise, the Carnegie Steel Company.
- John D. Rockefeller brought together many small, independent oil refineries and combined them into the giant Standard Oil Company.
- J. P. Morgan established the United States Steel Corporation in 1901; as a banker, he later financed several major corporations.

Monopolies

Large corporations such as Carnegie Steel and Standard Oil helped create economic growth, but they also created monopolies. A monopoly arises when one business is the only seller of a good or a service. Some business leaders formed trusts, in which a group of managers controlled rival businesses without formally owning the businesses.

Objections. Monopolies and trusts led to high profits and steady sales. However, they gave some companies so much power that they could take unfair advantage of others. Without competition, companies could charge high prices or reduce a product's quality without any consequences.

Soon the cry went up that the government must control the monopolies. Said one advocate of control, Henry Demarest Lloyd, "If the tendency of combination is inevitable, control of it is imperative."

Legislation. The federal government responded with legislation. Many of the laws were ineffective, however, since those in high government office had little interest in placing limits on large industrial corporations.

- The Interstate Commerce Act of 1887 established the Interstate Commerce Commission to keep railroads from giving lower prices to some large businesses.

- The Sherman Antitrust Act of 1890 was passed "to protect trade and commerce against unlawful restraints and monopolies."

- The Clayton Antitrust Act of 1914 protected the rights of labor unions to organize and negotiate.

Spotlight on... JOHN D. ROCKEFELLER

1839–1937

- John D. Rockefeller was one of the wealthiest men of his time, and a symbol of big business in America.

- He entered the oil refining business in 1863.

- By 1880, his Standard Oil Company controlled 90 percent of oil production in the country.

- His business tactics drew strong criticism from rivals.

- He gave away about $540 million during his lifetime, mostly through foundations he established himself and through other organizations.

GIBBONS V. OGDEN

Congress's right to pass laws restricting monopolies comes, in part, from the 1824 Supreme Court case *Gibbons v. Ogden*. The Court ruled

- that federal powers overrule state powers in all interstate (between states) commerce.

- that "commerce" could be broadly defined to include means and routes of transportation— namely, railroads.

- since large corporations such as Standard Oil traded between states, the government could regulate them.

Industrial Effects

Though the beginnings of industrial growth in the United States are usually traced to the 1830s and 1840s, the greatest surge of growth began after the Civil War. In the next 50 years, industrial expansion completely changed the United States—from agricultural to industrial, from rural to urban, from inward-looking to outward-looking.

Shifting Populations

In the years following the Civil War, the American population both grew and shifted. Immigrants poured in, especially from southern and eastern Europe. (See pages 148–149.)

Urbanization. Much of America's farmland had been settled by the late 1800s, so people flocked to cities. Cities had large, ready-made workforces available, and so that is where industrialists built their plants. Once opened, the plants drew in even more workers. Cities doubled or tripled in size. In 1880, less than a quarter of the American population lived in cities. By 1900, well over half of Americans did.

Cities such as Chicago, New York, and Philadelphia were exciting places—centers of theater, music, the arts, and sports. But they had their seamier sides, too. Poverty, crime, and disease were rampant. City governments paid little attention. Powerful political machines stole money from city treasuries and took bribes.

THE SOCIAL GOSPEL

In the late 1800s, some Christian leaders responded to changing social conditions.

- In 1891, Pope Leo XIII called on employers to pay their workers a just wage.
- In the United Kingdom, a movement began combining Christian and socialist policies.
- In the United States, such Protestant ministers as Walter Rauschenbusch preached the Social Gospel, which applied Christian teachings to labor issues and other social problems.

Life in Industrial America

Major industrial leaders—the Carnegies, the Rockefellers, the Fords—grew rich on the growth of their businesses. A comfortable middle class, made up largely of business managers and clerical workers, was growing as well. But a large mass of people were not benefiting from rapid industrialization.

The Working Class. Life for the working class was marked by hardship and uncertainty.

- Industrial laborers worked 70- and 80-hour weeks for less than 20 cents an hour, often in dirty and unsafe conditions.
- Immigrants made up a large percentage of laborers, as well as the children of the poor—as many as 2 million children worked in factories in 1900.
- An injury could throw a person out of work, and when it did, there was no pay.
- Economic depressions caused widespread unemployment every 10 years or so—with no unemployment compensation or other public assistance to replace wages.

Urban housing for the poor was dark and overcrowded. The mortality rate among tenement occupants, especially children, was shockingly high.

Early Labor Unions			
Union	**Founder**	**Members**	**Goals**
Knights of Labor (1869)	Uriah Stephens	700,000 by 1886	• Eight-hour workday • Strict laws against child labor • Protections for farmers, merchants, wage earners
American Federation of Labor (1886)	Samuel Gompers	Over a million by 1904	• Wage increases • Included only wage earners

Rise of Labor Unions

In response to low wages and dangerous working conditions, workers began to form labor unions. These unions lobbied for higher wages, shorter hours, better working conditions, and an end to child labor. Their members might strike (stop work) until conditions improved.

Reaction to Unions. Business owners and managers were generally hostile to labor unions. The government, too, disliked unions, because their strikes interrupted trade. Union supporters were accused of being socialists, communists, or un-American.

Strikes. Because of the strong opposition, strikes were often bloody.

- In 1892, a strike at the Carnegie Steel Works at Homestead, near Pittsburgh, resulted in nine strikers and three company guards dead.

- In 1894, at a strike at Pullman's Palace Car Company near Chicago, federal troops were brought in on the side of management.

▲ **Labor's struggle** for better wages and conditions would continue for many decades.

◄ **The Haymarket Riot** turned many Americans against the idea of labor unions.

THE HAYMARKET RIOT

On May 4, 1886, an unsuccessful general strike for an 8-hour workday led to bloodshed and death.

- Police tried to break up a meeting of anarchist workers in Haymarket Square in Chicago.

- A bomb exploded, killing seven policemen.

- The bomb thrower was never discovered; however, eight anarchists were tried and convicted.

- Seven were sentenced to death; one was given 15 years in prison.

Technology

In the late 1800s and early 1900s, rapid advances in technology revolutionized peoples' lives. New means of transportation and communication contributed to America's rapid industrial growth—and some, like the automobile, became booming new industries themselves.

Communication

Just as the printing press had done centuries before, the invention of the telegraph and the telephone brought about major social changes. For the first time, people could communicate with one another almost instantly across great distances.

The telegraph was developed by Samuel F. B. Morse in 1837 and introduced rapid communication before the Civil War. In 1866, Cyrus Field laid the first transatlantic cable, linking Europe and the United States. The transatlantic cable made it possible to send messages between the continents in minutes rather than days or weeks. In the 1870s, Thomas Edison introduced numerous improvements in telegraphy.

Spotlight on... THOMAS ALVA EDISON

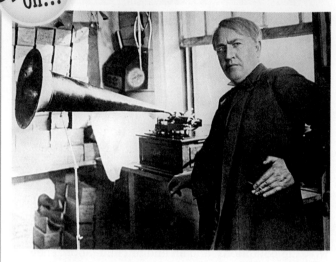

1847–1931

Thomas Edison was one of the greatest inventors in history. More than 1,000 inventions came out of his Menlo Park laboratory. He became known as the Wizard of Menlo Park.

- Edison patented his first invention, a vote recorder, in 1868.

- In 1876, he opened his laboratory at Menlo Park, New Jersey, where he invented the microphone and the phonograph (1877), which was the first device to play recorded sound.

- In 1879, he invented an incandescent light bulb, and the age of electricity began. (The first central electric power plant was the Edison General Electric Company.)

- In the 1890s, Edison's team invented the kinetoscope—the first practical motion picture machine.

The telephone arrived in 1876, when Alexander Graham Bell demonstrated his "speaking machine," or telephone. This device would one day form the basis of American Telephone & Telegraph (AT&T). At about the same time, Edison developed the carbon button microphone. The microphone turned Bell's telephone into a practical device.

Alexander Graham Bell gave his first telephone demonstration at the Centennial Exposition. The telephone would revolutionize businesses around the world.

Transportation

In the mid-1800s, expanding railroads revolutionized the way people moved around the country. By the early 1900s, transportation technology would go even further. Soon, Americans would get behind the wheel—and take to the skies.

Automobiles. People had been trying to build "horseless carriages"—automobiles—since the late 1700s. Initial designs ran on steam, like trains.

- Around 1891, William Morrison, an American inventor, built a successful battery-powered electric car.
- The Duryea brothers, Charles E. and J. Frank, built the first successful gasoline car in the United States in 1893.
- The 1901 Oldsmobile was the first mass-produced car.

Flight! While roads were filling up with cars, another form of transportation was literally spreading its wings. Two bicycle mechanics, Orville and Wilbur Wright, had developed an airplane.

- The first successful flight took place near Kitty Hawk, North Carolina, on December 17, 1903.
- In 1909, the U.S. Army Signal Corps bought a Wright machine. This was a sign that the airplane was more than just an interesting toy.

Air transportation did not affect the economy until after 1920. Nonetheless, the early success of powered flight gave people hope that one day no mountain, jungle, or ocean would stand between one person and another.

The first airplane, flown by the Wright brothers in 1903, is on display at the Smithsonian National Air and Space Museum.

HENRY FORD AND THE ASSEMBLY LINE

- In 1900, there were about 3,500 cars in the United States. By 1920, there were 9 million. This was due, in large part, to Henry Ford.

- In 1903, Ford organized the Ford Motor Company.
- To cut production costs, Ford adopted an assembly line method.
- Conveyor belts brought automobile parts to workers. Each worker

The Model T appeared in 1908.

performed a particular task, such as adding or tightening a part.

- This system helped reduce the assembly time of a Ford from about 12.5 worker-hours in 1912 to about 1.5 worker-hours in 1914.
- Ford's assembly line methods made the automobile affordable for the average family. Between 1910 and 1917, his company sold more than a million and a half Model T's, and each year the price went down—beginning at $950 and ending at $360.

now you know!

✔ After the Civil War, the United States developed into an industrial power.

✔ Large corporations began to form, especially in the steel, oil, and finance industries.

✔ Cities grew rapidly as new industrial plants were built and farmland became scarce.

✔ Labor unions formed and began agitating for safer working conditions and better pay.

✔ Inventions such as the automobile, the telephone, and the airplane began to change industry and daily life.

A CHANGING SOCIETY

In the late 1800s and early 1900s, changes in industry and technology went hand in hand with a shifting culture. Floods of new immigrants brought their own cultures to the American "melting pot." Many Americans called for changes in the country's economic, political, and social systems. They wanted to reduce poverty, improve the living conditions of the poor, and regulate big business. Meanwhile, segregationists in the South fought to maintain the economic and racial divisions of the era before the Civil War.

Immigration

Between 1815 and the 1920s, a flood of some 35 million immigrants—most of them Europeans—arrived on American shores. From 1815 to 1890, 15 million people came. The peak came in 1882, when 800,000 immigrants arrived in a single year. Yet the millions of immigrants who came during the early 1900s dwarfed even that figure.

Immigration Patterns

The United States has had four major waves of immigration. The migration before 1885 is often referred to as the "old migration." This migration began with the first colonists, and consisted mostly of people from northern and western Europe. The migration after 1885 is known as the "new migration." It consisted of many more immigrants from southern and eastern Europe.

Ellis Island. Newcomers from Europe typically landed at Ellis Island in New York Harbor. There they were questioned by government officials and examined by doctors before being allowed to enter the country.

Immigration to the United States			
Who	**When**	**How Many?**	**Why?**
Irish	1840 to 1850s	About 1.5 million	Famine resulting from potato crop failure
Germans	1840s to 1880s	About 4 million	Severe economic depression and unemployment; political unrest
Danes, Norwegians, and Swedes	1870s to 1900s	About 1.5 million	Poverty; shortage of farmland
Poles	1880s to 1920s	About 1 million	Poverty; political repression; cholera epidemics
Jews from eastern Europe	1880s to 1920s	About 2.5 million	Religious persecution
Austrians, Czechs, Hungarians, and Slovaks	1880s to 1920s	About 4 million	Poverty; overpopulation
Italians	1880s to 1920s	About 4.5 million	Poverty; overpopulation

Northern and Western Europe

In the 1840s, the surge of immigrants from northern and western Europe nearly tripled.

- In the 1840s, 1,700,000 immigrants—many from Ireland and Germany—arrived.
- In the 1850s, 2,600,000 more arrived.
- From 1860–1890, another 10 million arrived, mainly from Great Britain, Ireland, Germany, and Scandinavia.

Many of these groups migrated to the Midwest and West, where they built new farms.

Southern and Eastern Europe

The late 1800s brought a shift in the origins of Europeans emigrating to America.

- New arrivals continued to come from England, Scotland, Ireland, Germany, France, and other parts of northern Europe.
- A much larger number came from southern and eastern Europe—Italians, Poles, Russians, and others.
- Jews came to America from Russia and elsewhere in eastern Europe after 1880, largely to escape pogroms (massacres) and other anti-Semitic persecutions.

These immigrants tended to settle in ethnic neighborhoods in cities, rather than on farms, because much of America's farmland had already been settled.

China

San Francisco was the main port of entry for Chinese immigrants, many of whom came looking for work during the California gold rushes.

- They called the city "the Golden Mountain" (Jinshan or Gam Saan), and established the first Chinatown in America.
- Chinese immigrants generally planned on staying for only a few years, hoping to make enough money to return to China and live comfortably.
- Between 1850 and 1882, for example, some 322,000 Chinese arrived in the United States, but only about 100,000 actually remained. (See also page 141.)

European immigrants arrive in New York. Due to poor nutrition and disease on the long transatlantic voyage, a significant number never lived to see America.

Restrictions

The wave of immigrants from southern/eastern Europe and Asia led to a backlash of nativism—opposition to immigrants. Some feared the immigrants would threaten American unity. Others objected that immigrant workers kept wages low. For the first time, the United States began to restrict immigration.

- In 1882, Congress passed the Chinese Exclusion Act, which prohibited Chinese laborers from coming to the United States. Only certain "exempt" groups—such as clergy, scholars, and diplomats—were permitted.
- In 1907, the United States concluded a "gentlemen's agreement" with Japan to exclude any further immigration from that country.
- Legislation during the 1920s set up quotas that discriminated against immigrants not from northern and western Europe.

Segregation

The end of the Civil War brought about the end of slavery in the United States. The 13th, 14th, and 15th amendments guaranteed freedom, voting rights, and equal treatment for African Americans. (See pages 132–133.) African Americans, many of them freed slaves, were appointed to local offices. Some were also appointed to the U.S. Senate and House of Representatives. Despite this, former slaves continued to suffer widespread racial discrimination, especially in the South.

PLESSY V. FERGUSON

This Supreme Court case (1896) established what came to be known as the "separate but equal" doctrine.

- The case challenged the separation of black and white train passengers.

- The court ruled that separate facilities were legal, so long as they were "equal" to white facilities.

- Segregation became the law of the land, but black facilities were almost never truly equal to white ones.

"Separate but Equal"

White Southerners regained control of state governments in the South during the late 1870s, and reversed most of the gains made by former slaves. A series of legal actions—and some illegal ones—gradually stripped black citizens of their rights and segregated, or separated, them from white society.

The Black Codes

As the former Confederate states drew up their laws in 1865 and 1866, they incorporated a number of acts called Black Codes. The Black Codes

- forbade blacks from carrying arms.
- governed their employment.
- instituted curfews for African Americans.

In 1867 and 1868, many African-American voters worked to have the southern state constitutions revised, removing many of the Black Codes.

Jim Crow Laws

Beginning in 1882, southern states again began passing laws that enforced strict segregation between blacks and whites, and otherwise limited African-American civil rights.

- Segregation laws came to be called Jim Crow laws, after a black character in a popular song.

- Laws required segregation in nearly all public places.

- Poll taxes and other voting restrictions effectively prevented black citizens from voting.

The Supreme Court generally supported the existence of these laws.

◄ **Segregation.** Under Jim Crow laws, black citizens were restricted to separate public facilities or separate sections, from train cars to phone booths. Some courthouses even provided separate copies of the Bible for swearing in witnesses.

Spotlight on...

IDA B. WELLS-BARNETT

1862–1931

- A journalist and reformer, Wells-Barnett was known chiefly for her campaign against the lynching of African Americans during the late 1800s and early 1900s.

- Wells-Barnett was born a slave in Holly Springs, Mississippi.

- In 1889, she became part-owner and a reporter for *Free Speech*, a Memphis newspaper.

- In 1892, after three of her friends were hanged in Memphis, she began to investigate lynchings and other violence against African Americans.

- In 1909, Wells-Barnett helped found the National Association for the Advancement of Colored People (NAACP).

▲ **Ku Klux Klan** members threatened, beat, and killed many blacks and white sympathizers. The Klan terrorists hid their identities under white sheets and hoods.

THE KU KLUX KLAN

Some white Southerners wanted not only to maintain strict control over black citizens' activities, but also to end black participation in voting and government. The Ku Klux Klan formed to keep both blacks and white Republicans away from elections. To try to combat such actions, Congress passed the Force Bill in 1870 and the Ku Klux Klan Act in 1871.

Responses to Segregation

African Americans began organizing for greater rights even before the Civil War ended. In 1864, they formed the National Equal Rights League to press for voting rights. Later, free blacks successfully campaigned against segregated schools in Louisiana and South Carolina. As segregation worsened throughout the South, new organizations formed in response.

Freedmen's Bureau. In March 1865, Congress established the Freedmen's Bureau to help impoverished freedmen make new lives. The bureau offered

- funds for food and education.
- protection in labor contracts.
- help with local troubles.

But the bureau could not compete with widespread racial discrimination. Life remained desperate for the former slaves.

New Leaders, Different Approaches. Within the African-American community, a new group of leading voices called for solutions to the spread of segregation and increasing violence against African Americans.

- Conservative southern African Americans like Booker T. Washington favored accommodating whites and living with segregation until integration could be achieved.

- Leaders like W. E. B. Du Bois argued that accepting segregation would only make it permanent.

◄ **W. E. B. Du Bois** helped found the NAACP in 1909.

Populists and Progressives

At the end of the 1800s, the United States had grown into a world power. Industry was booming, the population was growing, and technology was advancing rapidly. At the same time, the working class suffered crushing poverty, natural resources were disappearing, and government corruption was rampant. The nation was ripe for reform.

CORRUPTION

Scandal, election disputes, and tragedy fueled demands for political reform.

Crédit Mobilier Scandal (1872). The owners of the Union Pacific Railroad diverted millions of federal loan dollars into their own construction company, Crédit Mobilier of America.

Tilden-Hayes Dispute (1876). Democrat Samuel J. Tilden won a majority in the 1876 popular vote, but the Republicans challenged the electoral votes. An electoral commission, voting along Republican party lines, gave Republican Rutherford B. Hayes the election.

Garfield's Assassination (1881). On July 2, President James A. Garfield was shot and killed by Charles J. Guiteau, a man who had been denied a government job. In 1883, the Pendleton Act reduced the practice of giving government jobs as political favors.

PROGRESSIVE POLITICAL REFORMS

- The secret ballot
- Initiative (the right of voters to suggest laws to their legislators)
- Referendum (the right of voters to vote directly on certain bills)
- Recall (the right of voters to remove officials)

Populists and Progressives

Two movements arose to deal with the problems of the new, industrial America: Populism and Progressivism. The Populist Party never really gained much power, but its ideas were taken up by the Progressives, who came from both the Republican and Democratic parties.

Movement	Goals
Populists	• Support for the interests of farmers • Currency backed by silver, to help farmers pay off debts • An 8-hour workday • Popular election of senators (the 17th Amendment, in 1913, made this law)
Progressives	• Improvement of living conditions for the poor • Building standards and sanitation in city tenements • Reduced workdays • Workplace safety and child labor laws

Strike! Unions such as the American Railway Union, founded by socialist activist Eugene V. Debs, fought for better working conditions and pay.

Theodore Roosevelt

The Progressives achieved real national power when one of their own, Republican Theodore Roosevelt, became president in 1901.

An Unexpected Presidency. Roosevelt's enemies in the Republican Party had tried to sidetrack his political career by making him William McKinley's vice presidential running mate in the 1900 election. McKinley won the election; however, the following September, he was shot at the Pan-American Exposition in New York. He died 8 days later, and Roosevelt took office.

Theodore Roosevelt. At age 42, Roosevelt was the youngest American president.

The Square Deal. Roosevelt firmly believed that all Americans should get what he called "a square deal"— fair treatment. This belief was put to the test by 150,000 striking coal miners in May 1902. In previous strikes, the federal government had sided with management rather than labor. But under Roosevelt, the government took the striking workers' side. They forced the reluctant owners to accept a commission's ruling, which awarded

- a shorter workday.
- a 10 percent pay increase to the miners.

Trust Busting. Roosevelt opposed "bad trusts"— business combinations that used their great financial power to kill competition and thus increase their profits. Under Roosevelt, the government brought many prosecutions against trusts.

- 44 cases were decided in the government's favor.
- Many railroads and shippers were convicted.
- Among the most famous "trust busts" was the suit against the Standard Oil Company, which was ordered to dissolve in 1907.

CONSERVATION

In 1908, Roosevelt's Conservation Congress met, with hopes of saving the nation's rapidly dwindling natural resources. The Congress called for

- the renewal of forests.
- the protection of wildlife.
- the development of waterpower.

THE JUNGLE

During the Progressive era, journalists called muckrakers worked to make the public aware of poverty, injustice, and other evils. One famous muckraker was the author Upton Sinclair. In 1906, Sinclair wrote The Jungle, which exposed unsanitary conditions in Chicago's meat-packing industry. The book led to two major acts:

- The Meat Inspection Act, giving government inspectors the right to inspect meat-packing plants
- The Pure Food and Drug Act, prohibiting the use of harmful ingredients in food and medicinal products

Chicago Cattle Industry. In 1903, Chicago was the hub of a vast railroad network that stretched across the country. Millions of head of cattle arrived on trains from western states to spend their final days in Chicago's Union Stock Yards. ▶

Social Reforms

Movements to improve American life began sweeping the country during the 1820s and 1830s. In the early 1900s, groups such as the Populists, the Progressives, and others brought about a number of social and political reforms—some more successful than others.

Education

In the early 1800s, most good schools in the United States were expensive private schools. Poor children went to second-rate "pauper," or "charity," schools, or did not go at all.

Public Schools

During the 1830s, Horace Mann of Massachusetts and other reformers began demanding better education and public schools open to both the rich and poor.

African Americans

Before the American Civil War, African-American children were not allowed to attend most schools in the North, and in the South it was a crime to teach slaves to read. As a result, it took longer for African Americans to benefit from the education reforms started in the 1830s. In 1881, Booker T. Washington founded the Tuskegee Institute in Alabama. Its aim was to provide education for young black men and women for immediate and practical application.

Reform	Result
Establishment of public schools	• More children enrolled • Students attended longer
Teacher training schools	• More standardized education system • Schoolchildren throughout the country learned the same things

Temperance and Prohibition

The drive for Prohibition began in the early 1800s, led by concerned women and churchmen who felt that alcohol harmed individuals and families.

- In 1874, the Woman's Christian Temperance Union (WCTU) was formed. Its members went into saloons, where they prayed and sang hymns to discourage drinking.

- Carry Nation, one of the most forceful crusaders, took a hatchet into saloons and smashed the liquor kegs.

- In 1919, the 18th Amendment was ratified and Prohibition began. It was now against the law to make, sell, or transport any alcoholic beverage.

- Americans found that they did not like living "dry," and in 1933, the 21st Amendment was passed. It repealed Prohibition.

Al Capone of Chicago was probably the era's most famous bootlegger. ▶

MCGUFFEY READERS

One thing that most American schools of the 1800s had in common was the McGuffey Reader. Written by a clergyman and teacher named William Holmes McGuffey, the Reader taught patriotism and morality as well as reading.

THE FLIP SIDE OF PROHIBITION

Prohibition made it illegal to sell alcohol, but not to drink it. Illegal liquor quickly became big business.

- Many people made their own beer, wine, or distilled liquor at home illegally.
- Illegal bars called speakeasies sold alcoholic drinks.

People called bootleggers met much of the demand for illegal alcoholic beverages. They battled each other for control of liquor supplies and markets. Violent gang wars erupted in many large cities, and gang members killed one another at a furious pace.

The Untouchables

The years of Prohibition pitted law enforcement against violent bootlegging gangs. Eliot Ness, a special agent with the U.S. Department of Justice, led investigations against gang leaders such as Al Capone. Ness and his squad were known as "the Untouchables" because they refused to accept bribes or give in to threats from mobsters.

- ✔ Millions of immigrants came to the United States during the late 1800s and early 1900s.
- ✔ After Reconstruction ended, segregation of blacks and whites spread throughout the South.
- ✔ The Populist and Progressive parties formed in response to widespread corruption and poverty.
- ✔ Theodore Roosevelt became president in 1901; he opposed monopolies and worked to conserve the country's natural resources.
- ✔ Reformers worked toward public education, Prohibition (1919), and women's suffrage (1920).

Women's Suffrage

The WCTU was helpful in working for another constitutional amendment, one that would not be repealed: extension of voting rights to women.

- The suffrage movement began in 1848 in Seneca Falls, New York.
- The Seneca Falls Convention, led by Lucretia Mott and Elizabeth Cady Stanton, demanded equal rights for women, including the right to vote.
- In 1869, Stanton and Susan B. Anthony formed the National Woman Suffrage Association. Its aim was to get Congress to pass an amendment giving women the vote.

The struggle was a long one. It was not until 50 years later, in 1920, that women got what they wanted—the 19th Amendment guaranteeing women's suffrage.

Votes for Women! Activists who campaigned for woman suffrage, nicknamed "suffragettes," were sometimes arrested and sent to jail for their marches and protests.

GLOBAL INFLUENCE

Prior to the Civil War, the United States took little part in world affairs. By the end of the 1800s, America had developed into a major economic and industrial power. This led to a demand for foreign markets and raw materials. The United States began to play an ever-increasing role in world affairs.

Rough Riders

The Spanish-American War

For economic and strategic reasons, many influential Americans wished to take over Spain's possessions in the Caribbean and the Pacific. Cuba, just off the Florida shore, had long been rebelling against Spanish rule. In 1895, Spain sent General Valeriano Weyler to crush the rebellion. Reports of his cruel treatment of the Cuban people earned American sympathy for the Cuban cause. (See also page 533.)

Causes

In 1898, riots broke out in Havana. President William McKinley sent the U.S. battleship *Maine* to the Havana harbor to protect American citizens and property.

- On the night of February 15, the *Maine* blew up in the harbor, killing 266 American sailors.
- It was never proven that Spain was responsible, but newspapers played up the incident. "Remember the *Maine*!" became a cry for war.
- On April 19, Congress recognized Cuban independence and authorized military intervention.

Roosevelt's Rough Riders. The First United States Volunteer Cavalry, led by Theodore Roosevelt, were nicknamed the Rough Riders. Their bravery at San Juan Hill helped make Roosevelt a hero and, later, president of the United States.

Events

On April 24, Spain declared war, and on April 25, the United States Congress did the same. The fighting was done by the end of July.

- On May 1, Commodore George Dewey destroyed the Spanish fleet at Manila Bay with no American losses.
- Commodore Winfield S. Schley effectively blockaded the harbor.
- On July 1, the Rough Riders helped storm and capture San Juan Hill.
- The U.S. Navy bombarded Santiago, and the city surrendered on July 17.

Results

On December 10, 1898, a peace treaty was signed in Paris.

- Spain gave up all claims to Cuba, Puerto Rico, and Guam.
- Spain sold the Philippine Islands to the United States for $20 million.
- Americans occupied Puerto Rico.

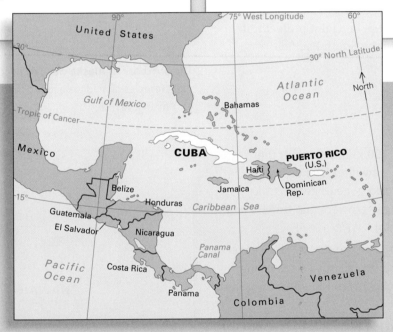

CUBA

In February 1901, Cuba framed a constitution patterned after the U.S. Constitution. As a condition of American withdrawal from the island, the Cubans added an amendment guaranteeing that Cuba would permit no foreign interference or control. The United States had the right to intervene, at its own will, on behalf of Cuba's peace or independence.

Under the military leadership of General Leonard Wood, education and sanitation on the island improved. Yellow fever was wiped out in Havana through the efforts of an Army commission headed by Major Walter Reed, a U.S. Army surgeon, and Major William C. Gorgas.

PUERTO RICO

Puerto Rico remained under U.S. military control until the Foraker Act of 1900 established a civil government with an American governor and executive council appointed by the American president, and a house of representatives elected by the inhabitants. Finally, an act passed in 1917 gave Puerto Ricans their own legislature and U.S. citizenship.

A World Power

Victory in the Spanish-American War (1898) gave the United States control of territories in the Caribbean and the Pacific. The nation was on its way to becoming an imperial power, with possessions scattered all over the globe.

Alaska

The first American stirrings toward empire occurred in 1867. Secretary of State William H. Seward prevailed on Congress to buy Alaska from Russia for $7.2 million. In 1867, Seward also arranged for the United States to buy the Midway Islands in the Pacific. In 1889, the United States joined Germany and Britain in a joint protectorate of the Samoan Islands in the South Pacific.

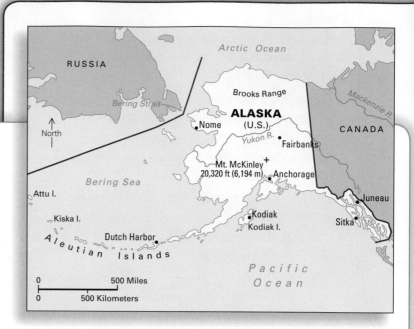

The purchase of Alaska was called "Seward's folly"—until great reserves of gold were found there 30 years later, setting off a mad gold rush.

Hawaii

Some 2,000 miles (3,200 kilometers) off the California coast lay the Hawaiian Islands, where American missionaries had gone to convert the islanders, and where sugar growers and traders had become rich and powerful.

- By the 1890s, these business interests were eager to take total control of the islands by removing the Hawaiian monarch, Queen Liliuokalani, from the throne.

- In January 1893, with the help of U.S. Marines, they achieved their goal.

- President Grover Cleveland restored Queen Liliuokalani as head of the new government and opposed annexation.

- In 1898, during the Spanish-American War, Congress annexed the Hawaiian Islands to the United States.

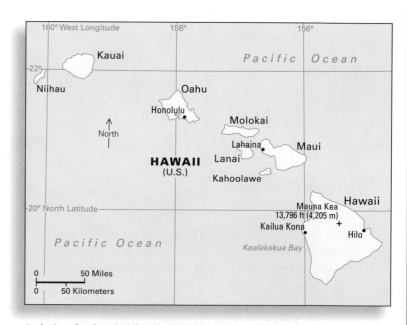

A chain of volcanic islands, Hawaii was attractive to the United States for its agricultural riches and strategic military position in the Pacific Ocean.

The Philippines

American overseas expansion met resistance in the Philippines. The islands' 80 tribes were united against foreign control.

- Under the leadership of Emilio Aguinaldo, the Filipinos tried, in February 1899, to oust the temporary American regime established in Manila.
- The United States engaged in a 3-year guerrilla war.
- Thousands of Filipinos were killed before U.S. forces put down the revolt.

Antiimperialists denounced U.S. occupation of the Philippines, but the imperialists argued that the occupation could

- promote new business enterprises.
- tap the expanding trade with the Orient.
- keep other expanding powers, particularly Germany, out of the Pacific.
- "uplift and civilize" the people of the islands.

The Jones Act of 1916 promised the Filipinos independence as soon as a stable civil government had been established, but independence did not arrive until 1946.

▲ **The Philippines.** At the end of the 1800s, some 7 million Filipinos lived on approximately 80 islands. The country lies more than 6,000 miles (9,654 kilometers) from America's west coast.

THE PANAMA CANAL

With political interests in the Atlantic and Pacific, the U.S. wanted to move ships more quickly between the oceans. Roosevelt hoped to dig a canal across the Isthmus of Panama, in Colombia.

- In 1903, Secretary John Hay concluded the Hay-Herrán Treaty, which would let the United States buy a strip of land across the isthmus. Colombia rejected it.
- Roosevelt secretly helped the inhabitants of Panama rebel against Colombia and establish an independent republic. This new government signed a treaty with the U.S. in 1904.
- The land cost $10 million, plus a perpetual annual payment of $250,000. The canal itself cost $400 million to build.

The Panama Canal. Construction on the "Big Ditch" began in 1904, but it would not be completed until 1914. During construction, thousands of lives were lost to accidents, yellow fever, and malaria.

At Home and Abroad

By the end of the 1800s, the United States had overseas possessions and global responsibilities. As the next century began, new foreign and economic policies were taking shape.

Foreign Policy

In the early 1900s, many countries in the Western Hemisphere were experiencing political and economic troubles. The United States, which now controlled Cuba and Puerto Rico, took a more militant approach to protecting its interests.

The Roosevelt Corollary

Beginning in 1823, the United States had operated under a foreign policy called the Monroe Doctrine. Established by President James Monroe, the doctrine stated that the Western Hemisphere was no longer open to European colonization. (See page 91.)

During Theodore Roosevelt's presidency, several European nations were threatening to use force against the Latin American countries that owed them large debts. In response to this threat, Roosevelt developed a new policy.

- The Monroe Doctrine made the United States the guardian of the Western Hemisphere.
- Therefore, it had the responsibility to police all of the international difficulties in the area.
- If any nation of the hemisphere were unable to meet its financial obligations, the United States would intervene.

Roosevelt and his successors, Taft and Wilson, used this policy to intervene in Nicaragua, Haiti, and the Dominican Republic—causing lasting resentment among Latin Americans.

TROUBLE IN MEXICO

In 1913, after a series of revolutions, General Victoriano Huerta seized control of Mexico's government.

- Both President Taft and his successor, Woodrow Wilson, refused to recognize Huerta's new regime.
- Wilson claimed that the regime did not represent the will of the Mexican people. He engaged in efforts to bring down the Huerta regime. This stand came to be called "moral diplomacy."
- Huerta retaliated in 1914.

War seemed imminent, but the so-called ABC Powers—Argentina, Brazil, and Chile—intervened and recommended Huerta's resignation. Huerta fled Mexico, and the U.S. recognized his replacement, reform leader Venustiano Carranza.

Pancho Villa, an anti-Carranza revolutionary, raided Columbus, New Mexico, in March of 1916, killing 17 Americans. With Carranza's permission, Wilson sent General John J. Pershing and his troops into Mexico to capture Villa, but Pershing failed.

Economics—Abroad

As American markets extended into Asia and the Caribbean, the nation developed policies to support its business interests as well as to build relationships with foreign economies.

- In 1899, United States secretary of state John Hay started the Open Door policy, in which powerful countries agree to allow each other to trade freely in an area. The policy initially applied to China.

- President William Howard Taft established a policy of "dollar diplomacy"—using superior economic power, instead of force, to spread American influence.

Economics—At Home

Under President Theodore Roosevelt, the government began to rein in the power of large corporations. Presidents Taft and Wilson continued these policies.

- Roosevelt, Taft, and Wilson all regulated trusts—business combinations that prevented competition in order to keep prices and profits high.

- Wilson lowered tariffs and established the Federal Reserve System, giving the government more control over finance.

William Howard Taft, 27th president of the United States, from 1909 to 1913, also served as chief justice of the Supreme Court from 1921 until his death in 1930. He considered his tenure on the Court as his highest honor.

BUSTING TRUSTS

In 1914, two new laws restricted corporate trusts.

The Clayton Antitrust Act

- listed in detail all trust practices condemned by the courts (such as secret agreements and price privileges)
- exempted labor and farm unions from antitrust laws, giving them new freedom to organize and operate

The Federal Trade Commission Act

- established the Federal Trade Commission (FTC)
- prevented unfair competition in interstate commerce

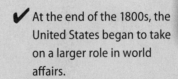

- ✔ At the end of the 1800s, the United States began to take on a larger role in world affairs.
- ✔ The Spanish-American War (1898) gave the U.S. control over Cuba, Puerto Rico, Guam, and the Philippines.
- ✔ The U.S. also added Alaska (bought in 1867) and Hawaii (annexed in 1898).
- ✔ The Roosevelt Corollary began a policy of having the U.S. intervene in events throughout the Western Hemisphere.

THE UNITED STATES AND WORLD WAR I

At the start of the 1900s, Europe dominated the world politically, economically, and culturally. The powerful European nations began building empires, leading to competitive rivalries. By 1914, rivalries between major powers had come to a boiling point. That year, Europe engulfed itself in a world war. The United States initially resisted involvement, but was eventually drawn into the fighting. For the first time in its history, the United States mobilized for a full-scale war on foreign territory.

War Begins in Europe

The drive for empire among European nations created bitter rivalries. Fearful of one another, the European countries formed alliances for their mutual protection. (See also pages 534–537.)

Alliances

By 1907, two major alliances faced each other.

- The Triple Entente, or the Allies, including Britain, France, and Russia
- The Triple Alliance, or the Central Powers, including Germany, Austria-Hungary, and, until 1914, also including Italy

The terms of these alliances were sometimes kept a secret, meaning that nations could not always predict the consequences of their disputes with other countries. The situation grew increasingly volatile as the nations built up their militaries.

WITH TWO SHOTS, A WORLD WAR

On June 28, 1914, Archduke Franz Ferdinand—the heir to the Austro-Hungarian throne—was riding in an open limousine through the streets of Sarajevo, Bosnia.

- Bosnia was a part of the Austro-Hungarian Empire.
- The Austro-Hungarian Empire and Serbia were enemies after years of war on the Balkan peninsula.

In the crowd stood a young student from Serbia, Gavrilo Princip. He thought Bosnia should be freed from Austria-Hungary and become a part of Serbia. As the limousine paused en route, Princip raised a gun and fired twice, killing both the archduke and his wife, Sophie. This single act propelled all of Europe into war.

A Political Assassination. Archduke Franz Ferdinand and his wife, Sophie, step toward the limousine in which they would be riding when they were shot.

Fighting Begins

The assassination of Austrian Archduke Franz Ferdinand caused Austria-Hungary to declare war on Serbia on July 28, 1914. A chain reaction followed throughout Europe.

- Russia (considering itself Serbia's protector) prepared to fight Austria-Hungary.
- Germany declared war on Russia on August 1, and on France 2 days later.
- Britain declared war on Germany on August 4. World war had begun between the two alliances.

Stalemate

By 1917, the two sides had reached a stalemate.

- The British had lost one-third of their troops, the French over half.
- In July, the Russians launched a major offensive that turned into a disaster.
- In November, the Bolsheviks seized power and took Russia out of the war.
- The Central Powers concentrated their forces on the western front.

EUROPE AT WAR

This map shows the movements of the Allies and the Central Powers throughout World War I. The war was fought along two major fronts.

Western Front

The two sides were locked in trench warfare along the western front by 1915. The western front remained deadlocked for nearly 3½ years.

Eastern Front

The eastern front swung back and forth until Russia agreed to stop fighting late in 1917.

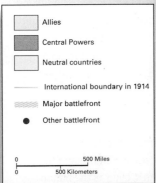

From Neutrality to War

World War I raged in Europe for over 2 years before the United States joined the Allies in the fight. By then, the Allies were in a desperate situation. They had been fighting for nearly 3 years, and were unable to break the stalemate.

In August 1914, President Wilson urged Americans to stay neutral: "Be impartial in thought as well as in action, neutral in fact as well as in name." Americans were willing to follow this course; most opposed any involvement in a European war. As the war went on, however, neutrality became increasingly difficult.

Woodrow Wilson. In 1916, Wilson won a close election over his Republican opponent, Charles Evans Hughes, using the slogan "He Kept Us Out of War."

Dangerous Waters

Orders for guns and food flooded the United States from both sides.

- Britain, however, was using its navy to set up a blockade of Germany in an effort to starve that nation out.

- Americans were angered when British ships harassed American shipping headed for Germany. In an effort to stay neutral, the United States took no action.

- To break the blockade, Germany resorted to its submarines, or U-boats, which could strike British ships and ships heading for Britain.

- The United States protested U-boat warfare, since it sometimes cost American lives and property.

The Sinking of the Lusitania
May 7th 1915

THE *LUSITANIA*

On May 7, 1915, a German U-boat sank the British passenger liner *Lusitania* off the coast of Ireland. Nearly 1,200 people were killed, including 128 Americans. The sinking of the *Lusitania* aroused great anger in the United States. In September 1915, Germany promised to stop sinking passenger ships without warning.

The sinking of the *Lusitania* stirred up anti-German sentiment in the United States, even as the nation attempted to stay neutral.

164

The End of Neutrality

Three events combined to end American neutrality.

Submarine Warfare

Germany returned to "unlimited submarine warfare" on February 1, 1917. Wilson broke off diplomatic relations with Germany.

The Zimmermann Telegram

This coded telegram came from the German Foreign Minister Arthur Zimmermann. It urged Mexico to join the Central Powers, promising to return former Mexican territories (Texas, New Mexico, and Arizona) after the U.S. was defeated.

The Russian Revolution

The opening phase of the Russian Revolution began in March of 1917.

- The czar was replaced by a pro-Allied provisional government.
- The new government declared its intention to continue the war against the Central Powers, but it was not in full control of the country.

On April 2, 1917, President Wilson asked Congress for a declaration of war against Germany. "The world must be made safe for democracy," he stated. On April 6, Congress declared war, and the United States joined the Allies.

PROPAGANDA

After declaring war, the U.S. government worked to stir up enthusiasm for the war effort. The major U.S. propaganda effort was handled by an agency called the Committee on Public Information.

- The committee distributed more than 100 million posters and publications designed to increase support for the war.
- Government propaganda pictured the war as a battle for liberty and democracy.
- People who still opposed the war faced increasingly unfriendly public opinion. They could even be brought to trial under certain wartime laws.

Posters such as this one stirred patriotic fervor during World War I, "the war to end all wars."

Preparing for Battle

After years of neutrality, the United States needed to raise an army and mobilize the nation for war.

- Within 3 months, over a million men had volunteered for the army, but many more would be needed.
- On May 18, 1917, the Selective Service Act was passed. Nearly 3 million men would eventually be drafted.
- Citizens were encouraged to save food by honoring "wheatless Mondays" and "meatless Tuesdays."
- Federal agencies also took control of the American economy, telling manufacturers what to produce for the war effort.

WOMEN AND WORLD WAR I

On the home front, women rushed in to fill the jobs left by departing volunteers and draftees. For the first time,

- women became auto mechanics, mail carriers, and trolley conductors.
- women lawyers and doctors were allowed to work for government agencies.

The Great War

President Wilson declared war in April of 1917, but it took time for the U.S. Army to mobilize. Relatively few American troops reached France until March of 1918. President Wilson chose General John J. Pershing, a veteran of the Spanish-American War, to head the American Expeditionary Force (AEF).

The Americans in Battle

In March 1918, a series of German offensives began.

- The Central Powers pushed the Allied lines back.
- The German forces formed two "bulges," called *salients*, which threatened Paris.

Search for a Just Peace

Before the war had ended, Wilson had proposed "Fourteen Points" on which he thought the peace should be built. Among them were

- a point stating that all peoples should have the right to choose how to govern themselves.
- a point proposing a League of Nations, where all nations might settle their differences peaceably.

Other Allied leaders were more interested in punishing Germany than in adopting Wilson's ideals. (See also pages 538–539.)

Major American Battles of World War I		
Battle Location	**Date**	**Outcome**
Cantigny, France	May 28, 1918	The Allied 1st Division overran the German defenses and held them against several fierce counterattacks.
Château-Thierry, France	June 4, 1918	Allied forces halt the German advance.
Belleau Wood, France	June 6–24, 1918	American troops drive out the German forces.
Marne River, France	July 15, 1918	● The Germans launch a last offensive. ● The Allies, including about 250,000 Americans, counterattack on July 18.
St.-Mihiel, France	September 12–13, 1918	Americans attack and destroy a German salient (a "bulge" in the opposing army's lines).
Argonne Forest, France	September 26, 1918	● U.S. troops attack German lines in the Argonne Forest. ● Over 1 million Americans fight there and triumph.

The Germans hoped to strike a devastating blow and end the war before the growing American forces could turn the tide against them. In a series of battles in France, however, the Allies triumphed. On November 11, 1918, Germany surrendered. The "war to end all wars" was over.

The Treaty of Versailles

The Treaty of Versailles did provide for a League of Nations, but

- it demanded huge reparations from Germany.
- it also stripped Germany of its colonies.

The bitterness created by these terms helped to ensure that European war would soon come again.

In the U.S., Wilson campaigned across the country building support for the League of Nations. But Congress would not approve the Treaty of Versailles. Wilson's hopes for a "just peace" were shattered.

A NEW KIND OF WAR

World War I was unlike any war before it. New developments in technology made weapons stronger, more accurate—and more deadly. This illustration shows four fighting machines that played significant roles in World War I (1914–1918): an airplane, a submarine, a tank, and a machine gun.

- The war marked the first time airplanes were used in combat.

- Submarines, like the German UB II, fired torpedoes that struck surface ships and then exploded.

- Tanks were a British invention. They were designed to crush barbed wire and cross trenches.

- The rapid fire of machine guns slaughtered attacking soldiers.

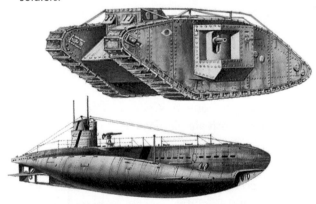

▲ **Machine Guns and Fighter Planes.** The Airco D.H.4, a British bomber (*top*), and the French army's 8-millimeter Hotchkiss gun (*below*) added to the carnage of World War I.

Trench Warfare. Much of the war was fought in a sprawling system of wet, cramped trenches.

- Front line trenches protected soldiers during battle.

- Support trenches housed off-duty soldiers between battles.

- Communications trenches were for moving soldiers and equipment from place to place.

The German UB II (*bottom*) and the **MK IV tank** (*top*) first saw action during World War I.

- ✔ World War I began in Europe in 1914; the United States remained neutral until 1917.

- ✔ The war was fought between the Allies (Britain, Russia, France, and the U.S.) and the Central Powers (Germany, Austria-Hungary, and Italy).

- ✔ Germany surrendered on November 11, 1918; the Allies had won the war.

- ✔ The Treaty of Versailles punished Germany heavily; this would later be one of the causes of World War II.

BOOM TIMES

After the end of World War I, the nation was in a mood to forget war, hardship, and troubles abroad. Americans welcomed the message of Warren G. Harding, Republican senator from Ohio: "America's present need is not heroics but healing, not nostrums but normalcy . . . not surgery but serenity. . . ." In 1920, the American people elected Harding president, hoping he would bring the nation "a return to normalcy." Instead, the 1920s saw rapid social and economic change. The nation swung from freewheeling prosperity to financial disaster.

The 1920s are often looked back on as a crazy, fun-loving era—the Roaring Twenties, the Era of Wonderful Nonsense, the Jazz Age. But the '20s had their deeply serious side as well. Recession, labor unrest, and paranoia lived side by side with tremendous wealth and technological wonders.

Political Scandals

It has been said that the only qualification Warren G. Harding had to be president was that he looked like one. During Harding's administration, cabinet and executive officers engaged in massive political corruption.

- His attorney general, Harry Daugherty, made a fortune by selling government favors.
- Harding's friend Charles Forbes, head of the new Veterans' Bureau, helped himself and his friends to $200 million of the bureau's funds.
- Secretary of the Interior Albert B. Fall took more than $400,000 in bribes in return for leasing government land, at Teapot Dome in Wyoming and Elk Hills in California, to private oil developers.

Word of all this corruption was just starting to come out when, on August 2, 1923, Harding died suddenly in San Francisco while on a trip to the West Coast. Vice President Calvin Coolidge became president.

SPECULATION

One of the causes of the seeming prosperity of the 1920s was the busy stock market.

- Speculation in stocks—buying shares in hopes of profiting when their price rose—had become nothing short of a national mania.
- Stock prices kept going up and up until they were dangerously overpriced.
- Speculators kept borrowing more money to buy more stocks, confident that their profits would pay off the loans.

The Business of America

The early part of Coolidge's presidency saw the rise of many business-friendly policies.

- Tariffs (taxes on imports) went up.

- Income tax rates went down.

- Antitrust legislation was not enforced.

Coolidge's attitude toward business could not have been more encouraging: "The business of America is business," he declared. During the 1920s, industrial production nearly doubled.

Silent Cal. The shy and serious Vice President Calvin Coolidge, nicknamed "Silent Cal," succeeded Harding as president. The beginning of his presidency was known as the age of "Coolidge prosperity."

Prosperity's Downside. Hostility toward organized labor unions ran high under Coolidge's big-business philosophy.

- During the Progressive Era, Congress had passed several laws protecting the rights of unions.

- The unions lost several of these safeguards as the Supreme Court found unions in violation of antitrust legislation.

The Red Scare

The recession following World War I led to labor strikes. Many Americans were quick to blame the strikes on communist influences within the labor unions. A wave of bombings, blamed on "foreign anarchists," fueled American fears that the "Reds" were plotting to overthrow the American government.

The Wobblies. A special target of the ensuing crackdown during this period was a Marxist-oriented labor organization called the Industrial Workers of the World (IWW). Members were sometimes called Wobblies.

- Formed in Chicago in 1905, its leaders included Eugene V. Debs and Elizabeth Gurley Flynn (shown here leading a strike).

- Many of its leaders were jailed, and its membership dwindled in the 1920s. Some joined the Workers (or Communist) Party, or the Communist Labor Party, both of which were founded in 1919.

The Jazz Age

Ragtime, blues, and jazz music, all of which originated in the South, flourished among African Americans in northern cities during the early 1900s. These new genres contributed to a uniquely American music.

- Ragtime king Scott Joplin, "father of the blues" W. C. Handy, and Dixieland jazz trumpeter Louis Armstrong all helped establish a permanent place for African-American musicians in popular music.

- In New York, pianist Fletcher Henderson organized the first big band in 1923, and musician Eubie Blake produced *Shuffle Along* (1921), one of the many African-American musicals that played on Broadway during the 1920s and 1930s.

- Thomas A. Dorsey, the "father of gospel music," wrote nearly a thousand gospel songs and popularized this type of music in the late 1920s.

THE HARLEM RENAISSANCE

The 1920s saw an African-American literary flowering, centered in New York, called the Harlem Renaissance. Among the many notable works were

- *Weary Blues* (1926) by poet Langston Hughes.
- *The Book of American Negro Poetry* (1922) by James Weldon Johnson.
- *Home to Harlem (1928)* by Claude McKay.

African-American musicians such as Eubie Blake (shown here) invented new styles of music during the 1920s and 1930s.

Flappers. With their shorter dresses and short hair, the young women known as "flappers" became a symbol of the Roaring '20s.

WOMEN IN THE ROARING '20S

The changes in American culture during the 1920s also brought about changes in peoples' values. The roles of women, especially, had begun shifting during World War I, and continued to shift afterward.

- **Economics.** The war opened up new professional opportunities outside the home. (See page 165.)

- **Politics.** The 19th Amendment, giving women the right to vote, was ratified in 1920.

- **Personal Life.** Before the war, women had worn long hair, ankle-length dresses, and long cotton stockings. Afterward, many wore short, tight dresses and rolled their silk stockings down to their knees. They cut their hair in a boyish style called the bob and wore bright lipstick and other cosmetics.

Many Americans embraced these changes, but some feared that morality would crumble completely.

TAKING TO THE SKIES

Aviation, introduced by the Wright brothers in 1903, advanced rapidly during the 1920s.

- The first coast-to-coast airmail service was introduced in 1920.
- The Air Commerce Act of 1926 provided federal aid for the development of airports and air transportation.
- Also in 1926, Robert H. Goddard opened the age of modern rocketry when he launched the first successful liquid-fuel rocket.
- On May 22, 1927, Charles A. Lindbergh, Jr., made the first nonstop flight from New York to Paris, France.

Amelia Earhart, as a member of a three-person crew, became the first woman to fly across the Atlantic in 1928. In 1932, she became the first woman to fly solo across the Atlantic.

Technological Developments

The 1920s were years of rapid technological growth. New discoveries—and improvements on older discoveries—helped create new industries and contributed to a booming economy. The growing American middle class snapped up new gadgets and innovative forms of entertainment.

The Age of Radio. Forms of radio communication had been around since 1895, but they were mostly used to send messages to and from ships. The 1920s turned radio into entertainment for the masses.

- In 1920, the first regular radio broadcasting station, KDKA in Pittsburgh, Pennsylvania, went on the air. It was joined by other stations.
- In 1926, the National Broadcasting Company (NBC) became the first radio network.
- The Columbia Broadcasting System (CBS) followed in 1927.
- Later, NBC was divided, and one part became the American Broadcasting Company (ABC).

Automobiles. More and more people could afford to buy the Model T, the inexpensive automobile that Henry Ford had developed in 1908. (See page 147.) The number of passenger cars in the United States jumped from fewer than 7 million in 1919 to about 23 million in 1929.

◀ **Broadcast radio** was a major source of family entertainment. Families gathered in their living rooms in the evening to listen to comedies, dramas, and other programs.

Fears and Liberties

In many ways, the 1920s were a time of great social progress. Women had won the right to vote, labor unions fought for the rights of workers, and groups like the National Association for the Advancement of Colored People (NAACP) worked to fight racial prejudice and segregation. Some Americans, however, feared the changes that were sweeping the nation.

The Tribal Twenties

The years after World War I saw a rise in nativism—fear and hostility toward foreigners. Nativist feelings were also directed at American minorities, such as African Americans, Jewish people, and people with certain political ideas.

THE PALMER RAIDS

Distrust of immigrants played a part in the "Red Scare"—a widespread fear of communists that arose during the 1920s.

- In January of 1920 Attorney General A. Mitchell Palmer ordered a series of raids on groups suspected of "un-American" ties, typically groups containing many immigrants.

- Some 6,000 suspects were arrested in 33 cities, and over 500 were deported.

No overthrow plots were ever uncovered, and many Americans began to feel that the raids were trampling on the Bill of Rights. By the end of the year, the Red Scare had died down. (See also page 169.)

Revival of the Ku Klux Klan. Fear of the new and the strange was especially strong in the small towns of the South and Midwest. There, prejudice against blacks had long been strong. After the Civil War, a group called the Ku Klux Klan (KKK) was formed. They threatened, beat, and killed African Americans.

- The original KKK had died out when Congress allowed the use of federal troops against the group.

- In 1915, it was reestablished in Georgia. Now Catholics, Jews, and new immigrants were also targets.

- By 1923, the Klan's membership had grown to 4 million people bent on preserving America for white, "native-born" Protestants.

The Ku Klux Klan aimed to terrorize those who did not fit their definition of an American; they also worked to elect politicians who shared their views.

Immigration. In the mid-1800s, large numbers of immigrants began arriving from southern and eastern Europe. Widespread distrust and dislike of these immigrants had increased by the 1920s.

Act	Date	Outcome
Emergency Quota Act	May 1921	• Congress passed the Emergency Quota Act, which severely limited, by nationality, the number of immigrants who could enter the United States.
Immigration Act of 1924	May 1924	• Congress passed this act as the Emergency Quota Act was about to expire. • Act decreed that only a small number of immigrants could enter the United States. • In 1929, the total number of immigrants allowed in annually was lowered to 150,000.

Organization/ Group	Date Founded	Goals and Achievements
Society of American Indians	1911	• Promote collective action by Indian tribes • Passage of a law granting Native Americans U.S. citizenship (1924)
National Association for the Advancement of Colored People (NAACP)	1909	• Fight the spread of laws supporting segregation • Work to prevent unjust legal penalties and job discrimination • Passage and enforcement of anti-lynching laws
American Civil Liberties Union (ACLU)	1920	• Provide lawyers and legal advice • Protect individuals' constitutional rights, such as freedom of speech and protection against unfair punishment

Fighting for Civil Liberties

During the early part of the 1900s, several groups formed to protect the rights of citizens, particularly minorities who suffered from discrimination. During the 1920s, these groups fought against the rising nativist sentiments. Many of these groups, such as the American Civil Liberties Union, are still active today.

Spotlight on...

MARCUS GARVEY

1887–1940
• Jamaican social reformer remembered for his "back to Africa" campaign in the United States.
• In 1914, he founded the Universal Negro Improvement Association, dedicated to promoting black business, cultural pride, and eventual resettlement in Liberia.
• By the early 1920s, Garvey had an estimated 2 million followers, chiefly poor blacks.
• Accused of fraud and eventually deported, Garvey continued to speak for black unity.

THE GREAT MIGRATION

Beginning in the late 1870s, southern state governments began reversing many of the gains made by former slaves. Jim Crow laws enforced strict segregation and limited many African Americans' civil rights.

African Americans responded to worsening treatment in the South by moving to New York, Chicago, and other northern cities. The migration began slowly at first. Between 1890 and 1910, about 200,000 African Americans moved north. From 1910 to 1930, however, about 1.25 million African Americans left the South for segregated neighborhoods in northern cities.

now you **Know!**

✔ During the 1920s, business-friendly policies led to high profits, low taxes, and high industrial production.
✔ People made millions of dollars speculating on the stock market.
✔ Immigration and anti-union feelings led to a backlash against communists called the Red Scare.
✔ Jazz, blues, and ragtime music flourished; the African American artists of the Harlem Renaissance produced famous works.
✔ The role of women—especially after the 19th Amendment gave women voting rights—began to change.
✔ The KKK and other nativist groups returned, but organizations such as the NAACP and the ACLU worked to protect the civil rights of minorities.

THE GREAT DEPRESSION

The giddy progress and profits of the 1920s came to a screeching halt in 1929. An economic crash led the nation into the worst and longest period of high unemployment and low business activity in the 20th century. Millions of people were left jobless and penniless. The Great Depression was felt around the world, although the impact varied from country to country. In Germany, for example, poor economic conditions contributed to the rise of the dictator Adolf Hitler, who would draw the world into another war. (See page 542.)

Falling stocks and failing farms led to the failure of banks throughout the country. Millions of Americans' savings were wiped out.

Crash and Collapse

During the 1920s, industrial production soared and many people profited. Americans bought millions of cars, radios, and other consumer goods, while stock prices rose. Beneath the prosperous surface, however, the American economy was beginning to weaken.

Building Economic Troubles

Under President Calvin Coolidge, big industrial businesses benefited from government policies that lowered taxes and lifted restrictions on corporations and trusts. Other areas, such as farming and trade, stumbled.

Farm Troubles. Agricultural production had grown impressively during World War I as American commodities entered world markets. After the war, however, came a long slump.

- Farmers had taken out mortgages on new land and put it under cultivation.
- As Europe got back on its feet and could meet much of its own agricultural needs, prices for American farm products fell.
- As a result, it was becoming increasingly difficult for American farmers to meet their mortgage payments.
- Banks began repossessing farms.

President Coolidge vetoed several measures authorizing federal aid to help support agricultural prices and find foreign markets for American products.

THE 1928 ELECTION

In 1928, Coolidge—grieving over the death of his son and his father—announced, "I do not choose to run." The Republicans nominated Herbert Hoover as their candidate. Satisfied with the prosperity under the two previous Republicans, the voters overwhelmingly elected Hoover.

The Democratic candidate, Alfred E. Smith, was the first Catholic to run for a major political party; prejudice against Catholics, especially in the South, hurt his candidacy.

The Market Crashes

Rising stock prices during the 1920s led to a rash of speculation. By 1929, a total of $9 billion was owed to banks as a result of stock speculation. Then the bubble finally burst.

- Prices had been going down steadily, as the Federal Reserve tried to rein in the market.

- Nervous speculators tried to sell their stocks as quickly as they could.

- On October 29, speculators dumped 16 million shares on the market—and there was no one who wanted to buy.

The stock market had crashed. Soon the nation's other economic ills would become apparent to all, and the worst depression in the nation's history was under way.

▲ **The Market Crash of 1929.** Police and crowds gather outside the New York Stock Exchange on October 24, 1929. On that day, called Black Thursday, stock prices fell rapidly. The following Tuesday, the market would crash.

TRADE TROUBLES

In 1930, Congress passed the highest protective tariff in its history, the Hawley-Smoot Tariff.

- Within 2 years, the United States lost over $5 billion in world trade.

- With its world trade down, the nation had an excessive supply of manufactured goods.

- Factories soon began cutting back on production, and then cutting back on manufacturing jobs.

Crash and Collapse

Brother, Can You Spare a Dime? Out of work, with savings lost to bank failures, many Americans were forced to rely on begging or charity programs. This image shows men waiting in a soup line.

Economic Breakdown

From October 1929 until early 1933, the U.S. economy slumped almost every month. Business failures increased rapidly among banks, factories, and stores, and unemployment soared. Millions of people lost their jobs, savings, and homes. The national situation became desperate and human suffering grew.

- Between 1929 and 1932, farm income shrank by 50 percent.
- Industry was operating at half its former rate.
- In 1932 alone, 32,000 businesses failed.
- Nearly 1,500 banks failed, wiping out the life savings of millions of Americans.
- The number of unemployed Americans reached over 12 million—fully one-quarter of the workforce.

One million Americans took to the road, trying to find work, and local and state charities could not deal with the widespread destitution.

THE DUST BOWL

Falling prices and overdue mortgages were not all that farmers had to worry about during the Great Depression. Severe droughts and dust storms hit parts of the Midwest and Southwest during the 1930s. The afflicted region became known as the Dust Bowl.

- Thousands of farm families were wiped out.
- Some farmers fled to the fertile agricultural areas of California to look for work.
- Most who found jobs had to work as fruit or vegetable pickers for extremely low wages.
- The migrant families crowded into shacks near the fields or camped outdoors.

Fallout of the Dust Bowl. The American author John Steinbeck's famous novel *The Grapes of Wrath* (1939) describes the hardships some farmers and migrant families faced during the Depression.

Hoover's Response

President Hoover's response to the ever-worsening economy was to let businesses solve the crisis themselves. He opposed measures that would have used the federal government to provide relief. Still, he did take some steps to end the Depression.

- In 1930, he launched a huge program of public works to try to stem unemployment.
- In 1932, he secured passage of the bill for the Reconstruction Finance Corporation, which lent $2 billion to banks, railroads, and other industries.

Unfortunately, because the Great Depression was worldwide, nothing short of world recovery could stem the economic disaster.

At Home in Hooverville. Some people who lost their homes during the Depression moved to a shabby section of town. There, they built shacks from flattened tin cans and old crates. Groups of these shacks were often called Hoovervilles, a name that reflected the people's anger and disappointment at President Hoover's failure to end the Depression.

THE BONUS ARMY

In 1932, ten thousand World War I veterans marched on Washington. They demanded payment of the $1,000 bonuses the government had promised them, although the bonuses were not yet due. President Hoover ordered U.S. Army troops to drive them away.

Migrant camps and shanty towns called Hoovervilles became home to many Americans who had lost their jobs and homes.

The Election of 1932

Despite the backlash against him, Republicans renominated Hoover for president in 1932. The Democrats chose New York governor Franklin D. Roosevelt.

- As governor, Roosevelt had set up a relief program for New York.
- He promised to set up relief programs on a national scale if elected.
- He toured the country promising a "New Deal."

Roosevelt won a landslide victory—472 electoral votes to Hoover's 59—as voters rejected Hoover's administration, which many blamed for their economic problems. The Democrats also gained firm control of both houses of Congress.

The New Deal

Roosevelt took office on March 4, 1933, saying: "The nation asks for action and action now. We must act and act quickly." He sought to assure Americans that the country's problems could be solved, and that "the only thing we have to fear is fear itself." It was exactly what the American people wanted to hear.

"Action and Action Now"

As soon as he was elected, Roosevelt and his advisers, called his "brain trust," began shaping a series of domestic, social, and economic programs—the New Deal. The New Deal had three main objectives: reform to prevent another depression; recovery for the nation's economy; and relief for those hit hardest by the Depression.

Reform. Many policies of the New Deal aimed to reform finance, since mass bank failures had worsened the effects of the Depression.

- Roosevelt's first act was to declare a "bank holiday": banks were closed and inspected, to determine which were sound enough to continue doing business.

- Then Congress passed the Emergency Banking Law, giving the president the power to reorganize insolvent national banks.

- The Securities and Exchange Commission (SEC) was founded to regulate the stock market.

Recovery. Several acts were passed to stimulate the economy and boost trade, which had fallen drastically under President Herbert Hoover. To help revive industry, Congress passed the National Industrial Recovery Act (NIRA). This act

- established codes for industries to eliminate unfair competition and abolish child labor and sweat shops.

- established minimum wages and maximum hours.

- created additional jobs for the unemployed.

- enabled labor to organize freely (labor unions) and bargain collectively.

Spotlight on... FRANKLIN D. ROOSEVELT

1882–1945

- 32nd president of the United States, 1933–1945

- Elected as a Democrat to the New York Senate in 1910

- Married to Eleanor Roosevelt (1884–1962) and had six children, one of whom died as an infant

- In 1921, he developed polio; it left him handicapped for life.

- The first U.S. president to use the radio to address the public directly on a regular basis

- The only U.S. president to serve more than two terms

To aid agriculture, Congress passed the Agricultural Adjustment Act (AAA). This act

- controlled the production of farm goods through subsidies aimed at lowering production.

- lent money to farmers.

Relief. Congress also passed a number of relief acts, some offering direct aid to the needy and some offering jobs in public works.

- The Civilian Conservation Corps (CCC) and Public Works Administration employed millions.

- The Tennessee Valley Authority (TVA) employed people to develop a depressed area covering parts of seven states.

The Bonneville Dam, on the Columbia River in Oregon, was one of many public engineering projects organized during the New Deal.

THE FIRST HUNDRED DAYS

Franklin D. Roosevelt took office on March 4, 1933. In the first months of his term, aided by a sense of crisis in the country and a Democratic majority in the Congress, he passed bills designed to help the needy and shore up the economic structure of the nation. Some of these acts were temporary and some provisions were later ruled unconstitutional; but many provisions endured and some agencies are still active and important. The major acts are in the chart below.

Major Acts — First Hundred Days	
Emergency Banking Relief Act, March 9	Imposed federal regulation on the banking business
Civilian Conservation Reforestation Relief Act, March 31	Provided jobs for young men on federal conservation projects
Federal Emergency Relief Act, May 12	Granted funds to states for relief money for the poor; provided 4 million civil works jobs
Agricultural Adjustment Act, May 12	Paid farmers subsidies for reducing production and made federal loans available
Tennessee Valley Authority Act, May 18	Created Tennessee Valley Authority to provide jobs, electrical power, and flood control for communities in the Tennessee Valley
Federal Securities Act, May 27	Tightened regulation of securities markets; required fuller disclosure about securities in order to protect investors
Home Owners' Refinancing Act, June 13	Provided federal mortgages to those in danger of losing their homes because of unemployment
Glass-Steagall Banking Act, June 16	Created the Federal Deposit Insurance Corporation to insure bank deposits up to $5,000
National Industrial Recovery Act, June 16	Suspended antitrust laws; granted new rights to labor; created the National Labor Board

The New Deal

Controversies and Opposition

Roosevelt's ideas were popular with many Americans, but he still faced strong opposition. Many of the New Deal measures were radical changes from previous governmental practices, and their constitutionality was questioned. Some felt Roosevelt's programs were wasteful and favored unions too much. Others, such as Huey Long and Father Charles Coughlin, criticized Roosevelt because his changes weren't radical enough.

Roosevelt and the Supreme Court. The Supreme Court found both the Agricultural Adjustment Act and the National Industrial Recovery Act unconstitutional. An angry President Roosevelt blamed this defeat of his policies on the fact that the Supreme Court was made up of "nine old men," six of them over 70 years old and seven of them appointees of Republican presidents.

- In February 1937, Roosevelt proposed that Congress reorganize the High Court, giving the president the right to name a new justice for each one who did not retire by age 70.

- This was intended to enable Roosevelt to install his own justices, who would be more likely to be sympathetic to the laws he proposed.

- Congress angrily accused Roosevelt of trying to "pack the court," and denied his proposal. The Court's membership remained as it had been.

Spotlight on... HUEY P. LONG

1893–1935

- Never finished high school, but eventually became the Louisiana governor and a United States senator
- Nicknamed the "Kingfish"
- Called for social reforms to benefit farmers and workers living in poverty
- Accused of using dishonest or unlawful methods to protect his political power
- Originally supported President Franklin D. Roosevelt; later attacked the New Deal for not being more radical
- Became a candidate for president in 1935
- Shot on September 8, 1935, in the state capitol in Baton Rouge, and died 2 days later

The Supreme Court. Roosevelt's attempts to change the structure of the Supreme Court met with severe criticism. ▼

CONSTITUTIONAL AMENDMENTS

Two constitutional amendments were passed during the years of the Great Depression.

Amendment	Date	Provision
20th Amendment	January 1933	• Moved the date of the presidential and vice presidential inauguration from March 4 to January 20 and also required sessions of Congress to open on January 3 of each year
21st Amendment	February 20, 1933	• Repealed the 18th Amendment and ended Prohibition (Roosevelt thought that Prohibition had been ineffectively enforced, had promoted the growth of organized crime, and had lost favor among many Americans.)

Effects of the New Deal

The New Deal did not return the nation to prosperity at once. In fact, its radical features and broad scope raised bitter and vocal opposition. It had significantly altered the government but had failed to reach the objectives it had set. When Roosevelt began his second term in 1937, he had to state that he still saw "one-third of the nation ill-housed, ill-clad, ill-nourished."

Reelection. The 1936 presidential election became a referendum on the New Deal. When the votes were counted, Roosevelt had beaten his Republican opponent, Alfred M. Landon, by 11 million popular votes, winning 523 electoral votes to Landon's 8.

New Deal projects employed workers in many different fields, such as engineering, construction, and even the arts. ▼

The Changing Role of Government. By 1938, the New Deal was running out of steam, but it had already made the most profound, dramatic, and lasting changes in government in American history.

- Government had grown larger than ever before.
- It had moved into many new phases of American life.
- Direct government intervention and regulation—in business, social welfare, and human security—reached heights undreamed of a few years earlier.

Even after the Depression ended, government's right to intervene and regulate was widely accepted.

THE SOCIAL SECURITY ACT

One of the most far-reaching laws enacted during the New Deal was the Social Security Act, which was passed by Congress on August 14, 1935. The Act provided the foundation for the nation's Social Security system, which still exists today. It authorized funds for these items:

- old-age benefits
- unemployment compensation
- aid to dependent children

To pay for the programs, the law also established equal taxes on employees and their employers based on the employees' wages.

DISCRIMINATION AND THE DEPRESSION

The Great Depression hit some groups harder than others.

- African Americans suffered higher unemployment than whites, with unemployment up to 50 percent in some areas.
- The 1930s brought heightened discrimination against Mexican Americans. Many people viewed them as a drain on the American economy.
- Thousands of Mexican Americans—including some citizens—were deported against their wishes.

✔ During the 1920s, economic problems began to build in spite of the nation's overall prosperity.

✔ On October 29, 1929, the stock market crashed, and thousands of people lost huge sums of money. This event began the Great Depression.

✔ Bank failures, business failures, and unemployment followed. Nearly one-quarter of Americans were unemployed.

✔ Franklin D. Roosevelt was elected in 1932; his New Deal programs began to alleviate some of the suffering of the Depression, but many people opposed them.

WORLD WAR II was the most destructive war in history. It killed more people, destroyed more property, and probably had more far-reaching consequences than any other war previously fought. The war brought about the downfall of western Europe as the center of world power. It led to the dominance of the Soviet Union and the United States and to their power struggle: the Cold War. (See also pages 552–563.)

Adolf Hitler. Germany had been punished severely for its role in World War I; Hitler rose to power by arguing that Germans were in fact a superior race.

Invasion and War

The end of World War I left many European nations in poor economic condition. Then, desperation caused by the worldwide Depression paved the way for the rise of rightist military dictators in Europe and Asia.

- Adolf Hitler and the Nazi Party took control of Germany.
- Benito Mussolini and the Fascists ruled Italy.
- In Japan, a military government came to power under Emperor Hirohito.

These dictators ruled with iron fists and crushed all dissent, but promised their nations new lands, wealth, and honor.

On the March

The German, Italian, and Japanese dictatorships were bent on expansion, and soon each was on the move: Japan into China in 1931, Italy into Africa in 1935, and Germany into Austria and Czechoslovakia in 1938. In the mid-1930s, the three signed a series of mutual assistance pacts and became known as the Axis powers.

The Munich Pact. In 1938, the Allied Powers, Britain and France, desperately hoped to avoid war. They signed the Munich Pact as part of a plan to appease Hitler and maintain peace.

- The pact gave Hitler the Sudetenland, part of Czechoslovakia.
- Hitler, in turn, promised not to claim any new territory.
- By 1939, however, Hitler had broken the pact and taken over the rest of Czechoslovakia.

War in Europe

On September 1, 1939, Hitler's tanks rolled into Poland, an ally of Britain and France. The Allied nations declared war on Germany.

- In the spring of 1940, Hitler conquered Denmark, Norway, the Netherlands, Belgium, and France, leaving Britain to fight alone.
- In 1941, Hitler broke a nonaggression pact with Stalin and attacked the Soviet Union.
- The Soviet Union immediately joined Britain as an ally.

Once again, all of Europe was at war.

German Invasion. The swift and brutal invasion that conquered Poland was called a *blitzkrieg*, or lightning war.

The U.S.: From Neutrality to Aid

As in World War I, popular sentiment in the United States favored staying out of war. In 1935 and 1937, Congress passed a series of Neutrality Acts to isolate the United States from the fighting overseas.

In November of 1939, a new Neutrality Act legalized the sale of arms and munitions to belligerents—warring powers—on a "cash and carry" basis: the nations had to pay for their purchases and transport them on their own ships.

The Arsenal of Democracy. In the fall of 1940, Roosevelt won an unprecedented third term as president. By that time, it had become clear that the nation could no longer remain uninvolved.

- On June 10, Italy had declared war on France and Great Britain.

- In September of 1940, the United States gave Britain 50 destroyers in return for leases for military bases.

- On December 29, Roosevelt told Americans that their nation must become the "arsenal of democracy," providing money and military equipment to nations resisting German forces.

- In March 1941, Congress approved the Lend-Lease Act, which supplied Britain with guns, tanks, ships, and planes.

- In November 1941, Congress repealed the Neutrality Acts.

A Testing Ground for Warfare. Many of the military tactics used during the Spanish Civil War would later play a role in fighting World War II.

THE SPANISH CIVIL WAR

In 1939, Francisco Franco and his Nationalists seized power in Spain after a 3-year civil war. Hitler and Mussolini had sent troops, weapons, aircraft, and advisers to aid the Nationalists.

At War, Again

By the end of 1941, the United States was providing arms and supplies to the Allies. Still, the nation had not joined the war. In the end, only a direct attack would bring the United States to take up arms.

Into War

Although the United States had become involved with the Allies' struggle in Europe, it was actually the conflict brewing in Asia that would boil over into declarations of war.

Conflict with Japan. The European colonial powers that had footholds in Asia were weakened by the war in Europe. Japanese militarists saw this as an opportunity to drive all colonial powers, including the United States, out of East Asia and establish their own "New Order." President Roosevelt and Secretary of State Cordell Hull resisted these efforts.

- The Japanese occupied French Indochina (Vietnam and Cambodia) in July 1941.

- The president froze Japanese assets in the United States and embargoed shipments of the oil and scrap iron that were desperately needed in Japan.

- Britain followed suit.

▲ **Hopes of Empire.** Japanese Emperor Hirohito and prime minister Hideki Tojo wanted to build an empire that would include China, Burma (now Myanmar), and Indochina (now Laos and Vietnam).

- In November 1941, negotiations over trade, the status of China, and territorial expansion in Asia began between the United States and Japan.

- Japan demanded an end to all U.S. and British influence in Asia.

While the talks were going on, however, a Japanese fleet set out across the Pacific toward Hawaii.

THE basics

WORLD WAR II: CAUSES AND BEGINNINGS

✔ Worldwide economic depression during the 1930s helped create military dictatorships in Europe and Asia.

✔ Germany, Italy, and Japan joined forces as the Axis powers.

✔ Britain, France, and the Soviet Union formed the Allies.

✔ War in Europe began when Germany, under Adolf Hitler and the Nazi Party, invaded Poland in 1939.

✔ War in Asia began when Japan invaded China in 1931.

✔ The United States entered the war in 1941, after the Japanese bombing of Pearl Harbor.

Strategy. After the German and Italian declarations of war, the United States found itself facing war on two fronts—in Europe and in the Pacific. Roosevelt determined that the situation in Europe was the more desperate: if Britain and the Soviet Union fell, the United States would be totally on its own.

The major disagreement among the Allies was the timing of the Allied invasion of Western Europe. The Soviet Union was suffering enormous losses on the eastern front. It insisted that Britain and the United States invade France without delay. But the Allied forces were not yet strong enough to invade Europe.

In January 1943, Roosevelt and Churchill met at Casablanca, Morocco, and agreed that the Allies would continue to prosecute the war until total and unconditional surrender by the Axis was achieved.

Allied Cooperation. Throughout the war, the leaders of the "Big Three"—Stalin for the Soviet Union, Roosevelt for the United States, and Churchill for Britain—as well as other Allied civilian and military leaders, met regularly to work out wartime strategy and to plan for postwar peace.

PEARL HARBOR

On the morning of Sunday, December 7, 1941, Japanese fighters, bombers, and submarines attacked the American naval base at Pearl Harbor in Hawaii.

- Nineteen U.S. ships were sunk or badly damaged.

- More than 2,300 Americans were killed.

- The following day, President Roosevelt spoke to Congress, referring to the "day which will live in infamy" and asking for a declaration acknowledging that a state of war existed between the United States and Japan.

Within a few hours, war was declared. Three days later, the other Axis powers, Germany and Italy, also declared war on the United States.

◀ **Pearl Harbor.** The Pearl Harbor attack was a great tactical success, but bringing the United States into the war would prove disastrous for the Japanese Empire and its citizens.

The War at Home

The United States initially attempted to stay out of the Second World War, and many people supported this position. When the nation finally entered the war in 1941, however, the American people were tireless in their support of the war effort. Some Americans would see economic and social benefits from the nation's wartime changes; other groups would suffer greatly.

The War Effort

As early as September 1940, Congress passed the Selective Service Act, the first U.S. peacetime draft. In December 1941, the limits were broadened to include men 20 to 44 years of age. In all, more than 16 million Americans served in military units during the war.

Economic Recovery. As World War II began, the United States was still struggling with high unemployment and low productivity as a result of the Great Depression. Suddenly, there was a need for tanks, ships, guns, and airplanes, and other military supplies.

Industry and agriculture mobilized to create a giant wartime production apparatus. Factories shifted from making consumer goods to producing military supplies and equipment.

- The wartime economy provided millions of new jobs, higher wages, overtime pay, and profitable war contracts for manufacturers.
- Many government agencies were set up to coordinate production and to regulate prices, wages, and rents.
- Rationing systems were set up for scarce goods such as gasoline, sugar, coffee, and rubber.

Victory Gardens. The American government encouraged civilians to plant their own gardens, which they called "Victory Gardens," in order to reserve as much food production, labor, and transportation as possible for the war effort.

Women in the War. With so many men in active service, factories, defense plants, and other businesses began hiring women. "Rosie the Riveter," described in a popular song as "making history working for victory," became the symbol of women workers.

In May 1942, Congress authorized the formation of women's noncombat branches in the Navy (WAVES), Army (WACS), Air Force (WAFS), Coast Guard (SPARS), and Marines. About 338,000 women served in the armed forces.

▲ **Women in the Workforce.** World War II brought millions of American women into defense plants and other industries. This would forever change the structure of American society.

African Americans in the War. African Americans had been hit hard by the Great Depression. They fared better on the job front during the 1940s, thanks to the wartime demand for labor.

- About a million more African Americans left the South, often for cities like Los Angeles, which had many war-related factory jobs.

- About 1 million African Americans served in the military during World War II.

In 1941, President Franklin Delano Roosevelt issued Executive Order 8802, which banned discrimination in the United States defense industries. The order also created the Fair Employment Practices Committee to help achieve its goals.

In 1948, President Truman desegregated the military, and Democrats adopted a strong civil rights plank. (See page 210.)

Highest Honors. In 2007, the United States awarded the Tuskegee Airmen (shown here in 1942) the Congressional Gold Medal, the highest civilian award given by Congress. ▼

WORLD WAR II AND JAPANESE AMERICANS

The attack on Pearl Harbor left many Americans, particularly on the West Coast, fearful of further Japanese attacks, enemy spies, and sabotage. Suspicion landed on all people of Japanese ancestry, even those born in the United States (known as the Nisei).

In 1942, President Roosevelt signed Executive Order 9066. Many Americans would later condemn this order.

- The order authorized inland "relocation camps" for purposes of military necessity.

- Over 100,000 Japanese Americans were forcibly removed from their homes and property and were interned in relocation camps.

- In 1944, the Supreme Court decision *Fred Korematsu v. United States of America* declared Executive Order 9066 constitutional.

DIVERSITY IN THE MILITARY

Despite the discrimination they often faced as American citizens, many minority groups made outstanding contributions to the American war effort.

- **The Tuskegee Airmen** were a group of African Americans who served in the Army Air Corps during World War II. Many became decorated war heroes.

- **Code talkers** were small groups of American Indians who served in the United States armed forces. Code talkers developed and used codes in Indian languages to send secret messages.

- **442nd Regimental Combat Unit.** Thousands of Japanese Americans served in the U.S. armed forces during World War II. Most were in the Army's 442nd Regimental Combat Unit. The unit fought bravely in Europe and suffered many casualties.

Theaters of War

BATTLE OF THE ATLANTIC

The Allied war effort depended on shipments of food, military equipment and supplies, and other provisions across the Atlantic Ocean from North America. Germany tried to stop the shipments. This struggle, the Battle of the Atlantic, lasted the entire war. The Germans launched nearly 1,200 submarines. Of these, close to 800 were sunk and about 200 were scuttled by their own crews. Out of about 40,000 submariners sent into action, 28,000 never returned—the highest death rate of any armed service in the history of modern warfare. About 3,000 Allied ships sank, taking more than 30,000 Allied sailors with them.

When the United States entered World War II, the nation faced war in three regions: Europe, North Africa, and the Pacific.

Europe and North Africa

Germany's powerful war machine brought much of Europe under Axis control during the early stages of World War II. By November 1942, Axis-controlled territory extended from Norway to northern Africa and from France to the Soviet Union.

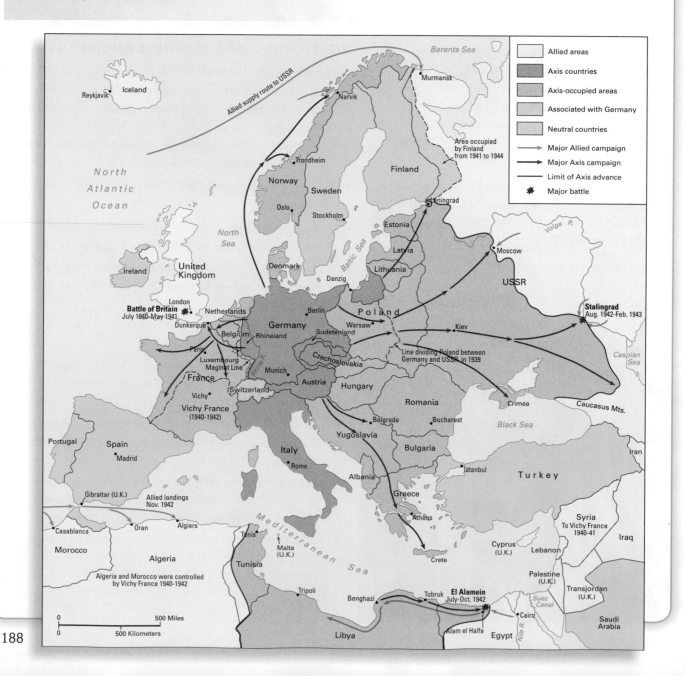

The Pacific

After Japan attacked Pearl Harbor on December 7, 1941, its forces rapidly advanced across Southeast Asia and the western Pacific Ocean. This map shows key battles in that campaign and the greatest extent of Japan's empire. The Allies halted Japan's expansion in the summer of 1942.

NAVAL WARHORSE

The aircraft carrier was a floating airfield that became the backbone of the U.S. Navy during World War II. Carrier-based planes took part in many battles in the Pacific and helped defeat Japan. The irregular pattern on the USS *Wasp, below,* made it hard for enemy submarines to determine the ship's course.

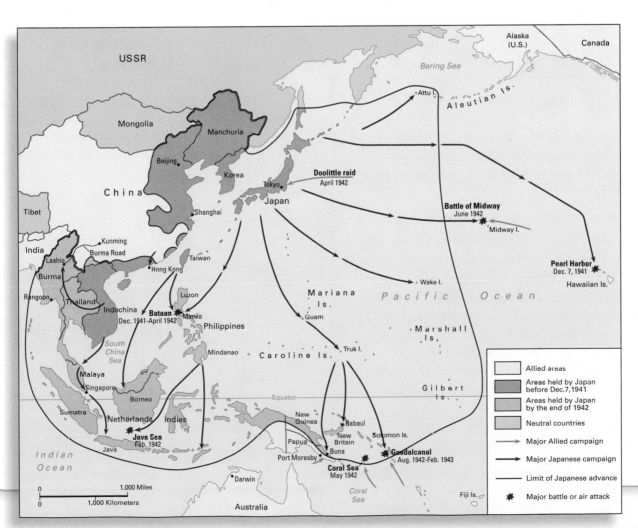

USSR

Alaska (U.S.)

Canada

Bering Sea

Mongolia

Manchuria

Attu I.

Aleutian Is.

Beijing

Korea

Doolittle raid
April 1942

China

Tokyo

Japan

Shanghai

Battle of Midway
June 1942

Midway I.

Tibet

India

Kunming

Burma Road

Taiwan

Lashio

Hong Kong

Burma

Rangoon

Thailand

Indochina

Luzon

Bataan
Dec. 1941-April 1942

Manila

Philippines

Mariana Is.

Guam

Pacific Ocean

Pearl Harbor
Dec. 7, 1941

Hawaiian Is.

Wake I.

Marshall Is.

South China Sea

Mindanao

Caroline Is.

Truk I.

Malaya

Singapore

Borneo

Equator

Gilbert Is.

Sumatra

Netherlands Indies

Java

Java Sea
Feb. 1942

New Guinea

Papua

Buna

Port Moresby

Rabaul

New Britain

Solomon Is.

Guadalcanal
Aug. 1942-Feb. 1943

Indian Ocean

Coral Sea
May 1942

Darwin

Coral Sea

Fiji Is.

Australia

	Allied areas
	Areas held by Japan before Dec. 7, 1941
	Areas held by Japan by the end of 1942
	Neutral countries

→ Major Allied campaign

→ Major Japanese campaign

— Limit of Japanese advance

✸ Major battle or air attack

0   1,000 Miles
0   1,000 Kilometers

Major Battles

World War II lasted from 1939 until 1945. Countless battles and campaigns were fought, both in Europe and in the Pacific. A few were important enough to change the course of the war, or—like the Pearl Harbor attack—to "live in infamy."

Europe

Allied troops had driven the Germans and Italians out of North Africa by 1943. This opened the way for Allied troops to move in on Europe. Their efforts began in Italy.

Battle/Campaign	Dates	Details	Results
Italy	1943–1944	• In 1943, Allied forces invaded Sicily. • Mussolini and the fascist government in Italy were overthrown. • Mussolini escaped to northern Italy and proclaimed a new fascist republic.	• Fighting continued into 1944. • On June 4, 1944, U.S. troops liberated Rome.
D-Day (see feature below)	June 6, 1944	• The invasion of Normandy, also called D-Day, began the invasion of western Europe. • With massive air support, American, British, Canadian, and other Allied troops moved across France.	• French forces led by Charles de Gaulle entered Paris in August. • The Soviet army moved on Germany from the east.
Battle of the Bulge	December 1944	• Hitler launched an all-out offensive in the Ardennes. • This caused a large bulge in the Allied lines.	• The battle sped up the invasion of Germany on both fronts.

D-DAY

The Germans expected an Allied invasion along the north coast of France in 1944, but they were unsure where it would occur.

- A chain of fortifications ran along the coast.

- Explosive mines and barbed wire had been placed in the water and on the beaches.

The night of June 5, thousands of Allied ships carrying amphibious (land and water) landing craft and more than 130,000 troops crossed the English Channel. About 23,000 paratroopers dropped behind German lines.

At dawn on June 6, battleships opened fire on the beaches. More than 50,000 Allied troops and aviators, and tens of thousands of German troops, died in the battle. (See also page 558.)

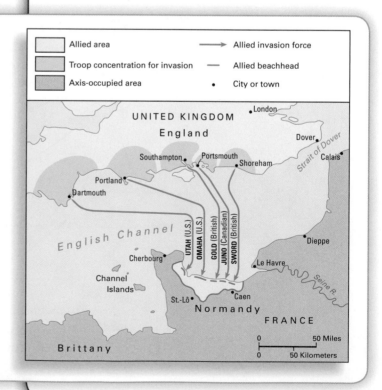

190

The Pacific

When war began, the Allied leaders—Churchill, Roosevelt, and Stalin—agreed that the Axis powers in Europe (Germany and Italy) were a greater threat than the Axis in the Pacific. Nonetheless, the Allies did undertake initiatives against the Japanese army.

The Bataan Death March. Thousands of American and Filipino soldiers died of abuse, starvation, or disease during the march to prison camps, which came to be known as the Bataan Death March. ▼

THE FIGHT FOR THE PHILIPPINES

The day after the bombing of Pearl Harbor, Japan began an invasion of the Philippines—which were still under American control. U.S. general Douglas MacArthur led the American and Filipino defense forces.

- In December, MacArthur was forced to abandon the capital city of Manila.
- For 3 months, his forces held off the Japanese Army on the Bataan Peninsula.

MacArthur was ordered to leave the Philippines in March of 1942. As he left, he promised the troops: "I shall return." The remaining Filipino and American troops surrendered. The Japanese led them on a forced march to Japanese prison camps—about 65 miles (105 kilometers) away.

Battle/Campaign	Dates	Details	Results
The Doolittle Raid	April 18, 1942	• Colonel James H. Doolittle led a squadron of carrier-based B-25 bombers in a raid on Tokyo. • All 16 planes were lost due to lack of fuel.	• The raid shocked the Japanese and helped to restore American confidence.
Battle of Midway	June 1942	• Allied forces halted a Japanese invasion of Midway Island.	• The battle was the first firm Allied victory in the Pacific. • The Japanese lost four aircraft carriers, and the tide began to turn against Japan.
Guadalcanal	August 1942–January 1943	• United States Marines invaded the island of Guadalcanal. • The surprise attack led to a 6-month fight for the Solomon Islands.	• The Allies cut off Japanese shipments, starving out the Japanese troops.

The Allied leaders—Roosevelt, Churchill, and Stalin—had agreed that they would fight until the Axis powers surrendered unconditionally. By early 1945, surrender in Europe finally began to seem possible. However, victory in the Pacific seemed further away.

Allied Infantrymen hold up a captured German Nazi flag during World War II.

Victory in Europe

The Allies began their final assault on Germany in early 1945. Soviet soldiers reached the Oder River, about 40 miles (65 kilometers) east of Berlin, in January. Allied forces in the west occupied positions along the Rhine by early March.

- British and Canadian forces cleared the Germans out of the Netherlands and swept into northern Germany.

- American and French forces raced toward the Elbe River in central Germany.

- The Allies left the capture of Berlin to Soviet forces. By April 25, 1945, Soviet troops had surrounded the city.

- At the end of April 1945, Hitler and many top Nazis committed suicide; others fled.

Germany surrendered unconditionally, and the war in Europe ended on May 8, 1945. The date is now known as V-E (Victory in Europe) Day.

PREPARING FOR PEACE

In February of 1945, at the Yalta Conference in the Crimea, Churchill, Roosevelt, and Stalin met once again. They would plan for the postwar occupation of Germany, the reorganization of Europe, the entry of Russia into the war against Japan, and a conference to draw up a charter for the United Nations. In July, the United States, Britain, and the Soviet Union met in Potsdam, near Berlin, to decide on how Germany would be occupied.

Planning the Postwar World. The Allied leaders (from left to right) Churchill, Roosevelt, and Stalin had met frequently throughout the war, planning campaigns and invasions. At Yalta and Potsdam, they planned for peace. ▶

Victory in the Pacific

The war in Europe had ended, but the war in Asia raged on with no sign of stopping. American forces moved on Japan from the east, "island hopping" in bloody campaigns that formed an ever-tightening ring around Japan. In October of 1944, the Battle of Leyte Gulf marked the end of Japanese naval power and cleared the way for the liberation of the Philippines. In November, large-scale bombing of Japan began.

- American bombers began to drop incendiary (fire-producing) bombs that set Japanese cities aflame. A massive incendiary raid in March 1945 destroyed the heart of Tokyo.

- In all, over 300,000 Japanese civilians were killed in American bombing raids.

- Devastating Allied invasions of the islands of Iwo Jima and Okinawa led some Japanese leaders to consider surrender, but others refused.

The Atomic Bomb. Meanwhile, Allied leaders, horrified by the heavy death toll at Okinawa, looked for a way to avoid a full invasion of Japan.

- On August 6, 1945, the newly developed atomic bomb was dropped on the Japanese industrial city of Hiroshima.

- Differing estimates show that between 70,000 and 140,000 people were killed in the explosion. Still, Japan did not respond.

- On August 9, a second bomb was dropped on Nagasaki.

Japan surrendered the next day, and Allied victory was declared on August 15. World War II was over, after the loss of over 405,000 American lives among millions of casualties worldwide.

V-J Day. General Douglas MacArthur accepted the surrender of the Japanese on September 2, 1945, now called V-J (Victory in Japan) Day. ▶

ROOSEVELT TO TRUMAN

President Roosevelt did not live to see the German surrender, the use of the atom bomb, or the Japanese surrender. In 1944, although aging and ill, Roosevelt had been elected to a fourth term. On April 12, 1945, less than 3 months after his fourth inauguration, Roosevelt died after suffering a stroke. He was succeeded by his vice president, Harry S. Truman, a blunt, plainspoken former senator from Missouri.

◀ **President Truman** made the difficult decision to use atomic weapons against Japan, "in order to save the lives of thousands and thousands of young Americans," as he explained in a speech given August 9, 1945.

A New Kind of War

By the time World War II finally ended in 1945, the world had been irreversibly changed. Europe was physically, economically, and psychologically shattered. The war had been unlike anything anyone had ever seen, with horrifying new military technology and evidence of unimaginable cruelty. Twelve million people had been displaced from their homes. The effects of aerial warfare, the Holocaust, and the atomic bomb would be felt for generations.

Aerial War

Airplanes were first used in combat during World War I; however, it was during World War II that they began to play a significant role in warfare. Whole cities were destroyed by bombs from the sky.

- **London Blitz.** From August of 1940 until May of 1941, Hitler unleashed his air force against English cities in what is known as the Blitz. German planes bombed cities from London to Manchester day after day, then night after night for months. More than 40,000 British civilians lost their lives.

- **V-1 and V-2 Attacks.** In September of 1944, the Germans launched the first V-2 rocket attack against London. This weapon caused even more damage than the V-1 "flying bombs," which had first been launched against London in June.

- **Dresden Bombing.** In February 1945, Allied bombing raids killed thousands of people in Dresden and destroyed much of the city

Air Raids. During World War II, squadrons of airplanes dropped bombs first on military targets, and later on civilians.

✔ Economic troubles in Europe and Asia led to the rise of rightist military dictators: Adolf Hitler (Germany), Benito Mussolini (Italy), and Emperor Hirohito (Japan).

✔ Germany, Italy, and Japan became known as the Axis powers.

✔ Hitler invaded Poland on September 1, 1939, and the Allied nations (Britain, France, and the Soviet Union) declared war.

✔ The United States entered the war on the Allied side after Japanese forces bombed Pearl Harbor in Hawaii.

✔ World War II was fought in Europe, North Africa, and the Pacific. It lasted until 1945; Germany surrendered on May 8, and Japan on August 10.

THE ATOMIC BOMB

In 1939, the German-born scientist Albert Einstein had informed President Roosevelt about the possibility of creating a superbomb. It would produce an extremely powerful explosion by splitting the atom. Einstein and other scientists feared that Germany might develop such a bomb first. In 1942, the United States set up the Manhattan Project, a top-secret program to develop an atomic bomb. The atomic age had begun, and the stage was set for a new kind of conflict.

Dawn of the Nuclear Age. The United States exploded the first atomic bomb in a test blast in the New Mexico desert in July 1945. Two atomic bombs, dropped on Hiroshima and Nagasaki in Japan, would end World War II.

The Holocaust

As the Allies liberated Nazi-controlled Europe, they made a horrifying discovery: concentration camps filled with starving prisoners—and corpses. These camps, and the people who survived them, were the evidence of Hitler's brutal "Final Solution."

Germany's Nazi government had based part of its ideology on racial purity and the elimination of people the Nazis considered inferior, particularly Jewish people. Persecution of Jews had begun in the early 1930s. Later, the Nazis had imprisoned and systematically killed the following groups:

- Jews
- Germans with physical handicaps or mental retardation
- Roma (sometimes called Gypsies)
- Poles and Soviet prisoners of war
- homosexuals
- Jehovah's Witnesses, priests, and ministers
- members of labor unions, Communists, and other political opponents

Historians estimate that perhaps as many as 11 million people were killed, including 6 million Jews.

The Holocaust. Victims were imprisoned in concentration camps, where many were killed in specially constructed gas chambers and their bodies burned. This system of state-sponsored murder is known as the Holocaust—a word meaning "a sacrificial offering that is completely burned." (See also page 559.)

World War II: Time Line

World War II began on September 1, 1939, when Nazi Germany invaded Poland. Over the next 6 years, the Allies and the Axis powers would fight in nearly every part of the world—from Southeast Asian jungles to frozen tundra in the Soviet Union.

The pictures across the top of the time line depict stages of the war. From *left* to *right*: German soldiers march in a victory parade in Poland, October 5, 1939; a British army soldier rescues a woman from the rubble; Allied troops land at Salerno, Italy, in September 1943.

1939–1941

German armies attack Poland on September 1, 1939. The Allied powers, led by Britain and France, declare war on the Axis (Germany and Italy). By July 1940, the Axis powers overrun Denmark, Norway, Belgium, Holland, and France, and threaten Britain. In June 1941, they invade the Soviet Union.

Meanwhile, the Japanese, allied with the Axis, take control of South Asia and the Pacific. On December 7, 1941, they attack Pearl Harbor, a U.S. Navy base in Hawaii. Within days, the United States declares war on all Axis nations.

1942

January–May
Japanese capture the Philippines and Burma.

May
U.S. forces drive off Japanese fleet in Coral Sea.

June
U.S. defends Midway Island, defeats Japanese fleet.

August
U.S. forces land on Guadalcanal, face bitter fight.

November
U.S. and Allied forces land in North Africa.

1943

February
- Soviets begin long offensive to retake Stalingrad and drive Germans from USSR in bloodiest campaign of war.
- U.S. completes conquest of Guadalcanal.

May
Allied forces drive all Axis troops from North Africa.

July–August
Allies invade and occupy Sicily.

July
U.S. begins drive on Solomon Islands.

September
Allies invade the mainland of Italy.

1944

January–May
- Allied air forces begin heavy bombardment of Germany.
- U.S. defeats Japanese in New Guinea.

June–August
- Rome liberated (June 4)
- D-Day: Allies invade France at Normandy beaches (June 6)
- Paris liberated (August 25)

June
U.S. forces capture Saipan and Guam.

October
U.S. fleet crushes Japanese fleet at Leyte Gulf, gains foothold in Philippines.

December
Battle of the Bulge; German counteroffensive drives Allies back in Belgium. Allies hold at Bastogne.

1945

February
Manila, capital of the Philippines, is liberated.

April–June
U.S. approaches Japan, captures Okinawa.

April–May
Fall of Germany
- British, U.S., and Soviet forces meet.
- Berlin falls (May 2).
- Germany surrenders (May 8).

May–June
U.S. bombards Japan.

August
- U.S. drops atom bombs on Hiroshima (August 6) and Nagasaki (August 9).
- Japan accepts terms of surrender (August 14).

POSTWAR AMERICA

The end of World War II had left much of Europe and Asia in ruins, while the United States enjoyed a period of prosperity. As the Allies began rebuilding, two nations—the United States and the Soviet Union—emerged as the world's leading powers. Their wartime alliance soon collapsed as the Soviet Union sought to spread Communism in Europe and Asia. The struggle between the Communist world, led by the Soviet Union, and the non-Communist world, led by the United States, became known as the Cold War.

Rebuilding

After the war, Americans found it impossible to return to the policy of isolation their country had followed before the war. They needed strong allies, and so they helped the war-torn nations—friend and foe alike—recover. Before long, however, the nation found itself locked in a power struggle with its old ally, the Soviet Union.

Postwar Policies

The Soviet Union insisted on keeping a tight hold on the nations of eastern Europe. In March 1946, Churchill warned that an "iron curtain" had descended across Europe, dividing eastern Europe from western Europe. Behind the Iron Curtain, the Soviet Union helped Communist governments take power in Bulgaria, Czechoslovakia, Hungary, Poland, and Romania. The other Allies opposed Communist expansion, and began working to prevent it.

The Truman Doctrine. In March 1947, in response to Soviet efforts at Communist expansion in Greece and Turkey, Truman announced what came to be called the Truman Doctrine.

- The doctrine stated that it "must be the policy of the United States to support free people who are resisting attempted subjugation."

- Truman asked Congress to authorize millions of dollars in economic and military aid for Greece, Turkey, and any other nation that wanted to fight Communist takeover.

Germany Divided. The Soviet sector of Berlin became known as East Berlin; the rest became West Berlin. ▼

THE BERLIN AIRLIFT

In June of 1948, a direct confrontation between the Western nations and the Soviet Union arose in Berlin.

- All of eastern Germany had been occupied by the Russians, with the exception of the German capital of Berlin.

- In Berlin, Americans, French, British, and Russians controlled different zones within the city.

To drive the Western nations out of this eastern area, Soviet troops blocked the highways and railroads in an effort to cut off the city's supplies. The Western powers mounted a massive airlift into Berlin, flying in enough cargo each day to keep Berlin's 2 million residents, as well as their own troops, supplied. In May of 1949, after 321 days, the Russians lifted the blockade.

The Marshall Plan. Truman's secretary of state, George C. Marshall, wanted to prevent Communist influence in the economically devastated countries of Europe. On June 5, 1947, he announced that the American government would provide economic aid to any country that agreed to work for its own recovery.

- For the European Recovery Plan (ERP), also called the Marshall Plan, Congress appropriated $12.5 billion in aid to countries in western Europe.

- The countries of eastern Europe were offered the same aid, but the Soviet Union did not allow them to accept.

AN INTERNATIONAL COMMUNITY

The end of World War II brought about new efforts at international cooperation and law. In 1945, representatives from 50 nations had come together to establish the United Nations (UN), an organization committed to maintaining a "just peace." Many of its actions after World War II have become lasting elements of the world community. (See also page 565.)

Universal Declaration of Human Rights

- Adopted by the United Nations in 1948

- Set forth the fundamental social, political, and economic rights of all peoples of the world

International Monetary Fund (IMF)

- Created in 1944 to develop international economic cooperation

- Became an agency of the UN

- Provides short-term credit to its approximately 185 member nations

World Bank

- Created in 1944 and began operating in the aftermath of World War II

- Its original objective was postwar reconstruction, but its focus soon shifted to development aid.

The United Nations has not always been able to maintain world peace, but it has helped to build productive relationships between nations.

The Cold War lasted from the end of World War II until the early 1990s. During that time, hostility waxed and waned, and more than once the world was on the brink of nuclear war. Several events and people eventually came to define the era, with all its suspicion, fear, and hope.

The Balance of Terror

As tensions with the Soviet Union built after World War II, President Truman established a policy of containment—halting the spread of Communist influence into new nations. Initially, this was done through economic aid programs, such as the Marshall Plan. Before long, however, military actions and nuclear threats would take the place of aid.

Both sides struggled constantly to maintain a "balance of terror"—equal destructive power, which would prevent any full-on attack.

TREATY ORGANIZATIONS

After World War II, Communist nations (known as the Eastern Bloc) and non-Communist nations (the Western Bloc) alike formed alliances for mutual protection.

Western Bloc	Eastern Bloc
North Atlantic Treaty Organization (NATO)	**Warsaw Treaty Organization (WTO)**
April 1949	May 15, 1955
• Security alliance for member nations • Original members: the U.S., Canada, and 10 Western European nations	• Sometimes called the Warsaw Pact • Provided mutual defense for members • Kept members under tight Soviet control • Dissolved in 1991

The nuclear arms race began on August 29, 1949, when the Soviet Union tested an atomic bomb. Until then, the United States had been the only nation that knew how to make the atomic bomb.

- The United States and the Soviet Union began competing furiously to build new and more potent nuclear weapons.

- In November of 1952, the United States tested a new type of atomic weapon, the hydrogen bomb, which had many times the destructive power of the first atomic bombs.

- In 1953, the Soviet Union exploded its first hydrogen bomb.

- Rockets carrying nuclear warheads and atomic submarines equipped with missiles were stockpiled in huge numbers.

The Nuclear Age. John Foster Dulles, the secretary of state under President Dwight D. Eisenhower, committed the United States to the theory of "massive retaliation"—under which the U.S. would respond to Soviet aggression with nuclear weapons.

THE SPACE RACE

In 1957, the United States was working to develop a satellite to send into orbit around Earth. Americans were stunned when they learned that on October 4 the Soviet Union had placed its own satellite, Sputnik, into orbit. Fearing that the United States was falling behind in rocket technology, the Eisenhower administration stepped up its space program. On January 31, 1958, it launched Explorer 1.

The Army-McCarthy hearings, shown on television, demonstrated to the American public McCarthy's unfair tactics. Public opinion began turning against him.

MCCARTHYISM

A fear of Communist activity both abroad and at home dominated much American thinking during the late 1940s and early 1950s.

- In 1950, Senator Joseph McCarthy of Wisconsin claimed to have a list of 205 Communists or Communist sympathizers working in the State Department.

- In that same year, former State Department official Alger Hiss, accused of spying for the Soviet Union 20 years earlier, was convicted of perjury.

- In 1953, Ethel and Julius Rosenberg, convicted of treason for stealing sketches of the atomic bomb, were executed.

Other private and public investigations went on throughout the country. Many people were unfairly dismissed from their jobs and labeled "security risks," though few charges were ever proved.

Then, in early 1954, McCarthy accused the U.S. Army of harboring known Communists. In December, McCarthy's colleagues in the Senate censured him for "conduct unbecoming a member," and "McCarthyism" faded away.

Into Outer Space. The United States and the Soviet Union competed with each other to see who could build more powerful (and potentially weapons-carrying) rockets.

The Cold War: Continues

The Cold War continued to develop throughout the 1950s and 1960s. After several close calls with nuclear annihilation in the early 1960s, tensions eased a bit. The nations began working toward treaties. Still, each nation kept a massive number of nuclear weapons.

The Cuban Missile Crisis

One critical moment of the Cold War was what is now called the Cuban Missile Crisis. For a week, the nation stood at the edge of total destruction. (See page 573.)

The Crisis. In October 1962, the United States learned that the USSR had secretly installed missiles and missile bases in Cuba, about 90 miles (140 kilometers) from Florida.

- President Kennedy demanded that the USSR remove them.
- He set up a naval "quarantine" of Cuba.
- The USSR said that it would not remove the missiles unless the United States removed its nuclear missiles from Turkey and promised not to invade Cuba.

After a week of extreme tension, Khrushchev removed the Soviet missiles.

▲ **President John F. Kennedy**, shown here with military officials, led the nation through the Cuban Missile Crisis in 1962.

The Aftermath. Following the Cuban missile crisis, Kennedy took steps to ease the threat of nuclear destruction.

- In the spring of 1963, the missiles in Turkey were withdrawn.
- A "hot line" was set up between Washington and Moscow, allowing direct communication between the two heads of state in times of crisis.
- The United States, the Soviet Union, and Great Britain signed a treaty in 1963 that banned testing of nuclear weapons in the atmosphere and underwater.

Soviet leader Joseph Stalin died in March 1953. Some leaders who followed him, such as Nikita Khrushchev, claimed to want "peaceful coexistence" with the West, but the arms race continued.

THE U-2 INCIDENT

In the mid-1950s, following the death of Stalin, there was a thaw in Soviet-American relations. The two nations planned a summit conference in 1960.

- Shortly before the meeting, however, an American U-2 reconnaissance plane was brought down inside the Soviet Union.
- The pilot, Francis Gary Powers, confessed to his spy mission but President Eisenhower refused to apologize.
- The Soviet Union angrily withdrew from the planned summit.

DUCK AND COVER

In 1961, the U.S. Office of Civilian Defense Mobilization began a public fallout shelter program. Its purpose was to identify— and stock with supplies—buildings and underground areas where people would be protected from the fallout of a nuclear explosion. (Fallout gives off radiation that can cause illness and death.)

The Civil Defense branch also provided the public with nuclear safety information. One 1952 filmstrip, titled *Duck and Cover*, was often shown in schools.

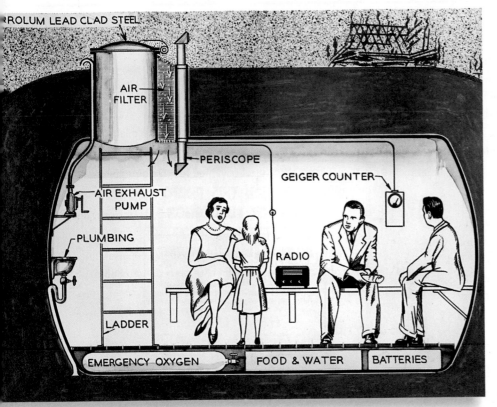

◀ **Shelter from the Bomb.** The federal government designated buildings and underground areas as fallout shelters throughout the 1960s. However, many people protested the program and refused to take part in national civil defense exercises.

Friendlier Relations

In the late 1960s and early 1970s, several Communist and democratic nations developed friendlier relations with one another.

- In November 1969, the United States and the Soviet Union ratified a nuclear non-proliferation treaty.

- In February of 1972, President Nixon became the first U.S. president to visit the People's Republic of China, ending nearly 25 years of diplomatic separation.

- Nixon and the Chinese leaders agreed to increase trade between the two nations and to allow journalistic, scientific, and cultural exchanges.

- In May 1972, Nixon visited the Soviet Union and signed a treaty limiting antiballistic missiles, a result of the Strategic Arms Limitation Talks (SALT).

The Cold War: A Time Line	
Year	**Location**
1946–1948	Communists take over eastern Europe.
1947	Truman Doctrine announced by the United States.
1948–1949	Berlin blockade and airlift
1949	NATO pact signed by 12 countries.
1949	Communists win control of China.
1950–1953	Korean War: first use of UN troops in battle (See pages 206–207).
1953	Death of Stalin alters Cold War.
1960	Soviet Union downs American U-2 spy plane.
1961	German Communists build Berlin Wall.
1962	Cuban Missile Crisis
1964	United States bombs bases in Communist North Vietnam.
1975	Communists win Vietnam War (See pages 216–217).
1979	Soviet Union invades Afghanistan.
1989	Communist rule ends in several eastern European countries.
1989	German Communists open Berlin Wall.

Postwar Prosperity

When World War II ended, the United States found itself the world's leading industrial and military power. Its wartime allies and the Axis nations were severely war-damaged and they faced the monumental task of rebuilding their industries and cities. The United States, on the other hand, was relatively untouched. Its most pressing problem (aside from the Cold War) was to convert from a wartime economy to a peace-time economy.

Adjusting to Peace

America was able to convert to peace with surprising ease. Presidents Truman and Eisenhower oversaw years of national prosperity. The period of readjustment, however, was not without its problems. For example, increased demand for consumer goods—and the lifting of wartime price controls—led to inflation. Within a single year, the cost of living rose by 50 percent.

THE G.I. BILL

Returning military personnel were aided by the so-called G.I. Bill of Rights, passed by Congress in 1944. The bill offered

- money for tuition
- living expenses to those who wanted to go to college or to training schools
- low-cost loans to those who wanted to buy homes or start up businesses
- unemployment benefits to those who were seeking jobs

Millions of veterans took advantage of these opportunities, at once raising the educational level of the nation and sending the building industry into a period of unprecedented boom.

The Election of 1948

In 1948, Truman offered a platform called the Fair Deal, which promised to extend many New Deal programs. The Fair Deal split the Democratic Party.

- Left-leaning Democrats, wanting more, formed the Progressive Party.
- Southern Democrats, rejecting Truman's insistence on equal rights for blacks and other minorities, broke away to form the States' Rights Party.

Republicans chose Thomas E. Dewey and awaited a landslide victory. But Truman began an extensive "whistle-stop campaign," traveling by train across the nation to address the voters. His victory over Dewey was one of the great comebacks in American political history.

▲ **Truman's victory** in 1948 was such an upset that many newspapers had already printed headlines declaring Dewey the winner. Truman had given 350 speeches around the country on his "whistle-stop campaign."

The Eisenhower Years

In 1952, the Republicans chose General Dwight D. Eisenhower as their candidate for president. A decorated war hero, he had commanded the D-Day invasion and had been given the newly created rank of five-star general. Adlai E. Stevenson, governor of Illinois, was the Democratic candidate. A respected liberal, Stevenson failed to overcome the popular sentiment for "Ike," and Eisenhower won by a large margin.

Eisenhower vowed that if he were elected, he would to go to Korea, where Communist North Korea had begun attacking non-Communist South Korea. His strong stance on Communism appealed to the American people.

▲ **Suburban housing developments** sprang up around American cities in the 1950s and 1960s. The homes were constructed using prefabricated units and assembly-line techniques, and therefore often looked much alike.

Domestic affairs. The Eisenhower years saw the development of unprecedented prosperity in the United States. Population growth, brought on largely by a "baby boom" after the war, encouraged tremendous building activity in many sectors, including:

- houses (mostly in new suburbs)
- highways
- schools
- shopping centers

Science and technology, pushed ahead by wartime research, helped industries such as plastics, electronics, and television to grow.

The demand for TV sets was enormous. In 1945, there were probably fewer than 10,000 sets in the country. This figure soared to about 6 million in 1950, and to almost 60 million by 1960. ▶

The Korean War

At the end of World War II, Korea had been divided into zones of occupation, with the United States controlling the country up to the 38th parallel and the Soviet Union controlling territory above the 38th parallel. Just as in Germany after the war, the Soviets and the Western powers could not agree on reunification, and two separate states were established. (See also page 572.)

The Cold War Turns Hot

In 1949, a long civil war in China had ended with Communist triumph. The People's Republic of China was now the ally of the Soviet Union and of North Korea. On June 25, 1950, Communist North Korean troops crossed the 38th parallel and attacked non-Communist South Korea.

The UN Intervenes. Fearful that if one Asian nation were conquered by communists, others would soon follow, the United States sent its troops as part of a UN force to aid South Korea.

- By November, the UN troops had driven the North Koreans back behind their border and were continuing north, almost to the Chinese border.

- At that point, the Chinese intervened, sending the UN troops retreating southward.

The fighting continued for the next two and a half years, until finally a cease-fire was signed on July 27, 1953, essentially restoring the old border between North and South Korea. The war cost 157,530 U.S. casualties, including 54,246 dead.

TRUMAN AND MACARTHUR

General Douglas MacArthur, famous for his service in the Philippines during World War II, was the commander of all UN forces in Korea.

- MacArthur publicly advocated air and naval strikes against targets in China in order to secure the defeat of Chinese and North Korean forces.

- President Truman opposed these measures. He feared they were likely to provoke a third world war.

This disagreement on the conduct of the war with President Truman led to MacArthur's removal from command. He was replaced by General Matthew B. Ridgway.

Removed from Command. The disagreement between MacArthur (*right*) and Truman highlighted the difficulty of balancing military needs with political needs during the tense years of the Cold War.

Effects

The Korean War demonstrated the strong determination of the United States to resist Communist aggression around the world, but it also revealed the dangers and the tremendous cost of American involvement in a land war in Asia. In the end, UN forces halted North Korean aggression, but the 1953 armistice produced little more than a fragile armed truce. Neither side had gained significant territory.

- ✔ After World War II, the United States and the Soviet Union became the leading world powers.

- ✔ The Communist Soviet Union controlled eastern Europe and helped to set up Communist governments in those nations.

- ✔ The U.S. and its allies worked to stop Communist expansion. This struggle between the U.S. and the Soviet Union became known as the Cold War.

- ✔ The Cold War became a "hot" war in Korea in 1950.

- ✔ For years, the U.S. and the Soviet Union stockpiled nuclear weapons, and were often on the brink of nuclear war; gradually, tensions eased.

MAJOR EVENTS OF THE KOREAN WAR

1950

- **June 25**
  North Korean forces invade South Korea.

- **June 27**
  UN authorizes the use of UN forces to repel the North Koreans. President Truman orders U.S. forces to South Korea.

- **June 28**
  Seoul falls to North Koreans.

- **July 8**
  General Douglas MacArthur is named UN commander in Korea.

- **August 6**
  North Koreans open a major drive to destroy UN forces.

- **September 15**
  UN forces land at Inchon, near Seoul and the 38th parallel, and drive the North Korean army north toward Manchuria.

- **November 24**
  General MacArthur launches an end-the-war offensive in northern Korea.

- **November 26**
  The Chinese launch a massive counterattack. UN forces begin retreat, then stabilize front near 38th parallel.

1951

- **April 11**
  General MacArthur is relieved of command. General Matthew Ridgway is named UN commander in Korea.

- **July 10**
  Armistice talks begin.

1953

- **July 27**
  Armistice is signed and goes into effect.

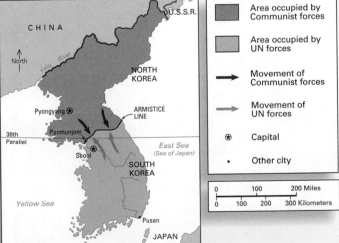

Korean War. This map illustrates the fourth and final stage of the Korean War—the advance north by UN troops starting in January 1951, and the battle line north of the 38th parallel where fighting continued between the Allies and the Communists until July 1953.

The Great Society

The 1960s began on a note of hope. In November 1960, Democrat John F. Kennedy, at age 43, became the youngest man ever elected to the American presidency, as well as the first Roman Catholic.

Kennedy chose Senator Lyndon B. Johnson of Texas, his main opponent at the Democratic convention, as his running mate. In the election in November, Kennedy narrowly defeated Republican Richard M. Nixon, Eisenhower's vice president.

Kennedy's victory was secured in part by his performance in four televised debates with Nixon, during which Nixon appeared to be less comfortable and less prepared than Kennedy.

The Kennedy Years

Kennedy staffed his cabinet with people distinguished by their youthfulness, academic background, and vigor. His inaugural address was an inspiring appeal to his fellow citizens to join him in pushing toward a "New Frontier," both at home and abroad.

He told Americans: "Ask not what your country can do for you—ask what you can do for your country."

The New Frontier. Kennedy offered several innovative programs.

- The Alliance for Progress (1961), a cooperative program to improve relations with Latin America

- The Peace Corps (1961), a program in which volunteers served overseas as teachers, agricultural advisers, public health workers, engineers, and community advisers

Giant Leap. As Armstrong set foot on the moon on July 20, 1969 he said, "That's one small step for a man, one giant leap for mankind."

TO THE MOON!

In an address to Congress on May 25, 1961, Kennedy announced a new goal for the space program: to land a man on the moon and return him safely to Earth.

- The Mercury program had launched the first American in space, Alan Shepard, on May 5, 1961.

- On February 20, 1962, John Glenn made the first U.S. orbital flight around Earth.

With the Apollo program, Kennedy's goal was achieved. In July of 1969, astronauts Neil Armstrong, Edwin Aldrin, and Michael Collins accomplished the first manned landing on the moon.

THE KENNEDY ASSASSINATION

On November 22, 1963, while riding in a motorcade in Dallas, Texas, Kennedy was shot by a gunman hiding in a nearby building. He died shortly afterward of a rifle bullet wound in his brain, the youngest American president to die in office.

- Police soon arrested 24-year-old Lee Harvey Oswald, a former Marine who had once defected to the Soviet Union. Two days later, the accused assassin was himself killed by Jack Ruby, a Dallas nightclub owner, as police were moving Oswald from one jail to another.

- Lyndon Baines Johnson, who had accompanied Kennedy to Texas, was sworn in as president aboard the presidential jet, Air Force One.

Lyndon B. Johnson frequently brought about agreement through clever planning and persuasion, which came to be known as the "LBJ treatment." Before running for president in 1960, he was known as the "Master of the Senate."

Johnson's Great Society

President Johnson pledged himself to carry out Kennedy's domestic program and to build a new momentum for social change in the United States. He did this through an ambitious program of domestic legislation:

- A 1964 tax cut that decreased individual and corporate income tax rates

- The 1964 Economic Opportunity Act, which began a federal "war on poverty"

- The Office of Economic Opportunity (OEO), which was created to operate a federal Job Corps

- VISTA (Volunteers in Service to America), community action programs, a program for migrant workers, and the Head Start program for disadvantaged preschool children

The 1964 Election. In August, Johnson won the Democratic nomination easily and chose Senator Hubert H. Humphrey of Minnesota as his running mate. The month before, the Republican Party had nominated Senator Barry M. Goldwater of Arizona, a staunch conservative. Johnson beat Goldwater by almost 26 million popular votes, in one of the great landslides in American political history.

A Mandate. Johnson considered the election to be a mandate for his domestic programs, which he believed would turn the nation into the "Great Society." He got Congress to pass many more programs to assist public schools, the aged, and the poor. Other measures increased Social Security benefits and the minimum wage.

MEDICARE

Perhaps the most ambitious program passed by Congress was the Medicare bill, which Johnson signed into law on July 30, 1965. The program was designed to make medical and hospital care affordable for all Americans aged 65 and older.

CIVIL RIGHTS are the freedoms and rights that a person should enjoy as a member of a community, state, or nation. Civil rights include freedom of speech, of the press, and of religion. Among others are the right to own property and to receive fair and equal treatment from government, other persons, and private groups. In the second half of the 20th century, many groups of Americans began to fight for civil rights—especially the right to fair and equal treatment—that they had been denied.

The movement for African-American civil rights had arisen in the days of slavery and made rapid strides in the years just after the Civil War. Then, in **1896**, the Supreme Court nearly crushed the movement with its ruling in the case of *Plessy v. Ferguson*. The court declared separation of the races legal—provided that blacks had access to "separate but equal" accommodations. (See page 150.)

The movement took on new life, however, in the **1940s** and **1950s**. In the **1960s**, President Lyndon B. Johnson's "Great Society" platform also sought to extend full civil rights to African Americans.

Ending Segregation

World War II had a lasting impact on the movement for African-American civil rights.

- The wartime economy had improved African Americans' employment options.

- Divisions of African-American soldiers, such as the Tuskegee Airmen, had become war heroes.

- The defeat of Hitler's racist ideology had given new strength to the movement for equality.

In **1948**, President Truman officially desegregated the military. Afterwards, the antisegregation battle took place on two fronts: the schools and public accommodations.

◀ *Plessy v. Ferguson* led to segregation of almost all public facilities, especially in the South.

Schools. On **May 17, 1954,** the Supreme Court handed down a momentous decision forbidding school segregation. The unanimous ruling in *Brown v. Board of Education of Topeka* held that "separate but equal" schools were "inherently unequal." The decision overturned the *Plessy v. Ferguson* ruling—upon which racial segregation had relied for almost 60 years. The High Court ruled that school desegregation should begin at once.

The Montgomery Bus Boycott. Popular protest against segregation began a year after the *Brown* decision. In Montgomery, Alabama, police arrested a seamstress and civil rights activist named Rosa Parks for refusing to give up her seat to a white person, as required by city law.

- To protest her arrest, blacks in Montgomery boycotted the city's bus system.

- Their protest lasted 382 days.

- It ended when the U.S. Supreme Court declared segregated seating on the city's buses unconstitutional.

▲ **Desegregation** met with strong resistance in many parts of the South. Federal troops and marshals were sometimes called in to enforce school desegregation.

THE FREEDOM RIDERS

In **1961,** several interracial groups calling themselves "Freedom Riders" traveled together on interstate buses through the South. They hoped to get the federal government to enforce a **1946** Supreme Court ruling that had ordered desegregation of long-distance buses.

The Freedom Rides sparked numerous violent confrontations, but they were ultimately successful, as were many "sit-ins" to desegregate restaurants and entertainment establishments in the South.

Sit-ins were a popular form of protest for the civil rights movements. Many restaurants and lunch counters refused to serve black customers. Protesters would sit at the counters until they were either served or arrested. Often, crowds would gather to assault or harass the protesters. ▶

Civil Rights: "I Have a Dream"

The Movement Spreads

The drive for African-American civil rights continued despite violent attacks by white segregationists. In **1957**, 28-year-old Dr. Martin Luther King, Jr., a clergyman who had helped lead the Montgomery boycotts, joined with other leaders to form the Southern Christian Leadership Conference (SCLC). Other groups would follow:

- The Student Nonviolent Coordinating Committee (SNCC)
- The Congress of Racial Equality (CORE)

Backlash. King and his followers preached nonviolent resistance; however, their nonviolent demonstrations often provoked brutal responses by local policemen in the South and by whites opposed to integration.

- In **1963**, an African-American church was bombed in Birmingham, Alabama. Four young girls attending Sunday School were killed; riots followed.
- On **June 12, 1963**, Medgar Evers—field secretary of the NAACP—was shot and killed outside his home.
- In **1964**, three civil rights workers engaged in voter registration in Mississippi were murdered.

These acts increased support for integration among whites outside the South. But the bloodshed also turned many African Americans, especially younger ones, toward organizations that advocated violence.

THE MARCH ON WASHINGTON

By **1963**, King was recognized as the major leader of the civil rights movement. On **August 28, 1963**, more than 200,000 civil rights supporters joined in a march on Washington to show Congress their desire for civil rights legislation. Standing in front of the Lincoln Memorial, King addressed the vast crowd, describing his dream of full equality and respect between blacks and whites.

Free at Last. In his famous "I Have a Dream" speech, King urged the nation to "make real the promise of democracy."

Malcolm X was assassinated in **1965**. Three black men, at least two of whom were Black Muslims, were convicted of the murder.

Black Militancy. During the height of the civil rights movement, some groups claimed that it was almost impossible to change white racial attitudes.

- The Black Muslims, organized in the **1930s**, advocated black separatism and openly opposed nonviolent tactics.
- Malcolm X promoted the Black Muslim cause in the **early 1960s**, but later started his own organization.
- The Black Panthers, formed in the **late 1960s** by Huey P. Newton and Bobby Seale, were initially even more militant.

CULTURAL CONTRIBUTIONS

Throughout the years of the civil rights movement, African Americans also continued to break down racial barriers in American cultural life.

- Popular singers like Nat "King" Cole and Ella Fitzgerald enjoyed widespread fame.
- Gospel singer Mahalia Jackson appeared on network television.
- Black music called rhythm and blues gave birth to rock and roll in the **1950s**.
- In **1963**, Sidney Poitier became the first African American to win the Academy Award for a leading role.

◀ **Breaking Barriers.** In **1947**, Jackie Robinson of the Brooklyn Dodgers became the first black player in modern Major League baseball.

Role of Congress

As a result of the civil rights movement, Congress passed several laws designed to eliminate discrimination based on race.

"Two Societies." Despite the laws passed by Congress, though, blacks still struggled for the opportunities that full civil rights were intended to give them. In **1967**, the Kerner Commission, a government group that had studied riots in black neighborhoods of Los Angeles and other cities, concluded that "Our nation is moving toward two societies, one black, one white, separate and unequal."

Still, the civil rights movement dramatically increased participation of African-American voters in both the South and the North. By the **mid-1970s**, some 4,000 African Americans had been elected to political office at all levels of government.

Major Civil Rights Laws	
The Civil Rights Act of 1964	Requested by President Kennedy in **1963** and signed by President Johnson, it outlawed racial discrimination in employment and public accommodations.
The Voting Rights Act of 1965	Provided for federal supervision to allow blacks to register where they had been previously denied the right to vote
The Civil Rights Act of 1968	Attempted to guarantee blacks the right to open housing

The activism of the **1960s** inspired other crusades for equal rights. In the **1960s** and **1970s** two movements—for women's rights and for gay rights—came into the public eye.

▲ **Betty Friedan** also helped organize the National Women's Political Caucus, which encourages women to seek political office.

Women's Rights

The official women's rights movement in America had begun with the Seneca Falls Conference in **1848**. The movement's chief goals were property rights and women's suffrage—the right of women to vote. The 19th Amendment, which took effect in **1920**, finally granted women the right to vote.

World War II brought women into the military and the workforce. But after the war ended, these women were urged to leave the workforce to make room for the returning servicemen, and the women's movement died down.

The Second Wave. Its revival during the **1960s** is sometimes called the "second wave" of feminism. The movement gained new momentum with the **1963** publication of Betty Friedan's book *The Feminine Mystique*. The book identified many of the inequalities women suffered in American life—social, political, and economic.

Three years later, Friedan founded NOW, the National Organization for Women. NOW demanded, among other things,

- equal educational opportunities for women
- equal pay for equal work
- wider job opportunities
- publicly funded day-care centers
- the repeal of laws banning abortion

In 1972, Congress passed the Equal Rights Amendment (ERA), which stated, "Equality of rights under the law shall not be denied or abridged by the United States or any state on account of sex." But the amendment failed to be ratified by the necessary 38 states, and it did not take effect.

Women's Rights—Milestones	
Equal Pay Act (1963)	Guaranteed equal pay for equal work
Civil Rights Act (1964)	Prohibited job discrimination on the basis of sex as well as race
Roe v. Wade, Doe v. Bolton (1973)	Ruled that states could not prohibit abortion during the first 3 months of pregnancy, due to the constitutional right to privacy
The Equal Credit Opportunity Act (1975)	Prohibited banks and other organizations from discriminating on the basis of sex or marital status in making loans or granting credit

Spotlight on...

HARVEY MILK

1930–1978

- First openly homosexual person to be elected to a government office in the United States
- Elected to the San Francisco Board of Supervisors in **1977**
- While in office, helped pass a gay rights law and establish alliances between the gay community and various other minority groups
- Shot and killed in **1978** by Dan White, a former board member, while serving on the board

Milk's political service and the circumstances surrounding his death brought widespread attention to the gay rights movement in the United States.

Gay Rights

During the 1950s and 1960s, the gay rights movement was small and consisted of local organizations or chapters. These early organizations protested against police harassment, used lawsuits to defend gay rights, and became active in political parties.

Present-Day Goals. Today, the gay rights movement seeks to educate society about gay issues and to encourage gay individuals to publicly declare their sexual orientation.

- The movement includes activist organizations, artists, journalists, politicians, and religious groups.
- Organizations associated with the movement include the International Lesbian and Gay Association; the Human Rights Campaign; and Parents, Families and Friends of Lesbians and Gays (PFLAG).

Opposition. Many opponents of gay rights argue that homosexual behavior is morally wrong. In addition, many question whether lesbians and gays have a legitimate claim to certain legal protections.

✔ The movement for African-American civil rights took on new life in the **1950s** and **1960s**.

✔ *Brown v. Board of Education of Topeka* (**1954**) declared racial segregation of schools to be unconstitutional.

✔ Landmark events in the civil rights battle included the Montgomery bus boycott, the Freedom Rides, lunch counter sit-ins, and the March on Washington.

✔ Dr. Martin Luther King, Jr., became the major leader of the movement; he preached nonviolent resistance. Malcolm X and the Black Panthers sought militant resistance.

✔ President Johnson signed the Civil Rights Act of **1964**, which outlawed racial discrimination in employment and public accommodations.

✔ The women's rights movement of the **1960s** and **1970s** fought for equal pay, equal education, and the repeal of laws banning abortion and contraception.

✔ In the **1970s**, the gay rights movement began fighting for equal civil rights.

THE VIETNAM WAR

was the longest war in which the United States took part. It began in 1957 and ended in 1975. Vietnam, which had been the French colony Indochina before World War II, was divided at the time into the Communist Democratic Republic of Vietnam, called North Vietnam, and the non-Communist Republic of Vietnam, called South Vietnam. North Vietnamese and South Vietnamese rebels (Vietcong) sought to overthrow the government of South Vietnam and to eventually reunite the country. The United States and the South Vietnamese army tried to stop them, but failed.

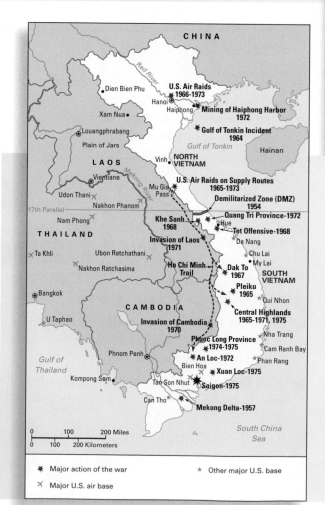

The Tet Offensive ranged from Hue in the northern part of South Vietnam to Saigon in the south.

The Domino Effect

Beginning in the late 1950s, North Vietnam backed Vietnamese guerrillas who were fighting to overthrow the regime of South Vietnam. The Northerners wanted to reunite Vietnam under a Communist government.

Concerned that if one country fell to Communism, others might also fall—like a "row of dominoes," Eisenhower said—Presidents Eisenhower and Kennedy had sent military advisers and supplies to help South Vietnam. (See also pages 574–575.)

Troops on the Ground

As South Vietnam's situation grew desperate, President Johnson increased American involvement.

- In August of 1964, North Vietnamese patrol boats attacked an American destroyer off the coast of North Vietnam, in the Gulf of Tonkin.

- Congress passed the Tonkin Gulf Resolution, authorizing the president "to take all necessary measures to repel any armed attack against the forces of the United States and to prevent further aggression."

Entering the War. Soon American planes were bombing targets in North Vietnam, and in March 1965, the first American combat troops were sent to South Vietnam.

THE TET OFFENSIVE

From 1965 to 1967, the war was a draw. In February of 1968, the North Vietnamese staged an ambitious offensive during the Vietnamese festival Tet, the lunar New Year celebration.

- North Vietnamese and Vietcong forces assaulted scores of towns and cities.

- It turned into a military defeat for the Communists.

The Tet offensive showed the American public how little control non-Communist forces had in South Vietnam.

▲ **Troops in Vietnam.** By the end of 1967, 500,000 troops were fighting in Vietnam. By 1968, the number had grown to 540,000.

▲ **The Vietnam War Memorial,** which lists the names of soldiers killed in the war, has helped to heal the emotional scars caused by the Vietnam conflict.

Ending the War

In March 1968, President Johnson, undermined by lack of success in Vietnam and by antiwar protests at home, announced that he would not seek reelection. Nixon came to office with the promise of ending the Vietnam War. "The greatest honor history can bestow is the title peacemaker," he said in his inaugural address.

Vietnamization. Nixon's original plan was to "Vietnamize" the war—to withdraw U.S. troops gradually and turn the war over to the South Vietnamese. In 1969, President Nixon announced plans to reduce troop levels by 110,000. Antiwar protestors, however, continued to demonstrate for an immediate end to American involvement, especially after details of an American massacre of Vietnamese civilians at My Lai were revealed that November.

Winding Down. In February of the next year, the American invasion of Laos triggered a number of reactions at home.

- Congress repealed the Tonkin Gulf Resolution, the original mandate for massive U.S. involvement.
- Bills were introduced to curb the president's power to commit the United States to war.
- Proposals were made for a fixed deadline for the withdrawal of all American forces.

Finally, on January 27, 1973, an agreement for peace was signed. Terms included a cease-fire, withdrawal of American troops, and return of all American prisoners of war.

Aftermath

- In January 1975, the Communists opened their final offensive in northern South Vietnam.
- Within 2 months, the South Vietnamese forces were in full retreat.
- In April, the last Americans were evacuated, and within days, South Vietnam was entirely in Communist hands.

U.S. involvement in the conflict had cost 58,000 American lives, many billions of dollars, and a crisis of confidence in government.

THE END OF OPTIMISM

The relative peace, prosperity, and optimism of the 1950s and early 1960s began to give way, in the late 1960s, to a much more troubled time. A long, drawn-out war in Vietnam divided the nation, while prominent leaders fell victim to assassins and scandals. New conflicts arose in the Middle East, creating an oil crisis that would hit the already-struggling American economy hard. As the 1970s came to an end, American confidence in the government was low, and political changes were on the way.

Antiwar protests occasionally led to violent clashes. The Kent State protests were commemorated in the protest song "Ohio," by the popular music group Crosby, Stills, Nash, and Young. The song's refrain, "four dead in Ohio," was a reference to the students who had been killed. ▼

Kent State to Watergate

The war in Vietnam and the struggle for civil rights had both brought about high levels of public dissatisfaction and protest. At times, the nation seemed to erupt into violence. Even the presidency was not immune to the upheavals of the era.

Assassinations

The nation had been stunned by the assassination of President John F. Kennedy in November of 1963. More tragedies were still to come.

- On April 4, 1968, Martin Luther King, Jr., was shot dead in Memphis, Tennessee, by James Earl Ray. Rage swept the nation and riots broke out in over 170 cities.

- On June 5, 1968, Robert F. Kennedy—brother of the slain President Kennedy—was shot by gunman Sirhan Sirhan, following Kennedy's victory in the California presidential primary. Kennedy died on June 6.

Protests

Protesters against the seemingly endless war in Vietnam portrayed the conflict as a civil war in which the United States should not be involved. They also called attention to the large numbers of Vietnamese civilians killed by U.S. bombings. Their disillusionment spread to other citizens, until the antiwar movement claimed millions of supporters.

"FOUR DEAD IN OHIO"

In April 1970, despite promises of troop withdrawal, Nixon sent American and South Vietnamese troops into Cambodia. The public's reaction to the move was intense.

- Antiwar demonstrations were held across the nation.

- Four students at Kent State University, in Ohio, were killed by National Guard troops during a demonstration on May 4, 1970, and 448 colleges closed down in protest.

- On May 14, two students were killed at Jackson State College, in Mississippi, in a violent confrontation with police.

Elections

In 1968, President Johnson announced that he would not seek reelection. Senators Eugene McCarthy of Minnesota and Robert Kennedy of New York were candidates for the Democratic nomination.

- After Kennedy's death, Vice President Hubert Humphrey won the nomination over McCarthy.
- The Republicans chose former vice president Richard M. Nixon.
- Governor George C. Wallace of Alabama was a major third-party contender.

Nixon won the election by one of the narrowest popular vote margins in U.S. history, receiving 43.4 percent of the popular vote to Humphrey's 42.7 percent.

The 1968 Democratic National Convention in August was marked by violent clashes between police and antiwar protestors.

WATERGATE

The Watergate crisis outraged the American public and brought about the first presidential resignation in the nation's history.

- On June 17, 1972, five men were arrested for breaking into the Democratic National Headquarters in the Watergate complex in Washington, D.C.
- The intruders were later connected to the White House and the Committee to Re-elect the President.
- President Nixon denied any involvement, but congressional and judicial investigations found proof of Nixon's participation.
- The House Judiciary Committee approved articles of impeachment, and Nixon resigned from the presidency.
- Gerald Ford succeeded him as president.

Richard M. Nixon resigned in August 1974. One of President Ford's first acts was to pardon Nixon for all federal crimes he "committed or may have committed or taken part in" while president. ▶

A SLUMP AND A CRISIS

As American participation in the Vietnam War wound down, the U.S. economy became the major political issue.

- In 1971, five million Americans were out of work.
- Inflation reduced the value of the dollar.
- Industry produced below capacity, and American goods were unprofitable on the world market.
- This period of economic stagnation combined with inflation was called "stagflation."
- In 1973, an oil crisis erupted. Oil shortages led to rising energy prices, and increased worldwide inflation.

The oil crisis of 1973 caused gas shortages and increased energy costs sharply. This created extra hardship for the already-struggling American economy.

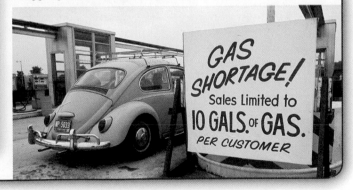

END OF A CENTURY

The last decades of the 20th century saw massive changes, both in the U.S. and abroad. The collapse of the Soviet Union finally brought an end to the Cold War, which had raged since the end of the 1940s. Conflicts that had been simmering in the Middle East, however, came to a boil again and again. The nation began to take on a role as global peacekeeper. During this time, the United States also experienced political shifts—both to the right and to the left.

Changing Direction

The years after Nixon's resignation were challenging years for the United States. President Ford—whose pardon of Nixon helped cost him a second term—and President Carter struggled to bring an end to the inflation and recession that were battering the American economy. Carter undertook many domestic programs, including civil service reform, promotion of energy conservation, and development of renewable sources of energy, but the economy continued to sputter.

The Reagan Years

By the time the election of 1980 approached, President Carter had the approval of only 21 percent of the American people. Energy shortages and high fuel costs, unemployment and inflation, and worsening relations with the Soviet Union and the Middle East had disillusioned the American electorate.

Election of 1980. Ronald Reagan won the Republican nomination and chose George H. W. Bush, one of his closest opponents, as his running mate. In November, Reagan defeated Carter in a landslide.

- Reagan's election brought the first basic change in federal government policy in nearly half a century.

- He promised to cut government spending, balance the budget, reduce taxes, and rebuild defense forces.

Guards kept constant watch all along the Berlin Wall, the division between East and West Berlin. Its dismantling in 1989 signaled the reunification of Germany and the end of the Cold War.

Reaganomics. Reagan's economic policy came to be known as "Reaganomics" or "supply-side economics."

- It called for tax cuts that would spur savings and presumably increase capital investment and create jobs.

- It was designed to reduce inflation, lower interest rates, and increase government revenues.

- The Reagan administration attempted to cut domestic programs such as social welfare and education, but were mostly stopped by Democrats in the House of Representatives.

The economy began to improve, but the budget deficit rose from $74 billion (under Carter) to $221 billion by 1986.

REAGAN AND GORBACHEV

The Reagan presidency faced numerous problems, including war in the Middle East, terrorism, and civil war in Nicaragua. Most significant, though, were Reagan's negotiations with the Soviet Union.

- Reagan held four summit meetings (in Geneva, Reykjavik, Moscow, and Washington) with General Secretary Mikhail Gorbachev of the Soviet Union.

- The meetings led to the first treaty in history to provide for nuclear arms reductions.

- Signed on December 8, 1987, and ratified by the U.S. Senate on May 27, 1988, the treaty called for the destruction of 2,611 U.S. and Soviet medium- and short-range missiles in Europe.

 On March 30, 1981, just a few months after his inauguration, Reagan survived an assassination attempt. He made a rapid recovery. The shooter, John W. Hinckley, Jr., was found not guilty by reason of insanity.

◀ **Negotiations** between the U.S. and the Soviet Union under Reagan and Gorbachev (shown here signing the 1987 treaty) helped bring about the end of the Cold War. The war would not officially end until 1991.

Iran-Contra Affair. During Reagan's second term, two different foreign policy problems intersected in a major scandal.

- The Reagan administration disliked the Marxist-oriented Sandinista regime in Nicaragua.

- Reagan sought to secure financial aid for the Contras, who opposed the Sandinistas, and whom he called "freedom fighters." At first Congress obliged, but later it resisted appropriations for any but humanitarian aid.

It was revealed on November 3, 1986, that the United States had been secretly selling arms to Iran in the hope of securing the release of American hostages in Lebanon. Some funds from the sales had been secretly diverted to the Nicaraguan Contras.

Both John M. Poindexter, the national security adviser, and his assistant, Marine colonel Oliver L. North, were convicted in 1990 on federal charges. In 1991, the convictions were overturned on appeal.

Bush's Presidency

In November 1988, Vice President George H. W. Bush was elected president, easily defeating his Democratic opponent, Governor Michael S. Dukakis of Massachusetts. In the election, Bush had taken advantage of his association with Reagan, who was an extremely popular president.

- *Before 1961, large numbers of East Germans crossed into West Berlin from East Berlin to escape Communist rule for a better living standard in the West.*

- *The Communists built the Berlin Wall to stop this emigration.*

- *More than 170 people died trying to escape from East Germany by crossing over the Berlin Wall. Most were shot by border guards.*

Bailouts, Recession, Trade. Early in his presidency, Bush had to deal with the worst crisis in the savings and loan industry since the Great Depression of the 1930s.

- Many savings and loan institutions had failed because of bad loans, poor management, and criminal activity.

- It was estimated that it would cost at least $300 billion to bail them out.

- On August 9, 1989, President Bush signed the bailout into law.

In 1990, a recession began to grip the country. It was marked by a high unemployment rate that did not go down until late 1992. Meanwhile, the annual federal deficit was about $300 billion, and the national debt by the end of 1992 was approaching $4 trillion.

On December 17, 1992, Canada, Mexico, and the United States signed the North American Free Trade Agreement (NAFTA), which would eliminate import taxes and other barriers to trade in all of North America. Congress approved NAFTA in 1993.

END OF THE COLD WAR

The Cold War finally came to an end under George H. W. Bush's presidency. (See also page 578.)

- Beginning in 1989, Communist rule came to an end in a number of eastern European countries, including Poland, Hungary, East Germany, and Czechoslovakia.

- In 1991, the Soviet Communist Party lost control of the Soviet government. The Soviet Union dissolved, and the republics that made up the nation became independent states.

- In 1992, Russian president Boris Yeltsin and U.S. president George H. W. Bush formally declared that their countries did not regard each other as potential enemies.

- The Strategic Arms Reduction Treaties (START and START II) were meant to reduce the number of nuclear weapons held by the U.S. and Russia.

▲ **The Berlin Wall** had been built in 1961 to prevent people from leaving Communist East Germany for the democratic West. In 1989, the wall was torn down. Some sections still remain as memorials.

The Clinton Years

With the Soviet Union dissolved and international relations improving, the 1992 presidential election focused on domestic issues.

- The Democratic Party nominated Governor Bill Clinton of Arkansas for the presidency and Al Gore of Tennessee for vice president.

- The Republican Party renominated President Bush and Vice President Dan Quayle.

- Texas billionaire businessman H. Ross Perot entered the campaign as an independent candidate.

The economic indicators did little to support Bush's argument that the recession was over. Clinton called for jobs training, education, technology, and a national health insurance program. In November Clinton defeated Bush. Perot won no electoral votes, but he received more than 19 million popular votes.

Second Term. In 1996, Bill Clinton became the first Democratic president to win a second term since Franklin D. Roosevelt in 1936. The Republicans gained control of Congress in 1994 (for the first time in 40 years) and kept their majorities in 1996. The Republicans and Clinton engaged in a lawmaking standoff that brought the federal government to a halt—twice.

Impeachment

- In December 1998, the House of Representatives voted two articles of impeachment against Clinton.

- He was charged with perjury and obstruction of justice relating to testimony about an extramarital affair.

- Clinton was only the second president in U.S. history to be impeached.

- In February 1999, the Senate acquitted Clinton on both counts.

Bill Clinton's presidency produced a strong economy, but was plagued by accusations of personal misconduct and gridlock in Congress. Eventually, laws were passed to balance the budget and reform the welfare system.

PEACEKEEPING

In the years following the end of the Cold War, the United States took part in two major peacekeeping missions with the United Nations.

Operation Restore Hope

In Somalia, civil war and drought had already cost some 300,000 lives, with another million in danger of starvation.

- U.S. armed forces landed in Somalia on December 9, 1992.

- The relief mission was a great success, but continuing conflicts between rival warlords slowed the withdrawal of U.S. military forces.

The Balkan Conflicts

In 1992, a civil war began in Bosnia-Herzegovina.

- Bosnian Serb rebels fought the country's government, which was dominated by Bosniaks (also called Bosnian Muslims).

- The United States attacked Serb forces to help the Bosniaks.

- In 1995, the Clinton administration brokered a Bosnian peace plan that called for a UN peacekeeping force of 60,000.

- President Clinton announced that 20,000 U.S. troops would take part in the mission, but would be withdrawn within a year.

During the second half of the 20th century, some nations in the Middle East experienced a rise of Islamism, or the desire to establish Islamic governments. Conflicts arose after the founding of Israel in the Arab region of Palestine in 1947. The United States became an ally of Israel, and was therefore considered an enemy by some Arab nations. The U.S. also supported certain changes of government in the Middle East—the overthrow of King Farouk in Egypt (1952), and the restoration of the Shah of Iran (1953).

Starting in the 1970s, the United States took an even more active role in the Middle East. At times, the United States was a peacemaker. At other times, it engaged in conflicts.

Oil Crisis

The United States incurred the wrath of the Arab nations, which provided 25 percent of all American oil, by supporting Israel after it was attacked by Egypt and Syria in October 1973.

- The Arab nations punished the United States by refusing to export oil to the country.

- Prices for petroleum and gasoline soared, raising inflation rates.

- When the oil embargo was ended in March 1974, the Organization of Petroleum Exporting Countries (OPEC), which had instituted steep price increases in 1973, continued to raise oil prices.

The Camp David Accords

Egypt and Israel had been in conflict with each other since Israel's creation. The United States had aided Israel with military equipment.

In April 1979, U.S. president Jimmy Carter called together Israeli leader Menachem Begin and Egyptian leader Anwar el-Sadat at the presidential retreat at Camp David, Maryland.

- There, for 13 days, the leaders worked out a treaty to end 30 years of war between Egypt and Israel.

- The treaty provided a framework for the Israeli return of captured land to Egypt, a process that was eventually completed in 1982.

This was the triumph of Carter's presidency.

Peacemakers. Menachem Begin, Jimmy Carter, and Anwar el-Sadat at the conclusion of the Camp David talks in September 1978. ▼

HOSTAGE TO IRAN

One of the staunchest allies of the United States in the Middle East was the Shah of Iran, Muhammad Reza Pahlavi. The Shah had sought to modernize his oil-rich country.

- In 1979, he was overthrown and exiled by opponents who believed modernization undermined the practices of Islam.

- The exiled Shah, dying of cancer, came to the United States for medical treatment.

- Iranian militants seized the American embassy in the capital at Tehran on November 4, 1979, and held 52 Americans hostage for 444 days.

THE IRAN-IRAQ WAR

In 1980, ten months of conflict between Iran and Iraq exploded into full-scale war. The war threatened to slow imports of oil into the United States.

- U.S. Navy ships were sent to the Persian Gulf in February 1984; they began to convoy neutral shipping.

- On May 17, 1987, an Iraqi warplane mistakenly fired a missile at the U.S. frigate *Stark,* killing 37 crewmen.

- An even greater tragedy came on July 3, 1988, when the U.S. cruiser *Vincennes* mistakenly shot down an Iranian passenger jet, killing all 290 persons aboard.

The Iran-Iraq War killed over 1 million people, but was largely considered a draw. (See also pages 582–583.)

The Persian Gulf War

In 1990, Iraq invaded the neighboring country of Kuwait. The United States responded to the invasion by leading a military coalition of soldiers from 30 nations against Iraq. The U.S. sent about 425,000 troops—the largest deployment since the Vietnam War. On January 16, 1991, coalition forces launched a 6-week military campaign that decisively defeated Iraqi forces and forced them out of Kuwait.

◄ **Saddam Hussein's** Iraqi forces were driven out of Kuwait, but he remained in power after the Persian Gulf War.

In the early 2000s, the United States ranked as the most powerful country in the world. It had the world's strongest military force, the richest economy, and the most influential popular culture. Americans had one of the highest standards of living in the world. Despite its power and influence, the United States faced many challenges. In particular, U.S. leaders grappled with a new kind of enemy, and decisions on when and where to involve U.S. military forces in international disputes.

The first years of the 21st century would bring the U.S. into new foreign and domestic struggles. Abroad, militant Islamic groups such as al-Qaeda gave rise to a new global crisis. At home, issues such as education, immigration, health care, and economic stability took center stage.

The 2000 Election

The first American election of the 21st century turned out to be one of the closest elections in U.S. history.

- Vice President Al Gore ran against Texas governor George W. Bush for the presidency.

- News networks predicted that Bush had won the election by capturing Florida's electoral votes, and Gore conceded.

- Hours later, the Florida vote looked too close to call, and Gore took back his concession.

- After weeks of legal wrangling, the Supreme Court ruled 5–4 to stop recounts in Florida, in effect giving the state to Bush by a margin of about 537 votes.

Thus, Bush won the electoral vote, but not the popular vote—the third time in history that this had happened. His presidency was barely underway before the nation faced a massive crisis.

Bush v. Gore, the Supreme Court decision that ended vote recounts in Florida in 2000, played a decisive role in George W. Bush's election to the presidency. Former vice president Al Gore would later go on to win the Nobel Peace Prize for his work on global climate change awareness.

The War on Terror

In response to the terrorist attacks in the U.S. on September 11, 2001, President Bush declared a "global war on terror."

- The United States launched a military campaign against Afghanistan's governing militia, the Taliban, which was protecting Osama bin Laden.
- The Office of Homeland Security was created to improve security and prevent future terrorist attacks.
- The Patriot Act was passed with the purpose of enhancing law enforcement investigatory tools.

▲ **U.S.-led coalition forces** remained in Iraq after the end of major combat operations in 2003. Subsequently, militants from both the Sunni Muslim and Shiite Muslim populations carried out guerrilla attacks, bombings, and other violent acts and called for a withdrawal of coalition troops.

The Iraq War of 2003

In March 2003, U.S. president George W. Bush launched a war against Iraq.

- He linked this war to the World Trade Center attacks in 2001.
- The intent was to disarm Iraq of weapons of mass destruction—that is, chemical, biological, or nuclear weapons.
- By mid-April, U.S.-led forces had toppled Saddam Hussein's government.
- United States and allied forces began working to rebuild Iraq—a task made difficult by numerous guerrilla attacks against them and against civilian targets.
- No weapons of mass destruction were found in Iraq.

▲ **The events of September 11,** which came to be known simply as "9/11," sent shock waves through American society. This image shows the World Trade Center towers shortly after the attack. (See also page 593.)

9/11/2001

On September 11, 2001, nineteen terrorists from the extremist group al-Qaeda—a group headed by Osama bin Laden—simultaneously hijacked four American airliners.

- One crashed into the Pentagon building, just outside Washington, D.C.
- Two planes crashed into the World Trade Center towers in New York City. The towers collapsed shortly after being hit.
- A fourth airliner crashed in a Pennsylvania field after its passengers attempted to overpower the hijackers.
- The attacks killed nearly 3,000 people, the largest loss of American lives in a single day since the Civil War.

Crisis and Change

The wars in Iraq and Afghanistan would continue throughout the rest of George W. Bush's presidency, but domestic struggles soon began to capture Americans' attention as well.

Domestic Issues

In 2004, President Bush ran for reelection against Massachusetts senator John Kerry. Both parties rallied aggressively to register voters, leading to the highest turnout at the polls since 1968. Bush won reelection with a majority of electoral votes and, this time, also the popular vote with 51 percent.

Reforms. Bush proposed several reforms for federal programs, with varying success.

- The No Child Left Behind Act on education reform passed with the support of both parties.

- Partial privatization of the nation's Social Security system did not pass.

- An immigration reform bill did not pass.

Immigration. Immigration had been an issue in the U.S. at various times throughout the nation's history.

- In the early part of the 20th century, immigration quotas favored immigrants from northern and western Europe, and limited immigration from other areas.

- In 1965, the nation ended quotas based on nationality.

- The Immigration Act of 1990 raised the number of immigrants allowed into the country.

During the spring of 2006, millions of immigrants and their supporters held rallies in several U.S. cities. They were protesting a proposed federal law that would increase penalties for undocumented immigration. Experts estimated that as many as 12 million illegal immigrants lived in the United States, most from Mexico and other Latin American countries.

In October, President Bush signed into law a bill that authorized the building of new fences along the United States–Mexico border.

HURRICANE KATRINA

In August of 2005, a massive hurricane struck the Gulf Coast.

- High winds and flooding caused heavy damage in Florida, Louisiana, Mississippi, and Alabama.

- In New Orleans, Louisiana, the levees—flood barriers—that protected the city failed.

- Most of New Orleans was submerged. Many residents were evacuated, and eventually relocated across the country. Others were stranded in the flooded city, waiting for rescue.

- About 1,800 people were killed, about 1,500 of them in New Orleans.

Hurricane Katrina overwhelmed rescue workers in the region. The Bush Administration was criticized harshly for its failure to prepare for the storm and to respond quickly in the aftermath. ▶

The Election of 2008

In 2008, the nation's economy took a sharp down-turn. (See pages 384–387.)

- Many financial firms suffered huge losses, largely related to the housing bubble (unrealistic home values).

- In September, several large firms failed or were bailed out by the U.S. government.

- The stock market plunged.

- In October, Congress passed a law that provided up to $700 billion for the government to purchase bad debts from troubled lenders.

By the summer of 2008, President George Bush's popularity was at an all-time low, due to the economy and the ongoing war in Iraq.

- The Democrats nominated Senator Barack Obama of Illinois for president.

- The Republicans nominated Senator John McCain of Arizona.

In the election, Obama defeated McCain with a decisive 52.9 percent of the popular vote and an electoral vote of 365 to McCain's 173.

President Barack Obama is the first U.S. president of African-American descent.

A New Administration. Shortly after taking office, President Obama began addressing domestic and foreign policy issues.

- A month after taking office, he signed a $787 billion economic stimulus bill meant to shore up the economy.

- He stated that all U.S. combat operations in Iraq would cease by August 31, 2010.

- In March 2010, he signed a historic health insurance reform bill.

THE U.S. AND THE ENVIRONMENT

The U.S. has taken steps to protect and conserve the environment since the late 1800s. The goals of environmentalists have changed over time, from conserving nature to protecting wildlife to developing safe, clean sources of energy.

- In 1970, the first Earth Day was observed and the Environmental Protection Agency (EPA) was established to protect the nation's environment from pollution.

- In 1973, the Endangered Species Act was passed.

- In 1990, concerns about the ozone layer led to pledges to reduce or stop producing ozone-destroying chemicals.

- The Clean Air Act of 1990 tightened pollution standards.

- In March 2001, President Bush rejected the Kyoto Protocol, an international agreement that calls for limiting the amount of greenhouse gases released into the atmosphere. Most of the world's nations have ratified the Protocol.

- In 2007, a 3-year study by the Intergovernmental Panel on Climate Change (IPCC) confirmed that human activity is likely causing global climate change.

- In April 2010, an explosion on an offshore oil rig resulted in the spillage of millions of gallons of oil into the Gulf of Mexico, about 50 miles (80 kilometers) off Louisiana. Officials called the spill one of the worst environmental disasters in U.S. history.

✔ During the last part of the 20th century, the U.S. became more involved in events in the Middle East.

✔ The U.S. and the Soviet Union began to negotiate in the 1980s; the Cold War finally ended in 1991.

✔ In 2001, terrorists used hijacked airplanes to attack the World Trade Center in New York City, and the Pentagon in Washington, D.C.

✔ The U.S. launched a military campaign against Afghanistan in 2001 and Iraq in 2003.

✔ In 2008, the world faced a serious economic collapse; later that year, Barack Obama became the first African-American president of the United States.

SOUTHWESTERN

George Washington, the first U.S. president and the foremost of the country's founding fathers, served from 1789 to 1797. More than any other individual, he was the architect of American government after the colonies broke away from British rule.

Born February 22, 1732, in Westmoreland County, Virginia, Washington was a key figure in the American Revolution. As commander in chief of the Continental Army, he was tasked with leading inexperienced troops through the bloody Revolutionary War.

After his victory in 1787, Washington presided over the Philadelphia Convention, where the Constitution was drafted. When the document was ratified, Washington was unanimously elected president. He took office April 30, 1789.

As the leader of a brand new country, Washington attended to a host of domestic issues. Foremost among them was passing tax legislation to pay the nation's mounting debts. But more than any single action he took as president, Washington's overarching contribution was setting a precedent for the executive branch. The way he handled certain aspects of government—for instance, cabinet appointments—still informs how the government operates today. The president carefully weighed all of his actions in light of this responsibility.

Washington's foreign policy was to remain neutral in international affairs whenever possible. He believed that the new country needed to focus its attention inward to grow stronger. It was a controversial position, particularly during the French Revolution, which some Americans felt obligated to support.

His long service took a toll on Washington, who retired after his second term. Three years later, in 1799, he died of a throat infection.

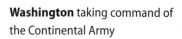
Washington taking command of the Continental Army

Thomas Jefferson, the nation's third president, held the office from 1801 to 1809. He is celebrated as the main author of the Declaration of Independence and for doubling the size of the country with the Louisiana Purchase.

Born April 13, 1743, in Shadwell, Virginia, Jefferson was a key figure on the political scene well before he became president. In 1776, he wrote the Declaration of Independence, which announced the American colonies' break from Great Britain. The principles he articulated in that document—including the belief that all men are created equal—informed Jefferson's political career. But many people question his personal commitment to those principles since he was a slaveholder.

In the years leading up to his presidency, Jefferson held a number of important political offices, including governor of Virginia, U.S. secretary of state, and vice president under John Adams. As president, two of his first acts were to slash spending and lower taxes.

Over time, Jefferson found himself drawn into international affairs despite his wishes. Sometimes the results were positive, like his triumphant Louisiana Purchase. Short on funds, the seller, Napoleon, was willing to part with much more land than Jefferson had anticipated going into negotiations.

But Jefferson made a major misstep in foreign affairs. In response to the French and English abuse of U.S. ships during the Napoleonic wars, he called for an embargo that blocked trade with Europe. The embargo backfired, seriously damaging the American economy.

After he retired, Jefferson lived at Monticello, his home, until he died in 1826.

Andrew Jackson, the founder of the Democratic Party, served from 1829 to 1837. His win in the election of 1828 represented a shift in the political landscape in many respects.

Born poor, Jackson was a self-taught lawyer with relatively little experience as a politician. Instead of working his way up to the presidency through the usual channels, he was propelled into the position by the American public.

Considering himself a mouthpiece of the people, Jackson took a heavy hand in domestic policy. His forceful agenda and penchant for veto earned him the nickname of King Andrew I among his critics.

Jackson shaped his policy around the national agenda, which he usually valued over the rights of individual states. One of the events that shaped Jackson's presidency was the nullification crisis, a rift with South Carolina that occurred when the state resisted a federally imposed tariff. The crisis was resolved before Jackson resorted to military force.

Another controversy during Jackson's presidency was his insistence upon moving federal funds from the centralized Second Bank of the United States to a variety of state-run banks. Many economists believe this incident, known as the Bank War, had a negative impact on the economy.

Jackson's largest failure as president was the Indian Removal Act, which he signed into law. It directly resulted in the Trail of Tears and other atrocities against Native Americans.

At the end of his second term, Jackson retired to his home outside of Nashville, Tennessee, where his health declined steadily until his death in 1845.

James K. Polk, a Democrat who served from 1845 to 1849, is remembered for his focus on westward expansion.

Polk, the eldest of 10 children, was born in Mecklenburg County, North Carolina, on November 2, 1795. He began moving in political circles as a young lawyer in Tennessee. After a stint in the state legislature, he served as Speaker of the House of Representatives from 1835 until he became governor of Tennessee in 1839.

Polk's close relationship with Andrew Jackson led to his nomination for the presidency in 1844. Polk is often referred to as a "dark horse" candidate because he wasn't well known to the American public at the time.

By the end of Polk's term, the country's footprint had grown by one-third. He acquired huge chunks of land in the west, including (but not limited to) Oregon, Texas, California, and New Mexico. He settled the boundaries of Oregon through peaceful negotiations with the British, but the other acquisitions were more difficult, resulting in the Mexican-American War.

While Polk's ambitious expansion was successful in terms of territorial gains, it ignited a national debate about whether or not slavery should be legal in the newly annexed areas. This issue deepened the divide between the North and the South, which eventually led to the Civil War.

Polk's reputation as a workaholic took a toll on his health during his one-term presidency. (He never intended to run for reelection.) He died just a few months after he left the White House in 1849.

Abraham Lincoln, known as the Great Emancipator for ending slavery in the United States, served from 1861 to 1865.

Born February 12, 1809, in Hardin County, Kentucky, Lincoln rose from humble beginnings to become a self-taught lawyer. One of the most widely admired figures in American history, his presidency was consumed by the Civil War. While he ultimately preserved the Union, the war lasted more than 4 years and left 1 million soldiers dead or wounded.

Lincoln's election precipitated Southern secession; seven states left the Union before he even took office. Worried that Lincoln would abolish slavery despite his pledge to the contrary, these states (and, eventually, four others) formed the Confederate States of America—an act that Lincoln considered illegal.

The Civil War began on April 12, 1861, when Confederates attacked Fort Sumter. Citing a national emergency, Lincoln expanded his powers as president. His goal was to reunite the country at all costs.

The war took a heavy toll on the country and on Lincoln, who made a point of being personally involved. He spent time with soldiers and considered their appeals for clemency. While his character is universally praised today, he was heavily criticized at the time.

On January 1, 1863, Lincoln signed the Emancipation Proclamation. It freed Confederate slaves and shifted the focus of the Civil War to freedom. Many black soldiers joined the Union Army.

Lincoln was shot and killed by an assassin, John Wilkes Booth, in April 1865, less than a week after Confederate forces surrendered.

Theodore Roosevelt, who became president after William McKinley was assassinated in 1901, spent his presidency expanding the government's reach to help more people at home and abroad.

Born in New York City on October 27, 1858, Roosevelt studied law, served in the Spanish-American War, and governed the state of New York before he became vice president under McKinley. At age 42, he became the country's youngest president.

Roosevelt developed a domestic agenda he nicknamed the Square Deal. His primary goals were to resolve disputes between laborers and employers, to oversee and regulate industry by enforcing antitrust laws, and to promote conservation by creating national forests and wildlife preserves. As he implemented the Square Deal, Roosevelt expanded the powers of the office of president.

At the same time, Roosevelt wanted the United States to become more involved in international affairs. To that end, he expanded the nation's role in Latin American countries and mediated a dispute between France and Germany. He also won the Nobel Peace Prize for mediating the Russo-Japanese War.

His biggest achievement in foreign affairs was developing the Panama Canal, a waterway that cut travel time between the Atlantic and Pacific oceans. Getting permission to build involved a complex series of negotiations with Great Britain, Colombia, and Panama.

After he left office in 1909, Roosevelt took a brief break from politics before running in the 1912 presidential election. (He lost to Woodrow Wilson.) He died in 1919.

Woodrow Wilson, who served from 1913 to 1921, is remembered for his ambitious domestic policy and for leading the country through World War I.

Wilson was born December 28, 1856, in Staunton, Virginia. He was a lawyer and an academic before he became a politician. As president, he aggressively pursued a progressive domestic agenda called the New Freedom program. A string of legislative victories—including labor regulations and bank reform—increased the government's influence over the American economy.

Wilson's early forays into foreign policy focused on promoting democracy in Latin America, but soon all of his attention was directed toward World War I. In the first years of the war, which began in 1914, Wilson tried not to take sides. He had little choice but to join the fray in 1917 when Germany continually attacked neutral ships. After the United States joined the war effort, the Allied forces (which included the United States, Great Britain, and France, among others) declared victory in 1918.

After the war, Wilson made many vital contributions to the Treaty of Versailles, an important peace agreement that created the League of Nations. A precursor to the United Nations, the League was an international peacekeeping organization. In 1919, Wilson tried (and failed) to rally support for the League in the United States. His exertions led to a debilitating stroke. While he carried out the remainder of his term, Wilson never fully recovered before he died in 1924.

Franklin Delano Roosevelt served from 1933 to 1945—the longest tenure of any American president. After he guided the nation through the worst of the Great Depression, he helped lead the Allies to victory in World War II.

Roosevelt was born January 30, 1882, in Hyde Park, New York. During his first years as president, he quickly developed and implemented a broad series of public programs called the New Deal. Designed to boost the economy and to broaden social benefits, the programs met with mixed success.

Initially, Roosevelt focused on emergency relief and preliminary steps toward recovery by stabilizing banks, giving cash to the poor, helping farmers, and creating new jobs. Later, he worked toward the broader goal of laying the foundation for a stable financial future for all Americans.

Ultimately, it was World War II that healed the economy as the country raced to manufacture materials for the war effort. Still, the soothing influence of Roosevelt's optimism over the American people through the darkest days of the Depression would be difficult to overstate.

Before the surprise attack on Pearl Harbor in 1941, Roosevelt had provided extensive aid to Great Britain while maintaining an official policy of neutrality toward the conflict. After the Japanese assault drew the United States into the fray, Roosevelt proved himself an effective wartime leader.

Roosevelt died of a cerebral hemorrhage on April 12, 1945, less than a month before the Germans surrendered and the Allied victory transformed the United States into a global power.

Harry S. Truman (born May 8, 1884) became president following the sudden death of Franklin Delano Roosevelt on April 12, 1945.

With the United States mired in World War II, the new leader faced many challenges. While the Germans surrendered mere weeks after Truman took office, Japan showed no sign of relenting. Appalled by the prospect of losing more American lives, he decided to hasten the end of the war by dropping atomic bombs on the Japanese cities of Hiroshima and Nagasaki. The bombs killed more than 100,000 people instantly, and the war was over within the month.

Truman continued to face tough foreign policy decisions throughout his presidency. He worked hard to contain the growing influence of the Soviet Union, which had become increasingly antagonistic toward the United States after the war. He supported countries in Europe that were vulnerable to Communist influence. He intervened in the Korean War with the support of the United Nations, which he had helped establish.

On the domestic front, Truman dealt with public unrest as the economy switched gears after the war. While the transition was shaky at first, it was ultimately successful. Truman started pursuing his domestic program, the Fair Deal, in 1949. It called for a wide variety of public programs and reforms, including civil rights and national health insurance. While most of his wish list never made it past Congress, Truman was successful in raising the minimum wage and expanding Social Security.

After Truman left office in 1953, he lived in Missouri until his death in 1972.

John F. Kennedy, who served from 1961 to 1963, is perhaps best remembered for his untimely death. The wildly popular president's assassination in Dallas, Texas, rocked and traumatized the nation.

Kennedy was born on May 29, 1917, in Brookline, Massachusetts. He was only 43 years old when he became president—the youngest person to be elected president in American history.

The threat of Communism was Kennedy's greatest challenge when he entered office. The Cold War was well under way, and Americans lived under the constant threat of nuclear attack by the Soviet Union. Kennedy tried to ease that strain by promising to eradicate Communism around the world.

In 1961, Kennedy secretly backed a group of Cuban rebels that tried to overthrow Fidel Castro. That failed attempt, known as the Bay of Pigs Invasion, was both an embarrassment and a setback for the American government.

In 1962, the Cuban Missile Crisis erupted when it became known that the Soviets were building stockpiles of missiles in Cuba. A tense standoff eventually gave way to an important nuclear weapons treaty between the United States and the Soviet Union.

At home, Kennedy's domestic agenda was thwarted somewhat by a lack of Congressional support. He enjoyed limited success in passing legislation that promoted economic and social programs.

While Kennedy supported civil rights for African Americans, he felt he had limited power to introduce legislation during his first term. He enforced desegregation in Southern schools with military troops and upheld other antidiscrimination laws, but leaders in the civil rights movement, including Martin Luther King, Jr., pressed him for further action. The president started making more progress on this front shortly before he was killed.

Kennedy giving his inaugural address. At his left is Vice President Lyndon Johnson.

Ronald Reagan, a popular Republican, focused on the economy and the strength of the U.S. military during his two-term presidency (1981 to 1989).

Born February 6, 1911, in Tampico, Illinois, Reagan spent his formative years in the Midwest before he moved to Hollywood to pursue a career in radio and film. As an actor and president of the Screen Actors Guild, he started moving in Republican circles. His anti-Communist stance helped launch his career as a politician. He served as governor of California from 1967 to 1975.

In 1981, just 2 months into his presidency, Reagan was shot in Washington, D.C. While he was gravely injured, his positive attitude and quick recovery cemented his popularity with the American public.

Throughout his presidency, Reagan's domestic policy was centered on economic reform. He decreased government spending on public programs and lowered taxes. While the U.S. economy rebounded from a recession during his watch, the national debt increased and homelessness became a prominent issue.

Reagan's foreign policy was based on a strong defensive stance. During his 8 years in office, the U.S. defense budget was increased by 35 percent. Where his predecessors carefully handled the country's strained relationship with the Soviet Union, Reagan was more bold. Still, by the end of his term, he had negotiated important arms reductions agreements with Mikhail Gorbachev, which helped end the Cold War.

In 1994, five years after he left the White House, Reagan announced that he had been diagnosed with Alzheimer's disease. He died in 2004.

George Herbert Walker Bush's presidency (1989 to 1993) coincided with a tumultuous time in history. His foreign-policy decisions helped the U.S. maintain its steady footing as the rest of the world changed.

Bush was born June 12, 1924, in Milton, Massachusetts. Before college, he served as a distinguished Navy pilot during World War II. After establishing himself in the oil industry in Texas, he held a wide variety of prestigious political offices, including Ambassador to the United Nations and Director of the Central Intelligence Agency. These appointments culminated in the two terms he served as vice president under Ronald Reagan.

His extensive experience in Washington proved valuable as Bush embarked upon his own presidency, when the world's political landscape was rapidly shifting. He skillfully handled the country's relationship with the East through the collapse of the Soviet Union in 1991. He also removed Communist dictator General Manuel Noriega from power in Panama.

Bush's biggest accomplishment was his victory in the Gulf War, which curtailed the aggression of Iraq against Kuwait. Bush organized an international coalition of countries in a war effort that lasted less than 2 months, temporarily restoring stability to the Middle East.

Meanwhile, on the domestic front, Bush faced challenges such as a large national deficit, a lack of funding for federal programs, and a failing economy. The public perceived him as placing too much emphasis on foreign affairs—a mistake that cost Bush the presidential election in 1992 to Bill Clinton.

THE PRESIDENTS: FREQUENTLY ASKED QUESTIONS

Forty-four presidents have served in the United States since 1789, for an average of about 5 years each. In recent times, as the United States has become a world power, the office of the president has become one of the most influential positions—as well as the most difficult to manage—in the world.

Looked at all together, the presidents of the United States are an interesting group. The following are some frequently asked questions about U.S. presidents, and the answers to those questions.

Which presidents served the longest and shortest times in office?

Longest: Franklin D. Roosevelt served from March 1933 to April 1945, a total of 12 years, 1 month. He had been elected for a fourth term and would have served 16 years had he not died in office. The 22nd Amendment (1951) limits presidents to two terms.

Shortest: William Henry Harrison served from March 4 to April 4, 1841. He caught a cold at his inauguration and died of pneumonia just 1 month after taking office. James A. Garfield, another president, died of gunshot wounds in September 1881. He had served only 6 months.

How many presidents died in office?

Eight. They are: William Henry Harrison, 1841, illness; Zachary Taylor, 1850, illness; Abraham Lincoln, 1865, assassination; James Garfield, 1881, assassination; William McKinley, 1901, assassination; Warren Harding, 1923, illness; Franklin D. Roosevelt, 1945, illness; and John F. Kennedy, 1963, assassination.

Were any presidents related to each other?

Yes. John Adams and John Quincy Adams were father and son. William Henry Harrison and Benjamin Harrison were grandfather and grandson. Theodore and Franklin Roosevelt were distant cousins. George H. W. Bush and George W. Bush are father and son.

Were all the presidents married?

All except one were married at some time in their lives. The exception is James Buchanan. Several presidents have been married more than once, usually after the death of their first wives. The only president who had been divorced was Ronald Reagan.

Did all presidents retire after serving as president?

Most presidents did retire after their terms ended, but not all.

- John Quincy Adams returned to the House of Representatives and served there for 17 years after his presidency.
- William Howard Taft became a law professor and later served 9 years as chief justice of the Supreme Court.

PRESIDENTIAL ELECTIONS: A SCHEDULE

Popular election	First Tuesday after first Monday in November	Candidate with plurality in each state wins that state's electoral votes.
Electoral College meetings	First Monday after second Wednesday in December	Electors meet in state capitals to cast their votes. States certify the votes and send them to Congress.
Counting the electoral vote		Results of the Electoral College vote are tallied by the president of the Senate (usually the vice president) at a joint session of Congress. If there is a tie in the electoral vote, the House of Representatives must elect the president, each state receiving one vote.
Inauguration	January 20	The president-elect is sworn in at noon and takes office.

FIRST NATIONS

The first human beings to inhabit what is now Canada were the ancestors of the present-day Indians and Inuit. They began arriving nearly 30,000 years ago from what today are known as Asia and Alaska. Over the centuries, some of these aborigines, moving south and east, spread themselves sparsely over the huge expanse of northern North America. These people came to constitute the tribes that the Europeans called Indians. The tribes developed distinctive languages, cultures, and ways of making a living. Today, Canada's native people are often known as *First Nations peoples* or *Aboriginals*.

Lands of the Inuit

Inuit culture developed over 1,000 years ago in the far northern areas of Canada, which consist mostly of treeless tundra. *Inuit* means *people* in the Inuit-Inupiaq language. The term is used today instead of the old term *Eskimos*, a word of Native American origin that could mean *eaters of raw meat*, *netter of snowshoes*, or *speaker of a foreign language*. Many Inuit consider the term Eskimo insulting.

Ways of Life

The Inuit have always lived in small groups scattered over a huge region.

- They lived in groups that varied in size from a single family to several hundred people.
- The size of the groups depended on the amount of food available in different seasons.

Igloos are built by stacking blocks of hard snow in coils to form a dome. Few Inuit would have lived in an igloo year-round, however. Igloos were mainly used for temporary shelter. The sled shown would have been the most common form of transportation in winter. ▼

Food and Shelter. The Inuit depended on fish, water-fowl, sea mammals, and the few land animals of the far north, such as bears and caribou, for food and for skins to be used for clothing and shelter.

Inuit families would have had both summer and winter housing:

- in summer, wood-frame tents covered with animal skins (probably seal or caribou)

- in winter, sod houses or snowhouses (igloos)

◄ **Today's Inuit** are partly integrated into the rest of the Canadian economy, as fishermen, fur traders, tour guides, and producers of arts and crafts.

Inuit Today

Of the 100,000 or so Inuit in the world today, more than 25,000 live in Canada. Because they were so isolated in the north, it took until the early 20th century for the Inuit to conveniently trade and live something like a modern life. Today, though, the traditional way of life has ended for most Inuit.

- They live in wooden homes rather than in snow-houses, sod houses, or tents. They wear modern clothing.

- Most Inuit speak English, Russian, or Danish in addition to their native language.

	Land inhabited by the Inuit today
	Land formerly inhabited by the Inuit

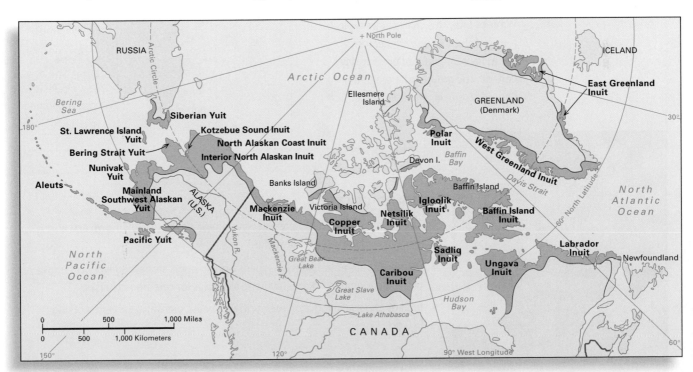

Inuit Lands. This map shows the regions currently and formerly lived in by the Inuit. Land inhabited by the Inuit today includes the northeastern tip of Siberia, the islands of the Bering Sea, and the coastal regions of mainland Alaska. They also include the north coast and islands of the Canadian Arctic and most of the west coast and part of the east coast of Greenland.

First Nations Peoples

Before the Inuit settled in Canada's northern regions, aboriginal groups populated the rugged, forest-filled areas further south, in the Canadian Subarctic region. Their descendants became known as Indians. (See also pages 22–27.)

Surviving the Subarctic

Most of the Indians lived by hunting and fishing. Although there was little agriculture, it was practiced to some extent in the warmer region of southern Ontario and in the valley of the St. Lawrence River.

- Animals, birds, and fish were plentiful, but the Indians had only crude tools and weapons for catching them.

- The great forests provided wood for fuel and housing, while animals provided skins for clothing and shelter.

- The caribou, a large animal that existed in enormous herds, was the chief prize of the hunt for both the Indians and the Inuit.

Finding enough food was a continuing struggle, and when different tribes met while on hunting expeditions, armed conflict over choice areas sometimes resulted.

Ways of Life. This chart shows typical forms of clothing and shelter for the Indians and Inuit of present-day Canada. The groups adapted to the natural resources available to them. ▶

	Arctic	Subarctic
Clothing	MacKenzie Inuit	Innu
Buildings and shelters	Polar Inuit sealskin tent	Cree bark tipi
	Iglulik Inuit snowhouse	Cree bark lodge
		Chippewa domed bark lodge

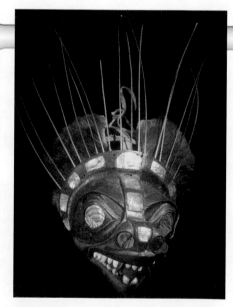

ART AND CULTURE

The aboriginal peoples of present-day Canada developed their own arts and cultures, as well as their own lifestyles.

- Inuit artists are noted for their superb work in bone, stone, and ivory carvings of the arctic animal life around them, as well as for ceremonial masks.

- Indians, especially those on the northwest coast, were also carvers, working in wood.

◀ **First Nations Art.** This mask was made by the Nootka of the western coast of British Columbia. The Nootka were also known for their elaborately carved totem poles.

Where They Lived

This chart lists some of the major tribes of the Sub-arctic and where they were located.

Location	Tribes
East	Micmac, Huron
West	Ottawa, Cree
Interior Prairie Region	Ojibwa (or Chippewa), Nipissing, Assiniboine, Blackfoot, Sioux, Athabascan, Gros Ventre
Far North	Dogrib, Nahani
Pacific Coast	Kwakiutl, Nootka, Tlingit, Haida

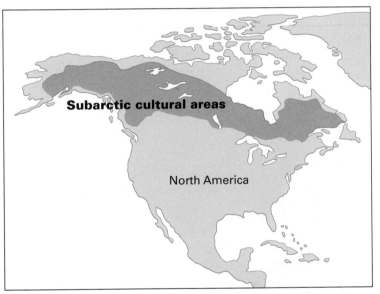

Subarctic cultural areas

North America

Contact with Europeans

The first Europeans to make contact with the Indians of Canada and the Inuit were the Vikings, who arrived in the late 900s. Other Europeans arrived in the 1500s. At that point, there probably were about 220,000 Indians and Inuit. It was the mid-1700s before there was much further contact, mostly with trading posts.

Effects. Unlike the Indian groups of the present-day United States, the Indians of present-day Canada had far fewer violent conflicts with the Europeans. They did, however, suffer from the coming of the Europeans.

- They had little resistance to European diseases, so epidemics such as smallpox wiped out half of the members of the tribes.
  - As in the United States, Indian groups in Canada also lost much of their lands. Today, many of Canada's Indians live on government reserves.

◀ **The Subarctic region** includes Alaska's interior and most of Canada.

✔ The first people to live in what is now Canada arrived nearly 30,000 years ago from what today are known as Asia and Alaska.

✔ These people were the ancestors of the present-day Indians and Inuit.

✔ The Inuit traditionally occupied the far northern areas of Canada, which mostly consist of cold, treeless land called tundra.

✔ The Indians of the Subarctic lived mostly by hunting and fishing.

✔ The first Europeans to make contact with the Indians of Canada were the Vikings, in the late 900s. Other Europeans began to arrive in the 1500s.

now you **Know!**

AGE OF EXPLORATION

Small groups of Europeans, such as the Vikings, had come to Canada around the year 1000, but none remained there permanently. In the 1400s, European explorers returned to the continent. They were looking for a fabled northwest passage—a direct westward route from Europe to Asia. They were also hoping to find rich kingdoms like the ones Spanish explorers had found in Mexico and Peru. After several tries, the French finally established permanent settlements and developed a rich fur trade in Canada.

Reaching Canada

The Europeans who landed in Canada during the 1400s came from many different nations. Most had no intention of staying in Canada—they were looking for a route around it, or through it. No northwest passage was ever found, but the explorers did find farmland, fishing, and a rich fur trade.

Vikings

The first recorded Europeans to land on the North American continent were the Vikings. The Vikings were Scandinavian warriors and traders, active from the 9th to the 12th centuries. Eric the Red (fl. 980–1000), a Norwegian explorer who named and settled Greenland, claimed he landed on what is now Baffin Island in AD 982.

Viking Settlements. Evidence suggests that it was Leif Eriksson (fl. ca. 1000), the son of Eric the Red, who first sailed to the region and landed there about 1001.

- He probably first touched the mainland on the coast of Labrador near Belle Isle.

- The best evidence indicates that the Vikings spent the winter in a settlement they built at l'Anse aux Meadows, on the northern coast of Newfoundland.

  The Vikings never established a permanent settlement, and knowledge of the European discovery of the continent was lost for nearly 500 years.

The Vikings were the best shipbuilders and sailors of their time. The remains of two large houses and of primitive ironworks uncovered at l'Anse aux Meadows suggest that the Vikings settled there temporarily.

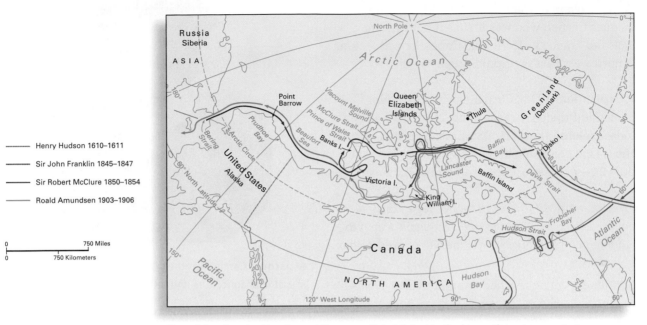

Henry Hudson 1610–1611

Sir John Franklin 1845–1847

Sir Robert McClure 1850–1854

Roald Amundsen 1903–1906

| 0 | 750 Miles |
| 0 | 750 Kilometers |

Searching for the Northwest Passage. Cabot failed to find a northwestern route to Asia. In later years, many other explorers would attempt the journey. This map shows routes traveled by explorers from the 1600s into the 1900s. (See also page 30.)

The Northwest Passage

The first of the explorers who tried to bypass the northern part of the Western Hemisphere was John Cabot (1450–1498). An Italian born in Genoa, Cabot sailed for Henry VII, king of England.

- On June 24, 1497, he landed on either the southwest corner of Newfoundland or the northern tip of Cape Breton Island.

- He took possession of the land in the name of the king—England's first claim to Canada.

Cabot was sure that he had reached Asia. He reported finding fish in great numbers. By the next year, English fishermen began to work the area around Newfoundland. Portuguese, French, and Spanish fishing boats soon joined them.

First Colonies. The first Europeans (after the Vikings) to establish a colony were the Portuguese, in 1521. Drawn by cod fishing, João Alvarez Fagundes transported Portuguese families to what is believed to have been Cape Breton Island, where a settlement was established.

This enterprise was abandoned for unknown reasons. The cartographers who joined them, however, brought back valuable maps of Nova Scotia and the southern shore of Newfoundland.

 *Some scholars claim that Irish monks, sailing by way of Iceland, settled on Cape Breton Island, northeast of Nova Scotia, in about AD 875. Legend has it that they joined the native population, and the settlement died out.*

Cartier and Champlain

France and Cartier

France's claim to Canada began with the voyages of Jacques Cartier, who was first sent out by King Francis I of France in 1534. Like Cabot, he was looking for a northwest passage from Europe to Asia.

First Expedition (1534). Cartier saw the Labrador coast, found Prince Edward Island and the Magdalen Islands, explored the Gulf of St. Lawrence, and landed on the Gaspé peninsula to take possession for France on July 24—in the presence of a band of Indians.

Second Expedition (1535). On this voyage, Cartier discovered the St. Lawrence River and sailed up it to the Indian village of Stadacona, the site of present-day Quebec City.

- Continuing on, he reached another village, Hochelaga, now the site of Montreal. Indians he met told him of three "kingdoms" farther west.
- Cartier and his men wintered near Hochelaga and returned to France the next spring.
- On the return voyage, Cartier determined that Newfoundland was an island.

Third Expedition (1541). On Cartier's third and final voyage, he went up the St. Lawrence to the Lachine Rapids, built a fort, and wintered at Cap Rouge.

▲ **Jacques Cartier** was the first to report that Canada might be useful for agriculture and settlement, in addition to fishing.

Cartier's Impact. Cartier refused to remain in Canada, having failed to find the Northwest Passage or the riches of Asia. He had, however, made important geographical discoveries and given the French a claim to the St. Lawrence River region.

The French continued to try—five times in all—to establish settlements during the rest of the century. The economic motive was the discovery of excellent furs, which were in high demand throughout Europe.

French colonists in this illustration are shown arriving in 1542 at the site of present-day Quebec City and being greeted by local Indian tribes.

Champlain

It was not until the early 17th century that France was able to establish permanent colonies in Canada. This was accomplished under the leadership of Samuel de Champlain (1567–1635), a naval commander and cartographer. He visited Canada in 1603 and returned the next year as joint leader of an expedition with Pierre du Gua, sieur de Monts (1558–1630).

Colonies. Champlain and du Gua founded a colony on Saint Croix Island (now a U.S. national monument) off the coast of Maine.

- In 1605, they moved the colony across the Bay of Fundy to found Port Royal (now Annapolis Royal, Nova Scotia).

- Port Royal was abandoned for a while in 1607, but in 1608, Champlain set up a fur-trading post at Quebec.

- Quebec became the first permanent establishment of France in Canada.

Champlain and the men he sent out also explored the interior of Canada and the New England coast as far south as Martha's Vineyard.

Later Explorers

During the 1600s, France and England began to compete for territory and resources in Canada. This led to a new wave of French exploration, with explorers claiming large areas for the French king. The chart below lists some key explorers and expeditions of that period.

▲ **Alliances and Conflicts.** Champlain's alliances with some Indian tribes caused a feud between the Iroquois and French.

THE IROQUOIS FEUD

Champlain's expeditions brought him into conflict with the Iroquois people.

- In 1609, French troops and their Indian allies fought a battle with some Iroquois. The guns of the French easily routed the Iroquois.

- The following year, Champlain wiped out another Iroquois band near the mouth of the Richelieu River.

- Champlain formed military alliances with the Algonquins of the Ottawa River, the Montagnais of the St. Lawrence River, and the Hurons.

✔ Around the year 1000, Vikings may have established a temporary settlement in Canada.

✔ Europeans who landed in Canada in the 1400s were looking for a northwest passage to Asia.

✔ Jacques Cartier, a French explorer, made three expeditions to Canada and gave France its first claim to the region.

✔ Samuel de Champlain founded the first permanent French settlements in Canada.

✔ Later, such explorers as Sieur de la Salle, Louis Jolliet, and Jacques Marquette expanded France's claim to the territory.

Louis Jolliet (1645–1700) Jacques Marquette (1637–1675)	• Led an expedition down the Mississippi River in 1673 • Explored present-day Illinois and Wisconsin
Sieur de la Salle (1643–1687)	• Established a fort at the mouth of the Niagara River in 1679 • Traveled to the mouth of the Mississippi in 1682
Louis Hennepin (1640–1701?)	• Explored the upper Mississippi River Valley in 1680

NEW FRANCE was

the name given to the North American lands claimed by French explorers and settlers. They helped develop a thriving fishing industry off the east coast. But they played an even more important role in Canada's growth by establishing the fur trade. The fur trade led to the development of a French colonial empire in North America. This empire lasted about 150 years and established the French culture and heritage in Canada.

Building an Empire

Formal government came to Canada on October 8, 1612, when Louis XIII, king of France, appointed his nephew Louis de Bourbon, comte de Soissons, governor and lieutenant general of New France. New France consisted at that time of fur traders, trappers, and Catholic missionaries operating along the St. Lawrence River.

Governing New France

Louis de Bourbon died on November 12, 1612, before he could really serve. Champlain had already been appointed deputy commander and so in effect became the first governor of New France. From 1633 until his death in Quebec City on December 25, 1635, Champlain held the title of commandant and acted as the French king's viceroy in New France.

Samuel de Champlain—naval commander, commandant and king's viceroy in New France, and cartographer—is here depicted against his map of the Gulf of St. Lawrence.

The Seigneurial System. Many aspects of French law and government were transferred to New France.

- A system akin to feudalism, called the seigneurial system, was introduced in the New World in 1623.
- The king gave land in the colony to several groups, including French military officers and merchants.
- Each seigneur, or landholder, brought in colonists at his own expense.

By 1760, there were about 250 landholdings, amounting to nearly 8 million acres (3.2 million hectares). Most of them were on the St. Lawrence River. Seigneurs were not actually liege lords of the king, but they had considerable authority over the lives of their tenants.

The Company of New France. Much of the power of government in New France was in the hands of trading companies, especially the Company of New France, or One Hundred Associates.

- This group, which consisted mostly of wealthy nobles, had been established in 1627 by Cardinal Richelieu, Louis XIII's chief minister.
- Iroquois attacks had destabilized the colony—farms had been abandoned and people were under a constant state of siege. The Associates had been unable to maintain order.
- As a result, in May 1663, Louis XIV declared New France was a royal province, instead of the property of a trading company.

Authority then was vested in the Sovereign Council (called the Superior Council after 1703).

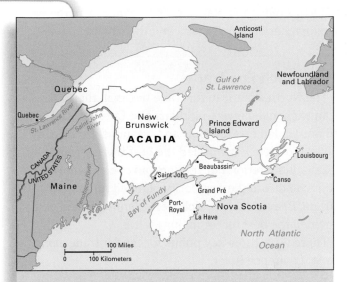

The Settlement of Acadia included what is today part of southeastern Quebec, New Brunswick, Nova Scotia, and Prince Edward Island.

ACADIA

In November 1635, the French set up a separate government for Acadia, where Pierre du Gua had established the first permanent settlement.

- Charles de Menou, sieur d'Aulnay-Charisnay, and Charles de Saint-Etienne de la Tour were named joint governors of Acadia.
- They quarreled to such an extent that civil war broke out, resulting in the recall of la Tour.
- La Tour was reinstated on February 25, 1651, following de Menou's accidental death by drowning in May 1650.

The Sovereign/Superior Council	
Governor	military and political chief; held the most power
Intendant	responsible for administration and finance
Bishop of Quebec	spiritual leader of the province

The Fur Trade

The fur trade industry was one of the first industries in North America. It played a significant role in the development of both Canada and the United States.

The French Fur Trade

The North American fur trade began in the 1500s as an exchange between Indians and Europeans. The Indians traded furs for tools and weapons. In the early 1600s, the French controlled the best trading routes in Canada's interior. Fur trading had become more profitable due to the popularity of felted fur hats in Europe. Beaver skins, which were plentiful in Canada, provided the best fur for making felt.

There were three key points for the fur trade along the St. Lawrence River.

- Tadoussac, at the mouth of the Saguenay River, was founded in 1600 by Pierre Chauvin.

- Trois-Rivières, Canada's second oldest city (after Quebec), was founded in 1634.

- The site of present-day Montreal was established in 1642.

Competition. As the French fur trade prospered, the competition grew. To the south of the French trade routes, Iroquois raided Huron canoes carrying furs. The Dutch and then the English began to give the French strong competition. Competition between the French and the English would be a major cause of the French and Indian War. (See pages 44–45.)

COUREURS DE BOIS

The French fur trade was officially a monopoly of the king, or his representatives. A large number of young Frenchmen, however, defied the monopoly laws and took to the fur trade on their own. They journeyed to the interior, lived like the Indians, and married Indian women.

After 1649, when the Huron were badly defeated by the Iroquois, these coureurs de bois—runners of the woods—took the place of the Indians as middlemen to deal with the tribes farther west. The descendants of these men and women, called Métis (mixed blood), later provided a large part of the fur trade's workforce.

THE HUDSON'S BAY COMPANY

The most important English explorer of northern North America was Henry Hudson (fl. 1607–1611). In 1609, Hudson, making a voyage for the Dutch East India Company, discovered the Hudson River in New York State. On his fourth and final voyage, in 1610, he discovered Hudson Bay. After the voyage, however, his crew mutinied, and set Hudson and his young son adrift in a small boat with six members of the crew. They were never seen again.

On May 2, 1670, Charles II, king of England, chartered the Hudson's Bay Company. This gave a group of courtiers and merchants the right to trade, settle, and search for the Northwest Passage in the lands explored by Hudson. The grant was known as Rupert's Land, after Prince Rupert, the leader of the company.

Indian Conflicts

The fur trade rivalries also brought Indian tribes into conflict with the French, and with each other.

- The Huron, as allies of the French, were a steady source of fur supply.

- The Iroquois, with guns supplied by the English, moved to seize the fur trade from the Huron. At one point, they blocked the Richelieu River and made the Ottawa River unsafe for Huron trappers.

- From 1640 to 1650, the Iroquois nearly exterminated the Huron living in the region of Huronia. Many of the French Jesuit missionaries in Huronia were killed as well.

- The Iroquois then went on to destroy their other rivals, the Petun, the Neutral, and the Erie nations. By 1660, Iroquois war parties were striking farms and settlements all over New France.

Military Action. In the face of the Iroquois threat to New France, Louis XIV moved decisively, sending the French military to Canada. In 1666, the Marquis Prouville de Tracy led his troops to victory over the Iroquois, destroying their villages and crops.

The Mohawks and other Iroquois tribes made peace with the French in the next year, but there would not be a lasting peace until 1701, when the Great Peace of Montreal was signed.

The North American Fur Trade.
This map shows the chief areas of the fur trade and the groups that controlled these areas in North America. Trappers sold their furs at trading posts, which were usually located on rivers, lakes, and bays. Furs were then exported overseas or to other parts of North America.

French
1500s to 1763

Colonial American
1600s to late 1700s

Hudson's Bay Company
1670 to 1850s

North West Company
1770s to 1821

Russian
1790s to 1850s

American
1820s to 1850s

→ Fur export route

■ Trading post

• City

0 ——— 1,000 Miles
0 ——— 1,000 Kilometers

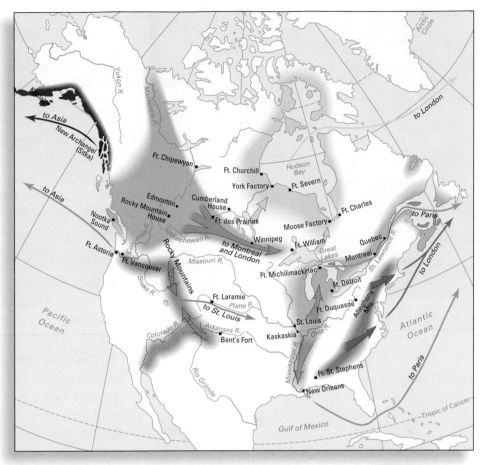

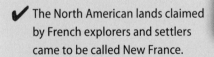

EFFECTS OF THE FUR TRADE

The fur trade contributed to the development of British and French empires in North America.

- The prospect of wealth brought many Europeans to the New World.

- Traders and trappers explored much of North America. They founded trading posts and settlements in the wilderness.

- Some of these settlements later became such major Canadian cities as Edmonton, Montreal, Quebec, and Winnipeg.

✔ The North American lands claimed by French explorers and settlers came to be called New France.

✔ In 1612, Louis XIII, king of France, established the first official government in New France, giving much of the power to trading companies.

✔ New France became a royal province in 1663, because the trading companies failed to maintain order.

✔ The fur trade played a large role in the development of both Canada and the United States.

✔ The success of the French fur trade in Canada led to competition with the Dutch, the English, and the Indians—especially the Iroquois.

CONFLICT WITH BRITAIN

Until the early 1600s, the French and English in North America had competed for the fur trade and made conflicting territorial claims, but they had not clashed directly. Eventually, however, the English colonies began to expand, filling with settlers. Several factors created tension between the two sides. Most of the French were Roman Catholics, and the majority of the English were Protestants. Most of the French wanted land for fur trading. The English wanted it for farming. These clashes, combined with rivalries in Europe, led to a series of bloody wars that ended France's claim to Canada.

France and Britain

Conflict began to build in the early 1600s, with overlapping land claims and occasional fighting. France and Britain were also rivals in Europe, and tensions in Europe added to the conflict growing in North America. In 1621, King James I disregarded French land claims and granted a Scotsman—William Alexander, later the Earl of Stirling—rights to the region from Cape Gaspé to the St. Croix River.

Following the outbreak of war between England and France in 1627, a group of London merchants organized an expedition against Canada and seized Quebec in 1629. (Quebec was returned to the French in 1632.)

French Policies. The French initially did little to bring in settlers or establish agriculture. During the 1600s, however, they did make an attempt to strengthen New France, as they called their Canadian lands.

- The Company of New France, or One Hundred Associates, took over the fur trade, and also arranged for 4,000 immigrants to come to Canada. In the end, however, far fewer than that came over. By 1663, the population of New France was only about 2,500.

- Count Louis de Frontenac, who was governor from 1672 to 1682 and again from 1689 to his death in 1698, established posts and forts in new French territory and resisted English pressure.

- Jean Baptiste Talon, who served as intendant from 1665 to 1668 and 1670 to 1672, sent out prospectors and explorers, and encouraged other enterprises.

Important Dates: Canada (1689–1791)	
Year	**Event**
1689–1763	A series of wars between British and French colonists ended with Great Britain in control of New France, the French empire in America.
1774	The Quebec Act gave French Canadians political and religious rights.
1775–1783	During the American Revolution, an American invasion of Canada in 1775 failed.
1784	The colony of New Brunswick was established.
1791	The Constitutional Act split Quebec into the colonies of Upper Canada and Lower Canada.

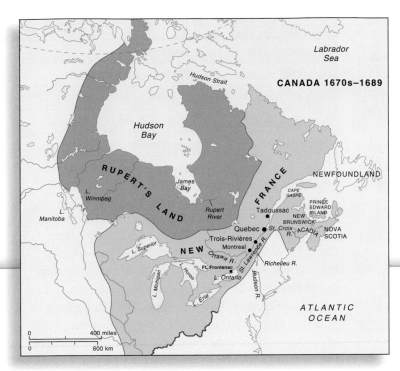

Canada 1670s–1689. In the late 1600s, the eastern part of Canada was divided between New France and Rupert's Land.

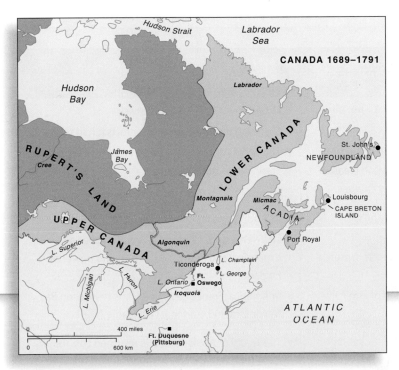

Canada 1689–1791. Over the course of nearly a century, French power in Canada was ended. The boundaries of what had been New France changed, and were divided into Upper and Lower Canada.

English Policies. Unlike the French, the English did encourage agriculture and settlement in Canada. They had also chartered the Hudson's Bay Company in 1670, with the help of two French traders, Médard Chouat, sieur de Groseilliers; and Pierre-Esprit Radisson. The region controlled by the company was called Rupert's Land (and was claimed by the French and the English at the same time). The company established trading posts all along Hudson Bay.

- The French tried to cut into this operation by intercepting the Indian traders as they went down the rivers to the bay.

- The Treaty of Neutrality in 1686 provided for a commission to settle the boundaries of New France and Rupert's Land.

The Colonial Wars

A Century of Wars

In 1689, the competition between England and France for land, fur, fish, and other commerce moved to the battlefield. That year saw the first of four wars that ended nearly a century later with the complete defeat of France. The wars were one part of a struggle for empire involving opposing groups of European nations. In fact, what the nations agreed on at the end of each war depended more on what had happened in Europe than in North America. (See also pages 44–45.)

Four Wars, Eight Names	
Canadian Name	**European Name**
King William's War	War of the Grand Alliance
Queen Anne's War	War of the Spanish Succession
King George's War	War of the Austrian Succession
Seven Years' War	Seven Years' War

In the United States, the four wars are known collectively as the French and Indian Wars.

Causes. Beginning in 1690, the English repeatedly sought to conquer the French settlements. They wanted total control of North America. The French, on the other hand, had little intention of conquering the more numerous English. Instead, they fought to preserve their control of the North American interior, which rested on a vast network of alliances with Indians. The alliances depended on trading furs and fighting each other's enemies.

Effects. While both King William's War and King George's War ended with little change in territorial boundaries, the losses from Queen Anne's War staggered New France. The immense fur-producing country around Hudson Bay was gone, and the English now had access to the Great Lakes, raising the threat of cutting off the route from Quebec to Louisiana. The loss of Acadia and Newfoundland meant that French control of the Gulf of St. Lawrence and the Atlantic coast was now also threatened.

The First Three Colonial Wars (1689–1763)			
	Dates	**Major Events**	**Results**
King William's War	1689–1697	• The French attacked Hudson's Bay Company posts in 1690. • The British took Port Royal, then in Acadia. • Strong French defense, fever, and bad weather prevented the English from taking Quebec.	• Ended with the Treaty of Ryswick • Each side returned all lands or forts it had taken. • The Great Peace of Montreal (1701) also ended the French war with the Indians.
Queen Anne's War	1702–1713	• In 1708, the French captured St. John's, Newfoundland. • After failing twice, New Englanders recaptured Port Royal in 1710. • British forces were a combination of English and American troops.	• In Europe, the French lost badly. • The Treaty of Utrecht in 1713 put an end to French expansion and indicated the growing power of England. • In America, France gave up claims to Hudson Bay, Newfoundland, and most of Acadia.
King George's War	1744–1748	• French troops failed to retake Port Royal. • British troops took Louisbourg in 1745. • French attempts to retake Louisbourg failed.	• The Treaty of Aix-la-Chapelle returned Louisbourg, Cape Breton Island, and Prince Edward Island to France. • All lands taken by the French were restored to England as well.

The struggle between the French and British for control of Canada was mounted at such forts as this one in Louisbourg, Nova Scotia.

ACADIAN EXPULSION

The region of Acadia had a large French population. In 1755, early in the Seven Years' War, the British demanded that the Acadians swear allegiance to Great Britain. The Acadians refused, although they wished to remain neutral in the conflict.

- In August, the British began rounding up Acadians to deport them.
- There was considerable delay and confusion and some families were separated.

- The British distributed these exiles among the English colonies along the Atlantic coast, and even in the Caribbean and England.
- Some ended up in Louisiana, where their descendants, known as Cajuns, still retain a separate culture.

In all, between 6,000 and 10,000 Acadians were exiled. Many eventually returned to the region.

Acadian Legends. Henry Wadsworth Longfellow's poem *Evangeline* (1847) tells the story of two lovers separated by the Acadian expulsion. Monuments to the Acadians often include the poem's heroine, Evangeline.

The Seven Years' War

The decisive conflict for control of North America was the Seven Years' War, which began in 1754. In the United States, it is known as the French and Indian War.

William Pitt (1759–1806), the British prime minister, planned to devote his war efforts to the defeat of the French Empire—and in particular, New France. He considered the French colonies, with their ability to attack the wealthy English territories, a menace to the British Empire.

Forts Changing Hands					
Fort	1755	1756	1757	1758	1759
Ft. Duquesne (Pitt)	France	France	France	Fort destroyed by the French	
Ft. Oswego	England	France (fort taken and destroyed by the French)			
Ft. William Henry	England	England	France (fort taken and destroyed by the French)		
Ft. Carillon (Ticonderoga)	France	France	France	France	Fort destroyed by the French
Ft. Louisbourg	France	France	France	England	England
Ft. Frontenac	France	France	France	England	England
Ft. Niagara	France	France	France	France	England
Ft. Saint-Frédéric (Crown Point)	France	France	France	France	Fort destroyed by the French
By 1760, three of eight major forts were in British hands. The French were in possession of none of them.					

Campaigns and Battles

The Seven Years' War began badly for the British. The French routed them at Fort Duquesne (present-day Pittsburgh, Pennsylvania) in 1755. This influenced the Indians of the Northwest to join the French side and left the English frontier settlements of Pennsylvania, Maryland, and Virginia open to attack.

Early French Victories. Under the leadership of Louis Joseph de Montcalm (1712–1759), the French took the initiative and gained some victories.

- In 1756, French forces captured Fort Oswego, on Lake Ontario, and destroyed it.
- In 1757, the French defeated a British plan to capture Louisbourg and took Fort William Henry in New York (Unfortunately, the Indian allies of the French massacred the British prisoners in spite of Montcalm's attempts to control them.)

Later British Gains. France's fortunes began to decline in 1758 as the British government increased its military strength in America. Although British forces failed in an attempt to capture Fort Carillon (Ticonderoga) in New York, they eventually took Louisbourg after a 7-week siege. Now the French had lost all control of the gulf and Atlantic coast. The English also took Fort Frontenac on the northeast shore of Lake Ontario. They now controlled the gateway to the St. Lawrence River. A final blow came in 1758: the French retreated from Fort Duquesne (present-day Pittsburgh).

The year 1759 was even more disastrous for France.

- In July, Fort Niagara, on the south shore of Lake Ontario, was captured by a force led by Sir William Johnson (1715–1774).
- At the same time, the French withdrew from Lake George and Lake Champlain, destroying Fort Carillon (Ticonderoga) and Fort Saint-Frédéric (Crown Point).

The Battle of Quebec

The military climax to a century of struggle between France and England for control of northern North America came in September 1759, with the fall of Quebec City. The British campaign to take this vital stronghold began with a naval blockade that closed the St. Lawrence River both above and below the city.

In June, 9,000 British troops landed opposite Quebec. They were commanded by James Wolfe (1727–1759), a young officer who had been second in command at Louisbourg's capture. Montcalm, meanwhile, had gathered a force of 10,000 to defend Quebec.

Wolfe's forces poured a heavy bombardment into the city, but the general could at first find no way to assault the French forces. At last, his troops reached the Plains of Abraham, outside the walls of the city under cover of darkness on September 12. The next day Montcalm decided to risk a battle. A French attack was quickly driven back. The British were victorious within 15 minutes. Quebec was forced to surrender on September 18.

▲ **The Battle of Quebec** was a swift victory for the British; however, the commanders for both sides—the Marquis de Montcalm of France and James Wolfe of the United Kingdom—were mortally wounded in the battle. This 1759 painting depicts Montcalm's death.

The End of the War. In 1760, the French made a futile attempt to retake Quebec, but they had to retreat to Montreal. In July, the French fleet in the St. Lawrence was destroyed, and on September 8, 1760, Montreal surrendered. After the final defeat of French forces in Newfoundland in 1762, the power of France in the New World was ended.

This defeat was acknowledged in the Treaty of Paris of 1763.

- France gave up Canada and ceded western Louisiana to Spain, its ally.
- Spain handed Florida over to England.
- France kept the islands of St. Pierre and Miquelon, and recovered Guadeloupe and Martinique in the West Indies.
- France ceded Grenada and the Grenadines to Great Britain.

The government of England now had to decide on important matters of policy affecting Canada. Most of the inhabitants were defeated enemies who spoke a different language and who were French Catholics rather than English Protestants.

now you **KNOW!**

✔ In the early 1600s, as Britain's settlements expanded, France and Britain began to clash over territory.

✔ In 1689, the first of four wars between France and Britain began. These wars were fought in Europe as well as in North America.

✔ The four wars are known as King William's War, Queen Anne's War, King George's War, and the Seven Years' War.

✔ The Seven Years' War finally ended France's control over Canada.

BRITISH CANADA

The shift from French to British rule brought economic changes as well as changes in the areas of law and government. British merchants followed the invading army and profited by supplying the soldiers and sailors with goods. In effect, Canada was now economically dependent on London rather than on Paris. The change of government replaced an absolute Catholic monarchy with a capitalistic system, which would lead to cultural and religious divisions between French and English Canadians. Still, most French Canadians benefited from an improvement in economic conditions.

Brigadier Thomas Gage became governor of Montreal in 1760. In 1775, he would give the orders that led to the first battle of the American Revolutionary War. ▶

Transfer of Power

Even before the signing of the Treaty of Paris in 1763, the British began installing new forms of government, gradually giving way to representative government.

Changes in Government

The governments—and boundaries—of the Canadian colonies would undergo a number of changes as British rule settled in. All the colonies, regardless of their specific form of government, fell under the ultimate authority of the British government.

Military Government. On September 8, 1760, after the French surrendered Montreal to British forces, Jeffrey Amherst, the British commander, was appointed governor-general of British North America. Canada was put under a military government reporting to Amherst in New York City. This military government consisted of three commands.

- Brigadier James Murray commanded in Quebec, which had been formed into a British colony on September 3, 1759.
- Brigadier Thomas Gage commanded in Montreal.
- Colonel Ralph Burton commanded in Trois Rivières.

After Amherst returned to England in 1763, civil government was again established in Canada under Murray, who was appointed governor on August 10, 1764.

Spotlight on...

SIR ALEXANDER MACKENZIE

1764–1820

- Canadian explorer, trader, and businessman
- Born in Scotland; went to Canada in 1778
- Made a fortune in the fur trade
- Discovered the Mackenzie River and followed it to the Arctic Ocean
- First European to cross the northern part of North America to the Pacific Ocean

Self-Government. A measure of self-government first came to Canada in 1758 when a legislative assembly met in Halifax as part of the government of Nova Scotia. Its members had been popularly elected by property owners. The government also consisted of

1. a governor, who served as the bridge between the British Parliament and the interests of the local population.
2. a council nominated by the governor, which shared his judicial and administrative duties.

Other colonies, such as New Brunswick and Prince Edward Island, eventually were granted similar governments. By 1867, most of what now constitutes eastern and central Canada had enjoyed some form of representative government for at least 20 years.

THE ENGLISH AND THE FUR TRADE

For a while, despite the British victory, the French continued to be the most important element in the fur trade. (See also pages 250–251.)

- The French traders and trappers had the experience to move confidently through western lands and to deal profitably with the Indian tribes.
- The tribes still disliked and distrusted the English and preferred to deal with the French.

Nevertheless, English merchants became involved in the Canadian fur trade, supplying credit and connections. In fact, the rivalry continued between the Canadian fur trade in the east, the Hudson Bay area to the west, and the trade centered on Albany, New York, to the south.

Conflicts in Quebec. In August 1764, the military government in Quebec was replaced by a new civil government. Soon after, problems arose because of the differences between the French and English legal systems. For example, the English had ruled that Catholics could not hold public office, but there were few Englishmen in Canada qualified to fill these positions. Governor Murray therefore allowed French citizens to serve on juries and to practice in the courts.

Murray also clashed with the growing merchant class. Several merchants asked London to recall Murray, and this was done in 1765.

Sir Guy Carleton (1724–1808), later Lord Dorchester, was Murray's successor. He was a distinguished veteran of the French and Indian Wars. Carleton replaced Murray's officials, and Quebec enjoyed a relatively peaceful period.

Not long after their victory in the Canadian colonies, the British found themselves dealing with the beginnings of a rebellion in the American colonies. In 1775, this rebellion would break out into the American Revolutionary War. Both the war and the peace that followed would have a significant impact on Canada and its borders.

The Quebec Act

The Quebec Act of June 22, 1774, was a milestone in the history of government in Canada. Made law by the British Parliament, it extended the boundaries of Quebec, restored religious freedom to the Catholic population of Quebec, and substituted French civil law for English law.

These changes irritated the American colonies. The act conflicted with American land claims. The predominantly Protestant population of the American colonies resented what they saw as favoritism to Catholics, whom they hated. The Quebec Act became one of the Intolerable Acts cited by American colonists against Great Britain and helped bring on the American Revolution.

The Canada Act. On June 10, 1791, the British Parliament passed the Constitutional Act of 1791, also known as the Canada Act. This was intended to mend the political divisions between French and English Canadians.

- It divided Canada into Upper and Lower Canada.
- Upper Canada was English-speaking, with English property and legal systems.
- Lower Canada was French-speaking, with a government based on French civil law, Catholicism, and the seigneurial system.

In the end, however, this system only resulted in further cultural conflicts.

This 1776 map shows Quebec, New England, and New York during the American Revolution. The boundaries of Quebec at that time had been set by the Quebec Act of 1774.

The American Revolution

When the First Continental Congress of the 13 American colonies met in 1774, a message was sent to Quebec. It invited delegates from Quebec to attend the next congress in 1775. No delegates came. Most of the French Canadians resented the anti-Catholic bigotry of the colonies and preferred to remain neutral. Many of the English inhabitants of Canada, especially in Nova Scotia, reacted the same way.

The Americans invaded Canada, partly in hope of changing the people's minds, partly to keep the British from using Canadian ports and strong points. The invasion focused on Montreal and Quebec.

The Congress authorized invasion in June 1775, but little progress was made until fall. To avoid a siege, Montreal surrendered to American forces under Richard Montgomery on November 12. A siege of Quebec led by Benedict Arnold and Montgomery failed, however, and Montgomery was killed. In May 1776, British reinforcements arrived, and the Americans retreated. (See also pages 56–59.)

After the Revolution. The Treaty of Paris, signed in that city on September 3, 1783, which gave the United States its independence, affected Canada in several ways.

- New boundaries greatly reduced Quebec's area: all the land north of the Ohio River, south of the mid-point of the Great Lakes (except for Lake Michigan), and east of the Mississippi River was now U.S. territory.

- The treaty also granted Americans the right to fish off Newfoundland and to cure fish in the uninhabited parts of Labrador and Nova Scotia, but not in Newfoundland.

◄ **Thayendanegea,** also known as Joseph Brant, led the Iroquois forces that fought on the side of the British in the American Revolution. He became a colonel in the British Army, and his raids on settlements in the Mohawk Valley caused great damage. After the war, Brant was a Mohawk leader in Canada.

THE LOYALIST MIGRATION

Canada benefited from the American Revolution in one unusual way. In the years during and following the war, about 50,000 Loyalists moved to Canada from the colonies. These were American colonists who had sided with the British and did not favor independence. They represented a wide and diverse group, from the rich and well educated to the farmer and artisan.

The government of Nova Scotia was supposed to supply these newcomers with land, tools, and help in the building of houses. However, it lacked the ability to provide this aid. Some of the refugees arrived in destitute condition; many had been town or city dwellers who were not equipped to deal with the demands of farming under pioneer conditions. Others settled in southern Ontario, but they suffered the same hardships as in Nova Scotia. In 1789, in fact, there was a near-famine situation.

In 1789, it was officially decreed that Loyalists who had come to Canada before 1783 were to be designated "United Empire Loyalists"; those who came after 1783 were known as "late Loyalists." Some of the late Loyalists had simply come from the United States to improve their economic prospects.

▲ **Nova Scotia** was a haven for most Loyalists because it was conveniently reached by sea and there were large areas of vacant land. By the end of 1783, an estimated 35,000 Loyalists had arrived, almost doubling the size of the provincial population.

The War of 1812

In 1812, Great Britain again went to war against the United States. Important engagements of the War of 1812 were fought on Canadian soil. In addition, several of the war's battles on American soil involved British forces operating out of Canada. A faction of American members of Congress, the "war hawks" who had agitated for the war, saw it as an excuse for conquering Canada. (See also pages 92–93.)

Battles

War was declared by the United States on June 18, 1812. American troops tried to capture Upper and Lower Canada during the war, but British and Canadian troops defeated two major invasion attempts. In July, General Isaac Brock (1769–1812), military commander and acting administrator of Upper Canada, declared martial law.

TECUMSEH

The English benefited considerably from the help of their Indian allies, especially those led by Tecumseh, the Shawnee chief. British and Canadian forces, along with the Indians, defeated the Americans on January 22, 1813, at Frenchtown, Ohio, but they were unable to dislodge the army of General William Henry Harrison (a future president of the United States), at Fort Meigs, Ohio.

On October 5, 1813, Tecumseh was killed leading his troops in Canada at the Battle of the Thames. This defeat put an end to the Indian confederacy that Tecumseh had formed in the United States.

Tecumseh. Before the War of 1812, Tecumseh had fought William Henry Harrison's forces in the Battle of Tippecanoe.

War of 1812: Canadian Involvement	
August 16, 1812	General Isaac Brock defeats American forces under General William Hull at Detroit.
October 13, 1812	American forces cross the Niagara River and occupy Queenston Heights, Ontario; Brock's forces defeat them, but Brock is killed in battle.
April 27, 1813	The Americans invade York (now Toronto); public buildings, including Parliament and the governor's residence, are burned.
September 10, 1813	At Lake Erie, Captain Oliver H. Perry (1785–1819) and his small American armada defeat a British fleet.
October 5, 1813	The Americans defeat English forces at the Battle of the Thames.
October 26, 1813	Charles de Salaberry and his small army of 460 Canadian Voltigeurs and some Indians defeat a much larger American force in Quebec. This victory ends American efforts to attack Montreal.
July 25, 1814	At Lundy's Lane, Americans attempt to advance into Ontario. They are fought to a standstill, with heavy casualties on both sides. The American force withdraws to Fort Erie, on the Canadian side of the Niagara River.
September 11, 1814	An American force under Thomas Macdonough defeats a British fleet near Plattsburgh, New York. This stops any plan to invade New York from Canada.

After the War

The War of 1812 spurred an arms race between Canada and the United States. Along the Great Lakes, each side built powerful battleships and giant fortifications. One of the most powerful ships built at this time was the 120-gun, three-decker *St. Lawrence* at Kingston, Ontario. However, by 1814, exhaustion was setting in on both sides of the border, with no real gains for either country.

The war formally ended with the Treaty of Ghent, signed in Belgium on December 24, 1814. The two nations agreed to restore each others' prewar territories. They also set up four commissions to settle the boundary line between Canada and the United States.

Rush-Bagot Agreement.
With peace declared, the U.S. and Canada began looking for a way to halt the expensive arms race—which was still continuing, though the war had ended. In 1817, the Rush-Bagot Convention brought this militarization to a halt.

The convention took its name from an agreement signed by Richard Rush (1780–1859), acting secretary of state of the United States, and Sir Charles Bagot (1781–1843), the British minister in Washington.

- Under the convention, each country was to have no more than four warships, not to exceed 100 tons each, on the Great Lakes.

- The agreement set a precedent for the settling of Anglo-American differences by negotiation.

- It also paved the way for an unfortified frontier between Canada and the U.S.

The London Convention.
In 1818, the London Convention was signed by Great Britain and the United States. By its terms

- the boundary between the United States and British North America would run from the Lake of the Woods (on the border of the present-day provinces of Ontario and Manitoba and the U.S. state of Minnesota), to the crest of the Rocky Mountains along the 49th parallel.

- the area west of there, known as the Oregon Territory, would be open to both countries for settlement and trade.

Fort McHenry. British forces operating out of Canada bombarded Fort McHenry in 1814. Observing the battle, Francis Scott Key wrote the words that became the United States' national anthem, "The Star-Spangled Banner."

now you **Know!**

- ✔ The shift from French rule to British rule brought changes to Canada's government and economy.

- ✔ Cultural and religious divisions developed between French and English Canadians.

- ✔ The Quebec and Canada Acts attempted to improve relations between French and English Canadians.

- ✔ During the American Revolutionary War, American forces invaded Canada to head off British attacks.

- ✔ Many British Loyalists emigrated from the American colonies to Canada during the Revolutionary War.

- ✔ Canadian forces participated in the War of 1812; the end of the war settled the boundaries between Canada and the United States.

FROM EXPANSION TO UNION

In the years following the American Revolutionary War and the War of 1812, Canada underwent a number of changes and upheavals. The population increased rapidly, due to immigration from Europe and the British Isles. In 1824, the Canadian population was 151,000. By 1867, it was 3,463,000. Explorers such as Alexander Mackenzie and Simon Fraser went westward in search of fur trading lands, and settlements gradually followed. In the 1820s and 1830s, political unrest and clashes over territory led to a movement to unify Canada.

Expansion and Conflict

The War of 1812 created considerable anti-American feeling in Canada. Many Canadians considered that they had been the victims of aggressors who sought to conquer and rule them. Some recent American settlers in Canada were believed to be outright disloyal.

Settlements Expand

In 1815, as a result of the anti-American sentiment, Canada banned the issuance of any more land grants to Americans. This inhibited the growth of Canada to some extent; nevertheless, Canada was growing. By 1825, the outlines of the eventual Dominion of Canada were becoming clearer. Canada now consisted of six settled areas: Lower Canada, Upper Canada, Newfoundland, Prince Edward Island, Nova Scotia, and New Brunswick. In the west, the Hudson's Bay Company continued to rule.

Canada's expansion began to escalate in the 1820s, and continued into the 20th century. The Dominion of Canada, which contained Ontario and Quebec, was officially established in 1867.

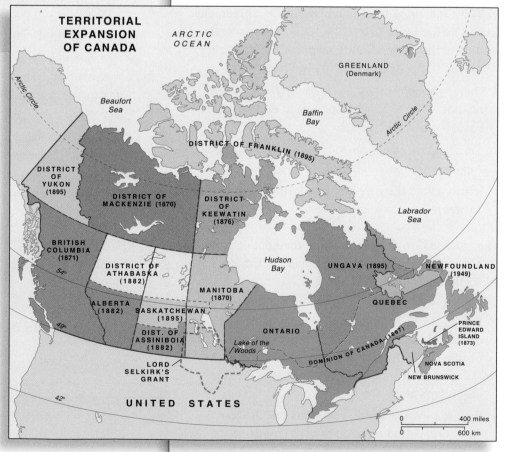

TERRITORIAL EXPANSION OF CANADA

Immigration. In the early 1800s, the flow of emigrants from Europe, chiefly from the British Isles, increased.

- Most of the immigrants followed the St. Lawrence River route into Lower and Upper Canada, with the number increasing from about 12,000 in 1828 to 66,000 in 1832.

- By 1838, the population of Upper Canada was almost 400,000, despite its distance from Europe.

- Settlement in Lower Canada was impeded somewhat by the seigneurial system, left over from French rule.

Immigrants also flowed into the maritime provinces.

- In the decade after 1815, nearly 40,000 arrived in Nova Scotia, the population of which was 200,000 by 1838.

- New Brunswick, with most of its immigrants coming from Ireland, had an average of 5,000 or more newcomers per year.

Obstacles. This influx of people was not without its problems.

- Many of those who came were destitute, or very poor, farmers or artisans; all were ill-equipped to become pioneers.

- In some areas, land was not easy to acquire. As a result, many immigrants who arrived in Canada continued on to the United States, where land was more easily available. (See also pages 148–149.)

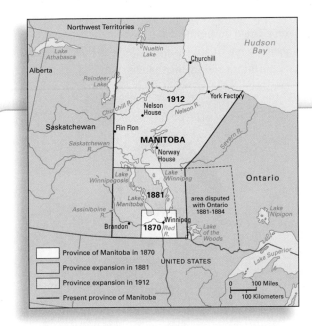

THE RED RIVER SETTLEMENT

Early in the period of Canadian expansion, an experiment in settling the west brought about clashes between fur-trapping and farming interests.

The Hudson's Bay Company and the North West Company were in constant competition for trade in the Canadian West. In 1811, Thomas Douglas (1771–1820), 5th Earl of Selkirk, secured a grant of 116,000 acres (300,000 square kilometers) from the Hudson's Bay Company. Selkirk then sent over groups of settlers from Scotland, and they founded the Red River settlement.

◄ **The Red River Colony,** as Selkirk's land was known, lay chiefly in present-day Manitoba, on the Red and Assiniboine rivers. It also extended south into parts of the present-day U.S. states of North Dakota, Minnesota, and South Dakota.

Hardship and Conflict. The early colonists suffered great hardships. Frosts, floods, and grasshoppers ruined many crops. At first, the settlers depended heavily on buffalo and other animals for meat. However, the colony lay in the heart of the North West Company's area of operations. As the colony expanded, there was much competition for food, especially buffalo meat.

Escalation. The North West Company became increasingly hostile after the colony's administrators issued the Pemmican Proclamation, which attempted to outlaw buffalo hunting in the Red River Valley. It turned local residents, including the Métis, against the colonists.

The Métis—descendents of white settlers and Native Americans, who depended on the buffalo for their livelihood—attacked the colony in 1815. In 1816, they killed Robert Semple, the colonial governor, and 20 others in the Battle of Seven Oaks. Peace came when the North West Company and the Hudson's Bay Company merged in 1821.

During the 1820s and 1830s, increasing unrest in both Lower Canada and Upper Canada led to a series of rebellions. The economic and political unrest stemmed from the fact that, in each province, economic and political power was held by a small group of individuals and families.

Discontent

Those in power were ultraconservative socially, economically, and politically. They worked in cooperation with the British-controlled government.

- In Upper Canada, the powerful faction was known as the Family Compact.

- In Lower Canada, a similar group was known as the Château Clique (the name was derived from the residence of the governor, the Château Saint-Louis).

Rebellion. On December 7, 1837, a minor armed rebellion broke out. The militia attacked a few hundred militants who had gathered near Toronto under the leadership of William Lyon Mackenzie. Some were captured; two were later convicted of treason and hanged on April 12, 1838.

Mackenzie, however, escaped to the United States. On Navy Island, in the Niagara River, he optimistically proclaimed a Canadian republic. He was arrested for violating the American neutrality laws, and in June 1839 he was sentenced to 18 months in prison.

William Lyon Mackenzie returned to Canada under the Amnesty Act of 1849 and was elected to the House of Assembly in 1851. He retired from politics in 1858. ▶

THE REFORMERS

Militant political reformers demanded self-government, which was not about to be granted by either the Canadian Tories (Conservatives) or the government in London.

- In Upper Canada, the leader of the reformers was William Lyon Mackenzie (1795–1861), a Scot who had come to Canada in 1820. In 1824, he had founded a journal, the *Colonial Advocate*. Many of Mackenzie's reform proposals were extreme.

- In Lower Canada, the reformers were led by Louis-Joseph Papineau (1786–1871), a militia officer in the War of 1812. In 1834, Papineau helped draw up the Ninety-Two Resolutions. The resolutions stated grievances with the existing government and advocated democratic government. They were also extreme in their bitter attacks on the British and colonial administrations.

Louis-Joseph Papineau took refuge in the United States after the rebellions of 1837; later, he went to Paris to live. He returned to Canada in 1845.

Fils de la Liberté. In Lower Canada, the unrest turned into more serious armed conflict. In the autumn of 1837, armed militants calling themselves Patriotes controlled some of the rural areas around Montreal.

- On November 6, 1837, rioting broke out between a Tory club and a Patriote group organized by Louis-Joseph Papineau, the Fils de la Liberté (Sons of Freedom).

- The Patriotes then massed in the Richelieu region and defeated a British force at Saint-Denis.

- On November 25, 1837, the British then routed the Patriotes at Saint-Charles, killing 56 while suffering 3 dead and 18 wounded themselves.

- At Saint-Eustache on December 14, the Patriotes were again defeated, suffering 71 dead to only 1 killed on the British side. Some of these rebels, Papineau among them, took refuge in the United States.

Other militants participated in incursions into Canada from the United States between February and December 1838. Further insurrections flared up in Lower Canada in 1838, with battles taking place during November and December; the Patriotes were defeated in all of them. Martial law was proclaimed and 733 rebels were taken prisoner. Of these, 28 were executed and more than 90 were transported to the penal colony in Australia.

Alexander Baring, 1st Lord Ashburton, negotiated the Ashburton-Webster treaty on behalf of Great Britain and Canada.

New Brunswick. The Ashburton-Webster Treaty gave more than half of the disputed area of 12,000 square miles (31,100 square kilometers) to the United States.

THE AROOSTOOK WAR

While rebellion was taking place in Canada and spilling over into the United States, a border dispute between the two countries brought about a minor clash that became known as the Aroostook War.

- Settlers from New Brunswick and Maine lived in the valley of the Aroostook River.

- The United Kingdom and the United States had never agreed on a boundary in this region, and disputes developed between New Brunswick and Maine loggers.

- The climax came in 1839 when militias from New Brunswick and Maine assembled to fight. No fighting took place, however. Sir John Harvey, lieutenant governor of New Brunswick, and General Winfield Scott, from the United States, agreed on a truce.

Daniel Webster (the American secretary of state) and Alexander Baring, 1st Lord Ashburton (representing Great Britain), settled the issue on August 9, 1842, in the Ashburton-Webster Treaty.

The treaty fixed the boundary between New Brunswick and Maine in part along the St. Croix River. It demonstrated the desire of Great Britain, representing Canada, to settle differences peacefully.

Act of Union

The Rebellions of 1837 made the British government aware of the need for a reform of the Canadian system of government. Those who had rebelled had been extremists, but many shared their general dissatisfaction. The need to replace the governing cliques with more democratic rule became evident.

Lord Durham's Report

The first step toward reform was the appointment of John George Lambton, 1st Earl of Durham, as governor-general and high commissioner to British North America. He arrived in Lower Canada on May 29, 1838, with colonial experts to help him determine a way to keep Canada a contented part of the British Empire. Between May and November 1, he studied the problems in both Upper and Lower Canada.

Durham submitted his "Report on the Affaires of British North America" to the Colonial Office on February 4, 1839. The report contained two significant recommendations.

1. The first, for "responsible government," meant that the government executive would be drawn from the party that held the majority in the elected Assembly.

2. The second held that Upper and Lower Canada would be united as the Province of Canada, containing Canada East (present-day Quebec) and Canada West (present-day Ontario).

On July 23, 1840, this resolution, known as the Act of Union, received royal assent. It became effective in Canada on February 10, 1841.

Union

Several changes followed the Act of Union.

- An elected House of Assembly was provided for, with an equal number of members from each of the two former provinces, as well as an appointed council.

- All legislative procedures were to be conducted in the English language.

- The British government still had the power to impose duties (taxes), but those duties, together with such other revenues as fines, land sales, and seigneurial dues, were to be used by the Province of Canada for its budget.

- Kingston was chosen as the capital on February 10, 1841. On May 10, 1844, however, the capital was moved to Montreal, where it would remain for $5\frac{1}{2}$ years.

Durham's report and the Act of Union did not win unanimous praise. The Tories in both England and Canada, and the members of the Family Compact and the Château Clique, opposed the changes. Nevertheless, the former Upper and Lower Canada consented to work within the act.

Spotlight on... LORD DURHAM

1792–1840

- Born John George Lambton

- Served as an outspoken liberal in the British Parliament from 1813 to 1832

- Played a leading role in the creation of the milestone electoral Reform Bill of 1832, giving most middle-class men the right to vote

- Earned the nickname of "Radical Jack" because of his activities and personality

The Beginning of Self-Government

During the 1840s, several colonial leaders fought for responsible government. These leaders included Robert Baldwin and Louis H. Lafontaine in the Province of Canada and Joseph Howe in Nova Scotia. The British government, however, initially resisted the change. It instructed its governors-general, such as Charles Poulett Thomson, Lord Sydenham, and Charles Theophilus Metcalfe, not to concede to the Reform Party's demands.

The situation was reversed after James Bruce (1811–1863), 8th Earl of Elgin, was commissioned governor-general of Canada on October 1, 1846. He carried new instructions from the British government to concede the right to govern. On December 6, 1847, Elgin dissolved the assembly and, in the following election, Reformers won a majority.

Baldwin and Lafontaine formed a ministry on March 11, 1848. Their government became known as the Great Ministry because of the reforms it undertook. The ministry passed a number of laws, some controversial.

- On August 14, 1848, it repealed the clause in the Act of Union that made English Canada's only official language.
- It passed the Amnesty Act of 1849, granting immunity to all persons who had fled the country after participating in the Rebellions of 1837.
- The Rebellion Losses Bill of 1849 was intended to repay people in Canada East whose property had been damaged during the Rebellion of 1837. (A previous bill in 1841 had compensated people in Canada West.)

Heads of Government, 1841–1867: Province of Canada		
Official	**Title**	**Years**
Charles Edward Poulett Thomson, 1st Baron Sydenham	Governor-General	Feb. 10, 1841–Sept. 19, 1841
Sir Richard Downes Jackson	Administrator	Sept. 24, 1841–Jan. 12, 1842
Sir Charles Bagot	Governor-General	Jan. 12, 1842–Mar. 30, 1843
Charles Theophilus, Baron Metcalfe	Governor-General	Mar. 30, 1843–Nov. 26, 1845
Charles Murray, 2nd Earl Cathcart	Administrator	Nov. 26, 1845–Apr. 24, 1846
	Governor-General	Apr. 24, 1846–Jan. 30, 1847
James Bruce, 8th Earl of Elgin	Governor-General	Jan. 30, 1847–Dec. 19, 1854
Sir Edmund Walker Head	Governor-General	Dec. 19, 1854–Oct. 24, 1861
Charles Stanley, 1st Baron Monck	Governor-General	Oct. 25, 1861–June 30, 1867

- ✔ The early 1800s were marked by an increase in immigration to Canada.
- ✔ Settlement in the Canadian West caused clashes between the settlers and the fur traders and Indians who already lived in the region.
- ✔ In 1837, political and economic unrest led to a series of rebellions, but these rebellions were unsuccessful.
- ✔ In 1839, Lord Durham's report recommended that Upper and Lower Canada unify under a responsible government.
- ✔ The Act of Union (1841) carried out Lord Durham's recommendations.

TOWARD CONFEDERATION

During the 1840s, leaders in some Canadian colonies pushed for responsible government in local affairs. In a system of responsible government, the executive is responsible (answerable) to an elected assembly. The United Kingdom gradually granted all the colonies such government. During the mid-1860s, some colonial leaders argued that Canada needed a strong central government to deal with domestic matters. They started a movement for a confederation (union) of the Canadian colonies. This movement led to the formation of the Dominion of Canada in 1867.

Caught in the Middle

In the middle of the 1800s, a newly united Canada found itself caught in a number of different conflicts—over territory and boundaries, over religious rights and land privileges, and over the role of government. Canada also found itself involved with the civil war that had broken out next door, in the United States.

Land Conflicts

In the 1840s and 1850s, the United States was gradually expanding northward and westward. This concerned Britain and its representatives in Canada. They worked to negotiate boundaries and rights.

Oregon Territory. In 1818, the southern boundary of the Oregon Territory was the 42nd parallel, and the 49th parallel was the northern boundary.

- The two countries agreed to joint occupation of the disputed territory for 10 years, and in 1827, this was extended indefinitely.

- On May 21, 1846, the United States gave England one year's notice that it would end the joint occupation agreement.

- On June 15, the Oregon Treaty defined the boundary from the Rockies to the Pacific along the 49th parallel and gave everything south of that line to the U.S., except for Vancouver Island. (See also page 101.)

British North America still contained sizeable First Nations populations as England and the United States discussed the control over their lands. Eventually, the Indians would lose most of their land to encroaching settlers.

THE NORTHWEST PASSAGE—AGAIN

The European explorers who came to Canada in the 15th century came looking for a northwest passage to Asia. They never found one. In the 19th century, a number of expeditions tried again. Sir John Franklin (1786–1847) of the British navy led several expeditions to explore the Arctic coast.

In 1845, Franklin sailed from England with two ships to seek the northwest passage. On July 26, a whaling ship met his ships in Baffin Bay. That was the last that was ever seen of Franklin, or of his expedition.

Franklin's two ships had become frozen in the ice between Victoria Island and King William Island, near waters that led directly to the Asian shore. They remained there for more than a year. Franklin had died on June 11, 1847. The other members of the expedition abandoned the ships in April 1848 and tried to make their way back to civilization, but all perished.

In 1984, the almost perfectly preserved body of the expedition's petty officer, John Torrington, was discovered in the ice of present-day Nunavut. Examination of the remains suggests that the men may, in fact, have died of lead poisoning from their canned foods.

The Far West. In 1849, Britain leased the colony of Vancouver Island to the Hudson's Bay Company for 10 years for development as an agricultural settlement. The population of the island and the adjacent mainland did not increase much for some time, largely because the Hudson's Bay Company was more interested in its fur trade than in bringing in farmers.

In 1858, however, a gold rush on the region's Fraser River brought an influx of miners to settle the west. This prompted the British Parliament to establish the colony of British Columbia on August 2, 1858. In 1866, Vancouver Island was made part of the colony.

◀ **Sir John Franklin** and his crew met with doom on their search for a northwest passage.

The Vancouver Island colony, which eventually was made part of the colony of British Columbia, is seen here as it appeared around the year 1800. ▼

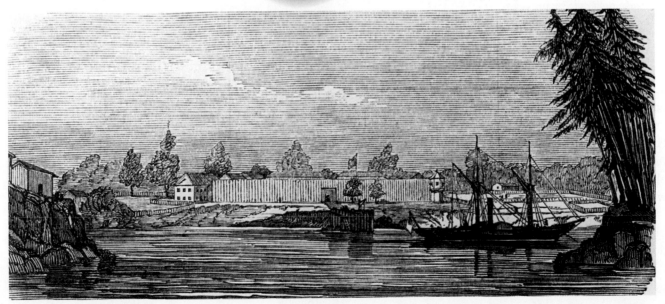

With the beginnings of responsible government in place, the ministries that governed the Canadian colonies began to tackle issues of development and policy. Conflicts continually arose between the liberal and conservative factions, as well as between religious groups.

Canada and the Railroad. Because of its vast distances and scattered population centers, Canada badly needed railroads. Railroad construction and financing would play a major role in Canadian politics for many years.

Domestic Issues

The arrival of the second half of the 19th century was marked by the end of the Baldwin-Lafontaine "Great Ministry." In 1851, Francis Hincks (1807–1885), a Reform leader in Canada West and inspector general in the ministry, replaced Baldwin as leader. Augustin-Norbert Morin (1803–1865), who had been speaker of the Assembly of Lower Canada, took Lafontaine's place.

Hincks and the Railroads. Hincks was interested in economic affairs, especially railroad promotion.

- In 1852, Hincks secured the incorporation of the Grand Trunk Railway.

- In 1867, it became the longest rail system in the world, running for 1,100 miles (1,770 kilometers) from Portland, Maine, westward to Sarnia, at the southern end of Lake Huron.

In 1854, Hincks's ministry with Morin ended when he was found to be involved in questionable financial transactions connected with the railway.

MacNab and Morin. Morin was a Reformer, an advocate of responsible government and of the political rights of French Canadians within Canada. He remained a leader in the next ministry with Sir Allan Napier MacNab (1798–1862), who had been elected to the provincial assembly in 1841. MacNab was a leader of the Tory and Conservative groups, and later, of the Liberal-Conservative coalition. Moderates on both sides, whether French or English, shared the desire for economic development.

Several important pieces of legislation were passed by the MacNab-Morin coalition.

MacNab-Morin Legislation	
Clergy Reserves	**Seigneurial Tenure**
• The Constitutional Act of 1791 had stated that one-seventh of all land granted to settlers was to be used for the support of a Protestant clergy. • This act greatly angered the Catholics of Upper Canada and even some Protestants.	• Those who had seigneurial tenure rights had certain judicial powers and were conceded privileges in church affairs.
• In 1854, a bill was passed that called for profits from the sale of these lands to be given to the municipalities instead.	• In 1854, these rights were terminated. • New laws permitted tenants to claim the rights to their lands.

CANADA AND THE AMERICAN CIVIL WAR

Because of its relationship with Great Britain, Canada became involved, involuntarily, in the American Civil War (1861–1865). (See also pages 128–131.)

- The British government supported the Confederacy in the South.

- The majority of Canadians favored the Union in the North and opposed slavery; however, a minority of Tories disliked the democratic North. They feared another attempt at invasion.

- England allowed armed ships for the Confederacy to be built in Canada's ports.

- Canada could not prevent agents of the South from using its ports as refuges and bases.

British support of the South outraged northern Americans, and they took out some of their resentment on their northern neighbor. When it seemed that Britain and the United States might go to war over English support of the South, 15,000 British troops were sent to Canada to ward off possible invasion.

Support for the Union. Though Great Britain had thrown its support to the South, Canada had actually made large contributions to the Union cause.

- Canada had long been the final haven on the Underground Railroad through which slaves escaped from the Southern states. About 40,000 African Americans ended up in Canada.

- According to one historian, 53,532 men of British North America served in the Union army. About two-thirds of them were French Canadians.

Effects of the Civil War. The American Civil War had some long-term effects on Canadian policies.

- Fear of U.S. invasion caused more people to support confederation, or uniting Canada under a central government.

- A long-standing trade agreement between Canada and the United States was cancelled, partly because of Great Britain's support for the South.

Confederate Raids. An extremist element among the Confederates slipped into Canada to use it as a base for raids into the United States. One plan was to free Confederate prisoners of war held in camps near the border. Another was to incite an uprising in Chicago.

In October 1864, a band of 40 Confederate soldiers, led by Bennett Young, raided St. Albans, Vermont, from Canadian soil. The men set fires, took $200,000 from three banks, killed one man, and wounded another. A Canadian judge, on technical grounds, ordered the raiders released after they had been captured (although the stolen money was returned to the banks).

Canada was one of the destinations for slaves escaping to freedom via the Underground Railroad.

Confederation

By the mid-19th century, both Canada and England sensed a need to consolidate British North America. They wanted to create a confederation that would eventually include the vast region from east coast to west coast, and from the U.S. boundary to the Arctic north. There was also a movement to bring the land of the Hudson's Bay Company under Canadian government control.

Causes of Confederation

Widespread support for confederation had several causes, both internal and external. The chief causes were political deadlock, the threat of U.S. expansion, and the threat of invasion.

Toward Confederation

The idea of confederation was not new. Proposals for different forms of union had been made as early as 1783.

- Lord Durham, the governor-general whose report resulted in the 1841 Act of Union, suggested in the report that confederation of British North America might be beneficial.

- In the early 1850s, there was a move for confederation of the maritime provinces, comprising New Brunswick, Nova Scotia, and Prince Edward Island.

- On August 7, 1858, George Etienne Cartier included the concept of confederation in his party's platform, but it was rejected on the grounds of "lack of support" in British North America.

ESSENTIALS

The benefits of union were considered to be

- more effective defense for the Canadian colonies.
- improved economic growth.
- improved relations between the French-speaking and English-speaking sections of the colonies.

Causes of Confederation	
Political deadlock	• Representation in the Legislative Assembly was inequitable for both Canada East and Canada West. • People thought that the number of seats in the legislature should be based on population.
U.S. expansion	• The U.S. adopted a policy of Manifest Destiny, or westward expansion. • Some in Canada feared the U.S. would attempt to take over Canadian lands.
Threat of invasion	• Beginning in June 1866, the Irish Fenian Brotherhood began conducting raids in Canada. • Fenian raids remained a threat for five years, illustrating the need for unified defense.

The Charlottetown Conference. During the mid-1860s, a group of political leaders in the Province of Canada finally decided that a strong union of all the colonies offered the best solution to their problems. The leaders of this group were

- Sir John A. Macdonald, a conservative from the old area of Upper Canada.
- George Etienne Cartier, a conservative from Lower Canada.
- George Brown, a liberal journalist and member of the colonial assembly.

In September 1864, they met with political leaders from New Brunswick, Nova Scotia, and Prince Edward Island in Charlottetown, Prince Edward Island. At this meeting, called the Charlottetown Conference, the delegates from the Province of Canada convinced the leaders of the other colonies that a confederation of the North American colonies should be created.

Delegates to the Quebec Conference, shown here, became known as the Fathers of Confederation. ▼

The Quebec Conference. The delegates agreed to hold another session in Quebec from October 10 to 27, 1864. Newfoundland joined this conference, with two delegates. Sir Etienne-Paschal Taché of Canada East led the conference.

By October 27, when the conference adjourned, it had adopted 72 resolutions on the matter of confederation. Still, disagreement remained over which kind of confederation would be best.

- One side wanted a national government that would leave the provinces with little power.
- The other side wanted to safeguard provincial rights.

In the end, the provincial rights advocates won out, but only the Province of Canada formally adopted the plan.

The British North America Act. On March 8, 1867, after a final conference in London with both the Canadians and the British represented, Parliament passed the British North America Act (since 1982, called the Constitution Act, 1867).

It received royal assent on March 29 and declared that on July 1, 1867, the Dominion of Canada would be established. (Read excerpts of the Act on pages 1006–1007.)

CONFEDERATION POETS

By 1888, a group of young poets called the Confederation poets began to be published. These writers described nature and regional scenes using forms and rhythms that showed a growing freedom from European styles. Pauline Johnson, daughter of a Mohawk chief and an English mother, became especially famous for her public performances and poetry about Indian life.

Other Confederation Poets

Duncan Campbell Scott

Sir Charles G. D. Roberts

Archibald Lampman

Bliss Carman

Wilfred Campbell

The original plan was to name the new confederation the Kingdom of Canada; however, some feared that there would be a hostile reaction to this name in the United States.

In 1867, the British North America act (now known as the Constitution Act, 1867) unified the Canadian colonies. The act established the Dominion of Canada, and was intended to improve the region's defenses, economy, and cultural relations.

The Dominion of Canada

In 1867, the new Dominion consisted of only four provinces.

- Ontario (formerly Canada West or Upper Canada)
- Quebec (formerly Canada East or Lower Canada)
- New Brunswick
- Nova Scotia

Although the other provinces, Prince Edward Island and Newfoundland, had participated in all the discussions of confederation, they did not join until 1873 and 1949, respectively. The city of Ottawa, in southeastern Ontario, just across the Ottawa River from the Province of Quebec, became the capital of the Dominion.

Government. The Dominion of Canada had an upper house, called the Senate, and a House of Commons.

Dominion of Canada—Government —1867		
	Senate	House of Commons
	72 senators, appointed by the governor-general	81 members, determined by population
Province	Number of Senators	Number of Seats
Ontario	24	82
Quebec	24	65
New Brunswick	12	19
Nova Scotia	12	15

Balance of Power. The British North America Act gave Canada internal self-government, but the British Parliament still held reserve powers, and could change the governmental system.

- Executive authority continued to be vested in the British monarch.
- In effect, Canada had to ask Great Britain for permission to amend its constitution.
- Foreign affairs remained in British hands.

Provincial Authority. The division of powers between the federal government and the provinces was also spelled out.

- Each province was to have a lieutenant governor appointed by the governor-general.
- Although the provincial lieutenant governor had extensive powers, each province had its own legislature. The provinces also had almost unlimited power over educational policy.
- Independence of judges was safeguarded. Provisions were made for admitting other colonies as provinces of the federal Dominion.
- Special provision was also made for "immediate construction" by the federal government of an intercolonial railway.

NATIVE AMERICANS AND CONFEDERATION

Under the Constitution Act of 1867, the new government of Canada continued the policy of confining Indians to reserves. The superintendent general of Indian affairs was placed in charge of the reserves and of government dealings with the Indians. Through the years, superintendents negotiated a number of treaties for western Indian lands. From then on, the Canadian government focused on assimilating (integrating) Indians into mainstream Canadian society.

JOHN A. MACDONALD

Dominion of Canada. In 1880, and again in 1895, Great Britain transferred to Canada territory it claimed in North America. The Dominion at that time included all of North America north of the United States, except for Alaska and Newfoundland, which remained a separate British colony.

1815–1891

- Born in Scotland, he came to Canada with his family as a child.

- He was elected to the Canadian legislative assembly in 1844 as a Conservative.

- In 1864, he became one of the leaders of the Great Coalition, a ministry that pledged to bring about confederation. (The other two leaders were George Etienne Cartier and George Brown—Brown, a Liberal, had resigned in December 1865.)

- Macdonald was one of the most influential members of the Charlottetown Conference in 1864 and at the Quebec conference that followed.

✔ The newly united Canada faced a number of conflicts over land, religious rights, and the role of government.

✔ The Grand Trunk Railroad, the longest rail system in the world at the time, demonstrated Canada's effort to consolidate its vast territory.

✔ Canada became involved in the American Civil War because of its relationship with Britain, which supported the South.

✔ After much negotiation, the Canadian colonies were consolidated under the British North America Act, 1867.

✔ The new Dominion of Canada consisted of Ontario, Quebec, New Brunswick, and Nova Scotia. John A. Macdonald became its first prime minister.

Macdonald and the New Dominion

John A. Macdonald became the first prime minister of the Dominion on July 1, 1867. Macdonald was eager to increase the influence of the Dominion. His first step was to acquire Rupert's Land, the land controlled by the Hudson's Bay Company.

In 1863, the company's shares were taken over by the International Financial Society. On June 22, 1869, this society agreed officially to sell Rupert's Land to the Dominion for £300,000. This land became much of the area of Canada's western provinces, the Northwest Territories, and later Nunavut. Gradually, the Dominion of Canada expanded from its initial four provinces.

MÉTIS REBELLIONS

The early days of the new Dominion of Canada were not entirely peaceful. The move to take over the Hudson's Bay Company land and to establish the new province of Manitoba aroused mixed feelings among the area's inhabitants, especially the Métis—people of mixed white and American Indian ancestry. (The word Métis comes from an old French word that meant mixed.) They thought, correctly, that the new settlers would disrupt their nomadic way of life, which was built around the fur trade and the hunting of buffalo. In two separate rebellions, the Métis attempted to resist the settlers.

Western Unrest

For the most part, the Métis did not hold any titles to the lands they used for hunting or farming. They feared that the Canadian government would not honor their informal claims. In 1868, a company of road builders came to the Red River area. In 1869, surveyors followed, to plan out townships. Both trespassed on farmland of the Métis, giving weight to their fears.

The Red River Rebellion

As the government takeover seemed more and more likely, a leader—Louis Riel—stepped forward and began organizing a resistance among the Métis.

- On December 1, 1869, William McDougall (1822–1905), representing the Dominion, crossed the border into what had been Rupert's Land and declared Canadian sovereignty.

- On December 8, Riel responded by proclaiming an independent provisional government. The rebellion had begun.

Uprising. Riel and his followers took possession of Fort Garry on the site of present-day Winnipeg. A pro-Canadian government group raided the fort. They were captured and imprisoned by the Métis. One of their leaders, Surveyor Thomas Scott, was executed by firing squad on March 4, 1870.

The government ordered Colonel Garnet Wolseley to lead troops into the Red River Valley, but Riel began negotiations with the government instead. The government agreed to set aside land for the Métis; still, many moved westward into Saskatchewan.

◄ **Buffalo** were the crux of nomadic ways of life in Manitoba and Saskatchewan. They provided food for people on the move.

Spotlight on...

LOUIS RIEL

1844–1885

Louis Riel led the Métis people in two rebellions against the Canadian government.

- Born in the Red River Settlement and educated in Montreal

- Elected to the House of Commons in 1873 and 1874, but was denied his seat

- Suffered a mental breakdown, and was in institutions in Quebec for 2 years, from January 1876 to 1878

- Hanged for treason after leading the Northwest Rebellion

Northwest Rebellion

In 1885, revolt flared up again with the start of the Northwest Rebellion. Louis Riel was again the leader of the Métis. This time, he was joined by two Cree Indian chiefs, Big Bear (d. 1888) and Poundmaker (c. 1842–1886).

The rebellion stemmed from discontent on the part of whites, Métis, and Indians in Saskatchewan.

- The Indians and Métis saw the buffalo, on which they depended for food, disappearing.

- Farms and railroads were destroying their way of life.

- The English population wanted representative government and a lowering of tariffs.

A petition listing all the grievances was sent to Ottawa on December 16, 1884. The federal government promised to investigate the issues.

Revolt. Riel talked again of forming an independent government, but he had lost the support of the English-speaking settlers and of many of the Métis.

- In March 1885, Riel and Gabriel Dumont seized a church and set up a provisional government. Riel surrendered less than 2 months later.

- On March 30, Poundmaker and his Indians overran a settlement. The residents escaped to safety.

- On April 2, Big Bear massacred all but four of the whites at Frog Lake.

Effects. Riel was condemned to death for treason and hanged on November 16, 1885. The two Indian chiefs were sentenced to prison.

Echoes of the rebellion and its aftermath were heard for some time in the east. Many in Quebec regarded Riel as a hero who had defended French-Canadian rights. His hanging caused tension between French- and English-speaking Canadians.

THE MOUNTIES

In 1873, partly as a result of the western rebellions, Canada established the North-West Mounted Police, often called the Mounties.

- Their original tasks were to control the Indians, to protect Indians from traders who supplied them with whiskey, and to police the new Dominion territory.

- In 1920 the official name became the Royal Canadian Mounted Police (RCMP).

◄ **The RCMP** now provides provincial police service for all but Ontario and Quebec, which have their own provincial police. Nationally, the RCMP investigates organized crime, narcotics, and fraud.

A CHANGING SOCIETY: 1885–1914

The young Dominion of Canada developed rapidly during the late 1800s. A railway connected western and eastern Canada, and courageous pioneers spread across the west. By the early 1900s, the Dominion had nine provinces spanning the continent. Huge wheat crops, rich mines, and new industries brought further economic expansion in this period. In addition, Canada became increasingly involved in international affairs.

Canada in the World

Although the Constitution Act of 1867 made Canada internally self-governing, it was still subordinate to Great Britain in foreign matters. In the late 1800s, however, issues arose between Great Britain and the United States that affected Canada directly. In dealing with these issues, Canada began to stake its claim in world events.

Disputes and Diplomacy

Canada's relationship to Great Britain was demonstrated during the negotiations of the Treaty of Washington in 1871. Prime Minister Macdonald attended the meetings, but only as a member of the British delegation. The treaty addressed two Canadian disputes (see chart).

In a gesture that acknowledged that Canada had an official part to play in such negotiations, the British asked the Canadian Parliament to ratify the treaty.

Treaty of Washington, 1871—Canadian Issues		
Issue	**Details**	**Solution**
Fishing Rights in Canadian Waters	• The Reciprocity Treaty of 1854 had given the United States certain rights. • The U.S. had repealed the treaty in 1866. • Canada imposed a license fee on American fishermen, which they tried to evade.	• The Americans were given inshore rights for a 12-year period in exchange for $5 million and free entry of Canadian fish to the U.S. market. • The British would reimburse Canadians for losses from the Fenian raids into Canada from the United States.
San Juan/ Northwest Boundary	• The line between British Columbia and the state of Washington was disputed. • There was a question of who owned several islands, especially San Juan Island. • The island had been occupied by U.S. troops in 1859.	• Joint occupation was agreed on. • The new treaty provided that Emperor William I of Germany would arbitrate the issue. • In 1872 he gave the island to the United States.

Early Diplomacy. In 1879, Canada began, in a small way, to have its own diplomatic representatives abroad. With the consent of the British government, Alexander Galt (1817–1893) was appointed to negotiate trade agreements with France and Spain.

- Galt had been a member of the Great Coalition cabinet, active in the movement for confederation, and minister of finance in the first federal cabinet.

- He was knighted for his work on the fishery settlement in the Treaty of Washington.

- He became Canada's first high commissioner in London, a post he held from 1880 to 1883.

In 1882, Hector Fabre (1834–1910) was named agent general for Canada in Paris. He held the agent general post until his death.

The Boer War. Canada's role in the British Empire became an issue with the outbreak of the Boer War (1899–1902) in South Africa. (See page 528.)

- English Canadians, for the most part, wanted to send troops to support the British cause.

- French Canadians opposed involvement.

The government, under Liberal prime minister Wilfrid Laurier, decided to send a token force of 1,000 infantrymen to join with the British forces. Some 7,000 Canadian volunteers eventually served there. Laurier's action caused a rift in the Liberal Party—the Quebec branch had opposed helping England.

THE ALASKAN BORDER

A long-standing dispute over the boundary between the Alaskan panhandle and British Columbia was settled in 1903 by a commission made up of two Canadians, three Americans, and Lord Chief Justice Alverstone of England.

The question of where the boundary should be located had become important in recent years because of the gold rush in the Yukon in 1896. The British representative sided with the Americans, and awarded the United States almost all it claimed.

The implication to the Canadians was that Great Britain was so eager to have America on its side in world affairs that it would sacrifice Canadian interests to do so.

◀ **The Yukon Gold Rush** brought thousands of prospectors, like the ones shown here, to the area. Great Britain had given the territory to Canada just before the rush; it soon became important to decide the region's Alaskan boundary.

Canada At Home

As the 20th century approached, Canada experienced a significant shift in political control. The Conservatives had dominated the country—with only a 4-year break—since Confederation in 1867. Wilfrid Laurier and the Liberal Party took control of the government in 1896 and brought a different outlook to the Dominion. Under Laurier, Canada enjoyed great prosperity, added new provinces, and experienced great technological progress.

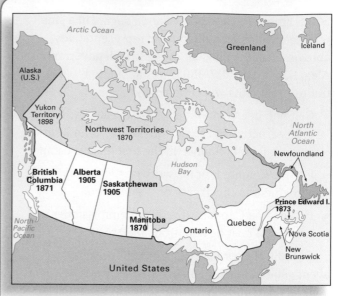

Canada in 1905. By 1905, Canada consisted of nine provinces and two territories. This map shows the date when each new province or territory became part of Canada.

fyi!

John A. Macdonald again became prime minister in 1878.

- *In 1880, the Canadian Pacific Railway Company was incorporated.*

- *The railway line was completed in 1885.*

THE CANADIAN PACIFIC SCANDAL

In 1871, British Columbia had joined the Dominion of Canada, but only on the condition that a transcontinental railroad be built, connecting them to the east. Prime Minister Macdonald's moves to carry out the promise to British Columbia ended in political disaster for him.

The government chose a company headed by Sir Hugh Allan to build the railway. Scandal broke out in 1873, stalling the project.

- It was revealed that Macdonald's Conservative Party had accepted a campaign contribution of about $300,000 from Allan in 1872.

- Leaders of the opposing Liberal Party charged that Allan's group got the railroad contract because of its campaign gift.

Macdonald had not used any of the money for his own election, but he resigned as prime minister. In November 1873, Alexander Mackenzie, leader of the Liberal Party, became prime minister.

The Canadian Pacific scandal, centered around the building of a transcontinental railroad, forced Prime Minister Macdonald's resignation.

Mackenzie's Government

Alexander Mackenzie (1822–1892), a Liberal, succeeded the disgraced Macdonald.

- Mackenzie's government introduced the secret ballot and the 1-day national election.

- He strengthened Canadian self-rule by dealing directly with the United States.

- In 1875, he established the Supreme Court of Canada. This decreased British control over Canada's legal matters.

Mackenzie was unable to complete the transcontinental railroad that had been started by Macdonald. British Columbia, to which the railway had been promised, threatened to secede. The public outrage, combined with an economic downturn, contributed to the end of his administration.

Laurier and the Liberals

Macdonald's death in 1891 resulted in a breakup of the Conservative Party. In the election of June 23, 1896, Wilfrid Laurier (1841–1919) became the first French-Canadian prime minister. Laurier saw the Dominion as more important than its parts, and Canada as a nation independent of British Empire interests though loyal to the Crown.

TECHNOLOGY MILESTONES

The beginning of the 20th century saw a number of Canadian technological advances.

- On December 12, 1901, the first wireless transatlantic communication in history—the Morse code letter *s*—was sent from Guglielmo Marconi's transmitting station in Cornwall, England, to St. John's, Canada.

- On February 23, 1909, John A. D. McCurdy, a Canadian engineering student, made the first successful Canadian airplane flight.

- In the early 1900s, Adam Beck helped bring public electrical service to Canada.

CANADA UNDER LAURIER

Immigration. Canada's population soared during Laurier's administration, encouraged in large part by his minister of the interior, Clifford Sifton. More than 2 million immigrants, most of them from Europe, flocked to Canada between 1896 and 1911. Many settled in such cities as Montreal, Toronto, and Winnipeg. But hundreds of thousands of others took up farming on the prairies.

Industry. Canada's economy flourished under Laurier.

- Farmers in the Prairie Provinces produced huge wheat harvests.

- Canada's flour-milling, steel, and textile industries grew quickly.

- Nova Scotia coal mines thrived, and mining areas opened or expanded in Ontario, British Columbia, and the Klondike region of northern Canada.

- New hydroelectric power plants and two new transcontinental railroads, the Grand Trunk Pacific and the Canadian Northern, contributed to the nation's prosperity.

Prime Minister Wilfrid Laurier, fluent in English and French, worked to unite French-speaking and English-speaking Canadians for the good of the country.

Reform and Rights

In the late 19th and early 20th centuries, some groups began to work toward reforming Canadian institutions, such as education and suffrage (voting rights). The rights of women and of First Nations peoples, as well as of French-speaking Canadians, became a matter of concern.

Education

Two major acts of the late 1800s led to changes in Canada's educational system. Both touched on the tensions that existed between different religious and cultural groups.

JESUITS' ESTATES ACT

On July 12, 1888, the Quebec provincial legislature, under Premier Honoré Mercier (1840–1894), passed the Jesuits' Estates Act. The law was meant to compensate the Jesuits, a Roman Catholic religious order, for land that had belonged to them before Britain awarded it to the Province of Canada in 1831.

- The land had been given to the Jesuits to provide funds for education, so in 1832 the revenues were assigned for educational purposes.

- Mercier's act appropriated $400,000 for this purpose and stipulated that the pope would decide how the funds were to be distributed.

Ultimately the Jesuits were to receive $160,000 to cover all claims; Université de Laval was to receive $140,000; and $100,000 was to be shared among certain dioceses. The act also granted an additional $60,000 to Protestant institutions of higher learning.

The act was popular in Quebec but not in Ontario, especially among the Orange Order, a militant Protestant group. Efforts were made to get Prime Minister Macdonald to cancel the act, but Macdonald refused, claiming that education was the responsibility of the provinces.

MANITOBA SCHOOLS ACT

The Manitoba Schools Act of March 31, 1890, ignited a similar controversy between the French- and English-speaking people of Canada. When the Province of Manitoba was created, the school system was to have both Protestant and Roman Catholic schools. As time went on, however, immigration into Manitoba became predominantly that of English-speaking (and generally Protestant) people. This migration changed the balance in the schools and other institutions.

- D'Alton McCarthy, a conservative Protestant who had voted against the Jesuits' Estates Act, opposed the use of French outside Quebec. He advocated for a monolingual (one-language) school system in Manitoba.

- Denominational schools and the use of the French language in schools were abolished.

- In 1897, a new Liberal ministry in Ottawa worked out an agreement: any school in Manitoba attended by 10 or more students who spoke a language other than English would provide instruction for those pupils in their own language.

In the long run, however, this arrangement did not work. In 1916, a new law made English the only language to be used in the schools for instructional purposes.

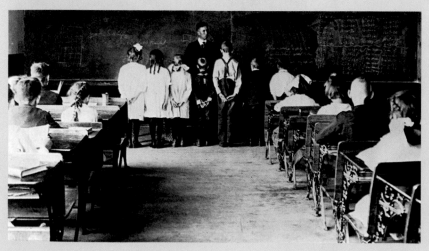

◀ **Schools in Canada** did not resolve the issue of bilingual education until the 1970s, despite efforts such as the Manitoba Schools Act.

Women's Rights

Like women in the United States, Canadian women had to fight for suffrage, or voting rights, as well as the right to serve in federal office. The fight was led by suffragists such as Nellie McClung of Manitoba and Ella Maud Murray of Nova Scotia.

- In January 1916, Manitoba was the first province to grant women voting rights.
- Saskatchewan and Alberta also granted women provincial (local) voting rights in 1916.
- In 1917, women in the military were permitted to vote in federal elections.
- In 1918, the Canada Elections Act gave all Canadian women over the age of 21 the right to vote.

The Famous Five. Women's rights groups also worked toward protecting women in other ways. For example, in 1928, the Canadian Supreme Court decided that "persons," as defined by the British North America Act of 1867, did not include women. Therefore, women could not be permitted to serve in the Senate. A group called the "Famous Five"—Emily Murphy, Irene Parlby, Nellie McClung, Louise Crummy McKinney, and Henrietta Muir Edwards—appealed the decision, and in 1929 "persons" was defined as meaning both men and women.

Nellie McClung, far right, attends the unveiling of a plaque commemorating the efforts of the "Famous Five."

- ✔ By the early 1900s, the Dominion of Canada had nine provinces.

- ✔ In the late 1800s, Canada slowly began taking part in international affairs; its relationship with Great Britain, too, began to shift.

- ✔ The political dominance of the Conservative Party ended with the elections of Alexander Mackenzie and Sir Wilfrid Laurier, both Liberals.

- ✔ Under Laurier, Canada enjoyed a period of growth and prosperity.

- ✔ Reform movements in the late 19th and early 20th centuries addressed education reform, women's rights, and First Nations rights.

First Nations Rights

The Canadian government focused on assimilating (integrating) Indians into mainstream Canadian society.

- Laws called for elected tribal governments to replace traditional hereditary leadership.
- Other laws allowed the government to order Indian children to be sent to boarding schools, where they could be taught white customs.
- Laws of the late 1800s banned certain Indian religious practices.

The Indian Act of 1876 summarized who could legally be considered an Indian. People who met the legal definition did not have to pay taxes on reserve property. But they could not vote in provincial and federal elections and were denied many other civil rights.

The Indian Act also offered *enfranchisement*. In choosing to become enfranchised, Indian men gained the right to vote and other privileges held by non-Indians—but lost their legal and treaty rights as Indians. An Indian woman became enfranchised if she married a non-Indian man.

WORLD WAR I AND AFTER

In 1914, the assassination of Austria-Hungary's Archduke Franz Ferdinand sparked a war throughout all of Europe. World War I would turn out to be the most destructive war the world had yet seen. (See pages 534–537.) On August 4, 1914, the United Kingdom declared war on Germany. This meant that Canada, as a dominion of the British Empire, was at war as well. Canada's contribution to the war effort would have long-term economic, social, and political effects on the Dominion.

World War I: Canadian Military Contributions		
Battle/Campaign	Date	Canadian Efforts
Ypres	April 1915	Canadian soldiers helped halt the first gas attack in the history of warfare.
Somme	July 1916	Canadians fought in several desperate battles, suffering high casualties. They established a reputation for valor here.
Vimy Ridge	April 9–10, 1917	Canadian troops stormed and captured Vimy Ridge, which the Germans had used to fire artillery at Allied troops.
Amiens	August 8, 1918	Canadian troops spearheaded breakthroughs at the Hindenburg line and Amiens, toward the end of the war.

Canada and the Great War

The war created a tremendous burst of patriotism in Canada. Thousands of Canadians rushed to volunteer for military duty. Many French-speaking Canadians, however, were less than enthusiastic about serving in the army. They felt that their language was a barrier to promotion. French speakers were underrepresented during the war, especially in the higher military ranks.

Participation

By the time the war ended in 1918, Canada had put 628,000 men and women in uniform, about two-thirds of whom saw service overseas. Casualties were high, with 59,544 dead or missing (almost identical in terms of lives and expense to that of the United States), and about 175,000 wounded—and Canada's population at the time was only 7.5 million people.

One reason for the high casualty totals was the way in which the Canadian troops were used—typically as shock troops, leading advances and attacks.

Battles. Canadian troops first saw combat in April 1915. They were quickly distinguished by their spirit and military skill.

Canada's World War I memorial stands on Vimy Ridge in France, which in 1917 was captured and held by a mostly Canadian force. The French had tried to capture the ridge since 1914.

CONSCRIPTION CRISIS

On the home front during the war, a bitter political battle arose over the issue of conscription (the draft).

When the war began, Prime Minister Sir Robert L. Borden had promised that there would be no drafting of troops. By 1917, however, the war had gone on longer than expected, with high casualties, and volunteer numbers declined.

Prime Minister Borden's government introduced the Military Service Bill in June 1917. The struggle over it was a main factor in bringing a new political party into power.

- An election on December 17 was fought between the Laurier Liberals, who opposed conscription, and the Unionists, led by Borden.

- The Unionists triumphed, winning 153 seats in the House of Commons.

628,000 Canadian soldiers, like the ones shown drilling here, fought in World War I. The need for more soldiers prompted a controversial draft law. Riots flared up over conscription during March and April of 1918, in Quebec City.

Postwar Canada

Canada's participation in the war enabled it to act more freely in establishing its own foreign policies.

- At the Paris Peace Conference in France, Canada had its own representatives.

- It signed the Versailles Treaty on June 28, 1919, as a full national state.

- Canada began to expand its own diplomatic service and first exchanged ministers with the United States in 1927.

Domestic Effects. The war also brought broad economic changes to the country.

- Agriculture expanded with the demand for food.

- Industry also grew with the building of steel mills and shipyards.

Overall, the economy grew by 20 percent in this period. On the other hand, a growing demand for goods and a high level of war debt brought about inflation. The cost of living increased by 60 percent between the start of the war and 1918.

THE HALIFAX EXPLOSION

- In Halifax, Nova Scotia, on December 6, 1917, two ships carrying out wartime efforts for the Allies collided, causing an explosion.

- The disaster killed more than 2,000 people, injured thousands, and wrecked much of the city.

- Every single building in Halifax was damaged.

The wartime atmosphere also speeded the granting of women's suffrage. The Prairie Provinces allowed it in 1916, and others followed. The right to vote in Canada-wide elections was granted in all provinces except Quebec by 1922. On April 13, 1925, Newfoundland granted the vote to women, though it did not attain provincial status until 1949. Quebec did not give the vote to women until 1940.

Between the Wars

After World War I, Canada found itself in a state of change. It was shifting out of its former position as a British Dominion, and coming into its own on the international stage. It was also entering into a new industrial age. Before long, however, the Great Depression would raise new questions about the role of government and Canada's vulnerability to hard times in other lands.

Domestic Troubles

In the years after World War I, unrest mounted at home.

- Inflation raised the cost of living.
- Workers throughout Canada demanded higher wages, better working conditions, and recognition of their unions.
- Farmers wanted relief from low crop prices.

Dissatisfied farmers formed political parties in almost every province. Farmer parties won control of the provincial government in Ontario in 1919 and in Alberta in 1921. In the national election of 1921, the Liberal Party gained a majority of the seats in the House of Commons, and William Lyon Mackenzie King became prime minister.

King and the Progressives. King was chosen leader of the Liberal Party in 1919 and rose to be prime minister after the election of December 6, 1921. King sought the support of the new Progressive Party.

This political group was organized in 1920, chiefly as the voice of western farmers who thought they were neglected by the government in Ottawa. The Progressives won 65 seats in the 1921 election, 15 more than the Conservatives, making them the second largest party in Parliament.

Scandal. King's government was soon threatened by scandal. Facing a vote of censure in 1926, King asked the governor-general, Lord Byng, to dissolve Parliament. Byng refused, and King responded by resigning—without a successor.

Conservative Arthur Meighen was chosen to replace King, but the Liberals later won a general election, and King became prime minister again.

The Great Depression

On October 29, 1929, the New York Stock Exchange experienced a record crash. (See page 175.) It was the beginning of a long period of worldwide depression, and Canada was not immune. Agriculture was hit especially hard.

- Wheat production shrank from 567 million bushels in 1928 to 182 million by 1937.
- The price of wheat by the end of 1932—38 cents a bushel—did not cover the cost of growing it.
- Drought in 1934 and 1937 ruined many crops.

The depression in agriculture had a ripple effect throughout the country: railroads lost millions of dollars in freight revenues because farm production was down. Demand for manufactured goods slumped drastically, and construction activity slowed. By 1935, fully one-tenth of the population, both urban and rural, was receiving some kind of government assistance.

William Lyon Mackenzie King (1874–1950) was the grandson of the 19th-century leader William Lyon Mackenzie. King entered Parliament as a Liberal in 1909 and the next year became a member of the cabinet as minister for labor.

The Great Depression. With an estimated 23 percent of the labor force out of work by 1933, many Canadians emigrated to the United States, where the situation turned out to be no better.

now you Know!

✔ When the United Kingdom declared war on Germany in 1914, Canada—as a dominion of the United Kingdom—was also at war.

✔ On the home front, a battle over conscription (the draft) led to a Unionist election victory as well as riots in Quebec.

✔ After the war, Canada took a larger part in international affairs.

✔ The Great Depression brought high unemployment and low productivity; Prime Minister Richard B. Bennett proposed sweeping reforms, but they were later found to be largely unconstitutional.

Bennett and the Conservatives. Unemployment was the chief issue in the election of 1930. King's government was defeated, and the Conservatives came to power under Richard B. Bennett. Bennett's government established more than 200 relief camps for single, unemployed men and spent hundreds of millions of dollars to aid the needy. The new administration promised to

- end unemployment by raising tariff barriers—eliminating competition from foreign goods.
- stimulate the economy by building railroads, starting work on the St. Lawrence Seaway, and constructing a national highway.

Bennett hoped that the higher tariffs would lead to new jobs; unfortunately, other nations had also raised their tariffs, hurting Canadian exports. The tariffs reduced imports and kept unemployment from being as high as it might have been, but raised costs and did not increase purchasing power.

Reform. In January 1935, Bennett suddenly announced a change of course: like President Franklin D. Roosevelt in the United States, he called for strong action by the federal government to deal directly with economic problems. Canada's Parliament enacted legislation that established

- minimum wages.
- hours of work per week.
- unemployment insurance.
- loans and credits for farmers.
- control of unfair trade practices.

These measures, however, did not remain in effect for long. Faced with court tests in 1937, they were held to be unconstitutional by the Privy Council in England.

Hard times continued, and many Canadians blamed Bennett. A federal election on October 14, 1935, put the Liberal Party in office with a large majority of the seats in the House of Commons. William Lyon Mackenzie King became prime minister once more.

WORLD WAR II

The 1920s and 1930s in Canada had been marked by economic instability and conflicts over the role of the federal and provincial governments. These conflicts, however, were soon overshadowed by World War II. Great Britain declared war on Germany on September 3, 1939, and Canada followed on September 10. The war—which ended with an Allied victory in 1945—would turn out to be the most destructive war in history. It would have long-term effects on Canada's economy, population, and role in the world.

World War II

In addition to providing troops overseas, the Canadian government lent billions of dollars to the war cause. It sent the British people large quantities of food during the Battle of Britain. Canadian factories built thousands of planes, ships, and weapons.

Military Involvement

At the outbreak of war, Canada's armed forces consisted of

- an army of 4,500 regular soldiers and 60,000 militia reservists.
- a Royal Canadian Air Force of about 4,500.
- a navy made up of 1,800 men and 13 ships.

In all, Canada put about 1 million men and women into uniform: nearly 700,000 in the ground forces, 220,000 in the air force, and 90,000 in the navy. By the end of the war, more than 90,000 had been killed or wounded. (See also pages 552–555.)

The War at Home. Canada's economy expanded greatly during World War II. By the end of the war, the government had invested $1.5 billion in the war industry. As a result, Canada grew into a fully developed industrial state. The wartime government also adopted several important social programs.

- Unemployment insurance (1940)
- Financial aid for children (1944)
- Veterans' benefits program (1945)

JAPANESE CANADIANS AND THE WAR

The war proved tragic for Canadians of Japanese descent. The Japanese bombing of Pearl Harbor had created widespread distrust. In February 1942, the Canadian government began to place about 21,000 Japanese Canadians in camps and isolated towns in Alberta, British Columbia, Manitoba, and Ontario. Their rights were not restored until 1949. Most of the Japanese Canadians lost their homes and businesses.

BUILDING THE CANADIAN ARMY

The issue of the military draft, or conscription, had led to a crisis during World War I. When Canada entered World War II, Prime Minister King pledged that there would be no conscription for overseas service (people could be drafted for training and service within Canada).

As the war went on, with Germany inflicting crushing defeats on the Allies in 1940 and Japan entering the war in December 1941, public support for conscription began to increase. In 1942, the nation voted by a large margin to release the government from its no-conscription pledge. Many French Canadians, however, opposed the measure. As a result, Prime Minister King avoided sending any drafted troops abroad until 1944.

Canadian troops advance through a flooded Dutch village during World War II. The retreating Nazis had blown up the dikes in an attempt to delay the Canadians, who would eventually fight their way through the Netherlands and into Germany. ▶

World War II: Canadian Military Contributions		
Battle/Campaign	**Date**	**Canadian Efforts**
Hong Kong	December 1941	● Two Canadian battalions attempted to defend Hong Kong, but it fell to the Japanese. ● The Canadians lost nearly as many men to harsh treatment in prison camps as in the battle.
Dieppe	August 19, 1942	● Two brigades and other units raided Dieppe, France. ● About 5,000 men took part; over 900 were killed and another 900 taken prisoner.
Sicily	July 10, 1943	● The 1st Division took part in the invasion of Sicily, and then in the invasion of Italy. ● Eventually, Canadians participated in the capture of Rome on May 23, 1944.
D-Day (Normandy invasion)	June 6, 1944	● The 3rd Canadian Division and the 2nd Armored Brigade took part in the initial assault on the beaches of Normandy. ● More Canadians were soon sent across the English Channel; in July, the 1st Canadian Army was activated.
Invasion of Germany	February 1945	● The 1st Army took part in the drive on the Siegfried Line and on into Germany. ● Some troops remained in Germany until April 1946, as part of the Allied occupation forces.

Postwar Canada

The end of World War II resulted in a number of changes for Canada, both at home and abroad. The industrial boom caused by the need to produce weaponry and goods for the war effort led to economic prosperity. Canada also took on a new role in the international community.

Canada at Home

Several amendments to the British North America Act, passed by the British Parliament between 1949 and 1960, allowed the federal government to legislate in new areas. The most important amendment was that of December 16, 1949. This amendment gave the Canadian Parliament the power to amend the constitution in matters that affected only the federal government (though formal assent of the British Crown was still required). Now, the British Parliament would only act on matters that affected both the nation and the provinces.

St. Laurent. Prime Minister William Lyon Mackenzie King decided to retire in late 1948. He selected as his successor Louis Stephen St. Laurent (1882–1973), a bilingual lawyer who had entered politics in 1942 as minister of justice in the King cabinet. St. Laurent was minister of external affairs from 1946 to 1948, when he became leader of the Liberal Party and prime minister of Canada.

Prosperity. Canada enjoyed an economic boom while St. Laurent headed the government. He and the Liberals sponsored more social insurance legislation and supported the growth of education facilities. Perhaps the most lasting achievement of the St. Laurent administration was the construction of the St. Lawrence Seaway, although it was not completed until 2 years after St. Laurent left office.

Louis Stephen St. Laurent was only the second French Canadian to hold the office of prime minister (the first was Sir Wilfrid Laurier). ▶

The St. Lawrence Seaway handles about 50 million short tons (45 million metric tons) of cargo annually.

THE ST. LAWRENCE SEAWAY

Built jointly with the United States, the St. Lawrence Seaway is a system of canals, dams, and locks that creates a shipping route from the Atlantic Ocean to the western end of the Great Lakes.

- In all, it is some 2,375 miles (3,821 kilometers) long.
- The Canadian government first approved the start of construction in 1951. It was formally opened on June 26, 1959.
- The initial cost to Canada was $330 million ($130 million to the United States); improvements cost another $300 million.

Political Shifts. Canadians were stunned when, in 1956, the government broke the rules of Parliament to push through a bill to finance construction of a natural gas pipeline. John G. Diefenbaker, leader of the Progressive Conservative Party, charged that St. Laurent's government had abused its authority and insulted Parliament. Many voters agreed. In the election of 1957, Diefenbaker led his party to a narrow victory.

The Diefenbaker government helped revitalize agriculture in western Canada. His "northern vision," a term often heard in his 1957 and 1958 election campaigns, led to economic development in the Far North. By 1962, however, his popularity had begun to decline.

- The economy had weakened and unemployment was high.
- A controversy had developed over the presence of nuclear weapons on Canadian soil.
- The government had cancelled the development of the Avro Arrow, a Canadian-designed supersonic fighter plane.

In the election of April 8, 1963, the Liberal Party won more seats than any other party, and Lester Bowles Pearson (1897–1972) became prime minister.

The Avro Arrow was the most advanced aircraft of its day. The cancellation of the project was a cause for heavy criticism of Diefenbaker's government.

Pearson's Canada. Pearson's legacy as prime minister mostly lies in the area of social welfare.

- In February 1965, the age of becoming a beneficiary of the Old Age Pension was lowered from 70 to 65 years.
- In April of that year, the Canada Pension Plan was established.
- In 1966, royal assent was given to the national Medicare Act, effective July 1, 1968, ensuring universal medical care. In addition, the Department of Regional Economic Expansion was set up to oversee the country's disadvantaged regions.

Canada in the World

After the war, both Canada's standing and its activity in international affairs increased.

- In 1945, Canada joined the United Nations (UN) and all its specialized agencies.
- On April 4, 1949, Canada became the first nation to ratify the North Atlantic Treaty (NATO).
- In the Korean War, which began in 1950, Canada furnished an infantry brigade to the United Nations forces. In 1954, Canada became one of three nations to supervise the Korean War armistice.
- Canada and the United States established a joint air defense command (NORAD, or North American Aerospace Defense Command) in 1958.
- In 1956, Lester Bowles Pearson proposed a UN peacekeeping force to serve in the Suez. For this, he was awarded the Nobel Peace Prize.

- ✔ Canada followed Great Britain in declaring war on Germany in 1939. The Dominion put approximately 1 million men and women into uniform.
- ✔ More than 90,000 Canadians were killed or wounded in World War II.
- ✔ Canada contributed to many crucial campaigns, such as D-Day and the invasion of Germany.
- ✔ The end of the war resulted in an economic boom and greater Canadian participation in world affairs.

SOVEREIGNTY

In 1763, the land now known as Canada came under the control of the British Empire. Over time, however, Canada gradually began to govern itself. First, the provinces established self-government. Then, in 1867, the British North America Act unified the provinces under a central government— but that government still answered to the British Parliament. Not until 1931 would Canada achieve sovereignty, or total independence from Great Britain.

Becoming a Nation

Beginning in the early 1800s, Canadian leaders worked to establish Canada's independence both politically and economically. Initially, this was done through policies and treaties that addressed Canadian interests separately from those of Great Britain. Later, Canadian independence would be written into law.

Early Steps

Under Alexander Mackenzie (in office 1873–1878), the Canadian government made several moves toward self-government.

- It won the United Kingdom's approval of a policy limiting the authority of the governor-general—the British monarch's representative in Canada.
- The new policy required the governor-general to respect decisions made by Canadian officials in the country's internal affairs.
- In 1875, Mackenzie established the Supreme Court of Canada. The court lessened British control over Canada's legal matters.

◀ **The Supreme Court of Canada**, established in 1875 by Prime Minister Alexander Mackenzie, gave Canada greater authority over its own legal matters.

Macdonald. The Mackenzie government became increasingly unpopular after 1875, and John A. Macdonald led the Conservatives to victory in the election of 1878. Macdonald worked toward making Canada self-sufficient economically.

In 1879, Macdonald began the National Policy, a program calling for high tariffs (taxes) on imported goods. The program was designed to help Canada's industries grow. The program raised the cost of foreign products and made Canadian products less costly by comparison. Macdonald was also determined to complete the stalled construction of the coast-to-coast railroad. In 1880, the government gave the Canadian Pacific Railway Company a contract to finish the job.

Changing Relations with Great Britain. Prime Minister Wilfrid Laurier (in office 1896–1911) took an active part in Canada's relations with Great Britain. At three colonial conferences in London, Laurier refused to commit Canada to action when the nation would not have a proper share in deciding on the policies involved, such as imperial defense.

- During the Boer War (1899–1902) in South Africa, English and French Canadians were divided on whether to support England. Laurier's government decided to send only a token force of 1,000 infantrymen to join with the British forces. Laurier's action caused a rift in the Liberal Party.

- In 1907, Laurier refused to allow Canada to contribute to the cost of the British navy. Three years later, however, he proposed that Canada build a small naval force of its own (this idea did not gain widespread support).

Centre Block of the Parliament Hill buildings in Ottawa was reconstructed in the Gothic Revival style after the first one burned down in 1916. Peace Tower (tallest, with the clock) rises from the middle of the symmetrical structure.

The 20th Century

After World War I, Canada's standing with the rest of the world—independent of Great Britain—improved. Canadian troops had contributed greatly to the war effort, and the government had participated in the peace process. Canada was beginning to be recognized as its own state.

Prime Minister William Lyon Mackenzie King was determined to establish Canada's independence in foreign affairs. On King's insistence, Canada signed its first treaty alone with another nation in 1923. The treaty, with the United States, regulated halibut fishing in the Pacific Ocean.

THE CANADIAN FLAG

- The original Canadian flag included the British Union Jack, signaling Canada's status as a British colony.
- After much debate, the new Canadian flag was raised on Parliament Hill for the first time in 1965.
- The maple leaf on the current flag has been the traditional emblem of Canada since the nation's early days.
- The flags of some provinces, such as Manitoba, still contain a Union Jack.

The Statute of Westminster. At the Imperial Conference in London in 1926, Prime Minister King led the drafting of the Balfour Report. The report stated that Canada—and other dominions—were autonomous communities. The conference also established a committee to carry out further study.

- In 1929, this committee made its report, which was adopted at the next Imperial Conference in 1930.

- The end result was the Statute of Westminster, an act of the British Parliament of December 11, 1931.

- This statute gave the dominions autonomous standing as full members of the Commonwealth with full control of their foreign and domestic policies.

- It also repealed some laws that had become obsolete in view of the new relationship between the mother country and the dominions.

The Statute of Westminster applied in part to Australia, New Zealand, South Africa, the Irish Free State, and Newfoundland. The British North America Act of 1867 remained in effect.

A New Constitution

Following the Statute of Westminster, the dominions could make their own laws without the British Parliament having to legislate for them or approve their actions. Still, the Canadian government needed parliamentary approval and royal assent in order to amend its own constitution.

A movement to change this situation had begun as far back as 1927, but the federal government and the provinces found it hard to agree on proposed constitutional revisions. Plans drawn up in 1961 and 1964 were withdrawn when the provinces were not unanimous in supporting them.

The Constitution Act, 1982

After Prime Minister Pierre Trudeau and the provincial premiers failed once again to agree on constitutional amendments during talks held September 8 to 13, 1980, the federal government began to prepare its own plan in October. A Special Joint Committee of the House of Commons and the Senate began televised hearings on November 6, 1980. On February 13, 1981, the report, advocating 65 constitutional amendments, was tabled, and on February 17, the final round of constitutional debates began in the Commons.

▲ **Queen Elizabeth II** signed the constitutional document in a formal ceremony in Ottawa, on April 17, 1982, where she proclaimed the Constitution Act, incorporating the Charter of Rights and Freedoms. This was 115 years and 19 days after her great-great-grandmother, Queen Victoria, had assented to the British North America Act.

Conflicts. The proposed new constitution was perceived as increasing the power of the federal government.

- The western provinces opposed the plan on the grounds that it would give too much control of their natural resources to the central government.

- Quebec feared that more federal power would bring domination by English-speaking Canada and lead to the decline of French culture.

In the end, the two major points of contention centered on a proposed bill of rights and on the process that Canada would employ to amend its constitution. The proposed rights bill was revised to make explicit the rights of Indians, Inuit, and women. Educational rights of the French-speaking minority outside Quebec and the English-speaking minority inside Quebec were extended.

The Charter of Rights and Freedoms. The most important new features of the 1982 Constitution Act are the amendment procedure and the Canadian Charter of Rights and Freedoms.

- The Charter gives all Canadian citizens the right to "enter, remain in, or leave Canada."

- Everyone is equal under the law without discrimination based on "race, national or ethnic origin, color, religion, sex, age, or mental or physical disability."

- English and French are now the official languages and have equal rights in government.

- Language rights in some of the provinces are spelled out; all provinces have spelled out language rights with regard to education.

- The existing aboriginal and treaty rights are affirmed. The term "aboriginal" here applies not only to Indians and Inuit but also to Métis.

Approval. After 18 months of debate, the House of Commons, on December 2, 1981, approved by a vote of 246 to 24 a resolution, the British North America Act, to patriate Canada's constitution from Great Britain, joining to it this new amending formula and the Charter of Rights.

- On December 8 the Senate approved the constitutional package by a vote of 59 to 23.

- In England, by a 177 to 33 vote, the House of Commons gave its approval on March 8, 1982, and the House of Lords on March 25.

- On the following day, March 9, Queen Elizabeth II gave her royal assent.

Elizabeth II remained queen of Canada and head of state, and Canada remained in the Commonwealth of Nations. (Text of the Constitution is on pages 992–1004.)

now you Know!

✔ Canada began to establish its political and economic independence from Great Britain as early as the 1800s.

✔ Under Laurier, Canada began reducing its involvement in British affairs, such as the Boer War.

✔ World War I improved Canada's standing with the rest of the world; the country began acting in its own right.

✔ The Statute of Westminster (1931) gave Canada and other dominions independence from Great Britain.

✔ The Constitution Act, 1982 gave Canada control over amending its own constitution, without British approval.

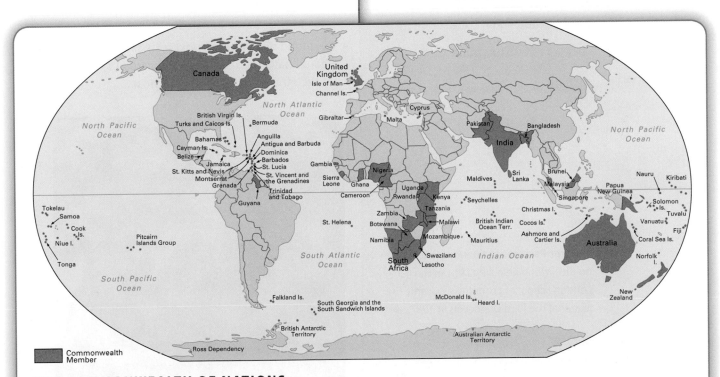

Commonwealth Member

THE COMMONWEALTH OF NATIONS

Canada is now part of the Commonwealth of Nations, an association of independent countries and other political units that have lived under British law and government. It includes the United Kingdom, about 50 independent nations that were once British colonies, and about 25 other political units, such as territories and dependencies. This map shows the location of all the Commonwealth members.*

*Fiji was suspended in 2009.

QUEBEC AND CANADA

Because it was colonized by two countries—Great Britain and France—Canada inherited two distinct cultures, languages, and civil systems. In 1763, Great Britain gained virtually all of France's possessions east of the Mississippi River. French Canadians were effectively cut off—economically, culturally, and politically—from their country of origin. Friction and conflict arose periodically between English-speaking and French-speaking Canada throughout the 19th and 20th centuries. In the early 1960s, French Canadians began rebuilding their cultural ties to France. Some began to seek separation from Canada.

Jacques Parizeau, a fluently bilingual politician who held a Ph.D. from the London School of Economics, became the leader of the Parti Québécois in 1987. ▶

Vive le Québec Libre!

The 1960s were a period of agitation. French-speaking Canadians, most of whom reside in Quebec, wanted to protect themselves from being overwhelmed by English-speaking Canada. The Francophones believed they were politically and economically disadvantaged, in part because the rest of Canada refused to adopt bilingualism.

Political Developments

As a result of the unrest, the federal government, in 1963, established the Royal Commission on Bilingualism and Biculturalism.

- In 1967, the commission recommended that both English and French be made official languages of the federal government.

- It also stated that in any province where the minority, either French or English, reached 10 percent, both languages should be official. This proposal was enacted into law in 1969.

- A second report in the next year said that children should have the right to be educated in whichever of the official languages they chose.

The Quiet Revolution. The 1960s also saw the beginning of what became known as the Quiet Revolution. Quebec Province was emerging from a period of economic hardship under the leadership of Premier Maurice Duplessis (1890–1959). Most industry at that time was owned by Anglophones—Canadian and American. Quebec's population was 80 percent Francophone, but there was no Francophone business class.

The Quiet Revolution sought to change all that. One of its leaders was Jacques Parizeau (1930–), a young politician. Another was Liberal provincial premier Jean Lesage (1912–1980), known as the father of the Quiet Revolution. The movement worked to increase Quebec's control over its own economy and to reduce such control by the federal government.

The Separatist Movement. A large number of Francophones in Quebec wanted to go even further than the Quiet Revolution. They wanted to declare Quebec independent of and separated from the rest of Canada. The situation was exacerbated when President Charles de Gaulle of France visited Quebec in July 1967. In a speech in Montreal, he seemed to promise support for independence, exclaiming, *"Vive le Québec libre"* (Long live a free Quebec).

Trudeaumania!

On April 6, 1968, Trudeau was elected leader of the Liberal Party, succeeding Lester B. Pearson. He took office as prime minister of Canada on April 20. Trudeau was a fervent nationalist whose success at the polls was rivaled only by that of Prime Minister King. His tide of popularity was known as "Trudeaumania." Trudeau worked hard to help preserve the French heritage in Canada. For example, he greatly expanded the use of the French language in government services.

Pierre Trudeau, Canada's third French-Canadian prime minister, served as prime minister almost continuously until 1984.

THE OCTOBER CRISIS

Terrorism by Quebec separatists in October 1970 forced Trudeau to make his most difficult decision as prime minister. Members of the Front de Liberation du Quebec (FLQ), an underground separatist group, kidnapped Pierre Laporte, the labor minister of Quebec, and James R. Cross, the British trade commissioner in Montreal. Trudeau suspended civil liberties and sent thousands of federal troops to Quebec. He invoked the War Measures Act, which permits police to search and arrest without warrants and to deny bail.

Laporte was murdered, and four men were later imprisoned for the crime. The government let Cross's kidnappers go to Cuba in return for his release. Trudeau's firm stand received strong popular support.

After the October Crisis, FLQ terrorism ended, but the separatist movement continued.

Trudeau had to deal not only with the demands of Quebec but also with dissatisfaction from other provinces on other issues. "Trudeaumania" began to fade. After the 1972 election, Trudeau had to form a minority government; however, he was returned with a majority in 1974.

At this point, he faced an economic crisis and burgeoning inflation. Wage and price controls were enforced in 1975, under much protest, and problems were compounded by the Quebec provincial election the next year.

Parti Québécois

The Quebec separatist movement scored a victory on its home territory on November 15, 1976, when the Parti Québécois won 89 of the 110 seats in the provincial legislature. René Lévesque (1922–1987), the leader of the Quebec nationalists, became premier of Quebec. In 1967, he had helped found the Mouvement souveraineté-association (Sovereignty-association movement), which became the Parti Québécois a year later.

As premier, he put through the provincial legislative measures intended to improve the status of the French language and culture—notably Bill 101, which made French the official language of Quebec—and other acts to increase the province's power in the fields of education and social welfare. Jacques Parizeau became minister of finance; he would revolutionize Quebec's economy.

Demands and Compromises

In June 1984, after struggling to persuade Quebec to approve Canada's 1982 Constitution Act, Trudeau stepped down as prime minister. John N. Turner (1929–) succeeded him, but served as prime minister for only a short time. An election on September 4, 1984, gave the Progressive Conservatives an overwhelming mandate—the largest majority won in a federal election in Canadian history.

▲ **René Lévesque** had formerly been a war correspondent in World War II. He had also served as an interpreter between the American forces and the Free French.

Leading Quebec. From the 1970s onward, the balance of power in Quebec has shifted between the Liberal and Québécois parties.

The 1980 referendum brought out strong opinions on both sides. In the end, however, a majority of voters rejected separation of Quebec from greater Canada.

THE INDEPENDENCE VOTE

The animosity between French- and English-speaking Canada, and between the provinces and Ottawa (the capital) over other issues, came to a head in 1980. In Quebec, Lévesque's government held a province-wide vote on a proposal to give provincial leaders authority to negotiate with the Canadian federal government for independence. The province would still maintain economic ties to Canada.

Even French-speaking citizens rejected this move, however, and about 54 percent of them joined the English-speaking minority (for a total of 60 percent) in voting no. In 1985, the Parti Québécois was voted out of office.

Mulroney and Quebec. The new prime minister was Brian Mulroney (1939–). Mulroney began a drive to persuade Quebec to sign the new constitution. Mulroney met on April 30, 1987, with the 10 provincial premiers, and the Meech Lake Agreement was worked out.

- The agreement provided that Quebec be labeled a "distinct society."

- Quebec would have three of the nine judges on the Canadian Supreme Court.

- No changes in federal institutions or provincial boundaries would be made without the unanimous consent of the federal government and the provinces.

- All the provinces would now have the right to nominate members of the Senate and justices of the Supreme Court.

On June 23, Quebec became the first province to ratify the agreement. The House of Commons on October 26 voted 242 to 16 to approve the agreement. However, Manitoba and Newfoundland did not ratify the agreement, and it failed.

The Charlottetown Accords. After the failure of the Meech Lake Agreement, Prime Minister Mulroney worked out a new agreement at Charlottetown, Prince Edward Island, on August 27, 1992.

- The new agreement again called for recognition of Quebec's distinctness.

- A new and elected Senate would replace the current one, whose members are appointed.

- Self-government would be established for indigenous people.

- The Supreme Court would adhere both to English common law and the Napoleonic Code of Quebec.

- The commitment of Canada to democratic values, sexual and ethnic equality, and respect for human rights would be reaffirmed.

A national referendum on October 26, 1992, resulted in rejection of these proposals. Quebec and the four western provinces voted against the scheme; the Atlantic provinces voted in favor of it. In all, five of the nine English-speaking provinces voted no.

Premiers of Quebec 1960–Present	Party	Term
Jean Lesage	Liberal	1960–1966
Daniel Johnson	Union Nationale	1966–1968
Jean-Jacques Bertrand	Union Nationale	1968–1970
Robert Bourassa	Liberal	1970–1976
René Lévesque	Québécois	1976–1985
Pierre Marc Johnson	Québécois	1985
Robert Bourassa	Liberal	1985–1994
Daniel Johnson	Liberal	1994
Jacques Parizeau	Québécois	1994–1996
Lucien Bouchard	Québécois	1996–2001
Bernard Landry	Québécois	2001–2003
Jean Charest	Liberal	2003–

now you Know!

- ✔ Canada developed with two distinct cultures—French and English—influencing it.

- ✔ Tensions between French-speaking and English-speaking Canadians have arisen frequently throughout Canada's history.

- ✔ Most of the French-speaking Canadians lived in Quebec.

- ✔ In the 1960s, a movement began to protect Quebec's French identity and culture; some advocated separation from Canada.

- ✔ A referendum to separate from Canada was voted down in 1980.

CANADA CURRENTLY

In the years since the Constitution Act, 1982, Canada has continued to develop its economy, address social issues, and adjust to the changing world around it. The nation has worked to establish greater rights for its Aboriginal population, expand its trading options, and continue its role in foreign affairs. The 1990s and early 2000s brought about significant changes in the country's political climate. Canada also faces a significant ongoing challenge in the onset of Arctic climate change.

Prime Minister Brian Mulroney spearheaded changes to Canada's trade policies with the United States and Mexico; however, these changes were not universally popular.

The 1980s and 1990s

The late 1980s and early 1990s, under Prime Minister Brian Mulroney (served 1984–1993), brought several major challenges. First was the ongoing challenge of Quebec separatism. Two of Mulroney's efforts at unity—the Meech Lake Agreement and the Charlottetown Accords—had failed to gain full approval. Secondly, Canada was suffering from prolonged economic troubles, with high unemployment.

Economics and Trade

Talks with the United States began June 17, 1986, with the goal of negotiating a free trade agreement between the two countries. After much difficulty, the talks resulted in a treaty that by the end of the century would

- eliminate tariffs and import quotas.
- end restrictions on investments in one country by businesses located in the other.
- increase trade between the two countries, which already amounted to $150 billion a year.

The agreement required ratification by Parliament, and this became the major issue in the election of November 21, 1988. Mulroney and the Progressive Conservative Party supported the pact. The Liberal and New Democratic parties thought it would threaten Canada's sovereignty. In the election, the Progressive Conservatives retained control of the House of Commons (though 56 percent of the votes were cast against them). The U.S.-Canada Free Trade Agreement was ratified by Parliament on December 30 and took effect on January 1, 1989.

NAFTA

On December 17, 1992, Canada joined Mexico and the United States in signing the North American Free Trade Agreement (NAFTA), which was implemented on January 1, 1994. The accord gradually eliminates virtually all import taxes and other trade barriers among the three countries.

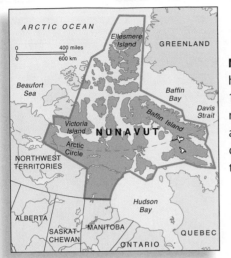

Nunavut is home to about 17,500 Inuit. The region comprises almost one-fifth of Canada's total territory.

ABORIGINAL RIGHTS AND NUNAVUT

Recent Canadian governments have made a great deal of progress in the area of Aboriginal rights.

- On September 5, 1988, the government agreed to give 390,000 Indians, Inuit, and people of mixed ancestry title to 200,000 square miles (518,000 square kilometers) of the Arctic region of the nation.

- The agreement also gave these groups a major role in the development of another 1.1 million square miles (2.8 million square kilometers) in northern Canada.

- The pact also included a provision for a cash settlement to Indians, Inuit, and people of mixed ancestry of $400 million, to be disbursed over a 20-year period.

In a further agreement, on December 16, 1991, the government granted the Inuit political rule over 770,000 square miles (1.9 million square kilometers) to be carved out of the Northwest Territories. In addition, the Inuit would be paid more than $1 billion over a period of 14 years. This area officially became a territory on April 1, 1999. The territory was named Nunavut, "our land" in the Inuit language.

In 2008, Prime Minister Stephen Harper apologized to Canada's native peoples for their suffering under the residential schools system. From the late 1800s to the late 1900s, thousands of native children were forced to attend boarding schools aimed at integrating them into mainstream society. Abuse and neglect often occurred at these schools.

Foreign Affairs

Canada has continued to play a role in international affairs, a role which began to take shape shortly after World War I. The nation remains an important participant in United Nations peacekeeping efforts.

- The Canadian Armed Forces took part in the Persian Gulf War of 1991. (See also page 225.)
- In August 1994, the last Canadian NATO troops in Europe were withdrawn, ending 27 years of Canadian service.

The Northwest Passage. In 2007, with the possibility of new shipping lanes opening due to global warming, the government asserted its claim to the Northwest Passage. The prospect of undiscovered oil and gas beneath the shrinking polar ice is also a consideration.

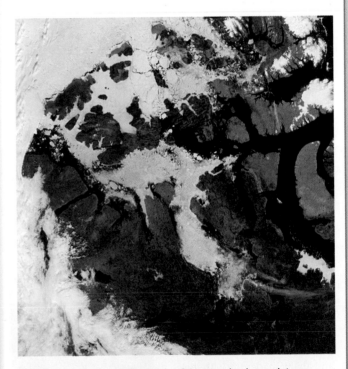

Russia, Norway, and the United States also have claims in the Arctic. Despite the majority worldview that these are international waters, Canada plans to establish a new army training center and deep-water port in the region.

Contemporary Leaders

In the 1990s, economic troubles continued to simmer. Dissatisfaction with the U.S.-Canada Free Trade Agreement—plus the government's implementation on January 1, 1991, of the unpopular Goods and Services Tax (GST)—all brought the Mulroney government to an all-time low in popularity in national opinion polls. A political shift was on its way.

Kim Campbell. In February 1991, Brian Mulroney announced his intention to resign as prime minister and federal Conservative Party leader. In June of that year, Kim Campbell (1947–) was elected Conservative Party leader and succeeded Mulroney as prime minister.

Voters rejected Campbell's attempts at a "fresh approach" in the federal election of October 25, 1993—an election that changed the country's political map completely.

The Conservatives won only two seats in Parliament, a humiliating blow. The electorate instead returned the Liberal Party to power with a full majority. The Bloc Québécois, the federal separatist party, under leader Lucien Bouchard (1938–), became the official opposition with 54 seats.

Kim Campbell was Canada's first female prime minister. Before that, she was also the nation's first woman minister of justice and attorney general.

Jean Chrétien. The new prime minister of Canada, Jean Chrétien (1934–), was sworn in on November 4, 1993. As prime minister, Chrétien took steps to fulfill his pledge of "good government," and his popularity in public opinion polls continued to rise. Nevertheless, solutions to difficult issues remained elusive. The country's high deficit continued to hamper economic growth.

Jean Chrétien's passionate patriotism, sense of humor, and ability to identify with the Canadian people made him one of the most popular political figures in English-speaking Canada. But his opposition to Quebec nationalism made him unpopular in his home province of Quebec.

fyi!

In addition to a prime minister, Canada also has a governor-general. The governor-general is appointed by the British monarch.

- *When a prime minister resigns, dies, or is voted out in an election, the governor-general fills the office temporarily.*

- *The governor-general has the ability to dissolve Parliament when requested by the prime minister. He or she also has the ability to refuse a request to dissolve Parliament.*

Paul Martin. After a decade in office, Chrétien, who had planned to retire in early 2004 before his term expired, stepped down on December 12, 2003. He was replaced as prime minister by the new leader of the Liberal Party, Paul Martin (1938–).

- Martin's plans included the creation of a cabinet-level national security department intended to deal with terrorism and disasters.
- Another plan called for a committee devoted to improving relations with the United States. The relationship had become strained when Chrétien refused to provide forces to the Iraq war in 2003.

Jean Chrétien and Paul Martin. In this photograph, Jean Chrétien—then the prime minister of Canada—at left, celebrates with Paul Martin, at right, after Martin was elected head of Canada's Liberal Party. Martin replaced Chrétien as prime minister in December 2003.

Stephen Harper. After 12 years of government rule by the Liberal Party, Conservative Stephen Harper (1959–) became prime minister in January 2006. Harper had cofounded the Conservative Party of Canada in 2003. Harper's government has had to contend with social and economic issues, including the worldwide economic crisis of 2008 and the ongoing issue of Quebec's identity.

Stephen Harper pledged, during his campaign, to repeal the Goods and Services Tax (GST) that had helped to make Prime Minister Mulroney's government unpopular.

now you know!

- From the 1980s through the present, Canada has worked to strengthen its economy and address global and social issues.
- The U.S.-Canada Free Trade Agreement and NAFTA eliminated the trade barriers between Canada, the U.S., and Mexico.
- Canada continues to play a role in UN peacekeeping efforts.
- In 1993, Canada elected its first female prime minister, Kim Campbell; however, she served only a short term.
- In 1999, the Nunavut region—controlled by Inuit groups—became an official territory.
- The balance of power shifted from the Conservatives to the Liberals and back again; in 2006, Stephen Harper became the first Conservative prime minister in 12 years.

CANADIAN IDENTITY

Over the past 60 years, Canada has grown into a multicultural society. As the population has grown, the nation has also become more industrialized and more urban. Today nearly 80 percent of the people live in urban areas. The people of Canada are striving to maintain control of their economy and to safeguard their Canadian identity, both of which tend to be overwhelmed by the influence of the much larger United States. Additionally, French Canadians continue to defend their French heritage and debate their role within Canada as a whole.

Life and Culture

Throughout its history, Canada has often been troubled by a lack of unity among its people. Clashes between the English and French traditions have persisted since the 19th century, as have clashes between provincial (local) and national interests. At the end of the 20th century, leaders such as Brian Mulroney and Jean Chrétien began to support resolutions recognizing Quebec's unique culture and promoting national unity. Despite these clashes, Canada has developed a vibrant and diverse culture.

French-Canadian Identity

Significant numbers of French-speaking people live in New Brunswick and Ontario. However, most of the French-speaking Canadians live in Quebec, and French is the official language of the province.

Bilingualism. The role of the French language and culture in Quebec has been controversial both within the province and within Canada as a whole. Quebec's legislature has passed a number of laws dealing with the uses of French and English in the province.

- In the 1970s, laws banned the use of English on commercial signs.
- English-speaking citizens of Quebec opposed these laws.

Through a series of court rulings and legislation, the laws were eventually changed. Today, bilingual advertising—in French and English— is allowed as long as the French lettering is larger than the English.

◀ **Quebec's French-speaking citizens,** called *Québécois*, consider themselves to be the guardians of the French language and culture in Canada.

Art and Culture

In Canadian literature, there are two major traditions: one primarily English, the other based in French-Canadian tradition. Canada exhibits distinct differences between the two language groups. For example, the theater of Quebec is often very different from the theater in other areas. Authors often have their work translated from one language to the other.

Literature. By the beginning of the 20th century, some Canadian novelists began to reach a wide audience outside their own land.

- *Anne of Green Gables* and its sequels by Lucy Maud Montgomery were bestsellers in Britain and the United States.

Some Modern Canadian Authors	
In English	**In French**
Margaret Atwood	Marie-Claire Blais
Morley Callaghan	Anne Hébert
Matt Cohen	André Langevin
Robertson Davies	Roger Lemelin
Margaret Laurence	Gabrielle Roy
Farley Mowat	Yves Thériault
Alice Munro	Michel Tremblay
Mordecai Richler	
Michael Ondaatje	

- In French, Louis Hémon found an international audience with his *Maria Chapdelaine* (1914).

In more recent years, many Canadian authors—both French- and English-speaking—have gained international recognition. (See pages 920–959.)

Visual Arts. Canada's visual arts, such as painting and sculpture, both reflect the nation's heritage and a distinctive Canadian style.

- Inuit artists are noted for their bone, stone, and ivory carvings of Arctic animal life, as well as for ceremonial masks.
- In the 1800s, Canadian painters such as Paul Kane, Cornelius Krieghoff, Horatio Walker, and Emily Carr used landscapes and ordinary life for their themes.
- In the 1920s, the Group of Seven, led by Tom Thomson, broke from the European tradition to emphasize Canada's unique natural features in landscapes.

▲ **The National Arts Centre,** shown here, presents drama, music, opera, ballet, and motion pictures.

GOVERNMENT AND CULTURE

The federal government has taken a positive role over the years in promoting Canadian culture.

- Canada Council grants, which are federally funded, assist various programs in the arts, as well as individual artists.
- In 1969, the federal government opened the National Arts Centre in Ottawa.
- The National Gallery, also in Ottawa, has an excellent collection of European art and a large number of Canadian works.

The CBC. The federal government organized the Canadian Broadcasting Corporation (CBC) in 1936 for radio broadcasting.

- The CBC (Radio-Canada is its French-language network) is government-owned but controlled by an independent board.
- It added television to its radio service in 1952.
- There are also private English and French networks, some associated with the CBC, others operating independently.

Select Prime Minister Biographies

Sir John Alexander Macdonald, Canada's first prime minister, served from 1867 to 1873 and 1878 to 1891. He was instrumental in the formation of the country and in facilitating its rapid expansion.

Macdonald was born January 11, 1815, in Glasgow, Scotland. In 1820, his family moved to what is now Ontario. At the time, Canada did not yet exist; it was a land of fragmented territories ruled by Great Britain.

In 1844, Macdonald, a lawyer, was elected as a government official in the Province of Canada. He quickly worked his way up through the Conservative Party. Increasingly, he recognized the need for centralized government. Macdonald helped draft the plans for confederation, which would bring the disparate provinces together as one country. He thought federal government should be limited and that provinces should govern themselves in most respects.

When Canada was formed by the British North America Act of 1867, Macdonald became its first prime minister. At the time, the country included New Brunswick, Nova Scotia, and the Province of Canada, with the expectation that more provinces would join later. Beginning in 1870, the provinces of Manitoba, British Columbia, and Prince Edward Island were added in quick succession, greatly expanding Canada.

Macdonald's first stint in office ended when he was forced to resign over a bribe scandal. When he regained power 5 years later, he enacted a new domestic agenda called the National Policy, which used steep taxes on foreign imports to build railroads and finance other government projects. He continued as prime minister until he died in 1891.

Sir Wilfrid Laurier, the first French-Canadian prime minister, served from 1896 to 1911. His long tenure coincided with a period of intense national growth.

Laurier was born November 20, 1841, in what is now Quebec. (The provinces did not come together to form a unified Canada until 1867.) Throughout his life, there was an informal divide between the French-speaking and English-speaking areas in Canada. As a politician, he tried to bridge that divide.

Laurier's years in office were a time of expansion and growth for the country. The population was on the rise as immigrants poured in, attracted by the prime minister's campaign to attract settlers away from the dwindling American frontier. The country added two new provinces, Saskatchewan and Alberta, in 1905. To accommodate and encourage further growth, Laurier funded more railroads.

His other focus was foreign policy. His main accomplishment was carefully managing Canada's relationship with Great Britain. The British Empire was keen to extend its reach into matters of Canadian government, but Laurier resisted. While he was never antagonistic toward the British government (in fact, he supported it in many ways), Laurier worked hard to maintain Canada's autonomy.

Laurier and his Liberal Party lost power due to his support of a controversial trade agreement with the United States. He remained active in the House of Commons until he died in 1919.

William Lyon Mackenzie King served longer than any other prime minister in Canadian history, totaling more than 21 years of service between 1921 and 1948. He was the country's most important political figure during that stretch, even though his time in office was divided into three distinct time periods (1921–1926, 1926–1930, and 1935–1948).

Born December 17, 1879, in Ontario, King spent his young adulthood immersed in his studies. He attended the University of Toronto and the University of Chicago before receiving his PhD from Harvard University. During his travels, King was exposed to the difficult conditions facing poor laborers. Their plight made a deep impression on him.

King's interest in labor issues led him down the path of government service. In 1900, he helped establish the Canadian government's first department of labor. Eventually, those interests would spill over into his domestic agenda as prime minister, when he promoted social programs such as unemployment insurance and welfare.

Foreign affairs—particularly Canada's relationships with the United States and Great Britain—were another area of focus for King. His administration worked closely with the U.S. government to establish a mutually beneficial trade agreement. As he led Canada through World War II, King managed to support Great Britain while asserting Canada's independence from the British Empire.

King died in 1950, two years after his retirement.

John George Diefenbaker, a Conservative who served as prime minister from 1957 to 1963, dedicated most of his term to promoting social justice.

The Ontario native was born September 18, 1895. After serving in World War I, he worked as a lawyer. He was a gifted orator known for his eloquent speeches. He was also known for his persistence; he lost five elections before he joined the House of Commons in 1940.

After a long career in politics and many years of service in Parliament, Diefenbaker became leader of the Progressive Conservative Party in 1956. His party swept the national election in 1957, gaining control of government after 22 years of Liberal leadership.

Diefenbaker's domestic policy was largely dedicated to social justice. Most importantly, he championed the Canadian Bill of Rights to promote equality and fair treatment. He reorganized federal programs to better help Canada's needy citizens. He also appointed the first woman to a prominent cabinet position and spoke out against apartheid in South Africa.

Foreign policy—particularly the way in which Diefenbaker handled the Cuban Missile Crisis—was the reason the public lost confidence in his administration. He resisted when the United States asked Canada to place its military on high alert in response to the threat of Soviet missiles in Cuba. While Diefenbaker ultimately agreed, his hesitation was widely perceived as tentative and indecisive.

After Diefenbaker lost power, he remained an active politician in the House of Commons until he died in 1979.

Lester Bowles Pearson served as prime minister from 1963 to 1968. While he had a strong background in foreign relations, he spent much of his time in office developing domestic programs.

Pearson was born in Ontario on April 23, 1897. He left college to serve in the military during World War I and then returned to his studies after he was injured. After a few years working in academia, he joined the foreign service in 1928. He spent the next 20 years in prestigious appointments in Great Britain and the United States.

Pearson was a prominent figure in international diplomacy long before he became prime minister. His most illustrious work was within the United Nations. As a Canadian delegate (1948–1956) and head of the General Assembly (1952–1953), he helped facilitate the end of the Korean War. He won the Nobel Peace Prize in 1957 for his contributions during the Suez Canal Crisis.

Pearson was also a key player in the North Atlantic Treaty Organization (NATO), a military alliance against the Soviet Union that was founded in 1949.

Much of Pearson's time as prime minister was devoted to domestic development, including a wide array of social programs. He broadened federally funded services and benefits, including the implementation of national medical care and a pension system. He also incited a fierce debate over the design of a new national flag, which was adopted in 1965.

After he retired from politics, Pearson resumed teaching until his death in 1972.

Pierre Elliott Trudeau served as prime minister from 1968 to 1984. His tenure was interrupted by a brief interval in 1979, when the Conservative Party controlled the government for less than a year.

Trudeau was born in Montreal on October 18, 1919. He was a lawyer and an academic until he began his career as a politician in 1965. A charismatic leader, he was already hugely popular by the time he took office in 1968.

One of the biggest challenges Trudeau faced was the independence movement championed by separatists who wanted Quebec to secede from Canada. In 1970, a terrorist group kidnapped two government officials. Trudeau, who was committed to a unified Canada, was largely praised for his forceful response to this event, which became known as the October Crisis.

Throughout his tenure, Trudeau continued his efforts to unify the country. He was a champion of multiculturalism and bilingualism, emphasizing that Canadian identity was broad enough to include speakers of both English and French. Under his leadership, Canada officially became bilingual.

Trudeau's other major accomplishments include severing ties with Great Britain by eliminating the British Parliament's influence over Canadian government, and establishing a diplomatic relationship with China.

After he retired from politics in 1984, Trudeau worked as a lawyer. He died in September 2000.

Kim Campbell became Canada's first female prime minister in 1993. She held the office for just over 4 months before power shifted to the Liberal Party.

Campbell was born March 10, 1947, in British Columbia. She was an academic and a lawyer before she turned to politics. After a stint in local government, she joined the House of Commons in 1988. There, she served as minister of State for Indian Affairs and Northern Development, minister of Justice and Attorney General, and minister of National Defense.

When Prime Minister Brian Mulroney retired in 1993, the Progressive Conservative Party chose Campbell to replace him. She assumed the office in June. While she was popular with the Canadian public at first, her party's standing was on shaky ground. (Mulroney had not been well liked.) When a national election was held in November 1993, the Conservatives lost almost all of their seats in Parliament.

Because of her limited time in office, Campbell's record as prime minister is relatively unremarkable. While her legacy as the first woman to serve in that role is important, her most substantial political accomplishments occurred during her time in the House of Commons. Since retiring from politics, Campbell has spent most of her time teaching at Harvard University.

Joseph Jacques Jean Chrétien served three terms from 1993 to 2003. Born January 11, 1934, in Quebec, Chrétien worked for many years as a lawyer and as a politician. He held a wide variety of important cabinet posts during the administrations of Lester Pearson and Pierre Trudeau.

When Chrétien took office, Canada had many financial problems, including a large national deficit. As prime minister, his first priority was to balance the budget. While he had to sacrifice federal programs and services along the way, the government had paid its debts by 1998.

One of the most difficult challenges Chrétien faced on the domestic front was the threat of secession from Quebec. The French-speaking province had long felt isolated from the rest of the country. In 1995, the people of Quebec voted to remain a province of Canada, but the vote was close. This was an embarrassment to Chrétien, a Quebec native who strongly believed in Canadian unity.

While Chrétien faced a number of domestic challenges, foreign policy issues led to his resignation. When the U.S. declared war on Iraq, he felt pressure from many sides to support the effort with troops. His flat refusal to participate was widely perceived as a good decision by the Canadian public, but it was less popular within the prime minister's own political party. As a result, Chrétien stepped down in 2003.

Government

FORMS OF GOVERNMENT

There are many ways in which forms of government can be different from each other—in the ways that leaders come to power, in the way the government is organized, in the way those organizations carry out responsibilities, and in the principles and procedures by which the governments operate. However, the greatest difference among forms of government is the degree to which the people participate in government.

Kinds of Government

Measuring Government

There are many different ways to measure governments. Political scientists study their economic policies, administrative organization, cultural aims, and many other aspects. But there are two scales of measurement that seem especially important. When trying to characterize existing governments, you need to ask

- What kind of authority does the government claim for itself? Some governments, including that of the United States, claim only conditional authority. Others, including those of China, North Korea, and many newly independent nations, claim unconditional authority.

- Is the government centralized or decentralized in its organization? Who makes policies and carries them out?

The Pharaoh of ancient Egypt exercised the unconditional powers of a god.

Kind of Government	Characteristics	Examples
Traditional	• Kings and emperors were seldom able to control and direct all the operations of the government. • Because communication and travel were slow, central authority was delegated to trusted administrators. Although communication and travel are much quicker today, traditional rulers still rely on administrators to help govern. • Usually, the unity of the State was based on shared religious values that frequently supported the spread of power among local groups.	*Historical* Ancient Egypt Roman Empire *Modern* Saudi Arabia
Democratic (Parliamentary form)	• There is little or no division of powers between the executive and legislative branches of the government. • The head of State, whether monarch or president, is little more than a figurehead, a national symbol.	England Canada Israel Germany Italy Scandinavia
Democratic (Presidential form)	• The president is elected by the people and is responsible only to them. • The legislature is also responsible to the people. • Sharp division of powers between the presidency and the legislature can cause serious conflict over policy, a development that is impossible in the parliamentary system.	United States France
Totalitarian	• Society gets its meaning and direction from an elaborate ideology. • Totalitarianism has always been associated with a new government that has arisen after a revolution or the achievement of national independence. • Totalitarian governments have so far appeared in two forms—democratic centralist (communist) and fascist (national socialist).	*Communist* China Cuba North Korea Soviet Union (1922–1991) *Fascist* Germany (1933–1945) Italy (1922–1943)
Authoritarian	• The election system does not allow for public policy debate or competition between candidates. • Some independent institutions—churches, labor unions, political organizations—are generally permitted. • In many cases, the regime cannot totally repress traditional institutions because the people are more loyal to the institutions than to the government.	Chile (1973–1990) Paraguay (1954–1993) Myanmar Syria Niger

Forms of Authority

Kinds of Government

Measuring governments on these two scales—centralized vs. decentralized and unconditional vs. conditional, we can divide them into four basic kinds (one kind has two types).

The following diagrams show the relationships among differing kinds of governments, and how levels of authority and degrees of organization shape the characteristics of specific governments. ▼

TRADITIONAL

Unconditional Authority

When a government claims unconditional authority, the State is the source of all values. Individuals have no real rights. Only the society as a whole has rights, and they are defined by the State. The best example of unconditional authority can be seen in the government of ancient Egypt. The Pharaoh was not simply installed by the gods—he was considered to be a god.

Decentralized Government

Governments that permit policy to be made at the regional or local level are decentralized. Decentralized governments usually have many centers of independent authority—states, cities, communities, business and labor organizations, political parties, special interest groups, and individuals. The United States is a good example of a decentralized system. (See pages 336–341.)

TOTALITARIAN ———————————— DEMOCRATIC

Centralized Government

Centralized governments usually try to control all phases of society. They may decide who will go to college and, in some cases, what will be studied. They decide what will be manufactured, where it will be manufactured, and how much it will cost at the retail level. The government requires its citizens to support and obey major government policies.

Conditional Authority

A government that claims conditional authority depends on the approval of its citizens for its survival. The primary role of the State is to protect the rights and values of its citizens. The most serious danger faced by a government claiming conditional authority is a dissatisfied citizenry that wants the State to adopt a set of religious or philosophical principles and claim unconditional authority.

AUTHORITARIAN

DECENTRALIZED GOVERNMENT

Traditional Government

From the empires of the ancient Near East through the Roman Empire to early czarist Russia, decentralized governments have been the most common. Populations under such governments were seldom politically active, leaving government to local or institutional leaders, such as nobles, provincial governors, priests, or tribal chiefs.

Democratic Government

There are two forms of democratic governments—parliamentary and presidential. In parliamentary government, the prime minister is the chief executive officer or head of government, but he is responsible to parliament. In a presidential system, the president is the chief executive officer, head of government and State, and wields a great deal of power.

UNCONDITIONAL AUTHORITY ———— CONDITIONAL AUTHORITY

Totalitarian Government

While the fixed, centralized form of government has existed in the past in some theocratic states (ruled by God or a priestly order), the truly totalitarian state is a modern development. True centralization, especially in a large country, depends on rapid communication and transportation systems.

Authoritarian Government

Authoritarian regimes are centralized like totalitarian regimes, but they lack an ultimate tradition or ideology that could provide the government with a sound base of authority. Power is concentrated in the hands of a single person or small group, and there is often a single major party that may be a small elite or a mass party with an elite leadership. If there is a legislature, it is powerless.

CENTRALIZED GOVERNMENT

✔ The principal difference among forms of government is the degree to which the governed people are able to participate in the government.

✔ The nature of a particular government is largely determined by the way the government exercises authority and the extent to which the government is centralized.

✔ Decentralized governments permit some policy to be made at local or regional levels.

✔ Centralized governments aim to control all aspects of the governed society.

✔ In unconditionally authoritarian governments, the State establishes all values and individuals have limited or no rights.

✔ In conditionally authoritarian governments, the State protects the rights of its citizens and survives only to the extent the citizens support it.

POLITICAL IDEOLOGIES

Governments make decisions for a society through a process called politics. Though the form and purpose of governments may vary, at the center of every kind of political system is power—government's capacity to get someone to do something willingly or because it can use force. Without power behind them, the decisions of government would not be binding.

Political scientists believe that modern communism was betrayed by its own leadership, resulting in inequality of ownership and power between Communist Party members and the people. The communist political system in the Soviet Union collapsed in 1991. Some of the key reasons for this were

- *government corruption.*
- *an inability of the economy to meet the needs of the people.*
- *the people's unwillingness to sacrifice for an abstract idea.*

How to Be Governed?

Anarchism

Anarchists propose an equal distribution of power to every citizen, each having the right to legislate for himself or herself and to maintain private ownership of material goods. Because anarchists see the state as a tool to dominate and exploit others, they advocate no state control. Some propose that anarchy can only happen after a violent overthrow of the state.

Communism

Communists argue that private ownership leads to inequality because unequal ownership implies unequal power. Communism prescribes a society where land, capital, and the means of production are collectively owned, and power is exercised by the masses. Built on the theories of Karl Marx and modified by V. I. Lenin, communist ideology was used to attack capitalism through doctrines of class conflict, historical inevitability, and economic determinism.

Karl Marx was an economist and philosopher. His works include *The Communist Manifesto,* which became the most influential document in the international communist movement.

Socialism

Socialists advocate government and group ownership of the means of production and the distribution of goods for the welfare of the individual members. It replaces competition with cooperation. Authoritarian socialist systems are run by a ruling elite who believe they know what is in the best interest of the people. In socialist democracies, the people elect representatives who decide on policies for regulating the economy and promoting general welfare.

Liberalism and Conservatism

American democracy is a system of government based on the ideologies of liberalism and conservatism. Liberalism is considered slightly "left" and conservatism is slightly "right." The American democratic system can be viewed as trying to find the balance between individual freedom and government authority. Democracies advocate equal access to opportunities. Other crucial freedoms in a democracy are based on civil rights and liberties such as freedom of speech, press, religion, assembly, and petition.

Fascism

In most cases, a fascist government is headed by a dictator. It involves total government control of political, economic, cultural, religious, and social activities. Unlike communism, which calls for the government to own all industry, fascism allows industry to remain in private ownership, though under government control. Other important features of fascism include extreme patriotism, warlike policies, and persecution of minorities.

The word *fascism* also describes any governmental system or political belief that resembles those of Benito Mussolini (*left*) and Adolf Hitler (*right*). Fascist governments ruled Italy under Mussolini from 1922 to 1943, and Germany under Hitler from 1933 to 1945. (See page 541.) ▶

Who Should Govern?

Bill Moyers is a journalist and commentator who has been an outspoken supporter of liberal ideals in the United States.

William F. Buckley was one of the best known writers and commentators on conservatism in the United States.

Concept	Liberalism	Conservatism
Government involvement	Favors more government regulations in promoting general welfare	Favors limits on what government can and should do to promote the general welfare
Reason in government	Assumes that human nature is rational and that people can make moral judgments and decisions for their lives	Believes that reason serves as an aid in making decisions, but reason is not trusted to be infallible
Tolerance	Assumes that social truths are relative and is more tolerant of differences of opinion	Reluctant to initiate changes and so relies more on what has worked in the past

Continuum of Ideologies		
Left	**Center**	**Right**
Anarchism **Communism** **Socialism**	**Progressive liberalism** **Conservative liberalism**	**Fascism**
Advocates radical or revolutionary change that gives all power to the masses and individuals; anarchism goes further to advocate dismantling of the State	Advocates moderate approaches to solving social and economic problems; seeks to balance individual rights, popular participation, and government authority	Advocates reactionary programs that restrict individual rights and gives all power to a ruling group or State (collective strength)

Ideologies prescribe *who* in the population should be responsible for governing.

Who Rules	Justifications	Critiques
The few		
Aristocracy	Rule by the better class of society will elevate the community to the highest level of achievement.	The interests of the many are sacrificed to the interests of the few.
Authoritarianism	A prince is necessary to organize and protect people, as well as create good laws and institutions.	The prince is a self-interested despot exercising power for power's sake.
Monarchy	Sanctioned by the Church, it is the monarch's "divine right" to rule. But the monarch has obligations to respect the rights of the people.	Fails to meet popular demands for political participation and can be despotic
Totalitarianism (communism and fascism)	Both communism and fascism seek absolute domination of all aspects of life to realize a perfect society, based on "scientific" theories of race or class.	Complete loss of individual liberty results in states that use absolute and arbitrary power, state terror, and genocide to dominate society.
The many		
Liberal democracy	Individual liberty is balanced with community needs through limited, representative government.	The elitist representative government is favored.
Participatory democracy	Ordinary people have an equal say in deciding issues that affect their lives.	Ordinary people are not competent enough to make complex political decisions.
Socialism	Public ownership of the means of production provides equal access to basic necessities such as education, health care, shelter, food, and transportation.	There is loss of individual control, liberty, and initiative.

✔ Politics is the process governments use to make decisions for a society.

✔ Political power gives governments the capacity to take action.

✔ Anarchism, communism, socialism, fascism, liberalism, and conservatism are political systems.

✔ Political systems are characterized in part by where they fall on the continuum of "left," "center," and "right."

✔ Liberalism and conservatism are distinguished from each other by their positions on government involvement in society, the function of reason in government, and the nature of social truths.

✔ Government may be conducted by the few, as in totalitarianism, or by the many, as in democracy.

AMERICAN DEMOCRACY took root in

traditions brought to North America by the first English colonists. The Revolutionary War in America began more than 150 years later, in 1775. The colonists wanted self-government and no taxation without representation. The Declaration of Independence, adopted by the Continental Congress in 1776, said that the people may change or abolish the government if it interferes with those rights. It established human rights as an ideal by which government must be guided. (See pages 64–67.)

The Magna Carta is an early example of limiting the arbitrary use of central power. It guarantees certain rights to a few subjects and sets a valuable precedent.

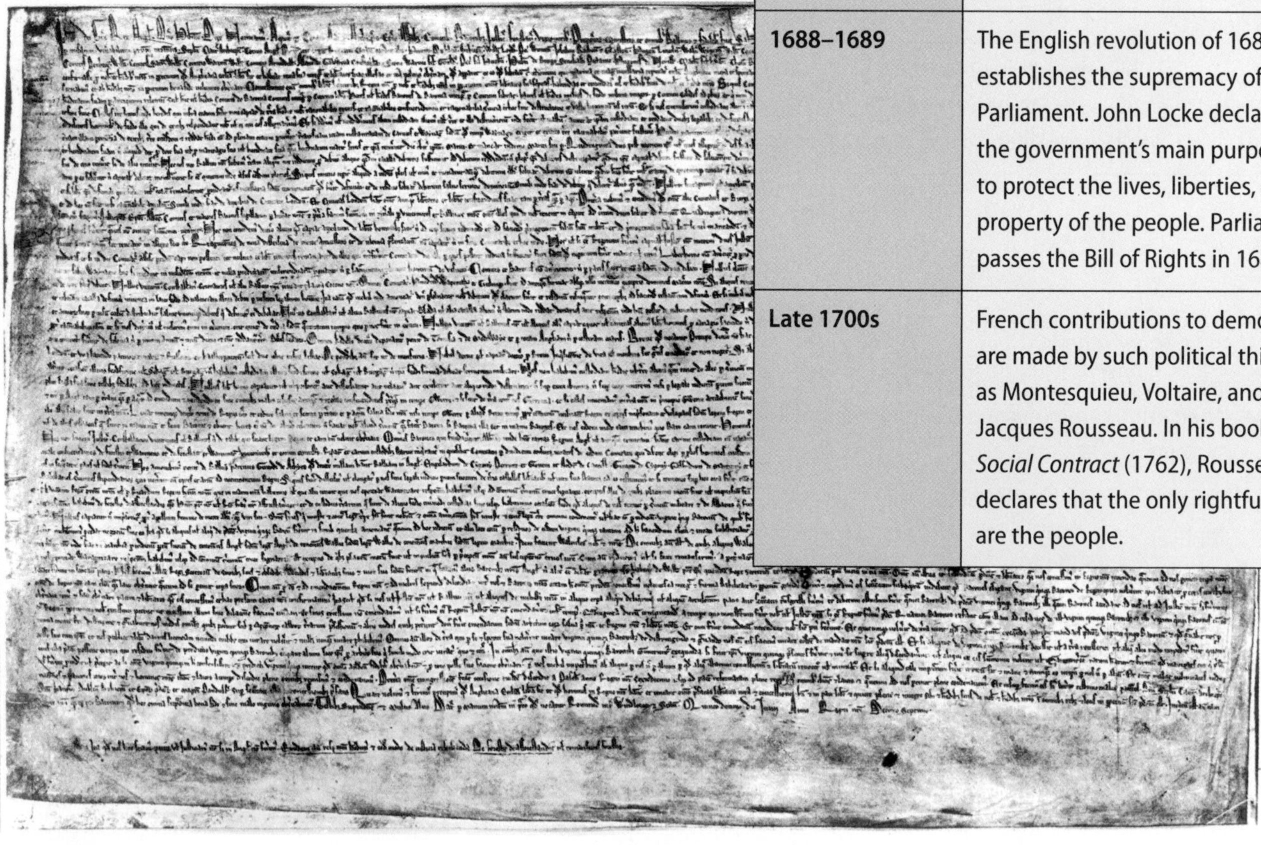

Important Influences

Influences on American Democracy

Modern Western democratic systems developed out of traditional governments. While the ideals of democracy have been discussed and attempted for thousands of years, true modern democracies are only a few hundred years old. The word democracy comes from the Greek words *demos*, meaning people, and *kratos*, which means rule or authority.

c. 500s–400s BC	In the Greek city-state of Athens, every male citizen has the right to vote in an assembly that passes laws and determines government policies.
c. 100 BC	The Roman statesman Cicero (106–43 BC) suggests that people have natural rights that every state must respect.
1215	English nobles force King John to approve the Magna Carta. This historic document is designed to keep the king from abridging the rights and privileges of feudal barons.
1688–1689	The English revolution of 1688 establishes the supremacy of Parliament. John Locke declares that the government's main purpose is to protect the lives, liberties, and property of the people. Parliament passes the Bill of Rights in 1689.
Late 1700s	French contributions to democracy are made by such political thinkers as Montesquieu, Voltaire, and Jean-Jacques Rousseau. In his book *The Social Contract* (1762), Rousseau declares that the only rightful rulers are the people.

JOHN LOCKE

THE INFLUENCE OF JOHN LOCKE

- People are capable of making rational decisions in their own self-interest.
- Government is indispensable for settling disputes and performing other activities that individuals could not handle easily on their own.
- Citizens should enter into a social contract with the government.
- The government breaks the contract whenever it trespasses on a citizen's natural rights, which include rights to life, liberty, and private property.

JEAN JACQUES ROUSSEAU

THE INFLUENCE OF JEAN JACQUES ROUSSEAU

- No government is legitimate unless all men (all classes) give their consent to it.
- All men are created equal, having equal right to participate in the making of law.
- There must also be initial agreement when establishing a government.

Fundamental Principles of American Government

Constitutional Authority. The national government gets its authority from the American people through a written document—the Constitution of the United States. The Constitution defines the goals of the national government and what it can and cannot do.

Federalism. There is a division of powers between a national or central government and local authorities. The Constitution divides powers between the national and state governments. In addition, the states share and divide powers with such local political subdivisions as counties, cities, and towns.

Representative Democracy. The United States government relies on the consent of the people. The people elect a certain number of their fellow citizens to represent them in making laws and in other matters. Federal, state, and local laws regulate elections.

Separation of Powers. Three separate branches share the powers of the United States government: the legislative branch makes the nation's laws, the executive branch enforces the laws, and the judicial branch interprets the laws if questions arise.

The Constitution

Constitutions embody the rights of citizens and describe the nature of the state's authority and power. In effect since 1789, the United States Constitution is the most successful written constitution in history. It set up a federal system, dividing responsibilities and authority between the new federal government and the individual states. Compared with other forms of government, the system was still decentralized, affording considerable independence to the states.

The Three Branches.
The Constitution further divided authority in the central government among three branches—the legislative, the executive, and the judicial—providing that each of these branches serve as a check on the others. The framers were fearful of two extremes:

- an executive so powerful that it might claim tyrannical power
- a legislature so driven by the majority that the rights of minorities might be overlooked

Growth and Change.
In the 200-plus years since the Constitution was written, the country has grown from a small coastal enclave with fewer than 4 million people to a giant superstate covering nearly half a continent and comprising more than 300 million people. During the 1900s, governmental power shifted to the federal government at the expense of the states. Within the federal establishment, the executive branch, headed by the president, has grown in importance at the expense of the legislative branch. Even under these changed conditions, however, the Constitution provides firm limits, and individual administrations may begin to shift power back to the states or back to the legislative branch.

Delegates gather to sign the new Constitution in this portrait by Howard Chandler Christy (1940). ▼

The Bill of Rights

The authors of the Constitution of the United States built a flexible document that has remained an effective government tool, requiring only 27 amendments in over 200 years.

The first 10 amendments to the Constitution were proposed—and adopted—together at the request of the states in 1791. The Bill of Rights has become an integral part of the Constitution, and its guarantees to individuals are still significant today.

▲ **The Bill of Rights** was adopted in 1791 in response to critics who claimed that the Constitution failed to address the principles of human liberty.

SIGNIFICANT AMENDMENTS

Freedom of expression

- First Amendment: freedom of religion, speech, press, assembly, and petition
- May result in innovative and useful solutions to political and social problems
- Criticisms can lead to reform.
- Censorship leads society toward totalitarianism.
- Maximizes freedom of expression but does not protect people from illegal acts

Rights of the criminally accused

- Fourth Amendment: security from unreasonable searches and seizures
- Warrants necessary before most seizures
- Fifth Amendment: protects against self-incrimination
- Defendants can't be forced to testify against themselves.
- Accused can't be tried for the same offense twice.
- Sixth Amendment: right to counsel
- Right to a speedy and public trial
- Eighth Amendment: protects those accused of a crime from cruel and unusual punishment
- Prohibits excessive bail

✔ American democracy is rooted in ideals first advanced by ancient Greek and Roman statesmen and expanded by European philosophers of the 17th and 18th centuries.

✔ The cornerstones of American government are constitutional authority; separation of powers among the executive, judicial, and legislative branches; federalism, or division of power between the federal and state governments; and representative democracy.

✔ The Constitution of the United States took effect in 1789 and, through its division of powers, reflects two great fears of its writers: a too-powerful executive and a too-powerful majority.

✔ The U.S. Constitution has proven to be a flexible tool of government, requiring only 27 amendments in more than 200 years.

✔ The first 10 amendments to the U.S. Constitution, adopted in 1791, comprise the Bill of Rights and ensure fundamental individual liberties.

FOUNDING PHILOSOPHIES

The emergence of the United States of America as an independent power would not have been possible without the contributions of some of the finest political minds in U.S. history. However, there was considerable friction and disagreement among them. The policies and philosophies they fought over determined the character of the government of this young country, and many of them still reverberate today.

Adams and Jefferson

John Adams (1735–1826)

John Adams was one of the key figures in the struggle for American independence. He served as vice president under George Washington and followed him as the second president. (See also page 89.)

Formation of Political Parties. During Washington's second administration, two political groups began to form in response to the French Revolution and to Washington's policies. Adams and Alexander Hamilton led the Federalists—supporters of Washington who favored a strong federal government.

The French Revolution. Many Americans saw the French Revolution (1789–1799) as an extension of the American Revolution, while others feared the overthrow of established order and the anarchy that might result. Washington and Adams were determined to keep the United States neutral.

Alien and Sedition Acts. During Adams's presidency, Congress passed laws designed to limit the criticism of their policies towards France. The Alien and Sedition Acts gave the president authority to banish or imprison foreigners and made it a crime to criticize the government, the president, or Congress.

These laws caused a storm of disapproval. Many people claimed they violated the guarantees of freedom of speech and of the press. Historians agree that the acts were unwise.

◀ **John Adams** spoke out boldly for separation from Great Britain at a time when many colonial leaders still hoped to settle their differences with the British.

Thomas Jefferson (1743–1826)

Thomas Jefferson was greatly influenced by the ideas of the English philosopher John Locke, who emphasized basic human rights and believed that people should revolt against governments that violated those rights. Jefferson believed the power of rulers, including monarchs, came from the people and should be limited. (See also page 90.)

Declaration of Independence. In the spring of 1776, Jefferson was part of the committee—along with John Adams, Benjamin Franklin, Roger Sherman, and Robert Livingston—that was charged with creating a Declaration of Independence. The committee unanimously asked Jefferson to prepare the draft and approved it with few changes. The Declaration affirmed belief in the natural rights of all people.

Thomas Jefferson favored a government that would pay more attention to the common citizen. After he became president in 1801, he spoke of his election as a "revolution."

Legacy. Jefferson's eloquent defenses of individual liberty and representative government continue to inspire people today. Jefferson felt that local governments—those closest to the people being governed—should be the most powerful, and that distant general governments should have only limited powers. He argued for freedom of speech, of the press, and of religion, and pressed for the addition of a bill of rights to the Constitution of the United States.

QUOTATIONS FROM THOMAS JEFFERSON

"...were it left to me to decide whether we should have a government without newspapers, or newspapers without a government, I should not hesitate a moment to prefer the latter."
—Letter to Colonel Edward Carrington, an American statesman, January 16, 1787

"...I have sworn upon the altar of God, eternal hostility against every form of tyranny over the mind of man."
—Letter to Benjamin Rush, American physician and political leader, September 23, 1800

"All, too, will bear in mind this sacred principle, that though the will of the majority is in all cases to prevail, that will, to be rightful, must be reasonable; that the minority possess their equal rights, which equal laws must protect, and to violate which would be oppression."
—First Inaugural Address, March 4, 1801

Madison and Hamilton

James Madison (1751–1836)

James Madison, the fourth president of the United States, is often called the Father of the Constitution. He played a leading role in the Constitutional Convention of 1787, where he helped design the checks and balances that operate among Congress, the president, and the Supreme Court.

Opposition to Washington and Hamilton. During George Washington's first administration, Madison supported many of the president's policies. But he gradually came to oppose the financial plans of Washington's treasury secretary, Alexander Hamilton. Madison believed that Hamilton's plans favored wealthy Easterners at the expense of ordinary citizens, particularly small farmers in what were then the southern and western United States. As a result, Madison turned against the Washington administration and Hamilton's Federalist Party. In 1791 and 1792, Madison and Jefferson formed the Democratic-Republican Party to oppose the Federalists.

JAMES MADISON
at the Constitutional Convention

Madison proved valuable to the Constitutional Convention in many ways.

- Madison had read deeply in political history and knew firsthand the weaknesses of the Articles of Confederation, the founding document that the Constitution later replaced.

- He kept a more complete record of the debates that took place at the convention than did anyone else who attended them.

- He proposed resolutions for organizing the Departments of State, Treasury, and War. He also drafted much of the first tariff act.

- He was largely responsible for drafting the first 10 amendments to the Constitution, the Bill of Rights.

INFLUENCE ON U.S. GOVERNMENT

Most of the Founding Fathers distrusted the Athenian version of direct democracy. They wanted to establish a republic because they feared that giving the people too much power would lead to mob rule. For this reason, the men who wrote the Constitution of the United States

- adopted a system that divided power between the federal government and the states.

- provided that the federal powers be divided among the legislative, executive, and judicial branches.

- provided that the president be elected by an electoral college rather than by the direct vote of the people.

James Madison coauthored *The Federalist,* a series of proratification letters that is considered the most authoritative explanation of the American constitutional system.

Alexander Hamilton (1755 or 1757–1804)

Alexander Hamilton served as the nation's first secretary of the treasury in President George Washington's cabinet. He also was a leader of the Federalist Party, one of the first political parties in the nation. (See also page 87.)

Strong Federal Government. Hamilton supported the establishment of a strong federal government and favored the development of manufacturing to achieve an economic balance between agriculture and industry. He worked to protect the interests of merchants and other business leaders and believed the nation could best be governed by people from these groups.

A National Bank. Hamilton proposed that Congress establish a national bank to handle the government's financial operations. This measure was opposed by Secretary of State Thomas Jefferson, who did not believe that Congress had the power to establish such an institution.

In the early 1790s, the conflicts between Hamilton and a group led by Jefferson and Madison resulted in the development of the nation's first two political parties. Hamilton led the Federalist Party, which favored a strong federal government. The Democratic-Republican Party, headed by Jefferson and Madison, wanted a weak national government.

Alexander Hamilton was a noted statesman and political leader during the early years of the United States.

✔ Historical events and differences of political philosophy among the American founding fathers prompted the development of political parties.

✔ John Adams, second president of the United States, and Alexander Hamilton, first secretary of the treasury of the United States, were leaders in the Federalist Party which favored a strong central government.

✔ Thomas Jefferson, third president of the United States, and James Madison, fourth president of the United States, founded the Democratic-Republican Party in support of limited central government.

TENSIONS IN U.S. DEMOCRACY

In democracies, all people are said to possess inalienable rights to freedom and equality before the law, but they are expected to cooperate in creating a healthy society. Democracies advocate equal access to opportunities. Other crucial freedoms in a democracy are based on such civil rights and liberties as freedom of speech, press, religion, assembly, and petition.

Conflict and Cooperation

Conflicting Interests

- **Majority Rule vs. Individual Rights.** Decision-making processes in a democracy are based on majority rule. However, in cases where majority rule is in conflict with the rights of a minority group, allowances need to be provided in order to protect the rights of that minority.

- **Liberty vs. Equality.** An individual's liberty needs to be balanced with community needs through limited, representative government. However, many believe this creates a climate in which the elitist representative government—working in support of community needs—will be favored.

- **State vs. National Authority.** Areas such as education and police protection, once the exclusive domain of the states and local governments, have become federal responsibilities, at least in part. However, state and local governments have grown, too.

- **Disobedience vs. the Rule of Law.** One way of getting attention from politicians is direct action techniques: marches, rallies, protests, demonstrations, picketing, boycotting, and strikes. A more controversial method is civil disobedience, the deliberate and public refusal to obey a law.

- **Freedom of the Press vs. Right to Fair Trial.** Journalists can show bias in many ways. In the case of a highly publicized trial, this bias can be used to sway public opinion and influence the outcome of the trial. It can be accomplished in more subtle ways as well.

Demonstrators in Oakland, California, protest school funding cuts and tuition increases.

A Source of Conflict

The First Amendment of the U.S. Constitution guarantees that "Congress shall make no law respecting an establishment of religion, or prohibiting the free exercise thereof . . . ." This provision originally protected religious groups from unfair treatment by the federal government only. Until the mid-1800s, New Hampshire and other states had laws that prohibited non-Protestants from holding public office. Since the 1940s, however, the Supreme Court of the United States has ruled that all the states must uphold the First Amendment's guarantees of religious freedom.

Today, freedom of religion remains an issue in the United States. Judges have struck down plans that called for the government to give financial aid to religious schools. The courts have also ruled unconstitutional a number of programs that teach the Bible or recite prayers in public schools. These rulings are highly controversial.

LIMITS ON RIGHTS

Even in democratic societies, there are limits to civil rights.

Civil Right	Limitations
Speech	Most democratic nations have four major restrictions on free expression. 1) Laws covering libel and slander prohibit speech or publication that harms a person's reputation. 2) Some laws forbid speech that offends public decency by using obscenities or by encouraging people to commit acts considered immoral. 3) Laws against spying, treason, and urging violence prohibit speech that endangers life, property, or national security. 4) Other laws forbid speech that invades the right of people not to listen to it. For example, a city ordinance might limit the times when people may use loudspeakers on public streets.
Search and seizure	In the Constitution of the United States, the Fourth Amendment states that no unreasonable searches or seizures may be made. The search warrant must describe the place to be searched and what is to be seized in the search. However, the Supreme Court has identified exceptions. • In 1982, the court ruled that police do not need a search warrant to accompany an arrested person into the person's home or to seize any possible criminal evidence in sight there. • In 1984, the court declared that evidence obtained with a search warrant later ruled to be defective may be used in court if the police reasonably believed they followed proper procedures in obtaining the search warrant.
Gun control	The Second Amendment to the U.S. Constitution reads: "A well-regulated militia, being necessary to the security of a free state, the right of the people to keep and bear arms shall not be infringed." • Gun control laws aim to reduce the criminal use of guns as much as possible. • Gun control laws try not to interfere with noncriminal gun use. • Some U.S. citizens argue that gun control laws violate their right to own guns.

U.S. GOVERNMENT

Although we seldom think about it, government touches each of our lives every day. When we consider government at all, we think of the president sitting in the Oval Office contemplating national policy or of the local mayor dealing with problems such as budgets or crime. However, the heads of governments are actually tiny parts of much larger institutions.

To understand the governmental system of the United States, it is important to consider the local, state, and federal governments in turn.

In small towns, legislative power may be in the hands of citizens at regular town meetings. ▶

Who Runs Local Government?

Form of Local Government	Description	Details
Strong mayor-council form	A miniature of state and federal government	The mayor acts as chief executive, appoints the heads of most major departments, drafts the budget, and has veto power over acts of the city council, which serves as a legislature. The advantages of this system include a division of powers and a system of checks and balances.
Weak mayor-council form	The power of the mayor is severely curtailed.	The council appoints administrators and drafts budgets. The mayor lacks veto power and sits at council meetings only as a moderator.
Commission form	A curious blending of administrative and legislative functions in one body	The commissioners—usually five in number—are elected at large and each assumes executive control of a department (public safety, public works, revenue, parks and recreation, public affairs). The commissioners also serve as a legislature, adopting budgets and ordinances.
Council-manager system	Usually consists of an elected council	The council passes ordinances and sets broad policies. A professional manager, who is appointed by the council, administers the daily business of government and gives advice to the council on matters of policy.
Mayor-manager system	The mayor, as chief executive officer, appoints the city manager to be chief operating officer.	In this model the manager serves at the mayor's pleasure rather than the council's. The voters can get rid of a manager whose actions are unpopular by voting against the mayor.

Functions of Local Government

Despite all the attention showered on national and state politics, local government probably affects more people in more ways than all federal and state government combined. Many local government functions are so familiar that we take them for granted.

Public Works. Perhaps the most visible of local governments' responsibilities lie in the area of public works. Local governments repair streets, remove snow and ice in winter, collect garbage, and dispose of sewage.

Public Safety. One of local governments' most important jobs is promoting public safety through police and fire protection. Not only must local governments prevent crimes, catch lawbreakers, and limit fire damage, they must do so publicly and visibly so that citizens feel secure.

Human Services. Many local governments operate public hospitals and medical clinics. Nearly all have health departments that enforce codes governing the cleanliness of restaurants, proper sewage disposal, inoculation against contagious diseases, and other public health concerns. Cities and counties also administer a variety of welfare services for the poor.

Culture and Recreation. Although many public libraries were built with the help of private contributions and local fund-raising efforts, their basic operating budgets come from local governments. Local governments also develop and maintain parks and other recreational facilities for local residents.

Regulation. Zoning is the determination of how land will be used. Local communities also enforce various building, housing, plumbing, electrical, health, and fire codes.

Education. In many areas, education costs more than all other local government activities combined. Local education is almost always supervised by a board of education that appoints a superintendent of schools, usually a professional educator, and supervises his or her work.

Five Basic Forms of Local Government

All cities with 1 million or more inhabitants use one of the mayor-council systems (see chart left). This form is also prevalent in large cities (500,000 to one million people) and some small towns (5,000 to 10,000). About half the municipalities between 10,000 and 500,000 use one of the city manager systems, about 40 percent employ mayors and councils, and about 10 percent retain commissions.

State Government

Structure of State Government

The differences among the states—in geography, population, and history—are so great that it is risky to generalize about them. However, the governments of the 50 states are remarkably similar in structure both to each other and to the federal government. Each has a governor, who serves as chief executive; a legislature, which has an upper and a lower house (except in Nebraska); and a judiciary, which may review legislation for its adherence to the state constitution.

Executive Branch. The governors are the chief executives of their states, but they face a variety of restrictions that limit their powers. Most states also elect

- a lieutenant governor.
- an attorney general—who is the state's attorney and the representative of the people in civil actions.
- a secretary of state, who oversees elections, licensing, corporate registrations, and other administrative functions.
- a treasurer, an auditor, or a controller, with various fiscal responsibilities.

Legislatures. The state legislatures pass legislation to create or amend programs, hold the power to appropriate money, and (at least in the upper houses) vote to approve gubernatorial appointments to cabinet offices and independent agencies. In practice, however, most legislatures have less real power than it appears. The leaders of the legislature include

- the lieutenant governor or senate president in the upper house.
- the speaker in the lower house.
- the majority and minority leaders in both houses.

All but the lieutenant governors are elected by the legislators themselves.

The Judiciary. Every state has a court of last resort, usually called the Supreme Court. The terms of the justices vary considerably. Some receive life tenure, but most are elected to terms ranging from 6 to 14 years. State courts suffer from two chronic ills.

- The caseload has increased far more rapidly than funds or court staff.
- Since they have jurisdiction over their own actions, they have assumed more responsibility at the expense of the legislative and executive branches.

The states are very involved in education, operating state university systems such as the University of Southern California. ▶

Responsibilities of State Government

State governments are specifically recognized in the U.S. Constitution, and their existence is independent of the federal government. The Constitution provides that powers not given to the federal government belong to the states. Each state has its own constitution that establishes the state's basic laws and administrative organization. The table at the right summarizes the responsibilities, taxing powers, and organization of state governments.

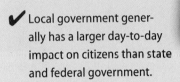

- Local government generally has a larger day-to-day impact on citizens than state and federal government.

- Local government is responsible for public works (for example, street maintenance), public safety, human services, culture and recreation facilities, regulation, and education.

- The five basic forms of local government are strong mayor-council, weak mayor-council, commission, council-manager, and mayor-manager.

- State governments have three branches, like the federal government: the executive (the chief executive is the governor), legislative, and judicial.

- State government maintains a court system to judge both civil and criminal cases and regulates such professionals as doctors and lawyers. Also, state government provides services similar to those of local governments in such areas as public safety and human services.

Police protection	Provide state police to patrol unincorporated areas, state highways, etc.
Court system	Maintain a system of courts to hear both civil cases (those between individuals, corporations, etc.) and criminal cases originating within state boundaries. State courts hear the vast majority of court cases in the United States. Parties to a case may appeal to federal courts only when federal laws or guarantees are at issue. (See Federal Government, Judicial Branch, page 337.)
Public safety	Establish laws and regulations governing certain areas of public safety; maintain state penal institutions for those sentenced to imprisonment for serious crimes.
Public works	Build and maintain state highways, buildings, universities, hospitals, parks, etc.
Education	Set minimum standards for local elementary and high schools; maintain state colleges and universities.
Social services	Provide assistance for needy citizens. States usually maintain public mental hospitals; set standards for other hospitals; and administer workers' compensation, unemployment, and welfare benefits, receiving partial funding from the federal government.
Recreation	Provide state parks and recreation areas.
Regulation	License corporations, drivers of motor vehicles, and practitioners of certain professions and occupations (doctors, lawyers, accountants, beauticians, etc.); regulate local tax rates and set minimum standards for certain local government services.
Representation	Represent state interests to private and other governmental organizations through elected and appointed state officials.

STRUCTURE OF THE U.S. FEDERAL GOVERNMENT

According to the Constitution of the United States (see pages 68–85), the federal government is responsible for four principal activities: regulation of affairs with other countries, defense of the country from foreign enemies and from civil disturbance, establishment of the monetary system, and regulation of relations among the states. The responsibilities of the government are carefully divided among the three branches: the legislative, the executive, and the judicial.

The United States Capitol, located in Washington D.C., is the meeting place for Congress.

Federal Government

President Barack Obama addresses a joint session of Congress in the House Chamber.

Legislative branch

The legislative, or lawmaking, branch consists of two elected bodies collectively called the Congress. Together, the Congress is responsible for considering and passing all laws and acts necessary to the operation of the government. In general, proposed laws or acts—called bills—may be first introduced in either house of Congress.

The House of Representatives. The larger of the two bodies is the House of Representatives, which consists of 435 voting members. The more populous states have a larger number of representatives. Representatives must be at least 25 years old and must run for reelection every 2 years.

The Senate. Two senators are elected from each state. Senators must be at least 30 years old. They serve 6-year terms, with approximately one-third up for election every 2 years. The Senate ratifies treaties with other nations negotiated by the president or his appointees, and it approves presidential appointments to major cabinet posts, diplomatic posts, and federal judgeships. If a president or other high official is impeached by the House, the Senate serves as a jury in the impeachment trial.

ORDER OF SUCCESSION TO THE PRESIDENCY
(in case of death or disability)

*The 25th Amendment to the Constitution provides a means by which a vice president who has succeeded to the presidency may nominate a new vice president with the advice and consent of the Senate. The order of succession above would take effect only if the vice president died at the same time as or soon after the president.

Barack Obama, the 44th president of the United States

1. Vice President*

↓

2. Speaker of the House

↓

3. President Pro Tempore of the Senate

↓

4. Secretary of State

↓

5. Secretary of the Treasury

↓

6. Secretary of Defense

↓

7. Attorney General

↓

8–16. Other cabinet secretaries

Executive Branch

The president and the vice president are the only two government officeholders elected by the whole electorate of the United States. The president and the vice president run on the same ticket and serve a 4-year term. They are elected in November of years divisible by four and take office the following January.

Presidential Responsibilities. The president serves in four important capacities.

- **Head of state.** The president serves as a symbol of national unity and directs the foreign relations of the United States.

- **Commander in chief of the U.S. armed forces.** The president has broad powers to direct the armed forces both in peace and in war. However, only Congress can officially declare war.

- **Chief political leader of the country.** As the chief officeholder elected by the whole country, he has broad powers to frame legislation and make policy.

- **Director of the executive branch of the government.** The president appoints the secretaries of each department and the heads of many independent agencies.

Judicial Branch

The Constitution gives the federal judiciary specific responsibility for hearing cases between states or residents of different states; cases involving other countries; and cases involving the breaking of federal laws. Today the court system consists of

- federal district courts, operating in every state.

- nine federal circuit courts, each hearing appeals from lower courts in a region of the country.

- several special courts for specialized cases.

- the Supreme Court, the final authority in the U.S. system of law. The Supreme Court consists of nine justices, one of whom serves as chief justice. They decide cases by vote, and a majority of justices present is required to reach a decision.

The Supreme Court is asked to decide thousands of cases each year, most of which come to it on appeal from state courts or lower federal courts.

Inside the Federal Government

Outline of the Three Branches

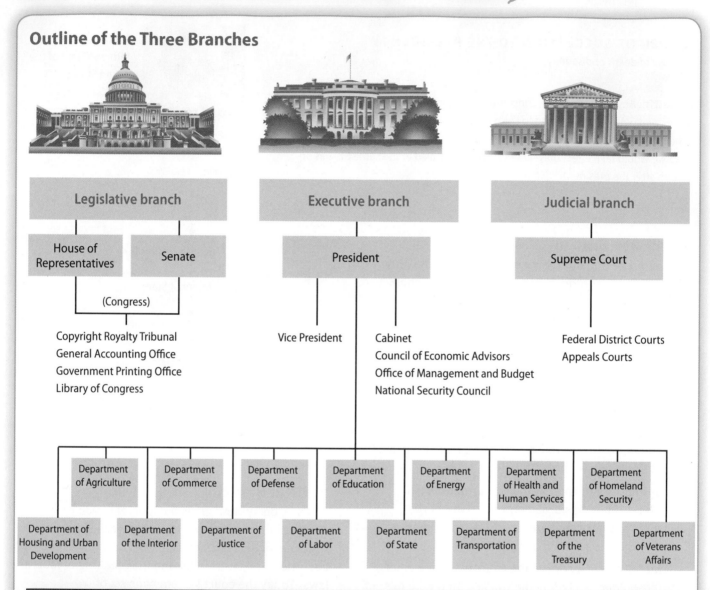

Legislative branch	Executive branch	Judicial branch
House of Representatives Senate	President	Supreme Court
(Congress)		

Legislative branch
- Copyright Royalty Tribunal
- General Accounting Office
- Government Printing Office
- Library of Congress

Executive branch
- Vice President
- Cabinet
- Council of Economic Advisors
- Office of Management and Budget
- National Security Council

Judicial branch
- Federal District Courts
- Appeals Courts

Department of Agriculture · Department of Commerce · Department of Defense · Department of Education · Department of Energy · Department of Health and Human Services · Department of Homeland Security

Department of Housing and Urban Development · Department of the Interior · Department of Justice · Department of Labor · Department of State · Department of Transportation · Department of the Treasury · Department of Veterans Affairs

Independent Establishments and Government Corporations

Central Intelligence Agency	Federal Reserve System	National Science Foundation
Consumer Product Safety Commission	Federal Trade Commission	National Transportation Safety Board
Environmental Protection Agency	General Services Administration	Nuclear Regulatory Commission
Equal Employment Opportunity Commission	National Aeronautics and Space Administration	Peace Corps
Federal Communications Commission	National Archives and Records Administration	Securities and Exchange Commission
Federal Deposit Insurance Corporation		Selective Service System
Federal Election Commission	National Foundation on the Arts and the Humanities	Small Business Administration
Federal Housing Finance Board	National Labor Relations Board	Social Security Administration
Federal Mediation and Conciliation Service	National Mediation Board	Tennessee Valley Authority
		United States Information Agency
		United States Postal Service

HOW A BILL BECOMES A LAW

House

1. Congressional sponsor introduces bill.
2. Bill is assigned to committee.

3. Committee reports bill to full House.

4. House approves.

Senate

1. Senate sponsor introduces bill.
2. Bill is assigned to committee.

3. Committee reports bill to Senate.

4. Senate approves.

When there are differences between House and Senate bills

Conference Committee
is formed to consider bill and revise.

Revised bill is returned to both Houses for final approval.

  Bill is printed, signed by **Speaker of the House.**

Bill is sent to **President** for signature.

Bill becomes a law on signature.

If President vetoes bill (refuses to sign it), it can be reconsidered by both Houses.

If it passes by two-thirds majorities in both Houses, it becomes law without President's signature.

The Distribution of Powers

Checks and Balances

The framers of the U.S. Constitution had a fundamental mistrust of government. This led them to distribute the powers of the federal government among three branches, with separate and distinct duties and responsibilities for each. In addition, the Constitution provides for checks and balances that offer each branch protection against the others.

Veto Power. The president has the power of veto over acts of Congress; he may simply refuse to sign into law a bill Congress has passed. The Congress, in turn, may override a presidential veto. If both the House and the Senate vote to override by a two-thirds majority, a vetoed bill becomes law despite the president's objections. The judiciary determines the constitutionality of laws passed by Congress and signed by the president.

Stalemates and the Limits of Power. The major complaint against separation of powers is that it breeds inefficiency. It is not uncommon for one political party to control the presidency while the other controls the Congress, or even for the House and the Senate majorities to be in the hands of different parties. This may lead to a frustrating stalemate on occasion, but the system was designed specifically to impose limitations on power.

Impeachment. The ultimate check in this system is that the president, the vice president, and federal judges are subject to impeachment and removal for violation of their oaths of office. Impeachment, while uncommon, is a potent threat to the overly ambitious. Impeachment is done by the House, and if it votes to impeach, the official is tried in the Senate with the chief justice of the Supreme Court presiding as judge.

No president has ever been removed from office by impeachment, but there have been several close calls.

1868. President Andrew Johnson was tried by the Senate, and the vote was only one short of the two-thirds majority required to convict.

1974. President Richard Nixon resigned in the face of almost certain impeachment and conviction.

1999. President Bill Clinton was tried on two Articles of Impeachment, charges of perjury and obstruction of justice with regard to a previous civil case against him. Without the two-thirds majority vote necessary, he was acquitted.

CHECKS AND BALANCES

may veto acts of Congress, delay execution of congressional programs

nominates all federal judges, may delay enforcement of judicial decrees

Executive branch

may override president's veto, refuse or reduce budget appropriation, delay consideration of executive initiative

rules on constitutionality of executive acts

rules on constitutionality of acts of Congress

approves court appointments, budgets

Legislative branch

Judicial branch

LANDMARK DECISIONS OF THE SUPREME COURT

1857, Dred Scott v. Sandford. Court ruled 6–3 that black slaves were property; that they had no rights of citizenship; and that Congress could not abolish slavery in a U.S. territory. The decision sharpened divisions that led to the Civil War in 1861. It was nullified by the 13th and 14th Amendments.

1896, Plessy v. Ferguson. Court ruled that "separate but equal" facilities for blacks and whites were constitutional. The decision was reversed in 1954 (see below).

1954, Brown v. Board of Education of Topeka. Separate but equal schools for blacks and whites are unconstitutional. (See page 211.)

1963, Gideon v. Wainright. The court ruled that a state must provide legal counsel for anyone who is accused of a felony and cannot afford a lawyer.

1966, Miranda v. Arizona. The court ruled that nothing arrested persons say can be used against them in their trial unless they have been told they have certain rights, including the right to remain silent and the right to be told they can have a lawyer present during questioning. If they cannot afford a lawyer, the court must appoint one.

1978, Regents of the University of California v. Bakke. The court ruled that university admissions policies may not use quotas to achieve racial balance. However, these policies may give special consideration to members of minority groups to achieve variety in a student body.

1995, Adarand Constructors, Inc. v. Pena. The court ruled in favor of a contractor in Colorado who sued the federal government, claiming his constitutional rights had been violated when an affirmative action program caused his company to lose a subcontract to install guardrails on a U.S. highway.

1996, United States v. Virginia (VMI). The Court ruled that the Virginia Military Institute's male-only admissions policy was unconstitutional.

U.S. Supreme Court and the Constitution

In addition to its constitutional responsibilities, the Supreme Court has two other important jobs:

- to decide the constitutionality of any act of Congress or the president. This power is seldom used, but it acts as a powerful check on both the Congress and the president.

- to review cases in which individuals or groups claim that their constitutionally guaranteed rights have been violated. These civil liberties, as they are called, are guaranteed by the first 10 amendments of the Constitution, called the Bill of Rights. These guarantees have been extended by later amendments to the Constitution.

now you Know!

✔ The three-part structure and checks-and-balances system of the U.S. federal government have their roots in the Founding Fathers' fear of too-powerful government.

✔ The three parts of the U.S. federal government are the legislative, the executive (the president is the head of state and of government), and the judicial.

✔ The Congress, the legislative branch, consists of the House of Representatives and the Senate, which are responsible for making all national laws.

✔ The president is commander in chief of the U.S. armed forces and the country's top political leader in addition to serving as head of state and manager of the executive branch.

✔ The U.S. federal courts and the Supreme Court comprise the judicial branch. The decisions of the Supreme Court are the final authority in the U.S. system of law.

CITIZEN PARTICIPATION

The government of the United States was organized to give the individual maximum power over government. The U.S. system encourages its citizens to help choose its leaders and to help determine government policies through voting, writing to elected officials, and direct political action—campaigning and demonstrating. An active citizenry is thought to be one of the best guarantees against corrupt and inefficient government.

The right to vote was extended through the passage of the following amendments.

- *The 15th Amendment (1870) extended the vote to males of all races and colors.*
- *The 19th Amendment (1920) extended the vote to women.*
- *The 26th Amendment (1971) extended the vote to 18-year-olds.*

What Can Citizens Do?

Voting

People can vote on a variety of issues. For example, they may vote on whether the government should build a school, expand the police force, or impose a tax. Under some systems, voters may approve or reject proposed laws through elections called referendums. A recall election allows voters to remove elected officials from office before the end of their term.

▲ **Informed citizens voting** by secret ballot in local, state, and national elections is the foundation of representative democracy.

Campaigning

Modern campaigns require a sophisticated team of "spinmeisters" and political consultants to keep up with technological advances and the fickle American public, whose opinions are subject to change with no notice. The presence of spinmeisters and consultants on the campaign trail has caused significant changes in the way that political campaigns are conducted. Formerly, campaigns revolved around amateur volunteers—people who had a personal interest in the candidate or the issues, and were vested in the outcome. Professional campaign workers, by contrast, operate at an emotional remove. Some observers believe that they have steril-ized campaigns, contributing to the apathy and general disillusionment felt by many citizens at election time.

Petitioning

The process known as *initiative* allows voters to introduce a law to the ballot through popular petition. In other words, it gives the electorate the ability to create laws independently of the official lawmaking body. In this way, initiative gives voters some amount of direct control over lawmaking, allowing independence from lawmakers who refuse to consider or enact a law that many people want.

Running for Political Office

If a voter is dissatisfied with the quality of elected officials, he or she does have a potentially powerful weapon: the ability to run for political office. However, elections have become increasingly expensive. A presidential campaign, for example, can cost hundreds of millions of dollars. This can make running for office very difficult for anyone who isn't wealthy, or doesn't have the backing of wealthy individuals or corporations. Recent campaign finance reform legislation has attempted to address some of these issues.

Lobbying

Today's lobbyists may seek to influence legislators, policy makers, or government administrators. They may even bring suit against the government to further their purposes. Many people imagine that such work only involves direct communication with legislators, but that is not the case. In fact, a lobbyist's interaction with elected officials is only a fraction of his or her job.

WHAT DO LOBBYISTS DO?

The bulk of lobbyists' work involves heavy research. They must become experts on the issue(s) in which they are involved. This entails several activities.

- researching the opinions and beliefs of the people or organizations they represent
- studying legislative proposals closely
- delivering opinions during congressional hearings
- monitoring and reporting on any developments in their issue
- communicating often with their employers to define goals

Protest demonstrations are one way for citizens to apply pressure on politicians.

Demonstrating

If lobbying proves ineffective, there are, of course, alternative ways that pressure groups can influence politicians. Direct action techniques such as marches, rallies, protests, demonstrations, picketing, boycotting, and strikes are all effective ways of reaching lawmakers. A more extreme (and controversial) method is civil disobedience. Direct action, while effective, is more difficult to implement, since it requires participation from a large group of willing volunteers. Lobbyists, by contrast, are efficient professionals.

THE U.S. POLITICAL SYSTEM

There is no mention of political parties in the United States Constitution. In fact, the Founding Fathers were against the development of parties, which they called "factions." Nevertheless, parties began to develop during the presidency of George Washington. Merchants and urban classes banded together as Federalists under the leadership of Alexander Hamilton, while the farmers of the South joined with less affluent urban dwellers in the North to form the Democratic-Republicans under Thomas Jefferson. (See page 67.)

Delegates at national political conventions will usually work together to ensure that ideological squabbles can't hurt their chances for electoral victory.

Inside the Political Parties

Political Parties

Political parties are organized groups of people who compete in governmental elections. They recruit candidates, organize campaigns, and raise money. They offer a banner under which candidates can run. The legends on those banners may be vague and sometimes even contradictory, but many voters have become so accustomed to them that it is very difficult for a candidate to win unless he or she is a Democrat or a Republican. Political parties serve other, more ideological purposes in representative democracies.

- They provide a direct link between people and their government, providing a forum where opinions are elevated into political action.

- They provide built-in opposition to the party in power, constantly giving critiques or suggesting alternatives.

- They help keep voters informed about current issues by staging public debates.

The Two-party System. The two modern parties—the Democratic and the Republican—initially attracted a broad spectrum of people with varying beliefs. The agrarian Democrats of the South tended to be more conservative than the urban Democrats of the North. Similarly, populist Republicans were more progressive than the business-oriented Republicans.

Today, American political parties are loosely organized at the local, state, and national levels. However, once a party nominates its candidate for the presidency, most members of the party unite for the duration of the campaign. The logic behind this phenomenon is simple: the presidency is too great a prize to risk losing to the opposing party over ideological squabbles. Divisions within the party can lead to resounding electoral defeats. This happened when moderate Republicans abandoned Barry Goldwater in 1964, and when conservative Democrats refused to support George McGovern in 1972.

▲ **The elephant** serves as the official symbol for the Republican Party. Like the Democratic donkey, it originated in the work of Thomas Nast, a popular political cartoonist.

◄ **The donkey** has long been the unofficial Democratic Party mascot. (It was never officially adopted by the Democratic Party.) The icon was originally used in conjunction with Andrew Jackson's campaign.

Growth of the Democratic and Republican Parties		
Historical Milestone	**Republican Party**	**Democratic Party**
Roots and origins	The roots of the Republican Party are in the antislavery movement. The first Republican presidential victory came in 1860, when Abraham Lincoln was elected president. His election spurred the secession of 11 states and, in effect, started the Civil War.	Although Thomas Jefferson formed the Democratic-Republican Party, many historians believe that the modern Democratic Party is rooted in the presidential campaign of Andrew Jackson. Jackson's constituents became known as Democrats around 1830.
After the Civil War	Republicans benefited from the bad reputation that Democrats secured during the Civil War. Republicans were particularly well received during the 1920s, when they were known as "the party of prosperity."	In the years following the end of the Civil War, it was widely remembered that Southern Democrats had been supporters of slavery. As a result, the Democratic Party became unpopular after the war.
Impact of the Great Depression	The Great Depression was a bleak moment in Republican history. Republican leaders were held responsible for the misery felt by those suffering in the wake of financial ruin.	In the depths of the Great Depression, Franklin D. Roosevelt was elected president (1932). His innovative New Deal revived the economy and established many important federal programs, such as Social Security.
Changes in the parties	In 1953, war hero Dwight Eisenhower became the first Republican president in 24 years. Republican candidates have won seven of the 13 elections since Eisenhower's presidency.	Beginning in the 1930s, many African Americans became involved with the Democratic Party. This marked a significant shift in party values, considering its history supporting slavery.
Recent presidential administrations	Ronald Reagan (1980–1988) George H. W. Bush (1988–1992) George W. Bush (2000–2008)	Jimmy Carter (1976–1980) Bill Clinton (1992–2000) Barack Obama (2008–)

Political Pressures

Interest Groups

Any group of individuals or institutions organized to influence public policy is an interest group. The power, or political clout, of an interest group depends on several variables. The most important of these are the size of its membership and the available financial resources. Their biggest weapon is the implied threat that their members will punish uncooperative politicians at the polls.

Economic Interest Groups. This category includes businesses, trade unions, and trade associations (which are often the largest and most active organizations). The National Association of Manufacturers, for example, represents more than 14,000 companies. Almost every industry, from mining to toy manufacturing, has an association representing its interests in Washington. This category also includes large private corporations, who often maintain their own lobbying offices in Washington. Many people believe that their immense financial resources gives economic pressure groups considerable (and sometimes unfair) access to the seats of power.

Public Interest Groups. In recent years, the State Public Interest Research Groups (PIRGs) have become an important presence in Washington. Each state operates a PIRG, which is funded by citizens. They work on issues such as public health, the environment, and the general well-being of people. Some public interest groups, such as the National Association for the Advancement of Colored People and the National Organization for Women, focus their attention toward a particular segment of society.

Single interest pressure groups include the American Civil Liberties Union, which defends the rights and freedoms of American citizens. The Sierra Club concerns itself with the environment. Mothers Against Drunk Driving works toward stricter punishments for those driving while intoxicated.

Ideological. The final type is the ideological pressure group. These organizations are based upon a particular ideology. Many of the most influential ideological pressure groups are based in conservative religion; the Christian Coalition and the Moral Majority are just two examples.

The Four Types of Interest Groups		
Type	**Description**	**Examples**
Economic	Profit-oriented organizations, including trade associations, large corporations, and professional associations	National Association of Manufacturers, General Motors, American Medical Association
Public interest	Nonprofit organizations working for the public's well-being	Common Cause, National Association for the Advancement of Colored People, National Organization for Women
Single interest	Organizations associated with a specific issue	American Civil Liberties Union, Sierra Club
Ideological	Organizations based around a particular ideology, often religious	Christian Coalition, John Birch Society

The Media

The press is one of the few institutions outside the government that is mentioned specifically in the Constitution. The Bill of Rights prohibits the government from abridging free expression of opinion on the theory that the press serves as a watchdog on government.

Adversaries. Since elected officials cannot actually regulate or restrict the press, they often employ subtle, but legal, forms of coercion. For instance, they might appeal to reporters' and editors' sense of patriotism to report a story in a certain way, or encourage reporters to become "insiders" who will not jeopardize a good source by criticizing him or her.

The FCC. The government possesses a particularly potent weapon against radio and television: the Federal Communications Commission, whose members are appointed by the president, licenses all radio and television stations. No station has ever lost its license for its news reporting, but the threat is implicit.

Citizens need to be able to depend on the media to provide them with honest reporting on the events of the day, unpressured by government influence or coercion. ▼

Biased Reporting. Politicians often complain that biased reporting can affect the outcome of an election. Indeed, reporters can show bias in many ways: the pictures, headlines, font sizes, page number, and length of pieces appearing in newspapers or magazines are ways in which a journalist can manipulate the image of a politician. On television, the amount of air time a candidate receives, the sound bites that are chosen, and coverage of his or her personal life also affect the way a public image is constructed.

Watchdogs or Entertainers? The press functions as an outside regulator of government. However, today there is some concern that the watchdog role of journalists has been compromised by concerns about profit. The most popular news source today is the televised news program. Like other entertainment programs, the success of these shows is measured by their popularity with viewers and, therefore, their ability to attract paying advertisers. As a result, news shows have been forced to conform to the features of entertainment programming to retain their viewers. News stories tend to be violent, lurid, and sensational; in other words, they are designed to attract attention (i.e., viewers and profits), rather than to inform.

now you **Know!**

✔ Political parties began to develop during the administration of George Washington.

✔ Today's two major U.S. political parties, the Democratic and Republican, have their roots in the 19th century.

✔ A political party helps to link individuals to their government, provides an opposition to a majority party, and keeps issues in front of voters.

✔ There are four types of interest groups: economic, public interest, single interest, and ideological.

✔ The media can be a force in political culture through imbalances, intentional or unintentional, that affect their coverage of political news.

CANADIAN GOVERNMENT

Although the Canadian and American systems of government stem basically from that of Great Britain, they exhibit certain differences. Canada's governmental structure is almost an exact copy of that of the mother country, with its Parliament, prime minister, elected House of Commons, and appointed Senate, which is similar to the unelected British House of Lords. Nevertheless, over the years the governments of Canada and the United States have developed along similar lines and have faced similar problems.

Canada: An Introduction

Canada's Unique History

The history of government in Canada differs from that of any other nation in the Western Hemisphere. South of what became the United States of America, Spanish and Portuguese rule prevailed. Their rule was monarchical, centralized, and bureaucratic. By contrast, the English colonies on the Atlantic seaboard from Georgia to Canada wished to run their own affairs. Their common heritage of language, culture, and government made for unity and consensus.

Two Cultures. England and France fought for control of Canada for nearly 100 years before Great Britain triumphed in 1763. Even then the strength of the French part of Canada was so great that England could not insist on anglicizing its new subjects. This fact was recognized in the Quebec Act of 1774, by which Protestant England allowed French-Canadians to continue their practice of the Roman Catholic religion. The need to recognize French-English differences has continued into the Canadian governmental system to this day.

Banff National Park is part of the Parks Canada Agency of the Ministry of Environment.

Structure and Functions

Canada today is a parliamentary democracy made up of 10 provinces and three territories, with its capital in Ottawa. At the formal head of the government, after the British monarch, is the governor-general, who is appointed by the monarch on advice of the Canadian prime minister.

The governor-general's duty is to see to it that the country has a government at all times. When a prime minister resigns, dies, or is voted out in an election, the governor-general fills the office. In practice, that official abides by the principle of majority rule in naming a new prime minister, but there can be complications requiring tact and diplomacy when no political party has a clear majority in the House of Commons.

The Queen's Privy Council. The Queen's Privy Council for Canada includes former cabinet ministers, the chief justice and former chief justices, former speakers of Parliament, and other distinguished persons. Membership is for life. The portion of the Privy Council that actually advises the government is the sitting cabinet.

The Prime Minister. The most powerful member of the government is the prime minister, who is leader of the party holding a majority of seats in the House of Commons. Following a general election the governor-general will ask the leader of the majority party to become prime minister, form a government, and select a cabinet.

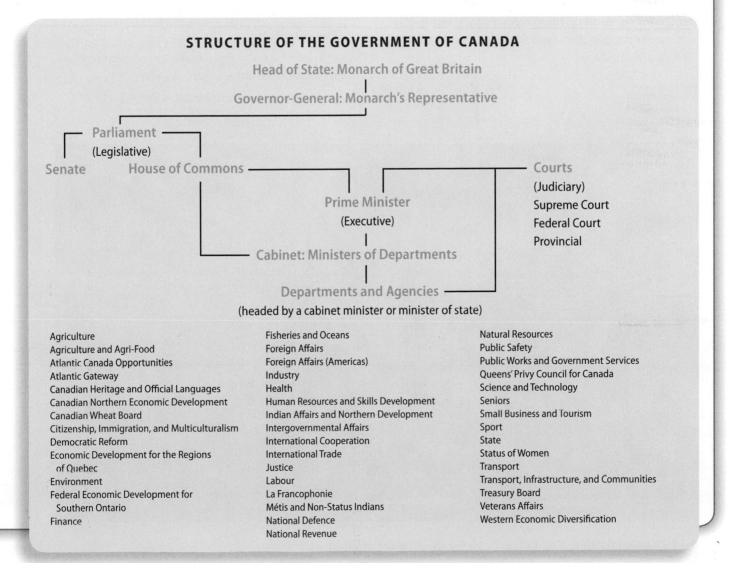

STRUCTURE OF THE GOVERNMENT OF CANADA

Head of State: Monarch of Great Britain

Governor-General: Monarch's Representative

Parliament (Legislative)

Senate   House of Commons

Prime Minister (Executive)

Cabinet: Ministers of Departments

Courts (Judiciary)
Supreme Court
Federal Court
Provincial

Departments and Agencies
(headed by a cabinet minister or minister of state)

Agriculture
Agriculture and Agri-Food
Atlantic Canada Opportunities
Atlantic Gateway
Canadian Heritage and Official Languages
Canadian Northern Economic Development
Canadian Wheat Board
Citizenship, Immigration, and Multiculturalism
Democratic Reform
Economic Development for the Regions of Quebec
Environment
Federal Economic Development for Southern Ontario
Finance

Fisheries and Oceans
Foreign Affairs
Foreign Affairs (Americas)
Industry
Health
Human Resources and Skills Development
Indian Affairs and Northern Development
Intergovernmental Affairs
International Cooperation
International Trade
Justice
Labour
La Francophonie
Métis and Non-Status Indians
National Defence
National Revenue

Natural Resources
Public Safety
Public Works and Government Services
Queens' Privy Council for Canada
Science and Technology
Seniors
Small Business and Tourism
Sport
State
Status of Women
Transport
Transport, Infrastructure, and Communities
Treasury Board
Veterans Affairs
Western Economic Diversification

Canadian Parliament

Parliamentary Structure

Parliament consists of two chambers, the House of Commons and the Senate, but Parliament often is used to refer only to the House of Commons. By law, Parliament must meet at least once a year. Legislation must pass both houses and then be given the royal assent, conveyed by the governor-general.

The House of Commons is by far the more important of the two bodies. All legislation having to do with government finance must start there. The House of Commons consists of 307 members, elected by popular vote from constituencies, based on population. Quebec has a fixed number of seats and each of the other provinces a number in relation to Quebec's (see table on facing page). Members are elected for terms of no more than 5 years, but the parliament is often dissolved for an election before 5 years are up.

The House of Commons elects a speaker, who presides over House sessions and rules on procedures. The cabinet appoints a speaker for the Senate. By custom, the speakers alternate between English- and French-speaking members.

The Senate has 99 members, who are appointed by the governor-general. They serve indefinite terms but must retire at age 75. Membership is based roughly on population.

HOW A BILL IS INTRODUCED TO PARLIAMENT

1. Permission to introduce the bill is requested.
2. The bill is printed and distributed to the legislators.
3. The bill is debated.
4. If the bill meets with approval, it is turned over to the appropriate committee, which may amend it.
5. It is brought to a vote and passed or rejected.

The Parliament Building, Ottawa, houses the Senate and House of Commons.

The Canadian Parliament		
Seats held by provinces and territories		
Province	**House of Commons**	**Senate**
Alberta	28	6
British Columbia	36	6
Manitoba	14	5
New Brunswick	10	10
Newfoundland and Labrador	6	5
Nova Scotia	11	10
Ontario	106	22
Prince Edward Island	4	4
Quebec	75	22
Saskatchewan	14	6
Northwest Territories	1	1
Nunavut	1	1
Yukon	1	1
TOTAL	307	99

Stephen Harper was elected prime minister of the Canadian government in 2006. (See page 305.)

Cabinet System

The prime minister names the members of the cabinet—usually between 25 and 30 members. Each province is represented in the cabinet. Ontario and Quebec have 10 or 12 members, depending on how many supporters of the party in power are elected from those provinces. One cabinet minister from Quebec will be an English-speaking Protestant, while another minister, usually from Ontario or New Brunswick, will be a French-speaking Catholic. A prime minister also may choose a minister for personal or geographic reasons.

Cabinet Ministers. There are three types of cabinet ministers.

- ministers who head a department with a given function, such as finance or agriculture
- ministers who have special parliamentary responsibilities
- ministers without portfolio, meaning no specific responsibility for any area of the government.

Ministers of State. In addition, there are two types of ministers of state, ranking somewhat below full cabinet members.

- ministers named for a designated purpose, such as a new or urgent project or policy
- ministers who assist a departmental minister

Other Governmental Bodies

In addition to the cabinet departments, there are a number of federal boards, agencies, commissions, Crown corporations, and councils. They include

- Canada Post.
- the Advisory Council on the Status of Women.
- the Commissioner of Official Languages.
- the International Joint Commission on the boundary water treaty of 1909 between the United States and Canada.

Provincial Governments

Each of the 10 provinces has a system of government that is essentially the same as that of the federal system. The lieutenant governor, appointed by the governor-general, is formally the chief executive. Each provincial government also has a political leader and a de facto executive, called premier. The premier represents the majority political party. In addition, there is a cabinet of department ministers.

Legislatures. The provinces have one-house legislatures. The membership varies considerably from province to province (see table below). Legislators are elected for terms of 4 years. Legislation must pass three readings and then have the assent of the lieutenant governor. Municipal governments are established by provincial laws that provide for mayors and other governing units. There now are about 5,000 municipalities.

Provincial Legislature	Number of Seats
Alberta	83
British Columbia	85
Manitoba	57
New Brunswick	55
Newfoundland and Labrador	48
Nova Scotia	52
Ontario	107
Prince Edward Island	27
Quebec	125
Saskatchewan	58

Territorial Governments

The territories have less self-government than the provinces. In large part, this is due to their vast expanses of land and small populations. Also, while there are many natural resources, they have not yet been developed and do not provide a basis for government support. The Northwest Territories and Yukon were joined by a third as of April 1, 1999. Nunavut (meaning "our land" in Inuktitut) is an Arctic area about the size of France that was carved out of the Northwest Territories. The area is populated mostly by Inuits (formerly referred to as Eskimos by many), who number around 25,000.

The Northwest Territories are governed by a federally appointed commissioner and a 19-member elected legislative assembly. The commissioner has final authority over legislation. On April 14, 1982, 56 percent of the voters favored separating the land into east and west units. On November 26, 1982, the federal government accepted this decision.

Yukon has a commissioner and a 18-member assembly, with all members appointed by the Dominion government.

Nunavut has a 19-member assembly that is elected by popular vote. Due to a land claims agreement forged prior to joining the Confederation, the Nunavut government has more input in decision-making than the other territories.

Legislative building for the territory of Nunavut. ▶

Territorial Issues

That Canada still has an English-French problem was demonstrated in 1986. On December 22 the Quebec Court of Appeals struck down a provision in a 9-year-old provincial language law requiring that public signs be written in French only.

Another debate centered on Sunday shopping laws. On December 18, 1986, the Supreme Court upheld an Ontario law that requires most retailers to close their businesses on Sunday. Debate continued for some time, but eventually Nova Scotia became the only province that had not legalized widespread Sunday shopping.

The Quebec legislature building houses a 125-seat legislature.

now you Know!

✔ Canada is a parliamentary democracy consisting of 10 provinces and three territories. Canada's head of state is the British monarch, represented in the country by the governor-general, and its head of government is the prime minister.

✔ Canada's federal government is patterned on the United Kingdom's government, with a prime minister and a parliament comprising a House of Commons and Senate (the House of Lords in the U.K.).

✔ Canada's House of Commons is the more important of the two bodies that make up the Parliament. Its 307 members are elected by popular vote.

✔ Canada's prime minister is the leader of the political party that holds a majority of House of Commons seats. The prime minister appoints members of a body called a cabinet to assist in the running of the government.

✔ The 10 Canadian provinces have governments that mirror the structure of the federal government, with a lieutenant governor and a premier, from the province's majority political party, as functioning chief executive.

✔ Because of their vast size and low population, Canada's three territories are less self-governing than its provinces.

✔ Colonial-era conflicts between the British and French segments of Canadian society continue into the present time.

Economics

ECONOMIC CONCEPTS: SUPPLY AND DEMAND

The supply of a product is the amount of it that businesses are willing and able to offer for sale at alternative prices. The demand for a product is the amount of it that users can and would like to buy at alternative prices. Because the amount that producers actually sell must be the same as the amount that users actually buy, the only price at which everyone can be satisfied is the one for which supply equals demand. This is called the *equilibrium price*.

The Meaning of Supply

Supply

Supply is the relationship between the price of a product and the quantity firms will produce and offer for sale. Given the assumption that a company will produce goods and services for profit, it will typically produce more of an item at a higher price than it will at a lower one. This direct relationship between price and quantity supplied is called the law of supply. It is reflected in the positive, or upward, slope of supply curves.

There are factors other than the selling price of the good or service that affect supply.

Alternative Outputs. The supply of one item can also be affected by the prices of other goods and services. Since resources can be used in different ways to produce different items, producers may allocate more of their resources toward the more profitable item(s).

For example, if the price of corn rises, farmers will dedicate more acreage to corn production and less to other crops such as wheat. This is true even if the price of wheat hasn't changed. In other words, a rise in the price of one product—corn—can reduce the supply of another product—wheat. It can also increase the supply of by-products—corn oil, for example, in this case.

What Affects Supply?		
Factor	**Typical Effect**	**Example**
Input costs	Negative	If labor costs rise, producers will reduce the quantity supplied at any given output price to avoid producing some units which were previously profitable but are now unprofitable because of higher labor costs.
Technology advance	Positive	If a technological advance (such as "smarter" equipment) reduces the cost of production, firms will produce more at any given output price.
Prices of related items	Negative	If, with the same or similar resources, a producer can shift production to a more profitable output, the quantity supplied for the original item will fall.

Consumers make choices in the marketplace by evaluating the tradeoffs between competing products. How much satisfaction will the consumer get from one product versus another? ▶

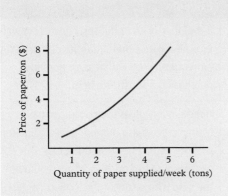

A graph that portrays all of the combinations of quantity supplied and price for a particular good or service is called a supply curve. Because producers are willing to supply larger quantities at higher prices, the supply curve has a positive, or upward, slope.

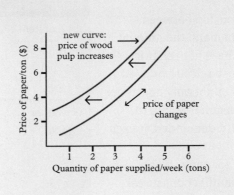

When a factor affecting supply other than price changes, it often causes a shift in the entire supply curve. This graph shows how a supply curve might move to the left, given that the price of a production input (wood pulp) increases. Now, at all the same prices as before, the quantity supplied decreases.

Utility

How does a consumer make any choice at all in an entire marketplace of products? To explain how individuals evaluate the tradeoffs among competing products, economists use the term *utility*. Utility describes the amount of satisfaction an individual gains from consuming a product.

Marginal utility is the extra satisfaction that an individual gets from consuming one more unit of an item. For most goods and services, marginal utility decreases as the number of units increases. For example, while the first ice cream sundae a day may be just the thing for a hungry consumer, chances are the fifth or sixth dish will be much less satisfying. As a result, the rational consumer will not be willing to pay as much for the sixth dish as for the first.

This idea—that satisfaction from marginal units decreases as more units are consumed—is called the law of diminishing marginal utility. It is one of the reasons why demand curves slope downward.

Changes in factors other than product price represent changes in supply that generate new supply curves. An increase in supply shifts the curve to the right; a decrease shifts the curve to the left. By contrast, when the price of a product changes, we move along the original curve to find the new quantity supplied.

The Meaning of Demand

Demand

Demand is the relationship between various prices of a product and the amount a consumer would purchase at each price. Demand is more than just a desire or need for an item. It must reflect not only consumer willingness, but also consumer ability to purchase the full quantity demanded at each price.

See the table at right for some of the factors besides price that affect consumer demand.

Demand Curve. In all cases, a change in any factor other than price is reflected as an entirely new demand curve, as shown on the graph on the next page. If higher quantities of products are demanded at each price (that is if demand increases), the demand curve shifts to the right. Changes that result in lower quantities shift the curve to the left.

A *new demand curve reflects a shift in demand. If price is the only factor that changes, no new curve is necessary. The quantity demanded is found by moving along the original curve.*

What Affects Demand?

Factor	Typical Effect	Example
Price of item	Negative	If the price of an item rises, consumers will typically reduce their quantity demanded, either getting by with less, or possibly purchasing a substitute item.
Consumer income	Positive	A raise in pay gives the consumer the ability to purchase more of a particular item without sacrificing something else. (An exception to this positive effect would be the case where consumers now consider the original item inappropriate to their real or perceived change in means and social status.)
Consumer wealth	Positive	This is similar to income. The distinction is that income is a measure of the flow of value into a household (hourly wages, monthly rents, quarterly dividends, profits, and so on), while wealth is a measure of the household's worth at one particular point. As with income, a consumer whose wealth increases can afford to buy more.
Price of complementary items	Negative	If the price of goods or services used along with the item rises (natural gas and gas stoves, staples and staplers), demand for the total "package" will decrease.
Price of substitute items	Positive	If the price of a reasonable substitute rises, consumers may begin to reduce their demand for the higher-priced good/service, choosing the now relatively lower-priced item.
Consumer preferences	Mixed	Consumer choices will vary, both from a society level (such as increased demand for low cholesterol foods, microwave meals, DVRs) and an individual level.
Consumer expectations	Mixed	Consumer expectations of how income, wealth, prices, and preferences will change also affect current demand. A consumer expecting income to rise steadily will typically purchase more of a particular item than if faced with imminent layoff.

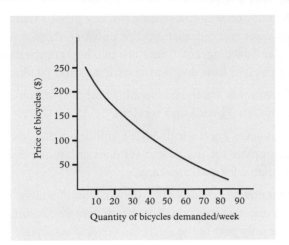

A graph that portrays all of the combinations of quantity demanded and price for a particular good or service is called a demand curve. Because the quantity demanded increases when price decreases, the demand curve has a negative, or downward, slope.

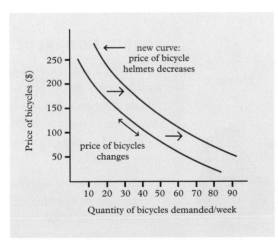

When a factor affecting demand other than price changes, it often causes a shift in the entire demand curve. This graph shows how a demand curve might move to the right, given that the price of a complementary good (bicycle helmets) decreases. Now, at all the same prices as before, the quantity of bicycles demanded increases.

Market Equilibrium

Now that we have a basic understanding of the individual factors that influence supply and demand, it's time to pull the pieces together and explore how they combine to influence overall behavior in a highly competitive market.

- The first step is the creation of market demand and market supply curves from the individual demand and supply curves already used.

- The next step is to bring consumers and producers together. For example, regardless of quantities that consumers have demanded, they will only be able to buy the amount firms actually produce. Likewise, just because firms produce and supply certain quantities, this doesn't guarantee that consumers will purchase in those quantities.

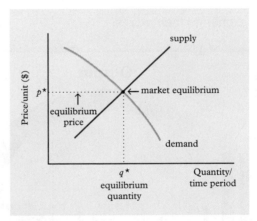

Graphing Equilibrium. In this step, we take the market demand and market supply curves and plot them on a single x/y graph. Recall that supply curves slope upward, demand curves downward. The point where the two curves intersect—where quantity demanded and quantity supplied are equal—is called market equilibrium. This point reflects equilibrium price and equilibrium quantity. At this point, there are no market forces prompting the price or quantity to change. Equilibrium is a point of natural rest.

ECONOMIC CONCEPTS: THE MARKET

No doubt you have heard the term "market," perhaps in reference to the stock market, the labor market, or to something as close to home as the supermarket. In economics, market—in its broadest sense—refers to the entire environment in which goods and services are produced, bought, and sold. It is not limited to a single location or industry. It may not even be housed in a physical structure; it could be simply a set of methods and rules by which buyers and sellers communicate with one another and exchange their wares.

How Markets Work

Circular Flow

A common way to illustrate the key groups within the market and the relationships between them is a circular flow diagram. There are two key groups in the basic circular flow diagram: consumers and producers.

- Consumers are the households that use, or consume, final goods and services.

- Producers are the individuals and organizations that create the goods and services and make them available for consumer use.

The obvious relationship, then, is one in which goods and services flow from producers to consumers. This is only part of the circle, however. Remember, the market is an environment for exchange, and so consumers typically pay a price or fee for the goods and services they receive.

This circular flow diagram includes two circles that reflect this close interdependency of consumers and producers. Goods and services provided are shown along the outer circle, with final outputs on the top half, production inputs on the bottom. Payments for all goods and services are shown within the inner circle.

PRODUCTION INPUTS

Because producers cannot produce goods and services out of thin air, there is another side to the circular flow of the market. This is the market for production inputs, which include

- **Labor,** the people who provide producers with needed skill, effort, and expertise.

- **Capital,** the supplies and equipment used by producers to create new goods and services.

- **Land,** the physical space on which producers locate their stores, offices, and factories, as well as the materials they can extract from that land.

Types of Markets

Every society has to deal with the three basic questions of economics.

1. What to produce?
2. How to produce it?
3. Who will get what is produced?

How different societies choose to answer each of these questions can be very different.

Command Economy. At one extreme, a society may choose to make its production and distribution decisions from one central, controlling point—usually a government agency. This type of economy is called a *command economy*. A command economy still has individual producers. However, these producers are not free to make production and distribution decisions on their own.

Laissez-faire Economy. At the other extreme of the market is the free or *laissez-faire economy*. The French term "laissez faire" literally means "allow them to do." In this type of economy, individual producers and consumers, acting in their own best interests, are expected to collectively produce a system that benefits all. As with the command economy, there is no perfect example of laissez-faire. Societies that are otherwise laissez-faire still may choose intervention through regulation, taxation, and so on.

Between the two market extremes, then, lies the wide expanse of real-world economies. Each economy is unique, defined by the manner and extent to which it implements the philosophies of one extreme or the other.

Market Comparison

Command

Definition: An economy in which a central organization plans and regulates the production and distribution of goods and services

Comments: Opposite extreme from laissez-faire. While a central authority plans output, consumers still determine demand; planners factor actual quantities purchased into future production goals.

Laissez-faire ("free market")

Definition: An economy in which individuals and firms are free to pursue their own self-interests without intervention by a central organization

Comments: Opposite extreme from command market. Derives from French phrase for "allow them to do." Relies on the market to bring consumers and producers together for exchange; the behavior of the market determines how goods and services will be produced and distributed.

Mixed

Definition: An economy that incorporates elements of both the command and laissez-faire economies

Comments: All real-world markets are mixed. The U.S.—primarily a free market—still includes substantial government purchases, employment, taxation, redistribution, and regulation.

✔ Supply is the economic relationship between the price of a product and the quantity of the product companies will make and offer for sale.

✔ Demand is the economic relationship between the various prices of a product and the amount of the product a consumer would purchase at each price.

✔ Such factors as the cost of labor (an input cost) can affect supply, and such factors as consumer income can affect demand.

✔ Market equilibrium happens when the quantity available of a product equals the quantity of demand for the product.

✔ Consumers make decisions among products and about how much of a product to buy on the basis of utility, which, as an economic term, means the amount of satisfaction the consumer gets from consuming the product.

ECONOMIC CONCEPTS: COMPETITION

Not all product markets are organized the same. They may differ by number of producers, by how unique the product is, or by the ease with which firms can enter and leave the market. All of these differences will affect market behavior.

Economists have developed several models to explain market differences. The most widely used are the extremes of perfect competition and monopoly. In addition, several intermediate models fall between these extremes on the competition continuum.

Perfect Competition

Perfect competition is a model of market organization where no firm controls or significantly impacts the market. Each firm is small compared to the size of the total market. (Refer to the table "Competition Comparison" for examples.) A perfectly competitive market has several distinguishing characteristics.

- The product of one supplier is virtually identical to that of another, so consumers can easily substitute one product for another. No producer enjoys the competitive advantage of brand recognition.

- There are no barriers to entry or exit. Firms can enter and leave the industry at will. No firm has an advantage that would preclude others from getting into the market (an exclusive patent, for example).

- Firms are unable to sell their products at higher than the market price because consumers will take their business elsewhere.

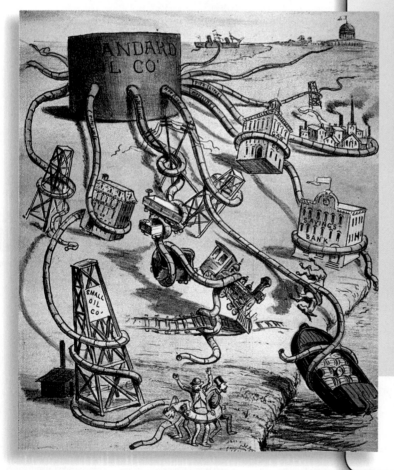

Monopoly

At the other extreme is the monopoly, a model of a market where only one firm (or a group of firms acting together) supplies a good or service. (Again, refer to the table "Competition Comparison" for examples.) A monopoly has these characteristics:

- There are no close product substitutes. Consumers either buy from the sole supplier or don't buy at all.

- There are barriers to entry and exit. One firm has an exclusive location or resource, or the government imposes barriers by protecting a patent or regulating an industry.

- The monopoly firm can set its own price. However, monopoly does not guarantee profits. The firm must still be able to produce its product at a cost below the price that consumers are willing to pay.

◀ **This political cartoon** from 1884 expresses the anger and frustration many people felt because of the monopolistic practices of the Standard Oil Company. (See page 143.)

Intermediate Models of Competition

Sometimes monopoly and perfect competition models do not adequately explain the behavior in a product market. As a result, a number of intermediate models have been developed.

Monopolistic Competition. In this particular model, many firms compete for the same consumer market, but the products they produce may have slight distinctions between them. Restaurants and publishing houses are examples of producers operating within monopolistic competition. Firms in this model try to establish name and brand recognition, so that at least for their particular product, they can act more as a monopoly (that is, they can exercise more control over the price of their product).

Oligopoly. In an oligopoly, there are only a few large firms that dominate the product market. Examples of oligopolies are the automobile, airline, and pharmaceuticals industries. On the competition continuum, an oligopoly is most like a monopoly.

GOT TO KNOW

Many intermediate models require that one firm take into consideration the action of the other firms. When an automobile manufacturer such as Honda sets the price for an Accord, it has to worry about Nissan's reaction to that price change and, in turn, General Motors' reaction to that price change, and so on. Thus, the firms in these intermediate models often place great importance on developing pricing and counterstrategies.

Competition Comparison			
Type	**Definition**	**Characteristics**	**Examples**
Monopoly	A market in which only one firm produces a good or service for which there are no close substitutes	Barriers to entry (natural or government-sponsored). Producer sets price, although still subject to market constraints. Often regulated by government.	Cable TV, public utilities
Oligopoly	A market where a few large firms dominate production	Competing firms typically take into account the actions and reactions of other firms in establishing pricing strategies. Limited market entry.	Automobiles, airlines
Monopolistic competition	A market in which there are many competing firms, but there are also slight distinctions among the products they produce	Many close substitutes. Firms try to induce brand loyalty—and thus, "mini monopolies"—by distinguishing their products from those of their competitors. No barriers to entry or exit.	Casual footwear, restaurants
Perfect competition	A market with many small firms (relative to the total market) whose products are completely interchangeable	Homogeneous, perfect substitutes. No firm can influence price. No barriers to entry or exit.	Farming, pencils

INFLATION

It is difficult to shop for anything today without noticing that prices have risen. But even though individual prices rise and fall in response to market behavior all the time, that is not inflation. Only when the overall price level rises do we have inflation.

Inflation occurs when many prices are rising at the same time. However, given the mix and weight of each of the goods measured by the Consumer Price Index (CPI), it is possible for some prices to fall even during a period of inflation.

"WHAT IS THE CPI?"

The most commonly used U.S. price index is the Consumer Price Index (CPI). It provides the average price change in a representative group of goods and services purchased monthly by a typical consumer. The CPI analyzes prices from all industries. It is compiled monthly by the Bureau of Labor Statistics.

To calculate the CPI, each of the goods and services is assigned a different weight according to the portion of income a typical consumer spends on that item. Those weights are updated every decade based on consumer surveys. Using this method, a rise in movie ticket prices won't affect the index as much as a rise in housing costs.

Economic Upheaval

Causes of Inflation

There are many possible causes of one-time inflation. Most are categorized as a source of either *demand-pull* or *cost-push* inflation.

- Inflation caused by an *increase in aggregate demand* (a country's demand for all goods and services) is called demand-pull inflation. Increases in aggregate demand can be brought about by increased government spending or measures intended to increase consumer and business spending, such as tax cuts or an increase in the money supply. Demand-pull inflation is often described as the condition in which too much money is chasing too few goods.

- Inflation can also be caused by an increase in input costs that is not matched by a comparable increase in demand. This kind of inflation is called cost-push, or supply-side, inflation. When possible, producers tend to pass these increased costs on to consumers in the form of higher prices. A sudden increase in the costs of production often can result from domestic or foreign economic or political disturbance.

Effects of Inflation	
People Affected	**Effect**
Those on fixed incomes	feel the squeeze because their incomes do not keep pace with rising prices
Workforce in the aggregate	usually does not experience a net loss in purchasing power as a result of inflation, since increases in general wage levels have typically outpaced inflation until recent years
Debtors	may benefit more than creditors, because the debtors are repaying their debts in cheaper currency
Creditors	tend to lose, since they are the ones who are receiving the cheaper currency
Those with savings accounts and other savings instruments that pay relatively low rates of interest	their investments or deposits become progressively less valuable in terms of purchasing power

Society suffers as a depression spreads mass unemployment, poverty, and despair. During the Great Depression, former homeowners resorted to living in "Hoovervilles" such as the one photographed here in Seattle in 1934. (See pages 176–177.)

Recession

Recession is a decline in overall business activity. During a nationwide recession, a country suffers a drop in buying, selling, and production, and a rise in unemployment. A recession may also hit an industry or a region. Recessions hurt countless people, especially the workers who lose jobs.

Causes. Most recessions occur because the total amount of spending in the economy drops. For example, if sales rise more slowly than usual, businesses may reduce their orders for new goods, causing manufacturers to cut back on production of those goods. They need fewer workers, and so unemployment increases. Workers have less money to spend, which further decreases the demand for goods. As this pattern spreads, a recession begins.

Reduced spending also may result if the government conducts a tight money policy, which makes bank loans harder to obtain. People's expectations also play a role in the decline of economic activity. If people believe conditions will worsen, they may cut back on their buying. By doing so, they can bring on the slump they were trying to avoid.

Depression

Depression is a deep, extended slump in total business activity. Buying and selling drop during a depression, causing a decline in production, prices, income, and employment. Many businesses fail, and many workers lose their jobs. This leads to further drops in sales, production, income, and employment.

The worst depression in history was the Great Depression, which struck in 1929 and continued through the 1930s. Depressions hurt great numbers of people, especially workers who lose their jobs. Bank failures wipe out the savings of depositors if such funds are not insured. Many people cannot meet rent or mortgage payments and lose their homes.

Causes. Economists disagree on what causes depressions. Theories on the causes include

- psychological factors determining decisions to save or to spend.

- population changes causing periods of expansion and contraction. When immigration or higher birth rates cause a population to grow, demand tends to increase. When population growth slows down, demand drops.

LABOR

The history of labor in the United States is the story of two struggles: of businesses struggling to adapt to changes in industry and technology, and the struggle between the management of those businesses and the employees, who seek to improve the quality of their lives. Although the objectives of managers and employees may differ, their interests oblige them to find ways to work together. The relationship between labor and management in the United States has often been adversarial, yet in the main both have cooperated to support the highly productive U.S. economy.

History of Organized Labor

Development

The improved technology of the Industrial Revolution, along with division of labor, made manufacturing more efficient and resulted in the development of the factory system. As a result, workers became specialized. Work was divided into small tasks, each of which was performed repeatedly by a worker. Rather than making an entire shoe, as a cobbler would, one worker in a shoe factory would cut the uppers, another would attach the heel, and so on.

Specialization of labor, although it increased efficiency, made workers dependent on the factories where they worked. They often lacked the training and variety of skills they would need to work anywhere else. If there was no factory work, employees lost their jobs.

Child labor and dismal working conditions contributed to the rise of labor unions.

Milestones in Organized Labor		
Milestone	**Year(s)**	**Event**
Early organization	1786	One of the first successful efforts came when Philadelphia printers banded together and secured establishment of the first minimum wage: 1 dollar a day.
Knights of Labor	1869	The first significant national union was the Knights of Labor. The organization comprised several craft unions, and membership eventually grew to over 700,000 workers. However, by the late 1880s, the Knights of Labor became fragmented, and conflict broke out among the various factions.
Haymarket riot	1886	The negative image of labor unions was solidified by violent incidents such as the infamous Haymarket riot in Chicago, in which a riot broke out as police attempted to break up a union rally. A bomb was thrown, killing 11 people, including seven police officers. Public outrage over the bombing made unions' attempts to secure better working conditions and a shorter workday even more difficult.
Worker exploitation	1900	In 1900, the average work week was about 60 hours. In some industries, such as steel production, it was even longer—12 hours a day, 7 days a week. Child labor was extensively used, as was the work of women, since employers usually paid them less. Workers who became sick or were injured on the job were fired and replaced. There were no pensions or workers' compensation programs.
American Federation of Labor (AFL)	1900–1920	Samuel Gompers wanted to make unions more effective. He concentrated on economic rather than social issues. Two major principles were advanced by the AFL under Gompers: Employees performing the same job should receive the same wage, and employee benefits should be based on seniority.
Congress of Industrial Organizations (CIO)	1935	As industries became more mechanized, more and more relatively unskilled workers, such as machine operators, were employed instead of skilled craftsmen. Some of the unions within the AFL began organizing workers in the automotive and steel industries, accepting both skilled and unskilled workers as members. In 1935, the industrial unions split from the AFL and formed the CIO under John L. Lewis (1880–1969).

Four Levels of Union Organization

There are four levels of union organization common in the United States: local, regional, national and international, and federation.

Local Unions. At the worker level are the local unions, which represent employees in a given geographic area. It is these local unions to which workers actually belong. The officers of local unions, as well as representatives sent to regional and national conventions, are elected by the members of the locals.

Regional Offices. At the regional level, most unions have state or district offices that coordinate the activities of local unions.

National and International Unions. National unions create the constitution and by-laws that local unions must abide by. It is often the national union that negotiates major issues with employers. Some unions, such as the United Auto Workers, have locals in Canada as well as the United States, making them international unions.

Federations. The highest level of union organization is the federation, the most significant of which in the United States is the AFL-CIO. The AFL-CIO is not itself a union, but an organization of unions. Federations mediate disputes between individual unions and provide a united labor front. They also work to get candidates elected to state and federal governments who are sympathetic to labor and lobby or otherwise press for favorable legislation.

Labor and Management

The Modern Era

In 1933, 2.5 million American workers belonged to labor unions. In the ensuing 20 years, favorable legislation and increased demand for workers during World War II helped union membership grow to more than 14 million, with the AFL and the CIO competing for membership. In 1955, the conflict ended, as the AFL and the CIO merged under George Meany (1894–1980) to form the AFL-CIO.

White-collar Workers. In the 1960s, government employees began to organize. Certain groups of white-collar workers, such as teachers, also formed unions. The two largest teachers' unions, the National Education Association (NEA) and the American Federation of Teachers, together now have almost 5 million members. (Although technically a teachers' association, the NEA is also considered a union, since it often acts as a collective bargaining agent and organizes strikes and pickets.) By the mid-1980s, more than 35 percent of all union members were white-collar workers.

Declining Membership. Double-digit inflation during the late 1970s made it more difficult for unions to demand increased benefits. Many workers were laid off, and others had to give up benefits to preserve their jobs. The air traffic controllers' union was effectively destroyed when President Ronald Reagan broke their strike early in his first term. This had a chilling effect on union efforts throughout the nation. Despite continued efforts to organize white-collar workers, membership declined into the 1990s. In 2010, total union membership was about 14.7 million, less than 12 percent of the workforce.

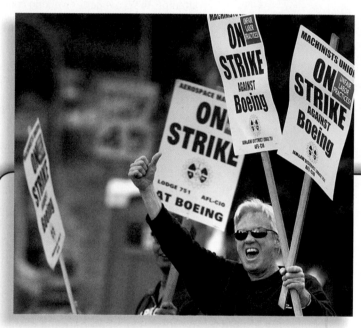

▲ **Going on strike** is one method unions can use to draw attention to disputes with management.

UNION TACTICS

- A *strike* deprives the employer of the services of its employees and draws public attention to the issues. In most cases, neither side wants or benefits from a strike. The company loses significant production and risks loss of customer loyalty. Profits may suffer dramatically. A prolonged strike usually causes hardship for the striking employees as well.

- Another major tactic used by union members is the *boycott,* a refusal of workers to use or buy products of the company with which the employees are in dispute.

▲ **Members** of the United Teachers Los Angeles union protest state and local budget cuts.

Collective Bargaining

Contract negotiations between a union and a company are referred to as *collective bargaining*. In this process, the emphasis is generally on such issues as wages, working conditions, grievance procedures, and fringe benefits.

Once a tentative agreement has been reached between union representatives and company management, the contract is presented to the union membership for ratification. If the workers vote in favor of the contract, it becomes legally binding on both parties for its duration, usually from 1 to 3 years.

Most labor-management negotiations result in a ratified contract without work stoppages. However, if an agreement is not reached, both labor and management have certain tactics available to them to pressure the other side to settle.

MANAGEMENT TACTICS

- A *lockout* occurs when the employer closes the business and refuses to allow the employees to work. Lockouts are rare and generally used only when a strike has already closed a plant.

- Employers may try to replace striking union workers with nonunion workers. Use of nonunion employees, called *strikebreakers* or *scabs,* is designed to put pressure on striking employees by making them believe they will lose their jobs if they do not return to work.

- In some instances, employers may secure a court order, called an *injunction,* forcing employees to cease certain activities. Excessive picketing or the use of pickets to intimidate those who attempt to cross picket lines may lead to court injunctions, as may activities that can result in damage to the employer's property.

- Management may also *outsource* work (contract it to other companies), transfer work from one of its plants to another, or even declare bankruptcy to end a union contract.

The Collective Bargaining Agreement

Contracts between employers and employees cover a wide variety of items, including wages, seniority rules, working conditions, work hours, personnel policies, and grievance procedures.

Cost-of-living clause

During the inflationary period of the 1970s, many collective bargaining agreements contained a cost-of-living adjustment (COLA) clause. A COLA clause calls for automatic wage increases when economic data indicate that the cost of living increases significantly prior to expiration of the contract.

Job security

During the recession of the early 1980s, high unemployment levels made job security a bigger issue than income in collective bargaining agreements, so unions pressed for job security guarantees. Management, however, was concerned with survival and pressed for union concessions, claiming that otherwise they could not compete successfully, particularly against foreign producers, and that many jobs would be lost. As a result, management often pressed for and received union concessions, sometimes called *givebacks*. Unions would agree to give up benefits and even accept lower wages to preserve jobs. Most collective bargaining agreements that included givebacks also included provisions specifying the conditions under which benefits would be reinstated.

Grievance resolution

Despite the comprehensive nature of employment contracts (some are more than 200 pages long), there is always the possibility that disputes will arise during the term of the contract. To handle these disputes, most collective bargaining agreements include a grievance procedure, a specified process by which complaints and disputes are aired and reconciled.

The Perils of Unemployment

Unemployment

Unemployment is the condition of a person who is out of work and actively looking for a job. Unemployment is commonly measured by a statistic called an *unemployment rate*. An unemployment rate is the percentage of jobless individuals in a community's total labor force—that is, in the segment of the population that is willing and able to be employed. Business executives, economists, and government officials use unemployment rates as indications of economic health.

Who Are the Unemployed? Unemployment statistics are compiled monthly by the Bureau of Labor Statistics, a branch of the U.S. Department of Labor. Anyone age 16 or older who has worked at least 1 hour as a paid employee in the previous month is considered employed. So too are individuals age 16 or older who have worked at least 15 hours in a family business, paid or not. Individuals on temporary leave are also considered employed. Full-time students and full-time homemakers are considered out of the workforce (and therefore not included in unemployment statistics).

WHAT IS THE UNEMPLOYMENT RATE?

The unemployment rate is a ratio of those who are unemployed compared to the total labor force, not the entire population.

total population = labor force + out of labor force
labor force = unemployed + employed
unemployment rate = unemployed / labor force

There are several difficulties in calculating an accurate unemployment rate.

- It is overstated to the extent that individuals say they are looking for work, but are not really doing so.
- It is understated to the extent that individuals unable to find work have become discouraged and stopped looking for work altogether.
- It does not reflect individuals who are underemployed (working fewer hours than they are willing and able to), nor the length of time that the average unemployed worker has no job.

Effects of Unemployment

Unemployment has a number of negative effects on society and the individual.

Effects on Society. From society's perspective, unemployment means loss of output. Every unemployed individual is someone who is willing and able to work, someone capable of producing output. What's more, the individual is not the only underutilized resource. So too are the supplies and equipment that now sit idle, producing nothing. Unemployment reflects resources that are not contributing to the nation's total output.

Effects on the Individual. From the individual's perspective, unemployment can be devastating. First, there is the loss of income. Not only are unemployed workers no longer producing, neither are they consuming (or at least not as much). Depending on the type and length of unemployment, the individual may also lose valuable job skills. The individual loses in terms of income and self-esteem.

Economists do not try to quantify the demoralizing effect that unemployment has on workers. However, economists do study the relationship between severe and prolonged unemployment on a host of social problems, including violence, crime, and poverty.

On August 13, 2010, several thousand people gathered ▶ outside City Hall in Los Angeles to protest unemployment and demand jobs. In the previous month, 131,000 jobs had been lost in the United States.

Causes of Unemployment. Economists generally classify unemployment into four categories.

1. *Seasonal unemployment* covers those individuals whose jobs require that they work only part of the year. Examples include construction work (less activity during bad weather months) and various retail stores that focus on holiday trade.

2. *Frictional unemployment* applies to individuals who are entering the job market for the first time or switching jobs. It is considered part of the normal employment process.

3. *Structural unemployment* reflects technological changes that make an existing group of workers' skills in a specific industry obsolete.

4. *Cyclical unemployment* is the type of unemployment associated with economic downturns (recessions and depressions). In times of cyclical unemployment, there are many layoffs and few job vacancies across all industries.

Unemployment insurance is a means of protecting workers who are out of work and looking for employment. These unemployed workers receive cash payments, usually each week, for a limited period. Besides aiding individual workers, unemployment insurance may help limit slumps in business activity by enabling unemployed people to buy goods and services. Such purchases help preserve existing jobs. Most industrial nations have government-sponsored unemployment insurance systems.

Unemployment insurance is financed chiefly by payroll taxes on employers. Both the federal and the state governments levy unemployment taxes.

- ✔ Two factors underlie the development of labor relations in the United States: The objective of business managers to make their companies profitable while adapting to economic and technological changes, and the objective of workers to improve the quality of their lives.

- ✔ The four levels of union organization in the United States are local (worker-level representation), regional (providing coordination of the local unions), national and international (providing overall governance), and federation (organizations of unions pursuing government relations and similar activities).

- ✔ Collective bargaining is the process by which business management and labor work out agreements about such matters as wages and working conditions which both groups follow for the period of time stated in the agreement.

- ✔ Types of unemployment include seasonal (work that by its nature lasts only part of the year), frictional (workers between jobs), structural (jobs made obsolete by technological advances), and cyclical (job loss because of economic downturns).

- ✔ The unemployment rate is the ratio of those who are unemployed compared to the total labor force, not the total population.

GOVERNMENT AND THE ECONOMY

One of the biggest areas of controversy in macroeconomics deals with the government's role in the economy. Some economists believe that government should play a major role by trying to smooth out the fluctuations in the economy. Their opponents claim that government actions are incapable of stabilizing the economy, and that such actions tend to overcompensate and just make matters worse.

Ferrari is an Italian manufacturer of sports cars. In order to promote the sale of automobiles manufactured in the U.S., the government imposes tariffs, raising the price of a Ferrari to a level that will encourage consumers to look more closely at American-made cars. ▼

Tariffs and Taxes

Fiscal Policy

How the government controls its budget—how it taxes and spends—is called *fiscal policy*. The government sets individual tax rates and controls spending decisions, but it does not set the total amount of government income and expenses. These are influenced more by the state of the economy.

Taxation. Taxes are meant to serve as an economic stabilizer. This is particularly true of progressive taxes, such as income tax, which increase in percentage as the base amount increases. Larger incomes result in larger tax revenues not only in amount but also in the percentage of income taken. As income increases, the proportion of it that is paid in taxes increases.

Tariffs are taxes that governments charge on imported goods. For example, the government can impose a tax on every foreign car that is brought in for sale from a foreign country. This tax raises the price of the item for consumers. Ultimately, the purpose of a tariff is to create a way to protect domestically made products (and domestic jobs) in a given industry.

Tariffs add to a foreign manufacturer's cost, making it less profitable for the foreign manufacturer to sell its goods in that country. If the foreign manufacturer is discouraged from exporting as many (or perhaps any) goods to that country, there is less competition for the domestic manufacturer. However, when competition decreases, prices rise. So, while tariffs seem favorable to the domestic manufacturer, they can be unfavorable to the consumer in the form of fewer choices and higher prices.

Government Spending. The other arm of fiscal policy is government spending. During a recession, a government may increase spending in an effort to increase total consumption. One goal here is that businesses will respond by increasing production and hiring more workers. However, an increase in government spending that is offset by an increase in taxes will reallocate national income but have little effect on the total amount of income. Taxpayers end up with a decrease in disposable income, but government suppliers realize an increase in income.

Government Borrowing. Governments borrow for many reasons. Large public works projects, such as interstate highways or mass transit systems, produce benefits for society over many years. If the government were to wait until it had sufficient funds to finance such projects, society would meanwhile be deprived of the benefits. Emergencies also force governments to borrow. In addition, war is a costly endeavor that ideally is financed immediately. Governments also use deficit spending—spending in excess of revenues—to stimulate a sluggish economy.

The Federal Deficit and Debt. In any year that government spends more than it receives, the result is a budget deficit. Alternately, if government receives more than it spends, the result is a budget surplus. Government must borrow money to finance deficits. It does this by selling government securities to the public, using the money received to pay off current bills, and promising to repay both principal and interest at some future date. The cumulative amount of money owed by the government at any point is called the federal debt. Each federal deficit adds to the federal debt.

FEDERAL DEFICIT/SURPLUS* AND DEBT

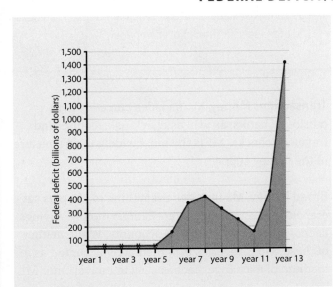

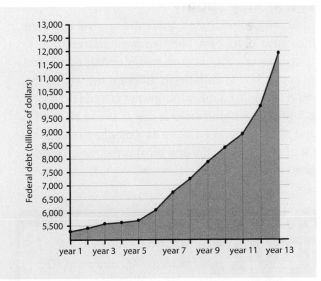

A federal deficit is not a cumulative figure. This graph represents how federal deficit figures might appear over a multi-year period.

*Note: The following years have surpluses: year 2 (69.3), year 3 (125.6), year 4 (236.2), and year 5 (128.2).

The federal debt is the total amount owed to corporations, banks, foreign lenders, and other government bondholders by the government at any point in time. Large federal deficits have resulted in a sharp rise in the federal debt.

Money

Monetary Policy

In the United States, monetary policy refers to actions taken by the Federal Reserve to control the supply of money. Deliberate expansion and contraction of the money supply are designed to control business cycles, maintain price stability, and contribute to full employment. When an economy is experiencing a recession, an increase in the supply of money can stimulate consumer demand. Such stimulation may result in increased productivity and employment as producers endeavor to meet the higher level of demand. As more people go to work, they spend more money, and the cycle continues. Also, as more people are put to work, tax revenues increase and welfare payments decrease, thus reducing the amount of money the government must borrow in order to operate. However, when the central bank increases the supply of money, inflation may result unless the supply of goods expands quickly enough to meet increased consumer demand.

The Money Supply

In the United States, there are several different measures of money. The two most common measures are *transactions money* or M1, and *broad money* or M2. Within these different measures, the main factor for determining what is and isn't money is liquidity. A liquid asset is one that can be used and accepted immediately as a medium of exchange. Currency (both coins and bills) is the most liquid asset of all.

One reason some econo- mists use M2 instead of M1 is that it is typically a more stable measure than M1. *This is because M2 is not affected by transfers between savings accounts and checking accounts or currency.*

THE FOUR ROLES OF MONEY

1. **Medium of exchange.** The primary role of money is to enable exchange of goods and services. Therefore, to be considered money, an item must be widely accepted in trade. The alternative to money as a medium of exchange is the barter system, where goods and services are exchanged directly for one another.

2. **Unit of account.** Money provides a way to meaningfully measure, compare, and add together different types of goods and services.

3. **Store of value.** Money provides a convenient way to hold value for future exchange; it's easier to store than lumber, yogurt, socks, or spaghetti! Because money has a fixed unit value, it is not the best store of value during periods of inflation; in such cases, the real value of money declines. However, during deflationary periods, money increases in real value.

4. **Standard for deferred payment.** Money provides a standard means for identifying the amount of a future payment. For example, if I loan you money today, I can get an I.O.U. for a specific future dollar amount.

Transactions Money. M1 includes currency held outside of banks, as well as checking accounts and traveler's checks. M1 is the most widely used measure of the money supply.

Broad Money. M2 includes everything in M1 plus several close substitutes for transactions money: savings accounts and money market accounts. While neither of these two categories is immediately accepted as a medium of exchange, each is easy to convert into M1.

Interest rates reflect the opportunity cost of holding currency. The relationship between the quantity demanded of money and the interest rate is inverse. For example, when interest rates rise, there is now more incentive for consumers and firms to save their dollars, removing them from the liquid money supply. Thus, when interest rates rise, the quantity demanded of money still in circulation falls.

The Federal Reserve Bank has three methods of controlling the money supply.

- changing reserve requirements
- changing the discount rate
- trading government securities on the open market

Changing Reserve Requirements. All banks are required to hold a percentage of the total value of their deposits with the Federal Reserve. (Deposits are what the banks "owe" their customers, such as savings and checking accounts.) This percentage is called the *reserve requirement.*

For example, if the reserve requirement is 10 percent, a bank with reserves of $100,000 is allowed to have up to $1 million in deposits (10 percent of $1,000,000 is $100,000). Any additional dollars held in reserves are called *excess reserves*. These can be used to cover additional deposits, as long as the required ratio (1:10 in this example) is not violated.

Changing the Discount Rate. Another tool the Federal Reserve has for affecting the money supply is the discount rate—the interest rate banks pay to borrow money from the Federal Reserve. There is an inverse relationship between discount rate and money supply. When the Federal Reserve lowers the discount rate, it expects that banks will borrow more. Adding the loan proceeds to its reserves, the bank can now make new loans of its own. The money supply increases.

Trading in the Securities Market. The tool most often used by the Federal Reserve to control the money supply is open market trading of government securities. The individual or organization that buys the security must pay for it, typically by writing a check on some type of bank demand deposit. That reduces the supply of money.

A similar type of process occurs when the Federal Reserve purchases government securities from the public, only this time it's in reverse. The check that the Federal Reserve writes to purchase the security is deposited in the seller's bank account, increasing the money supply.

Federal Reserve Board, Washington, D.C.

The Federal Reserve

In the United States, the money supply is controlled by the Federal Reserve. Founded in 1913, the Federal Reserve is the nation's central bank or "banker's bank." It regulates and supervises commercial banks, lends them money, acts as their clearinghouse, and assists banks in serious financial difficulty.

The Federal Reserve System is divided into 12 geographic districts, each served by a Federal Reserve Bank and subsidiary branch offices. All are governed by a seven-person Board of Governors. The chairperson of the board is appointed by the president for 4 years. The Federal Reserve banks are owned by the member banks in their districts; they are not government agencies.

Federal Reserve Districts			
District	**Headquarters**	**District**	**Headquarters**
1	Boston, MA	7	Chicago, IL
2	New York, NY	8	St. Louis, MO
3	Philadelphia, PA	9	Minneapolis, MN
4	Cleveland, OH	10	Kansas City, MO
5	Richmond, VA	11	Dallas, TX
6	Atlanta, GA	12	San Francisco, CA

Market Intervention

The Fair Labor Standards Act

The Fair Labor Standards Act is a law that sets the minimum wage and the length of the standard work week for most employees in the United States. Congress passed the Fair Labor Standards Act in 1938 as part of the New Deal, President Franklin D. Roosevelt's program to end the Great Depression.

Minimum Wage. The act originally set a minimum wage of 25 cents an hour. Amendments have raised the wage repeatedly. A 1963 amendment, the Equal Pay Act, requires that men and women be paid equally for doing equal work.

The Work Week. The act provided for the standard work week to be reduced to 40 hours—the current length—by 1940. For overtime, or the time worked beyond the 40-hour limit, employees are entitled to be paid wages at a rate of 1.5 times their regular rate.

Child Labor. The act bans the employment of children younger than 14 years old, except for certain agricultural jobs. Children 14 or 15 years old are prohibited from working in factories or during school hours. People younger than 18 years old may not work in jobs declared hazardous by the U.S. secretary of labor.

Consumer Safety

Legislation protects the consumer in a number of ways. Perhaps the most critical protection is consumer safety, the idea that consumers have the right to expect that they will not suffer injury because of negligently manufactured products.

Tort Law. A tort is a willful or negligent act, such as an assault, that results in harm to another. The aggrieved party must establish that the product was defective, that the product defect was the cause of some injury or damage, and that the product defect made the product unreasonably dangerous.

Pure Food and Drug Act. As early as 1906, the Pure Food and Drug Act prohibited adulteration of food and drug products. In 1938, this statute was expanded through passage of the Food, Drug, and Cosmetic Act, which prohibited false and misleading labels and established quality standards for food and cosmetic products.

Fair Packaging and Labeling Act. In 1966, Congress passed the Fair Packaging and Labeling Act, requiring that manufacturers identify the product, provide the name and address of the manufacturer, and also provide information relating to the quality of the product.

Consumer Product Safety Act of 1972. Enforced by the Consumer Product Safety Commission, the express purposes of this statute include

1. protection of consumers from risk of injury associated with the use of consumer goods.

2. assistance in evaluating the relative safety of various product offerings.

3. development of safety standards for consumer products.

4. promotion of investigation into the causes and prevention of injury, illness, and death that may be caused by consumer products.

◀ **Before child labor laws,** many boys and girls worked hazardous jobs, often operating machinery in factories. Seen here is a boy operating an automatic press at the Boston Index Card Company in 1917.

Regulation of Competition

Following creation of the Interstate Commerce Commission, Congress enacted its first major piece of antitrust legislation, the Sherman Antitrust Act of 1890. It prohibited the restraint of trade and banned monopolies and efforts to monopolize industries. More specific pieces of antitrust legislation were enacted.

Clayton Antitrust Act of 1914

This act prohibits certain actions meant to restrain trade, including

- tie-in contracts that require the seller of a product to carry other products of the manufacturer whether or not the seller wants to carry them.
- members of the board of directors of a company also serving on the board of a competing firm.
- a company acquiring a sufficient portion of the stock (ownership) of a competing firm, enabling it to guide the operations of that firm toward noncompetitive ends.

Federal Trade Commission Act of 1914

This act created the Federal Trade Commission (FTC), which investigates "unfair methods of competition in commerce." Today the scope of the FTC includes consumer protection as well as protection of competitors.

Celler-Kefauver Antimerger Act of 1950

This act expanded the prohibitions of the Clayton Act to include the purchase of major assets that would tend to decrease competition, such as the purchase of a production facility of a competing company.

Employee Relations

By the early 1960s, the face of the American workforce was transforming. In response, several important pieces of legislation were enacted to protect specific conditions and situations in the workplace.

The Civil Rights Acts deal in part with business practices that tend to discriminate against individuals because of personal characteristics, such as the individual's race, color, religion, sex, or national origin. (See page 213.)

Age Discrimination in Employment Act expands the provisions of the Civil Rights Act to include discrimination on the basis of age. Originally the act protected only workers between the ages of 40 and 65. The upper age limit was subsequently raised to 70 and then eliminated altogether in 1986.

The Americans with Disabilities Act prohibits employers from discriminating against any disabled qualified person. It also requires most employers to make existing facilities accessible to the disabled.

The Family and Medical Leave Act requires covered employers to grant an eligible employee up to a total of 12 work weeks of job-protected, unpaid leave for one or more of the following reasons: birth, adoption, or foster care of a child; care of a spouse, parent, or child with a serious health condition; or for the employee's own serious health condition. New military family leave requirements were added in 2008.

✔ Fiscal policy is the actions a government takes to control its budget by means of taxation, raising revenues, and regulating spending.

✔ Monetary policy, in the U.S., is the actions the Federal Reserve takes to control the money supply in the country.

✔ The Federal Reserve controls the money supply by establishing reserve requirements; adjusting the discount rate; and trading, buying, and selling government securities, such as bonds.

✔ Money has four roles. Money enables the exchange of goods and services; it provides a way to meaningfully measure different types of goods and services; it serves as an easy way to hold, or store, value; and it functions as a means of defining a payment to be made later, as in a loan.

✔ The government affects the market by making laws to regulate business and to protect consumers.

THE WORLD ECONOMY

Where does one begin when examining the economies of various countries? How many countries are there? The United Nations has 193 members. This number does not cover every country; in fact, determining how many countries exist also depends on how "country" is defined. Taiwan is not a member of the United Nations, nor do the U.S. and Taiwan have formal diplomatic connections. The Pitcairn Islands, with a population of fewer than 50 people, is classified as a dependency of Britain. Yet in all of these places an economy of one sort or another operates.

How is the United States economically tied to all of the other nations of the world?

Trade Between Nations

International Trade

International trade is the exchange of goods and services between countries. It is distinguished from domestic trade, which takes place entirely within a single country.

International trade permits countries to specialize in producing the things they are best suited to make with the resources they have. Countries benefit by producing the goods they can make most cheaply and buying the goods other countries can make more cheaply. International trade makes it possible for more goods to be produced and for more human wants to be satisfied than if each country tried to produce everything it needed within its own borders. The world's leading exporters of goods and services include China, France, Germany, Japan, and the United States. Most world trade is carried out by private exporters and importers, and only a small part is handled by governments.

Why Nations Trade. Trade takes place between nations for the same reasons it is carried on within a country. For example, trade between Australia and Japan is similar to trade between Wyoming and Rhode Island. In both cases, regions specialize in producing particular goods because they have resources that make such specialization sensible and profitable. Both Australia and Wyoming have abundant space and few people. This is the best combination of resources for efficient cattle raising. Japan and Rhode Island have little space, but they have much skilled labor and capital. Such a combination makes for efficient industrial production. Australia and Wyoming specialize in cattle and sell meat to Japan and Rhode Island, respectively. On the other hand, Japan and Rhode Island specialize in industrial products and sell them to Australia and Wyoming.

Benefits. International trade benefits people in two chief ways.

1. Consumers can get more goods at lower cost through specialization and exchange than if every country tried to be self-sufficient and make everything it needed.

2. Scarce resources can be used more efficiently if each nation makes mainly those things it can produce more efficiently than other countries. The economic principle of *comparative advantage* states that each country should concentrate on making those goods it can produce most efficiently and buy from other nations those goods it cannot make as efficiently.

Trade Barriers. In international trade, governments often place artificial barriers against the free movement of goods from one country to another. Two of the most significant trade barriers are

- tariffs, part of a system of import duties levied on goods coming into the country.

- quotas, which require an importer to get a government permit before bringing goods into the country.

The practice of establishing trade barriers to help domestic firms is commonly referred to as *protectionism.*

International trade gives consumers access to products that might otherwise be unavailable or only seasonally available.

WHY ARE THERE TRADE BARRIERS?

Trade barriers reduce the volume of international trade, raise prices to consumers, and deprive nations of the benefits of specialization. All nations create such barriers, however, for several reasons.

- Local producers and workers pressure their governments to protect them from foreign competition.

- Countries prefer not to be dependent on foreign sources in the event of war.

Although they were intended to help the U.S. domestic steel industry, tariffs on foreign steel ended up harming those domestic industries that use steel.

GLOBALIZATION

Do you enjoy sprinkling fresh blueberries on your morning cereal? In years past, you could savor those tasty treats during only a few weeks of the year. Blueberries have a short growing season. However, you can now eat those delightful berries all year long—even in the winter. In South America, seasons are the opposite of the seasons in North America. Fall and winter in the United States are spring and summer in Chile and Argentina. Farmers in Chile and Argentina know that millions of Americans want to eat those berries in January, so they began to grow that crop.

Interconnections

What Is Globalization?

Globalization is the interconnection of producers and consumers in today's world economy. A company can buy supplies and parts made in many different countries. They sell those goods to customers in their home country, as well as ship the products to buyers in other nations. In this way, factory workers and farmers in one country are closely linked to consumers in several other nations. Globalization means that a computer company in the United States buys hard drives made in Taiwan, memory chips manufactured in New Mexico, DVD drives made in China, and motherboards produced in South Korea. Then, workers in the company's U.S. factories assemble these parts to make a machine that is shipped to a store to sell.

How Extensive Is Globalization?

Globalization has linked all corners of the world. McDonald's has restaurants in more than 110 countries. Walmart has 225 stores in China alone. The popular sci-fi adventure movie *Avatar* earned more than $2.7 billion in ticket sales around the world—with more than 70 percent of that revenue coming from outside the United States. Meanwhile, Americans enjoy Japanese animé (animated films) and Mexican telenovelas (long-running television serials) and buy cars made by Japanese and German automakers that are built in Tennessee or South Carolina.

Trade is a growing share of the economies of countries around the world. In 1960, trade in goods accounted for only 10 percent of the world's total economic output. That percentage rose until the trade in merchandise equaled more than one-third of the world's economic output.

◀ **Farmers in Chile** saw a demand and began to produce blueberries to meet that demand. They didn't care that this demand originated in another country. They just wanted to take advantage of an opportunity. That's what globalization is all about—taking advantage of opportunities all around the world.

U.S. trade representative Ron Kirk. His responsibilities include advising the president and American citizens about trade issues.

REGIONAL TRADE ASSOCIATIONS

Regional trade associations are blocs of countries that join together to promote free trade among themselves. There are more than two dozen regional trade associations around the world. Among the largest are

- **The North American Free Trade Agreement (NAFTA).** In this treaty, leaders in the United States, Canada, and Mexico agreed to eliminate all trade barriers among their countries over the next several years. (See page 222.)

- **The European Union (EU).** This free trade zone covers most of Europe and includes the people of 27 nations. The nations of the EU account for more than $2.8 trillion in world trade, which is more than any single country except the United States.

- **The Association of Southeast Asian Nations (ASEAN).** This trade bloc includes 10 Southeast Asian nations, embracing more than 500 million people.

- **Mercosur.** This trade bloc links the economies of Argentina, Brazil, and several other nations in South America.

Overseeing the movement is the World Trade Organization (WTO), which helps countries work out free trade agreements. There are 153 member nations in the WTO.

Three Causes of Globalization

Globalization is not new. It has been happening for centuries. Merchants in China were sending caravans of valuable silk across Central Asia to the eastern edges of the Roman Empire 2,000 years ago. From there, the silk was sent to Rome, where the upper classes treasured the fabric for its lightness and vivid colors. Today, globalization takes place on an unprecedented scale. Networks of producers and consumers connect people in all nations.

There are three main causes for the spread of globalization.

Communication and Transportation Technologies. The growth of the Internet allows video game companies to create online games that are played by millions anywhere from Thailand to Bulgaria. Jet air travel means that farmers in Kenya can grow flowers that can be flown overnight to appear the next day in European florist shops.

Interconnected Financial Markets. Investors are now more willing to buy stocks and bonds issued in another country. If they see signs of a decrease in value in those investments, they can sell those investments and move their money to another country. The sell-off of investments can hurt the economy of the country where it occurs. Sometimes the economic bad news spreads around the globe. A sell-off of stocks in the United States can worry investors in other countries, who then sell stocks on their own exchanges.

The Spread of Capitalism. For much of the 20th century, many governments tried to control their economies. In these command economies, government officials decided what products businesses would produce and how they would produce them. But after decades of slow economic growth, the governments in many countries shifted to the market economic system in which individuals make the economic decisions.

Effects of Globalization

How Has Globalization Affected the United States?

Supporters of globalization say that the trend has produced many benefits for Americans:

- Americans now enjoy a greater variety of goods and services than ever before. Proponents of globalization say that many of these finished goods cost less than they would if globalization was not present.

- American workers earn higher wages than workers in other countries. By buying from foreign suppliers, American companies can hold down costs and make toys, T-shirts, and televisions available to American consumers for less than they would cost if made in the United States.

Critics say that these benefits have come with a significant cost. As companies move manufacturing operations overseas, they are closing American factories.

As a result, American workers are losing their jobs. This trend of locating operations overseas is called *outsourcing*.

How Has Globalization Affected Other Countries?

Economists and social scientists disagree about the impact of globalization on other countries. Many countries with fully developed economies, such as Japan and those in Western Europe, have seen some high-wage jobs lost to outsourcing, while consumers in those countries have had a dazzling array of goods and services available to them.

Beneficiaries. In the 1980s and 1990s, South Korea, Taiwan, Hong Kong (not part of China at that time), and Singapore all enjoyed tremendous economic growth. In more recent years, growth spurred by trade lifted Mexico and Brazil onto the list of the world's most productive economies. Now both China and India have enjoyed huge economic booms. This economic growth has raised incomes in these countries, fueling the growth of a middle class.

Problems with Economic Expansion. Critics believe that the growth in manufacturing in these countries has led to a number of problems. These include

- increased pollution and environmental damage.

- workers in developing nations being forced to work long hours under appalling conditions.

- the spread of products intended for Europe and North America, which has meant the destruction of locally produced products and local culture.

- multinational companies gaining too much power in countries with developing economies.

Trade has become a vital ingredient in the economies of many countries across the world.

What Is the Future of Globalization?

While opinion about globalization is divided, it is most likely here to stay. The close links forged between producers and consumers around the world in recent years are not likely to break.

In the 1930s, when the worst depression to date occurred, countries around the world moved to block trade in the hopes of protecting the industries in their own countries. (See pages 174–181.) However, the world has changed over the last 70 years. When a global financial crisis arose in 2008, the heads of the world's leading economies met to work out common efforts to meet the danger. None of the leaders moved to shut down trade or block the flow of money between countries. They realized that the world's economies were simply too closely linked.

Roses from Kenya wait to be sold at the Alsmeer Flower Auction in Amsterdam.

Tokyo, Japan. Japan's economy is highly industrialized and technologically advanced. It relies heavily on imported raw materials.

✔ Globalization, the worldwide interconnection of producers and consumers, is not new; it was in place even more than 2,000 years ago when Ancient Romans purchased textiles from China.

✔ The three causes of globalization are communication and transportation technologies that "shrink" the world; interconnected financial markets, where investors trade in stocks and bonds from many countries; and the spread of capitalism in a shift away from command economies.

✔ Globalization has both advantages and disadvantages. Among the advantages is a wider variety of goods, often at attractive prices; among the disadvantages is reduced demand for locally produced goods.

THE ECONOMIC MELTDOWN OF 2008

Monday, September 15, 2008, brought shocking news to the business world. Lehman Brothers, one of the nation's leading financial institutions, declared bankruptcy. The morning held another surprise: Merrill Lynch—the nation's leading stock brokerage—announced that it was being purchased by Bank of America for $50 billion, half of what it had been valued at only one year earlier. Across the country, Americans wondered what had happened—and why.

Traders working on the floor of the New York Stock Exchange on September 15, 2008. U.S. stocks declined sharply after news of Lehman Brothers' bankruptcy and Merrill Lynch's sale to Bank of America. ▼

Economic Crisis

A Crisis Builds

The problems of these two Wall Street giants had been building for years—and they were not alone. For months, Wall Street analysts had warned that the financial system was on the brink of collapse and pointed to several contributing factors.

Too Much Debt. In the 1990s, interest rates—the cost of borrowing money—had been low. At the same time, housing prices were rising. Banks happily gave out mortgages so people could buy new homes, confident that the value of the homes would keep rising and they would profit.

Subprime Mortgages. Yet, underlying this practice lurked a problem. Banks were providing mortgages to people who did not have enough income to afford them. These mortgages were called subprime mortgages because they were issued to borrowers who had lower-than-prime credit ratings. Some borrowers were allowed to obtain the full value of the home they bought without putting any money down. Many of these mortgages had very low interest rates in the first few years that adjusted upward in later years. In 2007, many of these mortgages began to rise, and the new payments were far higher than many homeowners could afford. Borrowers began to *default,* or fail to make payment, on their mortgages. By late 2007, almost one-fourth of those with subprime mortgages were either late on their payments or were in default.

Economic Effects. The subprime mortgage crisis had two damaging economic effects.

1. Banks raised interest rates and became less willing to lend money, which meant that houses were harder to sell. Housing prices fell. Many prime borrowers now wanted to sell their homes, but their homes were worth less than the amount they had borrowed.

2. In order to minimize the risk banks assumed when issuing subprime loans, the loans were bundled together and sold to other investors. These bundles—called collateralized debt obligations (CDOs)—spread the risk around, which would minimize the damage if there were widespread defaults on mortgages.

CDOs. The companies that bought CDOs borrowed the money to finance their purchase of bundled mortgages. As defaults escalated and housing prices fell, the financial companies that rate bonds began to view CDO-related bonds as having less value. As a result, the companies holding CDOs had lower assets and more liabilities. Investor confidence in these companies began to slip. Because CDOs were widely held—by banks, investment firms, and other companies—the whole financial system was at risk.

BANKRUPTCY

In *bankruptcy*, a company admits that its liabilities (what it owes to creditors) outweigh its assets (what it owns). Ordinarily, a company that files for bankruptcy has a chance to reorganize and continue business. However, bankruptcy means the end of business in the financial industry.

Angry Bear Stearns employees and other passersby wrote messages on this painted portrait of Bear Stearns CEO James Cayne. ▼

The Government Steps In

By March 2008, the investment firm Bear Stearns was reeling. Because it owned too many subprime mortgages, the company's value went from $170 a share in 2007 to less than $10 a share in March 2008. Worried that Bear Stearns would go bankrupt and cause panic, the government negotiated with investment bank J.P. Morgan to buy the firm for only $2 a share. As part of the deal, the government guaranteed to cover up to $30 billion in losses that J.P. Morgan might suffer from Bear Stearns' bad investments. It looked like a brilliant rescue—albeit one that risked taxpayer dollars.

Across the Country. Meanwhile, Americans were suffering. Gas prices rose to $4 a gallon by June. Automakers General Motors (GM) and Ford announced huge losses and some factory closings. The unemployment rate rose above 6 percent—higher than it had been in 5 years. The stock market steadily fell; the Dow Jones Industrial Average, an index used to monitor the stock prices of 30 of the largest and most widely held public companies in the United States, dropped from 12,650 points in January to under 11,200 points in early September.

An Ailing Financial System

Saving Fannie and Freddie

By September, there were new targets of investor alarm: the Federal National Mortgage Association, called Fannie Mae, and the Federal Home Loan Mortgage Corporation, or Freddie Mac. For years, Fannie and Freddie had been writing subprime mortgages at very low interest rates and buying mortgages originally issued by other lenders. They now either owned or guaranteed half of the outstanding mortgages in the nation. However, falling housing prices and rising defaults on mortgages hurt their balance sheets.

Drastic Action. By the first week in September, the two companies appeared to be on the brink of collapse. Fearful that such a catastrophe would bring down the nation's entire financial system, the Bush Administration acted dramatically. On September 7, Treasury Secretary Henry J. Paulson announced that the government was taking control of Fannie and Freddie. This was the most extreme move that the federal government had ever taken to intervene in the U.S. economy.

▲ **Private investors** owned Fannie Mae and Freddie Mac and shared in their profits. However, the federal government guaranteed the mortgages that the two companies wrote, which made Fannie and Freddie seem like perfectly safe investments.

MAIN STREET SUFFERS

In 2008, Wall Street turmoil hurt ordinary Americans in several ways.

- Banks tightened credit as they worried about the bad loans they held, which slowed consumer spending. Businesses could not obtain the money they needed to operate and so laid off workers.

- As the value of stocks plunged, so did the value of people's retirement funds and savings accounts.

- Two of the nation's big three automakers—GM and Chrysler—were teetering on the edge of collapse. Sales of cars had fallen drastically due to high gas prices and the credit crunch. Automakers needed billions of dollars in loans to stay afloat for a few months.

- The job market was collapsing. Slow sales and the prospect of low consumer spending caused an increasing number of companies to lay off workers—nearly 580,000 workers in December of 2008 and nearly 600,000 more the next month.

By January 2009, the unemployment rate had reached 7.6 percent; by August 2009, the rate stood at 9.7 percent.

The Government Stays Out

Following the Fannie and Freddie takeover on Monday, September 8, financial markets were jittery. Stock markets around the world fell as worried investors sold off shares. By Friday, Lehman Brothers' stock had dropped to a fraction of its former value.

That weekend, Paulson and other government officials met with the leaders of financial firms and delivered harsh news. The government would not step in to help Lehman Brothers. They believed that years of poor financial decision-making had caused Lehman's problems. They feared that if the government rescued Lehman, other companies would continue taking risks without worrying about the consequences.

Unfortunately, no company was willing to save Lehman Brothers by purchasing it. It had to go out of business.

Acting to Save the Financial System

After Lehman Brothers' bankruptcy, attention shifted to another financial giant. American International Group—A.I.G. for short—was the largest insurance company in the world. A.I.G. dealt with thousands of businesses in dozens of countries. It insured banks and companies that had invested in mortgages, CDOs, and other now shaky financial deals. If A.I.G. fell, the entire world financial system could collapse—and A.I.G. looked very vulnerable.

During that same September weekend, executives from A.I.G. asked the government for $40 billion in loans. However, Secretary Paulson and Federal Reserve Board chairman Ben Bernanke gave A.I.G. the same harsh news they had delivered to Lehman Brothers and Merrill Lynch. There would be no government rescue for bad investments.

Then came Monday's plunge in the stock market. This occurrence, combined with A.I.G.'s inability to raise private capital, changed Paulson's and Bernanke's minds. Late on Tuesday, they decided that the Federal Reserve Board would loan $85 billion to the insurance giant to prop it up.

The Bailout. Stock prices continued to fall, and concerns about banks and investment firms increased. Paulson and Bernanke put together an emergency rescue plan that used government money to buy bad investments from financial institutions. The price tag for this plan was $700 billion.

A majority of the House of Representatives balked at the bailout plan and voted against it on September 29, 2008. Wall Street reacted with a sell-off. By the end of the day, the Dow Jones average had plunged 777 points, with more than 400 points of that drop coming within the last few hours of the day during the House vote. Alarmed, Congress passed the bailout bill 4 days later. Wall Street rallied, but stock prices soon began to slide again.

A Worldwide Problem

While the recession that hit the United States was strong, some nations suffered more dramatically. Even China was suffering. For years, China had been the world's fastest-growing economy and had climbed to the second largest economy in the world. But China's economy depended on exports, and the United States was one of its major markets. As a result, economic growth in China in 2008 was nearly half of what it had been the year before. Unemployment rose. The Chinese government decided to pump about $585 billion into the economy to prevent a slowdown.

Nations from Great Britain to India, Russia to Brazil all boosted government spending in hopes of spurring demand and creating jobs. In February 2009, the U.S. government passed a $789 billion economic stimulus bill for the same reason. In addition, the Obama Administration also unveiled a $2.5 trillion plan to try to shore up the nation's financial system, aiming to convince investors that financial institutions were sound—and to push banks to start lending money again.

Know now you!

✔ A major cause of the economic meltdown of 2008 was the wide lending of money for purchases of homes to individuals who did not have the means to repay the loans. These loans are known as subprime mortgages. Because interest rates, the cost of borrowing money, had been low, lenders were eager to make loans.

✔ The problem of subprime loans was made worse by increasing interest rates, which made housing less attractive to buy and lowered the value of houses, sometimes to below the amount that had been paid for them. Also, as people failed to repay their loans, investments based on those loans lost much value.

✔ To prevent a total collapse of the country's financial system, the U.S. government acted to buy bad investments from financial firms such as banks and insurance companies and to spend large amounts of money to create jobs and fuel consumer demand for products.

✔ The financial difficulties in the U.S. reached into other countries around the world, affecting even strong economies like that of China. Like the U.S., these countries increased government spending to help their economies recover.

HISTORY OF ECONOMIC THEORY

Although distinctive economies have evolved over the years in numerous modern nations, including the United States, many of their philosophical bases came from British economists. The influences of Adam Smith, a Scot, and John Maynard Keynes, an Englishman, for example, are evident today, as are the theories of North American economists, such as Milton Friedman and Paul Krugman of the United States and the Canadian-born John Kenneth Galbraith.

Who's Who in Economics

Adam Smith (late 1700s)
Free Market Economy

Thomas Malthus (early 1800s)
Population and Resources

Karl Marx (late 1800s)
Class Struggle and Capitalists

John Maynard Keynes (early 1900s)
Fiscal Policy and Government Intervention

John Kenneth Galbraith (late 1900s)
Market Economy Driven by Big Business

Milton Friedman (late 1900s)
Equation of Exchange and Money Supply

Paul Krugman (early 2000s)
2008 Nobel Prize in Economics

Adam Smith was an 18th-century economist who coined the term "the invisible hand" to refer to the way markets regulate themselves through individual self-interest.

Adam Smith (1723–1790)

Adam Smith was born in Scotland, at a time when *mercantilism* was still the prevailing economic policy in Western Europe. Mercantilists stressed the importance of trade and commerce as the source of a nation's wealth and power by encouraging exports and discouraging imports in order to enable the country to amass quantities of gold.

Moral Sentiments and *Wealth of Nations*. In his first book, *Moral Sentiments,* Smith advanced the theory that men acting in their own self-interest are often led unknowingly by an "invisible hand" to "advance the interest of society." His next book, *Wealth of Nations,* described the forces that direct an economy. Smith's rejection of mercantilism in favor of *laissez-faire* policies provided the model of classical capitalism. Laissez-faire is a theory that private enterprise, competitive markets, and unimpeded international trade will lead to optimal consumer welfare and a rising standard of living.

Market Economy. Adam Smith believed that the free market and an individual desire for profit would direct the flow of scarce resources in a more efficient and effective manner than could a government. Self-interest, restrained only by competition, would result in full employment, price stability, and economic growth.

John Maynard Keynes asserted that individuals tend to save and to consume a relatively stable and predictable portion of any additional money they may acquire, whether through tax cuts, increased income, or other means.

John Maynard Keynes (1883–1946)

In 1935, the Englishman John Maynard Keynes published *The General Theory of Employment, Interest and Money*. In it he provided a new conception of the workings of a mature capitalist economy.

Interest Rates. According to Keynes, people save for a variety of reasons, many of them completely unrelated to interest rates. Individuals, he wrote, save to accumulate funds for a special purchase, for retirement, for emergencies, or simply out of habit. Is it reasonable to assume that, if interest rates decline, they will withdraw their savings from bank accounts, or that they will cash in their deposits and spend the proceeds? The Keynesian response is a resounding negative.

Fiscal Policy. Keynes believed that the level of business investment is the most volatile of the three determinants of national income. Therefore, the government must intervene, primarily through fiscal policy, to make up for insufficient investment by businesses. Deficit spending is far preferable to allowing an economy to languish in a recession.

Karl Marx based his economic theory on the belief that the value of goods and services depends solely upon the value of labor. Marxist theories provided the basis for the subsequent evolution of communist ideology.

Karl Marx (1818–1883)

The philosophy of Karl Marx, born in Germany, had elements in common with the philosophy of Adam Smith, since Smith felt that the self-interest motivation of individuals shapes the nature of social institutions and the way in which society is organized.

A Contribution to the Critique of Political Economy. In Marx's preface to this book, he wrote: "The mode of production in material life determines the general character of the social, political, and spiritual processes of life." But Marx believed wealth would accrue to the owners of the means of production, and that workers would be increasingly exploited.

Class Struggle. Marx suggested that workers produce goods and services of value, but because workers are paid less than the value they create, capitalists can appropriate much of this value for themselves as profits. He predicted that this exploitation would lead to ever-worsening crises. The resulting class struggle, Marx wrote, would inevitably result in revolution and the downfall of capitalism.

Thomas Malthus asserted that people have children and populations grow for reasons unrelated to economics.

Thomas Malthus (1766–1834)

Thomas Malthus is known best for advancing an economic theory unrelated to savings, investments, and interest rates. In 1798, he published *An Essay on the Principles of Population,* in which he asserted that the ultimate lot of mankind depends on the relationship between two factors—population and resources.

Population and Resources. Malthus contended that population tends to expand geometrically, for example, 1, 2, 4, 8, 16, 32, while the resources of the world are limited, and productivity from those resources grows arithmetically, 1, 2, 3, 4, 5. More and more food is needed to feed the growing numbers, and there is only so much new land that can be cleared to increase the food supply. Without more advanced and productive agricultural technology, Malthus wrote, famine, disease, and starvation would result even if population levels ceased increasing.

Critique of Malthus. While population growth is a severe problem in many underdeveloped nations, the world envisioned by Smith or Keynes is much more a reality than the world foreseen by Malthus. Many nations have experienced moderate population growth over the past decades. The two centuries since Malthus's time have witnessed greatly increased capital formation and higher standards of living.

Milton Friedman was a leading critic of government efforts to stabilize the economy. He argued that market-determined results are better than government-determined results.

Milton Friedman (1912–2006)

The model developed by Milton Friedman while working at the University of Chicago holds that monetary policy (money supply), not fiscal policy (government taxation and spending), is the most effective way to guide an economy toward its goals.

Equation of Exchange. At the heart of his monetarist theory is the equation of exchange: The level of national income is equal to the supply of money. Further, total income depends not only on how much money is in circulation, but on the velocity of money, that is, on how often it is spent. The monetarists also hold that the velocity of money is relatively stable, so the supply of money is the only variable that can be manipulated to affect national income. In the long run, according to this theory, an ever-expanding money supply will provide for economic growth in a steady fashion.

Critique of Monetarism. Critics of monetarism argue there is little evidence to support the position that changes in the money supply will always affect spending. Businesses, for example, often operate within negotiated credit lines with their banks. Changes in the money supply have no effect on these contractually established rights to borrow. Tight money may drive interest rates up, but it has little effect on access to credit.

John Kenneth Galbraith chastised his contemporaries for over-emphasis on the supply-demand relationship as a primary factor in the workings of an economic system.

John Kenneth Galbraith (1908–2006)

In his first book, *American Capitalism,* published in 1952, John Kenneth Galbraith declared that the traditional view of the importance of consumer sovereignty, the free-market mechanism, and the profit-maximization incentive are more an economist's dream world than the true basis of a capitalist economy. There is no true consumer sovereignty, he argued.

The Affluent Society. Galbraith believed that the real directors of a market economy are big labor, big government, and big business. In his book *The Affluent Society* (1958), Galbraith maintained that rather than being controlled by the market, big business replaces the free market to a great extent. The major power groups—managers, accountants, lawyers, and even the economists—actually manipulate the economy, especially in the area of consumer demand. He also argued that companies are actually run by managers whose interests are better served by corporate growth than by profit maximization.

Critique of Galbraith. One of the most prominent of Galbraith's critics has been Robert Solow of the Massachusetts Institute of Technology. Solow doubts that the profit motive plays the inconsequential role in business that Galbraith saw. He suggests that if managers do not seek to maximize profits, they may find themselves replaced by other managers.

Paul Krugman is also a prolific author of works on economic and political topics aimed at the general reader.

Paul Krugman (1953–)

Paul Krugman is an American economist who won the 2008 Nobel Prize in Economics. Krugman was awarded the prize for his work on economic geography and international trade patterns. Krugman's work analyzed such issues as the reasons nations produce and trade the things they do, and how urbanization and globalization affect international trade. In recognition of his work, Krugman had, in 1991, received the John Bates Clark Medal from the American Economic Association. This award is given every 2 years to an economist under 40 who has made a significant contribution to economic thought.

Speaking to a General Audience. In addition to producing academic books and articles, Krugman has spent a significant portion of his career writing for general readers. He has written for a number of magazines, and in 1999, he became a columnist for *The New York Times*. During the early 2000s, he became a well-known critic of the economic policies of President George W. Bush.

Publications. Some of Krugman's books include *Peddling Prosperity: Economic Sense and Nonsense in the Age of Diminished Expectations* (1994), *The Return of Depression Economics* (1999), *The Great Unraveling: Losing Our Way in the New Century* (2003), and *The Conscience of a Liberal* (2007).

World History

PRE-CIVILIZATION

The term *civilization* describes a culture that has reached a high degree of social, economic, and political development—one that has a system of writing, highly organized religion and government, advanced technology, and a high level of art. People have probably lived on Earth for about 2 million years. Human civilization, on the other hand, began at the earliest in about 3500 BC. The period before this is known as prehistory. Archaeologists have pieced together the story of prehistory by studying what the people left behind, including artwork, tools, ruins of buildings, fossils, and even their own skeletons.

Stone Age and Beyond

The Ice Age

During the Ice Age, Earth's climate was much colder than it is today.

- Giant glaciers, ice sheets sometimes several miles thick, spread out from the North and South poles.
- These glaciers covered large areas of northern Europe, Asia, and North America—one-third of Earth's surface.
- The Ice Age killed off many species of plants and animals and forced humans and surviving animals to migrate to ice-free areas closer to the equator.

Thaw. Gradually, though, Earth began to warm once again. The glaciers began melting and the ice receded toward the polar areas until it covered only one-twelfth of Earth.

Forests grew on the newly thawed land and animals multiplied, while other plant life—fruits, grains, and vegetables—flourished once again. People began to migrate back to the newly productive lands, following the food that was again available there.

Earth During the Ice Age.
This map shows the spread of glaciers across Earth during the most recent ice age. The melting of the glaciers led to big changes in human societies. ▶

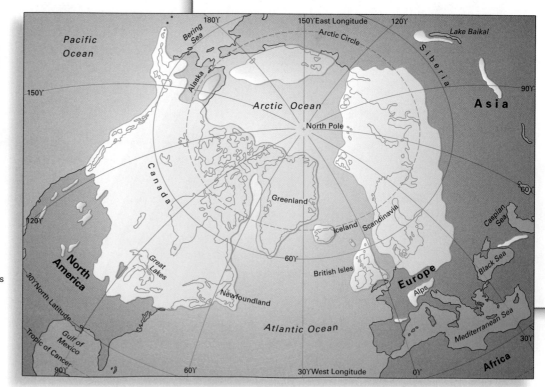

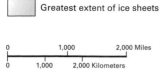

Greatest extent of ice sheets

Paleolithic and Neolithic People

The end of the Ice Age, about 11,500 years ago marked the end of a long period in human development: the Paleolithic Age, or Old Stone Age. The term *Stone Age* is used because during this period, in all human cultures, people used stone, rather than metal, tools.

Paleolithic people survived by hunting animals for meat and by gathering wild berries and grains. This hunter-gatherer way of life kept people on the move. To find the animals they hunted, they had to follow wandering herds and move on when they had picked an area clean of its edible plants.

The nomadic lifestyle of the Paleolithic people meant that they formed very small social groups. A social group needed to provide enough hands to do the work without presenting too many mouths to feed.

▲ **Paleolithic humans** lived in caves when they could find them, or in tents made of animal skins when they could not.

The Neolithic Age. As Earth entered the postglacial period, the Neolithic Age, or New Stone Age, began. This age saw the beginning of agriculture, or farming. Beginning about 11,000 years ago, many people across Earth discovered two things:

- They could domesticate animals such as cattle and sheep and keep herds of them, providing a steady supply of meat and milk.

- They could grow edible plants—grains, fruits, and vegetables—in large quantities to feed themselves.

As a result of these discoveries, people no longer had to travel continuously to find food.

 *Though the Stone Age in the Near East ended in about 3000 BC, not all societies left it behind at once. A few groups in New Guinea and Australia are still technically in the Stone Age today!*

THE AGRICULTURAL REVOLUTION

The discoveries of the early Neolithic Age marked the first great revolution in human history: the Agricultural Revolution. Some groups continued the hunter-gatherer lifestyle, but others settled in agricultural communities and built permanent homes. Soon villages appeared along river banks and in mountain valleys. By the time the Neolithic Age was ending in some parts of the world, about 5,500 years ago, human history was poised to begin a new and exciting era.

◀ **Neolithic villagers** began to develop new skills, like making pottery and weaving baskets and cloth. They created the wheel and learned that they could use animals to pull plows and wheeled carts.

THE RIVER VALLEYS

In the centers of early civilization, agriculture brought stability that freed many people from the daily toil of finding the food they needed to survive. Now farmers and herdsmen could produce the necessary food while others could specialize as craftspeople, such as weavers, potters, boat makers, or woodworkers. As the populations grew, basic economies and governing systems formed to organize agriculture and other group activities. Early civilizations flourished especially in four great river valleys: the Tigris-Euphrates in Southwest Asia, the Nile in North Africa, the Indus in South Asia, and the Huang He in East Asia.

TYPES OF SETTLEMENTS

Geographical factors can help determine where settlements will form. They can also help determine what those settlements will look like. Human settlements usually develop into one of three types: linear, nucleated (or clustered), and dispersed (or scattered). As they developed into the first cities, the early river valley settlements generally would have been linear settlements.

Type of Settlement	Description
Linear	• develops alongside a river, road, or canal • may have no obvious center
Clustered	• develops around a central point • houses and other buildings kept close together
Scattered	• no central point • buildings are randomly located; may not be close together

Early Settlements

Agriculture developed first in Southwest Asia, in the Fertile Crescent, an arc-shaped region stretching from the eastern Mediterranean to the Persian Gulf. It then spread west to North Africa and east to South and East Asia.

By around 8000 BC, inhabitants of China and parts of Central and South America had also established early forms of agriculture. Other peoples either independently developed agricultural systems at later dates, or formed them as other agricultural centers migrated or spread.

Major Events—Ancient Milestones	
c. 4500 BC	Copper replaces stone for tools and weapons in Mesopotamia and China.
c. 3500 BC	The wheel and the plow are invented in Mesopotamia; the sail is invented in Egypt.
c. 3100 BC	Menes unites Upper and Lower Egypt, establishing Egypt's first dynasty.
c. 3000 BC	Mesopotamian metalworkers discover bronze; major cities develop in Sumer; Sumerians invent cuneiform, a method of writing.
c. 2590 BC	The Great Pyramid of Cheops in Egypt is constructed.
c. 2300 BC	The cities of Harappa and Mohenjo-Daro emerge in the Indus Valley.
c. 1792 BC	Hammurabi comes to the throne of Babylon.
c. 1770 BC	The Code of Hammurabi is developed.
c. 1550 BC	The Hittites begin smelting iron and fashioning it into tools and weapons; a written language develops in China; the earliest form of steel is made by the Chalybes, subjects of the Hittites.
c. 1490 BC	Hatshepsut, the first woman ruler known to history, leads Egypt. (See image on page 407.)
c. 700 BC	The Aryans conquer Indus Valley cities.
c. 605 BC	The Hanging Gardens of Babylon are created.

Early Civilizations

Whether an agricultural settlement would develop into a major civilization depended much upon geography: the climate, physical features, and resources of an area.

Geography. The early human civilizations shared three common geographic factors.

- fertile soil
- available water supply
- favorable climate

Available water supply in the early civilizations came from major river systems: the Nile River, the Tigris and Euphrates Rivers, the Indus River, and the Huang He River. These rivers would flood each year, depositing silt in the surrounding soil. The silt made the soil fertile. These factors, combined with generally warm climates, made human efforts at farming more successful.

Elements of Civilization. While every society has a culture, not all societies are part of a civilization. Historically, civilizations have taken a wide range of forms, but they usually share several characteristics.

- **Government:** In the river valley cultures, governments generally consisted of a single leader or king. Wealthy landowners, priests, and government officials might also hold certain powers.

- **Religion:** The peoples of the river valley civilizations worshipped sets of gods and goddesses, as well as certain types of animals and even human ancestors.

- **Language and Art:** Archaeologists have uncovered evidence of written languages from each of these earliest civilizations. Works of art, from paintings and pottery to epic literature, have also been found.

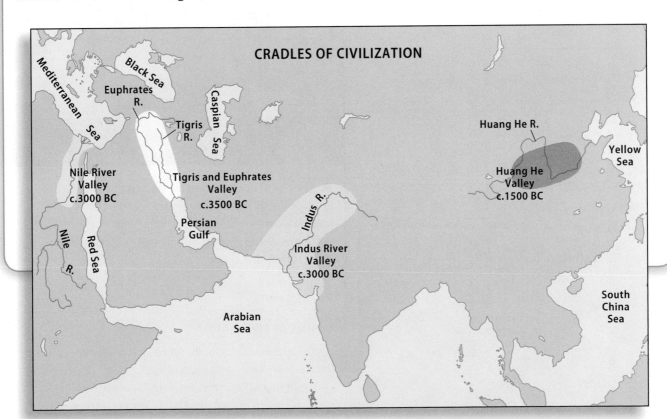

The Four Great River Valleys. This map shows the location of the world's four earliest civilizations. In each case, small agricultural villages became successful. Gradually, they developed into civilizations with organized systems of government, language, and economics.

TIGRIS-EUPHRATES VALLEY

In Greek, the word *Mesopotamia* means "the land between two rivers." This region, lying between the Tigris and Euphrates rivers, is sometimes called the "Cradle of Civilization"—it was home to the earliest known civilization.

Early Mesopotamian Milestones	
5000 BC	Farming villages appear.
4500 BC	Artisans learn to produce metal; metal tools replace stone.
3000 BC	Artisans learn to produce bronze; Mesopotamian Bronze Age begins.

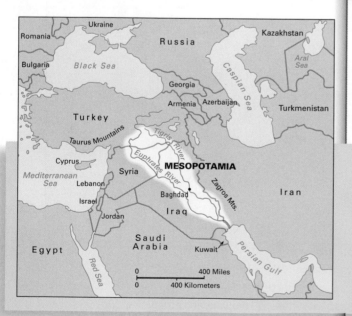

Cradle of Civilization

Sumerian Civilization

By 3500 BC, southern Mesopotamia, known as Sumer, was thriving.

- Irrigation canals transported water from the Tigris and Euphrates rivers to nourish the fields.
- Agricultural plenty triggered rapid population growth and the transformation of villages into cities.
- There were at least a dozen cities, with names like Kish and Erech and Ur.

With the appearance of cities, the world's first civilization developed. The people of this civilization are referred to as Sumerians.

▲ **The city of Ur** was a commercial center from about 3800 to 1850 BC. It included a temple area near the center and a residential area in the south. A canal ran from the North Harbor to the river, and to another harbor on the west side of the city. A wall surrounded most of the city.

CRADLE OF CIVILIZATION

Mesopotamia included the area that is now eastern Syria, southeastern Turkey, and much of Iraq.

The Tigris and Euphrates rivers run for more than 1,000 miles southward through the Fertile Crescent, in present-day Iraq, and into the Persian Gulf, carrying fertile silt with them. Each year, the rivers overflow their banks, flooding the land of Mesopotamia and renewing its soil with their silt.

Government. Sumer was organized into a number of powerful city-states, each ruled by a king. Each government directed the building of monuments and irrigation canals, oversaw the distribution of food, and provided for the city-state's defense.

Religion. The Sumerians believed in numerous gods and goddesses, each of whom represented a different aspect of nature. Some examples are

- An, the god of heaven.
- Ki, the god of earth.
- Enlil, the god of air.
- Enki, the god of water.

They also believed that each city-state had its own god or goddess who protected it.

As shrines to their deities, the Sumerians constructed temples, six or seven stories high, with broad stairways climbing to the top. In these temple towers, called *ziggurats*, priests presided over worship of the gods and goddesses.

Writing. The Sumerians developed a written language in about 3000 BC. Called cuneiform, it began as pictures of objects drawn with a sharp stylus into tablets of soft clay. When the clay tablets hardened, they became permanent records of business transactions, laws, and religious teachings.

In time, the pictures gave way to a simpler system of wedge-shaped symbols, more like the letters we know today. The name cuneiform comes from the Latin term for "wedge-shaped."

The Arts. The arts, a hallmark of civilization, also thrived in Sumer.

- Brightly colored friezes covered the ziggurats and beautifully sculpted statues of the deities filled them.
- Music composed and played on instruments like harps and lyres was a major part of festivals and religious ceremonies.
- Literature, in the form of epics, fables, and poems, has survived on clay tablets.

GILGAMESH

The longest and most famous example of literature from Mesopotamia is the *Epic of Gilgamesh*, the tale of a heroic ruler in search of everlasting life. The earliest verses were composed in southern Mesopotamia before 2000 BC. The most complete text comes from the library of the Assyrian king Ashurbanipal (668–627 BC).

The figure of Gilgamesh also appears in some art from the region.

▲ **Hundreds of thousands** of cuneiform tablets have survived. They provide information about Sumerian economy, law, literature, politics, and religion. The Sumerians also left writings about mathematics, anatomy, medicine, and magic.

For hundreds of years, the Sumerian city-states of Erech, Lagash, and Ur competed for control of neighboring lands. These bitter rivalries frequently resulted in war against one another. The chaos that followed left them vulnerable to conquest from the outside.

The Akkadian Empire

In about 2350 BC, the forces of Akkad, a city to the north, swept down upon the Sumerian city-states. The great Akkadian ruler Sargon unified the region and ruled from 2340 to 2305. He went on to conquer the lands surrounding his capital, Akkad.

Eventually, his empire included all of Mesopotamia, territories extending west to the Mediterranean, and lands as far north as the Black Sea. Later and weaker Akkadian kings allowed wars among Sumer's city-states to break out again. Destruction of the empire (c. 2180 BC) by barbarian tribes plunged Mesopotamia into a period of chaos.

CODE OF HAMMURABI

Hammurabi was one of the greatest rulers of the ancient world. A brilliant general, a wise administrator, and a generous patron of the arts, he is best remembered for the code of laws that he legislated for his empire.

Called the Code of Hammurabi, its nearly 300 laws covered all areas of life: trade; family life, including marriage and divorce; labor, including wages and working conditions; military service; personal property; and real estate. The code was harsh, demanding "an eye for an eye" and "a life for a life," but its purpose was to provide justice within the Babylonian Empire by applying the same laws to all.

Hammurabi ruled Babylonia from 1792 to 1750 BC. ▶

The city of Babylon was home to the famous Tower of Babel. This tower was a ziggurat, a style of temple tower (resembling a pyramid with wide terraces) that was popular with the peoples of Mesopotamia. ▼

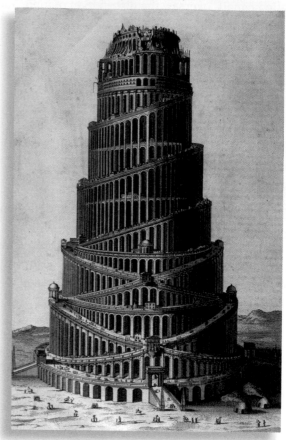

The Rise of Babylonia

In about 2000 BC, waves of nomadic invaders called Amorites swarmed into Mesopotamia from west of the Euphrates. Settling in a village called Babylon, they gradually gained power over their neighbors. Then, in 1792 BC, Hammurabi came to the throne. Over the next 40 years, he welded the city-states of Sumer into a new empire called Babylonia.

The Hittites. Hammurabi's weaker successors were not able to maintain Babylonian rule in the face of the militarily superior Hittites, warriors who conquered Mesopotamia from Asia Minor about 1550 BC. The Hittites were the first people in history known to smelt iron. With the Hittite conquest, the Bronze Age gave way to the Iron Age in Babylonia.

Assyrian Conquest

By 700 BC, Babylonia had been conquered by yet another invader, the mighty and fierce Assyrians. The great Assyrian empire began with the reign of Ashurnasirpal II (ruled 884–c. 860). He was followed by other conquerors, among them

- Tiglath-pileser III (ruled 745–728).

- Sargon II (ruled 722–705).

- Esarhaddon (ruled 681–668).

From their capital city at Nineveh on the upper Tigris River, these rulers created an empire that stretched from the Persian Gulf to the eastern Mediterranean Sea to Egypt.

The Assyrian political administration ruled with an iron hand and demanded tribute from its conquered provinces. The last great Assyrian ruler was Ashurbanipal (ruled 669–633), who organized a famous library of cuneiform tablets at his capital, Nineveh.

King Ashurbanipal made Assyria into a world power of its time. Much of what we now know about Mesopotamian history comes from writings he had preserved in his library. ▶

The Second Babylonian Empire (also known as the Chaldean Empire). In 626 BC, after more than a century of Assyrian domination, Babylon reestablished its independence (c. 625) under Nabopolassar (ruled c. 625–c. 605). Nabopolassar formed an alliance with the Medes and Persians, and together they brought down the Assyrian Empire by capturing its capital, Nineveh (612).

After the destruction of Assyria, Nebuchadnezzar II, Nabopolassar's son, came to the Babylonian throne in 605 BC.

- Nebuchadnezzar II made Babylon the most impressive urban center of its day.

- It is best remembered for the Hanging Gardens he had built there—one of the Seven Wonders of the Ancient World.

- Despite all the glory, the New Empire crumbled in 539 BC, less than 25 years after Nebuchadnezzar II's death.

now you **KNOW!**

✔ The end of the Ice Age, about 11,500 years ago, marked the beginning of the Neolithic era.

✔ Unlike the Paleolithic hunter-gatherers, Neolithic humans began to develop agriculture.

✔ The Agricultural Revolution led to permanent settlements and the development of other skills, such as pottery.

✔ Early civilizations began to form in fertile river valleys: the Tigris-Euphrates Valley, the Nile Valley, the Indus Valley, and the Huang-He Valley.

✔ The Mesopotamian civilizations of the Tigris-Euphrates Valley (Sumer, Babylonia, Assyria) had written language, systems of government, shared religious beliefs, and artistic achievements.

THE NILE VALLEY

At the same time that the Sumerian civilization was developing in the Tigris-Euphrates Valley, another powerful civilization was emerging 600 miles to the west. Ancient Egypt, one of the longest-lived civilizations in human history, rose along the banks of the Nile River of North Africa. The Greek historian Herodotus called Egypt "the gift of the Nile," for it could not have developed without that river's life-giving waters. This civilization would thrive for over 2,000 years and make significant contributions to the civilizations that followed it.

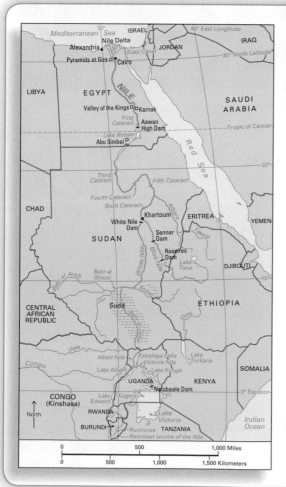

The Nile River. This map shows the location of the Nile River, the longest river in the world. The Nile rises near the equator and flows northward through northeast Africa into the Mediterranean Sea. Most ancient Egyptians lived along the Nile, in the river valley. Others lived in the fertile Nile Delta, or in the present-day Libyan Desert.

Ancient Egypt

In Egypt an advanced culture and a unified state developed early. Egyptian arts developed rapidly and hieroglyphic writing became widespread. Government, administrative, technical, and artistic skills were also developed. Still, like the other river valley civilizations, Egypt began its development with agriculture.

The Land

Ancient Egypt was a long, narrow country through which the Nile River flowed. Deserts bordered the country on the east, south, and west. The Mediterranean Sea lay to the north. The Nile River flowed north out of central Africa through the Egyptian desert to the Mediterranean.

The River. The annual Nile floods created a ribbon of fertile soil 5 to 15 miles wide through a sun-baked desert. The ancient Egyptians called their country *Kemet*, meaning *Black Land*, after the dark soil. At its mouth, the Nile empties into the Mediterranean Sea, creating a rich delta 100 miles long and 200 miles across.

During the Paleolithic Age, hunters and gatherers flocked to the generous food resources of the ancient Nile. During the Neolithic Age, they began to farm the fertile banks of the river, and by 4000 BC, the banks were lined with farming villages.

The People

Scholars believe the Nile River valley had from about 1 million to 4 million people, and possibly more, at various times during ancient Egypt's history. The ancient Egyptians spoke a language that was related both to the Semitic languages of southwestern Asia and to certain languages of northern Africa. They shared a set of religious beliefs as well.

Daily Life. Ancient Egyptian homes and clothing were designed with the region's hot climate in mind. Homes were built out of mud, with flat roofs. Small windows were placed high in the walls to help keep out the sun.

The type of home a person lived in depended upon his or her economic status.

- Poor Egyptians lived in small huts with only a few rooms.

- Middle-class Egyptians might have larger one- or two-story homes.

- Wealthy Egyptians often lived in large houses or estates, with dozens of rooms as well as orchards and gardens.

Egyptian clothing was typically made of white linen, which kept the wearer cool under the hot sun. Small children wore little, if any, clothing.

◄ **Wealthy Egyptians** might have lived on estates much like the one shown here.

EGYPTIAN RELIGION

Like the Sumerians, the Egyptians believed in several gods and goddesses that controlled the forces of nature. They also believed that their kings were gods.

Re: The most important god in this sun-baked land was the god of the sun, Re (sometimes spelled Ra).

Amon: A sun god worshiped in the city of Thebes, Amon was eventually combined with Re. The god was then called Amon-Re.

Osiris and Isis: Osiris was honored as god of the Nile, and his wife Isis was worshiped as the ideal wife and mother. The resurrection of Osiris, symbolized each year by the flooding of the Nile, convinced the Egyptians that they too would be reborn in a life after death.

Horus: The son of Isis and Osiris, Horus was god of the sky. He was called the lord of heaven and was often pictured with the head of a falcon.

▲ **Many Egyptian deities** were pictured with human bodies and the heads of animals. Such a head suggested a real or imagined quality of the animal and made identification of the deity easy.

The Kingdoms of Egypt

During the 2,000 years that ancient Egyptian civilization survived, 30 dynasties would rule its land, leading it through three major stages—the *Old, Middle,* and *New Kingdoms.*

By 3500 BC, the Nile region had progressed economically and politically to the point that two kingdoms had developed there: Upper and Lower Egypt.

- Upper Egypt lay to the south (because the Nile flows north, this is the upstream area).
- Lower Egypt lay to the north, bordering the Mediterranean Sea.

About 3100 BC, Menes, the king of Upper Egypt, united the two kingdoms and built his capital at Memphis, near the border between the two.

HIEROGLYPHICS

At the same time that Egyptians were establishing their new central government, they were inventing their written language, hieroglyphics. The image here shows an example of hieroglyphic script. Like the early Sumerian cuneiform (see page 399), hieroglyphics used pictures to convey information and ideas. However, it was often written on scrolls of papyrus, a kind of paper made from reeds, rather than on clay tablets.

The Old Kingdom (c. 2700–c. 2000 BC)

During this period, the kings of Egypt consolidated and strengthened their power over their people. Claiming descent from the god Amon-Re, they ruled as gods themselves. They owned all the land of Egypt, and their word was law.

Egyptian citizens paid taxes and rent to use the land. Many of them were also forced to contribute their labor to large building projects—particularly the building of the magnificent tombs called pyramids.

This period was marked by prosperity and cultural flowering. Trading expeditions traveled as far north as the Black Sea, where the Egyptians bartered for goods.

Decline. By about 2300 BC, Egyptians rebelled against the burdens of pyramid building, high taxes, and forced labor demanded of them. The governors who ruled the provinces of Egypt in the king's name also began to demand more power for themselves. In the face of such opposition, the central government weakened and the Old Kingdom fell, bringing on 150 years of disorder and disunion.

THE ROSETTA STONE

For over 1,000 years, scholars tried but failed to decipher the writing system of ancient Egypt. Then, in 1799, a rock slab with ancient Greek and Egyptian writing was found outside Rosetta, a city near Alexandria.

A French scholar named Jean-François Champollion began to compare the Greek and Egyptian words on the so-called Rosetta Stone. By 1822, he had deciphered the hieroglyphics. Dictionaries developed since then have helped scholars translate the writings on many monuments and in temples and tombs.

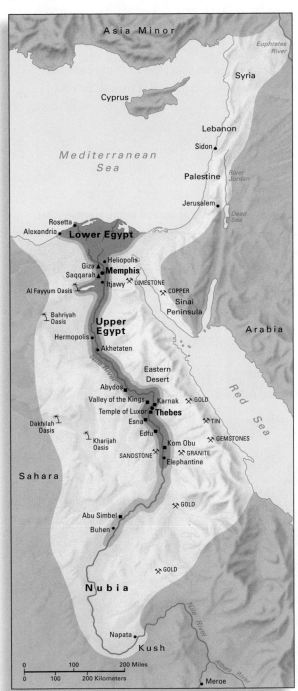

Old Kingdom
(about 2650 BC to 2150 BC)

Middle Kingdom
(about 1975 BC to 1640 BC)

New Kingdom
(about 1539 BC to 1075 BC)

▲ Major pyramid

■ Important temple or monument

● City or town

⚒ Mining site

Asia Minor

Euphrates River

Syria

Cyprus

Mediterranean Sea

Lebanon

Sidon

Palestine

River Jordan

Jerusalem

Dead Sea

Rosetta

Alexandria

Lower Egypt

Heliopolis

Giza ▲
Saqqarah ▲ **Memphis**
Itjawy ⚒ LIMESTONE
Al Fayyum Oasis ⚒ COPPER

Sinai Peninsula

Bahriyah Oasis

Upper Egypt

Hermopolis

Akhetaten

Arabia

Eastern Desert

Abydos

Valley of the Kings ■ Karnak ⚒ GOLD
Temple of Luxor ■ **Thebes**
Esna ⚒ TIN

Dakhilah Oasis

Edfu ⚒ GEMSTONES

Kharijah Oasis

Kom Obu ⚒
SANDSTONE ⚒ GRANITE
Elephantine

Red Sea

Sahara

⚒ GOLD

Abu Simbel ■
Buhen

⚒ GOLD

Nubia

Nile River

Napata

Kush

Atbara River

Meroe

0   100   200 Miles
0   100   200 Kilometers

The Middle Kingdom (c. 2050–c. 1800 BC)

About 2050 BC, King Mentuhotep II reunited Egypt and established a new capital at Thebes. Amenemhet I, a vizier in southern Egypt, began Dynasty XII around 1938 BC, when he seized the throne and moved the capital to Itjtawy, near Memphis.

Amenemhet and his strong successors, including Senusret I, Senusret III, and Amenemhet III, helped restore Egypt's wealth and power.

- They ordered the swamps of the Nile delta to be drained to increase agriculture.

- They opened a flourishing Egypt to greater contact with other parts of the ancient world, encouraging trade with ports on the Mediterranean and with Mesopotamia.

- They captured new lands, such as gold-rich Nubia to the south.

Culture. The Middle Kingdom also marked a golden age in Egyptian architecture and arts. Magnificent temples, which can still be visited today, rose at Karnak and Luxor, near Thebes. Literature flourished, including the *Tale of Sinuhe*, which gave rise to the familiar Sinbad the Sailor stories.

Decline. About 1720 BC, Asian invaders called the Hyksos overran Egypt with superior weapons of war—horsedrawn chariots, strong bronze swords, and metal armor. For the first time since its development, Egypt found itself under foreign rule. This ended the Middle Kingdom. The Hyksos people would control Egypt until 1520 BC; their empire was powerful and prosperous.

In an early example of one culture borrowing from another, however, the Egyptians studied the weapons and ways of warfare of their new rulers. Eventually, a group of princes from Thebes were able to turn these new military means against the Hyksos, expel them, and establish the New Kingdom.

▲ **A Growing Civilization.** This map shows the land occupied by ancient Egypt during the three major periods of the civilization: the Old Kingdom, Middle Kingdom, and New Kingdom.

The Kingdoms of Egypt

THE EGYPTIAN PYRAMIDS

The belief that the Egyptian kings were gods led to one of the Old Kingdom's greatest achievements: the construction of the pyramids. To live their lives after death in proper style, the ancient Egyptians believed they needed to be buried in magnificent tombs with lavish possessions. They also believed that the body needed to be preserved, because the person would need to use it in the next life as well. To do this, the Egyptians mummified—embalmed and dried—the bodies.

- The first pyramid was the Step Pyramid, designed for King Zoser about 2650 BC by the royal architect Imhotep. It stands over 200 feet tall.

- The largest pyramid was the Great Pyramid of Khufu, a king also known as Cheops, located at Giza. From a base that covered 13 acres, it rose to a point that reached 48 stories above the ground.

- It took 100,000 workers over 20 years to complete the Great Pyramid. It was completed in around 2600 BC.

◄ **Because of monuments** such as the great pyramids at Giza (shown here), the Old Kingdom of Egypt is sometimes referred to as the Age of Pyramids.

Building the Pyramids. A study of the Great Pyramid shows how these gigantic structures were built. The ancient Egyptians had no machinery or iron tools. They cut big limestone blocks with copper chisels and saws. Most of the stones came from quarries nearby. But some came from across the Nile River, and others came by boat from distant quarries.

1. Gangs of men dragged the blocks to the pyramid site and pushed the first layer of stones into place.

2. Then they built long ramps of earth and brick, and dragged the stones up the ramps to form the next layer.

3. As they finished each layer, they raised and lengthened the ramps.

4. Finally, they covered the pyramid with an outer coating of white casing stones. They laid these outer stones so exactly that from a distance the pyramid appeared to have been cut out of a single white stone.

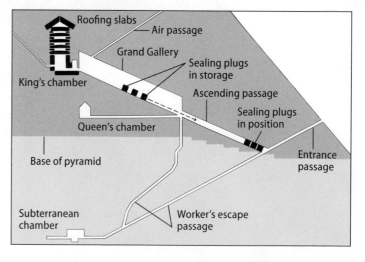

▲ **A cross section** of the Great Pyramid in Egypt shows the Grand Gallery, the King's Chamber, the Queen's Chamber, and various passages. Large blocks called sealing plugs were used to close the tomb.

The New Kingdom (c. 1539–c. 1090 BC)

The New Kingdom was a period of nearly 500 years in which ancient Egypt became the world's strongest power. During this period, the Egyptian rulers began to be called pharaohs, from the Egyptian term meaning "great house."

From the start of the New Kingdom, the pharaohs again consolidated their power and devoted their time to empire building. Amenhotep I, Thutmose I, and Thutmose III proved themselves great conquerors. They extended the Egyptian Empire far to the south in Africa and into Asia along the eastern Mediterranean and across to the Euphrates River.

Religious Reforms. Amenhotep IV weakened the empire when he attempted major religious reforms. This led to a bitter struggle with wealthy and powerful Egyptian priests.

- Amenhotep IV devoted himself to a sun god called the Aten.
- He changed his own name to Akhenaten.
- He declared that the Aten had replaced Amun and all other gods except Re.

King Tut. These religious reforms angered many Egyptians. Akhenaten's successor was 9-year-old Tutankhaten, the "boy king." King Tutankhaten removed -aten from his name and became Tutankh-amun. He restored the old state religion, allowing the worship of the old deities as well as the Aten.

Decline. By the 13th century BC, ancient Egypt was to know its last great period, under the rule of Ramses II, another great monument builder. Over time, the pharaohs' rule weakened, and again Egypt fell prey to invaders.

By 1090 BC, the power of ancient Egypt had collapsed. It would now be fought over and conquered by new empire builders—the Libyans, the Nubians, the Persians, the Macedonian Greeks, and finally the Romans (in about 30 BC).

▲ **Hatshepsut,** the mother of Thutmose III, reigned as pharaoh while Thutmose was a child. She was the first major woman ruler known to history. From 1490 to 1469 BC, she led Egypt through a period of foreign trade and monument building.

 *King Tutankhamun is best remembered today for the treasures of his burial place—"King Tut's tomb"—which would not be unearthed for another 2,500 years.*

✔ Civilization in the Nile Valley began to develop by about 3500 BC.

✔ The ancient Egyptian civilization lasted for 2,000 years. In that time, there were three major periods: the Old Kingdom, the Middle Kingdom, and the New Kingdom.

✔ Egyptians developed a writing system called hieroglyphics, which used pictures to convey stories and keep records.

✔ Because they believed their kings, or pharaohs, were gods, the Egyptians buried them in enormous tombs called pyramids. The largest of these is the Great Pyramid at Giza.

✔ Eventually, Egypt declined and was taken over by a series of invaders, ending with the Romans in 30 BC.

THE INDUS VALLEY

Over 2,000 miles to the east of Egypt, 1,500 miles beyond Mesopotamia, lies the Indus River. The river courses south 1,000 miles from the Himalayas to the Arabian Sea, which is an arm of the Indian Ocean. Its lower valley, located in what is now Pakistan, is one of the most fertile plains in the world. Here, about 2500 BC—roughly the time that the Old Kingdom was thriving in Egypt and Sumer was about to be made part of the Akkadian Empire—a civilization was emerging. In time, the Indus civilization grew to cover most of present-day Pakistan and parts of what are now Afghanistan and northern India.

▲ **Discovering the Indus.** In the 1920s, archaeologists began excavating huge earthen mounds where people had found artifacts and realized that they contained the remains of cities from a previously unknown civilization. Hundreds of Indus sites have been found since.

The Indus and Aryans

Settlement had begun in the Indus Valley, as it had elsewhere, when hunters and gatherers evolved into Neolithic farmers living in villages along the Indus River and its tributaries. By about 2300 BC, two of these villages had grown into the cities of Harappa and Mohenjo-Daro, with close to 40,000 people in each city.

Harappa and Mohenjo-Daro

Both of these cities were marvels of urban planning. At the center of each was a fortress, five stories high. From it, streets ran outward in a grid, making it easy to get around.

- Strict government regulations decreed neat and well-constructed houses, shops, and public buildings, including public baths.
- Many of the buildings were constructed on mud-brick platforms that protected the buildings from seasonal floods.
- Houses were made of baked or sun-dried brick. Beneath the streets, brick-lined sewers carried off waste, a sanitation measure unknown in other cities of the time.

Economy and Culture. Because of its bountiful agriculture, the Indus Valley developed a thriving economy. Here cotton was cultivated for the first time. Cotton cloth, as well as fine pottery and gold jewelry, was traded as far away as Mesopotamia.

Indus artisans also produced a variety of useful and decorative objects. They used copper and bronze to make tools, mirrors, pots, and pans. They also crafted silver and gold utensils and ornaments.

Writing System. Archaeologists have unearthed thousands of small clay figures and stone seals that carry pictures and a form of writing. The pictures indicate that the Indus people probably worshipped certain animals, like sacred bulls, and gods of nature. Unfortunately, scholars have not been able to decipher the writing and perhaps never will.

Aryan Conquest

The end of the Indus civilization came around the year 1500 BC, as warlike nomads from central Asia began streaming into the Indus Valley through mountain passes. The invaders called themselves Aryans, their term for "noble ones."

The Aryans quickly overran and looted the Indus towns and cities, as well as the societies of people called Dravidians. Soon they had conquered the entire northern plain of what is today India and Pakistan. By 700 BC, they had established a number of Aryan kingdoms across the Indian subcontinent, each kingdom ruled by a rajah.

Sanskrit is the basis for many modern Indian languages, including Hindi and Urdu. The name *Sanskrit* means *refined* or *polished*. ▶

SANSKRIT

The Aryans also developed a written language, Sanskrit. In it, they wrote the *Vedas*, books of sacred knowledge describing Aryan religious beliefs, known as Hinduism. The *Vedas* celebrated numerous gods and goddesses who personified natural phenomena, such as the sky, fire, or lightning. The most important Hindu sacred writings, called the *Upanishads*, appeared between 800 and 600 BC. (See also page 454.)

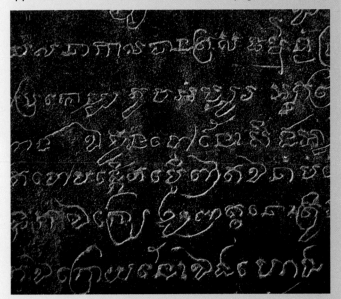

▲ **Indus sculptors** made clay figurines of animals and people, probably for use in religious rituals.

Decline. From about 1900 to 1700 BC, the Indus civilization gradually broke up into smaller cultures, called late Harappan cultures and post-Harappan cultures. The breakup was partly caused by changing river patterns that disrupted agricultural and economic systems.

Many people left the cities of the Indus Valley region. However, some aspects of Indus art, agriculture, and possibly social organization continued in the smaller cultures. Some of these aspects became incorporated into another civilization that began developing throughout the region about 600 BC.

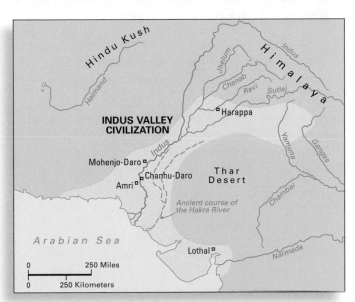

▲ **The Indus River Valley.** This map shows the location of the Indus Valley civilization, which flourished from about 2500 BC to about 1700 BC.

HUANG HE VALLEY

At the same time the Aryans were over-running the Indus Valley, a fourth river valley civilization was emerging 2,000 miles to the northeast, along the banks of the Huang He River, in today's northern China. The Huang He River rises in the mountains of central China and flows for 3,000 miles to the sea. As it does, it passes through the Loess Plateau, where it picks up tons of fertile silt, known as loess. The color of this rich silt gives the river the name by which it has been more commonly known, the Yellow River. The Huang He is also sometimes called *China's Sorrow* because of the many floods that have brought hunger and death to the people living along its banks.

ORACLE BONES!

Writing from the Shang period has been found on fragments of bones. Scholars have determined that such bones were "oracle bones," used to foretell the future. If a Shang king or indeed anyone wanted to know the answer to a question—"When is a good time to plant crops?"—he would have the question written on a piece of bone from a cow or pig. The bone was then thrown into a fire, which caused cracks to appear on it. A priest who could read such signs—an oracle—then interpreted the cracks, telling the future.

The Shang Dynasty

About 4500 BC, Neolithic farming villages began to appear in the Huang He Valley. Archaeologists have found shards of red pottery decorated with geometric designs left by this earliest Chinese culture, the Yang Shao. A second Neolithic culture, the Lung Shan, identified by shards of wheel-made black pottery, followed the Yang Shao.

Legend tells that kings of the Hsia dynasty ruled these Neolithic peoples and that these kings taught them astronomy, chariot and boat construction, and silk manufacture. But it was not until about 1500 BC, with the advent of the Shang dynasty, that the Chinese developed a written language and its recorded history could begin.

The "Mandate from Heaven"

The kings who founded the Shang dynasty believed that they were the "Sons of Heaven," that the god of the sky had given them the right to rule. They called this right a "Mandate from Heaven," and all succeeding dynasties would also claim it. The civilization that the Shang kings helped to found would become the longest continuous civilization the world has ever known.

▲ **China's first dynasty,** the Shang, arose in the Huang He Valley during the 1700s BC. It ruled China until about 1122 BC.

◀ **Shang scribes** often wrote by using sharp sticks or brushes to draw the characters on narrow strips of bamboo, which were then bound together. That is why, to this day, Chinese is written in vertical columns.

◀ **The artisans of the Shang dynasty** created beautiful works of metal, stone, and porcelain, some of which have survived to this day.

Kings and Priests. Shang government was not strongly centralized.

- The Shang kings ruled by granting land to supporters and making them a noble class.
- These nobles then governed their chiefdoms under the kings' direction.
- The Shang leaders organized armies of as many as 5,000 men and equipped them with bronze weapons and horse-drawn war chariots.

They ruled much of the valley in this way for about 600 years.

Shang kings also acted as chief priests, offering sacrifices to the many nature gods, as well as to their ancestors. (The Chinese believed that the spirits of their ancestors could intercede with the gods for help and protection.)

Written Language. Under the Shangs, the Chinese developed their complex written language. Like other early writing, it relied originally on pictures of objects to convey ideas. In time, these drawings changed into symbols, growing into a total of tens of thousands of characters, some representing whole words and phrases and some representing sounds. Gradually, this number was reduced to about 10,000 characters. In recent times, it has been reduced further still.

Culture and Art. The beginning of the Shang period also marked the start of the Bronze Age in China. Among the greatest of the works of the Shang period are bronze statues and vessels considered among the finest ever produced. They were widely used to offer sacrifices to ancestral spirits and to beautify the homes of the wealthy.

Shang artisans also developed white porcelain, the forerunner of modern "china" ware, and were master carvers in jade and ivory.

CULTURES OF THE MIDDLE EAST

As the four great river civilizations were reaching their heights, other civilizations were also emerging, especially in what we now call the Middle East: Southwest Asia, including Asia Minor, the eastern Mediterranean lands, and North Africa. Southwest Asia was already populated by Semitic peoples—for example, the Babylonians and the Assyrians, among many others. Now it also became a magnet for people from around the Black Sea, in what is today Ukraine, Russia, and Georgia.

The Phoenicians

About 2000 BC, groups of people now referred to as Indo-Europeans began leaving their homelands in one of the major human migrations in history. The Aryans who invaded the Indus Valley were one Indo-European people. The Hittites who invaded Babylonia, and the Medes and Persians who moved into what is modern Iran, were also Indo-Europeans. When the Indo-Europeans streamed into the Middle East, they brought major changes with them.

A Rising Power

About 2500 BC, a Semitic people known as the Phoenicians began establishing themselves along the Mediterranean's eastern shore, in the area that is roughly present-day Lebanon. The Phoenicians became the greatest traders and colonizers of the ancient Mediterranean world. By 1000 BC, their trading centers at Tyre, Beirut, Byblos, and Sidon dominated the commercial life of the Mediterranean.

Phoenician Lands. This map shows the location of Phoenicia, its colonies, and its trade routes. Phoenicia occupied the eastern coast of the Mediterranean Sea. It established colonies in southern Spain and northern Africa and on islands in the Mediterranean. Traders traveled to Egypt, western Europe, and throughout the Mediterranean region. ▼

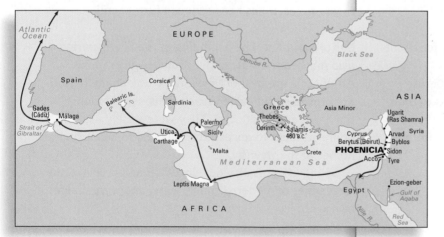

- Phoenician territory
- ← Phoenician trade route

0   500 Miles
0   500 Kilometers

Crossroads of the Middle East. With Egypt located to the south, Mesopotamia to the east, and Asia Minor to the north, Phoenicia became a crossroads of the ancient Middle East. Cultural influences poured into Phoenicia from all these areas, and Phoenicia's manufactured goods flowed out in a wealth-creating stream.

One of the Phoenician goods in high demand was a fine woolen cloth colored with a purple dye made from local shellfish and highly prized as the royal garb for the kings of the ancient world. Other Phoenician trade goods included

- furniture made from the famous cedars of Lebanon.
- wine, salt, and dried fish.
- glassware, metalware, and jewelry.

Major Events—Middle East	
c. 2500 BC	The Phoenicians establish themselves along the Mediterranean's eastern shore.
c. 2000 BC	The Indo-Europeans begin leaving the area around the Black Sea for the Middle East.
c. 1280 BC	The Hebrews return to Canaan from Egypt; they introduce the concept of monotheism.
c. 1100 BC	The Phoenicians develop an alphabet that will become the basis for all modern European alphabets.
c. 1025 BC	Hebrew tribes unite into the kingdom of Israel.
c. 600 BC	Cyrus the Great founds the Persian Empire.
c. 586 BC	Judah falls to Nebuchadnezzar, the king of Babylon; the Babylonian captivity of the Hebrews begins.
c. 536 BC	Cyrus the Great of Persia conquers Babylonia and frees the Hebrews.
c. 521 BC	The Persians build an advanced system of roads, providing a route to China and central Asia.

THE PHOENICIAN ABC'S

The Phoenicians' most memorable achievement as carriers of civilization was their improvement in written language. Having become familiar in their travels with both Mesopotamian cuneiform and Egyptian hieroglyphics, they developed a simpler form of writing, creating signs that stood for single speech sounds.

▲ **The Phoenician Alphabet.** The 22 consonant symbols that the Phoenicians created became the basis for the Greek alphabet—which in turn inspired the Roman alphabet and all Western alphabets.

Colonization. Phoenicia's daring sailors took their ships to the edges of the known world.

- They sailed across the Mediterranean, through the Strait of Gibraltar, and up the Atlantic coast as far as today's England.
- They may also have sailed down the west coast of Africa.
- They may also have been the first people to round Africa at the Cape of Good Hope and to sail north through the Indian Ocean.

As the Phoenicians traveled, they carried the civilization of the Middle East with them. They founded colonies throughout the Mediterranean world, in particular on the islands of Cyprus, Malta, Sicily, and Sardinia; on the southern coast of Spain; and on the northern coast of Africa. The greatest of all the colonies was Carthage, in North Africa, which grew into a major Mediterranean power, and which would later clash with Rome for control of the sea.

Decline. The Assyrians captured the Phoenician cities in 842 BC and controlled them for the next 200 years. After the downfall of the Assyrians in 612 BC, Phoenicia was briefly controlled by the Babylonians.

Later, Phoenicia would fall under the control of several foreign empires.

- It became part of the Persian Empire created by King Cyrus I in about 550 BC.
- It came under Greco-Macedonian rule when Alexander the Great captured the city of Tyre in 332 BC.
- The Romans would make Phoenicia part of the Roman Empire in 64 BC. (See also pages 436–437.)

The Iranian Plateau

Nomadic tribes of people known as the Medes and the Persians began settling on the Iranian plateau about 1500 BC. By the 7th century BC, united under Mede leadership, they were powerful enough to become part of an alliance with Babylon that overthrew the Assyrian Empire in 612 BC. Now, as they spread into northern Mesopotamia, they began building their own empire.

The Persian Empire

In the 5th century BC, a Persian prince overthrew the Medes and founded the Achaemenid, or Persian, Empire. As one of the finest military commanders and ablest organizers of the ancient world, Cyrus the Great (ruled 550–529 BC) succeeded in bringing Babylonia as well as all of the Fertile Crescent and Asia Minor under his control. The Greeks and Egyptians, however, held out against him.

Cyrus's successors would add Egypt and parts of southeastern Europe in the west, and territory as far east as the Indus River, making the Persian Empire the largest the world had yet known.

Governing the Empire. The Persians were excellent organizers and wise rulers. Darius I (ruled 522–486 BC) divided the empire into 20 provinces, called satrapies. Governing each was a satrap who collected taxes and enforced the laws. In an effort to discourage rebellion against Persian rule, the Persians allowed the different peoples of their empire to live under their own local laws, religions, and customs.

To bind the empire together, the Persian government built an advanced system of roads. These roads made contact between the emperor and the satraps easier, and served as arteries of trade throughout the empire. The roads also provided a route to central Asia and China over which silk and other valuable goods were traded.

This map shows the Achaemenid Empire at its peak about 500 BC, during the reign of Darius I. Persis, later called Persia, was the center of an empire that stretched west to the central Mediterranean Sea, east to northwestern India (now Pakistan), and from the Gulf of Oman in the south to the Caucasus Mountains and the Syr Darya River in the north. ▼

☐ Persia	•	City or town
▨ Persian Empire	×	Major battle
★ Capital		

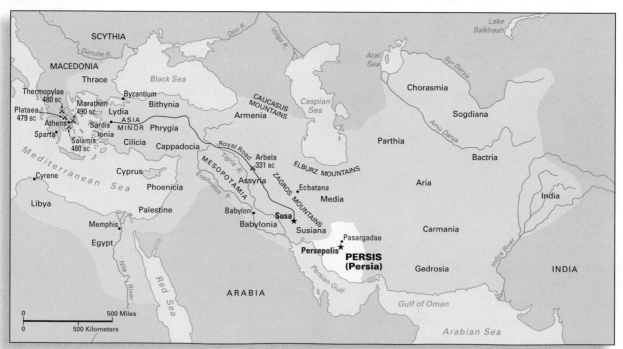

The Persian Wars

Darius I (522–486 BC) was determined to conquer the Greek city-states and launched the Persian wars. Darius's Persians invaded Greece in 490 BC; his son Xerxes I invaded in 480 BC.

- The first invasion was ended by the great Athenian victory at Marathon (490).
- The second invasion was turned back after the Persian fleet was destroyed at Salamis (480).

Following the Persian defeat in these wars, the empire sank into stagnation and collapsed before the armies of Alexander the Great.

Darius I, also called Darius Hystaspes or the Great, was one of the preeminent rulers of the Persian Empire. ▶

▲ **Xerxes I** ruled the Persian Empire from 486 BC until his death. He succeeded his father, Darius I, and spent several years trying to achieve his father's goal of conquering Greece. Xerxes failed in this attempt.

 *The Persians developed an efficient "pony express" system of mail delivery, built a highway and an irrigation system, and tried to standardize weights and measures.*

ZOROASTRIANISM

The earliest Persians believed in many gods of nature. However, about 600 BC, a religious prophet named Zoroaster began to preach a new set of beliefs.

- Life is a battle between good and evil. People must choose whether to join this struggle on the side of Ahura Mazda, the god of good, or on the side of Ahriman, the god of evil.
- Zoroaster predicted that good would win and that those who led moral lives would be rewarded with eternal life in paradise, while those who led evil lives would suffer eternity in hell.

Zoroastrianism set a high standard of honesty and other ethical behavior for the Persians. Many of its ideas would later be reflected in Judaism, Christianity, and Islam.

- ✔ As the river valley civilizations grew and prospered, other civilizations began to emerge in the region that we now call the Middle East.
- ✔ The Phoenicians established themselves in present-day Lebanon; they also founded colonies throughout the Mediterranean region.
- ✔ The Persian Empire began after tribes called the Persians and the Medes overthrew the Assyrians in 612 BC.
- ✔ Persian king Cyrus I and his successors would eventually make the Persian Empire the largest in history up to that point.

Israel and Judah

To the south of Phoenicia lay the land of Canaan, later known as Palestine. About 1200 BC, the Hebrews, a Semitic people, began returning to Canaan from a long exile. With them they brought a belief in a single, all-powerful god, and a clearly delineated code of ethics. These beliefs would profoundly affect later civilizations and would give rise eventually to three great world religions: Judaism, Christianity, and Islam.

Beginnings

The Jews (also referred to as the Hebrews or Israelites) trace their ancestry to a shepherd named Abraham, who lived sometime between 1800 and 1500 BC in southern Mesopotamia (now southeastern Iraq). According to the Bible, Abraham led his followers away from Sumer during a time of famine in about 1800 BC. They traveled northwest to Canaan. Famine there 100 years later drove the Hebrews south into Egypt, where they were enslaved by one of the Egyptian pharaohs.

Exodus. About 1300 BC, the Hebrew leader Moses led his people in a great exodus, bringing them out of Egyptian bondage and back to Canaan. The Hebrews' escape from Egypt is thought to have occurred during the reign of Ramses II (c. 1292–c. 1225 BC).

The Bible recounts the story in the book of Exodus, including Moses' efforts to win the release of the Hebrews, the escape and crossing of the Red Sea, the arduous journey to Mount Sinai, and the giving of the Ten Commandments.

After the Exodus. In Canaan, the Hebrews, loosely organized into 12 tribes, fought the Canaanites for control of the land and succeeded in subjugating them. Then a new and more powerful enemy appeared: the Philistines, a non-Semitic people who had been driven out of Asia Minor and settled in southwest Palestine. (The name Palestine derives from the Philistines.)

THE TEN COMMANDMENTS

According to the Bible, God revealed the Ten Command-ments to Moses on Mount Sinai, during the Hebrews' exodus from Egypt. The Commandments are rules for living and worship. Different versions of the Commandments appear in different parts of the Bible, as well as in different translations of the Bible.

Scholars have suggested several different ways of organizing and interpreting the list. Most people see the Ten Commandments as two natural groups: the first group deals with the relationships between people and God, while the second group deals with relationships among people.

▲ **A view from the Mount Sinai region** shows the rugged slopes in the Sinai Peninsula of Egypt. Debate continues over the exact location of Mount Sinai, but it is traditionally thought to be located on this peninsula, at Jebel Musa.

◀ **The Ten Commandments,** shown here written in Hebrew, are important to the religions of Judaism and Christianity. They are also parallel to certain parts of the earlier Code of Hammurabi.

לא תרצח	אנכי ד
לא תנאף	לא יהיה
לא תגנב	לא תשא
לא תענה	זכור את
לא תחמד	כבד את

The Kingdom of Israel

To overcome the Philistines, the Hebrew tribes united into the Kingdom of Israel, about 1025 BC, under the great warrior Saul. King Saul died in battle against the Philistines in 1000 BC, but his successor, King David, fought on and finally restricted this enemy to one small coastal area. David formed a strong kingdom with Jerusalem as the capital.

King Solomon's Rule. Under David, and later under his son Solomon, the Kingdom of Israel grew rich and powerful. Solomon inaugurated massive building projects, including a vast palace complex and the magnificent Temple of Jerusalem. He also brought great wealth to the kingdom by encouraging trade.

Soon after Solomon's death in 928 BC, the kingdom split in two. The north became the Kingdom of Israel and the south became the Kingdom of Judah.

Decline. Weakened by its split from Judah, Israel was crushed by the Assyrian Empire in 722 BC. The people of Israel were exiled and scattered. They became known as the ten lost tribes.

Judah fell to Nebuchadnezzar, king of Babylonia, in 586 BC. The king destroyed Solomon's Temple in Jerusalem and transported thousands of Jews back to Mesopotamia—the so-called Babylonian Captivity.

Fifty years later, when Cyrus the Great conquered Babylonia, the Persians freed the Hebrews, but both Israel and Judah came under Persian rule.

◀ **Kingdom of Israel.**
This map shows the location of the Kingdom of Israel during the 900s BC, at the height of its power.

◀ **The Divided Kingdom.**
This map shows the division between the Kingdom of Israel and the Kingdom of Judah. Jerusalem then became the capital of Judah, while Samaria became the capital of Israel.

JUDAISM

One major contribution of the Hebrews was the concept of monotheism, or the belief in a single god. In the period following the split of Israel and Judah, religious teachers, called prophets, began to develop many of the principles of the religion Judaism.

- The Hebrews believed that one god—Yahweh, or Jehovah—created and rules the universe.

- Yahweh demanded that the Hebrews live moral and ethical lives, following the laws revealed to the prophets and written down in the five books of the Torah (known to Christians as the Pentateuch, the first five books of the Old Testament).

- The Hebrews were to bring these laws to the rest of the world and encourage respect for the individual and toward justice and peace for all.

This ethical worldview greatly influenced the later world religions. (See pages 452–453.)

7 Wonders of the Ancient World

Have you ever heard something described as "the Eighth Wonder of the World"? If so, you might have wondered what the other seven were. The Seven Wonders of the Ancient World are notable objects built between about 2500 and 250 BC.

The practice of listing the seven wonders probably began in ancient Greece. The ancient Romans also listed memorable things that travelers should see. Different lists included different objects. But all the lists of ancient wonders included only

- objects made by human beings.
- objects considered notable because of their great size or some other unusual quality.

These are the seven most commonly listed wonders of the ancient world.

THE HANGING GARDENS OF BABYLON

The gardens were probably built by King Nebuchadnezzar in about 600 BC.

- They were laid out on a brick terrace 400 feet square and 75 feet above the ground.
- In order to irrigate the flowers and trees in the gardens, slaves worked in shifts turning screws to lift water from the Euphrates River.
- Archaeologists have not been able to find the remains of the gardens.

▲ **Babylon,** home of the famous Hanging Gardens, was located near modern-day Baghdad, Iraq.

THE STATUE OF ZEUS AT OLYMPIA

This statue showed Zeus, the king of the Greek gods, seated on a throne.

- The 40-foot-high structure was made by the Greek sculptor Phidias in about 430 BC.
- Though the statue had a wooden core, Zeus's flesh was made of ivory and his robe and ornaments were made of gold.
- The statue was taken to Constantinople in AD 391, where it was destroyed in a fire in 462.

◀ **The statue of Zeus at Olympia** was perhaps the most famous statue made by the ancient Greeks.

THE PYRAMIDS OF EGYPT

These pyramids were created as royal tombs for the Egyptian kings Khufu, Khafra, and Menkaure.

- The pyramids were built from about 2600 to 2500 BC.
- The largest of these structures, sometimes called the Great Pyramid, was dedicated to Khufu.
- They are the oldest of the seven ancient wonders, and the only ones that still survive.

For more on the pyramids, see page 406.

THE COLOSSUS OF RHODES

This was a bronze statue of the Greek sun god Helios. It stood on a promontory overlooking the harbor on the island of Rhodes, an island in the Aegean Sea.

- The Colossus was created between about 294 and 282 BC by the Greek sculptor Chares.
- It stood about 110 feet (34 meters) tall.

- Chares used stone blocks and about 8.5 tons (7.7 metric tons) of iron bars to support the hollow statue.
- In 226 BC, the Colossus was knocked down by an earthquake. It lay in ruins until the metal remains were sold for scrap in AD 653.

THE PHAROS OF ALEXANDRIA

This lighthouse was located on the island of Pharos off the coast of Egypt.

- The structure was designed around 270 BC by the Greek architect Sostratos.
- Its height was estimated to have been over 440 feet (134 meters).

- It became so famous that the word *pharos* came to mean lighthouse.
- The Pharos stood for about 1,500 years before it was finally toppled by an earthquake.

THE MAUSOLEUM AT HALICARNASSUS

This marble tomb was located in what is now southeastern Turkey.

- It was built for King Mausolus of Caria, who died in 353 BC.
- It became so famous that all large tombs are now called "mausoleums."

- The upper part of the mausoleum was destroyed by an earthquake in the AD 1200s, and only pieces of the building and its decorations remain.

◀ **Mausolus's tomb** was about 150 feet (46 meters) high. It had a rectangular base supporting a colonnade formed by 36 columns.

THE TEMPLE OF ARTEMIS AT EPHESUS

This enormous marble structure was one of the largest and most sophisticated temples built in ancient times.

- The temple was built in Asia Minor about 550 BC.
- It featured 106 columns 60 feet high, and was entirely made of marble (except for the roof).

- The temple burned down in 356 BC, and another one like it was built on the same foundation. The second temple was destroyed by invaders in AD 262.

ANCIENT GREEK HISTORY

Ancient Greece was the birthplace of Western civilization about 2,500 years ago. The Greek civilization developed in the form of several city-states, or self-governing towns and their surroundings. The most advanced city-states eventually developed the world's first democratic governments. Gradually, Greek culture spread to other lands, first through trade and later through conquering leaders such as Alexander the Great. The magnificent achievements of the ancient Greeks in government, science, philosophy, and the arts still influence our lives.

Major Events—Ancient Greece	
c. 2500 BC	A seagoing Minoan civilization develops on the island of Crete.
c. 800 BC	Homer produces the *Iliad* and the *Odyssey;* the city-state, or polis, begins to appear in Greece.
c. 776 BC	The first Olympic games are held in Greece.
508 BC	Athens becomes a democracy.
490, 479 BC	The Greeks defeat invading Persian armies on two separate occasions.
c. 458 BC	Aeschylus produces the *Oresteia*.
c. 450 BC	The Parthenon is built on the Acropolis in Athens.
c. 400 BC	Socrates introduces the cross-questioning (dialogue) method of teaching.
323 BC	Alexander the Great dies, and the Hellenistic Age begins.
146 BC	Greece is conquered by the Romans.

Early Greek Societies

Civilization derived from the Middle East, especially from Egypt, came to the island of Crete in the Mediterranean Sea as early as 2500 BC. From Crete, it gradually spread north to the Aegean Islands and the mainland of Greece.

Archaeology has revealed evidence of this Bronze Age culture. Because there are few written records, however, we do not have the same kind of detailed historical information on Crete and early Greece that is available from Mesopotamia, Egypt, and the Middle East in general. What we know about the Aegean culture we have learned from its material remains.

The Minoans

Early civilization in the Aegean is known as the Minoan period, named for the legendary King Minos of Crete. The culture appears to have been powerful until about 1500 BC.

- Enormous palace complexes, particularly at Knossos in Crete, show that the skills of Aegean artisans were the equal of those in the Middle East.

- Painted pottery and wall paintings were produced in a lively and elegant style. Marine motifs occurred frequently, an indication of the importance of the sea to these island people.

▲ **The Minoan culture** produced highly developed art and architecture, such as the dolphin fresco shown here. Some think that the tales of the lost city Atlantis may have had their roots in the destruction of the Minoan society.

*Some scholars believe Mycenae won a war against Troy, in Asia Minor (now Turkey), in about 1200 BC. The Trojan War, as it came to be called, inspired major works of classical literature, such as Homer's* Iliad *and Vergil's* Aeneid. *(See pages 920–921.)*

▲ **Early Greek Cultures.** This map shows the regions, cities, and sites of Aegean civilization, which existed on the island and shores of the Aegean Sea between 3000 and 1100 BC.

Mycenae

The final 300 years of the Bronze Age in the Aegean are known as the Mycenaean period, named for wealthy "golden" Mycenae, the leading Greek city of the time. There, modern archaeology has uncovered the finest examples of the crafts of the late Bronze Age, especially jewelry and decorative articles of solid gold buried in the royal tombs.

The Dark Age. The Bronze Age in Greece and Crete came to an end with barbarian invasions by a new wave of Indo-Europeans about 1200 BC. The invaders were Dorian Greeks from northwest Greece. These invaders completely destroyed the existing cultures, and for 400 years afterward Greece experienced a Dark Age. The splendid Mycenaean palaces were lost, as was the art of writing. The memories of the glorious past remained only in oral poetry.

Revival. Contact with the Phoenicians gradually stimulated a revival of civilized life. In about 800 BC, the Greeks borrowed an alphabet from the Phoenicians. They were soon on the road to the brilliant achievements that laid the foundations of Western culture. At this time, the earliest written literature—the *Iliad* and the *Odyssey* of Homer, which recount the great deeds of Bronze Age heroes—was produced.

THE LINEAR LANGUAGES

The only written records of Aegean civilization are a number of inscribed tablets.

- A few hundred tablets are written in a script called Linear A. They are found only on Crete and date from about 1500 BC.

- Another 3,000 are written in a somewhat different script called Linear B. They have been found at sites on both Crete and the Greek mainland. They date from about 100 years after the Linear A tablets.

Linear A is still a puzzle, but Linear B was deciphered in 1953; its language proved to be an early, primitive form of Greek.

▲ **The translated tablets** from Crete and Greece contain records that testify to the high degree of organization in the economies of the Cretan and Greek cities.

Growth and Glory

As ancient Greece climbed out of its Dark Age, which lasted from about 1200 BC to about 800 BC, a new form of political organization began to appear in the region. The city-state, or polis, would eventually become the basic political unit of Greece. Citizens were fiercely loyal to their own city-states, and ancient Greece was never voluntarily unified.

An Age of Expansion

In the 600s and 500s BC, Greece experienced rapid political and economic development. Stimulated by population growth as well as trade, the Greek cities sent boatloads of colonists throughout the Mediterranean, where they established scores of new city-states.

The following were the main areas settled by the Greeks.

- the shores of the Black Sea
- the Ionian coast of Asia Minor
- Sicily and southern Italy (these became known as Magna Graecia, or Greater Greece)

THE POLIS

At the height of its power, Greece consisted of more than a thousand city-states, most of them no more than towns, each with its small area of fertile farmland and separated from its neighbors by the rugged mountains that typify the Greek landscape.

- At first, kings ruled the city-states, with advice from wealthy nobles.
- By approximately 750 BC, the nobles in most city-states had overthrown the kings and become rulers.
- The nobility owned the best land and controlled the community.

The city-state was such an essential part of the Greek way of life that it was thought to be part of the natural world. The philosopher Aristotle's famous axiom that man is by nature "a political animal" is more correctly understood to mean that man is by nature "an animal who lives in a polis."

Government. As Greece expanded, the city-states changed from simple farming communities to dictatorships. These new, aggressive trading and manufacturing communities—complete with armies and navies—usually had written constitutions. They were controlled by a large class of wealthy people.

At the end of the 500s BC, however, Athens began one of the most adventurous political experiments in history: the creation of a direct democracy. All adult male citizens had an equal share in guiding the affairs of state. (Women and slaves, however, did not have these rights.) Public matters were decided by a majority vote of citizens in the assembly, which met every ninth day.

Ancient Greece consisted mostly of a peninsula that separated the Aegean and Ionian seas, nearby islands, and the coast of Asia Minor (now part of Turkey). This map shows important cities, regions, and historic sites of ancient Greece. ▼

The Classical Period

Ancient Greece reached its height during the 400s and 300s BC, a time often called the Classical period. Although this period is generally admired for its intellectual and cultural achievements, it is important to understand the political conditions that created the era. War, competition between city-states, and internal struggles for power were all significant political elements of classical Greece.

The Persian Wars (490–479 BC). For many years, the Greek city-states developed on their own and, apart from trade, were relatively isolated. In the early 400s BC, a series of invasions would force them to become aware of their power in a larger world.

- The Persian king Darius I, and later his son Xerxes, sought to add mainland Greece to the Persian Empire.
- Though greatly outnumbered, the Greeks inflicted crushing defeats on the Persians at the famous battles of Marathon, Salamis, and Plataea.

The Peloponnesian War (431–404 BC). After the Persian wars, Athens grasped the opportunity to grow. It rapidly built an empire over the Greek cities and islands of the Aegean. Sparta, on the other hand, had retreated into isolation and resented Athenian expansion.

- Sparta went to war against Athens, allying itself with Corinth and other polises of the Peloponnesus (the southern region of mainland Greece).
- The Peloponnesian War was fought for 27 years, on land and sea. It engaged the entire Greek world.
- Finally, Persia provided Sparta with the funds to build a naval fleet. In 404 BC, the Athenian fleet was destroyed and Athens unconditionally surrendered.

LEADERS AND LAWMAKERS

The city-state of Athens produced many powerful political leaders during its years of expansion and its "golden age," the Classical period.

Draco (c. 621 BC)

- Instituted the first legal code in Athens
- The notoriously harsh code prescribed the death penalty for even minor offenses.
- Today, the word *Draconian* means *harsh* or *cruel*.

Solon (c. 639–c. 559 BC)

- Reformed the Athenian constitution to allow all freemen to participate in the assembly
- Replaced the harsh Draconian code with a new law code and made other reforms that were the basis for democracy

Cleisthenes (c. 508 BC)

- Rose to power amid a political crisis in Athens and used the situation to institute reforms
- The father of Athenian democracy
- Broke the power of the landed aristocracy, which had previously controlled Athenian government

Pericles (c. 461–429 BC)

- Strengthened the Athenian democracy
- Brought about a period of peace and prosperity for Athens
- Became a great patron of the arts, and had the Acropolis of Athens built

Pericles tried to make Athens the most powerful of the Greek states. This led to conflict with the city-state of Sparta. ▶

Sparta and Athens

Two city-states—Athens and Sparta—had emerged from the Persian wars as the leading powers in Greece. Both were much larger and more powerful than any of the other Greek cities.

But Sparta and Athens were nearly opposites in their economic and political institutions, as well as in their cultural lives and in their goals. The history of Classical Greece is generally viewed as the story of the struggle between them.

Sparta

Sparta had long been recognized as the most powerful military state in Greece. It was entirely dedicated to military strength as the means of maintaining an authoritarian society. Life in this city-state was rigid and austere—even today, the term spartan refers to someone or something simple, frugal, or severe.

Land and Economy. Located in the Eurotas River valley, Sparta was protected on three sides by mountains. The climate was mild, and the soil was fertile and well watered. As a result, Sparta's economic focus was on farming.

- Spartan citizens were permitted to work only in agriculture.

- A few aristocrats owned their own land. However, a majority of the citizens held state-owned plots.

- The actual farm work was done by people called helots—Greeks who had been enslaved when Sparta conquered their lands.

- Because citizens could not carry on manufacturing or trade, the *perioeci*, a class of free people who were noncitizens, took over these industries.

The adjective "laconic," meaning "using few words, concise," comes from Laconia, the region in which Sparta was located. Spartans were famous for being men of few words.

Sparta and Athens: Side by Side

Sparta	Athens
Powerful oligarchy	Successful democracy
Focused only on the military and agriculture	Embraced trade, manufacturing, and the arts
Advanced land-based army	Advanced navy
Citizenship for the ruling class only	Citizenship and voting rights for all free adult males
Endurance, a scorn of luxuries, and unyielding firmness	Freedom, rationalism, individualism, and democracy

A Warlike People. Sparta was the only Greek city-state that maintained an army at all times. Every Spartan male belonged to the state from the time of his birth.

- At the age of seven, Spartan boys left home for military training.

- Between the ages of 20 and 30, Spartan men served as cadets who policed the country and kept the helots and other enslaved people in order.

- At 30, a Spartan male attained full maturity and enjoyed the rights and duties of citizenship.

- At 60, his military career ended.

Oligarchy. Sparta's government was an oligarchy, or a government in which a very small number of people hold power. Sparta had a citizen assembly. But citizens could not propose issues for debate in the assembly—and citizens made up only about 10 percent of the population.

- Two kings, who inherited their thrones, headed the army.

- Five officials, called *ephors*, and the *gerousia*, a council made up of 28 elders and the kings, governed the state.

- Citizens elected ephors to 1-year terms and members of the gerousia to life terms.

Athenian pottery became a valuable export throughout the Mediterranean region.

Athens

While Sparta was developing its state-controlled, military society, Athens was growing into something quite different. Athenian society was less controlled and more diverse; it also had a stronger focus on art, literature, and philosophy. Athens also sought to expand its territory and influence.

Land and Economy. Athens, like most of ancient Greece, enjoyed a mild climate that was favorable for farming. A shortage of good farmland in Athens, however, at times created conflict between the wealthy and the poor. Initially, wealthy aristocrats owned most of the land. Later, the leader Pisistratus (c. 546–527 BC) redistributed much of it to the poor.

- Most farmers worked alone or with the help of a few slaves.
- The entire family helped with planting and harvesting.

Athenians also produced a number of highly valued manufactured goods, especially pottery.

A Diverse People. While the Athenians became best known for their achievements in philosophy, science, and the arts, they also played a leading role in the Greek victories over Persia in the two Persian Wars (490 BC and 480–479 BC).

- Athens soon became head of the Delian League, a group of Greek states organized to continue to wage war against Persia.
- The league quickly developed into an Athenian empire.

While Sparta had a mighty standing army, Athens had built an impressive navy a few years before the final Persian attack. This navy proved to be the deciding factor in the repulse of Persia; after the war it became the most powerful fleet in the Mediterranean.

Democracy. Athens was governed by general assembly. The assembly passed laws and determined policies; the day-to-day government tasks were handled by a 500-person council.

- Every male Athenian citizen had the right to vote in the assembly.
  - The voters also elected Athenian generals.
  - Each year, the citizens drew lots to select the 500 men for the council.

◀ **In Athens,** trade was encouraged. This opened the city to the arts and crafts of a wide region. The Athenian *agora*, or marketplace, shown here would have been a center of commerce, political activity, and socializing.

The Hellenistic Age

For 70 years after the end of the Peloponnesian War, Greece was engaged in useless and destructive warfare. Each of several major Greek cities fought for leadership.

Inevitably, the weakened, internally warring cities were conquered by an outside power. As Greece declined, the bordering kingdom of Macedonia had been growing stronger.

- In 338 BC, Philip II, king of Macedonia, defeated the Greeks at the Battle of Chaeronea.

- Philip planned to unite the Greeks with the Macedonians and together conquer the Persian Empire.

- On the eve of his invasion, Philip was assassinated by a Macedonian. His 20-year-old son Alexander carried out his plans.

Greece's "Golden Age" came to an end, and all its cities eventually came under Macedonian rule.

Alexander the Great, and After

In the centuries that followed the Macedonian take-over, Greek culture continued, but with a difference. Alexander soon drastically altered the Greek world, earning himself the title "Alexander the Great."

In the 13 years between his taking over the Macedonian throne and his death at age 32 in 323 BC, Alexander led the combined Macedonian and Greek armies in conquering all of the Persian Empire. Greek and Middle Eastern culture would now influence each other across their shared lands.

Spotlight on... ALEXANDER THE GREAT

356–323 BC

As one of the greatest generals in history, Alexander the Great was responsible for the spread of Greek culture throughout western Asia and Egypt.

- He was educated by the famous Greek philosopher Aristotle.

- Legend says Alexander untied the famous Gordian knot—by cutting through it with his sword—and so fulfilled a prophecy to become king of Asia.

- After conquering Persia, he tried to integrate his own culture with the Persian customs; this caused conflict with his armies.

- He returned to Babylon to administer his vast kingdom, but died there in 323 BC of battle wounds and a fever. He was 32 years old.

The Empires of Persia and Alexander the Great. Alexander the Great conquered most of the territory from Egypt to India by 326 BC. He built Greek cities and introduced Greek culture wherever he ruled. ▶

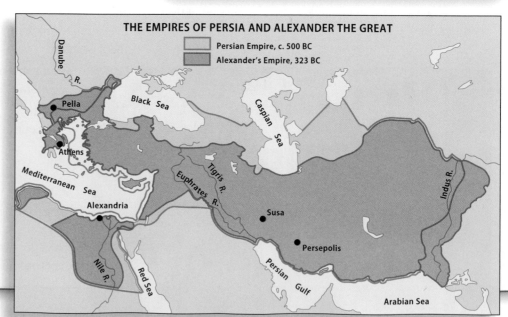

THE EMPIRES OF PERSIA AND ALEXANDER THE GREAT
- Persian Empire, c. 500 BC
- Alexander's Empire, 323 BC

Danube R.
Pella
Black Sea
Caspian Sea
Athens
Mediterranean Sea
Euphrates R.
Tigris R.
Alexandria
Susa
Indus R.
Persepolis
Nile R.
Red Sea
Persian Gulf
Arabian Sea

The Hellenistic World. The 300-year period that followed Alexander's death was called the Hellenistic Age. Because Alexander left no single successor to take his place, his huge empire was fought over by his generals, called the Diadochi. The Diadochi ultimately divided the empire among themselves and set up three major Hellenistic monarchies.

- The general Ptolemy named himself king of Egypt and founded the Ptolemaic dynasty there.

- A second general, Seleucus, founded a dynasty that ruled most of the Asian portions of Alexander's empire, the Seleucid Empire.

- Macedonia and Greece became the province of the Antigonids, descended from the general Antigonus.

To match these powerful territorial states, the old Greek city-states united in leagues. The Macedonian kings retained control, however, and in the end the leagues often ended up fighting each other.

Political Developments. Two important political developments occurred during this period:

1. People accepted the claim of divinity, similar to that of the Egyptian pharaohs, made by the Hellenistic monarchs.

2. The Greek Leagues began the first significant experiments in representative government, where people chose officials to represent them. This was distinct from the direct democracy of classical Athens, where each citizen voted on each issue.

Decline. The Hellenistic world's power was ultimately broken by conquest. The conqueror was Rome, the last and greatest organizer of the ancient world.

Through conquests, Rome had become one of the most powerful countries in the western Mediterranean by the 200s BC. The Romans then began to expand in the east. In the 140s BC, they took control of Greece and Macedonia.

Under Roman rule, the Greek city-states had no important military or political role. But trade, agriculture, industry, and intellectual activities flourished. (See page 440.)

▲ **The Romans** borrowed the art, religion, philosophy, and way of life of the ancient Greeks, and they spread Greek culture throughout their empire.

✔ Civilization began in the Aegean region in about 2500 BC, with the Minoans and later the Mycenaeans.

✔ In about 1200 BC, barbarian invasions brought about the Greek Dark Age, which lasted until about 800 BC.

✔ City-states, or polises, began to emerge toward the end of the Dark Ages.

✔ Athens and Sparta became the two most powerful Greek city-states. Sparta became known for its military; Athens became known for its cultural achievements.

✔ During the Classical period, the Greeks fought off two invasions by the Persians (490–479 BC). Athens and Sparta fought each other in the Peloponnesian War (431–404 BC); Sparta defeated Athens.

✔ Greece was conquered by Philip II, King of Macedonia, and his son, Alexander the Great. Alexander would go on to conquer most of the civilized world and bring Greek culture wherever he went.

ANCIENT GREEK LIFE AND CULTURE

Greek civilization reached its height in Athens during the mid-400s BC. Greek culture had been developing since the Greek Dark Age; then, the end of the Persian wars brought an era of relative peace and wealth. During this time, the work of Greek scientists, mathematicians, philosophers, poets, artists, dramatists, and historians surpassed that of earlier cultures. These works greatly influenced the development of Western civilization.

▲ **The *Odyssey*.** This mosaic depicts a scene from Homer's *Odyssey,* one of the most influential and popular works in ancient Greek literature.

The *Odyssey* and Beyond

In the Greek polis, public and private life were tightly interwoven. Religion, recreation, and entertainment, which today are considered private, were usually public activities for all.

The polis permitted a wide variety of governmental forms, customs, institutions, and attitudes, and it nourished freedom and a spirit of adventurous experiment. At the same time, its very smallness inspired an intense devotion in its citizens.

The Arts

In the 150 years from the Persian wars to the Battle of Chaeronea, when Macedonia took control of the region, Greece produced some of Western civilization's most precious intellectual, artistic, and literary heritage. The Athenian leader Pericles (495–429 BC), a great patron of the arts, made many of these works possible.

Literature. Greek literature more or less began with the *Iliad* and the *Odyssey* of Homer, which appeared at the end of the Dark Age. From there, it continued to advance.

- During the 600s and 500s BC, the Greeks began to produce lyric poetry with a wide variety of meters, subject matter, and imagery. This poetry would form the poetic tradition of the West.

- The writing of history also originated in Athens in the 400s BC. The accounts of Herodotus are still widely read. Thucydides' *History of the Peloponnesian War* is one of the most celebrated historical works ever written.

- The Hellenistic age produced new forms of literature: the comedy of manners; pastoral poetry; didactic poetry; and the prose romance or adventure (ancestor of the novel).

Drama. Greek drama evolved from ceremonies honoring the god Dionysus (Bacchus); it was raised to an art form by four masters of this period. Three of them, Aeschylus (525–456), Sophocles (c. 496–406), and Euripides (c. 480–406), developed the Greek tragedy. The fourth, Aristophanes (c. 448–c. 388), is known for his comedies and political satires. Many of their works remain enjoyable and relevant today.

Sculpture and Pottery. In the Classical Age, sculpture and vase painting advanced rapidly. Athenian vase painting was raised to the level of a fine art. Sculptors soon broke away from their Eastern models and developed characteristically Greek styles.

- Sculptures were freestanding, unlike earlier Egyptian statues.
- Muscles, features, and fabrics showed natural and realistic movement.

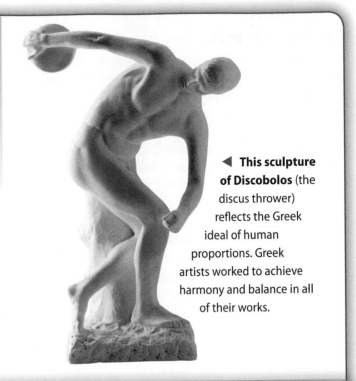

◄ **This sculpture of Discobolos** (the discus thrower) reflects the Greek ideal of human proportions. Greek artists worked to achieve harmony and balance in all of their works.

ANCIENT GREEK ARCHITECTURE

Ancient Greek architecture reached its peak in the 5th century BC, but it's been inspiring people ever since. You can see its influence in the grand columns of courthouses, public buildings—even the White House.

Greek architecture is best known for a set of styles, called orders: Doric, Ionic, and Corinthian. The orders used precise mathematical rules for the placement of walls and columns, which gave the buildings a look of balance and harmony.

- The Doric order was considered austere and masculine.
- The Ionic order was delicate and matronly.
- The Corinthian order was the ornate "young maiden."

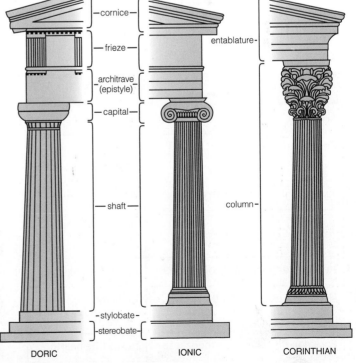

Labels: cornice, frieze, architrave (epistyle), capital, entablature, shaft, column, stylobate, stereobate

DORIC   IONIC   CORINTHIAN

▲ **The Parthenon,** the most brilliant surviving example of Greek architecture, was completed in 433 BC.

▲ **The columns** for each order have specific, distinctive shapes and decoration.

From Aristotle to Zeus

The Greeks at Home

In ancient Greece, men and women had specific roles. Men participated in public life and were the heads of their households.

Women were expected to remain mostly at home, managing the household and raising children. Wealthier women might have had slaves to do much of the work. Women in Sparta enjoyed more freedom than elsewhere in Greece; they could own property and run businesses.

Education. Schooling in ancient Greece was mostly done privately, except in Sparta (there, the state educated children from the age of seven). In Athens, students might learn reading, writing, arithmetic, and music. In Sparta, however, they would be trained mostly for intense military service.

Recreation. Greek men enjoyed sports, and they exercised and swam at public sports facilities. Greek women were permitted little entertainment outside the home, except for religious festivals.

In 776 BC, the Greek city-states held their first Olympic games (which took place at Olympia, in southern Greece). From then on, every 4 years, all wars and rivalries were temporarily put on hold so that athletes could compete in these sacred games. Discontinued in the 4th century AD, the Olympic Games were revived in 1896 and continue to this day.

Large crowds gathered for religious festivals in ancient Greece. At these festivals, athletes competed in such events as wrestling, boxing, foot and chariot races, jumping, and javelin throwing.

Marriage. Greek parents usually arranged their children's marriages. Most girls married in their mid-teens, but many men married around age 30. When a girl married, she received her share of the family's money or property as a dowry (gift). Her husband controlled the dowry but had to return it if they divorced. Normally, the dowry would pass on to her children.

The Olympians	
Gods	**Goddesses**
Zeus (ruler of the gods)	Hera (Zeus's sister and wife)
Apollo (light, music, poetry)	Artemis (hunting)
Ares (war)	Athena (wisdom, warfare)
Hephaestus (blacksmith of the gods)	Aphrodite (love)
Hermes (messenger for the gods)	Demeter (agriculture, fertility)
Poseidon (the ocean, earthquakes)	Hestia (the hearth)

THE GODS OF OLYMPUS

The Greeks were polytheists, or people who believed in many deities (gods and goddesses). Greek mythology tells the stories of these deities, who were immortal and powerful but behaved much like ordinary human beings otherwise. Families and city-states would honor particular deities with sacrifices and other offerings, as well as with large religious festivals. For example, the people of Athens worshiped Athena as their protector.

The most powerful gods in Greek mythology were the Olympians, gods who were said to live on Mount Olympus. The top rank of Olympians consisted of six gods and six goddesses.

The Sciences

During the Hellenistic Age, science made the most spectacular progress of any period of history until modern times. In Alexandria, the kings of the Ptolemaic dynasty founded the Museum, which was the first scientific institute in history.

- At this Museum, scholars were maintained at the expense of the state.
- A huge library was collected, laboratories and dissecting rooms were provided, and zoological and botanical collections were organized.
- Literary scholarship, textual criticism, and library science were developed.

The Hellenistic Greeks also made huge strides in mathematics, physics, astronomy, geography, botany, biology, and medicine.

ACHIEVEMENTS OF HELLENISTIC SCIENCE

- The properties of air were demonstrated.
- The heliocentric theory—that Earth revolves around the sun—was proposed.
- The circumference of Earth and the degrees of latitude were calculated.
- The motor and sensory nervous systems were discovered.
- The properties of cubes, cylinders, cones, and spheres were analyzed.

▲ **Plato's school of philosophy,** shown here, developed into what is believed to have been the first university.

PHILOSOPHY

Philosophy (literally, "love of wisdom") first appeared during the early 500s in the cities along the Ionian (Turkish) coast of the Aegean. There, a scholar named Thales (whom tradition calls the first philosopher), along with a group of other pioneers, used a systematic thought process to try to find a rational, non-supernatural explanation for all phenomena.

Philosophy came to maturity in the ideas of Socrates (469–399 BC), his student Plato (427?–347 BC), and Aristotle (384–322 BC). They examined the questions that human beings have probed ever since: the nature of the universe, of man, of God; the meaning of life; and the relation of the individual to the state.

During the Hellenistic Age, the formal schools focused their attention on ethics and their teachings began to emphasize the divine. For example, Stoicism, the most influential philosophy of the time, taught the immortality of the soul, the importance of doing one's duty on Earth, and the brotherhood of man.

✔ Greek civilization reached its peak during the 400s BC.

✔ Classical Age authors produced works of literature and drama that influenced all of Western culture.

✔ Three of the most influential Greek philosophers were Socrates, his student Plato, and Aristotle.

✔ Ancient Greek sculpture and architecture were based on ideals of harmony, proportion, and balance. The Parthenon is one of the best examples of Greek architecture.

✔ The Hellenistic Age saw great achievements in the sciences.

ANCIENT ROMAN HISTORY

is really the story of how a small farming community on the bank of the Tiber River in central Italy grew to become one of the greatest empires in history, and then collapsed. According to Roman legend, the city of Rome was founded in 753 BC by the brothers Romulus and Remus. By 272 BC, the Roman Republic controlled most of the Italian Peninsula. At its peak, in the AD 100s and 200s, the Roman Empire governed about half of Europe, much of the Middle East, and the north coast of Africa.

Major Events—Ancient Rome	
c. 433 BC	The first census of citizens and property is taken in Rome.
264–146 BC	The three Punic Wars bring Carthage under Roman control.
60 BC	The first triumvirate of Rome (Caesar, Pompey, and Crassus) takes power.
49–31 BC	Crassus's death leads to the Roman civil wars.
27 BC	The reign of Augustus begins.
c. AD 64	A great fire destroys large sections of Rome.
c. AD 161	The reign of Marcus Aurelius
c. AD 313	The Edict of Milan grants Christianity toleration in the Roman Empire.
AD 476	The western half of the Roman Empire collapses.

Birth of Rome

Archaeological research suggests that the early Romans were a local group of the Latins, one of the many Indo-European tribes who entered Italy shortly after 1000 BC. These tribes are known collectively as the Italic peoples.

Early Development

Until the late 300s BC, Rome was an insignificant state, largely agricultural and almost entirely illiterate. For a long period, the Romans were culturally influenced and even ruled by the Etruscans, their neighbors across the Tiber River. At that time, there were three powers in the western Mediterranean.

- The Etruscans
- The Greeks of southern Italy and Sicily
- The Phoenicians, whose major commercial city was Carthage, in North Africa (See pages 412–413.)

In this three-way struggle for land, trade, and power, the Etruscans were the losers. Their decline led to Rome's independence (traditionally dated at 509 BC).

▲ **Etruscan Lands.** This map shows the location of Etruria, the home of the Etruscans. The Etruscans ruled Rome for more than 100 years, from 616 to 509 BC. Rome took complete control of Etruria in the mid-200s BC.

Expansion. The newly independent Rome was slow to develop at first. As late as 390 BC, a tribe of barbaric Gauls from northern Italy sacked the city. Probably as a direct result of this event, Rome began to cultivate the military prowess that was responsible for its remarkable growth.

- By 338 BC, the Romans controlled the surrounding region of Latium.

- Latium's inhabitants had long been organized into the Latin League for military purposes; Rome now took control of the League.

- By the end of the 300s, the Romans ruled the peninsula south of the Po River.

In the following 150 years of uninterrupted military advance, Rome rose from a local power in Italy to the unchallenged ruler of most of the Mediterranean world, with direct control over all the rest.

The Punic Wars. A series of wars with Carthage, called the Punic Wars, began in 264 BC. In these wars, Rome opposed and then conquered the great empire of Carthage. With the destruction of Carthage in 146 BC, Rome's rule over the western Mediterranean was absolute.

In the same year, the Roman conquest of the Greek mainland was also completed. Rome added the last Hellenistic monarchy, Egypt, to its dominions in 30 BC.

▲ **Rome gained control** of the Italian peninsula through a series of military victories. This map shows the growth of Roman rule in the peninsula.

The Punic Wars: An Overview		
War	**Dates**	**Effects**
First Punic War	264–241 BC	• After some serious reverses, the Romans finally destroyed the Carthaginian fleet in 241. • Carthage was forced to give up Sicily.
Second Punic War	218–201 BC	• Carthaginian general Hannibal invaded and gained control of most of southern Italy. • He was defeated at the Battle of Zama in 202. • Carthage surrendered in 201 and never regained its former greatness.
Third Punic War	149–146 BC	• The Romans provoked the war and quickly laid siege to Carthage. • The city was destroyed, its inhabitants were sold into slavery, and the domain became the Roman province of Africa.

▲ **Hannibal,** shown here, crossed the Alps to invade Italy. He famously brought elephants with him to smash enemy lines.

Rise of the Republic

The nearly five centuries between Rome's independence from the Etruscans and its total control of the Mediterranean mark the period of the Roman Republic.

In theory, the structure of the republic emphasized the joint power of all classes in a unified citizenry. Contrary to legend, however, the plebeians, or common people, largely did not have rights equal to those of the patricians, or aristocrats.

Inequality and Unrest

The republic was intended to be a partnership between the Senate and the people of Rome. Instead, the political and judicial equality gained by the plebeians resulted in the formation of a joint patrician-plebeian aristocracy.

- This new aristocracy was composed of the wealthiest families in Rome, who intermarried among themselves and rigorously excluded outsiders.

- The aristocracy maintained a monopoly over the higher offices of state, and the holders of these offices filled vacancies in the Senate.

The tightly knit oligarchy directed Rome's triumphant territorial expansion, but it was motivated by a combination of patriotism and greed. Without any ideals or guiding philosophy, it treated conquest merely as an opportunity to gain unlimited wealth and power.

▲ **The motto of the Roman Republic** was *Senatus Populusque Romanus* (Senate and People of Rome). The initials SPQR appeared on the flags of the Roman legions and in official documents.

Spotlight on...

JULIUS CAESAR

100?–44 BC

Julius Caesar is considered one of Rome's greatest leaders and statesmen. His goals as dictator were eternal peace and stability, fair and equal treatment of conquered peoples, and no unnecessary taxation.

- Elected a consul in 59 BC—after bribery and some violence

- He was considered the second greatest orator, or speaker, of Rome (after Cicero).

- Initially he was made dictator for 10 years; later this office became dictator for life.

- He granted citizenship to many people in the conquered provinces and worked to control corruption.

- His assassination and its aftermath are the subject of William Shakespeare's play *Julius Caesar*.

The First Triumvirate. An alliance between the leaders Julius Caesar (100?–44), Pompey (106–48), and Crassus (115?–53), brought a brief lull in this turmoil. Though their arrangement was not a legal form of government, the three triumvirs overcame all opposition and made themselves masters of Rome. They remained in power until Crassus was killed in 53 BC.

The Roman Civil Wars

The death of Crassus pitted the two surviving members of the triumvirate, Caesar and Pompey, against each other. Over the next few years, Caesar defeated Pompey and his supporters. He had also made an alliance with Egypt, and restored Cleopatra as queen of Egypt. By 45 BC, Caesar had become sole ruler of the Roman world.

Death of Caesar. Resentment at Caesar's power soon grew to dangerous proportions in Rome, however, and many feared that he would crown himself king. On March 15, 44 BC, he was assassinated. The aristocrats Brutus, Cassius, Casca, and others stabbed him to death as a traitor to republican government. Caesar's death plunged Rome into a new and more deadly disorder.

The Second Triumvirate. In the turmoil following Caesar's assassination, Caesar's heir, Octavian (63 BC–AD 14), joined with Marc Antony (83–30 BC) and Lepidus (d. 13 BC) to form a second triumvirate to rule Rome. When they secured their position in Rome, Octavian and Antony pursued and defeated the armies of Brutus and Cassius (42 BC). The triumvirate was renewed in 37 BC, but in 36 BC Lepidus was ousted.

ANTONY AND CLEOPATRA

Marc Antony had been given control of the eastern part of the Roman provinces, which included Egypt. There he met Cleopatra; their love affair is among the most famous in history.

- From 42 to 40 BC, they remained in Egypt.

- When Antony returned to Rome, he was forced to marry Octavian's sister, Octavia, in order to keep his power. But he soon returned to Cleopatra.

- The lovers went into opposition to Rome and prepared for war.

- Octavian's Roman forces finally defeated them in the great naval battle at Actium, off the western coast of Greece, in 31 BC.

Antony and Cleopatra fled to Egypt. Pursued by Octavian, they committed suicide.

The tragic story of Antony's love affair with Cleopatra is at the center of William Shakespeare's famous play, *Antony and Cleopatra*.

Octavian, shown here, defeated Marc Antony's forces, and became the sole ruler of Rome.

- In 27 BC, he became the first Roman emperor.

- The Senate gave him the name Augustus, meaning "Revered One," a name that held religious meaning.

Emperor Augustus would realize Caesar's aims and establish the governmental structure of the Roman Empire.

The Roman Empire

More than a century of internal upheavals and civil war had destroyed the Roman Republic. The Roman Empire that took its place brought the civilized world under a single monarchic rule. Still, it used the political terminology of the Roman Republic and preserved the (by then obsolete) Senate. The empire tended toward authoritarianism and military despotism.

Governing the Empire

Although the early emperors of the 1st century AD led scandalous private lives, the empire they ruled actually prospered. During their reigns, Rome developed the centralized bureaucracy that would later make the empire a synonym for the art of government.

The Civil Service. By the middle of the 1st century AD, that government consisted of a permanent, highly organized civil service. Even the emperor considered himself the servant of his demanding office.

This government enabled a vast territory and a population of over 50 million people of different races, languages, cultures, and traditions to enjoy centuries of security, stability, peace, rational and disinterested administration, and almost impartial law.

Expansion. Augustus had left strict instructions to his successors not to expand the empire, but this was disregarded.

- Emperor Claudius invaded Britain in 43. He also added Mauretania (now northern Morocco and western Algeria) to the empire.

- Trajan seized Dacia in eastern Europe in 106.

Hadrian returned to the policy of Augustus. He marked the limits of Rome's empire with artificial frontiers on the Danube River, in northern Africa, and elsewhere. In northern England, he constructed Hadrian's Wall, parts of which still stand.

THE PAX ROMANA

The "good emperors" of the first century created the Pax Romana, or Roman Peace. Edward Gibbon, the great English historian of the 1700s, described this era as the period in which "the condition of the human race was the most happy and prosperous."

Civilization spread throughout the vast realm of the Roman Empire. Scores of cities were built where formerly there had been only barbarism. A Greek lecturer who came to Rome in the AD 150s praised Rome's accomplishment. He stated that the new unwalled cities were meant for a world at peace—for the first time in history cities needed no local defense.

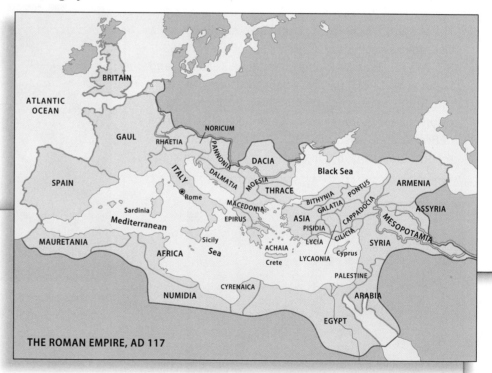

THE ROMAN EMPIRE, AD 117

▲ **Spread of the Empire.** The Roman emperor Augustus (63 BC–AD 14) added Egypt and most of southeastern Europe south of the Danube River. The Roman Empire reached its greatest size under Trajan, who ruled until AD 117.

Decline and Fall

Even at its peak, the Roman Empire already contained the seeds of its eventual collapse. The decline and fall of the Roman Empire is one of the most debated issues in history. Historians have offered several different types of explanations for Rome's decay.

- One explanation, called the moral explanation, blames personal failings—the greed of individual emperors, the decadent luxury of the wealthy, indifference to the misery of the masses, and so on.

- Another explanation emphasizes the divisions and conflicts of the empire—between rich and poor, urban and rural, military and civilian.

- A third explanation emphasizes economic issues, such as a devalued currency, growing taxation, and constant importation of luxuries.

Military Issues. The control of the armed forces remained a problem for centuries. There was a constant threat of coups and internal wars for control.

The pressure of two outside powers made a large military force a constant necessity:

- In the East, a revived Persian Empire

- In present-day Europe, a succession of Germanic tribes

Rome eased the threat in Europe in the 200s by admitting whole tribes into the empire.

Divided Empire

The problems in the 200s, and the decreasing power to deal with them, brought about an administrative revision around 395 that divided the empire into an eastern Greek-speaking half and a western Latin-speaking half.

In spite of the efforts of individual emperors, such as Diocletian and Constantine I, to restore unity, the two halves tended to grow further apart. By about 400 they were not only separate, but hostile.

Invasions. Weakened, the Roman Empire fell to a series of invading powers.

- Rome fell to the Visigoths in 410, the first time in 800 years that the city had been taken by foreign invaders.

- The Huns, under Attila, ravaged the East Roman Empire from 434 to 453. Attila reached the outskirts of Rome at one point.

- The Vandals, a Germanic people, sacked Rome in 455.

- Odoacer, a German chieftain, deposed Emperor Romulus Augustulus in 476, marking the end of the West Roman Empire.

- The East Roman Empire became known as the Byzantine Empire.

EMPEROR NERO

One of Rome's most notorious leaders was the emperor Nero (AD 37–68). Nero reigned from AD 54 until his death 14 years later. His scandalous life—he had two of his wives and many senators executed—made him unpopular.

His rule is perhaps best known for a fire that destroyed much of Rome in AD 64. Rumors circulated that Nero had started the fire so that he could build a grand palace on the ruins. However, Nero blamed the Christians, then an unpopular group in Rome, and persecuted them.

✔ Rome won its independence from the Etruscans in 509 BC.

✔ The period from 509 BC to Rome's total control of the Mediterranean is known as the Roman Republic.

✔ Civil war and rebellion led to the rise of the First Triumvirate—Julius Caesar, Pompey, and Crassus. Caesar was assassinated in 44 BC.

✔ The Roman Empire began with Emperor Augustus, in 27 BC.

✔ At its peak, the Empire controlled half of Europe, much of the Middle East, and the north coast of Africa.

✔ The Empire declined in the 200s and 300s. It collapsed finally in AD 476.

ANCIENT ROMAN LIFE AND CULTURE

The dramatic rise of the Roman Republic, its equally dramatic self-destruction, and its transformation into the Roman Empire were accompanied by a number of important cultural developments. At the empire's height, more than 50 million people lived there, mixing languages and cultures. Roman culture absorbed much from the conquered Greeks, but it also had its own unique qualities. Roman achievements in literature, architecture, engineering, and law survive to this day.

When in Rome

The daily lives of ancient Romans depended upon three things: their location, their citizenship status, and their social class. Rural and urban Romans lived differently, as did slaves and citizens.

Citizenship

People belonged to one of three groups in ancient Rome.

1. citizens
2. noncitizens
3. slaves

Citizens and noncitizens were free, while slaves were considered property. Citizenship gave protection under Roman law, and only a citizen could become a senator or government official.

At first, only those born in Rome could become citizens. As Rome expanded, it granted citizenship to more people in the empire. Women and children could become citizens, but they could not vote.

Wealthy, urban Romans might have lived in a large house like this one. Most people in Roman cities, however, lived in cramped apartment buildings three to five stories high. Many of these buildings had unsanitary conditions, and a number of them burned to the ground. ▼

Social Classes. The citizens of Rome were further divided into different social classes.

- At the top were members of the Senate, who were often wealthy landowners.
- Next were the equites, prosperous businessmen and merchants. Equites held important government positions and assisted in the running of the empire.
- At the bottom were farmers, city workers, and soldiers—the majority of Romans.

Daily Life. The large Roman cities—Rome itself, Alexandria, Athens, and so on—had large populations and served as trading hubs. The cities were carefully planned and full of vibrant culture. Public buildings and spaces, such as baths, theaters, and the Roman forum, were the centers of urban life.

In the country, small landholders were mixed in with large farms owned by the wealthy. The larger farms were worked by slaves. Small farmers would spend their summers in the army, and sometimes lose their lands.

Religion in Rome

Originally, the Romans adopted most of their gods from the Greeks, giving them Roman names. The Romans erected temples and shrines to honor their gods. The centerpiece of every Roman city was a temple to the three deities called the Capitoline triad: Jupiter, Juno, and Minerva.

Rulers of Rome were sometimes designated as gods. Romulus became the god Quirinus, and some emperors, including Augustus, Claudius, and Vespasian, were made gods after their deaths. Late in the empire, people began worshiping emperors as gods while they were still alive.

Christianity. In the 1st century AD, a new religion appeared and began to gain popularity in the Roman Empire—Christianity. The early church leaders borrowed many ideas from the Greek "mystery cults" and philosophers, which were already familiar to many Romans. By the AD 300s, Christianity had become the official religion of the empire. (See pages 456–457.)

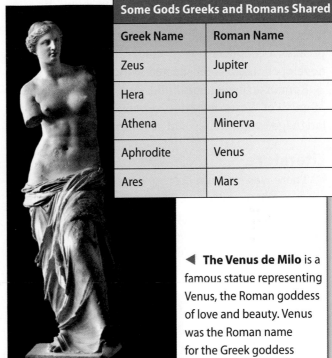

Some Gods Greeks and Romans Shared	
Greek Name	**Roman Name**
Zeus	Jupiter
Hera	Juno
Athena	Minerva
Aphrodite	Venus
Ares	Mars

◀ **The Venus de Milo** is a famous statue representing Venus, the Roman goddess of love and beauty. Venus was the Roman name for the Greek goddess Aphrodite.

POMPEII AND HERCULANEUM

Much of what we know about life in ancient Rome comes from the remains of Roman towns and cities. Archaeologists have excavated these remains and work to preserve them.

Two towns in particular have been valuable sources of information: Pompeii and Herculaneum. These cities were buried when the volcano Mount Vesuvius erupted in AD 79.

- Pompeii was buried in ash and stone.
- Herculaneum was buried in volcanic mud and lava.

Excavations of the cities began in the 1700s. Archaeologists have now uncovered about three-fourths of Pompeii and much of Herculaneum. Buildings, forums, streets, furniture, and utensils—even graffiti on the walls—have been preserved, giving us a model of life in ancient Roman times.

▲ **At Pompeii and Herculaneum,** visitors can walk through streets and buildings as they stood in AD 79.

Epics and Aqueducts

The Rome that embarked on world conquest after 300 BC was extremely primitive. It was a nation of simple and illiterate farmer-soldiers. Over time, however, and with the influence of the lands and peoples it conquered—especially Greece—Rome developed into a sophisticated world culture.

Roman achievements influenced the development of much of Western culture, especially in the areas of language, engineering, and government.

Literature

There was no Latin literature at all until 250 BC, when the first written work was produced. This work was a translation into Latin of Homer's *Odyssey* by Livius Andronicus, a Greek from southern Italy. Roman literature reached maturity only in the 1st century BC, with the works of great poets, prose writers, and historians.

THE INFLUENCE OF GREECE

The key to Rome's cultural achievements lay in its ability to absorb, adapt, preserve, and transmit the mighty cultural achievements of Greece.

- Rome adopted Hellenistic religious cults and ideas, philosophies, art, literature, and political institutions.
- Greek slaves were responsible for educating many Roman youths.
- Under the Roman Empire, Greek culture traveled even more quickly and widely, to the conquered lands of western Europe and Britain.

At its height, the Roman Empire's cultural values blended traditional Roman simplicity and dedication with Greek sophistication and creativity. To use the famous line of the Roman poet Horace, "Captive Greece captured her barbarian captor."

Poets. The Roman lyric poets Catullus and Lucretius used the Latin language to express a wide variety of mood, emotion, and thought. They often drew on the ideas of Greek philosophers in their works. The narrative poet Ovid collected mythological tales into his *Metamorphoses*, and was known for his witty love poetry.

The greatest of the Roman poets, however, was the epic poet Vergil. His works, especially the *Aeneid*, are still widely taught today. (See pages 922–923.)

Prose Writers and Historians. The writer and orator Cicero was responsible for the development of Roman prose. He gave Rome a language capable of expressing the complexity of Greek philosophy and Western civilization. His style has remained a popular educational model. The works of the great historian Livy are a valuable source of information on Rome's political and military history.

The *Aeneid* tells the story of Rome's founding while drawing on the Greek epics the *Iliad* and the *Odyssey*. It glorifies the achievements of Rome. ▶

ENGINEERING ROME

The ancient Romans adopted the basic forms of Greek architecture. But the Romans generally built larger structures than the Greeks. Two achievements of Roman engineering made larger buildings possible: the arch and concrete.

The Arch

Although the Romans did not invent the arch, they made better use of arches than previous cultures.

- Arches supported such structures as bridges and the aqueducts that carried water to Roman cities.
- Arched roofs known as vaults spanned the interior of buildings.
- Vaults eliminated the need for columns to hold up the roof and so created more open floor space.

Concrete

The Romans developed concrete.

- Concrete served as a strong building material for walls, vaults, and domed buildings.
- The most famous Roman building made with concrete is the Pantheon in Rome, which has a concrete dome about 142 feet (43 meters) in diameter.

▲ **The Pantheon** was built as a temple dedicated to all the Roman gods. (The word *pantheon* is from the Greek, meaning "place for all gods".) Today, many Italian national heroes are buried there.

▲ **The Pont du Gard,** part of a Roman aqueduct near Nimes, France, is a striking example of Roman engineering ability. Some Roman roads and aqueducts are still in use.

Art

After the Romans conquered Greece during the 140s BC, they adopted some of the styles of Greek art. Roman sculptors created realistic portraits that revealed individual personalities.

Roman sculptors also illustrated historical events through carvings on large public monuments.

Art at Home. Wall paintings decorated the houses of the wealthy. Paintings often showed garden landscapes, events from Greek and Roman mythology, historical scenes, or scenes of everyday life. Romans decorated floors with mosaics—pictures or designs created with small colored tiles.

now you Know!

- ✔ As Rome grew, it developed a sophisticated culture.
- ✔ Roman people were strictly divided into three groups: citizens, noncitizens, and slaves. There were also strict divisions between social classes.
- ✔ Initially, the Romans worshipped versions of the Greek gods; during the first century AD, Christianity began to spread.
- ✔ The Romans were heavily influenced by Greek literature, art, and architecture.
- ✔ The poets Catullus, Lucretius, Ovid, and Vergil produced a rich Latin literature.
- ✔ Roman engineering produced grand buildings, roads, and aqueducts—some of which still survive.

ANCIENT INDIA

As Greece was going through its Dark Age and the Latins were beginning to settle Rome, the Aryans were extending their kingdoms on the South Asian subcontinent, eastward along the Ganges River and southward across the Deccan Plateau. Along the way, they conquered the native populations. It was a period of political disunity as rival kingdoms warred frequently. India was entering its Epic Period (c. 1000–500 BC), a period named for the magnificent pieces of religious literature it produced. The Indian empires would also see great scientific progress and the rise of a new religion, Buddhism.

Major Events—Ancient India	
c. 1450 BC	The *Vedas*, the earliest Indian literature, are written.
c. 563 BC	Siddhartha Gautama, the Buddha, is born.
c. 500 BC	The caste system develops in India.
322 BC	Chandragupta Maurya overthrows the Nandas; Mauryan dynasty begins.
AD 1	Kushans rule India for two centuries.
c. 200	The great Indian epic poems, the *Mahabharata*, the *Ramayam,* and the *Bhagavad-Gita,* are completed.
320	The Gupta Empire begins to reunite India.
375	Chandragupta II subdues all of northern India.

The Indian Empires

The Persian Empire, under the rule of Darius I (50?–486 BC), annexed the Indus Valley region in what is now northwestern India. An alliance of Aryan kingdoms under the leadership of the kingdom of Magadha in northeastern India progressively reclaimed land from Persian control.

A Magadha dynasty, called the Nine Nandas, ruled northern India from 413 BC until 322 BC. The Nandas held on to their power in the region, even after the invasions of Alexander the Great in 326 BC, but they could not maintain power forever.

The Mauryan Empire

In 322 BC, an adventurous upstart named Chandra-gupta Maurya seized Magadha, overthrew the Nandas, and began to build India's first great empire under the Mauryan dynasty.

- Over the next 24 years, he brought all of northern India under his control.

- In 305 BC, in one of the first major battles between East and West, he defeated the Seleucids, and added parts of today's Afghanistan to his own empire.

The Mauryan Empire was the first to unite almost all of India under a single government.

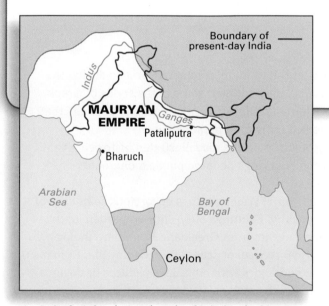

▲ **At its height,** during the rule of Ashoka, the Mauryan Empire stretched from the Hindu Kush mountains to the Bay of Bengal and covered nearly all of the Indian subcontinent.

Ashoka. The most famous of all emperors of ancient India was Ashoka. A grandson of Chandragupta, Ashoka ruled from 273 to 232 BC. Early in his rule, he led a campaign to add the east-central Indian kingdom of Kalinga to his empire. Over 100,000 were butchered in the battle. Horrified, Ashoka vowed this military campaign would be his last.

- He turned to the teachings of Buddhism, which he then propagated all over India.
- It was Ashoka who sent missionaries into other parts of Asia with the civilizing tenets of Buddhism.
- He did not persecute those who remained Hindu or followed other religions.

Collapse. Following Ashoka's death, the Mauryan dynasty began to disintegrate. Clashes within the empire, local rebellions, and outside invasions culminated with the assassination of the last Mauryan emperor in 185 BC.

For about the next 500 years, groups of central Asian peoples, including the Scythians and the Kushans, moved into northern India. The Kushans established a dynasty in northern India around AD 50.

▲ **Ashoka** was a humane ruler who is still revered for his religious toleration. He is also remembered for the 84,000 hemisphere-shaped relic mounds (shrines), called *stupas*, he built to honor Buddha.

The Gupta Empire

In AD 320, at about the time the Roman Empire started going into its decline, India was about to enter its "Classical Age." Chandragupta I (ruled 320–c. 330) began to reunite much of India once again from his base in Magadha.

Through conquest, his son, Samudragupta (ruled c. 330–c. 375), and grandson, Chandragupta II (ruled c. 375–413), subdued all of northern India from the Himalayas to the Deccan Plateau. The Gupta dynasty brought peace and stability. The trade they encouraged with the Roman Empire and with Southeast Asia brought great prosperity to India.

Collapse. However, the Guptas soon went into decline. Their rule ended in AD 535, when Hun invaders swept into India from the northwest. They destroyed the great urban centers of the Gupta dynasty and India's Classical Age came to an end.

▲ **The Gupta Empire** extended across present-day northern India and portions of present-day Pakistan and Bangladesh from about AD 320 to about 500.

India's Golden Age

SOUTHWESTERN

The empires of ancient India produced incredible works of art and culture. They also gave rise to two of the major world religions: Hinduism and Buddhism. Culture flourished, particularly during the peaceful and prosperous reign of the Guptas—India's "Golden Age."

THE BHAGAVAD-GITA

The *Mahabharata* tells the story of war among rivals for an Aryan throne and ennobles the Aryan warrior. Its final 18 chapters are called the *Bhagavad-Gita*. This is a philosophical dialogue that stresses the concept of *dharma*, the idea that performing one's moral duty is the fulfillment of life.

Literature

The literature of ancient India is generally divided into three periods: the Vedic period, the Epic period, and the Classical period.

Ancient Indian Literature		
Period	**Characteristics**	**Key Works**
Vedic Period (1400–500 BC)	• Mostly produced religious texts • Reflected the rituals of the early Aryan civilization of India	• The four *Vedas* (*Rig-veda, Sama-veda, Yajur-veda, Atharva-veda*) • The *Upanishads*
Epic Period (c. 1000–500 BC)	• Overlapped with the other two periods • Named for the epic poetry of the period	• The *Mahabharata* (the longest epic poem in world literature) • The *Bhagavad-Gita* (part of the *Mahabharata*) • The *Ramayana*
Classical Period (c. 400s BC–AD 500)	• Known for lyric and epic poems, as well as dramas	• Poems by Asvaghosa (c. AD 100) • Plays by Bhasa (c. AD 300) • *The Cloud Messenger*, a lyric poem by Kalidasa

Art

Painting and sculpture reached their heights during India's Classical Age. The Gupta emperors acted as generous patrons of the arts, and brilliant artists repaid them with magnificent works.

Gupta art is probably best exemplified by the 28 monasteries and temples carved out of solid rock cliffs at Ajanta in the Deccan Plateau. There, murals depict scenes from the life of Buddha as well as glorifications of the human form and human love. To the Gupta artist, the divine was not separate from the human.

Science and Technology

The Gupta era was also a golden age for learning in India. Universities attracted scholars from all over Asia. Mathematics and medicine were areas of special expertise.

- Indian mathematicians developed the 0 to 9 number system as well as the decimal system.
- Indian doctors devised means of sterilizing and keeping wounds clean, invented the scalpel, performed Caesarean sections, and even did plastic surgery.
- Indian metalworkers made the best iron and finest tempered steel in the world.

HINDUISM AND BUDDHISM

Two major religions have shaped Indian civilization: Hinduism and Buddhism. Hinduism remains the main religion of India today; Buddhism, on the other hand, has had its greatest influence outside of its native land.

Hinduism

Hinduism is a blend of many beliefs—the beliefs of the Aryans and of the peoples they conquered. One of its most important tenets is the idea that each soul must live through several reincarnations before earning salvation. (See page 454.)

Hindu Castes. The caste system begun by the Aryans became a pillar of Hinduism. Under this system, only the Brahmans, as the highest caste, could become priests and prescribe the rituals that helped people to earn salvation. This created some resentment.

Siddhartha Gautama became known as the Buddha, the "Enlightened One," and developed the religious philosophy that became Buddhism. ▶

Buddhism

The founder of Buddhism, a prince named Siddhartha Gautama (563?-483? BC), wanted to break the hold the Brahmans had over Hindu life and help people find their own way to salvation.

According to legend, Gautama renounced his luxurious life to go and learn the meaning of human suffering. After years of wandering and meditation, he achieved "enlightenment." (See page 455.)

The Spread of Buddhism. Buddha did not intend to replace Hinduism, only to reform its teachings. Nonetheless, Buddhism did become a movement separate from Hinduism after Buddha's death. Missionaries then spread the teachings of Buddha throughout Asia.

THE CASTE SYSTEM

The Aryans had been loosely divided into three social classes, from top to bottom: warriors, priests, and common people. Eventually the social structure became more rigid, and four major classes, or castes, emerged.

- The Brahmans, consisting of priests
- The Kshatriyas, or warriors
- The Vaisyas, or merchants
- The Shudras, or peasants and servants

At the very bottom of the social ladder were people not permitted in any caste. They were given the most degrading jobs, such as carrying away human and animal waste. These people were considered unclean and therefore "untouchables."

✔ The Mauryan Empire (c. 324–185 BC) first united much of India under one ruler.

✔ The Gupta Empire (AD 320–500) reunited northern India and ushered in a "Golden Age" of arts and sciences.

✔ Ancient Indian literature had three main periods: the Vedic, the Epic, and the Classical.

✔ The religions of Hinduism and Buddhism helped to shape Indian civilization.

ANCIENT CHINA

As India was entering its Epic Age in 1000 BC, China was also entering a period of growth and creativity. In 1045 BC, the Shang dynasty fell to the Zhou, a warrior tribe of north-central China. The Zhou claimed the "Mandate of Heaven" from the Shang, accusing the former rulers of having mismanaged it. The Zhou established their own dynasty, which would last longer than any other, 800 years, until 256 BC. This dynasty would be followed in turn by the powerful Qin and Han dynasties, and another age of invention and progress.

Major Events—Ancient China	
c. 551 BC	K'ung Fu-tzu, Confucius, is born.
c. 400 BC	Cast iron is developed in China.
c. 300 BC	Tsou Yen introduces the Yin-Yang school of philosophy.
221 BC	Qin dynasty comes to power under Shi Huangdi.
c. 206 BC	The Great Wall of China is completed.
141 BC	Wu Ti heads the Chinese Han Empire; Pax Sinica begins.
AD 105	Paper is invented in China.
c. AD 265	The Wei, Wu, and Shu dynasties are united in China.
AD 271	The Chinese begin to use the magnetic compass.

The Middle Kingdom

About 1045 BC, the Zhou people overthrew the Shang from the west and established their own dynasty. (See also pages 410–411.) They would rule until 256 BC. With most of northern China in their domain, the Zhou kings organized it into feudal states. They delegated rule of the states to relatives or local nobles, who, in turn, recognized the overlordship of the Zhou kings and promised them military support.

Life in the Zhou Dynasty

Under the Zhou, Chinese civilization made strides in its material and cultural development unrivaled by later dynasties.

- During the 6th century BC, iron production developed, leading to more efficient weapons and tools.
- With the iron plow, more land was put into farming.
- Canal-building projects irrigated the land and provided arteries for transporting farm produce and trade goods.
- The population grew and China became the most densely inhabited place on Earth.

Pleased with their progress as a civilization, they considered themselves high above peoples of other parts of the world—all of whom the Chinese considered "barbarians."

The rulers of the Zhou dynasty proclaimed China "The Middle Kingdom"— holding an exalted position between heaven and Earth.

Three Philosophies

Later Zhou rulers began to lose control of their empire as rivalry sent the feudal states into almost constant warfare. But within this political instability a flourishing intellectual life developed. Philosophers studied how to bring order back into Chinese life.

Three major schools of philosophy emerged, each with a different way to achieve societal order. Each would influence Chinese civilization profoundly.

CONFUCIANISM

The first and most influential of China's great philosophers was K'ung Fu-tzu, born in 551 BC, at about the time of Buddha in India, Zoroaster in Persia, and the early Greek philosophers. Christian missionaries to China, two millennia later, would call him Confucius.

- Confucius, as a secular rather than a religious thinker, taught that an orderly society is based on everyone having a clearly defined place, with clearly stated responsibilities.

- If everyone accepts those responsibilities and acts with loyalty, kindness, and hard work, society will be harmonious.

- Confucianism stressed the importance of the family as the basic unit of society and therefore encouraged filial piety—respect for one's elders—and ancestor worship.

- Confucius also taught that rulers must be both highly moral and well educated.

Chinese governments made Confucius's teachings the official state philosophy.

TAOISM

While Confucius called for people to take an active role in society, the semimythical philosopher Lao-tzu urged just the opposite.

- He taught that people should withdraw from such activity and instead contemplate the *tao*, which he defined as the universal force of nature.

- Only by living quietly, in harmony with nature, could people find happiness and end turmoil.

Confucianism and Taoism were rival schools of thought, yet the Chinese adopted elements of both. Confucian teachings had a strong influence on public life, while Taoism provided a comforting release in private life.

Taoism evolved into a religion in the 100s BC. Some scholars think that Lao-tzu is actually a mythical construction based on several philosophers and authors of the time.

LEGALISM

During the late Zhou period, yet another school of thought emerged: Legalism.

- Legalists shunned both Confucian ethics and Taoist meditation, because both assumed that human nature is basically good.

- The Legalists believed only a strong and efficient government that strictly enforces an elaborate code of laws and harsh punishments could maintain order.

Legalism stated that China needed to be unified and ruled by a strong central government. With the rise of the Qin dynasty, Chinese were about to get just that.

THE GREAT WALL OF CHINA

The Great Wall of China is the longest structure ever built.

- Construction on a major protective wall began under the Qin dynasty.

- Most of the existing wall was actually completed during the Ming dynasty.

- In practice, the wall protected only against minor attacks, not major invasions.

- Some commonly held beliefs about the Great Wall—for example, that it was built all at once, or that it can be seen from the moon—are false.

In 221 BC, the Qin dynasty came to power under the leadership of Shi Huangdi, who was able to subjugate the warring feudal states of China and unify them. He declared himself "the first universal emperor" of China. It was from the Qin dynasty that China took its name.

Qin Rule

With the help of his ruthless and efficient chief minister, Li Ssu, Shi Huangdi reorganized China along strict Legalist lines.

- He divided it into 36 provinces, after effectively breaking the power of the feudal states.

- He took land from the aristocrats for private ownership by the peasants who worked it.

- The peasants thus provided a broad tax base for the empire.

Under the Qin, provinces were governed by bureaucrats controlled by the empire's autocratic central government. A single, harsh, empire-wide legal code replaced local laws.

The Qin dynasty under Shi Huangdi had unified China, but its harsh laws, forced labor, and heavy taxation brought its downfall 3 years after Shi Huangdi's death in 210 BC. ▶

Engineering the Empire. Shi Huangdi recognized the need to protect the empire from invading nomads from Mongolia. The empire would also need to improve transportation and communication. To do this, he began a series of spectacular building projects using forced labor.

The first was an early version of the Great Wall of China. The wall connected the stone and earth walls that the northern feudal states had built. It was completed about 206 BC, 4 years after the emperor's death. Shi Huangdi also constructed roads and canals that rivaled those of Rome.

Great Wall of China

QIN

• Xianyang

The Han Dynasty

After the collapse of the Qin Empire, the Han dynasty ruled China for the next 400 years, to AD 220. This was one of ancient China's most glorious periods, a time that corresponded with the late Roman Republic and the rise of the Roman Empire.

Confucian Laws. Where the Qin rulers had based their government on the repressive philosophy of Legalism, the Han leaders introduced Confucian policies. They appeased the citizenry by lightening the burden of taxation and repealing the harsh Qin laws.

Former and Later Dynasties. Liu Bang (also spelled Liu Pang) became king of the Han in 206 BC, after the fall of the Qin dynasty. He became emperor in 202 BC. The Han rule was divided into two periods.

- The Former Han dynasty lasted from 206 BC to AD 8. Its capital was Chang'an (now Xi'an).

- The Later Han dynasty lasted from AD 25 to 220, and its capital was Luoyang.

Because Chang'an lay west of Luoyang, the two periods are also called the Western and Eastern Han dynasties.

▲ **This map shows the Han Empire** at its greatest size. The Han dynasty gained control of China in 206 BC. A major expansion occurred about 100 BC. Han warriors also conquered what are now North Korea and northern Vietnam.

THE SILK ROAD

During the Han dynasty, China and the West discovered each other. Wu Ti was quick to open trade relations between them.

Soon caravans were traveling the great Silk Road, leading from China across Central Asia to the Mediterranean.

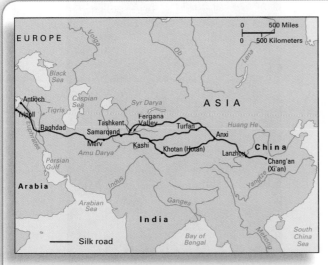

▲ **The Silk Road,** shown here, flourished primarily from the 100s BC to the AD 1500s. Romans and Greeks treasured fine Chinese silks and works in jade and bronze (at right), just as China treasured Western horses and Roman glass.

The Han dynasty ushered in an era of stability, advances in government, and creativity. Art, education, and science thrived. Writers produced histories and dictionaries. They also collected classics of literature from earlier times.

The Pax Sinica. The Han Empire reached its height under the "Martial Emperor," Wu Ti, who ruled from 141 to 87 BC.

- His conquering armies expanded China north to Manchuria and Korea and south to Indochina.
- He drove far into central Asia, annexing a long corridor to the west.

Having secured Chinese boundaries, Wu Ti ushered in the Pax Sinica, or Chinese Peace, at about the same time the Roman Empire was establishing the foundations for its Pax Romana. (See page 436.)

A Model Civil Service. Han emperors followed the Confucian ideal that government officials should be highly educated. To that end, they encouraged rigorous education in Confucian ethical standards.

The Han developed a system of choosing government officials based on a civil service examination that tested would-be bureaucrats on the teachings of Confucius. The civil service that resulted from this examination process lent a degree of social and political stability to Chinese life and became a model for governments elsewhere in Asia.

Fall of the Han. Political struggles at the royal court and administrative dishonesty plagued the last century of Han rule. In addition, powerful regional officials began to mistreat the peasants. As a result, large-scale rebellion finally broke out, and the Han dynasty fell in 220.

AN AGE OF INVENTION

Under the Han dynasty, China experienced a burst of inventiveness that made the Chinese technologically superior to any other people in the world.

- Paper made from cloth rags replaced bamboo strips for writing.
- The compass was developed.
- Iron smelting was improved by the use of the piston bellows.
- Steel manufacture began.

Other notable inventions of the Han dynasty included the wheelbarrow and the seismograph, an instrument that could measure earthquakes several hundred miles away.

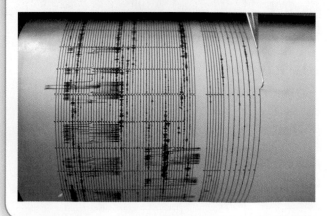

The seismograph built by the ancient Chinese (*above*) is the forerunner of the modern seismographs used to measure and predict earthquakes today (*left*).

ARTS OF THE HAN DYNASTY

The years of the Pax Sinica under the Han rulers led not only to scientific and technological innovation, but also to a burst of development in the arts.

- Chinese calligraphy (fine handwriting)—linked with the arts of poetry and painting—became common during this time.

- Han artisans created the world's first porcelain.

- Three main types of porcelain were "official ware" (*guanyao*), produced for the emperor's household; bluish-white *qingbai* ware; and crackled *ge* ware.

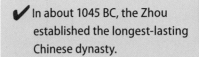

◄ **Han artists** produced exquisite glazed pottery like the container shown here. They were also known for large stone carvings.

✔ In about 1045 BC, the Zhou established the longest-lasting Chinese dynasty.

✔ Three philosophies—Confucianism, Legalism, and Taoism—developed late in the Zhou dynasty. They would influence China for centuries.

✔ The Qin dynasty (221–206 BC) under Shi Huangdi gave China its name.

✔ The Han dynasty (206 BC–AD 220) brought about an era of stability and peace called the Pax Sinica (Chinese Peace).

▲ **Early Chinese Buddhists** built temples in or near cities. In rural areas, they hollowed out cliffsides to form chapels. Sculptors decorated the chapels with figures of Buddha and his attendants.

Age of Disunity

Following the collapse of the Han dynasty, China broke up into three states—Wei in the north, Wu in the southeast, and Shu in the southwest. They were briefly united from 265 to 316, but a clash with Huns divided them once again.

For the next 270 years, southern China was ruled by a succession of five dynasties, but none were strong enough to control the territories they ruled. In northern China, dynasties rose and fell, most founded by conquerors from the north and from Tibet.

Foreign rule was a bitter pill for the Chinese to swallow, but as the conquerors came and went, the Chinese survived with their own civilization intact.

ARRIVAL OF BUDDHISM

Buddhism reached China during the 1st century AD, but did not affect Chinese life until the Han dynasty weakened and fell. The fall of the Han dynasty was followed by 350 years of disunion and civil war. During this time, the Buddhist promise of relief from pain and suffering attracted many converts.

WORLD RELIGIONS

For much of human history, religion has been a major driving force. Long before recorded history, ancient burials show evidence of a belief in an afterlife. The Egyptians and ancient Greeks left evidence of complicated religious practices, as did the Romans, Aztecs, Incas, and Hindus. The rise and spread of religions, new and old, brought change, conflict, and learning to the world's cultures. An understanding of the major religions of the world, past and present, can bring insight into the great wars, great art, and great movements of humankind.

Although smaller than the other major religions—with only about 15 million followers worldwide—Judaism is nonetheless considered a major world religion. Its followers are spread over much of the world.

Judaism is the religion of a people called the Jews. The Jews are a people or national group as well as a religion. A few followers of Judaism do not consider themselves to be a part of the Jewish people, and many who consider themselves Jews do not follow or practice the religion of Judaism.

Judaism

History

Judaism was probably the first truly monotheistic religion, devoted to the worship of a single all-powerful God. The Jewish faith holds that God acts through history to change events on Earth. Thus, history is important to Jews in a way that is different from its importance to people of other religions.

Christianity and Islam, both of which developed after Judaism, consider the history of the early Jewish nation to be part of the record of God's actions.

▲ **The Torah,** which is the first part of the Hebrew Bible (and which also makes up the first five books of the Christian Old Testament), reports the acts of God in the history of the Jews.

Ancient Hebrews. The Jews trace their history to a man named Abraham, a seminomadic shepherd who lived about 4,000 years ago. God told Abraham to take his family and followers (called the Hebrews) to Canaan, a land that today we identify with Israel. (See pages 416–417.)

God made a covenant, or solemn agreement, with Abraham: He would have descendants who would live in Canaan, and they would receive God's care if they followed his laws. With this covenant, the Hebrews (later known as Israelites and then as Jews) became God's chosen people—chosen to represent God to the rest of the world.

Essential Beliefs

The most important teaching of Judaism is that there is one God.

- This God, the creator of heaven and earth, wants people to do what is just and merciful.
- A Jew serves God by studying the Scriptures and fulfilling their divine commandments.
- A Jew who does these things is fulfilling the requirements of the religion.

Judaism allows believers to draw their own conclusions on many religious questions, so long as they fulfill the basic requirements. For example, some Jews believe in eternal life after death, while others do not. Many Jews believe that a messiah, or savior, will one day arrive on Earth.

THE JEWISH SCRIPTURES

Judaism has two major collections of sacred writings: the Hebrew Bible (Tanakh) and the Talmud.

The Hebrew Bible consists of several parts.

- The Torah contains five books—their English names are Genesis, Exodus, Leviticus, Numbers, and Deuteronomy—containing basic Judaic law and the Jewish history.
- The Prophets are books of history and moral teachings.
- The Writings are 11 books of proverbs and other teachings.

The Talmud was assembled in the **6th century AD**.

- It is a collection of legal, ritual, and ethical writings, as well as Jewish history and folklore.
- It serves primarily as a guide to Jewish civil and religious laws.

Jewish worship takes place in the home and in a house of worship called a *synagogue*. Important parts of home worship include daily prayers, the lighting of the Sabbath candles, and the blessing of the wine and bread at the Sabbath meal. Jews also observe many holiday rituals, such as Hannukah and Passover (Pesach) at home.

Jewish Denominations	Origins and Founders	Beliefs and Practices
Orthodox	Refers to the original form of Judaism	• Apply all ancient rules of worship • Conduct services in Hebrew, with women and men separate • Observe strict dietary laws (known as kashrut, or kosher) • Requires head coverings (yarmulke) for men and modest dress for women
Hasidic	1700s, Poland Founder: Israel Ball Shem Tov	• Observe the same laws as Orthodox Jews • Consider dancing, singing, and love of nature to be forms of worship • Maintain separate communities, many of them in New York City
Reform	1810, Germany Founders: Abraham Geiger, Samuel Holdheim	• Does not accept traditional interpretation of the Law • Services may be conducted in languages other than Hebrew • Dietary laws may not be observed • Houses of worship are called temples, not synagogues
Conservative	1845, Germany; early 1900s, United States	• Arose from a dispute about the use of Hebrew in services • Maintains Hebrew use • Attempts to balance Orthodox tradition and Reform spirit

Hinduism and Buddhism

Hinduism

Hinduism is the major religion of India. It has about 900 million followers. Although most Hindus live in India, Hindu literature and philosophy have influenced people throughout the world.

Hinduism represents a diverse group of beliefs, practices, and texts that have developed over thousands of years. No single authority exists in Hinduism.

History. Hinduism developed from the beliefs of the Aryan tribes who invaded India around **1500 BC**. The Brahmans, the priestly caste, preserved the sacred writings of the Epic Age and also interpreted them for the people.

The caste, or class, system of the Aryans also became a part of Hinduism. Each caste had its own strict social and religious rules, and living virtuously demanded complete acceptance of, and obedience to, these laws.

According to the Hindu law of karma, persons who live obediently as members of their caste would be reincarnated into a higher caste. If not, they would fall back into a lower caste in the next life, or even be reincarnated as a form of animal life.

Beliefs

In Hinduism there are many gods, but they are all manifestations of one supreme spirit, Brahma, the World Soul. Brahma is the Creator. United in the spirit is a trinity of main Hindu gods.

- Vishnu, the Preserver
- Shiva, the Destroyer
- Shakti, a goddess also known by the names Lakshmi, Kali, Durga, or Parvati

Reincarnation. Hindus believe that everyone has a soul that is part of the World Soul.

- The soul longs to become reunited with the World Soul.
- To do this, it must go through many reincarnations, becoming less worldly and more spiritual in each to earn salvation.
- A person must live a virtuous life to achieve greater spirituality.

▲ **Shiva, the Destroyer,** is one of the main Hindu gods. His destruction allows for things to be reborn. The goddess Shakti, in the forms of Kali or Durga, is also considered a goddess of destruction.

SACRED HINDU TEXTS

Hinduism has no single book that is the source of its doctrines, but it has many sacred writings that have contributed to its beliefs and practices. The great Hindu epics teach traditional Hindu values through their stories.

The *Vedas* are the oldest Hindu scriptures and include sections that are older than the sacred writings of any other major religion.

The *Puranas* are long verse stories that contain many important narratives about deities and the lives of great Hindu heroes.

The *Ramayana* is an epic that tells of Prince Rama and his attempts to rescue his wife, Sita, who has been kidnapped by the demon king Ravana.

The *Mahabharata* is an epic that describes a struggle for a disputed kingdom between the Pandavas and the Kauravas, two families who are cousins.

Buddhism

Buddhism was founded in India about **500 BC**, or shortly afterward, by a teacher called the Buddha. Today, Buddhism has about 350 million followers. Most live in Tibet and other regions of China, and in Japan, the Korean peninsula, Sri Lanka, and mainland Southeast Asia.

History. The founder of Buddhism, Siddhartha Gautama, was born in **563 BC**, the son of a wealthy rajah. According to legend, he had never known about the suffering of people until the age of 29. Shocked by what he saw, he renounced his life of ease to go into the outside world to learn why there was such suffering and how it might be cured.

After years of wandering and finding no answers, he sat down beneath a sacred fig tree to meditate. While there, he achieved "enlightenment," finding the knowledge he sought. From that experience, he became known as the Buddha, the "Enlightened One," and developed the religious philosophy that became Buddhism.

In some ways, Buddhism was a response to the Hindu caste system. Buddhists believe that anyone can achieve nirvana (peace), regardless of caste or status.

Beliefs

Buddhism is sometimes described as atheistic—believing in no god at all. The followers of Buddhism would dispute this. However, the Buddhist concept of God does not have the "personhood" concept found in other religions.

Over time, Buddhism became divided into two major branches.

- The Hinayana maintained the traditional Buddhist beliefs and honored Buddha as a great teacher.
- The Mahayana proclaimed Buddha a god and made Buddhism a religion of priests and temples.

THE NOBLE EIGHTFOLD PATH

Buddhists believe that eight behaviors will help a person avoid suffering:

1. Knowledge of the truth
2. The intention to resist evil
3. Saying nothing to hurt others
4. Respecting life, morality, and property
5. Holding a job that does not injure others
6. Striving to free one's mind of evil
7. Controlling one's feelings and thoughts
8. Practicing proper forms of concentration

OTHER WORLD RELIGIONS

Thousands of religions are practiced around the world. This chart lists some significant, though smaller, world religions.

Other Major Religions	Origins and Founders	Key Beliefs and Practices
Jainism	Mahavira, **500s BC**; India	• Every living thing has a soul; killing any living thing is prohibited.
Shinto	Unknown founders, main texts written **c. AD 600s**; Japan	• Worship many nature deities called kami
Baha'i	Baha'u'llah, **1863**; present-day Iraq	• Believe God wants a world of equality and acceptance; oppose all discrimination
Sikhism	Guru Nanak, **c. late 1400s**; India	• Monotheistic faith • Believers practice meditation and believe in reincarnation

Christianity

Today the Christian religion has the most followers worldwide, about 2 billion. Christianity is the dominant religion of Europe, both Americas, and Australia, with significant numbers of followers in Asia and Africa as well.

History

The earliest Christians were Jews who came to believe that Jesus of Nazareth was the Messiah the Jews had been awaiting. Jesus was born around 2010 years ago in a village called Bethlehem. He taught in the synagogues and outdoors, healing the sick and welcoming particularly the poor and the outcast. He said he had come to establish a new kingdom, in which people's wrongdoings would be forgiven, allowing them to achieve a new relationship with God.

The Crucifixion. When Jesus was about 33 years old, he was arrested by the official Jewish court and turned over to the Romans, who controlled the country as part of the Roman Empire. The Romans crucified Jesus on a wooden cross.

Three days after he died, according to the Gospels, he rose from the dead and visited many of his followers. Then he went to be with God the Father until the time for his return.

The New Covenant. The Gospels also say

- The night before his arrest, Jesus ate and drank with his closest followers. In this Last Supper, he told them to observe a similar meal to remember him.

- He suggested that his suffering, death, and resurrection would make a new covenant with God, replacing the covenant made between God and Abraham and Moses.

- In this new covenant, God forgives the sins of those who follow Jesus and offers them eternal life with God.

The Early Church. Early Christians thought of themselves as Jews who had recognized Jesus as the Messiah. Some Jews who did not recognize Jesus as the Messiah persecuted the early Christians.

One of the persecutors, Saul of Tarsus, had a vision of Jesus and was converted to Christianity. Under the name of Paul, he began converting non-Jews (Gentiles) in Syria, Greece, and Rome. The church began to separate from its Jewish beginning.

The religion spread rapidly through the Mediterranean. In **AD 325,** the Council of Nicaea affirmed its main beliefs, and named the pope its leader.

Major Christian Denominations	Origins and Founders	Beliefs and Practices
Roman Catholics	Formed by the Council of Nicaea, **325 AD**	• Pope (Bishop of Rome) has ultimate authority • Priesthood open to celibate men only • Seven sacraments: baptism, communion, ordination, confirmation, confession, last rites, and marriage • Transubstantiation: the bread and wine of communion become the literal body and blood of Christ
Eastern Orthodox	Split from the Roman Catholic Church in **1054 AD**	• Accepts the same sacraments as Catholics • Does not require celibate priests • Venerates religious paintings called icons
Lutherans	Martin Luther, **1517**	• The Bible, not the Pope, is sole authority • Salvation through God's grace alone • Two sacraments: communion and baptism • Rejects transubstantiation

▲ **The story of the Last Supper** is the source for the Christian practice of communion, though the exact practice varies among different Christian churches.

THE CHRISTIAN SCRIPTURES

Christianity has three major sets of sacred writings.

The Christian Bible is divided into two parts, which are in turn divided into books:

- The Old Testament (the Jewish Scriptures), which describes God's agreement with the Jewish people
- The New Testament, which describes Jesus' teachings and new covenant

Creeds are short statements of faith that set forth essential Christian beliefs. The oldest in use today are the Apostles' Creed and the Nicene Creed.

Catechisms are writings that present basic religious doctrines, often in a question-and-answer format, for teaching.

Essential Beliefs

Like Judaism, from which it grew, Christianity is monotheistic—its followers believe in only one God.

- Christians also believe that God acts in history and that He is the God of the early Jewish people.
- Early Christians came to believe that the one God expresses Himself through three different natures: God the Father, God the Son (Christ), and God the Holy Spirit. This is called the Trinity.
- The church and its members spread the gospel, or good news, about Christ.
- A few rites are basic to Christianity: baptism (ritual purification with water) and communion.
- Prayer to God is a part of the faith. The main symbol of the Christian religion is the cross, which signifies to Christians that Christ died for their sins.

Romans began persecuting Christians in AD 64, under the emperor Nero. This continued with varying degrees of severity for about 250 years. Despite the persecutions, the church grew. Persecution ended in AD 313, when the emperor Constantine made Christianity the state religion of the Roman Empire.

Major Christian Denominations	Origins and Founders	Beliefs and Practices
Calvinists/ Presbyterians	John Calvin, **1533**	• God's elect go to heaven; all others go to hell. • The elect cannot fall from grace; others cannot be saved. • Includes the Pilgrims and the Puritans • In Scotland, became the Presbyterian Church
Anglicans	King Henry VIII of England, **1534**	• Both Catholic and Protestant • Accepts all sacraments, but only communion and baptism are necessary • Sole authority is the Bible
Baptists/ Mennonites	Menno Simons and others, **1500s**	• Baptism must be chosen by an adult • Rejects transubstantiation
Methodists	John Wesley, **1738**	• Similar to Anglican beliefs • Focus on Jesus Christ as a guide to living

Islam

The second largest religion in the world, after Christianity, is Islam. Followers of Islam are called Muslims. Worldwide, over 1.3 billion people follow Islam. The largest Muslim populations are in Asia and Africa, but Muslims live in every nation in the world.

History

The founder of the Islamic religion is Muhammad, who lived in Arabia about 1,400 years ago (AD 570–632). When he was about 40, God began to speak to him. God told Muhammad to transmit His message to the people of Arabia and dictated a book to Muhammad, which was later written down and is known today as the Koran.

Hejira and Empire. In AD 622, the people of Mecca, where Muhammad and his wife and daughters lived, were so upset by Muhammad's teachings that he and his followers had to flee.

- His escape to Medina is known as the Hegira.

- The date of the Hegira is usually considered the beginning of Islam.

- Eight years after the Hegira, Muhammad returned to Mecca. By then, he had so many followers that he took over the city without a struggle.

From then on, the followers of Islam built a mighty empire that at its height stretched from Spain to India. Muhammad was effectively the ruler of Arabia as well as its religious leader when he died. Because the state and the religion were one, a separate church was not needed. (See pages 474–475.)

ISLAM'S SACRED WRITINGS

The Koran and the Sunnah make up the foundation of Islamic law.

The Koran is the collection of revelations Muhammad received from God. Muslims believe it contains God's actual words. The Koran also retells many stories that are familiar to Jews and Christians from the Bible. For example, it tells the stories of Jacob, Joseph, Moses, David, Solomon, and Jesus Christ.

The Sunnah is the example of the words and practices of Muhammad. It presents his sayings and acts in written collections called the Hadith.

From these collections and from the Koran, scholars in the 7th and 8th centuries developed a set of specific rules for worship and for life. These rules are called the Sharia, or Islamic law. The Sharia's relation to the Koran and to Muhammad's Sunnah is similar to that of the Talmud to the Torah.

After Muhammad. When Muhammad died, his followers were in control of Arabia. He had made it clear that the state and worship of God were to be unified but had left no instructions on how to achieve this.

Muhammad had not chosen anyone to take his place. The dispute over the *caliphs*, or successors, who followed Muhammad led to the first divisions of Islam—the Shiites and the Sunnites.

MECCA

Muhammad declared Mecca a holy city. When Muslims pray, they face Mecca. He also declared that the Kaaba, where Arabs had worshiped for many years, was to be a shrine for Allah.

- The Kaaba, shown here, is an empty cube-shaped building in the center of the Great Mosque in Mecca.

- Muslims believe Abraham and Ishmael built the Kaaba as the first house of worship.

- On the Muslim hajj, or pilgrimage, believers walk seven times around the Kaaba.

Beliefs

Like Judaism and Christianity, Islam is also a monotheistic faith. Islam is an Arabic word that means surrender or submission. Its main creed is simple: "There is no God but God, and Muhammad is His prophet." (A prophet is a human chosen by God to relate God's message on Earth.) In Islam, God is called *Allah*.

Muslims believe Muhammad was the last major prophet, but earlier prophets included those who founded Judaism and Jesus Christ. Thus, Muslims believe many of the same things that Jews and Christians do, although not always in exactly the same way.

Five Pillars of Islam. Islam is based on five principles, called the Five Pillars.

1. Faith that there is no God but God (Allah), and Muhammad is His prophet

2. Prayer to God five times daily

3. Charity, shown by helping the poor and providing upkeep for places of prayer

4. Fasting in two ways—by never drinking alcohol or eating pork and certain other foods; and by not eating, drinking, or smoking at all during daylight for 1 month each year (the Muslim month of Ramadan)

5. Pilgrimage to Mecca at least once in each Muslim's life

Muslims believe in a life after death in a paradise that is described in detail in the Koran. Paradise is for all who keep the faith. People who are evil will spend eternity in a fiery hell.

Major Denominations of Islam	Origins	Beliefs and Practices
Sunni	Original form of the religion	• Accept the first three caliphs, or leaders after Muhammad, as genuine • Claim to follow the Sunnah, or example, of Muhammad • Follow a traditional interpretation of Islam
Shia	Formed after **AD 632**	• Rejected the first three caliphs • Believe that Muhammad's son-in-law, Ali, was meant to be caliph • Refer to leaders as imam; imams must be direct descendants of Ali • Divided into two groups: Ismaili and Imami
Imami	Also known as the Ithna Ashari or Twelvers	• See authority as residing in 12 imams, or leaders, starting with Ali • Await the second coming of the "hidden imam," a caliph who disappeared in AD 873 • Believe this imam, Muhammad al-Mahdi, will return at the end of the world and rule the Earth along with Jesus
Ismaili	Broke away from the Imamis in **AD 700**	• Follow the Aga Khan, a religious leader based in France
Kharijites	Rejected Ali in **AD 657**	• Believe that the best Muslim should be caliph, regardless of status • Believe in equality under God • Initially elected their leaders

MEDIEVAL EUROPE

For Europe—the western half of the old Roman Empire—the Middle Ages began with disintegration and isolation. Germanic tribes—including Franks, Burgundians, Vandals, Visigoths, and Ostrogoths—overran Western Europe and set up a series of states to replace Roman rule. (See page 437.) The German tribes may have destroyed the Western Roman Empire as a political entity, but they did not destroy its civilization. They took over the administrative system, the taxes, the law, and the language of the culture they conquered.

After the Fall

Frankish Rule

The Franks were one of many tribes inhabiting northern Germany. As the Roman defenses on the Rhine gradually collapsed, Frankish war bands, each under an individual king, moved into northern Gaul.

The Franks first became politically significant under the Merovingians, the family of Clovis, who became the king of all Franks about AD 481.

Charlemagne. By the mid-700s, the Merovingians had declined and were replaced by the Carolingians, who inaugurated the most significant period in Frankish history. The greatest of the Carolingian kings was Charlemagne (ruled 768 to 814), grandson of Charles Martel, who had driven the Muslims back from southern France in 732, and the son of Pepin, who had overthrown the last of the Merovingians in 751.

Charlemagne unified a vast empire and the Roman Catholic Church under his leadership. In 800, he was crowned "Emperor of the Romans." Charlemagne's rule inspired a revival of learning and literacy and the copying of Latin texts to preserve the knowledge of classical antiquity.

Fall of Charlemagne's Empire. By the mid-800s, the empire consisted mostly of a landed society united by a loose and decentralized political system. Upon Charlemagne's death, internal struggles for power and land ensued, and in 843 the empire was partitioned into three portions by the Treaty of Verdun. Thus weakened, it was attacked by various barbarian groups: the Vikings from Scandinavia and the Magyars from Asia. By the early 900s, Charlemagne's empire had been shattered into more than 50 political units.

◀ **Charlemagne's empire** combined Roman unity, though on a much smaller scale, with Christianity and Germanic military power.

The Feudal System

Feudalism emerged in Europe because of the failure of the Frankish monarchy in the west to protect the kingdom from barbarian invaders. It was a time of military necessity that brought about a professional fighting class and a predominantly rural society.

Feudalism had several distinct features in Europe. The principal one was *vassalage*, a relationship in which one man placed himself at the service of another in return for maintenance and protection. As the position of the vassal rose in the social scale, he was supported by a grant of property, or a fief.

Feudalism was established by the mid-900s, at least in northern France. In the 1000s, it spread from France to England and, 100 years later, to Germany.

EUROPE IN 1000

Manorialism. The institution of feudalism was inseparable from its economic base, *manorialism*. The fief consisted of a large landed estate or estates called villas or manors that were cultivated by a peasantry in varying degrees of economic and legal servitude. It was from the manor that the vassal derived his income and over which he exercised his political jurisdiction.

Major Events—Medieval Europe	
c. 1100	The first universities in Europe are founded in Salerno (medicine), Bologna (law), and Paris (theology and philosophy).
1109	Henry I, of England, introduces a measure of length equal to the length of his arm—the yard.
c. 1154	Gothic architecture spreads throughout Europe.
1170	Thomas à Becket, the archbishop of Canterbury in England, is assassinated.
1189	The first paper mill in Europe is established in Herault, France.
c. 1202	The number zero is introduced in Europe.
1210	The teaching of Aristotle's works is forbidden at the University of Paris.
1253	The decimal system is introduced in England.
1271	Marco Polo begins his great journey to the Far East.
1290	Spectacles (eyeglasses) are invented in Italy.
c. 1347	Italian ships bring rats carrying fleas infected with the Black Plague to Europe, killing 25 million people.
1380	Forged iron guns, each weighing 600 pounds, are used by Richard II to defend the Tower of London.
c. 1387	Geoffrey Chaucer writes *The Canterbury Tales*.
1431	Joan of Arc is burned at the stake in France.

Feudal Monarchies

Although the political prospects everywhere in Europe looked bleak at the beginning of the 900s, by the end of the 900s, a revival began to take place in Europe. By the end of the 1200s, France and England had become similar to modern nation-states, and Germany only narrowly missed.

Germany. Beginning with Otto the Great, who ruled from 936 to 973, Saxon kings ruled Germany until they were replaced by the Salian dynasty (1024–1125). In 962, Otto was crowned Holy Roman Emperor, a title held by German kings for the next 300 years. But the power of the church soon overshadowed that of the German state.

During the Hohenstaufen dynasty (1152–1250), the German kings tried to unify Germany under a strong monarchy, but they met unmovable resistance from northern Italy, which was then part of the Holy Roman Empire, and from the church. Germany thus remained politically fragmented and weak.

France. The Capetian kings ruled France from 987 to 1328. A powerful, unified national state arose during this period. Philip IV (ruled 1285–1314) began a bitter struggle with Pope Boniface VIII over the royal right to tax the clergy. In 1303, Philip made an unsuccessful attempt to seize the pope, who died soon after. Two years later, a Frenchman was elected Pope Clement V, and in 1309, the papal seat was moved to Avignon. These events played a key role in the subsequent split within the church that came to be called the Great (or Western) Schism (1378–1417).

 *The Magna Carta is a document that English barons forced King John to approve in June 1215 at Runnymede, southwest of London. The Latin words* Magna Carta *mean* Great Charter. *The document limited royal power and made it clear that even the king had to obey the law.* Magna Carta *marked a decisive step forward in the development of constitutional government and legal ideas in England. The charter later became a model for those who demanded democratic government and individual rights for all.*

William of Normandy was a proud and ruthless ruler and a vassal of the king of France.

England. In 1066, William of Normandy (also known as William the Conqueror) invaded England from France and captured the throne at the Battle of Hastings. The Norman Conquest of England resulted in the establishment of a feudal system far more systematic and effective than any existing in Europe. The feudal aristocracy resented the power of the monarchy, but all benefited from the establishment of unified codes of law and general order. English medieval history thereafter became a record of attempts by the nobility to limit arbitrary monarchical power while preserving the benefits of strong central government.

Medieval walled city in France.

The High Middle Ages

Historians often divide the Middle Ages in Europe into two periods. The early half, from the collapse of the Western Roman Empire to the 1000s, a period when there was much barbarism and little education, has been called the Dark Ages. But following 1000, Europe experienced a revival in many areas, causing this period to be called the High Middle Ages.

The Revival of Commerce. One of the first signs of revival in medieval Europe was the development of towns and commerce. The source of commercial revival was Italy.

The Italians imported exotic goods from Africa and the East that were in great demand in medieval Europe: spices, cloth, precious stones, and perfumes. In return, they exported what was woven in towns like Bruges, Ypres, and Ghent in the Low Countries. The wool itself came from England, and the fine finished products were traded at the famous fairs of Champagne in France. Later, the Italians began to eliminate the middlemen in this prosperous trade by manufacturing their own woolen cloth.

✔ Charlemagne unified a vast empire and the Roman Catholic Church under his leadership. In 800, he was crowned "Emperor of the Romans."

✔ Feudalism emerged in Europe in order to protect the kingdom from barbarian invaders. This necessity resulted in a professional fighting class, and a predominantly rural society.

✔ The political picture in Europe looked bleak at the beginning of the 900s, but by the end of the 900s, a revival began to take place in Europe. By the end of the 1200s, France and England had become similar to modern nation-states, and Germany only narrowly missed.

✔ Italy led the revival of commerce through vigorous trade: importing exotic goods from Africa and the East (spices, cloth, precious stones, and perfumes) while exporting woven wool.

✔ Europe experienced an intellectual reawakening in the 11th century, beginning in monasteries, but in time, spreading to cathedral, and then secular, schools.

Medieval Life

The Growth of Towns. The revival of commerce stimulated the development of towns. Initially, merchants were itinerant, often traveling in caravans for mutual protection. Naturally, they sought out fortified centers as places of refuge and as markets for their goods.

Eventually, merchants began to settle in the most strategic locations. In due course, they were surrounded by people who catered to their needs, such as blacksmiths, bakers, and cobblers. As the population expanded, houses were built outside the original fortified center, and it became necessary to protect the people with another wall. At the same time, independent municipal governments were forming.

Thus, along with the rise of towns and commerce came the origins of a merchant class. The medieval merchant class and the social forms it produced were alien to the economic and social ethic of early medieval society. The feudal class resented the wealth and independence of merchants, and the church took a long time to recognize the activities of the marketplace and the countinghouse as Christian.

▲ **A street** of stone houses in the medieval French town of Belves.

Life in a Medieval Town	
Crowding	As towns grew larger, walls were built around them. The towns became crowded because the walls limited the amount of land available. Houses stood crowded together. The people had to build upward because land was expensive. Many buildings were five or six stories high.
Streets and sanitation	Streets were narrow, crooked, dark, and filthy. Until about 1200, they were not paved. People threw their garbage and rubbish into the streets, and disease spread quickly. During the 1200s, people in some towns began to pave their streets with rough cobblestones and take some steps toward increasing sanitation.
Safety	A citizen who went out at night took his servants along for protection against robbers. The servants carried lanterns and torches because no town had street lighting. The wide use of lamps, torches, and candles made fire one of the great dangers for a medieval town. Wealthy citizens had stone and brick houses, but most houses were made of wood. A large fire was likely to wipe out a whole town. The city of Rouen, in France, burned to the ground six times between 1200 and 1225.
Guilds	After the merchants and craftworkers settled in the towns, they set up organizations called guilds. A guild protected its members against unfair business practices, established prices and wages, and settled disputes between workers and employers.
Town government	Guilds played an important part in town government. When the first guilds were organized, the towns had few laws to protect merchants or craftworkers. Most laws were made and enforced by the lord who owned the land on which a town stood. As the townspeople gained power, they demanded the right to govern themselves. Often, a guild forced a lord to grant the people a charter that gave them certain rights of self-government. Guilds led the townspeople's fight for self-government, and so members of guilds often ran the new town governments.

The Medieval Church

Another aspect of revival was the change that began to take place within the medieval church. The first manifestation of change was the emergence of religious reform. One of the fundamental convictions of medieval popular Christianity was that the clergy ensured the salvation of the laity by leading moral lives and by administering the sacraments.

Reform Movements. The Cluniac reform movement, which began at the French monastery of Cluny in the early 900s, was an attempt to purify the church by restoring monastic discipline as exemplary of Christian life and by eliminating prevailing abuses in the church.

The Gregorian reform movement of the 1000s restored papal and church influence and expanded the authority of the pope while calling for state subordination to the church.

▲ **Notre Dame Cathedral,** in Paris, France, was built on what was once the site of a Roman temple to Jupiter. Notre Dame Cathedral construction began in about 1163. The towers were not completed until the mid-1300s.

▲ **Salisbury Cathedral,** in Salisbury, England, is an example of Early English Gothic architecture. Salisbury Cathedral construction began in 1220 and was mostly finished by 1284.

The Revival of Learning

The intellectual reawakening of Europe during the 1000s began in the monasteries, but in time, it was taken over by cathedral, and then secular, schools.

The new learning was not only intellectually stimulating, it was also immensely practical. The expanding bureaucracies of the church and government demanded men who could reason as well as read and write.

In the 1200s, there was a renewed interest in the philosophy of Aristotle (see page 431) insofar as it revealed religious truth as being compatible with human reason. St. Thomas Aquinas became a leading scholastic thinker of this age, arguing that Christian faith is a kind of supernatural knowledge.

HUNDRED YEARS' WAR (1337–1453)

The Hundred Years' War extended over the reigns of five English kings and five French kings who fought for control of France. This struggle between England and France actually consisted of a succession of wars broken by truces and treaties. Over the course of this multi-generational struggle, both sides had to battle not just each other but other factors: a cataclysmic outbreak of plague, revolts among the peasant population, and finally, military technologies that changed the nature of warfare.

War and Plague

Strife Between England and France

The war had several contributing causes. Efforts of the French kings to control the English-held province of Guyenne in southwest France angered the English. The French supported the Scots against England, and the French attempted to control Flanders and the English wool trade there. English and French sailors and fishermen quarreled over rights in the English Channel. In 1337, King Philip VI of France declared he would take over Guyenne, and King Edward III of England, whose mother was the sister of three French kings, claimed the French throne.

Effects. The war weakened the powers of the nobility and strengthened centralized government in both countries. The war also marked the decline of feudalism, the rise of French unity, the development of new military tactics, and the growth of English sea power.

Major Events of the Hundred Years' War	
1337	King Philip VI of France declares he will take over Guyenne. King Edward III of England, whose mother was the sister of three French kings, claims the French throne.
1346	Battle of Crécy: English archers and infantry win the war's greatest victory.
1356	Battle of Poitiers: The English are victorious.
1360	The Treaty of Bretigny begins a brief period of peace.
1415	Battle of Agincourt: Henry V of England renews the fighting and emerges triumphant.
1420	The Treaty of Troyes makes Henry V heir to the French crown.
1422	After Henry V dies, the French dispute the English claim to the throne, and war flares.
1428	The English sweep through northern France and lay siege to Orléans.
1429	Joan of Arc leads a French army and ends the siege. She becomes a prisoner of the English, who later execute her by burning her at the stake.
1453	England has lost all its territory on the continent of Europe, except Calais (which France would regain in 1558).

▲ **The Battle of Crécy** was the first important battle of the Hundred Years' War. English archers on foot proved more effective than armor-clad French knights on horses.

The Black Death

In 1347, at the Black Sea port of Caffa (in what is now Feodosiya, Ukraine) a ship, probably arriving from ports of call in Asia Minor, arrived carrying a deadly cargo: the Black Death. For the past year, stories about a horrible plague in the East had been filtering west, a disease that laid waste to cities with a fury no one had ever witnessed before. From Caffa, the disease spread quickly, from port city to port city throughout the Mediterranean, reaching the city of Messina, Sicily, in October of that year. From there it spread to the mainland, where it wrought devastation on small towns and major cities and made no distinctions between peasant and noble.

By 1400, the Black Death had killed off as many as 25 million people in Europe—roughly 40 percent of the population. It then lingered for several centuries, striking intermittently, culminating with the Great Plague of London in 1665.

Punishment from God? One of the major problems in fighting the plague was the fact that people at this time did not understand the cause of the disease (or of diseases in general), and so were incapable of systematic preventive measures. It was understood that contact with infected individuals spread the plague, so quarantines were enacted. But the knowledge that the disease was being spread by rats who carried the fleas that carried the plague bacterium was many hundreds of years away. Most Europeans of the time believed the plague to be divine punishment for the wickedness of the times.

Effects on Society. The catastrophic loss of life during the Black Death transformed European society in many ways. Villages and cities alike were hit hard, and some villages disappeared completely. The resulting shortage of skilled workers in the cities caused a hike in wages, which attracted many peasants from the country into the city—a further blow to villages already hit by heavy death tolls.

▲ **The Black Death** struck Europe in 1347 and lingered for the next 300 years, reappearing intermittently and decimating populations in villages and cities alike.

A DISEASE WITH A HISTORY

We now believe that the Black Death was actually the bubonic plague, an infectious disease caused by the bacterium *Yersinia pestis*. The Black Death is the second of three pandemics (diseases that affect an entire country or continent) that may have been caused by the bacterium.

The first occurrence began in the Middle East in the 6th century AD, and ravaged Egypt in the year 542. It swept through the Byzantine Empire during the reign of Justinian, killing off as much as half the population of the city of Constantinople, and then moved on across Europe. It was still active in 664, when it ravaged Ireland.

The third and most recent of these pandemics began in China in the mid-19th century. Outbreaks in India alone are believed to have killed 6 million, and the death toll worldwide was up to 20 million people. It reached San Francisco in 1899. The last urban plague epidemic in the U.S. occurred in Los Angeles in 1924–1925. Since then, human plague in the U.S. has occurred mostly as scattered cases in rural areas (on average, 10 to 15 cases per year).

The Crusades

The Crusades were partly the result of the transition of the European mind from the localism that had characterized the earlier period, to the realization that there was another world of other values. Specifically, it was the realization within Christian Europe that the soil where Jesus had trod was now ruled by Islam.

In 1095, Pope Urban II preached the call for the First Crusade. Europe's warrior class, the nobility, responded, eager to acquire new lands for themselves.

What Did the Crusades Accomplish? The First Crusade was sufficiently successful in the conquest of land that kings and emperors became involved in later crusades. However, by the end of 200 years of crusades, nothing had really been gained. Land won was eventually lost. Even though Crusaders at one time seized Jerusalem, the ability of Christians to journey to Jerusalem was finally achieved by treaty and not by war.

In retrospect, the Crusades accomplished very little. They appealed to mass hysteria and soured relations between Christians and Muslims.

▲ **A 14th-century manuscript** page depicting events from the First Crusade

The Crusades			
Crusade	Crusade Leader(s)	Destination	Results
First Crusade (1096–1099; "Crusade of the Princes")	Godfrey of Bouillon, Duke of Lower Lorraine; Raymond, Count of Toulouse; Stephen, Count of Blois	Jerusalem	Crusaders massacred inhabitants of Jerusalem, gaining control of the city.
Second Crusade (1147–1149)	Zanghi, Governor of Mosul; Louis VII, King of France; Conrad III, Emperor of Germany	Damascus	Sultan Saladin established control of Muslim Middle East; Christians lost control of the Middle East, controlling only Antioch, Tripoli, and Tyre by 1189.
Third Crusade (1189–1192)	Frederick I (Barbarossa), Emperor of Germany; Richard I ("Lion-heart"), King of England; Philip II, King of France	Port of Acre	Barbarossa drowned; Philip returned to France after the Port of Acre was captured; Richard negotiated with Saladin the right for Christian pilgrims to visit Jerusalem.
Fourth Crusade (1202–1204)	Pope Innocent III	Port of Zara	Crusaders were excommunicated because Zara was a Catholic city; subsequently, Crusaders successfully pursued the succession of the Byzantine throne and established a Latin kingdom of Constantinople that lasted until 1261.
Children's Crusade (1208)	Two contingents of children set off for the Holy Land.	Jerusalem	One contingent turned back; the other group was captured and sold into slavery.

Muslim Spain

In 711, Muslims from northern Africa invaded Spain. By 718, they had conquered almost all of the Spanish kingdom. At that time, the Muslims had a more advanced culture than did most of medieval Europe. They had made great discoveries in mathematics, medicine, and other fields.

Spanish Kingdoms. Christians in far northern Spain formed a series of kingdoms that extended from Spain's northwest coast to the Mediterranean Sea. These kingdoms now began to expand and push the Muslims southward. By the late 1200s, the Muslim territory in Spain had been reduced to the Kingdom of Granada in the south.

Expulsion of Muslims and Jews. In 1469, Prince Ferdinand of Aragon married Princess Isabella of Castile. Almost all of what is now Spain came under their rule.

Ferdinand and Isabella considered Jews and Muslims a threat to their goal of a strong monarchy. Their troops defeated the Muslims in 1492. That same year, the last of the Spanish Jews who would not convert to Christianity were expelled from the country.

now you Know!

✔ The Hundred Years' War had several contributing causes: French kings trying to control the English-held province of Guyenne in southwest France, the French supporting the Scots against England, and the French attempt to control Flanders and the English wool trade there.

✔ The Black Death (bubonic plague) reached Europe in 1347, at the Black Sea port of Caffa (in what is now Feodosiya, Ukraine). By 1400, it had killed an estimated 25 million people.

✔ Although the First Crusade was successful in the conquest of land, by the end of 200 years of crusades nothing had really been gained. Land won was eventually lost.

✔ Considering Muslims and Jews to be a threat, King Ferdinand and Queen Isabella of Spain had them expelled from the country in 1492.

History of the Inquisition

The Inquisition was an effort by the Roman Catholic Church to seek out and punish heretics. The Inquisition took place in many parts of Europe, but the Spanish Inquisition is the best known.

AD 392	Roman Emperor Theodosius I outlaws all non-Christian and non-Jewish worship. From this point on, heresy (holding unaccepted religious beliefs) becomes a crime against the state as well as the church.
1230	Pope Gregory IX introduces the Inquisition as a way to deal with heresy.
1237	At the Council of Lerida, responsibility for the Inquisition is given to the Dominican and Franciscan orders.
1252	In the Papal Bull *Ad exstirpanda*, Pope Innocent IV authorizes the use of torture in order to get confessions from heretics.
1478	The Spanish Inquisition is authorized by Pope Sixtus IV after the Catholic Church grows suspicious of "pseudo converts" to Catholicism from the Jewish and Islamic faiths.
1483	A Dominican monk, Tomas de Torquemada, is given the title Grand Inquistor. Over the next 15 years, 2,000 people are condemned for heresy by the Inquisition and executed.
1633	Galileo Galilei is brought before the Inquisition after the publication of his work *Dialog Concerning the Two Chief World Systems*. He spends the remainder of his life under house arrest.
1834	The Spanish Inquisition comes to an end.

THE BYZANTINE EMPIRE

Long before the Middle Ages in Europe began, the Roman Empire had been divided culturally into a Greek East and a Latin West. The East had a much larger population, many more cities, more commerce, industry, and wealth, as well as a richer heritage of art, literature, and philosophy. In AD 330, Emperor Constantine moved the capital to Byzantium, a small city located on the European side of the Bosporus that had been founded by Greek colonists in the 600s BC. The new capital was called Constantinople in honor of the emperor.

▲ **Emperor Justinian's** ambitious public building program is responsible for one of the most famous Byzantine structures still standing, the church of Hagia Sophia in Constantinople (now Istanbul).

The Eastern Empire

A Divided Empire

In 395, on the death of Emperor Theodosius I, the Roman Empire became divided and was ruled by two separate emperors. During the 400s, barbarians increased their pressure along the frontiers of both empires. The East Roman Empire was able to withstand the onslaught, but the West Roman Empire collapsed in 476 when its emperor was deposed.

Justinian. During the 500s, the Byzantine emperor Justinian (527–565) attempted to reconquer the West. Under the able generals Belisarius and Narses, the East was able to regain Italy, North Africa, and southeastern Spain. Justinian also fought a long war against the Persians, who had invaded the empire from the east.

A Divided Church. Justinian also made a major attempt to ensure the unity of the eastern and western Christian churches, which had been steadily growing apart. He suppressed heresy and paganism and sent out numerous missionaries. This action temporarily healed the breach, but the two churches quarreled continually, and the split between western Christianity, or Roman Catholicism, and eastern Christianity, or Eastern Orthodox Christianity, became irrevocable in what is known as the Schism of 1054.

THE CODE OF JUSTINIAN

In order to clarify the law, Emperor Justinian had the entire body of Roman law codified. The code clarified Roman laws and legal principles and illustrated them by cases. The code has served as a basis for the law codes of many countries. The Justinian Code was divided into four parts.

- The Codex consisted of a collection of imperial statutes.
- The Digest contained interpretations of many trials and decisions by lawyers of the AD 100s and 200s.
- The Institutes was a handbook for students and lawyers.
- The Novels were collections of legislation enacted after the publication of the Codex.

The Code of Justinian became eventually the basis of French, German, and Italian law.

Invasion and Expansion

Justinian was succeeded by a series of weak and ineffective emperors whose reigns were marked by internal unrest and renewed barbarian and Persian invasions.

Between 606 and 622, the Persians overran Syria, Asia Minor, Palestine, Mesopotamia, and Egypt. Slavs moved into the Balkans, and the Avars raided almost as far south as Constantinople.

In 610, Heraclius I, the son of the provincial governor of North Africa, seized the imperial throne and became the founder of a new dynasty. Heraclius reorganized the army and launched three brilliant campaigns against the Persians. By 628, the Persians were decisively defeated and the territory they had taken was regained.

◀ **This map** shows the expansion of the Byzantine Empire under Justinian I.

AD 476
AD 565

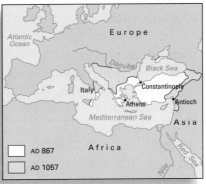

◀ **Under Basil I** and his descendants, 300 years of decline ended. By 1057, the empire controlled the rest of the Balkans and Asia Minor and more territory in Italy.

AD 867
AD 1057

◀ **By 1350,** the Byzantine Empire covered only a few small areas, including Thrace (now part of Turkey) and part of southern Greece.

AD 1350

Major Events—Byzantine Empire	
c. AD 286	Diocletian divides the Roman Empire into eastern and western halves.
c. 330	The capital of the Roman Empire moves to Constantinople.
c. 395	After the death of Theodosius I, the Roman Empire becomes completely divided and is ruled by two separate emperors.
404	The Latin version of the Bible is completed.
426	St. Augustine of Hippo completes *City of God*.
455	The Vandals sack Rome.
c. 867	Byzantine culture reaches a peak during the Macedonian dynasty; Constantinople becomes the artistic center and the marketplace of the Mediterranean.
1054	The Schism of 1054 splits the church between western Christianity (Roman Catholicism) and eastern Christianity (Eastern Orthodox Christianity).
1095	Pope Urban II, Peter the Hermit, and Walter the Penniless mount the First Crusade in order to take Jerusalem from the Arabs; it is the only successful crusade.
1250	The goose feather (quill) is used for writing.
1453	Constantinople falls to the Ottoman Turks.

At the Council of Clermont in 1095, Pope Urban II launched the First Crusade. ▼

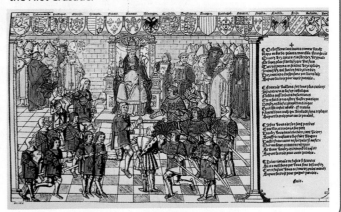

Rise and Fall of the Byzantines

The Middle Period

The middle period of Byzantine history lasted from the late 800s to the early 1200s. During this period, the Byzantine Empire reestablished itself as a significant economic and political power in the Balkan and eastern Mediterranean regions.

From 867 to 1056, the Macedonian dynasty, founded by Emperor Basil I, ruled the empire from Constantinople. Under this increasingly centralized and powerful regime, the Byzantines reestablished administrative and political control over a large geographical area. After many struggles, the Byzantines gained control over the Balkan region and extended their influence as far north as Russia. Military campaigns pushed the empire's eastern frontier back into Armenia and Syria. The Byzantines also regained control of the Aegean and Mediterranean seas from the Arabs.

A marked cultural and economic revival accompanied the development of political stability. Towns expanded, and trade flourished. Christian culture remained dominant, but some artists and writers developed a new interest in the traditions of ancient Greece and Rome.

▲ **A Byzantine church in Greece** called the Church of the Dormition of the Virgin was built in 874. Small towers called cupolas rest on the roof of the well-proportioned brick structure.

▲ **Byzantine architecture,** featuring ornate tile work, still remains more than 500 years after the collapse of the Byzantine Empire.

ISTANBUL, NOT CONSTANTINOPLE

The Byzantine Empire disappeared more than 550 years ago, but its capital city, Constantinople—now Istanbul—is still one of the world's great cities. It was the capital of the Ottoman Empire from 1453 to 1922. In 1922, Turkish nationalist forces gained control of the government of the Ottoman Empire and abolished the office of sultan. In 1923, Turkey became a republic and moved the capital to Ankara. In 1930, the Turkish government declared Istanbul to be the official name of the former capital. Until then, it sometimes still had been called Constantinople.

Decline of the Byzantine Empire

With the end of the Macedonian dynasty in 1057, the Byzantine Empire entered a period of decline that lasted until 1080. The empire was ruled by a succession of weak and inept emperors, and its territory was whittled away by Turkic raiders in the north, Normans in Italy, and Seljuk Turks in Syria, Palestine, and Asia Minor. The Seljuks won most of Asia Minor at the Battle of Manzikert in 1071.

The Crusades. Finally, in 1095, Emperor Alexius I asked the Roman Catholic pope in Rome, Urban II, to send military help to recapture Byzantine lands taken by the Seljuk Turks, pleading that they included the Holy Land of Palestine, sacred to Christians as the birthplace of Jesus Christ and a place of pilgrimage. So began the Crusades, a series of military expeditions from Europe to the Middle East. (See page 468.)

The first Crusades succeeded in winning back lands for the Byzantine Empire; but soon Crusaders grew envious of the empire's wealth. The decline of the empire was accelerated under the weak Angelus dynasty (1185–1195; 1203–1204). The Angeli lacked the power to stand against foreign enemies. The envious Europeans saw their chance.

The Latin Empire. In 1204, during the fourth Crusade, Venetian and French leaders attacked Constantinople on the pretext of intervening on behalf of Emperor Isaac II, who was deposed by his brother Alexius III. After a siege of 1 month, the city fell to the Crusaders and was sacked.

The Crusaders set up a feudal state under Baldwin of Flanders that was known as the Latin Empire. The French controlled most of the former Byzantine mainland possessions and the Venetians held most of the islands and coastal regions. Byzantine princes managed to retain control of Epirus in northwest Greece and of Nicaea and Trebizond in Asia Minor.

Now you Know!

- In AD 330, Emperor Constantine of Rome moved the capital to Byzantium, a small city located on the European side of the Bosporus that had been founded by Greek colonists in the 600s BC. The new capital was called Constantinople in his honor.
- In 395, on the death of Emperor Theodosius I, the Roman Empire became divided and was ruled by two separate emperors. The western empire collapsed less than 100 years later.
- The decline of the Byzantine Empire began with a series of inept emperors, coupled with rising threats from the Turks and Normans.
- The Byzantine Empire came to end with the fall of Constantinople to the Ottomans in 1453.

A Byzantine Restoration. These Byzantine princes continued to struggle against the Crusaders. Finally, in 1261, Michael VIII Palaeologus of Nicaea recaptured Constantinople and overthrew the Latin Empire. He founded the Palaeologian dynasty, which ruled for almost 200 years over a substantially reduced Byzantine Empire, consisting mainly of the area around Constantinople and parts of Greece.

Final Collapse. In May 1453, Constantinople fell to the Ottoman sultan Muhammad II; and the last of the Byzantine emperors, Constantine XI, was killed in the battle. Athens and the Peloponnesus continued to hold out against the Turks, but within a few years they were defeated. Trebizond fell in 1461. Constantinople, for more than 1,100 years the capital of the Byzantine Empire, became the Ottoman capital.

THE ISLAMIC WORLD

The civilization that would eventually produce an empire to rival the size of Rome at its height had its beginnings in a desert region that Roman legions never even tried to enter—the sandy reaches of the Arabian Peninsula. It began with the founding of the third great monotheistic world religion, Islam, meaning "surrender to God," and its followers, the Muslims.

The Story of Islam

Muhammad

The founder of Islam, Muhammad, was born about 570 in the city of Mecca, 50 miles inland from Jiddha, a busy port on the Red Sea. Mecca's location made it a center of caravan trade between southern Arabia and the Red Sea. As an Arabian merchant himself, Muhammad came into contact with Jewish and Christian traders and with the teachings of their religions.

A highly contemplative man, Muhammad often walked the foothills near Mecca to meditate. There, at age 40, he had a religious experience that convinced him that there is only one God, the God of the Jews and Christians, whom Muhammad called Allah. In his revelation, Allah called upon Muhammad to perfect the religion revealed to prophets such as Abraham, Moses, and Jesus, and to preach it to the world.

Medina. At first, Muhammad had little success among the Arabs, who worshipped many gods and spirits of nature. He received death threats for his preaching. He and his few followers fled to the coastal city of Medina, where he did succeed in making converts. His flight there, called the Hegira, became revered by Muslims as the turning point in the development of their faith; the Hegira's date, 622, became the first year of the Muslim calendar.

The Return to Mecca. By 630, Muhammad had attracted an army of followers and was able to march back to Mecca and force it to surrender to him. By the time of his death in 632, he had united all the nomadic tribes of Arabia, the Bedouins, under Islam.

◀ **The mosque** serves religious, military, and educational functions in Muslim life.

The Spread of Islam

Muhammad's successors sent out armies to spread both the faith and Muslim control over areas in the Middle East. By 636, Syria and Northern Palestine had fallen to Muslim forces, and by 641 all of Palestine, Mesopotamia, and Persia had also surrendered.

After the conquests of Egypt and islands in the Mediterranean, they swept west along the North African coast, capturing Carthage in 698 and making converts and allies of the Berber peoples of North Africa.

In 711, Muslim armies crossed from western North Africa over the Strait of Gibraltar to Spain, and within a decade the armies had captured nearly the entire Iberian peninsula. Muslim forces were also on the move eastward, reaching the Indus River by 724. By 750, the Islamic Empire had surpassed the size of the Roman Empire.

Division within Islam. The Umayyad dynasty came to power in 661 after the Arabic Umayyad tribe fomented a civil war against the fourth caliph, Ali, a son-in-law of Muhammad. Ali was assassinated and an Umayyad became caliph, establishing his capital at Damascus in Syria.

This dispute between Ali and the Umayyads created a schism in Islam. On one side were the Sunni Muslims, or Sunnites, who accepted the Umayyad succession; on the other were the Shiites, mainly non-Arabs, who believed only a relative of Muhammad could be caliph. The schism survives today—these two sects continue to be Islam's major groups, with the Sunnites more numerous by far.

The Umayyad dynasty was overthrown in 750. The Abbasids, an Arabic family tracing their descent from Muhammad's uncle, had joined the Shiites in their opposition to the Umayyad. They played upon discontent with Arab domination of Islamic government. The Abbasids and the Persians overran the Umayyad armies and an Abbasid was named caliph. Under the Abbasids, Islamic civilization became more Persian than Arabic.

The Dome of the Rock in Jerusalem is one of the holiest places in Islam. The dome encloses a rock from which the Prophet Muhammad is believed to have ascended to heaven. The dome was built between 688 and 691, during the rule of the Umayyad caliph Abd al-Malik ibn Marwan. ▶

Major Events—Growth of Islam	
c. 571	Muhammad is born.
c. 610–622	Muhammad preaches in Mecca.
622	The Hegira, Muhammad's flight from Mecca to Medina, marks the first year of the Muslim calendar.
630	Muslims conquer Mecca.
632	Muhammad dies.
650	Caliph Uthman, noting differences arising in versions of the Koran, has a standardized version of it written down.
661	A schism divides Islam into the Sunnites and the Shiites; the schism survives today.
711	Muslim armies enter Spain from North Africa.
732	Muslim armies are defeated at the Battle of Tours (in modern-day France).
c. 900	The golden age for Islamic civilization begins; Muhammad al-Razi produces over 100 treatises on disease; Muslim mathematicians perfect algebra; scientists develop the astrolabe, which measures the altitude of a star and helps sailors determine their position at sea.
1030	Christian armies capture Cordoba (Spain).
1071	The Byzantine army is defeated by the Seljuk Turks at the Battle of Manzikert.
1281–1324	The Reign of Osman, founder of the Ottoman Empire.
1453	Ottomans conquer the Byzantine Empire.
1492	All Muslims and Jews are expelled from Spain.

Islamic Achievements

Under the Abbasids, the Muslim economy achieved unprecedented prosperity. The Arabic language and commercial ties with the continents of Asia, Africa, and Europe gave the Muslim world tremendous cohesion.

The Abbasid Empire was ethnically and culturally diverse. Many people lived in large cities. Arabic was the language of government, religion, and intellectual life. The population was active in agriculture, the arts, industry, and trade. Literature, philosophy, and science also flourished. Sunni Muslim religious scholars developed a sophisticated body of Islamic law and theology during this period.

Borrowed Culture. The civilization that developed under these conditions was adept at borrowing the best from the diverse peoples whom it embraced; philosophy and science were borrowed from the Greeks, and mathematics from the Indians, for example. It kept classical learning alive and synthesized scholarship from wherever it was to be found, in turn making its own original contributions to scholarship and art.

A GOLDEN AGE FOR ISLAMIC CIVILIZATION (900 TO 1100)

- Mohammed al-Razi, known as Rhazes to Europeans, the greatest of Muslim physicians, produced over 100 treatises on disease.

- The Arab scholar Avicenna later organized all of al-Razi's learning, as well as all the contemporary knowledge about the symptoms and treatment of diseases, into the *Canon of Medicine,* which was the world's most widely used medical book for centuries.

- From Indian scholars, Muslim mathematicians adopted a numbering system (now called Arabic numbers) that included 0, which makes large numbers possible.

- Muslim mathematicians perfected algebra (from the Arabic al-jabr, meaning "reunion of broken parts").

- Among the most famous literary works of Islamic civilization are Omar Khayyam's long romantic poem, *The Rubáiyát,* and the collected stories that make up *A Thousand and One Nights.*

- The epitome of Muslim architecture is the mosque, with its domes borrowed from the Byzantines. Because Islamic law had strictures prohibiting depictions of the human form, calligraphy and geometric forms became mainstays of Muslim art.

Failure of the Abbasids

Once the Abbasid dynasty lost the ability to maintain political unity, the Islamic Empire began to break up into smaller Muslim states. In 1055, the Seljuk Turks, nomads from central Asia who had become Muslims, gained control of Baghdad and conquered Syria, Palestine, and Asia Minor. In the 13th century, Genghis Khan and his hordes swept out of Mongolia and began their conquest of central and eastern Asia. In 1258, his grandson captured Baghdad and ended the rule of the Abbasids. The Mongols ruled for only a short time. In the early 14th century, another Turkish force, the Ottomans, moved in.

◀ **Hārūn al-Rashīd** served as the ruler of the Islamic Empire from AD 786 to 809. He is also famous as a character in the *Arabian Nights,* also called *The Thousand and One Nights.*

The Coming of the Ottoman Turks

The Ottomans had been vassals of the Seljuks in northwestern Asia Minor, and like them had converted to Islam. The Turkish tribes led by Osman began to expand their small territory in the northwest corner of Anatolia (now Turkey) during the late 1200s. As Seljuk power declined, the Ottomans took over their territories and initiated more wars of expansion.

In 1326, the tribes captured the city of Bursa, which had been part of the Byzantine Empire. In the late 1300s, the Ottomans formed a group of highly trained soldiers called Janissaries.

OMAR KHAYYAM

Omar Khayyam was a Persian poet, astronomer, and mathematician. He was famous during his lifetime for his reform of the Islamic calendar. About 100 years after his death, collections of poems appeared bearing his name. A collection called the *Rubáiyát of Omar Khayyam, the Astronomer-Poet of Persia*, first attracted attention in the West in 1859, when English writer Edward FitzGerald published his free translation of a number of the stanzas arranged as a continuous poem.

Conquest of Constantinople. By the mid-1400s, the Ottomans had conquered the entire Byzantine Empire except for the city of Constantinople. Ottoman troops, led by Sultan Mehmet II, succeeded in capturing Constantinople in 1453.

From 1453 to 1520, they made all of the Balkans, Asia Minor, territory north of the Black Sea, Syria, Palestine, northwestern Arabia, and Egypt part of the Empire. Between 1520 and 1566, they added North Africa, more of Arabia, Iraq, and parts of modern Austria and Hungary, making the Ottoman Empire the world's largest at the time.

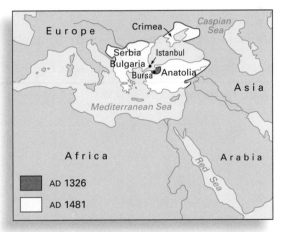

▲ **The Ottoman Empire** started as a small state around Bursa in Anatolia (now Turkey). By the late 1400s, the empire had expanded into eastern Europe.

now you know!

✔ Muhammad was an Arabian merchant who had a religious experience that convinced him that there is only one God: Allah. In his revelation, Allah called upon Muhammad to perfect the religion revealed to the prophets Abraham, Moses, and Jesus, and to preach it to the world.

✔ Scholars of the Abassid Empire kept classical learning alive, borrowing and synthesizing scholarship from wherever it was to be found: philosophy and science from the Greeks, and mathematics from the Indians.

✔ The Ottomans were a group of Turkish tribes who were converted to Islam. Under Osman, they began to expand their small territory in the northwest corner of Anatolia (now Turkey) during the late 1200s.

AFRICAN CIVILIZATION

At one time, Stone Age hunters and gatherers roamed the Sahara, which was then covered with grass, trees, rivers, and lakes. About 5000 BC, climatic changes began to dry the Sahara; by 1500 BC the Sahara had turned into the vast desert it is today. Its Stone Age inhabitants migrated, some toward the Nile Valley and some into the river valleys of Africa's south and west. When they became agriculturalists, the first civilizations began to emerge, some developing in isolation, in part because of the barrier created by the Sahara Desert.

▲ **The civilization of Kush** developed after 1000 BC and lasted until about AD 350 along the Nile River in what is now northern Sudan. Kush was an important trade center. The Kush temple pictured here shows the influence of Roman and Egyptian architecture.

East and Central Africa

Kush and Aksum

About 2000 BC, the kingdom of Kush emerged in the Upper Nile, south of Egypt in what is now Sudan. It developed as a major commercial center, using the Nile River and the Red Sea to trade goods with Egypt, Arabia, and Mesopotamia.

About 750 BC, the Kush were strong enough to conquer Egypt and a Kush dynasty ruled there until 671 BC, when the Assyrians invaded Egypt and drove them out. But Kush civilization quickly regrouped. Having learned how to make iron from the Assyrians, it became a center for iron making in Africa in its capital at Meroë.

The Rise of Aksum. About AD 200, Kush began to decline while its neighbor to the south, Aksum, in what is now Ethiopia, grew stronger. Aksum defeated Kush about 350, and took control of the area's thriving trade.

Twenty-five years earlier, King Ezana of Aksum had converted to Christianity along with many of his people. The scene was thus set for the development of Christian Ethiopia. Invasion by Muslims in the 7th century did not wipe out Christianity there, though it did cut off contact with the rest of the Christian world.

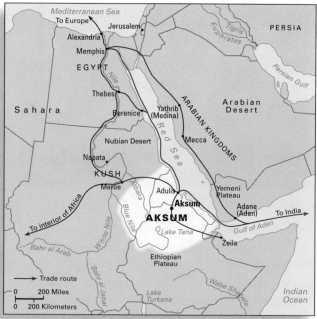

▲ **By the middle of the AD 300s,** Aksum had gained control of the land and sea routes from Africa to Europe and Asia. Present-day boundaries are shown as gray lines.

East African Trade

From ancient times, settlements along Africa's east coast had been involved in trade on the Indian Ocean. By 1200, numerous city-states lined the coast, combining the native Swahili-speaking culture with that of Muslim merchants, thus producing a synthesis of African and Middle Eastern civilization. Indian traders added elements of Hindu civilization.

The Swahili city-states reached their peak in the period from 1200 to 1500. Foremost among them were Malindi, Mombasa, and Kilwa. Rulers built elaborate stone mosques and enormous palaces lavishly decorated with gold and ivory. Swahili writers produced great literature; poems and ballads written in Arabic script abounded.

Central Africa and Zimbabwe

The Bantu-speaking peoples began a mass migration east and south from west-central Africa about 1000 BC. Over the next 2,000 years, they founded states along the Atlantic coast and in the Bantu interior.

One, founded near the Bantu homeland at the mouth of the Niger River, grew into the kingdom of Benin, celebrated for its incomparable iron and bronze sculptures. Farther south was the kingdom of Kongo, at the mouth of the Congo River. There, a bureaucratic monarchy ruled six provinces that engaged in a thriving trade between the interior and Africa's west coast.

Perhaps the most powerful was the inland kingdom of Zimbabwe, between the Zambezi and the Limpopo rivers in southern Africa. Here, about AD 1000, migrating Bantu had found gold; Zimbabwe became the major producer of gold for the East African trade.

Ruins in the valley of Zimbabwe give evidence of the wealth and power that gold brought to this kingdom, which peaked between 1250 and 1450. At the center lies the Great Zimbabwe, a spectacular fortress spread over 60 acres, with granite walls 20 feet high and 10 feet thick, a domed temple, and a mysterious stone tower.

Major Events—Africa	
c. 300–700	Rise of the kingdom of Aksum and conversion to Christianity
c. 600–1000	Migration of Bantu people and the spread of Bantu languages and culture throughout central and southern Africa
beginning c. 700	The Islamic faith makes inroads, beginning in North Africa and then extending into sub-Saharan Africa.
711	North African Muslims invade Spain.
c. 1000	Height of the kingdom of Ghana in western Africa
c. 1200	The decline of Ghana creates a struggle for power in western Africa, resulting in the rise of the Mali Empire.
c. 1200–1500	Swahili city-states thrive in eastern Africa on the coast of the Indian Ocean.
c. 1250–1450	Peak of the kingdom of Zimbabwe
1441	The European slave trade begins as the first shipment of African slaves is sent to Portugal.
1468	Following a string of military victories, the Songhai Empire becomes the most powerful kingdom in western Africa.

▲ **Great Zimbabwe,** the capital of the kingdom of Zimbabwe, was built about 1100 in the plains of southern Africa. The city was an important center of trade in the region. The ruins of the spectacular walls and buildings of the capital remain today.

West Africa

The Kingdoms of West Africa

As in East Africa, the development of great kingdoms in West Africa was profoundly affected by gold and trade. Trade began there in the 3rd century, when camel caravans began crossing the Sahara, north to south, exchanging salt that West Africa did not have for gold that it did have.

Highly organized states existed in Africa long before the European colonial period. This map shows the main states and trade routes of the 1400s. Islamic states were in northern Africa, along the Niger River, and along the east coast of Africa. West African states were located near the Gulf of Guinea. Bantu states were in areas that are now part of Nigeria and Cameroon in western Africa, Congo (Kinshasa) and Angola in central Africa, and Mozambique and Zimbabwe in southeastern Africa. A Christian state was located in what is now Ethiopia. ▶

Ghana. The first of West Africa's great kingdoms was Ghana, which began its development as a group of villages along the upper Niger River during the 4th century AD. According to legend, its first rulers were Berbers from North Africa who were overthrown about AD 700 by the indigenous people under Kaya Maghau, who founded a new dynasty and expanded the desert trade.

Ghana reached its peak during the 11th century. An Arabian visitor named al-Makri recorded that the gold-rich kingdom had a 200,000-man army and an all-powerful king, thought to be divine. Two centuries later, Ghana went into decline for unknown reasons, and by 1203, a new leader, Sundiata, overthrew the king and founded a new kingdom called Mali.

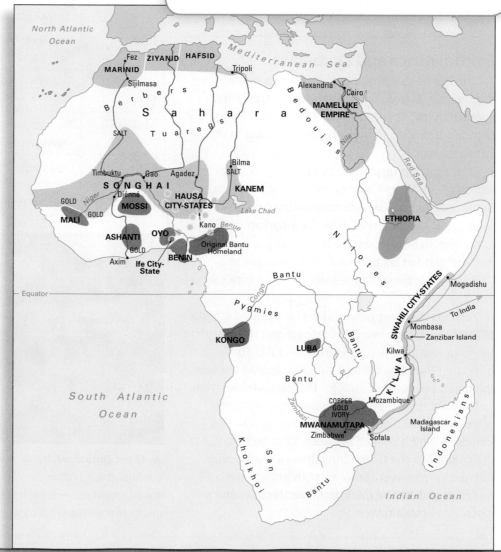

■	Islamic state
■	West African state
■	Bantu state
■	Christian state
Berbers	Major ethnic group
GOLD	Important trading product
——	Land trade route
----	Sea trade route

0   1,000 Miles
0   1,000 Kilometers

480

Mali. Sundiata took over Ghana's gold trade and founded a new dynasty, which, in the mid-13th century, converted to Islam, the religion of its North African trading partners. Mali continued to expand its empire. At its height in the 14th century, Mali's kings ruled 40 million people in West Africa from their capital at Timbuktu on the Niger River.

Mansa Musa, Mali's greatest ruler, held power from 1307 to 1332 and enlarged Mali's holdings. As a devoted Muslim, he invited Muslim scholars and architects to come to Timbuktu to promote learning and to build mosques for Muslim worship.

Mansa Musa gained fame throughout the civilized world when he made a pilgrimage to Mecca in 1324. With a retinue of 60,000 and with 500 slaves, each carrying a 4-pound bar of gold to pay expenses along the way, he cut a spectacular figure. The gold he spent in Egypt alone is said to have caused 20 years of inflation there.

Successors of Mansa Musa were not able to keep the Mali Empire together, as states within it went into rebellion. By the end of the 14th century, the eastern province of Songhai had won its independence; a century later, it had conquered most of Mali.

▲ **Mansa Musa** greatly expanded Mali and made it West Africa's political and cultural power.

now you Know!

✔ The kingdom of Kush emerged in the Upper Nile, south of Egypt, in what is now Sudan in about 2000 BC. It developed as a major commercial center, using the Nile River and the Red Sea to trade goods with Egypt, Arabia, and Mesopotamia.

✔ In about 1000 BC, the Bantu-speaking peoples began a mass migration east and south from west-central Africa. Over the next 2,000 years, they founded states along the Atlantic coast and in the Bantu interior.

✔ The kingdom of Ghana reached its peak during the 11th century. An Arabian visitor named al-Makri recorded that the gold-rich kingdom had an army of 200,000 men and an all-powerful king.

✔ In the 14th century, at the height of its power, Mali's kings ruled 40 million people in West Africa from their capital at Timbuktu on the Niger River.

Songhai. The Empire of Songhai reached its height from 1464 to 1492 under the rule of Sonni Ali II. He was followed by Askia Muhammad, from 1493 to 1528. Songhai became both the largest empire in West Africa and the best organized to maintain power. Timbuktu became a major center of Islamic learning, its university a magnet for scholars and students.

Songhai flourished until nearly 1600, when its wealth brought the envy of the king of Morocco. With weapons unknown to Songhai—cannons and muskets—the Moroccans broke Songhai's empire into a number of smaller, weaker states.

MEDIEVAL CHINA

In AD 580, Yang Chien, a northern Chinese general, began reunifying China after the 350 years of disorder ushered in by the collapse of the Han dynasty. (See pages 449–451.) In 589, he founded the Sui dynasty, which ruled China until 618. During that time, Sui kings created a centralized administration, reviving the civil service examinations begun by the Han to supply it with government officials. This reorganization provided a solid base on which two succeeding dynasties, the T'ang and Sung, could build. These dynasties brought China into two new golden ages, rivaling and surpassing that of the Han era.

China Under the T'ang

The T'ang Dynasty

During the T'ang period, 618 to 907, the Chinese Empire reached its greatest size yet. It subjugated two Turkic states in central Asia, made Tibet a dependency, became the overlord of Korea, and conquered Annam (modern northern Vietnam) in Indochina. The Chinese capital at Changan (modern Xian) grew to more than 2 million people, making it the world's largest city.

T'ang government closely regulated the economy and encouraged its prosperity by building roads and canals to facilitate trade. The most sweeping of its building projects was the Grand Canal, which stretched 650 miles from Hangzhou (Hangchow) to Tianjin (Tientsin), linking the rich rice-growing area along the Yangtze River with fast-growing population areas along the Huang He (Yellow River). Under the T'ang, foreign trade was also encouraged, as the Silk Road used during Roman times was reopened and the port of Canton along the southern coast welcomed 100,000 foreign merchants, from Persia, Arabia, India, and the East Indies.

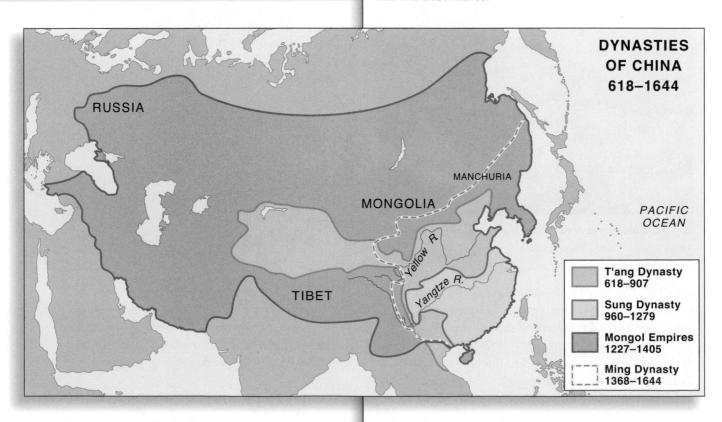

DYNASTIES OF CHINA 618–1644

RUSSIA

MANCHURIA

MONGOLIA

PACIFIC OCEAN

Yellow R.

Yangtze R.

TIBET

- T'ang Dynasty 618–907
- Sung Dynasty 960–1279
- Mongol Empires 1227–1405
- Ming Dynasty 1368–1644

Art and Technology. The T'ang era was especially brilliant in the art and technology it produced. Poetry flourished, most notably that of Li Po (c. 700–762), who wrote movingly of nature, human emotions, and life's mysteries. Interest in the possibilities of learning from history encouraged an outpouring of historical writing, leading to the improvement of papermaking and the invention of block printing, which had originated in China in about 600.

Decline. After two centuries, the T'ang dynasty went into decline, the result of weakened emperors and ill-conceived decisions, like overtaxing peasants and persecuting Buddhists. In 907, the last T'ang emperor was deposed. Fifty years of division and disorder ensued.

▲ **A depiction** of a foreign trader, as seen by a potter during China's T'ang dynasty.

Major Events—Medieval China	
618–907	The T'ang dynasty in China is especially brilliant at producing art and technology.
960–1279	The Sung dynasty increases the manufacture of silk, lacquerware, and porcelain, enabling China to prosper; paper money is in use for the first time.
c. 1050	Some Chinese books are printed with movable type.
1107	The Chinese invent multicolor printing, mainly to make paper money harder to counterfeit.
1206–1227	Mongol tribes are united under the rule of Genghis Khan in 1206, and in following years he and his savage bands of warriors sweep across Asia. Genghis Khan first attacks China and Korea.
1275	Marco Polo arrives in China.
1279–1290	The grandson of Genghis Khan, Kublai Khan (1215?–1294) brings the Eurasian Mongol empire to its height by conquering China in 1279. He makes China the seat of the Mongol empire. At what is now Beijing, he builds a magnificent city as his capital.
1368–1644	The Ming dynasty emperors end the period of Mongol rule begun by Kublai Khan. They expand their empire to include Korea, Vietnam, Burma, Turkistan, and Mongolia.

 *Gunpowder was another Chinese technological development under the T'ang dynasty. At first, it was used only for fireworks. The Chinese began to use gunpowder for military purposes in the 10th century, after which they developed explosive grenades and land mines. Firearms did not appear until the 12th century.*

The Sung Dynasty

In 960, Chao K'uang-yin, a northern Chinese leader, founded China's next dynasty, which would rule until 1279. Militarily weaker than its predecessor, the Sung kept out restless Mongol invaders like the Khitan by paying them tribute in the form of silk and silver. But in 1127, another invading group, the Jurchin, came down from Manchuria and captured northern China, driving the Sung out of their capital at Kaifeng and forcing them to flee south. Now China was divided in two—the Jurchin's Chin Empire in the north and the Sung Empire in the south, with its capital at Hangzhou.

ART AND LEARNING

Chinese art and learning continued to advance under the Sung. Landscape painting reached its height as artists plumbed the depths of their Taoist love of nature to capture the rugged beauties of China with delicate brush strokes on silk.

During the 12th century, philosopher Chu Hsi (1130–1200) developed Neo-Confucianism, which synthesized the teachings of Confucianism, Buddhism, and Taoism into a single school of thought. This philosophy characterized the universe as a self-regulating order to which human beings must learn to adjust rationally.

Trade and Commerce. Even with this turmoil, Sung civilization bloomed, thanks largely to continuing commercial success. By establishing commercial colonies throughout East Asia, the Chinese took over the rich trade of their southern ports, previously controlled by foreign merchants. Trade was conducted as far away as India, Persia, and the Middle East. Increased manufacture of such goods as silk, lacquerware, and porcelain enabled the Chinese to prosper as never before.

In their extensive dealings, they introduced the use of paper money for the first time in history. Sea trade also encouraged the development of water clocks and paddleboats, as well as a 24-point mariner's compass. Science and cartography also were enriched, as was medicine. The Chinese developed smallpox inoculation, another first.

Scholar by a Waterfall is an ink drawing on silk by the Sung dynasty artist Ma Yuan. ▶

The Mongol Empire

By the 13th century, Chinese civilization was no longer able to hold back the Mongols, with either military might or with tribute. The Mongols then began a series of conquests that created the Mongol Empire. In 1215, Genghis Khan and his fierce and powerful cavalries conquered northern China, occupying most of the Chin Empire and capturing Beijing, its capital.

For the next decade, he continued his empire building, taking his armies west and conquering parts of northern India as well as of Persia, Iraq, and southern Russia. After his death in 1227, his descendants continued to expand the Mongol Empire until it stretched from the Black Sea in the west to Korea in the east. It was Genghis Khan's grandson Kublai Khan who completed the conquest of China and the overthrow of the Sung dynasty in 1279. He also brought the Southeast Asian states of Burma, Annam, and Cambodia under Mongol control but failed in his attacks on Japan.

The Yuan Dynasty. Kublai Khan chose the Chinese name Yuan for the dynasty he founded in 1279, and which lasted until 1368. He made his capital at Beijing. Chinese officials were replaced with Mongols, who held themselves to one set of laws while holding the Chinese to another, harsher set.

Commercial and cultural contacts with the outer world increased under the Mongols.

▲ **Genghis Khan**

Restoration Under the Ming

Under Kublai Khan's successors, Mongol rule weakened and Chu Yüan-chang, a former Buddhist monk, led a successful rebellion. It culminated in 1368 with his establishment of the Ming dynasty, which ruled until 1644. The Ming rulers moved quickly to restore Confucian government and bureaucracy.

Early in their rule, the Ming encouraged foreign trade and sent voyages of exploration to Southeast Asia, India, the Persian Gulf, and East Africa. But in the mid-1400s, for unknown reasons, the voyages were ended and China cut off its foreign contacts and withdrew into itself. At this time, it was probably the most technologically advanced civilization on Earth, but with its turn inward, it gradually lost its technological edge.

now you Know!

✔ Between 618 to 907, during the T'ang period, the Chinese Empire reached its greatest size yet. It made Tibet a dependency, became the overlord of Korea, subjugated two Turkic states in central Asia, and conquered Annam (modern northern Vietnam) in Indochina.

✔ The Sung dynasty introduced the use of paper money for the first time in history. They were also responsible for several nautical innovations: the development of water clocks and paddleboats, as well as a 24-point mariner's compass.

✔ In 1215, Genghis Khan and his powerful Mongol cavalries conquered northern China, occupying most of the Chin Empire and capturing Beijing, its capital.

✔ The weakening Mongol rule was ended in 1368, when Chu Yüan-chang, a former Buddhist monk, led a successful rebellion that brought about the Ming dynasty, which ruled until 1644.

JAPAN AND SOUTHEAST ASIA

Developing in the shadow of China, and deeply influenced by it, was the civilization of Japan, just across the Sea of Japan from Korea and Manchuria. In ancient times, migrations of Asian peoples had come to Japan by way of Korea, gradually displacing the indigenous Stone Age Ainu population. By the 1st century AD, Japan's mountainous topography had encouraged these peoples to organize themselves into farming clans in numerous self-contained tribal states.

Japan Emerges

Early Japan

According to legend, the first emperor of Japan was Jimmu, a descendant of Amaterasu, the sun goddess. He is thought to have been a member of the Yamato clan, which in the early centuries AD extended their power over neighboring clans in central Japan. Traditionally called the "Sons of Heaven," the Yamato line of emperors of Japan is unbroken to the present.

Japan's religious beliefs were centered on the simple worship of gods and goddesses, known as *kami,* who controlled the forces of nature. Called Shinto, or "Way of the Gods," this religion advocated neither a system of ethics nor an organized priesthood.

Chinese Influences. Just as Korea had served as a land bridge for migrations to Japan, so it served as a cultural bridge from China. Strong Chinese cultural influences began to reach Japan during the Chinese Han dynasty, in the 3rd century AD. Soon the Japanese became avid cultural borrowers. Having no written language of their own, they adopted Chinese writing about 400. In 522, Buddhism reached Japan. (See page 455.) The Yamato rulers embraced it and encouraged its spread among the Japanese, eventually declaring it Japan's official religion. Confucian ideas about family loyalty and obedience to political authority were also embraced.

Japanese art and architecture, especially in Buddhist temples, also imitated Chinese styles. Japan adopted China's use of paper money and its system of weights and measures.

◄ **Originally** built in the 14th century, Japan's Himeji Castle has been remodeled many times and has survived natural disasters and extensive bombing during World War II.

The Heian Period

In 794, Japan entered the Heian period, a name taken from the Japanese term for "peace and tranquility." During this period, which lasted until 1185, Japan concentrated on evolving a distinctive Japanese culture. During the 10th century, a phonetic alphabet developed, freeing the Japanese from an unwieldy system of ideograms borrowed from the Chinese.

The period was marked by a change in the role of the emperor. A new clan, the Fujiwara, took control of the central government, mainly by marrying into the Yamato clan. Yamato emperors remained on the throne, but they were reduced to political figureheads as Fujiwara regents wielded the real political power.

Heian culture was centered largely in the new city of Heian (Kyoto), to which the imperial court moved in 794. Japanese poetry was enriched by the publication of the Manyoshu, a collection of over 4,000 poems that celebrate love of nature and human emotions. The study of human emotions was also at the heart of *The Tale of Genji*, a long novel in which Lady Murasaki of the imperial court depicted life there.

Feudal Society in Japan	
Shogun	The "great general"—Japan's military dictator
Daimyo	Local lords and great warriors who carved out huge estates
Samurai	Warrior knights who swore their loyalty to their daimyo and followed a strict code of conduct called bushido, meaning "the way of the warrior." Violation of this code of chivalry brought great disgrace and demanded harakiri, or ritual suicide.
Peasants, artisans	The farmers and craftspeople who worked the daimyo's land
Merchants	An influential group not honored in Japanese society, but whose influence grew as their wealth did, a result of growing foreign trade with China, Korea, and Southeast Asia

Feudal Japan

By the 12th century, Fujiwara political power was breaking down as the power of provincial lords was increasing. In 1185, following a period of warfare among clans over who was to replace the Fujiwara, Minamoto Yoritomo established a new capital at Kakamura on Tokyo Bay. He later declared himself shogun, or "great general," in effect, military dictator. The emperor's court remained at Kyoto, but political power now lay in the hands of the hereditary shogunate in its headquarters at Kamakura.

In 1333, an alliance of daimyo overthrew Kamakura. Five years later, the Ashikaga family claimed the shogunate and held onto it until 1573. But the Ashikaga never gained firm control over the daimyo, and they were not helped by a schism that erupted between rival houses of their family in 1467. This schism brought on civil war that continued on and off for the next century.

Even under these circumstances, agricultural production rose and prosperity brought population and urban growth. Buddhism, especially a new sect called Zen Buddhism, exerted a major influence on life and the arts. Highly stylized theater in the form of Nō and Kabuki plays emerged, as did the haiku form of poetry.

Major Events—Japan and Southeast Asia	
c. 400	Chinese influence in language, Confucian government, and art predominates in Vietnam; the Japanese adopt Chinese writing.
c. 522	Buddhism reaches Japan.
645	Japanese art and architecture imitate Chinese styles; Japan adopts China's system of weights and measures.
794	The Heian period begins in Japan; the Japanese concentrate on developing a distinctive culture and form a phonetic alphabet.
938	Vietnam gains independence from China.
c. 1150	The Hindu temple, or Wat, of Angkor is created.
1192	Minamoto Yoritomo became the first shogun. He established a military government headquartered in Kamakura.
1274	Japan defeats Mongol invasion.
c. 1470	Highly stylized theater emerges in Japan in the form of Nō and Kabuki; haiku poetry also emerges.

Southeast Asia

Southeast Asia: World Crossroads

Southeast Asia is a tropical area of peninsulas and archipelagos whose earliest peoples probably migrated from India, Tibet, and China. The peoples of the mainland and the Indochinese and Malay peninsulas developed mainly as agrarian peasants. Those on Pacific islands such as Sumatra, Java, Borneo, and the Philippines gravitated more toward livelihoods made from the sea, in occupations such as fishing and trade.

Foreign Influences. Southeast Asia was subjected to the strong cultural, political, and religious influences of its powerful neighbors, India and China. India exerted the earliest and most powerful influence, as Hindu traders and Buddhist missionaries colonized the area. Between the 4th and 15th centuries AD, Hindu-Buddhist culture—its religious beliefs, Sanskrit writing, and styles of art—came to dominate both the mainland and the islands.

Chinese influences—language, Confucian government, and art—became predominant only in Vietnam, which it conquered during the Han dynasty and ruled until the Vietnamese won their independence in the 900s.

The Khmer Empire

During the 8th and 9th centuries, several successful Hindu and Buddhist kingdoms emerged in Southeast Asia, often fighting one another for dominance. Perhaps the greatest was the Khmer Empire, which reached its height in 1200, when its rule included all of central Indochina, down to the Malay peninsula.

Prosperous and powerful, the Khmer emperors are said to have ruled in unimaginable magnificence.

Angkor. Between 820 and the 1100s, Cambodian kings built a large network of cities, villages, temples, artificial ponds, irrigation canals, and rice fields covering over 386 square miles (1,000 square kilometers) in the vicinity of the present-day city of Siem Reap. The city of Angkor was the most magnificent. It may have had a million people, more than any European city at that time. The city included Angkor Thom, which was actually a city within the city of Angkor, and covered 4 square miles (10 square kilometers). The city of Angkor also contained many temples and palaces. The city and its temples rank as one of the artistic and architectural wonders of the world. Carved scenes of Cambodian life and Buddhist or Hindu mythology decorate the walls of the temples.

Angkor is a group of temples in Cambodia. The temples, built of richly carved sandstone, were begun in the 1100s and show the Hindu influence on architecture outside India. ▼

Angkor Wat, Cambodia's fantastic temple city, was built in the 1100s, lost, reclaimed by the jungle, and rediscovered late in the 20th century. ▼

Angkor Wat. One of the temples, Angkor Wat, is probably the finest architectural monument in Cambodia. It covers nearly 1 square mile (2.6 square kilometers) and has a pyramidal form. This form imitates the mythological home of the Hindu gods. Angkor Wat was constructed in the 1100s to honor the Hindu god Vishnu. It was also used as an astronomical observatory. Angkor Wat later became the tomb of the Cambodian king who had ordered its construction.

Another temple, the Bayon, stands at the center of Angkor Thom. It was dedicated to Buddha and the reigning king. More than 200 giant stone faces adorn its towers.

The Coming of the Muslims

As early as the 13th century, Muslim traders had been putting in at ports in the Malayan, Indonesian, and even Philippine archipelagos. They were eager for the spices, tin, gold, and precious woods produced there. Proselytizing Islam was as successful there as it had been elsewhere in the world, and by the 1400s most of the Malay peninsula and Indonesian archipelago had become Muslim.

now you **Know!**

- ✔ China's cultural influences began to reach Japan during the 3rd century AD. Soon the Japanese became avid cultural borrowers, adopting Chinese writing about 400 and Buddhism in 522.

- ✔ During the Heian Period, from 794 to 1185, a distinctly Japanese culture emerged, including a phonetic alphabet to replace the unwieldy system of ideograms borrowed from the Chinese.

- ✔ In 1185, Yoritomo Minamoto established a new Japanese capital at Kakamura on Tokyo Bay. He declared himself shogun, or "great general," in effect, military dictator.

- ✔ The Khmer Empire reached its height in 1200, when its rule included all of central Indochina, down to the Malay peninsula.

- ✔ Angkor Wat, constructed in the 1100s to honor the Hindu god Vishnu, is probably the finest architectural monument in Cambodia. Covering nearly 1 square mile, it was used as an astronomical observatory and later became the tomb of the king who had ordered its construction.

◀ **The magnificent Bayon Temple,** seen in this photograph, stands at the center of Angkor Thom, a walled city built within the ancient city of Angkor. The limestone structure, built around AD 1190, is a Buddhist temple that incorporates elements of Hindu design.

DEVELOPING CULTURES OF THE AMERICAS

Cultures of the Americas developed independently of those in Europe, Africa, and Asia, without either side of the world being aware of the other. By about 1000 BC, their productive agrarian economy had acquired the essential features of civilization: occupational specialization; religious organization; effective government, in this case, run by a priestly ruling class; written language, in the form of hieroglyphics; and high artistic achievement, especially in architecture.

The Olmecs and the Maya

The Olmecs

One of the earliest of the American civilizations were the Olmecs, located along the Gulf Coast in southern Mexico. The Olmecs constructed a series of planned cities as religious centers, with stone pyramids nine and 10 stories high as altars to the gods. They were marvels of masonic skill and of decorative carving. Ruins of these pyramids can still be found, along with massive stone sculptures of grim-faced heads, some weighing 20 tons.

Olmec influence spread across all of Mesoamerica, perhaps reaching its height in the city of Teotihuacan, in the northeastern Valley of Mexico. There, a pyramid over 15 stories high honored the god Quetzalcoatl, pictured as a feathered serpent. By AD 500, this city had a population of somewhere between 100,000 and 200,000, making it the sixth largest city in the world at that time.

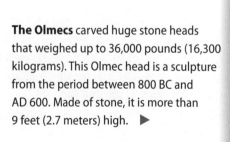

The Olmecs carved huge stone heads that weighed up to 36,000 pounds (16,300 kilograms). This Olmec head is a sculpture from the period between 800 BC and AD 600. Made of stone, it is more than 9 feet (2.7 meters) high. ▶

The Maya

South of Teotihuacan, in the Yucatán Peninsula in what is now Guatemala, the Mayan civilization arose in the first millennium BC. By AD 300, it had become the most splendid yet seen in the Americas.

Like the Olmecs, the Maya built magnificent religious centers that grew into major cities such as Tikal, Palenque, and Uxmal. The cities had royal palaces occupied by a hereditary priest-king, considered the descendant of the sun god, and the priests and warrior nobles, the ruling class. Each city also had pyramid temples, some 20 stories high, built to honor the many deities the Maya worshipped. Decoration included magnificent stone sculptures made with stone tools (the native cultures of the Americas never developed iron making). The art of mural painting reached great heights under the Maya.

Astronomy. Because Mayan scholars were avid students of astronomy, observatories were another feature of their cities. The Maya made astronomical discoveries that helped them to perfect a calendar they adopted from the earlier Olmecs but using an ingenious notational system of their own design.

Collapse. Mayan civilization collapsed in the 800s. The reasons are unknown, but overpopulation, rebellion, and attack from barbarian tribes were possible causes. By 900, their great cities were abandoned and new peoples, like the Toltecs, rose to power. These peoples absorbed Mayan influences as they gained control of Mesoamerican trade, and built spectacular urban centers at Tula, in the Valley of Mexico, and Chichén Itzá on the Yucatán Peninsula.

◄ **The Maya** built tall pyramids of limestone with small temples on top, such as the one shown here, at Chichén Itzá in northern Yucatán. Priests climbed the stairs of the pyramids and performed ceremonies in the temples.

Major Events—The Americas	
c. 1000 BC	The Olmecs found one of the earliest American civilizations along the Gulf Coast in southern Mexico.
c. AD 300	The Mayan civilization in Central America creates magnificent stone sculptures with stone tools.
c. 600	Incan villages begin to grow into cities in the highlands of Peru.
c. 1000	The Vikings, led by Leif Ericson, reach North America, perhaps at Newfoundland; the lack of archaeological evidence leaves doubt as to the exact location.
1300	The Aztecs dominate the central valley of Mexico.
1454	Italian navigator Amerigo Vespucci is one of the first Europeans to recognize that North and South America are undiscovered continents.
1492	Columbus reaches America. (See page 503.)
1525	Smallpox reaches the Incan Empire, killing Huayna Capac, the Incan king.

The Aztecs and the Inca

The Aztecs

By the 13th century, a new group of invaders, the warlike Aztecs, had migrated south from central Mexico. As they moved south, the Aztecs conquered other tribes, demanding tribute and enslaving some of the conquered people.

About 1325, the Aztecs founded their capital at Tenochtitlán, where Mexico City is located today. At that time, it was an island located in the center of a lake reachable only by causeways, making it highly defensible. Led by Montezuma I, who ruled from 1440 to 1468, the Aztecs fought for 20 years, until they had extended their empire into Guatemala, and along both the Gulf of Mexico and the Pacific coasts.

The hereditary Aztec ruler, whose people believed he was an incarnation of the sun god, governed as a despot, assisted by 38 provincial governors. A powerful military force held the system together, putting down any revolts by conquered peoples.

▲ **The Aztec Empire** had its capital at Tenochtitlán, which stood on the site of present-day Mexico City. The empire was established during the 1400s, when the Aztecs and their allies conquered much of central and southern Mexico.

Religion. Aztec religion was based on the worship of gods and goddesses of natural forces. Perhaps most important was the god of the sun, Huitzilopochtli. The Aztecs believed that this god demanded human sacrifice and so they built altars atop tall pyramids on which they tore out the living hearts of the hapless victims that they abducted from conquered tribes. Then they held the still-beating organs up to the sun.

Historians sometimes draw a parallel between the Maya and Aztecs and the Greeks and Romans. Just as the Romans borrowed much of their culture from the Greeks, so the Aztecs built their culture by borrowing from earlier Mayan and Toltec models. Also like the Romans, the Aztecs honored military discipline, direct action, and efficient imperial organization.

Aztec writing consisted of small pictures called pictographs. This page from an Aztec codex shows Xipe Totec, left, the god of spring, and the god Quetzalcoatl, who appears as a snake, right. ▼

The Inca

People began settling in villages in the Andes Mountains about 1500 BC. By AD 600, villages began to grow into cities. Over the succeeding centuries, rival kingdoms battled one another incessantly. In the 1100s, one group began to conquer and unite the area—the Inca. Under the leadership of Pachacuti, who reigned from 1438 to 1471, they brought all of the territory from northern Ecuador to central Chile, a length of 2,700 miles, and from the Pacific coast to the Amazon rain forests, into their empire.

Structure of the Government. The huge Inca Empire had a strong central government under the authority of the emperor, considered to be the son of the Inca's most important god, Inti, god of the sun. The empire was divided into four provinces, each governed by a viceroy and each divided into 40 subsections under subgovernors. Each of these was further divided into units of 10 families under the authority of a local official.

Engineering Marvels. The Inca built a system of roads and bridges that successfully linked the highly mountainous empire, enhancing its efficient rule. Even without the wheel, which Native American cultures failed to develop, they moved massive stones to build temples and fortresses, fitting the stones so closely together that they required no mortar.

By 1500, the Inca Empire had reached its zenith under the rule of Huanyna Capac. However, a dispute over the succession to the throne, and interference by Europeans, helped to set the stage for its rapid decline in the century that followed.

▲ **The empire of the Inca** lay along the western coast of South America. It included parts of what are now Colombia, Ecuador, Peru, Bolivia, Chile, and Argentina.

▲ **Machu Picchu,** built in the 1400s, probably served as an Inca royal estate. The Inca, who built Peru's last great indigenous (native) civilization, were conquered by the Spaniards in the 1530s.

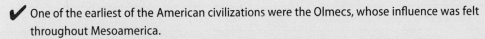

✔ One of the earliest of the American civilizations were the Olmecs, whose influence was felt throughout Mesoamerica.

✔ The Maya made astronomical discoveries that helped them to perfect a calendar they adopted from the earlier Olmecs but using a notational system of their own design.

✔ The Aztec capital was Tenochtitlán, where Mexico City is located today. At the time, it was an island located in the center of a lake reachable only by causeways, making it highly defensible.

✔ Although they had no knowledge of the wheel, the Inca were able to move massive stones to build temples and fortresses. These stones fit so closely together that they required no mortar.

THE RENAISSANCE IN EUROPE

The Italian Renaissance

In the traditional sense, the term *Renaissance,* which literally means rebirth, denotes the revival of classical learning and culture in Italy, mainly in the 1300s and 1400s, and its spread to other parts of Europe, mainly during the 1400s and 1500s.

The Renaissance was the first period in which people really considered themselves to be "modern"—that is, they believed their own age to be not only different from the preceding one but superior to it. The "Renaissance man" rejected the "barbarisms" and "corruptions" of the centuries since the decline of ancient Greece and Rome.

Scholars of the Renaissance scorned medieval "dog-Latin," and eagerly searched for old manuscripts from which they could recover the pure Latin of the ancient Romans. On a smaller scale, the study of ancient Greek was enthusiastically taken up, as was Hebrew.

Humanism. The medieval scholar had been concerned with the harnessing of reason in the defense and service of religion. The Renaissance scholar was more concerned with the secular side of things. His philosophy was humanism, which holds that the study of humankind and of the world is most important. Poets and philosophers concerned themselves with this world, not the next; with the world of nature, not that of theology; with men, not angels.

Painters and sculptors sought to capture real people rather than general types and individual personalities rather than universal human traits.

Major Events—Renaissance	
c. 1300	The Renaissance, a revival of classical learning and culture in Italy, begins.
1321	Dante writes *The Divine Comedy.*
1353	Boccaccio writes *The Decameron.*
c. 1450	Johannes Gutenberg develops a printing press that uses movable type.
1453	The Turks capture Constantinople; many Greek scholars escape to the west.
1506	Leonardo da Vinci completes the *Mona Lisa.*
1512	Michelangelo finishes painting the Sistine Chapel.
1517	Martin Luther posts the "95 theses," which sparks the Protestant Reformation.
1535	Sir Thomas More is beheaded by order of Henry VIII for refusing to swear allegiance to the Church of England.
1543	Copernicus publishes *On the Revolutions of Heavenly Bodies.*
c. 1559	Tobacco is brought to Europe from America.
1600	Shakespeare's *Hamlet* is first performed. (See pages 972–979.)
1609	The telescope is invented by Hans Lippershey, a Dutch scientist.
1620	The first weekly newspaper in Europe begins publication in Amsterdam.

The Secular Spirit. In fact, the spirit of the Renaissance was above all secular. Even the papal throne was usually occupied in this period by "Renaissance popes," such as Julius II (ruled 1503–1513), who divided his time between making war (as ruler of the Papal States) and sponsoring enormous art projects by Michelangelo and other masters. The universities were also more secular. As centers of the "new learning," they not only concentrated heavily on secular subjects but also produced large numbers of educated laymen, not just clergy. Even the "universal man" (one who is adept at a variety of pursuits, from scholarship and poetry to the art of war), who was the Renaissance ideal, was concerned mainly with secular activities.

The Birth of Vernacular Literature. The Renaissance period in literature includes some of the greatest literary figures in history: Dante, who wrote *The Divine Comedy*; Petrarch, famous for his sonnets and poems; and Boccaccio, author of *The Decameron*.

One of the greatest Renaissance achievements was the development of a superb vernacular (the language spoken by the people) literature that furthered the development of native languages such as Italian. Until then, most writing was in Latin. This change was helped along as books printed in the vernacular began to replace hand-copied classical manuscripts, thereby reaching a greater number and variety of people. (See pages 925–926.)

Renaissance art of both religious and secular subjects became more proportional, natural, and realistic. Among a host of great Renaissance painters were the versatile Leonardo da Vinci, best known for his paintings *Mona Lisa* and *The Last Supper*; Raphael, a remarkable master of color; and Michelangelo, famous for his fresco covering the entire ceiling of the Sistine Chapel in St. Peter's Basilica.

Mona Lisa, by Leonardo da Vinci

Masters of the Italian Renaissance	
Dante, 1265–1321	poet
Giotto, 1266–1337	painter
Petrarch, 1304–1374	poet and humanist
Donatello, c. 1386–1466	sculptor
Leonardo da Vinci, 1452–1519	painter, sculptor, engineer, scientist
Niccolò Machiavelli, 1469–1527	writer and political philosopher
Michelangelo, 1475–1564	painter, sculptor, architect
Raphael, 1483–1520	painter
Galileo, 1564–1642	scientist

Detail, Sistine Chapel, by Michelangelo

The Northern Renaissance

The Northern Renaissance in Europe was conspicuous during the 1300s for its growing religious mysticism, which favored direct worship of God without an intervening priesthood. This was fostered early in Germany by the writings of Meister Eckhart and Thomas à Kempis. Humanism was also influential, especially through the writings of Erasmus of Rotterdam and Sir Thomas More of England.

Literature. Rabelais and Michel de Montaigne represented French literary development in the Northern Renaissance, while Cervantes, who wrote *Don Quixote*, became Spain's master literary figure. (See page 930.)

The greatest literature of the Northern Renaissance came from England. Edmund Spenser wrote *The Faerie Queene*; late Renaissance writing included Milton's epic *Paradise Lost*. Perhaps the highest literary achievement of all came in the form of the English dramas written by Christopher Marlowe and those of the more famous William Shakespeare.

◀ *Feast of the Rose Garland* by Albrecht Dürer

▲ *The Blue Cloak* by Pieter Bruegel the Elder

▲ *Erasmus* by Hans Holbein the Younger

Art. Following the inspiration of the Italian innovations, painting flourished in northern Europe. Flemish painters popularized the use of oils in the 1400s. Flemish painters Hieronymus Bosch, Hans Holbein the Younger, Pieter Bruegel the Elder, and Peter Paul Rubens created some of the most memorable paintings in European history. Albrecht Dürer of Germany

visited Italy twice, and his later works reveal a strong influence from the Renaissance masters he met there. Dürer was not only one of the greatest painters and engravers of the period, he is largely responsible for the spread of the ideas and ideals of Italian art into northern Europe.

Masters of the Northern Renaissance	
Erasmus, 1466?–1536	Dutch humanist, scholar
Albrecht Dürer, 1471–1528	German artist
Nicolaus Copernicus, 1473–1543	Polish astronomer
Sir Thomas More, 1478–1535	English author
François Rabelais, 1494?–1553	French writer
Hans Holbein the Younger, c. 1497–1543	German artist
Pieter Brueghel the Elder, c. 1525–1569	Flemish artist
Michel Eyquem de Montaigne, 1533–1592	French essayist
Miguel de Cervantes, 1547–1616	Spanish writer
Francis Bacon, 1561–1626	English philosopher
William Shakespeare, 1564–1616	English dramatist

The Introduction of Printing

The spread of writing and widespread public literacy was amplified by the introduction of printing with movable type in Europe. In the mid-1400s, Johannes Gutenberg, a goldsmith, began casting individual letters of the alphabet in metal so they could be fitted together to print one page and then easily rearranged to print another.

Gutenberg spent a number of years in Strasbourg, carrying on experiments to develop a method for printing books that would replace handwritten copying. He produced types that could be arranged in even lines of composition. A number of pages containing thousands of types could easily be put on and taken off the press. After printing, the types could be separated and used again to set up other pages.

The Gutenberg Bible. Gutenberg and his associates, Johannes Fust and Peter Schoffer, printed a magnificent Bible, known as the Mazarin Bible and Gutenberg Bible, which shows that these pioneer printers had mastered every technical detail.

It is estimated that before Gutenberg there were no more than 100,000 books, all laboriously hand copied, in Europe. By 1500, there were perhaps 9 million. Although the vast majority of early printed books were theological works, including the Bible, Europe became a more literate society. The demand for knowledge increased greatly.

The Birth of Modern Astronomy

In the early 1500s, most astronomers still thought that Earth was motionless at the center of the universe. The Greek astronomer Ptolemy had developed this idea in the AD 100s.

A Polish astronomer, Nicolaus Copernicus, saw Ptolemy's system as a complicated mathematical invention with no basis in physical reality. He sought the simplest and most systematic explanation of heavenly motion. Copernicus realized that it required that every planet, including Earth, revolve around the sun. In developing his theory, he also accounted for Earth's rotation on its axis and the much slower wobble of that axis. These motions of Earth affect the paths that objects appear to follow in the sky.

In his masterpiece, *On the Revolutions of the Heavenly Spheres* (1543), Copernicus showed how Earth's motion could be used to explain irregularities in the movements of other heavenly bodies. In the early 1600s, the German astronomer Johannes Kepler showed that the planets follow elliptical (oval-shaped) orbits. Also in the early 1600s, the Italian scientist Galileo made discoveries with the telescope that supported Copernicus's theory.

◀ **Nicolaus Copernicus,** a Polish astronomer, proposed the theory that the planets, including Earth, revolve around the sun.

Renaissance Politics

The Renaissance State

The Renaissance state, in many ways a forerunner of the centralized, omnipotent modern state, developed rapidly, particularly in northern Italy's cities. Medieval republican city governments, which also ruled outlying territories, gave way to rule by an individual despot in Milan, by a wealthy oligarchy in Venice, by both in Florence, and by the pope in the Papal States around Rome.

Elsewhere, larger territorial states were being consolidated under strong monarchical rule, most importantly in England, France, and Spain. By the early 1500s, each of these countries had achieved, in rough form, its modern boundaries. Although each developed differently, royal power was markedly increased, and the centralized institutions characteristic of modern governments swiftly developed.

England and France. In England, strong government was established by the Tudor dynasty, especially by Elizabeth I (ruled 1558–1603). In France, centralization was slowed by almost constant foreign wars in the first half of the 1500s, and by civil wars in the second half. The Valois dynasty ended in 1589, and Henry IV (ruled 1589–1610) ushered in the Bourbon dynasty, which would rule France for the next 200 years.

A Short-lived Empire. In 1469, Spain was united under the strong rule of Ferdinand and Isabella. Maximilian I (ruled 1493–1519), the Holy Roman Emperor of the Hapsburg dynasty, inherited the Netherlands and Austria, and married his son into Spanish royalty. The resulting empire, greatest in Europe, split in 1556 between Austrian lands under Ferdinand I (ruled 1556–1564) and Spanish lands under Philip II (ruled 1556–1598). Philip brought the power of the Spanish crown to its highest peak.

The rivalry between the French crown and the Hapsburgs—especially the Spanish branch—continued until the Treaty of Pyrenees was signed in 1659, by which time French predominance in Europe had replaced Spanish.

Civic Humanism

Civic humanism originated in Florence between 1385 and 1425. Coluccio Salutati and Leonardo Bruni, the humanist chancellors of Florence during this period, were the leading practitioners of this school of thought, which extolled the republican form of government, liberty over tyranny, family values, and hard work. Important documents of civic humanism include Salutati's republican letters to Florentine allies in Italy, and Bruni's book *On the Family,* which became the basis of bourgeois-capitalist family values.

Civic humanism was also associated with republicanism, as these values formed the basis of republican traditions that developed elsewhere in Renaissance Italy, as well as in England and its North American colonies.

NICCOLÒ MACHIAVELLI

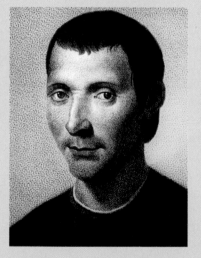

Niccolò Machiavelli (1469–1527), the well-known Renaissance humanist, is remembered for his book *Il principe (The Prince).* In the book, Machiavelli recommended the same principles for governing tyrannical and republican states: that is, that the government must exhibit virtù, or force and strength, in doing whatever is required to maintain its power. This advice has come down to us over the years in the phrase "the ends justify the means." Machiavelli wrote *The Prince* hoping he would be hired by the ruling Medici family; ironically, in spite of the attention the book has received over the years, the Medici chose to ignore the book and Machiavelli.

The Medici Family

The Medici were one of the ruling families of Florence, Italy. With their great wealth and influence as bankers, they were able to rule Florence, except for a few brief periods, from the early 1400s to 1737. Their cultural interests led them to become patrons of the arts, and Florence became an art center under their rule. Michelangelo and Raphael were among the artists the Medici helped.

Giovanni de' Medici is considered the first great Medici. He made a fortune in banking and commerce in the late 1300s. His son Cosimo de' Medici became the first Medici to win wide fame. He ruled Florence from 1434 to 1464 and gave large sums of money for the arts. Cosimo's grandson Lorenzo de' Medici was the most famous Medici. Called "Lorenzo the Magnificent," he ruled Florence from 1469 to 1492. Under him, Florence achieved its greatest splendor and was one of Italy's most powerful cities.

▲ **Lorenzo de' Medici** was the political and cultural leader of Florence when the city was the center of the Italian Renaissance in the 1400s. Lorenzo was called "the Magnificent" because of his achievements as a ruler, supporter of the arts, and author.

The Medici influence extended to Rome when three members of the family became popes. Leo X reigned from 1513 to 1521 and Clement VII from 1523 to 1534. Leo XI was pope for only 27 days in 1605. Two women of the Medici family became queens of France. They adopted the French spelling of the name, de Medicis. Catherine de Medicis, the wife of Henry II and mother of three French kings, was a powerful force in France from 1559 until her death in 1589. Marie de Medicis married Henry IV. After his death in 1610, Marie ruled until her son Louis XIII took over.

The Renaissance, the period following the Middle Ages, involved a rebirth of classical sensibilities. The Latin root of the word renaissance is the same as other English words involving birth, such as natal, nativity, and nascent. Thus, the word literally means "rebirth."

now you know!

✔ Many Renaissance scholars were humanists. Humanism holds that the study of humankind and of the world is most important. Poets and philosophers concerned themselves with this world, not the next; with the world of nature, not that of theology; with men, not angels.

✔ One of the most important Renaissance innovations was the development of a superb vernacular (the language spoken by the people) literature, furthering the development of native languages. Until then, most writing had been in Latin.

✔ Albrecht Dürer of Germany was a great painter and engraver. Having visited and studied in Italy himself, he is largely responsible for the spread of the ideas and ideals of Italian art into northern Europe.

✔ It is estimated that before Gutenberg built his movable type printing press in the 1450s, there were no more than 100,000 books, all laboriously hand copied, in Europe. By 1500, there were perhaps 9 million.

✔ Lorenzo de' Medici ("Lorenzo the Magnificent") ruled Florence from 1469 to 1492. Under him, Florence achieved its greatest splendor and was one of Italy's most powerful cities.

THE REFORMATION AND COUNTER REFORMATION

Humanist scholarship on the eve of the Reformation had established a list of complaints against the Church. Scholars such as Lefèvre d'Etaples and Erasmus had made major criticisms, not only of "Old Learning," but of the mechanistic religious practices of the day: salvation hinging on numbers of indulgences acquired, on pilgrimages, and on fasting. Erasmus criticized the ignorance and folly of the monks, whose religious lives were often less than spiritual, chaste, and impoverished.

Theology in Conflict

The Reformation

By the early 1500s, the Catholic Church was facing serious problems, including a growing secularism in its hierarchy, ignorance among the lower clergy, and widespread abuses, such as simony (sale of church offices), pluralism (holding of more than one church office), and violation of vows of celibacy.

Humanists pointed to errors of translation in the official Vulgate Bible. These errors destroyed the scriptural basis for some doctrines and opened the way for attack on others. In earlier periods of decline, the church had found the inner resources to reform itself; under the Renaissance papacy, it did not.

Martin Luther, a German religious reformer of the 1500s, became the leader of the Reformation, the movement that led to the birth of Protestantism. ▶

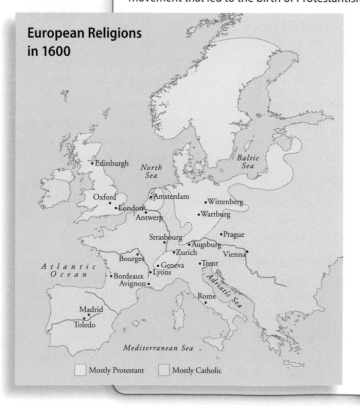

European Religions in 1600

Edinburgh
North Sea
Baltic Sea
Oxford
Amsterdam
London
Antwerp
Wittenberg
Wartburg
Strasbourg
Prague
Augsburg
Bourges
Zurich
Vienna
Geneva
Trent
Bordeaux
Lyons
Avignon
Atlantic Ocean
Adriatic Sea
Rome
Madrid
Toledo
Mediterranean Sea

☐ Mostly Protestant   ☐ Mostly Catholic

Martin Luther. The matter was brought to a head by Martin Luther, a German monk and professor of theology. In 1517, Luther posted a list of grievances against the church, the "95 theses," on the cathedral door in Wittenberg, Germany. Ordered by Pope Leo X to rescind this challenge to church authority, Luther refused, saying, "On this I take my stand. I can do no other. God help me. Amen."

Luther's stand sparked the Protestant Reformation, giving rise to a number of Protestant denominations that split off from Roman Catholicism. The first of them was Lutheranism, which quickly gained followers in Germany. In Geneva, French-born scholar John Calvin led one of these splinter movements, preaching against church dogma, ritual, and pomp.

The Counter Reformation

The Roman Catholic Church struggled to make internal reforms and to stop the spread of Protestantism, but initially it faltered. Many German princes adopted Protestantism, and Lutheranism was recognized in the Holy Roman Empire by the Peace of Augsburg (1555). The ruler's religion was to be the legal religion of each German state. As migration to another state was allowed, subjects could move to a state where the official religion was their own.

Religious and Political Violence. Civil war raged in France and the Netherlands. In France, thousands of Calvinists, called Huguenots, were butchered in the St. Bartholomew's Day Massacre in 1572. In the Netherlands, the Protestant rebels, led by William of Orange, were eventually joined by the Catholics of the Low Countries in opposing the unpopular Spanish rule. In 1581, the northern provinces, aided by the British, separated from the southern provinces.

In 1588, Philip II of Spain, incensed at British intervention, sent the great Spanish fleet—the Invincible Armada—to conquer England and depose Queen Elizabeth I. His costly undertaking was a dismal failure, and when Henry IV took the throne in France, Catholic Spain lost its last ally in its attempt to reconquer the rebel Dutch United Provinces.

Thirty Years' War

In Germany, the Counter Reformation had gained strength, and from 1608 to 1609, German princes formed rival military alliances, grouping themselves in the Protestant Union and the Catholic League. Religious and political hostility erupted into three decades of war (1618–1648).

In 1635, five years after Sweden's king Gustavus Adolphus had joined the Protestant cause in the war, peace was reached. But Cardinal Richelieu of France, wishing to destroy Austrian and Spanish Hapsburg power, plotted to prolong the war. He allied France with Sweden, the Dutch princes, Savoy, and numerous German princes and was successful in weakening Hapsburg strength.

The war ended in Germany and the Netherlands in 1648 with the Peace of Westphalia, which gave France important territories on its German frontier and made the German states practically independent of the empire—and most vulnerable to French influence. Secularized church lands in Germany were returned to their 1624 holders, while Calvinists were tolerated. Spain recognized the independence of the United Provinces. The war between France and Spain, however, dragged on until 1659.

▲ **John Calvin** was one of the leaders of the Reformation that led to the development of Protestantism. Calvin helped establish Protestantism in Geneva, Switzerland.

now you know!

✔ The Catholic Church was facing serious problems in the early 1500s: a growing secularism in its hierarchy, ignorance among the lower clergy, and widespread abuses, such as sale of church offices, holding of more than one church office, and violation of vows of celibacy.

✔ In 1517, Martin Luther, a German monk and professor of theology, posted a list of grievances against the Church on the cathedral door in Wittenberg, Germany. Luther's act sparked the Protestant Reformation, giving rise to a number of Protestant denominations.

✔ While the Roman Catholic Church struggled to make internal reforms and to stop the spread of Protestantism, Lutheranism was recognized in the Holy Roman Empire by the Peace of Augsburg (1555).

✔ From 1608 to 1609, German princes formed rival military alliances, grouping themselves in the Protestant Union and the Catholic League. Religious and political hostility erupted into the Thirty Years' War (1618–1648).

THE AGE OF DISCOVERY AND COLONIZATION

Europe's drive to explore and colonize overseas was as important as any other development given impetus by the Renaissance. By the end of the Middle Ages, Europeans had considerable knowledge of Asia, received from ancient writers, Crusaders in the Middle East, travelers to the Far East, and merchants involved in commerce with Muslim ports in the eastern Mediterranean and the Black Sea. But they knew little of sub-Saharan Africa and were totally unaware of the existence of the Americas, Australia, and Antarctica.

Over the 200-year period from 1450 to 1650, all this would change. (See also pages 28–33.)

Trade fueled the fires of curiosity and courage that drove early explorers into unknown waters and lands. Many did not return. ▶

Trade and Exploration

Portuguese Leadership

The desire of Europeans for goods available only from the Orient (such as spices, precious teak, and sandalwood from Southeast Asia, and silks and porcelain from the Far East) sent merchants in search of new and better trade routes.

Portugal, with its long Atlantic coastline on the Iberian peninsula, took the lead in searching for an all-water route to the Orient. The Portuguese hoped to reach the Indian Ocean by sailing south along the west coast of Africa, rounding its southern tip, and sailing north into the Indian Ocean. Prince Henry the Navigator sponsored a series of voyages during the first half of the 15th century that advanced this route until first Bartholomeu Dias and then Vasco da Gama rounded Africa's southern cape. In 1498, da Gama reached Calicut in India and opened up Portuguese trade there.

A Trading Empire. Portugal began building a maritime empire that would monopolize African and Asian trade for the entire 16th century. They had already set up trade with kingdoms in West Africa, such as Benin and Kongo, dealing largely in slaves. In East Africa, they conquered the Swahili city-states and established trading posts in Mozambique and Zanzibar. In 1511, they captured Malacca, a center of trade on the Malay peninsula. From there they moved on to dominate the Spice Islands in the Indonesian archipelago and to trade with Ming China and with feudal Japan.

By this time, Portugal had also gained a stake in the Americas. In 1500, a Portuguese fleet under the command of Pedro Cabral had been blown so far off course as it sailed down Africa's west coast that it crossed the Atlantic and reached Brazil. At first, the Portuguese used Brazil only as a penal colony, but soon the Portuguese king was granting tracts of lands to colonists who turned them into thriving sugar plantations, using slave labor.

Spanish Exploration and Conquest

Four years after Dias rounded the African cape, Christopher Columbus, an Italian sailing for Spain, set out to reach the East by sailing west across the Atlantic. In October 1492, he reached the Americas, though he thought it was Asia.

Hearing of kingdoms in Mexico, Central America, and South America that were rich in gold, Spanish *conquistadores* set out to conquer the native peoples and capture their wealth.

In 1519, Hernán Cortés launched his attack on the Aztec kingdom of Mexico. Within 2 years, he had destroyed the capital at Tenochtitlán, robbed the Aztecs of their gold and silver, and brought most of central Mexico under Spanish rule. Ten years later, Francisco Pizarro attacked the Inca Empire in South America. By 1535, he had overrun the empire. In a period of only about 15 years, the two most powerful civilizations of the Americas had fallen to superior weapons and Spanish domination.

Ferdinand Magellan was a Portuguese sea captain who led the first expedition that sailed around the world, from 1519 to 1522. He was the first European to cross the Pacific Ocean, Earth's largest ocean. Magellan did not live to complete the voyage around the world, but his leadership made the entire expedition possible. Many scholars consider it the greatest navigational feat in history. ▼

The Great Explorers	
1405–1434	Cheng Ho of China explores the coast of Vietnam, the Persian Gulf, the Red Sea, and East Africa.
1487–1488	Bartholomeu Dias of Portugal is the first European to round the Cape of Good Hope; he was originally part of the expedition that discovered Brazil.
1492	Christopher Columbus, an Italian sailing for Spain, lands in the Bahamas.
1497–1504	Vasco da Gama of Portugal is the first European to reach India by sea; John Cabot of Italy explores Newfoundland, Greenland, and the Chesapeake Bay for England; Amerigo Vespucci of Italy explores the eastern coasts of Central and South America.
1504–1520	Hernán Cortés explores the Yucatán and Mexican coasts and leads the Spanish conquest of Mexico.
1513	Ponce de León explores Florida and Vasco Núñez de Balboa crosses the Isthmus of Panama to the Pacific Ocean, both for Spain.
1519–1522	Ferdinand Magellan's ship *Victoria*, sponsored by Spain, is the first to circumnavigate the globe.
1531–1541	Francisco Pizarro of Spain explores the west coast of South America and conquers the Inca.
1534–1536	Jacques Cartier of France travels south on the St. Lawrence River as far as present-day Montreal.
1579	Francis Drake claims California for England.
1609–1611	Henry Hudson of England, sailing for the Dutch East India Company, explores the Chesapeake, Delaware, and New York bays.
1642	Abel Tasman of the Netherlands discovers Tasmania and New Zealand.
1768–1779	James Cook of England charts the coasts of New Zealand and the east coast of Australia; he also discovers the Hawaiian Islands.

Commence and Beyond

Spain's American Empire. Spain divided the vast American lands into five provinces and organized them under a central government ruled by the Council of the Indies from the Spanish capital at Madrid and by five viceroys, representatives of the king who each governed a province.

Spanish settlers arrived in America to exploit the rich silver mines of Mexico and Peru and to turn the Indian lands into giant plantations and ranches. For the Indians, life under foreign domination was a disaster. Diseases brought from Europe decimated their populations. Enslavement in Spanish mines and on Spanish plantations and ranches killed still more.

In the face of such a death toll and of Indian resistance to working for the Spanish, there was a severe labor shortage. Importation of slaves from Africa began in earnest, about 1510, and by 1650, nearly 200,000 Africans had been brought to Spanish colonies, particularly the Caribbean islands.

Dividing Up the World

England, France, and the Netherlands quickly joined Spain and Portugal in the exploration and colonization of the world. In 1497, England sent the Italian sea captain John Cabot in search of a north-west passage to the Orient through North America. England laid claim to much of North America and colonized small islands in the West Indies. France and the Netherlands soon joined England in claiming land and colonizing in both places.

Enter the English and the Dutch. Across the seas in Asia, English commercial interests struggled to establish trade with the Spice Islands. The British East India Company battled the Portuguese to win trading rights there and in India. With the British acquisition of the major ports of Bombay and Calcutta, England positioned itself for colonial predominance. The Dutch made gains in the Indonesian islands of Southeast Asia when they drove the Portuguese and the English out of the Spice Islands and won a monopoly over East Indian trade.

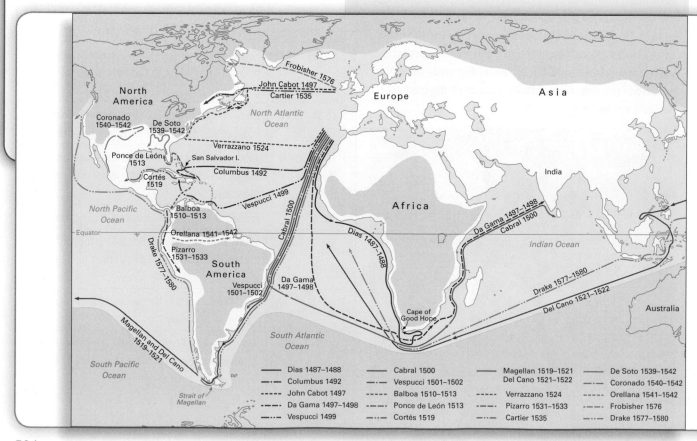

The Commercial Revolution

The revival of trade that began in medieval Europe was the first of the economic developments that constituted a full-scale revolution in the European economy. Urban commercial centers grew in size and number throughout Europe. Local and regional self-sufficiency was increasingly replaced by a geographical division of labor, in which regions concentrated on what they did best or what they seemed best suited for.

Long-distance commerce was stimulated by western Europe's penetration of overseas areas, which expanded the source of goods in demand and provided new markets, although both did not necessarily occur in the same area. The East, for example, had little desire for Europe's primitive exports, and demanded coined money in exchange for its spices, fine cloths, and other products.

Overseas shipping, banking, and commerce to handle increased trade volumes, stock companies to finance commercial ventures, and government protection of business and industry all increased dramatically. By 1750, small-scale medieval trading had developed into capitalism.

Linking the Globe

By 1600, the Spanish had explored Central and South America and parts of North America. Spain had established numerous colonies there. Spain tried to claim all of North America. But the French and English set up their own colonies and explored much of the continent themselves. Meanwhile, Russians moved east to explore Siberia and Alaska.

Changing Focus. During the European Enlightenment, a historical period from the late 1600s to the late 1700s, the goals of exploration began to change. Expeditions of the 1500s and 1600s focused on trade, religious missions, and colonization. By the 1700s and into the 1800s, exploration focused increasingly on science. However, European rulers did not support scientific expeditions simply to increase knowledge. Science offered the promise of more accurate maps, the discovery of new and valuable resources, and international prestige.

European explorers gradually filled in the outlines of the areas unknown to them. They mapped the Pacific Ocean, worked their way through the interiors of Australia and Africa, and reached the Arctic and Antarctic.

◄ **European knowledge of the world** expanded greatly in the 1400s and 1500s. European explorers sailed around Africa's tip to Asia and began mapping the Americas. In the late 1400s, expeditions departed from Spain seeking direct ocean routes to India. They visited South America's east coast, North America's northeast coast, and the Caribbean. Between 1400 and 1519, explorers sailed south around South America to the eastern shore of the Pacific Ocean. They also reached the southern United States and Central America. By 1535, expeditions had visited Indonesia and completed the first trip around the world. From 1539 to 1580, explorers searched northeast Canada for a northwest passage to Asia.

now you Know!

✔ The Portuguese hoped to reach the Indian Ocean by sailing south along the west coast of Africa, rounding its southern tip, and sailing north into the Indian Ocean. Prince Henry the Navigator sponsored a series of voyages during the first half of the 15th century that advanced this route.

✔ In 1519, Hernán Cortés launched his attack on the Aztec kingdom of Mexico. Within 2 years, he had destroyed the capital at Tenochtitlán, robbed the Aztecs of their gold and silver, and brought most of central Mexico under Spanish rule.

✔ The Spanish, suffering a severe labor shortage, began importing slaves from Africa in about 1510. By 1650, nearly 200,000 Africans had been brought to Spanish colonies, particularly the Caribbean islands.

✔ By the 1700s and into the 1800s, exploration focused increasingly on science, which offered the promise of more accurate maps, the discovery of new and valuable resources, and international prestige.

CHINA—FROM MING TO MANCHU

By the mid-1500s, China's Ming dynasty was in decline. (See page 485.) The population doubled between 1400 and 1600, from 75 million to 150 million. Slowing levels of production could not supply it. But China was strong enough to resist European domination. The Mings had expelled the Portuguese, the first European traders to reach China; by 1557, the Portuguese were restricted to the trading center of Macao. In the 1600s, other European traders were limited to the port city of Guangzhou, where they were forced to comply with severe trade restrictions passed by the Chinese.

▲ **Nurhachi,** first emperor of the Ch'ing dynasty

China in Decline

Rise of the Manchus

In the early 1600s, a new enemy threatened Ming rule—people from Manchuria who called themselves Manchus. In 1644, Manchu armies overwhelmed the Ming capital at Beijing. A Manchu emperor, Nurhachi, took the Chinese throne. The Manchus proclaimed themselves the Ch'ing (or Qing) dynasty and made Beijing their capital.

The Ch'ing dynasty, an empire established by the Manchu people of Manchuria, ruled China from 1644 to 1912. ▼

- — Boundary of present-day China
- Russian Empire
- Mongolia
- Beijing
- Korea
- **CHING (Manchu)**
- Japan
- Tibet
- India
- Guangzhou
- Taiwan
- Burma
- Hong Kong
- Annam

Manchu Rule. The Manchus comprised only about 2 percent of the population of China, so to rule in China, they had to have Chinese cooperation. To get it, the Ch'ing dynasty retained the Ming form of government, including the civil service examinations to select government officials.

By 1800, China covered the largest area in its long history and had a population estimated at 300 million, double its population of only 200 years before.

The White Lotus Rebellion. The population explosion placed great pressure on the peasantry, whose need for land grew with their numbers. In 1796, unhappy peasants supported a revolution mounted by the Buddhist White Lotus Sect against Manchu domination. They finally succeeded in putting down the White Lotus Rebellion but grew weaker in the process, setting the stage for more uprisings and for threats from trade-hungry Westerners.

The Opium War

In the last half of the 18th century, British traders had begun to use opium produced in India to pay for the tons of Chinese tea imported to Britain. As a result, a serious opium addiction infiltrated all strata of Chinese society. In 1800, the government forbade the foreign traders to bring any more opium into China.

For years, traders ignored the ban on opium importation. In 1838, the Ch'ing dynasty prescribed the death penalty for opium dealing. The following year, it captured and burned all the chests of British-owned opium it found in Guangzhou. Britain retaliated by sending its warships to fire on Guangzhou. The Opium War had begun. For the next 3 years, superior British forces humiliated the Chinese. In 1842, the Ch'ing rulers were forced to pay the British an indemnity, to cede Hong Kong to British control, and to open several ports to British trade.

But when the Chinese resisted implementing this first of a series of "unequal agreements," the Opium War roared to life again as France joined Britain in attacking China in 1856. A second Chinese defeat led to the Treaty of Tientsin in 1858. The treaty forced China to open many new ports to Westerners, including Americans and Russians, and allowed these foreigners to live and travel in China while gaining political and economic power.

National Disintegration

During this same period, internal dissension was wracking China. From 1850 to 1864, the Taiping Rebellion, a major uprising mainly of peasants, spread throughout China and took the lives of 20 to 40 million people. It so weakened the Ch'ing dynasty that it fell prey to still more foreign inroads.

China was forced to cede pieces of territory and spheres of influence to Western powers: Russia, Britain, France, Portugal, and Germany. From 1894 to 1895, Japan fought China for control of Korea. Japan forced the Ch'ing dynasty to pay a large indemnity and to cede it vast areas, including the island of Taiwan.

In 1899, the United States, having no sphere of influence of its own in China, convinced other powers to accept the Open Door Policy, which granted equal trading privileges to all powers in China.

The Boxer Rebellion. Angered at all these incursions, Chinese secret societies united. The Righteous Harmony Fists sought to drive all "foreign devils" out of China. In 1900, it staged the Boxer Rebellion, attacking the foreign quarter of Beijing. An army of 18,000 foreign soldiers defeated the Boxers, and once again, China had to pay reparations and grant concessions.

The Ch'ing dynasty was nearing its end. An uprising in 1912 would sweep the last Manchu emperor from the Chinese throne.

◀ **Fort Macao** on the Pearl River was the site of significant action during the Opium Wars.

JAPAN—FEUDALISM TO IMPERIALISM

In the century after the 1460s, Japan was an armed camp. Peasants in the countryside were forced to take up swords to protect their communities. Temples with large landholdings trained their own armies of warrior-monks to protect their assets. Some estate owners gathered private armies of samurai to guard their lands. Samurai without masters roamed the country offering to fight for pay. The most powerful samurai became regional lords called daimyo. They exercised control over many armed warriors, governed large areas of farmland, and fought each other for military supremacy during the 1500s.

Era of the Samurai

Reunification

Beginning in 1568, three military leaders who would reunite Japan emerged. The first was Oda Nobunaga, the son of a daimyo and a warrior of the Taira clan. After becoming master of three provinces, he made the shogun his puppet and became dictator of central Japan.

On his death in 1582, his lieutenant Toyotomi Hideyoshi, a peasant soldier who had risen to the rank of general, continued the drive to unify Japan. By 1590, military conquest had made him ruler of a united Japan. He led Japan in its war against China in 1592 over Korea, weakening the Ming dynasty there and supplying a foretaste of later Japanese expansionism.

In 1600, two years after Hideyoshi's death, his ally Tokugawa Ieyusu completed the work of Japanese unification by taking command of the new national government and having himself declared shogun.

The Tokugawa Shogunate

The Tokugawa shogunate would rule Japan for 250 years. The emperor continued to act as a figurehead from his imperial court at Kyoto. The Tokugawa shoguns governed from their capital at Edo.

The Tokugawa governed in two ways. They ruled directly the one-quarter of Japan they owned, and they ruled the rest through the nearly 300 daimyo who held individual feudal estates. The shoguns' extensive military power and ingenious checks on power kept the daimyo in line and ensured the peace. One check involved "alternate attendance," a system that demanded each daimyo to spend every other year at Edo. This regulation had the dual effect of keeping the daimyo under the shogun's close observation and of causing the daimyo to spend his money to support two residences rather than to build up military power.

Once peace was established among the daimyo, their samurai evolved from rugged warriors into an educated elite who administered their daimyos' estates and acted as local government officials. The samurai became Japan's learned professional class.

◄ **A samurai** wipes blood from his sword after a battle. The samurai were members of Japan's warrior class. They were known for their self-discipline and for their bravery in combat.

Western Impact

Japan had its first experience with Europeans when Portuguese merchant ships arrived there in 1542. Christian missionaries and more traders from Portugal and Spain arrived soon after. At first, the Japanese were tolerant of them. The Japanese learned about and traded for European firearms, such as muskets, which they used in their battles for reunification. In 1600, Dutch and English merchants began to arrive in Japan, introducing intrigues to help them beat their European competitors.

The Tokugawa soon grew wary of the influence the foreigners were having on Japan. In 1637, the government closed off all contact with the West. It expelled all foreigners—missionaries and traders—and allowed only one Dutch trading post to remain, at Nagasaki. The government forbade all Japanese to leave the country. Christianity was bloodily stamped out wherever it had taken root.

For the next 200 years, Japan enjoyed peace and prosperity as internal trade thrived, the merchant class grew, and commercial centers evolved into great cities. But then the West, once again, began to threaten in the same imperialist fever that had propelled it into India and China.

Perry Arrives in Japan

In 1853, the United States sent a naval mission, under Commodore Matthew C. Perry, to Japan to demand that the Japanese open their country to trade. As United States Navy guns pointed at them from Edo (now Tokyo) Bay, the Japanese were well aware of the fate the Chinese had suffered at the point of British guns in the Opium War. (See page 507.) In 1854, they reluctantly signed the Treaty of Kanagawa, agreeing to American demands. Within a period of 2 years, Japan had signed similar treaties with Great Britain, France, Russia, and the Netherlands.

Civil War. The Tokugawa shogunate's capitulation to the West stirred up fierce opposition to its continued rule in Japan. Opponents rallied around the emperor and the court at Kyoto, demanding that the emperor be returned to power and that Tokugawa military rule be overthrown. In 1866, civil war broke out between the imperial and shogunate factions, and in 1868, the imperial side won. The last Tokugawa shogun turned over his extensive estates to the 15-year-old emperor Meiji, who moved his court from Kyoto to Edo, which was renamed Tokyo. The emperor's long reign lasted until his death in 1912, a reign that was called the Meiji ("enlightened rule") Restoration.

◀ **Commodore Matthew C. Perry** led a naval mission to Japan in 1853. The United States government sent Perry to open diplomatic and trade relations with the Japanese. The mission ended Japan's isolation from the rest of the world. In 1854, Japan signed a treaty opening two ports to U.S. trade.

Japan Becomes a World Power

Restoration

The leaders who emerged during the restoration's early days were energetic young men from the samurai class. They believed that Japan's only defense against domination by Western powers was to modernize along the Western industrial model.

The Japanese now sent commissions to Europe and the United States to study Western railroad and telegraph systems, factories, munitions manufacturing sites, and shipyards. They studied Western military forces and chose to model a new Japanese army along German lines and a new Japanese navy along British lines, decisions that allowed them to easily defeat China in the Sino–Japanese War of 1894–1895.

Japan's rapid militarization and industrialization was really part of a complete social, political, and economic revolution. During this time, the new compulsory education program made Japan one of the only nations in the world with virtually no illiteracy. The universal draft calling all Japanese men to military service removed the monopoly by the samurai of that occupation and instilled in the draftees loyalty, obedience to the emperor, and the glory of death on the battlefield. The merchant class emerged with new power and prestige as the *zaibatsu,* family-owned industries, came to dominate the Japanese economy, Mitsubishi and Mitsui among them.

The End of Feudalism. In 1871, feudalism was officially abolished in Japan, and the central government under the emperor reorganized the old feudal estates into provinces that it could tax, legislate for, and administer uniformly. The abolition of feudalism was not without its opponents, mainly samurai bands who staged several uprisings. The most serious uprising was the Satsuma Rebellion of 1877, which the central government put down decisively, strengthening itself further.

The emperor and his cabinet formed an oligarchy that dominated the central government. Dissidents intent on even more Westernization agitated to break oligarchic control and introduce more democratic government. Once again, Japan sent out a commission, this time to study Western governments. The model they adopted was the German one, and in 1889, Japan got a constitution that established a bicameral legislature, the Imperial Diet, with an upper house of peers and a lower house elected by property owners of means. However, the Diet was given only limited powers, and the emperor and his ministers retained their oligarchic powers. Behind their powers lay the military, which wielded strong control over governmental policies.

Asian powers in 1900, a point at which Japan was just about to emerge as a rising world power ▶

Japanese Expansionism

Like the industrialized Western nations, Japan experienced rapid population growth and urbanization. And like them, Japan grew imperialistic for the same reasons: the desire for new markets in which to sell their goods and the need for industrial raw materials.

The Sino-Japanese War of 1894–1895 was the first step, and victory in it caused Westerners to begin viewing Japan as a power to be reckoned with. In 1903, Japan reinforced this view when it went to war against Russia over influence in Korea and Manchuria. Repeated Japanese victories forced Russia to accept the Treaty of Portsmouth in 1905, by which Japan took over Russian railroad and mining rights in Manchuria and paved the way for Japanese annexation of Korea in 1910. Japan had become a first-class world power.

▲ *Moonlit Street Scene in Edo* is one of many prints of the city created in the 1800s by the Japanese artist Hiroshige. Edo was renamed Tokyo in 1868, when it became Japan's capital.

Time Line—Japan's Rapid Modernization, 1854–1905	
1854	The United States forces Japan to reopen Japan to foreigners.
1868	With the end of the Tokugawa dynasty and the beginning of the Meiji Restoration, the capital moves to Edo, which is now called Tokyo.
1869	Yukichi Fukuzawa's 10-volume *Things Western* triggers a wave of Westernization.
1870	The first newspaper is published in Japan.
1871	The yen is adopted as the official currency.
1872	Japan's first railway line is opened. Built with technical advisors from Great Britain, it travels between Tokyo and Yokohama.
1877	The University of Tokyo is founded.
1894–1895	The Sino-Japanese war occurs, with Japan emerging victorious.
1899	Japan enters into its first joint venture with foreign capital: the newly founded Nippon Electric Corporation (NEC) and the United States' Western Electric.
1900	The population of Japan exceeds 44 million.
1904–1905	Japan defeats Russia in the Russo-Japanese War.

✔ The Ch'ing dynasty retained the Ming form of government, including the civil service examinations to select government officials.

✔ In the last half of the 18th century, British traders had begun to use opium to pay for the Chinese tea imported to Britain. When the Chinese tried to prevent it, Britain retaliated by sending in warships. The Opium War had begun.

✔ The Tokugawa shogunate ruled Japan for 250 years. While the emperor acted as a figurehead, the Tokugawa shoguns governed from their capital at Edo.

✔ In 1854, the Japanese signed the Treaty of Kanagawa, which opened two ports to American trade.

✔ During the restoration, the Japanese studied Western military forces and chose to model a new Japanese army along German lines and a new Japanese navy along British lines, decisions that allowed them to easily defeat China in the Sino-Japanese War of 1894–1895.

✔ In 1903, Japan went to war against Russia over influence in Korea and Manchuria. Repeated Japanese victories forced Russia to accept the Treaty of Portsmouth in 1905.

THE RISE OF DEMOCRACY AND NATIONALISM

The modern period began in the early 17th century with the dawn of the Enlightenment, which seemed to suggest an unalterable line of progress for humanity. These hopes have been dampened by the consequences of modern state formation and war, which have cast doubt on the future of the West. Even the hopeful nationalist movements of the 19th century only hid sectional animosities that still exist today.

▲ **René Descartes**

The Age of Reason

The Enlightenment

The Enlightenment was a period in history when philosophers emphasized the use of reason as the best method of learning truth. The philosophers of the Enlightenment believed that human beings have a unique advantage over all other creatures because they can reason. They contrasted reason with ignorance, superstition, and uncritical acceptance of authority—all of which they felt had dominated the Middle Ages. They blamed people in authority, particularly the leaders of the Roman Catholic Church, for keeping others in ignorance to maintain their own personal power.

The Power of Math. The philosophers of the Enlightenment were greatly influenced by discoveries in the physical sciences, such as the law of falling bodies discovered by Galileo in Italy and the laws of gravitation and motion formulated by Sir Isaac Newton in England. The philosophers saw that great discoveries such as these were made through the use of mathematics. Because of mathematics, scholars discovered laws of nature that otherwise would have remained unknown. As a result, the philosophers of the Enlightenment believed mathematics was the model that all other sciences should follow.

▲ **Sir Isaac Newton** invented a new kind of mathematics, discovered the secrets of light and color, and showed how the universe is held together.

Deism. The philosophers of the Enlightenment were convinced that the universe can be understood by the human mind. This is not an accident, the philosophers emphasized, because God could have created a universe too complex to be grasped by human beings. Instead, God created a universe ideally adjusted to the reasoning powers of people.

Most of the philosophers believed that after God had created the universe, He left it strictly alone. This idea, called *deism,* rules out the possibility of miracles or other special acts by God. According to deism, God regulated nature so that it proceeds mechanically. Future events are therefore fully predictable on the basis of earlier events. The philosophers liked to think of the universe as a clock that keeps perfect time because it was designed by a superior clockmaker.

Influence of the Enlightenment. The thinkers of the Enlightenment formulated ideals of human dignity and worth. In France, unjust social and political conditions were criticized by a group of philosophers known as the *philosophes.* This group, which included Diderot, Rousseau, and Voltaire, greatly influenced leaders of the French Revolution. The philosophes and, more importantly, the English thinker John Locke also influenced the leaders of the Revolutionary War in America. (See page 323.)

The urge to advance knowledge also explains why great effort was made to organize and circulate the results of the scientific research of the time. Many scholars gathered, organized, and published this knowledge. In fact, the Enlightenment could be called the "age of the encyclopedia." The most famous reference work was the French *Encyclopédie,* edited by Diderot and Jean d'Alembert and completed between 1751 and 1772.

Major Figures of the Enlightenment	
Thomas Hobbes (1588–1679)	English philosopher and author of *Leviathan*
René Descartes (1596–1650)	French mathematician and philosopher who devised analytical geometry and is the father of modern philosophy
Baruch Spinoza (1632–1677)	Dutch philosopher and author of *Ethics*
John Locke (1632–1704)	English philosopher; author of *An Essay Concerning Human Understanding*
Sir Isaac Newton (1643–1727)	English physicist and mathematician; achievements include the binomial theorum, the calculus, the reflecting telescope, the nature of light and color, and the law of gravitation; author of *Principia*
Charles-Louis Secondat Montesquieu (1689–1755)	French historian and philosopher and author of *The Spirit of the Laws*
Voltaire (pseudonym for François-Marie Arouet) (1694–1778)	French writer and philosopher; author of *Candide,* one of the most widely read satires of all time
Georges-Louis Leclerc, Comte de Buffon (1707–1788)	French naturalist whose writings helped advance the study of biology and geology
David Hume (1711–1776)	Scottish philosopher and historian and author of *Treatise of Human Nature*
Jean-Jacques Rousseau (1712–1778)	Swiss-born French philosopher who praised life uncorrupted by civilization
Denis Diderot (1713–1784)	French philosopher, writer, critic, and dramatist
Immanuel Kant (1724–1804)	German philosopher; author of *Critique of Pure Reason*
Edward Gibbon (1737–1794)	English historian; author of *Decline and Fall of the Roman Empire*
Thomas Paine (1737–1809)	English-born American political writer; author of *Common Sense* and *The Rights of Man*
Thomas Jefferson (1743– 1826)	Scholar, author, farmer, natural scientist, architect, and third president of the United States

American Revolution

Many historians trace the beginnings of the modern world to the revolutions of the late 1700s. The first of these was the American Revolution (1775–1781), in which 13 British colonies in North America declared their independence from the mother country and successfully resisted British military pressures for 7 years. (See also pages 56–61.)

The American patriots based their revolution on Enlightenment ideas, claiming that all men have certain God-given rights. In 1788, the new United States adopted a Constitution that offered political and civil rights to a much larger part of the population than in any European country. The new republic drew on both the political traditions of Britain and the philosophies of French thinkers (Montesquieu, Rousseau) of the mid-1700s. In turn, the American experiment inspired a new wave of revolution in Europe.

French Revolution

The year after the adoption of the U.S. Constitution, the French overthrew a government dominated by an absolute monarch, hereditary nobility, and higher clergy. The middle classes and landless peasants united in their opposition to the extravagance and arbitrary policies of King Louis XVI, the aristocracy, and the powerful French church.

Pressed by the need for money, Louis called the Estates-General (a weak parliamentary body) in 1789. The members began the revolution by forming the National Assembly, which they proclaimed the true representative of the French nation. The king recognized the assembly, but rumors about his intentions and serious food shortages in Paris led a mob to storm the Bastille on July 14, 1789. They freed the prisoners there (many of whom had been sentenced for political offenses). Violence soon spread to the provinces.

▲ *Liberty Leading the People* by Eugene Delacroix

The National Assembly abolished feudal privileges and enacted the *Declaration of the Rights of Man* (August 1789), proclaiming individual liberties for all. The king was driven from his palace at Versailles in October, and church lands were nationalized in November. The monarchy was finally abolished in 1792.

The Violence Intensifies. The revolution was applauded in America and by many in Europe. But other European monarchies feared the spread of revolutionary politics, and in 1792, they began a series of wars against the new French Republic. They attempted to invade France in 1792 and 1793, both times unsuccessfully.

Meanwhile, the revolution itself was entering its most radical and bloodiest phase. In January 1793, the king and his queen, Marie Antoinette, were beheaded. Then in September, Maximilien de Robespierre (1758–1794) and his radical Jacobin faction gained control of the government. They instituted the notorious Reign of Terror (1793–1794), in which some 17,000 persons were executed. Robespierre was overthrown in July 1794, and moderate elements again took control. By 1797, Napoleon had begun his rise to power, and in 1799, he took control of the government, ending the revolutionary period.

Napoleon

Napoleon reorganized France's administrative machinery to centralize control, stabilized its currency, and instituted sweeping legal reforms. By 1802, he had also made peace with the countries that had taken up arms against France.

Then, in December 1804, Napoleon proclaimed the French Empire and crowned himself emperor. The countries of Europe united against the new empire, and Napoleon soon faced great military challenges.

A Military Genius. By 1805, Napoleon was at war with an alliance that included England, Russia, Austria, and other powers. Napoleon conquered most of Europe in the ensuing years. At its height, his empire included most of present-day Germany, Austria, Italy, Belgium, the Netherlands, and Spain. But when he invaded Russia in 1812, his army was forced to retreat during a severe Russian winter, suffering disastrous losses. Then, in 1813, Napoleon was defeated at the Battle of Nations. Napoleon abdicated on April 11, 1814, and was exiled to the island of Elba in the Mediterranean. He escaped, however, and returned to France on March 1, 1815. Beginning his famous Hundred Days, Napoleon assumed power and again began the war against the allied European powers. He met final defeat in June 1815, at the famous Battle of Waterloo in Belgium.

▲ **Napoleon I** posed in his study for French painter Jacques-Louis David in 1812, above. David served as the court painter to the French emperor.

now you KNOW!

✔ A key tenet of the Enlightenment was that human beings have a unique advantage over all other creatures: they can reason. Enlightenment thinkers contrasted reason with ignorance, superstition, and uncritical acceptance of authority—all of which they felt had dominated the Middle Ages.

✔ Most of the philosophers of the Enlightenment believed in a theory called *deism*. According to deism, God regulated nature so that it proceeds mechanically. They liked to think of the universe as a clock that keeps perfect time because it was designed by a superior clockmaker.

✔ The French Revolution began when the National Assembly proclaimed itself the true representative of the French nation. Rioting in Paris ensued as a mob stormed the Bastille on July 14, 1789. Violence soon spread to the provinces.

✔ After seizing control of the government in 1799, Napoleon proclaimed the French Empire and crowned himself emperor in December 1804.

EUROPE IN TRANSITION

The revolutions in North America and France, along with the Napoleonic Wars that gripped Europe at the beginning of the 1800s, were only the harbingers of great change that would soon overtake the continent, fracturing empires and creating new nations in the process. As governments transformed, the relationship between rulers and the people was changing as well.

Political Transformations

Congress of Vienna

This historic conference in 1814–1815 met to decide the future of Europe following Napoleon's abdication. The purpose was to ensure a lasting peace by establishing a balance of power between rival nations. Monarchies in France, Spain, and Austria were restored, and a confederation of German states was organized. New kingdoms were set up in the Netherlands and Poland. Peace in Europe was maintained for some years following the congress, largely through the skillful diplomacy of the Austrian statesman Clemens von Metternich (1773–1859). But his repressive measures met increasing opposition.

The Congress of Vienna was bitterly criticized for many years because it ignored the strong democratic and nationalistic sentiments of many Europeans. These sentiments contributed to democratic revolutions in numerous European countries in 1830 and 1848 and to nationalistic movements in Germany and Italy. But some historians have praised the Congress of Vienna for creating a balance of power in Europe and for not treating defeated France too harshly.

The nations of Europe in the wake of Napoleon's defeat and the Congress of Vienna ▼

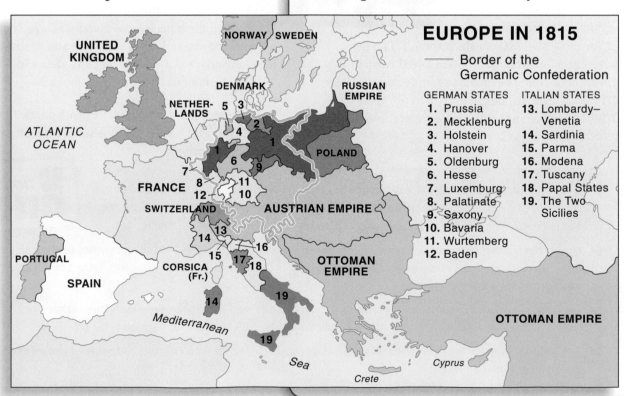

EUROPE IN 1815

— Border of the Germanic Confederation

GERMAN STATES	ITALIAN STATES
1. Prussia	13. Lombardy–Venetia
2. Mecklenburg	14. Sardinia
3. Holstein	15. Parma
4. Hanover	16. Modena
5. Oldenburg	17. Tuscany
6. Hesse	18. Papal States
7. Luxemburg	19. The Two Sicilies
8. Palatinate	
9. Saxony	
10. Bavaria	
11. Wurtemberg	
12. Baden	

PETER THE GREAT

Following a century of relative stagnation and political turbulence, the westward advance was renewed by **Peter I** ("the Great"; ruled 1682–1725), who Westernized many Russian institutions and cultural ideas.

His strong, centralized administration enabled Peter to seek "windows to the west." After two decades of war, Russia absorbed Sweden's Baltic lands, from Karelia to the Polish frontier, by the terms of the Treaty of Nystadt in 1721. In 1715, St. Petersburg became the new capital and Peter made advances into Turkish territories in search of a Black Sea outlet. Westernization continued during the reign of Elizabeth (1741–1762).

Emergence of Russia

By the 1400s, Muscovy, or Moscow, was the most important feudal principality in the Russian Empire. In this period, Prince Ivan III (the "Great"; ruled 1462–1505) increased the territory and position of Moscow, reduced the threat of the Mongols to the south, and laid the foundations of modern Russia. Ivan considered himself the heir of the Byzantine Empire, now lost to the Ottoman Turks, and successor to the Byzantine and Roman emperors. He assumed the title of czar, or Caesar.

Successive czars strengthened their power within the increasingly centralized state, while extending its territory. Ivan IV ("the Terrible"; ruled 1533–1584) ruthlessly subdued the nobles, or boyars, created a centralized state administration, and expanded the empire east and west.

Liberalism and Nationalism

With the defeat of Napoleon and the conclusion of the Vienna settlement in 1815, Europe settled down to enjoy the calm of peace. Although each nation reacted differently to the absence of war, the essential dynamic forces in every country were the same.

Despite its relative success, the Congress of Vienna totally ignored the vital issues of nationalism and liberalism. It was this shortsightedness that eventually destroyed the peace effected for some years by the settlement.

The liberal aspirations that had been created during the revolutionary era could not be eradicated by a stroke of the pen. As the groups to which liberalism appealed grew stronger, their challenge to the constituted governments became sharper, until they later exploded into revolution.

Similarly, the nationalism that had been aroused by French occupation could not be turned off with the departure of the French. This was particularly true in Italy and Poland, where the withdrawal of the French was followed by occupation by the Austrians and the Russians.

In the period 1815 to 1848, it was the challenge of liberalism that tended to provide the greatest impetus to change. After 1848, the situation became more complicated. In some countries, notably Great Britain and Italy, liberalism retained its vigor. In other countries, such as France, its suppression led to the rise of socialism. In Austria and Germany, liberalism was submerged in a wave of nationalism.

New Governments, New Nations

Great Britain. In Great Britain, the new class of industrial workers demanded representation in Parliament. The situation came to a crisis following passage of the Corn Laws, which worked to the advantage of the landed aristocracy and led to more misery for the industrial class. In 1819, riots broke out and several people were killed by government troops in the Peterloo Massacre.

In the following years, though, Parliament was finally brought around to reform. The Reform Bill of 1832 gave the industrial class much greater representation in Parliament, and by 1884, the urban workers had finally been enfranchised.

Austria. The rise of nationalism in Germany posed a constant threat to Metternich of Austria, who was trying to maintain Austrian rule over a weak and loosely organized German Confederation. The Hungarians, Italians, and Poles ruled by the Austrian Empire also seethed with discontent as nationalistic fervor rose to oppose foreign rule, especially that of Metternich's oppressive brand.

Metternich responded with determination. To keep the empire intact, he created a virtual police state and held back the growth of industrialism for fear that it would breed revolutionary discontent among the urban factory workers.

France. In France, the industrial class was small and weak, but tension grew when the Bourbons were restored to the monarchy by the Congress of Vienna in 1815. Both peasants and bourgeoisie were angered by the return to power of the monarch and the aristocrats. When Charles X (ruled 1824–1830) sought to restore the prerevolutionary power of Church and State by revoking the liberal rights granted by France's 1814 constitution, revolution broke out again. The July Revolution of 1830 only succeeded in turning the monarchy over to Louis Philippe of the House of Orléans; however, yet another revolution, in 1848, led to the establishment of the Second Republic.

The benefits of the new government of 1848 went to the bourgeoisie rather than to the industrial workers, who still lacked unity and influence. The working class, whose demands derived from the socialist Louis Blanc, was put down with brutal force during the June Days slaughter. This marked the origin of socialism as an active and potent force in French politics.

Louis Napoleon, the nephew of Napoleon Bonaparte, was elected president in 1848. In 1852, he led a coup d'état and declared himself Emperor Napoleon III of the Second Empire. The empire worked hard to establish an industrial base, but it suffered diplomatic catastrophes, was decisively defeated in the 1870 Franco-Prussian War, and was generally unpopular and weak.

▲ **Napoleon III, or Louis Napoleon,** ruled as emperor of France from 1852 to 1870. He was the nephew of Napoleon I.

1848 Uprisings

News of the French revolt of 1848 electrified all of Europe. The Hungarians seized the opportunity to break away from Vienna; the Romans overthrew papal power; people in northern Italy felt their day of liberation had come. Revolution even broke out in Vienna.

In Prussia, a state without a middle or industrial class, the powerful military machine was operated by king and nobles working together. Following the French Revolution, the state embarked on a liberal course, abolishing serfdom and granting various concessions to the free peasantry. The result was a liberal Prussian state that elicited fierce patriotism, national pride, and loyalty from all classes of people.

Spotlight on...

GUISEPPE GARIBALDI

Giuseppe Garibaldi was a military hero who fought to create an independent, united Italy.

Forced into exile as a young man, Garibaldi went to South America, where he aided the Brazilian province of Rio Grande do Sul in a revolt against the Brazilian government. Later, Garibaldi fought for Uruguay against Argentina.

In 1860, Garibaldi and his troops, called the red shirts, conquered the Kingdom of the Two Sicilies, which controlled much of southern Italy and the nearby island of Sicily. These areas became part of the Kingdom of Italy, proclaimed in 1861. During the 1860s, Garibaldi fought to bring Rome into the kingdom by ending the pope's rule there. But Garibaldi's efforts failed. In 1866, Garibaldi helped Italy gain the city of Venice from Austria. During the 1860s and 1870s, he was repeatedly elected to the Italian parliament.

National Unification

A major aspect of European development in the mid-1800s was the forging of two new national states in major geographical-cultural regions—modern Germany and Italy.

Germany. An industrial middle class began to emerge in Germany in the 1840s, and it was powerfully affected by the French revolution of 1848. At the Frankfurt Assembly, convened in May 1848, representatives from the numerous German states called for popular representation in a unified Germany—but Prussian assistance, which was needed to break Austria's control, was not forthcoming. The revolution was defeated in the spring of 1849.

Otto von Bismarck became the prime minister of Prussia in 1862. He began to build a liberalized state to enlist the support of the growing working and industrial classes. A constitution and progressive social legislation followed. In 1866, he forced Austria out of German affairs, and in 1870, he rallied the southern German states to victory in the Franco-Prussian War against the French. Germany was at last united under Prussian influence.

Italy. In Italy, Count Cavour, prime minister of Sardinia, forged the unification of much of Italy, using liberalism as a tool for popular support in much the same way that Bismarck had done. In inciting Austria, which controlled large portions of Italy, to war in 1859, Cavour was aided by Napoleon III of France. Austria was soundly defeated, and the national patriot Giuseppe Garibaldi then succeeded in forcing Sicily and southern Italy into the new union. The new nation of Italy was proclaimed in 1861, with Victor Emmanuel of Sardinia its new king.

Industrial Revolution

The Industrial Revolution grew from very humble beginnings in Britain, where its first impact was felt in the area of cotton textile manufacture.

During the 1770s and 1780s, a burst of inventive genius revolutionized the textile industry. From hand operations on simple machines, such as spinning a single thread or weaving only one bolt of cloth at a time, the industry progressed to multiple spindles and complicated looms.

As the machines grew larger and more complicated, they could no longer be run by human power. Instead, they were run by waterpower. Ultimately, even waterpower became insufficient. The development of the steam engine provided a solution to the power problem. Its application in the steam locomotive was to revolutionize transportation.

Areas rich in natural resources but without easy access to water transportation, the only economical method of transport before the railroad, gained new importance. When rail transportation was brought to those areas, they became centers of industrial activity and prosperity.

Social Effects. It was through industrialization that western Europe was transformed from a rural to an urban civilization. Factories drew formerly rural peoples together to one spot for the purpose of production of manufactured goods. Men, women, and children worked long hours for a salary, and labor abuses became prevalent. These abuses, including child labor, unsafe conditions, overwork, and underpayment, led to the growth of socialism.

Cities sprang up and grew in size by leaps and bounds. Urbanization increased political awareness and activity among the masses. The new industrial classes in Britain and France began gradually to undermine the power of the landed aristocracy. This was particularly true in Great Britain, the supreme industrial power of the world, where human labor became an important and valuable resource.

France industrialized much more slowly, and in Prussia, Austria, Russia, and most of the other nations of Europe, the time for industrialization had not yet come. Most nations feared the emergence of a working class that might clamor for equal rights and of subversive democracies resembling those of the tumultuous French Revolution.

▲ **The Industrial Revolution** caused profound changes in the workplace. Used to working on farms or in small shops, people increasingly were employed in large factories.

now you Know!

✔ The Congress of Vienna (1814–1815) was an effort to ensure a lasting peace in Europe by establishing a balance of power between rival nations. Monarchies in France, Spain, and Austria were restored and a confederation of German states was organized. New kingdoms were set up in the Netherlands and Poland.

✔ Peter the Great (ruled 1682–1725) Westernized many Russian institutions and cultural ideas. His modernized, strong, centralized administration enabled Peter to seek "windows to the West."

✔ One of the most significant effects of the wave of nationalism and liberalism that swept Europe in the mid-1800s was the forging of two new national states in major geographical-cultural regions—modern Germany and Italy.

✔ The Industrial Revolution began when the British textile industry was transformed by increasingly efficient machinery in the late 1700s. As the machines grew larger and more complicated, more power was needed to run them. Ultimately, it was the development of the steam engine that provided a solution to the power problem. Its application in the steam locomotive was to revolutionize transportation.

Key Innovations of the Industrial Revolution	
The Textile Industry	
One of the most spectacular features of the Industrial Revolution was the introduction of power-driven machinery in the textile industries of England and Scotland.	
Spinning machines	Between 1774 and 1779, Samuel Crompton developed the spinning mule, which efficiently spun fine yarn for high-quality cloth. During the 1780s and 1790s, larger spinning mules were built. They had metal rollers and several hundred spindles. These machines ended the home spinning industry.
Weaving machines	In the mid-1780s, steam-powered looms that made all the movements for weaving were introduced. By 1835, the United Kingdom had more than 120,000 power looms. Most of them were used to weave cotton.
The Steam Engine	
Many of the most important inventions of the Industrial Revolution required much more power than horses or water wheels could provide. Industry needed a new, cheap, and efficient source of power and found it in the steam engine.	
Early steam engines	In 1698, Thomas Savery patented a pumping engine that used steam. In 1712, Thomas Newcomen created an improved engine that came into general use during the 1720s. Newcomen's steam engine wasted much heat and used a large amount of fuel.
James Watt improves the steam engine	By 1785, a Scottish engineer named James Watt had eliminated many of the problems of earlier engines. Watt's engine used heat much more efficiently than Newcomen's engine and used less fuel.
Refining tools for precision work	Because Watt could not find a tool that drilled a perfectly round hole, his engines leaked steam. In 1775, John Wilkinson invented a boring machine that drilled a more precise hole. By 1825, English inventors had developed a planer to smooth the surfaces of steam engine metal parts.
Coal and Iron	
Coal provided the power to drive the steam engines and was needed to make iron. Iron was used to improve machines and tools and to build bridges and ships. Britain's large deposits of coal and iron ore helped make it the world's first industrial nation.	
The revolution in ironmaking	Between 1709 and 1713, Abraham Darby succeeded in using coke to smelt iron. Coke is made by heating coal in an airtight oven. Smelting with coke was much more economical and efficient than smelting with charcoal. The smelting, puddling, and rolling steps could be combined into a continuous operation near the coal fields.
Transportation	
The growth of the Industrial Revolution depended on industry's ability to transport raw materials and finished goods over long distances. Thus, the story of the Industrial Revolution is also the story of a revolution in transportation.	
Waterways	Until the early 1800s, waterways provided the only cheap and effective means of hauling coal, iron, and other heavy freight. In 1807, the American inventor Robert Fulton built the first commercially successful steamboat. Within a few years, steamboats became common on British rivers.
Roads	In the early 1800s, Scottish engineers John Loudon McAdam and Thomas Telford made important advances in road construction: the macadam type of road surface, which consists of crushed rock packed into thin layers; and a technique of using large flat stones for road foundations.
Railroads	In 1804, Richard Trevithick built the first steam locomotive. However, steam locomotives did not begin to come into general use for passenger and freight transportation until the late 1830s.

EUROPEAN IMPERIALISM

The exploration and colonization begun by Europeans around 1500, followed by industrialization in the late 1700s, brought the far-flung parts of the world into contact as never before. (See pages 502–505.) Their earliest forays into Asia had left Europeans in awe of the wealth and power they found in the courts and cities of Asia's oldest civilizations. Asians were not similarly impressed with the restless and upstart Europeans they encountered, and Asian rulers, convinced of their own civilizations' superiority, did not recognize and were therefore not prepared for the global revolution under way.

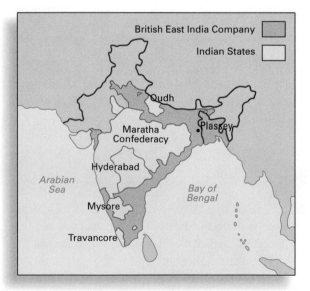

▲ **The British East India Company** controlled much of the Indian subcontinent by the early 1800s. The Indian states of Hyderabad, Mysore, Oudh, and Travancore were not directly held by the company but were allied states. Only the Maratha Confederacy in central India was not allied to the company.

Southeast Asia

Culture Clashes in Southeast Asia

In 1500, Southeast Asia was a complex mix of contending cultures. On the mainland, the influence of the formerly great Khmer Empire was limited to what is today southern Cambodia. To the west was the Thai kingdom of Ayutthaya, unified by Rama Thibodi in 1350 and ruled by the dynasty he founded until 1767. To the east was Vietnam. Under the Tranh dynasty (1225–1400), it had achieved some degree of political stability. Under the Le dynasty (1428–1788), it had absorbed Champa, its neighbor to the south, and had made its neighbor Laos a vassal state.

Burma was the third state vying for preeminence on mainland Southeast Asia. There, two brilliant kings, Tabinshweti (ruled 1531–1550) and Bayinnaung (ruled 1550–1581), unified the Burmese kingdoms under the Toungoo dynasty (1486–1752). Toungoo expansionism produced a series of wars against the Thais that went on from 1531 to 1605.

In 1767, the Burmese, under the Korbaung dynasty (1752–1885), invaded the Thais once again, but they were repelled. In 1782, a new Thai dynasty, the Chakkri (which rules Thailand to this day), came to power. It made its capital at Bangkok and then expanded to the east, occupying parts of Cambodia and Laos.

Prior to 1500, much of the Indian archipelago had been under the domain of the Hindu Majapahet Empire, based in Java. But the coming of Islam effected its demise in 1520. A number of maritime commercial states emerged under Muslim rule, notably Malacca on the west coast of the Malay peninsula, Aceh in northern Sumatra, Demek in northern Java, and Tidore and Ternate in the eastern islands of the Indonesian archipelago.

Enter the Europeans. It was into this complex of Southeast Asian states that the Europeans, led by the Portuguese, entered in the early 1500s, eager for trade and colonization. When the busy port of Malacca was conquered by the Portuguese in 1511, a new period began in the history of Southeast Asia, the period of European trade expansion and conquest.

Europeans were somewhat more successful in the archipelagos. By the late 1500s, Spain had gained control of the Philippines, first reached in 1521 by a Spanish expedition to circumnavigate the globe under the command of Ferdinand Magellan. Spanish missionaries succeeded in converting the majority of Filipinos to Christianity, and Hispanic culture became firmly entrenched.

The city of Rangoon in Burma (now Myanmar) was captured by the British in 1824. ▶

From Trade to Political Intervention. In the Indonesian archipelago, the well-financed Dutch East India Company was able to force the Portuguese out in 1641. After waging war against the local sultans, the company expanded its influence over the area for the next century and a half.

Western Domination. European governments themselves began taking over rule of the colonies from the trading interests. In 1799, the Dutch government revoked the Dutch East India Company's charter and declared the Dutch East Indies a royal colony. When Britain revoked the British East India Company's charter in 1858, taking control of the government of India, it also took responsibility for governing that company's interests in Southeast Asia. At the same time, the French government began to step up its efforts to gain imperial holdings in Southeast Asia.

- By the early 1900s, all of Southeast Asia was under Western domination.
- Great Britain controlled Burma, Malaya, Singapore, northern Borneo, and eastern New Guinea.
- The Dutch held Indonesia; the French held Indochina.
- The United States controlled the Philippine Islands, having won them in its war with Spain in 1898.
- Only Thailand retained its sovereignty.

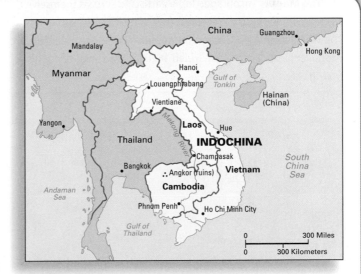

▲ **This map shows French Indochina,** which included Cambodia and Laos in the west, and Vietnam in the east. France divided Vietnam into Tonkin, Annam, and Cochin China. France gained control of Indochina in the 1800s.

India—from Moguls to the Raj

Of Asia's major civilizations, India was the first to be profoundly affected by contact with Europe. At the beginning of the 16th century, the Muslim Delhi Sultanate was crumbling and the Hindu Rajput princes were fighting among themselves to gain control.

▲ **The Moguls** encouraged India's artists to surpass themselves in creativity. Perhaps the greatest fruit of their artistic success is the Taj Mahal in Agra, a magnificent pink marble structure built by Mogul emperor Shah Jahan (ruled 1628–1658) as a tomb for his young wife.

The Mogul Empire. This upheaval made it possible for a small force of Mongols to capture Delhi in 1526 and subjugate the Rajput princes. This marked the beginning of India's glittering Mogul Empire. (Mogul is the Persian word for "Mongol.") Within 200 years, the empire covered nearly the entire Indian subcontinent.

The Mogul Empire flowered under the rule of Akbar, from 1542 to 1605. Though a Muslim himself, he worked to end Muslim discrimination against Hindus. His successors did not agree; they reinstated oppressive measures against the Hindus.

Challenges to the Empire. The Mogul Empire reached its height under the rule of Aurangzeb (ruled 1658–1707). However, his ceaseless wars to bring all of the Indian subcontinent under Muslim rule weakened the Moguls, encouraging others to challenge their reign.

In 1739, marauding Persians sacked the Mogul capital at Delhi, followed 18 years later by raiders from Afghanistan. Mogul monarchs retained the title of emperor for another century, but their realm shrank to the area surrounding Delhi, and their former empire disintegrated into hundreds of small states.

British Inroads. The British East India Company, which had prospered under the Moguls, took advantage of the political unrest to strengthen its position in India. In 1757, British military forces took control of Bengal, an important center of trade in northeastern India. Then, in 1784, the British government passed the India Act, which gave the British Parliament the right to share the power over East India Company policy in India and to name high company officials. For the next half century, the British continued to expand their control in India.

◄ **British India** was set up in 1858. The United Kingdom took over East India Company lands and also had indirect control of the remaining states of Baluchistan, Hyderabad, Kashmir, Mysore, Rajputana, and Travancore.

Colonial Rule. In 1857, Indian soldiers serving under the British rebelled. The Indian Rebellion convinced Parliament to revoke the British East India Company's charter and take control of India itself. In 1858, Parliament put India under full colonial rule. Great Britain continued the economic exploitation begun under the East India Company. Indian farmers were encouraged to grow cotton, rather than food, to supply cotton mills in England. Indian manufacture was discouraged in order to create a market for British manufactures in India.

▲ **The Indian Rebellion** spread throughout northern and central India. The rebellion began because Indian soldiers, called sepoys, had religious objections to some British Army orders. The sepoys captured several major cities, including Delhi, shown here, Kanpur, and Lucknow.

Westernization in India. The British directed the construction of a vast railroad system and telegraph network to link the sprawling subcontinent. British schools educated the sons of the higher castes, fostering an Indian professional class to assist the British in carrying out colonial rule.

Ironically, British education for young Indians helped launch a movement to rid India of British rule. Learning about the struggles of the English for democracy stirred Indians' desire for political freedom for themselves. In 1885, Hindu nationalists founded the Indian National Congress. By the early 1900s, it was advocating the total expulsion of the British from India.

✔ By 1500, the influence of the Khmer Empire was limited to what is now southern Cambodia. The empire was under increasing pressure from its expansionist neighbors: the Thai kingdom of Ayutthaya to the west and Vietnam to the east.

✔ By the late 1500s, Spain gained control of the Philippines. Spanish missionaries succeeded in converting the majority of Filipinos to Christianity, and Hispanic culture became firmly entrenched.

✔ By the early 1900s, all of Southeast Asia was under Western domination. Great Britain controlled Burma, Malaya, Singapore, northern Borneo, and eastern New Guinea; the Dutch held Indonesia; the French held Indochina; and the United States controlled the Philippine Islands. Only Thailand retained its sovereignty.

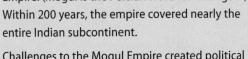

✔ In 1526, a small force of Mongols captured Delhi, marking the beginning of India's glittering Mogul Empire. (Mogul is the Persian word for "Mongol.") Within 200 years, the empire covered nearly the entire Indian subcontinent.

✔ Challenges to the Mogul Empire created political unrest that allowed the British East India Company, which had prospered under the Moguls, to strengthen its position in India.

✔ An uprising among Indian soldiers in 1857 convinced the British Parliament to revoke the British East India Company's charter and take control of India itself. In 1858, Parliament put India under full colonial rule.

EUROPEAN DOMINANCE IN THE SOUTHERN HEMISPHERE

Among the last places that European nations cast their considerable influence were the continents and islands in the Southern Hemisphere. While traders and explorers had sailed to and settled on the coast of Africa, it was many years before they began to explore and conquer the interior. As for New Zealand and the island continent of Australia, these were among the last places on Earth to be discovered by Europeans, and it wasn't long before their territorial ambitions were directed there.

The Last Distant Places

Australia, New Zealand, and Oceania

The last places in the world to be settled lay far from Earth's major landmasses. They included Australia, New Zealand, and the numerous islands of Oceania in the South Pacific that make up Micronesia, Melanesia, and Polynesia. Perhaps as long as 30,000 years ago, people from Southeast Asia began fanning out toward the northern coast of Australia and the western islands of Micronesia and Melanesia. Over the centuries, they continued their movement until, by the AD 700s and 800s, they had reached Australia and Tasmania. They also reached far enough east and south to inhabit Polynesia from the Hawaiian Islands and the area from Easter Island to New Zealand. In their far-flung domains, these migrants developed in isolation from outside cultural influences.

Early History. Australia's first settlers, the Aborigines, were a nomadic hunting and gathering people. One of the most culturally advanced of these island peoples were the Polynesian Maoris, who settled in New Zealand about 1,500 years ago.

Sea Explorers
——— Jansz 1606 (Neth.)
—·— Tasman 1642, 1644 (Neth.)
------- Cook 1770 (U.K.)
— — — Bass and Flinders 1798–1799 (U.K.)
——— Flinders 1801–1803

Land Explorers
——— Blaxland 1813
—·— Hume and Hovell 1824
------- Sturt 1829–1830
— — — Mitchell 1835
—·— Eyre 1840–1841
——— Leichhardt 1844–1845
—·— Burke and Wills 1860–1861
------- Stuart 1861–1862
— — — Warburton 1873
—·— Forrest 1874

0 ——— 500 Miles
0 ——— 500 Kilometers

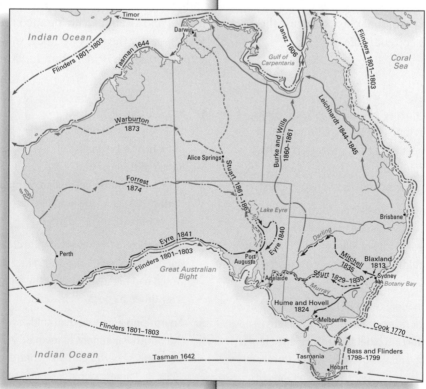

◄ **This map** shows the routes of some European expeditions to Australia. Exploration began with sea voyages to Australia during the 1600s and 1700s. Explorers crossed the interior of the continent in the 1800s.

Exploration by Europeans. Prior to 1500, Australia's existence was virtually unknown to the rest of the world. A Dutch ship, blown off its course, made the first European contact in 1616. From then on, Dutch navigators mapped the north and northwest coasts of New Holland, as they called the island continent.

Throughout this period, the islands of Oceania were gradually being reached by Europeans. Foremost among these explorers was Britain's James Cook. His expeditions, in the 1760s and 1770s, charted New Zealand and Australia's east coast. He also discovered New Caledonia in Melanesia and the Cook Islands in Polynesia, and visited Tonga and the Hawaiian Islands, where he was killed in a conflict with the islanders.

▲ **James Cook** explored much of the Pacific before his violent death on Hawaii.

National Development. Following the founding of Australia's first colony in New South Wales, the British divided the continent up into additional colonies—Tasmania, Western Australia, South Australia, and Victoria. In 1850, these independent colonies won the right to self-government from the British; 2 years later, New Zealand won the same right. In 1901, the Australian colonies federated under the Commonwealth of Australia Constitution Act and became a dominion of the British Commonwealth. In 1907, New Zealand achieved this same status.

Colonization of Australia. Cook's charting of eastern Australia led to its colonization by the British. The first settlers were convicts. The agriculturally minded British quickly took over the most productive land to grow crops and to graze sheep, driving the Aborigines back into the deserts of the interior.

By 1850, the colonial population reached 400,000. The next year, gold was discovered, setting off a rush that doubled that number in a decade. By 1900, the population had grown to 4 million.

Colonization of New Zealand. The earliest European settlers in New Zealand were sealers and whalers, sailors who had jumped ship, and convicts who had escaped the penal settlements of Australia. By 1820, the British had founded several settlements in New Zealand. Like the Aborigines, the Maori natives suffered at the hands of colonists. Diseases brought by the Europeans decimated their population. In addition, the Maoris adopted European muskets, using them in intertribal wars that wiped out still more of their number. By the 1850s, the estimated pre-European population of 100,000 had been cut nearly in half.

To stop further encroachment, the Maori tribes tried to unify under one king; this led to a long series of Anglo-Maori wars. The Maori presented formidable resistance, but by 1872, they were finally beaten and the colonists continued to take their land at will.

Colonization of Oceania. By 1850, Europeans were settling on the islands of Oceania, building plantations that raised and exported cocoa, coconuts, coffee, and sugar.

Americans joined in colonization as well, especially in the Hawaiian Islands. By 1893, the American planters there were powerful enough to depose the last Hawaiian queen, Liliuokalani, and 5 years later, the United States annexed her former kingdom. (See page 158.)

The Struggle for Africa

SOUTHWESTERN

Europeans in Africa

Africa became a magnet for European trade and territorial ambitions around 1500. However, disease and African resistance helped to discourage Europeans from penetrating the interior of the continent. Some Europeans did establish trading posts and forts in certain coastal areas. From these bases, they influenced African life to an extent far beyond what their small numbers would indicate. In 1870, the Europeans began coming in greater numbers. Their military and technical sophistication helped them to eventually overwhelm the Africans.

Know now you!

✔ Europeans first reached Australia in 1616. Dutch navigators subsequently mapped the north and northwest coasts of the island continent.

✔ By 1850, the colonial population in Australia was 400,000. When gold was discovered a year later, it triggered a rush that doubled the population in a decade. By 1900, the population had grown to 4 million.

✔ In 1893, Americans deposed the last Hawaiian queen, Liliuokalani. Five years later the United States annexed her former kingdom.

✔ One of the earliest European settlements in southern Africa was Cape Town, founded in 1652 to supply Dutch ships as they rounded the Cape of Good Hope.

✔ The Zulu Empire emerged in the late 18th and early 19th centuries. When they came in contact with the Boers, a conflict arose that neither side was able to win decisively, until the British sent in troops. European weapons won the day, and the Zulu Empire was destroyed.

✔ Cecil Rhodes pushed British expansion northward into Bechuanaland (modern Botswana), which Britain made a protectorate in 1885, and into the area named for him, Rhodesia (modern Zambia and Zimbabwe). In 1890, he became prime minister, virtually the dictator, of Cape Colony.

✔ By the early 1900s, all of Africa had been carved up and placed under European rule, with the exception of Ethiopia and Liberia.

Southern Africa

Rise of the Zulu Empire. By 1500, the Bantu migrations had finally reached southern Africa. The largest Bantu-speaking group to occupy southern Africa was the Nguni, subdivided into the Swazi, Zulu, and Xhosa peoples. The Bantu did not find it necessary to form strong centralized kingdoms, but in the 17th and 18th centuries, this changed because of the encroachment of European settlers. In the late 18th and early 19th centuries, the Zulu Empire emerged with the help of the brilliant military leader Shaka.

Clash Between the Boers and the British. One of the earliest European settlements in southern Africa was Cape Town, founded in 1652 to supply Dutch ships as they rounded the Cape of Good Hope. It grew into the thriving Cape Colony. As Dutch settlers pushed into the interior, they faced heavy resistance by Africans, many of whom they enslaved. During the Napoleonic wars, Great Britain seized control of Cape Colony, creating conflict between the descendants of the original Dutch settlers, the Boers, and incoming British settlers. Having abolished slavery themselves, the British wanted it abolished among the Boers. They also declared English the colony's official language.

In response, about 100,000 Boers left Cape Colony in 1836 and began a journey to the northeast to establish new colonies. They founded the Orange Free State, the Transvaal inland, and Natal along the southeast coast.

The Boers' expansion brought them into conflict with the Zulu Empire, a conflict neither was able to win decisively, until the British sent troops to battle the formidable Zulu warriors. European weapons won the day, and the Zulu Empire was destroyed.

Cecil Rhodes. In 1852, Great Britain had recognized the sovereignty of the Boer republics of Transvaal and Orange Free State, but in 1885, gold was discovered, whetting the British appetite for this land too. A guiding force behind Britain's drive for dominion over southern Africa was Cecil Rhodes, who had made a fortune in diamonds after coming to South Africa in 1870. He had pushed British expansion northward into Bechuanaland (modern Botswana), which Britain made a protectorate in 1885, and into the area named for him, Rhodesia (modern Zambia and Zimbabwe). In 1890, he became prime minister, virtually the dictator, of Cape Colony and began to plot the seizure of the Transvaal and Orange Free State for Britain as well.

The Anglo-Boer War. Rhodes's attempts to topple the Boer governments failed, but they created more conflict between the Boers and the British, and in 1899, the adversaries went to war. The Boer War was bitterly fought until 1902, when the Boers were forced to surrender. In 1909, the British Cape Colony and the Boer states were united into the self-governing British dominion of the Union of South Africa.

▲ **Boers (now called Afrikaners),** shown here, held the town of Mafeking (now Mafikeng) under siege for several months during the Anglo-Boer War of 1899–1902, or South African War. The siege lasted from October 1899 to May 1900.

Colonial Rule. By the early 1900s, all of Africa had been carved up and placed under European rule, with the exception of Ethiopia and Liberia, an independent West African state founded in 1821 by former slaves returned from the United States. For Africans, the adjustments were daunting. Large tribes were split up among different European colonies, and small tribes, often antagonistic to one another, were combined into one colony.

Tribal law was superseded by laws handed down from the colonial powers, and tribal rulers were replaced by European officials. Land was often taken from the Africans and given to European settlers to turn into plantations or mines. In some areas, Africans were restricted to "native reserves," similar to American Indian reservations. For the Africans, it was a bewildering time, as their traditional cultures were assaulted by the very different developed and industrialized European culture.

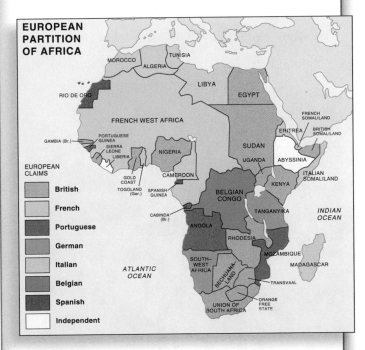

EUROPEAN PARTITION OF AFRICA

EUROPEAN CLAIMS
- British
- French
- Portuguese
- German
- Italian
- Belgian
- Spanish
- Independent

INDEPENDENCE IN LATIN AMERICA

Latin America denotes a vast area that includes Mexico, Central America, the West Indies, and South America. The name itself reflects the impact that Europeans speaking languages derived from Latin—Spanish, Portuguese, and French—had on the Americas beginning about 1500. Latin America had been carved into colonial empires by the European powers: Spain in the West Indies, Mexico, Central America, and much of South America; Portugal in Brazil; and France in Haiti in the West Indies. The colonial economies that developed during the 16th and 17th centuries were based mainly on plantation agriculture, herding, and mining, and they relied heavily on slave labor.

▲ **The slave revolt** in Haiti (1791–1801) was the first major revolution in Latin America.

The End of Colonial Rule

Colonial Times

During the 16th, 17th, and 18th centuries, Spain and Portugal were the major colonial powers in Latin America. During the 17th century, France, England, and the Netherlands also founded colonies, mainly in the Caribbean. (See also pages 504–505.)

Under the Spanish viceroys, individual government officials exercised great powers. Such personal government rooted Latin America in a form of autocracy that facilitated the rise of dictators.

Imbalance. Colonial society was essentially divided into a small and wealthy elite and a large and broadly impoverished lower class, in large part Indian and black. There was only a tiny middle class, mainly in the large cities. This dichotomy, with wealth in the hands of a few at the top and poverty the lot of the majority, would also far outlive the colonial period.

Revolution and Independence

By the 18th century, discontent with colonial rule began to rack Latin America. American Indians staged intermittent uprisings against their colonial masters. Enslaved blacks and the descendants of colonists, the Creoles, also rebelled. Educated Creoles were inspired by the writings of the Enlightenment's French philosophers and by the successful American Revolution to the north. The *mestizos,* people of mixed European and Indian blood, objected to what they saw as their treatment as third-class citizens.

Haiti. The first major revolution in Latin America occurred in the French colony of Haiti, the western half of the island of Hispaniola. In 1791, following the French Revolution, the slave population of the colony rebelled. They found a great leader in Pierre Toussaint l'Ouverture, a Haitian black who had been in the French army. By 1801, the slaves had gained control of all of Hispaniola. Napoleon sent troops to try to recapture the island, but they ultimately failed and Haiti became Latin America's first independent nation.

South America. When Napoleon invaded Spain in 1808, he declared his brother, Joseph Bonaparte, monarch. Spanish colonies in Latin America refused to accept this new king and responded by setting up autonomous governments in what are now Argentina, Chile, Colombia, and Venezuela. When Ferdinand VII returned to the Spanish throne in 1815, independence forces in Latin America resisted return to Spanish rule.

Simón Bolívar, a wealthy Venezuelan Creole, led the fight against Spanish forces in northern South America. In 1819, he led an army across the Andes Mountains to attack the Spanish at Boyacá in Colombia. This successful campaign led to the creation of the independent nation of Gran Colombia, made up of today's Ecuador, Venezuela, Colombia, and Panama.

At the same time, two other liberators, José de San Martín and Bernardo O'Higgins, led Argentina and Chile to independence by forcing Spanish withdrawal. In 1820, San Martín moved his troops north to Peru to drive the Spanish out of their last stronghold there. In 1825, the Spanish viceroy of Peru surrendered, ending Spanish rule in South America.

◄ **Simón Bolívar** has been called the "George Washington of South America" because his victories over the Spaniards led to independence for Bolivia, Colombia, Ecuador, Peru, and Venezuela. Bolivia, once part of Peru, was named in his honor.

Time Line—Latin American Independence	
1791–1801	The slave revolt in Haiti, on the western half of the island of Hispaniola, leads to its independence from France.
1810	The war for the independence of Mexico from Spain begins.
1811	Paraguay and Venezuela declare their independence from Spain.
1813	At the first Mexican Congress, Mexico is formally declared an independent nation.
1816	Argentina declares its independence from Spain.
1818	Chile declares its independence from Spain.
1822	Brazil declares its independence from Portugal.
1825	Bolivia declares its independence from Spain.
1836	Texas declares its independence from Mexico.
1846–1848	Mexican-American War
1862	The French Army invades Mexico.
1867	The French are driven from Mexico, Emperor Maximilian is executed, and the republic is reestablished.
1888	Slavery is abolished in Brazil.
1898	The Spanish-American War ends with Cuba gaining independence from Spain but succumbing to intervention from the United States. The U.S. also takes control of Puerto Rico.

Building New Nations

Mexico and Central America. Mesoamerica followed a somewhat different path toward independence. In 1810, Miguel Hidalgo y Costilla, a Mexican priest, led an army of Indian peasants against both Spanish officials and the Creoles of Mexico. The uprising failed, but it convinced the wealthier classes that they should retain Spanish rule, rather than risk social revolution.

However, in 1820, a liberal army rebellion against the king in Spain caused the conservative upper classes to change their minds, and they mounted an independence movement that succeeded. Mexico was declared a republic in 1824. In 1823, the states to the south had declared themselves the United Provinces of Central America, with their own constitution and president.

Brazil. Napoleon invaded Portugal in 1808, causing its king, John VI, to escape to Brazil and set up court in Rio de Janeiro. During his stay, he encouraged the colony's economic development. In 1821, he returned to Portugal to reclaim his throne, leaving his son Pedro to rule Brazil. In 1822, Pedro proclaimed Brazil's independence, overcame the resistance of Portuguese troops, and was crowned emperor of Brazil.

Miguel Hidalgo y Costilla is called "The Father of Mexican Independence." In 1810, he led a revolt against Spanish rule in Mexico. The heart in the upper right-hand corner of this portrait says *Libertad,* the Spanish word for liberty. ▼

Internal Strife

Simón Bolívar had hoped to unite the newly independent states into a league of constitutional republics, but clashing interests, bitter power struggles, and territorial disputes dashed this hope, and many separate nations emerged in Latin America. Though many adopted constitutions based on the United States model, true representative government would prove elusive.

Latin America's colonial background had not prepared it for democratic government. Land and wealth were concentrated in the hands of the few, mainly Creoles and the Roman Catholic Church. A great deal of political power lay in the hands of *caudillos*—tyrannical military leaders whose armies could make them dictators of the new republics. Power of any kind—political, social, or economic— totally eluded Indians, blacks, and poor mestizos, who made up the great majority of the population.

Economically, the new nations also faced formidable problems. The wars for independence had disrupted agricultural and mining production, on which the Latin American economies had been built. Foreign trade had withered, and roads and harbor facilities had fallen into disrepair. Industrialization, spreading rapidly through Europe and the United States, did not reach Latin America.

 *The United States favored Latin American independence from Europe and wanted to discourage any attempts by Spain to reestablish power in the Western Hemisphere. In 1823, U.S. president James Monroe proclaimed that "the American continents are henceforth not to be considered for future colonization by any European powers." Eager to increase its trade with the newly independent states of Latin America, Great Britain helped enforce the Monroe Doctrine by using its formidable navy to discourage any European moves in that area.*

National Development

It was this foreign industrialization that helped the nations of Latin America to strengthen themselves. Industrialized nations needed raw materials that Latin America could produce in abundance, as well as food products for growing populations.

Both foreign investment and waves of immigrants flowed into Latin America. Roads, bridges, railroads, telegraphs, and ports were built; mining methods were improved; and new agricultural areas were developed. The countries concentrated on exporting natural resources; they supplied industrialized economies without becoming industrialized themselves.

This economic development contributed to and grew out of the young nations' improved political stability. Argentina, Brazil, Chile, Uruguay, and Costa Rica were especially successful in achieving orderly governments, though they were more oligarchic than representative.

Foreign Relations. By and large, the nations of Europe honored the principles of the Monroe Doctrine. As the 1800s drew to a close, however, many Latin Americans began feeling that the United States was using the Monroe Doctrine to further its own dominance of the Western Hemisphere.

The Spanish-American War of 1898 fueled their fears. Cuban rebels had been fighting for independence from Spain. The United States declared war on Spain. Cuba won its independence from Spain, but the United States forced the Cubans to accept the Platt Amendment, giving the U.S. the right to intervene in Cuban affairs if they deemed it necessary. In addition to making

Mexico had a more difficult struggle toward stability. For much of the period from 1833 to 1855, it was led by a corrupt caudillo, General Antonio López de Santa Anna. During his rule, Mexico suffered the humiliation of losing Texas, California, and the rest of the Southwest to the United States. These losses resulted from the Texas war for independence in 1836 and the Mexican War of 1846–1848 (see also pages 102–103). A bitter civil war (1861–1867) eventually brought on the dictatorship of Porfirio Díaz, who ruled Mexico for nearly the whole period from 1877 to 1915.

▲ **The USS** *Maine* had gone to Havana to protect U.S. interests in Cuba, and its sinking was a precipitating cause of the Spanish-American War.

Cuba a virtual protectorate, the United States also took control of Puerto Rico.

As the 20th century began, Latin Americans became preoccupied with the further encroachments that the "Colossus of the North," as they called the United States, might make on them.

✔ In 1791, the slave population of the French colony Haiti rebelled. By 1801, the slaves controlled all of Hispaniola.

✔ Simón Bolívar led the fight against the Spanish in northern South America. A successful military campaign led to the creation of the independent nation of Gran Colombia, made up of today's Ecuador, Venezuela, Colombia, and Panama.

✔ In 1823, U.S. president James Monroe issued the Monroe Doctrine, which proclaimed that "the American continents are henceforth not to be considered for future colonization by any European powers."

✔ In 1810, Miguel Hidalgo y Costilla led a revolt against Spanish rule in Mexico. The uprising failed, but it set in motion the movement toward independence. Mexico was declared a republic in 1824.

✔ Under the rule of General Antonio López de Santa Anna, Mexico lost Texas, California, and the rest of the Southwest to the United States. These losses resulted from the Texas war for independence in 1836 and the Mexican War of 1846–1848.

now you know!

WORLD WAR I

In 1900, Europe dominated the world politically, economically, and culturally. Through its imperialism, it had carved up much of Asia and Africa into colonial preserves. Through its industrialism, it had developed prospering economies, unrivaled financial power, and formidable military might.

Yet within a short time, all this would change. In 1914, Europe engulfed itself in a world war that ultimately destroyed its world primacy. Conflicting interests among the nations of Europe created dangerous rivalries for colonies, greater national glory, and superior military might. Another matter was the "Eastern question" of who would control Eastern Europe, including the Balkan peninsula north of Greece.

Verdun. Row upon row upon row of crosses mark the graves of fallen soldiers in a cemetery at Verdun, France, where over 1 million died in February 1916.

The Great War: Time Line

June 28
Archduke Franz Ferdinand and his wife, the Duchess Sophie, are assassinated in Sarajevo. Gavrilo Princip, a Bosnian associated with a Serbian terrorist group called the Black Hand, would leap onto their car and shoot them both as they rode in the back seat. ▲

April 22
Poison gas is used for the first time by Germany.

1914

July 28
Austria declares war on Serbia.

August 1–4
Germany declares war on Russia (8/1) and France (8/3), then invades Belgium (8/4).

August 10
Austria-Hungary invades Russia, opening fighting on the Eastern Front.

September 6–9
The First Battle of the Marne: the Allies stop the Germans in France.

October 29
The Ottoman Empire enters the war on the side of the Central Powers.

1915

April 25
Allied troops try to open a new front at Gallipoli, at the mouth of the Bosporus. Unsuccessful, they pull out in December 1915.

May 7
A German submarine sinks the S.S. *Lusitania,* a British ocean liner, off the coast of Ireland. On the Eastern Front, the German and Austrian "great offensive" conquers all of Poland and Lithuania.

May 23
Italy declares war on Austria-Hungary.

August 20
At the Battle of Tannenburg, a vast Russian army is crushingly defeated by the Germans.

February 21
A strong German offensive begins at the Verdun fortress in France; the Battle of Verdun becomes the longest and bloodiest battle of World War I; over 1 million are killed.

April 6
The United States declares war on Germany.

June 24
American troops land in France.

October 24
Italians are forced to retreat in the Battle of Caporetto; 600,000 Italian soldiers are lost as prisoners, deserters, or casualties.

January 8
Woodrow Wilson introduces the Fourteen Points peace program.

March 3
With the Treaty of Brest-Litovsk, Russia's new Bolshevik government withdraws from the war.

March 21
Germany launches its last offensive on the Western Front.

1916   **1917**   **1918**   **1919**

May 31–June 1
The British fleet fights the German fleet in the Battle of Jutland.

July 1
Heavy fighting between British and German forces begins at the Battle of the Somme in northern France.

September
The Brusilov offensive costs the Russians over 1 million men.

December
The Romanian capital of Bucharest is captured by German troops.

November 20
Tanks are used en masse at Cambrai, France, by the British army.

December 7
The United States declares war on Austria-Hungary.

December 15
Russia signs an armistice with Germany, ending the fighting on the Eastern Front.

June 20
American troops face their first important battle at Château-Thierry; they join with the French to stop the German advance.

November 11
The armistice is signed by Germany and the Allies.

June 28
Five years to the day after the assassination of Archduke Franz Ferdinand, German representatives sign the Treaty of Versailles in its namesake palace. The treaty redraws the map of Europe and forces Germany to assume responsibility for the war. ▼

Unbalancing Alliances

A SYSTEM OF ALLIANCES

To understand how World War I came about, it is necessary to understand the European balance of power as the 20th century began.

Germany and Austria

Otto von Bismarck realized that Germany needed protection against a resurgent France, which was intent on recovering Alsace-Lorraine, which it had lost in the Franco-Prussian War (1870–1871). The Germans feared a two-front war, with Germany caught between Russia and France. To ensure his southern flank, Bismarck made a defensive treaty with the Austro-Hungarian Empire. This treaty, made in secret, guaranteed German support to Austria-Hungary if it was attacked by Russia. The loss of Austria's Italian territories had turned Austrian ambitions toward the Balkans, where they conflicted with Russian interests. Russia therefore found it against its interests to become friendly with any ally of Austria.

France and Russia

After its defeat by Prussia in 1870, France had learned the necessity of allies and set out to remedy the lack. France's natural ally was Russia, for the two had no areas of real conflict. The new power of a united Germany loomed ominously. Russia was desperately seeking capital to invest; France was as eagerly looking for good investments for its wealth. In 1894, the Dual Alliance, aligning France and Russia, became a reality.

Britain and Italy

The British felt secure behind their powerful navy and desired no permanent entanglements on the Continent. Only when its colonial empire was threatened did Britain begin to cast about for allies. By the end of the 1800s, the imperialist race had just about run its course, with France and Britain emerging the winners. Germany was a threat to both colonial empires; it was natural for Britain and France to turn to each other. In 1904, the Entente Cordiale between Britain and France came into being, reversing a diplomatic pattern existing since the 1300s.

Italy proved to be a special problem as it turned outward and entered the contest for colonies. The Italians were willing to sign treaties with everyone as long as they were permitted to create a colonial empire of their own. Italy finally allied itself with Germany and Austria-Hungary in the Triple Alliance in 1882. But a few years later, Italy's other obligations were practically to nullify its promise to support Germany and Austria.

The Great War Begins

By the early 1900s, two great power blocs, Germany and Austria-Hungary in central Europe, and a French-Russian alliance, supported by Great Britain, faced the center of Europe.

The Austrians were experiencing difficulties in the Balkans, a hotbed of nationalism. A number of small groups pledged to national liberation saw their mission in an almost messianic light.

One group in Austrian-held Bosnia, headed by a Serbian patriot and secretly backed by Serbia, assassinated the heir to the Austrian throne, Archduke Franz Ferdinand, on June 28, 1914, in Sarajevo.

The Austrians interpreted this as the first move in a new nationalist attack on the Austro-Hungarian Empire. Austria felt it had no alternative, if its empire was to survive, but to declare war on Serbia.

Outbreak. Austria declared war on Serbia on July 28. Russia, tied by treaty to Serbia, ordered a general mobilization of its armed forces. Germany felt it then had no choice, if the Schlieffen Plan was to be effective, but to throw its military machine into gear.

Germany declared war on Russia on August 1, 1914, and on France on August 3. According to the Schlieffen Plan, the Germans had to march through Belgium. Belgium, a neutral country, refused permission for German armies to cross its territory. The Germans denounced the treaties guaranteeing Belgian neutrality and marched in. This brought Great Britain into the war on August 4.

THE SCHLIEFFEN PLAN

Developed by Alfred von Schlieffen, the plan assumed Germany would have to fight both France and Russia. It aimed at a quick defeat of France while Russia slowly mobilized. But as Russian mobilization times improved, Germany came to rely on Austria-Hungary to cover the east. If war came, speed would be critical for Germany. Once it mobilized, it would have little option but to go to war.

Course of the War

Stalemate. During the first few weeks of the war, the Germans seemed about to prove the brilliance of the Schlieffen Plan. But French armies held at the Marne River, and the war on the Western Front settled down to static slaughter. An advance of 100 yards was hailed as a great victory and was purchased at a cost of thousands of dead and wounded. Machine guns, trenches, and barbed wire proved a match for the infantry and artillery. All that could be done was to wait and see which side bled to death first.

In the east the situation was more fluid. The Russian military machine began to collapse; the unpreparedness of the Russian imperial regime exposed shortages of supplies and a lack of organization.

Catastrophe was staved off for 3 years only because the main German force was busy in the west, and the Russian peasants were willing to die for their country. Finally, the peasants could take no more. The Russian armies dissolved at the front and revolution broke out in the Russian cities.

The deepest desire of most Russians was for peace. Vladimir Lenin, leader of the Bolshevik wing of the Russian Social Democratic Party, promised it.

With brilliant tactical insights, Lenin outmaneuvered rivals for power to bring the Bolsheviks to control of the Russian state. The net effect of the Russian Revolution in 1917 on the European conflict was to remove Russia from the war and permit the Germans one more year of battle.

War's End. In early April 1917, the United States, angered by Germany's unrestricted submarine warfare (under which it sank ships of belligerents and nonbelligerents alike), entered the conflict on the side of the Allies. This revitalization of Allied manpower, together with the cumulative effects of a British blockade of shipping in and out of German ports, brought Germany to its knees. (See also pages 164–167.)

On November 11, 1918, the war ended and the German Empire ended with it. It remained for the victors to pick up the pieces and to try to put Europe together again. A peace conference was convened in the great Palace of Versailles, outside of Paris.

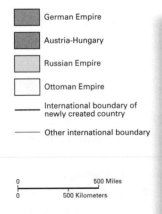

World War I (1914–1918) led to changes in many borders. Treaties that officially ended the war split Austria-Hungary and the Ottoman Empire into national states. Russia and Germany gave up territory. Although several states won independence, most Arab lands in the Ottoman Empire were placed under French and British rule. ▶

www.SWadvantage.com

Guilt and Punishment

The Treaty of Versailles

When the representatives of the Allied powers met at the Palace of Versailles on January 18, 1919, they shared, with few exceptions, a grim spirit of revenge. This reflected the changes both in governments and in warfare since the Congress of Vienna had met a century before. The Napoleonic wars had been made by governments, not by whole peoples, and had been considered instruments of national policy. Defeat merely closed off one avenue until the game could be played again.

World War I, in contrast, was waged on a mass basis by governments dependent on the support of their people. To gain this support, governments had to arouse mass emotions. No people could be expected to sacrifice its most vigorous generation just for some diplomatic goal or dynastic gain.

War on such a scale had to have a high moral justification, such as "to make the world safe for democracy," and it had to be directed against the forces of "evil." Only in such an atmosphere of intense and unreasoning emotion could so many millions be persuaded to believe that they were not to die in vain.

The greatest bloodletting in the history of Europe had just ended, and someone had to be punished.

Vladimir Ilyich Lenin

THE RUSSIAN REVOLUTION

The czarist regime in Russia had been weak and ineffectual for years, but it took the stresses of World War I to bring down the old regime. The Russian army lost disastrous battles against the Germans. The government and the economy under Czar Nicholas II (ruled 1894–1917) weakened steadily.

Workers took over St. Petersburg in February 1917. The czar was forced to abdicate, and a moderate provisional government was set up. Various Socialist parties opposed the government and undermined it and each other. Finally, the Bolshevik faction, led by Vladimir Ilyich Lenin (1870–1924), staged a coup in October, set up a Communist government with Lenin at its head, and made peace with Germany. Not all Russians went along with the Bolshevik government, and soon the Reds (Bolsheviks) and the Whites (anti-Bolsheviks) were involved in a bloody civil war. The war ended with the triumph of the Reds and the exile of the Whites in 1920. Lenin ruthlessly consolidated the rule of the Communist Party in the 4 years before his death.

▲ **Soldiers wore gas masks** for protection against poison gas attacks. Both sides used poison gas in World War I, and gas masks were important equipment in the trenches.

The Guilt Clause. The obvious candidate at Versailles for punishment was Germany, and the Treaty of Versailles contained a "guilt clause," under which the Germans were to assume ultimate responsibility for the war. All else followed from this. Germany was loaded with a reparations debt that it could not possibly pay and was stripped of its colonies. Territory in Europe was taken from Germany and given to the newly created states of Czechoslovakia and Poland.

The Treaty of Versailles was a bitter pill for the Germans to swallow, but they had no choice. The British refused to lift their blockade until Germany accepted the terms of the treaty. In June 1919, the German representatives signed.

The recognition of the principle of nationalism was the one pure principle embodied in the treaty, but this too proved to be a failure. Instead of removing the pressures caused by intense nationalism that had served so long to disturb the equilibrium of Europe, the terms of the treaty merely served to aggravate the pressures in such nations as Germany and Italy. Both saw their nationalist ambitions thwarted by the peace settlement. The League of Nations, an international peacekeeping body set up under the Treaty of Versailles, would later prove powerless to stop the aggression that grew out of these ambitions.

▲ **Prior to** the signing of the Treaty of Versailles, some of the peace conference attendees met at President Woodrow Wilson's Paris home, including (seated, left to right) Italian premier Vittorio Orlando, British prime minister David Lloyd George, French premier Georges Clemenceau, and President Wilson.

now you Know!

✔ By the beginning of the 20th century, Europe had two great power blocs: Germany and Austria-Hungary in central Europe, and a French-Russian alliance, supported by Great Britain.

✔ World War I was triggered by a Serbian patriot who assassinated the Austrian archduke, Franz Ferdinand, on June 28, 1914, in Sarajevo.

✔ The Russian Revolution in 1917 effectively removed Russia from the war and caused the war to drag on for another year.

✔ The "guilt clause" in the Treaty of Versailles placed responsibility for the war on Germany, which was then stripped of its colonies and loaded with a reparations debt that it could not pay.

BETWEEN THE WARS: EUROPE

The world that emerged after World War I was a far cry from "a world made safe for democracy." In Europe, victorious nations such as Britain and France were racked with disillusionment because much of their faith in reason and in the democratic process founded on reason had been destroyed. Deprived by the war of the generation that should have provided fresh leadership in the 1920s and 1930s, these two countries pursued listless and cynical courses.

In Russia, Italy, and Germany, also exhausted and embittered by war, totalitarianism found fertile ground as ruthless leaders offered new ideologies that promised a glowing future. When a worldwide and crushing depression struck in the 1930s, totalitarian regimes became even more despotic.

Rise of the Dictators

Totalitarianism on the Ascent

Propelling the world toward that war was a new kind of tyranny that took hold in parts of Europe. Authoritarian regimes exercised total control over their citizens' lives. (See page 315.) This new type of authoritarian government began with Lenin's Communist regime in Russia and climaxed with the fascist regimes of Italy and Germany.

Aftermath of the Russian Revolution. After Lenin's death in 1924, Joseph Stalin gained control of the Communist Party and began his dictatorial rule of the Soviet Union, which would last until his death in 1953. "The very essence and foundation of our policy," Stalin said, "is to transform our land from an agricultural to an industrial country." To do this, Stalin inaugurated a series of "5-year plans" under which the government set rigorous production quotas for farms and factories. Peasants or workers who objected were ruthlessly punished, often with exile or death. Other "enemies of the state," real or imagined political opponents, were likewise "purged." Under Stalinism, the Soviet Union did industrialize, but at a great cost.

Russian soldiers gathered in Moscow to support the Russian Revolution. ▶

Fascist Italy. Italy emerged from the war in frustration. In 1915, the country had finally decided to throw in its lot with Great Britain and France. Italian soldiers had fought bravely, but poor leadership and inadequate supplies had made the Italian front more of a liability than an asset to the Allies.

At the Versailles conference, Italy's demands were submerged beneath the demands of others. The Italians left Versailles convinced that they had been cheated of their just due only because they were not as powerful as Britain, France, or the United States.

This feeling of national humiliation, combined with the failure of unification to achieve any significant national or international goals, led to the rise in 1922 of Benito Mussolini, a young former socialist leading a national fascist movement.

At the heart of fascist political theory was a belief in the inability of the individual to run his own life satisfactorily. The leader, *il duce* in Italian, must assume the heavy burden of responsibility for the individual. Only thus would the sickness of society be cured.

Spotlight on... BENITO MUSSOLINI

1883–1945

Benito Mussolini, the founder of fascism, ruled Italy for almost 21 years, most of that time as dictator. Originally a socialist, Mussolini had a falling out with other socialists over his support of Italian involvement in World War I.

Mussolini organized the nucleus of his Fascist Party amid the strikes and unrest that overtook Italy after World War I. By appealing to nationalistic spirit and using brutal tactics against Communists and Socialists, Mussolini quickly became a formidable power in Italy. In 1922, the fascists forced King Victor Emmanuel III to appoint Mussolini prime minister.

In 1925, Mussolini declared a dictatorship. He abolished other political parties and imposed government control on industry, schools, the press, and police. In 1929, he signed agreements that settled long-standing disputes between the government and the Roman Catholic Church. He also sought to make Italy a corporate state, in which the government would help resolve disputes between employers and workers.

Mussolini sought to make Italy a major power and to create an Italian colonial empire. He invaded and conquered Ethiopia in 1935 and 1936. But this action was condemned by Britain, France, and other countries and drove Mussolini toward an alliance with the German dictator, Adolf Hitler. In 1936, he joined Hitler in sending troops to fight in the Spanish Civil War in support of the Nationalist leader General Francisco Franco. In 1939, Italy conquered and annexed Albania.

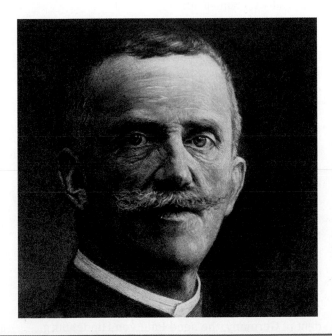

▲ **Victor Emmanuel III** (1869–1947) was king of Italy from 1900 to 1946. He became unpopular because of his cooperation with fascist dictator Benito Mussolini.

Failed Democracies

Germany: The Weimar Republic

The road back to normal life seemed incredibly long and difficult in Germany. After a series of short but violent revolutions, the country settled down under the ill-fated Weimar Republic.

The experiment in democratic republican government suffered from a dire lack of the most essential ingredient—believers in the democratic process. The upper classes sneered, and the lower classes looked to socialism for salvation.

During the 1920s, the German people attempted to dig out of the ruins of defeat. Fortunes had been wiped out, the savings of the middle class had disappeared in inflation, and the threat of socialism seemed ever-present. In a class-conscious society such as that of Germany, loss of social status was the ultimate evil and to be avoided at all cost.

The great achievement of the Weimar Republic was that it staved off a revolution for a decade. But the drain of reparations payments on Germany's financial resources prevented the revitalization of German business and, therefore, economic stability. As a result, the financial collapse in 1929 that marked the beginning of the world economic depression of the 1930s effectively sealed the doom of the Weimar Republic.

▲ **Paul von Hindenburg,** the president of Germany, named Hitler chancellor on January 30, 1933. By the summer of 1933, Hitler had made himself dictator.

Small splinter parties appeared like mayflies in the intense heat of opposition to the Weimar Republic. Among these small splinter groups was the National Socialist German Workers Party, the Nazis. Its only real resource was the oratorical talent of its leader, or *führer*, Adolf Hitler, who was an Austrian by birth.

Hitler drew broad support from the desperate middle class that was rapidly descending into the lower echelons of society. But in spite of inflation, chaos, the weakness of the Weimar Republic, and the fear of the dissolution of society itself, Hitler and the Nazis did not win a majority of votes in the elections held in November 1932. In fact, the Nazis actually lost seats in the German parliament, the *Reichstag*.

Hitler was brought to power by a right-wing cabal of men high in government who persuaded the president of Germany, the aged Paul von Hindenburg, to appoint Hitler chancellor. Once in power, Hitler lost no time in bringing his Nazi underlings into positions of power.

▲ **The boundaries of Germany after World War I.** Under the Treaty of Versailles, Germany lost some of its territory to Czechoslovakia, Lithuania, and Poland in the east, and to Belgium, Denmark, and France in the west.

Spain: The Spanish Civil War

The Spanish Civil War (1936–1939) was fought between the forces of Spain's democratically elected, liberal government and conservative rebels. The war cost the lives of hundreds of thousands and set the stage for a dictatorship that lasted more than 35 years.

The forces that fought against the government were known as Nationalists. They included military leaders, segments of the Roman Catholic Church, groups that wanted Spain to become a monarchy again, and fascists.

The forces that fought on the side of the government were known as Republicans. They included a variety of left-wing groups, such as socialists, Communists, and anarchists.

Failed Reforms. The government that ruled Spain between 1931 and 1933 attempted to transform Spain's social, economic, and political institutions. Some policies, including certain land reforms and the establishment of an 8-hour workday, threatened the upper classes who owned Spain's industries.

In the late spring of 1936, a series of strikes, violent public demonstrations, and political assassinations caused many to lose faith in the government.

- ✔ Joseph Stalin gained control of the Communist Party after Lenin's death in 1924 and began his dictatorial rule of the Soviet Union.

- ✔ Benito Mussolini was able to assume power in Italy by appealing to nationalistic spirit and using brutal tactics against Communists and Socialists.

- ✔ Adolf Hitler came to power in Germany because of a group of government officials who persuaded the president of Germany, the aged Paul von Hindenburg, to appoint Hitler chancellor.

- ✔ Nationalists in Spain included military leaders, segments of the Roman Catholic Church, groups that wanted Spain to become a monarchy again, and fascists.

Rebellion Leads to Civil War. On July 17, 1936, Spanish army units stationed in Morocco launched a rebellion against the Spanish government. The revolt spread to Spain itself, and within 4 days, the rebels controlled about a third of Spain.

In September 1936, the Nationalists chose Francisco Franco to serve as both commander-in-chief of the armed forces and head of the Nationalist government. Franco and his advisers based the new government on fascist principles and created a prominent role in the government for the Roman Catholic Church. By the end of 1937, all the forces on the Nationalist side had merged into a state system under Franco's leadership.

On March 28, 1939, Franco's troops began entering the capital. The remaining Republican forces throughout Spain surrendered, and Franco announced on April 1 that the war was over.

Francisco Franco ▶ **(1892–1975)** ruled Spain as dictator from 1939 until he died in 1975. He decided that Prince Juan Carlos would succeed him, with the title of king.

Results of the War. Estimates of the numbers of people killed during the Spanish Civil War vary. Many experts estimate that from 600,000 to 800,000 people died as a result of the war. Following the war, Franco established a harsh right-wing dictatorship. He had thousands of Republican supporters executed and outlawed all political parties but his own.

BETWEEN THE WARS: AFRICA AND LATIN AMERICA

Just as political change was in the air in Europe, so it was in the world outside. While European imperialism brought colonialism to much of the world, it transmitted ideas of Western democracy and nationalism as well. As the 20th century unfolded, such ideas created nationalist movements around the globe. People who wanted to break the shackles of colonialism, gain their independence, and establish their own political systems mounted rebellions in numerous nations.

Europe's Hold on Africa

Colonial Africa

The European colonization of Africa exacted a heavy cost in African lives. (See pages 528–529.) Millions were killed directly in wars of conquest and indirectly through the demands imposed upon them in colonial plantations. For example, historians estimate that the brutal regime of King Leopold II of Belgium in Congo Free State, now Congo (Kinshasa), caused the death of several million Africans.

The colonial period also witnessed social transformations that included changes in the patterns of urbanization, education, and religious practice. New urban centers emerged, and many old cities expanded. In these cities, Africans created new forms of social life and leisure activities. Many Africans educated by missionaries opposed colonialism and demanded higher education or pursued it abroad. During colonial rule, both Christianity and Islam expanded.

Beginning of the End. World War I marked the beginning of the end for colonialism in Africa. African soldiers had fought for both Great Britain and France in that war. When the soldiers returned home, they brought European ideas of nationalism with them. Then, too, some Africans were being educated in Europe, and they too returned with Western ideas of independence and self-government.

The European imperial powers were not going to give up their colonial possessions easily. Following the war, rule over colonies was simply shifted around. The Treaty of Versailles gave former German colonies in Africa as mandates to the British, French, and Belgians. German Southwest Africa (later Namibia) was given as a mandate to the Union of South Africa.

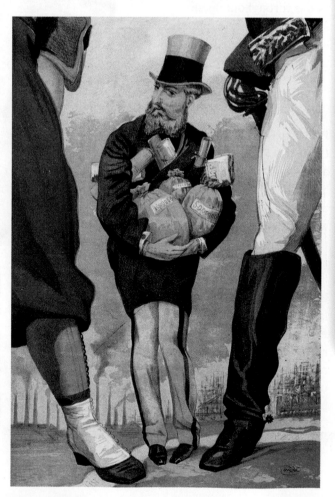

◀ **Leopold II** (1835–1909) was king of Belgium from 1865 until his death. Leopold built up a huge private fortune through control of the Congo's vast resources. However, many people of the Congo were used as forced labor, and millions died under the brutal conditions.

STRICT SEGREGATION IN SOUTH AFRICA

Africans in British colonies were governed by "indirect rule," that is, the British governed through the tribal chiefs. This worked for a time in West Africa, where the population was overwhelmingly black. In places like Kenya and Rhodesia, however, white rule was much more evident because great numbers of British had come to settle permanently.

In the British dominion of the Union of South Africa, life under white rule became the hardest for blacks. Though tensions between the British and the Boers remained high, the two white groups were united by uneasiness over the numerical superiority of the black population—three blacks to each white.

To hold onto their power, South African whites created a policy of strict segregation called *apartheid*. They relegated many blacks to tribal reservations; limited their movements and their permits to work; gave them only the lowest paying jobs; and barred them from all political participation.

North Africa. In 1919, Egyptian nationalists, chafing under their country's status as a British protectorate, staged a revolt that was put down by British troops stationed in the country. But in 1922, Great Britain did grant Egypt independence, though the British military presence remained strong. During the 1920s and 1930s, Algeria and Morocco staged unsuccessful revolts against their French rulers.

Sub-Saharan Africa. Independence for Africans south of the Sahara was still far in the future. In none of the African colonies were blacks really being prepared for self-government. Both the French and the Portuguese thought of their African colonies as overseas provinces, to be ruled by their countries' laws. They saw no reason to establish political institutions that were uniquely African. Neither did the Belgians, who ruled in a highly paternalistic way, improving medical services and elementary education but giving no encouragement to African political organization.

In the years preceding World War II, feelings of nationalism gradually gathered strength in black Africa, mainly among the small educated elite. Following World War II, this group would lead a drive to end imperialism.

Following the end of World War I, a black nationalist movement called Pan-Africanism emerged. Led by the black American leader Dr. W. E. B. Du Bois, it sought to end both colonialism and supremacy of whites in Africa, and to unite Africa under black rule. The movement did not call for immediate independence, however, but for a gradual shift toward self-government and equality of the races. Pan-Africanism's most valuable contribution to African nationalism was probably the scholarship it encouraged in African studies, which generated pride in African history and culture. Pan-Africanism also produced the future leaders of African independence—Jomo Kenyatta of Kenya and Kwame Nkrumah of Ghana among them.

An Uneasy Independence

Latin America

As the 20th century dawned in Latin America, people warily eyed the United States and Europe, both of which had invested heavily in Latin American nations. Revolutions, border disputes, and capricious dictators kept dissension within Latin America at a boil, inviting foreign interference.

Interventionism. Such interference became apparent in the early 1900s when both Venezuela and the Dominican Republic defaulted on European loans. British, German, and Italian ships blockaded Venezuela, a first step in getting Venezuela to pay its debt. President Theodore Roosevelt of the United States stepped in to bring the matter to arbitration. In 1904, he announced the Roosevelt Corollary to the Monroe Doctrine. From now on, it stated, the United States would exercise "international police power" in Latin America. If Europeans had a dispute with a Latin American nation, the American government would do what it deemed necessary to correct the problem, including sending American troops into Latin American countries and taking over tax collection in those countries.

To Latin Americans, this was another blatant example of "Yankee imperialism" on the part of the "Colossus of the North." They were still smarting over Roosevelt's intervention in the national affairs of Colombia. There, in 1903, the Colombian government had refused to sell the United States the right to build a canal across Colombia's northern province of Panama. Roosevelt encouraged Panama to rebel against Colombia and to declare its independence. The United States then promptly recognized Panama as a sovereign nation and bought permission to build the canal from it. (See page 159.)

Latin American-U.S. relations continued to deteriorate as the United States intervened several times in the affairs of Latin American nations. American Marines occupied and set up military governments in Nicaragua (1912–1925 and 1927–1933), Haiti (1915–1934), and the Dominican Republic (1916–1924). American troops were also sent into Mexico twice, in 1914 and 1916, as that country was torn by a highly destructive civil war. In addition, American presidents invoked the Platt Amendment to intervene in Cuba on four occasions between 1906 and 1922.

THE GOOD NEIGHBOR POLICY

In 1933, President Franklin D. Roosevelt sought to improve relations with Latin America by proclaiming the Good Neighbor Policy. Under this policy, the Platt Amendment and the Roosevelt Corollary were revoked and American troops were withdrawn. The United States committed itself to the principle of nonintervention, and a new era in relations began. As World War II loomed, the United States agreed to consult with the South and Central American countries on hemisphere defense, thereby modifying a policy of unilateralism that dated from the Monroe Doctrine (1823). The goodwill thus engendered provided a base for wartime solidarity. Only one Western Hemisphere country, Argentina, remained neutral.

▲ **Rafael Trujillo** (1891–1961) controlled the government and military of the Dominican Republic from 1930 to 1961. From 1930 to 1938 and from 1942 to 1952, Trujillo held the office of president. During periods when he was not president, Trujillo controlled the country through puppet governments.

Economic Developments. In the Latin American nations, the economic norm became dependency on producing one or two primary products for export. For example, Brazil depended on coffee, Venezuela on oil, Cuba on sugar, Chile on nitrates, Argentina on wheat and meat, Central American countries on bananas, and Bolivia on tin.

World War I created a boom for such products that lasted well into the 1920s. But as European agricultural production recovered, prices for Latin American foodstuffs fell. When the worldwide depression struck, between 1929 and 1932, the value of Latin American exports dropped 65 percent.

During this time, Latin American governments tried to encourage the development of industries to produce consumer goods to make their countries less dependent on imports and on the necessity of selling exports. The United States and Great Britain flooded Latin America with cheap imports to discourage the competition that Latin American industry might create. However, Germany under Hitler encouraged Latin American industrialization, bartering German factory machinery for commodities.

Authoritarian Regimes. During the 1930s, nearly every government in Latin America was overthrown as political power shifted from landed gentry and exporters, ruined by the depression, to the emerging middle class and the military.

The military establishments of Latin America believed that their interests were inseparable from those of their nations. In the 20th century, the military continued to exert a strong influence on government in Latin America by intervening in civil affairs. During the 1930s, several military officers emerged as dictators.

- Fulgencio Batista in Cuba
- Rafael Trujillo in the Dominican Republic
- Anastasio Somoza in Nicaragua

Social Reform. The revolution in Mexico in 1910 began a drive for social reform in Latin America. Mexico led the way in appropriating land from the large landowners and redistributing it among the peasants. It also encouraged the organization of trade unions as it sought to break the hold of foreign investors over national resources and workers.

Other Latin American nations also tried to improve life for both peasants and urban workers. But rapidly growing populations helped to ensure that widespread poverty would persist.

✔ African soldiers who had fought for Great Britain and France in World War I returned home with European ideas of nationalism, independence, and self-government.

✔ After an unsuccessful revolt against the British in 1919, Egypt gained independence in 1922, though the British military presence remained strong.

✔ Under the Good Neighbor Policy, the United States committed itself to the principle of nonintervention in Latin American affairs.

✔ The military in Latin America exerted a strong influence on government by intervening in civil affairs and even overthrowing governments.

BETWEEN THE WARS: ASIA

While India and Indochina struggled to gain their independence from their European rulers, the Chinese were feeling crushing pressure from the newest Asian power: Japan. Meanwhile, Japan's struggle toward a modern democracy was met with resistance in the form of the Japanese military, which scorned the civilian government and sought more and more military control of Japan's domestic and foreign affairs.

In China and Indochina, a new voice was entering the struggle for independence: the Communists.

▲ **Mohandas K. Gandhi** sailed to the United Kingdom in 1931 for talks with the British government on the status of India. The talks ended without an agreement to end British rule, and Gandhi returned to India to continue his efforts to achieve Indian independence.

India Against British Rule

As the 1900s dawned in India, stirrings against British rule grew violent. The central Indian government remained firmly under British control, and those who wanted Great Britain out of India completely found little to satisfy them.

To retain the support of India during World War I, the British promised that India would gradually be granted self-government within the British Empire. After the war, Britain passed the Government of India Act of 1919, granting Indians more control over provincial matters, but once again retaining control over such national matters as taxation, foreign policy, and justice. To the militantly nationalist Indian National Congress, this fell far short of expectations.

In 1920, Mohandas K. Gandhi became the leader of the Indian National Congress. Gandhi advocated civil disobedience against the British—hunger strikes, labor strikes, mass demonstrations, boycotts of British goods, and nonpayment of taxes.

Gandhi advocated other programs for India as well. These included ending the stigmatization of the caste system and freeing the untouchables, improving the status of women, and replacing the centuries-old conflict between Hindus and Muslims with a spirit of tolerance and cooperation.

HINDU–MUSLIM CONFLICT

Both Hindus and Muslims wanted Great Britain out of India, but antagonism between the two groups increased as they jockeyed for position in the Indian nation that would emerge after the fight for independence was won. Disputing the claim of the predominantly Hindu Indian National Congress to leadership of the independence movement, the Muslim League emerged in the 1930s under the leadership of Muhammad Ali Jinnah. The league wanted no part of an independent India dominated by Hindus, and the specter of a divided India, part Hindu and part Muslim, was raised.

In 1937, a new Government of India Act went into effect, providing another step toward self-government. Under it, a British viceroy remained India's chief executive, but Indians gained autonomy in provincial government and control over all central government matters except foreign affairs and defense.

Japan

Japan's designs on China began with the Sino-Japanese War of 1894–1895. In 1915, Japan presented China with the Twenty-One Demands. If China had been forced to comply, Japan would have obtained virtual control of the country. However, the United States was able to convince Japan to back down.

Both Japan and China entered World War I on the side of the Allies, but Japan profited from the war at China's expense. The victorious Allies agreed that Japan could take control of China's iron-rich Shantung Province from defeated Germany rather than return it to China itself. Japan also retained the rights it had won in coal- and iron-rich Manchuria as a result of the Russo-Japanese War.

Spotlight on... EMPEROR HIROHITO

1901–1989

Hirohito was born in Tokyo on April 29, 1901. He became regent for his father, Yoshihito, in 1921, and he became emperor in December 1926. Hirohito's reign began during the days of rising democratic sentiment. Japan had just granted all men the right to vote, and the country seemed likely to become increasingly democratic and internationalist. However, military leaders in Manchuria and elsewhere called for a stronger foreign policy. Within Japan, criticism of the political parties sharpened after economic crises struck. Military incidents abroad and assassinations in Tokyo soon reversed the democratic and internationalist trends of the 1920s.

Hirohito personally opposed the militarism of the 1930s. But his advisers kept him from making his wishes known, so that the radical militarists would not take direct action against the monarchy. As a result, Hirohito remained silent and approved the decisions that led to World War II.

Evolution in Government. In the decade following World War I, Japan seemed to be moving toward parliamentary democracy. In 1918, Hara Takashi became prime minister, the first commoner to reach such high office. In 1925, the Universal Suffrage Bill extended the vote to all males over age 25. But the Japanese military was scornful of democracy and eager for continued military expansion.

Military Takeover. Industrialization had paid big dividends for Japan, but the worldwide depression that struck in the 1930s shattered Japanese trade. The military saw its chance. In 1932, it had the new prime minister, Tsuyoshi Inukai, assassinated, ending civilian control of government. A military clique took control and set out to take from China the raw materials Japan needed. Japan's invasion of China in 1937 was part of its plan to drive all Western interests out of China, so that Japan, China, and Manchuria could become one economic unit under Japanese leadership.

▲ **This map** shows the stages of Japanese expansion as a result of three wars: the Sino-Japanese war of 1894–1895, the Russo-Japanese War (1904–1905), and World War I (1914–1918). Japan took control of Taiwan in 1895. By 1910, Korea and a small portion of Manchuria had fallen under Japanese control. Many islands in the Pacific came under Japanese rule in 1914.

China

In China, the Boxer Rebellion of 1900 signaled that the Chinese were now intent on driving out the foreign influences that dominated their land. This intent was voiced most strongly by young Chinese who had been sent to study in Western universities. They returned to China with ideas about nationalism, liberalism, and the democratic process.

▲ **Chiang Kai-shek** led the Nationalist Chinese from 1925 to 1949 but fled to Taiwan, still as leader of Nationalist China, when the Communist Chinese came to power.

Chiang Kai-shek. Sun Yat-sen's successor was Chiang Kai-shek. Under Chiang, the Nationalist armies began their drive north in 1926; within 2 years they occupied Beijing.

But by now, dissension had broken out between two wings of the Kuomintang. On one side were the conservatives under Chiang. On the other side were members of the Chinese Communist Party, which had been organized in 1921.

In 1927, Chiang took advantage of a Communist-inspired workers' uprising in Guangzhou to crush the left wing. Communists scattered to the hills and mountains of southeastern China, where they set up their own administration, calling it the Chinese Soviet Republic.

▲ **Sun Yat-sen** and his followers overthrew the Ch'ing dynasty but were unable to create a unified China.

Sun Yat-sen. Their leader was Sun Yat-sen, who founded the Kuomintang, or Nationalist People's Party. The first order of business was to overthrow the dying Ch'ing dynasty. This was accomplished in 1912, following a rebellion in southern China. The Kuomintang proclaimed China a republic.

Sun Yat-sen laid out his aims in the "Three Principles of the People": political unity for a China freed of imperialist domination; democratic government; and an economy that could provide a basic living for all Chinese people.

Meeting these ambitious aims soon proved impossible. The Kuomintang republic actually controlled only a small area of China. Powerful warlords—generals with their own armies—controlled much of the rest. When Sun Yat-sen died in 1925, his dream of a unified China was still unfulfilled.

Mao Zedong. The Chinese Communists were led by Mao Zedong, who had been a student at Beijing University when he became a founding member of the Chinese Communist Party. Mao was convinced that the way to create a Communist China was to win the support of the peasant population. To do this, the Communists made major reforms in the territories they controlled, seizing large landowners' estates, dividing them up, and distributing them to the peasants. They also reduced the peasants' onerous tax burdens. Mao's reforms succeeded in winning over many peasants.

Southeast Asia

As the 1900s began, Southeast Asia remained firmly under the control of Great Britain, France, and the Netherlands. One of the first nationalist movements arose in the Philippines. In 1896, Filipinos staged an uprising against the Spanish. Following the outbreak of the Spanish-American War in 1898, Filipino nationalists proclaimed the Republic of the Philippines. However, independence was short-lived as American rule replaced Spanish rule.

Nationalists in Burma took their cue from India in agitating for independence from Great Britain. In 1937, Burma gained a parliamentary system of government and chose a Burmese prime minister, but a British governor controlled foreign relations and defense.

In Indochina, France maintained an oppressive political and economic hold. The French did nothing to encourage education, so the Indochinese people remained almost entirely illiterate and bound to their traditional culture. This paved the way for anticolonial agitation.

Vietnam led the way in organizing nationalist movements. One of the earliest was founded in the 1920s by Vietnamese who had returned from France, where they had worked during World War I and had become acquainted with liberal ideas. This movement was overtaken by the Indochina Communist Party, founded in 1930 by Nguyen That Than, later known as Ho Chi Minh. The party attempted an uprising against colonial rule that year, but the French crushed it. Despite the defeat, Communism would remain at the center of the Vietnamese nationalist movement.

Anticolonialism followed a similar pattern in Dutch Indonesia. The first major nationalist movement there was mounted by the Islamic Union, founded in 1912. It had little success against powerful Dutch domination. Communist anticolonialism took the form of the Indonesian Communist Party, founded in 1920, but the uprising it staged in 1926–1927 was crushed just as the one in Vietnam had been.

Southeast Asian nationalist ambitions would have to wait for World War II before achieving success.

▲ **Mao Zedong** became leader of the Chinese Communist Party in 1934. He remained party leader until his death in 1976.

now you know!

✔ Mohandas K. Gandhi, who became the leader of the Indian National Congress in 1920, advocated civil disobedience against the British—hunger strikes, labor strikes, mass demonstrations, boycotts of British goods, and nonpayment of taxes.

✔ Even though the government in Japan was growing more democratic in the 1920s, the Japanese military was scornful of democracy and eager for continued military expansion.

✔ Mao Zedong was convinced that the way to create a Communist China was to win the support of the peasant population.

✔ The first Communist revolt against French rule in Vietnam occurred in 1930 and was organized by Nguyen That Than, later known as Ho Chi Minh.

WORLD WAR II

During the 1930s, events in Europe, Asia, and Africa were leading the world toward another world war. Although few people realized it at the time, Hitler's ascent to power in Germany was the decisive moment in the first half of the 20th century. He had spelled out his program in the 1920s in his book *Mein Kampf* (*My Struggle*), which underlined the necessity of a resounding German military victory in Europe to restore the honor and integrity of Germany.

Adolf Hitler speaks to the German Reichstag on September 3, 1939, two days after the German invasion of Poland and the same day that Britain and France declared war.

The War in Europe: Time Line

September 1
Germany invades Poland. ▲

May 10
Germany invades Belgium and the Netherlands.

1939

September 3
Britain and France declare war on Germany.

September 17
The Soviets (then allies of Germany) invade Poland from the east.

September
Germany and the Soviet Union divide up Polish territories.

October–April 1940
Germany, Britain, and France avoid fighting along the Maginot and Siegfried Lines in what was known as the Sitzkrieg, or Phony War.

1940

May 10
Winston Churchill replaces Neville Chamberlain as British prime minister.

May 12
Germans cross the French frontier using Blitzkrieg (air, tank, and infantry "lightning strike") tactics.

May 26–June 4
German victories force the evacuation of more than 300,000 Allied troops from the French port of Dunkirk.

June 10
Italy declares war on France and Great Britain.

June
France capitulates to German troops, and a puppet government under Marshal Henri Pétain is set up. The armistice between France and Germany is signed on June 22.

July 10
The Battle of Britain begins with German saturation bombings of British military installations, factories, and land and sea transportation sites; the British respond by destroying over 1,500 German Luftwaffe bombers.

March 11
The Lend-Lease Act becomes U.S. law. The act permits President Roosevelt to lend or lease raw materials or supplies to any nation fighting the Axis.

April 6
Germany invades Yugoslavia and Greece.

April
German field marshal Erwin Rommel takes over Axis forces in North Africa and begins a rapid German advance there.

August 14
The Atlantic Charter, a joint declaration of war policy, is signed by Roosevelt and Churchill. ▼

1941

September
Italy opens fighting in the North African desert by attacking British Egypt from Libya.

September
Beginning of the Blitz, German bombing campaigns against British cities.

May 20
German paratroopers land on the island of Crete and seize an airfield. The entire island is soon under German control, giving them a critical Mediterranean base.

May 27
German battleship *Bismarck* is sunk in a battle with British naval forces.

June 22
Germany invades the Soviet Union in Operation Barbarossa, ending the German-Soviet alliance and bringing the Soviets into the war against Germany.

September 8
German troops begin the siege of Leningrad (now St. Petersburg), which lasts until January 1944. More than 1 million Soviets die after years of shortages of food, water, and medicine.

September 19
The Soviet city of Kiev surrenders to German forces. Nearly 665,000 Soviet soldiers are captured by the Germans in their greatest single victory.

November 15
German forces attack Moscow. They are exhausted by their slow march through mud, however. The onset of bitter winter cold combined with fresh Soviet reinforcements freezes the German offensive 20 miles (32 kilometers) short of the city.

December 7
Japan bombs the U.S. Pacific Fleet stationed at Pearl Harbor, located on the Hawaiian island of Oahu. The United States, Canada, and the United Kingdom declare war on Japan the next day.

December 11
Germany and Italy declare war on the United States.

The War in Europe: Time Line

June 25
General Dwight Eisenhower becomes head of U.S. operations in Europe.

August–October
German eastward drive in the Soviet Union stalls at Stalingrad.

February 1
The German 6th Army surrenders at Stalingrad, a major turning point in the war in Russia.

April 19–May 16
Jews in the Warsaw ghetto (a section of the city) rise up against the Nazis until the Nazis crush the uprising, killing thousands of Jews and sending most survivors to concentration camps.

July 25
Mussolini is deposed; Badoglio is named premier of Italy.

1942

1943

August 25
Hitler orders his forces to capture Stalingrad.

October 23
British forces attack the Axis powers at El Alamein in Egypt. The tank battle rages until November 5, when German forces withdraw.

November 8
Allied troops land in Algeria and Morocco, beginning the invasion of North Africa.

November–March 1943
Soviet counterattack at Stalingrad drives Germans into retreat.

May 13
Axis forces in northern Africa surrender.

July 4
Germany opens an assault near the Soviet city of Kursk.

July 10
Allies invade the Italian island of Sicily. ▼

September 3
Italy secretly surrenders to the Allies, but the Germans refuse to surrender the Italian peninsula.

September 9
Allied troops land at Salerno, Italy, and begin a difficult, contested drive north to Rome. They reach the Gustav Line, Germany's defensive position 75 miles (120 kilometers) south of Rome, by early November, but the line holds.

January 22
Allied troops land in Anzio, Italy, but German forces pin them on the beaches for 4 months.

January 27
The siege of Leningrad ends with the retreat of Nazi troops.

February 20
Strategic bombing of Germany begins. Better bombsights, introduced by the U.S. Army Air Forces, allow bombers to target and hit military and industrial sites.

July 20
Plot to assassinate Hitler fails.

August 25
American and Free French forces liberate Paris. Resistance fighters had been battling the Germans street by street since August 19.

October 13
Athens is freed by the Allies.

March 7
Allies cross the Rhine in Germany.

April 25
Soviet forces surround Berlin.

April 28
Benito Mussolini is executed at Lake Como by Italian partisans.

April 30
Hitler takes his life in Berlin.

July 17–August 2
Potsdam Conference between Allied leaders. Germany is divided into four zones, one each to be occupied by the United States, the Soviet Union, the United Kingdom, and France. The four powers would jointly administer Berlin.

1944

1945

April 2
Russians enter Poland.

June 4
Rome captured by Allies after German defenses are punctured in May.

June 6
Allied troops land in Normandy for the D-Day invasion. ▼

December 16
Germans strike back at U.S. troops in the Battle of the Bulge—the last major German counteroffensive.

May 2
German forces in Italy surrender to the Allies. German positions in northern Italy hold during the fall and winter of 1944, but the following spring, the Allies sweep north to the Alps.

May 7
Germany surrenders unconditionally to the Allies in Reims, France, ending World War II in Europe.

May 8
The Allies declare V-E (Victory in Europe) Day. ▶

November 20
Nuremberg war crimes trials begin.

WORLD WAR II: EUROPE

Hitler began his expansion in 1936 by sending German troops into a section of western Germany called the Rhineland, in direct violation of the Treaty of Versailles. In that same year, Germany signed a pact with Italy, forming a military alliance called the Rome-Berlin Axis. The year 1936 also marked Italy's conquest of Ethiopia in Africa. In 1938, German troops marched into Austria and annexed it to Germany, another violation of the Versailles treaty. None of these actions met opposition from the Allied powers.

Europe in Peril

War Begins

In 1939, the Nazis occupied all of Czechoslovakia. It became clear that a line had to be drawn somewhere or Hitler would swallow all of Europe. Great Britain and France finally took a stand on the issue of Poland's territorial integrity.

The United Kingdom and France hoped that the Soviet Union would help defend Poland. Stalin recognized that Russia was unprepared for a Nazi assault should Hitler turn farther to the east and so signed a nonaggression pact with Germany that profoundly shocked the world. That pact sealed Poland's fate. On September 1, 1939, German forces began the dismemberment of Poland. On September 3, France and England declared war on Germany.

Overview of World War II in Europe. This map shows major offensives and the greatest extent of Axis domination. ▼

Fall of France

In May 1940, German tanks and aircraft passed around the Maginot Line as they swept through Luxembourg and Belgium and into northern France. On June 5, the Germans launched a major assault along the Somme River, which had been the scene of brutal slaughter in World War I. The blitzkrieg overwhelmed the French forces, driving them mercilessly backward. Seeing an opportunity to profit from Germany's success, Italy declared war on France and the United Kingdom on June 10. The French government fled from Paris to Bordeaux the same day.

German troops entered Paris on June 14, 1940. Paul Reynaud, the new French premier, wanted to fight on. But many of his generals and cabinet officers believed that the battle for France was lost. Reynaud resigned, and a new French government agreed to an armistice on June 22.

One of the French generals, Charles de Gaulle, escaped to the United Kingdom after France fell. In radio broadcasts to France, he urged the people to carry on the fight against Germany. The troops who rallied around de Gaulle became known as the Free French.

▲ **Paris falls, June 1940.** With the Arc de Triomphe in the background, General Kurt von Briesen (on horseback) salutes his soldiers as they parade down the Avenue Foch.

Battle of Britain

The British were determined to resist the Nazis and fought on alone. Hitler prepared to invade southern England in a military operation with the code name Sea Lion. But before an invasion force could safely cross the English Channel, Hitler had to clear the Royal Air Force from the sky. The Battle of Britain was to become the first battle ever fought solely for air supremacy.

Hitler had originally ordered that no civilian targets should be attacked. But in late August, a lost Luftwaffe pilot violated his orders and bombed central London. An outraged Churchill retaliated with a bombing attack on Berlin. Hitler then unleashed his air force against English cities, beginning what is known as the Blitz. German planes bombed cities from London to Manchester for months. Raids continued throughout the winter and spring until finally, in May 1941, Germany gave up its attempts to defeat the United Kingdom from the air. More than 40,000 British civilians had lost their lives.

Hitler's decision to switch attacks from Royal Air Force (RAF) bases to British cities effectively won the battle for the United Kingdom. It allowed the RAF to constantly replace both planes and pilots. The United Kingdom's survival became immensely important later in the war. The island itself served as a giant airfield and base for the Allied invasion of Europe, and the British Army and High Command made crucial contributions to the ultimate Allied victory.

THE UNITED STATES ENTERS THE WAR

On December 7, 1941, the Japanese launched a surprise attack upon the U.S. Pacific Fleet at Pearl Harbor, Hawaii.

The United States, Canada, and the United Kingdom declared war on Japan on December 8, 1941. Germany and Italy declared war on the United States on December 11. The world was now truly a world at war. (See also pages 184–197.)

A Hard-Won Victory

D-Day

Soon after British forces evacuated Dunkirk in their retreat from the continent in 1940, the United Kingdom started to plan a return to France. In 1942, the United States and the United Kingdom began to discuss a large-scale invasion across the English Channel. Throughout 1943, preparations moved ahead for an invasion of northern France the following year. The invasion plan received the code name Operation Overlord.

General Eisenhower, as supreme commander of the Allied forces, chose Monday, June 5, 1944, as D-Day—the date of the Normandy invasion. However, rough seas forced him to postpone until June 6. During the night, thousands of ships carrying landing craft and more than 130,000 landing troops crossed the channel. Minesweepers had gone ahead to clear the water. In addition, about 23,000 paratroopers and glider troops began dropping behind German lines to capture bridges and railroad tracks. At dawn, battleships opened fire on the beaches. At 6:30 a.m., soldiers from the United States, the United Kingdom, Canada, and France stormed ashore on a 60-mile (100-kilometer) front in the largest seaborne invasion in history.

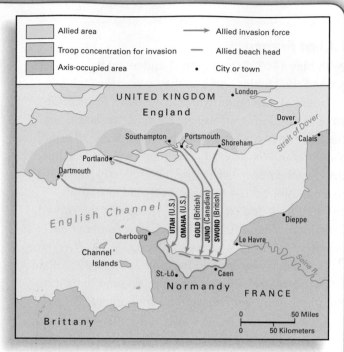

▲ **Hitting the beach,** Allied infantrymen swarmed ashore along the Normandy coast of northern France on D-Day—June 6, 1944. It was the largest seaborne invasion in history. Hitler had boasted that German defenses along the coast could resist any attack. But he was wrong.

D-Day took the Germans by surprise, but they responded fiercely. At one landing site, code-named Omaha Beach, U.S. troops came under heavy fire and barely managed to stay ashore. Nevertheless, all five Allied landing beaches were secure by the end of D-Day. By the end of June 1944, about 1 million Allied troops had reached France.

The Allied forces advanced slowly. During August, the Allies cleared the Germans out of most of northwestern France. Allied bombers hounded the retreating Germans. More than 50,000 Allied troops and aviators died in the Battle of Normandy.

Victory in Europe

The Allies began their final assault on Germany in early 1945. British and Canadian forces cleared the Germans out of the Netherlands and swept into northern Germany. American and French forces raced toward the Elbe River in central Germany. Hitler ordered his soldiers to fight to the death. But seeing the war was over, large numbers of German soldiers surrendered each day.

By April 25, 1945, Soviet troops had surrounded Berlin. From a bunker deep underground, Hitler ordered German soldiers to fight on. On April 30, however, Hitler killed himself rather than face defeat.

The Holocaust

When Adolf Hitler became dictator in 1933, he instituted a crackdown on the Jewish population. Hitler and the Nazis made it impossible for Jews to remain in the professions, businesses, or universities of Germany. In 1942, the Nazi elite gathered in Potsdam to put the finishing touches on a plan called the "Final Solution." This plan foresaw the killing of all Jews in lands controlled by Germany, as well as all physically and mentally handicapped people and all Gypsies. In death camps such as Auschwitz and Buchenwald, victims were led off to gas chambers or killed and then thrown into common ditches for graves. Six million Jews and about 2 million others died in this manner.

▲ **Survivors** of the Nazi concentration camp Buchenwald— some too weak to stand—provided proof of Nazi savagery. The Nazis imprisoned and murdered millions of Jews, Slavs, and members of other groups.

The fighting in Berlin claimed the lives of over 70,000 Soviet soldiers. The Germans propped up their ramshackle remaining units with children and elderly reservists. Thousands of them died in that last week of fighting.

On May 7, 1945, General Alfred Jodl, chief of staff of the German armed forces, signed a statement of unconditional surrender at Eisenhower's headquarters in Reims, France. World War II had ended in Europe. The Allies declared May 8 as V-E Day, or Victory in Europe Day.

Resistance. Initially, the Jews tried to thwart the Nazis by nonviolent means. Also, it was difficult and dangerous for the Jews to obtain weapons. Anti-Semitism was widespread, and Jewish resistance did not have popular support. Jewish fighters could not disappear among the population because non-Jews might betray them. But many Jews who managed to escape the ghettos joined secret bands of fighters against the Nazis. And some non-Jewish individuals risked their lives to smuggle Jews to safety.

Some Jews in ghettos, slave labor camps, and death camps did fight. In 1943, thousands of Jews revolted in the ghetto in Warsaw, Poland. Although the Jews were surrounded and poorly armed, they held out for about 4 weeks. But the Nazis either killed or sent to death camps all of the 60,000 Jews in the ghetto.

In 1943, uprisings took place at the Treblinka and Sobibor death camps. In 1944, prisoners at Auschwitz revolted and set fire to a crematorium. A few prisoners escaped during each uprising, but most were killed. Such revolts were often acts of desperation. They erupted when the Jews understood Nazi intentions and had abandoned hope of survival. The fighters also hoped to protect Jewish honor and to avenge Jewish death.

now you Know!

✔ German troops entered Paris on June 14, 1940, forcing the French government to sign an armistice on June 22.

✔ Before Hitler would commit troops to an invasion of southern England, he needed to clear the Royal Air Force from the sky. The result was the first battle ever fought solely for air supremacy: The Battle of Britain.

✔ The Allies' invasion of France on D-Day was the largest seaborne invasion in history.

✔ In 1942, the Nazis put the finishing touches on a plan called the "Final Solution," a plan that called for the killing of all Jews in lands controlled by Germany, as well as all physically and mentally handicapped people and all Gypsies.

WORLD WAR II: THE PACIFIC

The attack on Pearl Harbor on December 7, 1941, left the U.S. Pacific Fleet briefly powerless to halt Japan's expansion. During the next 6 months, Japanese forces swept across Southeast Asia and the western Pacific Ocean. Japan's empire reached its greatest size in August 1942. It stretched northeast to the Aleutian Islands of Alaska, west to Burma (now Myanmar), and south to the Netherlands Indies (now Indonesia). The Allies halted Japan's expansion in the summer of 1942. They hacked away at its empire until Japan surrendered in August 1945.

▲ **A Japanese kamikaze** (suicide pilot) flies toward a United States warship in this photograph. In a last desperate effort to win World War II, kamikazes crashed their planes into Allied ships.

The War in Asia: Time Line

February 15 ▲
The British surrender Singapore to the Japanese.

July 21
Japanese occupy French Indochina.

April 9
Bataan falls, ending resistance to the Japanese in the Philippines; U.S. general Douglas MacArthur vows, "I shall return."

October 18
Hideki Tojo becomes Japanese prime minister.

1941   1942

December 7
Japanese attack Pearl Harbor, beginning a rapid sweep through the Pacific region.

April 18
American bombers hit Tokyo in the Doolittle raid.

May 4–8
The Allies stop a Japanese assault in the Battle of the Coral Sea.

May 6
Americans and Filipinos on Corregidor Island in Manila Bay surrender to the Japanese.

December 8
United States enters the war; Japan lands troops in the Philippines. Britain and Canada declare war on Japan.

June 6
U.S. planes destroy the Japanese fleet at the Battle of Midway.

August 7
U.S. Marines land at Guadalcanal in the first amphibious assault that allows U.S. naval forces to push back the Japanese.

June 19–20
A U.S. naval force defeats the Japanese in the Battle of the Philippine Sea.

July 18
Japan's Prime Minister Tojo resigns.

February 9
Japanese resistance on Guadalcanal ends.

March 2–4
U.S. defeats the Japanese in the Battle of Bismarck Sea.

January 9
The Allies land on the Philippine island of Luzon and drive to Manila.

March 16
U.S. Marines capture Iwo Jima (an island now known as Iwo To).

March 26
U.S. forces land on the Japanese island of Okinawa.

June 21
Allied forces capture Okinawa.

August 8
The Soviet Union declares war on Japan and invades Manchuria.

August 9
A second atomic bomb is dropped, on Nagasaki, Japan.

September 2
Japanese sign surrender terms aboard the battleship *Missouri* as it lay at anchor in Tokyo Bay (V-J Day).

1943   **1944**   **1945**

June 1
U.S. starts using submarine warfare against the Japanese.

October 7
Approximately 100 American POWs are executed by the Japanese on Wake Island.

November 20
U.S. forces invade Tarawa in the Gilbert Islands.

December 26
The Allies launch a full assault on New Britain in the Solomon Islands.

October 20
The Allies begin landing in the Philippines.

October 23–26
The Allies defeat Japan's navy in the Battle of Leyte Gulf in the Philippines.

October
General MacArthur returns to the Philippines.

August 6
The United States drops the first atomic bomb, on Hiroshima, Japan; more than 78,000 people are killed in a single minute. ▼

Struggle in the Pacific

Early Japanese Victories

On December 8, 1941, Japanese bombers struck the British colony of Hong Kong on the south coast of China and two U.S. islands in the Pacific Ocean—Guam and Wake. The Japanese invaded Thailand the same day. Thailand surrendered within hours and began cooperating with the Japanese. Japanese troops took Hong Kong, Guam, and Wake Island by the end of the year.

By late January 1942, the Japanese had pushed the British forces back to Singapore, a fortified island off the tip of the Malay peninsula. The Japanese stormed the island on February 8, and Singapore surrendered a week later. Japan captured about 60,000 soldiers, making the fall of Singapore the United Kingdom's worst military defeat ever.

Japan began landing troops in the Philippines on December 8, 1941. American and Philippine forces commanded by U.S. general Douglas MacArthur defended the islands. In late December, MacArthur's forces abandoned Manila, the capital of the Philippines, and withdrew to nearby Bataan Peninsula. Although suffering from malnutrition and disease, they beat back Japanese attacks for over 3 months.

The Battle of Midway

Three events in 1942 helped turn the tide against Japan. The first was the Doolittle raid on April 18, 1942, in which the United States staged a daring bombing raid on Tokyo and other Japanese cities. The second was the Battle of the Coral Sea, in which American warships met the Japanese force northeast of Australia from May 4 to 8.

The third and most significant was the Battle of Midway. Japan sent a large fleet to capture Midway Island at the westernmost tip of the Hawaiian archipelago. The United States had cracked Japan's naval code and thus learned about the coming invasion. Admiral Chester W. Nimitz, commander of the U.S. Pacific Fleet, gathered the ships that had survived the raid on Pearl Harbor and the Battle of the Coral Sea and prepared to ambush the Japanese.

The battle opened on June 4, 1942. During the 3-day battle—also fought entirely by warplanes—the Japanese suffered great losses: 4 aircraft carriers, 275 aircraft, and around 3,000 sailors and aviators.

The Battle of Midway was the first clear Allied victory over Japan in World War II. The battle crippled the Japanese navy and stopped Japan's advances. Aircraft carriers had become the most important weapon in the war in the Pacific.

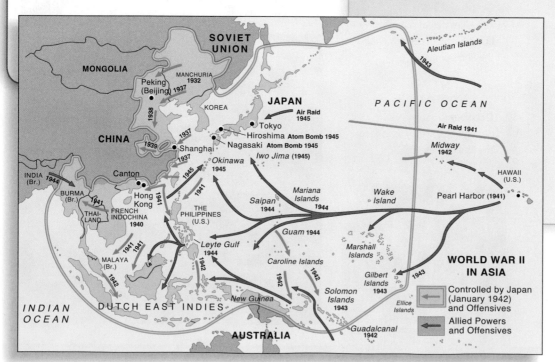

◀ **Overview of World War II in the Pacific.** This map shows major offensives and the greatest extent of Japanese control.

The Liberation of the Philippines

The campaigns in the Central Pacific brought the Allies within striking distance of the Philippine Islands. Expecting stiff Japanese resistance, the Allies assembled a landing force of more than 700 ships and pointed them at the island of Leyte in the central Philippines. On October 20, 1944, American troops poured ashore.

During the Battle for Leyte Gulf, the Japanese unleashed a terrifying new weapon—the *kamikaze* (Japanese for "divine wind") suicide pilot. Kamikazes intended to crash their planes filled with explosives into Allied warships, but most were shot down before they reached their targets. The few that got through, however, caused great damage, terror, and loss of life.

On January 9, 1945, the Allies landed on the island of Luzon and fought their way to the capital city of Manila, which was almost completely destroyed. Nearly 100,000 Filipino civilians died in the conquest of Manila. Eventually, the remaining Japanese troops on Luzon—50,000 of them—pulled back to the mountains and went on fighting until the war ended.

American losses in the Philippines were heavy, with 13,700 killed in action. Japanese losses were catastrophic, with at least 200,000 dead. Japan was doomed to defeat after losing the Philippines. But it did not intend to surrender.

The Atomic Bomb and Its Aftermath

On August 6, 1945, an American B-29 bomber called the *Enola Gay* dropped the first atomic bomb used in warfare on the Japanese city of Hiroshima. The explosion killed from 70,000 to 140,000 people, it is estimated, and destroyed about 5 square miles (13 square kilometers) of the city. After Japanese leaders failed to respond to the bombing, the United States dropped another bomb on Nagasaki on August 9. It killed about 40,000 people. Later, thousands more died of injuries and radiation from the two bombings. Meanwhile, on August 8, the Soviet Union declared war on Japan and invaded Manchuria.

Victory in the Pacific. Although Japan's emperors had traditionally stayed out of politics, Hirohito urged the government to surrender. On August 14, Japan agreed to unconditional surrender.

On September 2, 1945, representatives of Japan signed the official statement of surrender aboard the U.S. battleship *Missouri*, which lay at anchor in Tokyo Bay. Representatives of all the Allied nations were present. Truman declared September 2 as V-J Day, or Victory over Japan Day. World War II had ended.

ISLAND HOPPING IN THE CENTRAL PACIFIC

From late 1943 until the fall of 1944, the Allies hopped from island to island across the Central Pacific toward the Philippines. During the island-hopping campaign, the Allies became expert at amphibious invasions—seaborne operations that involve naval, air, and land forces. Each island they captured provided a base from which to strike the next target. But rather than capture every island, the Allies bypassed Japanese strongholds and invaded islands that were weakly held. That strategy, known as leapfrogging, saved time and lives. Leapfrogging carried the Allies across the Gilbert, Marshall, Caroline, and Mariana islands in the Central Pacific.

✔ On December 8, 1941, the day after they attacked Pearl Harbor, the Japanese invaded Hong Kong, Thailand, and the islands of Guam and Wake.

✔ The Battle of Midway was the first clear Allied victory over Japan. The battle crippled the Japanese navy and stopped Japan's advances in the Pacific.

✔ During the Battle for Leyte Gulf in the Philippines, the Japanese unleashed a terrifying new weapon: kamikaze suicide pilots, who intended to crash their planes filled with explosives into Allied warships.

✔ The war in the Pacific came to an end only after the United States dropped atomic bombs on Japanese cities: Hiroshima on August 6 and Nagasaki on August 9.

THE POSTWAR WORLD: THE AFTERMATH

Peace came in 1945 to a Europe that had suffered more than at any time since the barbarian invasions of Rome. A new word, *genocide,* was coined to describe the Nazi attempts to wipe out the Jews and other "inferior" races of Europe. The discovery that 6 million Jews, 6 million Slavs, and others had actually been killed in special extermination camps (the Holocaust) shocked a world that thought it had seen every imaginable kind of cruelty. The moral foundations of Europe had been severely battered by this display of barbarism.

WORLD WAR II	
TOTAL WAR DEATHS: 35,695,000	
Major Participants (total military and civilian deaths)	
Allied Powers	**Axis Powers**
Belgium (150,000)	Bulgaria (24,000)
Canada (39,000)	Germany (4,000,000)
France (675,000)	Hungary (836,000)
Great Britain (450,000)	Italy (220,000)
Netherlands (206,000)	Japan (2,000,000)
Poland (6,445,000)	Romania (626,000)
Soviet Union (15,000,000)	
United States (408,000)	
Yugoslavia (1,400,000)	

Staring Out from the Rubble

Rebuilding from Scratch

The physical state of Europe was no better. Strategic bombing had leveled cities, destroyed industries, and disrupted communications. Everything would have to be rebuilt, including the structure of governments.

Large parts of Asia also were devastated by war, especially China, which had been fighting for 8 years. Little pleasure could be taken in Japan's defeat there; it meant only that civil war between Nationalists and Communists could resume. Japan had suffered massive damage, and it also had been humiliated, its military ruling regime disgraced.

▲ **Hamburg, Germany,** sustained heavy Allied bombing. The buildings on this street were reduced to unrecognizable rubble by 1945.

A Struggle for World Peace

In the half century following World War II, the world was transformed more completely and dramatically than ever before in history. Established nations changed politically and economically; new nations emerged. Rapid technological advances in warfare, transportation, and communications altered people's general view of the world. In an age of potential universal annihilation, a new perception arose that all nations must work toward a common destiny, that humanity is, in fact, a sort of "global village."

The United Nations

Even before the war had ended, a new international organization was founded. It was pledged to establish and maintain a just peace in the postwar world. In April 1945, representatives of 50 nations met in San Francisco to draft a charter for the United Nations (UN). Their hope was that the UN could succeed where the earlier League of Nations had failed.

PREAMBLE TO THE CHARTER OF THE UNITED NATIONS

"We the peoples of the United Nations determined

- to save succeeding generations from the scourge of war, which twice in our lifetime has brought untold sorrow to mankind, and

- to reaffirm faith in fundamental human rights, in the dignity and worth of the human person, in the equal rights of men and women and of nations large and small, and

- to establish conditions under which justice and respect for the obligations arising from treaties and other sources of international law can be maintained, and

- to promote social progress and better standards of life in larger freedom,

and for these ends

- to practice tolerance and live together in peace with one another as good neighbors, and

- to unite our strength to maintain international peace and security, and

- to ensure, by the acceptance of principles and the institution of methods, that armed force shall not be used, save in the common interest, and

- to employ international machinery for the promotion of the economic and social advancement of all peoples,

have resolved to combine our efforts to accomplish these aims.

- Accordingly, our respective Governments, through representatives assembled in the city of San Francisco, who have exhibited their full powers found to be in good and due form, have agreed to the present Charter of the United Nations and do hereby establish an international organization to be known as the United Nations."

Rebuilding Europe

As Allied victory became assured in the closing months of World War II, there was no coherent plan for postwar Europe. During the war, the Allies had held top-level meetings at Tehran in Iran and at Yalta in the Soviet Union. At these meetings, the "Big Three"—Franklin D. Roosevelt of the United States, Winston Churchill of Great Britain, and Joseph Stalin of the Soviet Union—discussed the reconstruction of postwar Europe. The question of what to do with Germany was left open. All that was decided was that there would be occupation zones—the Russians would occupy eastern Germany; Britain, the United States, and France would share the western part.

Splitting Germany. The occupation zones hardened into two new countries. In 1949, the German Democratic Republic (East Germany) was established under Russian aegis. The Federal Republic of Germany (West Germany) was guarded by the British, French, and Americans. The creation of the two Germanies marked a larger phenomenon, the consolidation of Soviet rule in Eastern Europe, which, in effect, became a Soviet dependency. As Winston Churchill remarked, an iron curtain had fallen across Europe, dividing it into a Communist East and a democratic West and restricting communication and travel between the two.

▲ **The United Nations flag** has a map of the world surrounded by a wreath of olive branches on a light blue background. The olive branches symbolize peace.

Rebirth in Europe and Japan

Reviving European Economies

The political reorganization of Europe took place at the same time that attempts were being made to revive the European economy. In 1947, George C. Marshall, the American secretary of state, proposed a plan for the economic recovery of Europe that involved heavy American subsidies. The Marshall Plan was offered to all the nations that had suffered from World War II, including the Soviet Union and the countries of Eastern Europe. (See page 199.) The Soviet Union declined and also forced its satellites to forgo the benefits of the plan. The rest of Europe eagerly accepted the helping hand. The results were dramatic. Western Europe made a rapid economic recovery. By the 1950s, normality had been regained.

Things were different on the other side of the iron curtain. The Soviet Union determined to follow a socialist course in recovering from its terrible losses in the war, and could do it only by political and economic domination of the lands that had fallen under its control. Countries behind the iron curtain were drawn into a close economic embrace, and their economies subordinated to Russian needs. The standard of living in the Communist countries rose with glacial slowness, in contrast to the incredible rapidity with which the standard of living in the West shot up.

Europe after World War II. Communist and non-Communist states were positioned opposite each other across a basically east-west divide.

Western European Integration

The economic miracle achieved in postwar Western Europe owed much of its success to a growing spirit of unity among its nations. In 1949, the Council of Europe formed to link them socially, culturally, and economically. In 1951, Belgium, France, Italy, Luxembourg, the Netherlands, and West Germany forged the European Economic Coal and Steel Community, which served to unify these countries' coal, iron, and steel industries.

The Common Market. In 1957, these same nations signed the Treaty of Rome, which established the European Economic Community, or Common Market. Its aims were to eliminate barriers to free trade among its members and to facilitate the movement of labor and capital among them. The old economic walls that had served to separate the countries of Europe began to tumble down. There was not, however, universal agreement on the nature and scope of economic reforms. France, under Charles de Gaulle's leadership, played a leading role in the organization, and was able, at first, to exclude Great Britain from the Common Market. It was only in 1973 that Britain finally joined the European Community.

Japan

Unlike Germany, Japan was not divided into zones of foreign occupation after World War II. Only American forces occupied Japan.

The Allies had arrived at two major postwar aims for Japan: to eliminate any possibility of renewed Japanese militarism, and to turn Japan into a democratic state. To accomplish the first, Japan was totally demilitarized. The United States promised to provide defense for Japan should it be threatened militarily. Also, an emphasis was placed on the education of Japanese children away from militarism. For instance, textbooks were rewritten to eliminate any glorification of Japan's military tradition.

To accomplish the second goal, democratization, the Japanese emperor was required to renounce his claim to divinity; however, he was permitted to remain as a figurehead monarch. More importantly, in 1947 the Japanese adopted a new constitution that established a parliamentary form of government. It also granted women full equality, including the right to vote.

▲ **Cauldrons of molten steel** glow at the Yawata Steel mill in June 1952.

THE DOWNSIDE OF JAPAN'S ECONOMIC MIRACLE

Japan's economic miracle was achieved at high cost. Here are three of the biggest problems Japan has had to face in its quest for industrial preeminence.

- Industrialization has taken its toll on the environment and has concentrated more than half of Japan's population in a heavily overcrowded 350-mile industrial corridor on the island of Honshu.

- Economic success has also strained relations between Japan and other industrial powers, especially the United States. Japan has developed a huge trade surplus, annually exporting goods valued at billions of dollars more than the goods it imports.

- Industrial competitors accused Japan of maintaining trade policies that made it difficult or impossible for them to sell their products in the country.

Japan's Economic Miracle. By the time the American occupation ended in 1952, Japan was well on its way to not merely full economic recovery, but to creating the second highest gross national product in the world.

At first, Japan concentrated its resources on the development of heavy industry and textiles. By 1957, Japan had the most-modern steel mills in the world and surpassed France and West Germany in industrial production. Japan then turned to light industry, specifically high-technology products such as electronic equipment and components. By the 1970s, it had surpassed the former world leader in high technology, the United States, in many areas.

Japan's economic success resulted from three major sources: a stable, conservative government, mainly under the leadership of the Liberal Democratic Party, that fostered pro-business policies; a well-educated workforce; and a high personal savings rate, which helped to provide the capital needed for long-range business development.

Independence in India

The Indian Subcontinent

In 1945, the British government promised that the Indian subcontinent and the British colony of Ceylon, off India's southern coast, would be granted independence no later than 1948. But as the Indians tried to draw up a constitution, the centuries-old Hindu-Muslim conflict flared again. The Muslim League demanded that India be partitioned into two states: India for the Hindus and Pakistan for the Muslims. The British government acceded, and in August 1947, British rule ended in India. In 1948, Ceylon became independent. It was later renamed Sri Lanka.

The partition of India led to the displacement of millions and countless acts of violence, as Hindus fled Muslim Pakistan and Muslims fled Hindu India. In the exchange of more than 10 million people, about 500,000 were killed. Mohandas K. Gandhi, an opponent of partition, was another casualty, killed by an anti-Muslim Hindu fanatic in 1948.

Conditions did not improve between India and Pakistan in the decades that followed. Border disputes broke out regularly and violently, especially over the rich province of Kashmir, peopled mainly by Muslims but governed mainly by India.

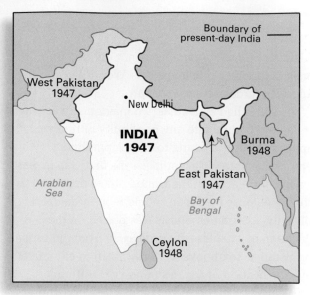

▲ **The independent country of India** was founded on August 15, 1947, the day after the northwestern and northeastern parts of the Indian subcontinent became the independent country of Pakistan. Burma (now Myanmar) and Ceylon (now Sri Lanka) won independence in 1948. East Pakistan broke away in 1971 and became the independent country of Bangladesh.

Internal Strife. Acrimonious disputes between groups within the newly independent states emerged as well. In 1971, civil war erupted in Pakistan, whose eastern and western sections were separated by a thousand miles on opposite sides of northern India. East Pakistan, angered at West Pakistan's dominance in government, gained India's support and fought off West Pakistani troops to become the independent state of Bangladesh in 1972.

In India, controversy over language and religion created internal dissension. When Hindi was declared the official language of India in 1965, speakers of India's 13 other major languages objected, especially the Tamil speakers of the south. The protesters saw it as an attack by the central government on provincial rights and traditions.

In the 1980s, the Sikhs, a religious sect based in the Punjab, stepped up their demands for independence from India. The violence peaked in 1984, with the bloody suppression in June of a Sikh uprising.

▲ **Mohandas Karamchand Gandhi** helped win freedom for India. He preached nonviolence in his long campaign for freedom and social reform.

568

ECONOMIC CHALLENGES

The rapidly growing population of South Asia puts a severe strain on the food production capabilities of the area. India's population alone, which grew from 350 million in 1947 to over 600 million in 1975, and over 1 billion in 2000, has been repeatedly threatened by famine. Only "Green Revolution" gains in food production have held it at bay. In Bangladesh, an extremely high population density and frequent devastating floods have repeatedly produced famine and homelessness. Other nations of South Asia are at risk as well.

This action led to Prime Minister Indira Gandhi's assassination in October 1984, by two militant Sikh members of her bodyguard. Bloody reprisals against Sikhs followed.

A civil war also erupted in Afghanistan, Pakistan's northern neighbor. In 1978, a coup put a pro-Soviet Communist government in power, leading to a revolt by anti-Communist Afghan rebels. The following year, the Soviet Union sent in an estimated 100,000 troops to bolster the Communist regime and help suppress the rebellion. During the 9 years of war that followed, about a million Afghans were killed and hundreds of thousands of Afghan refugees crossed the border into Pakistan, severely straining that country's resources. In early 1989, the last Soviet troops in Afghanistan were withdrawn. At first, it was believed that the Communist regime in Kabul would soon collapse without Soviet military aid, but Afghan guerrillas were unable to score a decisive military victory. The civil war continued unabated.

Know now you!

✔ In April 1945, representatives of 50 nations met in San Francisco to draft a charter for the United Nations (UN), which pledged to establish and maintain a just peace in the postwar world.

✔ The Marshall Plan was offered to all the nations that had suffered from World War II. The results were dramatic. By the 1950s, normality had been regained in Western Europe.

✔ Japan's economic success resulted from three major sources: a stable government; a well-educated workforce; and a high personal savings rate, which helped to provide the capital needed for long-range business development.

✔ British rule ended in India in August 1947 and resulted in the partitioning of India into two countries: the predominantly Hindu nation of India and the Muslim nation of Pakistan.

THE COLD WAR

The firm hold that the Soviet Union maintained on the countries of Eastern Europe convinced the West that the Soviets intended to expand Communist influence throughout the world. In 1949, the United States initiated the North Atlantic Treaty Organization (NATO), an alliance of the United States, Canada, and 10 Western European nations committed to mutual defense in the event of a Soviet attack. The Soviet Union countered by organizing the Warsaw Treaty Organization, or Warsaw Pact, a mutual defense alliance including the Soviet Union and the seven Eastern European nations it dominated. Europe was clearly split into two opposing camps, both armed but maintaining an uneasy peace.

THE NEW IMPERIALISM

▲ **Growing Russian imperialism** is depicted in this 1951 cartoon.

Communism in Europe

The Soviet Bloc

The Soviet Union had suffered during World War II more than any other nation, with an estimated loss of 20 million Russian lives. Eager to create a security zone of satellite states as a buffer between Western Europe and the Soviet Union, Stalin consolidated the Soviet hold over the Eastern European nations it had occupied during the war—Estonia, Latvia, Lithuania, Poland, East Germany, Czechoslovakia, Hungary, Romania, and Bulgaria. (Two others, Yugoslavia and Albania, succeeded in breaking away from Soviet domination, though they retained Communist governments.)

▲ **Winston Churchill,** photographed here in 1946 when speaking in New York City

The Iron Curtain Descends. During 1945 and early in 1946, the Soviet Union cut off nearly all contacts between the West and the occupied territories of Eastern Europe. In March 1946, Prime Minister Winston Churchill of the United Kingdom warned that "an iron curtain has descended across the Continent" of Europe. He made popular the phrase "iron curtain" to refer to Soviet barriers against the West. Behind these barriers, the Soviet Union steadily expanded its power.

In 1946, the USSR rejected a U.S. proposal for an international agency to control nuclear energy production and research. The Soviet Union believed the United States had a lead in nuclear weapons and would have a monopoly if controls were approved. The Soviet Union pictured itself as a defender of peace and accused the United States of planning a third world war. (See pages 200–203.)

▲ **President Harry S. Truman** is pictured signing the Unification Bill, which created the Department of Defense in 1947.

In March 1947, President Truman declared that the United States would help any free nation resist Communist aggression. Congress granted his request for $400 million for aid to Greece and Turkey. With this aid, both Greece and Turkey successfully resisted Communism. The new American policy became known as the Truman Doctrine. Aimed at Soviet expansion in Europe and the Middle East, the Truman Doctrine developed into the Containment Policy. The Containment Policy was designed to hold back the expansion of Communism throughout the world.

▲ **Nikita Khrushchev** in a show of solidarity with other eastern leaders in Bucharest, Romania, 1962

The De-Stalinization of the Soviet Union

Stalin died in 1953, and after a power struggle in the Communist Party, Nikita Khrushchev became the Soviet premier. In 1956, in a secret speech that stunned the party bureaucracy, Khrushchev denounced Stalinist tyranny. He then initiated a series of reforms that aimed at "de-Stalinizing" the Soviet Union. But Khrushchev had no intention of easing Soviet domination of the Eastern bloc. In 1956, Hungary made an effort to break away, but Soviet tanks rolled in to crush the revolt. Meanwhile, discontented East Germans were fleeing to West Germany by the thousands, many through Berlin, which was still under the joint occupation of the Allies. In 1961, the Berlin Wall was built through the city by the East German government to stop the flow of refugees. In 1968, Czechoslovakia tried to liberalize its Communist rule, only to be invaded and subdued by Warsaw Pact troops ordered there by Leonid Brezhnev, Khrushchev's successor.

Communism in China

At the close of World War II, civil war between Chiang Kai-shek's Nationalist forces and Mao Zedong's Communist "People's Liberation Army" resumed. Mao had gained the broad support of the peasants, and by 1948, the Nationalists were in full retreat and the Communists were gaining control of China. On October 1, 1949, Mao proclaimed the establishment of the People's Republic of China, with its capital at Beijing. Chiang and his remaining forces fled to the island of Formosa, or Taiwan, 100 miles off China's southeastern coast. There he proclaimed the Nationalist government of the Republic of China, with its capital at Taipei. Both claimed to be the sole legal government of all of China.

Mao Zedong, as depicted in a mural found on an old coal mine administrative building. ▼

The Korean War

Japan's defeat in World War II had freed Korea from 35 years of Japanese domination. At the end of the war, Soviet troops occupied the northern part of Korea and American troops the southern part. In 1948, the foreign troops pulled out, but they left a country divided into a Communist North Korea and a non-Communist South Korea.

In June 1950, North Korea invaded South Korea in an attempt to reunite Korea under Communist rule. The United States asked the United Nations (UN) to send in troops to defend South Korea. By November, UN forces, mainly comprised of U.S. troops, had driven North Korean forces to the Chinese border. Before the North Korean army could be completely defeated, however, some 200,000 Chinese troops swept across the border to join the conflict. The fighting continued until an armistice was signed in July 1953. It returned North and South Korea to their prewar borders and statuses.

THE CULTURAL REVOLUTION

By the **mid-1960s**, Communist leadership in China was divided between the pragmatists, who favored gradual economic development and social change, and Mao and his followers, who felt radical means had to be used to keep the process of revolution going.

In **1966**, Mao launched the Great Proletarian Cultural Revolution. Paramilitary groups of students, called the Red Guards, attacked the "elite"—government officials, managers, and intellectuals—declaring them enemies of the people. Chaos ensued all over China as violence disrupted government, industrial production, and education. Not until **1969** was the army able to restore order and bring the Red Guards under control.

The Berlin Wall

As Cold War tensions increased in 1961, the Communists moved in August to end the embarrassing flow of refugees from Communist East Germany into West Germany. The result was the Berlin Wall, a 29-mile-long barrier separating East and West Berlin. In the West, the wall quickly became a symbol of Communist oppression. (The wall was dismantled in November 1989, following the collapse of Communism in East Germany.)

Cuban Missile Crisis

One of the most serious incidents of the Cold War was the Cuban Missile Crisis of 1962. Communists had come to power in Cuba in 1959. In October 1962, the United States learned that the Soviet Union had installed missiles in Cuba that could launch nuclear attacks on United States cities. U.S. president John F. Kennedy's demand that the missile sites be dismantled and withdrawn brought the United States and the Soviet Union to the brink of nuclear war. After 6 days, the crisis passed. Soviet leader Nikita Khrushchev and President Kennedy agreed that the Soviets would remove their missiles from Cuba in return for the removal of U.S. nuclear missiles from Turkey and Kennedy's promise that the United States would not invade Cuba. The incident was a contributing factor to Khrushchev's fall from power in 1964. However, the crisis also served to heighten public awareness of the dangerous possibility of nuclear war.

SPUTNIK AND THE SPACE RACE

Sputnik, a 184-pound artificial satellite, was launched into orbit around Earth by the Soviets on **October 4, 1957**. The launch marked the beginning of the space age. On **April 12, 1961**, the Russian cosmonaut Yuri A. Gagarin became the first man to orbit Earth. U.S. astronaut John Glenn became the first American to orbit Earth, in **February 1962**. But on **July 20, 1969**, the United States won a clear victory by landing the first men on the moon (Neil Armstrong and Edwin "Buzz" Aldrin, Jr.). Meanwhile, satellites and other space vehicles were perfected for a wide range of peaceful and military purposes by both sides.

◀ **A missile launch site** in San Cristobal, Cuba, shown here in an aerial photograph, was part of the evidence that precipitated the Cuban Missile Crisis.

Communism in Southeast Asia

Vietnam

France was not willing to give up its colonial possessions in Indochina. In 1946, it granted some autonomy to Cambodia and Laos but did not grant them independence until 1953 and 1954, respectively, and only after becoming mired in a guerrilla war in another Southeast Asian colony, Vietnam. The Communist leader Ho Chi Minh, who had led the Viet Minh guerrilla resistance against the Japanese, had proclaimed Vietnam a republic in 1945, with himself as president. French military attempts to restore colonial rule ended with a major Viet Minh victory at Dien Bien Phu in 1954. The peace agreement that ended the struggle, the Geneva Accords, temporarily divided the country into a Communist North Vietnam and a non-Communist South Vietnam—pending elections leading to a reunified country. However, the regime in South Vietnam declined to hold elections, and the temporary division of Vietnam became permanent with the formation of two Vietnamese states. This division was a direct outgrowth of the Cold War.

The Vietnam War. Soon Communist guerrilla and regular forces from the north joined the southern guerrillas, called the Vietcong, and resumed the war. By 1960, open warfare against the South Vietnamese government began.

With Chinese and Soviet support, the North Vietnamese were able to keep the Vietcong supplied and fighting. The United States provided support for the South Vietnamese troops, at first sending financial aid, military equipment, and several hundred military advisers. In 1964, however, the United States decided to expand military assistance to South Vietnam, adding great numbers of combat troops. By 1968, half a million American troops were in Vietnam, saving South Vietnam from collapse but not defeating the Vietcong.

In 1968, American and Vietnamese diplomats began peace negotiations in Paris, but not until 1973 was a peace treaty signed. American forces withdrew from Vietnam. Shortly after, the fragile cease-fire was ignored by the North Vietnamese, who initiated a major offensive. In April 1975, Communist forces overwhelmed South Vietnamese units and took control of the south. In 1976, Vietnam was united under Communist rule and Saigon was renamed Ho Chi Minh City.

Important Dates in the Vietnam War	
1957	The Vietcong began to rebel against the South Vietnamese government headed by President Ngo Dinh Diem.
Nov. 1, 1963	South Vietnamese generals overthrew the government; Diem was killed the next day.
Aug. 7, 1964	Congress passed the Tonkin Gulf Resolution, which gave the president power to take "all necessary measures" and "to prevent further aggression."
March 6, 1965	President Lyndon B. Johnson sent U.S. Marines to Da Nang, South Vietnam.
Jan. 30, 1968	North Vietnam and the Vietcong launched a major campaign against South Vietnamese cities.
June 8, 1969	President Richard M. Nixon announced U.S. troop withdrawal.
Jan. 27, 1973	The United States, North and South Vietnam, and the Vietcong signed a cease-fire agreement.
March 29, 1973	The last U.S. ground troops left Vietnam.
April 30, 1975	South Vietnam surrendered.

▲ **The Vietnam War** was the longest war in which the United States took part. It lasted from 1957 to 1975. In the war, helicopters often ferried U.S. soldiers from one site to another. (See pages 216–217.)

Political Turmoil in Southeast Asia

Vietnam's neighbors in Indochina, Laos and Cambodia, were also wrenched by war, as the Vietnamese conflict escalated during the 1960s. Civil war raged in both countries as Communist forces fought pro-Western factions.

Simultaneously with the Communist triumph in Vietnam, Communist forces fighting in Laos and Cambodia found themselves in much stronger strategic positions.

In Cambodia, the Khmer Rouge routed government forces and captured Phnom Penh, the capital, in April 1975. Under Pol Pot, the Khmer Rouge forcibly removed Cambodia's urban population to the countryside and began a monstrous reign of terror that claimed about a million Cambodian lives. Border clashes with Vietnam led to a Vietnamese invasion of Cambodia in 1977. A new, pro-Vietnamese Communist regime was installed in Phnom Penh. However, Vietnamese forces remained in Cambodia until 1989.

▲ **The Khmer Rouge,** under Pol Pot, systematized the slaughter of hundreds of thousands of Cambodian citizens. This table and its burden was photographed in 1989 in Siem Reab, a former extermination center.

In Laos, the Communist Pathet Lao forces, backed by North Vietnam, scored major military gains in 1975, taking control of the country in December.

During and after these upheavals, hundreds of thousands of refugees fled from Vietnam, Cambodia, and Laos. Many unfortunate people fleeing their homes found their way to overcrowded refugee camps in Thailand, Malaysia, Indonesia, and Hong Kong. International organizations took up the complicated task of relocating the dispossessed to other countries, helping to reunite families, and aiding refugees in adjusting to life in unfamiliar surroundings and cultures.

Nearly all the countries of Southeast Asia faced problems of political stability. Burma (now Myanmar), for example, had to deal both with separatist movements launched by ethnic minorities and with Communist insurgents.

Malaysia faced conflict between its major ethnic groups—the Malays, Malaysia's largest ethnic group, and the Chinese and Indians, who dominated Malaysian business and commerce. In the Philippines, Communist guerrilla forces have been active for decades, and Muslim secessionists in the south have been fighting to establish an autonomous state in Mindanao.

now you **Know!**

✔ After World War II, Stalin consolidated the Soviet hold over the Eastern European nations it had occupied during the war.

✔ In 1949, the Communists gained control of China, forcing the Chinese Nationalists to retreat to the island of Taiwan.

✔ During the Cuban Missile Crisis in 1962, U.S. president John F. Kennedy demanded that Soviet missile sites on the Communist-controlled island of Cuba be dismantled and withdrawn.

✔ In 1964, the United States greatly expanded military assistance to South Vietnam. By 1968, half a million American troops were fighting in Vietnam.

END OF THE COLD WAR

At the heart of Cold War tensions was the threat of nuclear warfare. Both sides had built up their nuclear arsenals until each was capable of destroying the world many times over. The standoff created by the fear of nuclear attack came to be called the "balance of terror."

In the early 1970s, the United States and the Soviet Union began looking for ways to ease international tensions, a process that took the name *détente*.

The Soviet Union once covered more than half of Europe and nearly two-fifths of Asia. This map shows the country's 15 republics and the dates when they became republics. When the Soviet Union dissolved in 1991, these republics all became independent nations. ▼

A New Generation of Leaders

Attempts at Détente

Early efforts at détente centered on arms reduction, especially the Strategic Arms Limitations Talks (SALT), by which the superpowers agreed to limit the number of nuclear missiles and warheads each could stockpile.

However, détente began to collapse in the late 1970s. U.S. president Jimmy Carter strongly supported human rights. In late 1979 and early 1980, Soviet troops invaded Afghanistan to try to keep that country's pro-Communist government in power. Governments worldwide condemned the invasion. The United States protested the invasion by limiting shipments of wheat to the USSR and by boycotting the 1980 Summer Olympic Games held in Moscow.

Soviet-U.S. relations worsened in 1981. That year, U.S. president Ronald Reagan called for a U.S. military buildup to match an expansion of Soviet arms. Soviet leaders feared that this buildup would give the United States a military advantage. They also realized that the USSR could not compete with the U.S. economy.

The Rise of Gorbachev

The older generation of Soviet leaders, who had been trained under Stalin, were dying out by the mid-1980s. In 1985, Mikhail Gorbachev became head of the Communist Party. At age 54, Gorbachev became the first member of a new generation of Soviet leaders to head the country.

Gorbachev's Reforms. Under Gorbachev, the Soviet Union changed rapidly. Gorbachev sought to improve economic performance by means of the policy of *perestroika*. He wanted to restructure the economy to stimulate growth and increase efficiency in Soviet industry. The reforms failed: shortages increased, inflation grew, and hoarding became widespread.

The most striking change was a new policy of openness called *glasnost*. Gorbachev introduced glasnost to help win popular support for his policies and overcome resistance to perestroika in the Communist Party and the Soviet government. Glasnost made it possible to discuss political and social issues critically and with more freedom than ever before in the Soviet Union. Also, a new freedom of expression in literature and the arts developed, and books by opponents of Communism became available in stores.

U.S. president Ronald Reagan (on right) and Soviet leader Mikhail Gorbachev are shown here signing a treaty in 1987 that led to reductions of U.S. and Soviet nuclear arms. Reagan met with Gorbachev several times. (See page 221.) ▼

Party Resistance. The Communist Party resisted Gorbachev's reforms, and so he promoted a reduction in the role of the party. In March 1989, the Soviet Union held its first contested elections in history. These elections resulted in the defeat of many top Communist Party officials and several top generals. The Communist Party's role was further reduced in March 1990, when the Soviet government voted to permit the creation of non-Communist political parties in the Soviet Union.

Under Gorbachev, the Soviet Union's relations with the West improved. In 1987, Gorbachev and U.S. president Ronald Reagan signed a treaty that was the first of a series of agreements to reduce the size of U.S. and Soviet nuclear forces. Between May 1988 and February 1989, Soviet troops withdrew from Afghanistan. In 1991, Gorbachev and U.S. president George H. W. Bush signed the Strategic Arms Reduction Treaty (START). This agreement, which would take effect when approved by the legislatures of both countries, ordered a reduction in the numbers of U.S. and Soviet long-range nuclear weapons.

In March 1990, the Soviet government created the office of president. The president became the head of the central government and the most powerful person in the Soviet Union. The Congress of People's Deputies elected Gorbachev as the first president of the USSR.

The Hurdles of Change

The Empire Crumbles

Poland provided a striking example of growing popular discontent within the socialist countries. The unavailability of consumer goods, high food prices, low wages, and repressive government contributed to the general unrest. In the fall of 1981, a nationwide labor movement called Solidarity emerged. Through strikes and demonstrations, it gained power and popularity until Polish prime minister General Wojciech Jaruzelski, under pressure from the Soviet Union, declared martial law, banned Solidarity, and imprisoned its leaders. But by the end of the decade,

Poland's economic problems finally forced its Communist Party to alter its stance. Solidarity was legalized, and after elections in 1989, Solidarity and the Communist Party fashioned a fusion government.

Much of the impetus for change in Poland and other Eastern European countries came from the changes brought about by Mikhail Gorbachev.

Gorbachev permitted the countries of Eastern Europe to follow their own courses of development free of the threat of Soviet military intervention. The result was widespread repudiation of Communism by these countries.

▲ **In the fall of 1989,** East Germany, one of the last hard-line Communist countries, saw the disintegration of its Communist Party in the face of economic chaos and revelations of party corruption. The new East German government began dismantling the Berlin Wall, the symbol of the Cold War, and less than a year later the two Germanies were finally reunited. By the end of 1989, not only Germany had seen a revolution, but Czechoslovakia, Hungary, Romania, and Bulgaria had also disposed of their Communist governments.

The Failed Coup. To prevent further disintegration, Gorbachev proposed a union treaty designed to satisfy demands by the republics for more control over their affairs. In July 1991, Gorbachev and the leaders of 10 republics reached agreement on a treaty that would give the republics a large amount of independence. The treaty was to be signed by five of the republics on August 20.

On August 19, before the treaty could be signed, conservative officials of the Communist Party staged

a coup against Gorbachev's government. The coup leaders imprisoned Gorbachev and his family in their vacation home. The president of the Russian republic, Boris N. Yeltsin, led opposition to the coup, which collapsed on August 21. Yeltsin's role in defying the coup increased his power and prestige both at home and abroad.

After the coup, Gorbachev returned to the office of president but never regained full power. He then resigned as head of the Communist Party.

Modernizing China

In the late 1950s, ideological differences began to cause strains between China and the Soviet Union. In 1959, the Soviet Union halted all aid to China and in the 1960s, the two countries clashed in border skirmishes. However, as Chinese relations with the Soviet Union deteriorated, those with the United States warmed. In 1972, U.S. president Richard M. Nixon visited China, ending more than 20 years of hostility and opening diplomatic relations.

Both Mao Zedong and Prime Minister Chou En-lai, the central figures in the Chinese Communist Party for decades, died in 1976. Soon, a more pragmatic wing of the Communist Party gained control of the government. China declared its dedication to four modernizations.

- agriculture
- industry
- military
- science and technology

To achieve these aims, China moved away from Communist ideological purity and toward greater economic incentives for peasants and workers; less central planning and more entrepreneurial activity; and more contact with the West, encouraging Western investment in China and increased Western trade.

- Early efforts at détente between the United States and the Soviet Union faltered when the Soviets invaded Afghanistan in 1979–1980.

- Relations between the United States and the Soviet Union improved upon the rise of Mikhail Gorbachev.

- On August 19, 1991, conservative Communist Party officials staged a coup against Gorbachev's government. The president of the Russian republic, Boris N. Yeltsin, led opposition to the coup, which collapsed on August 21.

- In 1972, U.S. president Richard M. Nixon visited China, ending more than 20 years of hostility and opening diplomatic relations between the two countries.

▲ **On May 4, 1989,** thousands of students gathered in Tiananmen Square.

Tiananmen Square. However, political reforms did not keep pace with economic reforms in China. In December 1986, many Chinese university students began demanding increased freedom of speech and a greater voice in the selection of officials. Students held demonstrations in a number of cities to promote their demands. In January 1987, Hu Yaobang was removed from his post of Communist Party general secretary. Conservative leaders had criticized Hu for his liberal views on freedom of expression and political reform.

Hu Yaobang died in April 1989. University students held marches to honor Hu and mourn his death. They called for a reevaluation of Hu by the country's leaders. These events led to large demonstrations by students and other citizens in Beijing's Tiananmen Square and on the streets of other Chinese cities. The protesters called for more democracy in China and an end to corruption in government. The military crushed the demonstrations and killed hundreds of protesters. The government later arrested many people suspected of involvement in the pro-democracy movement. The government executed a number of those arrested.

CONFLICT IN THE MIDDLE EAST

As in Asia following World War II, Western colonialism was soon to end in the Middle East and North Africa. Yet the fortunes of Western industrialized nations remained closely tied to those of the oil-rich nations of the region. In the postwar era, conflicts in the region seemed always at the flash point and a repeated threat to world peace.

As these largely Arab nations became independent, they joined the Arab League, formed in 1945. Original members included Egypt, Syria, Lebanon, Jordan, Saudi Arabia, Iraq, and Yemen. The Arab League spearheaded opposition to the formation and existence of Israel.

Conflict and Détente

The Arab-Israeli Conflict

Since its founding in 1948, Israel has fought several times with its Arab neighbors.

- In 1948, armies from Egypt, Jordan, Lebanon, Syria, and Iraq invaded Israel on behalf of the Palestinians who rejected Israel's creation. The Israelis repelled the invasion and took control of a large part of Arab Palestine.

- The second war began in 1956, when Egypt seized control of the Suez Canal from Great Britain. British, French, and Israeli forces attacked Egypt in response. United Nations (UN) intervention ended this war.

- In 1967, Israel struck against Egyptian, Syrian, and Jordanian forces. In 6 days, Israel destroyed the Egyptian and Syrian air forces and captured extensive territory.

- The fourth war was launched by Egypt and Syria in October 1973, on the Jewish holy day of Yom Kippur. After initial success, Egyptian and Syrian forces were driven back.

- Israeli-PLO tension led to a limited war between Lebanon and Israel in 1978 and an Israeli invasion of Lebanon in 1982. Conflicts between the two countries arose again in 2006.

New Hopes. In 1993, Israel and the Palestine Liberation Organization (PLO), led by Yasir Arafat, reached an agreement to establish Palestinian civil autonomy in Gaza and the West Bank town of Jericho. In 1994, Israel extended Palestinian self-rule in the West Bank, and Jordan and Israel ended their official state of war. However, Israeli-Palestinian violence continues to disrupt attempts to bring peace to the region, thwarting Arabs' and Israelis' desires to live peacefully without fear of terrorist attacks.

◀ **Jews paraded a captured Arab vehicle** through Tel Aviv on May 14, 1948, the day the Jewish state of Israel was established in the historic region of Palestine. Zionists (Jewish nationalists) and Palestinian Arabs were fighting over the region, which they both claimed. Israelis and Palestinians continue to struggle over the region.

Egyptian-Israeli Détente

Originally, Egypt acted as the leader of Arab opposition to Israel. In 1952, Gamal Abdel Nasser, an Egyptian army officer, led a military coup that overthrew the Egyptian monarchy. Nasser became president of the new Republic of Egypt. Nasser, determined to eliminate all British influence from Egypt, ordered the seizure of the Suez Canal in 1956. Nasser also ordered the construction of the Aswan High Dam to control the floodwater of the Nile River.

When Nasser died suddenly in 1970, another army officer, Anwar el-Sadat, succeeded him as president. Under Sadat's leadership, Egypt fought the 1973 Yom Kippur War against Israel. In 1977, Sadat surprised the world by visiting Israel to address the Israeli parliament, the Knesset, and advance a new peace initiative. That effort foundered, but the following year, U.S. president Jimmy Carter invited Sadat and Israeli prime minister Menachem Begin to Camp David in Maryland to renew negotiations. In September 1978, the parties signed the Camp David Accords, which established the foundations for a peace treaty between Egypt and Israel. The treaty was signed in Washington, D.C., in March 1979.

OIL AND OPEC

In 1960, the oil-producing nations of the Middle East, as well as the North African nations of Libya and Algeria, joined with other oil-producing nations to form a cartel, the Organization of Petroleum Exporting Countries (OPEC), to regulate production and prices. Oil production has added immeasurably to the wealth of Middle Eastern and North African nations and has given them a powerful political tool—the potential to raise oil prices or cut off oil supplies as punitive measures against Western policies in the region.

Such an action occurred after the Yom Kippur War of 1973, when Arab oil producers placed an embargo on oil shipments to nations supporting Israel. After lifting the embargo in 1974, OPEC again showed its power by quadrupling the price of oil. Worldwide inflation and a crippling of Western industrial growth was the result.

◄ **Anwar el-Sadat,** photographed here on June 4, 1981, as he meets with Israeli Prime Minister Menachem Begin for the 10th time

Iran and Iraq at War

Iran-Iraq War, 1980–1988

The modern history of Iraq could just as easily be referred to as the rise and fall of the Ba'ath Party, which ruled from 1968 until 2003. In large part, it is also the story of Saddam Hussein, since he basically was the Ba'ath Party after becoming president of Iraq, chairman of the Revolutionary Command Council, prime minister, and commander-in-chief in 1979.

Around the time that Saddam came into power in Iraq, Iran went through a major political upheaval: revolutionaries changed Iran's government from a monarchy to an Islamic republic in 1979. The new government was composed of Shiite Muslims who were highly antagonistic toward Iraq's Sunni-led government. The ayatollah made no secret of his disdain for Saddam and the Iraqi government in general.

At the same time, Saddam felt that Iran would be particularly vulnerable to attack. There were several reasons for this.

- Iran's new government was both internally unstable and internationally disliked.
- The regime was not widely supported by the Iranian people.
- The military was disorganized.
- The Iranian hostage crisis had spoiled Iran's international relations, particularly with the United States.

Since Iran had such a bad image and had effectively alienated itself from all of the major world powers, Saddam thought it likely that the world would support his aggression, if reluctantly.

War. On September 17, 1980, Saddam abruptly announced that Iraq had exclusive control over the Shatt al-Arab waterway, a major shipping channel used by both countries, located where the Euphrates and Tigris rivers meet.

Saddam felt confident that his large and well-equipped army would easily defeat Iran's, which had not yet fully recovered from the 1979 revolution. Furthermore, he assumed that the Iranian people would side with Iraq, since the new Iranian regime was widely disliked. However, the people of Iran responded to the attack by uniting under their government instead of toppling it.

The Iran-Iraq War (1980–1988) cost the two countries billions of dollars, and hundreds of thousands of people were killed. This photograph shows Iraqi soldiers standing next to a military truck on September 25, 1980. ▶

The war lasted for almost a decade. It can be broadly sketched in four stages.

The Iraqi Offensive. Although it became immediately obvious that the war was not going to be resolved as quickly as Saddam had planned, Iraq was relatively successful in these first years of the conflict. At one point, Iraq occupied the Shatt al-Arab and a sizable area of Iranian borderland.

The Iranian Counteroffensive. In late 1981, Iran unleashed a particularly grisly force: the Basij Army, whose sole tactic was literally to run at Iraqi soldiers. Iran then moved the fighting inside Iraqi borders. Iraq, appalled by its turn of fortune, offered a cease-fire in 1982. Emboldened by their recent success, the Iranians refused.

The War of Attrition. By 1984, Iran was hoping to wear down Iraq to the point of surrender. By this point, both sides had endured heavy casualties.

International Intervention. When Iran began attacking neutral foreign ships that were doing business with Iraq, the United States and other prominent Western powers felt obliged to become involved. Since Iran remained isolated from the Western world, these powers sided predominantly with Iraq.

The international powers that aligned themselves with Iraq contributed greatly to Iran's decision to accept a cease-fire in August 1988. The terms were specified in Resolution 598 of the UN Security Council, which had come about the year before.

▲ **Saddam Hussein** was president of Iraq from 1979 to 2003.

Control of the Shatt al-Arab waterway, on the border between Iran and Iraq, was the central issue in the Iran-Iraq War. ▶

U.S. War with Iraq

The Persian Gulf War

In the aftermath of the Iran-Iraq War, Iraq needed Kuwait and other Arab countries to cancel debts that Iraq had incurred to fight the Iran-Iraq War. But Saddam Hussein disagreed with Kuwait's leaders over how much debt cancellation Kuwait should provide to Iraq. He also wanted to acquire Kuwait's oil wealth and to increase Iraq's power within OPEC.

Saddam ordered the Iraqi army to enter Kuwait on August 2, 1990. Kuwait's 20,000-man army did not stand a chance against the swarming Iraqi troops. One week after the invasion, Saddam declared that Kuwait was the 19th province of Iraq.

The International Coalition. After the invasion, President George H. W. Bush stated that the United States would not tolerate Iraq's aggression against Kuwait. The president began building a coalition against Iraq. More than 30 countries became part of this group.

The single purpose of the coalition was to force Iraq to leave Kuwait immediately and unconditionally. Many of the Western coalition countries wanted to overthrow Saddam's regime, but it is unlikely that the Arab countries would have agreed to such an agenda. In any case, Saddam's removal would have almost certainly extended the duration of the war—an unattractive possibility in the eyes of most coalition members. (See pages 224–225.)

Operation Desert Storm. On January 17, 1991, coalition forces attacked via air, beginning a treacherous bombing campaign that targeted military-related sites in Iraq and Kuwait. This air strike, which lasted about 6 weeks, had severe, long-term detrimental effects on the Iraqi economy.

The air strike ended and ground fighting began on February 24. Troops were organized under a joint command structure, with General Norman Schwarzkopf leading the non-Arab countries and Saudi lieutenant general Khalid ibn Sultan ibn Abd al Azizl al Saud commanding Arab troops.

The ground attack did not last long. Iraqi troops surrendered or fled within a few days, and the Iraqi army was quickly forced out of Kuwait. Military operations were officially over by February 28. Coalition casualties were less than 400, while tens of thousands of Iraqis had died.

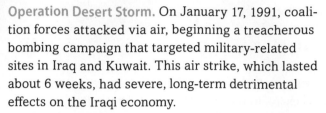

◄ **In one last ghastly act of defiance,** Iraqi troops dumped large amounts of Kuwaiti oil in the Persian Gulf and set fire to hundreds of oil wells as they left the country. While the fires were quelled relatively quickly (within months instead of years), the destruction was still significant. On top of the damage that Kuwait had already sustained during the war, its oil production facilities and the natural environment were further compromised.

Aftermath. Iraq accepted the terms of a cease-fire agreement a few months after its surrender. This agreement marked the beginning of the weapons inspection fiascos that would be the bane of the Western world for years to come. It also continued economic sanctions that would evolve into an utter humanitarian disaster for Iraqi citizens.

Operation Iraqi Freedom

As part of the cease-fire agreement that ended the Persian Gulf War of 1991, Iraq agreed to destroy all of its weapons of mass destruction—that is, biological, chemical, or nuclear weapons—and any facilities it had for producing such weapons. However, Iraq failed to cooperate with UN teams sent to inspect suspected weapons sites. Starting in 1998, the Iraqi government refused to allow UN weapons inspectors into the country.

U.S. president George W. Bush's justifications for a second war against Iraq were related to the threat of Iraq's presumed weapons stores. Many people believed that there was too much uncertainty surrounding past weapons inspections and recommended further investigation in Iraq before taking any drastic action. Ultimately, this caution proved to be well founded, since official investigations later discovered that there were no longer any weapons of mass destruction in Iraq.

▲ **Saddam** was dirty, disheveled, and graying when captured by U.S. forces near his hometown of Tikrit.

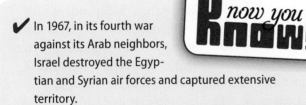

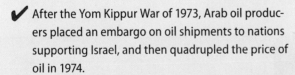

- ✔ In 1967, in its fourth war against its Arab neighbors, Israel destroyed the Egyptian and Syrian air forces and captured extensive territory.

- ✔ After the Yom Kippur War of 1973, Arab oil producers placed an embargo on oil shipments to nations supporting Israel, and then quadrupled the price of oil in 1974.

- ✔ The Iran-Iraq War began in 1980 when Iraq claimed exclusive control over the Shatt al-Arab waterway, a major shipping channel used by both countries, located where the Euphrates and Tigris rivers meet. The war lasted almost a decade.

- ✔ The most significant difference between the Persian Gulf War of 1991 and the second Iraq war was that in the latter, removing Saddam Hussein and the Ba'athist regime from power in Iraq was the primary objective.

The Bush administration was determined to go to war despite the proliferation of doubt both domestically and abroad. This resolve continued even after the UN did not mandate the second Gulf War. While the United States had deferred to the UN in the past, it did not do so in this instance.

The primary objective of the second Iraq War (also known as Operation Iraqi Freedom) was to topple the Ba'athist regime. The war was launched March 20, 2003. The explicit agenda for this war was to remove Saddam from power, a very different formulation than the stated goal of the Persian Gulf War.

U.S. forces seized control of Baghdad on April 9, only a few weeks after the start of the war. The first stage of Operation Iraqi Freedom was complete: Saddam had been removed from power.

By 2007, the U.S. Congress also began to exert pressure on the administration to set clear deadlines for the withdrawal of U.S. forces and to transfer security responsibilities to Iraqi units. Worldwide public opinion had increasingly come to oppose the continuing U.S. military presence in Iraq.

DEVELOPMENTS IN AFRICA

In the decades following World War II, nearly 40 newly independent nations emerged in sub-Saharan Africa, free from colonial rule but facing major political, economic, and social challenges. (See pages 544–545.) Many were very poor, making setting up the institutions of a modern nation—efficient executive, legislative, and judicial bodies as well as educational and health systems—exceedingly difficult. Achieving national unity was another challenge. Molding a variety of tribes, many with traditions of deep enmity toward each other, into a single, homogeneous state presented further serious problems. Establishing democratic government, an ideal of most African nationalists, proved elusive; either military dictatorships or one-party rules proliferated.

An Uneasy Transition

Independence

British colonies led the way in winning independence. In West Africa, the Gold Coast was the first to gain independence when it became the new nation of Ghana in 1957. Nigeria became independent in 1960, and Sierra Leone gained independence in 1961. In East Africa, independence came for Tanganyika in 1961. It joined with the island of Zanzibar to become Tanzania in 1964. Uganda, Rwanda, and Burundi became independent in 1962, and Kenya in 1963. In southern Africa, Northern Rhodesia became the Republic of Zambia in 1964. Southern Rhodesia remained a British colony until 1980, when it became the independent nation of Zimbabwe.

In 1958, Guinea became the first of several independent nations to be carved out of French West Africa and French Equatorial Africa. More new nations, including Senegal, the Ivory Coast (known now as Côte d'Ivoire), Mauritania, Mali, Niger, Chad, Cameroon, and Gabon, were formed in 1960. In the same year, the Belgian Congo became an independent nation, eventually called the Republic of Zaire (and now the Democratic Republic of the Congo).

Portugal, however, remained unwilling to give up its colonies, the oldest in Africa. Independence for these colonies came only after bitter guerrilla wars, begun in the early 1960s, and the overthrow of the government of Portugal in a military coup in 1974. The former colonies gained independence as the nations of Angola, Mozambique, and Guinea-Bissau.

◀ **The Gold Coast** gained its independence in 1957. It took the name Ghana, the name of an ancient African kingdom. Ghana was the first member of the Commonwealth of Nations to be governed by black Africans. A black star symbolizing African freedom is in the center of the middle yellow stripe of their flag.

Dates of African Independence			
Angola	1975	Libya	1951
Benin	1960	Madagascar	1960
Botswana	1966	Malawi	1964
Burkina Faso	1960	Mali	1960
Burundi	1962	Mauritania	1960
Cameroon	1960	Mauritius	1968
Cape Verde	1975	Morocco	1956
Central African Republic	1960	Mozambique	1975
Chad	1960	Namibia	1990
Comoros	1975	Niger	1960
Congo (Brazzaville)	1960	Nigeria	1960
Congo (Kinshasa)	1960	Rwanda	1962
Côte d'Ivoire (Ivory Coast)	1960	São Tomé and Príncipe	1975
Djibouti	1977	Senegal	1960
Egypt (African)	1922	Seychelles	1976
Equatorial Guinea	1968	Sierra Leone	1961
Eritrea	1993	Somalia	1960
Ethiopia	c. AD 1	South Africa	1931
Gabon	1960	Sudan	1956
Gambia	1965	Swaziland	1968
Ghana	1957	Tanzania	1964
Guinea	1958	Togo	1960
Guinea-Bissau	1974	Tunisia	1956
Kenya	1963	Uganda	1962
Lesotho	1966	Zambia	1964
Liberia	1847	Zimbabwe	1980

Struggles for Political Stability

The first major challenge following independence was the task of drawing ethnically diverse groups together and establishing a sense of national unity. Leaders urged their peoples to think of themselves as more than tribal members and to accept their responsibilities as citizens of a new nation. But ethnicity was not to be denied and civil wars broke out.

Nigeria. In Nigeria, bitter rivalry between the Hausa peoples of the north and the Ibo peoples of the east erupted in civil war, with the Ibo seceding from Nigeria and proclaiming the independent state of Biafra in 1967. After 3 years of war and famine, the starving Ibo surrendered and the work of reconciliation began.

Foreign Influence

The Cold War also contributed to political instability among the emerging nations of Africa. Zaire (present-day Democratic Republic of the Congo) and Angola were Cold War battlegrounds, with each superpower supporting opposing sides in civil wars.

Cold War competition in Ethiopia and Somalia was strong. Both countries are strategically located near the sea-lanes of the Red Sea and the Indian Ocean and the oil shipping traffic from the Persian Gulf.

By 1974, both Ethiopia and Somalia had forged close ties with the Soviet Union, accepting Soviet military aid and advisers and granting the Soviets permission to establish military bases in their territories. In 1977, Ethiopia and Somalia went to war over disputed land. The Soviet Union sided with Ethiopia, leading Somalia to expel the Soviets and welcome American military advisers and economic assistance.

Setbacks and Victories

Economic Challenges

Just as the newly independent African nations often lacked experience in government, they also lacked broad experience in establishing and running national economies. To overcome this obstacle, some of the new nations opted to retain close ties with the former colonial powers. Most of the former French colonies remained within the French community, and former British colonies joined the British Commonwealth.

However, there were enormous problems associated with attracting capital investment for the modernization and development of business and industry. The economies of many African nations remained primarily agricultural and extractive and therefore dependent on foreign trade. This, in turn, made them especially vulnerable to fluctuations in commodity prices and to protective measures against imports of their commodities.

Setbacks in Nigeria. Nigeria's experience illustrates the way price fluctuations can affect African economies. An oil-rich nation, Nigeria benefited from the Arab oil embargo of 1974–1975, during which it became the major shipper of crude oil to the United States and other Western nations. It used some of its newfound oil wealth to finance the construction and modernization of factories and to improve education and transportation. In the 1980s, when crude oil prices plummeted, Nigerian economic development suffered a major setback. Even Nigeria's vast oil reserves could not keep it from the fate of other African nations: a rapidly growing population fast outstripping the country's economic resources.

The economic instability in Nigeria helped foster political conflict. Attempts at civilian government have been thwarted repeatedly by the military. Since 1999, ethnic, religious, and political tensions in Nigeria have sparked outbreaks of violence, leaving tens of thousands of people dead. Many conflicts have been over access to land or other scarce resources. The adoption of the Sharia (Islamic law), also spelled Shari`ah or Shari`a, in several northern Nigerian states has led to clashes between Muslims and Christians.

UGANDA

Most of the new African states had little or no background in parliamentary democracy, which encouraged the rise of dictators, often by military coup. In Uganda, Idi Amin, an illiterate noncommissioned officer, ousted the elected president and became military dictator in 1971. In 8 years of brutal rule, some 300,000 Ugandans lost their lives. Amin further weakened his country by expelling all Asian citizens, who possessed the bulk of the nation's business expertise, and nationalizing all business. By the time Amin was deposed in 1979, Uganda was in deep economic trouble and mired in political and social instability.

▲ **Oil workers** steady a drilling pipe at an oil platform off the coast of southern Nigeria. Petroleum is Nigeria's most valuable natural resource.

South Africa

African independence did not automatically bring the peaceful end to white domination. In the Union of South Africa in particular, whites struggled to maintain their position of dominance.

The Union of South Africa continued to hold steadfastly to white rule, though whites made up only about 15 percent of the total population. In 1948, South Africa hardened its practices of racial segregation into the official policy of *apartheid,* or total separation of the races and denial of basic civil rights to blacks. Earning the scorn of the world for this action, South Africa withdrew from the British Commonwealth, declaring itself the Republic of South Africa in 1961. It also withdrew from the United Nations (UN) in 1962, after the UN imposed economic sanctions.

The struggle over apartheid gained momentum in the 1970s and 1980s. The white-controlled government of South Africa showed great reluctance to change its policies, even in the face of growing resistance at home—by white as well as black South Africans—and the institution of political, cultural, and economic sanctions by other countries.

The End of Apartheid. In February 1990, the new president, F. W. De Klerk lifted the ban on political organizations, including the African National Congress (ANC) and Pan-Africanist Congress (PAC). Later that month, de Klerk released Nelson Mandela, the most famous member of the ANC, from prison. Mandela had been arrested in 1962 and sentenced to life imprisonment in 1964 for sabotage and conspiracy against the South African government. While in prison, Mandela had become a symbol of the black struggle for racial justice. In May 1990, the government held its first formal talks with the ANC. Mandela met with de Klerk several times to discuss political change in South Africa.

In 1990 and 1991, the South African government repealed most of the remaining laws that had formed the legal basis of apartheid. In 1993, the government adopted an interim constitution that gave South Africa's blacks full voting rights. The country held its first elections open to all races in 1994. The ANC won nearly two-thirds of the seats in the National Assembly, and the Assembly then elected Nelson Mandela president. After the elections, politically motivated violence decreased. In 1994, South Africa resumed full participation in the UN.

▲ **Apartheid** was the South African government's official policy of racial segregation from 1948 until 1991. This sign, in English and Afrikaans (one of South Africa's official languages), designates a beach only white people were allowed to visit.

▲ **Nelson Mandela,** left, takes the oath of office for the presidency of South Africa in May 1994. Mandela was elected president in the country's first elections open to all races.

DEVELOPMENTS IN LATIN AMERICA

The nations of Latin America had supported the Allies during World War II (although Argentina did not declare war on Germany until 1945), and they benefited economically from Allied demand for their food exports and natural resources. But their basic problems remained— political instability; authoritarian governments; social unrest caused by the great disparity between the rich few and the many poor; and rapidly growing populations that increased by an average of 3 percent annually. Added to these woes were heavy foreign debts and high inflation. Though the nations of Latin America had been independent for over a century, they had more in common with the emerging nations of Asia and Africa than with the industrialized nations of the West.

Manuel Noriega, as photographed in 1982 ▶

A Plague of Dictatorships

Authoritarianism and Repression

In the postwar period, Latin American nations were plagued by military coups and authoritarian central governments. In Argentina, Juan Perón seized power through a military coup in 1946, but was ousted by another coup in 1955. In the succeeding 25 years, Argentina underwent 14 changes of government, nearly all of them accomplished through violence. Bolivia, Brazil, Chile, the Dominican Republic, Ecuador, Guatemala, and Honduras also suffered coups.

Repressive dictatorships were established in both Argentina and Chile. The military governments of these nations were ruthless in their suppression of dissent. Tens of thousands of citizens were seized by the secret police or the military and disappeared during the 1970s. After civilian control was restored, investigations revealed the magnitude of the crimes committed by the military governments against their own people.

Manuel Noriega. In Panama, a new kind of dictator arose, in the person of General Manuel Noriega. Charged with aiding international drug operations and harboring fugitive drug kingpins, Noriega maintained a stranglehold on Panama largely through power derived from drug money and a large, heavily armed, and personally controlled paramilitary force. Noriega's regime was toppled only with the aid of American military intervention.

Cold War Effects

Latin America became a battleground for the Cold War struggle between the United States and the Soviet Union. In 1954, the United States secretly supported a military coup that overthrew Guatemala's President Jacobo Arbenz Guzmán, a champion of economic and social reform. In the three decades following, Guatemala suffered numerous political upheavals.

▲ **Fidel Castro**

Cuba. In 1959, a guerrilla force led by Fidel Castro overthrew the Cuban dictator Fulgencio Batista. Castro soon brought Cuba squarely into the Soviet camp, receiving massive amounts of military and economic aid and actively supporting leftist or Communist-led guerrilla movements in other countries.

The Sandinistas. In Nicaragua, Cuba supported the Sandinista guerrillas during the 1979 popular uprising against the rightist dictatorship of Anastasio Somoza Debayle. The Sandinistas established a Marxist government. Soon an anti-Sandinista guerrilla movement was formed. The contras, or counterrevolutionaries, receiving U.S. aid, locked the Sandinistas in a fruitless and devastating civil war. (See page 221.) As economic and social conditions deteriorated, so did the Sandinistas' standing with the people, and in 1990 they were voted out of power in an upset election.

Emerging Trends

In the 21st century, there are signs that citizens are coming to play a larger role in the electoral process in many Latin American countries. Sentiments toward a greater degree of democracy have become increasingly pronounced, especially in Costa Rica, the Dominican Republic, Colombia, and Peru. Argentina, Brazil, and Mexico are making strides toward greater democracy.

In the face of widespread urban and rural poverty, the Roman Catholic Church has emerged as a strong advocate of action to improve the welfare and safeguard the human rights of the poor. Claiming 90 percent of Latin Americans as members, the church had long been considered a force of conservatism and support for the ruling elite. In recent years, however, church leaders in several Latin American countries have come to be viewed as champions of political, economic, and social reform.

now you Know!

✔ In Uganda, Idi Amin, an illiterate noncommissioned officer, ousted the elected president and became military dictator in 1971. Some 300,000 Ugandans lost their lives before Amin was deposed in 1979.

✔ In 1990 and 1991, the South African government repealed most of the laws that had formed the legal basis of apartheid. In 1994, Nelson Mandela won the presidential election.

✔ In 1959, a guerrilla force led by Fidel Castro overthrew the Cuban dictator Fulgencio Batista. An avowed Communist, Castro was able to get the Soviet Union to send massive amounts of economic and military aid.

✔ In recent years, the Roman Catholic Church has emerged as a strong advocate of action to improve the welfare and safeguard the human rights of the poor in Latin America.

GLOBAL ISSUES

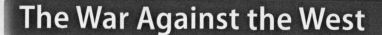

When the Soviet Union collapsed in 1991, effectively bringing to an end the Cold War that had gripped the world for nearly half a century, many believed that this was a sign that the world was entering a new historical period. For many in Western nations, genuine peace and prosperity seemed to be the inevitable consequence of this momentous event. The reality, as usual, turned out to be more complicated. Three of the most significant trends to emerge in the 1990s and take center stage after the turn of the century were the rise of religious extremism in the Middle East, the threat of global climate change, and great advances in computers and communications technology.

Rise of Extremism

During the last three decades of the 20th century, a religious revival began to sweep through much of the Muslim world. One aspect of this Islamic resurgence has been the growth of an ideology known as Islamism. Islamists believe that the social and political order should be based solely on the sharia (traditional Islamic law). A return to a fully Islamic society, they argue, would bring an end to government corruption, moral decay, and social injustice and would eventually restore the Muslim world to the preeminent position it once held centuries ago, before the rise of the West.

The outside world paid little attention to this until 1979, when a revolution in Iran toppled the Shah and led to the creation of the first modern Islamist state under the leadership of Ayatollah Khomeini. Encouraged by the events in Iran, Islamist groups became more assertive and saw their popularity surge during the 1980s. By 1989, Islamists had taken control of the government of Sudan. Two years later, an Islamist party won a free election in Algeria but was prevented from coming to power by the army. This led to a revolt by radical Islamists, which was suppressed by the government, but only after 6 years of civil war.

THE TALIBAN

The Taliban are a militant Islamic political group that gained control of most of Afghanistan beginning in the mid-1990s. The Taliban enforced strict adherence to their interpretation of Islamic laws.

In 1998, the United States accused the Taliban of harboring Osama bin Laden, wanted in connection with terrorist attacks against two U.S. embassies in Africa. Then, in 2001, the United States accused bin Laden and al-Qaeda of carrying out the September 11 terrorist attacks. The United States demanded that the Taliban hand over bin Laden. The Taliban refused to do so, and the United States and its allies launched a military campaign against the Taliban.

Many Taliban and al-Qaeda members went into hiding across the border in Pakistan. The Taliban began to regroup in Pakistan and clashed frequently with police and government troops.

The Road to 9/11. Many Islamists condemn the United States for its strong support of Israel and for its massive aid to certain Middle Eastern governments, which Islamists believe are corrupt, oppressive, ungodly, and illegitimate. Moreover, American society, in their view, is materialistic and morally lax, the epitome of everything that is wrong with secular Western culture.

The most notorious Islamic extremist was Osama bin Laden. Born to a wealthy family in Saudi Arabia,

bin Laden created an international network in the 1980s to raise funds and recruit volunteers for the war against the Soviets in Afghanistan. After the Soviet withdrawal in 1989, he began to use this network, now known as al-Qaeda ("The Base"), to conduct a series of terrorist attacks on American targets at home and abroad. By 1996, bin Laden, now an international outlaw, was living in Afghanistan under the protection of the Taliban, an Islamist militia that had taken control of most of that country.

On September 11, 2001, 19 al-Qaeda operatives simultaneously hijacked four American airliners and crashed one into the Pentagon and two into the World Trade Center towers in New York, killing nearly 3,000 people, the largest loss of American lives in a single day since the Civil War. A group of passengers on the fourth airliner, attempting to overpower the highjackers, forced the plane to crash in a field in Pennsylvania, far from any intended target.

By the start of 2008, most of the original leadership circle of al-Qaeda had been killed or captured, including Khalid Shaikh Mohammed, who was believed to be the mastermind of the 9/11 attacks, but bin Laden and his chief lieutenant, Ayman al-Zawahiri, remained at large, and the global jihad they had inspired still posed a serious threat to world stability.

America's attention began to shift back to Afghanistan, where the level of violence was increasing thanks to a resurgent Taliban. The situation was also worsening

◀ **Osama bin Laden,** a Saudi-born millionaire and radical Muslim, was the founder and longtime leader of al-Qaeda, a global terrorist organization.

The World Trade Center towers billowed flames and smoke on September 11, 2001, after terrorists crashed hijacked airliners into the two buildings. The towers were the tallest buildings on the New York City skyline until they collapsed a short time after the attack.

in neighboring Pakistan, where Islamist militants were believed to be responsible for the assassination of popular opposition leader and former prime minister of Pakistan Benazir Bhutto at the end of 2007 and for a series of attacks in the Indian city of Mumbai in November 2008. The possibility that all or part of Pakistan's nuclear arsenal might fall into the hands of Islamic extremists, coupled with North Korea's claim to possess nuclear weapons and Iran's determination to pursue atomic research despite opposition from the UN, the European Union (EU), and the United States, has revived fears that nuclear proliferation might someday provide terrorists with weapons vastly more destructive than any previously employed.

Battling Pollution

Environmental Issues

Environmental pollution is one of the most serious problems facing humanity and other life forms today. Badly polluted air can harm crops and cause life-threatening illnesses. Some air pollutants have reduced the capacity of the atmosphere to filter out the sun's harmful ultraviolet radiation. (See pages 628–629.)

Progress in controlling pollution has gained speed since the 1960s. Nearly all the industries in western Europe and the United States have switched from coal to cleaner-burning fuels, such as oil and natural gas. Today, cities in many parts of the world also treat their water and process their sewage, thus greatly reducing the problems caused by harmful bacteria.

Important progress has been made in other areas of pollution management. By the early 1970s, the Great Lakes were so polluted that the waters had turned green and smelled foul, and huge fish kills were common. In 1972, Canada and the United States signed the Great Lakes Water Quality Agreement. Since then, local governments around the lakes have improved sewage treatment plants, controlled the runoff of chemical fertilizers from farms, and worked to reduce the use of phosphate detergents. They have also forced industries to reduce the pollutants they dump into the lakes. Today, the Great Lakes are much cleaner.

▲ **Ward Island, off Toronto, Ontario,** littered with garbage that washed up from Lake Ontario, one of the Great Lakes.

The Kyoto Protocol

The Kyoto Protocol is an international agreement whose underlying purpose is to limit global warming. Global warming is an increase in the average temperature of Earth's surface since the late 1800s. The protocol requires many countries to limit their emissions (releases) of greenhouse gases. The Kyoto Protocol serves as an addition to the United Nations (UN) Framework Convention on Climate Change, a treaty adopted in 1992 to stabilize greenhouse gas concentrations. Delegates from more than 160 countries adopted the protocol at a 1997 meeting in Kyoto, Japan. To become legally enforceable, the protocol had to be ratified (formally approved) by at least 55 countries. In addition, the developed countries ratifying the protocol had to account for at least 55 percent of the total CO_2 emissions of all developed countries in 1990.

▲ **A United Nations conference met** in December 2008, in Poznan, Poland, to begin talks on a climate change agreement to succeed the Kyoto Protocol.

Rejection by the U.S. Delegates worked to complete the details of the agreement in a series of meetings. Most countries eventually agreed to the protocol, but some nations chose not to ratify it. These nations included the United States, whose 1990 emissions of CO_2 represented the highest share of the total for developed countries: 35 percent.

In 1997, the U.S. Senate voted unanimously not to sign any agreement that did not include emissions reductions for developing countries or that would seriously harm the U.S. economy. In 1998, the administration of President Bill Clinton signed the Kyoto Protocol but did not submit it to the Senate for approval. In 2001, President George W. Bush rejected the Kyoto Protocol.

The protocol entered into force in 2005. In the same year, the European Union began working to meet its obligations by establishing its Greenhouse Gas Emission Trading Scheme. The scheme sets limits on emissions by power plants and other large sources of greenhouse gases. It also enables facilities to buy and sell emissions allowances. The Kyoto Protocol also led to the creation of a global "carbon market" for the trading of greenhouse gas emissions. Developing countries began to participate in emissions reductions through hundreds of clean development projects.

In late 2005, delegates from the parties agreed to extend the Kyoto Protocol beyond 2012. Delegates at a conference in Bali in 2007 set a deadline to conclude negotiations for the next agreement by 2009, to ensure that there would be no gap between agreements. These negotiations took place in 2008 and 2009.

▲ **An Indiana coal-fired power plant** pumps pollutants into the atmosphere.

GULF OIL SPILL OF 2010

In April 2010, there was an explosion on the Deepwater Horizon oil rig in the Gulf of Mexico, off the coast of Louisiana. The explosion killed 11 people and blew out an underwater well pipe. For nearly 3 months afterward, about 206 million gallons (780 million liters) of oil poured from the well into the Gulf of Mexico. BP p.l.c., a major international oil company, was the well's principal owner.

BP had hired Transocean Ltd., the rig's owner and operator, to drill a well beneath the Gulf's surface. On April 20, gases building up in the well pipe ignited on the rig, causing the explosion and oil spill.

The leakage continued for months. Oil coated coastal lands and harmed birds, fish, and other wildlife. The spill also devastated fisheries and tourism-based businesses along the Gulf Coast.

On July 15, BP succeeded in capping the well. On September 19, BP engineers sealed the well using a relief well. The relief well intercepted the damaged well about 2.5 miles (4 kilometers) beneath the seafloor. Engineers then pumped cement through the relief well, permanently sealing the damaged well.

After the well was sealed, BP pledged $20 billion to help pay victims who lost work or property due to the spill. The federal government hoped to use any penalties collected from BP to establish a fund dedicated to restoring affected Gulf areas. Scientists warned that the full extent of environmental damage would not be known for years.

Technological Revolutions

Global Change

Social change has always been a factor in human history. Empires rise and fall; societies are modernized; communities are destroyed. What forces lead to such phenomena? How can these changes be explained? As advances in technology have sped up transportation and communication, changes seem to come rapidly, relentlessly—and their diffusion throughout world culture can be unpredictable. In weighing the past as a way of planning for the future, it is important to understand the factors that help to speed up social change.

▲ **The Face of Change in 1954.** This enormous machine is an IBM data processing machine used for aeronautical research computations.

CULTURAL DIFFUSION

Cultural diffusion—the adoption by one culture of elements from another—has had profound repercussions, especially since the expansion of Western culture in modern times. While today we think of examples like Coca-Cola in Kuwait and jeans in Japan, we tend to overlook earlier borrowings, such as "Arabic" numerals from India, steel from Damascus, and paper from China.

Technology as a Historical Force

Arguably, technology has become the single most important generator of social change in the world today. In the United States, the automobile helped bring about the development of the petroleum industry, the growth of suburbs, and a vast network of highways and shopping centers. It also led to air pollution, the destruction of neighborhoods, and the decline of railroads and other public transportation systems. Recent technological developments with far-reaching implications include television, computers, artificial organs, and improved medical diagnosis and treatment.

Rapid Communication. One of the greatest changes to occur in world culture is the increasing speed with which information could be transmitted across the globe. One early example of this change can be seen in two cataclysmic events of the 19th century: the eruptions of two volcanoes in Indonesia, Mount Tambora in 1815 and Krakatoa in 1883. The Tambora eruption is believed to be the largest volcanic eruption in recorded history. It caused massive devastation and affected world climate in 1815 and 1816. However, it happened in a place that was remote from the Western world, and many people at the time were unaware of the eruption—even as it was devastating crops in Europe and North America. The Krakatoa eruption occurred after the spread of telegraphy throughout the world. The people of Western Europe and North America—where the telegraph had the most impact—were able to follow events on Krakatoa, and scientists were ready to observe and measure the impact of the eruption. The telephone was still a brand-new invention, while radio, television, and the computer did not yet exist. But even without these, the revolution in global communication had already begun.

▲ **Touch screen technology** is a recent innovation.

Computer power is growing at a staggering rate, even as the cost of that power drops to new lows. Tens of millions of homes now have personal computers, and new computer trends promise to shape our lives and our world in the years to come. Miniaturization of hardware has allowed for the development of small handheld computing devices that are growing more powerful and versatile with each new release.

Future historians may view the development of the computer as the most important event of the 1900s. Some observers, in fact, say that the computer revolution is the most important technological advance in human history. But it is a revolution still in progress.

The Computer Revolution

The computer has changed the way we work, learn, communicate, and play. Virtually every kind of organization throughout the world uses computers to conduct business. Students, teachers, and research scientists use the computer as a learning tool. Millions of individuals and organizations communicate with one another over the Internet. Computer games entertain people of all ages.

The computer revolution shows no signs of slowing. Computers grow more powerful almost daily, offering vast amounts of information storage and ever-faster operating speeds.

Connecting Computers. Perhaps the invention that did the most to expand the usefulness of computers was the modem, a device that connects computers to other computers around the world. More and more computers in businesses, institutions, and private homes are being linked in this way, forming a global network of interconnected computer networks called the Internet. The Internet made possible the invention of the World Wide Web, a vast collection of documents, images, video, audio, and a variety of services, which has revolutionized the way people shop, get their news, and interact with each other.

now you **Know!**

✔ The Taliban are a militant Islamic political group that enforced strict adherence to their interpretation of Islamic laws. The Taliban gained control of most of Afghanistan beginning in the mid-1990s.

✔ The Kyoto Protocol is an international agreement that requires many countries to limit their emissions (releases) of greenhouse gases in an effort to limit global warming.

✔ In April 2010, an explosion on the Deepwater Horizon oil rig blew out an underwater well pipe, eventually pouring about 206 million gallons of oil into the Gulf of Mexico.

✔ The invention of the modem has made it possible for computers in businesses, institutions, and private homes to be linked, forming a global network of interconnected computer networks called the Internet.

Geography

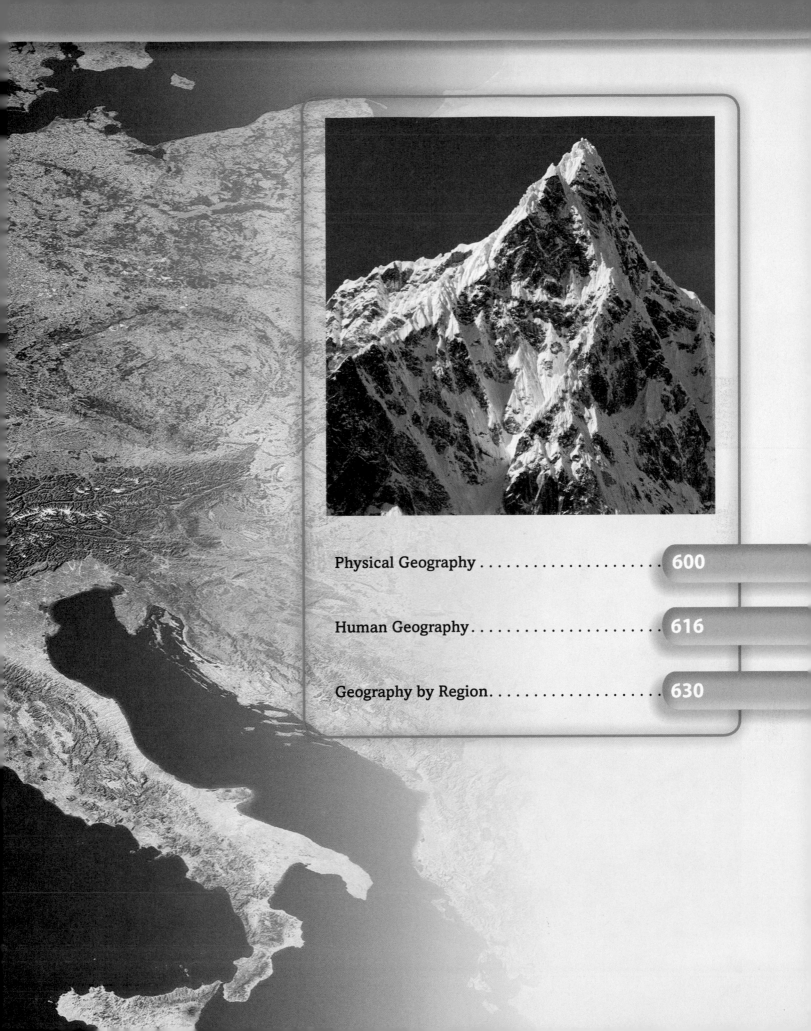

MAPS AND GLOBES

People have been making maps since ancient times. As the technology behind mapmaking advanced, maps became more accurate and more useful. Today, we use maps to locate places, measure distances, plan trips, and find our way. Pilots of ships and airplanes use maps to navigate. City planners and engineers use maps to decide where to put new buildings or roads. Maps can also help us understand patterns, such as how populations move or grow, and how boundaries and features change over time.

Making Maps

Mapping is one of the geographer's most basic activities. Making or studying maps is called *cartography*. A person who creates maps or knows a great deal about them is a cartographer.

- To design maps, cartographers use lines, colors, shapes, and other symbols.
- These symbols stand for such features as roads, rivers, forests, or cities.

A map is only a representation of an area. Therefore, it does not attempt to show everything that exists in the area. Instead, a cartographer decides which features a map should show by considering how people will use the map. For example, a road map used by drivers would need to show roads, highways, and cities.

Mapmaking Steps

1. **Observation and measurement:** Cartographers observe and measure geographic features to collect fundamental information called base data.
2. **Database development:** Data are stored in a *database,* or collection of computer records.
3. **Planning and graphic design:** The mapmaker (and often a graphic designer) decide what the map should include and how it should look.
4. **Production and reproduction:** Computer mapping programs, geographic information systems (GIS), or computer-aided design (CAD) programs are used to draw, label, and print the map.
5. **Revision:** Databases are updated and maps changed to reflect changes in the map's area, such as new borders or a growing population.

Globes can be found in homes, classrooms, and libraries.

Important Map Projections

Cartographers use mathematical methods called *projections* to make Earth look flat. Every type of projection distorts distances. Other features, such as land shapes or areas, may also be distorted. But each projection is useful in some important ways.

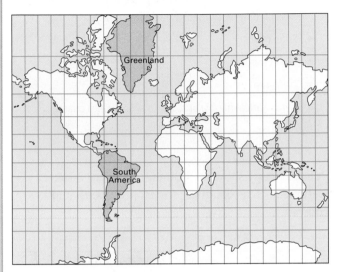

▲ **The Mercator projection** is also called a *conformal projection*.

Pro: shows the correct angles between directions at any point

Con: geographic areas do not have correct size relationships to one another (areas near North and South poles look larger than they really are)

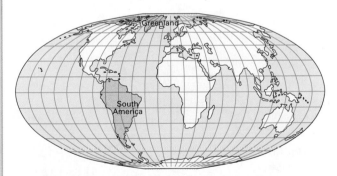

▲ **The Mollweide projection** is also called an *equal area*, or *equivalent*, projection.

Pro: areas are the correct size in relation to one another.

Con: some surface areas are the wrong shape.

The Robinson projection is also called a *compromise* projection. It attempts to correct the distortions of the other two projections as much as possible. Size relationships are more accurate than on a Mercator projection, and shapes are slightly more accurate than on a Mollweide map. ▼

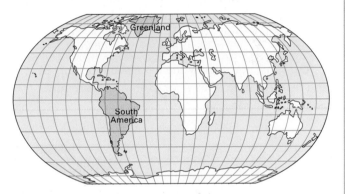

GLOBES VS. MAPS

Globes

Because Earth is round, the best way to represent it is on a round map called a globe.

- Globes of the earth are known as terrestrial globes.
- A globe shows the location and shape of geographic areas exactly as they are on Earth.
- They are also helpful in planning air and sea routes and in establishing satellite communications.

Maps

Most maps are flat because, unlike globes, flat maps are easy to carry and to print in books.

- Flat maps, however, are not completely correct.
- Representing the round Earth on a flat surface requires stretching some areas and shrinking others.
- This stretching and shrinking is called *distortion*.

Types of Maps

There are many different types of maps. Each type serves a specific purpose; the purpose affects how the map will look and what information it will contain. Two major categories of maps are general reference maps and thematic maps.

General Reference Maps

General reference maps are used to show the locations of different types of geographic features. Geographic features can be either natural (mountains, rivers, forests) or constructed (roads, bridges, towns and cities, borders).

Topographic maps show the details and heights of land features in an area—for example, mountain ranges or canyons.

NAVIGATION MAPS

Another type of map is the navigation map, which is used to show the route from one place to another. There are several different types of navigation maps.

- Road maps
- Street maps
- Transit maps
- Aeronautical (flight) and nautical (boating) charts

Political maps show the boundaries of constructed features such as counties, states, provinces, and countries.

This topographic map of Spain shows the land elevation throughout the country, as well as its various mountain ranges. Different colors are used to represent changes in elevation.

This political map of Spain and its surroundings shows the boundaries of the different nations, as well as the locations of major cities.

602

Thematic Maps

Like general reference maps, thematic maps represent a geographical area, and may identify the locations of certain features such as boundaries, roads, or natural features. Unlike general reference maps, however, they also illustrate how a particular feature, such as population, rainfall, or a natural resource, is distributed over an area. These types of maps are used to study patterns.

Elements of Thematic Maps. Many thematic maps express quantities by means of colors or symbols.

- *Isolines*, or *isograms*, are lines used to connect areas of equal value. Some specific types of isolines have special names. On a weather map, for example, isolines called isotherms are used to indicate areas of common temperature.

- Variations in size or shape may express quantities. A map of the international petroleum trade might indicate large exports of oil with thick arrows and small exports with thin arrows.

Land Use and Resources

Predominant land use
- Commercial agriculture
- Dairying
- Livestock ranching
- Nomadic herding
- Subsistence agriculture
- Primarily forestland
- Limited agricultural activity

Major resources
- Coal
- Natural gas
- Oil
- Au Gold
- Fe Iron ore
- Ag Silver
- U Uranium
- Al Bauxite
- Other minerals
- Fishing
- Major manufacturing and trade centers

In 1855, an English physician named John Snow used a thematic map called an inventory map to track victims of a cholera epidemic. (Inventory maps show the exact location of a particular type of featured item.) His map showed a large number of victims clustered around a water pump on Broad Street. It was soon found that water from that pump was the source of the infection.

▲ **This thematic map** illustrates the different patterns of land use throughout the continent of Europe.

- Colors are used to show the main use of each area.
- Symbols indicate the locations of different natural resources, such as oil or gold.

The combination of colors and symbols tells you, for example, that the United Kingdom has very little forested land, and that coal mining is common there.

Reading Maps

Maps often combine a number of symbols, colors, and lines, each of which expresses a different piece of information. To read a map effectively, the reader must know what each element means. This diagram shows elements common to many different types of maps.

Terrain map key

⬜ Ice cap		── Boundaries	
⬜ Tundra		── Rivers	
⬛ Mountains		▲ Mountain peaks	
⬜ Evergreen forest			
⬜ Mixed forest			
⬜ Grassland			
⬜ Arid			
⬜ Oceans and seas			

MAP LEGENDS

Map legends list and explain the symbols and colors used on a map. Some symbols resemble the features they represent. For example, a small tree might stand for a forest, an orchard, or a state park. But many symbols have little resemblance to the features they represent, as when a circle stands for a city.

SCALE

Because maps are much smaller than the area they represent, the features on a map are greatly reduced in size. For example, 1 inch (2.5 centimeters) on a map might represent a distance of 100 miles (160 kilometers) on Earth's surface. A tiny circle might represent a large city.

The scale of a particular map is often shown on a bar. The bar will indicate how much distance (in miles, kilometers, feet, etc.) is represented by each inch (or centimeter) on the map. This bar shows that each inch on the map represents 2,000 miles.

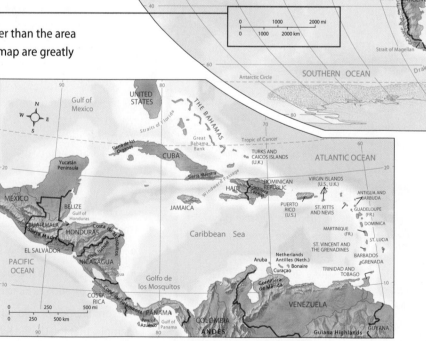

✔ Cartography, or the making and studying of maps, is one of the main activities of geography.

✔ Because the earth is round, different kinds of flat maps, called projections, distort shape, size, and distance. Three major map projections are the Mercator projection, the Mollweide projection, and the Robinson projection.

✔ General reference maps show the locations of natural and constructed geographic features.

✔ Thematic maps show the distribution of something, such as a population, a natural resource, or even a cultural idea, across a geographic area.

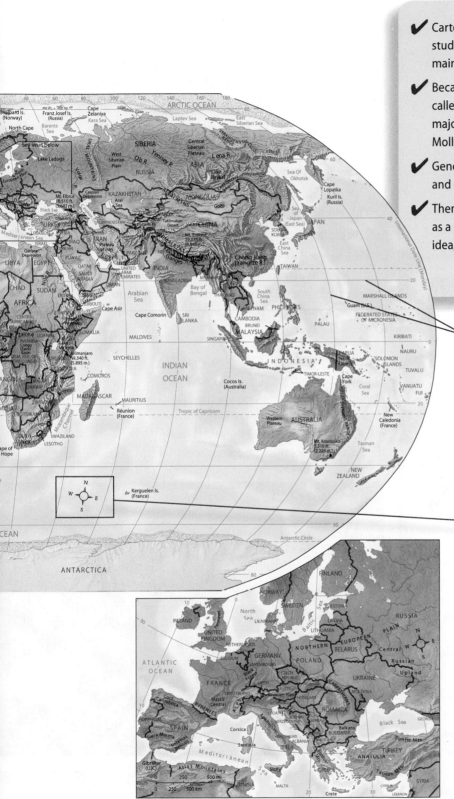

GEOGRAPHIC GRIDS

Maps often include networks of imaginary lines, called geographic grids, that help us find and describe places on Earth. The grid on this map is called a graticule. A graticule—the most common geographic grid—divides the globe using lines called parallels of latitude, which show north-south position, and lines called meridians of longitude, which show east-west position.

NORTH ARROW

A north arrow shows the direction of north on a map. The arrow often has the letter N or the word North written over it. Maps without a north arrow usually show north at the top of the map or include a geographic grid to orient the user.

PLANET EARTH

Geography is the study of locations and patterns on Earth, and of the forces that change the planet. The surface shown on a map or a globe is the result of many different processes. To understand these processes, and how they shape the world, one must understand the characteristics of Earth overall, including its position and movement in space.

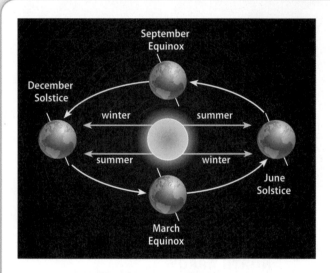

DAYS, YEARS, AND SEASONS

Every day, the sun appears to rise in the east and set in the west. Each year, the same seasons—winter, spring, summer, and autumn—repeat themselves much as they did the year before. These patterns are the result of Earth's movement in space.

Every 24 hours, Earth spins completely around its axis, creating our nights and days. The Earth also rotates around the sun on an elliptical path—a path in the shape of an oval.

- Because of this, different parts of the planet receive different amounts of sunlight throughout the year.

- When a hemisphere is tilted toward the sun, it receives more direct light, for a longer time each day; this is summer. In winter, the opposite is occurring.

- The seasons are reversed in the Northern and Southern Hemispheres.

What Is the Earth?

Earth is one of eight planets in our solar system—a group of planets and other objects orbiting a star in outer space. (The sun is the star at the center of our solar system.) Earth is the third-closest planet to the sun. The sun heats and lights the surfaces of all the planets in the solar system.

The Earth in Space

Earth's position in space affects conditions on its surface. The sun heats Earth's atmosphere unevenly, for two reasons.

1. The planet spins.
2. The planet is tilted at 23 degrees.

This uneven heat creates wind, and wind in turn contributes to erosion—one of the major forces that change the planet. Uneven amounts of heat and sunlight also contribute to the many different climates found on Earth.

The Solar System. Mercury, Venus, Earth, and Mars make up the inner planets of the solar system. Jupiter, Saturn, Uranus, and Neptune make up the outer planets. The planets nearest the sun are warmer than the outer planets. ▼

Earth's Structure

Earth is made up of several layers. The solid earth itself consists of four different layers (see diagram). In addition, there are four other layers, both inside and outside the solid planet, called spheres. Each of these spheres has an effect on the locations of features and patterns of life and movement studied by geographers.

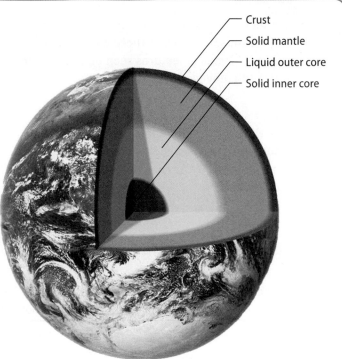

Crust
Solid mantle
Liquid outer core
Solid inner core

▲ **The biosphere** stretches from the ocean floor to a few miles out into the atmosphere. Living things can have a huge effect on geographic features.

Inner Earth. Earth's interior consists of four layers: 1) the solid inner core, 2) the liquid outer core, 3) the mantle, and 4) the crust. The lithosphere consists of the last two layers. The crust is what we see, in the form of rocks and soil. The mantle is mostly solid, but its upper layer is partially molten. This allows plates of the crust to move.

Earth's Spheres	Characteristics	Effects on Geographic Features
Atmosphere	• surrounds the planet and becomes thinner farther from the surface • contains different layers of air with different properties	• traps heat from the sun and warms the planet • creates weather with patterns of air movement, contributing to regions' climates
Hydrosphere	• covers much of Earth's surface • a layer of water (oceans, rivers, lakes) and ice	• erodes or dissolves rock on the planet's surface • stores heat and contributes to climate
Lithosphere	• part of the solid Earth • consists of a thin outer layer, the crust, with a thick rocky layer, the mantle, beneath it • crust is divided into constantly moving sections called tectonic plates	• plate movements create and change large landforms on Earth's crust
Biosphere	• portion of atmosphere, hydrosphere, and lithosphere where life exists	• creates and alters atmosphere • living creatures erode, change, or preserve existing landforms

The Changing Earth

Our planet is constantly changing, both from the inside and the outside. Many of these changes affect the location and types of features seen on Earth's surface—and studied by geographers.

Inside the Earth

Some of the largest geographical features—continents, mountain ranges, canyons, and trenches—are created and changed by forces inside the planet, in the mantle and crust.

PLATE TECTONICS

According to the theory of plate tectonics, Earth's crust is made up of pieces called plates.

- The plates are different shapes and sizes.
- They lie on a layer of molten rock that makes up the top part of Earth's mantle.
- Because this layer is molten, the plates shift.

When the plates shift, separate, and collide, the results are often visible on Earth's surface as mountain ranges, volcanoes, canyons, and trenches.

The continental drift theory says that the movement of tectonic plates has changed the look of Earth's landmasses over time. The continents are moving—for example, the Atlantic Ocean is growing wider—about 2 inches per year. Therefore, the Earth that geographers map today will not look the same in several million years.

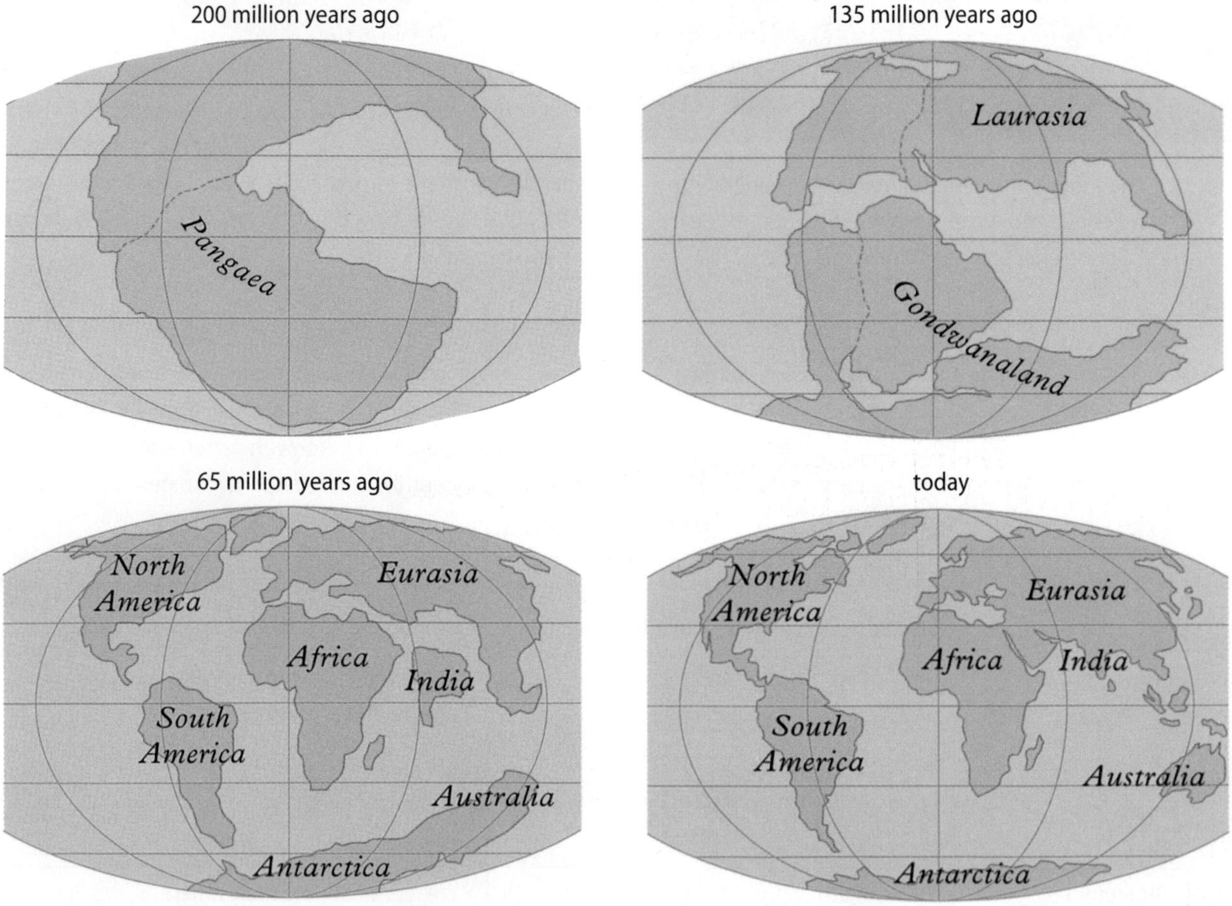

200 million years ago

Pangaea

135 million years ago

Laurasia

Gondwanaland

65 million years ago

North America   Eurasia

Africa   India

South America

Australia

Antarctica

today

North America   Eurasia

Africa   India

South America

Australia

Antarctica

On Earth's Surface

Forces on Earth's surface, and in its atmosphere, also produce geographical changes. Many major changes in the geographer's picture of Earth's surface come from erosion.

Erosion is the breaking down and removal of rock. The main agents of erosion are running water, ice, wind, and glaciers.

- Running water: The force of water on rock breaks rock fragments into smaller pieces and carries them away.

- Ice: As water freezes, it expands. When water inside a crack of a rock freezes, it can break the rock apart.

- Wind: Winds pick up fine particles from Earth's surface and carry them away.

- Glaciers: These huge masses of ice cover about 5.8 million square miles (15 million square kilometers) of Earth's surface. As they move and recede, they carry particles of soil and rock with them.

Over time, erosion changes the shapes of rock formations and even coastlines.

Humans and Animals. Some geographical changes can either be caused by or accelerated by human and animal behavior. The Sahara, a desert in Africa, has expanded as farmers have grazed their livestock too heavily on nearby grasslands. As the grasses disappear, the desert spreads.

▲ **Human projects** such as farming and mining can also speed up the process of erosion.

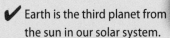

- ✔ Earth is the third planet from the sun in our solar system.

- ✔ Earth's position and movement in space help to create the planet's seasons and climate.

- ✔ Earth is made up of four spheres: the atmosphere, the hydrosphere, the lithosphere, and the biosphere. Changes in these spheres can result in changes to geographic features.

- ✔ Earth's surface is changed from within by the movement of tectonic plates, and from without by forces such as erosion and human activity.

▲ **One type of wind erosion** can be seen in sand dunes. These dunes slowly move in a downwind direction, as wind picks up their fine, round sand particles.

CLIMATE refers to the average weather conditions of a region over a long period of time. A region's climate includes its average temperature, rainfall, and humidity (the amount of water vapor in the air). Earth's climate varies from place to place, depending on several different factors. Climatology, which is a subfield of geography, is the study of patterns of climate, how climate changes, and how humans might affect it.

MAJOR FACTORS THAT CONTRIBUTE TO A REGION'S CLIMATE

- Latitude
- Bodies of water
- Altitude
- Mountains
- Winds
- Pressure belts

Winds and Weather

Latitude

Latitude refers to a location's distance from Earth's equator.

- Near the equator, the sun's rays are almost vertical.
- These regions also receive the same amount of sunlight per day throughout the year (other regions have longer and shorter daylight periods—for example, in the Northern Hemisphere, winter days are shorter).

As a result of these factors, average temperatures near the equator tend to be higher than those farther away from it. However, latitude alone cannot determine a region's climate.

Bodies of Water

Oceans and lakes make the air temperature less extreme in places downwind of them. These places have milder winters and cooler summers than places at the same latitude but well inland.

- An ocean or lake surface warms up and cools down more slowly than a land surface.
- Thus, between summer and winter, the temperature of the water varies less than the temperature of the land.
- The temperature of the water strongly influences the temperature of the air above it.
- Therefore, air temperatures over the ocean or a large lake also vary less than air temperatures over land.
- Ocean currents can also change temperatures in areas where the winds mostly blow in from the ocean.

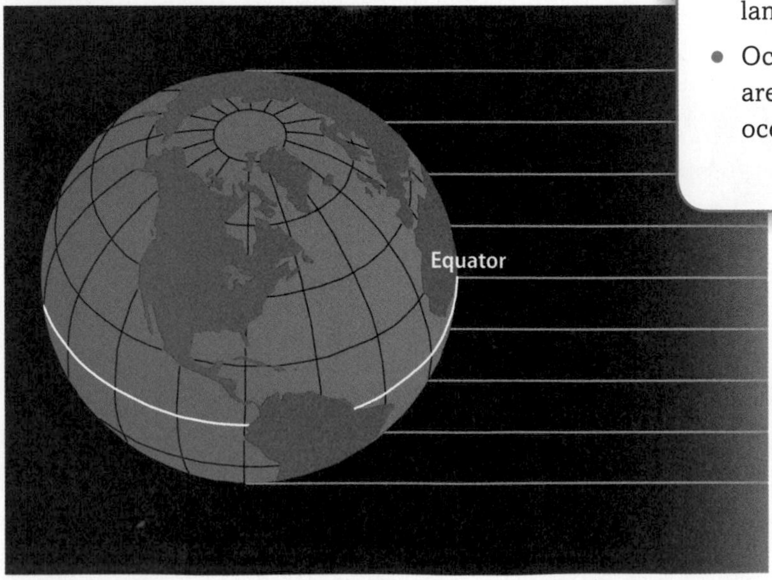

Equator

Latitude. This diagram shows the angles at which the sun's rays hit the Earth. Notice how the rays at the equator hit directly.

Winds

Wind comes from a difference in air pressure, caused by the unequal heating of Earth's atmosphere by the sun. Winds always flow from high-pressure areas to low-pressure areas.

Giant wind systems travel through the atmosphere, affecting weather in different ways. Winds can change the patterns of precipitation (rainfall or snow) in a region; they can also cause seasonal storms, such as monsoons. Local wind systems work the same way as global wind systems, on a smaller scale.

Altitude

Temperatures decrease as altitude increases; as a result, high-altitude locations tend to have cooler average temperatures than low-lying regions.

Mountains

Mountain ranges can affect a region's climate in different ways, depending upon whether the winds in that region are warm or cold.

- A warm wind blowing against high mountains will produce a high amount of precipitation, because warm air tends to contain more water vapor.

- A cold wind will produce relatively little precipitation.

- The side of a mountain sheltered from the wind will often have a dry climate, because the air has lost most of its moisture by the time it reaches that side.

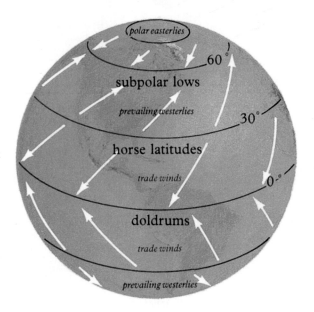

▲ **This diagram** shows the major wind belts, and the directions in which they flow.

Even at the equator, where average temperatures are higher, very tall mountains often have snow at their peaks due to their high altitudes.

World Climates

The earth's surface is a patchwork of climate zones. This map shows the distribution of different climates throughout the world. Notice how the regions near the equator tend to have hotter, more humid climates than regions farther north.

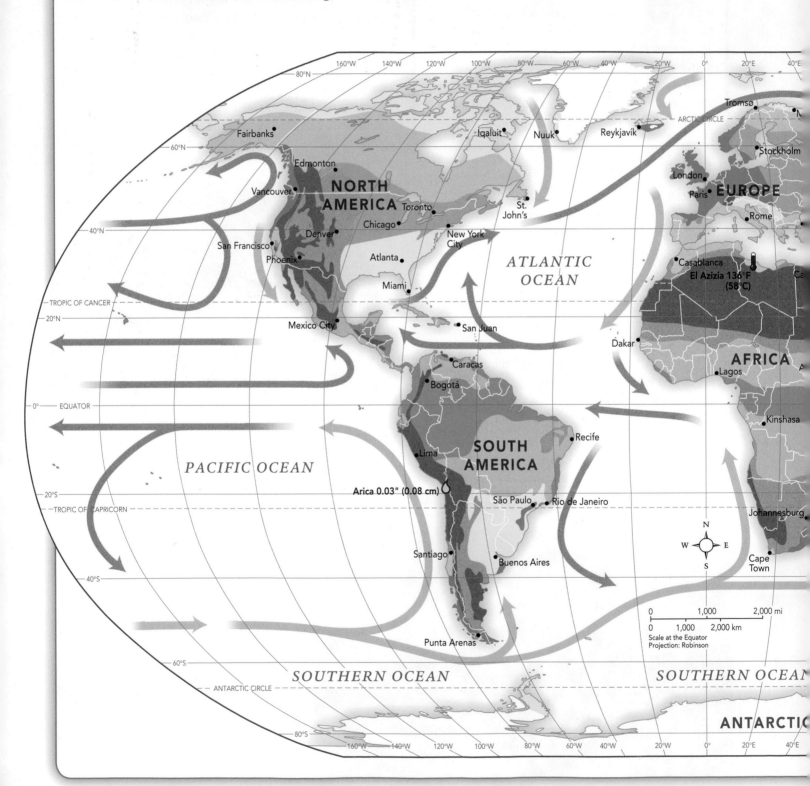

Climate varies from place to place because of distance from the equator and other factors. For example, in this satellite photo, the vast tan area at the north of Africa—the Sahara Desert—contrasts with the green equatorial regions farther south. ▶

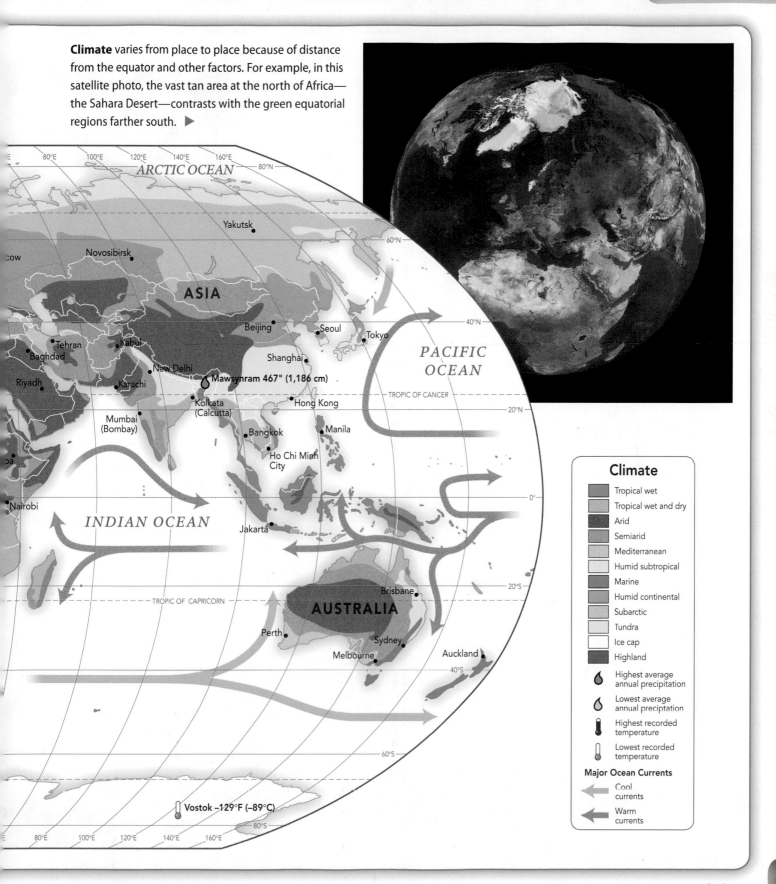

ARCTIC OCEAN

80°N

Yakutsk

60°N

Novosibirsk

cow

ASIA

Beijing

Seoul

40°N

Tokyo

Tehran

Kabul

Shanghai

PACIFIC
OCEAN

Baghdad

New Delhi

Riyadh

Karachi

Mawsynram 467" (1,186 cm)

TROPIC OF CANCER

Kolkata
(Calcutta)

Hong Kong

20°N

Mumbai
(Bombay)

Bangkok

Manila

a

Ho Chi Minh
City

0°

Nairobi

INDIAN OCEAN

Jakarta

Brisbane

20°S

TROPIC OF CAPRICORN

AUSTRALIA

Perth

Sydney

Melbourne

Auckland

40°S

60°S

Vostok –129°F (–89°C)

80°S

80°E   100°E   120°E   140°E   160°E

Climate

	Tropical wet
	Tropical wet and dry
	Arid
	Semiarid
	Mediterranean
	Humid subtropical
	Marine
	Humid continental
	Subarctic
	Tundra
	Ice cap
	Highland

Highest average
annual precipitation

Lowest average
annual precipitation

Highest recorded
temperature

Lowest recorded
temperature

Major Ocean Currents

Cool
currents

Warm
currents

PLANT REGIONS

Plants live everywhere except in regions that have permanent ice, such as Antarctica and much of Greenland. But not all plants grow in all regions of the world. This map shows the regions in which different types of plant life thrive.

- Tundra and high mountain plants grow near the poles and throughout Earth's mountainous regions.

- Forests thrive across broad regions of North and South America, Europe, northern Asia, and Southeast Asia.

- Vast grasslands cover central Africa and interior regions of most of the other continents.

- Desert plants, such as cacti, grow across a huge area of northern Africa, the Middle East, and central Asia as well as the interior of Australia.

- Aquatic plants, such as cattails, thrive in watery regions.

Growing on Earth

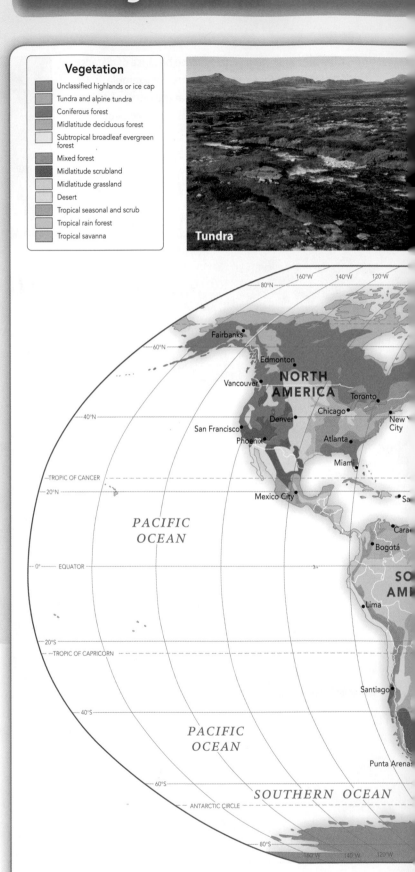

Vegetation
- Unclassified highlands or ice cap
- Tundra and alpine tundra
- Coniferous forest
- Midlatitude deciduous forest
- Subtropical broadleaf evergreen forest
- Mixed forest
- Midlatitude scrubland
- Midlatitude grassland
- Desert
- Tropical seasonal and scrub
- Tropical rain forest
- Tropical savanna

Tundra

Tropical rain forest

Savanna

Coniferous forest

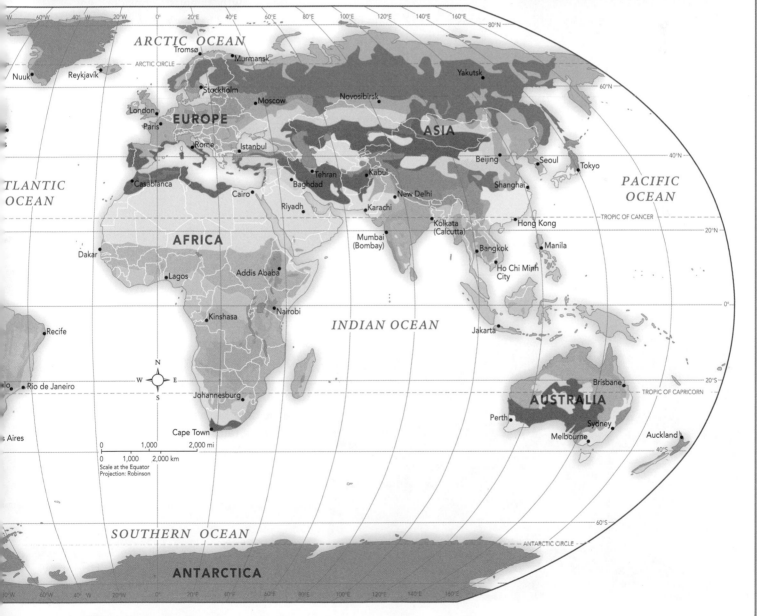

HUMAN GEOGRAPHY

People Everywhere!

studies patterns of human activity, including the locations and movements of populations. The population of a country or other area is the total number of people who live in it. Populations change as a result of migration—movement from one place to another—and a process called natural increase. Natural increase is the difference between births and deaths. Most countries have more births than deaths, and so their population increases, unless a net loss results from migration.

Historical Population Growth	
1650	550 million (estimate)
1850	1,100 million (estimate)
1927	2 billion
1974	4 billion
1999	6 billion
2010	7 billion

Scientists estimate that for thousands of years, the number of people in the world was fairly small and stable. During the shift from hunting and gathering to farming, around 8000 BC, the population started to grow. This growth was gradual until about AD 1650. At that point, population growth began to speed up.

By the early 2000s, the world's population had reached nearly 7 billion. The number of people is increasing at an annual rate of about 1.2 percent.

How Populations Change

To study population growth, scientists consider two main factors: birth and death. The *crude birth rate* is the ratio of births per 1,000 members of the population. The *crude death rate* is the ratio of deaths per 1,000 members of the population.

Factors affecting the birth rate

- number of women of childbearing age
- cultural factors such as marriage and birth control

Factors affecting the death rate

- infant mortality
- life expectancy

The net rate of population growth is calculated by subtracting the crude death rate from the crude birth rate. (In an individual society, the migration rate—number of people entering versus people leaving the society—is also counted.)

Growth Rates. Population growth rates vary throughout the world. Developing nations generally grow much faster than developed nations. This is largely because their birth rates remain high, while death rates have decreased, due to improved health care and sanitation.

High birth rates and low death rates have led to population explosions in some developing nations.

WHERE PEOPLE LIVE

Humans are not evenly distributed across the earth. Some areas have extremely high populations. Others, such as certain deserts and the continent of Antarctica, have no permanent settlers at all. The average number of people living in a particular area is called *population density*.

- A very densely populated region would have many people per square mile/kilometer of land.

- A thinly populated region would have few people per square mile/kilometer.

The most densely populated areas of the world are in Europe and in southern and eastern Asia. North America has dense populations in its central and northeastern regions, as well as along the Pacific coast. Africa, Australia, and South America have densely populated regions along their coasts, but not in their interiors.

The two countries with the largest populations are in Asia. They are China, which has about 1.33 billion people, and India, which has nearly 1.25 billion. The two next largest countries are the United States, with about 310 million people, and Indonesia, with about 240 million people.

World Population Density. This map shows how the world's population is distributed. About three-fourths of all people live in Asia and Europe. Regions with severe climates, such as desert areas, are thinly populated. The map also shows the location of some of the world's largest metropolitan areas. ▼

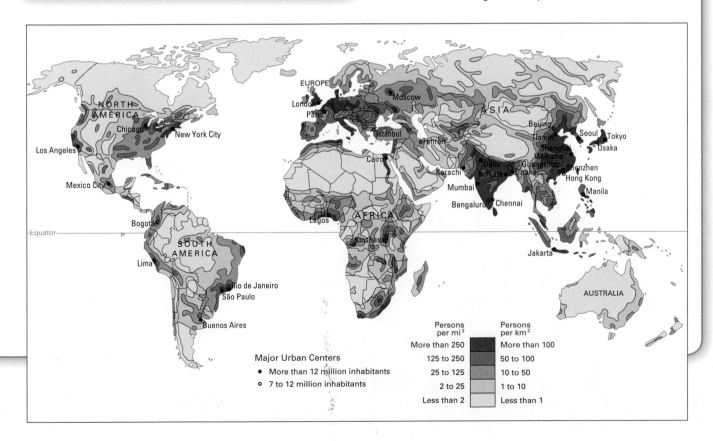

People on the Move

For thousands of years, populations of human beings have migrated, or moved from place to place. Early groups of people traveled in search of food sources, following herds of animals for hunting, or searching for edible plants and fruits.

Ancient Migrations

As agriculture, and later civilization, developed, tribes moved as a result of invasions and war. For example:

- in about 1500 BC, nomads called Aryans migrated into the Indus Valley (in modern-day India) and established kingdoms there. (See pages 408–409.)
- in about 1200 BC, a group called the Dorians invaded southern Greece.

These migrations resulted in the destruction of cultures and the foundations of new cultures.

THE BANTU MIGRATION

The Bantu are a large group of African peoples. (The word Bantu also refers to the related languages spoken by these peoples.) The first Bantu probably lived in what is now Cameroon. But sometime before AD 300, faced with a growing population, the Bantu began one of the greatest migrations in history.

- The migration occurred gradually, with small groups continually splitting off and moving to new regions.
- These groups slowly developed into the cultural units of today.
- By 1500, Bantu peoples had moved into most of central, eastern, and southern Africa.
- Such groups as the Ganda, Kongo, Luba, Lunda, Nyoro, and Rwanda established great kingdoms in central Africa.

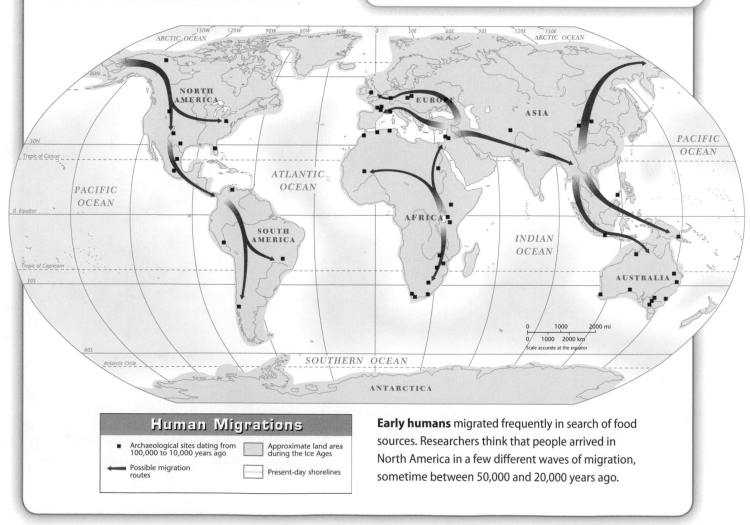

Human Migrations

- ■ Archaeological sites dating from 100,000 to 10,000 years ago
- ◄— Possible migration routes
- Approximate land area during the Ice Ages
- Present-day shorelines

Early humans migrated frequently in search of food sources. Researchers think that people arrived in North America in a few different waves of migration, sometime between 50,000 and 20,000 years ago.

Modern Migration

Migrations can be found at most stages of human history. One era of human migration began with the rise of European exploration in the 1400s and 1500s. This led to the settlement of large numbers of Europeans in Central and North America.

The past 300 years have been a period of several great migrations, including that of Europeans to the Americas and some Pacific areas. There have also been many migrations within a region; for example, between 1910 and 1930, many African Americans migrated from southern states to northern states.

Causes of Migration. There are many reasons for people to leave their homelands for new places. Some migrations are involuntary, meaning that people are forced to migrate elsewhere. For example:

- from the 1500s to the 1800s, Europeans shipped black Africans to the Western Hemisphere as slaves. (See page 39.)

- the United Kingdom transported convicts to Australia from the late 1700s to the 1860s to relieve overcrowding in British jails.

Push-Pull Factors. Other migrations are caused by bad conditions in a person's original home. One theory calls poor conditions that drive people from their home countries "push factors." For example:

- during the Great Irish Famine of 1845–1850, millions left Ireland for the United States and elsewhere.

- in the 1990s, millions of refugees fled their home countries of Bosnia-Herzegovina, East Timor (now Timor-Leste), Ethiopia, Iraq, Kosovo (then a province of Serbia), Liberia, and Rwanda due to war and genocide.

The main reason for immigration, however, has long been economic opportunity—the lure of better land, a better job, or a better life. Factors that draw people to a certain place are sometimes called "pull factors."

▲ **Many immigrants** are drawn to their new homes by economic opportunity. During the 1800s, the rich prairie land and growing industries of the United States and Canada attracted many European immigrants. Ellis Island, shown here, was for many years the entry point for immigrants to the United States.

✔ Human geography studies the movements of populations, as well as other human activities.

✔ A population is the total number of people belonging to a region or group. Population density refers to the average number of people living in an area.

✔ Population growth is determined by subtracting the crude death rate from the crude birth rate in an area.

✔ Migrations, or movements of populations from one place to another, have several causes, such as war and economic opportunity.

Urbanization

World population growth has been accompanied by a trend toward increasing urbanization, or development and growth of cities. Urban geography deals with cities and other urban areas.

- Urban geographers examine how location may be important in the development of cities and other communities.
- They may investigate where different groups live within a city or why slums develop where they do.

URBANIZATION IN ASIA

By 2012, researchers predict that the three largest urban centers in the world will be found in Asia. (An urban center is a city surrounded by a continuously built-up area having a high population density.)

1. Tokyo, Japan
(Estimated 2012 population: 36,823,000)
Tokyo, the capital of Japan, is part of a huge urban area that also includes the port city of Yokohama and the manufacturing cities of Chiba and Kawasaki. About one-fourth of Japan's population lives in the area.

2. Delhi, India
(Estimated 2012 population: 22,930,000)
The city of Delhi is currently the second largest in India—only Mumbai has more people. Delhi and its surroundings, however, are soon expected to exceed Mumbai's population. New Delhi is India's capital.

3. Mumbai, India
(Estimated 2012 population: 20,720,000)
Mumbai, formerly called Bombay, is currently the largest city in India, though Delhi's population may soon make it the second largest. Mumbai is an important financial center, the home of India's diamond-cutting industry, and the heart of the Indian film industry.

Rise of Cities

Cities have been particularly important in the development of civilization; they have served as centers of trade, government, and learning. But until the mid-1800s, they contained only a small proportion of the world's population. It is estimated that, even as late as 1850, only 5 percent of Earth's people lived in cities.

The massive industrialization that began in the 1800s led to rapid growth in the manufacturing and industrial centers of the world. Then the urbanizing trend began to gather force even in undeveloped countries. According to one projection, over 60 percent of the total population will live in cities by the year 2030.

City Growth in the U.S.

Like other industrialized nations, the United States is highly urbanized; almost three-fourths of its people live in urban settings. Metropolitan areas—central cities together with nearby suburbs and fringe exurban areas shading into open countryside—are the characteristic form urbanization now takes.

URBAN AMERICA

The shaded areas on this map outline the major metropolitan corridors, or regions, of the United States:

- BOS-WASH stretches from Boston, Massachusetts, to Washington, D.C., along the Atlantic coast. It includes such major cities as Providence, New York, Philadelphia, and Baltimore.

- CHI-PITTS stretches from Chicago, Illinois, to Pittsburgh, Pennsylvania, along the southern shores of the Great Lakes. It includes Detroit and Cleveland.

- SAN-SAN runs along California's Pacific coast from San Francisco to San Diego. It includes the sprawling Los Angeles region, which is made up of several metropolitan areas.

SUBURBANIZATION

The general trend in the United States over the last several decades has been for suburbs to grow at the expense of central cities. Unfortunately, the shift to suburbs involved mainly middle-class families. Increasingly, the population of central cities became comprised of low-income minority families.

As the urban tax base declined, commercial taxes rose, and businesses as well as families moved to suburbs. This situation in turn resulted in fewer jobs and economic opportunities in the city cores—a process that is sometimes called urban decay.

This pattern of wealth in outlying regions and poverty near the center of the city is a reversal of an earlier pattern. In the 1800s, the wealthy lived near the center of town, and the poor in outlying regions.

- Another cluster of large cities is growing up in Texas in a triangle whose corners are Houston-Galveston, Dallas-Fort Worth, and San Antonio.

- There are also three metropolitan areas in Florida with a million or more people: Jacksonville, Tampa, and Miami.

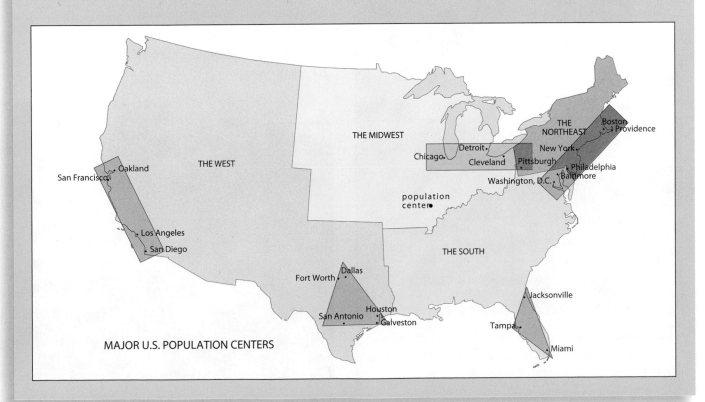

MAJOR U.S. POPULATION CENTERS

CULTURAL GEOGRAPHY

Culture is learned behavior, and it sets humans apart from animals. Humans act out of shared experience and have developed different patterns of living, ranging from that of the Arabian Bedouin to that of the Alaskan Inuit. The distinctive pattern of a particular group of people is called an individual culture. Cultural geography examines the location and historical spread of beliefs, customs, and other cultural traits. For example, cultural geographers might study the spread of a set of religious beliefs. Or they might explore how a people's cultural practices have changed the part of Earth where they live.

Nonmaterial culture refers to a society's behaviors and beliefs. For example, showing respect by greeting people with a bow is part of the nonmaterial culture of Japan. ▶

What Makes a Culture?

A group of people develops characteristic kinds of social arrangements and interactions, as well as its own way of manufacturing tools, of eating, of picturing the universe, of speaking and gesturing, and even of sitting or sleeping. Culture is all of the traits that humans learn from the other humans around them.

Culture and Society

The terms *culture* and *society* are often used to refer to the same thing, but they actually have slightly different meanings.

- Culture refers to all the products (material and nonmaterial) of a group.
- Society refers to the people (usually in a common territory) who share this way of life.

Western culture is a way of life shared by American society, French society, and so on. Every human society has a culture.

Cultural traits can be divided into two groups: material and nonmaterial culture.

- **Material culture** includes all the physical objects created by humans, from pizza and sneakers to calculators and hydrogen bombs.
- **Nonmaterial culture** consists of abstract creations, such as religious beliefs, language, and marriage customs.

▲ **A Multicultural Nation.** The United States is known for embracing many different kinds of cultures, thanks in part to a history of immigration that has brought many different ethnic groups to the country.

Multiculturalism. Some societies—such as those of Tibetans in Tibet and various peoples of the Pacific Islands—have traditionally been associated with a single culture. Other societies—such as those of the United States and Canada—are multicultural societies. They include many distinct cultures.

People of one culture who move to a country where another culture dominates may give up their old ways and become part of the dominant culture. The process by which they do this is called *assimilation*. Through assimilation, a minority group's members lose the cultural characteristics that set them apart. In a multicultural society, however, assimilation does not always occur.

SUBCULTURES

Subcultures are variations within a culture. Social groups often develop some cultural patterns of their own that set them apart from the larger society they are part of. Subcultures may develop in businesses, ethnic groups, occupational groups, regional groups, religious groups, and other groups within a larger culture.

One example of a subculture would be the Amish communities of Pennsylvania and the Midwest. Another example might be the members of a teenage street gang. ▼

LANGUAGE AND CULTURE

Humans transmit knowledge, whether it be tribal traditions or chemical formulas, using language. A culture's language expresses the concepts its people regard as important. For example:

- some cultures with strict systems of social status will have several pronouns that correspond to the English word "you," with different pronouns used for social superiors, equals, or inferiors. (One language that does this is Vietnamese.)
- nouns also reflect the needs and experiences of culture. You may have heard that the Inuit, who live above the Arctic Circle, have 20 words describing snow; the Aztecs, living in the tropics, had only one word that meant snow, frost, ice, and cold.

How Culture Spreads

No society is so isolated that it does not come in contact with other societies. When contact occurs, societies borrow cultural traits from one another. As a result, cultural traits and patterns tend to spread from the society in which they originated.

Contact and Change

The process by which cultural traits spread from one society to another is called *diffusion*. Corn growing, for example, began in what is now Mexico thousands of years ago and eventually spread throughout the world.

Western cultures adopted Arabic numerals from India, steel from Damascus, and paper from China. Today, we might think of examples like Coca-Cola in Kuwait and blue jeans in Japan.

Acculturation. When two cultures have continuous, firsthand contact with each other, the exchange of cultural traits is called *acculturation*.

- Acculturation has often occurred when one culture has colonized or conquered another, or as a result of trade.

- In addition to adopting each other's traits, the two cultures may blend traits, such as clothing, dances, music, recipes, and tools.

Through acculturation, parts of the culture of one or both groups change, but the groups remain distinct. (Unlike assimilation, in which one group becomes part of another group and loses its separate identity.)

Westernization has been rejected by some cultures and embraced by others. These Japanese young people have adopted American rockabilly fashions. ▶

CULTURAL DIFFUSION

Diffusion can occur without firsthand contact between cultures. Products or patterns may move from group A to group C through group B without any contact between group A and group C. This diagram gives some examples of how a cultural idea might spread. The arrow represents direct contact between two cultures.

Today, diffusion is rapid and widespread because many cultures of the world are linked through advanced means of transportation and communication.

Cultural Diffusion

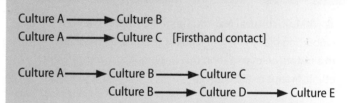

Culture A ⟶ Culture B
Culture A ⟶ Culture C   [Firsthand contact]

Culture A ⟶ Culture B ⟶ Culture C
        Culture B ⟶ Culture D ⟶ Culture E

WESTERNIZATION

In the past several hundred years, Western culture has come to influence virtually every other culture in the world. The culture has been carried by invading armies and imposed by political regimes. But it has also been adopted by choice in many areas since it promises material improvement and prestige.

People in remote corners of the world have learned about the West from radio, film, television, and visits from Western businesspeople. Where two cultures are of similar complexity and economic power, acculturation brings change to both. When the power of two cultures is unequal, however, the results are often tragic.

Many cultures have sought to reject westernization.

- In the United States, the resistance of American Indians to Western culture led to violent clashes, such as the Wounded Knee massacre. (See page 139.)

- The 1979 revolution in Iran sought to destroy Western cultural influence without giving up the advantages of Western technology.

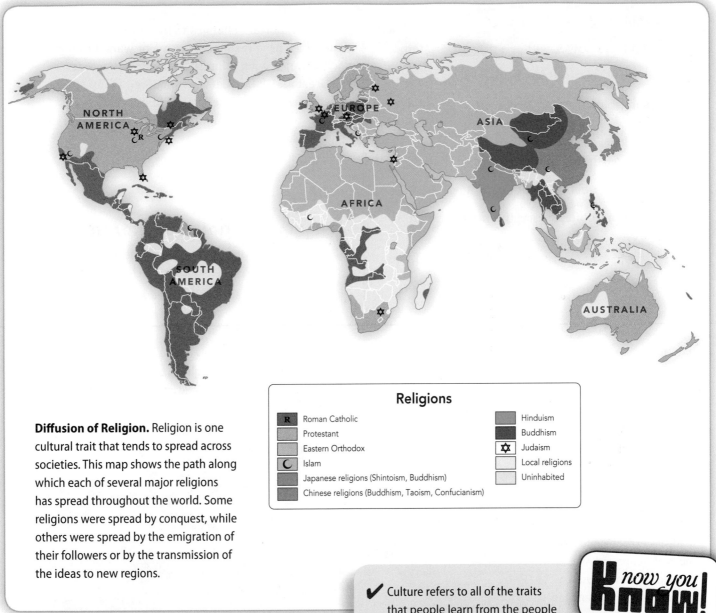

Religions

R Roman Catholic	Hinduism
Protestant	Buddhism
Eastern Orthodox	✡ Judaism
☾ Islam	Local religions
Japanese religions (Shintoism, Buddhism)	Uninhabited
Chinese religions (Buddhism, Taoism, Confucianism)	

Diffusion of Religion. Religion is one cultural trait that tends to spread across societies. This map shows the path along which each of several major religions has spread throughout the world. Some religions were spread by conquest, while others were spread by the emigration of their followers or by the transmission of the ideas to new regions.

now you **Know!**

✔ Culture refers to all of the traits that people learn from the people around them. Cultural geography examines the location and historical spread of beliefs, customs, and other cultural traits.

✔ Every human society has a culture; multicultural societies embrace several different cultures at once.

✔ Cultural diffusion occurs when cultures come into direct or indirect contact with each other, such as through conquest or communication.

✔ Acculturation is the blending of cultures through constant direct contact; assimilation is when members of one culture adopt a different culture entirely.

POLITICAL GEOGRAPHY

deals with the ways people in different places make decisions or gain and use power within a political system. Political geographers study such topics as changes in political boundaries, problems of political instability, and patterns of voting. Political maps show the boundaries of units of government, such as counties, states, and nations. Throughout history, the political map of the world has changed repeatedly.

Borders and Nations

Many important changes to the world's political boundaries have resulted from major wars. During ancient times, such military leaders as Alexander the Great and Julius Caesar conquered many groups of people and established vast empires. Numerous empires rose and fell later in history, and boundaries changed again and again.

CHANGING NATIONAL BOUNDARIES

The political map of the world continues to change, as a result of both peaceful and violent change.

- In 1991, the collapse of the Soviet Union led to a redrawing of many political boundaries in Eastern Europe (see map below).

- Yugoslavia began dissolving in 1991 as well; after many years of internal fighting between ethnic groups, it was finally divided into the nations of Serbia and Montenegro in 2006.

- In 1993, the nation of Czechoslovakia was divided into the Czech Republic and Slovakia.

Russia, Yesterday and Today.
This map shows how the nation of Russia developed over time, gradually expanding to include much of Europe and Asia. The thin red line shows Russia's boundaries as they stand today.

- - - - - - Boundary of Moscow 1462

Expansion 1462–1533

Expansion 1533–1584

Expansion 1584–1689

Expansion 1689–1914

──── Boundary of present-day Russia

365 Barack Obama   **173** John McCain

2008 PRESIDENTIAL ELECTION

*The 5 electoral votes from Nebraska were split, with four votes for McCain and one vote for Obama.

Political geographers also study political activity across and within regions. One example of this would be voting patterns. These maps show election results for two different U.S. elections; a political geographer would note the differences between the two and draw conclusions about the country's changing political climate.

286 George W. Bush   **252** John F. Kerry

2004 PRESIDENTIAL ELECTION

HUMAN IMPACT

Everything humans do has some kind of effect on the planet. The effects of our large—and growing—population and the growth of our industrial society have been drastic. The major environmental issues of today are large and complex. *Environmental conservation* combines information from both physical geography and human geography. Geographers study this information at the local, regional, national, and international levels. They can then draw conclusions about the ways in which human beings are changing Earth, and what we can do differently.

SHRINKING FORESTS

Many forest regions have been stripped of large areas of trees. In Brazil, for example, an average of 15,000 acres of forest are destroyed every day. The trees are cut down for timber, and also to clear land for crops.

- This leads to soil erosion and the destruction of plant and animal life.

- Trees remove carbon dioxide (CO_2) from the atmosphere, so reduced forests mean higher CO_2 levels.

Our Worldwide Footprint

For hundreds of years, people have used the world's natural resources to make their lives more comfortable. However, these resources are not always used wisely. Many different industries and activities drive the world's economy. Some of these, such as mining, logging, and farming, threaten the environment.

Global Warming. People often use the term *global warming* to refer specifically to the increase in Earth's average surface temperatures, observed since the mid-1800s.

Natural processes have caused Earth's climate to change in the distant past. But scientists have found strong evidence that human activities have caused most of the warming since the mid-1900s.

- Geographers gather sets of data on precipitation, temperature, wind speed, and other factors to create maps for studying future climate patterns.

- They use these models to predict the effects of changes in human activities.

Sustainability involves replacing harmful human activities with environmentally sound practices that protect natural resources.

For example, certain farming practices, including the use of chemical fertilizers and pesticides, pollute soil. Other farming methods reduce soil's fertility over time. Geographers at the local level might study these things:

- the ecological factors that influence natural farming methods.

- changes in agricultural land use.

- policies that influence farmers.

They can use the data to recommend more sustainable methods.

Energy Use. Geographers also study patterns of energy consumption, or use, both locally and around the globe. Because much of the energy humans use comes from burning fossil fuels, levels of energy consumption are tied to carbon dioxide emission levels.

CARBON DIOXIDE EMISSIONS

The major cause of the rise in global surface temperatures, or global warming, is the greenhouse effect.

- Atmospheric gases—methane (CH_4), nitrous oxide (N_2O), ozone (O_3), and carbon dioxide (CO_2)—trap the sun's heat.

- Carbon dioxide, which mostly comes from burning fossil fuels, produces the most warming.

- Many efforts at slowing global climate change center on reducing CO_2 emissions in the areas with the highest emission levels (see map).

Carbon Dioxide Emissions

Million tons, 2004

- More than 5,000
- 1,000–5,000
- 400–999
- 200–399
- 100–199
- Less than 100

Source: United Nations Statistics Division—Environmental Statistics

GLOBAL ENERGY CONSUMPTION

This map shows the energy consumed by all nations, in units called BTUs, or British Thermal Units. In 2006, the United States and China both consumed over 50 quadrillion BTUs of energy.

Energy Consumption

Quadrillion BTU, 2005

- More than 100
- 50–100
- 10–49.9
- 5–9.9
- 1–4.9
- Less than 1

Source: Energy Information Administration, United States Department of Energy

REGIONS OF THE WORLD

The phrase "the whole world" conjures up a picture of something huge, intriguing, colorful, and full of variety. The world around us is exactly that. Though the planet may be small in comparison with the universe—full of stars and other giant planets that may or may not support life—it is still a source of never-ending wonder, speculation, and possibilities. Geographers are engaged in the project of showing us the world as it is—all its different places and its many people.

The Seven Continents of the World. Asia is the largest continent, followed by Africa, North America, South America, Antarctica, Europe, and Australia. Geographers sometimes refer to Europe and Asia as one continent called Eurasia. The region known as the Middle East is technically part of the Asian continent, but is often considered to be a separate region. ▼

Looking at the World

When geographers look at the world, what do they see?

- The surface area of the world totals about 196,900,000 square miles (510,000,000 square kilometers).

- Water covers about 139,700,000 square miles (362,000,000 square kilometers), or 71 percent of the world's surface.

- Only 29 percent of the world's surface consists of land, which covers about 57,200,000 square miles (148,000,000 square kilometers).

The Continents

The land area of the world—29 percent of the total surface—consists of seven continents and many thousands of islands. The people of each continent and country have shaped the land to meet their needs and desires, but their customs and ways of life have also been shaped by the land.

From economies based on abundant natural resources to populations that grow, shrink, or move across great distances, the human world is a reflection of the natural one.

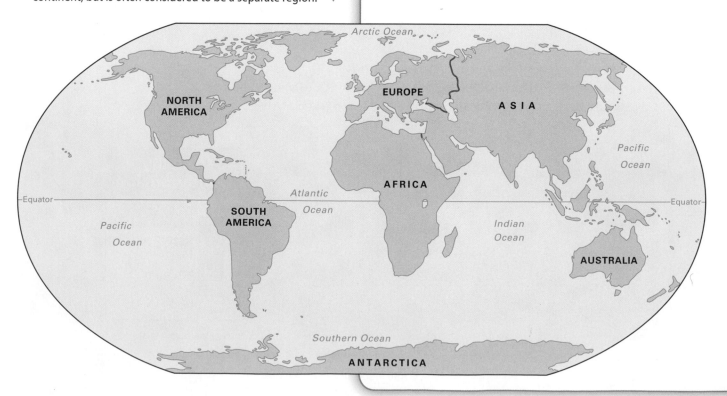

Characteristics. Each continent has certain physical characteristics, depending on a variety of factors.

- land formations, such as mountains or valleys
- nearness to the equator or either of the poles
- the people who live there
- the types of plants and animals found there
- the lack or abundance of mineral resources

Effects. The characteristics of each continent have an effect upon the people who live there. For example:

- if the land has expanses of territory that are not suitable for human habitation, only the most easily accessible areas will be developed and support large populations.
- where millions of people have congregated in big cities, they may face challenges supporting a population far from sources of food and other necessities.

The characteristics of any given region are a factor in determining the relative quality of life in that area. They can determine whether necessities and luxuries are easily obtained, or whether simply having adequate food and shelter is a constant struggle.

◀ **The equator** runs through the continent of Africa. This means that much of the continent has very high temperatures, though other factors affect the humidity and rainfall of different regions.

▲ **Antarctica** is mostly buried by thick ice; the only human inhabitants are researchers. The continent's deepest ice is more than 10 times the height of the Willis Tower, one of the world's tallest buildings.

North America

The North American continent includes Canada, Greenland, the United States, Mexico, the countries of Central America, and the islands of the West Indies in the Caribbean Sea. It is the third largest continent in landmass, covering about 9,360,000 square miles (24,242,289 square kilometers), and has the fourth largest population, with about 538 million people.

GEOGRAPHIC REGIONS

North America has eight major land regions.

▲ **The Rocky Mountains** are a popular destination for tourists and hikers.

North American Land Regions	
Pacific Ranges and Lowlands	• Two parallel mountain ranges separated by a series of valleys • Extends from Alaska to Mexico
Western Plateaus, Basins, and Ranges	• Between the Pacific ranges and the Rocky Mountains • Includes the Columbia Plateau, the Colorado Plateau, the Great Basin centered in Nevada, and the Plateau of Mexico
Rocky Mountains	• North America's largest mountain system • Runs from Alaska to New Mexico
Interior Plains	• Covers much of central Canada and the midwestern United States
Canadian Shield	• Huge area of ancient rock that covers most of Canada east of the Great Plains and north of the Great Lakes
Appalachian Highlands	• Extends from the island of Newfoundland to Alabama • Region includes low, rounded mountains; plateaus; and valleys
Coastal Lowlands	• Stretches along the Atlantic Ocean and the Gulf of Mexico • Runs from New York City to Mexico's Yucatán Peninsula
Central America and the Caribbean	• Consists of the narrow bridge of land at the southern tip of North America and the islands in the Caribbean Sea

POPULATION

About 538 million people live in North America, or about 8 percent of the world's population.

- The population of the United States in 2010 was 309,183,463.
- The population of Canada in 2010 was estimated to be 31,800,000.
- The population density for the United States is roughly 80 persons per square mile (31 persons per square kilometer).
- The population density for Canada is roughly 9 persons per square mile (3 persons per square kilometer).

CLIMATE

North America is the only continent that has every kind of climate, from the dry, bitter cold of the Arctic to the steamy heat of the tropics.

- The northern part of North America, including most of Alaska and interior northern Canada, is arctic or subarctic.
- The Pacific coastal region, from southern Alaska to northern California, has a much milder climate.
- Western Canada east of the coastal ranges has a milder climate than that of the northern interior.
- The eastern two-thirds of the continent has a generally moderate and moist climate.
- The southwestern United States and the Basin and Range region have the warmest and driest climates in North America.
- The climate of Central America varies depending on elevation and distance from moisture-laden Caribbean air masses.

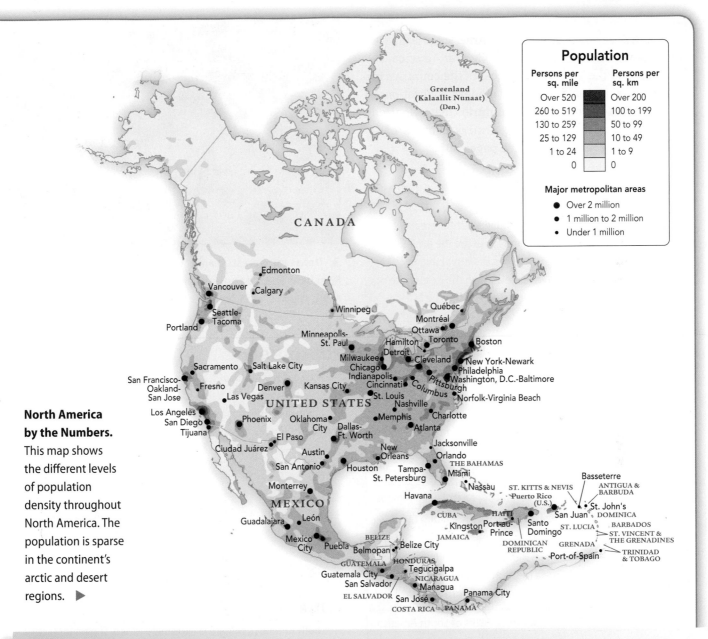

Population

Persons per sq. mile		Persons per sq. km
Over 520		Over 200
260 to 519		100 to 199
130 to 259		50 to 99
25 to 129		10 to 49
1 to 24		1 to 9
0		0

Major metropolitan areas

● Over 2 million

● 1 million to 2 million

• Under 1 million

North America by the Numbers.

This map shows the different levels of population density throughout North America. The population is sparse in the continent's arctic and desert regions. ▶

VEGETATION

North America has a broad variety of vegetation, from vast coniferous and broadleaf forests in Canada and the Pacific Northwest, to tundra along the continent's northern rim, to tropical rain forests in the Central American isthmus and the Caribbean coast of Mexico.

ECONOMY

North America possesses an abundance of natural resources, especially those needed to support a modern industrial economy.

The United States and Canada have a combined gross national product of over $6 trillion. Per capita incomes of both countries are among the highest in the world.

Mexico and Central America. In most Latin American countries, significant industrial development did not occur until the late 19th or 20th century. Mexico has a well-balanced and now growing economy, even though a combination of falling oil prices and large foreign debt caused severe economic difficulties in the past.

South America

South America is part of Latin America, a large cultural region that also includes Central America, Mexico, and the West Indies. Most of the countries in this cultural region derive their modern civilizations from Spain and Portugal, the countries that colonized them following discovery of the Americas by Europeans beginning in AD 1492. (See pages 502–505.)

▲ **Dense rain forests** blanket most of the warm, wet Amazon River basin and the northeast and northwest coasts of the continent. Many valuable forest products come from the lush Amazon region.

GEOGRAPHIC REGIONS

South America may be generally divided into three geographic regions. The two upland zones are the Andes mountain system, in the west, and the eastern highlands, which extend from eastern Venezuela along the northeastern and eastern edges of the continent. The third region is the Central Plains region.

South American Land Regions	
Andes mountain system	• extends along the entire western edge of South America • center of often devastating seismic and volcanic activity • frequently interspersed with deep river valleys and plateau regions
Eastern Highlands	• consists of several uplifted plateau regions • the Brazilian Highlands rise along the Atlantic coast • the Guiana Highlands extend from eastern Venezuela through Guyana, Suriname, and French Guiana and into northern Brazil
Central Plains	• covers about three-fifths of South America • consists of grasslands called the Llanos; a lowland region called Selva; the hardwood scrub forest Gran Chaco; and the vast grassland called the Pampas

POPULATION

The continent of South America has a population of about 396,258,000 people. Its population density is about 58 people per square mile (22 per square kilometer). It ranks fifth among the continents in population. (Asia, Europe, Africa, and North America all have more people.)

- South America covers about 12 percent of the world's land area and has about 6 percent of the total world population.
- Nearly all the peoples of South America live in highlands or plateau regions.
- In South America, these regions rarely extend over 200 miles (320 kilometers) from the coastlines.

CLIMATE

South America's climate is extremely varied. The major factors influencing climate in South America are latitude, elevation, and ocean currents and associated air masses.

- Temperature generally decreases toward the south and in the higher elevations.
- Freezing temperatures occur only in the upper elevations of the Andes and on the extreme southern tip of the continent.
- The warm Brazilian Current off the continent's Atlantic coast, coupled with warm steady breezes, provides heavy rainfall to the Amazon basin region, which has a tropical climate year-round.
- The Pacific coasts of Colombia, northern Peru, and southern Chile receive heavy rainfall.

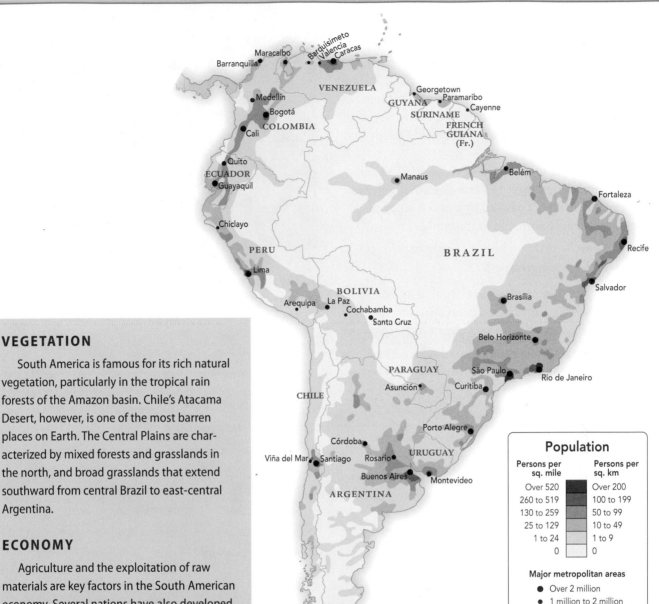

VEGETATION

South America is famous for its rich natural vegetation, particularly in the tropical rain forests of the Amazon basin. Chile's Atacama Desert, however, is one of the most barren places on Earth. The Central Plains are characterized by mixed forests and grasslands in the north, and broad grasslands that extend southward from central Brazil to east-central Argentina.

ECONOMY

Agriculture and the exploitation of raw materials are key factors in the South American economy. Several nations have also developed thriving industrial and manufacturing sectors.

- The processing of agricultural products remains the main industrial activity.

- The manufacture of such things as metals, chemicals, plastics, textiles, automobiles, electrical goods, machinery, and consumer goods has expanded rapidly in the last few decades.

- Most industries are located in or near the major urban centers.

Population

Persons per sq. mile	Persons per sq. km
Over 520	Over 200
260 to 519	100 to 199
130 to 259	50 to 99
25 to 129	10 to 49
1 to 24	1 to 9
0	0

Major metropolitan areas
- Over 2 million
- 1 million to 2 million
- Under 1 million

▲ **South America by the Numbers.** This map shows the different levels of population density throughout South America. The bulk of the population lives along South America's Atlantic coast and in the Andean highlands.

Europe

The continent of Europe is one of the smallest of the world's seven continents in area but one of the largest in population. All of the continents except Australia have more land than Europe. But only Asia and Africa have more people. The countries of Europe include the world's largest country, Russia, as well as the world's smallest, Vatican City. Russia lies partly in Europe and partly in Asia.

Europe has long ranked among the world's leading industrial and agricultural centers. The continent has many rich deposits of coal and iron ore. It also has some of the richest farmland in the world.

GEOGRAPHIC REGIONS

Europe can be divided into four topographical regions. These regions are large bands of territory running east to west.

European Geographic Regions	
Northwest mountains	• runs from the northern British Isles across Scandinavia • generally harsh climate and poor soil
Central Uplands	• plateau region stretching from Spain through central Europe • includes the Meseta, or central plateau, of Portugal and Spain and the Massif Central in France
Alpine mountain system	• stretches across the south from southern Spain to southeastern Europe • home to continuing volcanic and seismic activity
Great European Plain	• lowlands running through southeastern England, southern France, Belgium, the Netherlands, Denmark, northern Germany, Poland, Ukraine, and much of Russia • most fertile farmland in the region

▲ **The sharp peaks** and steep sides of the Alps are a sign that the mountain range is relatively young. Picturesque villages in the Alpine mountain region are popular tourist destinations.

POPULATION

Europe is a densely populated continent, though certain geographic factors cause the density to vary widely from place to place. For example, the mountainous interiors of Norway and Sweden are sparsely populated.

- In 2010, Europe's estimated population of 857,000,000 accounted for almost 13 percent of the world's population.
- On average, Europe's population is growing at a substantially slower rate than the world population.
- Industrialization and economic diversity help to support the large existing population.

CLIMATE

Europe has four basic climatic regions.

- The Mediterranean region, in the southern part of the continent, has hot, dry summers and wet, mild winters.
- The maritime climate regions have abundant rainfall year-round, and moderate temperatures in both summer and winter.
- The continental climate is mostly found in eastern Europe and most of Russia. It has lower precipitation and harsh winters. Rainfall occurs mostly in the summer.
- The fourth climate region occurs wherever the continental climate and the maritime climate merge. This climate is characterized by cold winters with heavy snowfall in the mountains, and generally warm and dry summers.

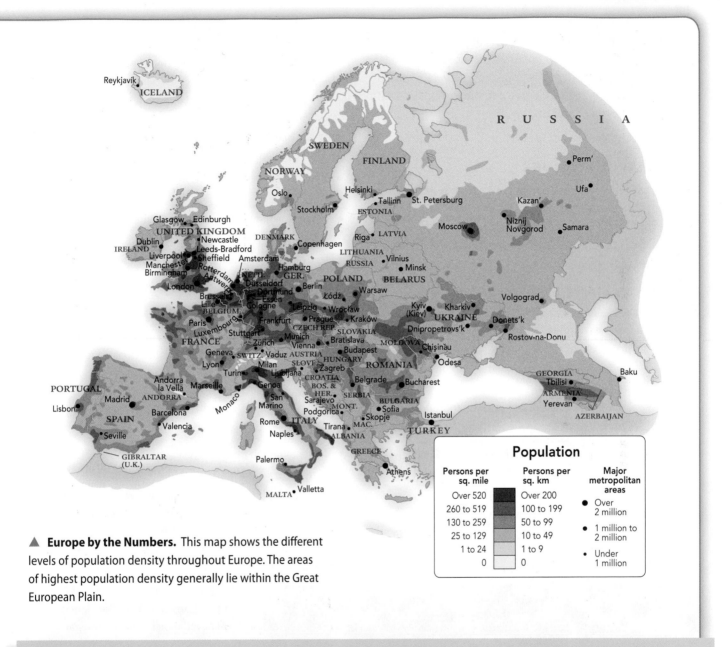

▲ **Europe by the Numbers.** This map shows the different levels of population density throughout Europe. The areas of highest population density generally lie within the Great European Plain.

Population

Persons per sq. mile	Persons per sq. km	Major metropolitan areas
Over 520	Over 200	● Over 2 million
260 to 519	100 to 199	
130 to 259	50 to 99	● 1 million to 2 million
25 to 129	10 to 49	
1 to 24	1 to 9	· Under 1 million
0	0	

VEGETATION

Most areas of Europe have substantial woodland. In northern coastal regions near the Arctic, only mosses, lichens, and small shrubs thrive. Coniferous and broadleaf forests are found in the middle of the continent. Large areas of the Mediterranean have been dedicated to the cultivation of olive, fig, citrus, and other fruit trees.

ECONOMY

The Industrial Revolution, which began in Great Britain in the mid-18th century, shifted the European economy from agriculture to industrial production. Today, manufacturing and high-technology industries—aerospace, electronics, and communications—play an important role in the economy.

The majority of countries in Europe belong to the European Union, which has a common market and uses a common currency, called the euro.

Africa

Africa is the second largest continent in area and in population. Only Asia covers a larger area and has more people. Africa covers approximately 11,684,000 square miles (30,262,000 square kilometers), about a fifth of the world's land area.

GEOGRAPHIC REGIONS

Africa is almost topographically homogeneous—that is, its surface is fairly consistent across the region. The vast majority of the continent is occupied by an enormous plateau. On this plateau, two major divisions order the continent into distinct areas: Low and High Africa.

African Geographic Regions	
Low Africa	• area north of the Congo River and west of the Nile River • includes about one-third of the continent's total area • extends through desert, grassland, and rain forest
High Africa	• area south and east of the Nile and Congo rivers • plateau interrupted by mountains, coastal plains, and the Great Rift Valley • Great Rift Valley cuts through the plateau from the Red Sea in the north to the Shire River in South Africa

POPULATION

Africa has a population of more than 1 billion, about one-seventh of the world's people.

The population is distributed unevenly. Large areas of the Sahara and other deserts have no people at all. On the other hand, the Nile River valley in Egypt is one of the most heavily populated regions on Earth.

- About 70 percent of all Africans live in rural towns and villages.
- Population growth is close to 3 percent and has been at that level for 30 years.
- Low population densities occur in the deserts, mountains, and forests.

CLIMATE

Most of Africa has a warm or hot climate, but the humidity and amount of rainfall vary dramatically from area to area.

- Tropical rain forests stretch across equatorial Africa to the lakes region of eastern Africa in a belt that extends about 400 miles (645 kilometers) north and 400 miles south of the equator.
- Temperatures in the rain forest rarely reach 100°F (38°C) or drop below 70°F (27°C).
- North and south of the rain forests are two parallel belts of grassland, or savanna. The grassland is known as the Sudan in the north and the veld, or bush, in the south. Temperatures here are high, reaching over 100°F (38°C) in the summer.
- The Sahara Desert has the region's hottest temperatures; it also has the highest level of variation between seasonal temperatures.
- Sea breezes in the coastal regions help provide milder climates. Some of the coastal regions have Mediterranean climates—dry summers and wet winters.

◀ **Mount Kilimanjaro,** the highest point on the African continent, is located in the country of Tanzania. The mountain rises to 19,331 feet (5,892 meters).

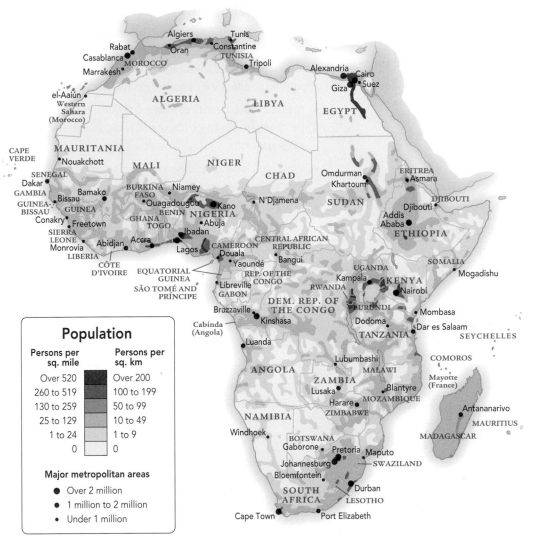

◀ **Africa by the Numbers.** This map shows population density across Africa. Areas of high population density exist in western Africa along the Niger; along the coast between Gambia and Cameroon; along the eastern coast from Kenya to South Africa; along the northern shores in Tunisia, Morocco, and the lower Nile; and on the East African Plateau in Ethiopia.

Population

Persons per sq. mile	Persons per sq. km
Over 520	Over 200
260 to 519	100 to 199
130 to 259	50 to 99
25 to 129	10 to 49
1 to 24	1 to 9
0	0

Major metropolitan areas

● Over 2 million

● 1 million to 2 million

• Under 1 million

VEGETATION

The tropical forests of equatorial Africa are dense with hundreds of different species of plants. Many grasslands and forests have been destroyed by agricultural and industrial development. Some regions have been turned almost entirely into deserts.

- Bamboo and oil palms are the most common plants.

- Mahogany, teak, ebony, and other hardwoods are the most valuable. Rubber, coffee, and cola nuts are also cultivated.

- The savannas have large numbers of acacia and baobab trees, thorny euphorbia bushes, and desert grasses.

ECONOMY

Despite Africa's mineral wealth and energy resources, the continent remains relatively poor. African countries, with the exception of South Africa, have been slow to develop modern industries and farming techniques.

- Agriculture employs three-quarters of the African workforce. Most is subsistence agriculture.

- The most significant contribution to the economic importance of Africa comes from the sizable oil and natural gas reserves of the Sahara.

Asia

Asia is the largest continent, both in land mass and in population. It covers about 30 percent of the world's land area and has about 60 percent of its people. Asia extends from Africa and Europe in the west to the Pacific Ocean in the east.

The northernmost part of the continent lies within the frozen Arctic. But in the south, Asia ends in the steaming tropics near the equator. It contains 50 different countries.

GEOGRAPHIC REGIONS

The continent of Asia often is divided into six subregions, each of which tends to be unified climatically, geographically, and culturally. Each subregion contains many different nations. The southwestern part of the continent is often referred to as the Middle East. (See pages 642–643.)

Asian Geographic Regions	
South Asia	• consists of Pakistan, India, Sri Lanka, Bangladesh, Bhutan, and Nepal • includes the Himalaya mountain range
Southeast Asia	• includes the Indochinese peninsula—Cambodia, Laos, Myanmar, Thailand, and Vietnam—Indonesia, and the Philippines • far eastern Indonesia considered to be part of Oceania rather than part of Asia
East Asia	• includes the eastern third of China, Korea, Taiwan, and Japan • 90 percent of the region is covered by China
Central Asia	• includes the western two-thirds of China, Mongolia, Tibet, Afghanistan, Kazakhstan, Kyrgyzstan, Tajikistan, Turkmenistan, and Uzbekistan
North Asia	• consists entirely of Siberia, which makes up about 75 percent of Russia

POPULATION

The countries of Asia are home, collectively, to about 4,186,414,000 people. Asia's population density averages about 250 people per square mile. However, local and regional population densities vary widely. For example:

- the population density of Mongolia, which has 2.7 million people in an area twice the size of Texas, averages 4 people per square mile.

- some mountainous and desert areas in central Asia have essentially zero population density.

- Singapore and Hong Kong have population densities approaching 12,000 and 14,600 people per square mile, respectively.

CLIMATE

Asia's weather is dominated by a pattern known as *monsoon*.

- During the winter, high-pressure areas form over the cold land (generally in Siberia), causing a flow of cold dry air toward the low-pressure areas over the warm seas and oceans.

- During the summer, the wind pattern of the monsoon is reversed. Low-pressure areas form over the land, particularly in the Punjab region of northern India and in the Gobi Desert region of China.

- Hot, moisture-laden air from the oceans and seas flows across the land toward the centers of low pressure.

- The mountain barriers force the air to rise and cool, thus reducing its ability to carry moisture.

- For this reason, the lands on the coastal side of the mountain barriers receive abundant monsoon rainfall and the inland regions of Asia receive very little precipitation.

Irrigated terraces for rice, such as this one, increase the amount of usable farmland in many Asian countries, which depend heavily on rice as a staple crop. ▶

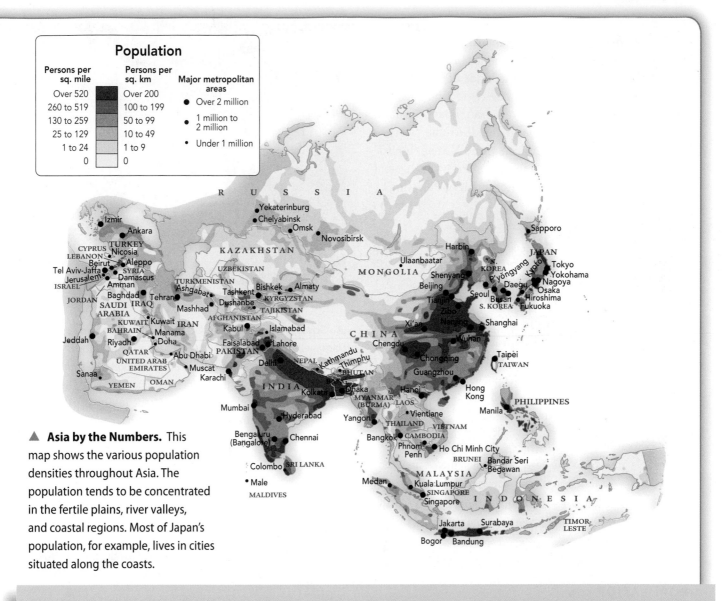

Population

Persons per sq. mile	Persons per sq. km
Over 520	Over 200
260 to 519	100 to 199
130 to 259	50 to 99
25 to 129	10 to 49
1 to 24	1 to 9
0	0

Major metropolitan areas
- Over 2 million
- 1 million to 2 million
- Under 1 million

▲ **Asia by the Numbers.** This map shows the various population densities throughout Asia. The population tends to be concentrated in the fertile plains, river valleys, and coastal regions. Most of Japan's population, for example, lives in cities situated along the coasts.

VEGETATION

Asia has a wide range of vegetation zones. Desert conditions prevail in central and west-central Asia. The lands to the north, east, and southeast of this region constitute a belt of low grassland called steppe. In eastern Asia, temperate grasslands merge into forest. In west-central Asia, the vast Plateau of Tibet, classified as Alpine tundra, gives way along the Himalayas to a tropical rain forest extending along the northern rim of the Indian subcontinent southeast through most of Southeast Asia.

ECONOMY

In economic development, Asia is a continent of contrasts. Countries that are desperately poor, such as Bangladesh, Cambodia, and Vietnam, exist side by side with wealthy countries, such as Japan, South Korea, and Singapore.

- The economy of Asia is dominated by agriculture, which employs more than 60 percent of the labor force.
- Countries that are not highly developed employ a greater percentage of their workforces in agriculture.
- Major industries in modern Asia include electronics, textiles, chemicals, petrochemicals, aluminum, steel, automobile manufacturing, and arms production.

Middle East

The Middle East, also called the Near East, is not a continent—it is part of the continent of Asia. The term refers to a region made up of the lands of southwestern Asia and northeastern Africa. The region includes the countries of Bahrain, Egypt, Iran, Iraq, Israel, Jordan, Kuwait, Lebanon, Oman, Qatar, Saudi Arabia, Syria, Turkey, the United Arab Emirates, and Yemen. It also includes the West Bank and the Gaza Strip, which, along with Israel, make up the historic region of Palestine.

GEOGRAPHIC REGIONS

Mountains and deserts dominate the topography of the Middle East. The region can be divided into northern and southern parts.

Middle Eastern Geographic Regions	
North	• mountains bordering interior plateaus • includes the Pontic Mountains and the Taurus Mountains in Turkey, and the Elburz and Zagros mountains across Iran
South	• vast dry plateau • several large deserts, including the Western and Eastern deserts of Egypt (part of the Sahara) • includes the Rub al Khali (Empty Quarter), a vast expanse of sand dunes across southern Saudi Arabia

POPULATION

The population of this region is over 230 million. The extreme aridity of the Middle East has caused the population to be distributed unevenly.

- Towns and cities have grown mostly around coastal areas, inland oases, and river valleys.
- The mountain regions have also created isolated communities.
- Most people are farmers, nomadic herders, or city dwellers.

A high population growth rate, above 2.5 percent, has put an enormous strain on the environment and the economy. The cities have been forced to adapt rapidly to constant growth and an influx of people.

▲ **Straits, Gulfs, and Canals.** The Bosporus (shown here) and Dardanelles straits in northwestern Turkey connect the Black and Mediterranean seas. The Persian Gulf is both the source of and chief waterway for the Middle East's rich oil trade. The Red Sea has become a major international trade route since the completion of the Suez Canal in 1869, which connects the Red and Mediterranean seas.

CLIMATE

The varying topography of the Middle East divides the region into discrete climatic zones.

- Most areas receive rain only during the winter months.
- The interior desert regions of the Middle East face some of the highest temperatures in the world during the summer months, often reaching above 135°F (57°C). The winters are much cooler.
- The shores of the Mediterranean, Black, and Caspian seas generally have a more temperate climate, with regular precipitation.
- In the northern mountains, winter temperatures average below 32°F (0°C).
- The mountains of Yemen and Lebanon receive snow regularly in the winter months, but their temperatures are generally not as low as in the northern ranges.

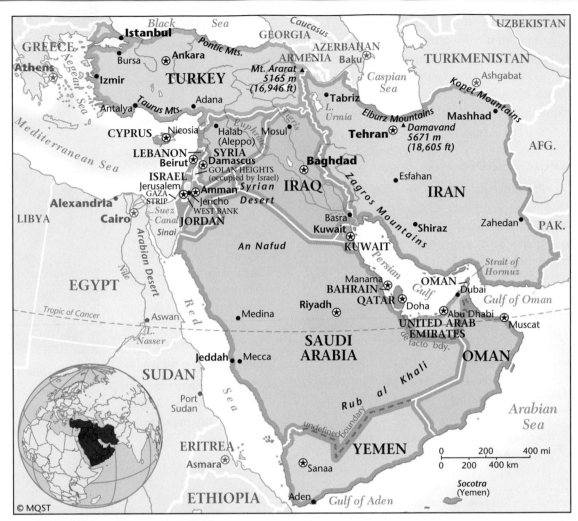

▲ **Nations that make up the Middle East** have an uneven distribution of people. Recently, the growth of urban areas has had the effect of bringing diverse cultures into close contact.

VEGETATION

The sandy soil of the Middle East's desert regions cannot support tree growth or most varieties of vegetation without irrigation.

- Some plants have adapted to the conditions and have formed small areas of vegetation.
- Overgrazing has depleted most areas of grassland and allowed desert expansion.
- Soil is also lost from wind and river erosion.
- Oranges, bananas, apricots, and dates thrive in the river valleys as well as in many coastal areas.

ECONOMY

Although the Middle Eastern economy has been revolutionized by the vast wealth earned from the oil industry, agriculture is still the region's main economic activity.

- Most of the people in the Middle East live by crude subsistence farming.
- The cash crops are cotton and tobacco.
- Nomads herd livestock in the deserts and grasslands.
- Over half of the world's known oil reserves are located here, mostly along the Persian Gulf coasts.
- Oil processing is the main industry in the Middle East.

Australasia

The last places in the world to be settled lie, not surprisingly, far from Earth's other major land masses. They include Australia, New Zealand, and the numerous islands of Oceania in the South Pacific that make up Micronesia, Melanesia, and Polynesia. The entire region is sometimes referred to as Australasia.

GEOGRAPHIC REGIONS

The smaller Pacific islands are generally divided into three groups based on their geography and cultural backgrounds: Polynesia, Micronesia, and Melanesia.

Australia is surrounded by water, like an island, but it is classed as a continent. It is the only country that is also a continent. Australia is divided into three land regions.

Australian Geographic Regions	
Eastern Highlands	• includes the highest elevations in Australia
	• extends from Cape York peninsula in extreme northeastern Australia to the south coast of Tasmania
	• includes a low plain bordered by sandy beaches and rocky cliffs along the Pacific coast
Central Lowlands	• the lowest elevations in Australia
	• generally flat, with many rivers after heavy (but infrequent) rains
	• riverbeds farther inland are dry most of the year
Western Plateau	• covers the western two-thirds of Australia
	• has a higher average elevation than the Central Lowlands
	• mostly consists of flat land, as in the lowlands

POPULATION

Australia is home to approximately 21,865,000 people. New Zealand has a population of 4,293,000, while Papua New Guinea's population is about 8 million.

- In Australia, the majority of inhabitants live in and around a half dozen major urban centers, which are all located along the coasts.

- Most of the people in New Zealand are descendants of British settlers who came there in the 1800s. The largest minority group is the Maoris, the Polynesian people who originally settled the islands.

- The inhabitants of the Pacific islands probably came from southeast Asia many thousands of years ago.

▲ **Australia** is home to many animals, such as this koala, that are found nowhere else in the world.

CLIMATE

Most of the islands of the Pacific lie between the equator and the Tropic of Capricorn and are considered tropical. Most enjoy a mild climate with temperatures that average about 75°F, with little fluctuation.

- Australia and New Zealand have seasons, although they are the reverse of seasons in the Northern Hemisphere.

- The northern part of Australia is warm or hot all year, with a wet season from November through April and a dry season from May through October.

- The southern parts of Australia have four seasons and occasional frosts.

- The climate of New Zealand is generally warm and moist, due to the ocean breezes, much like the northwest coast of the United States.

- There are basically two seasons in the smaller islands: the warm and humid period between November and April and the dry season between May and October.

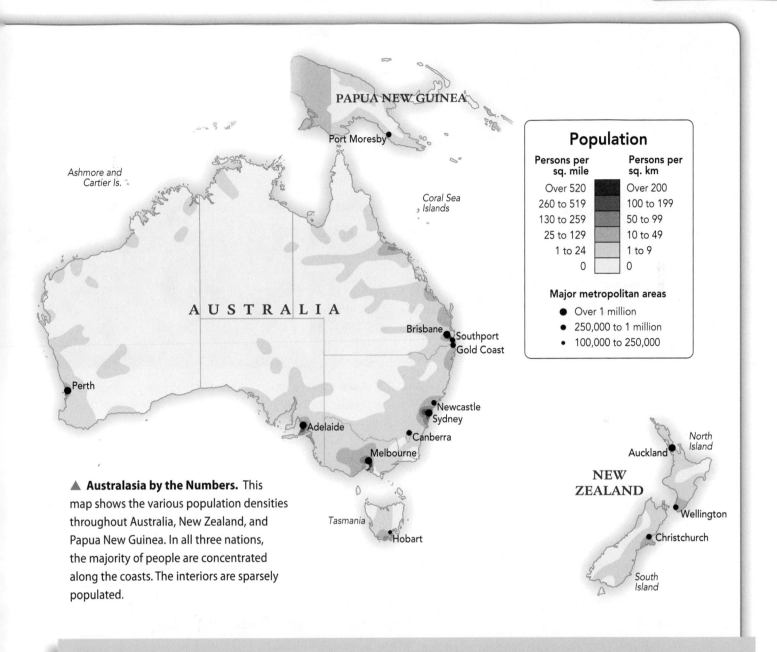

PAPUA NEW GUINEA

Port Moresby

Ashmore and Cartier Is.

Coral Sea Islands

A U S T R A L I A

Perth

Brisbane
Southport
Gold Coast

Newcastle
Sydney

Adelaide

Canberra

Melbourne

Tasmania

Hobart

Auckland
North Island

NEW ZEALAND

Wellington

Christchurch

South Island

Population

Persons per sq. mile	Persons per sq. km
Over 520	Over 200
260 to 519	100 to 199
130 to 259	50 to 99
25 to 129	10 to 49
1 to 24	1 to 9
0	0

Major metropolitan areas
- Over 1 million
- 250,000 to 1 million
- 100,000 to 250,000

▲ **Australasia by the Numbers.** This map shows the various population densities throughout Australia, New Zealand, and Papua New Guinea. In all three nations, the majority of people are concentrated along the coasts. The interiors are sparsely populated.

VEGETATION

The Pacific islands are largely tropical. Australia has extensive forests on its northern, eastern, and south-western coasts, changing inland to broadleaf shrub and savanna. From about the center of the continent to its western coast is a vast semiarid and desert region. New Zealand is predominantly forest and grassland and has a great variety of plant species found nowhere else in the world.

ECONOMY

Australia and New Zealand have well-developed economies. Australia depends largely upon agricultural and mining industries. New Zealand depends upon agriculture and manufacturing.

The economies of the smaller islands, however, are largely at the subsistence level. Tourism is becoming an important element in the economies of many of these countries, as they search for means to develop.

Antarctica

Antarctica is the ice-buried continent that covers and surrounds the South Pole. This dry and nearly barren land forms the coldest and iciest region in the world. It is colder than the region around the North Pole. The South Pole lies near the center of the Antarctic continent, on a high, windy plateau of ice and snow.

GEOGRAPHIC REGIONS

The Transantarctic Mountains cross the entire continent. They separate Antarctica's two ice sheets and form two regions: East Antarctica and West Antarctica.

Antarctic Land Regions	
East Antarctica	• covers more than half the continent • consists of rocks more than 570 million years old • coast marked by mountains, valleys, and glaciers
West Antarctica	• rock surface beneath the ice lies below sea level • includes the Antarctic peninsula, a mountainous, S-shaped finger of land (part of the Andes mountain chain) that points out from West Antarctica toward South America • includes several other mountain ranges and volcanoes

POPULATION

Recent human activity in Antarctica is mainly for scientific and tourism purposes. More than 40 year-round scientific stations operate on the continent and nearby islands. The National Science Foundation maintains the three year-round U.S. stations.

1. Amundsen-Scott South Pole Station
2. McMurdo Station on Ross Island
3. Palmer Station on Anvers Island near the Antarctic peninsula

McMurdo Station has Antarctica's largest community. About 1,000 scientists, pilots, and other specialists live there each summer. About 250 stay for winter.

▲ **Antarctica's** rugged coast features jagged mountain peaks and glacier-filled valleys. Ice and snow cover 98 percent of the continent.

CLIMATE

Antarctica's climate varies from extremely cold, dry conditions on the inland plateau to milder, slightly moister conditions along the coasts.

- Many people call the plateau a "polar desert." It has only about 2 inches (5 centimeters) of snowfall each year. Annual coastal snowfall averages 24 inches (61 centimeters).
- The Antarctic winter lasts from May through September.
- For several months of the year, the continent is in continual darkness.

Summer in the Antarctic lasts from November through February.

- July temperatures range from a low of –94°F to a high of –40°F (–70 to –40°C) inland and from –22 to –5°F (–30 to –21°C) on the peninsula's coast.
- January temperatures range from –31 to 5°F (–35 to –15°C) inland and reach 32°F (0°C) on the coast.
- Northern islands may have summer temperatures of up to 50°F (10°C).

Seven countries that built Antarctic bases claim parts of Antarctica as their national territory. The parts are shaped like pie slices, with the South Pole at the center. Many nations, including the United States, do not recognize these claims. ▶

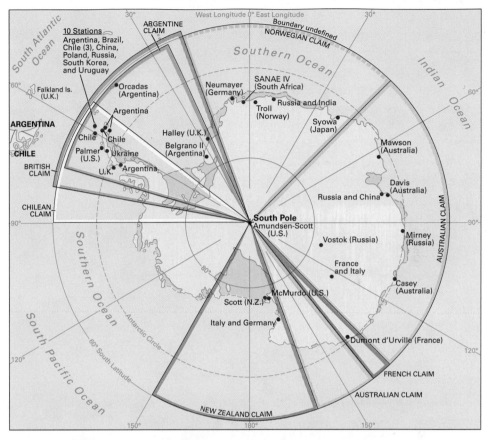

Year-round research station

Areas claimed by:
- Argentina
- Australia
- Chile
- France
- New Zealand
- Norway
- United Kingdom

0 — 1,000 Miles
0 — 1,000 Kilometers

THE SOUTH POLE EXPEDITIONS

In June 1910, Captain Robert Falcon Scott left London, hoping to win for the United Kingdom the honor of reaching the South Pole first. In October, while Scott was in Australia, he received a telegram from the Norwegian explorer Roald Amundsen—Amundsen, too, was going to Antarctica.

- Amundsen and his four assistants began on October 19, 1911.

- Scott set out with 15 other men on November 1, 1911, about 60 miles (97 kilometers) farther from the Pole than Amundsen's starting point.

- Amundsen's group arrived at the South Pole on December 14, 1911. They had lost several of their sled dogs, but all five men were in good health.

- Scott's group reached the pole with five men on January 17, 1912. Cold, hunger, and exhaustion had severely weakened the explorers. They were greeted by Amundsen's flag.

- Scott's men photographed themselves at the Pole and began their return. All five men perished on the way. The bodies of Scott and two of his assistants were found in a tent only 11 miles from food and supplies.

▲ **The race to the South Pole** became one of the most famous events in the history of Antarctica. Amundsen and Scott never met, but both knew that they were racing for the same prize.

Language Advantage

Grammar

Writing and Research

Vocabulary

Reading

Speaking

Literature

At a Glance

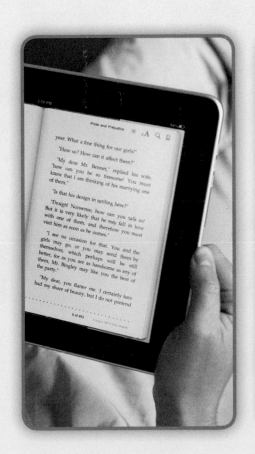

Grammar

PARTS OF SPEECH

are the word categories of language. Words belong to the same category if they show the same formal features or if they share a common function or position in a sentence.

Introduction

Every word in a sentence has a job. A word can change jobs depending on when, where, and how it's used. We use labels called *parts of speech* to show how words work in different surroundings. There are eight parts of speech: nouns, pronouns, verbs, adjectives, adverbs, prepositions, conjunctions, and interjections.

Once you know a word's job, you can classify it as a particular part of speech. Some words act as only one part of speech. Other words are like lizards that change color to fit their surroundings. For example, the word *down* may function as a noun, a preposition, or an adverb as shown in the examples below.

noun	The quarterback passed on third down.
preposition	The ball sailed down the field.
adverb	The receiver fell down.

Parts of Speech	Jobs	Examples
Nouns	name people, places, things, or ideas	Susan, city, Tuesday, liberty
Pronouns	replace nouns	he, she, it
Verbs	express action or a state of being	flip, draw, read, are, was
Adjectives	describe nouns or pronouns	ugly, tired, peaceful
Adverbs	describe verbs, adjectives, or other adverbs	sadly, nicely, soon
Prepositions	express a relationship between a noun or pronoun and another word in the sentence	of, to, forward
Conjunctions	connect words	and, or, but
Interjections	express strong emotion	Wow! Oh! Gosh!

The parts of speech are like building blocks for every sentence. Many kids enjoy playing with blocks to construct all kinds of things they have seen and learned about. They use blocks of different shapes, sizes, and colors to build houses, forts, castles, towers, bridges, and roads. By trial and error, they learn how to use the blocks correctly so the things they build will stand on a solid foundation and not wobble or fall down.

At first, the structures they build with their blocks are simple, using just a few pieces. But as children grow, so does their understanding of the physical principles involved in building with blocks, and the things they construct become more interesting and complex. They may create an entire city with schools, roadways, airports, office buildings, hospitals, houses, stores, streets, and parks.

When children start to speak, their sentences, like their early block structures, are simple and small and make use of only a few parts of speech. As young people grow, so does their ability to use words in speaking, writing, and reading.

If you want to communicate well, learning how to correctly put together the different parts of speech is as important as choosing the right sizes or shapes of building blocks to use. Learning the principal building blocks of language provides a firm foundation for logical thinking and for clear communicating.

TAKING APART A MAKE-BELIEVE SENTENCE

When you understand how a language functions, you can identify the parts of speech even if most of the words are nonsense.

The plomic basinkers pirked the lampix at the simter ciptically.

Except for **the** and **at,** the sentence is made up of words that have no dictionary meaning. Yet it still reads like a sentence. It begins with a capital letter and ends with a period.

Even though the words are nonsense, they follow a familiar pattern and rhythm. More importantly, the words act like an English sentence. The word **basinkers** is a noun because it has a plural ending, **-s.** It also is marked by the article **the.** In the same way, **lampix** and **simter** are nouns because both are marked by the article **the.**

The word **plomic** is probably an adjective because it appears between an article and a noun. **Pirked** is probably a verb because **-ed** is a characteristic ending of past tense verbs. The word also has a position in the sentence typical of a verb. We know that **pirked** is a transitive verb because it has an object, **lampix.**

At the simter can be identified as a phrase that modifies pirked, telling where. **At** is a preposition often followed by an object. **Ciptically** is probably an adverb because it ends in **-ly.** It may modify **pirked.**

Nouns

Nouns are words that name people, places, things, or ideas. Most nouns are either

- **Common or Proper**
- **Concrete or Abstract**
- **Singular or Plural**

Common or Proper?

All nouns are either common or proper.

Common nouns are people, places, things, or ideas that are general and vague.

> veterinarian   holiday   city   friend

Proper nouns are people, places, things, or ideas that are specific and particular.

> Dr. Fish   Halloween   Mumbai   Jesse

Notice that proper nouns start with a capital letter.

Nouns answer the question *who*, *what*, or *where*.

> Sally   ate   sushi   in   Sacramento.
>
> *who?*   *what?*   *where?*

Concrete or Abstract?

All nouns are either concrete or abstract.

Concrete nouns name things that you can see, touch, feel, taste, or smell.

> pickles   puppet   pony   picnic

Abstract nouns name things that cannot be seen or touched, like feelings or ideas.

> jealousy   justice   jaunt   joy

COOL COLLECTIVE NOUNS

A collective noun names more than one person or thing, but it's treated as a singular noun in a sentence. Collective nouns are often used in the animal kingdom to describe groups of creatures that live or travel together.

pride of lions	brood of chicks
gaggle of geese	pack of dogs
swarm of bees	flock of seagulls
murder of crows	litter of kittens

Common names are general	Proper names are specific
puppet(s)	Cookie Monster Pinocchio Punch and Judy
game	Monopoly Charades Boggle
country	Iceland Japan Argentina

Check the dictionary if you're not sure about the plural form of a word.

Singular or Plural?

Most nouns are either singular or plural.

Singular nouns name one person, place, or thing.

cat   circus   ship   match

Plural nouns name more than one person, place, or thing. Most plural nouns are formed by adding *-s* or *-es*.

cat**s**   circus**es**   ship**s**   match**es**

Other words change more in the plural form.

one mouse	three mice
a thief	many thieves
one child	two children

Some words just stay the same in the singular and plural forms.

one sheep	ten sheep
one fish	two fish
one moose	many moose

Nouns	
People	student scientist Jane Goodall
Places	wetland Central Park jungle
Things	binoculars birds tree
Ideas	exploration research environmentalism

WORDS AT WORK

This poem by Frank O'Hara is packed with nouns.

Today

Oh! kangaroos, sequins, chocolate sodas!
You really are beautiful! Pearls,
harmonicas, jujubes, aspirins! all
the stuff they've always talked about

still makes a poem a surprise!
These things are with us every day
even on beachheads and biers. They
do have meaning. They're strong as rocks.

Pronouns

Pronouns are words that take the place of nouns. They are often used to avoid repeating the same noun over and over.

> The ape used to live at the zoo, but the ape recently escaped.

> The ape used to live at the zoo, but it recently escaped.

The noun that a pronoun replaces is called an **antecedent.** In the sentence above, the noun *ape* is the antecedent of the pronoun *it*.

Types

There are five types of pronouns: *personal, relative, interrogative, demonstrative,* and *indefinite*.

COMPOUND SUBJECTS AND OBJECTS

Most people would not say, "Me have a new house." But a surprising number of people would say, "Jane and me have a new house." Whether a sentence has a single subject or a compound subject, the pronoun in the subject should be in the nominative case.

Similarly, to most people, "The rocks hit I" sounds wrong, while "the rocks hit Jane and I" sounds fine.

Whenever you have a compound object or subject including a pronoun, eliminate the other subject to see which case to use. If the pronoun is in the object position, receiving the action of the verb, or serving as the object of a preposition, use the objective case. (See also page 692.)

Personal pronouns refer to specific people or things. They can be

- the person speaking (first person):
  I think it's my fault.
- the person spoken to (second person):
  You should make yourself some cupcakes.
- the person spoken about (third person):
  Heather wants to teach her monkey some tricks.

Personal Pronouns

Number	Person	Nominative	Objective	Possessive
Singular	first	I	me	mine
	second	you	your	yours
	third	he	him	his
		she	her	hers
		it	it	its
Plural	first	we	us	ours
	second	you	you	yours
	third	they	them	theirs

Relative pronouns connect a noun in the main part of the sentence with another group of words.

> Mr. Baggins is the artist who paints peacocks.

> *Mr. Baggins* is the noun. *Who* is the relative pronoun.

> The mystery book, which was a gift from Claire's brother, held her spellbound from beginning to end.

> The committee that formulated this plan has been commended.

Interrogative pronouns are used to ask questions. The words are the same as relative pronouns.

> What does this word mean?

> Who is going with you?

Relative and Interrogative Pronouns

who	whom	whose
which	that	what

Case

Personal pronouns and the pronouns *who* and *whoever* change their form depending on how they are used in a sentence. These changes show the *case* of a pronoun. There are three cases: *nominative*, *objective*, and *possessive*.

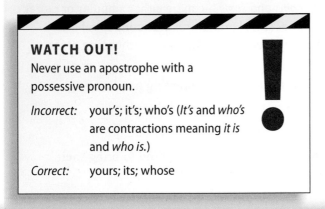

WATCH OUT!

Never use an apostrophe with a possessive pronoun.

Incorrect: your's; it's; who's (*It's* and *who's* are contractions meaning *it is* and *who is*.)

Correct: yours; its; whose

Demonstrative pronouns point out certain people, places, or things.

That is a huge pumpkin.

Those are my favorite colors.

This will be easy to fix.

Demonstrative Pronouns

this	that
these	those

Indefinite pronouns refer to people, places, or things in a more general (or vague) way than nouns do. Unlike other pronouns, indefinite pronouns have no antecedents. They are used when the appropriate noun is unknown or unspecified.

The Lions Club sent invitations to **everyone** in the community.

Indefinite Pronouns

all	either	most	other
any	everybody	neither	several
anybody	everyone	nobody	some
anyone	everything	none	somebody
anything	few	no one	someone

Nominative Case

A pronoun used as the subject of a sentence is in the nominative case.

I am the only one who knows how to get there.

Nominative Case Pronouns

I	we	you
he	she	it
they	who	whoever

Pronouns used as predicate nominatives are also in the nominative case.

It was **I who** called.

Increasingly, people don't use the nominative case in casual conversation. For example, many people say "it's me" instead of "it is I." It's also common to hear "that's him" instead of "that is he."

Objective Case

Use the objective case when a pronoun acts as a direct object, as an indirect object, or as an object of a preposition.

Kelly saw **him** at the dance.

Objective Case Pronouns

me	us	you
him	her	it
them	whom	whomever

Possessive Case

The possessive case indicates ownership.

My favorite number is four.

Possessive Case Pronouns

my	mine	your(s)
his	her(s)	it(s)
our(s)	their(s)	whose

Pronouns

Agreement

All pronouns must agree with their antecedents in number, gender, and person.

Agreement in Number

Use a singular pronoun to refer to or replace a singular antecedent.

> Kameko decided that she would pack a picnic lunch.

Kameko is the antecedent of the pronoun *she.*

Use a plural pronoun to refer to or replace a plural antecedent.

> Kameko's sisters decided that they would buy something there.

Sisters is the antecedent of the pronoun *they.*

Use a plural pronoun to refer to or replace two or more singular antecedents joined by *and.*

> Shannon and Travis have seen their favorite movie six times.

Use a singular pronoun to refer to or to replace two or more singular antecedents joined by *or* or *nor.*

> Either Shannon or Travis will bring his photographs to school.

Agreement in Gender

The gender of a pronoun is either masculine, feminine, or neuter. A neuter pronoun is neither masculine nor feminine.

Use a pronoun that agrees in gender with its antecedent.

> Dave leaned his bike against the fence.
>
> Myra painted her room blue.
>
> The cat licked its paw.

masculine	he	him	his
feminine	she	her	hers
neuter	it	it	its

Some indefinite pronouns—including *all, any, more, most, none,* and *some*—can be either singular or plural. Use either singular or plural pronouns to refer to or replace them, depending on the meaning of the sentence.

> All of the color in the painting had lost its glow.

All refers to *color,* which is singular; *its* refers to *all.*

> All of the students are required to bring their permission slips.

All refers to *students,* which is plural; *their* refers to *all.*

When an antecedent is a collective noun, decide whether the collective noun is singular or plural. If it is singular, use a singular pronoun to refer to it or replace it.

> The club voted to change its meeting time and location.

The singular is used because the meeting time and location are for the entire club as one unit.

If the collective noun is plural, use a plural pronoun.

> The city council argued among themselves.

The plural is correct in this example because the council members were arguing as individuals.

Agreement in Person

Use a pronoun that agrees in person with its antecedent. Pronouns can be in the first, second, or third person.

> First person: I get home before my parents do.
>
> Second person: Will you get home before your parents do?
>
> Third person: Noel will get home before his parents do.

SEXIST NOUNS AND PRONOUNS

Some writers use *mankind* as a term that includes both men and women. They use *he* as an inclusive pronoun and begin letters to unknown recipients with *Dear Sir.*

It is true that for centuries it was conventional to default to *he* in our language. More recently, however, people have become more aware of the unfairness of that practice. In today's world, traditional gender roles no longer apply. Doctors can be *shes* and nurses can be *hes,* so writers need to be careful about the pronouns they use.

Nonsexist language has evolved so that writers can use more inclusive neutral terms that apply to both sexes. Make sure you're careful to use nonsexist terms that apply to *people* in general.

- Use plural forms. "An engineer must pass his certification exam" becomes "Engineers must pass their certification exams."

- Add a pronoun. "An engineer must pass his certification exam" becomes "An engineer must pass his or her certification exam."

- Use another word that is not gendered. For instance, instead of fireman use firefighter. Instead of chairman use chairperson. Instead of mailman, use mail carrier. Instead of mankind, use humanity.

WHO VS. WHOM

Possibly someday the word **whom** will be obsolete. Already, there are many people who do not bother to distinguish between **who** and **whom.** But the rule that dictates which word to use is actually pretty simple.

Use **who** as a subject.

That is the boy who threw the rock.

Use **whom** as an object.

The girl for whom I bought the gift was delighted.

CLEAR PRONOUN REFERENCE

Incorrect pronoun usage will confuse your readers. Here are a few guidelines that will help you double-check your writing to make sure that all pronouns match their antecedents.

Do not use a pronoun that can refer to more than one antecedent, even if it means repeating the antecedent.

Unclear: Susan chose Lily to be on her team because she knows the game well.

Clear: Susan chose Lily to be on her team because Lily knows the game well.

In the first example, we are unsure of which of the two girls knows the game well.

Avoid using the pronouns *it, they, you,* or *your* without a clear antecedent.

Unclear: Before you give the baby its bottle, be sure to shake it.

Clear: Before you give the baby its bottle, be sure to shake the bottle.

In the first example, we do not know whether to shake the baby or the bottle.

Avoid unnecessary pronoun shifts that may change the meaning you intended.

Incorrect: I like summer best because **you** can swim in the ocean.

Correct: I like summer best because **I** can swim in the ocean.

Verbs

Verbs are words that express action or a state of being.

run appear sing seem hope

The verb is sometimes considered the part of speech that is at the heart of a sentence, mostly because it affects meaning more than any other element. It determines the number of nouns needed, and it guides the action that takes place. Verbs can indicate a state of being as well as a physical action. They can even focus a reader's attention on a particular part of a sentence.

Types of Verbs

There are two main types of verbs: **action verbs** and **helping verbs.**

TRANSITIVE OR INTRANSITIVE?

Many verbs can be either transitive or intransitive depending on how they are used in a sentence. If a verb takes a direct object, it is a transitive verb. If it does not take a direct object, it is an intransitive verb.

Transitive:	Mary writes a letter.
Intransitive:	Mary writes beautifully.
Transitive:	John walked his dog.
Intransitive:	John walked to the store.
Transitive:	I read three books a week.
Intransitive:	I read quickly.

Action Verbs

Action verbs describe the behavior, or action, of someone or something and may express either physical action or mental activity.

The band marched down Northfield Avenue.

He believes in working hard.

All action verbs are either **transitive** or **intransitive.**

Transitive verbs express an action that is performed on something. A transitive verb needs an object, called the object of the verb, to complete its meaning.

Michael bought a monkey.

Wally painted his house last summer.

Intransitive verbs have no direct object. (See page 676.)

The subway stopped abruptly.

Jane smiled with pleasure.

Linking verbs such as *be* and *have* are always intransitive.

Common Linking Verbs

appear	feel	look	seem
sound	taste	become	smell

Note: Most linking verbs can also be used as action verbs.

Linking verb: The hour grew late.

Action verb: The children grew quickly.

Helping Verbs

Sometimes a verb needs the help of another word called the **helping verb.** Together, a main verb and a helping verb form a *verb phrase*.

Will you be waiting for me after school?

Waiting is the main verb, *will* and *be* are the helping verbs, and *will be waiting* is the verb phrase.

Susan ought to study her grammar more.

To study is the main verb, *ought* is the helping verb, and *ought to study* is the verb phrase.

Common Helping Verbs

am	do	must	are	does	ought
be	had	shall	being	has	should
been	have	was	can	is	were
could	may	will	did	might	would

Adjectives that follow linking verbs are called predicate adjectives. *Nouns or pronouns that follow linking verbs are called* predicate nominatives *or* predicate nouns.

660

Tense

Verbs have several characteristics, like *tense,* that other parts of speech do not have.

The tense of a verb indicates the time of the verb's action. There are six verb tenses: *present, present perfect, past, past perfect, future,* and *future perfect.*

Future: The cat will run.

Present: The cat runs.

Past: The cat ran.

WHY ARE THERE SIX TENSES?

There are three major divisions of time: past, present, and future. In each of these time frames, the action may be considered as simple (simply occurring at the particular moment) or perfect (the action is completed or "perfected").

Present Tense

The present tense is used when something is happening now, in the present. It also indicates habitual action, which is something that happens regularly.

I see at least one movie a week.

Past Tense

The past tense is used when something happened before today, in the past.

I saw a good movie two days ago.

Future Tense

The future tense is used if something will happen later, in the future.

I will see the new Disney movie this weekend.

Present Perfect Tense

The present perfect tense is used when something was started in the past but completed in the present moment.

I have seen two movies so far this month.

Past Perfect Tense

The past perfect tense is used when something happened before another past action or event.

I had not seen many movies before last year.

Future Perfect Tense

The future perfect tense is used for actions that will be completed at some future time.

By the end of this year, I will have seen more than 50 movies.

Verbs

It's important to understand the difference between the words was and were. Use were to express doubt or a wish. Use was for statements of fact.

Mood

The mood of a verb suggests your attitude toward the sentence. There are three moods: indicative, imperative, and subjunctive.

Indicative Mood

The indicative mood is used for statements of fact or questions.

I **am coming**. **Are** you **coming**?

Imperative Mood

The imperative mood is used to give commands.

Come here!

Subjunctive Mood

The subjunctive mood is used to express wishes and statements contrary to fact.

I wish you **were** here.

If you **were** here, I would be happy.

REGULAR OR IRREGULAR?

- Verbs are either regular or irregular.

- Most verbs are regular verbs. They form their past and their past participle the same way, by adding *-ed* or *-d* to the infinitive.

- Irregular verbs do not follow the standard rules for forming the past and the past participle. The only way to master the past and past participial forms of irregular verbs is to memorize them or check the dictionary.

Common Irregular Verbs

Present	Past	Past Participle	Present	Past	Past Participle
beat	beat	beat, beaten	leave	left	left
bend	bent	bent	lend	lent	lent
bleed	bled	bled	lie	lay	lain
bring	brought	brought	make	made	made
build	built	built	pay	paid	paid
catch	caught	caught	read	read	read
cost	cost	cost	ring	rang	rung
creep	crept	crept	rise	rose	risen
dig	dug	dug	see	saw	seen
drink	drank	drunk	set	set	set
eat	ate	eaten	shake	shook	shaken
fall	fell	fallen	shut	shut	shut
fight	fought	fought	sit	sat	sat
forget	forgot	forgotten	speak	spoke	spoken
freeze	froze	frozen	spring	sprang	sprung
get	got	gotten	stick	stuck	stuck
grow	grew	grown	swim	swam	swum
hear	heard	heard	take	took	taken
hold	held	held	tear	tore	torn
keep	kept	kept	throw	threw	thrown
know	knew	known	wear	wore	worn

Modals

The auxiliary verbs *can, could, may, might, must, will,* and *should* are known as modals. These verbs are used with main verbs to add emphasis to a sentence or to provide shades of meaning.

Can and *could* express the ability to perform the action of the main verb.

We **can** walk faster if you like.

She **could** have walked with us yesterday if we had called her.

May and *might* express permission or possibility rather than ability.

The doctor said my mother **may** walk now that her ankle has healed.

The test **might** be canceled.

Must expresses a requirement or a certainty.

Sheila **must** call her parents immediately.

Gunnar **must** have been wrong about the date of the meeting.

Should suggests that something ought to happen.

Sheila **should** call home immediately.

CHOOSING EFFECTIVE VERBS

As you write, select specific verbs whenever you can. Strong verbs give your readers precise, clear images.

Dull: The puppy **walked** into the kitchen and **lay** down.

Vivid: The puppy **waddled** into the kitchen and **sprawled** on the floor.

Conjugation

To conjugate a verb means to list all of the forms for its six tenses. The conjugation of a verb also shows how the verb forms change for

- the first person, the second person, and the third person
- the singular and the plural

The full conjugation of a verb is the orderly presentation of all its forms.

The infinitive is the basic form of a verb. It usually begins with the word *to*.

to walk   to run

to win   to lose

CONJUGATION OF *TO FALL*

Principal parts

Present	Present Participle	Past	Past Participle
fall	(is) falling	fell	(has) fallen

	Singular	Plural
Present tense	I fall you fall he, she, it falls	we fall you fall they fall
Past tense	I fell you fell he, she, it fell	we fell you fell they fell
Future tense	I will fall you will fall he, she, it will fall	we will fall you will fall they will fall
Present perfect	I have fallen you have fallen he, she, it has fallen	we have fallen you have fallen they have fallen
Past perfect	I had fallen you had fallen he, she, it had fallen	we had fallen you had fallen they had fallen
Future perfect	I will have fallen you will have fallen he, she, it will have fallen	we will have fallen you will have fallen they will have fallen

Adjectives

Adjectives are words that make the meaning of a noun or pronoun more specific. Most adjectives are either *descriptive* or *limiting*.

Descriptive adjectives can be

- positive
- comparative
- superlative

Limiting adjectives can be

- numerical
- pronominal
- articles

Adjectives are words that modify nouns and pronouns. *Modify* means to change. An adjective changes the meaning of a noun or pronoun by describing it or making it more specific.

Use adjectives to add detail, to make distinctions, and to be precise when you write.

Adjectives answer the question *how many, what kind,* or *which*.

Two raccoons ate rotten red apples from the trash can.

how many?   *what kind?*   *which?*

Adjectives make descriptions sharper and more interesting.

They describe

- color
- smell
- number
- size
- taste
- feel
- shape
- age

Descriptive or Limiting?

Descriptive adjectives indicate a quality or condition of a noun. They provide additional information about the noun or pronoun that is being described.

strange   sad   stingy   super   simple

Limiting adjectives point out nouns or indicate their number or quantity.

ten   two   their   third   that

Limiting adjectives can be classified as **numerical, pronominal,** or **articles.**

Numerical adjectives can be cardinal or ordinal.

Cardinal adjectives are numbers that tell how many.

The manuscript contained ten pages.

Six people were in the room.

Ordinal adjectives are numbers that explain order.

Our team came in third place.

The second step is broken.

Pronominal adjectives are pronouns that are used as adjectives.

Welcome to our home.

Several questions came up.

Articles—the words a, an, *and* the—*used to be considered a separate part of speech, but now they're thought of as a special type of adjective. A and* an *are called indefinite articles;* the *is called a definite article.*

Degrees of Comparison

The degree to which a descriptive adjective indicates a quality or characteristic can be stated as a comparison. There are three degrees of comparison: *positive*, *comparative*, and *superlative*.

The positive degree states the quality or characteristic.

attentive   tall   good

The comparative degree expresses a degree higher or lower than the positive.

more attentive   taller   better

The superlative degree expresses the highest or lowest degree of the quality or characteristic.

most attentive   tallest   best

Downward comparisons use the words *less* or *least*.

Positive	Comparative	Superlative
tall	less tall	least tall
stubborn	less stubborn	least stubborn
reasonable	less reasonable	least reasonable

Upward comparisons use the word endings *–er* or *–est* when the word is one syllable.

Positive	Comparative	Superlative
tall	taller	tallest
high	higher	highest
sweet	sweeter	sweetest

Upward comparisons use the words *more* or *most* when the word is two syllables or more.

Positive	Comparative	Superlative
stubborn	more stubborn	most stubborn
attentive	more attentive	most attentive
reasonable	more reasonable	most reasonable

Occasionally, comparative adjectives are irregular.

Positive	Comparative	Superlative
good	better	best
bad	worse	worst
little	less	least

Placement

Adjectives usually precede the nouns and pronouns they modify.

The skinny young man always ate as much as he wanted.

Sometimes, an adjective is placed after the noun or pronoun for variety or for special emphasis.

The man, skinny and young, always ate as much as he wanted.

WATCH OUT!

Never use *more* or *most* when adding the suffixes *–er* and *–est* to adjectives. This is known as a double comparison.

Incorrect: Sandra was **more smarter** than Caroline.
Correct: Sandra was **smarter** than Caroline.

Incorrect: Harold is the **most tallest** person I know.
Correct: Harold is the **tallest** person I know.

WORDS AT WORK

This poem by Wallace Stevens is enlivened with adjectives.

The Emperor of Ice-Cream
Call the roller of big cigars,
The muscular one, and bid him whip
In kitchen cups concupiscent curds.
Let the wenches dawdle in such dress
As they are used to wear, and let the boys
Bring flowers in last month's newspapers.
Let be be finale of seem.
The only emperor is the emperor of ice-cream.

Take from the dresser of deal,
Lacking the three glass knobs, that sheet
On which she embroidered fantails once
And spread it so as to cover her face.
If her horny feet protrude, they come
To show how cold she is, and dumb.
Let the lamp affix its beam.
The only emperor is the emperor of ice-cream.

Adverbs

Adverbs are words that add interest and accuracy to your writing. They can be used to describe verbs, adjectives, or other adverbs. Adverbs answer one of the following five questions:

How?

Claus and Yoshio shook hands firmly.

When?

See you soon!

Where?

Nell looked everywhere for her lost bracelet.

How often?

Their family seldom eats dinner together.

To what extent?

Barry was very sure he would get a part in the play.

UNNECESSARY ADVERBS

Unnecessary adverbs can clutter and confuse a sentence. Often, a single specific verb can replace an adverb and sharpen an expression. *Hurried* is preferable to *moved quickly,* and *grasped* is better than *took eagerly.*

Adverbs like *hardly, barely,* and *scarcely* carry a negative meaning. Using the adverb *not* with these words is unnecessary and confusing, like a double negative.

Incorrect: The family did not have scarcely enough to eat.

Correct: The family had scarcely enough to eat.

Incorrect: I cannot hardly remember the incident.

Correct: I can hardly remember the incident.

Unnecessary adverbs often repeat the meaning of the words that they modify.

He advanced forward to his position in the line.

The word *advanced* already implies forward movement, so the word *forward* is redundant and unnecessary.

Types

There are four types of adverbs: *simple* adverbs, *sentence modifiers, conjunctive* adverbs, and *intensifiers.*

Simple adverbs are single words. Most of them end in *-ly,* as in *certainly* and *deeply.* However, not all words that end in *-ly* are adverbs. For example, *lovely* and *jolly* are adjectives.

Sentence modifiers are adverbs and adverb phrases that modify the whole action of a sentence or clause rather than a single word in it. They often appear at the beginning of a sentence.

Frankly, I don't want to hear about it.

As I recall, nobody asked any questions.

Fortunately, we could reach him before he had left town.

Conjunctive adverbs serve a double purpose. When they are used in a simple sentence, conjunctive adverbs act like sentence modifiers.

You have made a few payments. However, we must ask you to send checks regularly.

When they are with a semicolon, they serve as structure words—words that connect one part of a sentence to another.

You have made a few payments; however, we must ask you to send checks regularly.

Other words commonly used as conjunctive adverbs include *therefore, still, otherwise, also, moreover, nevertheless,* and *yet.* Phrases that are frequently used as conjunctive adverbs include *for example, that is, on the other hand,* and *in conclusion.*

Intensifiers do not alter the meaning of the words they modify, but they add emphasis to those words. For example, when intensifiers are added—as in *very* proud, *extremely* quiet, *quite* concerned, and *too* loud—additional force is given to the verbs they modify.

Degrees of Comparison

Like adjectives, adverbs that answer the question *how?* may be compared in three degrees: *positive*, *comparative*, and *superlative*. (See also page 665.)

Most adverbs are compared upward by adding the words *more* or *most*.

Positive	Comparative	Superlative
happily	more happily	most happily
quickly	more quickly	most quickly
accurately	more accurately	most accurately

A few adverbs are compared upward by adding the endings *–er* or *–est*.

Positive	Comparative	Superlative
soon	sooner	soonest
near	nearer	nearest
early	earlier	earliest

All adverbs are compared downward by adding the words *less* or *least*.

Positive	Comparative	Superlative
happily	less happily	least happily
quickly	less quickly	least quickly
accurately	less accurately	least accurately

Some adverbs are irregular.

Positive	Comparative	Superlative
badly	worse	worst
little	less	least
much	more	most

Placement

An adverb can appear in different positions in a sentence depending on the word it modifies.

Verbs. An adverb does not have to appear next to the verb that it modifies. Notice the different positions of the adverbs *silently* and *slowly* in these sentences.

Silently and slowly, the snow covered the yard.

The snow covered the yard silently and slowly.

Adjectives and Adverbs. An adverb often comes directly before the adjective or adverb that it modifies.

Josh discovered that the map was fairly easy to read.

Raisa crossed the balance beam quite slowly.

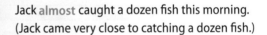

WATCH OUT!

Keep in mind that the meaning of a sentence may vary depending on where the adverb is placed. Putting modifiers in the wrong place can create unclear sentences.

Jack almost caught a dozen fish this morning.
(Jack came very close to catching a dozen fish.)

Jack caught almost a dozen fish this morning.
(Jack caught fewer than twelve fish.)

I just spoke with Sally.
(I spoke with Sally a few minutes ago.)

I spoke just with Sally.
(Sally was the only person with whom I spoke.)

Be especially careful with the placement of adverbs such as *almost, only, just, even, hardly, scarcely, merely,* and *nearly*. Place these adverbs as close as possible to the words they modify to make sure your meaning is clear.

More on Modifiers

Adjectives and adverbs expand our experience of language. These parts of speech are often called *modifiers* because they alter, refine, and sharpen our writing.

Sometimes it's hard to distinguish between adjectives and adverbs, which leads to usage problems.

The most important difference between these two parts of speech is the type of words that they modify. Adjectives modify nouns and pronouns, while adverbs modify verbs, adjectives, and other adverbs.

	Parts of Speech Modified	Information Provided
Adjectives	nouns pronouns	which? how many? what kind?
Adverbs	verbs adjectives other adverbs	how? when? where? to what extent?

WATCH OUT!

Don't craft adverbs that sound unnatural. As William Strunk wrote in his influential guide to writing, *The Elements of Style,* "Do not dress words up by adding –ly to them, as though putting a hat on a horse."

Awkward: Emily responded **hesitatingly** to her mother's question.

Clear: Emily **hesitated** before responding to her mother's question.

Placement

Putting modifiers in the wrong place can create confusing sentences. To avoid misplacing modifiers, put the adjective or adverb as close as possible to the word you wish to modify.

Unclear: Strolling by the lake, a family of geese walked in front of Jaime.

Clear: Strolling by the lake, Jaime noticed a family of geese in front of him.

Unclear. Grilled over charcoal, we particularly enjoy vegetables like zucchini.

Clear: We particularly enjoy vegetables like zucchini grilled over charcoal.

Consider the difference between these two sentences.

The **daily** newspaper has excellent local sports coverage.

The adjective *daily* modifies the noun *newspaper*.

Arden delivers the newspaper **daily.**

The adverb *daily* modifies the verb *delivers*.

Sometimes adverbs just don't work with nouns.

Jim is a **loudly** guy.

It's a **truly** story.

Choosing the right form can be tricky. Look at these two sentences. Which is right?

The pizza tasted **bad.**

The pizza tasted **badly.**

Bad is an adjective that modifies the noun *pizza*. The adverb *badly* doesn't work because it means the pizza isn't good at tasting.

Adjectives usually follow verbs that relate to the five senses—touch, taste, sound, smell, and sight. That's because sense words modify nouns, not verbs.

Your dog smells **funny.**

not

Your dog smells **funnily.**

Adverb or Adjective?

Many words that end in –*ly* are adverbs.

surely strongly sharply

However, some words that end in –*ly* are adjectives.

lovely manly friendly cowardly

And some adverbs do not end in –*ly*.

here there far soon

Some words can be used as either adverbs or adjectives.

Word	Adverb	Adjective
deep	Dig *deep* to find water.	We dug a *deep* well.
far	We walked *far* into the forest.	He came from a *far* country.
hard	Mark hit the ball *hard*.	It was a *hard* choice.
little, long	The world will *little* note nor *long* remember . . .	He had *little* feet and *long* legs.
near	The horse came *near*.	It was a *near* escape.
right	Turn *right* at the stop sign.	That was the *right* way to turn.
straight	He drew his lines *straight*.	He walked a *straight* line.

Other words that can be used as either adverbs or adjectives include *close, daily, first, hard, high, late, only,* and *tight*.

In some cases, usually in short commands, the two forms have the same meaning and can be used interchangeably. The shorter form is considered to be more informal.

Go **slow** around that curve. (adjective)

Go **slowly** around that curve. (adverb)

More often, the two forms have different meanings and cannot be used interchangeably.

Sam hit the ball **hard.** (adjective)

Nancy **hardly** had time to catch her breath. (adverb)

COMMONLY CONFUSED ADJECTIVES AND ADVERBS

Bad vs. Badly

Bad is an adjective. Badly is an adverb.

Use *bad* when you want to describe how you feel. If you're modifying a verb, use *badly*.

She sang so **badly** that the audience felt **bad.**

Good vs. Well

Good is an adjective. Well is an adverb.

Never use *good* as a substitute for *well*.

The team played **well,** which made me feel **good.**

Real vs. Really

Real is an adjective. Really is an adverb.

In conversation, *real* is often used for *really*. Be careful in writing, however, to distinguish between the two.

The test was a **real** challenge, but I think I did **really** well.

AVOID WEAK MODIFIERS

Use precise adjectives and adverbs to create colorful, vivid details. Avoid using vague adverbs such as *very, really, only, well, hard,* and *often*. Suppose a friend sent you an e-mail with the sentence:

Mel wore a **very nice** dress.

What does that really tell you about Mel's dress? "Very nice" could mean a lot of things. Was the dress expensive? Attractive? Flattering? Fancy?

Mel wore a **stylish red** dress.

Ah, so *that's* what your friend meant. Why didn't she just say so?

Prepositions

A preposition is a word that combines with a noun to form a phrase, or a small group of words. This phrase shows the relationship between a noun or pronoun and some other word in the sentence.

Prepositions usually state direction, time, or position.

Direction: The plane flew over the clouds.

Time: The audience became restless during his speech.

Position: Please place the book on that table.

Prepositional Phrase

Prepositions rarely stand alone. Together, the preposition, the object of the preposition, and the modifiers of that object form a *prepositional phrase*. A prepositional phrase works as an adjective to modify a noun. (See also page 678.)

The book with the torn cover is Henry's.

The prepositional phrase *with the torn cover* modifies the noun *book*.

The object of the preposition is the noun or pronoun that follows the preposition. The preposition describes the object's relationship to another word in the sentence.

The deer are running toward the woods.

The preposition is *toward*, while *woods* is the object of the preposition.

How Many Prepositions?

When two or more words associated with different prepositions appear before one object, do not delete any of the prepositions.

Charlie was interested in and curious about local politics.

When two or more words associated with the same preposition appear before one object, all but the last preposition may be deleted.

"Charlie was interested in and involved in local politics" may be written as, "Charlie was interested and involved in local politics."

WORDS AT WORK

Prepositions are important in this poem by William Carlos Williams.

The Red Wheelbarrow

so much depends
upon

a red wheel
barrow

glazed with rain
water

beside the white
chickens.

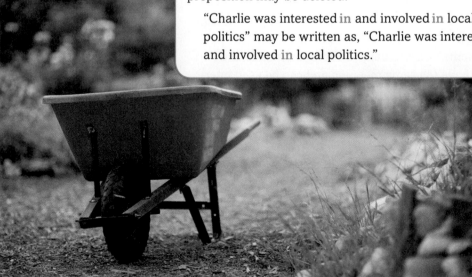

Preposition or Adverb?

Many words that are prepositions can also be adverbs. Sometimes it's hard to tell the difference. *Out* is an example of a word that can be a preposition or an adverb.

Preposition: The cat ran **out** the door.
The preposition *out* takes the object *door*.

Adverb: The cat ran **out**.
The adverb *out* modifies the verb *ran*.

Another example of a word that can do double-duty is *down*.

Preposition: We stumbled **down** the hill.
The preposition *down* takes the object *hill*.

Adverb: We stumbled **down**.
The adverb *down* modifies the verb *stumbled*.

When you're not sure whether the word functions as a preposition or an adverb, check if it takes an object. If it does take an object, it's a preposition. If it doesn't, it's an adverb.

Which Preposition to Use?

Specific prepositions are often closely associated with other nouns, adjectives, and verbs.

account for	foreign to	protest against
argue with	happy about	sensitive to
capable of	independent of	similar to
confide in	inseparable from	sympathize with
obedient to	tamper with	envious of

Other times, one word may be associated with several different prepositions. In this case, each preposition provides a slightly different shade of meaning.

angry at	careless about	free from
angry with	careless of	free of
apply for	concerned for	part from
apply to	concerned with	part with

In a good dictionary, the entry for the principal word will explain the subtle differences in meaning created by using different prepositions.

WATCH OUT!

The subject pronouns **I**, **he**, **she**, **we**, and **they** cannot be used with prepositions. Instead, use the object pronouns **me**, **him**, **her**, **us**, and **them**.

FREQUENTLY USED PREPOSITIONS

about	beneath	off
above	beside	on
across	between	out
after	by	over
against	down	throughout
around	during	to
as far as	except	toward
at	for	under
because of	from	until
before	in	up
behind	in spite of	with
below	of	

Conjunctions and Interjections

Conjunctions are connecting words. The three kinds of conjunctions are

- **coordinating**
- **correlative**
- **subordinating**

Conjunctions are like bridges that join words, phrases, or sentences.

Coordinating conjunctions connect words or sentence parts that are similar and equal.

Coordinating conjunctions connect words with words.

> It's raining cats *and* dogs.

The conjunction *and* connects the nouns *cats* and *dogs*. *Cats* and *dogs* are considered equal because it doesn't matter which one comes first.

Coordinating conjunctions connect phrases with phrases.

> Can you rub your stomach *and* pat your head at the same time?

The conjunction *and* connects the phrases *rub your stomach* and *pat your head*.

Coordinating conjunctions combine sentences.

> She wanted a cat, *but* she settled for a hermit crab.

The conjunction *but* connects the sentences *She wanted a cat* and *she settled for a hermit crab*.

Correlative conjunctions are pairs of words that work like coordinating conjunctions.

both/and	either/or	neither/nor
not only/but also	so/as	whether/or

Incorrect: Rita is both talented and makes friends easily.

Correct: Rita is both talented and friendly.

Incorrect: We went not only to the bank but also grocery shopping.

Correct: We went not only to the bank but also to the grocery store.

GOT TO KNOW

The word **FANBOYS** will help you remember the seven coordinating conjunctions.

For **A**nd **N**or **B**ut **O**r **Y**et **S**o

WATCH OUT!

Make sure you use correlative conjunctions to join words and phrases that are similar (nouns with nouns, adjectives with adjectives, etc.).

Incorrect: Kim will take **either** her bike **or** will drive to get down to the beach.

Correct: Kim will take **either** her bike **or** her car to get down to the beach.

Interjections are words or phrases that express emotions that are strong or sudden.

Interjections that stand alone are usually followed by exclamation points.

Wow! That's the biggest squirrel I've ever seen.

Other interjections are set off with commas within a sentence.

Oh, don't worry about it.

Common Interjections

oh	ouch	bravo
whoops	no	wow
whoa	stop	yikes

Subordinating conjunctions introduce dependent clauses, sometimes called subordinate clauses, which are phrases that cannot stand alone as a complete sentence. (See page 680.)

We will meet for practice on the field tomorrow unless it rains.

The subordinating conjunction *unless* connects the subordinate clause *unless it rains* to the main part of the sentence.

You must finish your homework if you want to go out.

The subordinating conjunction *if* connects the subordinate clause *if you want to go out* to the main part of the sentence.

Interjections are spoken more often than they are written. Try not to use them often in your writing. Using too many interjections will dull the very impact you are trying to create.

Some Subordinating Conjunctions

after	although	as	as if
because	before	but	how
if	in order that	since	so that
that	though	unless	until
when	where	while	why

GRAMMAR MYTHS

English grammar is based on a system of rules. But language is not static; it's a living, growing thing that changes all the time. That means the rules aren't all set in stone. Some grammatical habits have fallen out of fashion over time. (To see for yourself, read a novel that was written 150 years ago.) Other rules have changed. And many rules have wiggle room that allows writers to make choices based on the situation and their own preferences.

That means there are a lot of misconceptions in grammar—myths that have been passed down through the ages from the mouths of strict teachers or old textbooks. Here you'll read about the most common grammar myths and how to avoid them.

Bending the Rules

Myth: Never use contractions.

Actually, you can use contractions—words such as *can't,* for *cannot,* and *I'm,* for *I am*—as often as you like. Contractions give your writing a conversational feel. In an e-mail, for instance, contractions create a casual, friendly tone. However, academic writing often requires a more formal tone. And you should avoid contractions in some work situations, especially business letters and legal documents.

That is not to say that you can never use contractions in formal writing. When in doubt, read the sentence out loud. If it sounds too stiff, replace the offending words with a contraction. Of course, it works the other way around; if the contraction sounds too chatty, replace it with the full phrase.

Myth: Never use *a* before a vowel.

Some people believe that the article *a* comes before words that start with consonants, while *an* comes before words that start with vowels. But when it comes to choosing an article, it's the sound—not the letter—that matters.

Use *a* before words that begin with a consonant sound.

a horse   a star   a one-time deal

Use *an* before words that begin with a vowel sound.

an hour   an SUV   an offer

Myth: Never start a sentence with a conjunction.

Formal grammar rules state that sentences should not start with coordinating conjunctions like *and* or *but.* However, many sentences can communicate extra force and interest when this rule is bent.

Sandra thought she had solved the mystery. But she was wrong.

Keep in mind that starting a sentence with a conjunction creates a somewhat informal tone, so make sure not to overuse this technique.

Myth: Never shift verb tenses.

Occasionally, you'll find it necessary to shift verb tenses within a paper, a paragraph, or even a sentence.

It's important to keep the reader oriented in time. In general, try to make sure your verbs use a consistent tense. All actions occurring at the same time should be in the same tense. (See page 661.)

John **walked** into the study hall and **started** to complain about his grade on the test.

But some sentences describe a number of actions occurring at different times. When that happens, you need to make sure the tenses represent the sequence of events correctly.

Elaine **promised** to call when she **gets** home.

The sentence above describes the past and the future, so a shift in tense is necessary.

Myth: Never end a sentence with a preposition.

Your best guideline for whether or not to end a sentence with a preposition is to listen to how the sentence sounds. Some sentences sound stiff and unnatural when they don't end with a preposition.

Consider this sentence pair.

Stiff: That is the fence **over** which we climbed.

Natural: That is the fence we climbed **over**.

When you write, use your judgment and opt for the version of the sentence that sounds best. Remember Winston Churchill's complaint against rigidly following the rule forbidding end prepositions. "That," he said, "is the kind of nonsense up with which I will not put!"

Myth: Never split infinitives.

Contrary to popular belief, it's fine to split infinitives. A split infinitive occurs when an adverb comes between *to* and the stem of a verb.

Jack and Walter decided **to** simply **stay** home.

The recipe says **to** thoroughly **mix** the batter.

In the past, there was a hard-and-fast rule against splitting infinitives. And sometimes, split infinitives create awkward sentences.

Split infinitive: She wanted **to** quickly **paint** the kitchen.

Revised: She wanted **to paint** the kitchen quickly.

While most sentences can be rewritten to avoid split infinitives, it isn't always required. In fact, it may be preferable to split infinitives rather than to create awkward or confusing sentences.

Awkward: I was unable fully **to appreciate** the program.

Split infinitive: I was unable **to** fully **appreciate** the program.

Splitting an infinitive can also help avoid confusion. For example, it's unclear what *constantly* modifies in the following sentence.

Confusing: **To chew** gum constantly ruins your image.

Rewrite the sentence to clarify that *constantly* modifies *chew*.

Split infinitive: **To** constantly **chew** gum ruins your image.

SENTENCES

A sentence is a group of words that expresses a complete thought. Each sentence is a unit that begins with a capital letter and ends with a punctuation mark. Most sentences have several words. *(She was frightened by the rooster.)* Other sentences have just a noun and a verb. *(We ate.)* And occasionally, sentences have just one word. *(Hello!)* By understanding how sentences work, you will learn to choose the best ways to express your ideas.

A complete sentence has a subject and a predicate. These are the most basic units of a sentence.

Subject + Predicate = Sentence

Sentence Types

You can classify sentences according to the speaker's purpose. Most sentences just make a statement. Other sentences ask a question, express strong feelings, make a request, or give a command.

There are four basic types of sentences: *declarative, interrogative, exclamatory,* and *imperative.*

	Purpose	Punctuation
Declarative	to state something plainly	period (.)
Interrogative	to ask a question	question mark (?)
Exclamatory	to express a strong feeling	exclamation mark (!)
Imperative	to make a request or a command	period (.) or exclamation mark (!)

Sentence Parts

Subject

The **subject** of a sentence includes a noun or pronoun plus its modifiers. (Remember that modifiers are words that add to the meaning of nouns and verbs.) The subject names the person, place, thing, or idea that the sentence is about.

Every subject is built around a noun or a pronoun, which is the **simple subject.** It's easy to find the simple subject in a short sentence.

Jane hates strawberries.

This sentence is about Jane, so that is the simple subject.

Wordy sentences are more likely to have complex subjects.

Mr. Wong's fried dumplings are the best I've tasted.

In the sentence above, *Mr. Wong's fried dumplings* is the **complete subject** (the noun *dumplings* plus its modifiers). *Dumplings* is the noun at the heart of the sentence, so it is the simple subject.

The **stack of dirty dishes in the sink** must be washed.

Stack of dirty dishes in the sink is the complete subject (the simple subject *stack* plus its modifiers).

Direct Objects

A **direct object** is a part of the predicate that follows an action verb. It names the person or thing that receives the action of the verb.

John hits the **ball.**

The ball receives the action of hitting, so it is the direct object.

Margaret writes **letters** to her cousin.

The letters receive the action of writing, so they are the direct object.

An easy way to find the direct object in a sentence is to find the subject and verb and then ask *"what?"* or *"whom?"*

Dan likes **soccer.**

Dan likes what? He likes soccer, which makes that word the direct object.

Rachel called **Mitch.**

Rachel called whom? She called *Mitch,* which makes him the direct object.

Predicate

The predicate is the part of the sentence that explains what the subject is doing.

Penny went to clown school.

Every predicate is built around a verb, which is the **simple predicate.** It's easy to find the simple predicate in a short sentence.

He cooked dinner.

Long sentences are more likely to have complex predicates.

The eagle rose from the nest with stately grace.

Rose from the nest with stately grace is the **complete predicate** (the verb *rose* plus its modifiers). The verb *rose* is the simple predicate.

The track team ran at a slow pace.

Ran at a slow pace (the simple predicate *ran* plus its modifiers) is the complete predicate.

Compound Subjects and Predicates

A **compound subject** consists of two or more nouns or pronouns that are the subject of the same verb.

Sandra and Jim went to the movies.

Sandra and *Jim* are subjects of equal importance, so they form a compound subject.

A **compound predicate** consists of two or more verbs that have the same subject.

The soda bubbled and fizzed in the glass.

The verbs *bubbled* and *fizzed* form a compound predicate because they refer back to the subject *soda*.

Indirect Objects

An **indirect object** names the person or thing to whom or for whom the action of the verb is being performed. It comes immediately after the verb and before the direct object.

John threw the dog a bone.

To whom was the bone thrown? It was thrown to the dog, which makes *dog* the indirect object.

Jennifer sent her friend a letter.

To whom was the letter sent? It was sent to Jennifer's friend, which makes *friend* the indirect object.

An easy way to find the indirect object in a sentence is to find the direct object and then ask *to whom?* or *to what?*

Compound Objects

Just as there are compound subjects and predicates, there are compound objects. A compound object consists of two or more objects that complete the same predicate.

Jake read several books and articles about icebergs.

Books and *articles*—the things that are being read— form a compound direct object.

Marlene offered Carol and her brother tickets to the game.

The words *Carol* and *brother*—the people who receive the tickets—form a compound indirect object.

Phrases

A **phrase** is a group of related words that does not contain a subject or a predicate. (See pages 676–677.) A phrase is used in place of single words in a sentence. Together, the words in a phrase function as a single part of speech.

Some phrases are defined by the part of speech introducing the phrase.

Phrase Type		Part(s) of Speech
Prepositional Phrases	*function as*	Adjectives Adverbs
Appositive Phrases		Nouns
Participial Phrases		Adjectives
Gerund Phrases		Nouns
Infinitive Phrases		Nouns Adjectives Adverbs

Prepositional phrases contain a preposition, its objects, and any modifiers.

> between you and me
>
> through the dangerous intersection
>
> by the cool fountain

Prepositional phrases may be used as adjectives or adverbs.

An adjective phrase is a prepositional phrase that modifies a noun or a pronoun.

> The newspaper will list the location of the next meeting.

The prepositional phrase *of the next meeting* modifies the noun *location,* so it is an adjective phrase.

An adverb phrase modifies a verb, an adjective, or another adverb.

> Mr. Whiteside left before dinner.

The prepositional phrase *before dinner* modifies the verb *left,* so it is an adverb phrase.

A single sentence can contain both an adverb phrase and an adjective phrase.

> The entire class was curious *about methods of conserving energy.*

The adverb phrase *about methods* modifies the adjective *curious,* while the adjective phrase *of conserving energy* modifies the noun *methods.*

Appositive Phrases

An appositive is a noun that explains or elaborates on another nearby noun.

> The class secretary, Anton Berrioz, read the meeting notes aloud.

The appositive *Anton Berrioz* describes *secretary,* the noun that precedes it.

An appositive phrase is just a longer version of an appositive.

> I was surprised that the movie, a thriller with special effects, was so boring.

The appositive phrase *a thriller with special effects* elaborates on the noun *movie.*

An essential appositive phrase is an appositive that is vital to the meaning of the sentence. This kind of appositive should not be separated from the rest of the sentence with commas.

> Edgar Allan Poe's short story "The Tell-Tale Heart" has been adapted many times.

Poe wrote more than one short story. Therefore, the appositive "The Tell-Tale Heart" is necessary to identify which story has been adapted many times.

A nonessential appositive phrase is an appositive that is not vital to the meaning of the sentence. This type of appositive phrase is set off with one or more commas.

> "The Tell-Tale Heart," a story published in 1843, was written by Edgar Allan Poe.

In this case, the appositive *a story published in 1843* provides extra information that is not vital to the main thrust of the sentence.

 *Gerund phrases and participial phrases look just alike, but you can tell them apart by how they function in the sentence. Gerund phrases are used as nouns. Participial phrases are used as adjectives.*

Always place a comma after an introductory participial phrase.

Verbal Phrases

There are three types of verbal phrases: *participial* phrases, *gerund* phrases, and *infinitive* phrases. Verbals are verb forms that function as parts of speech other than verbs while retaining some characteristics of verbs.

Participial phrases are used as adjectives. A participial phrase contains a present or past participle, its objects, and any modifiers.

Participles are verb forms that are used as adjectives. They end with –*ing* or –*ed*. A word can often be identified as a participle only because it takes an object.

The shouting mob, hurling stones, moved forward.

In the sentence above, *shouting* is an adjective because it doesn't have an object. *Hurling* also modifies *mob,* but it is a participle because it has an object, *stones. Moved* is a verb.

In addition to the participle, the participial phrase contains objects and modifiers.

Cooing softly to herself, the baby played with her toes.

The participial phrase *cooing softly to herself* modifies the noun *baby.*

The boy covered with mud is my brother.

The participial phrase *covered with mud* modifies the noun *boy.*

Gerund phrases are used as nouns.

A gerund is a noun that looks like a verb. Gerunds always end with –*ing.*

Mike likes riding horses.

A gerund phrase contains a gerund, its objects, and any modifiers.

I hate cleaning my room.

The gerund phrase *cleaning my room* acts like a noun. It is the direct object of the verb *hate.*

The possessive form of a noun or a pronoun is used before a gerund and is considered part of the phrase.

Talia's winning the debate tournament was a shock.

His parents encouraged his studying chemistry.

Infinitive phrases are used as nouns, adjectives, or adverbs. An infinitive phrase contains the infinitive, its objects, and any modifiers.

To win at chess requires concentration.

The infinitive phrase *to win at chess* functions as a noun.

The best time to cut flowers is early in the morning.

The infinitive phrase *to cut flowers* is an adjective that modifies the noun *time.*

I run every day to stay in shape.

The infinitive phrase *to stay in shape* is an adverb that modifies the verb *run.*

Clauses

A **clause** is a group of related words that contains both a subject and a predicate. All clauses are either

- **independent or dependent**
- **restrictive or nonrestrictive**

Clauses show important relationships between ideas and help make your writing clear and direct.

A sentence must have at least one clause. Some sentences have only one clause.

She released the red balloon.

Other sentences have two clauses or more.

If he arrives in time, we can close the deal.

If he arrives in time and *we can close the deal* are clauses.

In the first clause, the subject is *he* and the predicate is *arrives*. In the second clause, the subject is *we* and the predicate is *can close*.

An independent clause can stand alone as a sentence because it expresses a complete thought. You can turn an independent clause into a simple sentence just by adding a period.

When an independent clause stands by itself, it is called a sentence.

I'll make the coffee.

When it appears in a sentence with another clause, it is called a clause.

I'll make the coffee; you flip the pancakes.

Independent clauses can be joined with a semicolon or a coordinating conjunction. If you use a conjunction, the conjunction is not part of either clause.

I ordered beef and she ordered lamb.

The conjunction *and* is not part of either clause. It is just a connecting word that ties the two independent clauses together.

Try to put the most important information in the independent clauses. Less important details can go in dependent clauses.

A dependent clause cannot stand alone as a sentence because it does not express a complete thought. This type of clause depends on the rest of the sentence to complete its meaning.

Because we were late,	we missed the kickoff.
dependent clause	independent clause

Because we were late can't stand alone as a sentence. It only makes sense when it's attached to the rest of the sentence. Since it can't stand alone, it is a dependent clause.

All dependent clauses are either adjective clauses, adverb clauses, or noun clauses.

An **adjective clause** functions in sentences exactly as a single-word adjective does. Adjectives and adjective clauses modify nouns and pronouns.

The package that Sue wrapped was the prettiest.

The adjective clause *that Sue wrapped* modifies the noun *package*.

An **adverb clause** works just like a single-word adverb does. It can modify any verb, adjective, or adverb in a sentence. Adverb clauses tell how, when, where, to what extent, and why.

We will go whenever you're ready.

The adjective clause *whenever you're ready* modifies the verb *will go*.

I baked enough cupcakes so that some people can eat two.

The adverb clause *so that some people can eat two* modifies the adjective *enough*.

A **noun clause** acts like a single-word noun. It may be used in a sentence in any situation where a noun or pronoun may be used.

What happened at the party surprised everyone.

The noun clause *What happened at the party* modifies the verb *surprised*.

A restrictive clause is essential to the meaning of a sentence. It identifies a specific person or thing.

>   The bike **that is in the shed** has a flat tire.

A restrictive clause contains important information, so it can't be deleted without changing the meaning of the sentence.

>   Computer manuals **that are badly written** are hard to understand.

If you remove the restrictive clause, the sentence would say that all computer manuals are hard to understand.

A nonrestrictive clause contains extra information. The details in a nonrestrictive clause are not vital to the meaning of a sentence.

>   The parade, **which is in its second year,** will start at noon.

If you removed the nonrestrictive clause, the meaning of the sentence would stay the same.

Nonrestrictive clauses are always introduced with *which*, *who*, or *whom*. A nonrestrictive clause should always be enclosed in commas unless it begins or ends the sentence.

WHICH VS. THAT

One of the most misunderstood topics in grammar is when to use *which* versus when to use *that*. The rule is actually pretty simple.

>   that = restrictive clause

>   which = nonrestrictive clause

A good rule of thumb is that phrases that start with *which* can be removed from a sentence without changing its meaning. In other words, phrases with *which* provide extra information.

Consider the differences between these two sentences.

>   The house **that I liked best** was not for sale.

>   My house, **which is old,** needs many repairs.

In the second sentence, you can remove the clause *which is old* without changing the meaning of the sentence.

WATCH OUT!
Never use a comma in front of a restrictive clause.

Incorrect: The dog, that doesn't behave, must always be kept on a leash.

Correct: The dog that doesn't behave must always be kept on a leash.

Diagramming is one way to grasp all the parts of a sentence and their relationship to each other. A sentence diagram is like a map of a sentence. It arranges the words in a way that makes it easy to see their relationships.

Always begin your diagram with a horizontal line crossed with a vertical line.

Simple Sentences

On the left side of the horizontal line, write the simple subject of the sentence. The simple subject is either the main noun in a noun phrase or a pronoun. On the right side of the line, write the verb, including any auxiliaries.

Snow is falling.

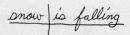

Direct Objects

When the verb is transitive, draw a vertical line to the right of the verb. The vertical line should meet but not cross the base line. To the right of this line, write the main noun or pronoun of the direct object.

Liz likes me.

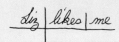

Linking Verbs

If the sentence has a linking verb, draw a diagonal line to the right of the verb. The line should meet but not cross the base line. To the right of this line, write the adjective complement or the predicate nominative.

People can be nice.

We are students.

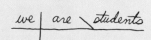

Modifiers

If there are adjectives (including determiners) modifying a noun, put them on a diagonal line beneath the noun. Do the same with adverbs modifying the verb.

A light snow fell softly.

Prepositions

When diagramming a prepositional phrase, write the preposition on a diagonal line beneath the word that the phrase modifies. Then write the noun or pronoun on a horizontal line, and put any adjective modifiers on diagonal lines below.

The woman in the red dress hurried from the room.

Indirect Objects

Diagram an indirect object as if it were a prepositional phrase with the preposition *to* understood. Put *to* in parentheses.

The experience taught my friend a hard lesson.

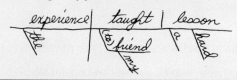

Compound Subjects or Predicates

To diagram compound sentence elements, place them on parallel lines. Connect the two lines with a dotted vertical line, and write the coordinating conjunction on it.

Ray and Bernice ate lunch together today.

The children washed the dishes and swept the floor.

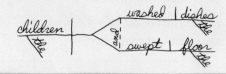

Compound Sentences

To diagram a compound sentence—that is, two simple sentences joined by a coordinating conjunction—diagram each of the simple sentences, one above the other. Then connect them with a vertical dotted line and write the conjunction on that line.

The mail has come, but that letter was not in it.

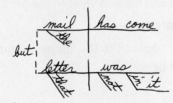

Appositives

To diagram an appositive, put the appositive noun or pronoun in parentheses after the noun that it renames or identifies.

Sam, an old friend of mine, sent this book.

Relative Clauses

To diagram a relative clause, diagram the clause on its own line below the main line. With a dotted line, connect the noun that's being modified to the relative pronoun or relative adverb.

Those apples that you sent me were delicious.

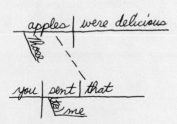

This is the place where we saw him last.

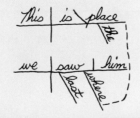

Participles and Participial Phrases

A participle is diagrammed in a curve along a diagonal and a horizontal line. The complement of the participle, if any, is to the right on the horizontal line.

Laughing, Judy handed me the squirming puppy.

The man scratching his head is your new teacher.

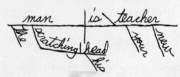

Gerunds

A gerund is diagrammed the same way as a participle, except that it is placed on a pedestal. The bottom of the pedestal rests on the base line in a noun's position.

His being the culprit surprised everyone.

Infinitive Phrases

An infinitive phrase occupying a noun position is diagrammed the same way as a gerund.

Nobody wants to leave the game yet.

Adverbial Clauses

An adverbial clause is diagrammed on a line below the base line. The subordinating conjunction is written along a diagonal dotted line that connects the word being modified to the clause's verb.

If I were you, I would be careful.

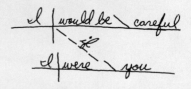

SENTENCE STRUCTURE

There are four types of sentences: simple, compound, complex, and complex-compound. Every sentence you read will fall into one of these categories. To determine a sentence's type, count the number of clauses it contains. (See pages 680–681.) Simple and compound sentences, for instance, will never have a dependent clause. As you write, use different sentence structures to keep things interesting.

Sentence Types

Simple sentences have only one independent clause and no dependent clauses.

> The toddler chased his puppy.

A simple sentence may contain a compound subject, a compound predicate, or both.

Compound subject

> The **man** and his **son** went to the park.

Compound predicate

> The pianist **bowed** to the audience and **sat** on the bench.

Both

> My **brother** and **sister love** to swim and **hate** to ski.

Compound sentences contain two or more independent clauses and no dependent clauses.

> Nathan is a born leader, and he will go far.
>
> The roast is burning; take it out of the oven.
>
> Carol made the lemonade, and Harry stirred the punch.

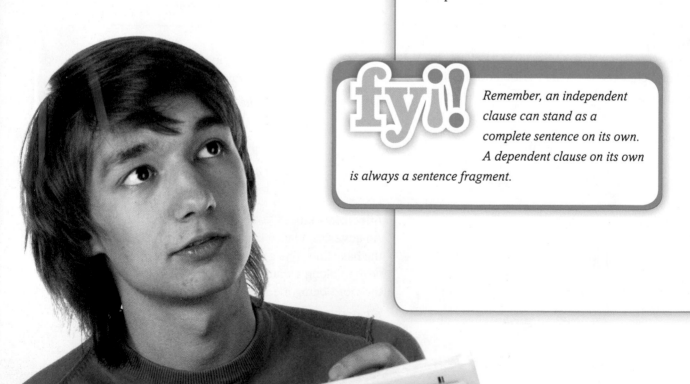

fyi! *Remember, an independent clause can stand as a complete sentence on its own. A dependent clause on its own is always a sentence fragment.*

Complex sentences contain one independent clause and one or more dependent clauses.

This complex sentence contains one independent clause and one dependent clause.

| She didn't say anything | while I was there. |
| independent clause | dependent clause |

This complex sentence contains one independent clause and two dependent clauses.

> After I finished my homework, I went to the store that you told me about.

After I finished my homework and *that you told me about* are dependent clauses.

I went to the store is an independent clause.

Complex-compound sentences contain two or more independent clauses and one or more dependent clauses. This complex-compound sentence starts with a dependent clause and concludes with two independent clauses.

> When the house gets cold in the winter, Mom lights the fireplace and Dad makes hot chocolate.

When the house gets cold in the winter is a dependent clause, whereas *Mom lights the fireplace* and *Dad makes hot chocolate* are independent clauses.

This complex-compound sentence alternates between dependent and independent clauses.

> If Sally can come to visit tomorrow, we'll go to the park; if she can't, I'll stay home and read.

If Sally can come visit tomorrow and *if she can't* are dependent clauses; *we'll go to the park* and *I'll stay home and read* are independent clauses.

> *A compound sentence can be divided easily into two separate sentences by taking out the comma between the independent clauses and using a period at the end of each new sentence.*

Sentence Type	Number of Independent Clauses	Number of Dependent Clauses
Simple Sentence	1	0
Compound Sentence	2 or more	0
Complex Sentence	1	1 or more
Complex-Compound Sentence	2 or more	1 or more

Writing would be boring if it were nothing but one simple sentence after another. Often, simple sentences can be combined to form more complex sentences.

There are many ways in which sentences can be combined, including compounding, complex transformations, and deletion transformations.

Compounding

Compounding is the simplest way of combining sentences. It's a way to join sentences together with coordinating conjunctions.

Consider these two simple sentences.

My mother is a dentist.

My father is a writer.

These two sentences can be smashed together by simply joining them with a comma and the word *and*.

My mother is a dentist, and my father is a writer.

Neither of the original sentences has been changed; they have just been joined together. Note that when two simple sentences are combined in this way, a comma usually comes before the word that joins them.

PARALLELISM

When you compound sentences, it's important that the sentence elements you combine are of the same type.

In the following pair of sentences, for example, a compound cannot be correctly formed by simply adding the word *and*.

He likes tennis.

He likes to swim.

It would be incorrect to say, "He likes tennis and to swim." That's because *tennis* is a noun and *to swim* is an infinitive; therefore, these two sentence elements are not parallel.

To combine the two sentences, you must make the related sentence elements match. In this case, you should change the infinitive *to swim* into the gerund *swimming*. Gerunds act like nouns in sentences, so the two elements are now parallel.

He likes tennis and swimming.

Now take a sheet of paper. Write out the combinations of each of these pairs of sentences using the conjunction given in italics.

Do not look at the combined versions until you have finished writing your own.

1. Combine these sentences using the word *but*.

   Yesterday was beautiful.

   Today is cold and rainy.

   Answer: Yesterday was beautiful, but today is cold and rainy.

2. Combine these sentences with the word *because*.

   We took a long walk.

   It was a lovely day.

   Answer: We took a long walk because it was a lovely day.

COMPOUNDING CONJUNCTIONS

and	because
or	nor
but	for
either/or	neither/nor
both/and	not only/but also

3. Combine these sentences with the words *either/or*.

   We shall leave today.

   We shall leave tomorrow.

   Answer: Either we shall leave today, or we shall leave tomorrow.

Compounding Sentence Parts

Take another look at that last pair of sentences. Notice that they are exactly the same except for the adverbs at the end.

We shall leave today.

We shall leave tomorrow.

When two sentences contain some words that are identical, the identical words can be crossed out of the second sentence and then the remainder of the sentence can be combined with the first.

We shall leave either today or tomorrow.

You can combine all kinds of sentence parts. For instance, these sentences are identical except for the subjects.

Jerry is ready.

I am ready.

Note that when the subjects are compounded, the verb must be changed to its plural form.

Jerry and I are ready.

The same principle works when you deal with three sentences that all contain some identical words.

The day was bright.

The day was cold.

+ The day was windy.

The day was bright, cold, and windy.

Another way to compound sentences is to use semicolons.

Finish your breakfast.

+ Then we can go.

Finish your breakfast; then we can go.

In the last example, it is important that the punctuation mark be a semicolon for the sentence to be grammatically correct. A comma just won't cut it.

WATCH OUT!

Make sure you watch your punctuation when you combine sentences. Often, a comma will need to be changed to a semicolon (or vice versa).

Incorrect: Burt wants to make the cookies first, he will make the cupcakes later.

Inez could have passed the ball; but she decided to shoot it instead.

Correct: Burt wants to make the cookies first; he will make the cupcakes later.

Inez could have passed the ball, but she decided to shoot it instead.

Combining Sentences

Complex Transformations

Complex transformations are a more complicated method of combining sentences. They can be performed by creating a relative clause. A **relative clause** helps identify or modify a noun. There are two types of relative clauses: nonrestrictive and restrictive.

Recall that a nonrestrictive clause adds information to a noun or pronoun. A restrictive clause is vital information that identifies a noun or pronoun. (For more on nouns and pronouns, see pages 654–659.)

Nonrestrictive clauses contain extra information, rather than essential information.

Consider these sentences:

Mr. Johnson is my teacher.

+ Mr. Johnson is standing on the corner.

Mr. Johnson is my teacher, and he is standing on the corner.

An even better way to combine the two sentences is to transform one of them into a relative clause.

First, change the part of one sentence that is the same as the part of the other sentence—in this case Mr. Johnson—to a relative pronoun. The relative pronouns are *who, whom, whose, which,* and *that.* In this case, use *who.* The second sentence of the pair should now read

who is standing on the corner

Now insert this group of words into the middle of the first sentence.

Mr. Johnson, who is standing on the corner, is my teacher.

The words *who is standing on the corner* simply add extra information, so they form a nonrestrictive clause.

Restrictive clauses contain vital information.

To perform this complex transformation, start with two different sentences:

The man is my teacher.

The man is standing on the corner.

Once again, you can transform the second sentence into a relative clause.

who is standing on the corner

Now insert this group of words into the middle of the first sentence.

The man who is standing on the corner is my teacher.

In this case, the clause tells us which man we are talking about. It suggests that the man standing on the corner, rather than the man walking down the street, is the speaker's teacher.

Deletion Transformations

Sometimes you can delete the beginning of a relative clause, producing a number of different kinds of sentence structures.

Deletion transformations are only possible when

- the relative pronoun is the subject of the relative clause.
- the word immediately following the relative pronoun is a form of *be*, such as *am, is, are, was,* or *were*.

You can use deletion transformations to create appositives and participles.

Remember that you may need to change the order of the words in a sentence when you make deletions.

Appositives

An appositive is a noun phrase that identifies or renames another noun phrase, which it immediately follows.

Kelly, **my sister,** went to the mall.

Now return to these two sentences.

Mr. Johnson is standing on the corner.

Mr. Johnson is my teacher.

Recall that by changing the second sentence to a relative clause *(who is my teacher)* and inserting it into the first sentence, we produce this combined sentence.

Mr. Johnson, **who is my teacher,** is standing on the corner.

A further change, a deletion transformation, is possible if we change the relative clause into an appositive.

Delete *who* and *is:*

Mr. Johnson, **my teacher,** is standing on the corner.

The noun phrase *my teacher* is an appositive. Notice that the appositive, like the nonrestrictive clause from which it was made, is set off from the rest of the sentence by commas.

Participles

Remember that every verb has two forms called participles. They are the present participle, or *-ing* form (seeing, showing, looking), and the past participle (seen, shown, looked).

Participles are used only with helping verbs. Often the helping verb is a form of *to be.*

Sentences that contain participles can be made into relative clauses and combined with other sentences. Consider this sentence pair.

The boy spoke to me.

The boy was standing.

If you change the second sentence to the phrase *who was standing,* you have

The boy **who was standing** spoke to me.

Because the relative clause begins with *who was,* those two words can be deleted.

The boy, **standing,** spoke to me.

Without its helping verb, the participle in the sentence on the left is now a word by itself, modifying the noun *boy.* It has, in fact, become an adjective. Since it is an adjective, it can be moved to a position before the noun.

The **standing** boy spoke to me.

Sentence Problems

There are two main types of sentence problems: fragments and run-ons. In general, fragments have too few words, while run-ons have too many.

Sentence Fragments

You have learned that the minimum requirements of a sentence are at least one subject and one verb. A common grammatical mistake is to punctuate a group of words that is not a sentence.

A **sentence fragment** is a piece of a sentence instead of the whole thing. The fragment can be a phrase or a dependent clause. Fragments can be a little mysterious because they're missing information.

After the storm.

What happened after the storm? We don't know because this fragment is missing a verb.

The tricky thing about fragments is that they are usually disguised as sentences. They can have all the dressings of a real sentence, like punctuation and capital letters.

If I leave tonight.

Thinking about it?

Swimming in the lake!

These fragments might look like sentences, but don't be fooled: they are incomplete. A good way to find sentence fragments is to read out loud. Sometimes it's easier to hear a bad sentence than to see it.

Correcting Sentence Fragments. Weed fragments out of your writing by transforming them into complete sentences. One way you can correct a sentence fragment is by tacking it onto another sentence. You can tack it onto the front end of a sentence.

Fragment:	After going to college for four years. I was ready to teach.
Correction:	After going to college for four years, I was ready to teach.

You can also tack the fragment onto the back end of a sentence.

Fragment:	Even though I awoke earlier than usual. I was late for work.
Correction:	I was late for work, even though I awoke earlier than usual.

Other times you can change the wording a little to make a fragment a complete sentence.

Fragment:	One of my friends who lost her ring in the swimming pool.
Correction:	One of my friends lost her ring in the swimming pool.

Some fragments will require additional information to correct.

Incorrect:	If I leave tonight.
Correction:	If I leave tonight, I'll be in Baltimore by breakfast.

---

fyi!

Remember, a phrase is a group of related words that does not have a subject or a predicate. A dependent clause is a group of words that can't stand alone.

THREE WAYS TO FIX A SENTENCE FRAGMENT

1. Tack it onto another sentence.
2. Change the wording.
3. Add more information.

Run-on Sentences

A sentence is supposed to be a unit of thought. A good sentence is a group of words that expresses an idea.

A **run-on sentence** has too many ideas. It is overloaded with subjects and verbs. A run-on sentence occurs when two or more sentences are improperly joined into a single sentence.

Many grown-ups think that children watch too much television and they think children do not read or exercise enough and grown-ups worry about this.

The tricky thing about run-on sentences is that you can't identify them by length. A long sentence can be grammatically correct, just as a run-on sentence can be short.

She lives in Maine he doesn't.

WATCH OUT!

A comma alone cannot be used to link two independent clauses. If you do join two sentences with a comma alone, you have created the dreaded comma splice.

Incorrect: Devin loves to play video games, Taylor would rather go outside.

Correct: Devin loves to play video games, but Taylor would rather go outside.

THREE WAYS TO FIX A RUN-ON SENTENCE

1. Separate it into more than one sentence.

2. Use a semicolon or a conjunction.

3. Change one of the independent clauses into a phrase or a dependent clause.

Correcting Run-on Sentences. There are several ways to fix a run-on sentence. Often, a sentence that is too long has to be separated into shorter sentences.

Run-on: Melissa won first place, her prize was $500.

Correction 1:   Melissa won first place. Her prize was $500.

You can also fix a run-on sentence by adding a semicolon or a conjunction.

Correction 2:   Melissa won first place; her prize was $500.

Correction 3:   Melissa won first place, and her prize was $500.

Another option for repairing a run-on sentence is to make one of its independent clauses a phrase or a dependent clause.

Run-on: The board is scheduled to meet tomorrow they have many matters to discuss.

Correction: Scheduled to meet tomorrow, the board has many matters to discuss.

Subject-Verb Agreement

For a sentence to be clear, the subject and its verb must agree. The forms of nouns, pronouns, and verbs can be changed to show whether they are singular or plural.

If the subject is singular, the form of the verb should be singular.

> **Peter lives** in a small town near the border of Tennessee.

If the subject is plural, the form of the verb should be plural.

> **Three of Peter's relatives live** in the same town.

This is called making the subject and verb agree in number.

Singular	Plural
I am at home.	We are at home.
You are at home.	You are at home.
He, she, or it is at home.	They are at home.

If the two subjects form a single idea or are thought of as a unit, they should take a singular verb.

SUBJECT

A subject that is joined to a group of words introduced by *with, together with, accompanied by, as well as, including,* and so on is not changed in number.

> The director, together with the department managers, *was* at the meeting.

> The department managers, accompanied by the director, *were* at the meeting.

Determining the Number of the Subject

In some sentences, you may find it difficult to determine the number of the subject. These guidelines will help you.

Compound Subjects. Remember that a compound subject consists of two or more nouns or pronouns that are the subject of the same verb.

> **Eddie** and **Steve** are roommates.

Eddie and *Steve* are nouns; *and* is a coordinating conjunction. The subjects are connected by a coordinating conjunction.

A compound subject may take a singular or a plural verb, depending on

- the coordinating conjunction
- the number of the words in the compound subject (whether they're singular or plural)

Use a plural verb with a compound subject that is connected by the coordinating conjunction *and*.

> The **coach and the principal** plan to attend the meeting.

Use a singular verb with a compound subject that has a singular noun or pronoun connected by the coordinating conjunctions *or* or *nor*.

> **Either her aunt or her cousin** plans to host the event.

Use a plural verb with a compound subject that connects plural nouns or pronouns with *or* or *nor*.

> **Neither the old televisions nor the broken radios** have been fixed.

If the compound subject is mixed in number—one subject is singular and the other subject is plural—use the subject that is closest to the verb in the sentence.

> Neither the cellists nor the **violinist has** sheet music.

> Neither the violinist nor the **cellists have** sheet music.

Collective Nouns. A collective noun is singular in form but refers to a group.

audience   cast   choir   majority   staff

A collective noun takes a singular verb when the group is regarded as a unit.

The audience was applauding.

But a collective noun takes a plural verb when emphasis is placed on the individual members of the group.

The audience were arriving.

Nouns with Plural Forms. Nouns such as *economics, mathematics, measles,* and *news* are plural in form but singular in meaning. Although they end in -*s*, they refer to a single thing or to a unit and therefore take a singular verb.

Physics is a challenging branch of science.

Other nouns, such as *clothes, congratulations, pants, pliers, shears,* and *scissors,* end in -*s* but take a plural verb, even though they refer to one thing.

His garden shears are on the porch.

Some nouns, such as *athletics, dramatics,* and *politics,* end in -*s* but may be singular or plural depending on their meaning in the sentence.

Politics is the art of the possible.

His politics are constantly changing.

Watch Out for Extra Words. Sometimes words and phrases come between a subject and its verb. These words or phrases do not change the number of the subject. Make sure the verb agrees in number with the subject of the sentence, not with some other word in another phrase.

Lisa, new to the life of babysitters, was unprepared for her lack of free time on weekends.

The contestants waiting backstage for a cue were becoming excited and restless.

Every and *Many A.* The words *every* and *many a* are adjectives that emphasize separateness when they modify subjects. *Every* means "every single one" and *many a* means "each one of a large number." Use a singular verb with a single subject or a compound subject modified by *every* or *many a(n).*

Every man, woman, and child has to be counted.

Many a student prepares thoroughly for tests.

A plural subject takes a plural verb, and a singular subject takes a singular verb.

PUNCTUATION is

the use of certain marks in writing. It has one purpose: to make writing clear and easy to read. Like traffic signs, punctuation tells readers when to slow down, when go carefully, and when to pause or stop. This section covers 13 types of punctuation.

- Periods
- Question marks
- Exclamation points
- Commas
- Semicolons
- Colons
- Dashes
- Hyphens
- Ellipses
- Parentheses
- Brackets
- Quotation marks
- Apostrophes

End Punctuation

There are three kinds of end punctuation: the period, the question mark, and the exclamation point. End punctuation brings the reader to a full stop. Every sentence must end with one of these marks.

Periods are at the end of an ordinary sentence.

Ben is a good dog.

We should leave.

Question marks ask for information instead of stating it.

Is Ben a good dog?

When should we leave?

Exclamation points give a sentence extra "oomph."

Ben is a good dog!

We have to leave now!

Punctuation marks are signals that tell readers to slow down, speed up, or take a break. ▼

Punctuation Mark	Meaning
Period (.)	Signals a strong pause
Comma (,)	Signals a weak pause
Semicolon (;)	Signals a medium-strength pause
Colon (:)	Introduces additional material
Parentheses (( ))	Sets aside information from the rest of the sentence
Brackets ([ ])	Sets aside information within parentheses
Dash (–)	Signals an interruption
Ellipsis points (…)	Signals an omission or a pause

Periods

Periods are plain punctuation placed at the end of sentences that are statements or commands.

Let's see a movie.

My cat caught a canary.

Dad sold three pies at the bake sale.

Periods signal the end of a thought, telling the reader to pause before moving on to the next sentence.

They are also used in certain abbreviations, including initials, months, countries, titles, and other commonly abbreviated forms.

T. S. Eliot

Feb.

Dr. and Mr. Green

Finally, periods are used after numbers and letters on outlines and lists.

Eating Contests

    I. Hot dog eating contests

      A. Dates

      B. Winners

Question Marks

Question marks are placed at the end of sentences that ask something. Use question marks whenever you need more information.

Were there lions at the circus?

What's your favorite book?

Is there time to stop for snacks?

Exclamation Points

Exclamation points are used at the end of sentences that show strong feelings. Use exclamation points for emphasis whenever you have a strong point of view.

I don't want to go camping!

Go away!

What a great party!

RIGHT AND WRONG PUNCTUATION

There are two issues in punctuation. The first is a simple question of right and wrong. A writer who ends each sentence with a colon rather than a period is just wrong because sentences cannot end with a colon. It's that simple.

The second issue is less clear-cut; it's more a matter of style. Sometimes, a writer is free to choose punctuation that suits his or her taste. For instance, one writer might choose to use a semicolon to separate two closely related thoughts, while another writer might choose to use a period. With practice, you'll learn which choices make your meaning most clear.

Pauses

Some punctuation marks stand in for the natural pauses or changes in inflection you would use if you were speaking instead of writing. Punctuation that asks readers to pause includes

- **Commas**
- **Semicolons**
- **Colons**
- **Dashes**
- **Hyphens**
- **Ellipsis points**

WORDS AT WORK

In this sentence from her short story "Average Waves in Unprotected Waters," Anne Tyler demonstrates how to use commas to organize details.

Most men came behind them, dressed in work clothes, carrying folding chairs, black trunklike boxes with silver hinges, microphones, a wooden lectern, and an armload of bunting.

Commas

Commas ask readers to pause briefly as they read a sentence. They separate certain parts of the sentence without interrupting the overall flow.

Commas are the most frequently used punctuation mark. You can use them in many different ways.

You can use commas to separate items in a series.

Penguins, polar bears, and peacocks are my favorite zoo animals.

Without commas, the same sentence would be much harder to read.

Penguins polar bears and peacocks are my favorite zoo animals.

You can also use commas to separate compound sentences joined by conjunctions such as *and, or,* or *but*.

Peacocks like popcorn, but they don't care for peas.

Additionally, commas set off parenthetical information and appositives.

The penguins' pen, which is north of the food court, is big and clean.

The new polar bear, Percy, likes to play hide and seek.

Use commas to set off an introductory modifier.

Feeling hot from the sun, Percy went for a swim.

Finally, use commas before or after the name of a person being spoken to.

Percy, please save some fish for me.

 *A good rule of thumb is to use a comma anywhere you might pause if you were saying a sentence out loud.*

Semicolons

Semicolons join two sentences without using a conjunction. They create a pause that is stronger than a comma and weaker than a period.

Use a semicolon to separate sentences that are, in your judgment, too closely related to be separated by a period.

I want to finish the article now; I'll go to lunch later.

A semicolon can be used when two sentences are joined by a transitional word like *however* or *therefore.*

Today is a holiday; therefore, the mail will not be delivered.

Semicolons are also used to separate items in a list when commas are used within the items.

Speakers at the town meeting included Mrs. Sloan, the butcher; Mr. Bates, the baker; and Mr. White, the candlestick maker.

Colons

Colons are used to introduce lists, examples, questions, or long quotes. Whereas semicolons tell readers to stop and separate, the colon says, "Go on; look ahead. Here comes something."

You will need the following items: a compass, a rope, and a water bottle.

The question is this: What should we do next?

The world's three largest countries in area are as follows: Russia, Canada, China.

It is also used after the salutation in a business letter.

Gentlemen:

Dear Mrs. Rogers:

To Whom It May Concern:

Another use for a colon is to separate a title from its subtitle and to separate hours from minutes.

Thanks a Lot: Mastering the Art of Faint Praise

6:30 p.m.

MARCEL PROUST

Marcel Proust, a French writer, was a wordy fellow. His famous novel *Remembrance of Things Past* was so long that it had to be published in seven parts. He is also known for having written one of the longest sentences in all of literature. Clocking in at 958 words in English, Proust had to use a lot of semicolons to make his supersized sentence hang together.

WORDS AT WORK

This excerpt from William Faulkner's short story "Barn Burning" uses two colons.

Hit's big as a courthouse, he thought quietly, with a surge of peace and joy whose reason he could not have thought into words, being too young for that: *They are safe from him. People whose lives are part of this peace and dignity are beyond his touch, he no more to them than a buzzing wasp: capable of stinging for a little moment, but that's all.*

Dashes

Dashes ask readers to pause before a sudden break in thought or an interruption.

> The best way to finish that—but no, you don't want my opinion.

Dashes are also used to emphasize or define part of a sentence.

> Margie Miller—the best writer at the paper—got a promotion.

To form a dash, you may need to type two hyphens together. A single hyphen is not a dash.

WORDS AT WORK

Emily Dickinson is famous for using many dashes in her poems. (See pages 946–947.)

After great pain, a formal feeling comes—
The Nerves sit ceremonious, like Tombs—
The stiff Heart questions 'was it He, that bore,'
And 'Yesterday, or Centuries before'?

The Feet, mechanical, go round—
A Wooden way
Of Ground, or Air, or Ought—
Regardless grown,
A Quartz contentment, like a stone—

This is the Hour of Lead—
Remembered, if outlived,
As Freezing persons, recollect the Snow—
First— Chill—then Stupor—then the letting go—

Hyphens

Use hyphens to form compound adjectives. A compound adjective is two or more words that modify a noun.

> I prefer up-to-date Web sites.

> A well-known painter will be there.

Note that compound adjectives are hyphenated only when they appear BEFORE the noun.

> The Web sites I prefer are up to date.

> The painter who will be there is well known.

Hyphens are also used to form compound nouns. Compound nouns are hyphenated regardless of their position in a sentence.

> father-in-law   great-grandmother
> jack-in-the-box

Hyphens are used to spell out compound numbers between twenty-one (21) and ninety-nine (99).

> twenty-four   sixty-one   twenty-ninth

Hyphens are used to spell out fractions that are used as adjectives.

> We saw a one-third increase in earnings this year.

Note that fractions that are used as nouns are NOT hyphenated.

> Two thirds were counted as present.

You should also hyphenate prefixes and suffixes to avoid confusion of words that are spelled alike.

> re-cover the sofa/recover from the loss
> re-count money/recount a story
> re-creation of the scene/recreation area

Ellipsis Points

An ellipsis can be used to indicate a pause or an unfinished thought.

Can this . . . really be true?

I'm not sure. . . .

The main use of ellipses, though, is to indicate that words have been deleted from a direct quote. You do not need to use an ellipsis if it is obvious you are using a partial quote.

William Price Fox told the interviewer that he "didn't like to think very much before writing."

An ellipsis can be three dots (. . .) or four dots (. . . .) depending on where it's placed in a sentence. If the omission occurs at the beginning of a quotation, or within a quotation, use three dots.

William Price Fox told the interviewer that he "didn't like to think . . . before writing."

Note that there is a space on both sides of the three dots.

When the omission occurs at the end of a quotation, use four dots. The extra dot is the period at the end of the sentence.

William Price Fox told the interviewer that he "didn't like to think. . . ."

> *Compound nouns can be two words joined by a hyphen (bull's-eye), two words smashed together (stepfather), or two separate words (vice president). Check the dictionary if you're not sure how a compound noun should look.*

WATCH OUT!

Make sure that you don't change the meaning of a sentence when you omit words.

For example, imagine you are going to use the following quote:

Mayor: "The budget committee is doing all it can to avoid having to raise taxes again for at least two years."

Incorrect: The mayor's last point about "… having to raise taxes again…" seemed to draw the most attention from the crowd.

Mixed Bag

Parentheses

Parentheses are used to set certain words apart from the rest of a sentence. Parentheses can be used to add commentary (like this) or other information that doesn't follow the flow of thought.

George Washington (1732–1799) was our first president.

Occasionally, parentheses are used to set off full sentences. (There are sentences like that.)

> *The punctuation always comes after the closing parenthesis unless the parenthetical material is a stand-alone sentence.*

Brackets

Brackets are used to enclose parenthetical matter within parentheses.

Shakespeare's most difficult tragedy (*Hamlet* [circa 1600]) is quite popular.

Brackets can also be used to flag information that has been added to a quote or to correct a mistake in a quote.

"Nothing was left for him [the president] to do but wait."

"The chocolate mous[s]e was delicious," he wrote.

Quotation Marks

Quotation marks are used to enclose someone else's exact words. Use them when you repeat the exact words spoken or written by an outside source.

Ralph Waldo Emerson said, "A foolish consistency is the hobgoblin of little minds."

"I think," she said, "that you are wrong."

"Who are you?" he asked.

Note that periods and commas fall inside quotation marks. Semicolons and colons, on the other hand, fall outside quotation marks.

"To be or not to be": this is one of Shakespeare's most famous lines.

Use single quotation marks to mark a quote within a quote.

John said, "To quote a famous president, 'I cannot tell a lie.'"

Apostrophes

Apostrophes are used to show possession. If the possessive noun is singular, just add an apostrophe followed by an s (*'s*).

Pete's father drove us to school.

Do you like Martha's dress?

If the possessive noun is plural, add only the apostrophe.

The boys' bicycles are all blue.

The editors' meeting is at 3:00.

The possessive case of pronouns does NOT use an apostrophe.

hers	theirs	ours
his	its	yours

Occasionally, you'll find a singular noun that already ends with s. When this happens, you can choose between adding an apostrophe and an -s or just an apostrophe.

It was Coach Woods' fault.

Yeats's poems are my favorites.

Apostrophes are also used to indicate missing letters in contractions.

I can't see what you're doing.

WATCH OUT!

Parentheses, brackets, and quotation marks always come in pairs.

Incorrect: (See also Farthingham's study of butterfly habits [2003].

Correct: (See also Farthingham's study of butterfly habits [2003]).

Any words that can be put into parentheses can also be put inside a pair of dashes. Parentheses suggest a quiet aside; they're often used for additional information that isn't that important. Dashes are more dramatic, calling attention to the material.

Cap It

Capital letters act as signals to readers. They distinguish proper nouns and adjectives from common nouns and adjectives. They announce new sentences and the beginning of direct quotations.

Here are some rules for using capital letters correctly. The subject pronoun *I* is always capitalized.

> I wish I could go back to bed.

A capital letter is always used at the beginning of a sentence.

> Do you think we should sell the cow?

The first word of a direct quote that is a complete sentence starts with a capital letter.

> He asked, "Do we have any homework?"

Proper nouns—the names of particular people, places, and events—always begin with capital letters.

> Billy and Barbara moved to Brazil.

The names of months and days of the week start with capital letters.

> School starts on the first Monday in September.

The names of holidays begin with capital letters.

> I only eat turkey on Thanksgiving Day.

PROPER ADJECTIVES

Proper adjectives are adjectives that have been formed from proper nouns.

> She studied Shakespearean drama.

The adjective *Shakespearean* is formed from the name Shakespeare, which is, of course, a proper noun. Similar examples include

American tourist	Elizabethan era
Chinese art	Iowa farmer
New England state	Texas chili

Over time, some proper adjectives become so common that they are no longer capitalized. Check a dictionary if you are unsure.

bohemian lifestyle	pasteurized milk
quixotic	

Titles of rank and office are often capitalized.

> President Lincoln met with General Grant.

All the major words in titles of books, movies, and TV shows are capitalized.

> My class is reading *The Catcher in the Rye*.

The first letter of the first word in a line of poetry is often (but not always) capitalized.

Knowing when to use capital letters and when to use lower-case letters can be confusing. Some words can go either way, depending on the context.

> I'm a citizen of the planet Earth.

> The worm burrowed into the earth.

When in doubt, decide whether the word in question is being used as a proper or common noun. Proper nouns always begin with a capital letter.

Have you ever referred to capital letters as uppercase or small letters as lowercase? There's a story behind those names. Back in the era of the printing press, typesetters stored their metal letters in a big drawer called the job case. Small letters were stored in the lower part of the case, so they became lowercase. Can you guess where the capital letters were stored?

Abbreviations

The United States Postal Service recommends two-letter capitalized abbreviations for each of the 50 states and the District of Columbia, Guam, Puerto Rico, and the Virgin Islands. No periods are used.

The Canada Post has done the same for its provinces and territories.

U.S. States and Territories

Alabama	AL	North Dakota	ND
Alaska	AK	Ohio	OH
Arizona	AZ	Oklahoma	OK
Arkansas	AR	Oregon	OR
California	CA	Pennsylvania	PA
Colorado	CO	Puerto Rico	PR
Connecticut	CT	Rhode Island	RI
Delaware	DE	South Carolina	SC
District of Columbia	DC	South Dakota	SD
Florida	FL	Tennessee	TN
Georgia	GA	Texas	TX
Guam	GU	Utah	UT
Hawaii	HI	Vermont	VT
Idaho	ID	Virginia	VA
Illinois	IL	Virgin Islands	VI
Indiana	IN	Washington	WA
Iowa	IA	West Virginia	WV
Kansas	KS	Wisconsin	WI
Kentucky	KY	Wyoming	WY
Louisiana	LA		
Maine	ME		
Maryland	MD		
Massachusetts	MA		
Michigan	MI		

Canadian Provinces and Territories

Minnesota	MN	Alberta	AB
Mississippi	MS	British Columbia	BC
Missouri	MO	Manitoba	MB
Montana	MT	New Brunswick	NB
Nebraska	NE	Newfoundland and Labrador	NL
Nevada	NV	Northern Territories	NT
New Hampshire	NH	Nova Scotia	NS
New Jersey	NJ	Nunavut	NU
New Mexico	NM	Ontario	ON
New York	NY	Prince Edward Island	PE
North Carolina	NC	Quebec	PQ
		Saskatchewan	SK
		Yukon	YT

Writing and Research

THE SEVEN-STEP SYSTEM

THE SEVEN-STEP SYSTEM is a process you can use for any writing project you're assigned, whether it's an informal essay or a long research report. The steps will help guide you through the process, including picking a good topic, constructing a strong thesis, and putting together your ideas in a logical order.

Every time you write for school, organize your work according to this system. Eventually, the steps will become second nature.

Where Am I in the Seven-Step System?

THE SEVEN-STEP SYSTEM

1. **Choosing a Topic**
2. Gathering Information
3. Constructing a Thesis
4. Outlining
5. Drafting
6. Revising
7. Proofreading

Some of the material in the Writing and Research section (pages 706–821) is reprinted with permission of Kendall Hunt Publishing Company, from Research for Writers: Advanced English Composition *by Florida Community College at Jacksonville. Copyright © 2002 by FCCJ Foundation. Further reproduction is prohibited.*

Choosing a Topic

The first step is to choose a good topic. Spending extra time to set up a good writing project at the front end will help the later stages move faster.

Most writing assignments demand a narrow topic so you have enough room for all the detail you need. For example, if you try to write a paper on a broad topic like the circulatory system, you will find yourself overwhelmed with information. A more manageable topic might be, say, how white blood cells fight disease.

Paper Topics

Too Broad	More Manageable
the circulatory system	how white blood cells fight disease
life in colonial America	tools used by colonial farmers
space travel	life aboard a space station

Background Reading

If you're having a hard time homing in on a topic, do some background reading to become more familiar with your subject. The *Southwestern Advantage Topic Source* is designed for this specific purpose. As you read, think about what kinds of information you would like to include in your report and what can be left out. It's natural to find some sections that interest you more than others. This will help you pinpoint the aspect of the subject you would most like to write about.

Make a list of points as you go to serve as a preliminary outline and research guide. Your list might just be a series of questions you hope to answer in your report. If you're reading about life aboard space stations, you might ask questions like

- What does the inside of the station look like?
- How big are the crew's quarters?
- How do astronauts eat?
- How do they spend most of their time?

Generating Ideas

Once you've settled on a topic, it's time to think things through. Jot down some notes as you go. At this point, you're just writing for yourself, so no one has to see.

Techniques you can use to guide your thinking include *brainstorming, freewriting,* and *cubing*. Give yourself about 15 minutes for each technique.

Brainstorming

Make a list of words and phrases that relate to the topic as they come to mind. Don't censor yourself. Just write down ideas without thinking about them too much.

Freewriting

Freewriting is another good way to generate ideas. The technique is based on the belief that we often limit or block our creativity by focusing on details like grammar and word choice. Let your ideas flow freely by concentrating on your subject and allowing yourself to write as fast as you can, without editing or evaluating your words as you go.

When your time is up, read over what you've written. You'll find that some ideas seem more useful than others. Circle or underline the words and phrases that seem to be headed in the right direction and ignore the rest.

Cubing

Cubing is like freewriting, but it's more directed. It allows you to explore a topic from six perspectives.

1. Describe it
2. Compare it to another topic
3. Associate it with another topic
4. Analyze it
5. Explain how it can be used
6. Evaluate it (argue for or against it)

Each perspective brings different questions into play. Freewrite on each perspective for three to five minutes. Don't worry if you find yourself writing more questions than answers. The idea is to generate lines of inquiry, which will give you different ways to approach your topic.

Keep in mind that there are other questions you can use to form the six sides of your cube. Journalists, for instance, often ask the questions *who, what, when, where, why,* and *how*.

Brainstorming is a great way to generate ideas as you try to choose a good topic. ▶

Gathering Information

Step 2 in the seven-step system is gathering information. This step is important enough to have its own section in this volume. (For more information, see the research section beginning on page 782.)

Finding Sources

Not all writing projects require research. For example, simple book reports rarely require you to consult outside sources. If you're not sure what your project requires, check with your teacher.

Most of the sources you use for your writing projects will be in the library or on the Internet. Common types of sources include

- books
- magazines
- newspapers
- encyclopedias
- Web sites
- dictionaries
- almanacs
- reference librarians
- original research (interviews, experiments, etc.)

Taking Notes

As you gather information, take notes about the different sources you consult. Make sure you differentiate between the ideas that belong to other people and the ideas you've had yourself. Also, be careful to mark direct quotes so you don't accidentally use someone else's words as your own.

Think about the kinds of evidence you might want to use to support your claim, which might include

- examples
- definitions
- statistics
- descriptions
- stories
- explanation

Where Am I in the Seven-Step System?

THE SEVEN-STEP SYSTEM

1. Choosing a Topic
2. **Gathering Information**
3. Constructing a Thesis
4. Outlining
5. Drafting
6. Revising
7. Proofreading

Process and Evaluate

Approach your research materials with a critical eye. As you read, digest the information by thinking about how you might use it in your writing project.

Questions you can ask yourself include

Does the author have a bias? Everyone has a point of view that informs their writing. Think about the perspective the author has on the material and how that perspective might have influenced his or her writing.

What kind of expertise does the author have? Does the writer have training or other credentials that make you trust (or distrust) his or her claims? Has the author written anything else on a similar topic?

How does the source relate to my topic? Think about how the source relates to your writing project. If the connection doesn't seem strong, drop what you're reading and move to the next thing.

How current is the source? Check the publication date. If it's recent, you're in good shape. If it's older, ask yourself how much the topic has changed over time. Some topics, like literature, probably haven't changed much. Others, like science, change so fast that an older source might contain outdated information.

Get Rid of Anything You Don't Need

Don't assume you can use every source you consult. It's important that you use good judgment to choose only the best and most relevant sources. Put aside any research material that isn't up to snuff; it will do more harm than good.

Document Your Sources

It's important that you show your readers where to look for information that you use in your paper. As you take notes for your writing project, make sure to take down the details that will be required on your works cited page. Typically, this includes author, title, publication date, publisher, and page numbers. Note the url, page/topic name, and author (if listed) for Internet sources.

GATHERING INFORMATION

The gathering information phase of your writing project should include the following steps.

1. **Find sources.**
2. **Take notes.**
3. **Process and evaluate the information.**
4. **Get rid of anything you don't need.**
5. **Document the sources you think you'll use.**

WATCH OUT!

For research projects, your teacher might base part of your grade on the sources you choose.

Constructing a Thesis

Writing the Thesis

As you read through the information you have assembled, you will begin to form certain opinions on your topic. You can use these opinions to develop a tentative thesis, which is a statement that summarizes the main thrust of the ideas in your paper.

Think of your thesis as a work in progress. It can grow and change as your paper develops.

The most important thing about a thesis is that it needs to make an argument. It would be difficult, if not impossible, to argue that the middle class pays 85 percent of the taxes in the United States. That statement is either correct or incorrect, so it is an ineffective thesis.

Changing the thesis to assert that the middle class should pay more in taxes would be an arguable point.

> *The most important thing about a thesis is that it needs to make an argument.*

Where Am I in the Seven-Step System?

THE SEVEN STEP SYSTEM

1. Choosing a Topic
2. Gathering Information
3. **Constructing a Thesis**
4. Outlining
5. Drafting
6. Revising
7. Proofreading

Testing Your Thesis

There are three conditions that a good thesis should satisfy.

The thesis should be news. Your thesis should not be accepted as common knowledge. Obviously, the audience in this regard is crucial. It would seem entirely unnecessary to argue, for instance, that Earth circles the sun unless your audience consisted of primitive tribesmen, the Flat Earth Society, or thirteenth-century popes.

A thesis must be understandable. Keep in mind that your readers probably don't know the topic as well as you do. Make sure you explain your ideas in terms that people will understand.

A thesis must be supportable. You already know you must support your thesis with evidence. But keep in mind that what seems like good evidence to one group of readers might not seem strong to another group. If your thesis depends upon support from data compiled by the American Veal Association, for instance, and your audience is People for the Ethical Treatment of Animals (PETA), you really do not have a supportable thesis because the veal industry, for that audience, is not an authority. (See pages 798–803.)

WRITING A STRONG THESIS

- Never write your thesis as a question. Instead, use a declarative sentence with a period (.) at the end. While many theses start with a question, by the time you're writing you should be able to frame it as an answer.

- Remember that your thesis cannot be a statement of fact. It should be an arguable statement *about* the facts.

- Make sure you can support your thesis with evidence.

- Be precise and specific. Your thesis is not the place for vague language.

- Make sure your thesis limits the range of topics and presents an idea manageable enough to guide the length and scope of your research paper. Remember you can tweak your thesis (or even make a major change) as you work your way through the seven-step process.

EVALUATING THREE THESIS STATEMENTS
The good, the bad, and the ugly

Thesis: Satan is the real hero of Milton's *Paradise Lost.*

Rating: *Good.* This argument works because it is arguable. Some people will disagree with it, naming another character as the hero.

Thesis: Lincoln's role in the Civil War was crucial.

Rating: *Bad.* No controversy here. Everyone knows that Lincoln was a crucial figure in the Civil War, so there's no point in arguing it. To improve this thesis, go against the flow by arguing that his role was less important or more important than most people think.

Thesis: I like chocolate.

Rating: *Ugly.* It's hard to argue with a personal preference. How can anyone else say that I don't like chocolate? Instead, try to make a universal statement, such as "Chocolate is beneficial to the diet as an aid in combating depression." Now you've got an argument because there is an opposing point of view.

WATCH OUT!

Remember the thesis statement should summarize the purpose of your paper. Make sure you have it right before you go any further.

MAKE A PLAN
The front end of your project is a good time to make a plan. Here are five steps you can follow to come up with a good one.

1. **Break the project down into small steps.**
   You already know that you need to write a paper by a certain date. Breaking up your project into chunks will make it easier to get started. It will also help you track your progress, which makes it easier to adjust your pace if you fall behind.

2. **Gather everything you need.**
   Make a list of the materials you need and gather them so you have everything in one place.

3. **Organize your time.**
   It's human nature to postpone working on dull or difficult assignments. Make yourself start early so time doesn't get away from you. Look at the list of steps you created in step one. Estimate how much time you need for each one. Try to be realistic!

4. **Coordinate your plan with your other activities.**
   Make a list of any other projects you have going on. This includes ongoing projects, such as music lessons and practice, or one-time-only events, like a test. When you have a complete list, assign each entry a number: 1 for most important, 2 for second-most important, and so on. This is called setting priorities, and it's a very important part of planning.

5. **Stick to your plan.**
   Just because you make a plan doesn't mean you're going to stick to it. Plenty of people make plans on paper but never follow through with them. Put your head down and work through the steps you listed.

   If you finish part of the project earlier than expected, go ahead and get a head start on the next phase. That way, if you fall behind later, you have time to get back on track.

Outlining

An outline is a short summary of your main topics and principal ideas. You can use your outline as an organization tool to order your thoughts and notes on the subject you're writing about.

An outline lists the main ideas you want to present in your report in the order in which you want to present them. The procedure for making an outline is the same whether it's short and simple or long and complicated.

1. First, list the important points about a subject.

2. Next, classify the items on the list into meaningful groups.

3. Finally, decide on a method for organizing the groups to present this information clearly and effectively. (For example, move from the least important to the most important points.)

Get Organized

When you feel like you have all the information you need, it's time to review and organize your notes. Read through your notes carefully; then look at your thesis statement. Does it still make sense? Should it be changed somewhat on the basis of what you have learned from your research? Remember, the thesis statement should summarize the purpose of your paper. Be sure you have it right before you go any further.

After you have arranged your information in logical order, group it into large, obvious divisions. These divisions will be your main topics. The number of main topics you include will depend on the assignment. Next, see how your main topics can be subdivided. These subtopics must relate to the main topic. You must have at least two subtopics under a main topic—or none at all.

Formatting

When it comes to outlining, consistency is more important than the particular formatting conventions you use. The final outline can be either a topic outline or a sentence outline, but not a combination of the two. A topic outline summarizes the main points in brief phrases. A sentence outline uses complete sentences for each topic and subtopic.

Whatever form you choose, all the headings in your outline must be expressed in parallel phrasing. That means all topics of equal importance must be equally indented; topics and subtopics are identified by Roman numerals, capital letters, Arabic numbers, and lowercase letters, in that order, followed by periods.

Where Am I in the Seven-Step System?

THE SEVEN-STEP SYSTEM

1. Choosing a Topic
2. Gathering Information
3. Constructing a Thesis
4. **Outlining**
5. Drafting
6. Revising
7. Proofreading

Content

Your outline can be as simple or as sophisticated as you want it to be. Its purpose is to get your thoughts organized and down on paper where you can look at them objectively.

An outline briefly states the main topics and subtopics. Each main topic will later become the main idea sentence for a paragraph. The subtopics will be used as supporting details.

If you discover any gaps in your research as you construct your outline, go back to gather more information.

An outline, like the paper itself, should have an introduction, a body, and a conclusion. The introduction should state the focus or purpose of the paper. Its purpose is to let the reader know what the rest of the paper will cover in detail, so it should contain an abbreviated version of your thesis statement. You can also briefly discuss some historical background and provide important definitions.

Most of your outline will be taken up by the body. Spell out the main ideas of your paper, along with the subtopics that support them, in the body. The body may include explanations, comparisons, contrasts, examples, analogies, facts, and historical details. The level of detail should depend on the length of the paper itself. A 25-page paper usually requires a longer outline than a 10-page paper.

A conclusion is also necessary. This can be a summary of points you have made in your paper, or it can be a restatement of your thesis. It shows the reader that you have demonstrated what you set out to prove. Neither the introduction nor the conclusion has to be spelled out in the outline, since the ideas they detail are covered in the body.

CONSTRUCTING YOUR OUTLINE

1. Place a Roman numeral and a period before each main topic.

2. Indent subtopics under main topics.

3. Place a capital letter and a period before each subtopic.

4. Capitalize the first word of both topics and subtopics.

TOPIC OUTLINE

A topic outline summarizes the chief topics and subtopics of the piece in brief phrases.

Thesis: Car ownership is not all it's cracked up to be.

 I. Introduction
 II. Reasons for buying a car
   A. Convenience
   B. Status
 III. Reasons for not buying a car
   A. Inconvenience
     1. High cost of fuel
     2. Crowded roads
     3. Parking problems
       a. Availability
       b. Weather
   B. Hazards
     1. Highways inadequate
     2. Accidents
   C. Poor financial investment
     1. Initial investment
       a. High taxes
       b. High interest rates
     2. Continuing investment
       a. Fuel
       b. Equipment
       c. Maintenance
       d. Fees (government agencies)
 IV. Conclusion

Drafting

Up to this point, you have jotted down notes and written your thoughts in outline form. The outline is the skeleton of your project. Now you will add the rest of its body and turn it into a living work of prose.

Writing the First Draft

When the time comes for you to write a first draft, do not sit with fingers poised waiting for the perfect sentence to come to mind. At this stage, you simply need to put down the information and ideas you have gathered. You don't even have to use complete sentences. Later, you'll have time to expand and elaborate on those efforts when you go back to change and improve your work. Think of the first draft as the dress rehearsal that comes before the real performance.

Don't feel like you have to begin with the introduction. It doesn't matter where you begin writing the paper.

Your options include

- starting at the beginning.
- starting with another area with which you feel comfortable.
- working on individual paragraphs.
- starting with the area you have the most interest in.

IDEAS FOR YOUR INTRODUCTION

- Begin with general lead-in statements to lead your reader up to the main point of the essay, then gradually focus on the specific thesis statement.
- Make a striking or astonishing claim.
- Begin with an anecdote that will be finished in the conclusion.
- Give an interesting statistic or quotation.
- Ask a provocative question.
- Identify the main points you will cover.

Where you start is up to you, but keep in mind that writing is more than just copying summarized and paraphrased notes in some logical order. Your writing has to have its own voice, which you can achieve by incorporating your own thoughts and ideas. These ideas can provide the direction for all the information on the note cards. Your interpretation of the information will help the reader make sense of it all. Otherwise, your paper will end up a jumble of miscellaneous ideas lumped together.

Where Am I in the Seven-Step System?

THE SEVEN-STEP SYSTEM

1. Choosing a Topic
2. Gathering Information
3. Constructing a Thesis
4. Outlining
5. **Drafting**
6. Revising
7. Proofreading

 *Many writers prefer to draft quickly and spend more time in revision.*

The Three-Part Plan

As you get ready to start writing, think of the three parts of your paper in terms of this simple formula:

- Tell the reader what you are going to say.
- Say it.
- Tell the reader what you said.

You can also think of these steps in terms of sections: *the introduction, the body,* and *the conclusion.*

In the introduction, you briefly introduce your topic, giving the reader a preview of what is to come. The body of the paper—the longest part by far—provides the facts, examples, and details that support the main idea expressed in the introduction. The conclusion summarizes and restates the main idea.

The three parts of your paper should work together to make an effective whole. Strive for an attention-getting introduction—one that will arouse interest and encourage your reader to read on. In the body, make sure each point relates to the subject you are discussing. Do not stray into unrelated material or get caught up in trivial details that do not support your main idea. Your conclusion is your last chance to impress the reader. Try to make it as strong and effective as you can.

1. The Introduction

The introduction is a paragraph that captures the attention of your audience by telling an interesting incident, giving background information, or explaining your interest in the subject. Include your thesis sentence in the introduction of your composition. (See pages 710–711.)

2. The Body

Draft the supporting paragraphs in your composition, making sure that each paragraph has its own topic sentence. The paragraphs should present your ideas in a logical order.

3. The Conclusion

The concluding paragraph of your composition should complete your composition and reinforce the main idea stated in the thesis sentence. A concluding paragraph often includes a clincher sentence that sticks in the mind of the audience.

WATCH OUT!

Set a goal for each writing session. Whether it's one paragraph or one page, having a goal will help you focus on that particular section.

Drafting

Get Organized

As the writer, you get to decide how you want to organize your paper. If you're not sure how to arrange your ideas, experiment by moving paragraphs around until an organizational pattern becomes clear. Different structures suit different topics, so there's no right way to draft.

The main types of organizational patterns include

- **Chronological:** arrange paragraphs according to how the events/ideas occur in time sequence

- **Emphasis:** arrange paragraphs according to how the ideas are presented in order of importance (least to most important, or most important to least)

- **Compare and contrast:** arrange paragraphs to show how two events/ideas are alike or different

- **Pros and cons:** arrange paragraphs to show the pluses and minuses of something

- **Spatial:** arrange paragraphs according to how the details occur with regard to location (left to right, front to back, top to bottom)

- **Cause and effect:** arrange paragraphs according to how the events/ideas relate (from effect to cause or cause to effect).

As you work, frequently look back at what you have already written. Looking back helps you to pick up the thread of your discussion and helps to reacquaint you with the thoughts you are about to pursue.

Make Your Point

Audiences are persuaded by three factors.

- their perception of the author
- their feelings about the message
- their understanding of the argument's logic

Perception. The audience's perception of your powers of persuasion will be based on many things. For instance, poor grammar and spelling mistakes might convince readers that your ideas aren't worthy of their consideration.

Feelings. Readers will often have an emotional response to your ideas. We sometimes imagine that we live in a world in which arguments are evaluated on the basis of the facts, but actually the facts themselves may be perceived differently by different audiences. As you write, consider where the audience is starting from emotionally so you can gauge how they might respond to what you're saying.

Understanding. Readers will also have an intellectual response to your ideas. Consider the logic of your argument, and how that logic will appeal to your audience. What will your audience accept as reasonable evidence?

WATCH OUT!

Begin a new paragraph whenever you want to

- switch to a new idea.
- show a change of time or place.
- emphasize a point.
- break up a large amount of text.

Ideas for Your Conclusion

The ending of an argument is at least as important as any other part. You can engage the reader's attention and pursue an intelligent and convincing thesis, but this success is for nothing if the conclusion goes off the rails. Imagine a movie that draws you in at first, thrills and fascinates you in the middle, but then ends in an entirely unconvincing way.

Ask yourself the following questions to evaluate your conclusion.

- Does the closing add something new? An extension, an application, a recommendation, a connection—some new idea based on the introduction and body?

- Does the closing give the reader a sense of closure? Is it clear that you have finished (and not just quit)?

- Have you avoided claims that are implausible or unwarranted?

TIPS FOR EFFECTIVE DRAFTING

- Don't stop to make spelling and grammar corrections. Put question marks or notes in the margins if you are unsure of a spelling or if you think you see some other error.

- Try not to worry about the way you're using language. Your main goal is to get your ideas on the page. You can make it sound better later when you revise.

- Remember that no one has to see the first draft but you.

- Leave wide margins and a space between each line so you can easily make changes later.

- Always keep your purpose and your audience in mind.

- Use your own language. Don't try to be "cute," but don't try to sound like a professor, either. Write as yourself, a person who is telling something interesting to another person, in as clear and uncomplicated a way as you can.

- Think of your reader. Remember that the reader is the person for whom you are writing in the first place.

Potential Pitfalls

When you transfer your notes into your rough draft, be sure there is a logical connection between your ideas. If you just cut and paste all your notes together, the result will be a paper that jumps from one idea to another without smooth transitions. Connective phrases can help bridge ideas together.

Connective phrases include

- for example.
- in contrast.
- on the other hand.
- in addition.

Linking Ideas	
If you want to...	**Use these words**
add ideas	and, again, moreover, furthermore, besides, too, in addition, also
compare or contrast	likewise, similarly, yet, nevertheless, on the other hand, on the contrary, however, although
prove something	because, since, obviously, in addition, indeed
show exceptions	yet, however, despite, occasionally, still
show time	therefore, soon, finally, previously, next, now, then, later
show cause and effect	therefore, consequently, as a result, thus
repeat an important point	as noted, in brief, as stated previously
emphasize something	obviously, in fact, unquestion-ably, certainly, indeed
give examples	for example, for instance, to illustrate, to demonstrate
conclude	thus, consequently, on the whole, hence, therefore

Revising

The literal meaning of *revise* is "to look again." During revision, your job is to rethink all that you have written to make sure your prose is as clear and effective as possible.

It's important that you approach your paper with an open attitude. Always assume that your writing can be improved. Be willing to make changes—even large ones. Sometimes, you might even have to throw a chunk of text away and start again.

Try to be playful with your text. Test out new things and fiddle around with what you've already written. The worst attitude for revising is to feel too attached to the way you said something the first time. For most writers, the first draft is rarely, if ever, perfect.

It won't hurt to change your words. View the revision process as a game or a puzzle—an opportunity to get something just right. And if you don't like the changes, no harm done; you can always put things back the way they were.

Good writing requires revision, so don't look at revision as an indicator that you didn't write the paper well the first time. It's normal—even expected—for your paper to go through several revisions before it is complete.

REVISION IS

- Removing words, phrases, sentences, or even entire paragraphs
- Adding words, phrases, sentences, or paragraphs
- Moving words, phrases, sentences, and paragraphs around
- Reworking sections and subsections
- Giving time and attention to the changes needed

REVISION IS NOT

- Simply running spell check and grammar check
- Quickly proofreading
- Having a friend glance over the paper

Where Am I in the Seven-Step System?

THE SEVEN-STEP SYSTEM

1. Choosing a Topic
2. Gathering Information
3. Constructing a Thesis
4. Outlining
5. Drafting
6. **Revising**
7. Proofreading

 *The first step in revising is to disown your draft. This may seem like a strange thing to do after all the work you have put into it, but it's necessary. If you let your rough draft cool off for a while, you can read it as if it were written by someone else.*

Reading for Sense

If you can't follow or don't understand what you have written, no one else will, either. Here are some questions you can ask as you read to help identify any trouble spots.

- Do I understand what I have written?
- Can I follow the stream of information?
- How well do my ideas flow?
- How well have I stated my case?
- Will someone new to the subject understand what I am trying to convey?
- Did I just read a rambling series of disjointed facts?

WATCH OUT!

Don't worry about problems with spelling and grammar yet. Revising includes substantial editing of your paper. The polishing stage (proofreading) happens separately in the next step of the writing process.

Development. Ask yourself if each paragraph has enough material to make sense to a first-time reader. Also ask yourself if any points have been raised that need more support or should be discussed more fully. Here are a few things you can try if your paper needs more development:

- Define any terms your readers might not know. As you review your writing, keep an eye out for any words that the reader might not be familiar with. This is especially important for papers about subjects that tend to use technical language, such as science.

- Add details to any description that seems incomplete. Descriptions make your writing more vivid because they help the reader envision what you're talking about. Try to provide examples and illustrations that appeal to the five senses: sight, smell, touch, sound, and taste. (See pages 762–763.)

Accuracy. Make sure your paper doesn't contradict itself. If you come across a contradiction, go back through your notes to resolve it. Sometimes a contradiction can't be corrected because the experts themselves may be in disagreement. If that is the case, it's important to point this out so that it doesn't look like a mistake.

Introduction and Conclusion. These elements of your paper are important because the introduction lures the reader into the paper and the conclusion leaves the reader with a final impression. As you review these sections carefully, ask yourself the following questions:

- How does the thesis expressed actually relate to the body of the paper?
- Does the conclusion relate back to your thesis?

Once you have confirmed that the introduction and conclusion stayed on point, it's time to refine those paragraphs so they become more than statements of intent or summation. In other words, you need to breathe some life into them. As in television commercials or magazine articles, your goal is to entice your reader by presenting your thesis in an intriguing or appealing form.

Revising

Reading for Organization

Writing is a building process with words, sentences, and paragraphs as building blocks. Your goal is to

- choose the best words.
- put them together in clear, grammatical sentences.
- form the sentences into logical, coherent paragraphs.
- arrange and link the paragraphs in a logical order.

Organize Paragraphs. Read through your paper and ask yourself if there is a line of reasoning you can follow.

Your readers need to understand how your ideas relate to each other. Organize your paper by making sure that each paragraph flows smoothly from one to the next in a logical order.

If the reasoning seems fuzzy, go through your paper paragraph by paragraph. The body paragraphs should begin with a topic sentence that all the other sentences support. When you stay on point and avoid rambling, your ideas will fall into place.

WATCH OUT!

If you stumble as you read, that's probably a sign that a sentence needs to be reworked. Don't make your reader work hard to understand you.

Organize Sentences. Use topic sentences to state your main ideas. All your other sentences should have details that support those ideas. Otherwise, your reader might become confused.

Follow these steps to make sure your sentences are well organized:

1. As you revise, circle any sentences that don't relate to the topic sentence.
2. If possible, rephrase those sentences so they fit with the topic sentence.
3. Remove any sentences that you cannot rephrase.

COMPARE AND CONTRAST

The following two paragraphs demonstrate different levels of paragraph organization. Notice that in the first paragraph, the topic sentence introduces a thought that is explored in greater detail through the rest of the paragraph. In the second paragraph, the topic sentence does not relate to the other sentences in the paragraph.

PARAGRAPH 1

I think summertime is the best of all. Because the weather is warm, I participate in many outdoor activities, such as swimming, biking, and hiking. I also like to see all the colorful trees and flowers, to hear the sounds of nature, and to make good use of the longer days.

PARAGRAPH 2

Interviewers judge a job applicant on the basis of two chief factors: the person's achievement and the person's personality. Of course, some interviewers consider other factors as well. It's also wise to learn as much as possible about a job before an interview.

720

Reading for Style

Look, too, for opportunities to say things more clearly and precisely than in the first draft. Look for words that may be unnecessary and take them out. Look for sentences that can be rewritten so that their relationship to what has gone before and to what follows will be as clear as possible. (See also pages 724–731.)

There are two common style errors—and two basic fixes—you should keep in mind as you revise.

Combine short, choppy sentences into one compound or complex sentence. As you wrote your rough draft, your main concern was getting your ideas on the page. Some of your sentences probably sound awkward—take this opportunity to smooth them out.

Break down long, complicated sentences into two or more sentences for easier understanding. When you're writing about a complicated or interesting idea, it's common to use long sentences. Watch for sentences that stretch across more than two lines. You might need to simplify the sentences so your reader doesn't get tangled up.

REVISION CHECKLIST

- Does my writing have a beginning, a middle, and an end?
- Is there a clear, specific thesis for the paper?
- Is the paper organized around the thesis?
- Does each paragraph have a topic sentence?
- Is the order of sentences in each paragraph planned or random?
- Do the sentences in the paragraph support the topic sentence?
- Do the paragraphs have a logical relationship with one another, or are they isolated blocks of information?
- Is the development of the ideas adequate?
- Is my stance on the subject apparent to the reader?
- Is the wording clear and exact?
- Is the introduction strong?
- Does the draft conclude or just trail off?
- Have I included enough facts, examples, and illustrations?
- Is my method of development clear and easy to follow?
- Will my audience be unclear or confused about any of the ideas in my paper?

READING YOUR DRAFT ALOUD

If you have time, set aside your first draft for a day or two after you write it. A short break will help you approach your writing with fresh eyes. When you return to your draft, try to imagine the paper is someone else's work so you can be more critical.

When you return to your paper, read it aloud. Hearing your words will help you catch mistakes and trouble spots—any sections that are unclear or confusing.

If you can, read your paper to a friendly listener. Usually, it's best to read the draft once straight through. When you finish, let your listener silently read the paper a second time. After that second reading, ask him or her to point out the strong and weak points in your writing.

Proofreading

You have gone over your rough draft, filling it in here and thinning it out there. You're satisfied you have included all the information you need to provide. You're also confident that everything in your paper is necessary, understandable, and in its proper place.

Now you're ready to proofread.

Proofreading is the final step; it's the time to check your writing for simple errors. In theory, proofreading should be an easy, straightforward process. Often, though, it can be difficult to spot errors because you have already spent so much time with the paper. You might have to make an extra effort to slow yourself down, reading your paper through, sentence by sentence, paragraph by paragraph, from beginning to end.

Spelling

Running the spell checker on your computer will not guarantee that your paper will be free of spelling errors. The computer only recognizes misspelled words. It cannot, however, decide if you have used an incorrect word. For instance, a spell check can't distinguish between homophones like *your* and *you're*.

Check a dictionary for any words you're not sure about. Verify proper nouns like names and places.

Fact Checking

If you include such items as birth and death dates or publication dates, make sure they are correct. It takes only a few minutes to make sure these details are accurate.

PROOFREADING CHECKLIST

- Spelling
- Fact checking
- Grammar
- Formatting
- Capitalization
- Punctuation

TRICKS OF THE TRADE

Here are some ideas you can try to boost your proof-reading power.

- Start at the end of your paper and read backwards to check for errors.

- If you're using a computer, change the way the document looks by altering the layout or the formatting. Giving your paper a makeover might trick your brain into thinking you're looking at something new.

- Stop yourself from skipping ahead by covering the page with a sheet of paper. Uncover each line of text one at a time to help focus on what you're reading.

- Try working from a printed copy of your paper instead of making corrections on the screen.

- Use a colored pen to mark your changes so you can see them better.

- Avoid distractions like music or television. Focus all your attention on your proofreading.

- Take a break if you find your attention wandering.

Where Am I in the Seven-Step System?

THE SEVEN-STEP SYSTEM

1. Choosing a Topic
2. Gathering Information
3. Constructing a Thesis
4. Outlining
5. Drafting
6. Revising
7. **Proofreading**

Grammar

Mistakes in grammar can confuse the reader and even change the meaning of what you write. Here are some of the most common grammatical errors you should watch for as you proofread your work.

- Run-on sentences
- Sentence fragments
- Subject-verb agreement
- Pronoun agreement
- Unclear pronoun references
- Dangling modifiers
- Misplaced modifiers
- Shifts in verb tense
- Comma splices
- Misplaced apostrophes

FREQUENTLY MISSPELLED WORDS

accommodate	definitely	management
accustomed	dilemma	omitted
Antarctic	eligible	peaceable
approximately	feasible	pneumonia
bankruptcy	fictitious	remembrance
bookkeeper	intermittent	restaurant
bureau	inalienable	scissors
candidate	handkerchief	synchronous
circuit	ninety	tourniquet
commitment	gauge	unmanageable
conscious	jeopardize	veil
correspondence	lieutenant	weird

Formatting

Make sure you use the appropriate format. (Common sense will help you here. Ask your teacher if you are unsure about it.) Your goal is to make a good impression. Your paper should be easy to read, so the reader can focus on what you're saying. The format should support, and not distract from, your ideas. Don't make the reader strain to see what you're saying. If you're writing by hand, skip lines and use your best handwriting.

If the report is for a school assignment, find out ahead of time what information needs to be included on the first page, and where. These items will probably include your name, the teacher's name, the course name and number, and the due date of the report. You should also learn what format to use for page numbering and whether you need to include your last name on every page.

The best starting point for a title page is usually one-third of the way down. Center the title, then skip a line and write "by" followed by your name. Remember to provide good margins on both sides of the page and at the bottom.

Strategic Proofreading

Target your personal problem areas to get more out of your proofreading time.

- Be aware of your writing weaknesses. Everyone has different problem areas. Think about the types of errors you make most often. Are you a bad speller? Do you frequently create comma splices? Do you write run-on sentences? If you're not sure, take a look at feedback you've received from teachers in the past.

- When you proofread your writing, do a separate read-through where you focus on your personal problem areas. If you have an issue with sentence fragments, check every sentence to make sure it has a subject and a verb. If you have trouble with pronouns, focus on those.

- Address the source of your mistakes by spending extra time learning how to fix your problem areas. While it may take some effort, it will save you time in the long run.

STYLE is not what you say, but how you say it. The writer David Foster Wallace said that every sentence communicates in at least two different ways. On one level, the words convey content, or raw data. But on another level, the words also express something about the speaker's personality or sensibility. As you write, think about what you want your words to say about you.

Style Basics

There are many different ways to say the same thing. Style is not a matter of correctness; it's about the words you choose and the way you arrange them into sentences.

As you write more and more, your style will naturally improve. Most writers think mainly about what they're saying; the options they have in saying it become secondary.

Finding Your Style

Understanding your own style in a specific way can be revealing, and comparing your style to that of other writers can also be helpful. For instance, to take the most obvious statistic, you could check to see how long your sentences are and compare your average to that of some other writers. Do your sentences tend to be shorter, longer, or about the same?

Here are some other things you can count and compare.

- Number of *to be* verbs
- Number of images or comparisons
- Number of modifying words (See pages 664–669.)
- Length of paragraphs (number of words and number of sentences)

David Foster Wallace (*above*) wrote *Infinite Jest,* a long novel noted for its different voices and word choices drawn from widely varying fields of study.

"If the writing is solid and good, the mood and temper of the writer will eventually be revealed and not at the expense of the work. Therefore, the first piece of advice is this: to achieve style, begin by affecting none—that is, place yourself in the background."

from *The Elements of Style* by William Strunk, Jr., and E. B. White

Finding a Rhythm

Parallelism can give your prose a pleasing rhythm. It can add force and elegance to your writing, and it's not that hard to create. Here's how.

- Nouns in a series should be in the same form. The phrase "dancing, eating, and movies" should be changed to "*dancing*, *eating*, and *watching* movies."

- Other parts of speech should also be parallel when they appear in a series. For example, "The actor moved *behind* the screen, *around* the column, and *under* the tree."

- Make the items in a list parallel. "The carpenter should follow the usual procedure: *dip* the furniture in solvent; *scrape* off the loose paint; *sand* out any large scratches."

- Parallel clauses are useful in placing ideas side by side for comparison, contrast, or connection.

> *Learning to recognize and write in different styles is an important life skill. You wouldn't want to use the same style for a casual e-mail and a cover letter for a job application. Using a casual tone in a formal situation is like wearing jeans to a fancy wedding.*

ACTIVE VOICE VS. PASSIVE VOICE

A verb is in the active voice when the subject of the sentence performs the action. The passive voice, on the other hand, features a subject that is acted upon. Most good writing is in the active voice because it produces prose that is clear, direct, and forceful. Consider the difference in directness and forcefulness in these sentences.

Active voice: He wrote it.

Passive voice: It was written by him.

Once in a while, though, you'll find that the passive voice is your best choice. For instance, it makes sense to use the passive voice whenever the person or thing receiving the action is more important than the one doing it.

He was shocked by her refusal to marry him.

You may also use the passive voice when you do not know who said or did something.

It's been said that there's no fool like an old fool.

Or when it's not important to know who did something.

The test tube was filled with nitrogen.

 *If you can't imagine yourself saying what you've written, ask yourself how you would say it in conversation. Then write it down and revise that instead of starting with the original written version.*

Cutting the Fat

Always assume that you can make your writing tighter and leaner. If you look close enough, you'll almost always find sentences, phrases, and words that you don't really need. Make sure that every word works hard. If a simpler word or phrase will do the same job, use that instead.

Your goal is to be as succinct as possible without sacrificing clarity.

Don't Repeat Yourself

One good way to cut the fat is to avoid redundancy. Writing becomes redundant, or repetitive, when you use more than one word that means the same thing. Consider how the following phrases each use two words that mean the same thing.

free gift	gifts are always free
advance forward	*advance* and *forward* are synonyms
circle around	*circle* and *around* are synonyms
current trend	trends are always current

Another way to tighten your prose is to cut extra prepositional phrases. Whenever you have a string of prepositional phrases, check if any can be collapsed or eliminated.

> The imbalance of chemicals in the liver of the patient caused problems for the intern on the evening watch.

Removing some of the prepositional phrases takes this sentence from 19 words to 14.

> The chemical imbalance in the patient's liver caused problems for the evening-watch intern.

Wordy	Lean
ahead of schedule	early
almost never	seldom, rarely
along the same lines	similarly
at a loss for words	speechless
at the present time	today, now
by and large	generally
center of attention	focus
due to the fact that	because
familiar landmark	landmark
few and far between	rare
have a need for	need
in terms of	regarding
in the event that	if
in the near future	soon
in this day and age	today, now
safe to say	reasonable

Speak Plainly

Don't try to dress up your writing to be something that it's not. Instead of making a special effort to use big words, try to explain things as simply as possible.

Avoid Foreign Language Expressions. Don't use non-English expressions unless a word or phrase is common enough in English to be found in a dictionary. You'll sound like you're putting on airs. Foreign language expressions are hard to understand, pretentious, and almost always unnecessary.

If you must use a foreign word or phrase because it doesn't translate into English, write the foreign word in italics followed by its rough English equivalent in parentheses.

Avoid Jargon, Slang, and Euphemism. Jargon and slang may not be understood by your reader. Even if it is understood, that kind of language will make the tone of your paper too informal. Euphemism, the substitution of a polite, roundabout way of referring to something disturbing or unpleasant, can make your paper sound prissy.

Avoid Informal Language. Informal language that might be okay in conversation is often unacceptable in writing. Make sure you use a word correctly when you write it.

Avoid Clichés. Clichés are worn-out words and phrases that have been used so often that they've lost their meaning. Writing with clichés is lazy and careless. It suggests that you haven't thought out exactly what you want to say.

> "Young writers often suppose that style is a garnish for the meat of the prose, a sauce by which a dull dish is made palatable. Style has no such separate entity; it is nondetachable, unfilterable. The beginner should approach style warily, realizing that it is an expression of self, and should turn resolutely away from all devices that are popularly believed to indicate style—all mannerisms, tricks, adornments. The approach to style is by way of plainness, simplicity, orderliness, sincerity."
>
> from *The Elements of Style* by William Strunk, Jr., and E. B. White

	What Is It?	Example	Better Choice
Jargon	the specialized language of a particular group or profession	BPO epidermis	business process outsourcing skin
Slang	language that is flashy or trendy	LOL (the acronym for laugh out loud)	That's funny.
Euphemism	an indirect expression	passed away	died

Phrasing

Say that ten different people bought the same shirt at a department store—same style, same color, same everything. One person might choose to wear the shirt untucked with jeans. Another person might roll up the sleeves. Someone else might wear a vest over it.

Similarly, the way you arrange words in a sentence is a matter of personal preference.

It's possible to phrase the same information in many different ways. The choices that you make as you arrange words into a sentence are probably different from the choices someone else would make. It's not that one form is more correct than another; it's simply a matter of taste.

While everyone's phrasing is different, there are a few techniques you can use to make your style more lively.

There are four simple ways you can "mix things up" as you write.

WATCH OUT!

Pay attention to shades of meaning. When you use a thesaurus, make sure that you fully understand the meaning of an alternate word before you use it. Some synonyms are closer in meaning than others. Mark Twain famously described the difference between the almost-right word and the right word as the difference between a lightning bug and lightning.

Vary Sentence Length

Mixing the length and the structure of your sentences keeps things interesting. Some sentences are short. Other sentences, like this one, are longer, so they will take longer to read. Still others can join with another sentence using a semicolon; they can run for several lines, as you see here.

Vary Paragraph Length

Ideally, the length of your paragraphs should reflect the ideas they contain. Very short paragraphs are dramatic. They draw attention to themselves by interrupting the flow and ending abruptly. Long paragraphs work well for sorting through a complex idea. They allow you to follow a line of thought for an extended meditation. But if every paragraph were long, reading would seem like hard work. Short paragraphs provide little mental breaks to keep your reader moving along at a satisfying pace.

Vary Word Choice

It's also important to vary your word choice. When you have been writing about a topic for a while, it can be tempting to use the same words over and over. Avoid repetition whenever you can. If you can't think of a synonym on your own, try using a thesaurus (or even a dictionary).

Watch Your Punctuation

Periods and commas are a dime a dozen, but make sure you use special punctuation sparingly. (See pages 694–701.) Beginning a paragraph with a question can be effective, but asking too many questions in a row is ineffective. Use an exclamation mark only when you really need one. Using too many can make your writing seem crazed.

"Who can confidently say what ignites a certain combination of words, causing them to explode in the mind? Who knows why certain notes in music are capable of stirring the listener deeply, though the same notes slightly rearranged are impotent? These are high mysteries."

from *The Elements of Style* by William Strunk, Jr., and E. B. White

Use Specific Details

One of the most common problems in writing is saying too little, taking for granted that the reader can see or understand whatever is clear to the writer. Consider the difference between these two sentences:

After a boring day, he went home.

After a lengthy discussion of the paper towel allotment, an unnecessary and uneventful meeting with his assistant, and four hours of staring out the window, he went home.

Good writing is a mixture of the specific/concrete and the abstract/general. Movement back and forth between the two sides of the spectrum is effective. So, if you want to talk about "the car," that's fine—just include some concrete discussion. And if you want to talk about the windshield-wiper design on your blue Honda Civic, that's fine too; just make sure you include some reference to the general big picture.

Instead of using general nouns and abstractions, try to use specific language and solid images. The phrase "the person" seems vague and hazy, but "the middle-aged farmer" provides a clear picture. Use analogies and anecdotes to make abstract concepts such as love, time, good, and evil come alive.

One way to add details to bland sentences is to use appositives. Appositives add information to a sentence by renaming a noun. Consider these two sentences.

Samuel Johnson said many witty things.

Samuel Johnson, the eighteenth-century author, said many witty things.

Adding the appositive *the eighteenth-century author* gives the reader more information about Samuel Johnson.

REPLACE WEAK VERBS AND AVOID UNNECESSARY MODIFIERS

Use more active, more vivid, and more precise verbs.

Instead of saying, "He walked slowly along," you might want to say, "He meandered."

Instead of, "The new recipe is better than the old one," you might want to say, "The new recipe grabs your taste buds, while the old one just teases them."

Most teachers and style guides will tell you to watch out for *to be* or linking verbs—*is, am,* or *was*. When most of your sentences simply say that "X is Y," then it is likely that your prose is not very vivid or active. So, when you're revising, enliven some of your linking verbs.

If you use the right noun or verb to begin with, you will not need many modifiers. Modifiers sometimes weaken prose. "The abandoned child was left behind" can be changed to "the child was abandoned." "He walked quickly" can be changed to "he hurried."

Integrating Quotes

Using quotes is a great way to add credibility to your argument. The key is to use enough quotes to support your ideas without letting someone else's voice take over your paper. It's important that you write in your own voice.

Try to find the middle ground between using too many and too few quotes. Quotes are meant to strengthen and validate your paper, not take over the content. Well-chosen and properly placed quotations will help you build credibility.

When to Use a Quote

Select quotes with care. Use them sparingly; often, you may choose to write a paraphrase or a summary instead.

Good reasons to use a direct quote include

- to present an important, significant, or key thought by an expert.

- to showcase language that is memorable or unique.

- to present an idea that conflicts with the main-stream thought.

- to share specialized or technical information, such as statistics.

OTHER GOOD WAYS TO INTEGRATE A QUOTE

- Comment on it
- Critique it
- Put it into context
- Connect it to something else

Integrating a Quote

As you are writing, there will be times you want to incorporate direct quotations into the body of your paper. Keep in mind that while you may understand the quotation and know exactly why you feel it belongs where it does, your reader might need some context. Don't just insert the quotation without explaining its purpose or introducing it. It needs to flow into the body of the paper just as if you had written it, or it needs to stand out as the authority and be introduced by whistles and bells.

Here's how.

Select Your Quote. First, make sure to choose a quote that illustrates the point you're trying to make. You might be tempted to pick a quote that sounds good, even when it doesn't relate to your topic. Don't!

Determine How the Quote Fits with the Rest of Your Writing. No quote stands alone; it must have some sort of context so it doesn't stick out like a sore thumb. Your job is to make any given quote feel like it belongs with the rest of your text.

Introduce the Quote. When you meet a new person, it's customary to introduce yourself before you launch into a conversation. Similarly, you need to introduce a quote into your paper before you begin the quote itself.

A simple way to fold in a quote is to signal the transition to your reader with a lead-in phrase. Much like when you introduce people in real life, you need to acquaint your reader with the source.

Explain the Quote Further, if Necessary. Occasionally, a quote will be so self-contained that it requires no further explanation. More often, you'll need to elaborate on your quote so your reader understands exactly how it relates to your point.

Lead-In Phrases

Look at the following excerpt from a student paper on organ donation, which shows how you can use lead-in phrases.

According to Lee Gutkind, author of *Many Sleepless Nights*, "Only one percent, or 25,000 of the 2.5 million people who die in this country each year, die under circumstances suitable to become candidates for organ donation. What is even more unfortunate is that only 15 percent of the possible 25,000 actually become donors" (77).

Transitional Phrases

Now look at the same example with the addition of material that comments on the quote. The comment helps ease the reader out of the quoted material and into a related topic.

According to Lee Gutkind, author of *Many Sleepless Nights*, "Only one percent, or 25,000 of the 2.5 million people who die in this country each year, die under circumstances suitable to become candidates for organ donation. What is even more unfortunate is that only 15 percent of the possible 25,000 actually become donors" (77). **These statistics suggest** that there will always be a shortage of donors using the current methods of procurement. Because of this, researchers are looking into alternative ways of providing viable organs to patients in need of a transplant.

PUNCTUATING QUOTES

There are special rules for quotation marks that adjoin other punctuation.

1. **Commas and periods are placed inside closing quotation marks.**

   "I will go now," she said, "and be back in an hour."

2. **Semicolons and colons are placed outside closing quotation marks.**

   She said, "I'll go to the store"; but then she stayed home.

3. **Quotation marks and exclamation points are placed inside the closing quotation marks if they belong to the quotation.**

   "What book are you reading?" he asked.

4. **If question marks and exclamation points are not part of the quotation, they go outside the quotation marks.**

   "Did they sing 'America the Beautiful'?"

TYPES OF WRITING

There are three basic kinds of writing: *argumentative, expository,* and *narrative.* Many writing projects will combine all three forms. It's important to understand these types so you have them at your fingertips, whether you're working on an essay, a test, a research paper, or another type of analysis.

Argumentative

Argumentative writing, also called persuasive writing, attempts to convince the reader to agree with the writer's ideas, opinions, or attitudes. Argumentative writing may also attempt to convince the reader to follow a particular course of action.

Arguing a Position

Use a variety of the following techniques when constructing an argument: give facts and/or examples, relate incidents, and present opposing views. An effective argument must be supported by evidence. (See pages 810–811.) It is not enough to simply give an opinion.

TIPS FOR ARGUMENTATIVE WRITING

- Choose a topic that has at least two clear sides.
- State your position clearly at the beginning of your text.
- Make sure you differentiate between facts and opinions.
- Be reasonable and maintain an even tone. If you sound angry or defensive, you may put readers on edge and make them less receptive to your ideas.
- Make sure you support your ideas. It's not enough to explain *what* you think; you need to explain *why* you think it.
- Don't get carried away with your claims. Try to be as specific as possible.
- Give some thought to the other side's position. It will help you explain why you disagree with it.
- Choose a topic you know something about or that you can research adequately in the amount of time you have.

Arguing for a Course of Action

Give special consideration to the audience when organizing an argument that tries to persuade people to take a course of action. Persuading people to do something is usually more difficult than persuading them to agree with an idea or an opinion. When arguing for a course of action, use the kinds of evidence used in arguing for a position. In addition, follow the guidelines below.

1. Avoid offending the readers with insults and abusive language.

2. Use language that readers can understand. Do not use language that is condescending or confusing.

3. Use facts to support your opinion. Facts are convincing evidence.

4. Organize your argument by giving the least important facts first and the most important facts last. That way, you will conclude with your most convincing evidence.

5. Summarize your argument at the end by stating the course of action you feel the readers should take.

WATCH OUT!

Make sure you can defend your argument. If you're having trouble thinking of or finding evidence to support your opinions, that's a good sign you need to rethink the issue.

WEAK ARGUMENT

The following argument is not convincing because it does not offer proof to support the writer's opinions.

Cultural exchange programs between countries are, in my opinion, of little value. This sending of a lot of singers, dancers, and musicians back and forth is not going to solve any problems. Maybe some good feeling is created, but the stage cannot take the place of the conference table. And just try to sing away a stockpile of atomic bombs. When foreigners see our entertainers—and our sports stars, too—they realize how much better we are, and this makes them jealous.

STRONG ARGUMENT

The following argument is convincing because it uses reasons and facts to support the writer's opinion.

Employers should be allowed to pay teenagers less than the minimum wage. Minimum wage laws were passed to protect workers trying to support themselves and a family. However, most teenagers are not self-supporting. Many employers are willing to hire teenagers but cannot afford to pay them minimum wage because of their inexperience. But how can young people get job experience if no one is willing to hire them? Permitting teenagers to work for less than minimum wage would allow them to gain valuable job experience. It would also reduce the high level of youth unemployment.

Expository

Expository writing is writing that explains something. You will probably work more with exposition than any other kind of writing. Expository writing answers questions such as

- Who or what is the person or thing under discussion?
- Why is that person or thing important?
- What does the person or thing do?
- How does the thing work?
- What is its origin?
- How did it develop?

Avoid using personal pronouns such as "I" and "my" in expository writing. Instead, focus on the question you're trying to answer for the reader: the who, what, how, or why.

Elements of Expository Writing

There are a number of different elements in expository writing. Ways of supporting the thesis statement will vary depending on your content. Not every technique will be used in every piece of exposition.

Thesis. The thesis states the main idea of the composition. All sentences in a piece of writing should support the thesis statement. Expository writing always requires a thesis statement.

Examples. Examples are a great way to support your thesis. They help illustrate abstract concepts for readers.

Comparisons and Contrasts. Another good way to support the thesis is to compare and/or contrast one thing with another. Explaining the similarities and the differences helps readers see how concepts relate to one another.

Cause and Effect. Often, some aspect of your thesis can be explained by using a cause-and-effect relationship. A cause is something that brings about some action or result. An effect is what happens as a result of the cause.

Definitions. You can use definitions to support the thesis statement. A definition explains something by telling what it is or how it works.

Processes. Support your thesis statement by explaining how something operates or works. Process explanations usually take the reader through a process step by step.

TIPS FOR EXPOSITORY WRITING

- Begin writing with a clear goal in mind.
- Try to stick with one idea per paragraph.
- The thesis is the only element of expository writing that is required. Don't feel like you have to cram all of the others into one essay.
- Instead, choose a few of the elements that work best with your material.

EXPOSITORY WRITING SAMPLE

1   Most Paris neighborhoods these days are a striking blend of the old and the new. Narrow nineteenth-century buildings still dot the residential streets, but they now coexist with towering modern apartment complexes. Down in the commercial areas, small decades-old shops specializing in one commodity—cheese, perhaps, or fish or fruit or baked goods—stand side by side with huge new supermarkets carrying every food imaginable.

2

3   Like the surreal paintings of the French masters, contemporary Parisian neighborhoods present a striking juxtaposition of contrasts: modern chrome and mottled wood, poured concrete and ancient stone. But, unlike the Surrealists' creations, Paris's transformation is far from fanciful. It is based on cold, hard economic facts.

Real estate prices are soaring in Paris, just as they are in most modernized countries. A lot that ten years ago would have sold for the equivalent of $500,000 in U.S. dollars now goes for at least three times that price. Rents, too, have increased accordingly, echoing the rising property values.

4   The increase in price of land has affected both residential and commercial patterns. Owners of older, smaller residences, tempted by the high prices offered by developers, sell their properties to the highest bidders. Often, neighbors sell en masse, thus opening up the large lots necessary for development of high-rise apartments.

1. THESIS

Notice how the author states the thesis up front, so it's hard to miss.

2. EXAMPLES

The author uses specific examples of old and new structures to support the thesis.

3. COMPARE AND CONTRAST

The author explains how the neighborhoods are like (and unlike) French surrealist paintings.

4. CAUSE AND EFFECT

In the final paragraph, the author explains the causes behind new development in Paris neighborhoods.

Narrative

Narrative writing tells about events that happen. Nonfiction narrative writing usually tells about personal events, incidents, or experiences.

Using Chronological Order

Chronological order is often the organizing principle in narrative writing. Chronological order starts at the beginning of a sequence of events and follows those events step by step until the conclusion.

Using Descriptive Writing

Descriptive writing paints word pictures of particular people, places, or things. It appeals to the reader's senses: sight, sound, touch, taste, and hearing. (See pages 762–763.)

Selecting Details. Limit your subject before choosing details. Since effective description calls for a selection of the most significant details, it is often better to tell less about a subject but to tell it well.

Concrete details are specific, precise details that create an impression. They are not general or abstract.

The concrete details in the following example are in **bold** type.

> I saw him standing outside the train station, clutching his **white cane** and rattling the coins in his **battered tin cup**. His clothes were **old and tattered**, and he wore a **thin coat** even though it was the dead of winter. The **tempting odors of bacon and eggs** drifted from a restaurant a few doors away, where customers sat eating their fill in **comfortable booths** near the window.

TIPS FOR NARRATIVE WRITING

- **Appeal to readers' senses.** Using vivid details helps readers form strong images as they read.

- **Keep the reader oriented in time.** Make it clear to the reader when you are talking about the past, present, or future.

- **Pretend that you're telling a story.** Is your story funny? Suspenseful? Sad? Or something else?

- **Stay focused.** The key to a good narrative is to stay on track and keep the story moving.

- **Make an emotional appeal.** Choose a subject you have strong feelings about. Your writing is more likely to be compelling if it has some heart.

- **Don't lose track of the reason you're writing the narrative.** Are you merely sharing information? Or is there some other goal?

WATCH OUT!

If you don't understand what you're describing, chances are that your reader won't understand, either.

Short stories are sometimes considered fictional narrative writing.

Notice how the descriptive language in the passage below appeals to three of the five senses.

TOUCH

TOUCH

SMELL

SIGHT

We reached the top of the hill, dropped our backpacks, and stretched out on the **soft** grass that covered the **cool** earth. The air was filled with the **fragrance** of hundreds of brilliant wild flowers, their dense pattern and colors—**purple, pink, red, orange, and blue**—spread out like Oriental carpets displayed at a bazaar.

Using Flash-Forwards and Flashbacks

Use flash-forwards and flashbacks to create a special emphasis. A flash-forward is a device that a writer uses to tell about an event before it happens in straight chronological order. A flashback tells about an event that happened at an earlier time in the narrative.

When I stepped on the stage at the age of six to give my first violin recital, my heart was racing and the blood was pounding in my throat. I walked timidly to the center of the stage, made a stiff bow, brought the instrument up to my shoulder, and started to play.

Had I anticipated the thunderous applause that would greet me at the end of my performance, I would have been less nervous. My mother and father leapt to their feet and cheered. There were even calls for an encore.

But all that possible adulation was far from my mind as I made those first scratchy noises on my half-size violin. At the start of the recital, all I wished for was its conclusion.

Writing Under Pressure

An essay exam or timed essay can be thought of as a particular kind of expository writing. The form usually requires you to recall information quickly, to present it in a logical, orderly fashion, and to draw conclusions. As you read an essay exam question, it is important that you know what you are being asked to do. Look for the strategy term or phrase, which tells you how to approach the task of writing.

Key words in the questions will dictate the way you answer the question. Words to watch for include

- analyze
- define
- compare
- contrast
- describe
- explain
- summarize

WATCH OUT!

Make sure you always answer the question that is being asked. Remember to look back at the question as you write to make sure you're on the right track.

Five-Step Process

Use a five-step process to write your exam essay.

Step 1: Identify Your Topic

Before you begin to write, examine the question to find your topic. Be sure you understand what you are being asked to define, analyze, discuss, evaluate, or explain. You may want to circle the key word.

Step 2: Plan Your Essay

Once you understand what you are being asked to do, spend about 10 percent of your time planning your essay. Once you have determined the strategy for your essay, you will begin the second component of your exam—content. Prepare a quick outline by jotting down important points.

Step 3: Develop Your Outline

One approach to beginning your outline is to make a list of the main points you plan to cover in your essay. Fill in the list with supporting examples. The examples you plan to include should be noted in your outline by jotting down important points and subpoints.

Step 4: Formulate Your Thesis

After you have developed an outline, you can formulate your thesis. This approach is different from the way you normally write an essay, in which you develop your thesis first. Because you are in a time-pressured situation, writing the outline first and developing your thesis from it saves time and keeps you from forgetting a key piece of information.

Step 5: Writing the Essay

Once you are ready to write, keep the following points in mind.

- Clearly state your thesis and establish the essay's structure.
- Be direct and to the point.
- Provide examples and clear explanations.
- Avoid digressions and generalizations.
- Do not restate the question in the essay.
- Follow your outline closely.
- Use transitional phrases to move from one point to another.
- Write neatly and leave room for editing corrections.

How to Take a Test

Test-taking in general requires a strategy. These four steps can help you organize your limited time.

1. **Take a moment or two to read through the whole test.** Read all the instructions carefully. Notice how many questions there are and try to get a sense of how much time you will have for each question. Decide how much time you'll spend on different sections of the test.

2. **Read each question carefully.** If you misunderstand the question, you will answer it incorrectly no matter how much you know about the subject. Some tests have questions with tricky wording just to test your understanding. If a question seems complicated, read it a second time.

3. **Skip questions you aren't sure about.** It's best to answer all the questions that seem easy first. Then you can use all the remaining time to consider the more difficult questions. This will keep you from getting a mental block and will assure that you answer everything you know best before time runs out.

4. **Take the last two or three minutes to read through your answers.** This is especially important on essay tests. When you write quickly, you may leave out an important word. In multiple-choice tests, make sure that you have put your answers in the right space or column and (if there's time) that each answer seems reasonable.

EDITING YOUR ESSAY EXAM

Remember that you need to save some time for revising and editing your answers. Follow the same guidelines as you would for any paper. Helpful questions include

- Does the thesis answer the question on the exam?
- Is the thesis clearly stated?
- Have all the major points been covered?
- Are the details specific?
- Is each sentence complete?
- Are the spelling and grammar correct?
- Is the writing legible and neat—even with cross-outs and inserts?

BEFORE THE TEST

- Take good notes during class.
- Take good notes as you read assignments.
- Review and outline your notes periodically.
- When the time for the test approaches, make detailed outlines based on your notes.
- Try to determine which points have been stressed and repeated most often in class. Have you noticed any recurring themes? Is there a thread that ties all the major points together?
- Write down several possible test questions, and try to answer at least one of them before the exam as practice.

EXAM TIPS

- Begin by reading all the questions.
- During the exam, take time to prepare each answer.
- If you have several questions from which to choose, answer only the required number.
- Devote the appropriate amount of exam time to your answers according to the point value of the questions. For example, on a 100-point exam, a 30-point question should be allotted one-third of the exam time since it is worth approximately one-third of the grade.

ESSAYS are short nonfiction compositions that present the writer's opinion or analysis of a particular subject. Essays make up a major form of literature that includes many types of writing, such as book reviews, magazine articles, and newspaper editorials.

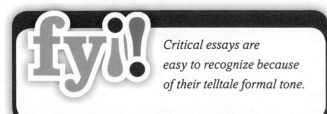

Critical essays are easy to recognize because of their telltale formal tone.

Critical Essays

Tracing Causes and Effects

Critical essays are typically formed around a central argument.

One good way to explain an argument is by demonstrating cause-and-effect relationships. A cause is something that brings about some action or result. An effect is what happens as a result of the cause.

In the paragraph below, every sentence describes some sort of cause or effect. Notice how those causes and effects relate to one another as you read.

1   **Interchangeable parts** and the assembly line increased auto production while decreasing the cost of manufacturing. This brought **car prices** 2 down. The installment plan helped people who could afford to buy a car only by making piece-meal payments. New oil discoveries kept the price of gasoline low. Responding to popular demand, states began extensive road-building programs. 3 By the 1920s, the **United States** was a nation on wheels. This, in turn, stimulated **growth** in auto 4 service businesses, and created motels, roadside restaurants and dance halls, and the drive-in movie.

1. Interchangeable parts are what caused the increase in auto production and the decrease in the cost of manufacturing.

2. Car prices went down because of the causes listed in the first sentence.

3. America became a nation on wheels because of installment plans, low gasoline prices, and road-building programs.

4. Growth was stimulated by all the drivers who were on the road by the 1920s.

ESSAYS IN HISTORY

Critical essays are a staple of academic life. When you write a literary analysis paper, for instance, you'll have to read through many critical essays in order to learn what the experts have said about your topic.

Formal essays were developed by Sir Francis Bacon, an English philosopher and statesman of the late 1500s and early 1600s. Bacon was the first English essayist. One of his major works was *Essays* (1597), a collection of 10 essays that explain how to lead a sensible life. These essays are short, impersonal, and informative, and they discuss such subjects as death, fear, truth, and wealth.

Essays have been important through literary and political history. The English poet and essayist John Milton wrote the *Areopagitica* (1644), one of the finest examples of a formal essay. It is a persuasive appeal to Parliament to protect freedom of speech and of the press. It was printed as a pamphlet and distributed in London.

▲ **John Milton** (1608–1674) also wrote *Paradise Lost* (1667, revised 1674), *Paradise Regained* (1671), and *Samson Agonistes* (1671). He composed the first two of these works, and probably also the last, when he was totally blind. (See also page 934.)

◄ **Francis Bacon** (1561–1626) believed all previous claims to knowledge, particularly of medieval science, were doubtful because they were based on poor logic.

Some writing assignments will require you to erase the "I" from your writing, favoring objective prose over the sharing of opinions, thoughts, and feelings. The personal essay asks you to do exactly the opposite. Its purpose is to relay a personal experience. The heart of its subject is you.

Finding the Point

Even though personal essays don't have a thesis, there should be a main idea. As you write, consider what your point is.

One way to approach the personal essay is by describing a "snapshot" from your life—telling a story about a single point in time. Your goal is to convince your reader of the importance of that experience. A good personal essay shows why the experience was important to you. It makes that experience relevant to readers by showing its importance to both you and them.

TIPS FOR WRITING A PERSONAL ESSAY

- If you don't find a topic interesting, your readers probably won't, either.

- Think of an experience that has been important to you in some way. Identify its significance.

- Think about ways in which you can describe the event's significance without stating it directly.

- Use descriptive language to make the experience seem vivid to your reader.

- Describe emotions and thoughts you had during the experience to draw your reader into the story.

- It's not enough to describe the experience; you also need to reflect on it and make that reflection part of your essay.

THE ORIGIN OF THE PERSONAL ESSAY

The first personal essay was crafted by Michel de Montaigne, a French writer of the 1500s. The word "essay" comes from *Essais* (1580), Montaigne's two-volume collection of writings.

Essais is a French word that means trials or attempts, which reflect the exploratory and informal nature of his compositions. His essays are based mainly on personal experience and discuss such topics as idleness, judgment, and lying.

"Write what you know" is a piece of advice often given to writers. A personal essay is a great way to practice writing because the topic is so familiar.

David Sedaris is an American essayist who is widely considered to be a master of the form. In his essay "The Youth in Asia," he talks about the lives and deaths of his pets over the years.

While you read, note the devices Sedaris uses as he tells his story. While humor is his trademark, there are a number of other effective techniques he uses to engage readers.

PERSONAL ESSAY EXCERPT

In the early 1960s, during what **my** mother referred to as "the tail end of the Lassie years," **my** parents were given two collies, which they named Rastus and Duchess. We were living in New York State, out in the country, and the dogs were free to race through the forest.

They napped in meadows and stood knee-deep in frigid streams, **costars in their own private dog-food commercial**. According to our father, anyone could tell that the two of them were in love.

Late one evening, while lying on a blanket in the garage, Duchess gave birth to a litter of slick, potato-size puppies. When it looked as though one of them had died, our mother arranged the puppy in a casserole dish and popped it in the oven, like the witch in **Hansel and Gretel.**

"Oh, keep your shirts on," she said. "It's only set on two hundred. I'm not baking anyone, this is just to keep him warm."

The heat revived the sick puppy and **left us believing that our mother was capable of resurrecting the dead.**

1

3

2

4

5

1. **POINT OF VIEW.** Personal essays generally use the first-person point of view, which is indicated by first-person pronouns like "my" and "I."

2. **TELLING DETAILS.** The reference to Hansel and Gretel emphasizes that the speaker is recalling a memory from childhood.

3. **HUMOR.** Sedaris uses humor to establish an intimate tone.

4. **DIALOGUE.** Use quotes to make the other people in your personal essay come to life.

5. **THOUGHTS.** Sedaris lets readers into his inner world by sharing his thoughts about his mother.

Process Essays

Process essays describe how something operates or works. At the most basic level, a process essay is a set of instructions.

> Threading a needle demands a sharp eye and a steady hand, but it is not a difficult task to accomplish. A right-handed person should hold the needle with the left hand; a left-hander should hold the needle with the right hand.
>
> Many people dampen the end of the thread before placing it through the needle's eye; this reduces friction and smooths out any loose ends. It is important to use a high-quality cotton or nylon thread so that the strands do not unravel as the thread is inserted into the needle's eye.

Notice that in the example above, the author explains both the steps as well as the reasoning behind the steps. The thread must be dampened because it smooths loose ends; good thread is needed to prevent unravelling.

For a process essay, you don't have to spend any time worrying about choosing structure or organization. It will always be chronological.

TIPS FOR WRITING PROCESS ESSAYS

- Take extra time with your outline to make sure you have all the steps in the right order. It will help the writing go faster.

- Use strong verbs. Most processes are driven by action, so make sure you choose the most descriptive, specific verb possible.

- If you think it will help the reader's understanding, explain the reasoning behind the steps you're describing.

- If you are giving someone directions, use the present tense. If you are describing a process you have already performed, use the past tense.

- Use clear, direct language. If someone gave you driving directions, you would probably prefer "turn left" to a more poetic description.

- Stick to the essentials. Don't get sidetracked by information that isn't related to the process you're trying to describe.

- Use words that indicate chronology, such as *first*, *second*, *next*, and *last*.

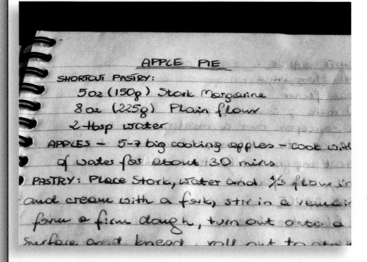

Process essays are like recipes in that they describe how to do something by breaking it down into logical steps.

In his essay "The Philosophy of Composition," Edgar Allan Poe discusses his theory of good writing, which he called the unity of effect. To illustrate his beliefs, Poe walks the reader through the choices he made as he wrote "The Raven," one of his most famous poems. (See pages 942–943.)

While it's unclear if the procedure that Poe describes is true to the actual process he followed as he wrote the poem, the piece stands as a strong example of a process essay.

PROCESS ESSAY EXCERPT

1 **I had now gone so far as the conception of a Raven—the bird of ill omen—monotonously repeating the one word, "Nevermore,"** at the conclusion of each stanza, in a poem of melancholy tone, and in length about one hundred lines. Now, never losing sight of the object supremeness, or perfection, at all points, **I asked myself—"Of all**

2 **melancholy topics, what, according to the universal understanding of mankind, is the most melancholy?" Death—was the obvious reply.** "And when," I said, "is this most melancholy of topics most poetical?" **From what I have**

3 **already explained at some length, the answer, here also, is obvious—"When it most closely allies itself to Beauty: the death, then, of a beautiful woman is, unquestionably, the most poetical topic in the world—equally is beyond doubt that the lips best suited for such topic are those of a bereaved lover."**

1. STEPS

As the essay progresses, Poe describes the steps he used to create his poem. After he selects the word "Nevermore," he sets about deciding on a melancholy topic.

2. LOGIC

Poe describes the reasons why he thinks the death of a beautiful woman is the most poetical topic.

3. QUESTION AND ANSWER

Throughout the essay, Poe asks himself questions and then provides the answers. This is a device that helps move the essay along; the questions stand in for those the reader might ask.

BOOK REPORTS

The book report is a standard school assignment from junior high on up. Just because it's common doesn't mean it has to be a dull, pointless exercise. Book reports can be surprisingly enjoyable to write. The process of writing book reports sharpens your ability to analyze books and recognize their strengths and weaknesses. They will also help you broaden and refine your writing skills. Remember, the deeper you explore a good book, the more interesting it becomes.

Reading the Book

A book report is not simply a point-by-point retelling of the book, nor is it a free-flowing presentation of your thoughts and opinions. Instead, it should have a definite form and structure.

Good book reports

- present a concise (yet thorough) description of the book.
- analyze the book's strengths and weaknesses.
- describe key plot points in general terms.
- avoid spoiling the ending for someone who hasn't yet read the book.

Choosing the Right Book

Perhaps the most common difficulty shared by book report writers is selecting the right book.

Consider Your Assignment. Are you required to write about a particular genre (such as fiction or nonfiction) or topic? If not, just choose something you think you'll enjoy.

Check the Book's Length. A 1,200-page novel may be so rich in characters and subplots that you can't treat it adequately in the limited space of a short book report. (If you're not a rapid reader, you may not even be able to finish the book in time.) On the other hand, a light novel may not provide enough material for any but the shortest book report.

Check the Cover. Sometimes you *can* judge a book by its cover. Read the blurb on the inside leaf of the dust jacket or the back cover of the book to see if it looks interesting.

Read a Little. Are the first few pages of the book interesting? Do they make you want to read more? Do the characters seem intriguing? If the answers are yes, consider using the book for your report.

Reading Tips

Read the Entire Book. You may be tempted to read the first few chapters and then skim the rest of the book to find out how it ends. Don't do it. You might think you'll save time, but the truth is that it is actually much more difficult to write a coherent, interesting book report about a book you aren't really familiar with.

Give the Book Your Full Attention. When the writer was laboring over the book you have selected, you can be sure that his or her attention was focused completely on the work at hand. When you settle down to read a book, try to do the same.

Give Yourself Plenty of Time to Read the Book. Once you've chosen your book, it's best to start reading right away. Estimate how long it will take you to read so you leave enough time to write the report.

Take Notes. One of the most useful things you can do while you read is to write down important ideas and good quotes as you come across them. Don't let the notes become a distraction. Write just enough to help you focus your attention on the material you're reading. Make sure you write down page numbers, especially for quotes.

Reread. Don't try to report on a book you read months or years ago unless you reread it. As you write the report, allow yourself time to skim or reread sections of the book as needed.

Always use the present tense when you write about characters and events in a work of fiction. Use the past tense when you write about the people and events in a nonfiction book.

Writing the Report

Ready, Set, Write!

When you finish reading, you may be tempted to sit down and immediately begin writing your paper. But you will find the writing task much easier if you first spend some time thinking about the book you have just read.

Collect Your Thoughts. Consider how much material the book offers for thought. A fast-paced suspense novel may not contain many deep thoughts to ponder. A book about American foreign policy in the nuclear age may contain so many ideas that it will take you some time to sort through them.

Refresh Your Memory. You may want to reread a paragraph or a page or two here and there. Review your notes. Soon you should begin to get a good idea of the important points you want to include in your report.

Ask Yourself Questions. There are three main questions you should consider when thinking about the book for your report: What is the book about? What is the author trying to say? What do you think about it, and why?

Write an Outline. If your book report is relatively short (say, five to seven paragraphs), you can just make a simple list of the facts and ideas you want to present.

Sample Book Report

1. OPENING PARAGRAPH

The first paragraph gives a general overview of the book you have read. Include the complete title of the work, the name of the author, what genre it is, and a general description of the book's contents, theme, or story line.

2. BODY (PARAGRAPHS 2–7)

Use the middle part of the book report to give a more fully developed description of the book's contents. Try to answer the basic questions, such as:

- Who?
- What?
- When?
- Where?
- Why?

Discuss the main characters and give a general but thorough synopsis of the plot and setting, telling what happens and when the story takes place. Also, discuss any important facts about the book's structure or the author's writing style and how these elements help advance the plot or the central theme.

3. CONCLUSION

Use the final paragraph to tell what you think about the book. Explain what you liked, what you disliked, and why. Decide whether the author accomplished whatever he or she set out to do.

WATCH OUT!

Think of your book report as a means of expressing your reasoned opinions about the book. Then, supply details to support your opinions. As you write, avoid using "I" statements. The elimination of the first person will make your sentences seem more direct and forceful.

1 When Stephen Crane wrote what was to become his best-known novel, *The Red Badge of Courage*, he had never personally witnessed the horrors of battle. Yet this psychological study of the effects of combat on a young recruit during the Civil War has become an American classic. Even today, a century after the novel was first published, it is noted for its realistic depiction of battle and its insight into the effects of warfare on human thoughts and actions.

2 All the events related in the novel center on and are seen through the eyes, thoughts, and emotions of Henry Fleming, a young Union volunteer, during a single, unnamed battle of the Civil War.

It could be any battle of any war, because Crane's real focus is on another battle: the hidden one raging within Henry Fleming as his romantic notions of war are crushed by the realities of fear, suffering, and death. Through Fleming's thoughts and actions, we see that the external conflict, the struggle between the Union and Confederate forces, is the foundation for his internal struggle to come to grips with his own fear and self-doubt.

Henry Fleming had dreamed of the glory of battle, but his first months in the army are filled with marches, encampments, and endless tedium. He spends much of his time wondering whether he will run from battle when the time comes.

The day finally comes when Fleming's regiment is sent into battle. The regiment repulses a Confederate attack, but when a second attack threatens to overwhelm the Union ranks, Fleming and some other soldiers panic and run. Separated from his regiment, Fleming feels burning shame when he learns that the Union line has held. He is ashamed again when he joins a group of wounded soldiers, one of whom keeps asking him, "Where yeh hit?" His shame burns yet again when he meets a mortally wounded friend, a tall soldier named Jim Conklin, who asks him, "Where yeh been, Henry?" Jim dies soon after this, beneath a highly symbolic "red sun . . . pasted in the sky like a wafer" that makes the scene one of blood sacrifice. Jim's death fills Fleming with silent rage.

Fleming meets a group of retreating soldiers, one of whom fells him with the blow of a rifle butt. That night a kind soldier, whose face Fleming never sees, helps him get back to his regiment. Fleming tells his comrades that he has been shot, and he accepts their warm approval and friendship.

The next day the Confederates attack again. Fleming, filled with rage and hatred, fights with an almost inhuman ferocity and shows great courage. When the fighting ends, Henry Fleming comes to terms with the personal shortcomings that the battle has revealed to him; he finally feels "a quiet manhood, nonassertive but of sturdy and strong blood."

3 *The Red Badge of Courage* is definitely not for the squeamish. Crane describes such gruesome details of war as ants swarming over the gray face of a dead soldier, and Jim Conklin's mortal wound, which looks "as if it had been chewed by wolves." Yet Crane's intriguing use of symbols and the sympathetic portrayal of Fleming's inner turmoil and ultimate triumph more than balance out the novel's grimness and make the book well worth reading.

LITERARY ANALYSIS

When you analyze something, you break it down into parts. By looking at its components, you hope to develop a better understanding of the whole. In literary analysis, your goal is to help your reader achieve a better understanding of a particular work of literature. To achieve this goal, you break a literary work into its components and choose the ones you want to discuss in depth.

Approaches

The act of interpreting a literary work is called literary analysis. The process involves

- reading a piece of literature carefully.
- drawing your own conclusions about the author's intent and message in the work.
- looking at the various elements of the work.
- determining which element would best help clarify that message for your reader.
- locating the references from the work itself that will justify your conclusions.

LITERARY ELEMENTS

The elements of literature include these concepts.

- Tone
- Mood
- Plot
- Character
- Setting
- Theme
- Imagery
- Style
- Symbols
- Point of view

Elements of Literature

Before you can analyze a work of literature, you need to know the elements that go into the making of that work. You need to be able to identify its basic components.

 *Sometimes, your assignment may require that you use outside sources to support the connections you make. If so, use those sources to confirm or support your own ideas.*

Analysis

Literary analysis—sometimes called an explication—is basically an *explanation*. It involves breaking down a work into various elements and analyzing those elements one at a time for the benefit of the reader. In most cases, the writing is organized around a thesis.

An explication is based on your analysis of the characteristics and meaning of the work. But, it is important to remain focused on the work you are explicating rather than straying to your own experience or opinions.

Although you will want to stay focused on the work you are explicating, this doesn't mean you will just be paraphrasing or rewording the original piece. Nor will you simply summarize the plot. Instead, you will need to logically analyze the various elements that contribute to the overall effect of the work.

For additional analysis, you can include the comments of a person who is an expert in the field. As with any paper, you will need to document the sources you use, in the proper format.

TIPS FOR LITERARY ANALYSIS PAPERS

- Write your literary analysis with the assumption that your reader is familiar with the work being analyzed. Don't provide extensive summaries of the work. Instead, use excerpts to support your points.

- Provide page numbers for your references whenever you're discussing a short story or a novel. For plays, provide the act and scene numbers. For poems, use stanzas and line numbers. Include these numerical references as part of the sentence introducing your textual example, or place them in parentheses after the example.

- For secondary sources, give the full textual citation for your source on the works cited page.

Three Ways to Understand Literature

Great works of literature can be understood in at least three ways.

Biographical: Literature gives us insight into the author's head and heart. In this sense, it can be approached as the study of great minds in human history.

Historical: Literature gives us insight into other times and places. In this sense, it can be approached as the study of the great movements in human history.

Interpretive: Literature gives us insight into enduring human problems. This approach focuses on the work itself, rather than biographical or historical distractions. The power of great literature lies in its ability to tell a reader what authors from other times and places understand about life's possibilities.

Orphaned Oliver Twist audaciously asks for another helping of gruel in the Charles Dickens classic *Oliver Twist*. (See also page 944.)

Tone and Mood

In writing, the terms *tone* and *mood* mean different things. The concepts are often related, but they are not interchangeable.

Tone	Mood
attitude	atmosphere
author	reader
voice	feeling

Tone

Often, in conversation, people communicate using their tone of voice. Sometimes we interpret whether someone is happy or angry or sad not by the words that they say, but by the way in which the words are said. In literature, too, writers communicate using tone.

Tone involves two main elements.

- Author's attitude toward the subject
- Author's attitude toward the reader

Words you might use to describe tone include serious, silly, formal, informal, sarcastic, humorous, wry, frustrated, academic, confident, confused, enthusiastic, and bored.

LITERARY ANALYSIS CORNER

To write about tone, follow these steps.

- Set aside your personal reaction.
- Focus on the author's attitude toward his or her topic.
- Pretend as if you're describing it to a friend. Think of at least three adjectives you would use in your description.
- Consider how the author's tone aligns with his or her subject matter. Does the tone seem like what you would expect, given the topic? Or is it surprising?
- Think about how the tone furthers the author's purpose. What kind of message does it help create?
- Now focus on the author's attitude toward the reader. Does it seem friendly? Hostile? Angry? Again, think of three adjectives you would use to describe it to a friend.

In his essay "A Modest Proposal," Jonathan Swift proposes that the disadvantaged people of Ireland fatten up their children and sell them as food to the rich. He uses a **mock serious tone** to underline how ridiculous the idea is.

I have been assured by a very knowing American of my acquaintance in London, that a young healthy child well nursed is at a year old a most delicious, nourishing, and wholesome food, whether stewed, roasted, baked, or boiled; and I make no doubt that it will equally serve in a fricassee or a ragout.

While *Moby-Dick* is a serious, dark novel, Herman Melville often uses a **light tone,** as in this excerpt. While the narrator is describing his depression, he uses humor to keep things from getting too dark.

Whenever I find myself growing grim about the mouth; whenever it is a damp, drizzly November in my soul; whenever I find myself involuntarily pausing before coffin warehouses, and bringing up the rear of every funeral I meet; and especially whenever my hypos get such an upper hand of me, that it requires a strong moral principle to prevent me from deliberately stepping into the street, and methodically knocking people's hats off—then, I account it high time to get to sea as soon as I can.

Mood

Mood is the emotional atmosphere of a story or poem. While tone focuses on the author's attitude, mood focuses on the reader's feelings about what he or she is reading.

Just as many different factors affect your mood on a given day, different literary elements contribute to the mood of a text, including

- Tone
- Characters
- Setting
- Theme
- Plot
- Imagery
- Setting

LITERARY ANALYSIS CORNER

To write about mood, focus on your own feelings and reactions to the story or poem. Then think about all the elements that contribute to those feelings.

- Characters: What are the characters' personalities? What are their moods?
- Setting: What kind of emotional charge do you get from the setting? Does it seem happy? Sad? Or something else?
- Theme: What is the message of the story or poem? Is it positive or negative?
- Plot: How does the end of the story make you feel? Was it satisfying? Upsetting? Or something else?
- How does the author's tone help create the atmosphere of the story or poem?
- What kind of images does the story or poem contain? What sort of emotional associations do those images call up?

The **mood** of this passage from Edgar Allan Poe's poem "Annabel Lee" (1849) is **dark and somber.**

The angels, not half so happy in heaven,
Went envying her and me—
Yes!—that was the reason (as all men know,
In this kingdom by the sea)
That the wind came out of the cloud by night,
Chilling and killing my ANNABEL LEE.

In sharp contrast, the **mood** of this passage from Lewis Carroll's *Through the Looking Glass* (1871) is **whimsical and silly.**

"The time has come," the Walrus said,
"To talk of many things:
Of shoes—and ships—and sealing wax—
Of cabbages—and kings—
And why the sea is boiling hot—
And whether pigs have wings."

"But wait a bit," the Oysters cried,
"Before we have our chat;
For some of us are out of breath,
And all of us are fat!"
"No hurry!" said the Carpenter.
They thanked him much for that.

Plot

Plot is the way that events are organized or ordered in a story. Traditionally, plots have a clear beginning, middle, and end that take place within a certain timeframe. Authors typically present a story's events to the reader in chronological order.

There are exceptions. William Faulkner's short story "A Rose for Emily" is a famous example of a story that jumps around in time, shaping the reader's response by rearranging the order of what happened.

Conflict

At the heart of every plot, there is a **conflict** between two forces. There are many types of conflict in fiction, including

- human vs. human
- human vs. society
- human vs. self
- human vs. nature
- human vs. animal
- human vs. supernatural
- human vs. technology

◀ **The central conflict** of *Beowulf*, the Old English epic poem, is human vs. supernatural.

LITERARY ANALYSIS CORNER

In literary analysis, writing about plot in a work of fiction means analyzing the conflict. Explain what the conflict is. Discuss the major events that illustrate the conflict. Describe the climax and its resolution. Since your goal is to help your reader understand the whole work, you must explain what the conflict means in terms of the theme or the message of the work.

OTHER PLOT-RELATED TERMS

Anticlimax:
a conclusion to the rising action that seems disappointing, sudden, or silly

Deus ex machina:
a plot resolution (usually considered "cheating") in which the conflict ends due to a new concept or character

Flashback:
when a story leaps backward to a scene that takes place earlier in time

Foreshadowing:
a clue in the plot that seems to predict or point toward an event that happens later in the story

In media res:
when a story begins in the middle of things instead of at the beginning

Subplot:
a side story that may involve supporting characters or weave in and out of the main plot

Macguffin:
a coveted object that drives a story's plot

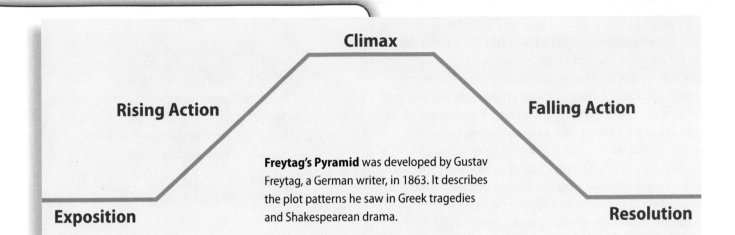

Climax

Rising Action

Falling Action

Freytag's Pyramid was developed by Gustav Freytag, a German writer, in 1863. It describes the plot patterns he saw in Greek tragedies and Shakespearean drama.

Exposition

Resolution

Exposition

The exposition reveals the background information that readers need to understand the story. In an artful exposition, this information seems to be a natural part of telling the story. Readers are often introduced to the setting and main characters.

Rising Action

The rising action describes conflict that arises when forces of some sort work against, or oppose, each other. It is a series of events that thicken, or develop, the story. A problem arises or comes to the forefront.

Climax

The climax is a moment of tension in the story when some decisive action is taken. It is the turning point for the main character, or protagonist.

Falling Action

The falling action shows the consequences, or results, of the climax.

Resolution

The resolution occurs when the conflict is resolved and the story draws to a close.

fyi! *Freytag's Pyramid doesn't apply to every story. Some writers avoid using this plot structure to play with readers' expectations.*

Character

Think about the people in your life and how well you know them. You could probably rattle off a lot of details about your family and close friends, such as their likes, dislikes, skills, and accomplishments. You know less about the lives of your acquaintances—people like your dentist or your neighbor. Then there are strangers that you cross paths with, like the people you pass in the street, about whom you know next to nothing.

Just as you have to pick and choose the people you want to get to know, authors must focus their attention on certain characters. In most stories, there are only a handful of characters you "get to know."

> The terms "round character" and "flat character" were coined by E. M. Forster, the English novelist who wrote Howards End.

Round Characters

The most complex people in a story are called round characters. Round characters are the objects of the author's (and the reader's) attention. They are the people we know the most about. Round characters usually change in some way over the course of the story.

Flat Characters

The simplest people in a story are called flat characters. They are the people we know the least about. Often, a flat character is defined by one major personality trait or feature. Flat characters rarely change over the course of the story.

	Round Character	Flat Character
also known as	main character	secondary character
characteristics	complex dynamic	simple static

LITERARY ANALYSIS CORNER

Ask yourself the following questions as you read and write to learn more about a character.

- How old is the character?
- What does he or she look like?
- What is his or her living situation?
- How would you describe the character's personality?
- Does the author tell you about the character using description, action, or dialogue?
- Is the character predictable?
- Did the character seem realistic? Why or why not?

- Do you recognize the character as a type that you've encountered in other works of fiction?
- What details brought the character to life?
- Do you like the character? Why or why not?
- What is the character motivated by? What does he or she care most about?
- What kind of relationships does he or she have with other characters?
- What do you know about the character's thoughts?

Loki is a shape-shifting trickster god in Nordic mythology. In addition to frequent cameos across the history of Scandinavian literature, Loki was featured as a character in Neil Gaiman's *Sandman* comic books.

Puck got his start in old English folklore, when he was a hobgoblin. Later, in medieval times, he became known as the fairy Robin Goodfellow. But the best-known Puck is probably the trickster in Shakespeare's *A Midsummer Night's Dream,* in which he appears as the mischievous servant of King Oberon. (See pages 964–965.)

Br'er Rabbit was immortalized by Joel Chandler Harris in the Uncle Remus stories, but long before that, the trickster was a folk hero in African-American storytelling. But the rabbit trickster's roots can be traced back even further than that to Africa, where the hare has long been part of oral tradition.

Trickster

The trickster is a type of character that has been around for a long time. When a certain type of character crops up in different forms across many cultures, it becomes known as an *archetype.*

All tricksters share similar characteristics. They live off their wits, getting through tough situations by tricking others. They're clever and foolish at the same time. They're cunning, prideful, and generally very entertaining.

By taking a closer look at three prominent tricksters—*Loki, Puck,* and *Br'er Rabbit*—you can get an idea of how that archetype has evolved over time and across cultures.

Fiction writers often invest meaning in their characters' names. For instance, in To Kill A Mockingbird, *the town eccentric was called Boo Radley, a name that implies he's scary.*

Setting

Setting refers to the location and the time period of the series of events. It can include

- Time of day
- Place
- Historical period
- Social environment
- Cultural environment
- Weather
- Neighborhood
- Geographic location
- Landscape
- Building
- Room
- Season

You may read a story that takes place in one particular location over a relatively short period of time or a story that takes place in multiple locations over an extended period of time. Stories can take place in the past, the present, the future, or in an alternate reality. Some stories may shift back and forth between multiple time periods.

What assumptions could you make about a story that is set during World War II? ▼

WORDS AT WORK

Writers are always looking for ways to convey information to readers without stating it directly. An author can accomplish many different goals by using a story's setting as shorthand. For example, setting can

- influence characters' thoughts, feelings, and actions.
- establish a particular mood or tone.
- reflect a character's emotions (for example, a story about someone who's down in the dumps might be set on a rainy day).
- foreshadow events that haven't happened yet.
- provide a framework for what happens.
- provide a historical context that creates a backstory.

Setting is an important element in "The Fall of the House of Usher," a short story by Edgar Allan Poe. Consider how the weather, season, landscape, time of day, and the house itself are described in this passage.

During the whole of a dull, dark, and soundless day in the autumn[1] of the year, when the clouds hung oppressively low [2]in the heavens, I had been passing along, on horseback, through a singularly dreary tract of country; [3]and at length found myself, as the shades of the evening[4] drew on, within view of the melancholy House of Usher. I know not how it was—but, with the first glimpse of the building, a sense of insufferable gloom pervaded my spirit.

1 **SEASON**

2 **WEATHER**

3 **LANDSCAPE**

4 **TIME OF DAY**

LITERARY ANALYSIS CORNER

Whatever the location or timeframe, when you write a literary analysis based on setting, you are discussing how the setting has an impact on the plot or on the characters.

Here are some questions you can ask about setting as you read.

- Have you been to the place where the story is set? If so, what do you know about that place?

- Is the story set in the past? If so, what do you know about that time in history?

- What kind of language does the author use to describe the setting? Does it seem positive or negative?

- Is the story set in the future? If so, what has changed? What has stayed the same?

- Is the setting realistic?

- What is the atmosphere of the story?

- How does that atmosphere affect (directly or indirectly) the series of events that occurs?

- How does the setting affect the behavior of the characters?

- How does the setting reflect the theme of the story?

- How does the author seem to feel about the setting? What about the narrator?

A shift to a scene in the past from the present is called a flashback. *(See page 737.)*

Theme

The theme is the main point or the central idea that the author is trying to convey to the reader. Every literary work has one, but some themes are more obvious than others.

Sometimes, you will walk away from a literary work with a strong sense of the author's message. You might finish a novel and feel like the writer banged you over the head with a message like, say, "crime doesn't pay" or "honesty is the best policy."

Other times, themes are subtle. A short story may illustrate a social injustice, for instance, without directly commenting on it. The theme may be an exploration of some part of the human life cycle, such as the end of a relationship or the transition into adulthood. Or the theme might just be a snapshot of a human characteristic, such as courage or pride.

While theme is an important element in literature, it doesn't exist in a vacuum; many different parts of a story or poem come together to help create it.

The most basic formula for theme is to consider a work's subject plus the author's attitude toward that topic.

Theme = Subject + Author's Attitude

Theme can be specific to a particular time and place. For instance, Charles Dickens often wrote about the mistreatment of children, a practice that clearly disgusted him, to illustrate his belief in social reform in Victorian England.

Often, enduring literature expresses a universal theme that resonates with readers, no matter who they are, or when they live(d).

LITERARY ANALYSIS CORNER

When you write a literary analysis paper on theme, your goal is to help readers achieve a better understanding of the overarching idea in a literary work. To analyze a theme, ask yourself the following questions.

- What is the main idea that the author wants his or her readers to walk away with?
- What elements of the story or poem contribute to that idea?
- What excerpts can you use to support your ideas about theme?

THEME-RELATED ELEMENTS

Other literary elements that contribute to theme include, but aren't limited to

- Characters
- Setting
- Plot
- Tone and Mood
- Symbols
- Imagery
- Style

UNIVERSAL THEMES

Some of the themes that have been explored by different authors over time include

- Alienation
- Loss of innocence
- Fate versus free will
- Futility of war
- Love and loss

When I Heard the Learn'd Astronomer
by Walt Whitman

1 When I heard the learn'd astronomer,

When the proofs, the figures, were ranged in columns before me,

2 When I was shown the charts and diagrams, to add, divide, and measure them,

When I sitting heard the astronomer where he lectured with much applause in the

    lecture-room,

3 How soon unaccountable I became tired and sick,

Till rising and gliding out I wander'd off by myself,

4 In the mystical moist night-air, and from time to time,

Look'd up in perfect silence at the stars.

The theme of this poem by Walt Whitman (see pages 946–947) is that the universe can't be adequately described by mere facts and figures. Different elements of the poem come together to create that theme.

1. Form. The poem is written in free verse, a type of poetry that isn't bound by rules. The form echoes the speaker's rejection of the proofs and figures of the astronomer.

2. Long lines are used to discuss the astronomer, suggesting that his lectures were tedious and boring.

3. Vivid language emphasizes the speaker's boredom. The phrase "tired and sick" appeals to the senses more than a simple statement of boredom.

4. Alliteration in the phrase "by myself in the mystical moist night-air" lends the end of the poem musical quality, which supports the speaker's preference of mystery over science.

Imagery is descriptive language that appeals to the five senses.

There are five types.

- Aural imagery
- Visual imagery
- Olfactory imagery
- Tactile imagery
- Gustatory imagery

Each type corresponds to one of the five senses.

- Sound
- Sight
- Smell
- Touch
- Taste

LITERARY ANALYSIS CORNER

As you read, pay attention to descriptive language in the text. Ask yourself the following questions if you want to analyze imagery in a literary work.

- Does the image relate to the theme?
- Which of your senses does the image appeal to?
- Why do you think the author chose to focus on that sense?
- What details are most important in the description?
- Is the image realistic? Or does it seem outlandish?
- What do you think the author feels about the thing he or she is describing? Is the description favorable or unfavorable?
- How do you feel about the image? Is it appealing or unappealing? Why?
- How does the image help you better understand the story or poem?

Aural Imagery

Aural imagery appeals to the reader's sense of sound. This excerpt from Edgar Allan Poe's poem "The Bells" (1849) appeals to readers' ears using rhyme and onomatopoeia.

> Hear the sledges with the bells—
> 　　　Silver bells!
> What a world of merriment their melody foretells!
> 　　How they tinkle, tinkle, tinkle,
> 　　　In the icy air of night!
> 　　While the stars that oversprinkle
> 　　All the heavens, seem to twinkle
> 　　　With a crystalline delight;
> 　　Keeping time, time, time,
> 　　In a sort of Runic rhyme

Visual Imagery

Visual imagery appeals to the reader's sense of sight. In his poem "Death Fugue" (1952), Paul Celan uses color to make a powerful statement about the persecution of Jews during the Holocaust.

> Black milk of daybreak we drink you at night
> we drink you at noon in the morning we drink you at
> 　　sundown
> we drink and we drink you
> a man lives in the house your golden hair Margarete
> your ashen hair Shulamith

WATCH OUT!

Sometimes, when an author spends a lot of time describing an object or a person, the image is a symbol. A symbol is something that has a level of meaning beyond the literal.

Marcel Proust, the celebrated French novelist, believed that the five senses were the gateway to memory. His most famous description of such a memory is that of a madeleine, a small cake that brings back his childhood when he dips it into a cup of tea. ▶

Olfactory Imagery

Olfactory imagery appeals to the reader's sense of smell. In this excerpt from his memoir, *Toast,* Nigel Slater sppeals to readers' sense of smell to make a scene from his childhood come alive.

Forget scented candles and freshly brewed coffee. Every home should smell of baking Christmas cake. That, and warm freshly ironed tea towels hanging on the rail in front of the Aga.

Tactile Imagery

Tactile imagery appeals to the reader's sense of touch. In this passage from *The Stranger* (1942), Albert Camus uses tactile imagery to help readers relate to the experience of the main character.

There was the same dazzling red glare. The sea gasped for air with each shallow, stifled little wave that broke on the sand. I was walking slowly toward the rocks and I could feel my forehead swelling under the sun. All that heat was pressing down on me and making it hard for me to go on. And every time I felt a blast of its hot breath striking my face, I gritted my teeth, clenched my fists in my trouser pockets, and strained every nerve in order to overcome the sun.

Gustatory Imagery

Gustastory imagery appeals to the reader's sense of taste. One of the most famous examples of gustatory imagery in literature is Marcel Proust's description of eating a madeleine in *Swann's Way* (1913).

And as soon as I had recognized the taste of the piece of madeleine dipped in lime-blossom tea that my aunt used to give me…immediately the old gray house on the street, where her bedroom was, came like a stage set to attach itself to the little wing opening onto the garden that had been built for my parents behind it. . . .

Style

Style is the particular way that a writer uses words. (See also pages 724–725.)

Style, like a signature or a voice, is very personal. It expresses something essential about the self. Think about what the word "style" means in other contexts, like fashion. What do you think the clothes you like best say about you?

In literature, many different elements contribute to a writer's style, including

- Language
- Characterization
- Plot
- Setting
- Tone or mood
- Point of view
- Subject

Good stylists convey something to their readers about their taste and views, even if they aren't stated directly.

This passage from *The Sun Also Rises* (1926) is representative of Ernest Hemingway's famously spare style.

> In the morning I walked down the Boulevard to the Rue Soufflot for coffee and brioche. It was a fine morning. The horse-chestnut trees in the Luxembourg gardens were in bloom. There was the pleasant early-morning feeling of a hot day.

This passage from *Mrs. Dalloway* (1925) showcases Virginia Woolf's stream-of-consciousness style, which follows the thoughts of a character.

> How fresh, how calm, stiller than this of course, the air was in the early morning; like the flap of a wave; the kiss of a wave; chill and sharp and yet (for a girl of eighteen as she was then) solemn, feeling as she did, standing there at the open window, that something awful was about to happen.

This passage from *The Great Gatsby* (1925) demonstrates F. Scott Fitzgerald's poetic style.

> On Sunday morning while church bells rang in the villages alongshore, the world and its mistress returned to Gatsby's house and twinkled hilariously on his lawn.

LITERARY ANALYSIS CORNER

As you analyze a work, ask yourself the following questions to gather information about the author's style.

- What makes the author's voice distinct or recognizable?
- Is there anything unusual about the way the words are put together?
- Is there a lot of dialogue? Or does the author focus on description?
- Does the tone seem conversational? Or is it more formal?
- How long are the sentences? Are they short and to the point? Or do they seem long and drawn out?
- Do any of the words seem outdated or unfamiliar?
- How does the author's writing sound different from your own? How does it sound different from the last text you read?
- What three adjectives best describe the author's style?
- Does the author follow the literary conventions of his or her time? Or does he or she try to do something different?

Recognizing Stylistic Differences

Artists often approach the same subject in different ways. In painting, as in writing, these differences can tell you a lot about an individual's views and feelings.

The painting below, *Scene from Shakespeare's The Tempest* (c. 1735), depicts a scene from Shakespeare's play. The people in the painting are recognizable as characters from the play. While there are some fantastical elements to the painting—the spirit Ariel and the beastlike Caliban are supernatural beings—the style is generally realistic. The colors and forms look like those we see in the real world. The painting and the play share a stormy setting.

The Jackson Pollock painting on the right, *Full Fathom Five* (1947), showcases a very different style. Instead of using recognizable forms to connect the painting to Shakespeare's play, Pollock's painting conveys a general sense of something dark, stormy, and wild. The title of the painting is taken from a line in the play:

Full fathom five thy father lies
Of his bones are coral made
Those are the pearls that were his eyes

Pollock was known for using thick drips and splashes of paint to create abstractions, or indirect depictions, of his subjects.

What can you guess about the artists based on the styles of these paintings?

These two paintings approach the same subject using two very different styles.

Symbolism

Sometimes an object or person can represent an idea or a concept. A symbol is an object that takes on a meaning beyond its literal significance.

Writers often use a person, place, or thing to stand in for something that is abstract. For example, trees are a commonly used symbol for life. Winter is often used as a symbol for death, and flowers are a common symbol for mortality.

In life, you encounter symbols every day. On the road, the color red means stop, while green is connected with go. Symbols in literature are similar. The words mean something beyond what they say on the surface.

In fiction and poetry, symbols are often open to interpretation. They can be slippery and complex.

Using Symbols

Writers like to use symbols as shorthand for complicated concepts. Symbols are often used in novels because part of an author's job is to show instead of tell.

The technique is simple in theory: use something literal to stand in for an abstract idea. In practice, however, symbolism can be tricky. Some symbols are common or generic; for instance, the spring season often symbolizes rebirth. Other times, writers create symbols that have meaning only within the context of a particular novel.

For writers, the difficulty lies in choosing a symbol that is not so generic so as to seem cliché, yet not so obscure that the reader becomes confused.

THE GREAT WHITE WHALE

When a whale appears in a story, it may be just a whale. Or, as in Herman Melville's *Moby-Dick,* it may be a symbol for something more. In the story, the whale symbolizes different things to different people. Here is a passage that describes what it meant to one character, Captain Ahab.

The White Whale swam before him as the monomaniac incarnation of all those malicious agencies which some deep men feel eating in them, till they are left living on with half a heart and half a lung. . . . All that most maddens and torments; all that stirs up the lees of things; all truth with malice in it; all that cracks the sinews and cakes the brain; all the subtle demonisms of life and thought; all evil, to crazy Ahab, were visibly personified, and made practically assailable in Moby-Dick. He piled upon the whale's white hump the sum of all the general rage and hate felt by his whole race from Adam down; and then, as if his chest had been a mortar, he burst his hot heart's shell upon it.

The white whale in *Moby-Dick* is an open symbol. Critics have different ideas about what it means; there is no one right answer.

Creating Meaning

Sometimes, a symbol means the same thing across different cultures. Other times, symbols may stand for different meanings depending on the context.

In many cultures, for example, the color red symbolizes war and violence. But in China, red represents marriage. Among American Indians, red stands for the east. Red symbolizes life in the Shinto religion of Japan, but in France it represents law schools.

A symbol has only the meaning that people have given it. Even a powerful symbol can lose its meaning if society dishonors or ignores it for a period of time. Take, for instance, the swastika. While it is a historical sacred symbol in many Eastern religions, it took on another meaning for most cultures when the Nazi Party adopted it in 1920. Now, for large parts of the world, the swastika symbol has come to represent the Nazi attempt to control Europe.

LITERARY ANALYSIS CORNER

When you write a literary analysis based on a symbol:

- Select an object or person that you find to be symbolic.
- Tell what that object or person represents.
- Explain your interpretation by using examples from the text.
- Show how the symbol relates or conveys the theme of the literary work.

In *The Scarlet Letter,* Hester Prynne is forced to wear a scarlet letter *A* on her dress to symbolize her shame as an adulteress.

READING LIST

Symbolism is an important part of these novels.

- *The Red Badge of Courage*
- *The Scarlet Letter*
- *The Picture of Dorian Gray* (See page 947.)
- *To Kill a Mockingbird*
- *The Great Gatsby*
- *The Adventures of Huckleberry Finn*

Many writers use symbols to help convey a work's theme. A symbol can be a person, a place, or an object.

Allusion

An allusion is a reference to something that is outside the world of a text. Allusions can refer to historical events in the real world or to fictitious stories in literature. These are examples of things to which an author may allude.

- persons
- places
- events
- ideas
- works of art
- musical compositions
- Bible or other religious writings

Recognizing Allusions

Like symbols, allusions are a form of literary shorthand. They use a few words to link the reader's prior knowledge to the text in which the allusion appears. Good writers manipulate this web of associations to add texture and layers of meaning to their works of fiction and poetry.

Usually, allusions are subtle and indirect. That means it's up to the reader to detect the reference and make the appropriate connection. The ability to recognize and "decode" allusions therefore requires a certain amount of cultural literacy.

Clever allusions do not depend solely on outside connections to help readers build meaning. Books and poems should make sense as self-contained entities. That way, meaning is deeper if the reader recognizes the allusion, but it is not taken away if the reader misses the connection.

LITERARY ANALYSIS CORNER

Ask yourself questions as you read and write to better understand the relationship between an allusion and the text in which it appears.

- Why did the author reference this particular person, event, or work of art?
- What does the reference have to do with the topic of the text it appears in?
- What images and associations does the allusion bring to mind?
- Would the text make sense by itself if you didn't recognize the allusion?
- How does the allusion contribute to the text? Does it add meaning? Does it contribute to the overall tone?

ALLUSION IN MODERNISM

Modernists like James Joyce, W. B. Yeats, and T. S. Eliot were big believers in the power of allusion, littering their works with references to old books, poems, and myths. Some critics believed this practice was snobby and ridiculous. How could regular readers be expected to recognize all those obscure references? How could readers find meaning in books and poems if they didn't have the right keys to unlock meaning?

Unlocking *The Waste Land*

Since *The Waste Land* was published in 1922, many people have approached T. S. Eliot's poem as if it were a code to be deciphered. To be sure, it contains a lot of obscure allusions that point to authors as diverse as Chaucer, Vergil, Ovid, Milton, Joseph Conrad, and many, many more.

In later editions of the poem, Eliot himself published footnotes that explained many of the poem's references. Do you think that you need a "key" to unlock *The Waste Land?* Is there a "right" way to read a poem? These are questions that critics still debate today.

T. S. Eliot referenced a wide variety of sources in his poetry.

ALLUSIONS ACROSS TIME AND PLACE

This passage from *The Waste Land* alludes to at least three different authors: Dante, an Italian poet from the Middle Ages; John Webster, a British writer in Shakespeare's day; and Charles Baudelaire, a 19th-century French poet.

DANTE

"I had not thought death . . ." alludes to Dante's *Inferno*. (See page 925.)

CHARLES BAUDELAIRE

These phrases refer to the French poet's famous volume, *Fleurs du Mal*.

> Unreal City,
> Under the brown fog of a winter dawn,
> A crowd flowed over London Bridge, so many,
> I had not thought death had undone so many.
> Signs, short and frequent, were exhaled,
> And each man fixed his eyes before his feet.
> Flowed up the hill and down King William Street,
> To where Saint Mary Willnoth kept the hours
> With a dead sound on the final stroke of nine.
> There I saw one I knew, and stopped him, crying 'Stetson!
> 'You who were with me in the ships at Mylae!
> 'That corpse you planted last year in your garden,
> 'Has it begun to sprout? Will it bloom this year?
> 'Or has the sudden frost disturbed its bed?
> 'Oh keep the Dog far hence, that's friend to men
> 'Or with his nails he'll dig it up again!
> 'You! hypocrite lecteur!—mon semblable,—mon frère!'

JOHN WEBSTER

"Oh keep the Dog far hence . . ." is a reference to the English playwright's revenge tragedy, *The White Devil*.

Point of View

When several people observe the same event, each has a particular perspective, or point of view. One observer may see something that no one else notices. Another person may have background information that makes him or her see the event in a different light than the other people watching.

In fiction, the term **point of view** describes the perspective from which a story is told. When we talk about point of view in literature, we are usually talking about the angle of vision of the voice telling the story: What can the storyteller see? What does the storyteller know?

The person who tells the story is the **narrator.** There are three main points of view: *first person, second person,* and *third person.*

First Person

A **first-person narrator** tells his or her own story. The reader sees all of the events of the story through the eyes of this person, who has his or her own biases and opinions. Events are either happening to this person or being witnessed by this person.

The use of the pronoun *I* is the trademark of the first-person narrator. Once in a while, you may find a first-person plural narrator. In this situation, the pronoun is *we.*

With first-person narration, the narrator can relate only the action that occurs when he or she is present and can relate only his or her own thoughts, and not the thoughts of other characters. The narrator can speculate as to what another person may be thinking, but it's just a guess.

fyi! *Stream of consciousness is a type of first-person narration that is supposed to look and flow like the thoughts of the narrator.*

"And then I asked him with my eyes to ask again yes and then he asked me would I yes and then his heart was going like mad and yes I said yes I will yes."

▲ **In his novel** *Ulysses,* James Joyce used stream-of-consciousness narration to present the thoughts, sensations, and memories that flow through a character's mind. This technique is illustrated in the quotation at left.

Second Person

Second-person narrators use the pronoun "you" to draw the reader into the action. Generally speaking, second-person narrators are more rare than their first- and third-person counterparts.

LITERARY ANALYSIS CORNER

Sometimes the narrator is a key participant in the story he or she tells. In that case, you can analyze the narrator just as you would any other character. Other times, the narrator is outside of the story. Think about the ways in which point of view impacts the story. Why did the writer choose that particular narrator instead of using someone else's perspective?

Points of View		
Point of View	**Pronouns Used**	**What the Speaker Tells**
first person	I, we	his or her own story
second person	you	the reader's story
third-person limited	he, she, they	another person's story
third-person objective	he, she, they	many people's stories from an outsider's perspective
third-person omniscient	he, she, they	many people's stories with an all-knowing perspective

Third Person

A **third-person narrator** tells a story about another person. These narrators are never characters within the story they're telling. They stand outside the story, like an observer. They typically use the pronouns *he, she,* and *they*.

There are three types of third-person narrators: third-person limited, third-person objective, and third-person omniscient.

Third-Person Limited

A **third-person limited narrator** tells someone else's story. This type of narrator is limited in that he or she only tells about the experience and thoughts of one character. It's as though the narrator is standing behind that one character throughout the whole story. As a result, the reader only knows about action that takes place when that particular character is present.

Third-Person Objective

A **third-person objective narrator** tells a story about many other people, instead of just one person (like a third-person limited narrator). This type of narrator tells the story as it unfolds and does not delve into the thoughts and motivations of the characters. He or she just stands back and conveys what happens from an outsider's perspective.

Third-Person Omniscient

A **third-person omniscient narrator** is all-knowing. This type of narrator has special knowledge of any number of characters. He or she can relate the action that happens to any character at any place at any time. Third-person omniscient narrators can also peer into the mind of any character and relate that person's thoughts.

RESEARCH PAPERS

are a great way to learn not only about the particular topic you're investigating, but also about the process of investigation itself. You must become a kind of detective to find the facts and theories needed to come to an informed conclusion. Putting the collected information together with personal ideas is the way all investigators solve mysteries. Unlike mysteries, however, research topics may have more than one possible conclusion.

Overview

Research paper: the very words fill some students with dread. Preparing a research paper is a big job. But if you go about it the right way, it is a manageable task. It helps to start out with a confident attitude.

Think of your research paper as a chance to learn a lot more about something that interests you. It's an opportunity to develop skills in information gathering, organization, and writing. These skills will make you better equipped to handle many other school assignments and even job responsibilities later in life.

A good research paper integrates information gathered from various sources with your own ideas. It demonstrates your ability to think and write clearly, as well as your skills in using the library and other sources to track information.

In writing a good paper, you learn how to argue your point fairly, yet persuasively.

Misconceptions

There are several common misconceptions about research papers. One is that a research paper is a collection of strung-together quotes and paraphrases from published sources with a lot of footnotes attached so no one can accuse you of plagiarism. Another is that it's a collection of uninformed opinions on a given topic.

In reality, a research paper is a combination of those two concepts—your informed opinions and ideas based on your investigation of published, and occasionally unpublished, information.

Another common misconception is to think of the research paper as strictly a writing project. While it's true that the final product you hand in will be a written paper, much work goes into the process before you ever pick up a pen or sit down at a keyboard to start writing.

Use interesting comparisons to bring statistics to life. For example, a figure for the population of India is much more interesting if you add the fact that more people live in India than in all countries of North and South America combined.

WATCH OUT!

Don't just regurgitate facts, figures, and other writers' opinions when you write a research paper. Show off your critical thinking skills by demonstrating that you've carefully considered the topic.

Making a Schedule

Planning ahead is a good idea for any writing assignment. For a research paper, it's a must. It's a good idea to go ahead and make a schedule as soon as you get the assignment.

Mark the due date on a calendar and count backwards to plan blocks of time for finishing the final draft, including

- research and note taking.
- preparing an outline.
- organizing note cards.
- writing the first draft.
- revising and proofreading.

The exact amount of time that goes into each of those blocks depends on the assignment and the speed at which you work.

Information Versus Evidence

Whenever you write a research paper, you will have to sort through and digest a large amount of information.

Your first task is to decide what information is relevant to your project. Facts, statistics, examples, and quotes are common types of information you will find. (See also pages 810–811.)

To write a successful research paper, your challenge will be to turn all that information into evidence or proof. Evidence is what information becomes when you use it to support your ideas.

If a piece of information does not help you make your point, think twice before you use it.

 *Plagiarism is presenting someone else's ideas as if they were your own. Changing words around is still plagiarism if you don't give the original author credit for the idea.*

Analytical Research Papers

There are two main types of research papers: argumentative and analytical.

What's the Difference?

An argumentative research paper is based on a thesis, a statement that argues a particular point of view. To write an argumentative paper, the process involves sifting through information from a variety of sources, digesting the material, and using it to support your thesis. Along the way, you can change that thesis if you need to, but there's always a guiding statement that you wish to prove in the paper.

Analytical papers, on the other hand, are more exploratory. Instead of starting with a thesis, they explore the topic with a more balanced, unbiased approach.

Analytical papers dealing with problems or events might be developed by discussing central issues first, then moving on to explore related side issues.

Argumentative Papers	Analytical Papers
persuasive	descriptive
starts with a thesis	starts with a question
carefully selected evidence	thorough, comprehensive evidence
focuses on answers	focuses on questions

FINDING THE RIGHT APPROACH

Before you begin writing, give some thought to how you want to approach your topic.

- If your subject inspires strong opinions, you may want to take a **pro or con approach,** in which you describe both sides of the issue.

- A **compare and contrast approach** is effective whenever you want to explain how two things are alike or different.

- A **chronological approach** traces the order in which events happened.

Writing the Paper

To write a successful analytical research paper, you'll need to learn how to find information from outside sources and explain the information they contain in your own words. Your topic needs to be thoroughly examined from all sides.

Start by completing the following steps.

1. Sifting through information from other sources
2. Reading and understanding the material
3. Developing a tentative thesis for your essay

Once you have your tentative thesis, you collect information to support it. To use the sources in your paper, you will paraphrase and organize the information and then reevaluate your thesis to see if it all works. Finally, you will write the paper.

For most research papers, you will have to use more than just one source, and for longer papers, keeping track of all the information can be intimidating. To tackle the challenge of keeping up with all the information you find during your research, you must have a system. As you start collecting reliable sources for any research paper, browse for ideas and skim some periodicals and book titles. Let your thesis grow as you learn more about the subject. Remember to be flexible; it is expected that your working thesis will change as the paper develops.

WATCH OUT!

Be sure to narrow the topic of your research paper to a manageable size. Do not be fooled into thinking you will have plenty of time and space to cover a broad topic. It is far better to cover a narrow topic in depth than to skim over a broad topic.

Finding a Good Topic

In most cases, your teacher will allow you to choose the topic for your research paper. Since you'll spend a lot of time working on it, it's important to choose a topic that you're really interested in.

Even if you don't like a particular subject, you can probably find a specific topic within the subject area that appeals to you. For example, perhaps you don't care much for United States history, but you love music. A U.S. history research paper on songs of the American Civil War might be a good choice.

The key to writing an analytical research paper is to keep an open mind as you research.

Argumentative Research Papers

Writing an argumentative paper involves taking one side of an issue and arguing it. To be effective, you must be able to

- make sure your thesis statement is arguable.
- identify an audience.
- establish credibility.
- find common ground.

If you can accomplish these four things, you will be well on your way to writing an effective argumentative paper.

Arguable Statements

There are two types of statements: factual and arguable. Every statement has to be one or the other; it can never be both.

Factual statements are plain truths that are verifiable and certain. Consider the reasons why the following examples are inarguable.

The temperatures this summer are hotter than they have ever been before.

The drought is causing millions of dollars in crops to be lost each year.

You could verify the first statement by comparing this summer's temperatures against the record. Similarly, the second statement describes a direct link that can be verified.

Now consider these statements:

The hot temperatures this year caused more incidents of road rage.

The loss of millions of dollars in crops each year due to drought could be eliminated if water preservation measures were strictly enforced.

The link described in the first sentence can't be proven because other factors might contribute to road rage. The second sentence is speculation.

If there aren't at least two sides to an issue, it isn't arguable. An arguable statement addresses a problem for which there is no absolute answer. It tries to convince the reader of something.

Audience

You should envision a specific, targeted audience for your argumentative paper. Assessing your audience is important in writing, speaking, and everyday interaction. Whenever you present information, spoken or written, you must always consider the receipients.

If you keep your audience in mind while you are writing, your paper will be more successful. Knowing the audience helps you decide what words, phrases, and research will be most convincing for your paper.

 *To make sure you have an arguable statement, try to write a sentence that summarizes the counterargument. If you can't think of one, that's a good sign you need to rework your thesis.*

AUDIENCE Q & A

Here are some questions to ask yourself before you begin writing.

What concepts and terms need to be defined for my audience?

- Are they experts who can handle technical words and complex concepts?
- Or are they beginners who require more explanation?

What is my audience's position on the topic?

- Are they already partially persuaded?
- Or are they defiantly opposed?
- Or do they have no opinion one way or the other?

What does my audience value?

The answers to these questions can help you decide

- what information to include.
- what deserves special emphasis.
- what kind of language to use.
- which sources will be most credible.
- what type of approach will be most effective.

Credibility

Once you have established your audience, you must work to build credibility with them. To establish credibilty, you must use reliable, relevant sources to support your position. You must be able to support your ideas with evidence through careful research.

To make your argument more believable, you must

- demonstrate your knowledge of the subject.
- establish common ground with the reader.
- demonstrate fairness to opposing viewpoints.

Establish Common Ground

To establish common ground with your audience, you can point out those elements of your argument on which all sides agree. For example, regardless of whether you're for or against mandatory drug testing in the workplace, everyone agrees that drug-related accidents should be minimized.

Other ways to establish common ground include

- using unbiased sources.
- refraining from being one-sided.
- acknowledging counterarguments.

ANATOMY OF A WORKING THESIS

A thesis is a statement that gives readers the main topic of a piece of writing. In an argumentative essay, the thesis states the central idea that the paper will prove.

A **working thesis** is the general, basic statement that you hope to prove in the paper or essay. Because it is a working thesis, it can be changed, expanded, strengthened, and modified during the writing process. (See also pages 710–711.)

BUSINESS WRITING

Letters and resumés are the two most basic forms of business writing. (That includes e-mail, the less formal little cousin of the letter.) Whether you're applying for a summer job during high school or a professional position after college, there are guidelines you can follow to make sure you represent yourself well and make yourself understood.

Letters

People write letters for business and pleasure. Business letters are generally more formal than personal letters. You might write a business letter to apply for a job or to make a complaint. Personal letters, including invitations and thank-you notes, are usually reserved for family and friends.

The following format applies to cover letters that you write to apply for jobs as well as regular business letters you might write in your role as a professional.

Addressing an Envelope

Two addresses are written on an envelope: the mailing address and the return address.

1. The **mailing address** is the address of the person receiving the letter. It is usually written in the middle of the envelope. Be sure to follow the custom of the country of the person you're addressing the letter to.

2. The **return address** is the address of the person sending the letter. It is usually written in the upper left-hand corner.

Leslie Ames
9816 Landis Street
Chicago, IL 60643

Mr. Eli Grant, Director
Customer Service Department
Acme Seed Company
350 Poplar Lane
Des Moines, IA 50336

WRITING A GOOD BUSINESS LETTER

- Be concise. Use simple, direct statements instead of long, involved sentences.
- Be exact. Make sure that every statement and detail is accurate.
- Don't use language that is overly stiff. Aim for a friendly, polite tone.
- Avoid slang and cliché.
- Organize your letter in a clear, logical manner.
- Try to stick to one main subject.

1 9816 Landis Street
Chicago, IL 60643

July 30, 2011

2 Mr. Eli Grant, Director
Customer Service Department
Acme Seed Company
350 Poplar Lane
Des Moines, IA 50336

3 Dear Mr. Grant:

4 On May 28, 2011, I received five rosebushes that I ordered from your current catalog. I planted the bushes promptly and cared for them according to the instructions that were enclosed. Within a month, however, four of the bushes had died. The fifth one died last week.

I would like a full refund in the amount of $35.50. I am enclosing my receipt.

Sincerely, **5**

6 *Leslie Ames*

Leslie Ames

Writing a Letter

1. The **heading** includes your full mailing address and the date. Don't use abbreviations except for the two-letter state postal abbreviation. For personal letters, just use the date.

2. The **inside address** includes the recipient's name, title, company name, and address. The first line of the inside address should be placed four lines below the date. You can omit this element from personal letters.

3. The **salutation** is the greeting. It appears two lines below the inside address. In business letters, it's followed by a colon. Personal salutations are followed by a comma.

4. The **body** contains the writer's message. Separate all paragraphs by a space of one extra line.

5. The **complimentary close** is the word or words that end the letter. Place it two lines below the body of the letter. Make sure it's consistent with the salutation in its degree of formality.

6. The **signature** is your name. Write it in ink four lines below the complimentary close.

Resumés

Writing a resumé is your first step toward finding a job. Your resumé introduces you to potential employers. It summarizes your work experience, education, interests, and achievements so your reader gets a good picture of what you're like at a glance. It's important that your resumé make a good impression.

A resumé includes four main sections.

- Heading
- Experience
- Education
- Activities and interests

It does NOT include

- your age, race, or religion.
- other personal information.
- references' contact information.

Jane Drummond
14 Elm Street
Jackson, Illinois 61531
312-555-1314

SKILLS: Good communication with children; patience and firmness in dealing with children; calmness in emergencies; capable of planning, following directions, and completing tasks

EVIDENCE: Have, from the age of 12, cared for younger brother and sister; have been in demand as a babysitter in the neighborhood; have taken charge of planning, buying, and cooking at least one family meal per week; have kept school marks at B average

Sample Resumé

1. The **heading** includes your name, your full address (including city, state, and zip code), and your phone number. Place the heading at the top of the page, either centered or at the left-hand margin.

2. The **experience** section lists the jobs you've held, beginning with the most recent position. Each entry should include the dates of employment, the name and location of your employer, your job title, and job description.

3. The **skills** section lists software proficiencies and other relevant skillsets (like language fluencies).

4. If you've had a job, the **education** section follows the experience section. List the school you attended most recently and work backward. The education section is also where you can list any additional courses or training programs that relate to the job you're seeking.

5. List any **activities and interests** that might be interesting to your potential employer. Include memberships in academic, professional, and business organizations. This is also the place where you can list foreign language fluencies or other skills that didn't fit under the experience or education sections.

NO WORK EXPERIENCE? NO PROBLEM.

When looking for part-time or summer work, your goal is not to begin or advance a career, but simply to make money. A resumé will help you show an employer what skills you have.

Think about all of your achievements in various fields. List them, and then write down the skills that were necessary to attain those achievements.

Match the skills that you have to the kinds of skills necessary and valuable for various jobs.

Use Skills and Evidence for headings on your resumé when you have no work experience.

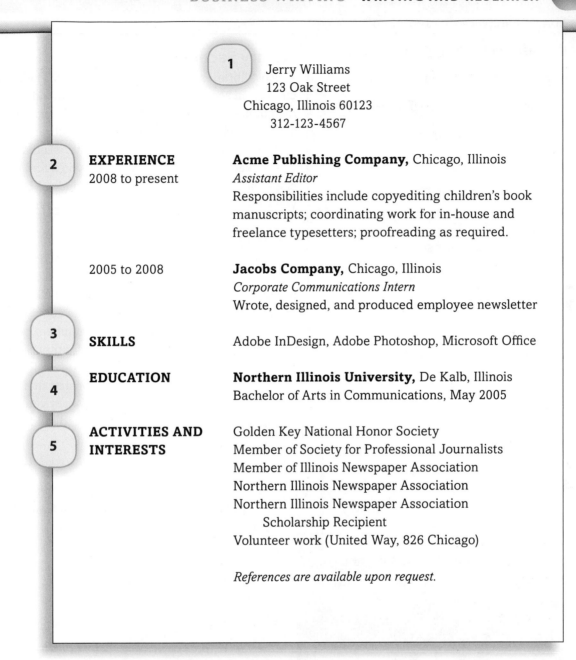

1 Jerry Williams
123 Oak Street
Chicago, Illinois 60123
312-123-4567

2 **EXPERIENCE**
2008 to present

Acme Publishing Company, Chicago, Illinois
Assistant Editor
Responsibilities include copyediting children's book manuscripts; coordinating work for in-house and freelance typesetters; proofreading as required.

2005 to 2008

Jacobs Company, Chicago, Illinois
Corporate Communications Intern
Wrote, designed, and produced employee newsletter

3 **SKILLS**

Adobe InDesign, Adobe Photoshop, Microsoft Office

4 **EDUCATION**

Northern Illinois University, De Kalb, Illinois
Bachelor of Arts in Communications, May 2005

5 **ACTIVITIES AND INTERESTS**

Golden Key National Honor Society
Member of Society for Professional Journalists
Member of Illinois Newspaper Association
Northern Illinois Newspaper Association
Northern Illinois Newspaper Association
   Scholarship Recipient
Volunteer work (United Way, 826 Chicago)

References are available upon request.

TIPS FOR WRITING A GOOD RESUMÉ

1. There are many different formats you can use. Choose one that you're comfortable with and that showcases your background and experiences.

2. Keep your resumé as short as possible. One page is ideal for most people. If you have a lot of experience, two pages is okay.

3. If you use two pages, include a heading on the second page with your name, phone number, and the page number.

4. Don't date a resumé, but make sure all the information you list is up to date and correct.

FINDING SOURCES

Today's libraries are very different than libraries of the past—not only in the resources and services they offer, but also in physical layout and atmosphere. And, since libraries constantly strive to expand and perfect the services they provide, they're still changing.

The principles behind finding quality sources, however, have changed very little. Once you learn how to scout for sources, you should be able to apply those skills in a variety of situations.

Using the Library

Library Sections

Most libraries have two major sections. The general circulation section contains all the fiction and most of the nonfiction books the library owns. You can almost always check these materials out of the library.

The reference section contains materials that can't be checked out of the library. There, you'll find encyclopedias, dictionaries, atlases—the kinds of books you wouldn't want to read from cover to cover.

Finding Books

Books are organized on the library's shelves by their call numbers. Each book has a call number printed on its spine. That call number is the key to the book's location in the library. Books about the same subject often have similar call numbers, so look around the surrounding shelves for other useful sources.

Your library should have a guide posted that directs you toward a range of call numbers. When you get to the right floor or section, a more detailed guide will direct you to the right shelf.

fyi!

The contents of libraries have changed so much over the years that the word library is, in a sense, inaccurate. It comes from the Latin word liber, *which means "book." Today, most research projects heavily rely on electronic resources.*

Libraries provide access to information in a wide variety of formats. Members can get information from many types of sources, including

- books
- magazines
- manuscripts
- newspapers
- pamphlets
- online databases

- CDs
- DVDs
- films
- maps
- paintings
- photographs

Most of your research will take place in libraries, so it's important to know how to use them.

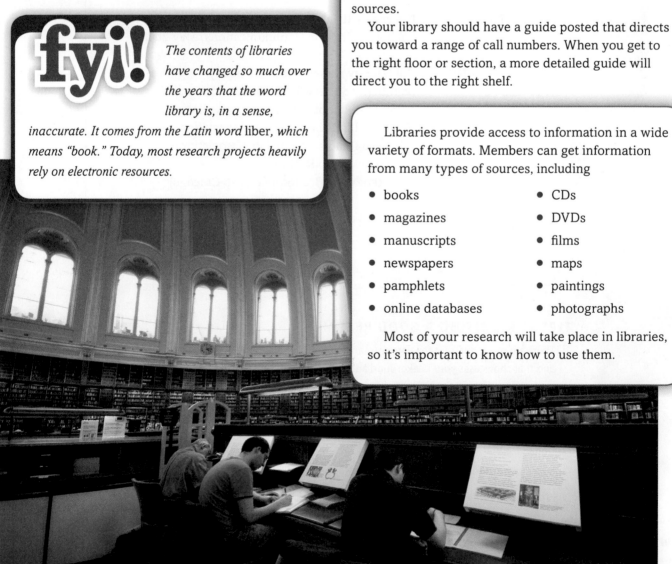

CLASSIFICATION SYSTEMS

The two main systems used in the United States for classifying books are the Dewey Decimal and Library of Congress systems. The first is used in most public libraries; the second, in many college libraries.

The Dewey Decimal system has 10 major divisions, from 000 for general reference works to the 900s for history. Each of these 10 main classes is broken up into more specialized fields. For example, class 600-699, Technology, is subdivided into 10 special classes. Each of these divisions is further subdivided. The numbers 630-639, for example, represent Agriculture, and are subdivided into such classes as Field Crops, Garden Crops, and Dairy and Related Technologies. When the classification becomes very fine, decimals are used to represent specific areas. For example, books on useful insects, such as bees and silkworms, are grouped under the number 638. Books on beekeeping are in 638.1, and those on silkworms in 638.2.

The Library of Congress system provides greater precision in most fields and more room for expansion than the Dewey Decimal system. Each Library of Congress classification is represented by a set of capital letters and numbers. The first letter in the set indicates one of 21 major areas of knowledge. The second letter stands for a subclassification. The numbers represent a specific topic.

Catalogs

The main types of library catalogs are card catalogs and online catalogs.

A card catalog is an index card filing system that tells you where to find the books you need. Most libraries have replaced their card catalogs with electronic catalogs, but you may have to use a card catalog in some libraries. Cards are arranged by title, author, and subject.

Electronic catalogs store information in computer files. Instead of searching through file drawers, you call up the information on a screen. The first screen should be the main menu, which will tell you exactly how to access the information you need. You can search by subject, author, title, or keyword.

Additional information in a catalog entry might include the birth and death dates of the author, the names of editors and translators, the place and date of publication, the publisher's name, a physical description of the book (including the size and number of pages), a short description of the book's contents, information on illustrations, photographs, bibliography, and explanatory notes.

Dewey Decimal System

000	Generalities
100	Philosophy and Psychology
200	Religion
300	Social Science
400	Language
500	Natural Science and Mathematics
600	Technology (Applied Science)
700	Arts
800	Literature
900	Geography and History

Library of Congress System

A	General Works
B	Philosophy, Religion
C	History
D	Foreign History
E,F	American History
G	Geography, Anthropology
H	Social Sciences
J	Political Science
K	Law
L	Education
M	Music
N	Fine Arts
P	Language and Literature
Q	Science
R	Medicine
S	Agriculture
T	Technology
U	Military Science
V	Naval Science
Z	Library Science, Bibliography

Library Resources

In addition to books you can check out, libraries offer many types of sources that can help with your research. Here's how to find them.

The Reference Section

Like the rest of the nonfiction collection, the reference section is arranged according to subject. Familiarize yourself with the part of the reference collection that contains materials for your research. Then you will be able to refer to it quickly when you need information.

Most libraries have hundreds or thousands of reference materials. You won't use all of them. But some will become reliable sources of information that you turn to again and again. The most frequently used reference works include

- Encyclopedias
- Yearbooks
- Dictionaries

You can find many answers to your research questions in reference materials. Some reference works, such as almanacs and encyclopedias, provide information directly. Others, such as indexes and bibliographies, tell you where to find information.

Encyclopedias are a good place to begin research. They contain thousands of articles on a variety of topics, so the subject you're interested in is likely to be covered in some form. Once you have an overview of your topic, you can determine the appropriate next steps in your research project.

Yearbooks are annual supplements to encyclopedias. Together with yearly almanacs, they provide up-to-date statistics and other facts on many topics, including business, politics, sports, entertainment, foreign countries, and population. These sources can be useful for information about current events. Archives, or collections of yearbook articles, can also be a good source of information on recent history.

Dictionaries. Most people think of a dictionary as a source to use when they want to know how to spell or pronounce a word or learn what it means. But if you take the time to become familiar with a good dictionary, you may find information about grammar, writing style, and how to proofread a manuscript.

Reference Librarians

All libraries are staffed by trained reference librarians who are experts in locating source material on any subject. Their purpose is to help people, so you should never hesitate to ask them questions. Librarians can help you find an answer to a specific question, such as when Babe Ruth was born. Or they can direct you to sources that contain information on a broader topic, like the history of baseball.

GETTING THE MOST OUT OF A REFERENCE WORK

To make full use of a reference work, take time to familiarize yourself with its organization before you plunge in to search for information.

- See if the book or Web site has an introductory section on how to use it, a key to abbreviations, or similar helpful information.

- Consult the table of contents to get an idea of what the reference work covers and how the material is organized. The table of contents lists chapter titles and features like illustrations and maps.

- Check materials in the front and back of the book. An introduction and author's foreword can have valuable information. Appendixes may include charts, tables, the text of documents, and author's notes. Bibliographies can provide you with titles of additional sources to check.

- When you're ready to find specific information, turn to the index. The index offers a far more complete guide to the book than the table of contents. Most reference books have one general index, which lists proper names, titles, and topics together. Some works have several indexes—for example, an author index, a title index, and a subject index.

Newspapers and Other Periodicals

Periodicals are a valuable source of information, especially for topics of current interest that may not be covered adequately in books. They can give you present-day views of events, issues, and important people.

Most libraries keep current issues of newspapers and magazines on shelves for easy access. Past issues may be kept as bound volumes or on microfilm. Bound volumes consist of all the issues for a particular period of time. On microfilm, pages are photographed and greatly reduced in size. The images appear on a reel or on a sheet called microfiche. A viewing machine enlarges the images and projects them on a screen so you can read the pages. Microfilm of newspapers and magazines is generally stored in file cabinets. You may be able to get bound volumes and microfilm yourself, or you may need to fill out a call slip. Many libraries also subscribe to databases that provide access to magazine and newspaper articles that are not freely available on the Internet.

Periodical and Newspaper Indexes

Periodical and newspaper indexes are reference tools that can tell you where to find articles on your topic. They organize articles from many different sources by subject and keyword so you can search the database easily and effectively. Many of these indexes are electronic. Print indexes can be found in the reference section of the library.

- To use an index, think of the word that most clearly identifies your topic. For information on the Nile River, look under "Nile," not "River." For information on the presidency of Nelson Mandela, look under "Mandela," not "presidency."

- After you've located the proper pages, skim the text to see if it has what you need. Look at headings, the topic sentence of each paragraph, and concluding summaries. This method should help you spot main ideas.

- Finally, if the source has useful information, fill out a source card (see pages 790–791), read the text carefully, and take notes.

In Addition to Newspaper Indexes

The Readers' Guide to Periodical Literature is a widely used index of magazine and journal articles. It is an organized list of articles from over 400 leading publications. The *Readers' Guide* is issued several times a year in paperback. Each year's issues are then reissued in a bound volume. (It's also available online.) The periodicals included may vary from volume to volume, so be sure to check the list that appears in the volume you're using. You'll also need to find out which periodicals your library has in its collection.

Specialized Indexes. In addition to the *Readers' Guide*, there are a number of specialized guides to periodicals, such as the *Art Index* and the *Business Periodicals Index*. Check with your librarian for more information.

A CLOSER LOOK AT *THE READERS' GUIDE TO PERIODICAL LITERATURE*

The entries in the *Readers' Guide* appear in alphabetical order by subject and author and sometimes by title. Abbreviations are used for many parts of the entry, including the name of the magazine and the date of the issue. An explanation of the abbreviations appears in the front of each volume of the guide. Be sure to read it so that you can understand the entry. Here's a sample entry on acid rain:

Acid Rain

When nitrate reigns [air pollution damage to forests; cover story] J. Raloff. il. *Science News* 147:90-1 F11, '95

The entry tells you that an article titled "When nitrate reigns," by J. Raloff, begins on page 90 of the February 11, 1995, issue of *Science News*. The illustrated story discusses damages to forests.

Writing for Information

Government agencies, businesses, organizations, and professional associations can be important sources of information. By contacting such organizations, you may be able to get reliable statistics and other facts that would be difficult to track down elsewhere.

For example, if you were writing a report about literacy in Canada, it might be helpful to e-mail Canada's provincial departments of education for the most recent statistics on literacy. Furthermore, these sources publish a variety of pamphlets and other materials you can use for research. Many of these materials are free.

Here are some tips for writing to organizations.

- Keep in mind that some groups are better equipped than others to handle requests.

- Make your request specific and reasonable.

- Use e-mail whenever possible. If you must write a letter, include a self-addressed, stamped envelope for the reply.

- Don't assume that the reply will arrive by the time you need it. (It might not.) Be prepared to use information from other sources if necessary.

Interviews

Conducting an interview can be an effective way to get facts and personal viewpoints that add special interest to your report. Begin with a courteous phone call or e-mail identifying yourself and requesting an interview. Explain what kind of information you need. Make yourself available at a time that is convenient for the person you are contacting.

Original Research

Conducting a survey is another way to get unique material. You can ask people questions in person or develop a questionnaire. Either way, phrase your questions carefully so people can respond easily and clearly. Surveys that use a "yes or no" or "for or against" format are the easiest to evaluate. You may want to include a "no opinion" category. Or you may prefer a format that allows for a range of opinion. Whatever method you choose, take care to record the results accurately.

Television

Television documentaries, news programs, and interview shows can give you access to expert opinions and valuable information. If you watch a program as part of your research, be prepared to take careful notes. Be sure to note the name of the program, the network, and the date of the broadcast for your list of sources and footnotes.

Exhibits

Museums, art galleries, and historical societies may enable you to explore your subject firsthand. For example, a report on the painter Vincent van Gogh could be enhanced by a visit to an art museum that exhibits some of his works. Many museums and other cultural centers have libraries or other research facilities open to the public. See what your community has to offer that can help you understand your topic better.

EFFECTIVE INTERVIEWING

A little planning will help you get the most from your question and answer session.

- Before the interview, read background material about the topic. That way, you'll be better able to ask intelligent questions and follow-ups.

- Prepare a list of questions ahead of time.

- Listen carefully during the interview.

- Take notes on important points and be careful to write direct quotations exactly as they are said.

- Be sure to ask permission to use a direct quote.

- Ask for clarification on points you don't understand and the spelling of unfamiliar terms or names.

- A recorder can eliminate the need for taking lengthy notes by hand. (Ask permission beforehand.)

- Before you leave the interview, be sure to accurately write the subject's name, position or title, and place of business. You'll need this information for your list of sources and footnotes.

- Don't forget to thank your subject at the end of the interview.

- Follow up with a thank-you note.

The Internet, CD-ROMs, and DVDs have drastically changed the way most people perform research inside and outside of the classroom. In order to research a subject effectively, you need to know how to find information electronically.

- The Internet is a network of computers that spans the globe. Government agencies, businesses, nonprofit organizations, and individuals provide free or fee-based access to their Web sites.

- CD-ROMs hold a lot of information and offer fast, interactive searches. Periodical indexes on CD-ROM allow you to quickly find recent articles by simply entering a keyword search.

- DVDs can hold the same information as CD-ROMs, but because their storage capacity is greater, they can also hold audio and video.

Search Engines

Web sites offer information on practically every subject. Unlike the knowledge in an encyclopedia, however, this information is not neatly organized. When you want information on a particular topic, you have to use a search engine such as Google to help locate that material.

To find what you need, search engines use indexes that summarize the contents of Web sites. You start by typing keywords or search terms that describe your topic or question. The search engine then returns a list of links to Web sites that relate to those words.

For example, say you need to research the Great Chicago Fire of 1871. If you begin with the keyword *Chicago*, the search engine will return millions of matches. If you add the keywords *fire* and *1871*, far fewer matches will result, and the information will probably be more relevant.

BOOLEAN SEARCH TERMS

AND (or +)

When you combine two words using AND, you will narrow your search to articles that contain both of these words. For instance, if you searched for "schools," you might get thousands of articles dealing with schools. A second search for "uniforms" would find similar, overwhelming results. However, if you combined the words with *and* to search for "uniforms AND schools," your choices would be narrowed down to articles that deal with the idea you wish to explore.

The more words you add, the more specific you can make your search. You could search for "uniforms AND schools AND mandatory policies" to get an even more specific search result.

NOT (or –)

Adding NOT will narrow your search, too, but by excluding words. For instance, if you found that too many articles for "uniforms AND schools" were about private schools, you could change your search to "uniforms AND schools NOT private."

OR

Using OR in the search will broaden your results if your search finds too few sources. It is best used with terms that have common synonyms, such as "elementary OR primary." OR is usually used in parentheses, so a search might look like this: "uniforms AND schools AND (elementary OR primary).

Many search engines will assume the OR when you enter keywords. This results in the search engine finding any site that has any of the words you entered.

The Boolean search is named after the logician George Boole, who founded the idea of symbolic logic.

Commercial Web Sites

Web sites that can be accessed for free are called general Web sites. Web sites that charge a fee for use are commercial Web sites. Many libraries purchase subscriptions to such sites, which members can then access for free. Commercial databases include periodical indexes as well as reference books such as encyclopedias, biographical directories, literary criticisms, and more.

If you're using the Internet for a research paper, the periodical index databases provided by your library should generally be your first stop. You can usually find them on your school or library's Web page. Some of the most popular databases include FirstSearch, InfoTrac, ProQuest, LexisNexis Academic Service, and EBSCOhost.

These resources allow you to enter key terms to find articles from well-known journals, magazines, government documents, and other reference works. Using these sources, you can be sure you're getting more reliable and timely information than you will find on most general Web sites.

EFFICIENT INTERNET SEARCHES

- Before you begin, think about your search strategy. There is a lot of information on the Internet, but much of it is unreliable or of poor quality. (See pages 802–803.)

- Start with a simple search. Each word you use limits the results the search engine finds. If you're too wordy, the search engine will filter out a lot of Web sites that might have been useful. You can always add more keywords if the results are too broad.

- Don't worry too much about getting the wording just right. There might be times where you can't remember how something is spelled or the full name of whatever you're searching for. Just take a shot—a good search engine like Google can often automatically correct your mistakes.

- Be as specific as possible. While your goal should be to use as few keywords as possible, your results will be better if you use descriptive words that link to your particular topic. Try to visualize the words that a Web site on your topic might contain.

- Keep in mind you can filter your search to return results for particular types of Web sites (for example, only sites that end with .edu) or file types (such as .pdf).

SEARCH ENGINE TIPS

Searches are case insensitive, so don't worry about capital letters. On the Web, *New York* is the same as *new york*.

Boolean search terms (AND, OR, NOT) DO need to be in all capital letters, though. Otherwise, common words like *a, an,* and *the* are usually ignored by search engines.

Punctuation is rarely important. The same goes for special symbols.

TAKING NOTES

Good research depends on good notes. The information you find must be recorded in your notes before it can become part of an organized and well-written report. Before you get started, make sure you read and grasp the source material you're writing about. You can't take useful notes on something that you don't understand.

Key your source cards to your notes by assigning each source a certain number. Write a new number in the upper right-hand corner of each source card. Then use that number on all the notes you take from that source. That way, you only have to write out the full source information once.

Source Cards

It's important to give credit to your sources. As you research your paper, keep careful notes about where you find particular quotes and ideas. That way, when it's time to write the paper, it will be easy to separate your ideas from other people's ideas.

A great way to track source information is by preparing a working bibliography using index cards.

Writing Source Cards

Whenever you find a source that looks interesting and relevant to your topic, make a new card for it. You may not use that source in the final paper, but it's important to write down all of the possible sources in the early stage of your research. Otherwise, it can be difficult to find the source again if you need it later.

Use one index card per source. Keep all the bibliography cards in an alphabetized stack organized by authors' last names.

Your source cards will be useful as you finish your paper, when you need to create a bibliography. Make sure you throw away the cards for sources that you didn't use in the final paper.

SOURCE CARD CHECKLIST

Each source card should include the following information:

- Author's name
- Editor's name (for compilations or periodicals)
- Title (of article and/or book)
- Publisher's name
- Publisher's location (city and state)
- Exact date of publication
- Page numbers (for periodicals or reference works)

- the author's name (last name first)
- the title
- the publication information (publisher, location, date)
- the library call number, www.address, or other detailed notes of exactly where the source can be found

Johnson, Charles
The Photography of Martin Luther King, Jr.
Penguin Group.
New York, New York. 2000
E 185.97.

A source card lists important information about your source that will help you (and your readers) track a source later.

WHY INDEX CARDS?

Index cards are better for note cards than regular notebook paper. Here's why.

- Using loose index cards allows you to order and reorder the way your notes are arranged.
- You can alphabetize the stack of index cards as you prepare to write your works cited page.
- You can easily add information about new sources without rewriting the whole list.

Preston Mafham, Ron and Ken.
Encyclopedia of Insects and Spiders.
Thunder Bay Press, San Diego, CA. 2005

QL463 .P714 2005   Carnegie Library of Pittsburgh

This source card is for a book. The information on your card will look a little different for each type of source you use.

Note Cards

As you take notes, remember that you are a filter for the information you read. With the exception of direct quotes that you want to include in your paper, your notes should be in your own words. You need to digest new concepts in order to write about them. You can't do this if you simply copy straight from the sources you're reading.

Write your notes on index cards, making sure to have only one note per card, even if there are two pieces of important information on the same page of your source.

There are four main types of note cards.

- Direct Quotes
- Paraphrases
- Summaries
- Personal Notes

It's important that you label each note card according to its type to prevent confusion.

WATCH OUT!

Too many direct quotes can work against your paper by causing you, the author, to have no voice. The paper is YOUR argument. The sources are there to back up and further your points.

Direct Quotes

Direct quotes add credibility to the information you present. (See pages 730–731.) Use them when you want to make sure the meaning of the author's words isn't lost. When you find a quote you might want to use in your paper, make sure you record

- the exact quote, word for word (copy it carefully).
- its page number.
- quotation marks (so you don't mistake the quote for a paraphrase).

Paraphrases

When you paraphrase, you put the author's ideas into your own words. Paraphrasing can be difficult because you have to really understand the source before you can explain it well.

Make sure that you write any comments or reactions to the material on a separate note card.

Summaries

Summaries are similar to paraphrases in that they put someone else's ideas in your own words. However, when you summarize, you condense that information, picking out the basics and leaving behind the rest of the detail. (Think the inside of a book jacket or the synopsis of a movie.) This means that an entire paragraph—or even a full-length book—could be summarized in one sentence.

Personal Comments

Personal notes help you remember your insights and impressions as you read. You might write, for example, a note about why you disagree with an author. It may seem silly for you to take the time to write down your thoughts, but if you don't write down those ideas as they occur to you, you may lose them.

Mark personal comments clearly to keep from confusing them later with the author's point of view.

Parts of a Note Card

1. **The heading** is a short description of the note that tells what kind of information is on the card.

2. **The body** of the note is the quote, paraphrase, summary, or personal comment that you might use in your paper.

3. **The source** is a way to indicate the origins of the information. It can be a number corresponding to a source card or the source's author.

4. **The page number** shows you exactly where to go if you need to return to the source.

Arachnid characteristics   **1**

Arachnids are often confused with insects, although they are built differently. Arachnids **2** have two body regions, whereas insects have three. Arachnids normally have eight legs instead of the insect's six. (paraphrase)
Note: Follow this with the different types of spiders.

Preston-Mafham, Ron and Ken.   p.248
            3   **4**

Writing a Note Card

- Limit yourself to one fact, idea, or quote per index card.

- Use only the front side of the index card.

- Double-check the source to make sure you included all the necessary information.

- Make sure you have stated the meaning completely in your own words (unless you're using a direct quote).

- Make sure to write down the page number on which the material was found.

fyi! *When you finish taking notes, shuffle your cards around according to topic. The paper could quickly order itself into a logical outline.*

INFORMATION LITERACY

When you choose to watch one TV show instead of another, your decision is based on which program you think will be the most informative, the most entertaining, or the most interesting. In the morning, you pick the day's outfit based on what's available, your preferences, and the weather forecast. All day, every day, you evaluate choices and make judgments.

Selecting research materials is a similar process. You choose sources and collect information based on what you think is important for your project. Inevitably, some sources will be more valuable than others. That's why it's important to be able to recognize the good ones (and the bad ones).

Critical Thinking

Each day, you're bombarded with information. You steadily receive data from a variety of sources, including computers, television, books, and other people. Whether or not you're aware of it, you're constantly processing and prioritizing that information in order to get through the day. You choose to ignore some things so you have time to pay close attention to other things.

You have to be similarly strategic with your research planning. You don't have time to find (much less read) every single thing that was ever written on your topic. At every stage of the research process, you must use critical thinking skills to determine how to make the most of your time.

As you begin your research, you will have to sift through a wide variety of sources to determine which ones you want to spend more time with later. Once you have compiled the best sources, study them with a critical eye. You can't believe everything you read; it's up to you to determine whether a source is accurate and useful.

Information literacy is about learning how to judge the worth of what you see, hear, and read. If you can easily identify valuable information, your work will be much easier.

The Medium Is the Message

Marshall McLuhan was a Canadian English professor who changed the way we think about mass media.

His most important idea was that each communication medium (such as books, television, and film) has certain characteristics that should be the object of study. He encouraged people to think critically about those characteristics and how they influence our thinking.

McLuhan believed that each major period in history takes its character from the medium of communication used most widely at the time. In other words, the dominant medium promotes certain values in society. For example, he called the period from 1700 to the mid-1900s the Age of Print. At that time, the printed word was the way that most people gained and shared knowledge.

Eventually, the Age of Print was replaced by what McLuhan called the Electronics Age. Computers have made communication so speedy that people in all parts of the world have become deeply involved in the lives of everyone else.

Marshall McLuhan (1911–1980) thought that the key to understanding mass communications was to study the tools we use to distribute information. ▶

Medium	Message
Print	individualism
	nationalism
	privacy
	specialization
Web	collaboration
	globalization
	community
	blending disciplines

MAKE THE MOST OF YOUR RESEARCH

- Engage with your sources.
- Reflect on what you read.
- Take notes as you go.
- Stay on topic.

Primary and Secondary Sources

There are two classes of sources you can use as you write a paper.

- Primary Sources
- Secondary Sources

The differences between these two source classes explain the author's relationship to the subject under discussion. If you read a novel, that book is considered a primary source. If you write a book report on that novel, that report is a secondary source because it is one step removed from the original material.

Primary Sources	Secondary Sources
first-hand	second-hand
unfiltered	filtered
direct	removed
in the moment or looking forward	looking back

Primary Sources

Primary sources are close to the subject you're researching. They are original sources, such as:

- creative works
- autobiographies
- diaries
- speeches
- lectures
- original research
- interviews

Primary sources give you a chance to interpret information for yourself. They can be powerful persuaders in your writing because readers know your information is coming straight from the source.

Secondary Sources

A secondary source refers to another source in some way; it cannot stand alone. Secondary sources comment on an idea that was originally presented in another piece of writing.

Any explication, analysis, interpretation, or evaluation is a secondary source because it must refer to something else.

 *Fictional works and poetry are always primary sources.*

PRIMARY SOURCE EXAMPLES

Catch-22 (novel)

"Lady Lazarus" (poem)

"A Good Man Is Hard to Find" (short story)

Speak, Memory (autobiography)

Anne Frank: The Diary of a Young Girl

Martin Luther King's "I Have A Dream" speech

SECONDARY SOURCE EXAMPLES

Journal articles

the "Romanticism" entry in an encyclopedia

Textbooks

Literary criticism (about a specific work)

Will in the World (Shakespeare biography)

Understanding the Past

The difference between primary and secondary sources makes a big difference to historians, who have the job of making sense of the past.

Whenever possible, historians use primary sources. To them, these documents and other accounts are raw data that hasn't been influenced or distorted by an added layer of interpretation.

Consider the kinds of witnesses a police officer might interview after a car crash. Which kind of witness is probably more reliable: someone who saw the car crash with his or her own eyes, or someone who just heard about someone else's account of the accident?

Like an eyewitness, a primary source speaks for itself. While that report isn't 100 percent reliable—it may, after all, contain inaccuracies—it is direct.

A secondary report, by contrast, introduces more opportunities for error. A secondary source is subjective. It views a primary source at a distance and through a particular lens. Since that primary source can no longer "speak for itself," there is an added layer of bias.

As you research, use primary sources whenever possible. If you're writing a paper about a novel, for instance, your best source is going to be the novel itself. As you gather secondary sources, keep in mind that you are looking at that novel through someone else's eyes. Does that secondary source discuss the primary source in a manner that seems accurate and unbiased? It's up to you to decide.

Writing a paper usually requires that you consult a variety of primary and secondary sources.

PRIMARY OR SECONDARY?

If you're not sure whether a source is primary or secondary, ask yourself the following questions.

- What is the author's relationship to the material? How does the author know about the subject? How far removed is he or she from the material?

- Where did the author find the information in the text? What kinds of sources, if any, did he or she use?

- Is the author saying something new or commenting on someone else's idea?

Evaluating Sources

In any research paper, the proof of your argument will depend heavily on the strength of your research and on how thoroughly you collect your information. After you gather your sources, you must selectively use that information to build your argument. Therefore, it's important to be able to evaluate your sources and to use them effectively.

You may need to examine various kinds of sources before you find the best possible ones. Books and articles are traditional sources, but you may discover your best information comes from a survey or interviews, the Internet, or a museum.

Valuable information may turn up where you least expect to find it. The notes on a record jacket, for example, could provide interesting details for a report on the origins of rock music.

View your research as an investigation. You are out to track down leads and find the facts you need to write the best paper you can.

Most research topics will have more sources than you have time to review. You must be strategic as you search. Maximize your time by focusing on the sources that seem to offer the most "bang for your buck."

Getting Started

Skim through your sources to find relevant material for your notes. Ask yourself questions as you read and review the material.

- Does the thesis of the source support my own thesis?
- Will this information help me make my case?
- Are there any specific examples or statistics that back up my argument?

If you answered no, it's time to move on to another source. If you answered yes, it's time to take a closer look at the source to see if it's going to be useful for your project.

Your next step will be to evaluate the source more carefully so you can be sure it contains good information.

Determining Value

It's important to remember that not all sources are created equal; some will be more useful than others. Some of the sources you find as you research may be off-topic, unreliable, or inappropriate.

To decide if a source is valuable, you must be able to assess the information it offers. This process calls for some judgment on your part.

After you've collected your sources, how can you judge if they're really useful? There are four factors to consider.

- Relevance
- Authority
- Bias
- Publication date

Relevance

Your first task is to make sure the source is relevant to your purposes. To know if a source is relevant, you must understand your own thesis statement. (See pages 710–711.) The best, most relevant sources are the ones that are most closely related to your thesis.

If you're in the early stages of your research project, you might check the preface and the table of contents. Turn to a book's index to see how much it covers your topic. If your topic appears on several pages, the work is worth checking carefully.

You might also skim the article to look for information that directly relates to the points you want to make in your paper.

Next, you need to make sure the source will be relevant to your audience. Often, it's easier to find information that gives you a general overview of a topic. You'll need to find specific material, too, but sources that are too specialized may result in a list of facts that are too narrow to give your reader the big picture. You need to make sure your reader understands your topic.

You don't want to get bogged down in technical, scientific, or medical terms that will confuse your readers. Ask yourself how much your readers know about the topic. You don't want to write over their heads, but you would also be making a mistake if you wrote in a style that was too simple.

In addition to considering the author's background, consider the publication in which your source appears. When using periodicals, for instance, consider the purpose and the target readership of the magazine.

EVALUATION CHECKLIST

- Is the source relevant?
- Does the information it contains support or oppose your own thesis?
- Will the source help you build your argument?
- Does the source contain information that is appropriate for your audience (not too general, not too technical)?
- Does your source have footnotes or a works cited page?
- Does the author or the publication have a known bias?
- Does the publication's audience have a particular point of view?
- Does the source contain current information?

fyi! *A source may be considered relevant even if it refutes or opposes your point of view. When you make an argument, it's often important to present the opposing viewpoints. In your paper, you can refute the opposition with your own argument, making your assertions even more valid.*

Evaluating Sources

Authority

Ask yourself about the credentials of the person who wrote the information you're considering.

- Is he or she an expert?
- Is the expert well known in the field?
- Has the author written other works on the subject?
- What is his or her experience with the issue?

The answers to these questions aren't always obvious. Almost every author has some sort of agenda. This doesn't mean the information isn't credible; it just means you need to to take the author's goals into consideration.

Are there footnotes, appendices, or other indications of careful scholarship? If you're consulting periodicals, it may be wise to avoid articles in popular magazines not recognized as authoritative. If you have doubts, check with a librarian to get a second opinion.

A little detective work can help you determine where an author is coming from. ▼

Bias

A writer who grew up on a family farm in Iowa and a writer who spent all her life in New York City may have different biases when writing about the value of small farms to the United States.

Everything you read is written by an author with a specific perspective and goal. Some authors may be better informed than others, and some may have a personal investment in the issue. As you might suspect, some authors may not care what opinion the reader forms as long as the author makes money from what is written.

Does the author have an apparent bias that could hamper the objectivity of the book or article? For example, if you're doing research on the 1967 Arab-Israeli war, a book, article, or Web site on the subject by either an Arab or an Israeli might be biased. Although it could be an interesting source to include among others, it would be unwise to use it as your main source.

BACKGROUND CHECK

Authors are not always upfront about their biases and agendas. You might have to do some detective work to learn more about an author's point of view. Here are a few ways you can go about getting more background information.

- Read the book jacket.
- Research the author on the Internet.
- Read the introduction to a source, if there is one.
- Use biographical reference tools such as *Who's Who in America* or *Current Biography*.
- Ask a librarian.

Publication Date

To determine if a source is current, you need to find out when it was published. Ask yourself these questions.

- How recent is the information?
- Is it current enough to be credible?
- Are there recent publications to help determine if the information is still valid?

To make sure you have the latest information, check magazine and journal articles on the subject first. They are usually the most up-to-date sources of information.

If you use a newspaper article as a source, keep in mind that the information presented is perishable. Ongoing events are covered in newspapers on a daily basis as more information comes to light. As a result, comprehensive coverage on a topic is seldom available in one newspaper article.

On the other hand, not all topics need up-to-the-minute information. If you're doing research in a rapidly developing field, such as technology, you'll want the latest materials available. But if you're dealing with a historical topic like the Korean War where the publication date may not be as important, you might use books and articles that are years old. In a book, the publication date often appears on the back of a title page.

STAYING UP TO DATE

It is important that you understand the changing nature of your topic when deciding if your source is current. Five years may not seem like a long time, but for dynamic topics like public policy or technology, if all the information you use is from years past, you could be overlooking new, relevant information, including laws, court cases, and recent examples. While you'll probably need to read and understand some background information and history of your topic, the focus of your argument can't be based on old information.

Two articles on the same topic can represent very different viewpoints. Consider the different kinds of articles you might see in magazines called *Lumber Digest* and *Saving the Forests*. ▼

Internet sources can be difficult to sift through because there is such a large amount of material. There are countless Web sites, so you must be thoughtful about the ones you use in your research. You also have to be careful; anyone can put anything on the Web, so you have to view every Web site with a critical eye.

When you go to the library for information, you know that librarians have carefully selected the books and journals inside. With online sources, there are no such safeguards. The Internet is like the Wild West of information. There are no rules. This often makes it difficult to verify the accuracy of a given Web site.

While you should carefully evaluate any source that you plan to use, it's especially critical to carefully evaluate online sources. While the same criteria—authority, relevance, bias, and publication date—apply to both print and electronic sources, the way you think about those categories is a little different.

A balanced approach to research involves different kinds of sources. Don't rely on the Internet for all your information. Make sure you review print sources, too.

Authority

Authority can be difficult to pin down on the Internet. When you read a book or an article, it's almost always obvious who the author is. On a Web site, that is often not the case. Often, no author is listed. And even when an author is listed, that person may fudge his or her credentials or other information.

As you browse the Web, keep an eye out for authoritative sources. The Web site of *The New York Times*, for example, is widely known as a reliable information source. Someone's personal blog, on the other hand, probably hasn't been established as a credible source, so facts and figures should be double-checked whenever possible.

You can ask questions to help determine whether or not a Web site is authoritative.

- Is the author of the page identified?
- What are his or her credentials?
- Who sponsors (or pays for) the Web site?
- What is that organization's (or author's) reputation?

Relevance

It can be difficult to stay on-task as you search for Web sources. There are a lot of distractions online, which makes it easy to lose time. You might become absorbed by a site that's interesting, but off-topic. Here are a few questions you can ask yourself to determine if a source is worthy of your valuable research time.

- What topics are covered?
- Are the topics explored in-depth?
- How does the page compare to print sources on the same topic?

STATIC AND DYNAMIC SOURCES

Print sources are static—they will always stay the same. A book will say the same thing today as it said 20 years ago. When you list a book on your works cited page, your reader has all the information she needs to find a source and read exactly the information that you read.

In contrast, Web sources are dynamic. While some sites are relatively stable, others change from moment to moment. Something you read on a Web site today might be different if you read that Web site tomorrow. Sometimes, the content—or even the Web site itself—will disappear. When you list a Web site on your works cited page, your reader has no guarantee that the source looks the same as it did when you reviewed it.

WATCH OUT!

When you use Web sites in your paper, make sure that you don't plagiarize. Web sites are copyrighted just like printed words, so be very careful that you cite the source accurately in the paper and include the source in your works cited list.

STRENGTHS OF THE WEB

- The Web is often more current than print sources because material can be published instantly. Print materials require more planning and lead time. Newspapers like *The New York Times* can publish breaking news stories in real time.

- The Internet is a great place to find factual information such as public documents and contact information for organizations and public figures.

- It can make you aware of other people who are doing similar kinds of research.

WEAKNESSES OF THE WEB

- The Internet is not as comprehensive as a library. Online research should be used to supplement (not replace) library research.

- Sources are not vetted or reviewed, so it can be difficult to confirm accuracy.

- Most copyrighted materials are not available for free. Some books and journals allow partial access or fee-based access.

Bias

Just as the writers of an advertisement have a different goal or purpose than the author of an encyclopedia article, different Web sites have different goals and purposes and points of view.

To determine if a site contains objective, unbiased information, you need to learn about the different types of Web sites. You can often learn something about a Web site by examining the last extension of its address.

Often, the most trustworthy and objective sites end in .edu or .gov. Their main purpose is to deliver information, and they are held accountable for the information that is disseminated.

Sites ending in .org are organizations, which tend to have bias on a subject. While an organization is most likely legitimate, you need to be aware of the organization's agenda in providing the information.

Sites ending in .com are commercial sites, and their main purpose is to sell products.

Publication Date

One of the Web's strengths is its ability to publish up-to-the-minute information, but that doesn't mean that all Web sites are current. The date that you visit a Web site is one thing, but the date that the Web site was created or updated is quite another. All of those dates are important, but they aren't always readily available.

Extension	Type of Site	Example
.com	commercial	www.apple.com
.edu	educational	www.uchicago.edu
.gov	governmental	www.whitehouse.gov
.org	organizational	www.redcross.org
.mil	military	www.navy.mil

Wikipedia can be a vital research tool, but you should avoid citing it as a source. Instead, you can use it as a starting point to get an overview of your topic or to find links to other valuable Web sites.

Analyzing the Argument

A good argument uses different kinds of information to support its central claim. The information that a writer uses to support an argument does the heavy lifting; without it, the claim would collapse and the argument would fail. (See pages 732–733.)

Often, authors use logic as that means of support. As you research a topic, you need to evaluate the logic of everything you read to make sure it's sound. Sometimes bad logic sounds right on the surface, but you can see the flaws when you look closely.

The two classical approaches to logic are *inductive* and *deductive* reasoning.

Inductive Reasoning

One way of thinking is called induction. People use inductive reasoning when they see a puddle of water and guess that it has rained recently.

Here's another simple example:

Observation 1: You bite into a green apple and observe that it's bitter.

Observation 2: You bite into another green apple and observe that it's bitter, too.

Observation 3: A third green apple also tastes bitter.

Conclusion: Based on your experience, you decide that all green apples taste bitter. You stop biting into them.

Science depends on this kind of thinking: making observations, taking them a step further, and drawing generalizations.

Deductive Reasoning

The other way of thinking is called deduction.

Statement 1: You know that apples are edible.

Statement 2: This thing is an apple.

Conclusion: Therefore, this thing must be edible.

As you can see, induction begins with particular observations and moves to a general conclusion.

Deduction is just the opposite: it begins with a generalization, or an assumption, and moves to a particular conclusion.

Both kinds of thinking are useful and valid.

Inductive	Deductive
informal	formal
common sense	scientific
probable	certain
guess	determine
inconclusive	conclusive

BUILDING A LOGICAL ARGUMENT

Induction begins with a particular observation and moves to a general conclusion.

Deduction begins with a generalization and moves to a particular conclusion.

Observation → Conclusion

Generalization → Conclusion

The Problem with Induction

The strength of induction is that it encourages a close observation of reality. Induction tries to make sense of new information without preconception.

Induction also has weaknesses, though. The first is that the reliability of an induction depends upon the reliability of the observation. Returning to the example of green apples, it's easy to find potential errors. The apples you bite may seem bitter to you, but what if there's something wrong with your taste buds? Or what if the apples have been washed with some sort of bitter solution? Or grown in bitter soil?

Even when the observation is correct, there is the possibility of error. How many green apples should one taste before concluding that all green apples are bitter? What if the fourth apple had been sweet? When a researcher gives a new drug to three patients and nothing bad happens, can she conclude that the substance is safe? Or should the new drug be given to 100 people? A thousand? While the probability of valid induction increases with the size of the sample, the results are never certain. That researcher will never be 100 percent sure that the drug is safe.

The Problem with Deduction

Deduction can be a powerfully persuasive tool because it appeals to reason and logic. But it's important to remember that there is considerable room for error.

Deduction begins with statements that are called premises. Logic tells us whether a deductive argument is valid or invalid based on those premises. That means that if you start with a false premise, deduction can lead to a perfectly logical, but false, conclusion.

Consider this example.

Premise 1: All Greeks have beards.

Premise 2: Zeno is a Greek.

Conclusion: Therefore, Zeno has a beard.

The conclusion is perfectly logical based on the premises. But take a closer look at the first premise. Do all Greeks really have beards? No, they don't. Therefore, the conclusion is called into question.

With deduction, where you start is just as important as where you end up. Your conclusion is only as correct as your premises.

Defective Arguments

There are probably as many ways to violate the rules of logic as there are people on the planet. But some logical errors are so common that they're especially familiar. They are commonly understood as a particular kind of error and have been given well-known names. Some have been around for so long that they've retained their original Latin names.

These defective arguments are called logical fallacies. Some of the best-known logical fallacies are listed on the chart at right.

The problem with bad thinking is that it isn't always immediately obvious to the reader. Logical fallacies, on the surface, can seem very convincing. Often, they appeal to emotion or common misconceptions instead of careful thinking. As you read, it's your job to evaluate the logic of a given argument.

WARNING BELLS

Here are some things to watch for as you check an argument for logical fallacies. These signals are often (but not always) a sign of bad thinking.

- Vague claims
- A defensive tone
- Overreliance on anecdotes instead of factual data
- Emotional appeals
- Personal attacks
- Abrupt topic change
- Broad judgments about a large group of people
- Assumptions (information that's taken for granted)

AVOIDING LOGICAL FALLACIES

Logical fallacies can be used purposefully to deceive people, as in misleading advertisements or dishonest political debates. Other times, logical fallacies are used accidentally. Avoid logical fallacies in your own writing by following these tips.

- Avoid sweeping conclusions. Be as specific as possible when you make a claim.
- Don't try to hide anything. Be upfront about any shortcomings in your argument.
- Stay on topic. Make sure any examples you use relate directly to your subject.
- Try to remain objective. Take a step back if you find yourself feeling emotional.
- Be honest about the opposing argument. Don't misrepresent the other side or fudge the facts.

WATCH OUT!

If you're having trouble understanding someone else's argument, or crafting your own argument, a logical fallacy might be the root of the problem.

An analogy *compares one thing with another thing.* A false analogy *results when the comparison is not based on any real similarities between the two items being compared. Watch for false analogies as you evaluate arguments.*

Fallacy	Definition	Cause	Examples	Dangers
Ad hominem argument	Latin for "to the person"	Discredits an argument with a personal attack	His argument is worthless because he has bad taste in movies.	Confuses the person with his or her argument
Circular argument	An assertion that appears to support an argument, but actually just repeats it in a different way	The respondent wants to evade the question.	She made an A in the course because she did very well.	The argument doesn't advance.
Generalization	The assumption that what is true for one person or thing is true for a group of people or things	Whenever people are organized into groups, people expect group members to share some common qualities.	People from Oregon State University are boring. I knew a student there who was really dull.	It's likely that someone or something in the group is exceptional.
Non sequitur	Latin for "doesn't follow"	Two unrelated statements appear to be connected.	The basketball team was playing well because the stock market was up.	Non sequiturs don't hold up to analysis, but they often sound plausible on the surface.
Polar thinking	Assuming that only one thing or its opposite can be true, allowing for only two options	Compromise can be difficult.	Either we should have a first-rate physics department, or we should just get rid of it.	Other possibilities are ignored.
Post hoc, ergo propter hoc	Literally, Latin for "after this, therefore because of this"	If one thing happens after another thing, we are tempted to see some causal relationship.	Don't cut the grass. The last time you cut the grass, the Braves lost the Series.	Sometimes things happen in a sequence even though they're unrelated.
Red herring	An irrelevant, distracting argument that takes attention away from the facts that matter	The respondent wants to evade the main point.	John doesn't deserve to be punished because he has volunteered for the Red Cross and his girlfriend just broke up with him.	Vital information is overlooked.
Stereotyping	Holding generalized, oversimplified, or incorrect beliefs about members of a group	Whenever people are organized into groups, people expect group members to share some common qualities.	All basketball players are tall. All actors are extroverts.	Stereotypes can be the basis of prejudice, which is negative attitudes or feelings directed at a group.
Straw man	Misrepresenting an opponent's position	As with the red herring, the respondent wants to evade the main point.	Real argument: arguing the SAT test should be eliminated. Straw-man argument: arguing that all college admissions requirements should be eliminated.	If the audience mistakes a straw man argument for the real one, then the false argument may be persuasive.

During your research, it's important to know the difference between facts and opinions.

A **fact** is generally accepted as something that has been documented and backed up by reliable, valid research and statistics.

An **opinion** is an individual conclusion formed after a person views and interprets the facts.

Fact	Opinion
Katie's hair is brown.	I like Katie's hair.
The president will spend three days in China next week.	The president's trip to China is long overdue.
Thursday night, I found a gray jacket in the auditorium.	The jacket probably belongs to Mike.

OPINION WORDS

When you see one of these words in a sentence, there's a good chance that what you're reading is an opinion.

bad	believe
best	better
effective	excellent
feel	good
great	guess
least	perhaps
probably	strange
suggest	terrible
think	wonder
worst	

Authors usually support their arguments and claims with both facts and opinions. During your research, you must scrutinize—that is, closely examine—an author's statements. Never accept a statement at face value without careful consideration.

Recognizing the Difference

Something that happened is a fact. Someone's thoughts or feelings about what happened is an opinion.

As you research a topic, pretend that you're a judge listening to a court case. Ask yourself: Am I reading about something that happened? Or am I reading about someone's perspective on what happened?

As you research, you have to judge which statements are facts and which are opinions.

Evaluating Facts

Not all facts are created equal. As you research a topic, it's your job to take a close look at the information and decide if it seems credible.

- Do other sources list the same facts?
- Are the facts presented objectively? Or does the author seem biased?
- Are the facts relevant to the argument? Or do they veer off track?
- What is the source of the facts? Does that source seem reliable?

 *As you take notes, make sure to mark the difference between fact and opinion.*

Evaluating Opinions

Opinions aren't necessarily a bad thing. Many, if not most, good sources state an author's opinion. Here are a few questions you can ask yourself as you decide whether or not to include a particular source in your paper.

- Who holds the opinion? Is it an expert? A witness? An author who has first-hand experience with a topic might have more perspective than another writer.
- Does the author try to disguise his or her opinion as fact? If so, the author might have a hidden agenda and the source might be unreliable.
- Is the opinion based on facts (such as statistics or dates)? Supporting an opinion with facts makes it seem stronger.
- Does the author include counterarguments? Including counterarguments suggests that the author has considered both sides of the issue.

Facts	Opinions
objective	subjective
evidence	judgmental
unbiased	biased
proven	unproven
unemotional	emotional
certain	beliefs
	attitudes
	thoughts
	personal
verifiable	guesses

Types of Evidence

SOUTHWESTERN

A good argument never stands alone. If it could, most of the things you read or write would be just one sentence long. The author would state his or her claim, and that would be that.

Arguments have to be supported by evidence that shows readers why they should (or shouldn't) believe the claim. As you research a topic, you're likely to come across many types of arguments in books and articles. One way to evaluate them is to examine the evidence the author provides.

There are many different types of evidence.

- Statistics
- Examples
- Anecdotes
- Reasons
- Definitions
- Descriptions

Most arguments will use more than one type of evidence to get the point across.

STATISTICS CHECKLIST

Ask yourself these questions to determine if a statistic is good evidence.

- Do you understand the statistic?
- Is the connection between the statistic and the argument clear?
- Is the source of the statistic reputable?
- Is the statistic relatively current? Or is it outdated?

Statistics

Statistics are numerical information that describes certain people or objects.

One in four people likes peanut butter better than jelly.

Thirty percent of American drivers sing along to the car radio.

Jolly brand paper towels are five times as absorbent as the leading national brand.

Statistics can be very convincing. You've probably noticed that they're used in advertisements like television commercials. But it's important to keep in mind that some statistics are more reliable than others.

That's because statistics can be collected in a variety of ways. For example, the statistic "one in four people likes peanut butter better than jelly" would seem meaningful if you knew that 4,000 people were surveyed. How might your opinion change if only four people were surveyed?

Examples

Specific examples are an effective way to support a claim or clarify a point.

The word *run* suggests rapid motion, but it has other meanings, too. A clock that runs is simply operating. A sore that runs is oozing. You find sheep in a run, run butter is melted, and run-down means exhausted.

Judge an example by how well it illustrates the author's point.

Anecdotes

Anecdotes are like little stories or short accounts of interesting or colorful incidents. A writer often uses an anecdote to illustrate his or her claim. Relaying them is often the best way of making a point because the story breathes life into a concept that might otherwise seem abstract.

> Mall parking lots are dangerous, especially after dark. Just last week, my neighbor was attacked by a group of teenage girls as he walked to his car. They knocked him down and stole his wallet.

While an anecdote might do a good job of illustrating a point, keep in mind that it's just one person's story. The point it illustrates might not apply to everyone.

Reasons

Authors often provide a list of reasons to support their beliefs and opinions.

> We live in the worst of times. The unemployment rate is high. Governments cannot be trusted. The high crime rate makes us fearful in our own homes. Worst of all, the possibility of nuclear war hangs over our heads.

Definitions

Many arguments will use definitions as support. A definition explains something by telling what it is or how it works.

> Every well-equipped kitchen should contain at least one meat cleaver. A cleaver is a large, wedge-shaped knife that can cut through almost any kind of bone and gristle.

Descriptions

Descriptions are easy to spot because they appeal to your five senses.

> Many people prefer Soft brand soap to other brands. Soft soap lathers easily, smells good, refreshes the skin, and cleans well. It costs less, too.

Descriptions might seem like good evidence because they are so vivid, but keep in mind that they can be subjective. There is a difference between saying the dog is brown and the dog is cute. "Brown" has a meaning that's similar in everyone's mind. "Cute" is a matter of taste.

EVALUATING EVIDENCE

In court, evidence is information that tends to prove or disprove a fact in question. Evidence may consist of documents, public records, or the testimony of witnesses.

Writing is similar. In both cases, the quality of the evidence is more important than quantity. As you research, consider the strength of the evidence as you read through different arguments.

Here are some questions you can ask yourself as you read.

- Is the evidence convincing?
- Is the evidence clear? Or is it confusing?
- Is it on topic?
- Is the evidence verifiable?
- Do other authors writing on the same topic use similar types of evidence?
- What kinds of evidence are most highly valued in the field?

MIX IT UP

Good writers use different kinds of evidence to support their arguments. Relying too heavily on one type can result in a weak argument. For example, a few well-chosen statistics are preferable to a long list; if you use too many numbers, they become less meaningful to the reader. Anecdotes, on the other hand, are a great way to make an argument more interesting and engaging, but they aren't a strong enough form of evidence to stand alone.

Whenever you read an argument that seems to focus on one area of evidence, stop to consider the author's motivation. You may uncover holes in the author's logic.

Letting Go

A research project involves gathering information and sifting through it to arrive at a conclusion. As you sift, two important categories will emerge: the research you want to use and the research you don't want to use.

Sometimes, when you read a book or an article, you quickly realize that the source is, for whatever reason, not right for your project. When that happens, you can set the source aside and move forward without another thought.

Other times, you might spend a lot of time with an unusable source. Since you had planned to use the source, you might have even taken detailed notes before you realized that it wasn't going to work out.

Plan of Action

The research you use includes the sources you plan to summarize, paraphrase, or quote in your paper. These sources will be mentioned in your writing and listed at the end of your paper.

The research you don't use will have to be discarded or set aside.

Throwing away a source can be more difficult than it sounds. You may feel frustrated that you wasted time with a source you can't use.

While it can be hard to let go of a source you have spent valuable time with, keep in mind that it's all part of the process. In fact, if you don't discard some of your sources, then you probably haven't researched the topic properly.

AVOID FORMING INCORRECT CONCLUSIONS

Being able to pick out the central idea in each source is crucial to the research process. Every source you read contains a thesis statement. It's your job to pick out the main point and decide how it relates to your own ideas.

As you read and evaluate sources, you are bound to draw conclusions. Make sure that yours are correct by asking yourself these questions.

- Do I have enough information to draw a conclusion?

- How does my conclusion relate to the author's main point? Do I agree or disagree with it?

- Which of the author's points shaped my conclusion?

When you finish reading, go back and skim the source to ensure you've correctly understood the author's main idea.

Common Reasons to Discard a Source

You found a similar source that works better.

You may find that two or more of your sources have similar messages. When this happens, you have two choices. The first is that you can list all the sources. This is a good idea when you want to show that more than one expert agrees on a particular point. Other times, you will need to choose the source that best presents the point you're making. For instance, you might select a single source when you need a direct quote.

The source seemed useful, but you never found a chance to mention it in your paper.

This often happens when the source has information that is too general or too specific. General information is so widely known that you don't need to attach it to any particular source. Specific sources might be too technical or too narrow for your purposes.

Your argument changed as you went through the research process.

Often, your thesis will change over the course of your research project. Don't worry; this evolution is natural and common. Often, when you begin your research, you don't know your topic very well. As you research, you become more informed. The sources you read influence your thinking. As a result, you might change your mind on a particular point or change your overall argument. Or maybe you decide to narrow your topic.

You discover the source is outdated.

A source can become outdated for many reasons. For instance, newspaper articles frequently become outdated as new information comes to light. They provide a good snapshot of a given topic at a particular moment in time, but the information they contain does not always hold up in the fullness of time.

You discover the source is incorrect.

Remember that the more you read about a topic, the more informed you become. A source that seemed reliable at first might be disproven over the course of your research project. When that happens, you have no choice but to let go of the bad source. (See pages 800–801.)

Resist the temptation to pad your works cited page with every source you can find. It's better to have a shorter list of carefully chosen sources.

DOCUMENTING SOURCES

Just like the credits at the end of a movie, a works cited list at the end of your paper gives proper credit to the people whose ideas and research contributed to the final product. Readers familiar with your subject can recognize sources they have encountered before. Readers unfamiliar with the topic are given information they can use to locate the source material themselves.

 *Consider your subject when you're deciding whether a source is current. Timely topics like technology change rapidly. Other topics, like literary criticism, are more static.*

Why Bother?

Plagiarism

The most important reason to document your sources is to avoid plagiarism.

One of the most common mistakes that beginning researchers encounter is knowing when to tell the reader that the ideas or the words in the paper belong to someone else. The rule is simple: If the ideas or words aren't your own, document them.

When you draw from someone else's work, credit for the borrowed information—whether it's a fact, an opinion, or a direct quote—must be clearly given to the original researcher. To assign credit, you must document all of your sources.

You must cite every quote, paraphrase, and summary you use from a book, periodical, interview, online database, Web site, and any other outside source you consult. You will need to use both an *in-text citation* and a full listing for that source for your *works cited* page.

Plagiarism is unethical. The copyright laws of many nations make plagiarism and other unauthorized copying a crime punishable by fine or imprisonment. In addition, the creator of a copyrighted work may sue anyone who plagiarizes it. Educational institutions prohibit plagiarism, and a student who plagiarizes will be subject to disciplinary penalties.

Plagiarism does not include the adoption of character types, general plots, or other ideas from existing works. Nearly all writers and artists do such borrowing, but they express the ideas in new ways. The great English playwright William Shakespeare took most of his plots from published historical and literary works. But he transformed the borrowed materials into works that were uniquely his own.

WATCH OUT!

When you take notes as you research, make sure you carefully mark anything that's a direct quote. Otherwise, it's easy to plagiarize when you start the writing process.

In-Text Citations

There are several ways to credit your sources. In the Modern Language Association (MLA) style, you need to acknowledge your sources by inserting brief parenthetical citations—in-text citations—within the text of the paper. This practice will help your reader differentiate between the ideas that are yours and the ideas that are someone else's.

In-text citations are shorthand versions of a more detailed entry that appears on the works cited list that appears at the end of the paper.

IN-TEXT CITATIONS: THE BASIC FORMULA

The exact form of an in-text citation depends on two things.

- the type of source (e.g., book or Web site)
- the source's entry on the works cited list

Most entries follow a simple formula:

(author's last name + page number)

(Chabon 81)

TERMS OF DOCUMENTATION

Crediting your sources
Giving credit to and recognizing the ideas and research of others

Plagiarism
Using other people's words and ideas, either accidentally or intentionally, as though they were your own

In-text citation
The author's name and page number following the text it references

Footnotes/Endnotes
Notes that refer the reader to other publications for further reading

Works cited entry
The full publication information of the sources you used in the in-text citations

The works cited list gives a detailed accounting to the reader of all the sources actually used in a paper. This list is easy to find because it is always the last page of the paper. It tells your reader about your research methods.

Your reader, in looking at your works cited list, will know the value of the publications you have used.

Stay Current

Consider the topic "current economic trends in technology stocks." The information you might find in a book on technology published in 1999 might be interesting, but it probably won't offer much useful information on the current trends.

Dig Deep

Your reader, in looking at your works cited list, will know the value of the publications you have used. For example, if you are writing about current economic trends in technology stocks, your first search might have turned up many articles in magazines like *Time, Newsweek,* and other popular periodicals. This kind of material might focus on the newest technology start-up companies, rather than the economic trends.

More specialized publications like *Forbes, The Economist,* and *Business Week* would probably offer more analysis addressing the business side of technology. It's likely that these sources delve deeper into your topic.

Other Information

Your works cited list also

- invites your reader to read more about the subject.
- tells your reader how to find source materials.
- allows the reader to review the source to see if he or she agrees with your particular interpretation of it.

In research, some publications are considered to be more valuable than others.

AT A GLANCE

The works cited list quickly identifies

- How many sources you consulted
- The types of sources you consulted
- Where those sources can be found
- How up-to-date your sources are
- What date you accessed information (for electronic sources)

BIBLIOGRAPHY FORMATTING

Works Cited

Adler, Alfred. *Cooperation Between the Sexes*. Eds. Heinz and Rowena R. Ansbacher. New York: Anchor

Books, 1978. Print.

---. *Superiority and Social Interest*. Eds. Heinz and Rowena R. Ansbacher. Evanston: Northwestern

University Press, 1964. Print.

Coomaraswamy, A. K. "Sir Gawain and the Green Knight: Indra and Namuci." *Speculum*. 19 January 1944:

104–125. Print.

Mythical Heroes Page. U of Oregon. Web. 5 April 2001.

1. Center the title of your bibliography at the top of the first page.

2. The author's name is always listed last name first. Entries should be arranged in alphabetical order.

3. Titles of long works like books and magazines should be italicized. Titles of shorter works like articles and poems should be in quotation marks.

4. The place, publisher, and date should be listed at the end of the entry. Make sure you use the correct punctuation.

5. If you list more than one work by the same author, use three dashes instead of writing the name out again.

6. Double space the entire works cited list. Make sure the second line of each entry (and each subsequent line) is indented.

7. Use alphabetical order throughout your bibliography.

Make the Grade

Your teacher will look at your works cited list to see how thorough your research was. For example, entries for electronic sources give the original publication information. This includes the author, title, periodical, date, and pages. It also includes information about the database name and your access date.

If your works cited list shows that you searched only one particular database for all your sources (as recorded in the entry by name), and that you found them all the same day (as recorded in the entry as the access date), your reader may conclude that you didn't spend enough time researching the topic.

MLA Works Cited Entries

Books

Book (One Author)

Author's last name, first name. *Book Title*. Edition [if stated]. Volume numbers(s) [if book is a multivolume work]. City of publication: publisher's name, year of publication. Publication medium.

Chabon, Michael. *The Amazing Adventures of Kavalier & Clay*. New York: Random House, 2000. Print.

Book (Multiple Authors)

List authors in the order they appear on the title page of the text.

Author's last name, first name, and second author's first and last name. *Book Title*. City of publication: Name of publisher, year of publication. Publication medium.

Strunk, William, Jr., and E. B. White. *The Elements of Style*. 3rd ed. New York: Macmillian Publishing Company, 1979. Print.

Edited Book

After the author's name, add the abbreviation "ed.(s)," separated from the name by a comma.

Kane, Thomas S., and Leonard J. Peters, eds. *Writing Prose: Techniques and Purposes*. New York: Oxford University Press, 1965. Print.

Information from a Reference Book

Author's name, last name first. "Article Title." *Publication title*. Edition. Year of publication. Publication medium.

Beller, Steven. "Vienna." *The World Book Encyclopedia*. 2009 ed. Print.

Unidentified Author

Book Title. Edition [if stated]. Volume numbers(s). City of publication: Publisher's name, year of publication. Publication medium.

Band on the Run: An Insider's Account. London: P.S. Press, 1987. Print.

Web Sites

Author's name, last name first. "Article or Web page title." *Web site title*. Publisher's name, date of publication. Publication medium. Access date.

Beasley, Maurine H. "Roosevelt, Eleanor." *World Book Student*. World Book, 2009. Web. 20 Jan. 2009.

Articles

Magazine Articles

Author's name, last name first. "Article Title." *Title of Magazine*. Date (day, month, year): page numbers. Publication medium.

Zakaria, Fareed. "A New Afghanistan Strategy." *Newsweek*. 9 Feb. 2009: 36-37. Print.

Scholarly Journal Articles

Author's name, last name first. "Article Title." *Title of Journal* volume and issue number (year of publication): page numbers. Publication medium.

Piper, Andrew. "Rethinking the Print Object: Goethe and the Book of Everything." *PMLA* 121.1 (2006): 36-37. Print.

Newspaper Article

Author's name, last name first. "Article Title." *Title of Newspaper* date (day, month, year), edition [if stated], section: page number(s). Publication medium.

Wronski, Richard. "Prairie Parkway Project on a Road to Nowhere?" *Chicago Tribune* 4 May 2009, sec. 1: 6. Print.

Microfiche Article

Original publication information. Microform. *Title of Source*, volume number, year, and microfiche number, grids.

Smith, John. "Welfare Reform Suffers Blow." *Spokane Journal* 25 Jan. 1990: A2. Microform. *NewsBank: Welfare and Social Problems*, 5 (1990): fiche 2, grids A9-11.

Other

Print Map or Chart

Title of Map or Chart. Map or Chart. City of publication: name of publisher, year published. Publication medium.

Southwest USA. **Map. Chicago: Rand McNally & Co., 1996. Print.**

Pamphlet

Author's name, last name first. *Pamphlet Title.* City of publication: Publisher's name, year of publication. Publication medium.

Modern Language Association. *Language Study in the Age of Globalization: The College-Level Experience.* **New York: MLA, n.d. Print.**

Radio or Television Program

"Episode or segment title." *Program Title.* Name of the network. Call letters, city of local station, broadcast date. Medium of reception.

"State of Denial." *60 Minutes.* **CBS. WBBM, Chicago, 1 Oct. 2006. Television.**

Government Publication

Government name. Issuing agency name. *Publication Title.* City of publication: Publisher, year of publication. Publication medium.

United States. Census Bureau. *Statistical Abstract of the United States: 2002.* **Springfield, VA: National Technical Information Service, 2001. Print.**

Interview

Interviewee's last name, first name. Personal interview. Date of interview (day month year).

Meyers, Davin. Personal interview. 4 May 2009.

Lecture or Speech

Last name, first name of speaker. "Presentation Title." Name of the meeting and the sponsoring organization. Location of meeting. Date. Descriptive label (address, lecture, keynote speech, reading).

Mason, Nathaniel. "Eliminating World Hunger." World Bank Forum. WBH Convention. Livingston Hotel, Denver. 2001. Address.

Films and DVDs

Program Title. Director. Producer. Original release date [if relevant]. Distributor, year of release. Publication medium.

America's Endangered Species: Don't Say Good-Bye. **Dir. Robert Kenner. National Geographic Society, 2008. DVD.**

WATCH OUT!

Use the following abbreviations for information you cannot supply.

n.p. No place of publication or publisher given

n.d. No date of publication given

n. pag. No pagination (page numbers) given

MLA REMINDERS

- Works with unknown authors are usually alphabetized by title.

- Make sure you note the medium of publication for every entry. Usually, the medium will be Print or Web. If the medium of publication is Web, you must include an access date.

- Don't include the Web address for a site unless your teacher asks you to. It isn't necessary since URLs frequently change.

- Watch your punctuation.

- There's a way to format almost any type of entry. If you can't find the format you need here, check online, with your teacher, or with a librarian.

APA Works Cited Entries

Books

Single-Author Book

Author's last name, first initials (Year). *Title of book* (Edition number). City of publication, state: Name of publisher.

Note: For first editions, no edition number is needed.

Turner, H. R. (1995). *Science in Medieval Islam* (3rd ed.). Austin, TX: University of Texas Press.

Book with More than One Author

Author's last name, first initials, & Author's last name, first initials (Year). *Title of Book* (Edition number). City of publication, state: Name of publisher.

Articles

Journal Article

Author's last name, first initials (Year). Title of article. *Name of Journal, volume number* (issue number), page numbers.

Note: Issue number is needed only when the journal is paginated by issue.

Journal Article with a Digital Object Identifier (DOI)

Author's last name, first initials (Year). Title of article. *Name of Journal, volume number* (issue number), page numbers. doi number.

Herbs-Damm, K. L. (2005). Volunteer support, marital status, and the survival times of terminally ill patients. *Health Psychology, 24*, 225-229. doi: 10.1037/0278-6133.24.2.22.

Online Journal Article Without a Digital Object Identifier (DOI)

Author's last name, first initials (Year). Title of article. *Name of Journal, volume number* (issue number), page numbers. Retrieved from URL.

Chandra, A., & Acosta, J. D. (2010). Disaster recovery also involves human recovery. *JAMA, 304*, 1608-1609. Retrieved from http://jama.ama-assn.org/cgi/content/extract/304/14/1608.

Magazine Article

Author's last name, first initials (Year published, month and day). Title of article. *Name of Magazine, volume number*, page numbers.

Newsletter Article

Author's last name, first initials (Year published, month and day). Title of article. *Title of the Publication, volume number*, page numbers.

Newspaper Article

Author's last name, first initials (Year published, month and day). Title of article. *Title of Newspaper*, page numbers.

Note: Page numbers should be preceded with p. or pp.

Jones, P. H. (1999, February 16). In forecasting emotions, most people flunk out. *New York Times*, pp. A20-23.

Newspaper Article, No Author

Title of article. (Year published, month and day). *Title of Newspaper*, page numbers.

Amazing Amazon region. (1989, January 12). *New York Times*, pp. D11, D14.

WORKING WITH APA GUIDELINES

Papers in the social sciences are written according to American Psychological Association (APA) guidelines. The works cited page is quite similar to MLA style, but there are subtle differences. These differences are captured in the examples shown on these pages.

- For citations for online resources, include the same citation elements and in the same order as you would for print, or other fixed-media, resources. The only addition is the retrieval information, such as the URL, that is needed to locate the resource.

- Access dates are not required for online resources.

Other

Encyclopedia Entry

Author's last name, first initials (Year). Title of article. *Title of encyclopedia* (Edition, volume number, page numbers). City of publication, state: Name of publisher.

Note: If the author is not provided, begin the reference with the entry title and date of publication.

Isenberg, G. I. & Netravali, A. N. (2009). Television. *The world book encyclopedia* (2009 ed., Vol. 26, pp. 110-128). Chicago, IL: World Book.

Technical and Research Reports

Author's last name, first initials (Year). *Title of work* (Report No. xxxx). City of publication, state: Name of publisher.

Published Doctoral Dissertation and Master's Thesis

Author's last name, first initials (Year). *Title of doctoral dissertation or master's thesis* (Doctoral dissertation or master's thesis). Retrieved from Name of database. (Accession or Order No.).

Unpublished Doctoral Dissertation and Master's Thesis

Author's last name, first initials. (Year). *Title of doctoral dissertation or master's thesis* (Unpublished doctoral dissertation or master's thesis). Name of institution, Location.

Motion Picture

Producer's last name, first initials. (Producer), & Director's last name, first initials (Director). Year of release. *Title of motion picture* [Motion picture]. Country of origin: Name of studio.

Musical Recording

Writer's last name, first initials. (Copyright year). Title of song [Recorded by Name of artist if different from writer]. On *Title of album* [Medium of recording: CD, record, cassette, etc.]. Location: Label (date of recording if different from song copyright date).

lang, k. d. (2008). Shadow and the frame. On *Watershed* [CD]. New York, NY: Nonesuch Records.

Vocabulary

WORD SCORE
TRIPLE LETTER SCORE
DOUBLE LETTER
L1 A1 T1 E1
TRIPLE LETTER SCORE
DOUBLE LETTER
D2 S1
TRIPLE LETTER
O1 Q10 U1

DICTIONARIES are books

that contain a select list of words arranged in alphabetical order. The first dictionary, which was created by an English schoolmaster in 1604, defined only the most difficult words—around 3,000 of them. It wasn't until Samuel Johnson's version was published in 1755 that dictionaries began to pin down the English language in a more holistic way. (See page 938.) Today, many dictionaries can be found online as well as in printed books.

Samuel Johnson (1709–1784) almost single-handedly published the *Dictionary of the English Language*.

USING GUIDE WORDS

Guide words make it easy and fast to find a word in the dictionary. For example, if the guide words at the top of a page are den/dinosaur, all the words in alphabetical order between these two guide words would be on that page. Some entry words might be *dentist, desert, detail, different, dig, dime*, and *dinner*.

The entry words *daisy, dare, date, deal*, and *deed* would appear before the den/dinosaur page. The entry words *dint, dip, diploma, direct, dirty*, and *disk* would appear later in the dictionary.

Look It Up

A **dictionary** explains the words of a language. It is an essential tool for finding out how to pronounce, spell, and learn the uses and meanings of words.

Good dictionaries include all known definitions of a word. They often include appropriate sentences to illustrate the word's meaning.

A **glossary** is an alphabetical list of difficult or special words used in a book. These definitions usually appear at the back of a book.

OTHER DICTIONARY ENTRY ELEMENTS

spelling	syllables	alternate definitions
inflections	illustrations	cross-references
abbreviations	synonyms	antonyms
homophones	homographs	usage examples
idioms	slang	figures of speech

1. Entry

Entries are the words explained in a dictionary. They're listed in alphabetical order with the word's meaning and information such as pronunciation and part of speech. Entries can be single words, compound words, abbreviations, affixes, or phrases.

2. Guide Words

The words explained in a dictionary are listed in alphabetical order, letter by letter. Two guide words, which are found at the top of each page, are the first and last entry words on that page.

3. Pronunciation

Most dictionaries list the pronunciation or phonetic spelling for each entry. Accent marks show which part of the word should be stressed when you say it. Many dictionaries include a small phonetic key on each page.

lizard / lock 2

388

during the day. **living wage,** a wage on which it is possible to live. **within living memory,** within the memory of people who are still alive.

liz·ard (liz-ărd) *n.* a reptile with a rough or scaly hide, four legs, and a long tail.

Lk. *abbr.* Luke.

LL *abbr.* Late Latin.

ll. *abbr.* lines.

lla·ma (lah-mä) *n.* a South American animal related to the camel but with no hump, kept as a beast of burden and for its soft woolly hair. ▷Do not confuse *llama* with *lama*.

lla·no (lah-noh) *n.* (*pl.* **-nos**) any of the treeless grassy plains of Latin America.

LL.B. *abbr.* Bachelor of Laws.

LL.D. *abbr.* Doctor of Laws.

LM *abbr.* lunar module.

LNG *abbr.* liquefied natural gas.

lo (loh) *interj.* (*old use*) see.

loach (lohch) *n.* a small edible freshwater fish of Europe and Asia.

load (lohd) *n.* 1. something carried. 2. the quantity that can be carried, as on a cart. 3. a unit of weight or measure for certain substances. 4. the amount of electric current supplied by a dynamo or generating station. 5. a burden of responsibility or worry or grief. 6. (*informal*) plenty, *loads of time.* **load** *v.* 1. to put a load in or on, to fill with goods or cargo etc., to receive a load. 2. to hil heavily. 3. to weight with something heavy. 4. to put ammunition into (a gun) or film into (a camera), to ready for use. 5. to add an extra

(a ball) slowly or in a high arc in tennis etc. **lob** *n.* a lobbed ball in tennis etc.

lo·bar (loh-băr, -bahr) *adj.* of a lobe, especially of the lung, *lobar pneumonia.*

lob·by (lob-ee) *n.* (*pl.* **-bies**) 1. an entrance hall used as a waiting room. 2. a body of people engaged in lobbying for a particular cause. **lobby** *v.* (**lob·bied, lob·by·ing**) to seek to persuade (a legislator) to support one's cause. **lob·by·ist** *n.*

lobe (lohb) *n.* a rounded flattish part or projection (especially of an organ of the body), the lower soft part of the ear.

lobed (lo̲____ having lobes.

lo·bel·ia (___el-yä) *n.* a low-growing garden plant w___ red, white, or purple flowers. 3

lo·bot·o___ (___bot-ŏ-mee) *n.* (*pl.* **-mies**) an incision int___ frontal lobe of the brain to relieve some cases ___ mental illness.

lob·ster (lob-stĕr) *n.* (*pl.* **-sters, -ster**) 1. a large shellfish with eight legs and two long claws that turns scarlet after being boiled. 2. its flesh as food. ☐**lobster Newburg,** a dish consisting of pieces of cooked lobster i___ a rich cream sauce contai___ brandy or sherry. ___**pot,** a slatted w___ box for trapping ___ **lobster therm___** a mixture of lob___, mushrooms, ___ egg yolks, and she___ ___ed in the lobster

lob·ule (lob-yool) *n.* ___all lobe. **lob·u·lar** (___ yŭ-lăr) *adj.*

lo·cal (loh-kăl) *n.* ___ place or a sm___

by sailors. [variant of *lob's couse;* origin uncertain. Compare *loblolly* gruel, *lob* boil with lumps (like porridge).]

Lob's pound (lobz), 1 *British Dialect.* jail or prison. 2 any situation of embarrassment or difficulty. [perhaps < *lob²* clown, bumpkin]

✱**lob·ster** (lob′ster), *n.* **1a** a sea animal about a foot long with two big claws and eight legs. Its shell turns a bright red when a lobster is boiled for food. Lobsters are crustaceans with compound eyes that grow on thick stalks. ___ flesh of a lobster, used as food. **2** any one ___us related crustaceans that lack an enlarg___ of claws, such as the spiny lobsters. **3** *Hi___.* a British soldier; redcoat. **4a** *Slang.* a gulli___ foolish, or stupid person. **b** a red-faced person. [Old English *loppestre,* probably alteration of Latin *lō·custa* locust, lobster] 5

✱**lobster**
definition 1a

lob·ster (lob-stĕr) *n.* (*pl.* **-sters, -ster**) 1. a large shellfish with eight legs and two long claws that turns scarlet after being boiled. 2. its flesh as food. ☐**lobster Newburg,** a dish consisting of pieces of cooked lobster in a rich cream sauce containing brandy or sherry. **lobster pot,** a slatted wooden box for trapping lobsters. **lobster thermidor,** a mixture of lobster meat, mushrooms, cream, egg yolks, and sherry cooked in the lobster shell. 1 4

4. Parts of Speech

Some words can be used as more than one part of speech. Dictionaries use abbreviations to indicate a word's part(s) of speech. These include

adj	adjective
adv	adverb
conj	conjunction
n	noun
prep	preposition
pron	pronoun
v or vb	verb

5. Origin

Many dictionaries tell what language a word originally came from. For example, the word *menu* might list an *F,* meaning it is from the French language.

SEARCH DICTIONARY: [_____] **GO**

Tools
Ⓓ Double-click a word to define it.   🖨 Print   • Dictionary help

You searched for **lobster**

lob|ster «LOB stuhr», *noun.*
  1. **a** a sea animal about a foot long with two big claws and eight legs. Its shell turns a bright red when a lobster is boiled for food. Lobsters are crustaceans with compound eyes that grow on thick stalks. **b** the flesh of a lobster, used as food.

  2. any one of various related crustaceans that lack an enlarged pair of claws, such as the spiny lobsters.
  3. *Historical.* a British soldier; redcoat.
  4. **a** *Slang.* a gullible, foolish, or stupid person. **b** a red-faced person.
[Old English *loppestre,* probably alteration of Latin *lōcusta* locust, lobster]

Wired Words. The same information found in heavy bound dictionaries can now be found quickly and easily online.

BUILDING VOCABULARY

A well-developed vocabulary is essential to all forms of communication, including writing, reading, and speaking. A good vocabulary is not just about knowing large, fancy words. It's also about using common words so other people can understand you better.

There are several methods you can use to develop your vocabulary. Don't be afraid to try different things to see what works best for you. Everyone learns differently, but patience and persistence go a long way.

Keep a Notebook

Your vocabulary expands a little every day. If you pay attention, you'll constantly encounter new words as you read books, magazines, and Web sites and listen to people talk in person and on TV.

A **vocabulary notebook** is a great tool that can help you expand your vocabulary quickly and effectively. The notebook is a place where you can write the correct spelling, definition, and part of speech for each new word, which will help you learn it (and also remember it later).

Make a point of writing all unfamiliar words in your notebook. That includes not only brand-new vocabulary, but familiar words that you might be a little unsure about.

MNEMONIC DEVICES

A mnemonic device is a memory aid. It is a mental trick or clue you can use to help recall important information. Here are a few mnemonic devices to try as you build vocabulary.

- make up a little rhyme that relates to the new word
- associate a mental picture with the word (the more vivid the better)
- think of a memorable sentence that tells you how to spell the word ("there is *a rat* in sep*arat*e" or "the princi*pal* is your *pal*")

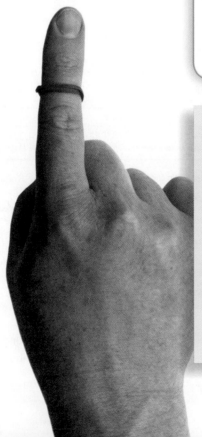

Learning New Words

Follow these eight steps to build vocabulary as you read.

1. When you come across a new word, guess its meaning.

You can often guess the meaning of an unknown word by examining its context in a sentence.

2. Check the meaning in a dictionary.

Sometimes, the actual definition of a word may differ from your guess. It's important to check the dictionary to make sure your guess was right. If you don't want to put down what you're reading, underline the word and come back to it later, or make a note of it on a separate sheet of paper.

3. Study the word's etymology, or origin.

The history of words is interesting in itself and can be a useful tool in learning new words.

4. Write the definition in your vocabulary notebook.

After you look up a new vocabulary word, it's helpful to copy out the definition. The act of writing can help crystallize a word's meaning in your memory.

5. Rephrase the definition in your own words.

Now that you've copied the exact dictionary definition, put its meaning into your own words. Thinking about the word in your own language will help you learn it faster.

6. Copy the sentence the word originally appeared in.

Make a note of the sentence in which you originally saw the new vocabulary word. That way, when you review your notebook, you'll be reminded of the word's context.

7. Write your own sentence using the new word.

Using the new word in your own sentence will help reinforce it in your memory.

8. Use the new word in your writing and in conversation.

Make a point of using new vocabulary words in your everyday life. The more often you use a word, the easier it will be to remember.

You can store your vocabulary notebook words in a computer file if you'd like to keep them in alphabetical order.

Make Flash Cards

Flash cards are another useful technique for memorizing new vocabulary. While some people prefer to simply write the word on one side of an index card and the definition on the other side, feel free to let your creative juices flow. Include drawings, paintings, or collages instead of limiting yourself to words.

Flash cards can be very convenient—you might run through them during a commercial break as you're watching television, or when you're in the car on the way to school.

Making Flash Cards

Start with a stack of index cards. Write the new vocabulary word on the front of the card and its definition on the back.

- Use a pen or a pencil. A heavy marker is likely to bleed through the paper.

- Print the vocabulary word in large letters. Make sure you use only one word per card.

- Use your best handwriting.

- Write the definition in your own words so you're more likely to remember it.

- Drill yourself with the flash cards frequently but for short periods of time.

- Use both sides of the card for practice. Switch things up by using the vocabulary word-side some times and the definition-side other times.

- Store all the flash cards together by grouping them with a rubber band or by placing them in an envelope.

- You can also use a Web site or software if you'd prefer to make flash cards on a computer.

- Make sure you write the words large enough that you can read them easily from a few feet away.

- Flash cards work best with straightforward definitions. It's more difficult to summarize complicated concepts. If you run out of room on the card, that's a good sign you should study in a different way.

HOW TO MAKE BETTER MEMORIES

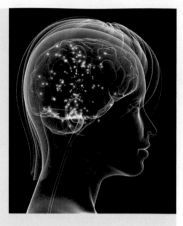

Whenever you try to learn something new, like a vocabulary word, try to associate it with something you already know. When you connect new knowledge to an old memory, you're more likely to retain it.

One reason that mnemonic devices—memory aids using rhyme, mental images, or other tricks—work is because they engage different areas of your brain. The more parts of the brain you engage in making a memory, the stronger that memory will be. (See page 826.)

"pessimist"

Vocabulary flash cards are easy to make. They're one of the best tools you can use to learn new words.

"a person inclined to look on the dark side of things and see all the difficulties and disadvantages"

OTHER WAYS TO BUILD YOUR VOCABULARY

- Always be on alert for new words.
- Read widely. Reading exposes you to new words in different contexts, which is a great way to learn new words.
- Read carefully. Close reading forces you to take notice when you encounter a word you're not familiar with.
- Keep a dictionary handy to make sure you can pronounce, spell, and correctly use any of the new words you have discovered.
- Try out new words when you speak and write.
- Set a vocabulary goal for yourself. Try to learn (and use!) at least one new word every day.
- As you read, ask questions about the author's words. Do you think those particular words make the material more interesting and colorful?

ETYMOLOGY is the study of the origin and development of words. Words, like people and places, have histories that can be traced and recorded. By studying the etymology of a word, you can trace a word back to its origin, see how its meaning has changed over time, and learn interesting facts about how people lived in the past. The English language has borrowed heavily from Latin and Greek. You can expand your vocabulary by learning more about those borrowed word parts.

To build vocabulary, you can analyze word structure, or the parts that make up words.

Long words are often made up of smaller pieces with meanings that are easy to learn. These parts are roots, prefixes, and suffixes.

Once you learn some of the common roots, prefixes, and suffixes, you can work out the meanings of many unfamiliar words.

A word consists of up to three parts

PREFIX + ROOT + SUFFIX

Roots

Using the Root

A root is a word or word part from which other words can be made. It is the base word to which beginnings or endings may be added. One root can be the source of many English words. For example, the root word *do* can become many different words, including

undo	redo
doing	doable

Understanding something about the function of roots can help you define words you have never seen before.

Common Latin Roots

Root	Meaning	Derivatives
acu, acr	sharp	acute, acrimony
aesthe	feel	aesthetic, anesthesia
ag, act	do, move	agility, activate
alg	pain	analgesic, nostalgia
am	love	amorous, amiable
anim	life, mind, soul	animal, inanimate
annu, enni	year	annual, bicentennial
anthropo	humanity	anthropology
aqu	water	aquarium
archa, arche	ancient	archaic, archaeology
aud	hear	auditory, audience
bel	war	bellicose, belligerent
bio	life	biology, biopsy
carn	flesh	carnivore
chron	time	chronology
clam, claim	shout	clamor, proclaim
cogn	know	recognize, incognito
cord	heart	accord, concordance
corp	body	corpse
cre, cresc	grow	increase, crescendo
culp	blame	culprit, culpable
cumb, cub	lie down	succumb, incubate
dict	say	dictator, dictionary
duc	lead	seduce, induct

Families of Meaning

Words that are members of the same family of meaning often are formed from the same root.

For example, many of the words dealing with believing and trusting are formed from the Latin root *cred*.

credit	credibility	creditor
incredible	incredulous	

The root *port* means "carry." Consider how these words relate to the concept of carrying.

import	export	deport
report	transport	portable

Root	Meaning	Derivatives
dyna	power	dynamite
fal, fals	deceive, fail	falsify
fer	carry	transfer, ferry
flect, flex	bend	flexible, reflect
flu, flux	flow	influence, influx
gest	produce, action	gesticulate, gesture
gno	know	diagnosis
grad, gress	step	grade, graduate
grat	pleasing	gratitude
grav	heavy	gravity
junc	join	juncture
jur	swear	jury, perjure
lect	gather	collect
loqu, locut	speak, rights	eloquent
mit, miss	send	transmit, emit
mon, monit	warn, advise	admonition
mor, mort	death	mortuary, mortal
mot	move	motor, motion
mut	change	mutate
nat	born	national, native
neg	deny	negative
path	feeling	pathetic
pel, pell, puls	push	propel, pulse
pend	hang, weight	pendant, appendage

Root	Meaning	Derivatives
plac	please	placate
ple, plen, plet	fill	complete, plenty
port	carry	transport
posit, pose	put, place	position
rog, rogat	ask	arrogance
rupt	burst	corrupt, erupt
scrib, script	write	scribble, scripture
sed, sid, sess	sit, settle	sedentary
spec, spic	look	spectacle, conspicuous
spir	breath	spirit, respiration
tang, ting	touch	tangible, contingent
temp, tempor	time	tempo, temporal
tort	twist	contort
tract	drag	tractor
trud, trus	push, thrust	protrude, intrusion
unda	wave	undulate
ven, vent	come	intervene, invent
ver	true	verify, veracity
vid, vis	see	evident, vision
viv	life	vivid, vivacious
voc, vok	voice, call	advocate, revoke
volv, volut	roll	revolve, evolution

Prefixes

A word consists of up to three parts

PREFIX + ROOT + SUFFIX

A **prefix** is found at the beginning of a word, before the root. (See page 830.) It can change or add to the meaning of the base word by indicating

attitude
number
position
direction

For example, the root of the word *introvert* is *vert*, which means "turn." The prefix *intro-* means "into," making the meaning of the word "turned inward." If we changed the prefix to *extro-*, the word would become *extrovert*, which means turned outward. Alternatively, switching the prefix to *a-* (meaning "away") changes the word to *avert* or "turn away."

Many prefixes change spelling depending on the sound that follows. This makes it hard to recognize certain prefixes in some words. Prefixes can also look similar but have different meanings; for example *ante-* means before and *anti-* means against.

A prefix changes the meaning of the word, sometimes to its opposite. The prefix *un-* means not.

happy	unhappy
fair	unfair
cut	uncut
kind	unkind
opened	unopened
used	unused

The prefix *mis-* means badly or wrongly.

fit	misfit
inform	misinform
fortune	misfortune
taken	mistaken
use	misuse

Common Prefixes

Prefix	Meaning	Examples
a-,	without	atheism, amoral
ab-, abs-	away	abjure, abnormal
ad-, a- ac-, af- ag-, al- an-, ap- as-, at-	to, toward	accord, affect, appear
an-	without	anonymous
ante-	before	antebellum
anti-	against	antitrust
auto-	self	automatic
bene-	well	benefit
circum-	around	circumference
com-, co- col-, con- cor-	together	companion, collect

832

Prefix	Meaning	Examples
counter-	opposite	contrary, controversy
contra-	against	
contro-		
de-	down, away	decay, defect, devolve
dem-	people	democracy
dia-	across, apart, through	diagonal, diagram
dis-, dif-, di-	not	dislike, differ
equ, equi-	equal	equation, equivalent
eu-	well	euphoria, eulogy
ex-, e-, ef-	out	exhale, eject
extra-, extro-	outside of	extrovert
hyper-	over	hyperbole
hypo-	under	hypocrisy, hypodermic
in-, em-, en-	in, against	intrude, embargo
in-, ir-, im-	not	inoffensive, imbalance
inter-	between	international
intra-, intro-	within	introspective
macro-	large	macroscopic
mal-, male-	bad, wrongly	malefactor, malign
micro-	small	microscope
multi-	many	multiple
neo-	new	neocolonial
non-	not	nonsense
ob-, oc-, of-, op-	to, against	occupy, offer, oppose
omni-	all	omniscient

Prefix	Meaning	Examples
para-	alongside	parallel, parody
per-	completely, through	perfect, perfume
poly-	many	polygamy, polygon
post-	after	postpone
pre-	before	preview
pro-	away, forward, in place of	proceed, pronoun
pseudo-	false	pseudonym
re-	again, back	reopen, receive
recti-	straight, right	rectify, rectangle
sub-, suc-, suf-, sug-, sum-, sup-, sur-, sus-	under, in place of	substitute, suffer, suggest, sustain
super-	above	superhuman
syn-, syl-, sym, sys	together	syllable, system, sympathy
trans-	across, over	translate, transcend
un-	not, reversal	unearthly, untie

When you see an unfamiliar word, try to break it down into parts. Chances are you know at least part of the word's meaning.

Suffixes

A word consists of up to three parts

PREFIX + ROOT + SUFFIX

A **suffix** is found at the end of a word. It indicates the root's number, tense, part of speech, and intensity.

WATCH OUT!

Any element of a word—prefix, root, or suffix—may change its form when it's used to make a word.

Tense

Familiar suffixes like *-ed* or *-ing* show you that a word is a verb in the past or present tense.

looked ——→ looking

Number

An *-s* or *-es* at the end of a noun usually means the word is plural.

cat ——→ cats
class ——→ classes

Part of Speech

Other suffixes indicate whether a word is being used as a verb, noun, adjective, or adverb. A word can be changed from one part of speech to another by altering its suffix.

Verb	Noun	Adjective	Adverb
motivate	motivation	motivational	motivationally
inspiring	inspiration	inspirational	inspirationally
loved	love	loving	lovingly

Intensity

Suffixes are also used with adjectives and adverbs to indicate increasing degree.

pretty ——→ prettiest

Suffix Spelling Rules

Understanding the way words are built can help you spell better. Often, the addition of a suffix doesn't change the spelling of a root word. In some cases, however, the suffix requires a variation in the spelling of the root word.

Rule 1: When the root word ends with a silent -e

When the suffix begins with a vowel, drop the silent *e*.

live ——→ living

When the suffix begins with a constonant, keep the silent *e*.

care ——→ careful
aware ——→ awareness

Rule 2: When the root word ends with a consonant

When the root word is one syllable and the final consonant is preceded by a single vowel, double the consonant.

hop ——→ hopping
win ——→ winner

When the root word has more than one syllable, and the accent does not fall on the final syllable, do not double the consonant.

travel ——→ traveler
panel ——→ panelist

Common Suffixes

Suffix	Meaning	Examples
-able, -ible	able, can do	reliable
-ade	result of action	blockade
-al	relating to	natural, artificial
-an, -ian	native of	American
-ant	state or condition of	defiant
-ary, -ery, -ory	relating to	visionary, olfactory
-arch	ruler	matriarch
-archy	government	anarchy, monarchy
-ary	place for	infirmary
-ate	having to do with	collegiate
-ation	act or process of	computation
-cide	murder	genocide
-cle	little, small	particle, molecule
-cracy	government	democracy
-dom	rank or realm of	kingdom
-ence	state of being	indifference
-er, -or	one who, that which	diver, doctor
-escent	in the process of	adolescent
-esque	in the style of	Romanesque
-ese	having to do with	Chinese
-et, -ette	small, group	midget, octet
-ful	full of	cupful, playful
-fy	make	simplify
-graph	writing	autograph, telegraph
-hood	condition, quality	manhood
-ment	state of, result	commitment
-ology	study of	biology, psychology
-ous	full of, having	gracious
-nomy	laws governing	astronomy, economy
-phile	lover	Anglophile
-ward	in the direction of	eastward, wayward
-y	inclined to, tend to	sleepy, needy

EDUCATED GUESSING

is a good way to improve your vocabulary skills. Many readers have trouble when they read passages about unfamiliar subjects. They may be able to recognize or pronounce all the words, but they cannot tell what a sentence means because they don't know the meaning of an essential word. But a new word can often be defined by paying close attention to clues that appear throughout the rest of the paragraph in which it appears.

Context Clues

Context clues are hints to the meaning of a particular word that are given in the sentence or paragraph that surrounds that word.

Readers can often learn a great deal about the meaning of a word simply by paying attention to what the rest of the passage says. Consider the word *perambulator,* in the following paragraph, for example.

> In the mornings, our nurse would take us to the playground in Central Park. I tagged along, holding onto her skirts, and she pushed my brother along in a great old-fashioned perambulator. It was much bigger and more luxurious than the baby carriages other nannies pushed, and the nurse seemed proud of it. She only complained when we went up the big hill, when she used to mutter over and over, "Too heavy! Too heavy!"

A reader who does not know the meaning of *perambulator* can learn a great deal about it from this paragraph. Here are some guesses you might make based on the context clues in the paragraph.

- The perambulator is compared with baby carriages, so it must be a thing of that kind.

- This perambulator is large and heavy, so it may be that in general perambulators are heavier than baby carriages.

- The language suggests that a perambulator is an old-fashioned kind of baby carriage.

 *Even if you can guess a word's meaning using context clues, check the dictionary to make sure your guess is right.*

Types of Context Clues

There are many other cases where the context will help define an unfamiliar word.

Type	Form	Example
direct definition	a direct statement that defines the word	An oyster is a *sea animal with a soft body inside a hard, two-piece shell.*
definition by example	an example built into the sentence or paragraph that helps define the new word	Erosion wears away the earth. *Running water, for example, carries loose soil, sand, gravel, and boulders and then deposits them in new places.*
definition by description	a description that helps you visualize the new word	The saber-toothed tiger was a catlike prehistoric animal with *long, pointed teeth* near the front of its mouth.
definition by simile	a phrase beginning with *like* or *as* that compares the new word to something else	Badminton is a game somewhat *like tennis.*
definition by comparison and contrast	compares and contrasts a word in greater detail than a simile	Badminton is a game somewhat like tennis. *But the shuttlecock (made of feather and cork) must be hit back and forth over the net without hitting the ground.*
definition by appositive	a word or phrase (usually set off by commas) that identifies a noun in the sentence	Schussing, *skiing straight down a slope without turning or stopping,* is the fastest form of skiing.
definition by origin	information about the language in which the word originated (see pages 830–831)	Do you know the drink of the gods? *It's an ancient Greek word we still use today: nectar.*
parenthetical definition	a clue set off from the rest of the sentence by parentheses	Amphetamine drugs may cause people to hallucinate *(see, hear, or feel stimuli that are not present).*
indirect definition	signaled by words such as *called, also called, or, known as, referred to,* and *that is*	Cameras control the amount of light passing through the lens with changeable openings *called stops.*

SHADES OF MEANING

Two Layers

If you've ever been to a hardware store, you've probably seen a paint strip: a thin strip of paper that shows different shades of the same color. The difference between, say, an orange chip and a blue chip should be obvious. Even when you're standing far away, it's easy to tell those colors apart. But the differences amongst the shades of orange on a paint strip are subtle and more difficult to distinguish. Similarly, in vocabulary, the difference between two similar words can be subtle. Good writers make a point of understanding those differences so they can get their point across effectively.

Most words have at least two layers of meaning: a denotation and a connotation.

Denotation

A **denotation** is the base layer of a word's meaning. It refers to a word's exact dictionary definition.

While every word has a denotation, some denotations are more specific than others.

There are three types of denotations: *concrete words*, *relative words*, and *abstract words*.

Concrete words have a core of meaning for anyone who reads or speaks them. They leave little room for guesswork or opinion.

dog   car   toaster

Proper names (names of people and places) are the most concrete, or specific, words of all.

Clark Kent   Belgium   Mount Rushmore

Types of Denotation		
	Definition	**Examples**
concrete word	a word with a specific, core meaning	milk, Elvis Presley, notebook
relative word	a word with a meaning that depends on context	heavy, quickly, wealthy
abstract word	a vague word that means different things to different people	culture, education

Relative words are descriptive words (usually adjectives or adverbs) that have shades of meaning. These words have a particular meaning, but there is more room for interpretation.

She wore a red dress to the party.

Consider all the shades of red. Is the dress you pictured fire-engine red? Or is it more of an orangish red? Or is it maroon?

My brother is the tallest person in our family.

If most of the members of your family are around 5'6", then 5'9" would be considered tall. To another family, 5'9" would not seem very tall.

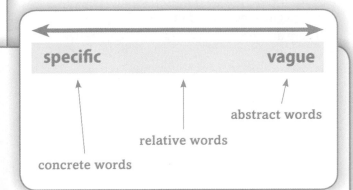

▲ **Some types of denotations** are more specific than others.

Abstract words do not refer to specific objects. They are concepts or ideas that can mean different things to different people. Consider how the following words can mean different things to different people.

justice   evil   success

Connotation

A **connotation** is an additional layer of meaning that a word suggests over and above its literal meaning. A word's connotation implies an emotion, a judgment, or an opinion.

Words that denote the same thing, or have the same dictionary definition, may have different connotations. Consider the similarities and differences among these synonyms.

home   house   address

You could use any of these words to refer to the place where you live, but each has a slightly different emotional charge or association. *Home* is the least formal of the three. *Address* is the most formal.

A writer who feels close to the place he or she grew up might call it "home," a word with a positive, warm connotation.

I can't wait to go home for the holidays.

Another writer who wants to express a more distant or formal feeling toward that place might refer to it as an "address."

The magazine was forwarded from my old address.

Connotations can be positive, negative, or neutral. A careful writer will choose a word with the connotation that is most appropriate for its purpose.

Types of Connotation		
Positve	**Neutral**	**Negative**
famous	well-known	notorious
slender	thin	skinny
normal	average	mediocre

Figures of Speech

A **figure of speech** is a word or phrase used in an imaginative, instead of a literal, way.

There are three main categories of figurative language.

- Comparison
- Contrast
- Association

METAPHORICALLY SPEAKING

Everyday speech is rich in metaphors. If we ask someone, "Did you land a job today?" the reply may be, "No, not even a nibble." These words from the special language of fishing are used to express thoughts about job hunting.

Metaphors are important in the speech of politicians, scientists, and journalists. In 1946, Sir Winston Churchill used the phrase "iron curtain" to describe an international problem. Scientists talk about the "wave theory of light." And the phrase "priming the pump" is sometimes used to refer to government spending to stimulate a nation's business and industry. In each case, metaphor has been an important tool of thought.

Figurative Comparisons

Some of the most widely used figures of speech work by comparing one thing to something else. Often, these comparisons are unexpected.

Similes are comparisons between two different things that uses the words *like* or *as*. The objects compared are different in most respects, except for one striking resemblance.

Metaphors make a comparison between two different things without using the words *like* or *as*. It is a word taken from one context and used in another.

Personification describes objects or animals as though they are people.

Figurative Contrasts

Other figures of speech contrast the literal meaning of a sentence with its intended meaning.

Hyperbole is an exaggeration used to emphasize or intensify a situation.

Irony is an expression that implies the opposite of what is actually said.

Figurative Associations

Some figures of speech take their meaning from the relationship between two objects, people, or concepts.

Metonymy is a figure of speech by which something or someone is called by the name of something else that's closely associated with it.

Synecdoche names a part when the whole is meant or names the whole when a part is meant.

Avoid mixing metaphors, which is combining two or more unrelated metaphors in the same expression:
"I smell a rat, but we shall nip it in the bud."

Figures of Speech

Figure of Speech	Type of Comparison	Example
simile	comparison using *like* or *as*	Sally is like a snake.
metaphor	implied comparison	Sally is a snake.
personification	giving an object human qualities	The sun was pale and tired.
hyperbole	exaggeration	I told you a million times to close the door.
irony	stating the opposite of what is meant	He's a terrible athlete—he only holds four school records.
metonymy	one word stands for another	The White House announced a press conference.
synecdoche	a part stands in for the whole or the whole stands in for a part	The rancher hired six hands. Chicago won the Stanley Cup.

IDIOMS

An **idiom** is a phrase or an expression with an understood meaning that differs from the literal meaning of the words. Idioms can't be interpreted word by word, so you have to learn the meaning of an idiomatic phrase just as you would learn any new definition.

The literal meaning of idioms is often silly or nonsensical. When you grow up with a language, you often use its idioms without thinking. But to someone who doesn't speak that language, the idiom might seem a little strange.

If you don't recognize an idiom, look up the key word of the expression in the dictionary. (See pages 824–825.)

Actual Meaning	English Idiom	Russian Idiom
I'm not kidding.	I'm not pulling your leg.	I'm not hanging noodles on your ears.
Don't be upset about something you can't change.	Don't cry over spilled milk.	Don't bite the elbow.

English contains more words than most languages. Because it is a rich blend of words from Latin, French, Greek, and other languages, English has many words with similar meanings. These words are called **synonyms.**

Using words with different shades of meaning adds richness, color, variety, and excitement to your language. (See pages 838–839.) The careful use of synonyms helps you communicate accurately and effectively. But wrong choices among words of similar meaning may leave a listener or reader with unclear or mistaken impressions.

Repetition of the same words makes reading and conversation dull and monotonous. Instead of always saying a person, thing, or event is *nice,* you can substitute more precise words such as *pleasant, enjoyable, delightful, attractive, lovely, charming, engaging, fascinating, thrilling, enchanting.*

Rather than repeatedly describing a food that you like as *delicious,* you can call the food *savory, tasty, palatable, piquant, delectable, elegant, scrumptious, flavorful, appetizing, mouth-watering,* or *luscious.*

Some synonyms are interchangeable. For example, either word can be used in a sentence without changing the meaning between "The small boy with the little dog lives in the red house" and "The little boy with the small dog lives in the red house."

Other synonyms are the same in one meaning of the words, but they differ in other meanings. You might say that a classmate is dull or stupid. You would not say that a knife is stupid or that a donkey is dull. You could mislay or misplace your wallet, but you only misplace your trust.

An **antonym** is a word that has the opposite meaning of another word.

USING A THESAURUS TO FIND SYNONYMS

To use a thesaurus, look up any word or term in the index to find the numerical category that contains related words and terms. Then turn to that category in the thesaurus.

red-handed
  murder 361
  in the act 680
  guilty 947
redict 905
redintegrate 660
redivivus 660
redness 382, 434 ←
redolence *odor* 398
  fragrance 400
redouble *increase* 356
  duplication 90
  repeat 104
  –one's efforts 686
redoubt 717
redoubtable 860

434. Redness

n.   **red**, scarlet, cardinal, cardinal red, vermilion, carmine, crimson, pink, rose, cerise, cherry, rouge, coquelicot, salmon, lake, maroon, carnation, *couleur de rose* [*F.*], *rose du Barry* [*F.*]; magenta, solferino, damask, flesh –color, –tint; color; fresh–, high-color; warmth; gules [*her.*].
redness etc. *adj.*; rubescence, rubicundity, ruddiness, rubefaction, rubrication, rubification; erubescence, blush.
[comparisons] ruby, *grenat* [*F.*], garnet, carbuncle; rust, iron mold *or* mould; rose, cardinal flower, lobelia; cardinal-bird, –grosbeak; red-start

Common Synonyms					
annoy	bother	fast	quick	shiny	bright
beautiful	lovely	finish	end	shut	close
	pretty	help	aid	skinny	thin
begin	start	hurt	injure	small	little
big	large	jump	leap		tiny
	huge	kind	gentle	smart	clever
	enormous	laugh	giggle	stiff	rigid
broad	wide	loud	noisy	story	tale
brook	stream	near	close	test	exam
cold	frigid	polite	courteous	tired	weary
cozy	snug	rock	stone	trail	path
easy	simple	run	jog	ugly	homely
famous	well-known	same	alike	unusual	strange

Common Antonyms					
begin	end	good	bad	over	under
clean	dirty	happy	sad	push	pull
come	go	hard	soft	quiet	noisy
dangerous	safe	heavy	light	rich	poor
dark	light	high	low	rough	smooth
day	night	hot	cold	smile	frown
empty	full	in	out	tall	short
far	near	kind	mean	up	down
fast	slow	laugh	cry	wet	dry
first	last	late	early	wild	tame
front	back	long	short	young	old
give	take	new	old		

SPELLING is the way we combine letters to write words. By following guidelines for improving spelling, becoming aware of common mispronunciations, and knowing which letter or groups of letters spell English sounds, you can become a better speller.

SPELLING WITH YOUR SENSES

See the word's beginning and ending letters, then the word as a whole. Close your eyes and try to remember how it looks.

Say the word, being sure to pronounce it correctly. Divide the word into syllables and say them distinctly. Then spell the word out loud.

Write the word a number of times until you can do it without really thinking about it.

Spelling Bee

The English language did not grow in an orderly way from one source. It came from many different languages, so many words are not spelled the way they sound.

Examples of words that aren't spelled by the sound of their letters include

bread (bred)

guest (gest)

knight (nite)

ocean (oshun)

some (sum)

The strange spelling of these words has to be memorized.

A good way to improve spelling skills is to keep a list of problem words in a notebook. A list of words that you repeatedly spell incorrectly may reveal a pattern. Once that pattern has been identified, you can try to correct it.

Reading also helps improve spelling. The more often a word is seen, the easier it becomes to remember its correct spelling.

Mispronunciation

Mispronounced words are the source of many spelling errors. This list shows some words that are often mispronounced and, as a result, misspelled.

ANTARCTIC	not antartic
ATHLETE	not athalete
BARBAROUS	not barbarious
BURGLAR	not burgaler
CANDIDATE	not canidate
CONGRATULATE	not congradulate
DIVIDE	not devide
DIVINE	not devine
DROWNED	not drownded
ESCAPE	not excape
EVIDENTLY	not evadently
FEBRUARY	not Febuary
GOVERNMENT	not goverment
HUNGRY	not hungery
JEWELRY	not jewlry
KINDERGARTEN	not kindygarden
LIBRARY	not libary
MISCHIEVOUS	not mischievious
NUCLEAR	not nucular
PERFORM	not preform
PERSPIRE	not prespire
POEM	not pome
PRACTICALLY	not practicly
PROBABLY	not probly
QUANTITY	not quanity
SIMILAR	not similiar
SOPHOMORE	not sophmore
STUDYING	not studing
SURPRISE	not suprise
TEMPERAMENT	not temprament
TEMPERATURE	not temprature

Spelling Tips

1. Consult a dictionary whenever you're not sure how a word should be spelled.
2. Use memory aids (like jingles, rhymes, and word games) to learn word spellings.
3. Keep a word list of all the words you misspell.
4. Proofread everything you write.

In 1938, the very first televised game show, Spelling Bee, *debuted in the United Kingdom.*

LEARNING TO SPELL A NEW WORD

Follow these steps whenever you have to look up the spelling of a word in the dictionary.

1. Write the word carefully.
2. Close your eyes and visualize the word in your mind.
3. Spell the word out loud.
4. Study the syllables if it has more than one.
5. Say the word out loud.
6. Study the word's meaning; it may have more than one.
7. Make up a sentence with the word.
8. Use the new word as often as possible.

Learning to Spell

Though the spelling of many English words does not follow any pattern, there are some basic rules that make it easier to spell correctly.

The difference between good spellers and poor spellers can often be traced to one problem: finding an effective method of learning to spell. You may have to experiment a bit to find the method that works best for you.

◀ **Even professional sign makers** can have spelling difficulties.

WATCH OUT!

Some words have two or more possible spellings. Usually, a dictionary gives the preferred spelling first, but that doesn't mean the alternate spelling is wrong.

Example: Gray can also be spelled *grey*.

Spelling Rules

Rule 1

The rule about when to use *ie* and when to use *ei* is explained in a poem.

> *Use i before e*
>
> *except after c*
>
> *or when it sounds like a*
>
> *as in neighbor and weigh*

Words like *friend*, *believe*, and *receive* follow this rule. Exceptions include *ancient*, *foreign*, and *weird*.

Rule 2

Most singular nouns are made plural by adding -*s* or -*es* to the end of the word.

pen	pens
match	matches

When a noun ends with a consonant and *y*, the is changed to *i* and -*es* is added to the plural.

baby	babies
candy	candies

But when a noun ends with a vowel (*a, e, i, o,* or *u*) and *y*, an -*s* is added to form the plural.

boy	boys
monkey	monkeys

Which is correct?	Correct spelling	This rule explains why	Some exceptions
tomatos or tomatoes	tomatoes	Nouns ending in *o* preceded by a consonant form the plural by adding *es*.	Some words add *s* only: *silos, dittos.*
brother-in-laws or brothers-in-law	brothers-in-law	Compound nouns add *s* to the main word to form a plural.	
cupsful or cupfuls	cupfuls	Add *s* to words ending in *ful*.	
desireable or desirable caring or careing	desirable caring	Words ending in *e* drop the final *e* before adding a suffix beginning with a vowel.	*mileage, saleable*

Rule 3

When verb endings that begin with a vowel, such as *-ing* or *-ed*, are added to verbs that end in silent *e*, the *e* is usually dropped.

bake + ed	=	baked
bake + ing	=	baking
plunge + ed	=	plunged
plunge + ing	=	plunging
salute + ed	=	saluted
salute + ing	=	saluting

The same rule applies when suffixes that begin with a vowel, such as *-able*, *-ical*, and *-ible*, are added to words that end in silent *e*.

live + able	=	livable
sphere + ical	=	spherical
sense + ible	=	sensible

However, most words that end with *ce* and *ge* do not follow this rule. The final silent *e* is needed to show that the soft sounds of *c* and *g* are used when saying certain words.

peace + able	=	peaceable
manage + able	=	manageable

A few words may drop the silent *e* before the suffix *-ment*.

judge + ment	=	judgment
acknowledge + ment	=	acknowledgment

Rule 4

For many words that end with a short vowel and a consonant, like *hop* and *step*, double the last consonant when a suffix is added that begins with a vowel, such as *-ed*, *-er*, or *-ing*.

hop	hopped	hopper	hopping

If a word consists of or ends in a long vowel and silent *e*, such as *hope*, the final consonant is not doubled.

hope	hoped	hoper	hoping

Consonant Endings		
bar	barred	barring
pin	pinned	pinning
scrap	scrapped	scrapping
star	starred	starring
Silent E Endings		
bare	bared	baring
pine	pined	pining
scrape	scraped	scraping
stare	stared	staring

Tricky Words

Frequently Misspelled Words

a lot	bicycle	descent	gauge	liable
absence	biscuit	desert, -ed	genuine	liaison
accident, -ally	bookkeeping	dessert	glamour	library
accommodation	boundary	diamond	government	license
achieve	brief	dilemma	governor	lightning
acknowledge	broccoli	disappear	grammar	liquefy
acquaintance	bureau	disappoint, -ed	grateful	literature
acquiesce	burglar	disease	grocery	lonely
adjacent	business	ecstasy	guarantee	loose
advice	calendar	effect, -ive	gymnasium	lose, -r
advise	campaign	eighth	handkerchief	machine
all right	candidate	either	harass, -ment	maintenance
already	cemetery	electricity	height	maneuver
altogether	census	embarrass, -ing	heroes	mediocre
among	certain, -ly	entrepreneur	hundredth	mileage
analyze	changeable	especially	immediate, -ly	millennium
ancient	chief	exaggerate	independent	miniature
anniversary	column	exceed, -ed	indispensable	miniscule
answer	committee	excellent, -ly	innocuous	miscellaneous
anxiety	compliment	exercise, -d	interest	mischief
apparel	confidence	existence	interim	mischievous
appear, -ance	congratulations	experience	irrelevant	misspell
appreciate	conscience	facsimile	itinerary	necessary
Arctic	conscientious	familiar	jealous	neighbor
article	conscious	fascinating	jeopardy	nickel
athlete	consensus	February	jewelry	niece
athletic	cooperate	foreign	journal, -ism	ninety
audience	courage, -ous	foresee	judgment	nuclear
auxiliary	courtesy	forfeit	juicy	nuisance
balloon	deceive	forty	khaki	occasion
basically	decision	fourth	knowledge	occur, -red
beginning	defense	freight	laboratory	omission
belief	definite, -ly	friend	league	ophthalmology
believe	definition	garage	leisure	pamphlet

paradigm	psychology	roommate	subtlety	truly
parallel	publicly	sandwich	subtly	twelfth
peculiar	pursue, -r	satellite	superintendent	tying
peninsula, -r	pursuit	schedule	supersede	usage
permissible	questionnaire	science	surprise	vaccinate
perseverance	queue	scissors	symbol, -ize	vacuum
physical	raspberry	seize	synonym	vegetable
picnic, -king	receipt	separate	technique	vicinity
plagiarism	receive	siege	temperament	Wednesday
possession	recommend	sieve	temperature	weight
precede	reinforce	similar	theater	weird
prefer, -red	religious	sincere, -ly	therefore	wholly
prejudice, -d	renaissance	solemn	though	wield
privilege	rescind	sophomore	thought	withhold
probably	restaurant	specific	threshold	yield
proceed	rhythm	strength	tomorrow	
pseudonym	ridiculous	strenuous	tongue	

SPELLING AND LOOKING UP WORDS

Almost everyone is unsure of how to spell some words, especially words that are pronounced one way and spelled another. The dictionary gives you the correct spelling. But how do you look up a word you can't spell?

Before you give up, think about what you already know about the word. If you want to spell the word *separate*, but you can't remember whether an *a* or an *e* follows the *p,* all you need to do is check *sep-*. If you want to spell the word *wagon*, but you can't remember whether to use one *g* or two, look up *wag-* and see what you find. (See also pages 824–825.)

Sounds

Homophones are words that sound alike but are spelled differently. Homophones are the source of many spelling mistakes. If you are unsure which word is which in a pair, look the word up in a dictionary.

Homophones											
aisle	isle	fir	fur	meat	meet	some	sum				
ant	aunt	flea	flee	night	knight	son	sun				
ate	eight	flour	flower	one	won	stair	stare				
bare	bear	great	grate	pail	pale	stake	steak				
be	bee	guest	guessed	pain	pane	steal	steel				
beat	beet	hair	hare	pair	pear	tail	tale				
blew	blue	heal	heel	peace	piece	their	there	they're			
board	bored	hear	here	plain	plane	threw	through				
brake	break	heard	herd	pray	prey	to	too	two			
buy	by	heir	air	rain	rein	toe	tow				
capital	capitol	hole	whole	read	red	vain	vane	vein			
cell	sell	hour	our	real	reel	waist	waste				
cellar	seller	in	inn	right	write	wait	weight				
cent	sent	knew	new	road	rode	way	weigh				
cord	chord	knot	not	role	roll	weak	week				
dear	deer	know	no	sail	sale	whole	hole				
dew	do	lead	led	scene	seen	whose	who's				
die	dye	loan	lone	sea	see	wood	would				
fair	fare	made	maid	sew	so						
feat	feet	mail	male	soul	sole						

A bare bear

A sail sale

Vowel Sounds

Many English sounds can be spelled several different ways. Although there are no rules to tell you how a given sound will be spelled in any particular case, it's helpful to know the possible ways a sound may be spelled. The following table shows some possible spellings for many English sounds.

Sound		Letters that can make this sound (example)
a	as in cat	a, ai (plaid)
a	as in cake	a, ai (paid), ea (break), ey (obey), ay (say)
a	as in care	a + r, ai + r (fair), ea + r (wear), e + r (there)
a	as in father	a, o (stop)
a	as in saw	a, au (caught), oa (broad), ou (fought)
e	as in bed	e, ea (heavy), ie (friend), ai (said)
e	as in we	e, ei (receive), ey (key), ie (field)
i	as in it	i (mitt), u (busy), ui (build), y (hymn)
i	as in kite	i, ie (tie), ei (height), ey (eye), uy (buy), y (fly)
o	as in go	o, oa (goat), oe (toe), ou (soul), ew (sew), ow (grow)
oo	as in tool	oo, ue (blue), ui (fruit), ew (threw), ough (through)
oo	as in book	oo, o (wolf), ou (would), u (pull)
ow	as in now	ow, ou (out), ough (bough)
oy	as in boy	oy, oi (toil)
u	as in cuff	u, o (son), oo (flood), oe (does), ou (double)
u	as in hurt	u + r, ea + r (heard), i + r (bird), o + r (worry), ou + r (courage)
u	as in fuse	u, ue (cue), eau (beauty), ew (few), iew (view), yu (yule), you (youth)
ə	(unaccented uh sound)	a (asleep), e (voted), o (confession), u (focus), etc.

THE GREAT ENGLISH VOWEL SHIFT

The way a vowel sounds in English is not always consistent with the way it is written. This inconsistency was caused in large part by the Great English Vowel Shift, a major change in English-language pronunciation that took place mainly in the 1400s and 1500s.

The Great Vowel Shift coincides with the transition from Middle English to modern English. Scholars do not know why it occurred, but before the shift, the letter *e* was pronounced with the sound it has today in *ballet*. After the shift, the "long" pronunciation of *e* was as in *beet*, and its "short" pronunciation was as in *bet*. Other English vowels underwent similar changes in pronunciation.

Reading

AUTHOR AND AUDIENCE work together to

build meaning. As you read, it's important to recognize the contributions of both the writer and the reader (that's you). If you ignore one side of the equation, your understanding of a text will be incomplete. By considering both author and audience, you'll learn more about the things you read—and more about yourself.

The Author

Creating Context

When you read a note from someone you know, there's a strong connection between the words you read and the person who wrote them. You know how to decipher your friend's messy handwriting. You might even understand what she means when the message itself isn't clear.

When you receive an e-mail from a stranger, it's more difficult to picture the flesh-and-blood person who typed the words on your screen. It's harder to guess at the writer's meaning when something seems unclear. Was that last line a joke or an insult? Without context, you're forced to speculate.

The same goes for a book or an essay written by someone who died centuries before you were born. Getting to know the author will help you better understand what you read.

MEET THE AUTHOR

You can learn more about an author by asking questions about his or her life and times.

- When and where did the author live?
- What do you know about the author's personality?
- What was the author's role in society? Did he or she have another job or public identity?
- What was his or her financial situation?
- What do you know about the author's childhood?
- What were the author's religious beliefs?
- What else do you know about his or her personal background?
- What was the political climate when the author was writing?
- How did other authors explore the same ideas?
- Is the author's perspective representative of his or her age? Or did the author go against the grain?
- What is the author's relationship to the tradition or genre in which he or she works?

Author's Intention

All authors have at least one purpose that shapes the content and style of their work.

- Journalists want to inform, so they focus on facts.

- Novelists want to entertain, so they use their imaginations.

- An advertising agency wants to sell something, so its writers use their powers of persuasion.

It's possible for an author have more than one purpose. Charles Dickens, for instance, wanted to entertain his readers while educating them about social injustice.

Identifying the author's intention is another good way to create the context that is critical to understanding. Consider *A Modest Proposal*, a satirical essay in which Jonathan Swift suggested that Irish babies be killed, sold, and eaten. (See page 937.) Swift hoped the essay would shock his readers so they would be encouraged to strive for change in their lives. Knowing his intention helps today's reader interpret the essay. You can imagine the misunderstandings that would result from a literal reading.

CASE STUDY: EZRA POUND

Ezra Pound, a 20th-century poet, is a controversial figure in literary history. His value as a writer is at odds with his reputation as a person.

Pound is known not only for his own poetry (particularly his epic work *The Cantos*), but for his influence over other important writers. As an editor, he played an important role in discovering unknown writers and helping them shape their work. He influenced heavyweights like T. S. Eliot, James Joyce, and Ernest Hemingway.

But he has another legacy that makes people uncomfortable. As he was crafting *The Cantos*, Pound, an American, was politically active in Italy, the country that became his adopted home in the 1920s. He followed the fascist dictator Benito Mussolini, who was aligned with Hitler in World War II. Pound was also known for his vocal anti-Semitism and anti-Americanism.

As a result, many readers who admire Pound's poems feel conflicted about his legacy. There's little doubt the poet's personal and political views are appalling. But how much should our knowledge of his personal beliefs factor into our consideration of his poetry? That question remains up for debate.

Some scholars believe that writers are shaped and moved by intentions the writers themselves aren't consciously aware of. These secret forces are part of what Sigmund Freud called the unconscious—mental processes and feelings that are buried way below the surface of our everyday thoughts.

Some of the material in the Reading section (pages 854–895) is reprinted with permission of Kendall Hunt Publishing Company, from Research for Writers: Advanced English Composition *by Florida Community College at Jacksonville. Copyright © 2002 by FCCJ Foundation. Further reproduction is prohibited.*

The Audience

SOUTHWESTERN

General Audience

As you read, the author's biography and intentions shouldn't be your only considerations. Another way you can create context is by thinking about the author's audience.

Sometimes an author writes with a particular audience in mind. It can be helpful to know who exactly is in that intended audience. For instance, we can expect to see differences between a book review that appears in a scholarly journal and a review of the same book that runs in a popular magazine. That's because the audiences of those two publications consist of different types of readers.

It's important to note that an author's intended audience does not always align with the text's actual readers. For example, in the 1660s, Samuel Pepys wrote his *Diary* with an unusual honesty, but he never intended for it to be read by the public. (He wrote it in a combination of code, shorthand, and foreign words and phrases.) More than a century after his death, Pepys's actual audience turned out to be the reading public.

THINKING ABOUT AUDIENCE

It's easy enough to figure out what you think about a text. But what about everyone else? Here are some questions you can ask to further your thinking about audience.

- How was the text received in its time?
- How have critics responded to the text over time?
- Who was the author writing for?
- Who actually read the text? The general population? Scholars?
- Was the text influential?
- Did it inspire change?
- Does the text remain relevant today? Why or why not?

▲ **William Empson,** along with I. A. Richards, developed the systematic textual analysis of literature that became known as New Criticism.

A DIFFERENT PERSPECTIVE

Before the world began to recognize the reader's role in building meaning, there was a group of thinkers called the New Critics. They believed that a text's meaning exists in a vacuum. To them, author and audience were not important considerations. Nothing mattered except the texts themselves, which are completely self-contained.

The New Critics thought the idea that we could determine an author's true purpose or intention was problematic. How could anyone really know what was in a given writer's head and heart? Their solution was to disregard the author altogether. A poem, for instance, is an artifact that belongs to the world instead of to the author. This represented a big shift in the way people thought about literature.

New Critics also did not believe that readers play an active role in building meaning. Instead, they argued that a given poem has a single correct interpretation. The reader's job, therefore, is to tease that meaning out. Meaning lies within the words on a page, waiting to be unlocked.

Reader Response

For hundreds of years, literary critics focused on the importance of the author in creating meaning. In this model, understanding is a one-way street. It is something that the author gives and the reader takes.

In the 20th century, attention shifted to the importance of the reader as an active participant in building meaning. In this model, the meaning of a text is never static or fixed. It is something that each reader builds from scratch.

Every time you read, your own experience and beliefs come to bear on the text. For example, you might

- read a newspaper editorial with your own opinion in mind.
- like a particular character in a novel because she reminds you of someone you know.
- dislike a writer's style based on your personal preferences.

Your unique perspective will affect your interpretation of everything you read. You do not just receive information when you read; you also filter it and process it.

In other words, the same text can mean different things to different readers. In this way, readers play an active role in the creation of meaning.

WATCH OUT!

Remember that the author and the audience work together to build meaning. Try to maintain a balanced approach; don't place too much focus on one or the other.

ACTIVE READING

As you read, it's important to engage with the text. One way to do that is to ask questions as you go.

- How does the text relate to my own experience?
- How does the world being described relate to my own world?
- What were my thoughts about this topic before I began reading? Have those thoughts changed?
- In what ways can I relate to the author? In what ways is his or her life different than my own?
- What about the characters (if it's fiction) or protagonists (if it's nonfiction)? In what ways are we alike or different?
- Do I belong to the author's intended audience?
- What techniques does the author use to get his or her point across? Are those techniques affecting my reading experience?
- Do I have an emotional reaction to this text?
- Have I learned anything new?

DESIGN is the way in which words, images, forms, and colors are arranged and organized on the page or screen. According to the old saying, you can't judge a book by its cover. But in reading, the way something looks can tell us a lot about what it means. To read well, it's important to understand that information does not just appear in the content of words, but also in how those words are ordered and presented.

Text	Graphics
in-depth	at-a-glance
shows detail	give an overview
holds readers' attention	draw readers in

GOOD REASONS TO USE TEXT

- List details
- Provide context and analysis
- Tell a story
- Explain the significance of something
- Make a subtle distinction

GOOD REASONS TO USE GRAPHICS

- Emphasize and reinforce an important point
- Explain how something works
- Summarize a complicated idea
- Break up long chunks of text
- Add visual interest

What You See

We tend to think of reading as a word-based activity, a process of seeing text and decoding its meaning. Actually, when we read, the words themselves are just one way that we make sense out of what we see. In addition to reading words, we read many kinds of visual cues.

Visual Vocabulary

As you read, visual cues provide information you need to help process the text.

When you learn a new vocabulary word, you have to memorize its definition. Your visual vocabulary is more intuitive; often, when you see a visual cue, you will understand its meaning instinctively, without having to think about it carefully.

Text size can be used to summarize key points and tell readers what is important. For example:

- Headlines in newspapers are in large letters to catch your eye. They summarize articles in a few words.
- In books, footnotes, which contain extra information, are in small letters.

Graphics, such as photographs, tables, and diagrams, help bring text to life. For example:

- A catalog contains photographs of the goods it sells to help convince readers to make purchases.
- A medical textbook contains diagrams and photographs to show readers how the body works.
- Advertisements feature models and celebrities to make their products seem more appealing.

Many other visual cues, including color and placement, affect the way you read books, magazines, Web sites, and other media. These cues give you important information such as

- what you should read first.
- which information is most important.
- what something or someone looks like.
- where to find information.

Thinking About Design

Babies look at picture books before they learn how to read.

- Why do you think children's books have more illustrations than adult books?

Novels have covers designed to appeal to certain kinds of readers.

- What are you drawn to when you browse a shelf for something to read?

- How might the cover of a science fiction novel look different than the cover of a romance novel?

Magazines use colorful pictures to draw readers into the text.

- Why do you think so many magazine advertisements rely on images more than text?

Scholarly journals contain long articles with long lines of text and few images.

- What do you think readers of these journals value most?

Manuals have diagrams to show you how something works.

- How do diagrams help readers understand the directions in a manual?

Look carefully at this page. Notice that some words are bigger than others. Notice that some words are in black and that other words that are in different colors. Notice where the paragraphs begin and end and the white space that appears in between them.

Now imagine a page where all the words looked exactly the same—just one long line of black letters that are all the same size and color.

Textual Features

That imaginary page would be difficult to read without textual features. Textual features are the visual cues that help you navigate your way through the words. They tell you where you are and where you're going.

Table of Contents. The table of contents appears toward the front of a publication. You can read the table of contents to get an overview of the text, or you can use it like a map to help direct you to the information you need most.

Chapters represent the main divisions in a text. Each chapter deals with a certain part of the story or topic. Chapters help organize information into chunks so readers can better understand how ideas relate to one another.

Headings and titles are descriptive phrases that appear in big bold letters. Typically, they're used to summarize a text in some way. For example, newspapers use headlines to tell readers what the rest of the article will be about. Some authors title the chapters of nonfiction books so readers have a better idea of what to expect as they progress through the text.

Subheadings are used to organize sections of text that are particularly long or complicated. They help indicate to the reader what the main concepts are within a given section.

Captions are the lines of text that appear under images and other visual features. Captions help explain the visual content of photographs, diagrams, and charts. Sometimes captions contain information that doesn't appear elsewhere in the text. Other times they repeat a point in the text to add emphasis.

Footnotes or endnotes are remarks printed in small type at the bottom of a page or at the end of a chapter or book. They contain extra information such as

- information about sources (citations).
- comments that don't fit in the main text.
- other people's opinions.
- other references.

Glossary. Textbooks and other specialized texts often contain glossaries, lists of words that are technical or difficult. In the main text, a glossary word might appear in **bold** or *italics*. Those words are usually defined in a special section at the back of the book.

Index. An index is an alphabetical listing at the end of a book that gives all the main topics included in the book and the page numbers on which they can be found. Using an index is a quick way to find specific information without reading every page.

Entries in an index might look like this

Adam, 195
Diamond, 502
Emerald, 409
Gem, 111, 213, 409

◀ **Cover copy** on a book's dust jacket will help you learn what a book is about and tell you something about the author.

CHAPTERS IN *THE GRAPES OF WRATH*

Like most novels, John Steinbeck's *The Grapes of Wrath* is organized into chapters. But a closer analysis of its chapters reveals a special system of organization that helps create meaning.

In between the chapters chronicling the Joad family's Depression-era struggles, Steinbeck interspersed more general chapters dealing with the larger forces and events that affected the lives of millions of people during that time in history. This structure helps the reader to understand more fully the events that shape the Joad family's lives, and it also elevates their sufferings and triumphs to a universal level.

The novel's structure plays an important role in the development and exposition of Steinbeck's theme. (See pages 760–761.)

TEXTUAL FEATURES IN POSTMODERN FICTION

During the 20th century, some fiction writers became interested in the ways in which textual features build meaning. Prose works became more playful. Some writers played with structure as a way to say something about how we experience the world and as a way to question literary traditions.

- Jorge Luis Borges wrote short stories that looked like essays to blur the line between fact and fiction.

- William Burroughs experimented with a technique called cut-up; he said the chapters of his novel could be read in any order.

- David Foster Wallace used footnotes to replicate the fractured way in which we experience reality.

◄ **Postmodern** writers such as Jorge Luis Borges (*left*) played with the textual features of prose works to call attention to the ways in which readers construct meaning.

Formatting

When you write a paper for an assignment, your teacher probably asks you to format the pages in a certain way. Those requirements might include guidelines for

- font
- margins
- page numbers
- line spacing
- a separate title page

Each of these requirements serves a particular purpose. Collectively, they make papers easier to read.

Font

Your teacher might require you to use a particular font. Like different kinds of handwriting, some fonts are easier to read than others. Your teacher likely wants something that's clear and easy to read. By asking everyone to use the same font, the teacher can tell just by looking if your paper is the right length.

Margins

A margin is the white space around the border of the words on your paper. Leave a wide enough margin for your teacher to have room to write comments.

CREATING EMPHASIS

There are a variety of formatting techniques that create emphasis. Whenever you read something with special formatting, you can assume that it's important or special in some way.

ITALICS

Italics is the style of type in which this sentence is printed. It's based on an old style of handwriting.

BOLDFACE

Boldface is the style of type in which this sentence is printed. It makes words stand out.

UNDERLINED TEXT

<u>This sentence is an example of underlined text.</u> It's another way of marking words to get the reader's attention.

Page Numbers

Page numbers help keep readers oriented as they make their way through a text. The numbers help you dip in and out of the text when you're looking for something specific (such as when your teacher tells you to turn to a certain page of your textbook). They also let you know how far you've come and how many pages you have left.

Line Spacing

Many teachers require students to double-space the lines of a paper. This makes papers easier to read and also leaves room for any comments and corrections the teacher needs to write.

Title Page

When you begin a book, you turn to the title page to learn basic information about what you're reading. The title page of a paper does the same for your teacher; he or she knows at a glance who is writing and what the subject of the paper is.

 *Keep an eye out for special formatting whenever you read an advertisement in a magazine, in a newspaper, or online. What information does the company want to highlight to readers? What information does it want to downplay?*

CAPITAL LETTERS

CAPITAL LETTERS are another way to get your reader's attention. SOMETIMES WHEN YOU WRITE IN ALL CAPITAL LETTERS IT "SOUNDS" LIKE SHOUTING.

SIZE

Big letters are another way to emphasize important text.

COLOR

Using a different color draws the reader's eye.

THE PRINTING PRESS

Printing, the process by which words and images are reproduced on paper and other materials, is one of our most important means of mass communication. It more or less began in Europe around 1436, when a German goldsmith named Johannes Gutenberg experimented with movable type.

With movable type, letters and other symbols are carved or stamped on individual plates that can be arranged and rearranged to form words and sentences using a printing press.

Before the printing press, books were expensive treasures, and monks labored for years copying each one by hand. The printing press changed history by making written knowledge cheaper and more accessible. Reading and writing spread widely and rapidly.

◀ **Gutenberg's press** probably looked like this drawing. It was adapted from a cheese or wine press and could print about 300 sheets a day. It produced the Gutenberg Bible.

E-BOOKS

An electronic book, or an e-book, is a collection of digital files that contain the text, and sometimes the illustrations, of a book. E-books can be viewed on computer monitors, cell phones, and special handheld devices called e-readers. E-readers can hold the files for many books, so it's possible to carry one device in place of hundreds—even thousands—of books.

E-books first appeared in 1998, but they didn't become popular until Amazon introduced its e-reader, the Kindle, in 2007. Today, e-books are available for purchase in online bookstores and on other Web sites. Some libraries offer e-books over the Internet at no cost.

The ways in which people read have changed so much since the advent of the Internet that many people wonder if printed books will become obsolete.

E-readers solve several problems for users—portability, notation, search—but are still challenged to elegantly reproduce drawings, photographs, and other images. ▶

Graphic Features

Graphic features like graphs, charts, photographs, illustrations, icons, maps, and other images help increase readers' understanding.

Graphs and Charts

Graphs are used to present facts in picture form to make them clear and easy to understand. Many readers find it helpful to see information instead of (or in addition to) reading it.

- Use a line graph to compare numbers.
- Use a bar graph to compare increases and decreases over a period of time.
- Use a circle graph to show how a part relates to its whole.
- Use a picture graph when you want the graph to provide as much information as possible at a glance.

Line graphs are the simplest type of graph. They are also one of the easiest ways to compare numbers.

Line graphs are made using a grid. The vertical axis (scale) indicates frequency, and the horizontal axis shows the categories being considered. For example, the frequency could be the number of pupils present, and the categories could be dates. Points on such a graph would indicate how many pupils were present on each date.

Line graphs can be used to present many kinds of data, such as

- statistics
- population
- production
- performance

Bar graphs are a good way to compare increases and decreases in quantity over a period of time. They work best when you're trying to measure data that fluctuates. For example, you could use a bar graph to show sales figures, your weight, or any kind of figure that goes up or down. Bar graphs are not useful for showing data that is relatively stable over time.

There are two kinds of bar graphs: horizontal and vertical.

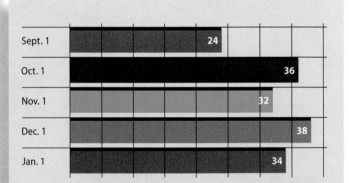

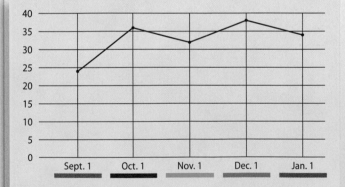

These three graphs all illustrate the same attendance record in different ways.

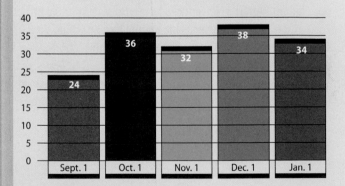

▲ **Bar graphs** make it especially easy to compare and contrast different data points.

Circle graphs (which are also called pie charts) show the relation of parts to the whole.

A long list of figures in paragraph form can be difficult and tedious to read. Suppose, for example, the cost of education in the U.S. is $2 billion divided as follows: general control, 3.4 percent; instruction, 61.9 percent; operation, maintenance, and auxiliary agencies, 19.1 percent; capital outlay, 8.8 percent; interest, 6.8 percent.

If you were to make a circle graph that showed the same figures, the percentages would appear as wedges that look like slices of a pie. At a glance, it would be immediately obvious that the "instruction" piece of the pie was much bigger than all the others.

A circle graph works well for showing the relationship between a part and its whole.

Picture graphs convey information through symbols instead of lines or bars. The pictorial form of these graphs helps readers understand the meaning of data without having to examine lists of figures. Picture graphs are most often used in magazines and newspapers. This type of graph is akin to the earliest form of writing, originating in the pictographs used by primitive people.

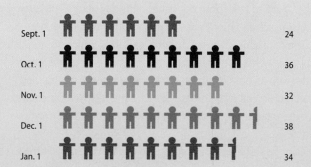

Sept. 1	24
Oct. 1	36
Nov. 1	32
Dec. 1	38
Jan. 1	34

▲ **In this picture graph,** each symbol represents the presence of four students.

WATCH OUT!

Make sure you choose the correct form of graph for the data you're depicting. A circle graph, for instance, is like a snapshot in time; it can't show how something changes over time.

Graphs do a great job of presenting complex numerical data in a way that's easy to digest, but they can't provide the same level of nuance and detail as written text. Don't forget to read the text that accompanies a graph to make sure you understand its context and its significance.

Icons and Illustrations

Icons and illustrations are also types of graphic features.

Icons

An icon is an image that symbolizes or embodies something. Icons are effective and economic communication tools. They're used in a variety of situations in which pictures convey information more quickly than words.

For example, icons help people

- recognize brands
- use computers
- read maps
- navigate roads

If you were to visit another country where you didn't speak the language, icons would help you make your way around. Icons help people find train stops, locate restrooms, and stay safe.

Icons make it easy for people to interact with computers.

Illustrations

An illustration is a picture that explains and adds interest to the written part of a text. There are many kinds of illustrations, and many processes that reproduce them. Types of illustrations include

- paintings
- drawings
- photographs
- maps
- engravings
- diagrams
- time lines

Illustrations may be done in black and white, in color, or in a combination of both.

While one purpose of illustrations is to decorate or draw attention to the story or text, they can also help the reader better understand the writing.

PUNCH MAGAZINE

Punch, a weekly magazine that ran from 1841 to 1992, was the longest-running publication of its type in the English language. Its mode was radical satire. *Punch* used funny illustrations to talk about the issues of its day, such as poverty, and to attack and mock politicians and other public figures.

The magazine invented editorial cartoons, which accomplish in pictures what editorials do in words. They encourage readers to develop an opinion about someone or something that has been prominent in the news. *Punch* frequently used caricature, an exaggerated way of drawing, to poke fun at well-known people.

Famous cartoonists, including Richard Doyle, Harry Furniss, Charles Keene, David Low, Phil May, Gerald Scarfe, Ronald Searle, John Tenniel, and Bill Tidy, drew for the magazine during its long life.

Reading Maps

People probably made rough maps even before they began to use written language some 5,500 years ago. We use maps to locate places, measure distances, plan trips, and find our way.

Using a map requires certain skills. To read a map, it is necessary to understand how map legends and scale work. It's also important to consider the map's date and purpose. (See also pages 604–605.)

Legends list and explain the symbols and colors used on a map. Some symbols resemble the features they represent. For example, a small tree might stand for a forest, an orchard, or a state park. But many symbols bear little resemblance to the features they represent, as when a circle stands for a city. The same symbol may represent different features on different maps. For example, a triangle might represent a mobile home park on one map and an eagle's nest on another. Such differences make it important to read the map legend to find out what each symbol means on a particular map.

Scales show the mathematical relationship by which distances on a map reduce actual distances on Earth. Many maps illustrate scale by marking off distances on a straight line. Each mark shows how distance on the line corresponds to miles, kilometers, or other units of measurement on Earth. Other maps state the scale in words and figures. Such a scale might appear as 1 inch: 16 miles. In this relationship, 1 inch on the map represents a distance of 16 miles.

Date. Our Earth changes constantly as a result of geographic and political events. For example, changes may occur in the population of cities, the shape of coastlines, or the acreage of forests. Keep in mind that old maps might be out of date.

Purpose. Mapmakers create many types of maps for a variety of purposes.

This map was designed to provide information about wind distribution. If it were to give information about a different topic (like crops or crime), the map would look different.

United States—Annual Average Wind Speed at Height of 80 Meters

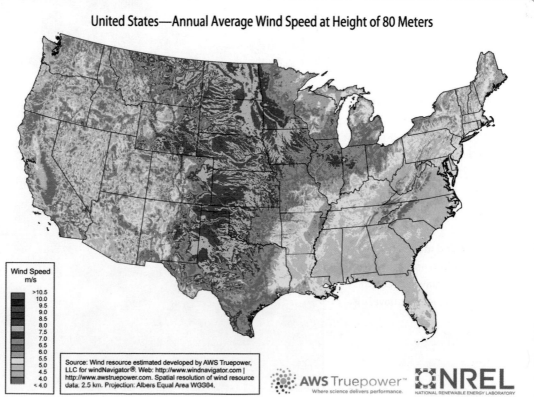
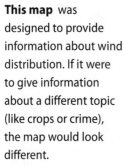

Wind Speed m/s

>10.5
10.0
9.5
9.0
8.5
8.0
7.5
7.0
6.5
6.0
5.5
5.0
4.5
4.0
< 4.0

Source: Wind resource estimated developed by AWS Truepower, LLC for windNavigator®. Web: http://www.windnavigator.com | http://www.awstruepower.com. Spatial resolution of wind resource data: 2.5 km. Projection: Albers Equal Area WGS84.

AWS Truepower™
Where science delivers performance.

NREL
NATIONAL RENEWABLE ENERGY LABORATORY

Exploring Graphic Features

These pages contain a variety of graphic features relating to the London Underground, the subterranean train stations in Great Britain's capital. As you examine the features, think about the particular ways in which each form presents information.

The icon for the London Underground is a symbol that's highly recognizable. It is used on signs and in stations because it's easy for everyone to see and to identify—even for people who can't read or who don't speak English. Why do you think it's important to use a symbol that's easy to recognize? ▼

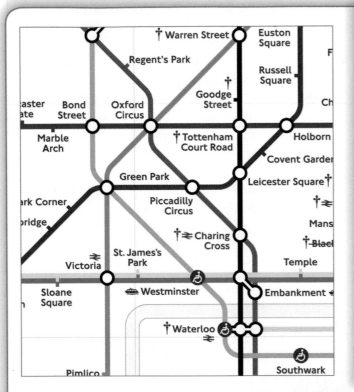

▲ **This map of the Underground** is specially designed for people who use the trains. How is it different from other maps? What features make it easy for travelers to use?

This above-ground map shows where Underground stations are in the "real" world. Why might a traveler need this map in addition to the one above? ▶

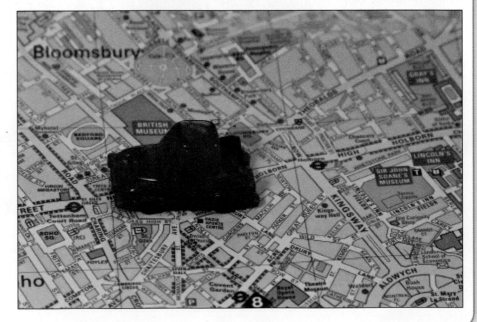

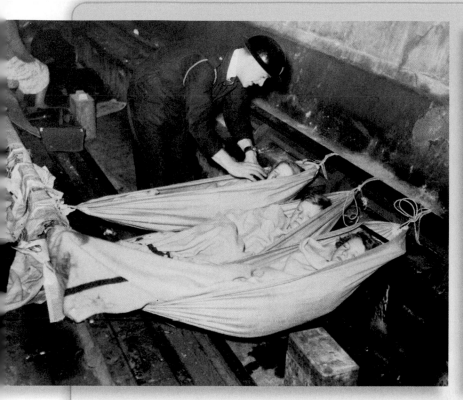

▲ **This photograph** reflects an important moment in the Underground's history: when its stations were used as public shelters during air raids throughout World War II. Do you think this picture is worth 1,000 words? Why or why not?

▲ **Thousands of advertisement posters** have been commissioned by the London Underground since the beginning of the 20th century. Why do you think most posters feature illustrations instead of photographs?

1850	1900	1950	2000

1845
Charles Pearson puts forward the idea of "trains in drains." Aboveground railroads were still relatively new at the time; the first public railroads began in the U.K. in the 1820s and '30s.

1908
Stations are marked with the famous London Underground icon.

1940–1945
Underground stations are used as air raid shelters.

1863
The first stretch of subterranean tracks—the Metropolitan line—opens.

▲ **A time line** is a good way to give an overview of a story that unfolds over time. It shows information that might otherwise take many paragraphs—or pages—to explain in writing.

STRATEGIES

Reading abilities and habits vary from person to person. Some people can read remarkably fast while understanding the main points and remembering key examples. Others read at a snail's pace, trying to absorb every word without ever evaluating the worth of the information. A good reader uses a variety of reading techniques. The technique you choose depends on the type of material, its difficulty, the reason you're reading, and your familiarity with the subject.

Types of Reading

Reading for Fun

Recreational reading is important for the practice it gives. Like swimming or playing a musical instrument, reading is a skill that improves with use—the more you do it, the more you improve. Like other skills, reading becomes more natural and easy over time.

Reading Textbooks

Much of the reading you do for school is for the purpose of extracting information. Some schoolbooks are very dense, which means they aren't meant to be read through quickly. Often, you read only a page or two at a time, and you may have to read a given section more than once.

Reading for Book Reports

Another kind of informational reading is the kind you do for a book report. With this type of assignment, you can save time by taking a few minutes before starting the first chapter to preview the book to see what it covers.

Reading for Research Papers

When you consult reference books with a specific purpose in mind, you might need to sort through large amounts of material to find what you need.

When you're sorting through a stack of potential sources, it's a good idea to preview a book before you invest time in it. If you just start reading, you may have to go through dozens of pages before you find what you need. Or, worse, what you need might not even be there. (See also page 785.)

Reading Tests

Many tests check reading comprehension by asking you to read a passage and to answer questions about it. Many students find it helpful to read such a passage twice—once very quickly to get the general idea, then a second time more slowly to get more detailed information. When answering the questions, read them carefully and be sure you understand them.

How to Preview a Book

You will understand the material in a book much more quickly if you examine it before you start to read. Follow these steps to make the most of your reading time.

1. **Look at the jacket.** If the book has a jacket, its illustration may help you to understand the mood or content of the book. On the flaps—the parts that fold inside the front and back covers—there is often a brief description of the book and a brief biographical sketch of the author.

2. **Look at the title page.** The title page might have a subtitle that is not on the cover of the book. The title page will also provide information such as the publisher and the date of publication.

3. **Look at the copyright page.** The copyright notice almost always appears on the back of the title page. It will tell you when the book was originally published. This might be very important if you are looking up the latest information on astronomy, for example. If the book was first published in 1945, it will not have up-to-date information.

4. **Study the table of contents.** The table of contents is the framework of most books. A few minutes spent studying it will show you how the book is put together. It will often show where the material you are looking for can be found. If you are doing research for a report and you only need a few facts, the contents can help lead you straight to your material.

5. **Look for a foreword or an introduction.** Writers often put important information in the introduction. They may tell you how to use the book, or that they have left out certain topics—perhaps even those you're most interested in.

6. **Page through the book quickly.** Starting at the front, turn the pages, familiarizing yourself with the look and feel of the volume. Pay special attention to chapter headings and to other headings in the text; they will help you see how the material is organized. Note the pages of any chapters or headings you want to go back and read later.

7. **Check the back of the book.** Several kinds of information can be found there. Often you'll find a bibliography, which lists books on related topics. In most nonfiction books, you'll find an index. The index can be especially helpful if you're looking for specific information.

8. **Choose your own adventure.** After you've been through these steps, it's up to you to decide how to use the book. If you plan to read it through, you already have a road map—you know where the book starts and where it's going. If you're using the book for reference, you may not start at the beginning, opting to turn directly to the chapter or page that interests you.

Comprehension

The first goal of reading is comprehension. Without comprehension, reading is a meaningless experience. The best test of your comprehension is to ask yourself if you can restate the idea presented in a unit of writing, whether it's a paragraph, a chapter, or an entire book.

Almost any idea can be expressed in a number of ways. If you have understood an author's message, you should be able to restate it in your own words—words that come naturally to mind, just as the original words of the author came to him or her.

Improving Comprehension

There are four ways you can improve your understanding of difficult reading material.

- Concentrate
- Sit up straight
- Pre-read
- Take notes

Concentrate. As you advance in your studies, you will have to pay close attention and apply your mental energy in subject areas that may not give you immediate satisfaction. While your mind tells you that you must read well, an inner voice may tell you that you would rather be doing something else. The result is a lack of concentration. What can you do about this problem?

First, pick a good place to do your reading. Our minds and thought processes are affected by our physical surroundings. Certain surroundings suggest certain activities. For example, a school gym in which a basketball game is going on suggests physical exercise—not reading or study. Libraries, on the other hand, suggest quiet reading and study.

WATCH OUT!

If you can't restate the author's ideas in your own words, you have failed to understand the text. Try reading it again.

Sit Up Straight. A soft armchair suggests relaxation, not active reading. A straight, hard chair suggests active reading. When you attempt to do serious reading in an armchair, you are fighting your natural tendency to relax. At a table, you don't have to fight that tendency. Take advantage of your physical surroundings.

Pre-read. To pre-read a book, first run down its table of contents to see what the book contains and how the subjects it covers are organized. Then skim the preface or introduction, which may give further information on the content and structure, as well as the author's purpose.

Next, skim through the chapters of the book. Read the main headings in the chapters and the introductory and closing paragraphs. Finally, find out whether there is an index at the end of the book that shows the topics that are covered. (See also page 871.)

Pre-reading is especially useful for studying high school and college textbooks. The time you'll spend pre-reading is only a small fraction of the total time it will take to read the book.

Take Notes. For serious students, reading and study mean almost the same thing. High school and college reading means using textbooks and challenging books effectively. The task is always to learn what an author has said and to make careful notes for review.

It is well known that we learn by repeated exposure to the material that is to be learned. The combination of careful initial reading plus review makes for good learning.

When you gather information for a report, it's always best to read a whole passage or chapter first before writing anything down, to make sure you understand what the writer is saying. After reading the whole passage, go back and summarize it in your mind. Put down this summary in your notes. Then, if there is particular information—a date, a name, or a specific idea—write it down afterward. Be sure that each note has the name of the book and the pages you read in case you need to find the passage again later.

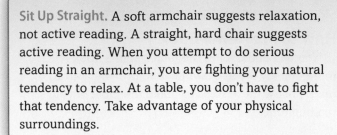

Good Reading Habits

Small changes can make a big difference in your reading habits. Make sure you set yourself up for success each time you sit down with a book.

Setting. Pick a comfortable, quiet place to read, away from distractions. Can you concentrate on reading if someone is watching television in the same room or playing a video game? If you are among the majority who cannot, find a comfortable chair in another room and read there.

Posture. Good posture promotes good reading. Many people find that sitting up in a chair with both feet flat on the floor is a comfortable position that promotes concentration. Stretching out on a sofa to read or settling deep into a soft chair may be too comfortable, making you drowsy and causing your thoughts to wander.

Lighting. Good lighting is also important. Make sure you have adequate light that is not too harsh.

Good reading requires an attitude of mental alertness that is hard to manage when your body is relaxed. When your body is relaxed, your brain tends to relax as well. Try to choose surroundings that invite good reading.

THE THREE STEPS TO UNDERSTANDING

1. **Word recognition:** At the heart of the reading process is the recognition of printed symbols. This involves translating printed symbols into the sounds we use in speaking.

2. **Comprehension:** Readers must understand vocabulary words and what they mean.

3. **Fusion:** Readers have to understand what vocabulary words mean when they are put together in various ways.

Your reading will improve if you find a place to read without distractions. ▼

Reading Rates

Most people use different reading techniques for different reading situations. For example, a mystery you read for entertainment may move more quickly than a classic Russian novel you read for a class.

Good readers can easily shift from one kind of reading to another. Reading flexibility improves with experience.

The Three Speeds

Alternating between three rates will help you become a more efficient reader. Your natural reading pace is fine for everyday materials like most books and magazines. Whenever you find yourself struggling to understand something, slow down. Reread sentences or even sections if you find your attention wandering. On the other hand, if you're reading something with a particular purpose in mind, feel free to speed up and skip any parts you don't need to read.

Flexibility

Good readers do not read everything at the same rate. When material is easy to understand, they read rapidly. When material is more difficult to understand—like a set of complex instructions—good readers slow down.

But there is more to reading rate than that. For example, when good readers wish to prolong their pleasure in reading stories or novels, or when the stories or novels must be considered with great care, good readers reduce their speed.

The quality that all good readers share is flexibility. This means they are able to adjust their reading rate to the difficulty of what they are reading and to their purpose in reading. Less efficient readers lack this flexibility. They tend to read everything, from the easiest children's book to the most exciting detective story, at a single speed.

THE THREE SPEEDS

Careful Rate

Use a careful rate in the following situations.

- to master details in a textbook
- to evaluate arguments
- to follow detailed instructions
- to read complex technical material
- to appreciate literary works that demand close attention

Slow

Normal Rate

Your normal rate is whatever reading pace feels comfortable. Use it for most purposes, including

- to read something that isn't very complex
- to find answers to broad questions
- to identify important details
- to get the overall meaning of a text

Medium

Skimming

Skimming is a reading technique used for specific tasks such as

- answering a particular question
- finding the main idea
- previewing a book or magazine
- refreshing your memory on material that you've already read

Fast

Pushing Yourself

The most effective method for increasing your reading speed is to push yourself to read a little faster than feels comfortable. Keep doing so until you find that you can't read any faster.

Keep in mind that comprehension is more important than speed. If your understanding is poor, you need to slow down in the next session of practice reading. Reading quickly doesn't serve a purpose if you can't follow the ideas in the text.

If you understood what you read, repeat the timing and the reading for five more pages. Remember that the idea is to read at a rate that is slightly difficult. About an hour of such practice each day is enough. Soon, you will read faster.

PRACTICE READING FASTER

1. Mark off the fifth page in a book you want to read.

2. Write your starting time in a notebook.

3. Begin to read a little faster—only a little faster—than is comfortable for you.

4. When you have finished the fifth page, note the time.

For Reluctant Readers

Does reading seem like a chore? The following suggestions may help.

List your interests. Make a list of the three subjects in which you are most interested. There are magazines and books available on almost every conceivable subject.

Look for reading material on your interests. If you like mystery stories, look for mysteries in comic book form. If you want to know more about cars, look for magazines and easy books on the subject. Ask a librarian or a friend who is interested in the same field for recommendations.

Read every day. Take 20 minutes each day just for reading. You can read almost anywhere, any time. Take a magazine to read on the bus or in the car. Put a book by your bed and read before you go to sleep. Once you get in the habit, you won't want to stop.

Find a friend with the same interests. Friends who are reading about the same subject have lots to talk about. Your friends may know of books you might like.

Reading Assignments

A fundamental problem of student writing is the failure to carry out the assigned task.

Whether you're working on a casual homework assignment or answering an essay question on a big exam, it's important to read the question carefully. If you misinterpret the question, chances are you will choose the wrong answer.

To help you focus on the task and execute it successfully, you need to carefully consider the way an assignment is worded.

The Topic

The first part of the assignment you need to consider is the topic. It's a good idea to circle the noun or the noun phrase that names the subject of the assignment, just to focus your attention.

Also notice any qualifiers or specifiers. If the assignment says, "Discuss the causes of the Civil War," for instance, make sure that you focus on specific causes, not just the Civil War in general.

ANSWERING THE QUESTION

1. Read the question carefully.

2. Note the topic and the verb. Underline or circle key words to help you focus.

3. Take a minute to collect your thoughts. Consider how you want to answer the question.

4. Before you answer, read the question again to make sure you're on the right track.

WATCH OUT!

Don't stray off-topic. It's easy to lose your way, especially if your assignment is about a topic you're interested in. Make sure to focus on whatever the assignment asks for, not the part of the topic that you like best. After you begin working, periodically reread the assignment to make sure you're on track.

 *When teachers give you an assignment, they are usually more interested in getting you to think than in having you adopt a particular viewpoint. Exploring both sides of an issue gives you a chance to show off what you know.*

The Verb

Every assignment should have a verb that tells you what you need to do. Some assignment verbs are more specific than others.

Analyze. When you are asked to analyze, divide the topic into categories and examine each aspect one at a time. Analysis of a problem forces the writer to examine all sides of an issue.

Compare and/or Contrast. Show the similarities and differences between two or more topics. *Compare* means focus only on similarities, while *contrast* means focus only on differences.

Define. To define something, you need to spell it out in specific terms. You may need to explain an abstract concept (like justice) or to interpret the meaning of a particular term.

Describe. In writing a description, the opportunity presents itself for you, the writer, to take the reader on a visual journey. A description provides details about how something feels, looks, tastes, smells, or sounds, or how it makes you feel.

Discuss. This verb can mean just about anything. Read the rest of the assignment carefully to make sure you understand what you're being asked to do.

Evaluate. An evaluation requires you to make a judgment about the value or significance of a topic. Don't limit your discussion to only descriptions and definitions. Evaluations require you to draw conclusions.

Explain. To explain something, you need to clarify the term or the concept by using examples or reasons. You may define how it works or why it exists.

Summarize. To summarize a topic, you should outline the major points in a short but thorough manner. List major points of the topic. Provide specific details in your answers.

Be sure to use clear, direct sentences that outline the structure of the piece being analyzed.

This is an open-ended word. You could use any writing strategy successfully.

Look for several examples of how the pieces being analyzed are alike and different.

Write a **well-organized** essay **discussing** the **similarities and differences** in both theme and style of the following **two poems**.

Make sure you give equal time to both pieces being discussed.

▲ Here's how one assignment might be analyzed.

POETRY, the oldest literary form, grew from the ancient combination of music and speech. Studying poetry is much like solving a puzzle: analyzing the pieces, fitting them together, and appreciating the whole. And while poems can be enjoyed without analysis and analyzed without enjoyment, the analyzed poem, like the completed puzzle, increases understanding, satisfaction, and pleasure.

Poetry	Prose
Indirect	Direct
Slippery	Specific
Figurative	Literal
Fanciful	Practical

Poetry is the oldest type of literature. The first poems are probably written versions of legends and stories that were originally sung or chanted by generations of traveling entertainers.

What's a Poem?

It's difficult to pin down the difference between poetry and prose. How poetry is defined depends in part on the perceptions of the reader.

You Can't Sound It Out

You may think of a poem as something that uses words that rhyme. But you can't recognize a poem just by the presence (or absence) of rhyming words. Plenty of poems don't rhyme at all.

Appearance Isn't Everything

Poetry often looks different from prose. Poems generally leave more white space on the page than prose. Also, poetry isn't always in sentences like you would read in a novel. Poems don't have to follow the established conventions of grammar, spelling, and punctuation. And lines are arranged according to the preference of the poet instead of being placed in orderly paragraphs.

Poetry That Looks Like Prose. But you can't always recognize a poem just by looking at it. Some poems are written in sentences. Charles Baudelaire, an important French poet, developed a type of literature called *prose poems* in the 19th century. His poems look like prose, but they contain characteristics of poetry, such as allegorical features, rhythm, and imagery.

Prose That Looks Like Poetry. On the other hand, a poem is more than just the way the words are arranged on the page.

> **Ask yourself what happens if a piece**
> **Of Prose**
> **Is arranged like**
> **A Poem.**
> **Does it become poetry?**

The Best Definition

Poetry may be difficult to define, but we can say that it is a special reading experience in which the style of expression is as important as the content of the words. An important part of the experience of reading a poem is comparing its style with its subject.

Common Poetic Devices

Poetry has a reputation for being hard to understand. That's because the purpose of poetry is to present a thought that can never be paraphrased fully in prose. Its language is often compressed and "difficult," requiring close reading.

Figurative language, imagery, and ambiguity are three important characteristics of poetry.

Figurative Language. Poems frequently contain figurative language—comparisons or other words and phrases that shouldn't be read literally. (See pages 840–841.) Figurative language helps poets express complex thoughts in an economical way. One example would be this well-known William Wordsworth simile, a comparison which uses "like" or "as."

I wandered lonely *as* a cloud

Literally, those words don't make much sense; a cloud can't be lonely. But figuratively, the poet's comparison suggests a web of associations, including detachment, thoughtfulness, and creativity.

Figurative language, of course, varies from poem to poem. Other common types of figurative language include metaphors, comparisons without *like* or *as*, and personification, giving human attributes to inanimate objects.

Imagery. Poetic language often includes imagery. Imagery is a type of description that forms strong pictures in the reader's imagination. It can help poets express their thoughts and feelings indirectly. A simple example is Robert Burns's famous simile

My love is *like* a red red rose.

As you read a poem, try to "see" its images in your mind's eye.

Ambiguity. Whenever a text has the possibility of two or more meanings, it is considered ambiguous. One example would be a symbol, such as the bird in Edgar Allan Poe's poem "The Raven," which represents a variety of associations rather than a single, static meaning.

Poetry is more open-ended than prose, which means that different people can interpret the same poem in different ways. Often, the purpose of prose is to inform, which means that the author wants readers to interpret the text in a certain "correct" way. Poets, on the other hand, often want their words to carry many layers of meaning.

In his poem "Richard Cory," Edwin Arlington Robinson contrasts the style of the poem—which has a formal, singsong quality—with its subject. The tension between style and content is what makes the dark turn in the final line so surprising.

Whenever Richard Cory went down town,
We people on the pavement looked at him:
He was a gentleman from sole to crown,
Clean favored, and imperially slim.

And he was always quietly arrayed,
And he was always human when he talked;
But still he fluttered pulses when he said,
"Good-morning," and he glittered when he walked.

And he was rich—yes, richer than a king—
And admirably schooled in every grace:
In fine, we thought that he was everything
To make us wish that we were in his place.

So on we worked, and waited for the light,
And went without the meat, and cursed the bread;
And Richard Cory, one calm summer night,
Went home and put a bullet through his head.

Types of Poetry

There are many kinds of poetry, but they can be reduced to three principal categories.

- Lyric
- Narrative
- Dramatic

Type	Characteristics	Some Forms
Lyric	personal intimate emotional short	odes sonnets hymns elegies haiku
Narrative	plot-driven long	epics ballads
Dramatic	theatrical; identifiable speaker tells (or acts out) the story	dramatic monologues plays

Lyric Poetry

Lyric poetry is the most emotional and musical of the three types. It expresses personal feelings, such as the hopes, joys, sorrows, and wishes of the speaker. The speaker might also share reactions to the things he or she sees, hears, thinks, and feels.

Lyric poetry is named for the Greek lyre, a stringed musical instrument. Like a song, lyric poems are often short and musical.

The focus of lyric poetry is emotion. Some poets express emotion more directly than others. This is one of the reasons that so many people find poetry confusing or mysterious: when they read a poem, they expect it to contain a story with a beginning, middle, and end. Lyric poets often ask readers to imagine the world of the poem instead.

Keep in mind that these three categories are fluid. Some poems might readily fit into more than one type. A dramatic poem, for instance, often has lyric elements. Still, understanding how the three categories break down will help you better understand poetry. When you have a good idea of what a poem is trying to do, you will be better equipped to respond to it thoughtfully.

As poets experiment with language, more and more poems fall outside of the lyric, narrative, and dramatic categories. Throughout the 20th century, a growing number of poets became interested in working outside the boundaries of traditional forms. For example, the Language poets in the U.S. crafted strange-looking poems to draw readers' attention to the ways that people create meaning as they read.

LYRIC POETRY

This excerpt from "The Skunk Hour," by Robert Lowell, is an important work from the Confessional poetry movement of the 1950s and '60s. The Confessional poets were known for their personal approach to the lyric tradition.

nobody's here—

only skunks, that search
in the moonlight for a bite to eat.
They march on their soles up Main Street:
white stripes, moonstruck eyes' red fire
under the chalk-dry and spar spire
of the Trinitarian Church.

I stand on top
of our back steps and breathe the rich air—
a mother skunk with her column of kittens swills the garbage pail.
She jabs her wedge-head in a cup
of sour cream, drops her ostrich tail,
and will not scare.

Narrative Poetry

The second category is narrative poetry, which tells a story. Like a novel or a film, narrative poems have a plot. Often, they consist of

- exciting adventures.
- strange events.
- historical happenings.

There are many types of narrative poems, ranging from ancient Greek epics to modern songs by Bob Dylan and Johnny Cash. The roots of narrative poetry are in ancient traditions. One narrative form, epics, dates back to prehistoric times, when poets accompanied themselves on stringed instruments. Epics had no established text; the singers composed each line as they sang it, following the outline of a traditional tale. Similarly, ballads, another form of narrative poetry, were sung before people could read or write. Rhyme and other poetic devices probably helped the singers remember the stories.

NARRATIVE POETRY

This excerpt from Edmund Spenser's epic poem, *The Faerie Queen,* is about adventures in a mythical world. While the spelling may look unfamiliar, the words are easy to sound out.

Upon a great adventure he was bond,
That greatest Gloriana to him gave,
That greatest Glorious Queene of Faerie lond,
To winne him worship, and her grace to have,
Which of all earthly things he most did crave;
And ever as he rode, his hart did earne
To prove his puissance in battell brave
Upon his foe, and his new force to learne;
Upon his foe, a Dragon horrible and stearne.

Dramatic Poetry

Like narrative poetry, dramatic poetry tells a story. The difference is that in dramatic poetry, a speaker tells the story or acts it out.

Dramatic poetry is distinct for being able to present more than one speaker. Most dramatic poems, however, are monologues, which means they are spoken by just one person.

The difference between drama and dramatic poetry is a matter of degrees. A play is considered dramatic poetry if the dialogue features rhymes, repeating rhythms, or other distinct poetic elements. William Shakespeare is the most famous dramatic poet. (See pages 960–983.)

DRAMATIC POETRY

This excerpt from Robert Browning's poem "My Last Duchess" is an example of dramatic poetry because the speaker delivers it as a monologue.

That's my last Duchess painted on the wall,
Looking as if she were alive. I call
That piece a wonder, now; Fra Pandolf's hands
Worked busily a day, and there she stands.
Will't please you sit and look at her? I said
"Fra Pandolf" by design, for never read
Strangers like you that pictured countenance,
The depth and passion of its earnest glance,
But to myself they turned (since none puts by
The curtain I have drawn for you, but I)
And seemed as they would ask me, if they durst,
How such a glance came there; so, not the first
Are you to turn and ask thus.

Fixed Forms and Genres

Poets give form to their verse in various ways. The most common means of creating poetic form is rhyme. Some rhyme schemes have been used so often that they have become standard verse forms.

A poem's meter, its line arrangement, and its number of stanzas also may determine its form.

Some forms are more fixed than others. The haiku form, for instance, has very formal requirements, while the romance genre is more of an approach or a sensibility than a set of strict guidelines.

Sonnets

Type: Lyric

Subtypes/Forms:

- Petrarchan / 2 quatrains plus 1 sestet
- Shakespearean / 3 quatrains plus couplet rhyming abab; cdcd; efef; gg
- Spenserian / Shakespearean, but rhyming abab; bcbc; cdcd; ee

Length: 14 lines

Characteristics: Focus on a single thought or feeling with a turn of thought in the final two lines

Odes

Type: Lyric

Subtypes: Pindaric odes, Horatian odes, Sapphic odes, stanzaic odes, irregular odes

Form: Varies by subtype

Length: Moderate

Characteristics: Formal, celebratory, complimentary, ceremonious

Example: "Ode on a Grecian Urn" by John Keats

Haiku

Form: 17 syllables in 3 lines; 5 syllables in the first line, 7 syllables each in the second and third lines

Length: Very short

Characteristics: Moody; impressionistic; indirect; simple; traditionally relates to one of the four seasons

SONNETS

Wilfred Owen's "Anthem for Doomed Youth" is a Petrarchan sonnet.

What passing-bells for these who die as cattle?
 Only the monstrous anger of the guns.
 Only the stuttering rifles' rapid rattle
Can patter out their hasty orisons.
No mockeries now for them; no prayers nor bells,
 Nor any voice of mourning save the choirs,—
The shrill, demented choirs of wailing shells;
 And bugles calling for them from sad shires.

What candles may be held to speed them all?
 Not in the hands of boys, but in their eyes
Shall shine the holy glimmers of good-byes.
 The pallor of girls' brows shall be their pall;
Their flowers the tenderness of patient minds,
And each slow dusk a drawing-down of blinds.

Romance

Type: Narrative

Length: Long

Characteristics: Based on legend

Example: *Sir Gawain and the Green Knight* (See page 925.)

HAIKU

Below is a haiku by Kobayashi Issa.

Even with insects—
some can sing,
 some can't.

Villanelle

Form: Two rhyming lines are frequently repeated in an intricate pattern

Length: 19 lines (five 3-line stanzas and a final quatrain)

Characteristics: Elaborate

Limerick

Type: Lyric

Form: 5 lines; first, second, and fifth lines rhyme; third and fourth lines rhyme

Length: Short

Characteristics: Humorous

RONDEL

"The Roundel" by Charles Swinburne is a rondel.

A roundel is wrought as a ring or a starbright sphere,
    With craft of delight and with cunning of sound unsought,
That the heart of the hearer may smile if to pleasure his ear
    A roundel is wrought.
Its jewel of music is carven of all or of aught—
    Love, laughter, or mourning—remembrance of rapture or fear—
That fancy may fashion to hang in the ear of thought.
As a bird's quick song runs round, and the hearts in us hear
    Pause answer to pause, and again the same strain caught,
So moves the device whence, round as a pearl or tear,
    A roundel is wrought.

VILLANELLE

Dylan Thomas's "Do Not Go Gentle into That Good Night" is a villanelle.

Do not go gentle into that good night,
Old age should burn and rave at close of day;
Rage, rage against the dying of the light.

Though wise men at their end know dark is right,
Because their words had forked no lightning they
Do not go gentle into that good night.

Good men, the last wave by, crying how bright
Their frail deeds might have danced in a green bay,
Rage, rage against the dying of the light.

Wild men who caught and sang the sun in flight,
And learn, too late, they grieved it on its way,
Do not go gentle into that good night.

Grave men, near death, who see with blinding sight
Blind eyes could blaze like meteors and be gay,
Rage, rage against the dying of the light.

And you, my father, there on the sad height,
Curse, bless, me now with your fierce tears, I pray,
Do not go gentle into that good night.
Rage, rage against the dying of the light.

Rondel

Type: Lyric

Form: Initial couplet repeated in the middle and at the end; two rhymes

Length: Short (often 14 lines)

Characteristics: Focuses on a single thought or feeling with a turn of thought in the final two lines

Sestina

Form: Six 6-line stanzas and one concluding triplet; last words of the first stanza are repeated in the other five stanzas in different order and in the concluding triplet

Length: 36 lines

Characteristics: Complex, clever

Unfixed Forms

There are two types of unfixed forms in poetry: blank verse and free verse.

Blank Verse

Blank verse is poetry written in unrhymed lines of iambic pentameter. It is not written in stanza form. Instead, the poem is developed in verse paragraphs that vary in length. Because of its flexibility, blank verse is especially appropriate for narrative and dramatic poetry.

Iambic Pentameter. Unrhymed iambic pentameter is the most common metrical form in English dramatic and epic poetry. Shakespeare's plays, for example, are written in blank verse. It was first used by Henry Howard, Earl of Surrey, in his translations of the *Aeneid* in the 16th century. The first English drama written in blank verse was Sackville and Norton's tragedy *Gorboduc* in 1562. Christopher Marlowe made masterly use of it in his tragedy *Tamburlaine*, written in 1587. Shakespeare adopted and perfected it.

	Blank Verse	Free Verse
rhyme scheme	none	none
meter	iambic pentameter	none
stanzas	paragraphs	irregular

WATCH OUT!

Blank verse is often confused with free verse. The two forms are similar insofar as neither requires a regular rhyme scheme. You can usually tell the difference by counting the beats in each line of the poem. Blank verse uses 10 syllables (or 5 beats) per line.

BLANK VERSE

"The Second Coming"
by William Butler Yeats

Turning and turning in the widening gyre
The falcon cannot hear the falconer;
Things fall apart; the centre cannot hold;
Mere anarchy is loosed upon the world,
The blood-dimmed tide is loosed, and everywhere
The ceremony of innocence is drowned;
The best lack all conviction, while the worst
Are full of passionate intensity.

Surely some revelation is at hand;
Surely the Second Coming is at hand.
The Second Coming! Hardly are those words out
When a vast image out of Spiritus Mundi
Troubles my sight: somewhere in sands of the desert
A shape with lion body and the head of a man,
A gaze blank and pitiless as the sun,
Is moving its slow thighs, while all about it
Reel shadows of the indignant desert birds.
The darkness drops again; but now I know
That twenty centuries of stony sleep
Were vexed to nightmare by a rocking cradle,
And what rough beast, its hour come round at last,
Slouches towards Bethlehem to be born?

Free Verse

Free verse is a style of poetry that doesn't follow the traditional rules of composition. In writing free verse, poets avoid common elements like regular meter and rhyme. Instead, they vary the lengths of lines, use irregular numbers of syllables in lines, and employ odd breaks at the end of each line. They also use irregular accents and rhythms and uneven rhyme schemes.

Still, free verse is not free from all form. It does use basic techniques such as alliteration and repetition.

Free verse first flourished during the 1800s when the romantic poets adapted the style. The American poet Walt Whitman is often considered the father of free verse. By the mid 1900s, free verse had become the standard verse form in poetry, especially in the works of American poets such as Robert Lowell, Theodore Roethke, and William Carlos Williams.

 *Free verse is not exactly new. The King James Bible is an early and influential example of free verse in English.*

FREE VERSE

from "Song of Myself"
by Walt Whitman

I celebrate myself, and sing myself,
And what I assume you shall assume,
For every atom belonging to me as good belongs to you.

I loafe and invite my soul,
I lean and loafe at my ease observing a spear of summer grass.

My tongue, every atom of my blood, form'd from this soil, this air,
Born here of parents born here from parents the same, and their parents the same,
I, now thirty-seven years old in perfect health begin,
Hoping to cease not till death.

Creeds and schools in abeyance,
Retiring back a while sufficed at what they are, but never forgotten,
I harbor for good or bad, I permit to speak at every hazard,
Nature without check with original energy.

Rhythm

Poetry is musical language. When you read a poem, you have to think about how the poet meant for it to sound.

Each poem has its own rhythm. For some poems, it is a fairly regular beat such as de-*dumm* de-*dumm* de-*dumm* de-*dumm* de-*dumm* de-*dumm*. For others, there is no regular pattern.

Rhythm in poetry means the flow of sound produced by language. The word rhythm *comes from the Greek word* rhein, *which means "to flow." Rhythm fills the world with repetition and flow, from the beat of our hearts to the rise and fall of ocean tides.*

Rhythm and Meaning

There are many tools that poets can use to control the rhythm of a poem. Certain techniques can

- encourage the reader to speed up or slow down.
- emphasize important words or phrases.
- guide the reader's expectations.
- go against the reader's expectations.
- sound soothing (like a lullaby).
- signal a change or shift.
- create meaning.

Poets can control the rhythmic patterns in poetry by using

- stressed syllables (feet).
- meter.
- enjambment.
- stanzas.
- caesura.

The poet Langston Hughes experimented with meter by using the rhythm of jazz and blues music in his verses. (See page 948.)

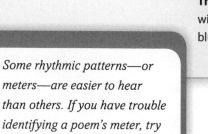
Some rhythmic patterns—or meters—are easier to hear than others. If you have trouble identifying a poem's meter, try reading the poem aloud slowly.

Feet

Units of a line of poetry are syllabic groups called **feet.** A foot is the basic unit of meter.

People tend to hear the syllables of a line of poetry in groups of twos and threes. A foot usually consists of two or three consecutive syllables put together. At least one syllable in a foot must be accented.

Stress. The placement of a stressed syllable in a foot determines its rhythm and gives the foot its name. Words in poetry generally carry the same syllabic stress that they have in speech.

Scansion is the analysis of metrical patterns of a poem by organizing its stressed and unstressed syllables into feet and showing the major pauses, if there are any. Scansion also involves the classification of a poem's stanza, structure, and rhyme scheme.

Foot	Formula	Examples
iambic	1 unaccented syllable + 1 accented syllable	agree above
anapestic	2 unaccented syllables + 1 accented syllable	insincere
trochaic	1 accented syllable + 1 unaccented syllable	daily humor
dactylic	1 accented syllable + 2 unaccented syllables	desperate murmuring
spondee	2 accented syllables	this team thirteen
pyrrhic	2 unstressed syllables	in the

COMMON MEASURE

Common measure is a folk meter that alternates four-beat and three-beat lines. It is used in ballads, hymns, lyric poems, and nursery rhymes. This poem by Emily Dickinson is in common measure:

"I heard / a Fly buzz /—when / I died—
The Stillness / in the / Room
Was like / the Stillness / in the / Air—
Between / the Heaves / of Storm—
The Eyes / around /—had wrung / them dry—
And Breaths / were gath / ering firm/
For that / last Onset /—when / the King
Be witnessed /—in the / Room—
I willed / my Keepsakes /—Signed away/
What / portion / of me / be
Assign / able /—and then / it was
There / interposed / a Fly—
With Blue /—uncertain / stumbling / Buzz—
Between / the light /—and me—/
And then / the Windows / failed /—and then
I could / not see / to see—

SCANSION MARKS

These are the marks that readers use to scan poetry.

´ = stressed syllable   ^ = pause
˘ = short syllable   / = foot division

When we read this poem, we pause at the end of each three-beat line. We pause because we tend to hear beats in pairs. The first line of the poem has two pairs of beats, so we expect the following lines to repeat this pattern. Such pauses are called musical pauses because they are created by the meter of the poem. This poem has many kinds of pauses. Each pause adds to the poem's effect.

Rhythm

Meter

In many poems, we can sense something repeating in the rhythm. *Meter* refers to the pattern of rhythm in a poem.

Meter gives form to what we hear in a poem by telling us what to expect the flow of language to do from line to line. A sudden change in rhythm can be jarring because it goes against readers' expectations. Poets can change the rhythm in a poem to emphasize something important or to signal a turn of thought.

Meter varies according to the sounds of the language in which a poem is written. The ancient Greeks based their meter on the long and short vowels in their words. Cheyenne, an American Indian language, has whispered syllables as well as spoken ones, which the meter of the language's poetry reflects.

The musical qualities of poetry in English are created by the length of a single line and the arrangement of stressed syllables within it.

METER TERMS

Falling meter: a rhythm that uses trochees or dactyls (stressed to unstressed)

Foot meter: a rhythm determined by the number of feet a line contains

Rising meter: a rhythm that uses iambs or anapests (unstressed to stressed)

Stress meter: a rhythm based on the number of stressed syllables in a line

Syllabic meter: a rhythm based on the number of syllables in a line

READING FOR METER

Follow these steps to determine a poem's meter.

- Mark the accented and unaccented syllables in several lines.
- Count the syllables.
- If the number is divisible by two, it is either iambic or trochaic.
- If the number is divisible by three, the foot is anapestic or dactylic.
- If the first syllable of each line is unaccented and the last is accented, it is iambic or anapestic.
- If the line is stressed at first and unstressed at the end, it is trochaic or dactylic.
- Put a slash between every foot.
- Count the number of feet. The type of foot plus the total number of feet per line equals meter.

Meter	Formula	Example
monometer	one foot	Thus I
tetrameter	four feet	The stag / at eve / had drunk / its fill
pentameter	five feet	That time / of year / thou mayest / in me / behold
hexameter	six feet	Fierce warres / and faith/full loves / shall mora/lize my song

WATCH OUT!

Poets may not follow a chosen meter exactly. The poet's decision to follow the meter closely or to vary from it greatly depends on the particular effects the poet wants to create.

Stanzas

Stanzas are groups of lines in poetry similar to the concept of paragraphs in prose. Stanzas are another tool that poets can use to control the rhythm of their words since readers tend to pause and reflect between groupings.

Note the characteristics of a poem's stanzas as you read, including:

- number of stanzas.
- shifts in topic, speaker, or mood.
- similarities or differences in length, meter, or rhyme scheme.

Wallace Stevens crafts meaning by manipulating stanzas. What significance might the number 3 have in this poem about blackbirds?

Caesura

Caesura is a pause created by commas, periods, and other punctuation marks. In English verse, both old and modern, the caesura often comes around the middle of a line.

Gwendolyn Brooks creates pauses using periods. Why do you think she arranged the poem this way instead of putting a full sentence on each line?

Enjambment

Enjambment is the continuation of a sentence from one line to the next. This device allows Brooks to start her sentences with "We" on one line and continue the thought on the next line.

Sound and Sight

In addition to rhyme, poets use other sound effects to help structure poems and create meaning.

Onomatopoeia

Onomatopoeia is the use of words to both imitate and refer to natural sounds. The simplest examples are the sounds that animals make. The word *hoot* both suggests and refers to the sound made by owls. Other examples are *mooing* cows or *quacking* ducks.

People make onomatopoeic sounds, too, such as *achoo* for sneeze and *haha* for laugh.

In poetry, letters and syllables can be used to imitate the sound of something the poem describes. (This technique also applies to rhythm. For instance, the beat of a series of dactyl feet recalls a horse's gallop.) The use of z-sounds, for example, creates a buzzing quality.

Alliteration

Alliteration is the repetition of consonant sounds that start words. For example, in "Peter Piper picked a peck of pickled peppers," alliteration is created by the occurrence of a *p* sound at the beginning of every accented syllable. "Now or never" and "time and tide" are examples of alliteration in everyday phrases.

In Old English verse, alliteration was used to form the poem's backbone. (Old English poetry didn't use rhyme.) Each line broke into two halves, with most of the accented syllables beginning with the same sound. While it's no longer used as a structural base, alliteration remains a common and effective device in poetry.

Onomatopoeic words for animal sounds vary widely from culture to culture. For instance, English speakers use "bark" or "ruff ruff" for the sound a dog makes. Spanish speakers, on the other hand, use "guau guau." English roosters say "cockadoodledoo," while their Spanish counterparts say "kikiriki."

ONOMATOPOEIA

"Cynthia in the Snow," a poem by Gwendolyn Brooks, uses onomatopoeia to describe snow. Read it out loud. Which words remind you of snow?

It SHUSHES.
It hushes
The loudness in the road.
It flitter-twitters,
And laughs away from me.
It laughs a lovely whiteness
And whitely whirs away,
To be
Some otherwhere,
Still white as milk or shirts.
So beautiful it hurts.

ALLITERATION

"Pied Beauty," a poem by Gerard Manley Hopkins, uses alliteration to give his words a sing-song quality.

Glory be to God for dappled things—
  For skies of couple-colour as a brinded cow;
    For rose-moles all in stipple upon trout that swim;
Fresh-firecoal chestnut-falls; finches' wings;
  Landscape plotted and pieced—fold, fallow, and plough;
    And all trades, their gear and tackle and trim.

All things counter, original, spare, strange;
  Whatever is fickle, freckled (who knows how?)
    With swift, slow; sweet, sour; adazzle, dim;
He fathers-forth whose beauty is past change:
      Praise him.

Assonance and Consonance

Assonance is the repetition of vowel sounds. Assonance can be used as an alternative to rhyme. Examples of assonance include the long *a* sound in brave/vain, the long *o* in lone/show, and the short *a* in man/hat.

Consonance is the repetition of consonant sounds. It can also be used as an alternative to rhyme. Examples include bake/strike and mad/bud.

Sight

Poets use visual effects to build layers of meaning and to draw readers into the world of the poem. These effects can range from the way the words and lines are arranged on the page to the language within the poem.

The way a poem looks can provide important clues to its meaning. The number of lines, or the way those lines are arranged, can help you decode a poem's meaning.

When you read a poem for the first time, pay attention to what you see. Take note of any unusual formatting or line breaks and ask yourself what they might signal in terms of meaning. Also note the images that you "see" in your mind as you read.

In his poem "Easter Wings," George Herbert creates meaning using both content and form. What do you see when you look at the poem?

Lord, who createdst man in wealth and store,
Though foolishly he lost the same,
Decaying more and more,
Till he became
Most poore:
With thee
O let me rise
As larks, harmoniously,
And sing this day thy victories:
Then shall the fall further the flight in me.

My tender age in sorrow did beginne
And still with sicknesses and shame.
Thou didst so punish sinne,
That I became
Most thinne.
With thee
Let me combine,
And feel thy victorie:
For, if I imp my wing on thine,
Affliction shall advance the flight in me.

"**Constantly Risking Absurdity**," a poem by Lawrence Ferlinghetti, uses form to reflect the action of the poet and the tightrope walker in the poem.

Constantly risking absurdity
                         and death
        whenever he performs
                  above the heads
                           of his audience
    the poet like an acrobat
              climbs on rime
                  to a high wire of his own making
and balancing on eyebeams
                  above a sea of faces
          paces his way
              to the other side of day
    performing entrechats
                  and sleight-of-foot tricks
and other high theatrics
                  and all without mistaking
          any thing
              for what it may not be

    For he's the super realist
                  who must perforce perceive
        taut truth
              before the taking of each stance or step
in his supposed advance
                  toward that still higher perch
where Beauty stands and waits
              with gravity
                  to start her death-defying leap

    And he
        a little charleychaplin man
                      who may or may not catch
              her fair eternal form
                  spreadeagled in the empty air
        of existence

Rhyme

Rhyme is a sound effect that occurs when two or more words sound alike. Poets often use a rhyme pattern to create an overall form for a poem. They may also use individual rhymes that aren't carried through the poem in a systematic way.

Poets can use rhyme to

- unify a poem
- emphasize a word or idea
- force associations

Types of Rhyme

In poetry, rhyme usually occurs at the end of lines, as in this couplet by William Butler Yeats:

**O body swayed to music, O brightening glance,
How can we know the dancer from the dance?**

Glance and *dance* form an end rhyme, which is when like-sounding words close out two lines. But there are many other types of rhymes.

Rhymes are typed according to how similar the words are and where exactly the rhyming words appear in the poem.

Rhyme Schemes

The rhyme scheme is the arrangement of rhymed lines in a poem. Some poems, like sonnets and villanelles, have a fixed rhyme scheme.

While many people think of rhyme as an essential ingredient of poetry, rhyme is not necessary in poetry. Many poems don't use rhyme at all, including blank verse and much free verse.

1. RHYME	2. ASSONANCE	3. CONSONANCE

Michael Palmer uses rhyme and other sound effects in his poem "Song of the Round Man."

The round and sad-eyed man puffed cigars as if
he were alive. Gillyflowers
to the left of the apple, purple bells to the right

and a grass-covered hill behind.
I am sad today said the sad-eyed man
for I have locked my head in a Japanese box

1
and lost the key.
I am sad today he told me
for there are gillyflowers by the apple

and purple bells I cannot see
Will you look at them for me
he asked, and tell me what you find?

2
I cannot I replied
for my eyes have grown sugary and dim
from reading too long by candlelight.

Tell me what you've read then
said the round and sad-eyed man.
I cannot I replied

for my memory has grown tired and dim
from looking at things that can't be seen
by any kind of light

and I've locked my head in a Japanese box
and thrown away the key.
Then I am you and you are me

said the sad-eyed man as if alive.
3
I'll write you in where I should be
between the gillyflowers and the purple bells

and the apple and the hill
and we'll puff cigars from noon till night
as if we were alive.

Common Types of Rhymes

Type	Definition	Examples
eye rhyme (also sight rhyme)	the rhyme of words of similar spelling but different pronunciation	near/bear
end rhyme	rhymes occuring at the ends of lines (note: end rhymes can be masculine or feminine)	motion/notion nail/pail
feminine rhyme	a rhyme of unstressed syllables	motion/notion happily/snappily
identical rhyme	the rhyme of two words that are exactly the same (in sound, spelling, and sense)	buzzard/buzzard
imperfect rhyme (also slant rhyme or near rhyme)	words that almost rhyme	have/grave wake/late
internal rhyme	the rhyme of a word within a line of verse with a word at the end of the line	Once upon a midnight dreary, while I pondered weak and weary
masculine rhyme	the rhyme of one-syllable words or of stressed final syllables	compare/despair nail/pail
perfect rhyme	rhyme between two words having the same pronunciation but different meanings	bear/bare

READING FOR RHYME

You can use one letter (A, for instance) for the first rhyme, another letter (B) for the second sound, and so forth. For example, the rhyme of the following Shakespearean sonnet can be summarized as ABAB; CDCD; EFEF; GG.

Sonnet 116

Let me not to the marriage of true minds	(A)
Admit impediments. Love is not love	(B)
Which alters when it alteration finds,	(A)
Or bends with the remover to remove.	(B)
Oh no! It is an ever-fixed mark	(C)
That looks on tempests and is never shaken	(D)
It is the star to every wandering bark,	(C)
Whose worth's unknown, although his height be taken.	(D)
Love's not Time's fool, though rosy lips and cheeks	(E)
Within his bending sickle's compass come.	(F)
Love alters not with his brief hours and weeks,	(E)
But bears it out even to the edge of doom.	(F)
If this be error and upon me proved,	(G)
I never writ, nor no man ever loved.	(G)

Meaning

How to Read a Poem

One of the joys and frustrations of reading poetry is that a poem does not necessarily reveal its meaning to you on the first read. If you don't understand a poem the first time you read it, relax; it doesn't mean you're doing something wrong.

Often, you'll need to read a poem at least four or five times—maybe more—to understand it well. Take your time.

First Read. Read the poem through once at a normal rate. Pay attention to your first impressions. What makes sense? What seems confusing? You will want to target the confusing bits in the next rounds of reading.

Second Read. Read the poem again more carefully. Watch for words or allusions you don't understand. Look up unfamiliar words and write down their meanings. Check allusions by looking them up in an encyclopedia or using some other resource (like your teacher, librarian, friends, or parents).

Third Read. Read the poem again. This time, try to translate it into your own words. Write the meaning of each line. Recognize that your paraphrase cannot mean the same thing as the poem itself—just as reading a description of a hamburger does not have the same taste as eating the hamburger.

Fourth Read. Read the poem again. Assume there is something wrong with your translation. Try to explain on paper what that problem might be. How is your paraphrase different? What are the problems with the poem that the paraphrase does not solve? This strategy may help you see the poem in a different way.

Fifth Read. Finally, read the poem again. This time, relax and enjoy the experience of moving through it. Write out (or underline) any words or phrases you find particularly effective or important. Now you're ready to analyze the poem.

Maya Angelou, a celebrated American poet, reads her piece "On the Pulse of Morning" at President Clinton's inauguration, in 1993.

How to Analyze a Poem, Step by Step

Here are some guidelines you can use to get to know a poem better. If you can't answer a question, move on to the next step. You can always ask for help later.

See the Obvious

1. Look at the title. What does it tell you about the poem?

2. Find out a little about the poet, such as when and where he or she lived.

3. Count the number of lines in each verse. This will help you determine what kind of poem it is.

4. Read the poem.

5. Look up words you don't know in the dictionary.

6. Write a one-sentence summary of what the poem is about.

Now you should know the subject, the historical context, the form, the words, and the theme of the poem.

Listen Carefully

7. Read the poem out loud. Listen for sound effects.

8. Assign letters to each end rhyme. Each word that rhymes gets the same letter. Each new sound gets a new letter.

9. What form does the rhyme scheme support?

10. Circle any example of alliteration.

11. Underline examples of consonance.

12. Note internal rhymes.

13. Find any instances of onomatopoeia.

14. Think about how these sounds support the poem's meaning.

Feel the Rhythm

15. Count the number of syllables in each line.

16. Mark stressed and unstressed syllables.

17. Draw a slash between feet.

18. Note any additional feet, such as a double stress or single syllable.

19. Name the feet and meter.

Dig for Meaning

20. Reread the poem.

21. Identify images and figures of speech in each verse.

22. Explain how those images and figures of speech support the meaning of the poem.

23. Paraphrase each verse or section of the poem in your own words.

The key to analyzing a poem is to take your time.

FOUR SCORE AN
GO OUR FATHERS
N THIS CONTINE
ONCEIVED IN LIF
ED TO THE PRO
MEN ARE CREA
NOW WE ARE
CIVIL WAR TES
NATION OR A
CEIVED AND S
ENDURE

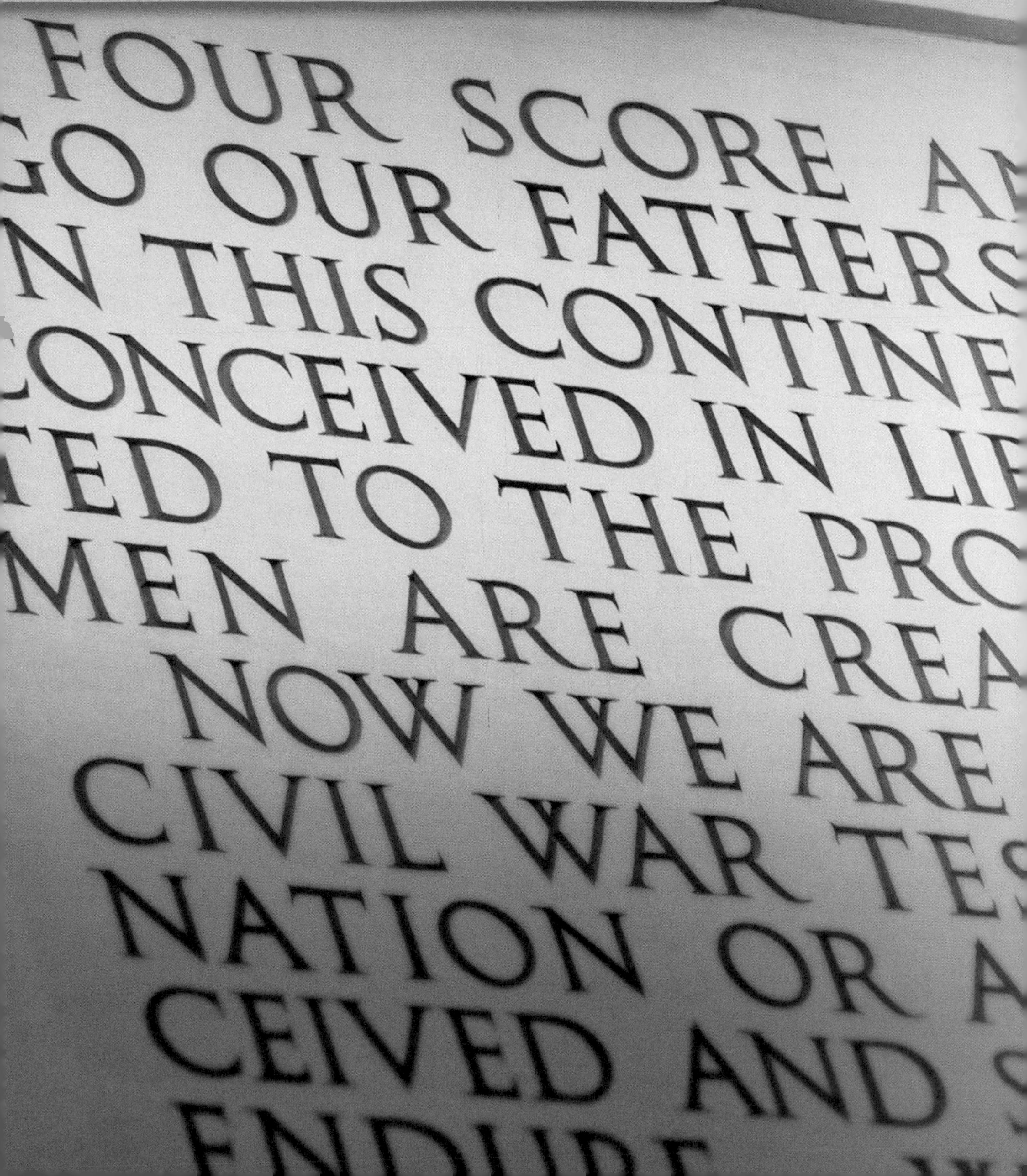

SPEAKING well is a great asset, whether you are in class, talking on the phone, or speaking before a group. It is also a vital component of most careers. Whether you're interviewing for a job, giving a formal speech, or making a call, being an effective speaker will help you accomplish your purpose.

Speaker's Tool Box

Speakers use many tools—those of the body and those of the intellect. You can sharpen these tools to improve your conversation skills as well as your public speaking ability.

Body Language

Much of the success of a good speaker has nothing to do with his or her words. Listeners are alert not only for what is said but for the way the speaker stands and how the words are delivered. Whether addressing a friend in conversation or an audience during a formal presentation, make sure your body language indicates that you are engaged, alert, and confident.

Your body contributes to effective speaking in a number of important ways. Your eyes, facial expression, posture, movements, gestures, and general appearance all help convey your message.

For example, many students are nervous about oral presentations, and they let the audience know this before they speak a word. They may slouch, sway back and forth, crack their knuckles, or keep their eyes down on their notes to avoid looking at anyone. This kind of behavior detracts from a speech. It says to an audience, "I don't really care that you're here, and I don't have anything I want to tell you." If you are in the audience when someone does this, you probably had a similarly negative reaction.

Facial Expressions. Your facial expressions should be appropriate to the topic and the occasion. In general, you want to appear pleasant and look pleased to be speaking to your audience.

Keep your facial muscles relaxed. This will keep your expression natural and make it easier for your vocal cords to do their best work. Allow your expressions to vary with what you are saying, just as you would in conversation.

Eye Contact. Look at individual members of the audience as you speak. Establish eye contact with as many people and as many parts of the audience as you can. Eye contact shows the people in the audience that you are interested in communicating with each one of them.

Good eye contact also helps you get feedback from the audience. You can see their reactions and, if necessary, make changes in your speech according to the reactions you're getting.

Posture. Your posture should show that you are alert, confident, and energetic. Stand up straight, but stay relaxed. Many speakers find that standing with feet slightly apart and one foot a little ahead of the other is most comfortable.

If you're stiff, your audience might think you're nervous. If you're so relaxed that you slouch or slump, they might think that you're bored.

Gestures. Gestures are another important tool. For a class report, throwing your arms around and jumping up and down may not be appropriate, but if there is something visual in your report that you want to explain—a spiral staircase, the size of the fish you caught—use your hands to help.

Gestures can be made with your hands, your arms, or your head. You can emphasize important points or show transitions through proper gestures.

- Try to make your gestures as natural as possible. Though dramatic gestures can be effective, fist waving or podium pounding can be seen as overly dramatic.

- Let your arms rest naturally at your sides unless you are gesturing to make a point. If you have a podium, you may want to rest your hands on it. Clutching the podium will cause unwanted tension in your upper body and may be seen by the audience as a sign of insecurity.

- If you're holding written notes or another speaking tool, such as a pointer, keep your grip firm but relaxed. Make only necessary movements and gestures with them. Flipping pages carelessly or tapping a pointer against your leg will distract your audience.

Other Movements

Any movements you make during a speech should be related to the speech. Moving forward or sideways a step or two could catch the audience's attention when you're making an important point or moving on to a new idea. But pacing back and forth will distract the audience from what you're saying.

Appearance

Your dress and appearance should be appropriate for the occasion, the audience, and the setting. Wear something comfortable. A belt or collar that is too tight, bracelets that jangle, or shoes that make you fidget will distract you.

Voice

The way you use your voice can add greatly to the impression you make when delivering your speech. As you speak, pay special attention to the volume, speed, and pitch of your voice.

Volume. Obviously, you will want to speak loudly enough so that the audience can easily hear you. You will have to consider such factors as the size of the room, whether you will be using a microphone, and whether there are outside noises you must speak over. Try to vary your volume to make your voice sound more interesting.

Speed. Do not speak so fast that you slur your words or become difficult to understand. If you have a time limit, pace yourself so that you can finish your speech without having to hurry at the end. Varying your speed from time to time can make your speech more effective. You can slow down to emphasize a point. And a dramatic pause at the end of a particularly important statement can be an effective technique.

Pitch is how high or low your voice sounds. You vary your pitch automatically during normal conversation. Your voice sounds higher when you are excited and lower when you are serious. During a speech, your voice should follow this natural pattern of pitch variation. Try to avoid speaking in a monotone.

WRITING A SPEECH

is very similar to writing an essay. There is, however, one important difference: oral language requires far more elaboration than written language. That's because people generally absorb more information through reading than through listening. In general, you'll want to include more examples in a speech than you might in an essay on the same topic. Important points should be stressed through repetition.

Preparation

There are five basic steps in the preparation of a speech.

Analyze the Audience

In deciding what to say on a given occasion, there are two things a speaker must consider: the listener and the subject of the speech. Aristotle said, "Of the three elements in speech making—speaker, subject, and person addressed—it is the last one, the hearer, that determines the speech's end and object."

Consider Your Listeners. Listeners have their own concerns and problems that color and prejudice everything they hear and see. Unless great care is taken, people will not understand everything you say because they will filter it through their own perceptions. Therefore, it is useful to know as much as possible about your audience.

Here are some things you might want to know about the members of your audience.

- size of the group
- age
- level of education
- occupation
- social background
- common interests, values, and goals
- reason the group is gathered

Make Adjustments. What you know about your listeners will help determine what kind of language you use, the mood you adopt, and the approach you take to a subject. As you gain experience as a speaker, you will make these decisions more and more deliberately.

Choose a Topic

Choose a topic that interests you and is suitable for the occasion and the audience. You'll usually choose a topic that you already know something about. If your topic requires research, be sure that the necessary sources of information are available. Make sure you choose a topic you can adequately cover in the time allowed for your speech. (See also page 706.)

Determine Your Purpose

Every speech has one of three main purposes

- to inform
- to persuade
- to entertain

Before you prepare the speech, decide what effect you want to have on your audience. Then write the specific purpose of your speech in a single sentence.

Gather Information

Begin by taking inventory of what you already know about the subject.

- Jot down whatever comes to mind. You may find that you have a sizeable list.
- Refine the list by asking yourself what your audience needs to know. Circle those items on your list.
- Look at your list again and decide if there are any large gaps in it that need to be filled with information from other sources. Make a note of anything you need to double-check.
- Do whatever research is necessary. Go to the library or talk to people who have special knowledge about your subject.

WATCH OUT!

Never read from your speech. Instead, use note cards for reference.

!

Get Organized

Any talk has three sections, which we can think of as the beginning, the middle, and the end. For a formal address, these sections are called the introduction, the body, and the conclusion. You'll want to consider these sections carefully before you start writing your speech.

Introduction. The beginning of a speech must be calculated to capture the listener's attention. If you fail to capture the listener's attention, your message will not matter.

How can you capture their attention? Try opening with a joke, a dramatic story, or a startling statistic. In any case, you want to make sure to introduce the material you will be talking about in an engaging and informative manner.

Body. The middle of a speech must explain the theme and establish it in the minds of listeners. There are a number of ways to organize the body of your speech. Such a choice is often dictated by the subject matter. For instance, if you are speaking about inflation, a logical way to organize your speech would be by its economic, social, and political consequences.

Conclusion. The end of a talk leaves the final impression. A speaker wants people to remember the speech and to leave in a certain frame of mind. If the purpose is to entertain, the audience should leave feeling happy. If the message is serious, the speaker wants listeners to feel moved. An effective conclusion will quickly review points discussed and emphasize the importance of the speech.

DELIVERING A SPEECH

After you've developed the content of your speech, you will need to rehearse it. Rehearsal is the step in which you improve and polish the speech. Allow plenty of time for this important part of preparation.

Getting Ready

Prepare Note Cards

Before you ever begin rehearsing a speech, you should develop note cards. These note cards are a form of insurance. Even if you don't plan to use them, they will be there in case you forget something or lose your train of thought.

Most people prefer placing notes on index cards. Apart from first and last sentences, you should not write in complete sentences. Instead, use keywords that will trigger your memory. You may also want to write notes to yourself in brackets, such as [Look up at audience].

There are a few things you can do to make sure that your note cards are as helpful as possible.

- Limit each card to one idea or point to make sure that they are easy to read.

- Write on only one side of the index card.

- Number the cards in case they get shuffled out of order.

WHAT TO WRITE ON NOTE CARDS

- Statistics
- Dates
- Cues
- Quotations
- Names
- First sentence
- Last sentence
- Keywords
- Bracketed notes to self

 *Look at your note cards only when you need to. Try to look at your audience about 95 percent of the time, reserving only 5 percent for consulting your notes.*

Practice

The single best way to make sure that your presentation goes smoothly is to practice it as much as possible. Extensive rehearsal will ensure that you know the material thoroughly and will help ease your fears on the day of the presentation. You may want to devote extra attention to your introduction, since this is when you are likely to be most nervous when you deliver a speech.

If possible, you should rehearse your entire speech at least three times. First, practice in front of a mirror. This will help you achieve eye contact and alert you to any distracting gestures you make. Next, deliver your speech into an audio recorder or a video camera. Play the recording for yourself and note your strengths and weaknesses. Finally, give your speech in front of a small group of friends or family members. They will probably be able to offer valuable advice, and it will accustom you to speaking in front of a group of people.

As you practice, pay attention to the way you talk. Your tone, word choice, and cadence should match your everyday speech. Enunciate clearly and speak loudly. Most importantly, keep an eye on the clock to make sure that your speech falls within the time constraints.

Visit the Setting

If you can, visit the setting where you'll give your speech. It determines the kinds of speaking tools that you can use as well as the type of presentation you should make. Do this job yourself. No one else knows the details that are important to you.

Use your visit to gather information such as

- the size of the room.
- the type of lighting in the room.
- the noise level (indoor noises like air conditioners or outdoor noises like traffic).
- where you will stand or sit.
- location of electrical outlets.
- availability of electronic equipment.

RELAXATION EXERCISES

These relaxation exercises will help you reduce tension. Do them in a quiet place that is out of sight of your audience.

1. Breathe deeply four or five times. Hold each breath for a count of 5.

2. Drop your head forward. Move it slowly in a circle—first from left to right, then right to left. Repeat 5 to 10 times.

3. Hold your arms out from your sides as far as you can. Then slowly rotate your arms in larger and larger circles. Repeat 10 times.

4. Keep your lips closed as you drop your jaw. Then open your mouth and yawn.

5. Open your mouth wide as you say the following sounds, using different rhythms and volumes.

   bah-bah-bah-bah-bah

   fah-fah-fah-fah-fah

   hah-hah-hah-hah-hah

   mah-mah-mah-mah-mah

Keep Your Cool

It is common to become nervous prior to giving a speech. It is comforting to remember two things: your audience wants you to do well, and you will always look better than you feel. Occasionally, something will go wrong. This happens to even the most experienced, well prepared speakers.

If you mess up, continue without acknowledging your mistake. Take a few deep breaths, or pause to collect your thoughts. A blunder that seems large to you is probably unnoticeable to most of the people in your audience.

Build Confidence

Confidence comes with experience. Each successive speaking situation will build your confidence as you prove to yourself that you can cope successfully. And if a particular speech doesn't go well, think of it as a chance to learn from your mistakes.

Raise your confidence by involving yourself in relatively unthreatening speaking situations at first. For instance, you can

- make a motion at a meeting.
- contribute an idea in a class discussion.
- volunteer to make telephone calls for an organization.

Make a list of the types of speaking situations in which you can gain confidence and experience. Use this list until you feel ready to give a short talk. Then use every opportunity you can get to gain experience in speaking for longer intervals.

 *When you watch others speak, pay attention to the things they do well and the things they could improve upon. You can learn from their successes and mistakes.*

Think Positively

Some people talk themselves into stage fright. They destroy their confidence by saying negative things to themselves, like, "I don't really know enough about this subject" or "no one in the audience will like what I say."

If you're in the habit of doing this, fight your negative thinking with logic. Tell yourself the facts.

- I know my subject matter.
- Many people are interested in this subject.
- I am well prepared.
- I have selected good examples to support my points.

Overcome Nervousness

Even good speakers are normally a little nervous when they stand up in front of a group. Chances are you will feel much more nervous than you look. Walk with confidence toward the front of the room, put your notes on the lectern, and look out into your audience, waiting until everyone is paying attention before beginning.

Watch Your Audience

One of your most valuable tools as a speaker is your awareness of yourself and others. Good speakers are sensitive to their listeners.

Even if you are reading from notes, look up at the audience once in a while. Your glance tells the audience that you are thinking about them. You may also notice some reaction that will tell you how you are doing. If half the room is yawning, perhaps you have gone on too long. If people look puzzled, perhaps there is some important fact you have left out or not explained clearly.

With your eyes, you can stay in contact with your listeners and can encourage them to stay in contact with you. Eyes both send and receive messages. Looking someone in the eye gives a speaker an immediate idea of the effect she is having on the listener. Is the message getting through? Is the listener bored and restless? A speaker who is looking down at the floor or up at the ceiling may not know until it is too late.

Make a Good Impression

There are many techniques you can use to ensure that you are making a positive impression on your audience.

- Stand up straight.
- Speak slowly, even if it seems forced.
- Make eye contact with people in your audience, or fake it by looking at their foreheads.
- Pause when you make an important point.
- Talk loudly and gesture to enforce key points.
- Smile as much as possible.

Be Realistic

Learn to be reasonable about what is expected from you as a speaker. What your listeners want to hear is organized remarks that will amuse them, give them helpful information, or stimulate them with new ideas. They do not expect perfection. They want you to succeed, not fail.

Remember, too, that failure to speak well in one situation, while unfortunate, is not usually going to embarrass you forever, cause you to lose friends, or ruin your career. Learn from your mistakes and resolve to do better next time.

Release Tension

Try to be physically and mentally relaxed before going into a speaking situation. Some speakers meditate before they speak. Others might drink a glass of water or listen to soothing music. Try different techniques until you find one that works well for you.

Move Naturally

If you move as you speak, you will use up some of the extra nervous energy stage fright gives you. Remember, though, that all your movements should be natural and appropriate to your speech.

Use the following movements when you practice so they'll feel natural when you give your talk.

- Step forward to stress a point if you are standing.
- If appropriate, write on an available chalkboard.
- Point to parts of a model or a chart.
- Change your position from time to time.
- Drink water if it is provided.

Concentrate

Put your mind on the message you are communicating to your listeners rather than on yourself and your nervousness. Check the faces and body language of your listeners to see if they seem to understand what you're saying.

Study your audience carefully. If they are restless, give them a break, change the pace of your speech, introduce new material or a story, use audio or visual tools, or conclude your speech.

Maintain Your Composure

If your mind suddenly goes blank, your listeners will not immediately notice that anything is wrong. They will assume you are taking a natural pause. You have time to do several things to get yourself back on track.

- Take a deep breath to reduce your tension.
- Check your notes if you are using notes. This will usually solve the problem.
- Continue your speech with confidence.

Handle Distractions

A distraction is anything that draws your audience's attention away from what you are saying. Decide on the spot whether to ignore the distraction or handle it in some way. Some distractions you may encounter include

- coughing
- talking
- sneezing
- cell phone ringing

If you are well prepared, you will be able to handle a distraction and then get right back to where you were before the interruption.

Cope with Equipment Failure

If you can think of a way to solve the problem quickly and efficiently, do it. If you know the problem will be temporary, wait until it disappears. When you cannot get equipment to function, continue without it.

Tricks and Tools

Tricks

In informal situations, people don't have to be careful about how they speak. Friends can often interpret what we say regardless of grammatical mistakes or poor pronunciation. With strangers or acquaintances, however, bad speech habits can be a serious handicap. Rooting out these habits can be very difficult, but very rewarding.

Avoid Meaningless Fillers. Many people are impatient with their speech. Instead of saying what is really on their minds, they habitually use interjections such as "you know" and "um." This is because many people distrust silence and feel obligated to fill in pauses in their speech.

Use Good Grammar. Grammar for speech need not be as strict as written grammar. Still, you should always make an effort to use good grammar whenever you speak. Grammatical mistakes may lead strangers to misjudge a speaker. Make sure you pay attention to subject-verb agreement, adjective and adverb use, and tense usage. (See pages 692–693.)

COMMON GRAMMATICAL FAULTS

Wrong	Right
hisself	himself
I ain't	I'm not
I been	I have been, I've been
I done	I did
irregardless	regardless
nowheres	nowhere
out loud	aloud
out of the door	out the door
overly	over
over with	over
supposing	suppose
theirselves	themselves
them people	those people
them things	those things
this here	this
thusly	thus
unawares	unaware

There is a wrong way (*left*) and a right way (*right*) to give an oral report. Which speaker would you rather listen to?

Tools

A speaking tool is anything other than words that a speaker uses to make the major points of a speech more clear and interesting. Speaking tools include visual aids and audiovisual tools.

Speaking tools are helpful in speeches that persuade or entertain. They are almost essential in speeches that inform. It's difficult to understand how a food processor works, how to make a quilt, or how to change an oil filter without looking at the actual objects or pictures of them.

Visual Tools. Visual props like posters or slides are an easy way to reframe information for your listeners. They make ideas more understandable and interesting, and they serve as a memory aid for you.

Visual tools you can use include

- charts or graphs
- chalkboard or dry erase board
- maps
- real objects
- models
- handouts
- projectors
- presentation software (like PowerPoint)

Keep visual aids simple. Be sure to practice with them.

Audiovisual Tools. The most important audiovisual tool is video, which includes films, TV shows, and other recordings.

The biggest advantage of video is that it shows motion. It's the next best thing to reality.

If you plan to use video in your presentation, make sure you prepare in advance.

- Preview programs before you use them in front of an audience.
- Make sure all the equipment you need is available.
- Adjust the sound level and other controls ahead of time.
- Make sure the video is set to begin in the right place.

The best time to distribute handouts is after you have finished speaking. If you distribute them beforehand, your audience will read them as you speak. If you distribute them during the session, the flow is disrupted.

GUIDELINES FOR USING SPEAKING TOOLS

- Use a speaking tool only if it will assist the purpose, message, or outcome of your speech. A tool should carry part of the message, not simply provide entertainment.
- Plan when and how you're going to use the tools. If you're speaking from notes, mark the places in the notes.
- Rehearse with the tools.
- Display or use a speaking tool only when it is needed. If people are looking at a model or chart before it's used, they are not giving you their full attention.
- Set up machinery and other equipment, such as an easel, before you begin speaking.

- Learn how to operate any special equipment before your presentation.
- Arrange things so that everyone in the audience can see what you are showing.
- Be sure images are large enough for everyone to see or read.
- Stand out of the way so your audience can see what you are talking about.
- Keep your focus on your audience. Glance at the visual you are showing only when you must.

The Gettysburg Address

A Speech to Rally the Nation

The Gettysburg Address is a short speech that President Abraham Lincoln delivered during the American Civil War at the site of the Battle of Gettysburg in Pennsylvania. (See also page 130.)

Setting. Lincoln delivered the address on November 19, 1863, at a ceremony to dedicate part of the battlefield as a cemetery for those who had lost their lives in the battle. He wrote the address to help ensure that the battle would be perceived as a great Union triumph and to define for the people of the Northern States the purpose in fighting the war.

Purpose. Lincoln's task was to prop up Northern morale through the horrible war in which many relatives in the North and South fought against one another and hundreds of thousands died. He understood that the Union's resources vastly exceeded those of the Confederacy and that the Union would eventually triumph if it remained dedicated to victory. For this reason, Lincoln used his great writing and speechmaking abilities to spur on his people.

Significance. If the Union had been destroyed, the United States could have become two, or possibly more, nations. These nations separately could not have become as prosperous and powerful as the United States is today. By preserving the Union, Lincoln influenced the course of world history. By ending slavery, he helped assure the moral strength of the United States.

Some historians think his simple and inspired words, which are among the best remembered in American history, reshaped the nation by defining it as one people dedicated to one principle—that of equality.

Lincoln spoke for only a couple of minutes at the Gettysburg battlefield dedication—Edward Everett, the main speaker, orated for 2 hours—but his words have been long remembered. ▶

Lincoln held a draft of the speech in his hand during the address, but he made several changes as he spoke. The most important change was to add the phrase "under God" after the word "nation" in the last sentence. ▼

1

Four score and seven years ago our fathers brought forth upon this continent, a new nation, conceived in liberty, and dedicated to the proposition that all men are created equal.

2

Now we are engaged in a great civil war, testing whether that nation, or any nation so conceived and so dedicated, can long endure. We are met on a great battlefield of that war. We have come to dedicate a portion of that field, as a final resting place for those who here gave their lives that this nation might live. It is altogether fitting and proper that we should do this.

3

But in a larger sense, we cannot dedicate—we cannot consecrate—we cannot hallow—this ground. The brave men, living and dead, who struggled here, have consecrated it, far above our poor power to add or detract. The world will little note, nor long remember what we say here, but it can never forget what they did here. It is for us, the living, rather to be dedicated here to the unfinished work which they who fought here have thus far so nobly advanced.

4

It is rather for us to be here dedicated to the great task remaining before us, that from these honored dead we take increased devotion to that cause for which they gave the last full measure of devotion; that we here highly resolve that these dead shall not have died in vain; that this nation, under God, shall have a new birth of freedom, and that this government of the people, by the people, and for the people shall not perish from this earth.

1. POETIC LANGUAGE

Consider the pleasing rhythm of the phrase "four score and seven years ago." How would the speech sound different if he had said "eighty-seven years ago" instead?

2. EMOTIONAL APPEAL

Lincoln's speech was made during a ceremony honoring the dead, which gave his words additional weight they might not have had in another setting.

3. ARGUMENT

Lincoln's speech had more than one purpose: he wanted to honor the dead and to rally the living behind the Union's cause. He introduces his second agenda at the end of this paragraph.

4. DURATION

Lincoln's speech is very brief. Both the simplicity of his language and the speech's short length heightened the impact of his words.

A Speech to Define a Movement

Martin Luther King, Jr., an African-American Baptist minister, was the leader of the civil rights movement in the United States during the 1950s and 1960s. He had an extraordinary speaking ability that enabled him to effectively express the demands of African Americans for social justice. King's eloquent pleas won the support of millions of people—blacks and whites—and made him internationally famous.

Setting and Purpose. King and other civil rights leaders organized a massive event in Washington, D.C., called the March on Washington. The purpose of the event was to highlight African-American unemployment and to urge Congress to pass a special bill. On August 28, 1963, over 200,000 Americans, including many whites, gathered at the Lincoln Memorial in the capital. The high point of the rally was King's stirring "I Have a Dream" speech, which defined the moral basis of the civil rights movement.

Significance. The speech helped achieve a major victory in 1964, when Congress passed the civil rights bill that President John F. Kennedy and his successor, President Lyndon B. Johnson, had recommended. The Civil Rights Act of 1964 prohibited racial discrimination in public places and called for equal opportunity in employment and education. King later received the 1964 Nobel Peace Prize.

1. SETTING

King's speech took place in front of the Lincoln Memorial. The giant statue of Lincoln, the president who helped end slavery, invoked the historical figure and set the tone for the event.

2. ALLUSION

When King said, "Five score years ago," he echoed the language Abraham Lincoln used at the beginning of his Gettysburg Address. King also mentions the Emancipation Proclamation.

3. IMAGERY

King used figurative language throughout his speech. His use of imagery—such as when he refers to segregation and discrimination as manacles and chains—helped listeners form mental images as he spoke.

4. COMPARISON

King explained how modern-day America is not living up to the promises made by the Founding Fathers.

5. EXTENDED ANALOGY

King compared the civil rights movement to "cash[ing] a check," emphasizing his point that equal rights was a broken promise, not a new concept.

6. REPETITION

King repeated the phrase "now is the time" throughout this paragraph. A Baptist minister, King knew that repeating key phrases emphasized his point and created a rhythm that pleased the ear.

7. ALLITERATION

"Sweltering summer" is one example of the small bursts of alliteration that King used throughout his speech. (See page 890 for more on alliteration.)

▲ **Martin Luther King, Jr.,** was known as a gifted orator. He was assassinated at age 39. (See also page 212.)

1 I am happy to join with you today in what will go down in history as the greatest demonstration for freedom in the history of our nation.

2 Five score years ago, a great American, in whose symbolic shadow we stand today, signed the Emancipation Proclamation. This momentous decree came as a great beacon light of hope to millions of Negro slaves, who had been seared in the flames of withering injustice. It came as a joyous daybreak to end the long night of their captivity.

3 But one hundred years later, the Negro still is not free. One hundred years later, the life of the Negro is still sadly crippled by the manacles of segregation and the chains of discrimination. One hundred years later, the Negro lives on a lonely island of poverty in the midst of a vast ocean of material prosperity. One hundred years later, the Negro is still languished in the corners of American society and finds himself an exile in his own land. And so we've come here today to dramatize a shameful condition.

4 In a sense we've come to our nation's capital to cash a check. When the architects of our republic wrote the magnificent words of the Constitution and the Declaration of Independence, they were signing a promissory note to which every American was to fall heir. This note was a promise that all men, yes, black men as well as white men, would be guaranteed the "Unalienable Rights of Life, Liberty, and the pursuit of Happiness." It is obvious today that America has defaulted on this promissory note insofar as her citizens of color are concerned. Instead of honoring this sacred obligation, America has given the Negro people a bad check, a check which has come back marked "insufficient funds."

5 But we refuse to believe that the bank of justice is bankrupt. We refuse to believe that there are insufficient funds in the great vaults of opportunity of this nation. And so we've come to cash this check, a check that will give us upon demand the riches of freedom and the security of justice.

6 We have also come to his hallowed spot to remind America of the fierce urgency of now. This is no time to engage in the luxury of cooling off or to take the tranquilizing drug of gradualism. Now is the time to make real the promise of democracy. Now is the time to rise from the dark and desolate valley of segregation to the sunlit path of racial justice. Now is the time to lift our nation from the quicksands of racial injustice to the solid rock of brotherhood. Now is the time to make justice a reality for all of God's children.

7 It would be fatal for the nation to overlook the urgency of the moment. This sweltering summer of the Negro's legitimate discontent will not pass until there is an invigorating autumn of freedom and equality. Nineteen sixty-three is not an end, but a beginning. And those who hope that the Negro needed to blow off steam and will now be content will have a rude awakening if the nation returns to business as usual. There will be neither rest nor tranquility in America until the Negro is granted his citizenship rights. The whirlwinds of revolt will continue to shake the foundations of our nation until the bright day of justice emerges.

But there is something that I must say to my people, who stand on the warm threshold, which leads into the palace of justice: In the process of gaining our rightful place, we must not be guilty of wrongful deeds. Let us not seek to satisfy our thirst for freedom by drinking from the cup of bitterness and hatred. We must forever conduct our struggle on the highest plain of dignity and discipline. We must not allow our creative process to degenerate into physical violence. Again and again, we must rise to the majestic heights of meeting physical force with soul force. The marvelous new militancy, which has engulfed the Negro community, must not lead us to a distrust of all white people, for many of our white brothers, as evidenced by their presence here today, have come to realize that their destiny is tied up with our destiny. And they have come to realize their freedom is inextricably bound to our freedom. We cannot walk alone. And as we walk, we must make a pledge that we shall always march ahead. We cannot turn back.

There are those who ask in the devotees of civil rights, when will you be satisfied? We can never be satisfied as long as the Negro is the very victim of the unspeakable horrors of police brutality. We can never be satisfied as long as our bodies, heavy with the fatigue of travel, cannot gain lodging in the motels of the highways and the hotels of the cities.

We cannot be satisfied as long as the Negro's basic mobility is from a smaller ghetto to a larger one. We can never be satisfied as long as our children are stripped of their selfhood and robbed of their dignity by signs stating "for white only."

We cannot be satisfied as long as the Negro in Mississippi cannot vote and the Negro in New York believes he has nothing for which to vote. No, no, we are not satisfied and we will not be satisfied until "justice rolls down like waters and righteousness like a mighty stream."

I am not unmindful that some of you have come here out of great trials and tribulations. Some of you have come fresh from narrow jail cells. Some of you have come from areas where your quest for freedom left you battered by the storms of persecution and staggered by the winds of police brutality. You have been the veterans of creative suffering. Continue to work with the faith that unearned suffering is redemptive. Go back to Mississippi, go back to Alabama, go back to South Carolina, go back to Georgia, go back to Louisiana, go back to the slums and ghettos of our northern cities, knowing that somehow this situation can and will be changed. Let us not wallow in the valley of despair.

I say to you today, my friends, so even though we face the difficulties of today and tomorrow, I still have a dream. It is a dream deeply rooted in the American dream.

I have a dream that one day this nation will rise up and live out the true meaning of its creed: "We hold these truths to be self-evident that all men are created equal."

I have a dream that one day on the red hills of Georgia the sons of former slaves and the sons of former slave owners will be able to sit down together at the table of brotherhood.

I have a dream that one day even the state of Mississippi, a state sweltering with the heat of injustice, sweltering with the heat of oppression, will be transformed into an oasis of freedom and justice.

I have a dream that my four little children will one day live in a nation where they will not be judged by the color of their skin but by the content of their character. I have a dream today.

I have a dream that one day down in Alabama, with its vicious racists, with its governor having his lips dripping with the words of "interposition" and "nullification," one day right down in Alabama little black boys and black girls will be able to join hands with little white boys and white girls as sisters and brothers. I have a dream today.

I have a dream that one day "every valley shall be exalted, every hill and mountain shall be made low; the rough places will be made plain and the crooked places will be made straight and the glory of the Lord shall be revealed, and all flesh shall see it together."

This is our hope. This is the faith that I go back to the South with. With this faith we will be able to hew out of the mountain of despair a stone of hope. With this faith we will be able to transform the jangling discords of our nation into a beautiful symphony of brotherhood. With this faith we will be able to work together, to pray together, to struggle together, to go to jail together, to stand up for freedom together, knowing that we will be free one day. This will be the day, this will be the day when all of God's children will be able to sing with new meaning:

My country, 'tis of thee, sweet land of liberty, of thee I sing. Land where my fathers died, land of the pilgrim's pride, From every mountainside, let freedom ring!

And if America is to be a great nation, this must become true. And so let freedom ring from the prodigious hilltops of New Hampshire. Let freedom ring from the mighty mountains of New York. Let freedom ring from the heightening Alleghenies of Pennsylvania. Let freedom ring from the snowcapped Rockies of Colorado. Let freedom ring from the curvaceous slopes of California. But not only that: Let freedom ring from Stone Mountain of Georgia.

Let freedom ring from Lookout Mountain of Tennessee. Let freedom ring from every hill and molehill of Mississippi. From every mountainside, let freedom ring.

And when this happens, when we let freedom ring, when we let it ring from every village and every hamlet, from every state and every city, we will be able to speed up that day when all of God's children, black men and white men, Jews and Gentiles, Protestants and Catholics, will be able to join hands and sing in the words of the old spiritual:

Free at last! Free at last! Thank God Almighty, we are free at last.

Here King used sensory language ("sweltering with the heat") to emphasize his point about injustice and oppression.

King alluded to the Bible with a quote ("every valley shall be exalted . . .") from the book of Isaiah.

Notice how King repeated the phrase "with this faith" throughout this section.

His use of repetition grew stronger toward the end of the speech.

King closed with the words from an old African-American spiritual song.

Lou Gehrig's Farewell Speech

A Speech to Say Good-bye

Lou Gehrig was one of the greatest players in baseball history. He played his entire Major League career—from 1923 to 1939—for the Yankees. He played in 2,130 consecutive games from 1925 to 1939. This total was a Major League record for 56 years, until Cal Ripken, Jr., of the Baltimore Orioles broke it in 1995.

Illness forced Gehrig to retire in 1939. He was suffering from amyotrophic lateral sclerosis, a rare and incurable nerve disease that is now commonly referred to as Lou Gehrig's disease. He died on June 2, 1941.

fyi! *Amyotrophic lateral sclerosis, also called ALS, is a rare, incurable disease of the nervous system. ALS gradually destroys the nerves that control the muscles. Weakness, paralysis, and eventually death result. ALS develops when certain nerve cells in the brain and spinal cord break down and die.*

Setting and Purpose. Gehrig delivered his speech in front of more than 60,000 fans at Yankee Stadium on July 4, 1939. The occasion was "Lou Gehrig Appreciation Day," a celebration of his retirement that included a special ceremony sandwiched between two games.

Significance. Gehrig's brief, powerful speech was a poignant moment in baseball history. He's remembered not only for his baseball career, but for his grace in the face of a terrible situation.

Lou Gehrig read his farewell speech between the two games of an Independence Day doubleheader. His nickname had been "The Iron Horse." ▶

1 Fans, for the past two weeks you have been reading about the bad break I got. Yet today I consider myself the luckiest man on the face of this earth. I have been in ballparks for seventeen years and have never received anything but kindness and encouragement from you fans.

2 Look at these grand men. Which of you wouldn't consider it the highlight of his career just to associate with them for even one day? Sure, I'm lucky. Who wouldn't consider it an honor to have known Jacob Ruppert? Also, the builder of baseball's greatest empire, Ed Barrow? To have spent six years with that wonderful little fellow, Miller Huggins? Then to have spent the next nine years with that outstanding leader, that smart student of psychology, the best manager in baseball today, Joe McCarthy? Sure, I'm lucky.

3 When the New York Giants, a team you would give your right arm to beat, and vice versa, sends you a gift—that's something. When everybody down to the groundskeepers and those boys in white coats remember you with trophies—that's something. When you have a wonderful mother-in-law who takes sides with you in squabbles with her own daughter—that's something. When you have a father and a mother who work all their lives so you can have an education and build your body—it's a blessing. When you have a wife who has been a tower of strength and shown more courage than you dreamed existed—that's the finest I know.

4 So I close in saying that I may have had a bad break, but I have an awful lot to live for.

1. DRAWING IN THE AUDIENCE

Gehrig began by addressing his fans directly. This helped draw his listeners into the speech.

2. EMOTIONAL APPEAL

Gehrig spends most of his speech thanking the people in his life. His gratitude is especially moving in light of what he calls his "bad break."

3. REPETITION

Gehrig repeated the phrase "that's something" throughout this portion of his speech to emphasize his point and to create a pleasing rhythm.

4. LENGTH

The short speech is well under 300 words. By keeping things simple and straightforward, Gehrig maximized the impact of his comments.

LISTENING

Wherever there's a speaker, there is also a listener.

When that listener is you, make sure you lend an ear. Paying attention will help you learn better, of course, but it will also make you a better speaker in the long run. You'll get a sense of what works well in front of an audience—as well as what doesn't work well.

Active Listening

Speaking is just one half of communication. Listening is the other half. Some people assume that listening is a natural ability rather than a skill that can be improved with practice. But it's becoming more and more clear that many communication problems can be solved by improving listening skills.

Improving Listening Skills

Train yourself to be an active listener. Learn to focus your sense of hearing along with your attention.

Approach every lecture, speech, or conversation with an open mind. Be receptive to the ideas of others. Be responsive to the person who is speaking—laugh, smile, frown, nod your head, or lean forward in your seat. Be able to reflect back to people what they have said to you. Look the speaker directly in the eyes. This will be taken as a sign that you care about what is being said.

Pay Attention. Concentrate on what the speaker says. Tune out everything—sights, sounds, and your own thoughts—except the speaker's voice. Try repeating to yourself what was said.

Listen for Main Ideas Rather Than Isolated Words and Phrases. Ask yourself, "What is the speaker getting at?" If possible, ask questions that will help clarify what the other person is saying. Be sure you have really heard and understood what was said.

Solving Listening Problems

If something about the way a speaker looks or sounds irritates you, try to tune out those distractions. Concentrate on the ideas.

If your mind begins to wander because you feel a speaker is telling you things you already know, concentrate on staying alert for details that may be new to you or provide a new way of looking at familiar information.

It is easy not to give your full attention to a speaker who says something with which you disagree. Make the effort to hear the speaker out with an open mind. In many situations, you will have an opportunity to discuss controversial statements after the speaker has finished. If you find a speaker's ideas difficult to understand, stay with it. Try to take notes about especially difficult points. Your goal should be to learn enough about the topic to ask intelligent questions. In that way you may eventually understand the subject.

Taking Notes

One of the best ways to improve your listening is to get in the habit of taking notes. Writing what you hear reinforces new information. Reading those notes again later, of course, reinforces what you've learned even more.

The secret of taking good notes is that you must first understand what the person is saying. Unless you can take shorthand, you won't be able to copy down even half of what is said. Even if you could, the results would probably not be worthwhile. Instead, you must get a sense of how the speaker's material is organized.

Mark What's Important. You may want to adopt some personal code to help distinguish between important and less important points. For example, the most important points might be written in all capitals. Many note-takers prefer to work in outline form.

Take Different Kinds of Notes. In a complicated presentation, you may even want to distinguish between several kinds of notes. For a very important phrase, you might take down the speaker's exact words and put them in quotation marks. Sometimes you might try to rephrase an idea in your own words and underline it as a reminder. There may also be times when you put down your reactions to the teacher's point (whether it's agreement, disagreement, or questions). You might want to put these reactions in parentheses so that you don't confuse your own ideas with your teacher's when you review your notes.

> 11/17   History
>
> About Abraham Lincoln
>   President 1861
>   born 1809 Kentucky
>   moved to Indiana
>   moved to Illinois
>   occupations, he had many
>   odd jobs on farms
>   clerk in store
>   law clerk (really a student of law)
>   became a lawyer by studying on his own

▲ **Notes** from a speaker's presentation may look like an informal outline, with each thought or topic on a new line.

Engage with the Material. As in all listening skills, the important part of note-taking is to remain active—staying alert for the important points, framing questions about the material, and trying to make connections. If you merely write down an odd part of what you hear now and then, your notes will almost certainly be useless.

Ways that you can engage with the material include

- identifying the speaker's argument.
- writing questions you want to research later.
- marking unfamiliar vocabulary words.
- making connections between the new material and something you already know.

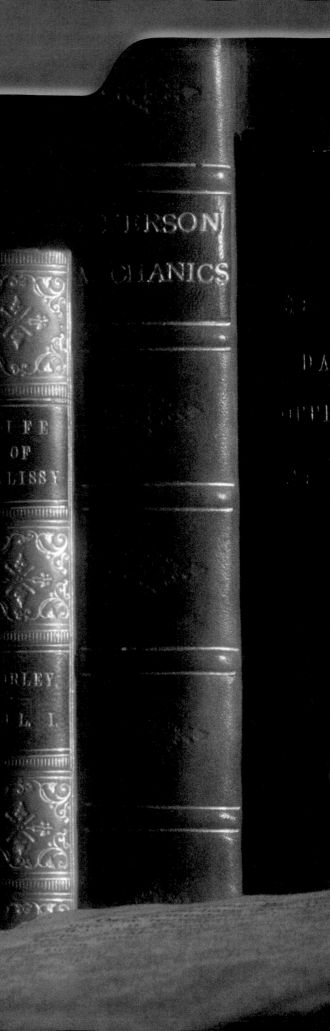

Literature

Literature: 800 BC to 330 BC

SOUTHWESTERN

Ancient literature has deep, but largely undocumented, roots in the East. China's first surviving documents date to around 1400 BC. The high level of skill involved suggests written Chinese already had a long history at the time. (See page 411.)

Greek literature is the oldest and most influential national literature in the Western world. It became the model for all later literature in the West, starting with Latin literature. Greek writers introduced many significant forms, including lyric and epic poetry, tragic and comic drama, philosophical essays and dialogues, critical and biographical history, and literary letters. Drama achieved preeminence during the Golden Age.

Use the legend, found on each two-page section, to easily identify entries belonging to a particular literary tradition. For example, on this page, green boxes hold information about Greek literature. Boxes with a gold background present information that offers historical context.

Legend
- Britain
- Greek
- Roman
- World

Period Facts

| 800 BC | 550 BC | 500 BC | 485 BC |

---

c. 800 BC
● **Homer** writes the *Iliad* and the *Odyssey*. After Homer's time, the two poems were recited as part of religious festivals in Greece. Copies of the poems became the basic textbooks that Greek children used to learn to read and to study legends and myths. As a result, the Greeks formed their religious views from Homer's portrayals of the gods and goddesses. His poems also furnished characters and plots for the great tragic dramatists of the 400s BC—Aeschylus, Euripides, and Sophocles.

c. 565 BC
● **Aesop,** the Greek slave credited with writing Aesop's fables, dies. Most of the characters in Aesop's fables are animals that talk and act like humans. They show the failings and good qualities of human nature in a simple, humorous way.

c. 500 BC
● **The poet Valmiki** writes the first version of the *Ramanyana*, one of the two great epic poems of India.

c. 500 BC
● **Sun Tzu** writes *The Art of War*, the first manual of military strategy, in China. Today, many people apply *The Art of War* to such fields as business, diplomacy, politics, and sports.

c. 483 BC
● **Siddhartha Gautama,** the founder of Buddhism, dies, spawning a major area of Indian literature on his life and teachings.

c. 490 BC
● **Pericles,** the Greek statesman whose name was given to the greatest period in the history of ancient Athens, is born. The Age of Pericles came to stand for all that was highest in the art and science of the Ancient World.

c. 479 BC
● **Confucius,** the most influential and respected philosopher in Chinese history, dies. From about 100 BC to AD 1911, his ideas about the relationship between morality and society served as the single strongest influence on Chinese life.

c. 600 BC
● **Sappho** writes lyric poetry that shows controlled, yet intense, emotion in direct language. While only fragments of her work survive, they demonstrate her keen power of observation and her ability to capture in a few words insights into the world of both nature and human nature. Later poets, especially the Roman poets Catullus and Horace, imitated Sappho's four-line stanza, a form known as Sapphic.

c. 420 BC
● *Oedipus Rex,* a tragedy by Sophocles, is first performed. Like most of his plays, it's about an individual who chooses a course of action that the chorus does not support. Sophocles was known for glorifying individuals over the state.

458 BC
● *The Oresteia* trilogy is first performed in Athens. The playwright, Aeschylus, changed the face of Greek tragedy by adding a second actor, which created dialogue between characters. Before that, a single actor was limited to interacting with the chorus.

404 BC
● **Athens** is defeated in the Peloponnesian War, effectively limiting freedom of speech. (See page 423.) Government leaders no longer permitted Old Comedy, with its elements of political and social satire.

356–323 BC
● **The Alexandrian Age** describes the era of Alexander the Great's rule. As Alexander's empire grew, Greek ideas and culture spread throughout the East.

c. 355 BC
● **Xenophon,** a Greek soldier, historian, and writer, dies. His book *Hellenica* is the major source for Greek history from 411 to 362.

---

440 BC   415 BC   400 BC   330 BC

---

431 BC
● *Medea,* a tragedy by Euripides, is first performed. The playwright was known for showing heroes as ordinary people. He used his plays to criticize political, social, and religious ideas of the time.

415 BC
● **Aristophanes's comedy** *The Birds* is first performed. His plays are some of the earliest and best examples of political and social satire, combining bawdy humor and pointed topical reference.

399 BC
● **Socrates,** the Greek philosopher and teacher, dies. He was one of the most original, influential, and controversial figures in ancient Greek philosophy and in the history of Western thought. Before Socrates, Greek philosophy focused on the nature and origin of the universe. He redirected philosophy toward a consideration of moral problems and how people should best lead their lives.

323 BC
● **Alexander the Great** dies, marking the beginning of the Hellenistic Age. Athens lost its dominant role as the center of Greek culture, and the city of Alexandria in Egypt became the new capital of Greek civilization.

427 BC
● **Plato,** an influential philosopher, is born. He invented a new literary form called the dialogue, dramatic conversations in which two characters argue about philosophical ideas.

411 BC
● **The point at which** *The Peloponnesian War,* a history book about the unfinished war of the same name, ends. The writer, Thucydides, was an Athenian general in the war between Athens and Sparta.

384 BC
● **Aristotle,** a philosopher who studied under Plato, is born.

330 BC
● **Euclid,** the Greek mathematician, is born. Widely considered the father of geometry, he wrote a textbook that probably had a greater influence on scientific thinking than any other work.

Literature: 250 BC to AD 100

70 BC
- **Cicero,** a Roman orator and statesman, gains fame when he successfully prosecutes Gaius Verres, a corrupt former governor of Sicily. Cicero's victory in this trial earned him the approval of the Roman aristocracy. His written orations and philosophical and religious essays made him one of the most influential authors in Latin literature.

250 BC — **200 BC** — **150 BC** — **50 BC**

c. 254 BC
- **Plautus,** an important Roman writer of comedy, is born. His plays are versions of Greek New Comedy, which emphasized young men in love with slave girls, mistaken identities, cunning servants, and deceived masters. Plautus added earthy Italian comic elements and his own boisterous wit.

c. 200 BC
- **Quintus Ennius** writes a historical epic, the *Annals*, whch describes Roman history from the founding of Rome to his own time. He adopted Greek dactylic hexameter, which became the standard verse form for Roman epics.

146 BC
- **The Greco-Roman Age** begins when Rome conquers Greece. During the Roman rule, prose again became the most prominent literary form.

c. 55 BC
- **Lucretius,** a Roman poet and philosopher, dies. His only surviving work is a philosophical and scientific poem called *De rerum natura* (*On the Nature of Things*). Lucretius wrote the poem to free humanity from religious superstition and the fear of death. The poem's vivid language helps contribute to its emotional power.

160 BC
- **Cato the Elder** writes the best-known prose piece of the period, *On Agriculture*. Cato also wrote the first Latin history of Rome and of other Italian cities. He was the first Roman statesman to put his political speeches in writing as a means of influencing public opinion.

240 BC
- **Latin literature** formally begins when a Roman audience sees a Latin version of a Greek play. The adaptor was Livius Andronicus, a Greek who had been brought to Rome as a prisoner of war in 272 BC. Andronicus also translated Homer's Greek epic the *Odyssey* into an old type of Latin verse called *Saturnian*.

c. 159 BC
- **Terence,** the Roman comic playwright, dies. His plays were essentially Latin versions of Greek plots, more refined than those of Plautus and marked by pure style, careful construction, and fine characterization.

c. 54 BC
- **Gaius Valerius Catullus,** a Roman lyric poet, dies. He was known for his personal and passionate poetry. His best-known poems tell of his love for Clodia, an aristocratic Roman called Lesbia in his poems.

c. AD 100
● **Plutarch,** a Greek biographer and essayist, becomes famous for his work, *Parallel Lives of Illustrious Greeks and Romans*. Plutarch wrote these biographies in pairs, each comparing one Greek and one Roman statesman or general. The comparisons are often forced, but the *Lives* constitute an important source of historical information. Twenty-three pairs of the *Lives* have survived. They became the basis of many stories and poems of the Middle Ages. William Shakespeare and other Elizabethan dramatists used them as source material for many of their historical plays.

27 BC
● **The Augustan Age** begins. The emperor Augustus took a personal interest in the literary works produced during his years of power, which stretched through AD 14. This period is sometimes called the Golden Age of Latin literature.

8 BC
● **Horace,** one of the greatest poets of ancient Rome, dies. He is most famous for *Odes*, a collection of short, songlike poems. Some are personal poems about love, friendship, and natural beauty. Others express Horace's love for his country and his religion, using myths and tales of national heroes.

25 BC	10 BC	AD 50	AD 100

Ovid

1 BC
● **Ovid,** the Roman poet, writes *The Art of Love*. It mocks the prevailing Roman tradition of didactic poetry by providing a handbook on the art of seduction, down to the minutest of details.

c. AD 100s
● **Lucius Apuleius** writes the only completely preserved novel in ancient Latin, *Metamorphoses*, also called *The Golden Ass*. This 11-part work is written in an elaborate, flowery style. It describes the adventures of a young man named Lucius who is accidentally turned into a donkey.

19 BC
● **Vergil** dies before he can finish the *Aeneid*, an epic poem describing the events that led to the creation of Rome. Centuries later, the Italian poet Dante Alighieri based his great epic *The Divine Comedy* (1321) on the sixth book of the *Aeneid*. In Dante's poem, it is Vergil who guides the poet on his journey through Hell and Purgatory.

c. AD 65
● **Lucius Annaeus Seneca,** a Roman statesman and author, dies. Seneca's tragedies adapt subjects used by the Greek playwrights. They influenced tragic drama in Italy, France, and Elizabethan England. He also wrote works on natural science and Stoic philosophy.

Legend
● Britain
● Greek
● Roman
● World
Period Facts

Literature: 600 to 1500

Medieval civilization reached its highest point of achievement between the 1000s and the late 1200s. This period is called the High Middle Ages.

Learning and the arts during the High Middle Ages were devoted to glorifying God and strengthening the power of the church. From 1100 to 1300, almost all the great ideas and artistic achievements reflected the influence of the church.

Morality plays, a form of drama, flourished in the 1400s. They developed from the mystery play, which dramatized Biblical events, and the miracle play, which dramatized the lives of saints. Morality plays were essentially dramatized sermons. Their general theme was the struggle between good and evil for the allegiance of the human soul. Unlike the mystery plays, which were performed by amateurs, morality plays were performed by professional and sometimes traveling actors.

600	800	1100	1200

618
● **The first year of the Tang Dynasty,** a series of rulers who governed China until 907. Many historians consider this period the golden age of Chinese civilization. (See also pages 482–483.)

814
● **Charlemagne** (Charles the Great), the most famous ruler of the Middle Ages, dies. As emperor, he revived the political and cultural life of Europe, which had declined after the fall of the Roman Empire in the 400s.

c. 1100
● **An unknown French author** writes *The Song of Roland*, an epic poem about Charlemagne's nephew. Most early medieval poems were about heroic figures like kings and warriors.

c. 1005
Murasaki Shikibu, lady-in-waiting to a Japanese empress, writes *The Tale of Genji*. Considered by some to be the oldest novel in the world, it portrays aristocratic life in Japan.

c. 1140
● ***The Song of the Cid,*** an epic poem about an 11th-century Spanish hero, is written. Almost all of it has survived, even though most of the epics from this era have since been lost.

c. 700s
● *Beowulf*, an Old English poem in alliterative verse, is written. It's the oldest epic in a European vernacular.

c. 1100
● **Pedro Alfonso** publishes *Scholar's Guide*, a collection of moral tales called *apologues*. It's the earliest known prose fiction in Spain.

c. 1200
● *Nibelungenlied,* a German epic poem, is written by an unknown author. It combines legends about the hero Siegfried, who slays the dragon Fafnir to gain possession of a treasure, with legends about the destruction of the rival Burgundians.

1096
● **The Crusades**, a series of religious wars proclaimed by the pope, begin in Europe.

Legend
● Britain
● Europe
● World
Period Facts

1308

● **Dante** begins writing *The Divine Comedy*, an allegorical poem that relates his spiritual development and focuses on the theme of life after death. He finishes it just before his death in 1321.

c. 1350

● **Giovanni Boccaccio** writes *The Decameron*, a collection of 100 short tales ranging from tragedy and romance to popular farce.

1348

● **Black Death,** the second strain of pandemic plague, hits London. By 1400, it had killed about 40 percent of the European population—around 25 million people.

c. 1440

● **Johannes Gutenberg** develops movable type and starts producing books with a printing press. Before the printing press, books were expensive treasures. Monks labored for years copying each one by hand. The printing press changed history by making written knowledge cheaper and accessible.

1304

● **Petrarch,** a great Italian lyric poet and scholar, is born. His love poetry, heavily influenced by the classics, is an important influence on world literature.

| 1300 | 1350 | 1450 | 1500 |

c. 1293

● **Dante Alighieri** writes *La Vita Nuova* (*The New Life*), a collection of poems about his beloved Beatrice. It shows the influence of troubadour poetry, a style that flourished in southern France in the 1100s and 1200s.

1337

● **The Hundred Years' War,** a long struggle between England and France, begins. The war marked the decline of feudalism, the rise of French unity, the development of new military tactics, and the growth of English sea power.

late 1300s

● **Sir Gawain and the Green Knight**, one of the most important medieval English verse romances, is written. Sir Gawain represents the chivalrous ideals of truthfulness and loyalty.

c. 1470

● **Sir Thomas Malory** writes *Le Morte d'Arthur* (*The Death of Arthur*), a long poem that tells the whole story of King Arthur of Britain and the careers of such Knights of the Round Table as Lancelot, Gareth, and Tristan. It provides the fullest version of the legends of Arthur and his court ever written in English.

c. 1387

● **Geoffrey Chaucer** begins writing *The Canterbury Tales*, a collection of 24 stories that he works on until he dies in 1400. They're about a company of pilgrims who share stories on their way to Canterbury. Like their tellers, the tales display diverse subjects and styles. Most tales reflect the personalities of the pilgrims who tell them.

1492

● **Antonio de Nebrija** publishes *Castilian Grammar*, the first book written on the rules of a modern European language.

The Monk, teller of one of the *Canterbury Tales*

Literature: 1500 to 1545

English literature, in deep hibernation from the time of Chaucer, emerged with startling suddenness at the beginning of the 1500s. The preceding century had seen the culmination of the long religious tradition of the miracle play, preserved in several separate but related collections, and the introduction of the vice-and-virtue homilies of the morality play.

Lyric and dramatic poetry flourished. The middle 1500s brought the first native English comedies and tragedies. Playwrights had the luck of a theater that almost accidentally made its way to a wide audience, leaving court performances for special occasions. Even toward the end of the century, during its greatest period, the theater never won the academic respectability of poetry, but it could earn a living for a playwright.

Writers like Marlowe and Shakespeare gave the West its most basic types of character and conscience.

William Shakespeare

1500   **1510**

c. 1500
● *Everyman,* an English morality play, is first performed. As in other morality plays, the characters are abstractions that personify concepts like sin, hate, and pride. It was designed to teach its audience about virtue and other Biblical values.

c. 1500
● *Arabian Nights,* a collection of folktales and romances from Arabia, Egypt, India, Persia, and other countries, is written. The stories had long been part of oral tradition.

19th century engraving from *Arabian Nights*

1503
● **Leonardo da Vinci** begins painting the Mona Lisa.

1506
● **Christopher Columbus** dies. (See page 503.)

1511
● **Desiderius Erasmus,** a Dutch scholar and humanist, publishes *In Praise of Folly,* a satire on human nature. Though he wrote it in just 1 week, it's considered one of the most important works of the Renaissance.

1513
● **Niccolo Machiavelli,** an Italian statesman-philosopher, writes *The Prince,* a political treatise. The experience he acquired as a government official and his study of history led him to view politics in a new way. The political writers of the Middle Ages treated politics idealistically, within the framework of religion. But Machiavelli sought to explain politics realistically, based on his view of human nature within the framework of history. *The Prince* was influential throughout Renaissance Europe.

1532
● **François Rabelais,** a French humanist, begins publishing *Gargantua and Pantagruel,* a comic narrative about French society in the 1500s, in a series of books. He used humor to play with such serious subjects as education, politics, and religion.

1542
● **Sir Thomas Wyatt**, an English poet who was active during the first phase of the English Renaissance, dies. While most of his important works were written for lute accompaniment, he was credited (along with Henry Howard) with introducing Petrarch's sonnet techniques into English literature.

1520　　　　　　　　　　　1530

1516
● **Sir Thomas More**, an English author, statesman, and scholar, writes *Utopia* in Latin. It's an account of an ideal society with justice and equality for all citizens. More's writings combined intense concern for the problems of his day and spiritual detachment from worldly affairs. He was beheaded in 1535 for refusing to accept Henry VIII as the head of the English Church.

1517
● **The Protestant Reformation** begins when Martin Luther, a German monk, protests certain practices of the Roman Catholic Church. It has a tremendous impact on social, political, and economic life.

1528
● **Baldassare Castiglione** publishes *The Courtier,* a book in which he set forth standards of conduct for the perfect courtier. Once it was translated into other languages, it became very influential across Europe.

1534
● **King Henry VIII** forces Parliament to pass the Act of Supremacy. The act declared the king to be head of the Church in place of the pope, who wouldn't grant Henry's request to end his marriage to Catherine of Aragon.

1536
● **Anne Boleyn,** King Henry VIII's second wife, is condemned on a charge of adultery and is beheaded.

1543
● **Nicolaus Copernicus,** a Polish astronomer, publishes *On the Revolution of the Heavenly Spheres.* Before Copernicus, most astronomers thought that a motionless Earth was the center of the universe.

Legend
● Britain
● Europe
● World
　Period Facts

1546
- **Martin Luther,** one of the main leaders of the Reformation, dies. By this time, he has been recognized as a major figure in the history of Christianity and the world. He symbolizes the split within western Christianity between Protestants and Roman Catholics. This split has affected the political and cultural development of Europe and North and South America. Luther continues to be the source of some of the most powerful ideas in Christianity.

1561
- **Francis Bacon,** an English philosopher, essayist, jurist, and statesman, is born in London. As one of the earliest and most influential supporters of empirical science, he helped develop the scientific method of solving problems.

c. 1580
- **Thomas Kyd,** an English playwright, publishes *The Spanish Tragedy,* which was the most popular tragedy of the 1500s. He created a new style of drama by bringing classical influence to popular drama. His work was based on the revenge play genre, in which the main character seeks vengeance for a crime.

1545	1555	1565	1575

1547
- **Ivan the Terrible** becomes the first Russian ruler to be crowned csar. He created a stronger and more centralized government and expanded Russia's territory.

1558
- **Elizabeth Tudor** becomes Queen Elizabeth I at age 25. Her court becomes a center for musicians, scholars, and writers. Her reign is often called the Golden Age or the Elizabethan Age because it was a time of great achievement in England.

1578
- *Holinshed's Chronicles,* a history by English author Raphael Holinshed, is published. This book was later used by Shakespeare as the chief historical source for his plays.

1550
- *Piers Plowman,* the Middle English satirical and allegorical poem of the 14th century, is printed for the first time. The main theme of *Piers Plowman* is the need to reform England spiritually through Christian faith and love.

c. 1580
- **Sir Philip Sidney,** an English author, courtier, and soldier famous for his literary criticism, fiction, and poetry, writes *The Defense of Poesie.* It was the first piece of major literary criticism in English.

1554
- *Lazarillo de Tormes,* the first picaresque novel, is published. This type of novel was the most important contribution of Spanish Golden Age fiction to world literature. This anonymous work was written in the form of a short autobiography.

c. 1580
- **Torquato Tasso,** an Italian poet, publishes *Jersualem Delivered,* an epic poem on the events of the First Crusade.

Legend
- Britain
- Europe
- World

Period Facts

928

1594
● **William Shakespeare's** *Romeo and Juliet* is first performed.

1594
● **Thomas Nash** writes *The Life of Jack Wilton*, a forerunner of the English novel that combines colorful fictional characters with references to actual people and events. Nash wrote some of the first works of prose fiction in English literature.

1599
● **Ben Jonson,** an English playwright and poet, writes *Every Man in His Humour*, a realistic and satiric comedy of London life in which each character is motivated by a single obsession, such as jealousy. (In his later satiric comedies, the humours are generally an aspect of human failings like greed, ignorance, or superstition.) For nearly 100 years after his death, Jonson's reputation and influence on English drama at least equaled that of his friend William Shakespeare.

c. 1587
● **Christopher Marlowe,** the first great Elizabethan writer of tragedy, establishes his reputation with *Tamburlaine the Great,* a play about an awe-inspiring conqueror of the same name. The play reflects the widespread fascination in his time with the reach and limits of the human will's desire for dominion. With this play, Marlowe influenced later drama with his concentration on a heroic figure and his development of blank verse as a flexible form for tragedy.

1585   **1595**   **1600**

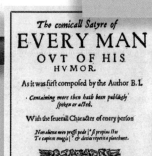

The comicall Satyre of
EVERY MAN
OVT OF HIS
HVMOR.

As it was first composed by the Author B. I.

Containing more then hath been publikely spoken or acted.

With the seuerall Character of euery person

Non aliena meo preffi pede | si propius stes Te capient magis | & decies repetita placebunt.

LONDON,
Printed for Nicholas Linge.
1600.

1588
● *Endymion*, a play by English playwright John Lyly, is published. Lyly was important in the development of Elizabethan popular comedy of high literary quality. His comedies, which influenced Shakespeare, treat idealized love and flatteringly reflect attitudes of the Elizabethan courtier.

1590
● **Edmund Spenser** publishes the first three books of his epic romance, *The Faerie Queen*. (He would only finish six out of the 12 planned books before he died.) The poem is an allegory filled with personifications of abstract ideas such as pride, hypocrisy, and faith; the faerie queen is a symbol for both the abstract notion of glory and for Queen Elizabeth I, to whom the poem is dedicated. Spenser blended classical themes and conventions with Christian moralism and strong English patriotic feelings. Influenced by Geoffrey Chaucer and the Italian epic romances of the 1500s, Spenser invented a unique form for his work, writing in a distinctive pattern now called the Spenserian stanza. His work is distinctive for its deliberate use of old-fashioned language and its rich visual imagery.

1588
● **Marlowe** writes *The Tragical History of Doctor Faustus*. Never before in English literature had a writer shown the soul's conflict with the laws defining the place of human beings in a universal order. The play's subject was typical of Marlowe's later plays, which focus on what were considered the dangerous and subversive elements of Renaissance culture, such as atheism, witchcraft, and homosexuality.

1593
● **Christopher Marlowe** is killed in a bar fight. In the years before his death, there was evidence of duels and reports of his unconventional, skeptical political and religious thought.

1599
● **Thomas Dekker** writes *The Shoemaker's Holiday*, a zestful picture of Elizabethan life that combines patriotism and romance with a favorable portrayal of the rising merchant and artisan classes. Dekker wrote all or part of more than 40 plays, but most of them have been lost.

Miguel de Cervantes published the first part of *Don Quixote*, his long novel, in 1605. Its hero is a Spanish landowner who enlivens his boring life by reading fictional tales about knights, tales he believes to be true and accurate. Wishing to live like the knights, he dresses in armor and sets out to gain fame by performing heroic deeds. He attacks windmills he thinks are giants and flocks of sheep he thinks are armies.

The peasant Sancho Panza serves as his squire during the hero's adventures. He stands for the real in life, while Don Quixote stands for the ideal. Their conversations make up a large part of the novel.

Until the 1800s, *Don Quixote* was thought of as a humorous story of a madman's adventures. After that, it became a model for a new type of fiction with heroes who do not conform to their times. Cervantes's work has been a major influence in the development of the novel.

Cervantes.

1600 ———————————————————————— **1605**

c. 1600
● **William Shakespeare** writes *Hamlet, Prince of Denmark*. The full version of the play didn't appear until 1623.

c. 1600
● **English society** begins looking for a less spontaneous, more ordered universe. It sought to deny parts of the Renaissance and to freeze the rest in a new classicism. The class of businessmen, professionals, and civil servants would try to emulate the old nobility in some respects, but it would also seek to recreate the literary world of its own lively middle-class image.

1601
● **The Russian famine** begins. Over the next 2 years, it will kill one-third of the population.

1603
● **Queen Elizabeth I** dies.

1604
● **King James I of England** authorizes a committee of about 50 scholars to prepare a revision of earlier English translations of the Bible. The new version will appear in 1611 and became known as the King James, or Authorized, Version. The beauty and grace of the translation establishes it as one of the great treasures of the English language. It will remain the most widely used translation in the English-speaking world for more than 200 years after its publication.

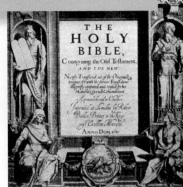

THE HOLY BIBLE,
Conteyning the Old Testament,
AND THE NEW:
Newly Translated out of the Originall tongues; & with the former Translations diligently compared and reuised, by his Maiesties speciall Commandment.
Appointed to be read in Churches.
Imprinted at London by Robert Barker, Printer to the Kings most Excellent Maiestie.
ANNO DOM 1611.

1607
● **Captain John Smith** establishes Jamestown, Virginia, the first English colony in the new world. Back on the continent, Europeans closely read his written accounts of the new settlement. The 104 original colonists were all men and boys.

1608
● **John Milton** is born in London. He attends St. Paul's School and then Christ's College at Cambridge University. Although his early training prepared him for a religious career, he came to believe "tyranny had invaded the church." So he decided to dedicate himself to God's service as a poet.

The period names Jaco-bean *and* Caroline *refer to reigns of English monarchs, just as* Elizabethan *refers to the years of Elizabeth I's reign, 1558–1603.*

Jacobean: the reign of James I, 1603–1625

Caroline: the reign of Charles I, 1625–1642

1600–1628

● **François de Malherbe** composes his *Odes and Stanzas,* a collection of poems on the themes of love and death, the great moral truths, and patriotic subjects of his day. Critical of flowery vocabularies and elaborate sentences, he insisted upon simplicity, clarity, force, and dignity. He was the first poet of France's Classical age, which lasted until the early 1700s.

1620

● **The Pilgrims** establish Plymouth Colony, the second permanent English settlement in America. Many of the Pilgrims belonged to a group of English Protestants called Puritans, who were followers of reformer John Calvin. (See pages 34–37.)

1610	1615	1620

---

c. 1610

● **English drama** began to change significantly as Jacobean and Caroline tragedies gained prominence. The tragicomedy, a serious play with a happy ending, increased in popularity. Many plots were artificially arranged and contained sensational, rather than genuinely tragic, elements. The obsession of much Jacobean and Caroline tragedy with violence, dishonesty, and horror has appalled many critics. But these plays have also been greatly admired for their magnificent poetry, their dramatic power, and their unflinching view of human nature and the human condition.

Important Jacobean playwrights included Francis Beaumont, John Fletcher, Thomas Middleton, Cyril Tourneur, and John Webster. Philip Massinger and John Ford were among the important Caroline playwrights.

After Charles I was deposed in the 1640s and the Puritans gained control of Parliament, theatrical performances were prohibited. The Puritan government closed the theaters in 1642, ending the richest and most varied era of English drama.

1613

● **The English kidnap Pocahontas,** the daughter of an important Native American leader, with the intention of using her as a hostage in negotiations with the Indians. She would go on to become a key figure in the relationship between the Indians and the settlers at Jamestown.

1613

● **John Webster** finishes *The Duchess of Malfi,* a revenge tragedy. Its power lies in the complexity of the characters' motives for acting as they do, the physical horror of the situations, and the poetic dialogue.

1616

● **William Shakespeare** dies.

1616

● ***The Alchemist,*** a comedy of humours by English playwright Ben Jonson, is performed. The play is an example of Jonson's use of characters dominated by humours. According to a Renaissance medical concept, everyone had four humours (fluids) in his or her body. Good health depended on a proper balance among them. An excess of one humour might dominate a person's disposition. An excess of bile, for example, supposedly made a person melancholy.

1620

● **William Bradford,** the English-born governor of Plymouth County, begins keeping a journal about Pilgrims that provides details on their day-to-day lives. It will be published posthumously in 1856.

1621

● **Robert Burton,** an English scholar, writes *The Anatomy of Melancholy,* a medical text. For him, melancholy includes all states of mind from pessimism to insanity. Burton's wit and interest in curious facts will help this book long outlive its medical usefulness.

c. 1621

● **Philip Massinger,** an English playwright, writes a comedy, *A New Way to Pay Old Debts.* The play's chief character, the monstrous villain Sir Giles Overreach, so appealed to actors and audiences that the play was performed longer than any other non-Shakespearean play of the 1600s.

SOUTHWESTERN

1624
● **Cardinal Richelieu** begins his reign as prime minister of France, which will last until 1642. He and King Louis XIII worked closely to govern the country. Richelieu strengthened the king's rule and helped make France the most powerful country in Europe.

1626
● **Thomas Middleton,** a leading playwright of the Elizabethan and Jacobean periods in English drama, dies. His comedies, which include *A Mad World, My Masters*, and *A Trick to Catch the Old One*, are a realistic portrayal of London life during his time. Middleton collaborated with a number of noted dramatists, including William Rowley on *The Changeling*, one of the great tragedies of Jacobean drama.

1632
● **John Ford** writes *'Tis Pity She's a Whore*, a sensational tragedy. Ford was strongly influenced by the idea of melancholy, a name given in his time to a disease of the mind. This modern psychological aspect of Ford's play has contributed greatly to its success with modern readers.

1635
● **Spanish dramatist Pedro Calderon de la Barca** writes his best-known play, *Life Is a Dream*. It explores the mysteries of human destiny and the conflict between free will and predestination. Calderon, who wrote about 200 plays, was the last great writer of Spain's Golden Age. He often dealt with traditional Roman Catholic moral and religious attitudes.

1625   **1630**   **1635**

1621
● **John Fletcher,** an English playwright, writes *The Wild Goose-Chase*, a comedy of manners. Like similar Restoration plays written later, this play was meant to please a sophisticated, upper-class audience. For many years, Fletcher's plays were as highly praised as Shakespeare's and Ben Jonson's. He collaborated with a number of other playwrights over the course of his career and probably helped Shakespeare write *The Two Noble Kinsmen* and *Henry VIII*.

1632
● **John Milton** writes "L'allegro" (Italian for the "cheerful one"), a short joyous poem. The piece praises the delights of life in country and town.

1633
● *The Temple,* a poetry volume by English writer George Herbert, is published just after his death. It includes more than 150 short lyric poems on religious subjects.

1633
● **John Donne,** an English poet and preacher, begins producing his *Holy Sonnets*, a series of religious poems. Donne's language is dramatic, witty, and sometimes shocking. He used a variety of images and based his rhythms on everyday speech. At times, the complexity of his thought makes his meaning difficult to understand, but his poems always unfold in a logical way.

1635
● **The French Academy** is founded by Cardinal Richelieu. It gave France the first "official" court of usage and literary style. The academy fixed both the language and the literary forms, insisting on the virtue of "correctness." It's often referred to as "L'Académie Française."

1633
● **Donne** is the most famous of the **Metaphysical poets,** a group of writers whose work was characterized by intellectual complexity. Metaphysical poetry contains irregular, "unpoetic" rhythms and colloquial language. It also sometimes uses far-fetched or outlandish comparisons, either similes or metaphors, called metaphysical conceits. The metaphysical conceit often extends a comparison to great length to describe an emotion, idea, or situation. Other writers associated with this movement include Andrew Marvell, Abraham Cowley, Richard Crashaw, George Herbert, and Henry Vaughn.

Legend
● American
● Britain
● Europe
● World
Period Facts

1641
- **Descartes** writes his most important work, *Meditations on First Philosophy*. In it, he sought to provide the foundations of human knowledge.

1648
- **Robert Herrick** publishes "To the Virgins, to Make Much of Time," a short lyric poem about seizing the day. Herrick, a clergyman, wrote in the tradition of the Cavalier poets, a group of English courtiers who supported King Charles I in his struggle with Parliament. Herrick's poems, which were often about nature, were heavily influenced by Roman poets.

1650
- **Poet Anne Bradstreet** publishes the first volume of American poetry, *The Tenth Muse Lately Sprung Up in America*. Although life as a settler was hard, she found time to write poetry, chiefly for her father and husband.

1640   **1645**   **1650**

1637
- **René Descartes,** the father of modern philosophy, publishes *Discourse on Method,* a collection of essays that opened up questions of belief and meaning itself to the logical processes implicit in mathematical thought. The French thinker was a pioneer in the attempt to formulate simple, universal laws of motion that govern all physical change.

1638
- **Galileo,** an Italian astronomer, finishes his final scientific masterpiece, the *Discourse on Two New Sciences*. Many consider him the founder of modern science.

1642
- **Civil war** breaks out in England between Parliament and the monarch. People who supported King Charles I were called *Royalists* or *Cavaliers*. Many of Parliament's greatest supporters were Puritans, who were called *Roundheads* because they cut their hair short. The Puritans closed the theaters in 1642, changed the structure of the Church of England, and tried to force many of their religious beliefs on the people. Theaters would remain closed for 18 years, effectively shutting down the development of English drama.

1649
- **Charles I** is beheaded. England becomes a republic called the Commonwealth of England. This period of English history, between 1649 and 1660, is called the *Interregnum*.

1651
- **Thomas Hobbes,** a British philosopher, publishes *Leviathan,* a highly influential political piece. In this work, he denied that people are naturally social beings. He argued instead that people's most basic motives are selfish considerations.

1653
- **Oliver Cromwell** ends the Commonwealth and establishes a dictatorship called the Protectorate, with himself as Lord Protector. He dies in 1658.

Literature: 1660 to 1700

Restoration is the period of English history beginning in 1660 when Charles II was reestablished on the throne. After the 20-year Puritan revolution, literature came back into favor and the light spirit of comedy replaced the solemnity preferred by the Puritan rulers. Among the comic dramatists of the age were William Congreve and William Wycherley, whose polished, somewhat cynical comedies of manners have remained in the English theatrical repertoire for 300 years.

The greatest literary name of the era was John Dryden. He, too, was an active dramatist, but he is best remembered for his literary criticism and his accomplished verse translations. Dryden's broad and generous appreciation of the literature of the past set the stage for the neoclassical age of Pope and Swift.

John Dryden

1660	1665	1670

1660
● **Samuel Pepys,** a British public official, begins keeping a diary in which he records the events of his daily life. When it's eventually published in the 19th century, it provides an intimate self-portrait and a vivid picture of an exciting period in English history.

1660
● **In England,** a new Parliament abolishes the Protectorate and restores the monarchy in the name of Charles II.

1662
● **Michael Wigglesworth** writes his somber poem, *The Day of Doom.* A Puritan pastor, doctor, and poet of colonial New England, Wigglesworth presented theology to the colonists in a form they could easily read and memorize.

1664
● **Molière,** the greatest French writer of comedy, writes *The Misanthrope,* his play about human failings. His plays emphasize one broad principle: the comic contrast between how people see themselves and how others see them.

1665
● **The Great Plague,** a disease carried by fleas that lived on black rats, hits London. The total number of deaths was about 70,000. (See pages 466–467.)

1666
● **The Great Fire of London** destroys large parts of the city. London houses in the 1600s were built mainly of wood, and they crowded so tightly over the narrow streets that the upper stories almost touched. There was no effective firefighting system, and a strong wind from the east fanned the flames through houses made abnormally dry by a long, hot summer.

1667
● **John Milton** writes *Paradise Lost,* an epic poem in blank verse. It relates how some of the angels revolted against God and were cast out of Heaven and into Hell. While Milton was heavily influenced by classical Greek and Latin authors, he emphasized the Bible as interpreted by the individual believer.

1667
● **Jean Racine,** a French playwright, writes *Andromache.* Racine was known for his simplicity. He followed the classical rules for composition, including the use of a single concentrated plot that takes place in a short time frame.

1672
● **John Milton** writes *Samson Agonistes,* which tells the Biblical story of Samson in the style of Greek tragic drama.

1672
● **John Dryden,** an English poet, dramatist, and literary critic, writes *Marriage à la Mode,* a comedy. He believed that the individual is part of a society that has its roots in ancient Greece and Rome, so many of his works deal with social and political issues.

1672
● **Peter the Great** becomes czar of Russia. Because of his admiration for European society, Peter forced Russia's nobility to adopt many Western customs. He also laid the basis for the Russian Academy of Sciences, started Russia's first newspaper, and founded technical schools, a museum, a public library, and an art gallery.

1673
● **Molière** publishes his last work, *The Imaginary Invalid*. He died while playing the role of Argan.

1681
● **William Penn** establishes Pennsylvania. (See page 37.)

c. 1690
● *The New England Primer*, a popular Puritan children's book in the colonies, is published. It taught colonial American children the alphabet through crude illustrations and brief rhymes.

1690
● **John Locke,** an English philosopher, publishes *Two Treatises of Government*, a book that strongly influenced Thomas Jefferson in the writing of the Declaration of Independence.

1675	1680	1690

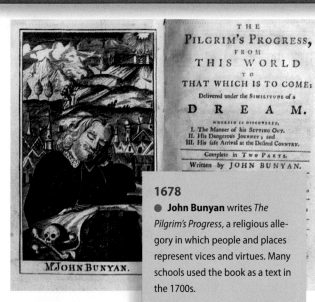

1678
● **John Bunyan** writes *The Pilgrim's Progress*, a religious allegory in which people and places represent vices and virtues. Many schools used the book as a text in the 1700s.

1675
● **King Philip's War** begins. King Philip, an Indian leader, formed an alliance with neighboring Indians and almost succeeded in wiping out the settlements. But after the defeat of his forces by the English colonists, Philip was hunted down and killed in a swamp near present-day Bristol, Rhode Island, on August 12, 1676.

1682
● **Mary Rowlandson's** description of her capture by Indians is published. It's the first of many captivity stories.

1682
● **Edward Taylor,** a pastor, begins writing his *Preparatory Meditations*, a collection of private poems. Taylor represented his complex thought in a few words. His work shows the influence of the intricate style of the English metaphysical poets of the 1600s. Although his language is complicated, Taylor's use of examples from everyday life makes his poetry understandable.

1690
● **Locke** also publishes *An Essay Concerning Human Understanding*, his major work. It describes his theory of how the mind functions in learning about the world. Locke declared that there were two kinds of experience, outer and inner. Outer experience was acquired through the senses of sight, taste, hearing, smell, and touch, which provide information about the external world. Inner experience was acquired by thinking about the mental processes involved in sifting these data, which furnished information about the mind.

1692
● **The Salem witchcraft trials** begin in Salem, Massachusetts. Nineteen people, both men and women, were convicted and hanged as witches. About 150 other people were imprisoned on witchcraft charges.

Legend
● American
● Britain
● Europe
● World
Period Facts

The Enlightenment, or the Age of Reason, was a period in history when philosophers emphasized the use of reason as the best method of learning truth. (See also pages 512–513.) Philosophers of the Enlightenment believed that nature is vast and complex but well ordered. The English poet Alexander Pope described nature as "a mighty maze, but not without plan."

Literature in the Enlightenment questioned accepted thinking. Writers portrayed human life as changeable and human understanding as partial. Much of the literature was written with self-consciousness and irony. It called attention to conventions and provoked skeptical awareness.

Alexander Pope

1700	1710	1720	1725

1700
● **William Congreve,** an English dramatist, writes *The Way of the World*, an outstanding comedy of the Restoration period. Like most plays of the period, its plot is fantastically complicated.

1702
● **Cotton Mather,** a Puritan historian, writes *Magnalia Christi Americana*, a religious history of New England. He wrote about 450 works on many subjects, including a defense of the witch-craft trials of the 1690s in Salem, Massachusetts.

1704
● **Jean Antoine Galland** translates *Arabian Nights* into French, bringing the most famous piece of Arabic literature into the Western world.

1712
● **Alexander Pope** publishes the first part of his mock-heroic epic, *The Rape of the Lock*. The poem uses all the conventions of the heroic epic—an invocation to the muse, supernatural intervention—to embellish the story of Lord Petre's theft of a lock of hair. Pope wrote in heroic couplets, with two rhymed lines of 10 syllables each. His polished, concise verse shows a keen feeling for sound and rhythm.

1719
● **Daniel Defoe,** an English novelist and journalist, writes *Robinson Crusoe*, one of the first English novels and one of the most popular adventure stories in Western literature. Critics have debated what role Defoe played in the development of the English novel, but he was undoubtedly a great master of realistic narrative and had a remarkable sense of detail in his work.

1726
● **Jonathan Swift** writes *Gulliver's Travels*, a satire with such a strong story that even the people Swift attacked failed to realize its meaning at first. In four parts, it tells of Lemuel Gulliver's voyages to imaginary lands.

1726–1729
● **Voltaire,** the French writer and philosopher, lives in exile in England. There, he met the writers Alexander Pope and Jonathan Swift and was attracted to the ideas of the philosopher John Locke and the scientist Sir Isaac Newton. It has been said that Voltaire went into exile a poet and came back a philosopher.

1729
- **Jonathan Swift** writes *A Modest Proposal*, a satirical essay. With a series of carefully reasoned arguments, he suggests that the children of the poor, properly cooked and seasoned, would make tasty dishes at a gentleman's table and at the same time be a source of profit rather than a burden to their parents.

1733–1734
- **Alexander Pope** writes *An Essay on Man*, an essay in rhymed couplets. It attempts to explain the nature of man, his place in the universe, and his relationship to mankind and to God. Many of its lines have become familiar quotations.

1745
- **Jonathan Swift** dies.

1744
- **Alexander Pope** dies.

1730 **1735** **1740** **1745**

1728
- **John Gay** writes *The Beggar's Opera*, a ballad opera. Two hundred years later, German dramatist Bertolt Brecht would adapt Gay's play for his satire on capitalism, *The Threepenny Opera*.

1748
- **Tobias George Smollett** writes *The Adventures of Roderick Random*, a picaresque novel important for its descriptions of 18th-century British navy life.

1731
- **George Lillo's** *The London Merchant* popularizes domestic tragedy, becoming a model for playwrights in France and Germany as well as England. Domestic tragedy, an ancestor of serious drama, substituted middle-class characters for the kings and nobles of earlier tragedy.

1740
- **Frederick the Great** of Prussia begins his reign. Frederick has been called an "enlightened despot" because he supported the progressive ideas and reforms of the period of history called the Enlightenment, or Age of Reason. Voltaire lived at Frederick's court as a guest from 1750 to 1753.

1749
- **Henry Fielding** writes *Tom Jones*, a comic novel remarkable for its vitality and its sweeping picture of 18th-century London and country life.

1732
- **Benjamin Franklin** begins writing *Poor Richard's Almanac*. The famous American statesman created the almanac early in his career, when he was a printer and publisher in Philadelphia. He issued the almanac for every year from 1733 to 1758. Many of the best-known American proverbs are from this source.

1740
- **Samuel Richardson,** an English novelist, publishes *Pamela*, the first epistolary novel. Richardson is considered one of the founding fathers of the novel. Richardson's books brought a number of new elements to the novel form. While they're not often read today, they've been extremely influential.

Legend
- American
- Britain
- Europe
- World

Period Facts

Literature: 1750 to 1800

1759
● **Voltaire** writes *Candide*, the satirical novel that would become his best-known work. On the surface, the work describes the adventures of an inexperienced young man as he wanders around the world. Philosophically, *Candide* is recognized as a complex inquiry into the nature of good and evil.

1776
● **Edward Gibbon,** the British scholar, begins publishing *The History of the Decline and Fall of the Roman Empire.* This classic work in six volumes considers the fall of Rome and traces the dissolution of the empire over more than a thousand years. Gibbon attributed the decline of Rome primarily to the corruption of classical Greco-Roman rational ideals by the emotional appeal of Christianity and other Eastern religions.

1751
● **Thomas Gray,** an English poet, writes his masterpiece, "Elegy Written in a Country Churchyard," which will become one of the best-known poems in the English language. Its theme is the common fate of common people, who live and die unnoticed and unremembered.

1755
● **Samuel Johnson** finishes his massive *Dictionary of the English Language*, which would establish his fame as a scholar.

1750   **1760**   **1775**

1754
● **Jonathan Edwards,** the famous minister of Puritan New England, writes *Freedom of Will*, his major philosophical work. As a philosopher, preacher, revivalist, and theologian, he was the leading intellectual figure in colonial America. During the 1730s and 1740s, Edwards's sermons contributed to a series of religious revival movements that spread through New England. These movements became known as the Great Awakening. They led to a new, more spiritual understanding of the church.

1760–1767
● **Laurence Sterne,** an English clergyman, becomes famous as the author of *The Life and Opinions of Tristram Shandy, Gentleman.* Its popularity reflects the growing regard for humor and laughter and for feeling and sentiment during that period.

1769
● **Frances Brooke** writes the first Canadian novel, *The History of Emily Montague*.

1773
● **English dramatist Oliver Goldsmith** writes *She Stoops to Conquer*. He would go on to produce a variety of works marked by a charming, lively style.

● **The Gothic novel** was a type of fiction that became popular in England during the late 1700s and early 1800s. The plots of Gothic novels included mysterious and supernatural events intended to frighten the reader. The stories were called Gothic because most of them took place in gloomy, medieval castles built in the Gothic style of architecture. Such buildings had many secret passageways, dungeons, and towers that provided ideal settings for strange happenings. Most Gothic novels were set in Italy or Spain because those countries seemed remote and mysterious to the English.

1776
● **Thomas Paine,** a political agitator and writer, writes *The American Crisis*, a series of revolutionary pamphlets written for the American colonists. His writings greatly influenced the political thinking of the leaders of the American Revolution.

1754
● **Horace Walpole** writes *The Castle of Otranto*, the first Gothic novel.

1777
● **Richard Brinsley Sheridan** writes *The School for Scandal*, one of the great comedies of English drama. With glittering wit, it exposes society people who love malicious gossip.

Legend
● American
● Canada
● Britain
● Europe
● World
Period Facts

938

1783
- **The Revolutionary War** ends. The American Revolution fundamentally changed life in America and stood as an example to peoples in many lands who later fought to gain their freedom. (See pages 56–61.)

1789
- **The French Revolution** begins.

1790
- **Robert Burns,** the national poet of Scotland, writes *Tam O'Shanter*, a narrative poem based on local legend.

1794
- **William Blake** writes *Songs of Experience*, the companion volume to *Songs of Innocence* (1789). In these works, he shows symbols of what he calls "the two contrary states of the human soul." Blake thought that we have war, injustice, and unhappiness because our way of life is founded on mistaken beliefs and that we cannot truly know reality through our five senses.

1780	1790	1795

1782
- **Jean-Jacques Rousseau's** *Confessions* is published 4 years after his death, creating a fashion for intimate autobiographies. The French philosopher's ideas foreshadow Romanticism.

1791
- **James Boswell** publishes *The Life of Samuel Johnson*, a biography of the English man of letters. Boswell preserved the wit and brilliance of Johnson's conversation; the sharpness of his opinions on people, politics, and literature; and the vigor of his personality.

1795–1796
- **Johann Wolfgang von Goethe,** the German poet, novelist, and playwright, publishes *Wilhelm Meister's Apprenticeship*, a novel that shows the gradual, sometimes painful, process by which a young man interested in the arts gains maturity, self-knowledge, and a sense of social responsibility. It is a typical Bildungsroman (a novel about an individual's educational development). It was much imitated.

1781
- **Johann Christoph Friedrich von Schiller's** Sturm und Drang tragedy *The Robbers* enjoys sensational success. His dramas are pleas for human freedom and dignity that inspired German liberals in their fight for liberty during the early 1800s and during the Revolution of 1848.

- **The Sturm und Drang (Storm and Stress) movement,** which began about 1770, emphasized strong emotion, originality, and rebellion against authority. Sturm und Drang was a rebellious, often chaotic movement that protested against middle-class social values, tradition, and authority in politics, art, and theology. Two of Germany's greatest dramatists, Schiller and Johann Wolfgang von Goethe, were prominent members of this movement as young men.

1798
- **The English Romantic movement** begins with the publication of *Lyrical Ballads* by William Wordsworth and Samuel Taylor Coleridge. They believe that poetry should be for (and about) everyone, so they often write about nature and rural life.

Literature: 1805 to 1830

Romanticism—a style that emphasizes passion over reason and intuition over logic—was a strong force in English and American literature in the 19th century. Romanticism favors full expression of the emotions and spontaneous action.

During the Romantic movement, most writers were discontented with their world. It seemed commercial, inhuman, and standardized. To escape from modern life, the Romantics turned their interest to faraway places, the medieval past, folklore and legends, and nature and the common people. The Romantics were also drawn to the supernatural.

Just as the Romantic hero is in revolt against social conventions, the Romantic artist is in revolt against artificial ideas of good form. In drama, for example, Romantic writers reject the classical unities of time, place, and action.

Jakob and Wilhelm Grimm

1805   1810   1815

1807
● **William Wordsworth** publishes one of the most famous poems in English literature, "Ode: Intimations of Immortality." Its argument for immortality rests on the poet's belief that our childhood is filled with memories of preexistence that fade as we grow old.

1807
● **Jakob and Wilhelm Grimm,** the brothers who collected Grimm's Fairy Tales, began gathering fairy tales from storytellers across the German countryside in an effort to preserve oral tradition. Folklore was an important element of the Romantic movement.

1808
● **Johann Wolfgang von Goethe** publishes the first part of *Faust*, a drama about a deal with the devil, in Germany. He ranks among the most important and influential writers of modern European literature.

1811
● **Jane Austen** writes *Sense and Sensibility*. Austen wrote with a keen sense of irony about the social institutions of her time. In each of her six novels, a woman meets and marries an eligible man after a series of usually comic difficulties. Overcoming these obstacles helps one or both of the characters gain the self-knowledge required for a happy marriage.

1814
● **Sir Walter Scott** publishes *Waverly*, the first in a series of romances that popularized historical novels. He was the first novelist to portray peasant characters sympathetically and realistically, and he agreed with the poet William Wordsworth's glorification of common people.

1815
● **Napoleon** is defeated at the Battle of Waterloo, ending nearly 20 years of war in Europe.

1817
● **Lord Byron** writes *Manfred*, a dramatic poem. The underlying theme in Byron's work is his insistence that people be free to choose their own course in life.

1817
● **William Cullen Bryant** becomes one of America's leading poets with the publication of his first poem, "Thanatopsis." Bryant was an influential newspaper editor and played a leading role in public affairs for almost 50 years. He also wrote essays on poetry that are among the earliest examples of literary criticism in American literature.

1819
● **English poet John Keats** publishes "Ode on a Grecian Urn." Like many Romantic writers, Keats often wrote about the fleeting nature of beauty.

1821
● **Thomas de Quincey,** an essayist, writes *Confessions of an English Opium Eater,* an account of his own experience. His prose was as much musical as literary in its style and structure and anticipated such modern narrative techniques as stream-of-consciousness.

1818
● **Mary Shelley** publishes *Frankenstein,* a novel about a gentle monster that was shunned by society. Gothic fiction was a popular form with Romantic writers.

WASHINGTON IRVING.

1820   **1825**   **1829**

1820
● **Washington Irving** publishes *The Sketch Book.* The rural settings of stories like "Rip Van Winkle" and "The Legend of Sleepy Hollow" puts his native country, the United States, on the map with literary critics across Europe.

Irving was one of the first American authors to win recognition in Europe as well as the United States. He became famous for his humorous stories and for his satirical essays, which poked fun at New York City's fashionable society. At various times, Irving also was a lawyer, a businessman, and a United States diplomat to England and Spain.

1820
● **Lyric poet Percy Bysshe Shelley,** Mary Shelley's husband, publishes *Prometheus Unbound,* a long poem that praises the power of the individual. (Individualism was highly valued by Romantic writers.) Shelley experimented with many literary styles and had a lasting influence on many later writers, particularly Robert Browning, Algernon Charles Swinburne, William Butler Yeats, George Bernard Shaw, and Thomas Hardy.

1823
● **James Fenimore Cooper** becomes the first successful American novelist with the publication of *The Pioneers,* the first of his Leatherstocking Tales. The adventures of Natty Bumppo, a hunter, explored the conflict of wilderness versus civilization, a popular theme in early American literature.

1824
● **Lord Byron,** the flamboyant front man of the Romantic movement in England, dies. He leaves his comic masterpiece, the epic poem *Don Juan,* unfinished.

1827
● **Alessandro Manzoni** writes *The Betrothed,* his only novel. A long historical story set in Lombardy during the 1600s, it set the standard for modern Italian prose.

1828
● **Noah Webster** publishes *An American Dictionary of the English Language* in two volumes.

1829
● **Honoré de Balzac** publishes the first novel in *The Human Comedy,* his series of nearly 100 works. He wanted to portray the private dramas of all aspects of life across France.

Legend
● American
● Canada
● Britain
● Europe
● World
Period Facts

American Transcendentalism, Romanticism's very serious little cousin, was a literary movement that developed in New England in the 1830s.

Transcendentalist writers—including Ralph Waldo Emerson, Henry David Thoreau, George Ripley, Margaret Fuller, and Bronson Alcott—shared some of the core values of Romantic writers in England and America. For instance, they all believed in the power of the individual. In general, though, the Transcendentalists wrote non-fiction essays that were more earnest than the flamboyant fiction of the Romantics.

Transcendentalism also has close ties to German thinkers like Immanuel Kant, who believed there were limits to what people can learn by observing the outside world.

In its day, some people considered Transcendentalism to be a threat to mainstream values. Other people just thought it was a joke. But the fullness of time has shown that the movement's legacy has been both lasting and positive, influencing the work of environmentalists and civil rights activists through the present day.

Edgar Allan Poe was the rock star of the American Romantic movement. His biography and body of work still have a strong hold on people's imaginations more than 150 years after his death.

His work was strongly influenced by Gothic novels, which were fashionable in Europe. Gothic novels featured exotic, gloomy settings and mysterious or supernatural happenings. Poe adapted these elements in his short

---

1830   **1840**

1830
● **Stendhal,** a French novelist, writes *The Red and the Black*, a powerful psychological portrait of a social outsider. Ambitious, romantic, and sensitive, its hero, Julien, heralded a new type of fictional hero.

In his writings, Stendhal was concerned basically with the search for happiness, which he believed could be achieved by the exercise of physical energy and will. Elements of realism and romanticism can be found in his work.

1830
● **Victor Hugo's** play *Hernani* announces the end of classical restraints on French drama. It also establishes him as the leader of the French Romantic movement.

1837
● **Victoria** becomes queen of the United Kingdom. Her 63-year reign will see the expansion of the U.K.'s colonial empire abroad as well as industrial expansion at home.

1837
● **Alexander Pushkin,** widely considered the father of Russian literature, is mortally wounded in a duel. Pushkin wrote in a wide variety of poetic and prose styles. He first achieved fame for long, narrative poems similar to those of the English poet Lord Byron, but he was also a master of lyric poetry and wrote plays in verse. In the late 1820s, Pushkin turned to prose and produced a series of outstanding short stories, novellas, and novels. He was also a brilliant literary critic, letter writer, and historian. In addition to his unparalleled influence on Russian literature, Pushkin's works provided subjects and inspiration for Russia's leading artists, composers, and choreographers.

1841
● **Edgar Allan Poe** publishes the first modern detective story, "The Murders in the Rue Morgue." His haunting poems and stories reflect his belief that works of literature should focus on a single effect or emotion.

1841
● **Ralph Waldo Emerson** publishes his essay *Self-Reliance*. His celebration of individuality (and rejection of conformity) is the cornerstone of Transcendentalist thought.

Emerson was the Transcendentalist movement's informal leader. His 1836 book *Nature* set its tone. (The other landmark text of the Transcendentalist movement was Henry David Thoreau's *Walden*, which was published in 1854.) Emerson's prose style was simple and straightforward. He urged people to think for themselves, stressing self-reliance, intuition, and independence. He also believed in a strong connection between truth and nature.

1842
● **In Russia, Nikolai Gogol** publishes the first part of *Dead Souls*, a novel about a swindler who cheats the government using the name of dead serfs, and "The Overcoat," his best-known short story.

Legend
● American
● Canada
● Britain
● Europe
● World
Period Facts

Edgar Allan Poe

stories, filling his tales with decaying castles, forbidden passions, and insane criminals. Unlike most American writers at the time, he preferred to set his stories in faraway lands instead of stateside locations.

While that all sounds very serious, Poe seemed to have a sense of humor. His nickname for the nature-loving Transcendentalists, a group of writers he strongly disliked, was "Frogpondians." And while most of Poe's work was filled with deranged characters doing horrible things, many critics detect a tone of amused distance in even his most melodramatic work.

1855
● **Walt Whitman** publishes *Leaves of Grass* with his own money. His use of charged free verse in sprawling poems such as "Song of Myself" earned him his reputation as one of the masters of lyric poetry.

1856
● **Charles Sangster** celebrates the beauty of the Canadian landscape in his poem "The St. Lawrence and the Saguenay."

1845   **1850**   **1855**

1845
● **Henry Wadsworth Longfellow,** the most beloved American poet of his time, brought the poetry of Europe to American readers with his anthology, *The Poets and Poetry of Europe.*

1845
● **Frederick Douglass** publishes his autobiography, the first of three. Born a slave, Douglass would become one of the most influential Americans of the 19th century. (See pages 114–115.)

1847
● **Henry David Thoreau** ends his 2-year residency in a cabin he built at Walden Pond. He recorded his retreat from consumer society in journals, which were published as *Walden* in 1854.

1850
● **Nathaniel Hawthorne** publishes *The Scarlet Letter*, a dark novel about sin and redemption set in Puritan times.

1851
● **Herman Melville** publishes *Moby-Dick,* a maritime adventure based on the author's 2-year voyage on a whaling ship. Captain Ahab's wild obsession with the great white whale embodied the Romantic movement's dark and stormy sensibility.

1852
● **Abolitionist Harriet Beecher Stowe** publishes her antislavery novel *Uncle Tom's Cabin.* Her account of an old black slave was so popular that many people believe it ushered in the Civil War.

1856
● **Gustave Flaubert** publishes *Madame Bovary* in France. The novel is known for its contrast of a romantic subject matter with bleak notes of realism. It introduced a new element of realism into Western literature, making it a landmark in the history of fiction.

1857
● **French poet Charles Baudelaire** publishes *The Flowers of Evil.* The collection shocked readers with its focus on death, decay, and the rebellion against middle-class values. Baudelaire's bold poetry inaugurated a European literary revolution, and his art criticism and literary essays anticipate modern theories of painting and poetry.

Literature: 1858 to 1880

1859
● **Naturalist Charles Darwin** publishes his theories of evolution in *On the Origin of Species*, marking a general shift from Romanticism to Realism.

1863
● **Edward Everett Hale** writes "The Man Without a Country," a short story about a young Army officer. Hale's story caused such a sensation that many people failed to realize that it was fiction.

1865
● **Lewis Carroll**—the pen name of Charles Lutwidge Dodgson, a matematician—writes *Alice's Adventures in Wonderland*.

1858   **1865**

1860
● **Charles Dickens** begins publishing *Great Expectations*. (Most of his novels were published in serial form.) Dickens was a keen observer of life and had a great understanding of humanity, especially of young people. He sympathized with the poor and helpless, and mocked and criticized the selfish, the greedy, and the cruel.

1861
● **The U.S. Civil War** begins when Confederate troops fire on Fort Sumter, a U.S. military post in Charleston, South Carolina. (See pages 118–131.)

1864
● **John Greenleaf Whittier** publishes "Barbara Frietchie," a poem. His best-known poems fall into two groups—those attacking slavery, and those praising the charms of New England country life.

1864
● **Fyodor Dostoevsky** writes *Notes from the Underground*. The underlying theme in his books is the struggle between good and evil for dominance of the human soul. Dostoevsky attempts to resolve this struggle by leading his characters to salvation through purifying suffering.

1866
● **Dostoevsky** writes *Crime and Punishment*, a novel about redemption through suffering.

1867
● **Matthew Arnold,** the most important literary critic of his time, publishes his poem "Dover Beach." It voiced the anxieties people felt about the industrial, political, and social upheaval that characterized Victorian England.

1867
● **Henrik Ibsen,** a Norweigan playwright who is recognized as the father of modern drama, writes *Peer Gynt*. Over the course of his career, Ibsen would write 26 plays with complex characters, lifelike dialogue, believable social and psychological motivation, and stories that addressed important issues.

Legend
● American
● Canada
● Britain
● Europe
● World
[Period Facts]

1862
● **Ivan Turgenev** writes *Fathers and Sons*, a novel that depicts Russian society on the eve of emancipation of the serfs. He was the first Russian writer to achieve substantial recognition in the West.

Charles Dickens

1873

● **French poet Arthur Rimbaud** publishes *A Season in Hell*. In this tortured, allegorical autobiography, the writer celebrates himself as an outcast. Rimbaud wrote his major verse between the ages of 15 and 20. He then abandoned his literary career and became a trader in what is now Ethiopia.

1870

● **Jules Verne,** a French novelist, writes *Twenty Thousand Leagues Under the Sea*. Verne wrote some of the first science-fiction stories.

1868   1875

1869

● **American novelist Louisa May Alcott** publishes the second part of *Little Women*, a loosely autobiographical story that traces the lives of four sisters. G. K. Chesterton later wrote that Alcott "anticipated realism by 20 or 30 years." Alcott also worked to gain voting rights for women and was active in the temperance movement.

1872

● **George Eliot** finishes publishing her serialized novel *Middlemarch: A Study of Provincial Life*. It explores the moral and social problems surrounding life in the English countryside.

1875

● **Leo Tolstoy** begins publishing *Anna Karenina*. The novel explores broad social, moral, and philosophical issues of Russia and its aristocracy in the 1870s. These issues include the hypocritical attitude of the upper class toward adultery and the role of religious faith in a person's life.

1880

● **French writer Émile Zola** publishes *Nana*, a novel that's part of his long series of novels, *The Rougon-Macquart*. He made Naturalism the leading form of literature in France in the late 1800s.

1872

● **German philosopher Friedrich Nietzsche** writes *The Birth of Tragedy*. It presented a new theory of the origins of classical Greek culture. His work would deeply influence many philosophers, artists, and psychologists of the 1900s.

● 1875

Writer and editor William Ernest Henley publishes *Book of Verses*, a collection of poetry that contains his popular poem "Invictus." It was written while he was in a tuberculosis hospital.

1868

● **Robert Browning** starts publishing his long poem, *The Ring and the Book*, in four installments. The 12 books, each spoken by a different narrator involved in a murder trial in 17th-century Italy, epitomize his dramatic monologue style.

Literature: 1880 to 1900

Walt Whitman was a real people person. He was fond of crowds and he often rode on stagecoaches and ferries just to talk with people. He loved life in all its variety and thrived on the strong connection he felt that all living things share. He celebrated difference and the power of the individual, but he also believed in an essential spirit that binds everyone together. Many of his poems explore the push and pull between those two forces.

Whitman expressed American values like diversity and democracy in long lyric lines that sounded like singing. He wrote in free verse, a style of poetry that doesn't follow a particular meter or rhyme scheme. Many of his poems sound like rhythmic lists.

"Song of Myself," the longest poem in *Leaves of Grass*, is widely considered Whitman's best work. It described spirituality as a force grounded in the earth, the body, and day-to-day life, a viewpoint that was very different from most organized religions' focus on the unseen world.

The other major force in American poetry in the 19th century was Emily Dickinson. On the surface, she was the polar opposite of her contemporary, Walt Whitman.

1881   **1885**

1881
● **Joel Chandler Harris** begins to publish his Uncle Remus stories. The tales, which are reworkings of authentic African folk tales, offer evidence of the extensive African culture brought to the New World by slaves.

1882
● **Walt Whitman** writes a book of essays, *Specimen Days*.

E. W. Kemble
·1884·

1885
● **William Dean Howells** writes *The Rise of Silas Lapham*. Howells played an important part in the rise of the Realism movement in the U.S., discouraging artificial sentimentality and romanticism in American fiction.

1881
● **Robert Louis Stevenson** amuses his stepson, Lloyd Osbourne, with a little tale about pirates and the buried treasure of Captain Kidd. The story grew into *Treasure Island*, which was published as a book in 1883. Stevenson fought illness constantly, writing many of his best books from a sickbed.

1884
● **Mark Twain** publishes *The Adventures of Huckleberry Finn*, a novel that describes the adventures of two runaways—the boy Huck Finn and the black slave Jim. Twain contrasted the natural life on the river—where a white boy and a black man can become friends—with the hypocrisy, moral decay, and corruption of society along the shore. Through his adventures and observations, Huck learns about the value and dignity of every human being.

1886
● **Emily Dickinson** dies.

Legend
● American
● Canada
● Britain
● Europe
● World
Period Facts

Where Whitman sought the company of others, Dickinson kept to herself. For most of her life, she limited her social circle to only close family members, shunning the outside world in favor of the life of the mind. This solitude gave her plenty of time to work—she wrote more than 1,700 poems—but only 11 of them were printed during her lifetime.

Dickinson's verse is terse where Whitman's sprawls, yet their subjects were largely the same. They both wrote about spirituality, immortality, and nature. If you look closely, Dickinson shared Whitman's spirit of openness and his bright eye for wonder. Her controlled meters and prim rhymes are punctuated by little surprises on almost every line. Her unconventional use of Capital Letters and dashes makes even her most straightforward poems seem a little bit slippery and sly.

1890 — **1895**

1891
● **Oscar Wilde** writes *The Picture of Dorian Gray*, his only novel. It describes a man whose portrait ages and grows ugly as a reflection of his moral corruption while his actual appearance remains the same. The book seems to show the destructive side of a devotion to pleasure and beauty similar to Wilde's own. Wilde preached the importance of style in both life and art, and he attacked Victorian narrow-mindedness and complacency.

1893
● **Sir Arthur Conan Doyle** writes a story in which Sherlock Holmes, the world's best-known detective, is killed. Readers forced Doyle to bring Holmes back to life in another story. To his admirers, Holmes in his lodgings at 221-B Baker Street, London, was as real as any contemporary celebrity. Doyle may have been the highest paid short-story writer of his time.

1894
● **Rudyard Kipling** writes *The Jungle Book*, a children's story that gained a wide international audience. Kipling is best known for his stories about India during the late 1800s, when India was a British colony. In 1907, he became the first English writer to receive the Nobel Prize in Literature.

1895
● **Stephen Crane** writes *The Red Badge of Courage*. It is one of the first books to treat battle realistically rather than as a theater for displays of gallantry; Crane, however, had never been in a war. He pioneered psychological realism, often exploring the thoughts of fictional characters facing death.

1896
● **A. E. Housman** writes *A Shropshire Lad*, a cycle of poems. Their tone is overwhelmingly nostalgic and elegiac; they deal with the passing of youth, and the transience of love and glory. Housman's outlook on life was pessimistic, and his poems characteristically express the fleeting quality of love and beauty.

1897
● **French playwright Edmond Rostand** writes *Cyrano de Bergerac*. Rostand wrote Romantic plays in verse during a period when most dramatists preferred a style known as Naturalism.

1898
● **H. G. Wells** writes *The War of the Worlds*, a science fiction novel. It simulates the horror of a Martian invasion that fails only because the invaders can't tolerate Earth's bacteria. A radio version in 1938 by Orson Welles and the Mercury Theatre Players caused a great panic among listeners who thought the play was an actual news broadcast.

Literature: 1900 to 1915

During the early 1900s, particularly in the 1920s, African-American literature began to flourish in Harlem, a district of New York City. This movement became known as the Harlem Renaissance. (See also page 170.)

The movement was not organized in any strict sense, but the writers, artists, and performers who contributed to it shared a pride in their cultural traditions and heritage as African Americans.

Major writers of the Harlem Renaissance included Sterling A. Brown, Countee Cullen, Jessie Redmon Fauset, and Langston Hughes. Other important writers were Zora Neale Hurston, James Weldon Johnson, Alain Locke, Claude McKay, and Jean Toomer.

Zora Neale Hurston

1900

1900
● **Joseph Conrad** publishes *Lord Jim*, a novel about a young English seaman who impulsively abandons his sinking ship. Conrad, a captain in the British Merchant Navy, used his own voyages as the basis for some of his best-known novels.

1900
● **American Theodore Dreiser** publishes *Sister Carrie*, a novel based on the experiences of one of his sisters. Dreiser is one of the most important writers in the Naturalism movement, a pessimistic take on Realism.

1900
● **Sigmund Freud** publishes *The Interpretation of Dreams*. He showed the crucial importance of unconscious thinking to all human thought and activity. Critics often analyze art and literature in Freudian terms.

1901
● **Anton Chekhov,** the Russian playwright and short-story writer, publishes his play *The Three Sisters*. Chekhov's works showed the stagnant, helpless quality of Russian society, especially the rural landowners, in the late 1800s.

1901
● **Booker T. Washington,** the most influential black leader and educator of his time in the U.S., describes his rise from slavery to national prominence in his autobiography, *Up from Slavery*. The son of a slave and a white man, Washington stressed the importance of better education and better jobs for blacks.

Naturalism began as a movement of the late 19th century that adapted the theories of science and the objectivity of the scientific method to literature and art. The naturalistic novel was often a case history in which the character's heredity and environment, rather than his own will, determined his fate. In exploring the effects of environment on personality, the naturalists often chose extreme environments, such as slums or the underworld, and thus introduced new areas of subject matter to fiction.

1902
● **Joseph Conrad** publishes *Heart of Darkness*, a novella that would become one of the most important works of the 20th century.

1902
● *The Lower Depths,* a play by Russian writer Maxim Gorki, is performed. Gorki vividly portrayed the poverty of peasants and workers, as well as the decay and narrow-mindedness of the middle class before the Communist Revolution of 1917.

1903
● **Henry James** publishes his novel *The Ambassadors*, which explores the contrast between European and American values. James was known for writing about characters of great psychological complexity.

1903
● **Jack London** publishes *The Call of the Wild*. London was fascinated with an idea called environmental determinism, which states that the world shapes us in ways we are powerless to resist. He also believed in survival of the fittest.

1907
● **John Millington Synge,** an Irish dramatist, writes *The Playboy of the Western World*. His plays, which portrayed the rugged life of Irish peasants in the 19th century, were written in poetic language based on folk speech.

1911
● **Edith Wharton** publishes *Ethan Frome*, a short novel sketching cramped and shattered love in New England.

1914
● **The assassination of Franz Ferdinand** sparks World War I. (See pages 534–539.)

1910
● **Colette,** the French writer, publishes *Vagabond*. She is known for her insights into women's struggles for independence and identity.

1913
● **D. H. Lawrence** publishes *Sons and Lovers*, an autobiographical novel. Like most of Lawrence's other works, it criticizes social attitudes that he believed were filled with hypocrisy and self-deception.

1904
● **Chekhov's** *The Cherry Orchard* premieres in Moscow.

1905 ——————————————————————————— **1915**

1905
● **American writer O. Henry** publishes *The Gift of the Magi*. In most of his nearly 300 works of fiction, O. Henry showed his mastery of mechanical plots that build to sharp, unexpected endings.

1908
● ***The Ghost Sonata,*** a play by Swedish author August Strindberg, is first presented. Strindberg, one of the most influential dramatists of his time, was hugely influential, second only to Norwegian playwright Henrik Ibsen in the development of modern drama.

1912
● ***Edna St. Vincent Millay,*** at the age of 19, writes "Renascence," a poem about a personal religious experience. She wrote about love and death, about the self and the universe, and about the feelings of rebellious youth, combining sentimentality with wit and sophistication.

1915
● ***Poetry* magazine** publishes T. S. Eliot's "The Love Song of J. Alfred Prufrock." The poem is an ironic commentary on the crippling power of social convention and the unheroic quality of modern man.

1905
● **Edith Wharton** writes *The House of Mirth,* a savage look at upper-crust New York society and what it does to the heroine, Lily Bart. Wharton, herself a product of that society, couched her biting criticisms in the polite form of a novel of manners.

1908
● **G. K. Chesterston** writes *The Man Who Was Thursday*.

1908
● **Lucy Maud Montgomery** publishes *Anne of Green Gables*, one of the most beloved Canadian novels.

1912
● **German writer Thomas Mann** publishes *Death in Venice*, a novella. Mann's intellectual scope, keen psychological insight, and critical awareness of cultural and political conditions made him one of the foremost humanistic writers of his time.

1915
● **Edgar Lee Masters** publishes *Spoon River Anthology*, a collection of poetry. Masters's work consists of more than 200 short poems spoken by a former resident of the village, now dead and buried in the Spoon River cemetery. The work was part of a movement to debunk the myth of life in rural and small-town America.

Legend
● American
● Canada
● Britain
● Europe
● World
Period Facts

Literature: 1915 to 1928

1916
● **James Joyce** writes *A Portrait of the Artist as a Young Man*, a largely autobiographical novel in which Joyce appears as the character Stephen Dedalus. In tracing Stephen's growth to young manhood, Joyce mixed conventional realist prose with passages using techniques known as interior monologue and stream-of-consciousness. These techniques give the reader the illusion of following the character's thoughts.

1919
● **H. L. Mencken,** an American journalist, critic, and editor, publishes *The American Language*. In it, he examined the development of the English language in America, praising the acceptance of new words and forms of expression as a reflection of the American lifestyle.

1922
● **T. S. Eliot** publishes his poem, *The Waste Land*, which became one of the major works in modern English poetry. Its theme explores a culture in distress, presented in a series of disjointed images and scenes drawn from modern daily life as well as ancient, obscure fertility rituals. While this long, complex poem includes many obscure literary references, many in other languages, its main direction is clear. It contrasts the spiritual bankruptcy Eliot saw in modern, post–World War I Europe with the values and unity of the past.

1916   **1920**

1917
● **Luigi Pirandello,** an Italian dramatist, writes *Right You Are (If You Think You Are)*. Pirandello, who is known for his philosophic plays, claimed we assume numerous roles or masks in our daily lives, none of them our true self.

1919
● **Sherwood Anderson** publishes a collection of poetic short stories called *Winesburg, Ohio*. Anderson was a major influence on the generation of American writers who came after him, including Ernest Hemingway, F. Scott Fitzgerald, and William Faulkner.

1922
● **James Joyce** publishes *Ulysses*, a novel that takes place in Dublin in one day. The book would be banned in the United States until 1933.

1918
● **Willa Cather,** an American novelist, writes *My Antonia*. Her writing expressed a deep love of the land and a strong distaste for the materialism and conformity she saw in modern life.

1920
● **F. Scott Fitzgerald** writes his first novel, *This Side of Paradise*. It brought him sensational fame and made him the spokesman for the Jazz Age generation.

1923
● **e. e. cummings** publishes his first book of poems, *Tulips and Chimneys*. He is especially known for violating the rules of composition, rejecting punctuation and capitalization, distorting syntax, and experimenting with typography.

1920
● **Sinclair Lewis** publishes *Main Street*, a satirical novel about small-town life. He went on to become the first American author to win the Nobel Prize in Literature.

1923
● **Robert Frost,** the most popular American poet of his time, writes "Stopping by Woods on a Snowy Evening." His poetry is noted for its plain language, conventional poetic forms, and graceful style. He was deeply influenced by classical poets, especially Horace.

Legend
● American
● Canada
● Britain
● Europe
● World
Period Facts

1924
- **Pablo Neruda,** a Chilean poet, gains recognition with the lyrical and romantic *Twenty Poems of Love and One Desperate Song*.

1924
- **Billy Budd,** a novella by Herman Melville, is published more than 30 years after it was written.

1925
- **Virginia Woolf** publishes *Mrs. Dalloway*. Woolf was a leading figure in the literary movement called Modernism. Woolf used a literary technique called stream-of-consciousness to reveal the inner lives of her characters and to criticize the social system of the day.

- **The Jazz Age,** also known as the Roaring Twenties, was the period of the 1920s in the United States. It was a time of rapid economic growth, rising prosperity, and far-reaching social changes for the nation.

1927
- **German author Hermann Hesse** publishes his novel *Steppenwolf*. Hesse's view of life was influenced by the German romantic writers and the Hindu philosophy of India. His novels concern the spiritual loneliness of people in a mechanized urban society, the conflict between intellect and sensuality, and the problems of society's outsiders.

1925

1928

1924
- **British writer E. M. Forster** writes *Passage to India*. Set in colonial India, it explores the enormous gulf of misunderstanding that exists between the Indians and their British rulers.

1925
- **Theodore Dreiser** writes *An American Tragedy*, a novel based on an actual murder case.

1925
- **F. Scott Fitzgerald's** greatest novel, *The Great Gatsby*, is published. Set in New York, it is an exposure of the boredom and spiritual bankruptcy of the Jazz Age and of the thoughtless cruelty of great wealth, false glamour, moral emptiness, futility, and boredom.

1926
- **Irish playwright Sean O'Casey** publishes *The Plough and the Stars*, which portrays some quarrelsome, gossiping, heavy-drinking occupants of a Dublin tenement. His plays deal with the violence in Ireland during and after its fight for independence from England. O'Casey's plays are full of colorful characters and speech and are written in a vivid, realistic style.

1927
- **Virginia Woolf** publishes *To the Lighthouse*, her most famous novel. It shows the fragility of human relationships and the collapse of social values. Some readers believe the portrait of Mr. Ramsay in this novel resembles Woolf's father, the critic Leslie Stephen.

- **The Bloomsbury Group** was a group of talented English intellectuals who began meeting in 1906, in the Bloomsbury district of London, to discuss philosophy and the arts. Among others, the group included Virginia Woolf; her husband, writer Leonard Woolf; economist John Maynard Keynes; biographer Lytton Strachey; artist Vanessa Bell; art critic Clive Bell; novelist E. M. Forster; painter Duncan Grant; and art critic/painter Roger Fry.

1928
- **D. H. Lawrence** writes *Lady Chatterley's Lover*. His frank discussion of sexual passion shocked many readers, and the work was banned in the U.S. until 1959.

1929
● **Stephen Vincent Benét** writes *John Brown's Body*, a modern epic poem. This book-length narrative of the Civil War wins him the Pulitzer Prize.

1929
The stock market crash marks the beginning of the Great Depression.

1929
● **Ernest Hemingway** writes *A Farewell to Arms*. Hemingway's style, which has been widely imitated, used a plain, forceful prose style characterized by simple sentences and few adjectives or adverbs. He wrote crisp, accurate dialogue and exact descriptions of places and things.

1932
● **Aldous Huxley** writes *Brave New World*. It reflects Huxley's concern over the impact of science and technology on society.

1932
● **James T. Farrell** writes the first of his *Studs Lonigan* trilogy. They explore the impact of urban industrial life on a boy growing up in a poor Chicago neighborhood.

1929   **1930**   **1933**

1929
● **Erich Maria Remarque,** a German-American author, writes *All Quiet on the Western Front*. This antiwar story relates the shattering experiences of a group of German soldiers in World War I. It shocked the world because it dealt with the everyday horrors in the trenches in a cool, matter-of-fact style.

1929
● **Thomas Wolfe** publishes his autobiographical novel, *Look Homeward, Angel*. Wolfe claimed that all great art was necessarily autobiographical, so the story of his childhood and youth assumes a symbolic significance in his novels.

1929
● **William Faulkner** publishes *The Sound and the Fury*, a novel that recounts the last stages in the decline of one proud Southern family, the Compsons. It is told in an involved fashion that skips back and forth in time through the complex interior monologues of the three Compson brothers. Faulkner's work is characterized by a remarkable range of technique, theme, and tone.

1930
● **Hart Crane** publishes *The Bridge*, his long poem. The mystical work explores modern American consciousness through images of the subway, the airplane, and most importantly, the Brooklyn Bridge. Historical and legendary characters such as Rip Van Winkle, Emily Dickinson, and Walt Whitman are united in this effort to understand a national, democratic spirit.

1930
● **Dashiell Hammet** publishes his classic detective novel, *The Maltese Falcon*. The work was influential in removing the mystery story from the genteel country house to a realistic underworld setting.

1931
● **Pearl Buck** writes *The Good Earth*. Based on the author's observations during nearly 40 years of study of China, this story of a Chinese peasant family's struggles for survival became the most famous of the author's many works on that country.

1933
● **Nathanael West,** an American novelist noted for a brilliant but bitter view of modern American life, writes *Miss Lonelyhearts*.

1933
● **Franklin D. Roosevelt** becomes president of the U.S. and begins to implement the New Deal. (See also pages 178–181.)

1933
● **Spanish poet and playwright Federico García Lorca** writes *Blood Wedding*, a rural tragedy. His plays are filled with violent passion and poetic symbolism.

1933
● **Gertrude Stein** writes *The Autobiography of Alice B. Toklas*. She introduced a unique style of writing that influenced writers such as Sherwood Anderson and Ernest Hemingway.

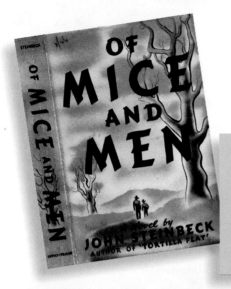

1937
● **John Steinbeck** publishes *Of Mice and Men*. The story portrays the friendship between Lennie Small and George Milton, two migrant workers in California during the Great Depression.

1939
World War II begins when Nazi Germany invades Poland. (See pages 552–563.)

1939
● **Dorothy Parker,** an American poet and short-story writer, publishes *Here Lies*, a collection of stories. She also won fame for her witty conversation and literary criticism.

1934   **1936**   **1939**

1934
● **Dylan Thomas** publishes his first book, *Eighteen Poems*. The volume bewildered and fascinated readers with its extraordinary verbal and musical energy and with its exploration of emotional extremes.

1934
● **F. Scott Fitzgerald** writes *Tender Is the Night*, a novel about the marriage of a young psychiatrist, Dick Diver, to one of his mental patients, Nicole. The book failed because readers during the Great Depression were not interested in Jazz Age frivolity.

1934
● **Evelyn Waugh** writes *A Handful of Dust*, a biting commentary on social mores among England's upper classes.

1936
● **Stephen Vincent Benét** writes "The Devil and Daniel Webster," a short story that combines a folktale with New England history. Benét was very interested in American history and folklore.

1938
● **Thornton Wilder** writes *Our Town*, a Pulitzer Prize–winning play that deals with the cycle of life in a small New England town.

1938
● **Marjorie Kinnan Rawlings** writes *The Yearling*. Rawlings often wrote about the conflict between people and nature in the Florida backwoods.

1938
● **Jean-Paul Sartre,** a French philosopher, publishes his first novel, *Nausea*. The bare existence of things fascinated and horrified Sartre, because there seems to be no reason why anything should exist.

1939
● **Steinbeck** writes *The Grapes of Wrath*. He effectively demonstrates how the struggles of one family mirror the hardships of the entire nation during the Great Depression.

1939
● **James Joyce** publishes *Finnegans Wake*. Joyce portrayed one family and at the same time all families, everywhere, at all times in history. In the story, Dublin symbolizes all cities. Joyce crammed the book with topical and historical names, events, myths, songs, jokes, and gossip. His goal was to make all people, places, things, and times repeat and resemble each other.

Legend
● American
● Canada
● Britain
● Europe
● World
Period Facts

Literature: 1940 to 1955

1948
● *Cry, the Beloved Country* is published by South African writer Alan Paton, a South African author, social critic, and educator who wrote about the tragic consequences of rigid racial segregation.

1946
● **Eugene O'Neill** writes *The Iceman Cometh*.

1940
● **Richard Wright** publishes *Native Son*. The powerful, realistic novel tells the story of Bigger Thomas, a young man living in the Chicago ghetto. It was the first work of African-American prose fiction to become a best-seller with a white audience.

1941
● **James Agee** writes *Let Us Now Praise Famous Men*, a landmark in literary journalism. The work grew out of a routine magazine assignment that required Agee to live for a time among white sharecroppers of Alabama during the Depression.

1947
● **Yasunari Kawabata** writes *Snow Country*. He will become the first Japanese author to win the Nobel Prize in Literature.

1948
● **Shirley Jackson** writes "The Lottery," a tale of psychological horror. The story is about gruesome human sacrifice in a seemingly ordinary small American town.

1940	1945	1948

1940
● **Graham Greene** writes *The Power and the Glory*. Greene's serious novels are set in varied and remote places and deal with troubled individuals. Many of his characters are mentally disturbed, suffering a religious crisis, or engaged in criminal activities. To Greene, these people are both victims and heroes.

1942
● **Albert Camus** writes *The Stranger*. Camus was concerned with the freedom and responsibility of the individual, the alienation of the individual from society, and the difficulty of facing life without the comfort of believing in God or in absolute moral standards.

1947
● **Tennessee Williams** writes *A Streetcar Named Desire*. His dramas portray the loneliness and isolation of life.

1947
● **W. H. Auden** writes *The Age of Anxiety*, a book-length poem.

1948
● **Norman Mailer** writes *The Naked and the Dead*. In his novels and essays, Mailer analyzed the myths and unconscious impulses that underlie human behavior. He often stressed sex and violence, but he used these elements for artistic purposes and not merely to shock.

1940
● **Carson McCullers** writes *The Heart Is a Lonely Hunter*. Known for her stories of small-town life in the South, many of her characters are lonely, disappointed people.

1944
● **Jorge Luis Borges** writes *Ficciones*, a collection of short pieces. The term *ficcion*, coined by the author, represents a new genre in which the story is disguised as essay. Historical and imaginary characters, their works, and events are discussed in such a way that the reader no longer knows what is historically verifiable. It's a metaphor for a universe in which we never know what is real and what we have imagined.

1948
● **German playwright Bertolt Brecht** writes *The Caucasian Chalk Circle*. Brecht believed that an audience's emotional involvement in the characters and action tends to cloud its grasp of the play's message, so he tried to shatter traditional stage illusions of reality by using special visual techniques and an unemotional acting style. His goal was to show that social forces determine human nature, and that the evils of capitalism brutalize the poor and make the rich corrupt.

1952
● **Samuel Beckett** publishes *Waiting for Godot*, a classic of the Theater of the Absurd. Beckett's drama created great controversy when it first opened because the work departed so radically from traditional drama. Many spectators objected that the play made no sense. It lacked physical action, and the plot did not seem to tie the events together. The mixture of philosophy, Biblical references, broad comedy, and nonsense dialogue also confused many people.

1949
● **Arthur Miller's** *Death of a Salesman* opens on Broadway. Miller describes the play as "the tragedy of a man who gave his life, or sold it" while pursuing the American dream. The play typifies Miller's belief that the common man is the modern tragic hero.

1954
● **William Golding** writes *Lord of the Flies*, a novel in which a group of English schoolboys stranded on an island seemingly reenact the Fall of Man. The story implies that civilization is merely a covering for people's natural violence.

1950

1955

1951
● **J. D. Salinger** writes *Catcher in the Rye*, a novel about a teenager's disenchantment with a hostile adult world. In that book and much of the fiction that followed, Salinger humorously and convincingly captured the speech, gestures, and feelings of the young.

1952
● **Ralph Ellison** writes *The Invisible Man*, which tells the story of a young black man's quest for identity and meaning. Ellison's novel is a complex work that integrates symbolism, African-American folklore, and references to music, myth, and classic literature.

1955
● **Vladimir Nabokov** writes *Lolita*. It was the first of his works in English to reach a wide popular audience. Nabokov's novels are noted for their complicated plots and the complex attitudes they express toward their subjects.

1951
● **Julio Cortázar** publishes his first book, a short-story collection called *Bestiary*. Cortázar was a leading figure in the Boom, a period in Latin American literature from the late 1950s to the early 1970s.

1955
● **Flannery O'Connor** publishes *A Good Man Is Hard to Find*, a collection of short stories. Her stories are filled with characters who are physically deformed or emotionally or spiritually disturbed. O'Connor was strongly influenced by her Southern heritage and her Roman Catholicism.

1953
● **Gwendolyn Brooks** writes *Maud Martha*. The novella, comprised of 34 short pieces, tells the growing-up story of a black girl in 1940s Chicago. It is Brooks's only prose work, the rest being well-known poetry.

Legend
● American
● Canada
● Britain
● Europe
● World
Period Facts

Literature: 1955 to 1965

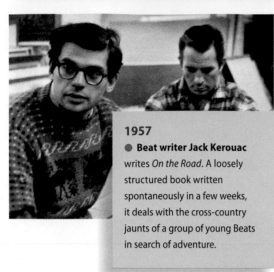

Allen Ginsberg, Jack Kerouac

1957
● **Beat writer Jack Kerouac** writes *On the Road*. A loosely structured book written spontaneously in a few weeks, it deals with the cross-country jaunts of a group of young Beats in search of adventure.

● **The Beat movement** refers to a set of literary, political, and social attitudes principally associated with certain American writers and artists during the 1950s. It was characterized by personal alienation and a contempt for convention. The literature of the movement celebrated stylistic freedom and improvisation. Its influences and themes included jazz, mystical Asian religions, drugs, and sexuality. Because the Beat movement advocated peace and civil rights, it helped set the stage for the radical protests of the 1960s.

1960
● **Yukio Mishima,** a Japanese novelist, playwright, and essayist, writes *Confessions of a Mask*, an autobiographical novel. He was one of Japan's most famous literary personalities and shocked the nation by committing ritual suicide in public view in Tokyo.

1960
● **Harper Lee** writes *To Kill a Mockingbird*.

1955   **1958**   **1959**   **1960**

1956
● **Allen Ginsberg** publishes *Howl and Other Poems*. "Howl" attacks the forces of conformity and mechanization that he believed destroyed the best minds of his generation. It ranks among the most significant expressions of the Beat movement of the 1950s.

1958
● **Brendan Behan** writes *The Hostage*, a play about a young English soldier held prisoner by the IRA. His colorful personality as well as his deep commitment to the ideals of a free Ireland helped make him one of the best-known Irish writers to emerge after the end of the Second World War.

1959
● **French playwright** Jean Anouilh writes *Becket*, a play that concerns the friendship and estrangement of the king of England and the archbishop of Canterbury. T. S. Eliot's *Murder in the Cathedral* tells the same story.

1960
● **Harold Pinter** writes *The Caretaker*, a play about the barriers to communication between humans in contemporary society. Pinter's dramas emphasize a sense of unspoken and sometimes unexplained tensions between the characters.

1959
● **Günter Grass** writes his first novel, *The Tin Drum*. Grass was a prominent member of "Group 47," an association of writers who helped restore substance and integrity to German literature after the Nazi period.

1956
● **John Osborne** writes *Look Back in Anger*, a play credited with revolutionizing modern English drama. It earned Osborne immediate fame and made him a leading spokesman for a group of young English writers labeled the "Angry Young Men," who identified themselves with the lower classes in English society and looked on the upper classes and national institutions with resentment and suspicion.

1958
● **Shelby Foote** publishes the first of three volumes in his epic history, *The Civil War: A Narrative*. Foote, also a novelist, told the story of the Civil War in minute detail, at times seemingly as though each campaign were its own novella.

1960
● **Polish-born author Isaac Bashevis Singer** writes *The Magician of Lublin*. Many of his works combine modern realism with Jewish folklore and fantasy.

1959
● **Isaac Asimov, Ray Bradbury, and Robert Heinlein** all publish collections of science fiction short stories: *Nine Tomorrows, A Medicine for Melancholy,* and *The Unpleasant Profession of Jonathan Hoag,* respectively.

Legend
● American
● Canada
● Britain
● Europe
● World
Period Facts

1961
● **Saul Bellow** writes *Herzog*, a novel about alienation in modern life.

1961
● **Edward Albee** writes *Who's Afraid of Virginia Woolf?*, a moving examination of the combination of cruelty and love in marriage. Albee often wrote about the need for human contact and the illusions his characters embrace to face the meaninglessness of existence.

1964
● **Frank O'Hara** publishes *Lunch Poems*. His poems read like casual records of urban life.

1963
● **Thomas Pynchon** publishes his first novel, *V.*

1965
● *Everything That Rises Must Converge* is published 1 year after author Flannery O'Connor's death.

1961

1963

1965

1961
● **V. S. Naipaul,** a West Indian–born writer, first gains recognition with his satirical novel *A House for Mr. Biswas*. Naipaul writes about many cultures and societies throughout the world, often exploring the theme of the clash of older traditions and practices with the raw aggressiveness of modern political life.

1963
● French dramatist **Eugène Ionesco** writes *A Stroll in the Air*. His unconventional plays often are filled with decaying or lifeless objects that grow until they suffocate the human characters.

1963
● **William Carlos Williams,** an American poet, dies. Williams wrote about American themes in the language of common speech. His poetry sought to discover the essence of everyday objects and experiences.

1963
● **President John F. Kennedy** is assassinated. (See pages 208–209.)

1965
● **Sylvia Plath's** poetry collection *Ariel* is published 2 years after her suicide. Her poetry and prose explored with humor the dark side of modern life.

1965
● **Truman Capote** writes *In Cold Blood*, a book that combines fact with fiction to tell about two drifters who murder a family in Kansas. Capote was a leading celebrity of his day, and his friendships with rich and famous people were widely reported.

1961
● **Joseph Heller** writes *Catch-22*, a dark comedic novel about World War II. The book satirizes the military and the ideals of war and is remarkable for its vivid comic characters and situations.

Literature: 1965 to 2005

1968
- **American Joan Didion** writes *Slouching Towards Bethlehem*, a collection of essays. Her style is characterized by a combination of social analysis and personal confession.

1973
- **Thomas Pynchon** writes *Gravity's Rainbow*, a huge novel that takes place in London at the end of World War II in 1945 and in postwar Germany. Pynchon is known for a dense style that makes extreme demands on the reader.

1980
- **John Kennedy Toole's** novel *Confederacy of Dunces* is published more than a decade after the author's death.

1986
- **Rita Dove** writes *Thomas and Beulah*. The collection is based on the lives of Dove's grandparents and tells the moving story of the couple's tragedies, struggles, and enduring love. The poems richly portray the history of African Americans who hoped to find a better life by migrating from the rural South to the urban North.

1967   **1975**   **1985**

1967
- **Gabriel García Márquez** writes *One Hundred Years of Solitude*. The novel has been interpreted as a symbolic history of Latin America told with mythical characters and places. It brought worldwide attention not only to its author, but also to the neglected literature of Latin America.

1967
- **Tom Stoppard** writes *Rosencrantz and Guildenstern Are Dead*. In this play, he used two minor characters from William Shakespeare's *Hamlet* to probe the meaninglessness he saw in human existence.

1969
- **Kurt Vonnegut** writes *Slaughterhouse-Five*. Although the tone of his fiction is often playful, he was a moralizing writer with a gloomy view of humanity.

1969
- **Philip Roth** writes *Portnoy's Complaint*. He's known for his frank, comic, and often satirical portraits of modern Jewish society and family life in the United States.

1970–1975
- **Canadian Robertson Davies** first gains fame for his Deptford trilogy—*Fifth Business* (1970), *The Manticore* (1972), and *World of Wonders* (1975).

1982
- **Alice Walker** writes *The Color Purple*, an epistolary novel. It tells about a Southern black woman who overcomes the pain of sexual and domestic abuse by forming strong bonds with other women.

1985
- **Canadian Margaret Atwood** writes *The Handmaid's Tale*, a dystopian novel about women who have been stripped of all their rights.

1985
- **Don DeLillo** writes *White Noise*, a novel about death and technology. DeLillo often interweaves historical facts with fictional characters in his writing. His themes include the excesses of consumption, mass culture, and politics in American society.

Legend
- American
- Canada
- Britain
- Europe
- World
- Period Facts

1987
● **Toni Morrison** writes *Beloved*. The novel tells the story of a former slave haunted by memories of her life in bondage and the baby she killed to save the child from slavery.

1989
● **Amy Tan** writes *The Joy Luck Club*. She's known for her novels dealing with the lives and concerns of Asian women in America.

1994
● **Japanese writer Haruki Murakami** publishes *The Wind-Up Bird Chronicle*.

1996
● **David Foster Wallace** writes *Infinite Jest*. He gained fame for his highly personal books that feature the energetic and complex use of language as well as an exuberant and offbeat sense of humor.

2002
● **Lydia Davis** writes *Samuel Johnson Is Indignant*.

2001
● **Jonathan Franzen** writes *The Corrections*. The story tells about two generations of the offbeat and troubled Lambert family—father Alfred, mother Enid, and their three adult children, Chip, Denise, and Gary.

1988

1990

2000

1988
● **Salman Rushdie** publishes *The Satanic Verses*, sparking international controversy. The novel plays upon the legend that Satan inserted certain verses into the revelation of the Koran, the sacred book of Islam. In 1989, Iran's spiritual leader, Ayatollah Ruhollah Khomeini, pronounced a *fatwa* (death sentence) on Rushdie. Fearing assassination, the writer went into hiding for several years.

1988
● **Ian McEwan** writes *Amsterdam*. McEwan's works often examine the psychological effects that an event has upon people and their relationships.

1990
● **Octavio Paz** became the first Mexican to win the Nobel Prize in Literature. Paz's works reflect a range of influences, including Aztec mythology, Marxism, Asian philosophy, surrealism, and symbolism.

1991
● **Michael Ondaatje** gains international acclaim with his novel *The English Patient*.

2000
● **Michael Chabon** writes *The Amazing Adventures of Kavalier and Clay*, a novel that describes the adventures of two Jewish cousins, an American named Sammy Klayman and a Czech named Josef Kavalier. Chabon has been praised for the way he blends styles, ranging from history and a longing for the past to science fiction, fantasy, and realism.

1999
● **J. M. Coetzee,** a South African writer, publishes *Disgrace*. Coetzee writes with brutal honesty about society's outcasts and outsiders, including those victimized by the former South African system of segregation called apartheid. Many of Coetzee's characters experience crises in their lives that mirror the larger social crises of the time and place where they live.

THE FIRST PERIOD

In Shakespeare's time, the English didn't care about keeping careful records about matters that didn't relate to the affairs of the Church or State. The information we have about Shakespeare's life has been culled from records that are few and incomplete by modern standards, including church registers and accounts of business dealings. By relating these records to what they know about English history, scholars have put together a fairly comprehensive account of his life. Still, gaps remain.

The Shakespeare Memorial Fountain rests in Leicester Square, the epicenter of London's West End theater district. ▶

Shakespeare's birthplace is located on Henley Street in Stratford-upon-Avon, Warwickshire. ▼

Shakespeare's Life

1564: William Shakespeare was born in the small market town of Stratford-upon-Avon, the third of eight children.

1569: Traveling companies of professional actors began performing in Stratford.

1573: He began attending the Stratford grammar school. Students spent around 9 hours a day studying mostly Latin. This might have been Shakespeare's first exposure to ancient Roman authors like Cicero, Ovid, Plautus, Seneca, and Vergil, who were major influences on his work later in life.

1582: Shakespeare received a license to marry Anne Hathaway, the daughter of a local farmer.

1583: Anne gave birth to the couple's first child, Susanna.

Play	Type	First Performed	First Published
The Comedy of Errors	Comedy	1589–1594	1623
Richard III	History	1592–1594	1597

1585: Anne gave birth to twins, Judith and Hamnet.

1585–1592: The so-called lost years. Scholars have proposed a number of theories about Shakespeare's activities during this time, but no one knows exactly what he was up to.

1592: Shakespeare arrived in London and began to work in the theater.

1593: Turning to poetry because of the frequently closed theaters, Shakespeare published *Venus and Adonis*, a volume of poetry that drew on the Ovid's *Metamorphoses*. It was so popular that it was reprinted at least 15 times during his life.

1594: Shakespeare became a shareholder in the Lord Chamberlain's Men, a theater company in London. His position as a shareholder helped him achieve a level of financial success unmatched by the dramatists of the age, many of whom lived in poverty.

1594: He published *The Rape of Lucrece*, another volume based on the works of Ovid. Despite the commercial success of these early publications, Shakespeare made no effort to make a career as a poet.

1596: Shakespeare's son, Hamnet, died.

1597: The playwright purchased New Place, one of Stratford's two largest townhouses.

1599: Shakespeare became one of six shareholders who signed The Globe Theatre's lease.

1603: Queen Elizabeth I died. She was succeeded by her cousin King James I, who actively supported the theater. He issued a royal license to Shakespeare and his fellow players that allowed the company to call itself The King's Men. In return, the actors regularly entertained the king at court.

1609: *Shakespeare's Sonnets*, a collection of more than 150 poems, was published. In the late 1500s, it was fashionable for English gentlemen authors to write sequences of sonnets.

1612: Shakespeare became widely known as England's most successful playwright.

1613: The writer bought a house in London.

1616: Shakespeare died.

Source Material	Plot	Notes
Menaechmi, a play by Plautus	The action in *The Comedy of Errors* takes place in the ancient Greek city of Ephesus. The plot deals with identical twin brothers, both named Antipholus. Each brother has a servant named Dromio, who also happen to be twin brothers. The twins of each set were separated as children, and neither twin knows where his brother is living. After a series of mistaken identities and comical mix-ups, the twin brothers are reunited.	*The Comedy of Errors* focuses on intrigue, broad humor, and physical comedy instead of characterization or fine poetry.
Partly based on Hall's *The Union of the Two Noble and Illustrious Families of Lancaster and York* (1548); Holinshed's *Chronicles* (1577)	The play deals with the end of the Wars of the Roses. It opens with the hunchbacked Richard, Duke of Gloucester, confiding his villainous plans to the audience. As King Edward IV lies on his deathbed, Richard plots a way to secure the throne for himself. To eliminate any competition, Richard has his brother, the Duke of Clarence, killed. When Edward dies, Richard sends the dead king's sons to the Tower of London, where they are executed. Shortly after seizing the throne, Richard's allies turn against him. Richard's army is defeated at the Battle of Bosworth Field.	Shakespeare's portrayal of Richard as a villain whose character is as twisted as his back was very popular in Tudor England. It gave Richard a reputation for evil that can't be wholly supported by historical fact. While Richard is thoroughly wicked, his soliloquies give his character depth and his frequent asides engage the audience.

1590–1591

The plays of William Shakespeare's first period tend to follow their sources more closely than the plots of Shakespeare's later works. Generally, the plots consist of a series of loosely related episodes, rather than a tightly integrated dramatic structure. Generally, the plays emphasize events more than the portrayal of character.

In his first period, Shakespeare's use of language indicates that he was still struggling to develop his own flexible poetic style. For example, his descriptive poetry in this period is more flowery than directly related to the development of the characters of the story. Speeches often use highly patterned schemes that involve word and sound repetitions.

The First Period

Play	Type	First Performed	First Published
The Taming of the Shrew	Comedy	1593	1623
King John	History	1594	1623
Titus Andronicus	Revenge tragedy	1594	1594
The Two Gentlemen of Verona	Comedy	1594	1623

Source Material	Plot	Notes
The Taming of the Shrew, unknown English playwright; *Supposes* (1566), a comedy by the English author George Gascoigne	This play dramatizes how Petruchio, an Italian gentleman, woos the beautiful but bad-tempered Katherine, whose biting tongue has discouraged other suitors. Petruchio marries her. Before and after the wedding, he systematically humiliates Katherine to cure her of her temper. After many comical clashes between the two, Petruchio's strategy succeeds and Katherine becomes an obedient wife. At this point, Petruchio reveals himself to be genuinely fond of Katherine.	*The Taming of the Shrew* is a broad and vigorous comedy that provides two outstanding roles in the characters of the battling lovers. The parts of Petruchio and Katherine have been a showcase for generations of gifted actors.
The Troublesome Reign of John, King of England (1591), a play by an unknown English author	The story concerns the efforts of England's King John to defend his throne against the claims of his older brother's son, Arthur, the young Duke of Brittany. John defeats and captures Arthur, who is supported by the king of France. When the young prince dies under suspicious circumstances, many of John's nobles abandon him and join an invading French force. The rebellious English lords only return to John when they learn that the French, if victorious, will execute their English supporters. A long war is avoided by the intervention of Pandulph, the papal representative, just as King John dies either from poison or illness.	Shakespeare focuses less on aesthetics in this work and chooses, rather, to retell the political events in a pragmatic tone. Though the play is not entirely historically accurate, it is based on some actual events in King John's reign. Philip Faulconbridge, the illegitimate son of Richard I, is arguably the moral center of the play. His witty comments on the action orient the audience's response to the play, which is deeply concerned with loyalty, allegiance, and legitimacy.
Possibly based in part on *The History of Titus Andronicus*, a story by an unknown English author	The action takes place in and around ancient Rome and involves a series of violent acts. The central conflict is between Tamora, the captured queen of the Goths, and Titus Andronicus, a Roman general. The exchange of insults and injuries reaches its climax at a feast in which Titus serves Tamora a pie containing the remains of her two sons.	In spite of the play's emphasis on spectacular violence, it does have moments of highly charged poetry. The most complex character is Aaron the Moor, Tamora's love interest and a self-declared villain in the mold of Richard III. Aaron's plotting drives much of the action, but when the child he has fathered with Tamora is threatened with death, he displays an unexpected warmth and humanity.
Diana (c. 1559) by Jorge de Montemayor; *The Book of the Governor* (1531) by Sir Thomas Elyot	The play is a witty comedy of love and friendship set in Italy. Two friends from Verona, Valentine and Proteus, meet in Milan. They soon become rivals for the love of Silvia, the daughter of the Duke of Milan. Valentine then tells his friend that he can have Silvia, but his generosity becomes unnecessary. Proteus learns that Julia, his former mistress, has followed him to Milan disguised as a page. Proteus realizes that he really loves Julia. He marries her at the end of the play, and Valentine marries Silvia.	Shakespeare introduced several features and devices that he later used so effectively in the great romantic comedies of his second period. For example, he included beautiful songs, such as "Who Is Silvia?"; scenes in a peaceful, idealized forest; and a young woman, disguised as a page, braving the dangers of the world.

1595-1600

The focus of Shakespeare's second period was historical drama and Elizabethan romantic comedy. Particularly in his histories and comedies of this period, Shakespeare demonstrated his genius for weaving various dramatic actions into a unified plot, rather than writing a series of loosely connected episodes. Throughout the second period, Shakespeare steadily developed the matchless gift for characterization that marks the great tragedies he produced in the early 1600s.

The Second Period

Play	Type	First Performed	First Published
A Midsummer Night's Dream	Comedy	1599	1600
Richard II	History	1595	1597
Love's Labour's Lost	Comedy	1596	1598

◄ **A Queen Loves a Donkey.** Shakespeare's plays are constantly being performed. This production of *A Midsummer Night's Dream,* with Dame Judi Dench as Titania, was staged in 2010.

Source Material	Plot	Notes
No chief sources	In an enchanted forest outside of Athens, two young men, Lysander and Demetrius, and two young women, Hermia and Helena, wander about together after they become lost. Lysander and Demetrius both love Hermia and ignore Helena, who loves Demetrius. Oberon, king of the fairies, orders the mischievous elf Puck to anoint Demetrius's eyes with magic drops that will make him love Helena. However, Puck mistakenly anoints Lysander's eyes, creating much comic confusion. Puck finally straightens out the mix-up. In a subplot, Oberon quarrels with Titania, his queen. He anoints Titania's eyes with the magic drops while she sleeps so that when she awakens, she will love the first living thing she sees. At this time, Nick Bottom, a weaver, and his comical friends are rehearsing a play. When Titania awakens, she sees Bottom and falls in love with him. Aided by her fairy attendants, Titania woos Bottom until Oberon takes pity on her and has Puck remove the spell.	Shakespeare wrote some of his most richly lyrical poetry for this play. He balanced the romantic fantasy with the rough humor of Bottom and his friends. The self-absorbed Bottom ranks as one of Shakespeare's finest comic figures. While the comedy has a serious side, it also makes fun of romantic love.
Holinshed's Chronicles	As the play begins, King Richard exiles his cousin Bolingbroke from England. Later, Richard seizes Bolingbroke's property. While Richard fights rebels in Ireland, Bolingbroke returns to England and demands his property. Richard hurries back to England to find his cousin leading a force of nobles who are unhappy with Richard's rule. Richard gives up his crown to Bolingbroke without a fight. Bolingbroke then orders that Richard be put in prison. After Bolingbroke is crowned Henry IV, the imprisoned Richard is killed by a knight who mistakenly believed that the new king wanted Richard murdered. At the end of the play, Henry vows to make a journey to the Holy Land to pay for Richard's death.	In *Richard II,* Shakespeare seriously explored for the first time the idea that a person's character determines his fate. The play is a study of a weak, self-centered man. Richard becomes so out of touch with reality that his only defense of his kingdom is the hope that his "master, God omnipotent, / Is mustering in his clouds on our behalf / Armies of pestilence." When he faces the certain loss of his crown, Richard compares himself to Christ, who "in twelve, / Found truth in all but one; I, in twelve thousand none."
No chief sources	King Ferdinand of Navarre and his friends, Berowne, Longaville, and Dumain, vow to live in seclusion without the company of women for 3 years to pursue philosophical study. But the princess of France unexpectedly arrives at the king's court with three female companions. The comedy centers on the efforts of the men to woo the women while pretending to keep their vow. At the play's end, the men propose to their visitors, who promise to give their answer in a year and a day.	This witty comedy has more references to events of the day than do any of Shakespeare's other plays. Many of these references have lost their meaning for modern audiences, which makes some passages difficult to understand. In addition, much of the language is elaborate and artificial. But Shakespeare included two simple songs—"When Daisies Pied and Violets Blue" and "When Icicles Hang by the Wall."

fyi! *In Shakespeare's time, most playwrights were freelancers who were paid a one-time fee for their plays. They usually worked for several companies. After 1594, Shakespeare maintained a relationship with a single company.*

Theater Companies

After arriving in London, Shakespeare began an association with one of the city's repertory theater companies. These companies consisted of a permanent cast of actors who presented a variety of plays week after week. The companies had aristocratic patrons, and the players were technically servants of the nobles who sponsored them. But the companies were commercial operations that depended on selling tickets to the general public for their income.

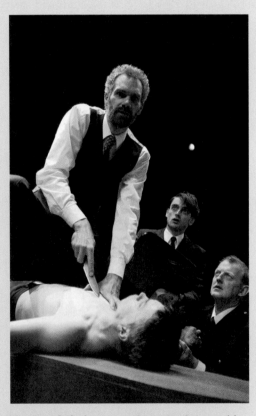

The Royal Shakespeare Company's ensemble actors perform in a production of *The Merchant of Venice*. This company, with stages in London and Shakespeare's birthplace, Stratford-upon-Avon, is perhaps the world's best-known theater company.

Play	Type	First Performed	First Published
Romeo and Juliet	Tragedy	1596	1597
The Merchant of Venice	Comedy	1597	1600
Henry IV (Parts I and II)	History	1597 (Part I) 1598 (Part II)	1598 (Part I) 1600 (Part II)

Source Material	Plot	Notes
The Tragicall Historye of Romeus and Juliet (1562), a poem by Author Brooke	*Romeo and Juliet* deals with two teenage lovers in Verona, Italy, who are caught in a bitter feud between their families, the Montagues and the Capulets. Romeo, a Montague, and his friends come uninvited to a masked ball given by the Capulets. At the ball, Romeo meets Juliet, a Capulet, and they fall in love. The next day, the couple are secretly married by Friar Laurence. Juliet's father, unaware that she is already married, tries to force her to marry a kinsman named Paris. To allow Juliet to escape from her father's demand, Friar Laurence gives Juliet a drug that puts her into a deathlike sleep for 42 hours. The friar sends a messenger to the exiled Romeo to tell him of the drug, but the messenger is delayed. Romeo hears that Juliet is dead and hurries to the tomb where she has been placed. There, he takes poison and dies by Juliet's side. Juliet awakens to find her husband dead and stabs herself. The discovery of the dead lovers convinces the two families that they must end their feud.	The popularity of *Romeo and Juliet* owes much to Shakespeare's sympathy for the young people in the play. Although the play does suggest that the boldness of young love is dangerous, Shakespeare does not present Romeo and Juliet as responsible for their fate. Instead, the play draws attention to the violence and aggressiveness that shapes the adult world. The success of the play also comes from effective characterizations and intensely lyrical poetry. Shakespeare's language shows signs of the simpler, more direct style he would use in his later tragedies.
A story in *Il Pecorone,* a collection of tales written circa 1378 by the Italian author Giovanni Fiorentino	Antonio, a merchant in Venice, Italy, borrows money from the Jewish moneylender Shylock to help his friend Bassanio. Antonio has promised Shylock a pound of his flesh if he does not repay the loan in 3 months. Three months later, when Antonio can't pay, Shylock demands the pound of flesh. Meanwhile, Bassanio has courted and married the beautiful and gifted heiress Portia. In court, disguised as a lawyer, she asks Shylock to reconsider. He remains firm. Portia then explains that he can, according to the contract, take one pound of flesh but not a drop of blood. If Shylock spills any blood, he will not only forfeit his own property but his life as well. Shylock drops his demand, and Antonio is saved.	In *The Merchant of Venice,* Shakespeare combined comic intrigue with a vivid portrait of hatred and greed. Although the play ends happily for everyone except Shylock and the melancholy Bassanio, it is not a light-hearted comedy. In Shakespeare's time, both the Church and the State considered lending money with a high interest rate a crime. Shylock was thus a natural object of scorn. On the surface, Shakespeare's view of him reflected the attitudes of the day. But the dramatist treated him with sympathy.
Two related histories: *Holinshed's Chronicles* and *The Famous Victories of Henry the Fifth* (1598), a play by an unknown English author	The two parts of *Henry IV* dramatize events that follow the murder of England's King Richard II. In Part I, the guilt-ridden Henry IV wants to go to the Holy Land to repent for Richard's death. But political unrest in England prevents him. At the same time, Prince Hal, his son, leads an apparently irresponsible life with his brawling friends, led by the fat, jolly knight Sir John Falstaff. The king quarrels with Henry Percy, known as Hotspur, the fiery young son of the powerful Earl of Northumberland. As a result of the quarrel, the Percy family revolts. At the Battle of Shrewsbury, Hal reveals himself to be a brave warrior and kills Hotspur. Part II of *Henry IV* also has many scenes of Falstaff's clowning. These scenes are set against the background of the continuing Percy rebellion and the approaching death of Henry IV, who is ill. Hal's brother, Prince John, finally defeats the rebels. The king dies, and Hal, as Henry V, takes the throne. He quickly reveals his royal qualities and rejects Falstaff and his friends, telling them to stay away until they have abandoned their wild living.	Of the two plays, Part I is more memorable. It introduces Falstaff, a bragging, lying, and thievish drunkard whose clowning provides most of the play's humor. Falstaff's faults are balanced by his clever sense of humor, his contagious love of life, and his refusal to take either himself or the world seriously.

The Second Period

Shakespeare's England

- During most of Shakespeare's lifetime, England was ruled by Queen Elizabeth I. Her reign is often called the Elizabethan Age.

- Shakespeare's works reflect the cultural, social, and political conditions of the Elizabethan Age. Knowledge of these conditions can provide greater knowledge of Shakespeare's plays and poems.

- Elizabethans believed in ghosts, witches, and magicians. No biographical evidence exists that Shakespeare had such beliefs, but he used them effectively in his works. Ghosts play an important part in *Hamlet, Julius Caesar, Macbeth,* and *Richard III.* Witches are major characters in *Macbeth.* Prospero, the hero of *The Tempest,* is a magician.

- Elizabethans were keenly aware of death and the brevity of life. They lived in constant fear of plague. When an epidemic struck, they saw victims carted off to common graves.

- Yet death and violence also fascinated many Elizabethans. Londoners flocked to public beheadings of traitors, whose heads were exhibited on poles. They also watched as criminals were hanged, and they saw the corpses dangle from the gallows for days.

- Elizabethan literature mirrored the violence and death characteristic of English life. Shakespeare's tragedies, like other Elizabethan tragedies, involve the murder or suicide of many of the leading characters.

- In spite of their tolerance of cruelty, Elizabethans were extremely sensitive to beauty and grace. They loved many forms of literature, including poetic drama, narrative and lyric poetry, prose fiction, and essays. People of all classes enjoyed music, and English composers rivaled the finest composers in all of Europe.

Play	Type	First Performed	First Published
As You Like It	Comedy	1599	1623
Henry V	History	1599	1600
Julius Caesar	Tragedy	1599	1623

▲ **In the Forest of Arden.** An 1890 book of Shakespeare plays included this drawing of a scene from *As You Like It.*

Source Material	Plot	Notes
Partly based on *Rosalynde* (1590), a novel by the English author Thomas Lodge	Rosalind and her cousin Celia leave the court of Celia's father, Duke Frederick, after he unjustly banishes Rosalind. Accompanied by Touchstone, the court jester, the two young women take refuge in the Forest of Arden. Also in the forest are Orlando, who loves Rosalind; Jaques, a melancholy philosopher; Audrey, a goatherd; Silvius, a shepherd; and Phebe, a shepherdess. Duke Frederick's brother, who is Rosalind's father and the rightful ruler of the land, also lives in the forest with a band of merry outlaws. Rosalind, disguised as a young shepherd named Ganymede, meets Orlando in the forest. Not recognizing the young woman in disguise, Orlando agrees to pretend that Ganymede is Rosalind so he can practice his declarations of love. Rosalind finally reveals her identity and marries Orlando. Oliver, Orlando's formerly wicked brother, marries Celia, Touchstone marries Audrey, and Silvius marries Phebe. The news that Rosalind's father has been restored to his dukedom completes the comedy's happy ending.	Like many other Elizabethan romantic comedies, *As You Like It* concerns young lovers who pursue their happy destiny in a world seemingly far removed from reality. Although evil threatens, it never harms. Shakespeare consistently balanced the merry laughter of *As You Like It* with notes of seriousness and even sadness. Touchstone's wit and Jaques's remarks question the nature of love and the values of society. Jaques adds a strong note of melancholy to the play with his famous description of the seven ages of man.
Partly based on *Holinshed's Chronicles* and *The Famous Victories of Henry the Fifth*	The king decides to press a claim he believes he has to the French throne. He heads an army that lands in France. Inspired by Henry's leadership, the outnumbered English troops defeat the French at the town of Harfleur. The two armies then meet in battle near the village of Agincourt. Against overwhelming odds, the English win a great victory. The triumphant Henry is received at the French court. There he is promised the throne and the hand of Katherine, the French princess.	Henry claims to hate war in general. Yet he finds himself carried away by the glamour and glory of the French campaign. Although the play occasionally seems to glorify war, Shakespeare sets the heroics against a background of political treachery and empty honor. Comic scenes mock the vanity of the royal court. These scenes remind audiences that monarchs and their councils plan wars, but ordinary people must fight and die in them.
Parallel Lives of Illustrious Greeks and Romans by the ancient Greek biographer Plutarch	The play takes place in ancient Rome. In spite of its title, the play's central character is Brutus, a Roman senator and Caesar's best friend. Brutus reluctantly joins a plot to murder Caesar because he believes Rome's preservation requires Caesar's death. Brutus defends the assassination to a crowd of Romans. But he unwisely allows the clever and eloquent Mark Antony to deliver a funeral speech over Caesar's body. Antony tells the people, "I come to bury Caesar, not to praise him." He then describes the plotters with heavy sarcasm as "honorable men." At the same time, Antony points out Caesar's virtues and thus gradually turns the crowd into a mob ready to avenge Caesar's death. The conspirators are forced to flee Rome. Mark Antony leads an army that defeats the conspirators at the Battle of Philippi. At the end of the battle, Brutus commits suicide.	*Julius Caesar* has become a popular play because of its innovative use of language and sharp character portraits. (For example, Caesar describes the plotter Cassius as having a "lean and hungry look.") But the play's real interest centers on the character of Brutus. A thoughtful, withdrawn man, he is torn between his affection for Caesar and his strong sense of duty to the Roman Republic.

The Second Period

Shakespeare's Style

- In Shakespeare's time, early modern English was still assuming its fully modern form.

- Shakespeare and other Elizabethan writers looked upon the English language as alive and changing. They did not consider it fixed for all time in a set of correct, unbreakable rules.

- Shakespeare experimented freely with sentence structure and vocabulary to create special effects. He also used various literary devices to present information.

- His style is probably best known for its brilliant use of language to create vivid pictures in the mind.

- Since his death, Shakespeare's style has helped shape the language of all English-speaking countries. Many later writers in English have accepted the Elizabethan style as their model. As a result, a large chunk of English and American literature reflects certain characteristics of Elizabethan writing.

- Shakespeare's vocabulary of about 29,000 words is remarkably rich. Like his fellow writers, he put old words to new uses, borrowed from other languages, and invented new terms.

- What sets apart Shakespeare's verbal creativity is that so many of his innovations were adopted by English speakers. Thomas Nashe, a contemporary of Shakespeare's, also freely invented words, but most of them are now forgotten.

- The richness of Shakespeare's vocabulary sometimes raises difficulties for modern readers. Not all the words and meanings used by Shakespeare remain current.

Play	Type	First Performed	First Published
Much Ado About Nothing	Comedy	1599	1600
Twelfth Night	Comedy	1600	1623
The Merry Wives of Windsor	Comedy	1600	1602

▲ **Patrick Stewart is Malvolio.** Stars of television and screen often test their mettle in a Shakespeare production.

Source Material	Plot	Notes
Partly based on *Orlando Furioso* (1516), an epic poem by the Italian author Ludovico Ariosto; and *Novelle*, a story in a collection of tales by the Italian author Matteo Bandello	The plot concerns the attempts by the villainous Don John to slander the virtue of Hero, the daughter of the governor of Messina, Italy. Hero is about to be married to Claudio, a young lord from Venice. Don John manufactures an accusation of infidelity that causes Claudio to jilt Hero at the altar. After much intrigue, Don John's plot is exposed and the couple happily marry. Much of the interest in the play centers on the relationships between Beatrice, Hero's cousin, and Benedick, a lord of Padua. These two witty characters trade insults for much of the play, but they come together in an attempt to restore Hero's damaged honor and soon realize that they are themselves in love.	The play's combination of sharp intelligence and lack of self-knowledge produces rich comedy. Broad humor is supplied by the talkative village constable, Dogberry, and his assistant, Verges.
Partly based on a story in *Barnabe Riche: His Farewell to Military Profession* (1581), a collection of tales by the English author Barnabe Riche	Viola and Sebastian, who are twins, become separated during a shipwreck. Stranded in the country of Illyria, Viola disguises herself as Cesario, a page, and enters the service of Duke Orsino. The duke sends the page to woo Countess Olivia for him. But the countess falls in love with Cesario. Meanwhile, Viola falls in love with the duke. The romantic action alternates with scenes of realistic comedy involving the fat knight Sir Toby Belch and his friends. Maria, Countess Olivia's lady-in-waiting, tricks the countess's steward, Malvolio, into thinking that Olivia loves him. The plot becomes increasingly tangled when Sebastian, Viola's twin brother, appears and agrees to marry Olivia. In the final scene, Viola, still disguised, is confronted by Olivia, who is confused by the youth's refusal to acknowledge their recent marriage. Duke Orsino is enraged by the treachery of "Cesario" and threatens violence. But all is resolved when Sebastian reappears and Viola reveals her identity. Viola and Orsino then declare their mutual love, and the play concludes anticipating their marriage. Only Malvolio is left unhappy.	*Twelfth Night* offers a blend of sentiment and humor. Feste, Olivia's clown, makes witty comments about the foolish ways of people. Feste's songs contribute both gaiety and sadness to the mood of the play. Only Malvolio, who thinks he is more moral than other people, spoils the gentle mood of the play.
Unknown	According to a popular (if unproven) story, Queen Elizabeth requested the play. She so enjoyed the comic character Sir John Falstaff in the *Henry IV* plays that she asked Shakespeare to write a comedy portraying Falstaff in love. The comedy dramatizes Falstaff's efforts to make love to Mistress Ford and Mistress Page, two honest housewives in the town of Windsor. Instead of winning their love, Falstaff ends up the victim of a number of comical tricks invented by the women.	Although *The Merry Wives of Windsor* lacks the romantic poetry of most Shakespearean comedies, the play is highly entertaining. The Falstaff in this work has less imagination and wit than the Falstaff in the *Henry IV* plays. But the character remains theatrically effective, even though the audience laughs at him rather than with him, as in the earlier plays.

1601–1608

Shakespeare wrote his great tragedies during this period of his artistic development. With the possible exception of *Pericles,* every play of this period shows Shakespeare's awareness of the tragic side of life. Even the period's two comedies—*All's Well That Ends Well* and *Measure for Measure*—are more disturbing than amusing. For this reason, they are often called "problem" comedies or "bitter" comedies. *Pericles* was Shakespeare's first romance—a drama that is serious in tone, but has a happy ending.

During this period, Shakespeare's language shows remarkable variety and flexibility, moving easily back and forth between verse and prose. The verse shows an increasing tendency to allow sentences to extend past the end of the verse line. The writing of this period is also marked by especially dense descriptive language. Shakespeare's language becomes a flexible dramatic tool that makes possible the skillful psychological portraits that mark this period.

The Third Period

Play	Type	First Performed	First Published
Hamlet	Tragedy	1601	1603
Troilus and Cressida	Comedy	1602	1609

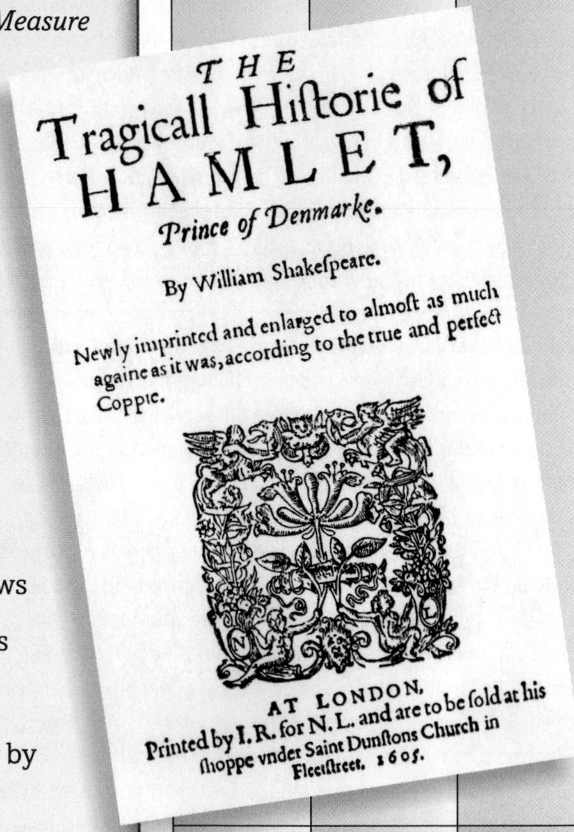

THE
Tragicall Historie of
HAMLET,
Prince of Denmarke.

By William Shakespeare.

Newly imprinted and enlarged to almost as much againe as it was, according to the true and perfect Coppie.

AT LONDON,
Printed by I. R. for N. L. and are to be sold at his shoppe vnder Saint Dunstons Church in Fleetstreet. 1605.

Source Material	Plot	Notes
Partly based on *Hamlet*, a lost play by an unknown English author, and on a story in *Histoires Tragiques* (1559–1580), a collection of tales by the French writer François de Belleforest	Prince Hamlet of Denmark deeply mourns the recent death of his father. He also resents his mother's remarriage to his uncle Claudius, who has become king. The ghost of Hamlet's father appears to the prince, tells him he was murdered by Claudius, and demands that Hamlet take revenge. Hamlet broods about whether he should believe the ghost. He decides to test his uncle's guilt by arranging the performance of a play that reenacts the murder. The king's violent reaction convinces Hamlet that the ghost has told the truth, but Hamlet rejects a chance to kill Claudius while the king is on his knees in prayer. Hamlet kills Polonius, the king's adviser, when Polonius eavesdrops on Hamlet and his mother in her sitting room. Claudius exiles Hamlet to England for killing Polonius. He also sends secret orders that the prince be executed after he arrives in England, but Hamlet intercepts the orders and returns to Denmark. He arrives in time to see the burial of Ophelia, the young woman whom Hamlet had loved, who killed herself following her father Polonius's death. Laertes, Ophelia's brother, blames Hamlet for the deaths of his sister and father. He agrees to a plot suggested by Claudius to kill Hamlet with a poisoned sword in a fencing match. Laertes wounds Hamlet during the duel and, in turn, is wounded himself by the poisoned weapon. While watching the match, Hamlet's mother accidentally drinks from a cup of poisoned wine Claudius had prepared for Hamlet. Hamlet finally kills his uncle, forgives Laertes, begs his friend Horatio to tell the true story of what has happened in order to clear his name, and dies.	The basic Hamlet story is a tale of revenge that goes back to ancient Scandinavian sources. But in making Hamlet a character whose actions are ruled by his thoughts and not just his emotions, Shakespeare created a character that modern readers and playgoers can appreciate. The play is noted for the depth of its characters. Hamlet, a soldier and scholar, is by nature a man of action, yet he is driven to inaction and even to the brink of suicide by his own thoughts. Claudius, a thorough scoundrel, is haunted by the horror of his own crimes and even tries to pray for forgiveness. Hamlet's mother reveals her own humanity when she recoils in horror at Hamlet's fierce rebukes.
No chief sources	The story takes place during the Trojan War, fought between ancient Greece and the city of Troy. It dramatizes the disastrous love affair between two Trojans: Troilus, one of the king's sons, and Cressida, a woman whose father has joined the Greeks. Cressida is suddenly sent to the Greek camp in exchange for a Trojan prisoner. Despite her promise to be faithful to Troilus, she accepts the love and protection of the Greek warrior Diomedes in the enemy camp. The play ends with the death of Troilus's brother, the great Trojan hero Hector.	In spite of its heroic setting, *Troilus and Cressida* is neither noble nor stirring. The play's satirical account of the heroic virtue associated with the epic tradition results in dark cynicism. No single character provides an authoritative vision of the events shown. This atmosphere of moral confusion and the play's extreme shifts between sexual humor and psychological realism have led many critics to classify it as one of Shakespeare's "problem plays" because it does not seem to fit neatly into any recognized dramatic category.

Shakespeare's London

The city of London experienced exceptional growth in Shakespeare's time. It had grown from 120,000 inhabitants in 1550 to 200,000 by 1600. By 1650, London contained 375,000 people. This growth is remarkable considering London's high mortality rate. The crowded and unsanitary city often experienced outbreaks of plague that regularly reduced the population. Sewage flowed in open ditches that drained into the Thames, and overbuilding led to slum conditions in many parts of the city. However, London continued to grow as the result of a massive flow of migrants, like Shakespeare himself, from the English countryside.

The crowded streets helped give London an air of bustling activity. But other factors also made London an exciting city. It was the commercial and banking center of England and one of the world's chief trading centers. The queen and her court lived there much of each year, adding to the color and excitement. The city's importance attracted people from throughout England and from other countries. Artists, teachers, musicians, students, and writers all flocked to London to seek advancement.

Although large for its day, London was still small enough so that a person could be close to its cultural and political life. The wide range of knowledge that Shakespeare showed in his plays has amazed many of his admirers. The range of Shakespeare's learning and the variety of his characters owe something to his involvement in London life.

Play	Type	First Performed	First Published
All's Well That Ends Well	Comedy	1603	1623
Measure for Measure	Comedy	1604	1623
Othello	Tragedy	1604	1622

The Globe. Built in 1599, burned in 1613 but quickly reconstructed, then demolished in 1644, the Globe Theatre was Shakespeare's theatrical home.

Source Material	Plot	Notes
Partly based on a story in *The Palace of Pleasure* (1567), a collection of tales by various European authors	This play takes place in France and Italy. Helena, the beautiful orphaned daughter of a physician, loves Bertram, a nobleman. In Paris, Helena cures the French king of an illness and wins Bertram as her husband in reward. But Bertram considers Helena beneath him socially and deserts her immediately after the wedding. He tells her in a letter that she can never call him husband unless she gets a ring from his finger and becomes pregnant by him. In Florence, Bertram attempts to seduce the young Diana. But Helena, having followed her husband, intervenes. She has Diana demand Bertram's ring in exchange for meeting him. Helena substitutes herself for Diana and spends the night with Bertram. When Bertram finds that Helena has fulfilled both conditions, he is forced to accept her as his wife.	On the surface, *All's Well That Ends Well* resembles other Elizabethan comedies of romantic intrigue. But unlike Shakespeare's earlier comedies, it has little gaiety and romance. Helena has many of the virtuous traits found in other Shakespearean heroines, but her pursuit of the unworthy Bertram puzzles some critics. Although the play does not emphasize character development, Helena's struggle to save Bertram from his own worst inclinations does present a complex vision of human nature. The play anticipates elements of the late romances in its use of such fairy-tale elements as miraculous cures and its emphasis on reconciliation.
Partly based on *Promos and Cassandra* (1578), a play by the English author George Whetstone	Vincentio, Duke of Vienna, turns over the affairs of the city to Angelo, his stern deputy. The duke hopes Angelo will introduce needed moral reforms in Vienna. In one of his first acts, Angelo sentences Claudio to death for making Juliet, his fiancée, pregnant. Claudio's sister, Isabella, pleads with Angelo for Claudio's life. Overcome by her beauty, Angelo agrees to save Claudio if she will allow him to sleep with her. Isabella refuses, preferring to let her brother die rather than yield her honor. After much intrigue and plotting, Claudio is saved, Isabella keeps her virtue, and Angelo's wicked deeds are exposed.	Many critics have objected to the happy ending of *Measure for Measure*. They consider it false to the spirit of the play. The first part of the play is serious, almost tragic. The latter part becomes a typical romantic intrigue. This lack of artistic unity creates problems. The first part of the play, for example, raises serious questions about the nature of justice that remain unanswered at the play's end. Because of these perplexing moral entanglements, *Measure for Measure* is often classified as a "problem play."
Partly based on a story in *Hecatommithi* (c. 1565), a collection of tales by the Italian author Giambattista Giraldi, who wrote under the name Cinthio	Othello, a Moor, is serving in Venice at the time when Cyprus is invaded by the Turks. He elopes with Desdemona, a general's daughter. Iago, Othello's evil aide, persuades him that Desdemona is unfaithful, and gets the trusting Desdemona to enhance the falsehood by convincing her to help the good-natured Lieutenant Cassio. Othello's judgment becomes clouded by jealousy, and he eventually smothers the guiltless Desdemona. When he realizes Iago's villainous influence, Othello kills himself with his sword. Iago is finally punished, but it's too late to bring back the deceived lovers.	*Othello* is one of Shakespeare's most powerful tragedies. The action moves rapidly without any unimportant plot developments. The language is also direct and forceful. Both Othello and Iago use especially vivid images, but when Othello is enraged, his language becomes fractured and incoherent. The play is centered on the impossibility of truly knowing the mind of another and insists on the fragility of human goodness and love.

The Third Period

Shakespeare's Poetry

- From mid-1592 to 1594, London authorities frequently closed the theaters due to outbreaks of plague.

- Without the income provided by acting and playwriting, Shakespeare turned to poetry.

- In 1593, *Venus and Adonis* became the first of his long poems to be published. It drew on Ovid's *Metamorphoses* and represented the kind of love poetry that was fashionable in court circles.

- *Venus and Adonis* was so popular that it had to be reprinted at least 15 times during Shakespeare's lifetime.

- In 1594, his second volume of poetry, *The Rape of Lucrece,* was published. It was more serious in tone than *Venus and Adonis,* describing a violent event that has enormous consequences.

- The second volume wasn't as popular, but it still sold well.

- Despite the commercial success of these early publications, he made no effort to make a career out of poetry.

- When the theaters reopened, he returned to acting and playwriting.

- In 1609, *Shakespeare's Sonnets,* a volume of 154 poems, was published.

- The first 126 sonnets addressed a young nobleman; the next 26 concentrate on a woman.

- The sonnets' most common themes concern the destructive effects of time, the quickness of physical decay, and the loss of beauty, vigor, and love.

- The individual poems have no titles.

- Shakespeare probably wrote the sonnets over several years, but the exact dates are uncertain.

- Scholars have tried to learn about Shakespeare's life from the poems because, in the late 1500s, it was fashionable for English gentlemen to write autobiographical sonnets.

Play	Type	First Performed	First Published
King Lear	Tragedy	1605	1608
Macbeth	Tragedy	1606	1623
Timon of Athens	Tragedy	1607	1623

Throne of Blood. Japanese director Akira Kurosawa adapted *Macbeth* in his 1957 masterpiece starring Toshiro Mifune.

Source Material	Plot	Notes
Holinshed's Chronicles; *The True Chronicle History of King Leir*, a play by an unknown English author; and *Arcadia* (1590), a romance in prose and verse by the English author Sir Philip Sidney	In his old age, Lear announces to his daughters that he will retire and divide his kingdom among them according to how each professes her love for him. Goneril and Regan announce that their love for him is endless and beyond price, greater than life itself. Cordelia says that indeed she loves him as her father, but not more than life itself. Lear, whose ego has been puffed up by people in his court, cannot accept this clear and separate person as his daughter, and he falls apart with rage. He disinherits Cordelia and turns to Goenril and Regan for comfort, planning to divide his time and kingdom between them. But they are full of greed and murder, and as Lear realizes their treachery, he goes mad on the heath in a terrific storm, accompanied by his Fool. In a parallel, intertwining plot, another old man, the Earl of Gloucester, cannot distinguish between his faithful son and his treacherous son.	In *King Lear*, Shakespeare created the brilliant characterizations that mark his dramas at their best. The characters realize their mistakes, which reflects Shakespeare's basic optimism. But they do so too late to prevent their destruction and that of the people around them. The play is widely regarded as the bleakest of Shakespeare's tragedies.
Holinshed's Chronicles	*Macbeth* is the story of a man who destroys himself when he chooses the forces of evil to shape his destiny. As the play opens, Macbeth and Banquo, two Scottish nobles, are returning from battle after defeating the rebellious Thane of Cawdor and a Norwegian army. They come upon three witches, who tell them that Macbeth is to become Thane of Cawdor and king. Macbeth is astonished when a messenger from the Scottish King Duncan tells Macbeth that he has been made the new Thane of Cawdor. Macbeth sacrifices his own sense of morality to his overpowering ambition to be king. When Duncan visits Macbeth's castle, Macbeth murders him in the night. Duncan's sons escape. Macbeth also murders Banquo. Macbeth and Lady Macbeth are tormented over his evil deeds, but he continues his bloody tyranny. Eventually, Macbeth loses all desire for the crown, and life itself has lost all meaning and value. Still, he fights on, even after Lady Macbeth kills herself. Macduff confronts Macbeth and kills him.	In *Macbeth*, Shakespeare wrote a tragedy of a man's conscience. During the course of the play, Macbeth changes from a person of strong but imperfect moral sense to a man who will stop at nothing to get and keep what he wants. By the play's end, he has lost all emotion. He cannot even react to his wife's death. On the other hand, Lady Macbeth encourages murder in the beginning. But her conscience grows as her husband's lessens. The play is also noted for its bitter humor, which reinforces the tragic action.
Parallel Lives of Illustrious Greeks and Romans by the ancient Greek biographer Plutarch	Timon is a nobleman in ancient Athens. Surrounded by flatterers, he spends his money extravagantly. But after he becomes penniless, his friends desert him. Their ingratitude turns Timon into a bitter person who hates humanity. Timon leaves Athens and goes to live in a cave near the sea, where he finds a buried treasure. But his new-found wealth brings him no happiness. He dies, still bitter, in his cave.	Although *Timon of Athens* has flaws, it also has passages of great eloquence. Several such passages occur when Timon pours out his scorn for humanity. Throughout the play, Shakespeare portrays people at their worst, with few of the noble qualities that lighten the gloom in his great tragedies.

Theater Life

- Acting companies consisted of only men and boys because women weren't allowed to perform.

- Salaried workers called hirelings took minor roles in the plays, performed the music, served as prompters, and did odd jobs.

- Each major actor in the company specialized in a certain type of role. For example, one played the leading tragic characters and another played the main comic characters.

- Elizabethan actors spoke their lines more rapidly than modern performers do. They had an especially clear and musical speaking style.

- Disguise was important. Audiences enjoyed comic situations in which a boy played a girl character who disguised herself as a boy.

- Elizabethans recognized sharp distinctions between social classes and occupations. These were emphasized by striking differences in dress.

- Nobles were immediately recognized by their clothing, as were doctors, lawyers, merchants, and pages.

- Characters could easily disguise themselves by wearing the garments of a certain social class or occupation.

Play	Type	First Performed	First Published
Pericles	Romance	1607	1609
Antony and Cleopatra	Tragedy	1607	1609
Coriolanus	Tragedy	1608	1623

The Merry Wives of Windsor was staged in 2008 in the newly rebuilt (1997) Shakespeare's Globe Theatre.

Source Material	Plot	Notes
Confessio Amantis (1390), a collection of European tales retold by the English poet John Gower	This play consists of many loosely related episodes. The action covers many years and ranges over much of the ancient Mediterranean world. The plot deals with the adventures of Prince Pericles of Tyre. Upon discovering that the beautiful woman he has been courting is corrupt and vicious, Pericles flees, only to become shipwrecked. Poor and unknown, he comes ashore at Pentapolis. Despite his tattered appearance, the king's daughter, the virtuous Thaisa, recognizes his basic nobility, and they marry. They have a daughter, Marina, but soon the three family members are separated. The loss of his wife and daughter causes Pericles to fall into a deep melancholy from which he recovers only when reunited first with his daughter and then with his wife.	Pericles shares a number of qualities with the later romances *Cymbeline*, *The Winter's Tale*, and *The Tempest*. Character development is less important than a complex plot that threatens to end in tragedy, only to come to an almost miraculous happy conclusion. Along the way, there is real suffering and even death, but all difficulties are redeemed by the joy of recovery and reunion. The two characters who are most fully portrayed are Pericles and Marina, whose radiant and saintly virtue protects her from the evils of the world.
Parallel Lives of Illustrious Greeks and Romans by Plutarch	Mark Antony shares the rule of the Roman Empire with Octavius Caesar and Lepidus. Antony lives in Roman-conquered Egypt, where he pursues a love affair with Cleopatra. Political problems in Rome and the death of his wife force Antony to leave his life of pleasure and return home. In Rome, he marries Octavius's sister Octavia for political reasons. But Antony soon returns to "his Egyptian dish." Octavius then prepares for war against him. Antony fights Octavius at sea. During the battle, Cleopatra's fleet deserts him, and Antony flees with the queen. After Cleopatra's ships desert him in a second battle, Antony finally realizes that he has lost everything. Cleopatra deceives him into thinking that she is dead, and Antony attempts suicide. But before he dies, he learns that Cleopatra is still alive. Antony returns to her and dies in her arms. Cleopatra is captured by Octavius, who plans to lead her in triumph through Rome. Although under guard, Cleopatra obtains poisonous snakes and uses them to commit suicide. She dies anticipating her reunion with Antony in the afterlife.	Early in the play, Enobarbus, one of Antony's officers, gives a famous description of Cleopatra that begins, "The barge she sat in, like a burnished throne, / Burned on the water." Cleopatra is a complex character. She goes from playfulness to irritation, from sweet intimacy to fierce anger, all in an instant. At the same time, she shows courage and determination.
Parallel Lives of Illustrious Greeks and Romans by Plutarch	Caius Marcius, a general in ancient Rome, wins the name Coriolanus after he captures Corioli, the capital city of a people known as the Volscians. Coriolanus returns to Rome in triumph and is nominated for the important office of consul. But he cannot hide his scorn for the common people, whose support he needs to become consul. Coriolanus's superior attitude leads to his exile. He joins forces with his old enemy, the Volscian general Tullus Aufidius, and heads an army against Rome. Coriolanus's mother, wife, and young son meet him outside the city and beg him to spare it. Moved by their pleas, Coriolanus withdraws his troops. Aufidius denounces him as a traitor and has him murdered.	In *Coriolanus*, Shakespeare raised issues that remain particularly important today. The tragedy questions the values of personal popularity and political success. It also debates the conflicting interests of public and private life. Shakespeare's direct and dramatic verse contributes to the play's power.

1609–1614

During his final period, Shakespeare wrote five plays—four romances and a history. Scholars believe the playwright collaborated with John Fletcher on two of these plays—*Henry VIII* and *The Two Noble Kinsmen*.

Unlike the masterpieces of the third period, the four romances seem detached from reality. Scholars disagree on the reason for this change. Some claim he was calmly looking back on his life and philosophically summing up his career. Other scholars believe that the romances are a response to the growing popularity of plays that mixed comic and serious elements and that in writing them Shakespeare was adapting his work to the changing tastes of his audience. These claims are not, however, mutually exclusive. Throughout his career, Shakespeare was attentive to the desires of his audience. At the same time, his work never appears merely commercial.

Shakespeare in South Africa. Cape Town's Baxter Theatre Centre staged *The Tempest* in 2009; then it toured Britain.

The Fourth Period

Play	Type	First Performed	First Published
Cymbeline	Romance	1609	1623
The Winter's Tale	Romance	1610	1623
The Tempest	Romance	1611	1623

Source Material	Plot	Notes
No chief sources	Cymbeline, king of Britain, exiles the poor but honorable Posthumous after the young man marries Imogen, the king's daughter. The treacherous Iachimo bets Posthumous that Imogen is not virtuous. Iachimo then tries to seduce her. He fails but tricks Posthumous into believing that he succeeded. Posthumous orders his wife killed, but she escapes disguised as a court page. After many adventures, Imogen and her husband are happily reunited. Iachimo, filled with regret, confesses his wickedness.	*Cymbeline* was once grouped with Shakespeare's tragedies, but it's now widely considered a romance. With its clumsy language, it is not thought of as one of Shakespeare's better works. Though seldom performed now, it was very popular in the 19th century. *Cymbeline* is a lively mix of historical elements. It includes portrayals of ancient Britons, classical Romans, and, in Iachimo, an Italian plotter who appears modern. Cymbeline's queen is the sort of wicked stepmother found in fairy tales. Her son, Cloten, is a cowardly clown.
Pandosto (1588), a prose romance by the English author Robert Greene	Leontes, king of Sicilia, becomes uncontrollably jealous of his wife, Hermione. He suspects her of sleeping with his friend Polixenes. Leontes tries to have Polixenes murdered, but he escapes and returns to Bohemia. Leontes then orders his wife to prison, where she gives birth to their daughter, Perdita. Leontes declares the child illegitimate and orders that she be abandoned in a deserted place. Leontes learns that his young son has died of grief. At this news, Hermione falls into a deathlike faint. Suddenly convinced of his error, Leontes is left to mourn the loss of his wife, daughter, and son. Meanwhile, Perdita has been saved by an old shepherd. She grows into a lovely young woman and wins the love of Florizel, prince of Bohemia. But Florizel's father, Polixenes, angrily disapproves of their romance, and the couple flee to Leontes's court for protection. There, Leontes discovers that Perdita is his daughter. The king's happiness is complete when he is also reunited with his wife, who was thought to be dead. Instead, with the help of a lady-in-waiting, she had been living in seclusion, hoping for Perdita's return.	Like *Cymbeline*, *The Winter's Tale* concerns exile, women suffering from male jealousy, and the reuniting of loved ones. Also like the earlier play, *The Winter's Tale* takes a potentially tragic situation and uses it to stress recovery rather than destruction. Still, there is loss. The young prince and the lord sent to dispose of Perdita are both dead. The conclusion is finely balanced between the joy of reconciliation and the painful knowledge of loss.
No chief sources	Prospero, the wrongfully deposed Duke of Milan, Italy, lives on an enchanted island with his beautiful daughter, Miranda. The mischievous spirit Ariel and the monster Caliban serve Prospero, who is a skilled magician. Using magic, Prospero creates a storm that causes a ship carrying his enemies to be wrecked on the island. The ship also carries the young prince Ferdinand. Miranda loves him at first sight. With his magic, Prospero brings Miranda and Ferdinand together and upsets plots laid against him by his shipwrecked enemies. Prospero appears before his enemies and forgives them. He decides to give up his magic and return to Italy, where Ferdinand and Miranda can marry.	Like *Cymbeline* and *The Winter's Tale*, *The Tempest* tells a story in which old injuries are forgiven and the characters begin a new and happier life. In *The Tempest*, Shakespeare blended spectacle, song, and dance with a romantic love story, beautiful poetry, and broad comedy. Many scholars have interpreted the play as Shakespeare's farewell to his profession, but no one knows if he intended it to be autobiographical.

The Fourth Period

Shakespeare's Actors

- Shakespeare wrote his plays to suit the talents of specific performers.

- He knew when he created a Hamlet, Othello, or King Lear that the character would be interpreted by Richard Burbage, the company's tragic actor.

- Shakespeare's comedies reveal the influence that specific actors had on the creation of his plays.

- From 1594 to 1599, the company's leading comic actor was Will Kemp. During that time, many of the comedies seem designed to take advantage of Kemp's talents as a physical comedian who specialized in playing rustic characters.

- After Kemp left the company, Robert Armin took his place and the style of Shakespeare's comedy shifted noticeably.

- The playwright skillfully used Armin's more sophisticated and intellectual comic talents in such lively but thoughtful comedies as *Twelfth Night* and *As You Like It*.

- Elizabethan acting companies were eager to stage plays that had roles for all their major performers. In part, this explains the appearance of comic characters—such as the gravedigger in *Hamlet,* the porter in *Macbeth,* and the fool in *King Lear*—in even the most violent and severe of his plays.

Play	Type	First Performed	First Published
Henry VIII	History	1613	1623
The Two Noble Kinsmen	Romance	1613 or 1614	1634

Will Kemp. This 1893 drawing depicts Kemp "morris dancing" (folk dancing) from London to Norwich on his "Nine Days' Wonder" in 1600.

Source Material	Plot	Notes
Holinshed's Chronicles and *The Book of Martyrs* (1563), a religious work by the English author John Foxe	The play dramatizes the events that led to England's break with the Roman Catholic Church. It deals with King Henry VIII's annulment of his marriage to Catherine of Aragon (spelled *Katherine* in the play) and his marriage to Anne Boleyn. The play also covers the fall of Cardinal Thomas Wolsey as the king's adviser and the rise of Archbishop Thomas Cranmer as Wolsey's replacement.	*Henry VIII* is a loosely constructed drama and better known for its pageantry than for its characterization. The play attempts to move beyond the anger found in almost all the historical accounts of England's split from Catholicism available during Shakespeare's lifetime. The play's alternate title, *All Is True*, suggests a mildly ironic attempt to create an account of the country's recent past that covers all the major events and invites agreement among the various sides.
Chiefly based on "The Knight's Tale" from Geoffrey Chaucer's *Canterbury Tales*	The play tells the story of two young aristocrats from Thebes, Palamon and Arcite. Although Thebes is ruled by the tyrant Creon, the two friends decide that loyalty requires them to help defend their city against the attack of Theseus, king of Athens. The two are captured in battle and taken to Athens. In prison, Palamon sees and falls in love with Emilia, the sister of Hippolyta, the wife of Theseus. Arcite, too, falls in love with Emilia. The two friends argue bitterly over their claims to Emilia. Arcite is released from prison and exiled, but he remains in Athens in disguise. Palamon manages to escape from prison and encounters the disguised Arcite in the woods. The two are about to fight a duel over Emilia when they are discovered by Theseus, who condemns them both to death. The king is talked into sparing the two on the condition that they return in a month to fight each other. The winner will marry Emilia, and the loser will be executed. In preparation for the fight, Arcite prays to Mars, the god of war. Palamon prays to Venus, the goddess of love, and Emilia prays to Diana, the goddess of virginity. Arcite wins the fight but afterward is thrown from his horse and fatally injured. Palamon, on the verge of execution, is permitted a final interview with his dying friend, who confesses that he has wronged Palamon and urges him to take Emilia. Theseus spares Palamon and agrees to his marriage to Emilia.	The *Two Noble Kinsmen*, like other late romances, has an artificial quality and an improbable plot designed to highlight the guiding role of Providence in human affairs. Like *Henry VIII*, the play emphasizes courtly ceremony and pageantry. However, the play's central focus is on a friendship between two men that is jeopardized by their rivalry for the same woman. Some of the play's best dialogue concerns the qualities and claims of friendship.

fyi!

No manuscripts in Shakespeare's handwriting exist, making it difficult to know what he wrote. Much research has been devoted to determining the order in which his plays were written and first performed, including records of performances, mentions of his works by other writers, references to current events, and analysis of each play's literary style.

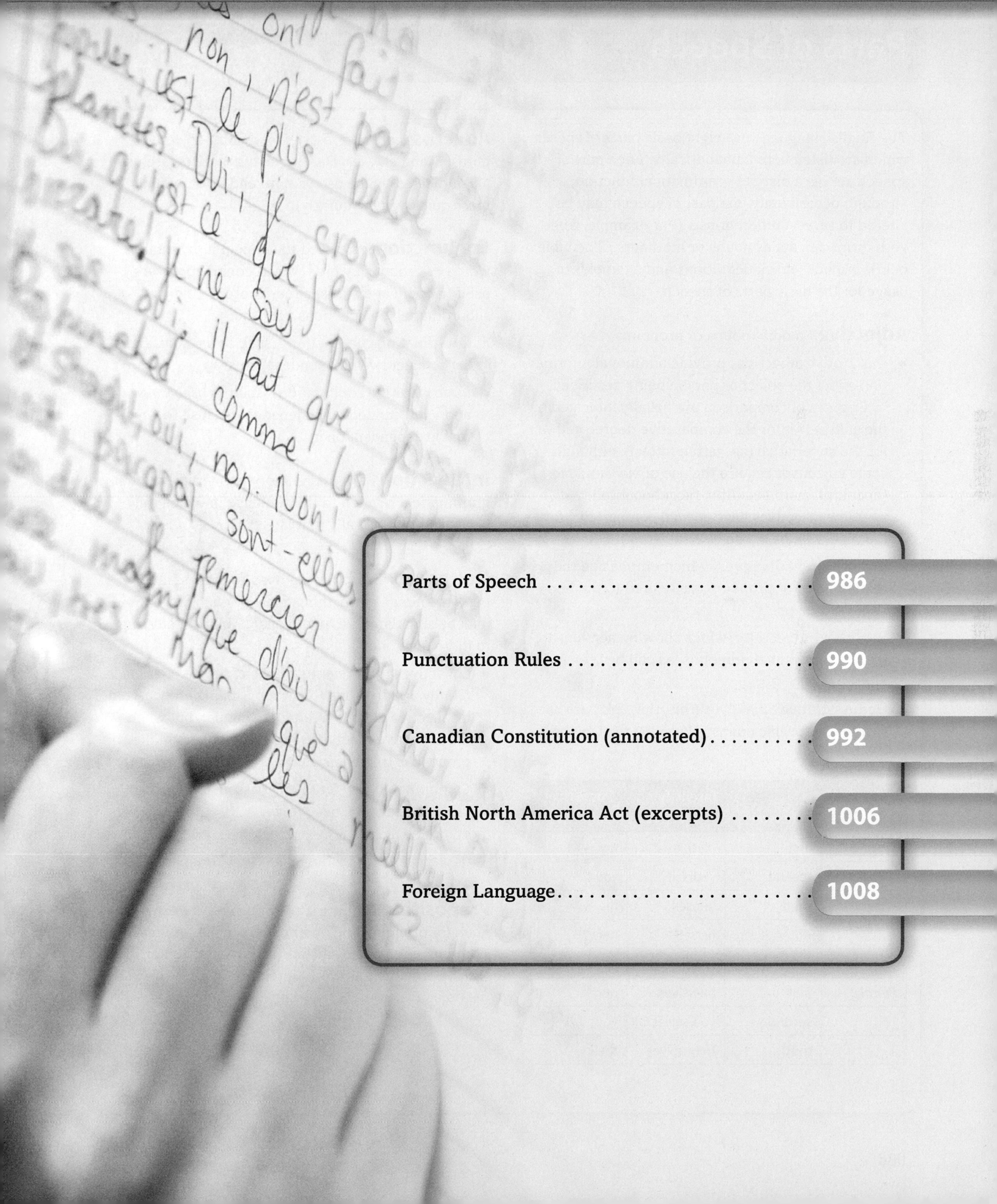

Parts of Speech

SW SOUTHWESTERN

The English language has eight basic parts of speech, which are listed here alphabetically. Each part of speech serves a distinct grammatical function, although occasionally one part of speech may be altered to serve a different use. (For example, some verb forms can act as nouns or modifiers.) The table below provides quick definitions and examples of usage for the basic parts of speech.

Adjectives modify nouns or pronouns.

- Descriptive adjectives provide additional information about the object or person being described.

   Degrees of comparison are usually indicated by the suffixes *-er* for the comparative degree and *-est* for the superlative (fat, fatter, fattest), although some adjectives require the use of *more* and *most* (beautiful, more beautiful, most beautiful).

   A few adjectives have special comparative forms (good, better, best; bad, worse, worst).

- Intensifying adjectives, which emphasize the related noun or pronoun, are related to the personal pronouns.

- Possessive adjectives, which show ownership, are related to personal pronouns, as can be seen in the chart below.

- Demonstrative adjectives (this, that, etc.) are used to indicate specific nouns. (Have you read *this* book?)

Number	Person	Intensifying Adjective	Possessive Adjective
Singular	first	myself	my
	second	yourself	your
	third	himself	his
		herself	her
		itself	its
Plural	first	ourselves	our
	second	yourselves	your
	third	themselves	their

Adverbs modify verbs, other adverbs, adjectives, phrases, and clauses. Degrees of comparison are usually indicated by the use of more and most (quickly, more quickly, most quickly).

Conjunctions are used to connect individual words or groups of words. When conjunctions are used to connect clauses, either coordinating or subordinating conjunctions are used.

- Coordinating conjunctions (such as *and*, *but*, and *or*) connect two independent clauses.

- Subordinating conjunctions (such as *as*, *because*, and *until*) connect an independent clause to one that is dependent on it.

Interjections are exclamatory expressions with no grammatical relation to the sentence in which they occur. (*Gosh*, is it really that late?)

Nouns are words that are used to represent a person, animal, place, thing, idea, or quality. Nouns may be singular (referring to one) or plural (referring to more than one).

- Collective nouns refer to groups of people or animals (family, herd). When the group is being emphasized, a collective noun is treated as singular, but when the collective noun refers to the members in the group, it is treated as plural.

- Common nouns refer to any person, animal, or place (a relative, a pet, a town).

- Proper nouns refer to a particular person, animal, or place (Uncle Charlie, Fido, New York City).

Prepositions show the relationship between a noun (or pronoun) and another part of the sentence. Common prepositions include at, between, for, of, and with. A pronoun following a preposition is always in the objective case.

Pronouns are words that can be used instead of nouns. The noun replaced by a pronoun is called the antecedent.

- Indefinite pronouns (each, all, etc.) do not have a clear antecedent. (*Each* tried to succeed, but none did.)
- Interrogative pronouns (who, whom, whose, what, which) are used to ask questions about unknown nouns. (*Who* came? *What* did she say?)
- Personal pronouns are listed in the chart at right.
- Reflexive pronouns (myself, yourself, himself, herself, itself, ourselves, yourselves, themselves) refer back to the person performing an action. (He taught *himself*.)
- Relative pronouns (who, whom, whose, that, what, which) introduce subordinate clauses and replace nouns or pronouns in the main clause. (He is the man *who* tried to help me.)

Personal Pronouns				
		Case		
Number	Person	Nominative	Objective	Possessive
Singular	first	I	me	mine
	second	you	you	yours
	third	he	him	his
		she	her	hers
		it	it	its
Plural	first	we	us	ours
	second	you	you	yours
	third	they	them	theirs

Verbs are used to express an action or a state of being. There are four types of verbs: *transitive, intransitive, linking,* and *auxiliary*. All verbs have four forms: the *infinitive* (to sing), the *present* (sing), the *past* (sang), and the *past participle* (sung).

Types of Verbs

- **Transitive verbs** show an action that has an effect on an object. (John *sang* the song.)
- **Intransitive verbs** do not have an effect on an object. (John *swam*.)
- **Linking verbs** equate a subject and its predicate. (John *is* good.)
- **Auxiliary verbs** are used with other verbs to indicate tense. (John *has* sung the ballad many times. John *will* swim tomorrow.)

Verbs vary according to tense, mood, and voice.

Tense. The tense of a verb indicates time. *Past, present,* and *future* are the three main tenses in English. In addition, English uses the *present perfect,* the *past perfect,* and the *future perfect*. The present and past perfect tenses are used to give more information about the past. The present perfect indicates that something has occurred at some indefinite time in the past, while the past perfect indicates that something has occurred at a particular time in the past. Similarly, the future perfect indicates that something will occur at some particular time in the future. (She has taken a nap. By teatime, she had taken a nap. By dinnertime, she will have taken her nap.) These tenses are formed by combining auxiliary verbs with the past participle.

Mood. English has three moods: *indicative, imperative,* and *subjunctive*. The indicative is used for statements of fact or questions (I am coming. Are you coming?); the imperative to give commands (Come here!); and the subjunctive mainly to express wishes (I wish you were here) and statements contrary to fact (If you were here, I would be happy).

Voice. Verbs may either be *active* or *passive*. A verb in the active voice shows that the subject has performed the action, while a verb in the passive voice shows that the subject has received the action. (I threw the ball. The ball was thrown.)

Punctuation Review

Questions of punctuation are always a serious concern in formal writing. The following pages provide a brief review of major types of punctuation.

Good style in punctuating, especially in the use of commas, often depends on a grasp of English grammar.

There are two issues in punctuating. The first is a simple question of right and wrong. A writer who ends each sentence with a colon rather than a period is simply wrong. Sentences cannot end with a colon.

The second issue is less clear-cut. For example, in some cases, the writer may choose punctuation to suit his or her taste: a semicolon to separate two closely related thoughts, or a period. Writers learn with practice which possibility to choose to make their meaning clearest.

End punctuation.
There are three kinds of end punctuation: the *period*, the *question mark*, and the *exclamation point*. Every sentence must end with one of these marks.

The exclamation point ends an exclamatory sentence, and the question mark is at the end of a question. All other sentences end with a period.

> *What a good boy Paul is!*
> *Is Paul a good boy?*
> *Paul is a good boy.*

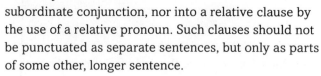

The most common mistake in end punctuation usage is to punctuate as a sentence a group of words that is not a sentence. A sentence must, as a minimum, have a subject and a verb. In addition, it must not have been transformed into an adjective clause by the addition of a subordinate conjunction, nor into a relative clause by the use of a relative pronoun. Such clauses should not be punctuated as separate sentences, but only as parts of some other, longer sentence.

Commas.
The most common mistakes in comma usage are using too many and using commas instead of semicolons to join two independent clauses.

- **Compound sentences.** When two simple sentences are joined together by a coordinating conjunction, put a comma before the conjunction. (This comma is often omitted when the clauses being joined are especially short.) Do not use commas when only a part of the sentence has been compounded.

  > *She got up to close the window, but he asked her to sit down again.*

- **Adverbial clauses.** An adverbial clause at the beginning of a sentence is set off from the rest of the sentence by a comma. Such a clause at the end of a sentence is not set off.

  > *When we got back from the beach, we were too tired to eat dinner.*

  > *We were too tired to eat dinner when we got back from the beach.*

- **Clarity.** Sometimes—but very rarely—a comma is needed to avoid confusion and to make a sentence clearer:

  > *To John, Matilda would always be a mystery.*

Sentence Fragment
Although I like the design.

Corrections
(1) *I like the design.*
(2) *Although I like the design, I don't care to use it in a living room.*

Periods.
Besides its use at the end of a sentence, the period is used after initials (*T. S. Eliot*) and after many other abbreviations, including those of months (*Feb.*), countries (*U.S.A.*), states (*Tenn.*), and other commonly abbreviated forms (*St., Ave., Dr., Mr.,* and so on).

- **Parenthetical expressions.** Parenthetical expressions are set off by commas. These include yes, no, and mild interjections (those not followed by an exclamation point), such as *well* and *oh*,

  Well, it's time to leave

  nouns of address,

  How is your garden growing, Mary?

  and such expressions as *of course* and *however*.

  We will, of course, be ready; others, however, may not be.

- **Series.** Use commas after all but the last item in a series.

  Her Russian was barely passable, but she was fluent in English, French, Italian, and Mandarin.

- **Nonrestrictive relative clauses.** A nonrestrictive relative clause is set off from the rest of the sentence by commas. So, too, are expressions that derive from nonrestrictive clauses, such as appositives and nonrestrictive participles and participial phrases.

  Mr. Jackson, standing on the makeshift platform, gave a rousing campaign speech.

Semicolons. Use a semicolon to join two sentences without using a conjunction. The semicolon is also used when two sentences are joined by such an expression as therefore or however.

Two plus two equals four; therefore, five is not an acceptable answer.

The semicolon is also used to separate the items in a series when there are already commas within individual elements of the series:

He has lived in Moline, Illinois; Boulder, Colorado; and Seattle, Washington.

Colons. The main use of a colon is to introduce a list, an example, a question, or a long quotation.

The question is this: What should we do next?

A colon used in this way should always follow a noun or a pronoun, never a verb or a preposition. It may also come after the expressions *as follows* and *the following*.

Dashes. The dash indicates a sudden break or change of emphasis in a sentence:

I have here a—now, where did I put that thing?

Dashes can also be used to set off an appositive when the appositive is to be emphasized or when it contains commas within it.

Parentheses. Parentheses set off material in a sentence that is separate or apart from the main thought.

She traveled through Davenport (a city in which she once lived) and on toward Chicago.

Quotations. A direct quotation—the exact words that someone has said or written—is enclosed in quotation marks. If the quotation is included within another sentence, it is set off from the rest of the sentence by commas:

"I think," he said, "that you are on the right track."

When more than one person is being quoted, as in a conversation, begin a new paragraph for each change of speaker.

Question marks and exclamation points are placed inside the quotation marks if they are part of the quote

"Who are you?" she asked

and outside if they apply to the sentence as a whole

Who was it that said, "I shall return"?

Periods and commas are always placed inside quotation marks, while the semicolon and colon are always placed outside.

Do not use quotation marks for an indirect quotation, that is, one that does not report someone's exact words:

He said that it was raining.

Punctuation Summary

Italics. Words to be set in italics are indicated in typed or handwritten material by an underline. Italics are used to single out words, phrases, or even sentences for special emphasis. Titles of books, plays, magazines, and newspapers, and the names of ships, trains, and airplanes, are italicized. (Shorter works like poems and stories are put in quotation marks.)

> *The Adventures of Tom Sawyer*
> *Hamlet*
> *National Geographic*
> the *Titanic*
> "Annabel Lee"
> "The Masque of the Red Death"

Capitalization. All proper nouns (names of specific persons, beings, places, or things) are capitalized. In addition, capitalize the first word of every sentence; the first word of a direct quotation embedded in another sentence; the names of groups, associations, and businesses; the letters of some abbreviations; and all historic events, buildings, monuments, and documents:

> *General Motors*   *Grant's Tomb*
> *NASA*   *Declaration of*
> *Independence*
> *World War II*

Titles used with proper nouns are capitalized:

> *Dr. Brown*
> *Senator Douglas*

Also capitalized are the first, last, and important words in titles of printed texts. Prepositions, articles, and conjunctions are not capitalized unless they are the first or last word of the title.

Symbol Name	Use
. period	Placed at end of statements.
	Used after initials.
	Used after abbreviations.
? question mark	Placed at end of sentences that ask something.
	Used in parentheses to express doubt.
! exclamation point	Placed at end of statements that show strong feelings.
, comma	Used to separate items in a series.
	Used to separate two clauses of a compound sentence joined by a coordinating conjunction.
	Used to set off parenthetical information.
	Used to set off appositives.
	Used to set off an introductory modifier.
	Placed after or before the name of someone being addressed.
	Used before an exact quotation or to conclude a statement in quotation marks.
	Placed after *yes, no, oh,* and *well,* and also after interjections.
	Used in dates to separate the day and year.
	Used to separate the name of a city and state or province.
" " quotation marks	Used to set off someone's exact words.
' ' single quotation marks	Used for quoted speech within a quoted sentence.
; semicolon	Used to separate independent clauses closely related to each other.
	Used to separate items in a series when the items include commas.
: colon	Used before a list.
	Used to separate independent clauses when the second clause provides additional information about the first.
	Used before a character's lines in a play.
	Used to separate the hour from the minutes when writing the time.
— dash	Placed before a sudden break in thought or an interruption.
	Used to add emphasis to part of a sentence.
' apostrophe	Used to indicate a missing letter in contractions.
	Used to show possession.
( ) parentheses	Used to set off additional information from the rest of a sentence.
	Used to set off sentences that are separate from the main sentence.
[ ] brackets	Used to set off information inserted to clarify quoted material.

Example
Grandfather is old.
J. F. K., T. S. Eliot
Ph.D.
Is your grandfather very old?
Chaucer, born in 1340(?), died in 1400.
Wow! Grandfather is old!
My mom is young, witty, and attractive.
My dad is old, but he is in good health.
Fred, who is quite old, is still in good health.
Grandfather, a most generous man, is well regarded in our town.
Despite all her hardships, she remains optimistic.   Hurt by her taunts, he left abruptly.   Politically, his future is not rosy.
Jane, please come here.   We'll miss you, Emma.
He said, "We'll miss you."   "We'll miss you," he said.
Well, the food finally arrived.   Yes, food is what we need.
My grandfather was born on May 7, 1910.
Duluth, Minnesota   Toronto, Ontario
"Grandfather is old," Dad said.
"I use the words attributed to Caesar, 'Et tu, Brute,' to express my dismay," said John.
Grandfather is old; his face is very wrinkled.   Grandfather is old; however, I'm not sure when he was born.
He has traveled to London, England; Paris, France; and Munich, Germany.
You will need the following items: a pen, a pencil, and an eraser.
I now have time to travel: I visit Italy to see Renaissance art. I visit England to see my grandchildren.
Peter: We'll fly away.   Wendy: But, Peter, I can't fly.
6:30
I want to finish—but first I must tell you how it all began.
Anne was influential in our community— she was the leading physician and an inspiring speaker—and could be counted on to lead us to victory.
He's no friend of mine.   She's running for office.
Peter's father treats us badly.   The Smiths' station wagon was damaged.
He has traveled to two cities (London and Paris) and enjoyed them both.
The president campaigned vigorously. (In fact, he made appearances in all 50 states. According to most reports, he was well received.)
"Nothing was left for him [the president] to do but await word from his ambassador."

The Canadian Constitution

Address to Her Majesty

THAT, WHEREAS in the past certain amendments to the Constitution of Canada have been made by the Parliament of the United Kingdom at the request and with the consent of Canada;

AND WHEREAS it is in accord with the status of Canada as an independent state that Canadians be able to amend their Constitution in Canada in all respects;

AND WHEREAS it is also desirable to provide in the Constitution of Canada for the recognition of certain fundamental rights and freedoms and to make other amendments to that Constitution;

A respectful address be presented to Her Majesty the Queen in the following words:

To the Queen's Most Excellent Majesty: Most Gracious Sovereign:

We, Your Majesty's loyal subjects, the House of Commons of Canada in Parliament assembled, respectfully approach Your Majesty, requesting that you may graciously be pleased to cause to be laid before the Parliament of the United Kingdom a measure containing the recitals and clauses hereinafter set forth:

An Act to give effect to a request by the Senate and House of Commons of Canada

Whereas Canada has requested and consented to the enactment of an Act of the Parliament of the United Kingdom to give effect to the provisions hereinafter set forth and the Senate and the House of Commons of Canada in Parliament assembled have submitted an address to Her Majesty requesting that Her Majesty may graciously be pleased to cause a Bill to be laid before the Parliament of the United Kingdom for that purpose.

Be it therefore enacted by the Queen's Most Excellent Majesty, by and with the advice and consent of the Lords Spiritual and Temporal, and Commons, in this present Parliament assembled, and by the authority of the same, as follows:

Constitution Act, 1982 enacted

1. *The Constitution Act, 1981* set out in Schedule B to this Act is hereby enacted for and shall have the force of law in Canada and shall come into force as provided in that Act.

Termination of power to legislate for Canada

2. No Act of the Parliament of the United Kingdom passed after the *Constitution Act, 1981* comes into force shall extend to Canada as part of its law.

French version

3. So far as it is not contained in Schedule B, the French version of this Act is set out in Schedule A to this Act and has the same authority in Canada as the English version thereof.

Short title

4. This Act may be cited as the *Canada Act*.

CONSTITUTION ACT, 1982

Part 1, Schedule B

Canadian Charter of Rights and Freedoms

Whereas Canada is founded upon principles that recognize the supremacy of God and the rule of law:

Guarantee of Rights and Freedoms

1. The *Canadian Charter of Rights and Freedoms* guarantees the rights and freedoms set out in it subject only to such reasonable limits prescribed by law as can be demonstrably justified in a free and democratic society.

Rights and freedoms in Canada

Fundamental Freedoms

2. Everyone has the following fundamental freedoms:

    (a) freedom of conscience and religion;

    (b) freedom of thought, belief, opinion and expression, including freedom of the press and other media of communication;

    (c) freedom of peaceful assembly; and

    (d) freedom of association.

Fundamental freedoms

Democratic Rights

3. Every citizen of Canada has the right to vote in an election of members of the House of Commons or of a legislative assembly and to be qualified for membership therein.

Democratic rights of citizens

4. (1) No House of Commons and no legislative assembly shall continue for longer than five years from the date fixed for the return of the writs of a general election of its members.

Maximum duration of legislative bodies

    (2) In time of real or apprehended war, invasion or insurrection, a House of Commons may be continued by Parliament and a legislative assembly may be continued by the legislature beyond five years if such continuation is not opposed by the votes of more than one-third of the members of the House of Commons or the legislative assembly, as the case may be.

Continuation in special circumstances

5. There shall be a sitting of Parliament and of each legislature at least once every twelve months.

Annual sitting of legislative bodies

Mobility Rights

6. (1) Every citizen of Canada has the right to enter, remain in and leave Canada.

Mobility of citizens

    (2) Every citizen of Canada and every person who has the status of a permanent resident of Canada has the right

    (a) to move to and take up residence in any province; and

    (b) to pursue the gaining of a livelihood in any province.

Rights to move and gain livelihood

| Limitation | (3) The rights specified in subsection (2) are subject to |

Limitation

(3) The rights specified in subsection (2) are subject to
   (a) any laws or practices of general application in force in a province other than those that discriminate among persons primarily on the basis of province of present or previous residence; and
   (b) any laws providing for reasonable residency requirements as a qualification for the receipt of publicly provided social services.

Affirmative action programs

(4) Subsections (2) and (3) do not preclude any law, program or activity that has as its object the amelioration in a province of conditions of individuals in that province who are socially or economically disadvantaged if the rate of employment in that province is below the rate of employment in Canada.

Legal Rights

Life, liberty and security of person

7. Everyone has the right to life, liberty and security of the person and the right not to be deprived thereof except in accordance with the principles of fundamental justice.

Search or seizure

8. Everyone has the right to be secure against unreasonable search or seizure.

Detention or imprisonment

9. Everyone has the right not to be arbitrarily detained or imprisoned.

Arrest or detention

10. Everyone has the right on arrest or detention
    (a) to be informed promptly of the reasons therefor;
    (b) to retain and instruct counsel without delay and to be informed of that right; and
    (c) to have the validity of the detention determined by way of *habeas corpus* and to be released if the detention is not lawful.

Proceedings in criminal and penal matters

11. Any person charged with an offence has the right
    (a) to be informed without unreasonable delay of the specific offence;
    (b) to be tried within a reasonable time;
    (c) not to be compelled to be a witness in proceedings against that person in respect of the offence;
    (d) to be presumed innocent until proven guilty according to law in a fair and public hearing by an independent and impartial tribunal;
    (e) not to be denied reasonable bail without just cause;
    (f) except in the case of an offence under military law tried before a military tribunal, to the benefit of trial by jury where the maximum punishment for the offence is imprisonment for five years or a more severe punishment;
    (g) not to be found guilty on account of any act or omission unless, at the time of the act or omission, it constituted an offence under Canadian or international law or was criminal according to the general principles of law recognized by the community of nations;
    (h) if finally acquitted of the offence, not to be tried for it again and, if finally found guilty and punished for the offence, not to be tried or punished for it again; and
    (i) if found guilty of the offence and if the punishment for the offence

has been varied between the time of commission and the time of sentencing, to the benefit of the lesser punishment.

12. Everyone has the right not to be subjected to any cruel and unusual treatment or punishment.

Treatment or punishment

13. A witness who testifies in any proceedings has the right not to have any incriminating evidence so given used to incriminate that witness in any other proceedings, except in a prosecution for perjury or for the giving of contradictory evidence.

Self-incrimination

14. A party or witness in any proceedings who does not understand or speak the language in which the proceedings are conducted or who is deaf has the right to the assistance of an interpreter.

Interpreter

Equality Rights

15. (1) Every individual is equal before and under the law and has the right to the equal protection and equal benefit of the law without discrimination and, in particular, without discrimination based on race, national or ethnic origin, colour, religion, sex, age or mental or physical disability.

Equality before and under law and equal protection and benefit of law

(2) Subsection (1) does not preclude any law, program or activity that has as its object the amelioration of conditions of disadvantaged individuals or groups including those that are disadvantaged because of race, national or ethnic origin, colour, religion, sex, age or mental or physical disability.

Affirmative action programs

Official Languages of Canada

16. (1) English and French are the official languages of Canada and have equality of status and equal rights and privileges as to their use in all institutions of the Parliament and government of Canada.

Official languages of Canada

(2) English and French are the official languages of New Brunswick and have equality of status and equal rights and privileges as to their use in all institutions of the legislature and government of New Brunswick.

Official languages of New Brunswick

(3) Nothing in this Charter limits the authority of Parliament or a legislature to advance the equality of status or use of English and French.

Advancement of status and use

17. (1) Everyone has the right to use English or French in any debates and other proceedings of Parliament.

Proceedings of Parliament

(2) Everyone has the right to use English or French in any debates and other proceedings of the legislature of New Brunswick.

Proceedings of New Brunswick legislature

18. (1) The statutes, records and journals of Parliament shall be printed and published in English and French and both language versions are equally authoritative.

Parliamentary statutes and records

(2) The statutes, records and journals of the legislature of New Brunswick shall be printed and published in English and French and both language versions are equally authoritative.

New Brunswick statutes and records

Proceedings in courts established by Parliament

19. (1) Either English or French may be used by any person in, or in any pleading in or process issuing from, any court established by Parliament.

Proceedings in New Brunswick courts

(2) Either English or French may be used by any person in, or in any pleading in or process issuing from, any court of New Brunswick.

Communications by public with federal institutions

20. (1) Any member of the public in Canada has the right to communicate with, and to receive available services from, any head or central office of an institution of the Parliament or government of Canada in English or French, and has the same right with respect to any other office of any such institution where

(a) there is a significant demand for communications with and services from that office in such language; or

(b) due to the nature of the office, it is reasonable that communications with and services from that office be available in both English and French.

Communications by public with New Brunswick institutions

(2) Any member of the public in New Brunswick has the right to communicate with, and to receive available services from, any office of an institution of the legislature or government of New Brunswick in English and French.

Continuation of existing constitutional provisions

21. Nothing in sections 16 to 20 abrogates or derogates from any right, privilege or obligation with respect to the English and French languages, or either of them, that exists or is continued by virtue of any other provision of the Constitution of Canada.

Rights and privileges preserved

22. Nothing in sections 16 to 20 abrogates or derogates from any legal or customary right or privilege acquired or enjoyed either before or after the coming into force of this Charter with respect to any language that is not English or French.

Minority Language Educational Rights

Language of instruction

23. (1) Citizens of Canada

(a) whose first language learned and still understood is that of the English or French linguistic minority population of the province in which they reside, or

(b) who have received their primary school instruction in Canada in English or French and reside in a province where the language in which they received that instruction is the language of the English or French linguistic minority population of the province

have the right to have their children receive primary and secondary school instruction in that language in that province.

Continuity of language instruction

(2) Citizens of Canada of whom any child has received or is receiving primary or secondary school instruction in English or French in Canada, have the right to have all their children receive primary and secondary school instruction in the same language.

(3) The right of citizens of Canada under subsections (1) and (2) to have their children receive primary and secondary school instruction in the language of the English or French linguistic minority population of a province

    (a) applies wherever in the province the number of children of citizens who have such a right is sufficient to warrant the provision to them out of public funds of minority language instruction; and

    (b) includes, where the number of those children so warrants, the right to have them receive that instruction in minority language educational facilities provided out of public funds.

Application where numbers warrant

Enforcement

24. (1) Anyone whose rights or freedoms, as guaranteed by this Charter, have been infringed or denied may apply to a court of competent jurisdiction to obtain such remedy as the court considers appropriate and just in the circumstances.

Enforcement of guaranteed rights and freedoms

    (2) Where, in proceedings under subsection (1), a court concludes that evidence was obtained in a manner that infringed or denied any rights or freedoms guaranteed by this Charter, the evidence shall be excluded if it is established that, having regard to all the circumstances, the admission of it in the proceedings would bring the administration of justice into disrepute.

Exclusion of evidence bringing administration of justice into disrepute

General

25. The guarantee in this Charter of certain rights and freedoms shall not be construed so as to abrogate or derogate from any aboriginal, treaty or other rights or freedoms that pertain to the aboriginal peoples of Canada including

Aboriginal rights and freedoms not affected by Charter

    (a) any rights or freedoms that have been recognized by the Royal Proclamation of October 7, 1763; and

    (b) any rights or freedoms that now exist by way of land claims agreements or may be so acquired.

26. The guarantee in this Charter of certain rights and freedoms shall not be construed as denying the existence of any other rights or freedoms that exist in Canada.

Other rights and freedoms not affected by Charter

27. This Charter shall be interpreted in a manner consistent with the preservation and enhancement of the multicultural heritage of Canadians.

Multicultural heritage

28. Notwithstanding anything in this Charter, the rights and freedoms referred to in it are guaranteed equally to male and female persons.

Rights guaranteed equally to both sexes

29. Nothing in this Charter abrogates or derogates from any rights or privileges guaranteed by or under the Constitution of Canada in respect of denominational, separate or dissentient schools.

Rights respecting certain schools preserved

Application to territories and territorial authorities	**30.** A reference in this Charter to a province or to the legislative assembly or legislature of a province shall be deemed to include a reference to the Yukon Territory and the Northwest Territories, or to the appropriate legislative authority thereof, as the case may be.
Legislative powers not extended	**31.** Nothing in this Charter extends the legislative powers of any body or authority.

Application of Charter

Application of Charter	**32.** (1) This Charter applies

    (a) to the Parliament and government of Canada in respect of all matters within the authority of Parliament including all matters relating to the Yukon Territory and Northwest Territories; and

    (b) to the legislature and government of each province in respect of all matters within the authority of the legislature of each province.

Exception	(2) Notwithstanding subsection (1), section 15 shall not have effect until three years after this section comes into force.
Exception where express declaration	**33.** (1) Parliament or the legislature of a province may expressly declare in an Act of Parliament or of the legislature, as the case may be, that the Act or a provision thereof shall operate notwithstanding a provision included in section 2 or sections 7 to 15 of this Charter.
Operation of exception	(2) An Act or a provision of an Act in respect of which a declaration made under this section is in effect shall have such operation as it would have but for the provision of this Charter referred to in the declaration.
Five-year limitation	(3) A declaration made under subsection (1) shall cease to have effect five years after it comes into force or on such earlier date as may be specified in the declaration.
Re-enactment	(4) Parliament or the legislature of a province may re-enact a declaration made under subsection (1).
Five-year limitation	(5) Subsection (3) applies in respect of a re-enactment made under subsection (4).

Citation

Citation	**34.** This Part may be cited as the *Canadian Charter of Rights and Freedoms*.

Part II Rights of the Aboriginal Peoples of Canada

Recognition of existing aboriginal and treaty rights	**35.** (1) The existing aboriginal and treaty rights of the aboriginal peoples of Canada are hereby recognized and affirmed.
Definition of "aboriginal peoples of Canada"	(2) In this Act, "aboriginal peoples of Canada" includes the Indian, Inuit and Métis peoples of Canada.

Part III Equalization and Regional Disparities

Commitment to promote equal opportunities	**36.** (1) Without altering the legislative authority of Parliament or of the provincial legislatures, or the rights of any of them with respect to the exercise of their legislative authority, Parliament and the legisla-

tures, together with the government of Canada and the provincial governments, are committed to

    (a) promoting equal opportunities for the well-being of Canadians;

    (b) furthering economic development to reduce disparity in opportunities; and

    (c) providing essential public services of reasonable quality to all Canadians.

(2) Parliament and the government of Canada are committed to the principle of making equalization payments to ensure that provincial governments have sufficient revenues to provide reasonably comparable levels of public services at reasonably comparable levels of taxation.

Commitment respecting public services

Part IV Constitutional Conference

37. (1) A constitutional conference composed of the Prime Minister of Canada and the first ministers of the provinces shall be convened by the Prime Minister of Canada within one year after this Part comes into force.

Constitutional conference

(2) The conference convened under subsection (1) shall have included in its agenda an item respecting constitutional matters that directly affect the aboriginal peoples of Canada, including the identification and definition of the rights of those peoples to be included in the Constitution of Canada, and the Prime Minister of Canada shall invite representatives of those peoples to participate in the discussions on that item.

Participation of aboriginal peoples

(3) The Prime Minister of Canada shall invite elected representatives of the governments of the Yukon Territory and the Northwest Territories to participate in the discussions on any item on the agenda of the conference convened under subsection (1) that, in the opinion of the Prime Minister, directly affects the Yukon Territory and the Northwest Territories.

Participation of territories

Part V Procedure for Amending Constitution of Canada

38. (1) An amendment to the Constitution of Canada may be made by proclamation issued by the Governor General under the Great Seal of Canada where so authorized by

General procedure for amending Constitution of Canada

    (a) resolutions of the Senate and House of Commons; and

    (b) resolutions of the legislative assemblies of at least two-thirds of the provinces that have, in the aggregate, according to the then latest general census, at least fifty per cent of the population of all the provinces.

(2) An amendment made under subsection (1) that derogates from the legislative powers, the proprietary rights or any other rights or privileges of the legislature or government of a province shall require a resolution supported by a majority of the members of

Majority of members

each of the Senate, the House of Commons and the legislative assemblies required under subsection (1).

Expression of dissent

(3) An amendment referred to in subsection (2) shall not have effect in a province the legislative assembly of which has expressed its dissent thereto by resolution supported by a majority of its members prior to the issue of the proclamation to which the amendment relates unless that legislative assembly, subsequently, by resolution supported by a majority of its members, revokes its dissent and authorizes the amendment.

Revocation of dissent

(4) A resolution of dissent made for the purposes of subsection (3) may be revoked at any time before or after the issue of the proclamation to which it relates.

Restriction on proclamation

39. (1) A proclamation shall not be issued under subsection 38(1) before the expiration of one year from the adoption of the resolution initiating the amendment procedure thereunder, unless the legislative assembly of each province has previously adopted a resolution of assent or dissent.

Idem

(2) A proclamation shall not be issued under subsection 38(1) after the expiration of three years from the adoption of the resolution initiating the amendment procedure thereunder.

Compensation

40. Where an amendment is made under subsection 38(1) that transfers provincial legislative powers relating to education or other cultural matters from provincial legislatures to Parliament, Canada shall provide reasonable compensation to any province to which the amendment does not apply.

Amendment by unanimous consent

41. An amendment to the Constitution of Canada in relation to the following matters may be made by proclamation issued by the Governor General under the Great Seal of Canada only where authorized by resolutions of the Senate and House of Commons and of the legislative assembly of each province:

(a) the office of the Queen, the Governor General and the Lieutenant Governor of a province;

(b) the right of a province to a number of members in the House of Commons not less than the number of Senators by which the province is entitled to be represented at the time this Part comes into force;

(c) subject to section 43, the use of the English or the French language;

(d) the composition of the Supreme Court of Canada; and

(e) an amendment to this Part.

Amendment by general procedure

42. (1) An amendment to the Constitution of Canada in relation to the following matters may be made only in accordance with subsection 38(1):

(a) the principle of proportionate representation of the provinces in the House of Commons prescribed by the Constitution of Canada;

(b) the powers of the Senate and the method of selecting Senators;

(c) the number of members by which a province is entitled to be represented in the Senate and the residence qualifications of Senators;

(d) subject to paragraph 41*(d)*, the Supreme Court of Canada;

(e) the extension of existing provinces into the territories; and

(f) notwithstanding any other law or practice, the establishment of new provinces.

(2) Subsections 38(2) to (4) do not apply in respect of amendments in relation to matters referred to in subsection (1).   **Exception**

(a) the office of the Queen, the Governor General and the Lieutenant Governor of a province;

(b) the right of a province to a number of members in the House of Commons not less than the number of Senators by which the province is entitled to be represented at the time this Part comes into force;

(c) subject to section 43, the use of the English or the French language;

(d) the composition of the Supreme Court of Canada; and

(e) an amendment to this Part.

43. An amendment to the Constitution of Canada in relation to any provision that applies to one or more, but not all, provinces, including   **Amendment of provisions relating to some but not all provinces**

(a) any alteration to boundaries between provinces, and

(b) any amendment to any provision that relates to the use of the English or the French language within a province,

may be made by proclamation issued by the Governor General under the Great Seal of Canada only where so authorized by resolutions of the Senate and House of Commons and of the legislative assembly of each province to which the amendment applies.

44. Subject to sections 41 and 42, Parliament may exclusively make laws amending the Constitution of Canada in relation to the executive government of Canada or the Senate and House of Commons.   **Amendments by Parliament**

45. Subject to section 41, the legislature of each province may exclusively make laws amending the constitution of the province.   **Amendments by provincial legislatures**

46. (1) The procedures for amendment under sections 38, 41, 42 and 43 may be initiated either by the Senate or the House of Commons or by the legislative assembly of a province.   **Initiation of amendment procedures**

(2) A resolution of assent made for the purposes of this Part may be revoked at any time before the issue of a proclamation authorized by it.   **Revocation of authorization**

47. (1) An amendment to the Constitution of Canada made by proclamation under section 38, 41, 42 or 43 may be made without a resolution of the Senate authorizing the issue of the proclamation if, within one hundred and eighty days after the adoption by the House of Commons of a resolution authorizing its issue, the Senate has not adopted such a resolution and if, at any time after the   **Amendments without Senate resolution**

expiration of that period, the House of Commons again adopts the resolution.

Computation of period

(2) Any period when Parliament is prorogued or dissolved shall not be counted in computing the one hundred and eighty day period referred to in subsection (1).

Advice to issue proclamation

48. The Queen's Privy Council for Canada shall advise the Governor General to issue a proclamation under this Part forthwith on the adoption of the resolutions required for an amendment made by proclamation under this Part.

Constitutional conference

49. A constitutional conference composed of the Prime Minister of Canada and the first ministers of the provinces shall be convened by the Prime Minister of Canada within fifteen years after this Part comes into force to review the provisions of this Part.

Part VI Amendment to the Constitution Act, 1867

Amendment to Constitution Act, 1867

50. The *Constitution Act, 1867* (formerly named the *British North America Act, 1867*) is amended by adding thereto, immediately after section 92 thereof, the following heading and section:

"Non-Renewable Natural Resources, Forestry Resources and Electrical Energy

Laws respecting non-renewable natural resources, forestry resources and electrical energy

92A.(1) In each province, the legislature may exclusively make laws in relation to

(a) exploration for non-renewable natural resources in the province;

(b) development, conservation and management of non-renewable natural resources and forestry resources in the province, including laws in relation to the rate of primary production therefrom; and

(c) development, conservation and management of sites and facilities in the province for the generation and production of electrical energy.

Export from provinces of resources

(2) In each province, the legislature may make laws in relation to the export from the province to another part of Canada of the primary production from non-renewable natural resources and forestry resources in the province and the production from facilities in the province for the generation of electrical energy, but such laws may not authorize or provide for discrimination in prices or in supplies exported to another part of Canada.

Authority of Parliament

(3) Nothing in subsection (2) derogates from the authority of Parliament to enact laws in relation to the matters referred to in that subsection and, where such a law of Parliament and a law of a province conflict, the law of Parliament prevails to the extent of the conflict.

Taxation of resources

(4) In each province, the legislature may make laws in relation to the raising of money by any mode or system of taxation in respect of

(a) non-renewable natural resources and forestry resources in the province and the primary production therefrom, and

(b) sites and facilities in the province for the generation of electrical energy and the production therefrom,

whether or not such production is exported in whole or in part from the province, but such laws may not authorize or provide for taxation that differentiates between production exported to another part of Canada and production not exported from the province.

(5) The expression "primary production" has the meaning assigned by the Sixth Schedule.

(6) Nothing in subsections (1) to (5) derogates from any powers or rights that a legislature or government of a province had immediately before the coming into force of this section.

51. The said Act is further amended by adding thereto the following Schedule:

"The Sixth Schedule Primary Production from Non-Renewable Natural Resources and Forestry Resources

1. For the purposes of section 92A of this Act,

(a) production from a non-renewable natural resource is primary production therefrom if

(i) it is in the form in which it exists upon its recovery or severance from its natural state, or

(ii) it is a product resulting from processing or refining the resource, and is not a manufactured product or a product resulting from refining crude oil, refining upgraded heavy crude oil, refining gases or liquids derived from coal or refining a synthetic equivalent of crude oil; and

(b) production from a forestry resource is primary production therefrom if it consists of sawings, poles, lumber, wood chips, sawdust or any other primary wood product, or wood pulp, and is not a product manufactured from wood."

Part VII General

52. (1) The Constitution of Canada is the supreme law of Canada, and any law that is inconsistent with the provisions of the Constitution is, to the extent of the inconsistency, of no force or effect.

(2) The Constitution of Canada includes

(a) the *Canada Act 1982*, including this Act;

(b) the Acts and orders referred to in Schedule; and

(c) any amendment to any Act or order referred to in paragraph *(a)* or *(b)*.

(3) Amendments to the Constitution of Canada shall be made only in accordance with the authority contained in the Constitution of Canada.

Margin notes: "Primary production"; Existing powers or rights; Idem; Primacy of Constitution of Canada; Constitution of Canada; Amendments to Constitution of Canada

Repeals and new names

53. (1) The enactments referred to in Column I of the Schedule are hereby repealed or amended to the extent indicated in Column II thereof and, unless repealed, shall continue as law in Canada under the names set out in Column III thereof.

Consequential amendments

(2) Every enactment, except the *Canada Act 1982*, that refers to an enactment referred to in the Schedule by the name in Column I thereof is hereby amended by substituting for that name the corresponding name in Column III thereof, and any British North America Act not referred to in the Schedule may be cited as the *Constitution Act* followed by the year and number, if any, of its enactment.

Repeal and consequential amendments

54. Part IV is repealed on the day that is one year after this Part comes into force and this section may be repealed and this Act renumbered, consequential upon the repeal of Part IV and this section, by proclamation issued by the Governor General under the Great Seal of Canada.

French version of Constitution of Canada

55. A French version of the portions of the Constitution of Canada referred to in the Schedule shall be prepared by the Minister of Justice of Canada as expeditiously as possible and, when any portion thereof sufficient to warrant action being taken has been so prepared, it shall be put forward for enactment by proclamation issued by the Governor General under the Great Seal of Canada pursuant to the procedure then applicable to an amendment of the same provisions of the Constitution of Canada.

English and French versions of certain constitutional texts

56. Where any portion of the Constitution of Canada has been or is enacted in English and French or where a French version of any portion of the Constitution is enacted pursuant to section 55, the English and French versions of that portion of the Constitution are equally authoritative.

English and French versions of this Act

57. The English and French versions of this Act are equally authoritative.

Commencement

58. Subject to section 59, this Act shall come into force on a day to be fixed by proclamation issued by the Queen or the Governor General under the Great Seal of Canada.

Commencement of paragraph 23(1)(a) in respect of Quebec

59. (1) Paragraph 23(1)*(a)* shall come into force in respect of Quebec on a day to be fixed by proclamation issued by the Queen or the Governor General under the Great Seal of Canada.

Authorization of Quebec

(2) A proclamation under subsection (1) shall be issued only where authorized by the legislative assembly or government of Quebec.

Repeal of this section

(3) This section may be repealed on the day paragraph 23(1)*(a)* comes into force in respect of Quebec and this Act amended and renumbered, consequentially upon the repeal of this section, by proclamation issued by the Queen or the Governor General under the Great Seal of Canada.

Short title and citations

60. This Act may be cited as the *Constitution Act, 1981*, and the Constitution Acts 1867 to 1975 (No. 2) and this Act may be cited together as the *Constitution Acts, 1867 to 1982*.

In late 1981 and early 1982, the Canadian and British governments approved the Constitution Act. The constitutional package consisted of 18 acts of the British Parliament, 8 acts of the Canadian Parliament, and 4 British orders-in-council. Elizabeth II remained queen of Canada and head of state, and Canada remained in the Commonwealth of Nations.

As part of these actions, the British North America Act, 1867 was renamed the Constitution Act, 1867.

▲ **This London** conference was one of several meetings held to frame the British North America Act and established the Dominion of Canada

Excerpts of the British North America Act, 1867 (renamed the Constitution Act, 1867, in 1982)

Whereas the Provinces of Canada, Nova Scotia, and New Brunswick have expressed their Desire to be federally united into One Dominion under the Crown of the United Kingdom of Great Britain and Ireland, with a Constitution similar in Principle to that of the United Kingdom:

And whereas such a Union would conduce to the Welfare of the Provinces and promote the Interests of the British Empire:

And whereas on the Establishment of Union by Authority of Parliament it is expedient, not only that the Constitution of the Legislative authority in the Dominion be provided for, but also that the Nature of the Executive Government herein be declared:

And whereas it is expedient that Provision be made for the eventual admission into the Union of other Parts of British North America:

Be it therefore enacted and declared by the Queen's most Excellent Majesty, by and with the Advice and Consent of the Lords Spiritual and Temporal, and Commons, in this present Parliament assembled, and by the Authority of the same, as follows: . . .

II. UNION

3. It shall be lawful for the Queen, by and with the advice of Her Majesty's Most Honourable Privy Council, to declare by Proclamation that, on and after a Day therein appointed, not being more than Six Months after the passing of this Act, the Provinces of Canada, Nova Scotia, and New Brunswick shall form and be One Dominion under the Name of Canada; and on and after that day these Three Provinces shall form and be One Dominion under the name accordingly. . . .

Canada shall be divided into Four Provinces, named Ontario, Quebec, Nova Scotia, and New Brunswick.

6. The Parts of the Province of Canada (as it exists at the passing of this Act) which formerly constituted respectively the Provinces of Upper Canada and Lower Canada shall be deemed to be severed, and shall form two separate Provinces. The Part which formerly constituted the Province of Upper Canada shall constitute the Province of Ontario; and the Part which formerly constituted the Province of Lower Canada shall constitute the Province of Quebec. . . .

9. The Executive Government and Authority of and over Canada is hereby declared to continue and be vested in the Queen. . . .

12. All Powers, Authorities, and Functions which under any Act of the Parliament of Great Britain, or of the Parliament of the United Kingdom of Great Britain and Ireland, or of the Legislature of Upper Canada, Lower Canada, Nova Scotia, or New Brunswick, are at the Union vested in or exercisable by the respective Governors or Lieutenant-Governors of those Provinces, with the advice, or with the Advice and Consent, of the respective Executive Councils thereof, or in conjunction with those Councils, or with any Number of Members thereof, or by those Governors or Lieutenant-Governors individually, shall, as far as the same continue in existence and capable of being exercised after the Union in relation to the Government of Canada, be vested in and exercisable by the Governor General, with the Advice or with the Advice and Consent of or in conjunction with the Queen's Privy Council for Canada, or any Members thereof, or by the Governor General individually, as the Case requires, subject nevertheless (except with respect to such as exist under Acts of the Parliament of Great Britain or of the Parliament of the United Kingdom of Great Britain and Ireland) to be abolished or altered by the Parliament of Canada. . . .

17. There shall be One Parliament for Canada, consisting of the Queen, an Upper House styled the Senate, and the House of Commons.

18. The Privileges, Immunities, and Powers to be held, enjoyed and exercised by the Senate and by the House of Commons and by the members thereof respectively shall be such as are from Time to Time defined by Act of the Parliament of Canada, but so that the same shall never exceed those at the passing of this Act held, enjoyed, and exercised by the Commons House of Parliament of the United Kingdom of Great Britain and Ireland and by the Members thereof.

19. The Parliament of Canada shall be called together not later than six Months after the Union.

20. There shall be a Session of the Parliament of Canada once at least in every Year, so that Twelve Months shall not intervene between the last sitting of the Parliament of one Session and its first Sitting in the next Session.

21. The Senate shall, subject to the Provisions of this Act, consist of Seventy-two Members, who shall be styled Senators. . . .

37. The House of Commons shall, subject to the Provisions of this Act, consist of One hundred and eighty-one Members, of whom Eighty-two shall be elected for Ontario, Sixty-five for Quebec, Nineteen for Nova Scotia, and Fifteen for New Brunswick. . . .

58. For each Province there shall be an Officer, styled the Lieutenant-Governor, appointed by the Governor General in Council by Instrument under the Great Seal of Canada. . . . .

91. It shall be lawful for the Queen by and with the Advice and Consent of the Senate and House of Commons, to make Laws for the Peace, Order and good Government of Canada, in relation to all Matters not coming within the Classes of Subjects by this Act assigned exclusively to the Legislatures of the Provinces: . . .

93. In and for each Province the Legislature may exclusively make Laws in relation to Education, . .

95. In each Province the Legislature may make Laws in relation to Agriculture in the Province, and to Immigration into the Province; and it is hereby declared that the Parliament of Canada may from Time to Time make Laws in relation to Agriculture in all or any of the Provinces, and to Immigration into all or any of the Provinces; and any Law of the Legislature of a Province relative to Agriculture or to Immigration shall have effect in and for the Province as long and as far only as it is not repugnant to any Act of the Parliament of Canada. . . .

102. All Duties and Revenues over which the respective Legislatures of Canada, Nova Scotia, and New Brunswick before and at the Union had and have Power of Appropriation, except such portions thereof as are by this Act reserved to the respective Legislatures of the Provinces, or are raised by them in accordance with the special Powers conferred on them by this act, shall form One Consolidated Revenue Fund, to be appropriated for the public Service of Canada in the Manner and subject to the Charges in this Act provided. . . .

145. Inasmuch as the Provinces of Canada, Nova Scotia, and New Brunswick have joined in a Declaration that the Construction of the Intercolonial Railway is essential to the Consolidation of the Union of British North America, and to the assent thereto of Nova Scotia and New Brunswick, and have consequently agreed that provision should be made for its immediate Construction by the Government of Canada: Therefore, in order to give effect to that Agreement, it shall be the duty of the Government and Parliament of Canada to provide for the Commencement within Six Months after the Union, of a Railway connecting the River St. Lawrence with the City of Halifax in Nova Scotia, and for the Construction thereof without Intermission, and the Completion thereof with all practiable Speed.

146. It shall be lawful for the Queen, by and with the Advice of Her Majesty's Most Honourable Privy Council, on Addresses from the Houses of the Parliament of Canada, and from the Houses of the respective Legislatures of the Colonies or Provinces of Newfoundland, Prince Edward Island, and British Columbia, to admit those Colonies or Provinces, or any of them, into the Union, and on Address from the Houses of Parliament of Canada to admit Rupert's Land and the Northwestern Territory, or either of them, into the Union, on such Terms and Conditions in each case as are in the Addresses expressed and as the Queen thinks fit to approve, subject to the Provisions of this Act; and the Provisions of any Orders of Council in that Behalf shall have effect as if they had been enacted by the Parliament of the United Kingdom of Great Britain and Ireland. . . .

French

Note: A powerful language-learning tool is included in **www.SWadvantage.com**. Called "Language Learning," it features multiple translation tools and vocabulary learning accelerators.

Verbal Spelling Irregularities

Spelling changes often occur in regular verbs. These changes appear to be needed to retain the original sounds within the infinitive forms. As you will shortly see, for example, by adding a cedilla to *c*, the soft *c* of verbs ending in *cer* is retained before vowels that normally would make the *c* hard.

Verb ending	Change	Present Participle	Present Indicative	Imperfect Indicative	Past Definite	Imperfect Subjunctive
-cer avancer (*to advance*)	requires the soft *c* sound throughout the conjugation	avançant	avance avançons	avançais avancions	avançai avançâmes	avançasse avançassions
-ger manger (*to eat*)	requires the soft *g* so *g* followed by *a* or *o* becomes *ge*	mangeant	mange mangeons	mangeais mangions	mangeai mangeâmes	mangeasse mangeassions

		Present Indicative	Future	Conditional	Present Subjunctive	
-oyer **-uyer** netoyer (*to clean*)	*y* changes to *i* before *e* in conjugation, but not elsewhere	nettoie, etc.	nettoierai	nettoierais	nettoie, etc.	
-ayer **-eyer** payer (*to pay*)	may either retain *y* throughout, or change to *i* before *e*	paye paie	payerai paierai	payerais paierais	paye paie	
-er when unaccented and followed by a single consonant mener (*to lead*)	*e* changes to *è* when the ending begins with an unstressed *e*	mène mènes mène menons menez mènent	mènerai mèneras mènera mènerons mènerez mèneront	mènerais mènerais mènerait mènerions mèneriez mèneraient	mène mènes mène menions meniez mènent	
-eter **-eler** (most verbs) appeler (*to call*) jeter (*to throw*)	the *l* or *t* is doubled to cause the first *e* to be stressed	appelle appelles appelle appelons appelez appellent jette	appellerai appelleras appellera appellerons appellerez appelleront jetterai	appellerais appellerais appellerait appellerions appelleriez appelleraient jetterais	appelle appelles appelle appelions appeliez appellent jette	
-eter **-eler** (some verbs) acheter (*to buy*)	follows the rule for unaccented *e*, as in *mener* above	achète	achèterai	achèterais	achète	

Irregular Verbs

Conjugation of Irregular Verbs							
Infinitive Present participle Past participle	Person	Present Indicative	Imperfect Indicative	Future Indicative	Past Indicative	Present Subjunctive	Imperative
aller (*to go*) **allant** **allé**	je tu il/elle nous vouz ils/elles	vais vas va allons allez vont	allais allais allait allions alliez allaient	irai iras ira irons irez iront	allai allas alla allâmes allâtes allèrent	aille ailles aille allions alliez aillent	 va allons allez
asseoir (*to seat*) **asseyant** **assis**	je tu il/elle nous vouz ils/elles	assieds assieds assied asseyons asseyez asseyent	asseyais asseyais asseyait asseyions asseyiez asseyaient	assiérai assiéras assiéra assiérons assiérez assiéront	assis assis assit assîmes assîtes assirent	asseye asseyes asseye asseyions asseyiez asseyent	 assieds asseyons asseyez
asseoir (*to sit*) **assoyant** **assis**	je tu il/elle nous vouz ils/elles	assois assois assoit assoyons assoyez assoient	assoyais assoyais assoyait assoyions assoyiez assoyaient	assoirai assoiras assoira assoirons assoirez assoiront	assis assis assit assîmes assîtes assirent	assoie assoies assoie assoyions assoyiez assoient	 assois assoyons assoyez
avoir (*to have*) **ayant** **eu**	je tu il/elle nous vouz ils/elles	ai as a avons avez ont	avais avais avaint avions aviez avaient	aurai auras aura aurons aurez auront	eus eus eut eûmes eûtes eurent	aie aies ait ayons ayez aient	 aie ayons ayez
battre (*to beat*) **battant** **battu**	je tu il/elle nous vouz ils/elles	bats bats bat battons battez battent	battais battais battait battions battiez battaient	battrai battras battra battrons battrez battront	battis battis battit battîmes battîtes battirent	batte battes batte battions battiez battent	 bats battons battez
boire (*to drink*) **buvant** **bu**	je tu il/elle nous vouz ils/elles	bois bois boit buvons buvez boivent	buvais buvais buvait buvions buviez buvaient	boirai boiras boira boirons boirez boiront	bus bus but bûmes bûtes burent	boive boives boive buvions buviez boivent	 bois buvons buvez

French

Irregular Verbs

Conjugation of Irregular Verbs							
Infinitive Present participle Past participle	Person	Present Indicative	Imperfect Indicative	Future Indicative	Past Indicative	Present Subjunctive	Imperative
conduire (*to lead;* *to take; to drive*) **conduisant** **conduit**	je	conduis	conduisais	conduirai	conduisis	conduise	
	tu	conduis	conduisais	conduiras	conduisis	conduises	conduis
	il/elle	conduit	conduisait	conduira	conduisit	conduise	
	nous	conduisons	conduisions	conduirons	conduisîmes	conduirons	conduisons
	vouz	conduisez	conduisiez	conduirez	conduisîtes	conduirez	conduisez
	ils/elles	conduisent	conduisaient	conduiront	conduisirent	conduiront	
connaître (*to know*) **connaissant** **connu**	je	connais	connaissais	connaîtrai	connus	connaisse	
	tu	connais	connaissais	connaîtras	connus	connaisses	connais
	il/elle	connaît	connaissait	connaîtra	connut	connaisse	
	nous	connaissons	connaissions	connaîtrons	connûmes	connaissions	connaissons
	vouz	connaissez	connaissiez	connaîtrez	connûtes	connaissiez	connaissez
	ils/elles	connaissent	connaissaient	connaîtront	connurent	connaissent	
coudre (*to sew*) **cousant** **cousu**	je	couds	cousais	coudrai	cousis	couse	
	tu	couds	cousais	coudras	cousis	couses	couds
	il/elle	coud	cousait	coudra	cousit	couse	
	nous	cousons	cousions	coudrons	cousîmes	cousions	cousons
	vouz	cousez	cousiez	coudrez	cousîtes	cousiez	cousez
	ils/elles	cousent	cousaient	coudront	cousirent	cousent	
courir (*to run*) **courant** **couru**	je	cours	courais	courrai	courus	coure	
	tu	cours	courais	courras	courus	coures	cours
	il/elle	court	courait	courra	courut	coure	
	nous	courons	courions	courrons	courûmes	courions	courons
	vouz	courez	couriez	courrez	courûtes	couriez	courez
	ils/elles	courent	couraient	courront	coururent	courent	
couvir (*to cover*) **couvrant** **couvert**	je	couvre	couvrais	couvrirai	couvris	couvre	
	tu	couvres	couvrais	couvriras	couvris	couvres	couvre
	il/elle	couvre	couvrait	couvrira	couvrit	couvre	
	nous	couvrons	couvrions	couvrirons	couvrîmes	couvrions	couvrons
	vouz	couvrez	couvriez	couvrirez	couvrîtes	couvriez	couvrez
	ils/elles	couvrent	covraient	couvriront	couvrirent	couvrent	
craindre (*to fear*) **craignant** **craint**	je	crains	craignais	craindrai	craignis	craigne	
	tu	crains	craignais	craindras	craignis	craignes	crains
	il/elle	craint	craignait	craindra	craignit	craigne	
	nous	craignons	craignions	craindrons	craignîmes	craignions	craignons
	vouz	craignez	craigniez	craindrez	craignîtes	craigniez	craignez
	ils/elles	craignent	craignaient	craindront	craignirent	craignent	

Conjugation of Irregular Verbs							
Infinitive Present participle Past participle	Person	Present Indicative	Imperfect Indicative	Future Indicative	Past Indicative	Present Subjunctive	Imperative
croire (*to think,* *to believe*) **croyant** **cru**	je tu il/elle nous vouz ils/elles	crois crois croit croyons croyez croient	croyais croyais croyait croyions croyiez croyaient	croirai croiras croira croirons croirez croiront	crus crus crut crûmes crûtes crurent	croie croies croie croyions croyiez croient	 crois croyons croyez
devoir (*to owe;* *to have to*) **devant** **dû**	je tu il/elle nous vouz ils/elles	dois dois doit devons devez doivent	devais devais devait devions deviez devaient	devrai devras devra devrons devrez devront	dus dus dut dûmes dûtes durent	doive doives doive devions deviez doivent	 dois devons devez
dire (*to say; to tell*) **disant** **dit**	je tu il/elle nous vouz ils/elles	dis dis dit disons dites disent	disais disais disait disions disiez disaient	dirai diras dira dirons direz diront	dis dis dit dîmes dîtes dirent	dise dises dise disions disiez disent	 dis disons dites
dormir (*to sleep*) **dormant** **dormir**	je tu il/elle nous vouz ils/elles	dors dors dort dormons dormez dorment	dormais dormais dormait dormions dormiez dormaient	dormirai dormiras dormira dormirons dormirez dormiront	dormis dormis dormit dormîmes dormîtes dormirent	dorme dormes dorme dormions dormiez dorment	 dors dormons dormez
écrire (*to write*) **écrivant** **écrit**	je tu il/elle nous vouz ils/elles	écris écris écrit écrivons écrivez écrivent	écrivais écrivais écrivait écrivions écriviez écrivaient	écrirai écriras écrira écrirons écrirez écriront	écrivis écrivis écrivit écrivîmes écrivîtes écrivirent	écrive écrives écrive écrivions écriviez écrivent	 écris écrivons écrivez
être (*to be*) **étant** **été**	je tu il/elle nous vouz ils/elles	suis es est sommes êtes sont	étais étais était étions étiez étaient	serai seras sera serons serez seront	fus fus fut fûmes fûtes furent	sois sois soit soyons soyez soient	 sois soyons soyez

French

Irregular Verbs

Conjugation of Irregular Verbs							
Infinitive Present participle Past participle	Person	Present Indicative	Imperfect Indicative	Future Indicative	Past Indicative	Present Subjunctive	Imperative
faire (*to do; to make*) **faisant** **fait**	je	fais	faisais	ferai	fis	fasse	
	tu	fais	faisais	feras	fis	fasses	fais
	il/elle	fait	faisait	fera	fit	fasse	
	nous	faisons	faisions	ferons	fîmes	fassions	fasions
	vouz	faites	faisiez	ferez	fîtes	fassiez	faites
	ils/elles	font	faisaient	feront	firent	fassent	
lire (*to read*) **lisant** **lu**	je	lis	lisais	lirai	lus	lise	
	tu	lis	lisais	liras	lus	lises	lis
	il/elle	lit	lisait	lira	lut	lise	
	nous	lisons	lisions	lirons	lûmes	lisions	lisons
	vouz	lisez	lisiez	lirez	lûtes	lisiez	lisez
	ils/elles	lisent	lisaient	liront	lurent	lisent	
mentir (*to lie*) **mentant** **menti**	je	mens	mentais	mentirai	mentis	mente	
	tu	mens	mentais	mentiras	mentis	mentes	mens
	il/elle	ment	mentait	mentira	mentit	mente	
	nous	mentons	mentions	mentirons	mentîmes	mentions	mentons
	vouz	mentez	mentiez	mentirez	mentîtes	mentiez	mentez
	ils/elles	mentent	mentaient	mentiront	mentirent	mentent	
mettre (*to put; to set*) **mettant** **mis**	je	mets	mettais	mettrai	mis	mette	
	tu	mets	mettais	mettras	mis	mettes	mets
	il/elle	met	mettait	mettra	mit	mette	
	nous	mettons	mettions	mettrons	mîmes	mettions	mettons
	vouz	mettez	mettiez	mettrez	mîtes	mettiez	mettez
	ils/elles	mettent	mettaient	mettront	mirent	mettent	
mourir (*to die*) **mourant** **mort**	je	meurs	mourais	mourrai	mourus	meure	
	tu	meurs	mourais	mourras	mourus	meures	meurs
	il/elle	meurt	mourait	mourra	mourut	meure	
	nous	mourons	mourions	mourrons	mourûmes	mourions	mourons
	vouz	mourez	mouriez	mourrez	mourûtes	mouriez	mourez
	ils/elles	meurent	mouraient	mourront	moururent	meurent	
offrir (*to offer; to present*) **offrant** **offert**	je	offre	offrais	offrirai	offris	offre	
	tu	offres	offrais	offriras	offris	offres	offre
	il/elle	offre	offrait	offrira	offrit	offre	
	nous	offrons	offrions	offrirons	offrîmes	offrions	offrons
	vouz	offrez	offriez	offrirez	offrîtes	offriez	offrez
	ils/elles	offrent	offraient	offriront	offrirent	offrent	

Conjugation of Irregular Verbs							
Infinitive Present participle Past participle	Person	Present Indicative	Imperfect Indicative	Future Indicative	Past Indicative	Present Subjunctive	Imperative
ouvrir (*to open*) **ouvrant** **ouvert**	je	ouvre	ouvrais	ouvrirai	ouvris	ouvre	
	tu	ouvres	ouvrais	ouvriras	ouvris	ouvres	ouvre
	il/elle	ouvre	ouvrait	ouvrira	ouvrit	ouvre	
	nous	ouvrons	ouvrions	ouvrirons	ouvrîmes	ouvrions	ouvrons
	vouz	ouvrez	ouvriez	ouvrirez	ouvrîtes	ouvriez	ouvrez
	ils/elles	ouvrent	ouvraient	ouvriront	ouvrirent	ouvrent	
partir (*to leave;* *to go away*) **partant** **parti**	je	pars	partais	partirai	partis	parte	
	tu	pars	partais	partiras	partis	partes	pars
	il/elle	part	partait	partira	partit	parte	
	nous	partons	partions	partirons	partîmes	partions	partons
	vouz	partez	partiez	partirez	partîtes	partiez	partez
	ils/elles	partent	partaient	partiront	partirent	partent	
pleuvoir (*to rain*) **pleuvant** **plu**	je	——	——	——	——	——	
	tu	——					
	il/elle	pleut	pleuvait	pleuvra	plut	pleuve	
	nous	——					
	vouz	——					
	ils/elles	pleuvent	pleuvaient	pleuvront	——	pleuvent	
pouvoir (*to be able*) **pouvant** **pu**	je	peux, puis	pouvais	pourrai	pus	puisse	
	tu	peux	pouvais	pourras	pus	puisses	——
	il/elle	peut	pouvait	pourra	put	puisse	
	nous	pouvons	pouvions	pourrons	pûmes	puissions	——
	vouz	pouvez	pouviez	pourrez	pûtes	puissiez	——
	ils/elles	peuvent	pouvaient	pourront	purent	puissent	
prendre (*to take*) **prenant** **pris**	je	prends	prenais	prendrai	pris	prenne	
	tu	prends	prenais	prendras	pris	prennes	prends
	il/elle	prend	prenait	prendra	prit	prenne	
	nous	prenons	prenions	prendrons	prîmes	prenions	prenons
	vouz	prenez	preniez	prendrez	prîtes	preniez	prenez
	ils/elles	prennent	prenaient	prendront	prirent	prennent	
recevoir (*to receive*) **recevant** **reçu**	je	reçois	recevais	recevrai	reçus	reçoive	
	tu	reçois	recevais	recevras	reçus	reçoives	reçois
	il/elle	reçoit	recevait	recevra	reçut	reçoive	
	nous	recevons	recevions	recevrons	reçûmes	recevions	recevons
	vouz	recevez	receviez	recevrez	reçûtes	receviez	recevez
	ils/elles	reçoivent	recevaient	recevront	reçurent	reçoivent	

French

Irregular Verbs

Infinitive Present participle Past participle	Person	Present Indicative	Imperfect Indicative	Future Indicative	Past Indicative	Present Subjunctive	Imperative
rire (*to laugh*) **riant** **ri**	je	ris	riais	rirai	ris	rie	
	tu	ris	riais	riras	ris	ries	ris
	il/elle	rit	riait	rira	rit	rie	
	nous	rions	riions	rirons	rîmes	riions	rions
	vouz	riez	riiez	rirez	rîtes	riiez	riez
	ils/elles	rient	riaient	riront	rirent	rient	
savoir (*to know;* *to know how*) **sachant** **su**	je	sais	savais	saurai	sus	sache	
	tu	sais	savais	sauras	sus	saches	sache
	il/elle	sait	savait	saura	sut	sache	
	nous	savons	savions	saurons	sûmes	sachions	sachons
	vouz	savez	saviez	saurez	sûtes	sachiez	sachez
	ils/elles	savent	savaient	sauront	surent	sachent	
sentir (*to feel;* *to smell*) **sentant** **sent**i	je	sens	sentais	sentirai	sentis	sente	
	tu	sens	sentais	sentiras	sentis	sentes	sens
	il/elle	sent	sentait	sentira	sentit	sente	
	nous	sentons	sentions	sentirons	sentîmes	sentions	sentons
	vouz	sentez	sentiez	sentirez	sentîtes	sentiez	sentez
	ils/elles	sentent	sentaient	sentiront	sentirent	sentent	
sortir (*to leave*) **sortant** **sorti**	je	sors	sortais	sortirai	sortis	sorte	
	tu	sors	sortais	sortiras	sortis	sortes	sors
	il/elle	sort	sortait	sortira	sortit	sorte	
	nous	sortons	sortions	sortirons	sortîmes	sortions	sortons
	vouz	sortez	sortiez	sortirez	sortîtes	sortiez	sortez
	ils/elles	sortent	sortaient	sortiront	sortirent	sortent	
souffrir (*to suffer;* *to bear*) **souffrant** **souffert**	je	souffre	souffrais	souffrirai	souffris	souffre	
	tu	souffres	souffrais	souffriras	souffris	souffres	souffre
	il/elle	souffre	souffrait	souffrira	souffrit	souffre	
	nous	souffrons	souffrions	souffrirons	souffrîmes	souffrions	souffrons
	vouz	souffrez	souffriez	souffrirez	souffrîtes	souffriez	souffrez
	ils/elles	souffrent	souffraient	souffriront	souffrirent	souffrent	
tenir (*to hold*) **tenant** **tenu**	je	tiens	tenais	tiendrai	tins	tienne	
	tu	tiens	tenais	tiendras	tins	tiennes	tiens
	il/elle	tient	tenait	tiendra	tint	tienne	
	nous	tenons	tenions	tiendrons	tînmes	tenions	tenons
	vouz	tenez	teniez	tiendrez	tîntes	teniez	tenez
	ils/elles	tiennent	tenaient	tiendront	tinrent	tiennent	

Conjugation of Irregular Verbs							
Infinitive Present participle Past participle	Person	Present Indicative	Imperfect Indicative	Future Indicative	Past Indicative	Present Subjunctive	Imperative
vendre (*to sell*) **vendant** **vendu**	je	vends	vendais	vendrai	vendis	vende	
	tu	vends	vendais	vendras	vendis	vendes	vends
	il/elle	vend	vendait	vendra	vendit	vende	
	nous	vendons	vendions	vendrons	vendîmes	vendions	vendons
	vouz	vendez	vendiez	vendrez	vendîtes	vendiez	vendez
	ils/elles	vendent	vendaient	vendront	vendirent	vendent	
venir (*to come*) **venant** **venu**	je	viens	venais	viendrai	vins	vienne	
	tu	viens	venais	viendras	vins	viennes	viens
	il/elle	vient	venait	viendra	vint	vienne	
	nous	venons	venions	viendrons	vînmes	venions	venons
	vouz	venez	veniez	viendrez	vîntes	veniez	venez
	ils/elles	viennent	venaient	viendront	vinrent	viennent	
vêtir (*to dress*) **vétant** **vétu**	je	vêts	vêtais	vêtirai	vêtis	vête	
	tu	vêts	vêtais	vêtiras	vêtis	vêtes	vêts
	il/elle	vêt	vêtait	vêtira	vêtit	vête	
	nous	vêtons	vêtions	vêtirons	vêtîmes	vêtions	vêtons
	vouz	vêtez	vêtiez	vêtirez	vêtîtes	vêtiez	vêtez
	ils/elles	vêtent	vêtaient	vêtiront	vêtirent	vêtent	
vivre (*to be alive, to live*) **vivant** **vécu**	je	vis	vivais	vivrai	vécus	vive	
	tu	vis	vivais	vivras	vécus	vives	vis
	il/elle	vit	vivait	vivra	vécut	vive	
	nous	vivons	vivions	vivrons	vécûmes	vivions	vivons
	vouz	vivez	viviez	vivrez	vécûtes	viviez	vivez
	ils/elles	vivent	vivaient	vivront	vécurent	vivent	
voir (*to see*) **voyant** **vu**	je	vois	voyais	verrai	vis	voie	
	tu	vois	voyais	verras	vis	voies	vois
	il/elle	voit	voyait	verra	vit	voie	
	nous	voyons	voyions	verrons	vîmes	voyions	voyons
	vouz	voyez	voyiez	verrez	vîtes	voyiez	voyez
	ils/elles	voient	voyaient	verront	virent	voient	
vouloir (*to want; to wish*) **voulant** **voulu**	je	veux	voulais	voudrai	voulus	veuille	
	tu	veux	voulais	voudras	voulus	veuilles	veuille
	il/elle	veut	voulait	voudra	voulut	veuille	
	nous	voulons	voulions	voudrons	voulûmes	voulions	veuillons
	vouz	voulez	vouliez	voudrez	voulûtes	vouliez	veuillez
	ils/elles	veulent	voulaient	voudront	voulurent	veuillent	

Strong and Irregular Verbs

In German, verbs that form the past stem by changing the vowel of the infinitive stem are known as strong verbs. Both the principal parts and the endings of these verbs must be known in order to derive all their conjugational forms. For most such verbs, the principal parts consist of the infinitive, the third person singular of the past tense, and the past participle. For some of these verbs, the third person singular of the present tense (which also provides the stem for the second person singular) is needed; for a few others, the general subjunctive stem is needed.

In German, most strong verbs follow one of the patterns in the table. Two regular verbs for each class are given. Some common verbs that conform to the classes (except for minor irregularities) are shown. Unclassified strong verbs and the irregular weak verbs are also given.

The examples in the table are given in the following order: **A** is the infinitive; **B** is the third person singular, present tense, indicative; **C** is the third person singular, past tense, indicative; and **D** is the past participle.

	Class I	II	III	IV	V	VI	VII
	Stem Vowel						
A	ei	ie	i {nd, ng} i {nn, mm}	e	e	a	a
B	ei	ie	i {nk} i	(a)i (b)ie	(a)ie (b)i	ä	a
C	(a)ie (b)i	o	a a	a	a	u	ie
D	ie i	o	u o	o	e	a	a
A	bleiben (*to stay*)	bieten (*to bid; to offer*)	finden (*to find*)	helfen (*to help*)	lesen (*to read*)	wachsen (*to grow*)	lassen (*to leave*)
B	bleibt	bietet	findet	hilft	liest	wächst	läßt
C	blieb	bot	fand	half	las	wuchs	ließ
D	geblieben	geboten	gefunden	geholfen	gelesen	gewachsen	gelassen
A	greifen (*to grasp*)	gießen (*to pour*)	beginnen (*to begin; to start*)	stehlen (*to steal*)	messen (*to measure*)	fahren (*to go; to travel; to drive*)	raten (*to guess; to advise*)
B	greift	gießt	beginnt	stiehlt	mißt	fährt	rät
C	griff	goß	begann	stahl	maß	fuhr	riet
D	gegriffen	gegossen	begonnen	gestohlen	gemessen	gefahren	geraten
A				nehmen (*to take*)		schaffen (*to manage*)	
B				nimmt		schafft	
C				nahm		schuf	
D				genommen		geschaffen	

Conjugation of Classified Strong Verbs *(table title)*

Conjugation of Unclassified Strong Verbs				
A	kommen (*to come*)	gehen (*to go*)	stehen (*to stand*)	tun (*to do*)
B	kommt	geht	steht	tut
C	kam	ging	stand	tat
D	gekommen	gegangen	gestanden	getan

NOTE: **Class I** verb stems ending in a vowel change the vowel of the past tense and of the past participle to *i* before -en.

Note: A powerful language-learning tool is included in **www.SWadvantage.com**. Called "Language Learning," it features multiple translation tools and vocabulary learning accelerators.

Conjugation of Irregular Strong Verbs						
Class I	**II**	**III**	**IV**	**V**	**VI**	**VII**
Stem Vowel		⎰nd ⎰nn				
A ei	ie	i⎰ng i⎰mm	e	e	a	a
B ei	ie	i⎱nk i⎱	(a)i (b)ie	(a)ie (b)i	ä	
C (a)ie (b)i	o	a a	a	a	u	ie
D ie i	o	u o	o	e	a	a
A schneiden (*to cut; to divide; to separate; to slice; to chop*)	ziehen (*to pull*)	erlöschen (*to go out; to die*)	treten (*to kick*)	geben (*to give*)	heißen (*to be called*)	laufen (*to run*)
B schneidet	zieht	erlischt	tritt	gibt	heißt	läuft
C schnitt	zog	erlosch	trat	gab	hieß	lief
D geschnitten	gezogen	erloschen	getreten	gegeben	geheißen	gelaufen
A leiden (*to suffer*)	heben (*to lift*)	saufen (*to drink*)	essen (*to eat*)	sitzen (*to sit*)	stoßen (*to push*)	fangen (*to catch*)
B leidet	hebt	säuft	ißt	sitzt	stößt	fängt
C litt	hob	soff	aß	saß	stieß	fing
D gelitten	gehoben	gesoffen	gegessen	gesessen	gestoßen	gefangen
A	schmelzen (*to melt*)	betrügen (*to cheat*)		liegen (*to lie—on a bed*)	hauen (*to hit; to carve*)	hängen (*to hang*)
B	schmilzt	betrügt		liegt	haut	hängt
C	schmolz	brtrog		lag	hieb	hing
D	geschmolzen	betrogen		gelegen	gehauen	gehangen
A	lügen (*to lie—tell an untruth*)			bitten (*to ask*)		rufen (*to call*)
B	lügt			bittet		ruft
C	log			bat		rief
D	gelogen			gebeten		gerufen
Conjugation of Irregular Weak Verbs						
A bringen (*to bring*)	denken (*to think*)	kennen (*to know*)	senden (*to send*)	NOTE: **Class IV** verbs, helfen (*to help*), sterben (*to die*), verderben (*to ruin; to spoil*), and werfen (*to throw*), have the umlauted vowel *ü* in the general subjunctive. The unclassified verb stehen (*to stand*) has *ü* for *ä*.		
B bringt	denkt	kennt	sendet			
C brachte	dachte	kannte	sandte			
D gebracht	gedacht	gekannt	gesandt			
* brächt-	dächt-	kennt- *also:* brennen (*to burn*) nennen (*to call*) rennen (*to run*)	sendet- *also:* wenden (*to turn*)	*general subjunctive stem		

Latin

Note: A powerful language-learning tool is included in **www.SWadvantage.com**. Called "Language Learning," it features multiple translation tools and vocabulary learning accelerators.

Conjugation of Irregular Verbs

Some Latin verbs have irregular principal parts; some lack one or two of the principal parts altogether; some lack some forms that are found in the conjugations of other verbs. Aside from its inherent importance, the forms of the irregular verb "to be" must be mastered because they are used to build the perfect tense system.

fero, ferre, tuli, latum (*to bear; to carry*)						
Indicatve (Active)	**Present**	**Imperfect**	**Future**	**Perfect**	**Pluperfect**	**Future Perfect**
	fero	ferebam	feram	tuli	tuleram	tulero
	fers	ferebas	feres	tulisti	tuleras	tuleris
	fert	ferebat	feret	tulit	tulerat	tulerit
	ferimus	ferebamus	feremus	tulimus	tuleramus	tulerimus
	fertis	ferebatis	feretis	tulistis	tuleratis	tuleritis
	ferunt	ferebant	ferent	tulerunt	tulerant	tulerint
Subjunctive (Active)	feram	ferrem	——	tulerim	tulissem	——
	feras	ferres	——	tuleris	tulisses	——
	ferat	ferret	——	tulerit	tulisset	——
	feramus	ferremus	——	tulerimus	tulissemus	——
	feratis	ferretis	——	tuleritis	tulissetis	——
	ferant	ferrent	——	tulerint	tulissent	——
Indicative (Passive)	feror	ferebar	ferar	latus sum	latus eram	latus ero
	ferris	ferebaris	fereris	latus es	latus eras	latus eris
	fertur	ferebatur	feretur	latus est	latus erat	latus erit
	ferimur	ferebamur	feremur	lati sumus	lati eramus	lati erimus
	ferimini	ferebamini	feremini	lati estis	lati eratis	lati eritis
	feruntur	ferebantur	ferentur	lati sunt	lati erant	lati erunt
Subjunctive (Passive)	ferar	ferrer	——	latus sim	latus essem	——
	feraris	ferreris	——	latus sis	latus esses	——
	feratur	ferretur	——	latus sit	latus esset	——
	feramur	ferremur	——	lati simus	lati essemus	——
	feramini	ferremini	——	lati sitis	lati essetis	——
	ferantur	ferrentur	——	lati sint	lati essent	——
Active		**Participle**			**Infinitive**	
Present		ferens			ferre	
Future		laturus			laturus esse	
Perfect		——			tulisse	
Passive		**Participle**			**Infinitive**	
Present		——			ferri	
Future		——			latum iri	
Perfect		latus			latus esse	

Conjugation of Irregular Verbs						
sum, esse, fui, ˙, (*to be*)						
Indicative (Active)	**Present**	**Imperfect**	**Future**	**Perfect**	**Pluperfect**	**Future Perfect**
	sum	eram	ero	fui	fueram	fuero
	es	eras	eris	fuisti	fueras	fueris
	est	erat	erit	fuit	fuerat	fuerit
	sumus	eramus	erimus	fuimus	fueramus	fuerimus
	estis	eratis	eritis	fuistis	fueratis	fueritis
	sunt	erant	erunt	fuerunt	fuerant	fuerint
Subjunctive (Active)	sim	essem	——	fuerim	fuissem	——
	sis	esses	——	fueris	fuisses	——
	sit	esset	——	fuerit	fuisset	——
	simus	essemus	——	fuerimus	fuissemus	——
	sitis	essetis	——	fueritis	fuissetis	——
	sint	essent	——	fuerint	fuissent	——
Active		**Participle**			**Infinitive**	
Present		——			esse	
Future		futurus			futurus esse/ fore	
Perfect		——			——	
eo, irte, ii, itum (*to go*)		* The *v* of the perfect, pluperfect, and future perfect tenses may be omitted.				
Indicatve (Active)	**Present**	**Imperfect**	**Future**	**Perfect***	**Pluperfect***	**Future Perfect***
	eo	ibam	ibo	ivi	iveram	ivero
	is	ibas	ibis	ivisti	iveras	iveris
	it	ibat	ibit	ivit	iverat	iverit
	imus	ibamus	ibimus	ivimus	iveramus	iverimus
	itis	ibatis	ibitis	ivistis	iveratis	iveritis
	eunt	ibant	ibunt	iverunt	iverant	iverint
Subjunctive (Active)	eam	irem	——	iverim	ivissem	——
	eas	ires	——	iveris	ivisset	——
	eat	iret	——	iverit	ivisset	——
	eamus	iremus	——	iverimus	ivissemus	——
	eatis	iretis	——	iveritis	ivissetis	——
	eant	irent	——	iverint	ivissent	——
Active		**Participle**			**Infinitive**	
Present		iens, euntis			ire	
Future		iturus			iturus esse	
Perfect		——			ivisse	

Conjugation of Irregular Verbs

fio, fieri, factus sum (*to be made; to become*)

Indicatve (Active)	Present	Imperfect	Future	Perfect	Pluperfect	Future Perfect
	fio	fiebam	fiam	factus sum	factus eram	factus ero
	fis	fiebas	fies	factus es	factus eras	factus eris
	fit	fiebat	fiet	factus est	factus erat	factus erit
	fimus	fiebamus	fiemus	facti sumus	facti eramus	facti erimus
	fitis	fiebatis	fietis	facti estis	facti eratis	facti eritis
	fiunt	fiebant	fient	facti sunt	facti erant	facti erunt
Subjunctive (Active)	fiam	fierem	——	factus sim	factus essem	——
	fias	fieres	——	factus sis	factus esses	——
	fiat	fieret	——	factus sit	factus esset	——
	fiamus	fieremus	——	facti simus	facti essemus	——
	fiatis	fieritis	——	facti sitis	facti essetis	——
	fiant	fierent	——	facti sint	facti essent	——

Active		Participle			Infinitive	
Present		——			fieri	
Future		——			factum iri	
Perfect		factus			factus esse	

malo, malle, malui, -, (*to prefer*)

Indicative (Active)	Present	Imperfect	Future	Perfect	Pluperfect	Future Perfect
	malo	malebam	malam	malui	malueram	maluero
	mavis	malebas	males	maluisti	malueras	malueris
	mavult	malebat	malet	maluit	maluerat	maluerit
	malumus	malebamus	malemus	maluimus	malueramus	maluerimus
	mavultis	malebatis	maletis	maluistis	malueratis	malueritis
	malunt	malebant	malent	maluerunt	maluerant	maluerint
Subjunctive (Active)	malim	mallem	——	maluerim	maluissem	——
	malis	malles	——	malueris	maluisses	——
	malit	mallet	——	maluerit	maluisset	——
	malimus	mallemus	——	maluerimus	maluissemus	——
	malitis	mallemus	——	maluerimus	maluissetis	——
	malint	mallent	——	maluerint	maluissent	——

		Participle			Infinitive	
Present		——			malle	
Future		——			——	
Perfect		——			maluisse	

Conjugation of Irregular Verbs						

nolo, nolle, nolui, -, (to be unwilling; to not want; to not wish)

Indicatve (Active)	Present	Imperfect	Future	Perfect	Pluperfect	Future Perfect
	nolo	nolebam	nolam	nolui	nolueram	noluero
	nonvis	nolebas	noles	noluisti	nolueras	nolueris
	nonvult	nolebat	nolet	noluit	noluerat	noluerit
	nolumus	nolebamus	nolemus	noluimus	nolueramus	noluerimus
	nonvultis	nolebatis	noletis	noluistis	nolueratis	nolueritis
	nolunt	nolebant	nolent	nolerunt	noluerant	noluerint
Subjunctive (Active)	nolim	nollem	——	noluerim	noluissem	——
	nolis	nolles	——	nolueris	noluisses	——
	nolit	nollet	——	noluerit	noluisset	——
	nolimus	nollemus	——	noluerimus	noluissemus	——
	nolitis	nolletis	——	nolueritis	noluissetis	——
	nolint	nollent	——	noluissent	noluissent	——
		Participle			**Infinitive**	
Present		nolens			nolle	
Future		——			——	
Perfect		——			noluisse	

possum, posse, potui, -, (to be able to)

Indicatve (Active)	Present	Imperfect	Future	Perfect	Pluperfect	Future Perfect
	possum	poteram	potero	potui	potueram	potuero
	potes	poteras	poteris	potuisti	potueras	potueris
	potest	poterat	poterit	potuit	potuerat	potuerit
	possumus	poteramus	poterimus	potuimus	potueramus	potuerimus
	potestis	poteratis	poteritis	potuistis	potueratis	potueritis
	possunt	poterant	poterunt	potuerunt	potuerant	potuerint
Subjunctive (Active)	possim	possem	——	potuerim	potuissem	——
	possis	posses	——	potueris	potuisses	——
	possit	posset	——	potuerit	potuisset	——
	possimus	possemus	——	potuerimus	potuissemus	——
	possitis	possetis	——	potuerimus	potuissemus	——
	possint	possent	——	potuerint	potuissent	——
		Participle			**Infinitive**	
Present		——			posse	
Future		——			——	
Perfect		——			potuisse	

Conjugation of Irregular Verbs

volo, velle, volui, -, (to be willing; to want; to wish)

Indicatve (Active)	Present	Imperfect	Future	Perfect	Pluperfect	Future Perfect
	volo	volebam	volam	volui	volueram	voluero
	vis	volebas	voles	voluisti	volueras	volueris
	vult	volebat	volet	voluit	voluerat	voluerit
	volumus	volebamus	volemus	voluimus	volueramus	voluerimus
	vultis	volebatis	voletis	voluistis	volueratis	volueritis
	volunt	volebant	volent	volerunt	voluerant	voluerint
Subjunctive (Active)	velim	vellem	——	voluerim	voluissem	——
	velis	velles	——	volueris	voluisses	——
	velit	vellet	——	voluerit	voluisset	——
	velimus	vellemus	——	voluerimus	voluissemus	——
	velitis	velletis	——	volueritis	voluissemus	——
	velint	vellent	——	voluerint	voluissent	——

	Participle			Infinitive	
Present	volens			velle	
Future	——			——	
Perfect	——			voluisse	

Numbers

	Cardinal Numbers	Ordinal Numbers	Roman Numerals		Cardinal Numbers	Ordinal Numbers	Roman Numerals
1	unus, una, unum	primus, -a, -um	I	11	undecim	undecimus	XI
2	duo, duae, duo	secundus	II	12	duodecim	duodecimus	XII
3	tres, tria	tertius	III	13	tredecim	tertius decimus	XIII
4	quattuor	quartus	IIII or IV	14	quattuordecim	quartus decimus	XIIII or XIV
5	quinque	quintus	V	15	quindecim	quintus decimus	XV
6	sex	sextus	VI	16	sedecim	sextus decimus	XVI
7	septem	septimus	VII	17	septendecim	septimus decimus	XVII
8	octo	octavus	VIII	18	duodeviginti	duodevicensimus	XVIII
9	novem	nonus	VIIII or IX	19	undeviginti	undevicensimus	XVIIII or XIX
10	decem	decimus	X	20	viginti	vicensimus	XX

Nouns

In Latin sentences, each noun has number (singular or plural), gender (masculine, feminine, or neuter), and case (grammatical role). Gender is a fixed quality, while number and case change depending on how the noun is being used.

Case. A declension is a pattern of case endings. There are five declensions; each noun may belong to only one. The dictionary entry for a Latin noun gives you first the nominative case, then an abbreviation for the genitive case, and then the gender.

Declensions									
	1st	**2nd**			**3rd**			**4th**	**5th**
Singular:									
Nominative	carta (*charter*)	dominus (*lord, master*)	puer (*boy*)	vinum (*wine*)	rex (*king*)	civis (*citizen*)	ius (*right; justice*)	redditus (*rent*)	res (*object; thing; matter*)
Vocative	carta	domine	puer	vinum	rex	civis	ius	redditus	res
Accusative	cartam	dominum	puerum	vinum	regem	civem	ius	redditum	rem
Genitive	carte	domini	pueri	vini	regis	civis	iuris	redditus	rei
Dative	carte	domino	puero	vino	regi	civi	iuri	redditui	rei
Ablative	carta	domino	puero	vino	rege	cive	iure	redditu	re
Plural:									
Nominative	carte	domini	pueri	vina	reges	cives	iura	redditus	res
Vocative	carte	domini	pueri	vina	reges	cives	iura	redditus	res
Accusative	cartas	dominos	pueros	vina	reges	cives	iura	redditus	res
Genitive	cartarum	dominorum	puerorum	vinorum	regum	civium	iurum	reddituum	rerum
Dative	cartis	dominis	pueris	vinis	regibus	civibus	iuribus	redditibus	rebus
Ablative	cartis	dominis	pueris	vinis	regibus	civibus	iuribus	redditibus	rebus

Case	
Case	**Major grammatical role**
Nominative	Subject of a verb
Genitive	Possession
Dative	Indirect object
Accusative	Direct object / Object of a preposition
Ablative	Adverbial use / Object of a preposition
Vocative	Direct address

Conjugation of Stem-Changing Verbs

First class. Certain verbs of the first and second conjugations with stem vowels *e* or *o* change *e* to *ie*, *o* to *ue* when stressed. Note that **jugar** (*to play*) is conjugated as if it were a first class stem-changing verb with stem vowel *o*.

EXAMPLES:

pensar (*to think*)	volver (*to return*)	Present participle	
		pensando	volviendo

Present indicative		Present subjunctive		Imperative	
pienso	vuelvo	piense	vuelva		
piensas	vuelves	pienses	vuelvas	piensa	vuelve
piensa	vuelve	piense	vuelva	piense	vuelva
pensamos	volvemos	pensemos	volvamos	pensemos	volvamos
pensáis	volvéis	penséis	volváis	pensad	volved
piensan	vuelven	piensen	vuelvan	piensen	vuelvan

Second class. Certain verbs of the third conjugation with stem vowels of *e* or *o* change *e* to *ie*, *o* to *ue* when stressed. Changes are the same as those listed above with the addition of *e* changing to *i*, and *o* to *u*, when the following syllable contains a stressed *a*, *ie*, or *io*.

EXAMPLES:

(ie) sentir (*to feel*)	(ue) dormir (*to sleep*)	Present participle	
		sintiendo	durmiendo

Present indicative		Present subjunctive		Preterite	
siento	duermo	sienta	duerma	sentí	dormí
sientes	duermes	sientas	duermas	sientas	dormiste
siente	duerme	sienta	duerma	sintió	durmió
sentimos	dormimos	sintamos	durmamos	sentimos	dormimos
sentís	dormís	sintáis	durmáis	sentisteis	dormisteis
sienten	duermen	sientan	duerman	sintieron	durmieron

Imperfect subjunctive		Imperative	
sintiera	durmiera		
sintieras	durmieras	siente	duerme
sintiera	durmiera	sienta	duerma
sintiéramos	durmiéramos	sintamos	durmamos
sintierais	durmierais	sentid	dormid
sintieran	durmieran	sientan	duerman

Third class. Certain verbs of the third conjugation with stem vowel *e* change *e* to *i* in all forms affected in the first and second classes of stem-changing verbs.

EXAMPLES:

(i) pedir (*to ask for*)		Present participle		
		pidiendo		

Present Indicative	Present subjunctive	Preterite	Imperfect subjunctive	Imperative
pido	pida	pedí	pidiera	
pides	pidas	pediste	pidieras	pide
pide	pida	pidió	pidiera	pida
pedimos	pidamos	pedimos	pidiéramos	pidamos
pedís	pidáis	pedisteis	pidierais	pedid
piden	pidan	pidieron	pidieran	pidan

Note: A powerful language-learning tool is included in **www.SWadvantage.com**. Called "Language Learning," it features multiple translation tools and vocabulary learning accelerators.

Spelling Change Verbs

This class of verbs undergoes changes in spelling during conjugation, with the effect of preserving the sound of the consonant found in the infinitive.

The chart below has examples of changes in the verbs **buscar** (to search), **jugar** (to play), **averiguar** (to find out), **vencer** (to conquer), **conocer** (to know), **leer** (to read), **escoger** (to choose), and **seguir** (to follow).

Verb ending	Spelling change	Examples
in verbs ending in **car**	*c* changes to *qu* before an *e*	buscar → busqué
in verbs ending in **gar**	insert *u* before an *e*	jugar → jugué
in verbs ending in **guar**	put *dieresis* over *u* before an *e*	averiguar → averigüé
in verbs ending in **cer** or **cir** preceded by a consonant	replace the *c* by *z* before an *a* or *o*	vencer → venzo
in verbs ending in **cer** or **cir** preceded by a vowel	insert *z* before *c* when followed by an *a* or *o*	conocer → conozco
in verbs ending in **er** or **ir**	change the *i* of the endings *ie* and *io* to *y*	leer → leyó
in verbs ending in **ger** or **gir**	replace the *g* with *J* before an *a* or *o*	escoger → escojo
in verbs ending in **guir** when the *u* is silent	drop the *u* before an *a* or *o*	seguir → sigo

Irregular Verbs

Irregular verbs are the most difficult verbs to learn. Yet, perhaps unfortunately, they describe actions and states of being that are most frequently needed in speaking and writing Spanish. The verb forms given in the chart below and on the following pages take thirty-eight irregular verbs through nine tenses. As you will see, the verb endings for certain tenses are the same as those you will encounter in conjugating regular verbs.

	Conjugation of Irregular Verbs								
Infinitive	Indicative				Conditional	Subjunctive			Imperative
	Present	Imperfect	Preterite	Future	Present	Present	Imperfect (1st form)	(2nd form)	
abrir (*to open*)	abro	abría	abrí	abriré	abriría	abra	abriera	abriese	
	abres	abrías	abriste	abrirás	abrirías	abras	abrieras	abrieses	abre
	abres	abría	abrió	abrirá	abriría	abra	abrira	abriese	abre
	abrimos	abríamos	abrimos	abriremos	abriríamos	abramos	abriéramos	abriésemos	abramos
	abrís	abríais	abristeis	abriréis	abriríais	abráis	abrierais	abrieseis	abrid
	abren	abrían	abrieron	abrirán	abrirían	abran	abrieran	abriesen	abran
andar (*to go; to walk*)	ando	andaba	anduve	andaré	andaría	ande	anduviera	anduviese	
	andas	andabas	anduviste	andarás	andarías	andes	anduvieras	anduvieses	anda
	anda	andaba	anduvo	andará	andaría	ande	anduviera	anduviese	ande
	andamos	andábamos	anduvimos	andaremos	andaríamos	andemos	anduviéramos	anduviésemos	andemos
	andáis	andabais	anduvisteis	andaréis	andaríais	andéis	anduvierais	anduvieseis	andad
	andan	andaban	anduvieron	andarán	andarían	anden	anduvieran	anduviesen	anden

Spanish

Irregular Verbs

	Conjugation of Irregular Verbs								
Infinitive	**Indicative**				**Conditional**	**Subjunctive**			**Imperative**
	Present	**Imperfect**	**Preterite**	**Future**	**Present**	**Present**	**Imperfect (1st form)**	**(2nd form)**	
buscar (*to search*)	busco	buscaba	busqué	buscaré	buscaría	busque	buscara	buscase	
	buscas	buscabas	buscaste	buscarás	buscarías	busques	buscaras	buscases	busca
	busca	buscabas	buscó	buscará	buscaría	busque	buscara	buscase	busque
	buscamos	buscábamos	buscamos	buscaremos	buscaríamos	busquemos	buscáramos	buscásemos	busquemos
	buscáis	buscabais	buscasteis	buscaréis	buscaríais	busquéis	buscarais	buscaseis	buscad
	buscan	buscaban	buscaron	buscarán	buscarían	busquen	buscaran	buscasen	busquen
caer (*to fall*)	caigo	caía	caí	caeré	caería	caiga	cayera	cayese	
	caes	caías	caíste	caerás	caerías	caigas	cayeras	cayeses	cae
	cae	caía	cayó	caerá	caería	caiga	cayera	cayese	caiga
	caemos	caíamos	caímos	caeremos	caeríamos	caigamos	cayéramos	cayésemos	caigamos
	caéis	caíais	caísteis	caeréis	caeríais	caigáis	cayerais	cayeseis	caed
	caen	caían	cayeron	caerán	caerían	caigan	cayeran	cayesen	caigan
cerrar (*to close*)	cierro	cerraba	cerré	cerraré	cerraría	cierre	cerrara	cerrase	cierra
	cierras	cerrabas	cerraste	cerrarás	cerrarías	cierres	cerraras	cerrases	cierre
	cierra	cerraba	cerró	cerrará	cerraría	cierre	cerraras	cerrase	cerremos
	cerramos	cerrábamos	cerramos	cerraremos	cerraríamos	cerremos	cerráramos	cerrásemos	cerrad
	cerráis	cerrabais	cerrasteis	cerraréis	cerraríais	cerréis	cerrarais	cerraseis	cierren
	cierran	cerraban	cerraron	cerrarán	cerrarían	cierren	cerraran	cerrasen	
conocer (*to know*)	conozco	conocia	conocí	conoceré	conocería	conozca	conociera	conociese	
	conoces	conocías	conociste	conocerás	conocerías	conozcas	conocieras	conocieses	conoce
	conoce	conocía	conoció	conocerá	conocería	conozca	conociera	conociese	conozca
	conocemos	conocíamos	conocimos	conoceremos	conoceríamos	conozcamos	conociéramos	conociésemos	conozcamos
	conocéis	conocíais	conociesteis	conoceréis	conoceríais	conozcáis	conocierais	conocieseis	conoced
	conocen	conocían	conocieron	conocerán	conocerían	conozcan	conocieran	conociesen	conozcan
dar (*to give*)	doy	daba	di	daré	daría	dé	diera	diese	
	das	dabas	diste	darás	darías	des	dieras	dieses	da
	da	daba	dio	dará	daría	dé	diera	diese	dé
	damos	dábamos	dimos	daremos	daríamos	demos	diéramos	diésemos	demos
	dais	dabais	disteis	daréis	daríais	deis	dierais	dieseis	dad
	dan	daban	dieron	darán	darían	den	dieran	diesen	den
decir (*to say; tell*)	digo	decía	dije	diré	diría	diga	dijera	dijese	
	dices	decías	dijiste	dirás	dirías	digas	dijeras	dijeses	di
	dice	decía	dijo	dirá	diría	diga	dijera	dijese	diga
	decimos	decíamos	dijimos	diremos	diríamos	digamos	dijéramos	dijésemos	digamos
	decís	decíais	dijisteis	diréis	diríais	digáis	dijerais	dijeseis	decid
	dicen	decían	dijeron	dirán	dirían	digan	dijeran	dijesen	digan

	Conjugation of Irregular Verbs								
Infinitive	Indicative				Conditional	Subjunctive			Imperative
	Present	Imperfect	Preterite	Future	Present	Present	Imperfect (1st form)	(2nd form)	
empezar (*to start*)	empiezo	empezaba	empecé	empezaré	empezaría	empiece	empezara	empezase	
	empiezas	empezabas	empezaste	empezarás	empezarías	empieces	empezaras	empezases	empieza
	empieza	empezaba	empezó	empezará	empezaría	empiece	empezara	empezase	empiece
	empezamos	empezábamos	empezamos	empezaremos	empezaríamos	empecemos	empezáramos	empezásemos	empecemos
	empezáis	empezabais	empezasteis	empezaréis	empezaríais	empecéis	empezarais	empezaseis	empezad
	empiezan	empezaban	empezaron	empezarán	empezarían	empiecen	empezaran	empezasen	empiecen
encontrar (*to find*)	encuentro	encontraba	encontré	encontraré	encontraría	encuentre	encontrara	encontrase	
	encuentras	encontrabas	encontraste	encontrarás	encontrarías	encuentres	encontraras	encontrases	encuentra
	encuentra	encontraba	encontró	encontrará	encontraría	encuentre	encontrara	encontrase	encuentre
	encontramos	encontrábamos	encontramos	encontraremos	encontraríamos	encontremos	encontráramos	encontrásemos	encontremos
	encontráis	encontrabais	encontrasteis	encontraréis	encontraríais	encontréis	encontrarais	encontraseis	encontrad
	encuentran	encontraban	encontraron	encontrarán	encontrarían	encuentren	encontraran	encontrasen	encuentren
escoger (*to choose*)	escojo	escogia	escogí	escogeré	escogería	escoja	escogiera	escogiese	
	escoges	escogías	escogiste	escogerás	escogerías	escojas	escogieras	escogieses	escoge
	escoge	escogía	escogió	escogerá	escogería	escoja	escogiera	escogiese	escoja
	escogemos	escogíamos	escogimos	escogeremos	escogeríamos	escojamos	escogiéramos	escogiésemos	escojamos
	escogéis	escogíais	escogisteis	escogeréis	escogeríais	escojáis	escogierais	escogieseis	escoged
	escogen	escogían	escogieron	escogerán	escogerían	escojan	escogieran	escogiesen	escojan
estar (*to be*)	estoy	estaba	estuve	estaré	estaría	esté	estuviera	estuviese	
	estás	estabas	estuviste	estarás	estarías	estés	estuvieras	estuvieses	está
	está	estaba	estuvo	estará	estaría	esté	estuviera	estuviese	esté
	estamos	estábamos	estuvimos	estaremos	estaríamos	estemos	estuviéramos	estuviésemos	estemos
	estáis	estabais	estuvisteis	estaréis	estaríais	estéis	estuvierais	estuvieseis	estad
	están	estaban	estuvieron	estarán	estarían	estén	estuvieran	estuviesen	estén
haber (*to have*)	he	había	hube	habré	habría	haya	hubiera	hubiese	
	has	habías	hubiste	habrás	habrías	hayas	hubieras	hubieses	he
	ha	había	hubo	habrá	habría	haya	hubiera	hubiese	haya
	hemos	habíamos	hubimos	habremos	habríamos	hayamos	hubiéramos	hubiésemos	hayamos
	habéis	habíais	hubisteis	habréis	habríais	hayáis	hubierais	hubieseis	habed
	han	habían	hubieron	habrán	habrían	hayan	hubieran	hubiesen	hayan
hacer (*to make; to do*)	hago	hacía	hice	haré	haría	haga	hiciera	hiciese	
	haces	hacías	hiciste	harás	harías	hagas	hicieras	hicieses	haz
	hace	hacía	hizo	hará	haría	haga	hiciera	hiciese	haga
	hacemos	hacíamos	hicimos	haremos	haríamos	hagamos	hiciéramos	hiciésemos	hagamos
	hacéis	hacíais	hicisteis	haréis	haríais	hagáis	hicierais	hicieseis	haced
	hacen	hacían	hicieron	harán	harían	hagan	hicieran	hiciesen	hagan

Spanish

Irregular Verbs

Infinitive	Indicative				Conditional	Subjunctive			Imperative
	Present	**Imperfect**	**Preterite**	**Future**	**Present**	**Present**	**Imperfect (1st form)**	**(2nd form)**	
ir (*to go*)	voy	iba	fui	iré	iría	vaya	fuera	fuese	
	vas	ibas	fuiste	irás	irías	vayas	fueras	fueses	ve
	va	iba	fue	irá	iría	vaya	fuera	fuese	vaya
	vamos	íbamos	fuimos	iremos	iríamos	vayamos	fuéramos	fuésemos	vamos
	vais	ibais	fuisteis	iréis	iríais	vayáis	fuerais	fueseis	id
	van	iban	fueron	irán	irían	vayan	fueran	fuesen	vayan
jugar (*to play*)	juego	jugaba	jugué	jugaré	jugaría	juegue	jugara	jugase	
	juegas	jugabas	jugaste	jugarás	jugarías	juegues	jugaras	jugases	juega
	juega	jugaba	jugó	jugará	jugaría	juegue	jugara	jugase	juegue
	jugamos	jugábamos	jugamos	jugaremos	jugaríamos	juguemos	jugáramos	jugásemos	juguemos
	jugáis	jugabais	jugasteis	jugaréis	jugaríais	juguéis	jugarais	jugaseis	jugad
	juegan	jugaban	jugaron	jugará	jugarían	juguen	jugaran	jugasen	jueguen
lavar (*to wash*)	lavo	lavaba	lavé	lavaré	lavaría	lave	lavara	lavase	
	lavas	lavabas	lavaste	lavarás	lavarías	laves	lavaras	lavases	lava
	lava	lavaba	lavó	lavará	lavaría	lave	lavara	lavase	lave
	lavamos	lavábamos	lavamos	lavaremos	lavaríamos	lavemos	laváramos	lavásemos	lavemos
	laváis	lavabais	lavasteis	lavaréis	lavaríais	lavéis	lavarais	lavaseis	lavad
	lavan	lavaban	lavaron	lavarán	lavarían	laven	lavaran	lavasen	laven
leer (*to read*)	leo	leía	leí	leeré	leería	lea	leyera	leyese	
	lees	leías	leíste	leerás	leerías	leas	leyeras	leyeses	lee
	lee	leía	leyó	leerá	leería	lea	leyera	leyese	lea
	leemos	leíamos	leímos	leeremos	leeríamos	leamos	leyéramos	leyésemos	leamos
	leéis	leíais	leísteis	leeréis	leeríais	leáis	leyerais	leyeseis	leed
	leen	leían	leyeron	leerán	leerían	lean	leyeran	leyesen	lean
llegar (*to arrive*)	llego	llegaba	llegué	llegaré	llegaría	llegue	llegara	llegase	
	llegas	llegabas	llegaste	llegarás	llegarías	llegues	llegaras	llegases	llega
	llega	llegaba	llegó	llegará	llegaría	llegue	llegara	llegase	llegue
	llegamos	llegábamos	llegamos	llegaremos	llegaríamos	lleguemos	llegáramos	llegásemos	lleguemos
	llegáis	llegabais	llegasteis	llegaréis	llegaríais	lleguéis	llegarais	llegaseis	llegad
	llegan	llegaban	llegaron	llegerá	llegarían	lleguen	llegaran	llegasen	lleguen
mirar (*to look at*)	miro	miraba	miré	miraré	miraría	mire	mirara	mirase	
	miras	mirabas	miraste	mirarás	mirarías	mires	miraras	mirases	mira
	mira	miraba	miró	mirará	miraría	mire	mirara	mirase	mire
	miramos	mirábamos	miramos	miraremos	miraríamos	miremos	miráramos	mirásemos	miremos
	miráis	mirabais	mirasteis	miraréis	miraríais	miréis	mirarais	miraseis	mirad
	miran	miraban	miraron	mirarán	mirarían	miren	miraran	mirasen	miren

	Conjugation of Irregular Verbs								
Infinitive	**Indicative**				**Conditional**	**Subjunctive**			**Imperative**
	Present	**Imperfect**	**Preterite**	**Future**	**Present**	**Present**	**Imperfect (1st form)**	**(2nd form)**	
oir (*to hear*)	oigo	oía	oí	oiré	oiría	oiga	oyera	oyese	
	oyes	oías	oíste	oirás	oirías	oigas	oyeras	oyeses	oye
	oye	oía	oyó	oirá	oiría	oiga	oyera	oyese	oiga
	oímos	oíamos	oímos	oiremos	oiríamos	oigamos	oyéramos	oyésemos	oigamos
	oís	oiais	oísteis	oiréis	oiríais	oigáis	oyerais	oyeseis	oíd
	oyen	oian	oyeron	oirán	oirían	oigan	oyeran	oyesen	oigan
olvidar (*to forget*)	olvido	olvidaba	olvidé	olvidaré	olvidaría	olvide	olvidara	olvidase	
	olvidas	olvidabas	olvidaste	olvidarás	olvidarías	olvides	olvidaras	olvidases	olvida
	olvida	olvidaba	olvidó	olvidará	olvidaría	olvide	olvidara	olvidase	olvide
	olvidamos	olvidábamos	olvidamos	olvidaremos	olvidaríamos	olvidemos	olvidáramos	olvidásemos	olvidemos
	olvidáis	olvidabais	olvidasteis	olvidaréis	olvidaríais	olvidéis	olvidarais	olvidaseis	olvidad
	olvidan	olvidaban	olvidaron	olvidará	olvidarían	olviden	olvidaran	olvidasen	olviden
pagar (*to pay*)	pago	pagaba	pagué	pagaré	pagaría	pague	pagara	pagase	
	pagas	pagabas	pagaste	pagarás	pagarías	pagues	pagaras	pagases	paga
	paga	pagaba	pagó	pagará	pagaría	pague	pagara	pagase	pague
	pagamos	pagábamos	pagamos	pagaremos	pagaríamos	paguemos	pagáramos	pagásemos	paguemos
	pagáis	pagabais	pagasteis	pagaréis	pagaríais	paguéis	pagarais	pagaseis	pagad
	pagan	pagaban	pagaron	pagarán	pagarían	paguen	pagaran	pagasen	paguen
perder (*to lose*)	pierdo	perdía	perdí	perderé	perdería	pierda	perdiera	perdiese	
	pierdes	perdías	perdiste	perderás	perderías	pierdas	perdieras	perdieses	pierde
	pierde	perdía	perdió	perderá	perdería	pierda	perdiera	perdiese	pierda
	perdemos	perdíamos	perdimos	perderemos	perderíamos	perdamos	perdiéramos	perdiésemos	perdamos
	perdéis	perdíais	perdisteis	perderéis	perderíais	perdáis	perdierais	perdieseis	perded
	pierden	perdían	perdieron	perderán	perderían	pierdan	perdieran	perdiesen	pierdan
poder (*to be able*)	puedo	podía	pude	podré	podría	pueda	pudiera	pudiese	
	puedes	podías	pudiste	podrás	podrías	puedas	pudieras	pudieses	puede
	puede	podía	pudo	podrá	podría	pueda	pudiera	pudiese	pueda
	podemos	podíamos	pudimos	podremos	podríamos	podamos	pudiéramos	pudiésemos	podamos
	podéis	podíais	pudisteis	podréis	podríais	podáis	pudierais	pudieseis	poded
	pueden	podían	pudieron	podrán	podrían	puedan	pudieran	pudiesen	puedan
poner (*to put*)	pongo	ponía	puse	pondré	pondría	ponga	pusiera	pusiese	
	pones	ponías	pusiste	pondrás	pondrías	pongas	pusieras	pusieses	pon
	pone	ponía	puso	pondrá	pondría	ponga	pusiera	pusiese	ponga
	ponemos	poníamos	pusimos	pondremos	pondríamos	pongamos	pusiéramos	pusiésemos	pongamos
	ponéis	poníais	pusisteis	pondréis	pondríais	pongáis	pusierais	pusieseis	poned
	ponen	ponían	pusieron	pondrán	pondrían	pongan	pusieran	pusiesen	pongan

Spanish

Irregular Verbs

	Conjugation of Irregular Verbs								
Infinitive	Indicative				Conditional	Subjunctive			Imperative
	Present	Imperfect	Preterite	Future	Present	Present	Imperfect (1st form)	(2nd form)	
quedar (*to stay*)	quedo	quedaba	quedé	quedaré	quedaría	quede	quedara	quedase	
	quedas	quedabas	quedaste	quedarás	quedarías	quedes	quedaras	quedases	queda
	queda	quedaba	quedó	quedará	quedaría	quede	quedara	quedase	quede
	quedamos	quedábamos	quedamos	quedaremos	quedaríamos	quedemos	quedáramos	quedásemos	quedemos
	quedáis	quedabais	quedasteis	quedaréis	quedaríais	quedéis	quedarais	quedaseis	quedad
	quedan	quedaban	quedaron	quedarán	quedarían	queden	quedaran	quedasen	queden
querer (*to want; love*)	quiero	quería	quise	querré	querría	quiera	quisiera	quisiese	
	quieres	querías	quisiste	querrás	querrías	quieras	quisieras	quisieses	quiere
	quiere	quería	quiso	querrá	quirría	quiera	quisiera	quisiese	quiera
	queremos	queríamos	quisimos	querremos	querríamos	queramos	quisiéramos	quisiésemos	quieramos
	queréis	queríais	quisisteis	querréis	querríais	queráis	quisierais	quisieseis	quiered
	quieren	querían	quisieron	querrán	querrían	quieran	quisieran	quisiesen	quieran
saber (*to know*)	sé	sabía	supe	sabré	sabría	sepa	supiera	supiese	
	sabes	sabías	supiste	sabrás	sabrías	sepas	supieras	supieses	sabe
	sabe	sabía	supo	sabrá	sabría	sepa	supiera	supiese	sepa
	sabemos	sabíamos	supimos	sabremos	sabríamos	sepamos	supiéramos	supiésemos	sepamos
	sabéis	sabíais	supisteis	sabréis	sabríais	sepáis	supierais	supieseis	sabed
	saben	sabían	supieron	sabrán	sabrían	sepan	supieran	supiesen	sepan
sacar (*to take out*)	saco	sacaba	saqué	sacaré	sacaría	saque	sacara	sacase	
	sacas	sacabas	sacaste	sacarás	sacarías	saques	sacaras	sacases	saca
	saca	sacaba	sacó	sacará	sacaría	saque	sacara	sacase	saque
	sacamos	sacábamos	sacamos	sacaremos	sacaríamos	saquemos	sacáramos	sacásemos	saquemos
	sacáis	sacabais	sacasteis	sacaréis	sacaríais	saquéis	sacarais	sacaseis	sacad
	sacan	sacaban	sacaron	sacarán	sacarían	saquen	sacaran	sacasen	saquen
seguir (*to follow*)	sigo	seguía	seguí	seguiré	seguiría	siga	siguiera	siguiese	
	sigues	seguías	seguiste	seguirás	seguirías	sigas	siguieras	siguieses	——
	sigue	seguía	siguió	seguirá	seguiría	siga	siguiera	siguiese	——
	seguimos	seguíamos	seguimos	seguiremos	seguiríamos	sigamos	siguiéramos	siguiésemos	——
	seguís	seguíais	seguisteis	seguiréis	seguiríais	sigáis	siguierais	siguieseis	——
	siguen	seguían	siguieron	seguirán	seguirían	sigan	siguieran	siguiesen	——
salir (*to go out*)	salgo	salía	salí	saldré	saldría	salga	saliera	saliese	
	sales	salías	saliste	saldrás	saldrías	salgas	salieras	salieses	sal
	sale	salía	salió	saldrá	saldría	salga	saliera	saliese	salga
	salimos	salíamos	salimos	saldremos	saldríamos	salgamos	saliéramos	saliésemos	salgamos
	salís	salíais	salisteis	saldréis	saldríais	salgáis	salierais	salieseis	salid
	salen	salían	salieron	saldrán	saldrían	salgan	salieran	saliesen	salgan

Conjugation of Irregular Verbs									
Infinitive	Indicative				Conditional	Subjunctive			Imperative
	Present	**Imperfect**	**Preterite**	**Future**	**Present**	**Present**	**Imperfect (1st form)**	**(2nd form)**	
ser (*to be*)	soy	era	fui	seré	sería	sea	fuera	fuese	
	eres	eras	fuiste	serás	serías	seas	fueras	fueses	sé
	es	era	fue	será	sería	sea	fuera	fuese	sea
	somos	éramos	fuimos	seremos	seríamos	seamos	fuéramos	fuésemos	seamos
	sois	erais	fuisteis	seréis	seríais	seáis	fuerais	fueseis	sed
	son	eran	fueron	serán	serían	sean	fueran	fuesen	sean
tener (*to have*)	tengo	tenía	tuve	tendré	tendría	tenga	tuviera	tuviese	
	tienes	tenías	tuviste	tendrás	tendrías	tengas	tuvieras	tuvieses	ten
	tiene	tenía	tuvo	tendrá	tendría	tenga	tuviera	tuviese	tenga
	tenemos	teníamos	tuvimos	tendremos	tendríamos	tengamos	tuviéramos	tuviésemos	tengamos
	tenéis	teníais	tuvisteis	tendréis	tendríais	tengáis	tuvierais	tuvieseis	tened
	tienen	tenían	tuvieron	tendrán	tendrían	tengan	tuvieran	tuviesen	tengan
traer (*to bring*)	traigo	traía	traje	traeré	traería	traiga	trajera	trajese	
	traes	traías	trajiste	traerás	traerías	traigas	trajeras	trajeses	trae
	trae	traía	trajo	traerá	traería	traiga	trajera	trajese	traiga
	traemos	traíamos	trajimos	traeremos	traeríamos	traigamos	trajéramos	trajésemos	traigamos
	traéis	traíais	trajisteis	traeréis	traeríais	traigáis	trajerais	trajeseis	traed
	traen	traían	trajeron	traerán	traerían	traigan	trajeran	trajesen	traigan
valer (*to be worth*)	valgo	valía	valí	valdré	valdría	valga	valiera	valiese	
	vales	valías	valiste	valdrás	valdrías	valgas	valieras	valieses	val
	vale	valía	valió	valdrá	valdría	valga	valiera	valiese	valga
	valemos	valíamos	valimos	valdremos	valdríamos	valgamos	valiéramos	valiésemos	valgamos
	valéis	valíais	valisteis	valdréis	valdríais	valgáis	valierais	valieseis	valed
	valen	valían	valieron	valdrán	valdrían	valgan	valieran	valiesen	valgan
venir (*to come*)	vengo	venía	vine	vendré	vendría	venga	viniera	viniese	
	vienes	venías	viniste	vendrás	vendrías	vengas	vinieras	vinieses	ven
	viene	venía	vino	vendrá	vendría	venga	viniera	viniese	venga
	venimos	veníamos	vinimos	vendremos	vendríamos	vengamos	viniéramos	viniésemos	vengamos
	venís	veníais	vinisteis	vendréis	vendríais	vengáis	vinierais	vinieseis	venid
	vienen	venían	vinieron	vendrán	vendrían	vengan	vinieran	viniesen	vengan
ver (*to see*)	veo	veía	vi	veré	vería	vea	viera	viese	
	ves	veías	viste	verás	verías	veas	vieras	vieses	ve
	ve	veía	vio	verá	vería	vea	viera	viese	vea
	vemos	veíamos	vimos	veremos	veríamos	veamos	viéramos	viésemos	veamos
	veis	veíais	visteis	veréis	veríais	veáis	vierais	vieseis	ved
	ven	veían	vieron	verán	verían	vean	vieran	viesen	vean

Photo and Illustration Credits

10–11   Shutterstock; SuperStock/Getty Images; Interfoto/Alamy

12–13   Marka/SuperStock; The Print Collector/Alamy; Iain Masterton/Alamy; Digital Stock

14–15   Nik Wheeler/Corbis

16–17   Steve Skjold/Alamy; Antiques & Collectables/Alamy

18–19   Bettmann/Corbis; All Canada Photos/SuperStock; National Archives of the United States; Photolibrary; Petr Svarc/Alamy; Jon Arnold Images Ltd./Alamy

20–21   Jan Sandvik/Alamy; Bettmann/Corbis

22–23   Smithsonian American Art Museum, Washington, DC/Art Resource, NY; Christie's Images Ltd./Superstock; The Granger Collection, NYC; The Southwestern Company map

24–25   Chris Williams/Alamy; Museum of the American Indian, New York City; World Book illustration

26–27   North Wind Picture Archives/Alamy; North Wind Picture Archives/Alamy; Visions of America, LLC/Alamy; Burstein Collection/Corbis

28–29   The Southwestern Company map; Shutterstock; Shutterstock

30–31   after Theodore de Bry/Getty Images; Getty Images

32–33   World Book map; Classic Image/Alamy

34–35   The Southwestern Company map; North Wind Picture Archives/Alamy; Getty Images; Classic Image/Alamy; Classic Image/Alamy; The Print Collector/Alamy; Portrait of Anne Hutchinson (1591–1643) by American School (20th century)/Schlesinger Library, Radcliffe Institute, Harvard University/The Bridgeman Art Library

36–37   Getty Images

38–39   Mary Evans Picture Library/Alamy; North Wind Picture Archives/Alamy; World Book map

40–41   Museum of the City of New York/Corbis; North Wind Picture Archives/Alamy; 19th era/Alamy

42–43   Chris Howes/Wild Places Photography/Alamy; Getty Images

44–45   World Book map

46–47   Bettman/Corbis

48–49   World Book illustration; North Wind Picture Archives/Alamy

50–51   Getty Images; Currier & Ives/Getty Images

52–53   SuperStock/Getty Images; SuperStock; North Wind Picture Archives/Alamy

54–55   SuperStock/Getty Images

56–57   PhotoDisc, Inc.; The Southwestern Company map

58–59   Photos.com; World Book map; World Book illustration

60–61   North Wind Picture Archives/Alamy; North Wind Picture Archives/Alamy; The Art Archive/Alamy; The Art Archive/Alamy

62–63   The Granger Collection, NYC; Shutterstock

64–65   Getty Images; SuperStock/Getty Images

66–67   North Wind Picture Archives/Alamy; FPG/Getty Images; North Wind Picture Archives/Alamy

86–87   North Wind Picture Archives/Alamy; Niday Picture Library/Alamy; Robert Harding Picture Library Ltd./Alamy; North Wind Picture Archives/Alamy

88–89   Lebrecht Music and Arts Photo Library/Alamy; Photos 12/Alamy

90–91   dbimages/Alamy; GL Archive/Alamy

92–93   Stock Montage/SuperStock; World Book map; Bettmann/Corbis

94–95   World Book map; The Granger Collection, NYC

96–97   The Granger Collection, NYC; Getty Images; The Granger Collection, NYC

98–99   Stock Montage/SuperStock; The Granger Collection, NYC

100–101   World Book map; PhotoDisc, Inc.

102–103   The Granger Collection, NYC; Shutterstock; World Book map; The Granger Collection, NYC

104–105   Planet Art; World Book map; The Granger Collection, NYC; Bettmann/Corbis

106–107   The Granger Collection, NYC; The Granger Collection, NYC; The Granger Collection, NYC

108–109   Paul A. Souders/Corbis; The Granger Collection, NYC; Corbis; The Granger Collection, NYC

110–111   Slaves dance to their own music on a Southern plantation, c. 1852, (colour litho) by American School (19th century)/Private Collection/Peter Newark American Pictures/The Bridgeman Art Library

112–113   The Granger Collection, NYC

114–115   Bettmann/Corbis; The Granger Collection, NYC; The Granger Collection, NYC; The Granger Collection, NYC; The Granger Collection, NYC

116–117   World Book map; Photos.com; Photos.com

118–119   The Granger Collection, NYC; Library of Congress; The Granger Collection, NYC

120–121   The Granger Collection, NYC

122–123   Niday Picture Library/Alamy; Getty Images; Getty Images

124–125   Mary Evans Picture Library/Alamy; Getty Images; Getty Images

126–127   The Granger Collection, NYC; The Granger Collection, NYC; The Granger Collection, NYC; The Granger Collection, NYC

128–129   Niday Picture Library/Alamy; SuperStock; The Southwestern Company map

130–131   PhotoDisc, Inc.; World Book illustration

132–133   Getty Images; Corbis

134–135   Getty Images; Archive Pics/Alamy

136–137   The Granger Collection, NYC; The Granger Collection, NYC; The Granger Collection, NYC

138–139   PhotoDisc, Inc.; Pictorial Press Ltd./Alamy; Getty Images; The Granger Collection, NYC

140–141   The Granger Collection, NYC; Bettmann/Corbis

142–143   Culver Pictures/SuperStock; SuperStock

144–145   The Granger Collection, NYC; Getty Images; Getty Images

146–147   The Granger Collection, NYC; Getty Images; Library of Congress/Getty Images; Getty Images

148–149   PhotoDisc, Inc.; Bettman/Corbis

296–297   AP Photo/Canadian Press, Ron Poling; World Book map

298–299   Time & Life Pictures/Getty Images; AFP/Getty Images; AP Photo

300–301   J. P. Laffont/Sygma/Corbis; J. P. Laffont/Sygma/Corbis

302–303   Bettmann/Corbis; The Southwestern Company map; NASA

304–305   Vernier Jean Bernard/Corbis Sygma; The Canadian Press/Tom Hanson/AP Images; J. P. Moczulski/Reuters/Corbis; Jim Young/Reuters/Corbis

306–307   Stock Connection Blue/Alamy; Caroline Commins/Alamy

308–309   Photos.com; Canadian Consulate General; Time & Life Pictures/ Getty Images; Time & Life Pictures/Getty Images

310–311   Bettmann/Corbis; AFP/Getty Images; Chris Wattie/Reuters/ Corbis; AFP/Getty Images

312–313   Tetra Images/Alamy; National Archives of the United States

314–315   PhotoDisc, Inc.

318–319   Getty Images; Photos.com

320–321   Time & Life Pictures/Getty Images; The Granger Collection, NYC

322–323   The Granger Collection, NYC; Rue des Archives/The Granger Collection, NYC; The Granger Collection, NYC

324–325   The Granger Collection, NYC; The Granger Collection, NYC

326–327   The Granger Collection, NYC; The Granger Collection, NYC

328–329   The Granger Collection, NYC; The Granger Collection, NYC

330–331   Getty Images

332–333   Getty Images

334–335   Photos.com

336–337   Shutterstock; Kristoffer Tripplaar/ Alamy; Pete Souza/Obama Transition Team/Handout CNP/Corbis

338–339   The Southwestern Company illustration; The Southwestern Company illustration

340–341   The Southwestern Company illustration

342–343   Getty Images; AFP/Getty Images

344–345   Ralf-Finn Hestoft/Corbis; The Granger Collection, NYC; Bettmann/Corbis

346–347   Tom Carter/Alamy

348–349   David Noton Photography/Alamy; The Southwestern Company illustration

350–351   Shutterstock; Getty Images

352–353   AFP/Getty Images; PhotoDisc, Inc.

354–355   Idealink Photography/Alamy; Photolibrary

356–357   Blend Images/Alamy; The Southwestern Company illustration; The Southwestern Company illustration

358–359   The Southwestern Company illustration; The Southwestern Company illustration; The Southwestern Company illustration

360–361   The Southwestern Company illustration

362–363   The Granger Collection, NYC

364–365   Bettmann/Corbis

366–367   Getty Images

368–369   Getty Images; Getty Images

370–371   AFP/Getty Images

372–373   Car Culture/Corbis; The Southwestern Company illustration

374–375   Lance Nelson/Corbis

376–377   The Granger Collection, NYC

378–379   Rudy Sulgan/Corbis; Pat Canova/ Alamy; Getty Images

380–381   Cephas Picture Library/Alamy; AFP/Getty Images

382–383   Photos.com; Jose Fuste Raga/ Corbis; Getty Images

384–385   Getty Images; Getty Images

386–387   AFP/Getty Images

388–389   The Granger Collection, NYC; Time & Life Pictures/Getty Images; The Granger Collection, NYC

390–391   The Granger Collection, NYC; Roger Ressmeyer/Corbis; Bettmann/ Corbis; David Brabyn/Corbis

392–393   Carmo Correia/Alamy; Petr Svarc/ Alamy

394–395   World Book map; www.Bibleland-Pictures.com/Alamy; The Granger Collection, NYC

396–397   The Southwestern Company map

398–399   World Book map; Nik Wheeler/ Alamy; The Art Gallery Collection/ Alamy; www.BiblelandPictures.com/ Alamy

400–401   Interfoto/Alamy; Mary Evans Picture Library/Alamy; www.BiblelandPictures.com/Alamy

402–403   World Book map; World Book illustration; World Book illustration; The Art Gallery Collection/Alamy

404–405   Egyptian/Getty Images; Peter Horree/Alamy; World Book map

406–407   Richard Nowitz/Getty Images; World Book illustration; PCL/Alamy

408–409   Borromeo/Art Resource, NY; Figure of an animal, from Mohenjo-Daro, Indus Valley, Pakistan, 3000–1500 BC (terracotta) by Harappan/Musee Guimet, Paris, France/Bonora/ The Bridgeman Art Library; Eye Ubiquitous/Alamy; World Book map

410–411   World Book map; The Granger Collection, NYC; Philip Game/Alamy

412–413   World Book map

414–415   World Book map; Photos.com; Achaemenid/Getty Images

416–417   PhotoDisc, Inc.; PhotoDisc, Inc.; World Book map

418–419   World Book illustration; World Book illustration; World Book illustration; World Book illustration; World Book illustration; World Book illustration; World Book illustration

420–421   Jane Hinshaw; World Book map; Mycenaean Clay Slab with an Inscription in Linear B (clay) by Mycenaean/Crete, Greece/ Bildarchiv Steffens/Henri Stierlin/ The Bridgeman Art Library

422–423   World Book map; North Wind Picture Archives/Alamy

424–425   Lebrecht Music and Arts Photo Library/Alamy; World Book illustration

426–427   The Southwestern Company map; Ancient Art & Architecture Collection Ltd./Alamy; Stefano Politi Markovina/Alamy

428–429   World History Archive/Alamy; Digital Stock; PhotoDisc, Inc.; The Southwestern Company illustration

430–431   Roman/Getty Images

432–433   World Book map; Eye Ubiquitous/ Alamy; World Book map

434–435   AFP/Getty Images; Peter Horree/ Alamy; Peter Horree/Alamy; Mary Evans Picture Library/Alamy

436–437   The Southwestern Company map

438–439   World Book illustration; Peter Horree/Alamy; Mark Coran/Alamy

440–441   The Granger Collection, NYC; David Pearson/Alamy; PhotoDisc, Inc.

442–443   World Book map; Sherab/Alamy; World Book map

444–445   PhotoDisc, Inc.

446–447   Jack Hollingsworth/Getty Images; Lao-Tzu (c. 604–531 BC), illustration from 'Myths and Legends of China,' by Edward T. C. Werner, pub. by George G. Harrap & Co., 1922 (colour litho) by English School (20th century)/Private Collection/ The Bridgeman Art Library

448–449　Photos.com; World Book map; World Book map; World Book map; TAO Images Limited/Alamy

450–451　Roger Ressmeyer/Corbis; Keren Su/China Span/Alamy; Jar from the Han Dynasty (206 BC–AD 220). Proto Porcelain by Private Collection/The Bridgeman Art Library; China Images/Alamy

452–453　The Granger Collection, NYC

454–455　AFP/Getty Images

456–457　Lebrecht Music and Arts Photo Library/Alamy

458–459　Shutterstock

460–461　Stefano Bianchetti/Corbis; The Southwestern Company map

462–463　Mary Evans Picture Library/Alamy; Bruno Barbier/Robert Harding World Imagery/Corbis

464–465　Peter Richardson/Getty Images; Shutterstock; Digital Stock

466–467　The Granger Collection, NYC; Getty Images

468–469　Photos.com

470–471　Latitudestock/Getty Images; World Book map; Ancient Art & Architecture Collection Ltd./Alamy

472–473　PhotoDisc, Inc.; SEF/Art Resource, NY

474–475　Shutterstock; Shutterstock

476–477　The Granger Collection, NYC; Lebrecht Music and Arts Photo Library/Alamy; World Book map

478–479　F. Jack Jackson/Alamy; World Book map; Robert Harding Picture Library Ltd./Alamy

480–481　World Book map; Look and Learn/Mansa Kankan Musa I, 14th century king of the Mali empire (gouache on paper) by Angus McBride (1931–2007)/Private Collection/Look and Learn/The Bridgeman Art Library

482–483　The Southwestern Company map; Werner Forman/Art Resource, NY

484–485　The Granger Collection, NYC; The Granger Collection, NYC

486–487　Asia Photopress/Alamy

488–489　World Book map; F1online digitale Bildagentur GmbH/Alamy; PhotoDisc, Inc.; Shutterstock

490–491　World Pictures/Alamy; City Image/Alamy

492–493　World Book map; Aztec Codex Borbonicus, 'Tonalamatl,' detail depicting Quetzalcoatl and Tezcatlipoca (vellum) by Pre-Columbian/Bibliotheque de l'Assemblee Nationale, Paris, France/Giraudon/The Bridgeman Art Library; World Book map; nagelestock.com/Alamy

494–495　Planet Art; Jim Zuckerman/Corbis

496–497　Planet Art; The Blue Cloak (De Blauwe Huik), 1559 (oil on panel) by Pieter the Elder Bruegel (c. 1525–69)/Staatliche Gemaldegalerie, Berlin, Germany/The Bridgeman Art Library; Archivo Iconographico, S. A./Corbis; The Granger Collection, NYC

498–499　Interfoto/Alamy; Classic Image/Alamy

500–501　The Southwestern Company map; The Granger Collection, NYC; Interfoto/Alamy

502–503　PhotoDisc, Inc.; Mary Evans Picture Library/Alamy

504–505　World Book map

506–507　The Granger Collection, NYC; World Book map; Photos.com

508–509　The Granger Collection, NYC; The Arrival of the Squadron of Commodore Perry into a Japanese Port in 1853 (colour woodblock print) by Japanese School (19th century)/Private Collection/Archives Charmet/The Bridgeman Art Library

510–511　The Southwestern Company map; Victoria and Albert Museum, London/Art Resource, NY

512–513　Classic Image/Alamy; Lebrecht Music and Arts Photo Library/Alamy

514–515　Reproduced by permission of The State Hermitage Museum, St. Petersburg, Russia/Corbis; Interfoto/Alamy

516–517　The Southwestern Company map; Lebrecht Music and Arts Photo Library/Alamy

518–519　The Granger Collection, NYC; The Granger Collection, NYC

520–521　Photos.com

522–523　World Book map; Rangoon: The Storming of one of the Principal Stockades on July 8th 1824, plate 15 from 'Rangoon Views" engraved by George Hunt, 1825 (aquatint) by Joseph Moore (fl. 1825) (after)/Private Collection/The Stapleton Collection/The Bridgeman Art Library; World Book map

524–525　Shutterstock; World Book map; The Granger Collection, NYC

526–527　World Book map; Photos.com

528–529　Popperfoto/Getty Images; The Southwestern Company map

530–531　The Granger Collection, NYC; North Wind Picture Archives/Alamy

532–533　The Granger Collection, NYC; Time & Life Pictures/Getty Images

534–535　DC Premiumstock/Alamy; Bettmann/Corbis; Rue des Archives/The Granger Collection, NYC; Trinity Mirror/Mirrorpix/Alamy; Mary Evans Picture Library/Alamy

536–537　World Book map

538–539　Bettmann/Corbis; Photos.com; Time & Life Pictures/Getty Images

540–541　Rue des Archives/The Granger Collection, NYC; Classic Image/Alamy; Lebrecht Music and Arts Photo Library/Alamy

542–543　World Book map; Hulton-Deutsch Collection/Corbis; Rue des Archives/The Granger Collection, NYC

544–545　Getty Images; The Granger Collection, NYC

546–547　The Granger Collection, NYC; Bettmann/Corbis

548–549　Dinodia Photos/Alamy; Rue des Archives/The Granger Collection, NYC; World Book map

550–551　Getty Images; Getty Images; Interfoto/Alamy

552–553　World History Archive/Alamy; ullstein bild/The Granger Collection, NYC; History/Alamy; Corbis; RIA Novosti/Alamy

554–555　Everett Collection Inc./Alamy; Bettmann/Corbis; Photos 12/Alamy; U.S. Coast Guard; Corbis; Trinity Mirror/Mirrorpix/Alamy; Bettmann/Corbis

556–557　The Southwestern Company map; ullstein bild/The Granger Collection, NYC

558–559　ullstein bild/The Granger Collection, NYC; World Book map; Time & Life Pictures/Getty Images

560–561　Corbis; Mary Evans Picture Library/Alamy; Corbis; Interfoto/Alamy; Time & Life Pictures/Getty Images; Corbis

562–563　The Southwestern Company map

564–565　Hulton-Deutsch Collection/Corbis; Tomasz Piotrowski/Alamy

566–567   The Southwestern Company map; Margaret Bourke-White/Getty Images

568–569   Interfoto/Alamy; World Book map; Karen Kasmauski/Science Faction/Corbis

570–571   The Granger Collection, NYC; Bettmann/Corbis; Corbis; Bettmann/Corbis

572–573   Victor Paul Borg/Alamy; Bettmann/Corbis; Bettmann/Corbis

574–575   The Granger Collection, NYC; Jacques Langevin/Sygma/Corbis

576–577   World Book map; Corbis

578–579   AFP/Getty Images; Peter Turnley/Corbis

580–581   Hulton-Deutsch Collection/Corbis; Alain Keler/Sygma/Corbis; Alain Nogues/Sygma/Corbis

582–583   Henri Bureau/Sygma/Corbis; Peter Jordan/Alamy; Shepard Sherbell/Corbis SABA

584–585   Corbis; Handout CNP/Corbis

586–587   Shutterstock

588–589   Bettmann/Corbis; Eye Ubiquitous/Alamy; David Turnley/Corbis; Louise Gubb/Corbis SABA

590–591   Bettmann/Corbis; Bettmann/Corbis

592–593   Getty Images; Sygma/Corbis; Getty Images

594–595   Win Initiative/Getty Images; Xu Jinquan/XinHua/Xinhua Press/Corbis; Joel W. Rogers/Corbis; Bevil Knapp/epa/Corbis

596–597   NASA Archive/Alamy; Shutterstock

598–599   Worldspec/NASA/Alamy; Jon Arnold Images Ltd./Alamy

600–601   Westend61 GmbH/Alamy; World Book map; World Book map; World Book map

602–603   World Book map; World Book map; Antenna International

604–605   Antenna International

606–607   The Southwestern Company illustration; World Book illustration; Shutterstock; The Southwestern Company map

608–609   The Southwestern Company maps; Shutterstock; Shutterstock

610–611   World Book illustration; Shutterstock; The Southwestern Company illustration

612–613   Antenna International

614–615   Antenna International; Shutterstock; Shutterstock; Shutterstock; Shutterstock

616–617   Shutterstock; World Book map

618–619   Antenna International; Archive Pics/Alamy

620–621   Shutterstock; Robert Harding Picture Library Ltd./Alamy; Shutterstock; The Southwestern Company map

622–623   Shutterstock; Christian Kober/Alamy; Compassionate Eye Foundation/joSon/Getty Images; Martin Thomas Photography/Alamy

624–625   J. Marshall-Tribaleye Images/Alamy; Antenna International

626–627   World Book Map; Antenna International;

628–629   Peter Arnold Images/Photolibrary; Antenna International

630–631   Antenna International; Shutterstock; Shutterstock

632–633   Shutterstock; Antenna International

634–635   Shutterstock; Antenna International

636–637   Shutterstock; Antenna International

638–639   Shutterstock; Antenna International

640–641   Shutterstock; Antenna International

642–643   Shutterstock; Antenna International

644–645   Shutterstock; Antenna International

646–647   Robert Harding Picture Library Ltd./Alamy; World Book map; Classic Image/Alamy

648–649   David Young-Wolff/PhotoEdit; Shutterstock; Susan Findlay/Masterfile; Iain Masterton/Alamy; Image Source/Alamy; SuperStock

650–651   PhotoAlto/Sigrid Olsson/Getty Images; David Young-Wolff/PhotoEdit

652–653   Shutterstock

654–655   Shutterstock; Shutterstock; Shutterstock

658–659   The Southwestern Company illustration

660–661   The Southwestern Company illustration; Shutterstock

670–671   Shutterstock

672–673   Shutterstock

674–675   Shutterstock; Shutterstock

680–681   Shutterstock

684–685   Shutterstock

686–687   Shutterstock

688–689   Shutterstock

690–691   Shutterstock

692–693   Shutterstock

694–695   Shutterstock

696–697   Time & Life Pictures/Getty Images; Bettmann/Corbis

698–699   Shutterstock

700–701   Shutterstock

704–705   Pressmaster/Superfusion/SuperStock; Shutterstock

706–707   Alibi Productions/Alamy

708–709   Shutterstock; Shutterstock

712–713   Shutterstock

714–715   David Grossman/Alamy

716–717   Shutterstock

720–721   Shutterstock

724–725   Redferns/Getty Images

732–733   Bob Handleman/Alamy; Photos.com

736–737   Richard Mittleman/Alamy

740–741   Bettmann/Corbis; Mary Evans Picture Library/Alamy; Getty Images

742–743   Getty Images

744–745   Shutterstock; Classic Image/Alamy

746–747   Shutterstock

748–749   James Woodson/Getty Images

750–751   Interfoto/Alamy

754–755   Mary Evans Picture Library/Alamy

756–757   Bettmann/Corbis; Lebrecht Music and Arts Photo Library/Alamy; Brer Rabbit by English School (20th century) /Private Collection/Look and Learn/The Bridgeman Art Library

758–759   Shutterstock; Trigger Image/Alamy

760–761   Shutterstock

762–763   Popperfoto/Getty Images

764–765   National Trust Photographic Library/John Hammond/The Tempest, c. 1730–35 (oil on canvas) by William Hogarth (1697–1764)/Nostell Priory, Yorkshire, UK/National Trust Photographic Library/John Hammond/The Bridgeman Art Library; SuperStock

766–767   Bettmann/Corbis; North Wind Picture Archives/Alamy

768–769   Shutterstock; Time & Life Pictures/Getty Images

770–771   Roger Viollet/Getty Images

772–773   Shutterstock

774–775   Shutterstock; Shutterstock

776–777   Shutterstock; Shutterstock

778–779   Shutterstock; Shutterstock

782–783   David Pearson/Alamy; The Southwestern Company illustration

784–785   Stockbyte/Getty Images

786–787   David Pearson/Alamy; Claudia Wiens/Alamy

788–789   Shutterstock

790–791   Shutterstock

792–793   David L. Moore-Studio/Alamy

794–795   Iain Masterton/Alamy; Bettmann/Corbis

Index

Index

Index

Index

Index

reform, 154
revival of learning in medieval
    Europe, 465
segregation, 151
teachers' unions, 368
U.S. local government, 333
U.S. state government, 334, 335
education section of a resumé,
    780, 781
.edu Web sites, 803
Edwards, Henrietta Muir, 285
Edwards, Jonathan, 38
Egypt
    ancient, 402–407
    Antony and Cleopatra, 435
    Egyptian-Israeli détente, 581
    Hebrews escape from, 416
    Pharos of Alexandria, 419
    Ptolemaic dynasty, 427
    pyramids, 406, 418
    revolt against Britain, 545, 587
    spread of Islam, 475
Eightfold Path, 455
Eisenhower, Dwight D., 205
    Cold War, 200
    presidential elections, 205, 345
    space race, 201
    World War II, 558
electoral college, 74
electric lighting, 146
electronic catalog (library), 783
electronic sources of
    information, 788–789
Elgin, James Bruce, 8th Earl of, 269
Eliot, George, 945
Eliot, T. S., 768, 769, 855, 949, 950,
    956
Elizabeth I (Queen of England)
    Anglicanism, 32
    death, 930
    Elizabethan Age, 928, 931, 968
    Renaissance state, 498
    Shakespeare's *The Merry Wives of
    Windsor,* 971
    Spanish Armada, 501
Elizabethan Age, 928, 931, 968
ellipses, 694, 699

Ellis Island, 148, 619
Ellison, Ralph, 955
Elyot, Sir Thomas, 963
Emancipation Proclamation
    (1863), 129, 132
Embargo Act (1807), 90, 93
Emergency Banking Relief Act
    (1933), 178, 179
Emergency Quota Act (1920), 172
Emerson, Ralph Waldo, 942
emphasis
    formatting for, 862
    organization of a paper, 716
Empson, William, 856
encyclopedias
    APA works cited lists, 821
    reference section of a library, 784
Encyclopedie (Diderot and
    d'Alembert), 513
Endangered Species Act (1973), 229
endnotes, 815, 860
end punctuation, 694–695
end rhyme, 892, 893
energy use, 628, 629
engineering
    Inca, 493
    Roman, 441
England. *See* Great Britain
enjambment, 886, 889
Enlightenment, the (Age of
    Reason), 52, 504, 512–513,
    514, 936–937
Ennius, Quintus, 922
envelopes, addressing, 778
environment
    conservation, 153, 229
    human impact, 628–629
    pollution, 594–595
Environmental Protection
    Agency (EPA), 229
epic poetry, 881
equal area projection, 601
Equal Credit Opportunity Act
    (1975), 214
equality
    Fourteenth Amendment, 80, 133
    versus liberty, 330

Equal Pay Act (1963), 214, 376
equation of exchange, 390
equator, 631
Equatorial Guinea, 587
equipment failures while
    speaking, 905
"Era of Good Feelings," 96
Erasmus, Desiderius, 496, 497,
    500, 926
Erie Canal, 91
Eritrea, 587
erosion, 609
Eskimos, 240
essay exams, 738–739
essays, 740–745
essential appositive phrases, 679
Estonia, 570
Ethiopia
    Christianity, 478, 479
    Cold War, 587
    independence, 529, 587
Etruscans, 432
etymology (word origins), 830–835
    building vocabulary, 827
    definition by, 837
    dictionaries, 825
    prefixes, 832–833
Euclid, 921
euphemism, avoiding, 727
Euripides, 429
Europe, 636–637
    See also Austria; Belgium;
        Bulgaria; Czechoslovakia;
        France; Germany; Great
        Britain; Hungary; Italy;
        Netherlands; Poland; Portugal;
        Russia; Spain; Sweden;
        Yugoslavia
    age of trade and exploration,
        28–31, 502–505
    continents, 630
    diffusion of religion, 625
    human migrations, 618
    imperialism, 522–529
    integration in Western, 565
    Medieval, 460–469
    plant regions, 615

Index

Index

Index

Index

four humours theory, 931
Sung dynasty China, 484
Medieval Europe, 460–469
Black Death, 461, 467
Crusades, 29, 468, 471, 473
High Middle Ages, 463
Hundred Years' War, 466
life in, 464–465
literature, 924–925
major events, 461
map of Europe in 1000, 461
Medina (Saudi Arabia), 458, 474, 475
Meech Lake Agreement (1987), 301
Meighen, Arthur, 288
Meiji Restoration, 509, 510
"melting pot," 148
Melville, Herman, 752, 766, 943, 951
Mencken, H. L., 950
Menes, 404
Mennonites, 457
mercantilism, 388
Mercator projection, 601
Mercier, Honoré, 284
Mercosur, 381
Mercury space program, 208
Merovingians, 460
Merrimack (ironclad), 128
Mesoamerican cultures, 490–493
Mesopotamia, 398–401
messiah, 453
metaphors, 840, 841
Metaphysical poets, 932
Metcalfe, Charles Theophilus, Baron, 269
meter, 886, 888
Methodism, 32, 457
Métis, 265, 278–279, 296
metonymy, 840, 841
metropolitan corridors, 621
Metternich, Clemens von, 516, 518
Mexican Americans, 181
Mexican War, 103, 531, 533
Mexico
Aztecs, 492
building a new nation, 532, 533
California lost to U.S., 100, 101, 533

democratic government, 591
France invades, 531
independence from Spain, 531, 532
Mexican War, 103, 531, 533
Olmecs, 490, 491
social reform, 547
Spain's American empire, 504
Spanish conquest, 503
Texas independence, 102, 531, 533
U.S. intervention, 160
Michelangelo, 494, 495
Michigan, 63, 95
Mid-Atlantic states
See also Delaware; Maryland; New Jersey; New York State; Pennsylvania
colonial economy, 39
early events, 37
first permanent settlement, 34
regional economy develops, 96
Thirteen Colonies, the, 34
Middle Ages (European)
See Medieval Europe
Middle East
See also Egypt; Iran; Iraq; Israel
ancient civilizations, 412–419
ancient Mesopotamia, 398–401
conflict, 580–585
regions of the world, 642–643
spread of Islam, 475
U.S. policy, 224–225
Middle Kingdom (Egypt), 405–406
Middle Passage, 39
Middleton, Thomas, 932
Midway Island, 158
Midway Island, Battle of (1942), 191, 562
Midwest
See also Illinois; Kansas; Missouri
immigration to, 148
Indiana, 63, 95
metropolitan corridors, 621
Michigan, 63, 95
Nebraska, 136
Ohio, 63, 95
South Dakota, 106, 137
Wisconsin, 63, 95

migration, human, 618–619
See also immigration
Milan, Edict of, 432
military, the
See also draft (military); soldiers
desegregation of U.S., 187, 210
Japanese militarization, 510, 549
president of the U.S. as commander-in-chief, 75
in Roman Empire, 437
women's branches formed, 186
Milk, Harvey, 215
Millay, Edna St. Vincent, 949
Miller, Arthur, 955
Milton, John, 496, 741, 930, 932, 934
.mil Web sites, 803
Minamoto Yoritomo, 487
Ming dynasty (China), 483, 485, 508
minimum wage, 178, 209, 289, 376
mining, 137, 283
Minneapolis, 375
Minoan civilization, 420
Minuit, Peter, 42
Miranda v. Arizona (1966), 341
Mishima, Yukio, 956
mispronunciation, 845
missions, Spanish, 38
Mississippi, 118, 126, 135
Mississippi River, 31, 32
Missouri
Bleeding Kansas, 113
Pony Express terminus, 140
St. Louis, 108, 375
secessionist groups in, 126
Missouri Compromise (1820), 112, 117
Missouri River, 94
mixed economies, 361
MLA (Modern Language Association) works cited lists, 815–819
mnemonic devices, 826, 828
mock serious tone, 752
modals, 663
Model T Ford, 147, 171
modems, 597

Index

Index

Index

figures of speech, 840, 841
poetry, 879
Simons, Menno, 457
simple adverbs, 666
simple sentences, 682, 684, 685
simple subjects, 676
Sinclair, Upton, 153
Singapore, 523
Singer, Isaac Bashevis, 956
single interest pressure groups, 346
single quotation marks, 701
singular nouns, 655, 693
singular personal pronouns, 656
Sino-Japanese War (1894–1895), 510, 511, 549
Sioux Wars, 104
Sir Gawain and the Green Knight, 882, 925
sit-ins, 211
Sitting Bull, 138
sitting up straight for reading, 872, 873
skills section of a resumé, 780, 781
skimming while reading, 874
"Skunk Hour, The" (Lowell), 880
slang, avoiding, 727, 779
Slater, Nigel, 763
Slater, Samuel, 96
slavery, 110–111
abolitionism, 114–115
ancient Greece, 424
ancient Rome, 438, 440
colonial America, 39, 40
Dred Scott v. Sandford, 113, 133, 341
Emancipation Proclamation, 129, 132
escapes to Canada, 273
human migration, 619
Latin America, 530
Lincoln's policy, 124
nineteenth-century South, 97, 110–111
Northwest Ordinance on, 63

outside U.S., 112
political and legal conflict over, 112–113
revolt in Haiti, 530, 531
seeking freedom, 116–117
Spain's American empire, 504
Thirteenth Amendment abolishes, 80, 132
trade, 39, 479
Slovak immigration, 148
smallpox
Native American deaths, 26, 42, 491
Sung dynasty China inoculates against, 484
Smith, Adam, 388
Smith, Alfred E., 174
Smith, Captain John, 33, 34, 35, 930
Smollett, Tobias George, 937
Snow, John, 603
social class
See also labor
Elizabethan England, 978
Marx on class struggle, 389
Roman Empire, 438
social contract, 322, 323
Social Gospel movement, 144
socialism, 319
continuum of ideologies, 320
France, 517
who rules, 321
Social Security, 181, 209, 228
social (human) services
U.S. local government, 333
U.S. state government, 335
Society of American Indians, 105, 173
society versus culture, 622
Socrates, 420, 431, 921
solar system, 606
soldiers
African American Buffalo soldiers, 137
Civil War, 131
Civil War generals, 127
quartering, 78
Revolutionary War, 59

Solidarity trade union, 578
Solomon, King, 417
Solon, 423
Solow, Robert, 391
Somalia, 223, 587
Somme, Battle of the (1916), 286
Somoza, Anastasio, 547
Songhai Empire, 479, 481
"Song of Myself" (Whitman), 885, 946
Song of the Cid, 924
"Song of the Round Man" (Palmer), 892
Songs of Roland, 924
Sonnet 116 (Shakespeare), 893
sonnets, 882
Sons of Liberty, 48
Sophocles, 429, 921
Sostratos, 419
sounds, spelling and, 850–851
source cards, 790–791
sources
analytical research papers, 775
central idea, 812
discarding, 812–813
documenting, 709, 814–821
evaluating, 798–803
finding, 708, 782–789
note taking, 790–793
primary and secondary, 796–797
processing and evaluating, 709
static and dynamic, 802
South, the (U.S.)
See also Florida; Georgia; Louisiana; North Carolina; South Carolina; Virginia
Alabama, 118, 126, 135
American Revolution, 58
Arkansas, 126, 135
"carpetbaggers," 134
Civil War, 118–133
colonial economy, 39
cotton production, 97, 110
desegregation, 211, 212
early events, 37
first permanent settlement, 34
Kentucky, 126, 136

Index

Index

right to vote in Canada, 285, 287

right to vote in Japan, 567

right to vote in U.S., 68, 82, 155

World War I, 165

World War II, 186, 214

women's rights movement

Canada, 285

United States, 214

Woman Suffrage Movement, 155

Wood, Leonard, 157

Woolf, Virginia, 764, 951

Worcester v. Georgia (1832), 105

word choice

varying, 728

wordiness, 726

word origins. *See* etymology (word origins)

Wordsworth, William, 879, 939, 940

working class. *See* labor

working thesis, 777

workplace

See also labor

transformation of, 520–521

works cited lists

APA format, 820–821

defined, 815

MLA format, 815–819

work week, 376

World Bank, 199

World Trade Center, 227, 593

World War I, 534–539

Canada, 286–287

Germany, 162–166, 534–537

map, 157

Remarque's *All Quiet on the Western Front,* 952

United States, 162–167, 537

World War II, 182–197, 552–563

begins in Europe, 182

Canada, 290–291

causes and beginnings, 184

Europe, 188, 190, 192, 552–559

Germany, 182, 183, 185, 188, 190, 192, 556–559, 564

home front, 186–187

major battles, 190–191

new kind of war, 194

the Pacific, 184, 189, 191, 193, 560–563

theaters, 188–189

time line, 196–197

total war deaths, 564

United States enters the war, 184–185

United States moves from neutrality to aid, 183

victory in Europe, 192, 558

victory in the Pacific, 193, 563

World Wide Web. *See* Web sites

Wounded Knee massacre (1890), 105, 139, 624

Wright, Richard, 954

Wright, Wilbur and Orville, 147

writing

Aztec, 492

Egyptian hieroglyphics, 404

Greek alphabet, 421

Japanese alphabet, 487

Linear A and Linear B, 421

Native American, 24

Phoenician alphabet, 413

quills used for, 471

Shang dynasty China, 410, 411

Sumerian, 399

writing and research, 704–821

7-step system, the, 706–723

finding sources, 708, 782–789

information literacy, 794–813

speeches, 900–901

style, 724–731

types of writing, 732–781

writing your thesis, 710

Wu Ti, 446, 450

Wyatt, Sir Thomas, 927

Wycherley, William, 934

X

Xenophon, 921

Xerxes I, 415, 422

XYZ Affair, 89

Y

Yalta Conference (1945), 192

Yamassee War (1715), 42

Yang Chien, 482

yearbooks, 784

Yeats, William Butler, 884, 892

yellow fever, 157

Yellow River (Huang He) valley civilization, 410–411

Yin-Yang philosophy, 446

Yorktown, Battle of (1781), 58

Ypres, Battle of (1915), 286

Yuan dynasty (China), 485

Yugoslavia

Bosnia, 223

Serbia, 162, 163, 536

World War II, 564

Yukon Territory

becomes part of Canada, 282

Canadian Parliament, 351

gold rush, 107, 281

territorial government, 352

Z

zaibatsu, 510

Zambia, 529, 586, 587

Zen Buddhism, 487

Zenger, John Peter, 49

Zeus, 418

Zhou dynasty (China), 446–447

ziggurats, 399

Zimbabwe

African civilizations, 479

independence, 586, 587

Rhodesia, 529

Zimmermann Telegram, 164

Zola, Emile, 945

zoning, 333

Zoroastrianism, 415

Zulu empire, 528

www.SWadvantage.com

How to Use Social Studies and Language Advantage

Strand/Subject color bars and names

Strand/Subject color bar

Social Studies

- UNITED STATES HISTORY
- CANADIAN HISTORY
- GOVERNMENT
- ECONOMICS
- WORLD HISTORY
- GEOGRAPHY

Language

- GRAMMAR
- WRITING AND RESEARCH
- VOCABULARY
- READING
- SPEAKING
- LITERATURE

- AT A GLANCE

THE NILE VALLEY

At the same time that the Sumerian civilization was developing in the Tigris-Euphrates Valley, another powerful civilization was emerging 600 miles to the west. Ancient Egypt, one of the longest-lived civilizations in human history, rose along the banks of the Nile River of North Africa. The Greek historian Herodotus called Egypt "the gift of the Nile," for it could not have developed without that river's life-giving waters. This civilization would thrive for over 2,000 years and make significant contributions to the civilizations that followed it.

Ancient Egypt

In Egypt an advanced culture and a unified state developed early. Egyptian arts developed rapidly and hieroglyphic writing became widespread. Government, administrative, technical, and artistic skills were also developed. Still, like the other river valley civilizations, Egypt began its development with agriculture.

The Land

Ancient Egypt was a long, narrow country through which the Nile River flowed. Deserts bordered the country on the east, south, and west. The Mediterranean Sea lay to the north. The Nile River flowed north out of central Africa through the Egyptian desert to the Mediterranean.

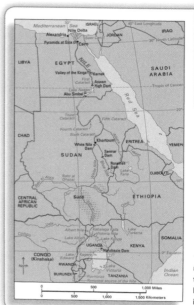

The River. The annual Nile floods created a ribbon of fertile soil 5 to 15 miles wide through a sun-baked desert. The ancient Egyptians called their country *Kemet*, meaning *Black Land*, after the dark soil. At its mouth, the Nile empties into the Mediterranean Sea, creating a rich delta 100 miles long and 200 miles across.

During the Paleolithic Age, hunters and gatherers flocked to the generous food resources of the ancient Nile. During the Neolithic Age, they began to farm the fertile banks of the river, and by 4000 BC, the banks were lined with farming villages.

◀ **The Nile River.** This map shows the location of the Nile River, the longest river in the world. The Nile rises near the equator and flows northward through northeast Africa into the Mediterranean Sea. Most ancient Egyptians lived along the Nile, in the river valley. Others lived in the fertile Nile Delta, or in the present-day Libyan Desert.